GW00696517

BACKEBERG

CACTUS LEXICON

Northern Argentina: typical *Helianthocereus* landscape (Photo: Rausch).

CACTUS LEXICON

Enumeratio diagnostica Cactacearum

by Curt Backeberg

with descriptions of many newer species (1966–73) by Walther Haage, Erfurt

With 543 illustrations, mostly in colour; and 18 Distribution Maps

Blandford Press
Poole   Dorset

All photographs by the original author, unless stated otherwise. A number of photographs were made available for the earlier German editions by the late J. Marnier-Lapostolle, in whose cactus collection, "Les Cèdres", the photographs by L. Schattat were also taken.

1st Ed. KAKTEENLEXIKON: 1966
2nd Ed. KAKTEENLEXIKON: 1970
3rd Ed. KAKTEENLEXIKON, with Appendix by W. Haage: 1976

Blandford Press Ltd.
Link House, West Street
Poole, Dorset BH15 1LL
First published in England 1977
Originally published in Germany 1966

All rights reserved
ⓒ VEB Gustav Fischer Verlag Jena, 1976

Translation based on the German 3rd Edition (1976)
by Lois Glass   Copyright ⓒ Blandford Press

ISBN 0 7137 0840 9

CONTENTS

Preface to the First Edition by Curt Backeberg 6

Foreword to the German Third Edition by Walther Haage 7

Translator's Introduction to the English Edition 8

Principles of Systematic Classification 9

Notes on Cultivation 17

Classification 21

Abbreviations and Symbols used in the text 62

Alphabetical List of the Genera, with the Species and Varieties 63

Distribution of the Cactaceae 517

Distribution Maps 519

Illustrations 545

PREFACE TO THE FIRST EDITION

The CACTUS LEXICON is intended to serve a dual purpose: in the first place it will provide the botanist and the specialist nurseryman with a handy work of reference covering all known species of the Cactaceae and their main characteristics, including the latest discoveries, many of them illustrated in black and white or colour. At the same time, descriptions of the newest finds will supplement my Handbook. Where it has been necessary, within the framework of the present edition, to treat systematic questions in a manner which is at variance with the views of some authors, my reasons have been stated in the introductory remarks to individual genera.

Secondly it is hoped the CACTUS LEXICON will provide the hobbyist, who has no need of the detailed Handbook, with the maximum of information about the plants he collects so that he can find answers to the following questions: to what genus do the relevant species belong, where do they originate, how are they recognised and distinguished from other closely related species, how should they be named, and what are the significant points about the various complexes of species?

Illustrations have been provided for almost all the genera so as to provide the reader with a comprehensive insight into the entire family. These photographs have great value in showing the widely differing forms which Nature has conferred upon the Cactaceae, and the colour plates in particular convey an impression of their full beauty as well as presenting numerous newer discoveries which are often objects of special interest to the collector.

The alphabetical arrangement of all the descriptive text enables any plant to be referred to quickly; to simplify identification or the checking of any name, diagnoses give only distinguishing characters: in other words, just those points of difference which are used to separate the species and varieties within any given genus. The concise presentation of the most essential data will enable even the non-German user to find the information he wants.

The diagnostic characters of taxa above specific rank are also clearly set out in the Systematic Survey. To simplify the finding of any genus therein, the descriptive text in each case gives a reference figure in brackets after the generic name.

Since there is no other complete classification based on the sum-total of our current knowledge, and because the phytographic system used here, with its reliance on clear natural divergences, is based on geobotanical considerations (cf. the distribution maps) so that it avoids uncertainties and theories, it has been possible to restrict the descriptions of genera and species to those names which can be considered valid and which are in general use. It is therefore hoped that the present work may contribute a much-needed standardisation and stabilisation to the nomenclature.

Hamburg-Volksdorf,   Curt Backeberg
August 1965.

"There cannot be excessive haste in scientific matters. Anything we have observed accurately will have a thousandfold effect on others before being reflected back to us. *If we have overlooked some fact, or pursued another too precipitately, this should not cause us too much regret.*"
Goethe to Alexander von Humboldt, 18. 6. 1795.

FOREWORD TO THE THIRD GERMAN EDITION

Curt Backeberg died on 14th January 1966, shortly before publication of his KAKTEENLEXIKON. A life devoted to studying the Cactaceae came to a sad and unexpected end. Since then, cactophiles have come to a growing realisation of how much he had crowded into those decades of work and the extent of his contribution to the enrichment of their hobby.

Of course there are amateurs and experts who do not always share his views, their criticism being directed against some aspects of his classification which he based fundamentally on geographical considerations. They may have had justification at times in protesting that his first descriptions failed to provide full details of flower and seed structure; but these observations could well have entailed years of delay, and it is readily understandable that a 72-year-old author is anxious to conclude his work. In a case of this kind it falls to his successors to resolve outstanding problems. His work nonetheless remains a complete whole, and even where time has brought new knowledge it should not be fragmented or amended.

VEB Gustav Fischer Verlag are to be congratulated for their farsighted decision to allow an Appendix to the Third Edition, summarising the many new discoveries of the years 1966–73.

Admittedly it is not always clear how far such finds can be considered valid species; the important thing is to let the reader have information about them, under the names currently attached to them. As to Friedrich Ritter's discoveries of the last decades, we often have no description and no certainty as to whether he will publish, while many of these plants have in the meantime been recollected and described under other names.

Obviously it is essential for scientific purposes that detailed descriptions should be supplied, especially of seeds, but these have been curtailed in the new text in order to conform to the general form of the original LEXIKON.

I take this opportunity of thanking the successful plant-hunters of our day who have provided me with their original descriptions and good colour photographs of these discoveries, since it has been one of my main objects to ensure that colour pictures of at least some of these novelties should be made available to the reader.

My warm thanks go to the following :–

A. F. H. Buining, Leusden, Holland — Figs. 460 – 464, 468 – 470, 473, 486 – 494, 496, 522 – 527

Fred. H. Brandt, Paderborn, Federal Republic of Germany — Figs. 497 – 521

Walter Rausch, Vienna, Austria — Figs. 465 – 467, 471, 472, 474 – 485, 528 – 534

D. J. Van Vliet, Scheveningen, Holland — Fig. 495.

At the same time I extend my gratitude to all those who provided me with foreign literature which I might otherwise have been quite unable to obtain.

Erfurt,
Spring 1974.

Walther Haage

TRANSLATOR'S INTRODUCTION TO THE ENGLISH VERSION

It was with very mixed feelings that I undertook to translate Backeberg's unique KAKTEENLEX-IKON. I know its usefulness to me, as the ordinary collector's reference book, and that many non-linguists have struggled with Backeberg's often very difficult prose. On the other hand I am well aware that no translation – good or bad – will be acceptable to the professional botanist, for cogent reasons: firstly because Backeberg created innumerable small genera ("splitting") in conformity with his principles of classification, and this runs strongly against the current of present-day think-ing where the larger genus ("lumping") is preferred; secondly, Backeberg's work contains many invalid names, which burden the synonymy.

This being so, I have assumed the present need to be for a cactus-collector's translation, and I have avoided most technical botanical terms where accuracy did not suffer, or the requirements of bre-vity were not overriding; in any case the reader is referred to Dr. R. B. Ivimey-Cook's invaluable aid: "Succulents: A Glossary of Terms and Descriptions", published in 1974 by the National Cac-tus & Succulent Society.

The next word of explanation concerns the German-language Third Edition on which the present translation is based. Backeberg died just before his KAKTEENLEXIKON was first published; and Walther Haage of Erfurt (German Democratic Republic), well known as the author of many popu-lar books on cacti, undertook an updating of the work, to cover most newer discoveries up to 1973. He believed the original text should stand unaltered, so that his additional information came in four separate sections: small addenda (e. g. type-localities); then a score of name-changes, mainly based on the work of Dr. H. Friedrich; some 50 printed pages describing more recently iscovered plants; and finally the valuable colour photographs which now complete the illustrated section.

The English translation provided an opportunity to incorporate these separate items into a single sequence (more difficult than it sounds!) for easier reference, but there need be no confusion as to who is responsible for additions th the Backeberg text. Mr. Haage's main addenda are indicated by a black line down the left margin; his brief amendments are given in square brackets and prefix-ed by his name. The colour photographs he provided are those of the second and third sequences, as explained on the introductory page of the Illustrated Section. My own rather motley and minor addenda are all labelled as such – in some cases providing the only information on some plant where it seemed a pity not to give details from my own collection, despite the known danger of generalising from one or two samples.

The reader may at first sight wonder about the inclusion of many names where Mr. Haage says only: "no description available"; these I have retained because of the FR numbers (field collection numbers of Friedrich Ritter) which I consider deserve mention; the ordinary collector may well not learn when his "FR such-and-such" has received baptismal rites, and one can envisage success-ive generations of field-numbered plants. Perhaps some of these can now be named.

In conclusion I thank my friends for information of detail they have so willingly provided, and I hope that they – as well as other expectant cactophiles at home and abroad – will find this English translation meets their expectations.

High Wycombe,   Lois Glass.
February 1977.

PRINCIPLES OF SYSTEMATIC CLASSIFICATION

No comprehensive description of all the members of the Cactaceae would be possible nowadays without a comprehensive classification; and the decision has to be taken as to whether genera shall be treated in the wider or the narrower sense. The former is more artificial, so that its delimitation is thereby open to various interpretations. Earlier attempts on these lines gave no guarantee of an ultimately more satisfactory general classification; indeed, in the light of the very extensive accumulation of material, it appears virtually impossible to range the entire family covering all the species of the Cactaceae, into extended genera under some unified principle of classification which would not be liable to create intolerable confusion and yet still offer a really convincing and serviceable advance on existing work. Only in this context is there any justification for "revisions" of the type recently undertaken on individual genera in Europe and the United States. A piecemeal approach can achieve nothing. The authors of these "partial treatments" have not suggested how they envisage any overall classification.

Other authors have attempted a new arrangement on the basis of phylogenetic considerations, but these, over a period of time, have only led to repeated amendments and produced no conclusive results; moreover, it is clearly beyond the powers of one individual to extend investigations of this type over the entire family, because of the impossibility of assembling sufficient living material, and such treatments thus depend heavily on theoretical reasoning. All this proves it to be merely a specialist field of phylogenetic study which cannot, at least in the foreseeable future, provide any complete and satisfactory systematic treatment of all members of the Cactaceae: fundamentally, this is not its purpose. The American phylogeneticist, G. Ledyard Stebbins Jr., long ago pointed out that phylogenetics and descriptive botany are two separate and distinct disciplines, each working at its own tasks with its different methods. Failure to observe this maxim has often produced needless conflict instead of leading to meaningful collaboration.

The narrowly conceived genus has always been accepted, since it is the one best suited to a systematic arrangement of the Cactaceae, seen overall and taking into account all the differences and varieties of form, for it is based on the facts of Nature and always relates to a group of plants with unified generic characteristics, so that it is the most "natural" genus of all, and at the same time, also the only one to which the concept of "type" may be applied without ambiguity. A further consideration is that within the cactus family we find a conspicuous concentration of genera and species in two widely separated centres of highest concentration, one in each of the Tropics. It has been shown that a satisfactory classification must correlate with geobotanical facts and recognise this phenomenon of bicentrism. Taking just the highly succulent Cereoideae, there is no other method of reflecting accurately in any classification the two centres of their distribution; and for the globose forms, the two geographically separated major groups each have their distinctive characters.

With a genus in this restricted concept, furthermore, Nature has provided her own delimitation in natural and practical fashion since there is a simple demarcation between genera, according to the stages of reduction observed in the shoot-reduction of the flower, with differentiated floral zones also requiring consideration. This systematic method thus reflects the present state in the evolutionary process, and also simplifies diagnosis by its reliance on simply observable characters.

In the light of the foregoing it is remarkable that objections are still raised against the small genus, because the latter is the most natural one and relies least on speculation; above all, no fundamental solution of any other kind has yet been put forward.

There is a tendency for the generic dispute to be exaggerated, as though this were the most important problem of our time. Systems have come and gone since the days of Salm-Dyck, and doubtless changes will still be made in times to come, although it seems probable that the science of the Cactaceae now holds few major surprises in store. Certainly the genus plays an important role in comprehensive classification, but without clear guide-lines as to its rôle in demarcation among other things, it may be short-lived, as with Buxbaum's recent division of Mammillaria. At the present time, by far the most important task is careful recording of the most essential details of all currently known species and their varieties. It must also be remembered that the larger a work, the more important it becomes to utilise readily understandable concepts and methods of classification. For practical tasks, involuted or purely theoretical approaches serve little purpose. This fact acquires a special significance at a period like the present, with the discovery of innumerable new species which it is of universal interest to treat immediately, even if additional work is later required, so as to ensure they are neither overlooked nor given several different names. At the same time a solution has to be found to the problem of centralised information, which can only be achieved by a complete descriptive summary, supplemented by later editions, in order to assemble the data often scattered here and there in the literature, and not always readily accessible. All such considerations demand a basic classification which can be readily understood and used by every reader, and it is hoped the present volume will satisfy these requirements, but it cannot be expected to give much weight to every new amendment concerned only with a narrow field, sufficient unto itself and with no concession to any kind of unified system.

Next to the systematic considerations, the vital question to be clarified in this Lexicon was the following: where does one small genus end, and the next begin? It is essential that the whole family should be treated identically, avoiding the illogical approach of some authors who regard such items as floral hairs and bristly cephalia, for example, as a diagnostic character within their chosen genera (*Pilocopiapoa* and *Cephalocleistocactus*), but refuse to accept it in the genera of other authors (*Submatucana* and *Seticereus*).

Another tangible advantage of the "small genus" is that it ensures careful investigation of each natural species complex and its differences, often compelling the worker to go more closely into the minutest differentiations. This method most closely reflects natural phenomena, permitting the most careful phytographic treatment, and providing new knowledge. This is the only way we can gain a proper insight into the marvellous creative forces of Nature – which is the ultimate goal of our investigations. To call division into small genera "splitting", as has been done by a few authors who do not always admit varieties, shows a superficial judgement which does not correctly represent the facts.

In certain species we cannot faithfully show the extent of the differences without resorting to the segregation of varieties. Here the *Tephrocactus articulatus* complex provides a convincing example. Britton and Rose wrongly named the species *Opuntia glomerata*, and they used this name to include every variant. However, even the vars. *calvus, inermis, ovatus, polyacanthus* and *syringacanthus* represent plants so divergent in appearance that it is impossible for any single description faithfully to reflect the entire swarm of varieties, thus there would be no real reflection of the range of variability, let alone any understanding of it. A more thorough treatment of the whole complex of varieties may indeed, in some species, require profound knowledge of the subject, and this is not always easy to acquire; and collection into larger groups may then be seen as the simple solution.

"Lumping", which seems particularly common in the USA, is open to objection, and is not very logical (what point is there in quoting a type-species in many such cases?) when one reflects that over there even naturally-occurring hybrids have been given hybrid-names, e. g. X *Myrtgerocereus* R. Moran, and X *Pachgerocereus* R. Moran, individual natural crosses of *Bergerocactus* with *Myrtillocactus* and *Pachycereus*. To be consistent, all other inter-generic hybrids should also be named, with consequences which are well-nigh unthinkable. Since the successful crossing of *Aporocactus* and *Trichocereus*, we know it is possible to achieve the most unlikely hybrids; and from the scientific

Inside one of the greenhouses in the late J. Marnier-Lapostolle's Botanical Garden, "Les Cèdres", at St. Jean, Cap Ferrat (France), which is one of the largest collections of succulents in the world.

point of view these are interesting, but many other hybrid genera can be imagined. On the Côte d'Azur, for instance, hybrids have been raised from *Cleistocactus, Oreocereus, Morawetzia* and *Denmoza*, as well as *Seticereus* – some of them extremely floriferous and vigorous. Since a number of them are of considerable interest to the horticulturist, closer consideration should be given to the question of their nomenclature and that of all inter-generic hybrids. As an example, I raised crosses of *Arthrocereus microsphaericus* and *A. campos-portoi* (now in the Exotic Gardens of Monaco), which far exceeded the parents in vigour and floriferousness. The Code makes provision for naming, such as that already practised in the case of the so-called "Epicacti"; but this has not yet been extended to the very succulent Cactaceae, even although here too there are many instances of outstanding and valuable hybrids which are of even more interest than the above to the breeder. However, hybrids of this kind have no place in a Handbook of naturally-occurring species, and they can therefore be mentioned here only in certain instances.

The maps showing distribution simplify understanding of the geographical areas occupied by the main categories and call attention to the duality of their occurrence. This formed the basis of the present systematic classification.

In the Subfamily *Opuntioideae* it was necessary not only to consider other diagnostic characters used to divide the genus (e. g. unsegmented stem-structure), but also to segregate groups of very divergent habit (cylindrical, ± globose, flat but more or less rounded segments); this acquires even greater importance by reason of the clear duality of geographical distribution seen in each case, where there is one major area in the north and another in the south of the American continent; this is even more marked in the genera of the *Cereoideae*. In a few cases generic demarcation was possible along conventional lines, as with *Trichocereus* and *Echinopsis*, where certain factors made this seem necessary (e. g. *Pseudolobivia*; and the geobotanical segregation of the genera of globular cacti in South America, according to their location west or east of the Andes).

11

Opuntias growing in the open in one of the finest collections of the genus, belonging to F. Rivière de Caralt, at Pinya de Rosa, Blanes (Spain).

In conclusion, attention is drawn to the fact that the systematic survey, arranged in the form of a key, gives all the principal characteristics of the individual categories and their subgroups, so that these are in most cases not repeated in the descriptive text which can then more readily emphasize the differentiating characters. The characteristics of the higher categories should be presumed in each of the relevant diagnoses.

In special cases, where species are commonly known under different generic names (e. g. *Chileorebutia*, and the "*Pyrrhocactus*" species of the Pacific distribution area), references are given so that they can readily be found in the Lexicon.

The foregoing explanations seemed to me necessary for a better understanding of the new systematic survey employed here, as well as the considerations mentioned under individual genera, for these are questions of interest to a wide readership in the present state of our knowledge of the Cactaceae and of the cactus-hobby.

Entrance to the Morawetz Garden, South Carolina, USA, notable for the uniformly large plants of *Carnegiea gigantea*.

For various reasons I have not been able to dispense with author-citations, especially since they are sometimes indispensable if confusion is to be avoided. In every case the author quoted in parentheses was responsible for first describing the species under some other generic name; and the name given after the brackets is that of the author responible for what is now regarded as the valid name. In most instances these names will be familiar to the reader, even in their abbreviated form; but if not, the information is available in the specialist literature.

Above: A modern Dutch nursery which raises 2-3 million young cactus plants a year.

Below: *Selenicereus grandiflorus* grown for medical use in the greenhouses of a pharmaceutical company in S. Germany; these plants produce a drug which has a spasmolytic effect on the coronary arteries and promotes circulation.

View of a Japanese nursery specialising in raising hybrids. Y. Ito reared many fine cultivars with magnificent blooms (Photo: Yoshio Ito).

Seedling-grafting on *Peireskiopsis* stock has made it possible to speed up very considerably the growth of young plants:

Left: Micropuntia gracicylindrica Wieg. & Backbg. grafted on *Peireskiopsis spathulata* (Photo: Schattat).

Right: Flowering 2-year seedling of *Lobivia arachnacantha* Buin. & Ritt., on the same stock (Photo: J. Marnier-L.).

CULTIVATION

The present chapter will be brief since most cactus-books discuss questions of cultivation, and it is assumed that most users of this work will be experienced cactophiles or else professional growers, both of whom will be so well versed in growing under their own conditions that "culture" scarcely worries them. I know of many collections where the plants, if the owner has time to give them sufficient care, are in such prime condition that they equal those of the "old hands". The importance of fertilisers was long ago appreciated, along with the fact that there are many types of artificial fertiliser with a low nitrogen-content which are rich in potassium and phosphorus as well as trace elements; and special composts are now on the market; even the grower of moderate experience knows that cacti require a winter-rest, that they need more water in summer, but that in spring and autumn watering must depend on visibly active growth; that the root-system needs to be inspected, to ensure surgery can be resorted to in time to prevent the spread of infection to healthy tissue; and that grafting is not an aesthetic disaster but an essential method of preserving and propagating valuable plants, and of ensuring that seedlings more quickly reach flowering size—the point at which they become a source of real pleasure. Of course one expects the professional to give his plants all the usual care, and it is reasonable to hope he will extend this to the care of his soil, i.e. to controlling root mealy bug and nematodes (eel-worms). Special preparations are readily available for these purposes but alas, their use is time-consuming. Unfortunately nematodes are becoming an increasing menace, as the buyer soon realises to his cost. Root mealy bug, scale insects or red-spider mite, unwittingly introduced with new acquisitions, can spread rapidly and eradication is far more time-consuming than a single treatment of new plants on arrival. Scale insects and ordinary mealy bugs are less of a worry; it is pests hidden in the soil which always constitute the major danger because they are not noticed immediately; their numbers then increase, and serious attacks require painstaking treatment.

Advances in chemistry and new techniques have dramatically affected the cultivation of cacti, especially in the case of hydroponics (more accurately, semi-hydroponic culture). Speedy and accurately controlled flooding of the gravel-base makes it easy to apply treatments for preventing the invasion of moulds and pests, and so greatly speeds the processes of plant-raising that the bigger nurseries are turning to it more and more, particularly since the resulting plants look more attractive, while transplanting and re-rooting in a "sales-compost" offer no problems; it is rare to find development checked in any way. It seems probable that the reduction of plant-losses by the large-scale grower is mostly due to his use of larger amounts of suitable inorganic fertilisers with a low nitrogen-content, provided precautions are also taken in good time against fungal infections; with these methods the plants are sturdier than under the older systems.

It is no surprise that many an amateur practises hydroponics in his greenhouse since the nutrient salts, equipment and trays he needs are now generally available.

It seems likely that the clay pot will disappear completely from use. Modern plastic pots have proved their worth: they are virtually unbreakable, and fine hair-roots do not cling to their walls as happened with clay pots, so that the root-ball more or less slides out for inspection or repotting, and so remains virtually intact; the plastic material warms up quickly, so that embedding is advisable, but if the compost is suitable root-formation will be hastened. The plastic pot retains moisture longer, reducing the frequency of watering, although obviously sufficient water must still be given during the growing period, and towards its close care is required to ensure the amount of moisture present is not excessive. Where these pots are in use, I have noticed that rooting is particularly rapid and the condition of the plants is outstanding. A new type of compost has been put on the market which is suitable for all plants but is particularly beneficial to those which cannot tolerate too much humus; this is a no-soil compost known as "Chemieerde", made up of quartz-sand and gravel, with added nutrient salts. I have seen for myself the excellent results which are obtained with this material; even rather sensitive species can be grown without grafting, while valuable rarities are cultivated with greater success.

In addition to the appropriate treatment the fundamental requirement for good results, as always, is a light position with all the available sunshine. For cultivation in less favourable positions such as on windowsills, the "sensitive" species are in any event not suitable. The no-soil compost I have mentioned comes with instructions for testing the pH-value so as to obtain the correct reaction; the most beneficial is an acid reaction of 5–6 (acid indicator on Litmus paper = red), thus avoiding both alkalinity or excessive acidity. While it is true that our predecessors, using no more than instinct and rule of thumb, managed to raise some fine plants, the proportion of losses is reduced with today's careful soil-control which is specially important for any collection of the many new, costly and sometimes difficult species. Verification of the pH-value is particularly important where there is any evidence of spine-calcification, or where hard water is used for the plants; the simplest procedure here is to add sulphuric acid, drop by drop, until the required reaction is obtained.

Grafting can never be entirely superseded, especially in cases where large plants are wanted for planting out in a short space of time. To take one example, the impressive display of plants in the Marnier collection ("Les Cèdres") would never have been possible without resort to grafting on vigorous stocks.

It is regrettable that far too few of such grafting stocks are grown for sale. It is particularly difficult to obtain *Peireskiopsis* cuttings which are used by professionals and amateurs alike for seedling-grafts, but this approach certainly offers exciting prospects. Here it is clearly important growers should ensure adequate supplies of this type of grafting stock. The speed with which minute seedlings develop, when grafted on *Peireskiopsis*, borders on the miraculous (see illustration), and they soon reach a size where they have to be regrafted onto robuster stocks; and these too must be available in sufficient quantity at the right time. The professional grower sometimes already turns this speedier seedling-growth to good account, since the stumps remaining after regrafting rapidly send out fresh shoots in turn, and so provide another generation of plants. This is an essential precondition for the successful propagation of the rarer species or of those which do not grow as well or as rapidly on their own roots. It is precisely these rarities or new species of particularly attractive appearance which appeal to collectors, and thus stimulate sales. The question deserves much more attention than it has hitherto received.

It would be pointless to devote space here to hints on grafting for experienced amateurs. Their numbers already include true masters of the grafter's art, and I owe them many invaluable tips, observations and illustrations for my work, particularly in the case of some new discoveries which could not otherwise have been brought to a size where they could serve for descriptions or illustrations. For older plants, *Trichocereus pachanoi* which I originally imported from Ecuador proved to be the best stock because it offsets sufficiently freely to ensure a succession of plants; it is virtually spineless (making grafting a less painful procedure); it increases in diameter as the scion develops; it remains green; the nature of its sap ensures that it readily accepts a graft and feeds it well; and it does not become as woody or exhausted as *Trichocereus spachianus*, once the most popular grafting-stock. One exception is in collections on the Riviera, where sturdy specimens of this latter species can be raised or bought, and considerable successes have been recorded with "on-the-spot" grafting: here, square stakes with an oblique bevel are pushed into the ground alongside the plants, and these stakes have metal strips arched over the grafts to provide the necessary pressure, while the crowns of the scions are protected by a piece of felt; since no transplanting of the stock is called for when using this procedure, the development of the scion is not retarded. *Eriocereus jusbertii*, which is rarely of a size to suit the scion and is also more prone to shrivel, is not now often used, or at most for species which remain fairly small. It has long been accepted that the plants in amateur collections do particularly well when planted out in trays so that the pots can be embedded, but space sometimes forbids this. Planting out in summer is beneficial even where the owner has a greenhouse. Epiphyllums and *Nopalxochia* ("leaf"-cacti), *Zygocactus* (segmented or Christmas cactus), *Epiphyllopsis* (Easter cactus) and above all *Rhipsalis* thrive much better when left in the open air during the main growing period; more buds form and when the plants are brought indoors no stem-segments are dropped, because the shoots have ripened; *Rhipsalis* fills out well, and when it is brought back into the greenhouse or placed on the windowsill the greater warmth induces flower-development. These plants can be suspended from fruit-trees, or placed on a patch of grass provided slug-bait is sprinkled round them. Grown thus *Rhipsalis*—a plant which is not much favoured by collectors—does so much better that these slender-stemmed and relatively hardy specimens become more interesting.

In the light of the foregoing, the reader will see why I do not propose going more deeply into "hints on cultivation". Many books are available on the subject and they provide all the necessary information. I will content myself in the present work with providing for each genus a symbol indicating the appropriate cultural requirements, also notes on any special treatment which may be necessary.

(These symbols are given on page 62, together with the abbreviations used in the text.)

CLASSIFICATION

(*Key to the Categories*)

Leaves present:
    Glochids absent; seeds with soft testa,
      large . . . .   SFam. 1 : **Peireskioideae** K. Sch.
    Glochids present, in part reduced; seeds
      hard, fairly large . . . .   SFam. 2 : **Opuntioideae** K. Sch.
Leaves absent:
    Glochids absent; seeds smaller, not ex-
      tremely hard . . . .   SFam. 3 : **Cereoideae** K. Sch.*

SFam. 1 : Peireskioideae K. Sch.
Key to the Tribes:

Leaves ± normal, not cylindrically reduced;
    flowers not terminal . . . .   Tribe 1 : Peireskieae Br. & R.
Leaves cylindrically reduced; flowers (al-
    ways?) terminal . . . .   Tribe 2 : Maihuenieae Backbg.

Tribe 1 : Peireskieae Br. & R.
Key to the Genera:

Shrubby or tree-like; ovary superior. . . .   1 : **Peireskia** (Plum.) Mill.
    Flowers fairly large, not sessile, clust-
      ered . . . .   SG. 1 : Peireskia
    Flowers small, sessile, 5-lobed . . . .   SG. 2 : Neopeireskia Backbg.
Tree-like; ovary ± inferior . . . .   2 : **Rhodocactus** (Berg.) Knuth

Tribe 2 : Maihuenieae Backbg.
One genus:

Low cushions; leaves not early deciduous,
    short, terete . . . .   3 : **Maihuenia** Phil.

SFam. 2 : Opuntioideae K. Sch.
Key to the Tribes:

Shrubby to tree-like; leaves ± normal or
    veinless and succulent. . . . .   Tribe 1 : Phyllopuntieae Backbg.

---

* In accordance with changes required by the Code of Nomenclature 1961 the SFam. should now be called "Cactoideae". This misleading name will not be used in the present work, so as not to confuse non-specialist readers; instead I have retained the much more appropriate name introduced 70 years ago; after all, the idea of "nom. alt." is a familiar one and it may be possible to protect the older term—which in this case is essential since the members of SFam. 3 are not the only "cactus-like" plants.

Dividing into fleshy shoots; leaves greatly
    reduced, rather small . . . .   Tribe 2: Euopuntieae Backbg.
Shrubby, branches long, slender-cylindric,
    inclined; leaves considerably reduced
    (sole night-flowering taxon) . . . . .   Tribe 3: Pseudopuntieae Backbg.

Tribe 1: Phyllopuntieae Backbg.
Key to the Genera:

With slender subsidiary spines (true glochids
    absent?)
    Flowers completely terminal
        Ovary narrow, sessile . . . .   4: **Quiabentia** Br. & R.
Glochids present
    Flowers not completely terminal
        Ovary in part stalked . . . .   5: **Peireskiopsis** Br. & R.

Tribe 2: Euopuntieae Backbg.
Key to the Subtribes:

Stems cylindrical; if spherical, not con-
    stantly so in cultivation . . . . . .   Subtribe 1: Cylindropuntiinae
                                      Backbg.

Stems spherical, clavate or short-cylindric;
    forms constant in cultivation . . . .   Subtribe 2: Sphaeropuntiinae Backbg.
Stems ± flattened . . . .   Subtribe 3: Platyopuntiinae Backbg.

Subtribe 1: Cylindropuntiinae Backbg.
Key to the Groups*:

Stems cylindric, without sheathed spines . .   Group 1: Austrocylindropuntiae
                                      Backbg.

Stems cylindric, with sheathed spines (in
    part from newer areoles only) . . . .   Group 2: Boreocylindropuntiae
                                      Backbg.

Group 1: Austrocylindropuntiae Backbg.
Key to the Genera:

Flowers not truly terminal; seeds not winged   6: **Austrocylindropuntia** Backbg.
Flowers truly terminal; seeds winged . . .   7: **Pterocactus** K. Sch.

Group 2: Boreocylindropuntiae Backbg.
Key to the Genera:

Flowers not truly terminal, at most subapi-
    cal; ribs not continuous
    Spines sheathed and glochids present . .   8: **Cylindropuntia** (Eng.) Knuth
                                      emend. Backbg.

---

* For the sake of uniformity the term "Sippe" (in English literally meaning "kin" or "clan", but translated for the present work as "Group") used by Alwin Berger in "Die Entwicklungslinien der Kakteen" has been retained here for the relevant taxon, since this was the word then in normal use. Nowadays "Natio" (and "Subnatio") would be preferred.

Flowers apical or terminal
    Spines with reduced sheaths; glochids, if
        present, clearly reduced except those
        of the newer areoles and the ovary
        Flowers apical; ribs continuous . . .   9: **Grusonia** F. Reichenb.
        Flowers and fruits terminal and sun-
          ken; shoot-tip enveloping the fruit,
          clavate at maturity and splitting
          laterally; ribs not continuous . . .   10: **Marenopuntia** Backbg.

Subtribe 2: Sphaeropuntiinae Backbg.
Key to the Groups:

Stems spherical or short-cylindric. . . . .   Group 1: Austrosphaeropuntiae
                                       Backbg.

Stems clavate to ± elongated . . . . . .   Group 2: Boreosphaeropuntiae
                                       Backbg.

Group 1: Austrosphaeropuntiae Backbg.
Key to the Genera:

Stem-segments never united at the base . .   11: **Tephrocactus** Lem. emend.
                                         Backbg.

Stem-segments united at the base . . . . .   12: **Maihueniopsis** Speg.

Group 2: Boreosphaeropuntiae Backbg.
Key to the Genera:

Large taproots not present
  Glochids present
    Spine-sheaths reduced ± to rudiments   13: **Corynopuntia** Knuth
Large taproots present; bodies minute . .
  Glochids ± absent (reduced?)
    Spine-sheaths clearly much reduced   14: **Micropuntia** Daston

Subtribe 3: Platyopuntiinae Backbg.
Key to the Groups:

Main stem continuous . . . .   Group 1: Cauliopuntiae Backbg.
Main stem not continuous, irregularly
    branched
    Flowers of normal structure . . . . .   Group 2: Platyopuntiae Backbg.
    Flowers almost closed, anthers pro-
      jecting . . . .   Group 3: Nopaleae Backbg.

Group 1: Cauliopuntiae Backbg.
Key to the Subgroups:

Branches ± in whorls; flowers with hair-like
    staminodes; seeds few, in part woolly   Subgroup 1: Brasiliopuntiae
                                         Backbg.

Branches ± cruciform; flowers without
    staminodes; seeds woolly (always?)   Subgroup 2: Consoleae Backbg.

Subgroup 1: **Brasiliopuntiae** Backbg.
One Genus only:

Main stem cylindric; new shoots thin . . .   15: **Brasiliopuntia** (K. Sch.) Berg.

Subgroup 2: **Consoleae** Backbg.
One Genus only:

Main stem ± flattened; new shoots thicker   16: **Consolea** Lem.

Group 2: **Platyopuntiae** Backbg.
One Genus only:

Shoots flat; flowers open, without stami-
     nodes; seeds mostly not woolly
     (woolly seeds commoner in spec. of
     southern distribution) . . . . . .   17: **Opuntia** (Tournef.) Mill.

Group 3: **Nopaleae** Backbg.
One Genus only:

Stems elongated; floral limb closed; seeds
     not woolly . . . .   18: **Nopalea** SD.

Tribe 3: **Pseudopuntieae** Backbg.
One Genus only:

Stems thin, long-cylindric; glochids readily
     dropped; leaves minute; flowers with
     long ovary, nocturnal, with revolute
     petals, with hair-development at base
     of inner petals . . . .   19: **Tacinga** Br. & R.

Subfamily 3: **Cereoideae** K. Sch.
Key to the Tribes:

Aerial roots present; plants epiphytic, semi-
     epiphytic or climbing . . . . . .   Tribe 1: Hylocereeae Backbg.
Aerial roots absent; plants terrestrial, except
     low-growing *Pfeiffera*. . . . . . .   Tribe 2: Cereeae Br. & R. emend.
                                                 Backbg.

Tribe 1: **Hylocereeae** Backbg.
Key to the Subtribes:

Mostly pendulous epiphytes with pre-
     dominantly smaller flowers and
     fruits; shoots mostly articulated into
     annual growths . . . .   Subtribe 1: Rhipsalidinae Backbg.
Plants more bushy-erect, with flat shoots;
     flowers and fruits mostly larger
     (fruits never smallish); shoots usually
     not articulated into annual growths   Subtribe 2: Phyllocactinae Backbg.

Plants with long shoots; bodies not flat but cereoid, with several ribs or angles, except for 2 modified flattened and clinging or twining, 3–4-winged plants; flowers with ± longer tubes   Subtribe 3: Hylocereinae Backbg.

Subtribe 1: Rhipsalidinae Backbg.
Key to the Groups:

Flowers appearing laterally (normal flower-insertion) . . . .   Group 1: Rhipsalides Backbg.

Flowers (and shoots) developing from the apex . . . .   Group 2: Epiphylloides Backbg.

Group 1: Rhipsalides Backbg.
Key to the Subgroups:

Flowers tubeless; stem-segments variable in shape . . . .   Subgroup 1: Eurhispalides Backbg.

Flowers with short tubes; segments flat . .   Subgroup 2: Pseudorhipsalides Backbg.

Subgroup 1: Eurhipsalides Backbg.
Key to the Genera & Subgenera:

Flowers tubeless
  Ovary free . . . .   20: **Rhipsalis** Gärtn.
    Stem-segments terete, bristles absent (*Eurhipsalis* K. Sch.) . . . .   SG. 1: **Rhipsalis**
    Segments terete or slightly furrowed, with many bristles . . . .   SG. 2: **Ophiorhipsalis** K. Sch.
    Segments distinctly angled or ribbed   SG. 3: **Goniorhipsalis** K. Sch.

    Segments flat, leaflike or 3-sided, without bristles . . . .   SG. 4: **Phyllorhipsalis** K. Sch.
  Ovary sunken . . . .   21: **Lepismium** Pfeiff.
    Segments narrow and flat or 3-sided; areoles sunken, very bristly (*Eulepismium* Knuth) . . . .   SG. 1: **Lepismium**
    Segments terete . . . .   SG. 2: **Calamorhipsalis** K. Sch.
    Segments 3-angled, articulated, angles and faces then alternating . . . . .   SG. 3: **Epallogogonium** K. Sch.

    Segments continuous, 3-angled; areoles not bristly . . . .   SG. 4: **Trigonorhipsalis** Berg.

    Segments polymorphic, at first slender, 5-angled, later stouter and 3(–4)-angled, in part rounded or the faces sunken; areoles bristly at first, later with only occasional bristles, with thick white woolly flock . . . . . .   SG. 5: **Heteropodium** Backbg.

Subgroup 2: Pseudorhipsalides Backbg.
Key to the Genera:

Flowers with short tubes
    Stem-segments spiny, flat to 3-winged   22: **Acanthorhipsalis** (K. Sch.)
                                                      Br. & R.
    Segments always spineless, flat . . . .   23: **Pseudorhipsalis** Br. & R.

Group 2: Epiphylloides Backbg.
Key to the Subgroups:

Areoles variously situated
  Stem-segments cylindric, clavate or with
    several angles
    Flowers normal, considerably reduced
      in size . . . . SG. 1: Mediorhipsalides Backbg.
  Segments small-opuntioid (rarely
    cylindric-elongated)
    Flowers greatly modified, zygomorphic   SG. 2: Epiphyllanthi Backbg.
Areoles lateral and/or apical
  Segments zygocactoid, offset one above
    the other
    Flowers normal (in part small) to
      greatly modified . . . . SG. 3: Epiphylli Backbg.

Subgroup 1: Mediorhipsalides Backbg.
Key to the Genera:

Stems rounded to clavate, abbreviated or
    elongated
  Areoles mostly minute, indumentum $\pm$
    only on abbreviated new growths;
    flowers from larger apical areoles;
    fruit $\pm$ glabrous . . . . 24: **Hatiora** Br. & R.
Stems terete, articulated
  Areoles more strongly hairy; fruits larger
    than in *Rhipsalis*, bristly . . . . . . 25: **Erythrorhipsalis** Berg.
Stems 2–3–5-angled, usually branching from
    the apex; flowers larger than in the
    preceding
  Areoles situated on the angles, $\pm$ bristly   26: **Rhipsalidopsis** Br. & R.

Subgroup 2: Epiphyllanthi Backbg.
One Genus only:

Stems mostly dwarf-opuntioid, in one in-
    stance cylindric and elongated (only
    an ecotype? acc. Voll), not con-
    spicuously branching from the apex,
    $\pm$ finely spined
  Flowers borne close to the apex, larger,
    zygomorphic . . . . 27: **Epiphyllanthus** Berg.

Subgroup 3: Epiphylli Backbg.
Key to the Genera:

Flowers regular, without a true corolla-tube
    Flowers reduced and Rhipsalis-like, small   28: **Pseudozygocactus** Backbg.
    Flowers larger
        Filaments grouped, stigma-lobes spreading; fruit acutely 5-angled (apical areoles often with many long bristles). . . . .   29: **Epiphyllopsis** (Berg.)
                                    Knuth & Backbg.
        Filaments in 2 groups, stigma-lobes capitate and connivent; apical areoles less bristly; fruit 4-angled . .   30: **Schlumbergera** Lem. non E. Morr.
    Flowers strongly zygomorphic, with a true corolla-tube
        Filaments (and style) curved and projecting, inner series with a basal fine recurved annular membrane; fruit top-shaped, not angular. . . . . .   31: **Zygocactus** K. Sch.

Subtribe 2: Phyllocactinae Backbg.
Only 1 Group: Phyllocacti Backbg.
Key to the Subgroups:

Flowers normal, funnelform . . . .   Subgroup 1: Euphyllocacti Backbg.
Flowers ± modified . . . .   Subgroup 2: Wittiae Backbg.

Subgroup 1: Euphyllocacti Backbg.
Key to the Genera:

Flowers funnelform
    Ovary with bristles and spines . . . . .   32: **Cryptocereus** Alex.
    Ovary with ± stiff bristles . . . .   33: **Marniera** Backbg.
    Ovary only felty . . . .   34: **Lobeira** Alex.
    Ovary glabrous . . . .   35: **Epiphyllum** Haw. (Phyllocactus)
Flowers ± bellshaped-funnelform
    Ovary faintly angular, axils somewhat felty, sometimes with little bristles (night-flowering). . . . .   36: **Eccremocactus** Br. & R.
    Ovary scaly, with 1–4 whitish bristles (day-flowering) . . . .   37: **Pseudonopalxochia** Backbg.
    Ovary small, glabrous (day-flowering). .   38: **Nopalxochia** Br. & R.

Subgroup 2: Wittiae Backbg.
Key to the Genera:

Flowers slender, medium-sized
    Flowers bellshaped-funnelform; ovary spherical . . . .   39: **Chiapasia** Br. & R.
    Flowers not bellshaped, offset above the tube, petals lax, narrow; tube shorter; ovary elongated . . . .   40: **Disocactus** Lindl.

27

Flowers rather small
  Tube narrow, thin
    Limb little opening, not revolute . . .   41 : **Wittia** K. Sch.

Subtribe 3 : Hylocereinae Backbg.
Key to the Groups :

Stems modified and clinging, flat or 3-winged   Group 1 : Strophocerei Backbg.
Stems not modified and clinging, angular or
    many-ribbed; not thin and pen-
    dulous . . . .   Group 2 : Nyctohylocerei Backbg.
Stems thin, pendulous . . . .   Group 3 : Heliohylocerei Backbg.

Group 1 : Strophocerei Backbg.
Key to the Subgroups :

Stems flat, clinging (rarely 3-angled)   . . .   Subgroup 1 : Nyctostrophocerei
                                                    Backbg.
Stems typically 3-angled, winged . . . . .   Subgroup 2 : Heliostrophocerei
                                                    Backbg.

Subgroup 1 : Nyctostrophocerei Backbg.
One Genus only :

Night-flowering; ovary and fruit with felt
    and bristly spines . . . .   42 : **Strophocactus** Br. & R.

Subgroup 2 : Heliostrophocerei Backbg.
One Genus only :

Day-flowering; ovary with hairs and bristles;
    Fruit very spiny . . . .   43 : **Deamia** Br. & R.

Group 2 : Nyctohylocerei Backbg.
Key to the Subgroups :

Ovaries not noticeably scaly, with spines or
    stiff bristles in the axils . . . . . .   Subgroup 1 : Selenicerei Backbg.
Ovaries noticeably densely scaly, axils ± or
    completely glabrous . . . .   Subgroup 2 : Hylocerei Backbg.

Subgroup 1 : Selenicerei Backbg.
Key to the Genera :

Corolla-tube more strongly spiny
  Fruits or ovary not bossed, strongly spiny
    Tube short, stout; ovary with many
      sharp black spines . . . .   44 : **Werckleocereus** Br. & R.
    Tube longer, with ± long hair and
      spines . . . .   45 : **Selenicereus** (Berg.) Br. & R.
  Corolla-tube with a few spines or bristles
    only at the base (47)

Fruits (or ovary) ± bossed at first, laxly
spiny or only hairy (47)
Tube longer, funnelform, scales small,
ovary and fruit spiny . . . . . .   46: **Mediocactus** Br. & R.
Tube shorter, scales curved, ovary with
stiff bristles; fruit hairy . . . . .   47: **Weberocereus** Br. & R.

Subgroup 2: Hylocerei Backbg.
Key to the Genera:

Flowers ± glabrous
Flowers rather small, with almost no tube,
± glabrous . . . .   48: **Wilmattea** Br. & R.
Flowers large, funnelform, glabrous . .   49: **Hylocereus** (Berg.) Br. & R.

Group 3: Heliohylocerei Backbg.
One Genus only:

Stems thin, pendant; flowers ± zygomorphic, diurnal
Tube bristly, or ovary only; fruit
similarly . . . .   50: **Aporocactus** Lem.

Tribe 2: Cereeae Br. & R. emend. Backbg.
Key to the Semitribes:

Southern taxa, having floral characters
differing from those of the north;
many spines or bristles still present
on flowers and fruits of spherical
forms . . . .   Semitribe 1: Austrocereeae Backbg.
Northern taxa, having floral characters
differing from those of the south;
flowers and fruits of the spherical
forms never spiny or bristly . . . .   Semitribe 2: Boreocereeae Backbg.

Semitribe 1: Austrocereeae Backbg.
Key to the Subtribes:

Cereoid forms, in some instances much
reduced: dwarf-cereoid (*Chamaecereus*) and ± spherical (*Pseudo-
lobivia* . . . .   Subtrike 1: Astrocereinae Backbg.
Cactoid forms, ± elongated only in in-
termediates or in older plants . . .   Subtribe 2: Austrocactinae Backbg.

Subtribe 1: Austrocereinae Backbg.
Key to the Groups:

Small, semi-epiphytic to epiphytic shrubs;
ovary and fruit spiny . . . .   Group 1: Pfeifferae Berg.
Small, terrestrial colonies; ovary with some
indumentum, fruit glabrous . . . .   Group 2: Milae Backbg.

29

Erect or rarely prostrate cerei; flowers with ovaries or fruits ± spiny, in part from modified areoles.	Group 3: Corryocerei Backbg.
Erect, tree-like cerei; ovaries and fruits glabrous	Group 4: Gymnanthocerei Backbg.
Erect to prostrate cerei; flowers specialised, narrow-limbed or zygomorphic. . .	Group 5: Loxanthocerei Backbg.
Erect cerei; flowers ± funnelform, hairy; only intermediates with ± bristly but never spiny ovary; fruit ± hairy . .	Group 6: Trichocerei Berg. emend. Backbg.

Group 1: Pfeifferae Berg.
One Genus only:

Plants with small flowers and fruits; fruit spiny, small-spherical.	51: **Pfeiffera** SD.

Group 2: Milae Backbg.
One Genus only:

Plants with small flowers and fruits; fruits almost completely naked; stems soft-fleshy	52: **Mila** Br. & R.

Group 3: Corryocerei Backbg.
Key to the Subgroups:

Flowers diurnal, not constricted; in 2 genera from modified areoles.	Subgroup 1: Heliocorryocerei Backbg.
Flowers nocturnal, constricted; areoles never modified.	Subgroup 2: Nyctocorryocerei Backbg.

Subgroup 1: Heliocorryocerei Backbg.
Key to the Genera:

Flowering areoles not modified	
Flowers borne high on the flanks, mostly larger, fruits likewise; tube bell-shaped, not spiny	53: **Corryocactus** Br. & R.
Flowers (usually) borne near the apex, smaller, the rather thin-skinned fruits similarly; tube not bellshaped, spiny	54: **Erdisia** Br. & R.
Flowering areoles modified	
Areoles large and bulbous to cylindrically elongated	
Flowers shortly funnelform; tube not clearly spiny	55: **Neoraimondia** Br. & R.
Areoles somewhat round and thickened	
Flowers more cylindric; tube with long spines	56: **Neocardenasia** Backbg.

Genera which have not been described or are insufficiently known:
(Day or night flowering?)

Flowers bellshaped, white; plants forming
      branching trees . . . .   57: **Yungasocereus** Ritt.
Flowers black and white(?), tubular, with
      dense wool and bristles; tree-like . .   58: **Lasiocereus** Ritt.

Subgroup 2: Nyctocorryocerei Backbg.
Key to the Genera:

Large, erect columns, with constrictions
      marking annual growth
    Buds of normal structure
      Inner petals not very narrow
        Fruit fairly large, spiny . . . . .   59: **Armatocereus** Backbg.
    Buds enclosed within the ovary-envelope
      Fruit long, angular, ± spineless . .   60: **Calymmanthium** Ritt.
Slender, low-growing columns, in groups;
      no demarcation of annual growth
    Inner petals very narrow
      Fruit rather small, only 1.3 cm $\varnothing$
        (2.5–4 cm long) . . . .   61: **Brachycereus** Br. & R.

Group 4: Gymnanthocerei Backbg.
Key to the Genera:

Flowers at most with traces of felt
    Scales small, especially on ovary . . .   62: **Jasminocereus** Br. & R.

Flowers completely glabrous
    Limb straight; fruit not dry
      Scales larger
        Scales densely imbricate. . . . . .   63: **Stetsonia** Br. & R.
        Scales laxly outspread, elongated . .   64: **Browningia** Br. & R.
        Scales broad, shrivelling after an-
          thesis, ± absent on the fruit . . .   65: **Gymnocereus** Backbg.
    Limb somewhat oblique; fruit dry
      Scales dense on tube and ovary . . . .   66: **Azureocereus** Akers & Johnson

Group 5: Loxanthocerei Backbg.
Key to the Subgroups:

Juvenile forms always cereoid . . . . . .   Subgroup 1: Euloxanthocerei
                                         Backbg.
Juvenile forms in part spherical or short . .   Subgroup 2: Brachyloxanthocerei
                                         Backbg.

Subgroup 1: Euloxanthocerei Backbg.
Key to the Genera:

Flowers always cylindric; limb straight,
      moderately broad, not opening to
      funnelform; tube straight, in part

31

with hairs inside (larger shrubs). . .   67: **Clistanthocereus** Backbg.

Flowers not always cylindric; opening ± funnelform in 68–70, ± oblique and narrower in 71–73, 77 and 78, cleistocactoid-cylindric and with short narrow limb in 74–76

  Stems hairless (at most with apical hairy felt)

    Flowers (perianth) broader, ± zygomorphic

      Flowering areoles without bristle-zone

        Flowers with a funnelform throat, ± zygomorphic

          Tube round, mostly ± bent

            Perianth without inner, shorter series ± pressed against the style . . . .   68: **Loxanthocereus** Backbg.

            Perianth with an inner, shorter series pressed against the style; petals lax and longer or more widely spreading. . . . .   69: **Winterocereus** Backbg. nom.
                             nov. (Winteria Ritt.)

      Flowers very zygomorphic

        Tube compressed . . . . . .   70: **Bolivicereus** Card.

      Tube circular, throat rather narrow, not opening to funnelform   71: **Borzicactus** Ricc.

      Flowering areoles with bristle-zone

        Tube-indumentum lacking bristles

          Tube ± compressed . . . . .   72: **Seticereus** Backbg.

        Tube-indumentum with bristles

          Tube round . . . .   73: **Akersia** Buin.

    Flowers opening only very slightly

      Tube and fruit bristly . . . .   74: **Seticleistocactus** Backbg.

      Tube and fruit without bristles

        Tube in part curved or bent, or sometimes ± straight

          Flowering-zone not bristly. . .   75: **Cleistocactus** Lem.

          Flowering-zone bristly . . . .   76: **Cephalocleistocactus** Ritt.

Stems usually hairy

  Cephalium absent . . . .   77: **Oreocereus** (Berg.) Ricc.

  Cephalium apical . . . .   78: **Morawetzia** Backbg.

Subgroup 2: Brachyloxanthocerei Backbg.

Key to the Genera:

Flowers hairy

  Plants eventually columnar

    Floral limb ± closed, not oblique; anthers projecting; tube-base with woolly ring . . . .   79: **Denmoza** Br. & R.

    Floral limb open, oblique; without

woolly ring at tube-base. . . . . . 80: **Arequipa** Br. & R.
Plants remaining ± spherical
  Floral limb oblique; anthers directed
    upwards . . . . 81: **Submatucana** Backbg.
Flowers glabrous
  Plants spherical to ± elongated
    Floral limb ± oblique; petals mostly
    rather strongly recurved. . . . . . 82: **Matucana** Br. & R.

Group 6: Trichocerei Berg. emend. Backbg.
Key to the Subgroups:

Tall, erect or lower, more slender columns;
  flowers nocturnal, in part open the
  next day, the tubes then not abbrev-
  iated and broadly funnelform . . . Subgroup 1: Nyctotrichocerei
                            Backbg.

Erect, stoutly columnar and medium-tall, or
  dwarf, slender and basally offsetting
  cerei, with abbreviated, broadly funnelform, diurnal flowers; or bodies
  ± cylindrically reduced, the flowers
  then open only during the day . . . Subgroup 2: Heliotrichocerei
                            Backbg.

Subgroup 1: Nyctotrichocerei Backbg.
Key to the Genera:

Floral tubes ± bristly, ± hairy
  Flowers narrowly cylindric, tubes with a
    few bristles; fruit with some in-
    dumentum only at the base . . . . 83: **Samaipaticereus** Card.
  Flowers bellshaped, with fairly dense
    bristles (fruit similarly above) . . . 84: **Philippicereus** Backbg.
  Flowers long-tubed, slender, medium-
    sized, mostly autogamous, petals
    narrow; ovary sometimes bristly;
    fruit not bristly; body slender, dwarf-
    cereoid. . . . . 85: **Setiechinopsis** (Backbg.) De Haas
Flower-tube never bristly, only hairy (fruit
  similarly)
  Body never cactoid in juveniles
    Limb never conspicuously oblique
      Stouter columns with funnelform
        flowers
        Scales not very large or not pro-
          jecting, those on the fruit not
          conspicuously triangular . . 86: **Trichocereus** (Berg.) Ricc.
        Taller cerei; flowers more large-
          funnelform, more nocturnal   SG. 1: **Trichocereus**
        Medium-tall to lower-growing
          or colony-forming cerei;
          flowers shortly funnelform,

remaining open next day (in
part for several days) . . . .   SG. 2: **Medioeulychnia** Backbg.

Scales on ovary large, ± projecting, those on the fruit triangular and red (inclined
plants; intermediate to *Erio-
cereus*?), axils strongly hirsute   87: **Roseocereus** (Backbg.) Backbg.

Tree-like cerei, flowers shortly campanulate, with silky hairs (hairs
in part very short), nocturnal,
remaining open the next day (as
in SG. 2 of *Trichocereus*)

Scales fairly dense on tube and
fruit . . . .   88: **Eulychnia** Phil.

Lower or slender columnar cacti
Flowers bellshaped to funnelform,
densely scaly . . . .   89: **Rauhocereus** Backbg.

Flowers funnelform, slenderer
than in *Trichocereus*, only
slightly hairy . . . .   90: **Haageocereus** Backbg.

Dwarf plants; floral tube long, thin   91: **Pygmaeocereus** Johns. & Backbg.

Floral limb mostly ± oblique, tube
bent ± to S-shape, densely scaly;
fruit only slightly hairy
Nocturnal and also diurnal? . . .   92: **Weberbauerocereus** Backbg.

Body at first ± cactoid (reduced), in part
columnar
Floral limb straight
Flowers long, ± slender funnelform,
with hairs only . . . .   93: **Echinopsis** Zucc.

Subgroup 2: **Heliotrichocerei** Backbg.
Key to the Genera:

Body thick-columnar, eventually branching
Floral tube or fruit bristly; flower broadly
funnelform
Flowers borne near the apex . . . .   94: **Leucostele** Backbg.
Floral tube and fruit not bristly. . . . .   95: **Helianthocereus** Backbg.
Flowers apical or high on the body   SG. 1: **Helianthocereus**

Body slenderer, forming lower colonies
Flowers borne high on the sides . .   SG. 1: **Neohelianthocereus** Backbg.

Body dwarf-cereoid
Flowers slender-funnelform . . . .   96: **Chamaecereus** Br. & R.
Body ± flattened-spherical and reduced,
never elongated
Flowers slender-funnelform, similar
to *Echinopsis*, rather slenderer,
mostly shorter; ribs ± notched to
hatchet-shaped . . . .   97: **Pseudolobivia** (Backbg.) Backbg.

34

Subtribe 2: Austrocactinae Backbg.
Key to the Groups:

Flowers from older areoles, ± on the sides or lower; ± elongated-funnelform	Group 1: Lobiviae Backbg.
Flowers from younger areoles nearer the apex, never low on the body, mostly shorter	Group 2: Austroechinocacti Backbg.

Group 1: Lobiviae Backbg.
Key to the Subgroups:

Tube and fruit hairy (fruit in one case spiny)	Subgroup 1: Eriolobiviae Backbg.
Tube and fruit hairy, with slender bristles .	Subgroup 2: Chaetolobiviae Backbg.
Tube and fruit glabrous	Subgroup 3: Gymnolobiviae Backbg.

Subgroup 1: Eriolobiviae Backbg.
Key to the Genera:

Flowers funnelform, nocturnal, self-fertile or autogamous; fruit spiny	98: **Acantholobivia** Backbg.
Flowers wide-funnelform; fruit hairy	
Scales of the tube mucronate	
Flower-base with a ring of hairs . . .	99: **Acanthocalycium** Backbg.
Flowers funnelform, opening variously, ring of hairs absent; fruit hairy	100: **Lobivia** Br. & R.
Inner petals ± erect to incurved, outer ones recurved	SG. 1: **Lobivia**
Corolla broadly funnelform to rotate . .	SG. 2: **Neolobivia** Backbg.

Subgroup 2: Chaetolobiviae Backbg.
Key to the Genera:

Flowers slender-funnelform, sparsely hairy and bristly	101: **Mediolobivia** Backbg.
Tubercles replacing ribs; plant spherical	
Style completely free	SG. 1: **Mediolobivia**
Ribs tuberculate but clearly discernible, or long-cylindric species in part with small tubercles	
Style mostly ± united	SG. 2: **Pygmaeolobivia** Backbg.
Flowers appearing to be stalked, petals projecting	
Style completely united with the tube .	102: **Aylostera** Speg.

Subgroup 3: Gymnolobiviae Backbg.
Key to the Genera:

Flowers slender-funnelform, without hairs or bristles	
Taproot and furrow absent; spines only fine, bristly; areoles circular	103: **Rebutia** K. Sch.

Style entirely free . . . . SG. 1: **Rebutia**
Style somewhat united . . . . . . SG. 2: **Neorebutia** Bewge.
Taproot present; spines ± stiffer; areoles
    narrow, long . . . . 104: **Sulcorebutia** Backbg.

Group 2: Austroechinocacti Backbg.

The primary task of phytography (plant-description) is to record accurately the overall picture of natural objects. However, systematic arrangement nowadays requires that factors of geographical distribution should be taken into consideration as well, related both to the occurrence of the individual, and its place in the distribution overall. Phylogenetic considerations are more a theoretical specialism, whereas any phytographic classification must be based on a carefully considered and deliberate arranging of the facts. Systematic recognition must be given on the one hand to the clearly discernible dual nature of the total distribution, into a major northern, and a major southern zone (see the taxa bearing the prefixes "Austro" and "Boreo"). On the other hand it is essential, for the sake of clarity, to retain some of the conventional distinctions, e.g. the generic segregation of *Trichocereus* and *Echinopsis*, which have long been seen as vital. For the same reason the genus *Pseudolobivia*—some of whose species bear a closer resemblance to *Lobivia* than to *Echinopsis*—has been kept distinct. Nature's inventiveness obviously transcends the production of forms and transitional stages; her works take no account either of human theoreticians or of our urge to classify. Nevertheless she presents us with sufficient data to enable us to perform the task—e.g. the duality of the total distribution referred to above. Because of earlier failure to recognise this, no convincing systematic arrangement has yet been developed. The most conspicuous difficulty has been a satisfactory arrangement to deal with the globular cacti of the Pacific zone and their East Andean relatives (*Pyrrhocactus*). The southern Andean elevation is very ancient, so that from time immemorial it has prevented any spread from east to west. Moreover we have no precise knowledge of the genesis of the Pacific species. Phytographic classification, relying on facts and ignoring theory, requires us to assume that the genera or species of the South American west coast have evolved along their own separate lines for long periods of time, possibly from a common ancestral population, and this has sometimes led to certain similarities. If this line of reasoning is accepted, the distinctions are more sharply focussed and the systematic arrangement of this group of the Cactaceae becomes much simpler. Care is of course still needed in diagnosis; the characters of the northern and southern genera must be compared; and the features established as separating the East Andean group from that of the Pacific must be given full weight.
For this reason I have separated the "Austroechinocacti" into an "Eastern Branch" and a "Western Branch", since this harmonizes the systematic arrangement with the geological or phylogenetic facts.

(Group 2: Austroechinocacti): Eastern Branch

Key to the Genera:
Flowers (or ovary and fruit) spiny (spines in
    part bristly
Flowers funnelform, conspicuous; body
    soft . . . . 105: **Austrocactus** Br. & R.
Flowers short, conspicuous, ± urnshaped
    (spines bristly). . . . . 106: **Pyrrhocactus** Berg. emend.
                                   Backbg.

36

Flowers small, spiny, ± tubeless, inner
   petals curved inwards . . . . . .   107 : **Brasilicactus** Backbg.
Floral tube ± bristly (reduced in *Blossfel-*
   dia); tube ± hairy
   Flowers ± funnelform to small and ±
     tubeless
    Flowers conspicuous; fruits drying to
     thin-membranous . . . .   108 : **Parodia** Speg.
    Flowers short, moderately large, set
     in a woolly crown; fruit berry-like,
     lengthening at maturity . . . . . .   109 : **Wigginsia** D. M. Port.
                      (Malacocarpus SD. non Fisch. &
                                Mey.)

    Flowers quite large, short-tubed, open-
     ing fully; fruit fleshy, spherical,
     splitting basally; crown woolly . . .   110 : **Eriocactus** Backbg.
    Flowers funnelform, medium-large to
     quite large, tube usually longer . . .   111 : **Notocactus** (K. Sch.) Berg.
                                      emend. Backbg.

     Fruit small-spherical, fleshy, splitting   SG. 1 : **Notocactus**
     Fruit elongated at maturity, in part
      becoming soft or disintegrating. .   SG. 2 : **Neonotocactus** Backbg.
    Flowers small, somewhat funnelform,
     with bristles above; fruit small-
     spherical, with bristles above; seeds
     not dust-fine (flowers often cleisto-
     gamous or autogamous). . . . . .   112 : **Frailea** Br. & R.
    Flowers minute, funnelform to bell-
     shaped (mostly autogamous?),
     bristles missing on tube and fruit;
     seeds dust-fine, with a larger hilum   113 : **Blossfeldia** Werd.
Flowers and fruit without bristles, only hairs
   or traces of felt present
   Flowers stoutly funnelform, hairy, the
    spherical desiccating fruit similarly
    (body large, spherical) . . . . .   114 : **Soehrensia** Backbg.
   Flowers slender, inner petals incurved;
    tube, ovary and fruit with traces of
    felt only; fruit dehiscing basally,
    seeds falling out . . . .   115 : **Oroya** Br. & R.
Flowers and fruit glabrous, only scaly
   Flowers larger, ± funnelform, tube with
    larger scales, fruit similarly . . . .   116 : **Gymnocalycium** Pfeiff.
   Flowers larger, ± urnshaped, tube absent
    Fruit stout, scaly. . . . .   117 : **Brachycalycium** Backbg.
   Flowers ± small, fruit similarly
    Bodies in part separated from the tap-
    root by a stalk-like section
    Fruit small-spherical, indehiscent   118 : **Weingartia** Werd.
    Bodies flat, on a thick taproot
    Fruit minute, with very few seeds   119 : Neowerdermannia Frič
                        (now classified as **Weingartia**
                                 Werd.)

(Group 2: Austrocechinocacti): Pacific Branch
Key to the Genera:

Plants eventually stout-cylindric, apex not
    felted; up to 1½ m; fruit fleshy . . .   120: **Rodentiophila** Ritt. (not
                                           described)

Plants never becoming stout-cylindric; fruit
    not fleshy
  Apex ± felted, sometimes ± glabrous
    Flowers funnelform, opening fully
      Bristles present on the flower
        Flowers not tubeless, not dioe-
          cious
          Tube ± hairy, ovary and fruit
            similarly . . . .   121: **Neochilenia** Backbg.
          Tube, ovary and fruit with only
            traces of felt. . . . . . .   122: **Horridocactus** Backbg.
        Flowers tubeless, dioecious . . .   123: **Delaetia** Backbg.
      Bristles absent on the flower
        Tube fairly short; ovary and
          fruit densely hairy . . . .   124: **Reicheocactus** Backbg.
    Flowers with a stalk-like tube; inner
      petals connivent
      Bristles present on upper part of tube
        and fruit
        Tube, ovary and fruit with only
          traces of felt. . . . . . .   125: **Neoporteria** Br. & R.
                                          emend. Backbg.

Plants large, robustly spherical, with apical
    felt
  Flowers bellshaped-funnelform, with de-
    nse white hairs, with bristles above,
    fruit similarly and dehiscing basally .   126: **Eriosyce** Phil.
Plants spherical to elongated; apex felted
  Flowers short-funnelform, rather small,
    laxly hairy, bristly above (fruit sim-
    ilarly)
    Fruit ± elongated at maturity; seeds,
      in part, in a membranous pocket . .   127: **Islaya** Backbg.
  Flowers and fruits with woolly hairs,
    otherwise similar to *Copiapoa* . . .   128: **Pilocopiapoa** Ritt.
  Flowers ± tubeless
    Flower and fruit glabrous
      Fruit splitting above at maturity (two
        forms: cereoid and cushion-
        forming plants) . . . .   129: **Copiapoa** Br. & R.

Semitribe 2: Boreocereeae Backbg.
Key to the Subtribes:

Cereoid forms, in some genera (*Echino-
    cereus*, *Arthrocereus*) greatly reduced
    to dwarf; with one ± cactoid but

cephalium-bearing branch (*Cepha-locacti*) . . . . Subtribe 1: Boreocereinae Backbg.

Cactoid forms (without cephalium), varying in size from the giant to the dwarf (parallelism to the southern zone of the cactoid plants); flowers never with spines or bristles (as in many S. American genera), in some cases borne in the axils (never known in the S. American genera) . . . . . . Subtribe 2: Boreocactinae Backbg.

Subtribe 1: Boreocereinae Backbg.
Key to the Groups:

Shrubby to tree-like
> Flowers with a line of reduction: tube with spines to bristles or only hairs
>> Tubes broadly funnelform; if more cylindric, then the limb is shorter; fruit in part glabrous (nocturnal and diurnal flowers) . . . . Group 1: Leptocerei Berg.
> Flowers ± cylindric-bellshaped, small, with or without a ring of hairs inside
>> Tubes densely set with scales, hairs and bristles
>> (Flowers nocturnal?) . . . . Group 2: Leocerei Backbg.

Small cerei, grouped or laxly branching, with soft flesh
> Flowers funnelform, spiny to ± bristly (diurnal) . . . . Group 3: Echinocerei Backbg.

Shrubby, larger to small
> Flowers ± slender-funnelform, larger (nocturnal)
>> Tubes spiny-bristly to only hairy . . . Group 4: Nyctocerei Berg.
>> emend. Backbg.

Shrubby, erect to prostrate
> Flowers variously sized, ± funnelform, the limb in part narrow and oblique, with spines or bristly spines (diurnal)
>> Tubes long to short. . . . . Group 5: Heliocerei Backbg.

Large, erect columnar cacti (only *Hertricho-cereus* is bushy and lower)
> Flowers varying from funnelform to bellshaped or more cylindric, moderately large, medium-sized to smaller, in one case (*Polaskia*) quite small
> Tubes with a complete line of reduction from spiny-bristly to glabrous or naked; fruits similarly, although in part spiny at first; in one branch of the Group which has bristly, hairy or glabrous flowers, various types of cephalium-development occur: lat-

39

eral and sometimes eventually encircling or apical, in part with subsequent growth continuing beyond (parallelism to some genera of *Cephalocerei*; day or night-flowering (in some cases not known)	Group 6: Pachycerei Berg. emend. Backbg.

Broadly branching, semi-treelike to erect-shrubby
  Flowers small, glabrous, usually several together from one areole
    Tubes very short, glabrous (day or night-flowering)	Group 7: Polyanthocerei Backbg.
Bushy-shrubby, erect to inclined, or tree-like
  Flowers funnelform, ± scaly; tubes and ovaries glabrous (night-flowering) .	Group 8: Gymnocerei Berg. emend. Backbg.

Shrubby to tree-like, erect
  Flowers from ± modified areoles, ± bellshaped to funnelform-bellshaped or ± cylindric; flowering zone with longer bristles, with ribs in part dissolving, with hair-development (up to complete reduction), with cephalia of various types (parallelism to corresponding stages in the *Pachycerei* although here the cephalia are much more compact, corresponding to the stout stems), lateral, in part in a groove, or apical
    Tubes with felt, hairs, bristles, to glabrous and naked, with all intermediate stages; in one case [*Castellanosia*: bellshaped flowers] day-flowering, otherwise always nocturnal	Group 9: Cephalocerei Backbg.
Spherical plants with apical cephalia (branch of the *Cephalocerei*?)
  Flowers small to fairly large; fruit a berry
    Tubes glabrous (day or night-flowering)	Group 10: Cephalocacti Backbg.

Group 1: Leptocerei Berg.
Key to the Subgroups

Flowers funnelform or (*Neoabbottia*) more cylindrical (nocturnal)	Subgroup 1: Nyctoleptocerei Backbg.
Flowers bellshaped-cylindric, stout, rather short (diurnal).	Subgroup 2: Helioleptocerei Backbg.

Subgroup 1: Nyctoleptocerei Backbg.
Key to the Genera:

Tall, bushy shrubs with curving shoots and few prominent ribs
 Flowers large, mostly spiny, fruit similarly; perianth funnelform . . . . .   130: **Acanthocereus** (Berg.) Br. & R.
Sparsely shrubby to (in part dimorphic) plants with virgate shoots; with taproots (in part stouter)
 Flowers slender-funnelform, with downcurving perianth; tube, ovary and fruit with ± stiff bristly spines . . .   131: **Peniocereus** (Berg.) Br. & R.
Tree-like plants with few ribs
 Flowers large-funnelform, with spines on the tube ± reduced; with a ring of felt above the nectary
  Fruit pear-shaped, glabrous . . . .   132: **Dendrocereus** Br. & R.
 Flowers cylindric, short-limbed, with only short hairs
  Fruit ovoid, glabrous (flowers borne either high on the flank or apically, in part from a ± felty zone); buds bristly-spiny . . . .   133: **Neoabbottia** Br. & R.

Subgroup 2: Helioleptocerei Backbg.
One Genus only:

Prostrate and bushy to tall-shrubby and ± tree-like, mostly with thin ribs
 Flowers bellshaped-cylindric, spiny
  Fruit ± spiny . . . .   134: **Leptocereus** (Berg.) Br. & R.

Group 2: Leocerei Backbg.
Key to the Genera:

Plants with thin stems (night-flowering?)
 Flowers small, no ring of hairs inside
  Tube hairy and in part spiny-bristly, with dense scales (flowering areoles with thicker wool) . . . .   135: **Leocereus** Br. & R.
Plants tree like
 Flowers small, with interior ring of longer hairs
  Tube only hairy (flower short-limbed)   136: **Zehntnerella** Br. & R.

Group 3: Echinocerei Backbg.
Key to the Genera:

Plants low-growing, robust, erect, solitary (cylindric), to ± prostrate, more slender and quite strongly branching to colony-forming

Flowers shortly to long-funnelform,
spiny; fruits similarly . . . . . .   137: **Echinocereus** Eng.
Plants slender, with flexible, thin to long and
branching stems; with tuberous
roots
Flowers quite small-funnelform, they and
the fruits with ± stiff bristly spines .   138: **Wilcoxia** Br. & R.

Group 4: Nyctocerei Berg. emend. Backbg.
Key to the Genera:

Shrubs with fairly slender branches or
shoots, ± erect to prostrate
Flowers funnelform, apical, or in part
from the apex of the previous year
which is marked by a thickening of
the stem
Tube ± long, bristly-spiny
Fruit bristly-spiny . . . .   139: **Nyctocereus** (Berg.) Br. & R.
Flowers conspicuously or fairly large-
funnelform
Tube and ovary ± hairy
Fruit red, ± slightly hairy, in part
spiny, dehiscent . . . .   140: **Eriocereus** (Berg.) Ricc.
Fruit yellowish, with felt only, inde-
hiscent . . . .   141: **Harrisia** Britton
Low-growing plants, in part arising from
larger woody roots
Flowers ± slender-funnelform, ± hairy
(fruit similarly) . . . .   142: **Arthrocereus** Berg.
Tube thin, faintly hairy . . . . . .   SG. 1: **Arthrocereus**
Tube stouter, fairly densely hairy . . .   SG. 2: **Cutakia** Backbg.
Plants stouter, low and bushy or prostrate
Flowers with a slender tube
Tube spiny only below
Fruit or ovary spiny . . . . . .   143: **Machaerocereus** Br. & R.

Group 5: Heliocerei Backbg.
Key to the Genera:

Flowers straight-limbed
Stems fairly soft, with few angles (3–4 or
somewhat more), inclined-shrubby
Flowers large-funnelform
Tube medium-long, spiny
Fruit or ovary spiny . . . . . .   144: **Heliocereus** (Berg.) Br. & R.
Stems more rigid, thin to stouter, ±
prostrate, freely branching to form
colonies
Flowers rather small
Tube short, densely spiny
Fruit or ovary spiny

(Fruit spherical, densely spiny) 145: **Bergerocactus** Br. & R.
Flowers ± zygomorphic
  Stems slender, weaker, in part erect or
    curved
    Flowers with a narrow tube
      Ovary only sometimes spiny
        Fruit spiny . . . . 146: **Rathbunia** Br. & R.

Group 6: **Pachycerei** Berg. emend. Backbg.
Key to the Genera:

Plants without cephalium-development
  Stems robust, erect
    Flowers without parchmenty scales
      Flowers small; petals recurved
        Tube very short
          Ovary densely scaly
            Fruit shortly spiny 147: **Polaskia** Backbg.
      Flowers larger
        Tube or flower not constricted
          Flowers bellshaped, apical
            Tube and ovary hairy and
            bristly
              Fruit spiny . . . . 148: **Lemaireocereus** Br. & R.
                                          emend. Backbg.

          Flowers funnelform-bellshaped
            Tube densely felty
              Ovary densely felty, ±
              bristly
                Fruit with ± long bristly
                  spines or only felty . . 149: **Pachycereus** (Berg.) Br. & R.
        Flowers funnelform
          Tube with long hairs and
          dense bristles
            Ovary hairy and bristly
              Fruit spiny . . . . . 150: **Heliabravoa** Backbg.
          Tube with felt and short hairs,
           sometimes with a bristle in
           the axils
            Ovary bristly-spiny
              Fruit spiny . . . . . 151: **Marshallocereus** Backbg.
          Tube glabrous, distantly scaly
           Ovary spiny above
            Fruit (shortly) spiny 152: **Rooksbya** Backbg.
          Tube ± glabrous or shortly
           felty
           Ovary shortly felty
            Fruit spiny . . . . . 153: **Rittereocereus** Backbg.
          Tube with traces only of felt
           Ovary similarly
           Fruit only sometimes
             with minute spines . . 154: **Carnegiea** Br. & R. non Perkins
        Flowers cylindric-bellshaped to

more broadly limbed
Tube glabrous, scaly
    Fruit ± glabrous to in
    part with bristly spine-
    lets and a ± felty pad .   155: **Neobuxbaumia** Backbg.
Ovary not constricted;
    scale-axils on fruit ±
    felty, sometimes bristly
    or ± reduced; scales in
    part with a desiccating
    appendage and then de-
    ciduous (Dawson) . . .   SG. 1: **Neobuxbaumia**
Ovary constricted; flowers
    cylindric-bellshaped, not
    cylindric-tubular; ovary
    with fairly large scales
    but indumentum com-
    pletely reduced . . . .   SG. 2: **Crassocereus** Backbg.
Flowers cylindric-funnelform
Tube with thick, fleshy scales,
    strongly felty, spiny
Ovary felty, spiny
    Fruit with fleshy wall,
    with felt and spines . .   156: **Pterocereus** McDoug. & Mir.
Tube or flower constricted
Flowers rather narrow-cylindric,
    shortly hairy
Tube with solitary bristles
Ovary only felty
    Fruit spiny (aroles bear-
    ing more than one
    flower each). . . . .   157: **Marginatocereus** (Backbg.)
                                         Backbg.

Tube not bristly
Ovary bristly
    Fruit spiny . . . . . .   158: **Stenocereus** (Berg.) Ricc.
    Fruit (and ovary) felty,
    only sometimes with a
    few bristles . . . . .   159: **Isolatocereus** (Backbg.)   Backbg.
Flowers with parchmenty scales
Flowers quite large, broad-
  funnelform
    Tube with dense, recurved
    scales, felty
    Ovary similarly, bristly
    Fruit (felty, with
    bristly spines?) re-
    putedly dry . . . .   160: **Anisocereus** Backbg.
Flowers shortly bellshaped, smaller
    Tube with triangular scales,
    glabrous
    Ovary and fruit with dry
    scales, glabrous

Fruit fleshy . . . . . 161: **Escontria** Rose
Stems thinner, arching to prostrate
Flowers funnelform, only medium-sized (morning-flowering)
Tube with few scales, glabrous
Ovary (scales) slightly felty, with tiny spines (Br. & R.), but these not constant or developing later (as the fruit starts to ripen?)
Fruit tuberculate, small, spiny, drying up and splitting basally ("like *Oreocereus*": Br. & R., The Cact. IV: 274) . . . 162: **Hertrichocereus** Backbg.
Plants with cephalioid development
Stems large, erect
Apical tufts or cephalia of felt, hairs or modified spines
Cephalium of hairy felt and/or more strongly modified spines
Flowers bellshaped, with dense hairs and bristles
Ovary and fruit similarly . . 163: **Mitrocereus** (Backbg.) Backbg.
Cephalium apical, hairy, with new growth extending beyond it
Flowers ± bellshaped to cylindrical-funnelform
Tube with small scales, some felt and sometimes short bristles
Ovary and fruit hairy, fruit with short spines. . . . . 164: **Neodawsonia** Backbg.
Cephalium lateral or encircling stem, of hairs or in part bristles
Cephalium widening to eventually encircling, of white wool with bristly spines
Flowers broad-funnelform, yellowish to pink, hairy
Fruit violet-red, slightly hairy 165: **Cephalocereus** Pfeiff.
Cephalium of long bristles, later irregularly widening, also decurrent laterally, interspersed only with short wool
Flowers ± cylindric
Tube with flaky felt and few bristles
Ovary similarly but bristles mostly in the upper part
Fruit with a few scales, with wool and longer bristles above (seeds comma-shaped) . . . 166: **Backebergia** H. Bravo
Cephalium of hairs and bristles, always(?) on one side only, on

45

tapering shoot-tips
Flowers shortly bellshaped
Tube ± scaly, glabrous
Ovary (probably also fruit)
naked . . . .   167: **Haseltonia** Backbg.

Group 7: Polyanthocerei Backbg.
Key to the Subgroups:

Tree-like plants with broad crowns, generally branching more freely above
Without longer spines from flowering
areoles (day-flowering) . . . . . .   Subgroup 1: Heliopolyanthocerei
Backbg.

Broadly bushy plants with stouter stems,
mostly branching from the base
In some cases with longer spines from
flowering areoles (night-flowering) .   Subgroup 2: Nyctopolyanthocerei
Backbg.

Subgroup 1: Heliopolyanthocerei Backbg.
One Genus only:

Flowers small, sometimes several simul-
taneously
Tube ± absent
Ovary spherical, with rudimentary
scales
Fruit naked . . . .   168: **Myrtillocactus** Cons.

Subgroup 2: Nyctopolyanthocerei Backbg.
One Genus only:

Tube short but present, slender, shortly
scaly
Ovary with several tiny scales
Fruit small, glabrous or sometimes
with tiny spines . . . .   169: **Lophocereus** (Berg.) Br. & R.

Group 8: Gymnocerei Berg. emend. Backbg.
Key to the Genera:

Flowers ± curved or bent, bellshaped above
the tube
Tube with large scales, stoutly short-
funnelform, scaly, glabrous
Ovary short, densely scaly, glabrous
Fruit small, with protuberances,
glabrous, with semilunate scales .   170: **Brasilicereus** Backbg.
Flowers slender-cylindric, glabrous,
medium-sized; the entire dried-up flower
persisting and not just the style . . . . .   171: **Monvillea** Br. & R.
Tube with small scales, glabrous

Ovary and fruit ± spherical . . . .   SG. 1 : **Monvillea**
Ovary and fruit slender-oblong (fruit
  ± clavate or ellipsoid) . . . . .   SG. 2 : **Ebneria** Backbg.
Ovary and fruit oblong to ± ovoid   SG. 3 : **Hummelia** Backbg.
Flowers very large, falling after anthesis;
  style persisting
Tube only slightly scaly; fruit smooth . .   172 : **Cereus** Mill.
Fruit dehiscent . . . .   SG. 1 : **Cereus**
Fruit indehiscent. . . . .   SG. 2 : **Neocereus** Backbg.

Group 9: **Cephalocerei** Backbg.
Key to the Subgroups:

True cephalium absent, but with longer
  spines from flowering areoles, or with
  ± areolar hairs in the flowering zone   SGr. 1 : Acephalocerei Backbg.
Mass of wool or hairs from normal areoles,
  forming a pseudocephalium; ribs not
  resolving; with lidded fruit (flowers
  very small) . . . .   SGr. 2 : Hemicephalocerei Backbg.
Cephalia of different types, lateral, zoned, in
  part from a furrow, or as a thickened
  mass of hairy felt and bristles, or as
  an apical tuft with hairs and bristles,
  or developed afresh each year, grown
  through, and persisting as a kind of
  ring . . . .   SGr. 3 : Eucephalocerei Backbg.

Subgroup 1: **Acephalocerei** Backbg.
Key to the Genera:

Without cephalioid flowering zones
  Without hair-development, but with lon-
    ger spines
    Flowers bellshaped (diurnal!)
      Tubes densely scaly, with felty pads
        Ovary and fruit similarly (elon-
          gated spines bristly; seeds small;
          fruit subspherical) . . . . . .   173 : **Castellanosia** Card.
With ± strongly developed hair in the
  flowering zone, in part reduced (all
  night-flowering)
  Fruits oblong
    Areolar hairs very slight
      Flowers funnelform-bellshaped,
      ± constricted at midway
      Tube glabrous
        Ovary oblong
          Fruit thick-walled; seeds
          large, matt . . . . . .   174 : **Subpilocereus** Backbg.
Fruits depressed-subspherical, ±
  wrinkled
  Areolar hair mostly more strongly

developed (reduced only in the transitional SG. *Mediopilocereus*, or tubes still with traces of felt)

Flowers bellshaped to bellshaped-funnelform

Tube not conspicuously constricted

Ovary subspherical

Fruit glabrous; seeds small, shiny . . . . 175: **Pilosocereus** Byles & Rowl.

(Areolar hairs reduced)

Tube with traces of felt . . . . SG. 1: **Mediopilocereus** Backbg.

(Areolar hairs not reduced, in part long and dense)

Tube glabrous . . . . SG. 2: **Pilosocereus**

Subgroup 2: Hemicephalocerei Backbg.
One Genus only:

With a mass of wool or hairs forming a pseudocephalium, bristles absent, longer spines present

Flowers very small

Tube minute, with a ring of tiny scales inside below

Fruit very small, lidded (Seedlings with long bristles below) . . . . 176: **Micranthocereus** Backbg.

Subgroup 3: Eucephalocerei Backbg.
Key to the Genera:

With true cephalia of wool and/or bristles, or as rings of hairs

Cephalia lateral, never encircling the stem-apex

Cephalium superficial, in part slightly depressed, but not to the axis and without a groove

Flowers small, abbreviated cylindric-bellshaped, with a very short limb; nectary ± closed

Cephalium consisting of a mass of brownish-reddish wool

Seeds lacking a large hilum

Plants tree-like, without a basal ring of bristles when young . . . . 177: **Facheiroa** Br. & R.

Flowers larger, ± funnelform to bellshaped-funnelform; nectary not completely closed

Cephalium of yellowish-white
wool with long black bristles
Seeds with a large hilum
Plants shrubby, at first with a
basal ring of bristles . . . 178: **Trixanthocereus** Backbg.
Cephalium of brownish-white
wool; bristles absent
Seeds without a large hilum
Plants shrubby, branching
from the base, with no ring
of bristles at the base . . . 179: **Pseudoespostoa** Backbg.
Cephalium lateral only in youth, even-
tually encircling the apex,
not depressed, in part with
long bristles (180) . . . .
Flowers ± cylindric, short-limbed
Tube, ovary and fruit with long
silky brownish hairs and
bristles . . . . 180: **Vatricania** Backbg.
Flowers ± bellshaped, rather short-
limbed
Tube or fruit glabrous . . . . . 181: **Austrocephalocereus**
(Backbg.) Backbg.

Flowering zones stepped or ± encircling
to decurrent, of woolly flock,
in part furry and dense
Flowers ± bellshaped-funnelform
Tube, ovary and fruit laxly hairy

182: **Neobinghamia** Backbg.
emend. Backbg.

Cephalium grooved, often depressed on
the flank of the stem, of wool
and in part (184) with bristles
Flowers funnelform, medium-sized
Tube, ovary and stout berry-like
fruit laxly hairy . . . . . . 183: **Espostoa** Br. & R. emend.
Werd.

Flowers ± bellshaped
Tube and ovary ± scaly, glabrous
Fruit a naked lidded fruit . . . 184: **Coleocephalocereus** Backbg.
Cephalium lateral, of wool and bristles
(later grown through, remaining
capable of flowering for some time)
Flowers medium-sized, ± bent outwards and down
Tube, ovary and the oblong or
compressed fruit smooth (cephalium more a crown of bristles,
with wool) . . . . 185: **Stephanocereus** Berg.
Flowers rather small, with a narrow
tube; the limb expanding fully at
anthesis
Tube, ovary and lidded fruit ±

smooth (fruit spherical to top-
shaped, with flower-remains
persisting) . . . . 186: **Arrojadoa** Br. & R. non Mattf.

Group 10: Cephalocerei Backbg.
Key to the Subgroups:

Day-flowering
 Cephalium at maturity prominent to
  cylindric
  Flowers small, fruits resembling those
   of *Mammillaria* . . . . SGr. 1: Heliocephalocacti Backbg.
Night-flowering
 Cephalium at maturity never cylindric,
  always broad
  Flowers quite large or long; fruit a
   rather thick berry . . . . SGr. 2: Nyctocephalocacti Backbg.

Subgroup 1: Heliocephalocacti Backbg.
One Genus only:

Body spherical to ± elongated
 Cephalium apical, at first ± flat, eventually mostly taller and in part
  cylindric, mostly of dense reddish
  bristles and felt (day-flowering)
  Flowers small, short, naked, petals
   often ± revolute at anthesis
   Fruits like those of *Mammillaria*,
   clavate-oblong, white and red,
   naked, with a small lid, with
   persistent floral remains . . . . . 187: **Melocactus** Lk. & O.

Subgroup 2: Nyctocephalocacti Backbg.
One Genus only:

Body only spherical
 Cephalium apical, never cylindric or
  elongated, tending to widen at
  maturity, of white wool with some
  bristles, these in one case absent
  (night-flowering)
  Flowers long, with a narrow tube; all
   petals long, curving outwards,
   those nearer the ovary shorter;
   tube naked towards the base
  Fruit a subspherical naked berry . . 188: **Discocactus** Pfeiff.

Subtribe 2: Boreocactinae Backbg.
Key to the Groups:

Flowers from the areoles, these in part ±
 elongated . . . . Gr. 1: Boreoechinocacti Backbg.

Flowers from the axils or in part from the
base of furrows half or all the length
of the tubercle (areoles not long) . .   Gr. 2: Mammillariae Berg.
emend. Backbg.

Group 1: Boreoechinocacti Backbg.
Key to the Subgroups:

Flowers from areoles, glands absent; fruit
not watery . . . .   SGr. 1: Euboreoechinocacti Backbg.
Flowers from the base of long areoles with
glands, or from long areoles which
are glandless, the fruit in that case
watery (intermediate to the
Coryphanthae) . . . .   SGr. 2: Mediocoryphanthae Backbg.

Subgroup 1: Euboreoechinocacti Backbg.
Key to the Genera:

Floral tubes ± funnelform, in part bell-
shaped, woolly, fruit similarly
Spines firm, never hooked
Scales rather dense, firm, pointed
Ovary and fruit (oblong) quite
woolly; fruit dehiscing basally .   189: **Echinocactus** Lk. & O.
Ovary very felty
Fruit (spherical) at first similarly
felty, eventually ± glabrous,
dehiscing irregularly . . . . .   190: **Homalocephala** Br. & R.
Spines mostly less rigid or absent (rigid
only in *A. ornatum*)
Scales less dense or firm
Ovary and fruit (spherical) more
laxly hairy . . . .   191: **Astrophytum** Lem.
Fruit opening stellately above   SG. 1: **Astrophytum**
Fruit opening basally . . . . . .   SG. 2: **Neoastrophytum**
Backbg.

Floral tubes or flowers ± bellshaped, with
only traces of felt, fruit similarly
Spines mostly flexible, central spines in
part hooked
Scales thin, lax
Ovary and fruit with traces of felt
Fruit ± oblong, splitting basally   192: **Sclerocactus** Br. & R.
Floral tubes ± funnelform, glabrous but ±
scaly
Bodies firm
Spines long, papery
Tubercles long, angular (± keeled
below), firm
Flowers with a long tube
Tube with larger scales
Fruit dry, scaly, spindle-

shaped, opening basally . . . 193: **Leuchtenbergia** Hook.
Spines very short, or absent
 Ribs replaced by greatly elongated, angular tubercles (rounded below), weak
  Flowers with a long tube, arising centrally from the newest areoles
   Tube smooth
    Fruit clavate, ripening rapidly 194: **Neogomesia** Castañ.
Spines firm, not very short
 Ribs not tuberculate
  Spines in part hooked
   Flowers or tubes strongly scaly; fruit opening basally . . . . 195: **Ferocactus** Br. & R.
   Flowers or tubes less strongly scaly
    Fruit small, only slightly scaly, opening basally. . . 196: **Hamatocactus** Br. & R.
 Ribs mostly narrow, ± wavy
  Spines never hooked
   Flowers mostly shorter
    Tube and fruit with small scales, opening basally (spines extremely variable) (ribs acute, broader in only one case) . . . . 197: **Echinofossulocactus** Lawr.
 Ribs conspicuously transversely furrowed
  Spines never hooked
   Flowers or tubes scaly
    Fruit subspherical, splitting irregularly(!) . . . . . . 198: **Coloradoa** Boiss. & Davids.
 Ribs ± tuberculate (areoles ± elongated)
  Ribs stouter or higher (than in *Echinomastus*)
   Flowers conspicuous, larger, more widely opening
   Fruit with few scales, opening basally . . . . 199: **Thelocactus** (K. Sch.) Br. & R.
  Ribs more slender, more numerous, tubercles slighter (than in *Thelocactus*)
   Flowers smaller, not widely opening
   Fruit with few scales, opening basally
    Spines more strongly interlaced throughout . . 200: **Echinomastus** Br. & R.
 Tubercles replacing ribs (ribs resolved into free-standing tubercles)

Flowers smaller, indistinctly funnelform, ± scaly
   Tube densely set with dry, ciliate scales (flower ± rotate)
      Ovary with ciliate scales .   **201: Utahia** Br. & R.
   Tube-scales not ciliate
      Ovary and fruit naked . .   **202: Pediocactus** Br. & R.
   Tube and fruit naked, fruit berry-like, mostly concealed in the apical wool, dehiscing laterally above .   **203: Gymnocactus** Backbg.
ines weak, lower ones mostly falling
   Fruits opening variously: basally in part, splitting or disintegrating (but never forming slender, long-projecting berries as in *Mammillaria*)
   Tubercles unusually shaped: truncated transversely or prominent and 4-sided
   Flowers opening to ± bellshaped
      Tube with dry-edged scales above
         Fruit ± naked, splitting laterally (seeds, here only, dust-fine). . . . . . .   **204: Strombocactus** Br. & R.
   Tubercles scale-like and up-curved
   Flowers ± trumpet-shaped
      Tube glabrous, apart from perianth remains above
         Fruit clavate, glabrous, splitting basally . . . . . .   **205: Obregonia** Frič
   Tubercles minute, round
   Spines flattened, papery-thin, longer persistent
   Flowers cylindric-bellshaped, opening fairly wide
   Ovary ± scaly, with traces of felt, in part with minute flat spines above
      Fruit fairly dry, spherical, thin-walled, dehiscing lengthwise, with 1–2 residual scales above. . . . . .   **206: Toumeya** Br. & R.
   Tubercles short-cylindric, truncated, small
   Spines corky, the exterior in part ± hairy-felty but with a firm core, terete to compressed-terete, longer persisting
   Flowers small, ± bellshaped-funnelform, tube absent

Ovary naked(?)
  Fruit semi-dry, top-shaped
    with one or more minute
    scales . . . .   207: **Navajoa** Croiz.
Spines thin, soon becoming hair-like
    and long, persisting
  Flowers small, naked, widely
    opening
  Tube short, robust
    Fruit dry, obovoid, forming a
      widely gaping lateral split
      at dehiscence . . . . . .   208: **Pilocanthus** B. W. Benson
                                         & Backbg.

Tubercles broad, low, small
  Spines ± compressed to bristly,
    usually soon falling
  Flowers ± funnelform, appearing
    stalked, in part opening
    laxly, ± naked
    Tube with only traces of scales
      above
      Fruit a naked berry, fleshy at
        first, with a minute lid,
        splitting across (in part
        with traces of scales above)   209: **Turbinicarpus** (Backbg.)
                                             F. Buxb. & Backbg.

Fruits berry-like, very prominent
  Ribs folded, abbreviated, with sub-
      sidiary ribs; spines small,
      soon falling
  Flowers trumpet-shaped, with few
      petals
    Tube stalk-like . . . .   210: **Aztekium** Böd.
Body soft
  Ribs spineless
    Flowers small
      Tube short, with minute scales
        (only the first seedling-spines
        are ± feathery, soon falling;
        spines often replaced by tufts
        of longer felt)
      Fruit berry-like, prominent . .   211: **Lophophora** Coult.
Body of *Mammillaria*-type, with minute
      tubercles and fine spinelets
  Flowers minute, set in apical wool
      (some species with longer
      roots)
    Fruit berry-like, protruding . .   212: **Epithelantha** (Web.) Br. & R.

Subgroup 2: Mediocoryphanthae Backbg.
Key to the Genera:

Body eventually oblong
  Ribs ± prominent and tuberculate
    Central spine long, hooked
      Areoles long, glandular
        Flowers arising from the base of
          the areole
          Tube with triangular scales
            Fruit oblong, fleshy
              (edible), scaly . . . . .   213: **Glandulicactus** Backbg.
Body eventually ± oblong or else remain-
    ing ± spherical
  Ribs clearly divided into tubercles
    Central spine hooked
      Areoles not glandular
        Flowers small, short funnel-
          form
          Ovary with a few thin, small
            scales
            Fruit watery, as in *Cory-*
              phantha (Br & R.)
              Seed brown or black
                (root, in one species
                forming a stouter tap-
                root, connected to the
                body by a thin neck) .   214: **Ancistrocactus** Br. & R.

Group 2: **Mammillariae** Berg. emend. Backbg.
Key to the Subgroups:

Flowers from furrows or rudiments thereof,
  ± central. . . . .   SGr. 1: Coryphanthae (Berg.) Backbg.
Flowers only from the axils, ± lateral to
  forming a coronet
    Flowers hairy . . . .   SGr. 2: Mediomammillariae Backbg.
    Flowers glabrous . . . .   SGr. 3: Eumammillariae Backbg.

Subgroup 1: **Coryphanthae** (Berg.) Backbg.
Key to the Genera:

Flowers from the furrow-base
  Fruits never splitting basally
    Tubercles of normal shape
      Fruit not watery, drying up and
        becoming thin
      Seeds hard
        Flowers somewhat larger, apical
          Ovary somewhat scaly . . .   215: **Neolloydia** Br. & R.
          Flowers from the base of a
            distinct furrow . . . .   SG. 1: **Neolloydia**
          Flowers from irregularly
            developed furrows
            (pseudo-axillary), in part
            with hooked spines (as

also found in *Eumam-millariae*, in correspond-ing stages) . . . . .   SG. 2: **Cumarinia** (Knuth)
                                           Backbg.

Fruit ± red, juicy and fleshy, not quick-ripening
  Seeds hard, ± black
    Flowers close to the apex, larger
      Ovary naked
        Tubercles later shrinking
          Seeds with a large aril   216: **Neobesseya** Br. & R.
    Flowers apical, small
      Tubercles persisting
        Seeds with a small aril
          Fruit sometimes with a little scale. . . .   217: **Escobaria** Br. & R.
Fruit greenish, watery, ripening quickly
  Seeds soft, (yellow-) brown
    Furrows only half the length of the tubercle
    Flowers apical, usually larger
      Ovary with traces of scales, axils slightly felty . . .   218: **Lepidocoryphantha** Backbg.
    Furrows the full length of the tubercles . . . . . .   219: **Coryphantha** (Eng.) Lem.
    Flowers medium to very large
    Ovary often with 1–2 spine-like scales, glabrous . .   SG. 1: **Neocoryphantha**
                                           Backbg.

      Ovary (and fruit) quite naked . . . .   SG. 2: **Coryphantha**
Tubercles not normally shaped, seeds not soft, not imbricate, not laterally compressed, ± wrinkled, with an areolar cleft
  Fruit becoming dry
    Flowers from a furrow (in part abbreviated), or its base, central . . . .   220: **Roseocactus** Berg.
Tubercles imbricate, scale-like
  Fruit naked
    Flowers axillary (?pseudo-axillary, i.e. from a rudimentary furrow). . . . . . .   221: **Encephalocarpus** Berg.
Tubercles laterally compressed, in part firm and woody; furrowed at the tip
  Fruit dissolving (in the crown)
    Flowers ± bellshaped-funnelform, with a short tube, from the newest tubercles or

undeveloped furrows? . . . 222: **Pelecyphora** Ehrenbg.

Subgroup 2: Mediomammillariae Backbg.
One Genus only:

Flowers axillary, hairy
  Tubercles unfurrowed
    Fruit dry, hairy . . . . 223: **Ortegocactus** Alex.

Subgroup 3: Eumammillariae Backbg.
Key to the Genera:

Flowers axillary, glabrous
  Tubercles unfurrowed
    Flowers lacking a stouter, longer tube
    Fruit not splitting basally
      Tubercles ± modified, firm
        Plants with milky sap, spherical
          Tubercles laterally compressed and truncate, small
            Flowers borne more on the flanks
              Fruit naked, elongated
                Berry prominent when ripe . . . . . . 224: **Solisia** Br. & R.
        Plants without milky sap, low-growing
          Tubercles horn-shaped, 3-sided, large
            Flowers large (areoles minute, in part suppressed)
            Fruit naked, oblong . . 225: **Ariocarpus** Scheidw.
      Tubercles normal, firm, smaller, more slender, conical, terete or ± angular, not connected at the base
        Plants with or without milky sap, ± spherical or ± elongated
          Flowers mostly small; tube ± absent; borne around the apex
            Style free
              Fruit ripening after a ± long rest, often only the next year, then protruding

      Section 1:
      Galactochylus
              K.Sch.
      With milky sap ap-

57

pearing from damaged tubercles

Section 2:

Subhydrochylus

Backbg.

Milk-sap vessels within the body; milky sap not appearing on damaged tubercles

Section 3:

Hydrochylus

K. Sch.

With watery sap

Subsection 1:

Parviflorae

Backbg. With small flowers

Subsection 2:

Grandiflorae

Backbg. With fairly large flowers

All Sections show some stages with hooked spines . . .   226: **Mammillaria** Haw.

Plants with milky sap, flat in shape, arising from a stouter taproot

Flowers conspicuous, short-tubed

Style free

Fruit always ripening in the same year(?) . . .   227: **Porfiria** Böd.*

Plants without milky sap, ± spherical

Flowers larger; tubes rather slender

Style free

Seeds lacking a large corky hilum . . . . .   228: **Krainzia** Backbg.

Seeds with a large corky hilum . . . .   229: **Phellosperma** Br. & R.

Tubercles mostly elongated, soft

Plants without milky sap, ± subspherical, low-growing

Flowers sometimes larger funnelform, sometimes smaller; tube neither very long nor stout

---

* Shown separately, since the name is in common use; I consider it referable to Mammillaria.

Style partly united with the tube (in all cases?)
Fruit greenish, long to short-clavate or very elongated or stout and spherical, protruding when ripe; spines not stiff at first, rather laxly arranged, in part hooked. . . . . . 230: **Dolicothele** (K. Sch.) Br. & R. emend. Backbg.

Fruit drying up when ripe and splitting basally; seeds then remain in a cavity
Tubercles broadly terete, firm, $\pm$ connected at the base
Plants without milky sap
Flowers fairly large, funnelform
Style in part united with the tube . . . . 231: **Bartschella** Br. & R.
Flowers with thicker longer tubes
Fruit not splitting basally when ripe
Tubercles not soft, not connected at the base
Plants without milky sap, subspherical, forming large cushions or colonies
Floral limb normal
Flowers with long, stout, densely scaly tube, ovary similarly . . . . . . 232: **Mamillopsis** (Morren) Web.
Plants without milky sap, cylindric, branching
Floral limb oblique
Flowers with longer naked tube and ovary . . . . 233: **Cochemiea** (K. Brand.) Walton

CATALOGUE OF THE GENERA, SPECIES AND VARIETIES

The preceding Classification briefly sets out the diagnostic differences between the genera, and to supplement this they and their species are given below in greater detail, with their main characteristics. In general, new discoveries have been examined in greater detail.

"Differential diagnoses" are not intended as a substitute for the longer botanical descriptions, but they have the advantage that—just as in a Key—they show clearly the "distinguishing characters" used for separating one species from another. The abbreviations in heavy type, used in the following pages for the most important parts of the plants, make it possible to find quickly whatever information is wanted; in the case of larger genera, any subdivisions given in the generic description are either repeated in the subsequent text, or they are shown by figures in brackets after the specific name. This arrangement ensures that in some cases only the descriptions relevant to the subgenus or series need be studied.

It is hoped that the Lexicon, with its very concise presentation, will simplify the task of identifying particular species, and summarise their distinctive characters, especially in the case of the most recent discoveries; at the same time it should help the user to find the correct name, either by checking an existing designation or, in the case of an unnamed plant, first to find the appropriate genus by means of the Classification and then to identify the species in question. Specific names which are not found under the relevant genus are invalid designations in the sense of this Lexicon, and may have to be sought under related genera. In many such cases an indication has been included in the text.

A number of Ritter's new names (e.g. *Pyrrhocactus*, *Chileorebutia*) as well as those of other authors have been referred here to the genera in which they belong under my Classification. Where descriptions have been reproduced (as in the case of Ritter), this does not constitute any sort of judgement on the validity of the plant's specific status etc.; they are simply recorded in the form in which they were published, in accordance with the aims of the Lexicon.

ABBREVIATIONS USED IN THE TEXT

acc.	= according to	n.prov.	= *nomen provisorum*, provisional name	
An.	= anther(s)	non	= not	
Ar.	= areole(s)	n.sp., n.v.	= new species, new variety	
Ax.	= axil(s)	Ov.	= ovary, ovaries	
Bo.	= body, bodies	p.	= page	
br.	= broad	Per.	= perianth	
Br.	= bristle(s)	Pet.	= petal(s)	
c.	= *circa*, approximately	p.part.	= *pro parte*, in part	
Ceph.	= cephalium, cephalia	R.	= root(s); rows	
Cor.	= corolla	Rec.	= receptacle	
Csp.	= central spine(s)	Ri.	= rib(s)	
Dept.	= Department	Rsp.	= radial spines	
E.	= east, eastern	S.	= seed(s); south, southern	
emend.	= *emendatus*, corrected	Sc.	= scale(s)	
f.	= *forma*, form	Sect.	= Section	
Fam.	= Family	Seg.	= (stem) segment(s)	
Fig.	= figure, illustration	sensu	= in the sense used by	
Fil.	= filament(s)	Sep.	= sepals, outer perianth segments	
Fl.	= flower(s)			
Fr.	= fruit(s)	Ser.	= Series	
G.	= Genus	SFam.	= Subfamily	
Gl.	= gland(s)	SG.	= Subgenus	
Glo.	= glochids	Sp.	= spine(s)	
Gr.	= Group (used to represent Backeberg's "Sippe": kin, clan)	spec.	= species	
		SSect.	= Subsection	
h.	= high	SSer.	= Subseries	
H.	= hair(s)	SGr.	= Subgroup	
Isp.	= intersecting spirals	Sh.	= sheath(s)	
lg.	= long	Ssp.	= subsidiary spine(s)	
L.	= leaf, leaves	St.	= stem(s)	
l.c.	= *loco citato*, in the publication already quoted	Sti.	= stigmas	
		STr.	= Subtribe	
M.	= median, middle	sv.	= subvariety	
N.	= north, northern	T.	= type-species	
n.comb.	= *nova combinatio*, reclassification in a new genus	Tr.	= Tribe	
		Tu.	= floral tube	
n.nud.	= *nomen nudum*, name not validly published	Tub.	= tubercle(s)	
		v., var.	= variety	
		W.	= west, western	

SYMBOLS, including cultural indications

∅	= diameter
±	= more or less
○	= grow in full sun
●	= grow in shade
◖	= grow in half-shade
(R)	= grow on own roots
(G)	= grafting advisable
✳	= care necessary with watering
///	= in summer, preferably grow in the open, or give more water.

Where the name of a publication is quoted after any generic or specific name, the genus, species or variety was only published after the appearance of my Handbook.

Acanthocalycium Backbg. (99)

Plants spherical to elongated. Flowers white, pink, red or yellow, funnelform; with the scales on the tube and ovary modified above into spines; with a small wool-ring at the tube-base.—Distribution: N. Argentina.[○. (R) (G)].

A. aurantiacum Rausch 1968
Bo. simple, 5 cm h., to 9 cm $\varnothing$, greyish-green, strongly frosted; **Ri.** 10–16, straight, slightly tuberculate; **Ar.** c. 2 cm apart, with white felt, later becoming glabrous; **Rsp.** 5(–7), spreading, 3–4 cm lg., straight, sharp; **Csp.** rarely 1; all **Sp.** whitish or yellowish, pink at midway and black-tipped; **Fl.** lateral, 5 cm 1g. and br.; **Tu.** olive-green or olive-brown, with brown Sc. and H.; **Sep.** orange-red with a brown or dark green M.-stripe, lanceolate; **Pet.** lanceolate or spatulate, orange-yellow bordered orange, red or pink; hymen, throat and **Fil.** light yellow; **style** green, with a ring of brown wool below; **Sti.** 10, green or yellow; **Fr.** spherical; **S.** 1.5 mm lg., testa glossy black, tuberculate.—Argentina (Catamarca, Mina Capillitas, 3000 m).

A. brevispinum Ritt.—"Taxon", XIII: 4, 144. 1964.
Bo. to 50 cm lg.; **Ri.** 14–25, to 1.5 cm h.; **Ar.** sunken, to 8 mm apart; **Csp.** 2–6 (in A. thionanthum 1–4, **Rsp.** as in last-named); **Tu.** with narrow Sc. (broader in A. thionanthum); **Fl.** as in A. thionanthum except that **Tu.** and **Pet.** are shorter; **Fr.** dark green, 1.5 cm lg.; **S.** 1.5 mm lg., dark, hilum white.—Argentina (Prov. Salta, S. of Cafayate, near Prov. Tucuman) (FR 968). In the absence of an illustration, the description is not sufficient to establish this as a valid spec.

A. catamarcense Ritt., not described: plants raised from Winter's seed are more grey, not green; **Ri.** 13; **Sp.** black at first, red below, later ± pink or horn-colour; **Rsp.** to c. 9, radiating, projecting, rather long; **Csp.** 1, same length as Rsp.; **Fl.** ?.—Argentina (Catamarca). It is not clear whether this spec. is sufficiently distinct from A. glaucum Ritt.

A. chionanthum (Speg.) Backbg.
Bo. spherical to cylindric, grey-green, to 7 cm h. and 6.5 cm $\varnothing$; **Ri.** 13–15, low, rounded; **Ar.** elliptical; **Sp.** 7–9, all radial, straight, stiffly subulate, ashen; **Fl.** 4.5 cm lg., white; **style** green; **Sti.** 13, white; wool-**ring** brown.—Argentina (Salta: near Cachi).

A. glaucum Ritt.—"Taxon", XIII: 4, 143. 1964.
Bo. blue-green, to 7 cm $\varnothing$, 15 cm h.; **R.** stout; **Ri.** 8–14, obtuse, to 1.5 cm h., notched; **Ar.** 1.5–2 cm apart, white; **Sp.** black throughout, thicker below; **Rsp.** 5–10, 5–20 mm lg., subulate, straight; **Csp.** 0,

sometimes 1–2, in upper part of Ar.; **Fl.** 6 cm lg. and $\varnothing$, with white flock; **Tu.** with elongated Sc. which are bristle-tipped; **Pet.** golden-yellow, rounded above; wool-**ring** white; **Fr.** to 2 cm $\varnothing$, dark green, spherical; **S.** 1.5 mm lg., brown to darker, hilum white.—Argentina (Prov. Catamarca, N. of Belén) (FR 970).

A. griseum Backbg.—Descr. Cact. Nov., III: 5. 1963 (Pyrrhocactus griseus n.nud., "Die Cact.", 3907, Pl. 3548, 1962).
Bo. spherical at first, later elongated, to 15 cm $\varnothing$, lead-grey; **Ri.** c. 11; **Sp.** 3 at first, later 5, fairly stout-subulate, thickened basally, to c. 1.5 cm lg., directed sideways, 1 downwards, all at first black, reddish below when moist, light at the base; **Fl.** c. 4 cm lg. and $\varnothing$, stout, with upwardly directed, ± appressed, grey-brown H. and fine, dark, spine-tipped Sc.; **ring** short, fine, brownish, at the base of the Fil.; **Pet.** yellow, to 9 mm br.; **Sep.** brownish, with a M.-line.—N. Argentina (exact locality not given; found by Fechser). (Fig. 1.)
v. rubriflorum n.nud., with red Fl., has been reported.

A. klimpelianum (Weidl. & Werd.) Backbg.
Bo. flattened-spherical, dark green, to 10 cm $\varnothing$; **Ri.** c. 19, narrow, slightly notched; **Ar.** elliptical, with yellow-brown felt, 6 mm lg.; **Sp.** straight, subulate, brown-tipped at first; **Rsp.** 6–8 (–10), unequal; **Csp.** (1–) 2–3 (–4), the bottom one longest and directed downwards; **Fl.** 3–4 cm lg., white; **Fil.** white; **ring** white.—Argentina (near Córdoba).

A. peitscherianum Backbg.
Bo. flattened-spherical, grey-green, c. 8 cm h., 10 cm $\varnothing$; **Ri.** 17, 1 cm h.; **Ar.** 2 cm apart, light yellow; **Sp.** to 2 cm lg., subulate, pale to light brown, black-tipped; **Rsp.** 7 (–9); **Csp.** 1; **Fl.** 6 cm lg.; **Tu.** campanulate, 4 cm lg., constricted above the Ov.; **Sc.** brownish; **Pet.** spatulate, c. 2.5 cm lg., whitish to lilac-pink; **style** 1.5 cm lg.; **Sti.** 10–12, yellowish; **ring** whitish-yellow.—Argentina (near Córdoba?).

A. spiniflorum (K. Sch.) Backbg. (T.)
Bo. spherical to elongated, dark green, to 60 cm h., 15 cm $\varnothing$; **Ri.** to 20 or more, acute, to 1.5 cm h.; **Ar.** 7–8 mm apart; **Sp.** 14–20, stiffly subulate, ± brownish to reddish-yellow; **Csp.** scarcely distinguishable; **Fl.** 4 cm lg., c. 4 cm br., bellshaped-funnelform, pink; **ring** yellow; **Sc.** yellowish.—Argentina (NW Córdoba).

A. thionanthum (Speg.) Backbg.
Bo. spherical to shortly cylindric, green, to 12 cm h. or more, 6–10 cm $\varnothing$; **Ri.** c. 14; **Ar.** shortly elliptical; **Rsp.** to 10; **Csp.** 1–4; **Sp.** strongly subulate, all ± equally long, to 1.5 cm lg., grey to

pale horn-coloured, at first mostly brownish above; **Fl.** 4.5 cm lg., sulphur to lemon-yellow; **style** whitish-green; **Sti.** 12, ± reddish; **ring** brownish; **Tu.** more strongly hairy.—Argentina (Salta: Cachi) (Fig. 2). A. brevispinum Ritt. may be a form of this spec.

A. variiflorum Backbg. n.sp.
Bo. solitary, spherical to ± elongated, green, to c. 8 cm ∅ has been noted; **Ri.** c. 17, rounded above, c. 1 cm br. at midway, swollen around the Ar.; **Sp.** mostly horn-coloured or somewhat darker, becoming paler, sometimes ± spotted, straight or usually ± curved to bent above; **Rsp.** c. 9, to c. 1.8 cm lg.; **Csp.** 1, to c. 2.2 cm lg.; **Fl.** variable in colour, yellow to ± orange-red to carmine; **Fil., An.** and **Sti.** yellowish-cream; **ring** ?; **Fr.** ?.—N. Argentina (locality not known). (U 2174 in collection Uhlig and Backeberg; found by Fechser.) (Fig. 3.)

Another spec. found by Fechser:
A. spec., somewhat resembling A. thionanthum; **Bo.** grey-green, to 7 cm ∅ reported; **Ri.** c. 14–15, rounded, thickened around the Ar.; **Sp.** when dry grey-black at first, darker above, or grey-brown above, at first uniformly so, soon lightening apart from the tip, projecting rigidly, laxly radiating to densely interlacing, the **Rsp.** to c. 2.3 cm lg., **Csp.** somewhat shorter, all rather stoutly subulate, thickened at the foot; **Rsp.** 9, radiating, projecting, only in part ± curved; **Csp.** 2, arranged one above the other, scarcely thicker, occasionally ± compressed laterally; **Fl.** unknown.—N. Argentina (U 2175 in the Uhlig and Backeberg collection; collected by Fechser, no data on locality). Variable in spination.

A. violaceum (Werd.) Backbg.
Bo. becoming elongated, dull light green, to 20 cm h., 13 cm ∅; **Ri.** c. 15 or more, to 1.8 cm h.; **Ar.** 2 cm apart, white; **Sp.** 10–12 (–20), yellowish to horn-coloured; **Csp.** scarcely distinguishable, 4 sometimes more distinct; **Fl.** to 7.5 cm lg., pale lilac; **ring** white.—Argentina (Córdoba, 1000 m).

Acanthocephala Backbg.: **Brasilicactus** Backbg.

Acanthocereus (Berg.) Br. & R. (130)

Squarrose shrubs, variable in size; shoots 3–4-sided, rarely more; ribs mostly thin, spines stout. Flowers fairly large, expanding fully and stoutly funnelform, the long tube not down-curving; flowers and fruits mostly spiny, but the spineless fruit of A. horridus shows the progressive reduction in flower-spination; in the Brazilian species A. albicaulis flower and fruit are not known; the genus is thus not fully clarified. Rare in cultivation.—Distribution: Warm, drier zones of Central America (not positively identified in the W. Indies), from Mexico and Florida to Colombia, Venezuela and Brazil. [(R.) ○.].

A. acutangulus (O.) Berg.
Bo. glossy green; **St.** 4 cm br.; **Ri.** (3–)4, angles acute, compressed, ± sinuate; **Ar.** 9–11 mm apart; **Rsp.** 4–6, the lower 2 only 2–3 mm lg.; **Csp.** 1, subulate, 11–17 mm lg.; **S.** smooth, with 5-angled tessellations, smaller than that of A. maculatus Wgt.—Mexico(?).

A. albicaulis Br. & R.
Bo. whitish; **St.** fairly slender; **Ri.** (3–)4; **Ar.** brown: **Sp.** 2–6, stiffly acicular, to 2.5 cm lg., brownish but often darker at first.—Brazil (Bahia).

A. baxaniensis (Karw.) Borg
Bo. shrubby; **St.** thicker and deeper green than in A. tetragonus; **Ri.** mostly 4, broad, winged; **Rsp.** 5 or more, brownish, c. 1.5 cm lg.; **Csp.** 1–3, yellowish-brown, to 3 cm lg., straight; **Fl.** 20 cm lg., white; **Sep.** brownish-green; **Ov.** spiny.—Mexico (warm NE. coast).

A. brasiliensis (FR 1230): no description available.

A. colombianus Br. & R.
Bo. fairly robust, with erect branches, to 3 m h.; **St.** to c. 9 cm br., acutely 3-winged; **Ar.** large, 5 cm apart; **Rsp.** 5–8, less than 5 mm lg.; **Csp.** 1–2, very robust, to 5.5 cm lg.; **Fl.** 25 cm lg., white; **Tu.** stout, c. 12 cm lg.; **Fr.** large, red, spiny.—Colombia.

A. griseus Backbg. n.sp.
Bo. tall, shrubby, branching, to c. 3–4 m lg.; **St.** 3–4-angled, curving and then bent upwards, to c. 6 cm ∅, green at first, soon whitish-grey, tapering towards the tip; **Ri.** to 2.5 cm h., laterally compressed in the upper part; **Ar.** 6 cm apart; **Sp.** carmine at first, light at the tip, thickened at the base, soon becoming whitish with a dark tip; **Rsp.** (5–)6, to 1.4 cm lg.; **Csp.** 1 (rarely 3–4), porrect, to c. 2.2 cm lg.; **Fl.** c. 9 cm lg. and ∅, Per. spreading laterally, the borders curved ± upwards; **Sep.** reddish-green; **Pet.** pale greenish-white; **Tu.** c. 7 cm lg., it and the green **Ov.** with carmine Sp. and white felt; **Fr.** ?—Mexico. (Fig. 4, 5 left). Discovered by MacDougall; sent under No. A 201 to the Botanical Garden, "Les Cèdres", where I saw it in flower.

A. horridus Br. & R.
Bo. robustly shrubby; **St.** acutely 3-angled or 3-winged but 5-angled at first, the angles very sinuate, with projections below the Ar.; **Ar.** large, 3–6 cm

apart; **Rsp.** 1–6, conical, less than 1 cm lg.; **Csp.** mostly 1(–2), very robust, to 5–8 cm lg.; **Sp.** brownish to blackish at first; **Fl.** 18–20 cm lg., white; **Sep.** brown or greenish; **Tu.** with the constricted section only 4 cm lg., with a funnelform opening c. 12 cm lg.; **Fr.** 3.5 cm lg., glossy light red, Ar. only white-felted, pulp red.—Guatemala, (to?) Mexico (Oaxaca?).

A. maculatus Wgt.
Bo. tall, shrubby, to over 3 m h., also arching over; **R.** carrot-like or more spherical; **St.** dark olive-green, marbled or in part concolorous green; **Ri.** 3–4, ± sinuate; **Ar.** small, white; **Rsp.** c. 8, 1–8 mm lg., the lower ones (only sometimes present) 2–3, longer, acicular; **Csp.** usually 1, thickened at the base, sometimes 2, porrect; **Sp.** all rather short, inconspicuous, brown; **Fl.** to 10 cm lg., cream-coloured; **Tu.** pink inside, reddish-brown outside, Ar. distant, with only a few pale Sp.; **Ov.** green, with narrow Ri. like those of the Tu., with a few short Sp.; **Fr.** c. 5 cm lg., ± pear-shaped, red inside and out; **S.** large, 4.5 mm lg., glossy black, with fine 5-angled tessellations.—Mexico (Guerrero, Campo Morado and near Mezcala in the Canyon del Zopilote). (Fig. 6.) In the collection of J. Marnier-Lapostolle it was observed that the perianth, at anthesis, is funnelform. The spec. does not therefore, as held by Cutak, belong to Peniocereus; the stouter roots are of as little significance here as in the small-flowered Peireskiopsis, so that Weingart's referal to Acanthocereus was correct, even although he never saw an open flower; he based his view principally on the seeds. We now know that in Peniocereus at anthesis all spec. have the inner Per.-segments directed stiffly downwards.

A. pentagonus sensu Br. & R.: **Acanthocereus tetragonus** (L.) Humlk.

A. princeps (Pfeiff.) Backbg.—Descr. Cact. Nov., III: 5. 1963 (Cereus princeps Hort. Würzburg, briefly described and illustrated by Weingart in MfK., 20–21. 1922, must be attributed to Pfeiffer because of the latter's description in En. Diagn. Cact., 108. 1837.)
Bo. shrubby, arching, 3(–4–5)-ribbed; **Ri.** compressed, not sinuate, thickened below the Ar.; **Ar.** whitish, relatively distant, shortly felty; **Sp.** 1.2–1.6 cm lg., straight, yellowish or white, with 7–8 radials, 3 centrals, the upper one very short or even absent.—Guatemala.
Acc. Weingart, Kaktkde. 15. 1933, this is a valid spec., particularly since the S. are moderately glossy and faintly divided into 6-sided depressions. Acc. Weingart, its S. were the largest he had seen. The smallest S., acc. Weingart, were those of

"Cereus variabilis Eng., which is closest to C. pentagonus Haw.", but unfortunately no-one now knows which spec. this was. Weingart said his spec. had "seeds with fairly flat, oval podaria". This may enable a determination to be made of the spec. in question.

A. tetragonus (L.) Humlk. (T.)
Bo. initially erect, then arching, to 6 m h.; **St.** to 8 m lg.; **Ri.** 4–5(–6), (more rarely 3), with deep furrows and the angles winged, deeply sinuate and indented; **Ar.** 3–6(–7) cm apart, stout; **Rsp.** (4–)5–7(–9), to 2.5 cm lg.; **Csp.** 1(–3), to 4 cm lg.; all **Sp.** grey with a dark tip, in part spotted; **Fl.** to 19 cm lg., white; **Tu.** somewhat spiny; **Fr.** spinier, red; **S.** glossy black, 4 mm lg.—Occurs throughout the entire range of the G. Previously incorrectly known as A. (Cereus) pentagonus.

The following are probably seldom, if ever, seen in collections:
A. brasiliensis Br. & R.: **St.** 3 cm ∅; **Ri.** 5–7; **Sp.** 9–20, acicular to bristly, white, yellowish-grey or greyish-brown; **Fl.** to 15 cm lg.; **Tu.** spineless; **Fr.** with greenish pulp.—Brazil (Catinga of Bahia).
A. floridanus Small: **St.** to 10 m lg., 3–5-angled, dark green; **Sp.** 4–7, thin or subulate.—USA (Florida, Hammocks).
A. occidentalis Br. & R.: Forming thickets; **St.** 4.5 cm ∅; **Ri.** 3–5; **Sp.** numerous, equal, to 7 cm lg.; **Fl.** 14–18 cm lg.—Mexico (Sinaloa, Nayarit, Durango).
A. sicariguensis Croiz. & F. Tamayo: **Bo.** to 2 m lg.; **Ri.** 2–5-winged, ± serrate; **Ar.** 2 cm apart; **Sp.** greyish-white, ± sharp; **Rsp.** 5–7, to 2 cm lg.; **Csp.** 1–3, to 2 cm lg.; **Fl.** 16 cm lg., to 8 cm ∅, white, with pink tips.—Venezuela (Lara, Sicaragua).
A. subinermis Br. & R.: differs in that the Sp. are missing, or only short, less than 1.5 cm lg., 6–10 in number; **St.** 5–7 cm br., 3–4-angled; **Fl.** 15–22 cm lg.; **Ov.** with few Sp. and those on the **Fr.** very short.—Mexico (between Mitla and Oaxaca).

Acantholobivia Backbg. (98)

Plants spherical, sometimes offsetting, related to Lobivia but night-flowering. Flowers (very variable in colour in one species) show an increasing spination as the ovary ripens; fruit spiny. Flowers self-fertile, autogamy having sometimes been observed. Seeds black, ± glossy.—Distribution: Peru (highlands of the centre and south). [(R) (G)].

A. incuiensis (Rauh & Backbg.) Rauh & Backbg.
Bo. dark green, to c. 11 cm ∅; **Ri.** 18–20, with hatchet-shaped Tub.; **Ar.** 2 mm apart; **Sp.** c. 24, spreading, tangled, centrals probably 8–10 but

scarcely differentiated, all greyish-violet-brown to horn-coloured, becoming grey to dark, some sometimes ± angular; **Fl.** c. 4 cm lg.; **Sep.** brownish-red; **Pet.** true red, but more bricky-orange below; **Fil.** pale carmine; **style** and 4 **Sti.** greenish.—S. Peru (near Incuio). (Fig. 7.)

A. tegeleriana (Backbg.) Backbg. (T.)
Bo. pure green, offsetting; **Ri.** 16 at first; **Ar.** to 17 mm apart, oblong; **Sp.** dissimilar, to 12, to 6 mm lg., radiating, mostly ± curved, all ± horn-coloured, darker above, the longest sometimes ± hooked; **Csp.** scarcely distinguishable; **Fl.** 4 cm lg., ± pinkish-orange in the T.; **Fr.** green, 2.5 cm ∅.— Central Peru (near Huancayo at 3500 m).
    v. **eckardtiana** Backbg. has remarkably long **Sp.**; v. **medingiana** Backbg., has **Fl.** sulphur-yellow to white, while those of v. **plominiana** Backbg. are pure red.

Acanthorhipsalis (K.Sch.) Br. & R. (22)

Plants resembling Rhipsalis in habit, but clearly differentiated by the spiny stems. Flowers only 1.5–2.5 cm long, white, orange or red, with a minute tube.—Distribution: Peru, E. Bolivia and NE. Argentina. [Epiphytes, rare in cultivation.]

A. crenata (Britt.) Br. & R.
Bo. bushy, branching laterally; **St.** sinuate, to 30 cm lg., to 6 cm br., thin, with a stout M.-rib; **Ar.** rather large, felty; **Sp.** 3–8, 2–4 mm lg.; **Fl.** small, red; **Fr.** 7 mm ∅.—Bolivia (Yungas).

A. incahuasina Card.
Bo. pendant, densely branching, to 60 cm lg., pale green; **St.** 3-angled, to 3 cm br., to 4 mm thick; **Ar.** 2 cm apart; **Sp.** 8–13, radiating, 2–12 mm lg., yellowish, 2–3 sometimes arranged ± centrally; **Fl.** ?; **Fr.** to 1.5 cm ∅, pinkish-carmine; **S.** 1 mm lg., brown, kidney-shaped.—Bolivia (Santa Cruz, Incahuasi).

A. micrantha (Vpl.) Br. & R. (T.)
Bo. shrubby, branching; **St.** to 20 cm lg., mostly with 3 Ri., rarely with only 2 wings; **Ri.** compressed, c. 1 cm h.; **Ar.** 1 cm apart; **Sp.** 3–10, somewhat flattened and tortuous, to 1.5 cm lg.; **Fl.** c. 2.5 cm lg., purple; **Ov.** somewhat felty, with scattered small Br.; **Fr.** spherical or ± oblong, 1 cm lg., ± winged, with a few Sc., brownish felt and sometimes Br. up to 2 mm lg.; **S.** black.—Peru (Sandia, on rocks, 2100 m).

A. monacantha (Griseb.) Br. & R.
Bo. mostly pendant; **St.** 2–3 cm br., to 45 cm lg., flat or 3-angled, serrate; **Ar.** to 1.2 cm apart; **Sp.** 1–6, to

1 cm lg., also a few Br.; **Fl.** to 1.5 cm lg., waxy orange, with small Sc. and felt; **Fr.** spherical, to 1 cm ∅, orange at first, then orange-red or paler, scaly; **S.** dark brown.—Argentina (Jujuy, Oran). Br. & R. incorrectly state the Fl. to be "white". (Fig. 8.)
    v. **samaipatana** (Card.) Backbg.: **St.** more conspicuously notched; **Ar.** more distant; **Fr.** pinkish-lilac, without Sc.—Bolivia (Santa Cruz, Baño del Inca, 1500 m).

A. paranganiensis Card.
Bo. shrubby, pendant, densely branching; **shoots** terete, 1 cm ∅, 2–3-winged, 2–4 m lg., aerial-R. absent; **Sp.** 2–4, whitish, 5 mm lg., fine, bristly, later also 1 white Sp. to 6 mm lg., also 1–3 short Br.; **Fl.** numerous, rotate, apical, to 2 cm lg., creamy white; **Ov.** 5 mm lg., 5-angled, with acute Sc., with a few short little Br.; **Fr.** ?—Bolivia (Cochabamba, Parangani, 2600 m).

| A. samaipatana Ritt. (FR 888): **A. monacantha** v. **samaipatana** (?).

Akersia Buin. (73)

Slender-stemmed, erect Cerei with fine, dense, yellow spines. Finer, longer spines and/or bristles develop in the flowering zone. Flowers pinkish red, bent, zygomorphic, with bristles on the tube and ovary; no wool-ring is present inside. At first considered to be a hybrid, but this appears improbable since no similar Cerei with floral bristles occur in the Andes.—Distribution: apparently N. Peru, in the interior. [(G).]

A. roseiflora Buin. (T.)
Bo. slender, 4–5 cm ∅, fresh green; **St.** to more than 1 m h.; **Ri.** 16–17, very low; **Ar.** c. 2.5 cm lg., flowering ones somewhat larger; **Sp.** in clusters of 30–40, to 1 cm lg., yellowish to lighter, dark at the base, those in the flowering zone finer, in part bristly, to 3.5 cm lg.; **Fl.** 5 cm lg., 3 cm br., lilac-pink, with several blackish-brown Br.; **Fr.** c. 1.5 cm lg., hairy, with a few Br.; **S.** 1.5 mm lg.—Peru(?), in the interior to the N., or in the S. near Chala(?). (Fig. 9.)

Ancistrocactus Br. & R. (214)

Plants spherical to elongated, in part constricted at the base and with larger napiform roots; with ribs ± conspicuously tuberculate. One central spine is always hooked. The relatively small flowers are cream-coloured, greenish or lemon-yellow, or pink. Seeds brown to dark brown or black. 4

species.—Distribution: USA (Texas) and N. Mexico (Chihuahua, Nuevo León, Tamaulipas). [(G).]

A. brevihamatus (Eng.) Br. & R.
Bo. spherical to ovoid, to 10 cm h., 7.5 cm ∅, dark green; **Ri.** mostly 13, strongly tuberculate; **Rsp.** 12–14, 1–2 cm lg., white; **Csp.** 4, the lowest one to 3 cm lg., stronger, brown or black, hooked, the lateral Csp. to 4.5 cm lg., less strong; **Fl.** to 3.2 cm lg., 2 cm ∅, pale pink with a dark M.-line; **Fr.** almost naked, c. 1.5 cm lg., thin-walled; **S.** 2 mm lg., blackish-brown.—USA (S. Texas) to N. Mexico (Chihuahua, Nuevo León, Tamaulipas).

A. megarhizus (Rose) Br. & R. (T.)
Bo. solitary or several-headed, to 8 cm. h.; **R.** large, fleshy; **Ri.** spiralled, conically tuberculate; **Rsp.** 20 or more, yellowish at first, radiating, appressed; **Csp.** 4, the upper three directed upwards, the lowest one strongest, 1.5–2 cm lg., hooked; **Fl.** 2 cm lg., greenish-yellow; **Fr.** green, clavate; **S.** black, glossy.—Mexico (Tamaulipas).

A. scheeri (SD.) Br. & R.
Bo. spherical, oblong or clavate, over 10 cm h., to over 6 cm ∅; **Ri.** c. 13, tuberculate; **Rsp.** 15–18, white to straw-coloured, spreading; **Csp.** 3–4, 2–5 cm lg., the lowest and longest one hooked, all blackish-brown with white marks; **Fl.** 2.5 cm lg., greenish-yellow; **Fr.** small, green; **S.** 2 mm lg., brown.—USA (Texas), N. Mexico (Chihuahua). (Fig. 10.)

A. tobuschii Marsh.
Bo. two-thirds hidden in the soil, to 7 cm lg. and br., the part above-ground hemispherical, dark green; tubercles in 5–8 R.; **Rsp.** 7, acicular, sharp, white at first, 1–1.5 cm lg.; **Csp.** 3, 2 of them directed upwards, one porrect, hooked, 3 cm lg., all flattened, light yellow, dark-tipped; **Fl.** 4 cm lg.; **Pet.** cream to lemon-yellow; **style** green; **Sti.** yellow; **Fr.** green to pink; **S.** dark brown.—USA (Texas, Vanderpool).

Only A. megarhizus has a napiform root with neck-constriction; A. brevihamatus (Eng.) Br. & R. has been regarded as a var. of A. scheeri, but it has pink Fl., weaker Sp., and only 12–14 Rsp.

Anhalonium Lem.: **Lophophora** Coult., in part also referable to **Ariocarpus** Scheidw. or **Roseocactus** Berg.

Anisocereus Backbg. (160)

Genus probably not found in cultivation; the

unusual diurnal flowers are funnelform, with thin dry scales, with bristles on and near the ovary; probably the fruit also is fairly dry; the seeds are glossy blackish-brown. Sometimes included, in addition to the shrubby-erect type-species which grows to 4 m high, is A. gaumeri (Br. & R.) Backbg. which grows to 7 m high and has similar flowers, but other authors attribute it, because of its 4-winged ribs, to Pterocereus McDoug. & Mir. (see Pterocereus), which also has similar flowers, but was only described much later. [(R).]

A. lepidanthus (Eichl.) Backbg. (T.)
Bo. bushy, to 4 m h.; **St.** dark leaf-green, to 8 cm ∅; **Ri.** 7–9, low; **Ar.** small; **Rsp.** c. 10, to 1.5 cm lg., thin, some also longer, to 4 cm lg., or often also 1–2 distinguishable as centrals, one of these to 6 cm lg.; **Sp.** cherry-red at first, dark-tipped, then canary-yellow and finally grey, black-tipped, all with a thickened base, the centrals also angular and compressed; **Fl.** 7 cm lg., 2.5 cm ∅, sepia-brown above, flame-coloured below, opening by day (acc. Eichlam), shrivelling when open; **Tu.** fairly densely set with revolute Sc., those towards the Ov. with awns (Br.) 1.5 cm lg.; **Sc.** drying to straw-like; **Fr.** not fleshy, dry, whitish; **S.** glossy blackish-brown.—Guatemala (Rancho San Agustin). (Fig. 11.)

I also refer the following spec. to this G.:

A. gaumeri (Br. & R.) Backbg.
Bo. to 7 m h., erect solitary or ± branching; **St.** with winged Ri.; **Ri.** (3–)4, to 4 cm h.; **Ar.** large, light brown; **Sp.** 3–6, ± subulate, brownish or light and dark-tipped, 1 Sp. ± central, 1–3 cm lg.; **Fl.** 5 cm lg., and acc. Marshall's illustration open at least during the day, yellowish-green; **Tu.** with black Sc., drying to become thin; **Fr.** becoming dry, spherical, to 4 cm ∅, **Ax.** felty, with 8 very short black Sp.; **S.** brown, 4 mm lg.—Mexico (Yucatán, Zenote Hondo, E. of Izamal). Nothing known of any awns or Sp. on the Fl., or of any Sp. on the Fr. of A. lepidanthus. In the light of the above data, no inclusion in Pterocereus is possible at present.

Aporocactus Lem. (50)

Epiphytes, predominantly creeping or pendant, the thin stems with quite marked development of aerial roots; flowers attractive, medium-sized, ± zygomorphic. The type-species has become one of the commonest of all cacti, and deserves to be even more widely grown; it was also one of the parents of the Heliaporus hybrids, some of them raised as early as 1830. Grows well on its own roots.—Distribution: Mexico (Oaxaca, Hidalgo,

Chihuahua ?) (Plant for the hanging basket; take precautions against red-spider mite!)

A. conzattii Br. & R.
Bo. pendant or creeping, with few aerial R.; **St.** 1.2–2.5 cm $\emptyset$; **Ri.** 8–10, with low Tub.; **Sp.** 15–20, needle-like, to 12 mm lg., light brown; **Fl.** to 9 cm lg., only slightly curved, $\pm$ zygomorphic, brick-red.—Mexico (Cerro San Felipe). (Fig. 12.)

A. flagelliformis (L.) Lem. (T.)
Bo. to 2 cm $\emptyset$; **Ri.** 10–12, inconspicuous, scarcely tuberculate; **Ar.** 6–8 mm apart; **Rsp.** 8–12, acicular, thin, reddish-brown; **Csp.** 3–4, brownish, yellow-tipped; **Fl.** 7–8 cm lg., open for up to 4 days, crimson; **Sep.** revolute, narrower than the Pet., the latter less spreading; **Fr.** small, spherical, to 12 mm $\emptyset$, pulp yellowish.—Mexico (Hidalgo).

One well-known hybrid is $\times$ Cereus smithii Pfeiff. (C. mallisonii hort.), also known as Heliaporus smithii (Pfeiff.) Rowl. Probably Schumann's v. leptophis of A. flagelliformis is identical with this.

A. flagriformis (Zucc.) Lem.
Bo. similar to the preceding; **Ri.** 11; **Rsp.** 6–8; **Csp.** 4–5, darker brownish; **Fl.** dark crimson, 10 cm lg., 7.5 cm br.; **Pet.** 1 cm br.; **Fil.** red, erect, projecting. Distinguished from the preceding also by the Sp. on new growth which are more reddish.—Mexico (Oaxaca).

Aporocactus knebelii Kneb.: garden form with tuberculate Ri.

A. leptophis (DC.) Br. & R.
Sp. yellowish; **Ri.** only c. 8; **Fl.** down-curving above the Ov.; **Pet.** narrow, red, Per. $\pm$ oblique.—Mexico (locality not known).
Distinguished from A. flagriformis by the lower Ri.-count; A. conzattii differs from the present spec. by the outer Pet. not being noticeably recurved.

A. martianus (Zucc.) Br. & R.
St. to 18 mm $\emptyset$; **Ri.** c. 8; **Ar.** 1.2 cm apart; **Sp.** 6–8, bristly; **Fl.** deep pink, to 10 cm lg.; **Tu.** with projecting bristly Sp. in the upper part; **Fr.** greenish, spherical, 2 cm $\emptyset$.—Mexico (Central Highlands?).
Rowley has raised a magnificent hybrid with pink Fl.

Arequipa Br. & R. (80)

Plants at first spherical, becoming elongated to semi-columnar or cereoid and then often prostrate; spines mostly strong; flowers red, zygomorphic, hairy, with the tube $\pm$ long. Fruits dehisce basally. Seedling plants particularly attractive.—Distribution: S. Peru to N. Chile. [(R).]

Arequipa aurantiaca (Vpl.) Werd.: **Submatucana aurantiaca** (Vpl.) Backbg.

A. australis Ritt. (FR 1080): no description available.

A. erectocylindrica Rauh & Backbg.
Bo. cereoid, even in juveniles, dull to greyish-green, to 50 cm lg.; **Ri.** 15–17(–18); **Ar.** to 6 mm br., yellowish-grey at first; **Rsp.** 12–14, acicular to slender-subulate, whitish to horn-grey; **Csp.** 7(–12), horn-coloured, with dark (brownish) tips, stout-subulate, to 4.5 cm lg.; **Sp.** on new growth in cultivated plants $\pm$ equal, more reddish-brown; **Fl.** c. 7 cm lg., red; **Fr.** elongated-cylindric, lemon-yellow.—S. Peru (volcano Chachani).

A. hempeliana (Gürke) Oehme
Bo. elongated, greyish-green, somewhat pruinose; **Ri.** 14–20; **Ar.** to 15 mm apart, light yellowish, becoming glabrous; **Rsp.** 8–12, amber-coloured, $\pm$ spotted, 1–3 cm lg., mostly curving; **Csp.** 3–4, yellowish-red at first, with a dark brown tip, to 5 cm lg., very flexible, $\pm$ interlacing; **Fl.** 7.5 cm lg., vermilion, more carmine at the tip, zygomorphic; **Ov.** green, it and the **Tu.** white-hairy; **Sti.** yellow.—Chile (N.). Has become very rare.

A. leucotricha (Phil.) Br. & R. was a spherical several-headed plant with 15 **Ri.**, with long white thin **Br.** and c. 6 rather long, light brown **Sp.**; **Fl.** scarlet.—Chile (Tarapacá, near Naquira and Usmaga). Not identical with A. rettigii, from Arequipa. Uncertain spec. Echinocactus leucotrichus sensu Soehrens was perhaps A. weingartiana.

A. mirabilis (Buin.) Backbg. n.comb. (Matucana mirabilis Buin., Sukkde. (SKG), VII–VIII, 39–41. 1963).
Bo. columnar, to 60 cm lg., 12 cm $\emptyset$; **Ri.** c. 12, tuberculate because of transverse furrows, eventually becoming flatter; **Ar.** to 1.5 cm apart, oval, 8 mm lg., 5 mm br., yellowish at first, then white; **Rsp.** c. 12, projecting, c. 1 cm lg., hyaline; **Csp.** c. 3, the 2 upper ones to 1.3 cm lg., the lowest one stouter, to 2 cm lg., brown above; **Fl.** 8.5 cm lg., 4 cm $\emptyset$, $\pm$ zygomorphic; **Sep.** green, to violet on the margins; **Pet.** light red, with violet margins; **Tu.** $\pm$ hairy; **style** white below, $\pm$ pink above; **Sti.** greenish; **Fr.** light yellow, dehiscing basally.—Peru (Dept. Lima, between Churin and Oyon, 3–3500 m). This must be the plant I saw in Buining's

collection, see plate in "Die Cactaceae" VI: p. 3680, Fig. 3342, or l.c. p. 3700, Fig. 3358; this, like the preceding spec., came from Akers. The illustrations clearly show that these are distinctly cereoid plants, referable to Arequipa. Matucana, acc. to the generic diagnosis of Br. & R., has a glabrous Tu. and Ov. The only other possibility would be my G. Submatucana, but this is not cereoid. Buining's remarks (l.c.) against Submatucana are inapplicable, as I have shown in my work "Kritisches zu den Kakteenbeiträgen in Sukkde. (SKG), VII–VIII. 1963".

Arequipa myriacantha (Vpl.) Br. & R.: **Submatucana myriacantha** (Vpl.) Backbg.

A. rettigii (Quehl) Oehme (T.)
Bo. ± spherical at first, eventually elongated and columnar and ± prostrate; **Ri.** 10–20; **Ar.** to 5 mm apart, grey-felty at first; **Rsp.** 20–30, thin, hyaline, to 1 cm lg.; **Csp.** to 10, the strongest one up to 3 cm lg., not all of them as robust as in the preceding spec.; **Fl.** to 6 cm lg. or somewhat more, scarlet, limb only slightly oblique; **Pet.** moderately long; **Tu.** slender, its length almost twice that of the Fl.—Ø; **Fr.** spherical.—S. Peru (around Arequipa). (Fig. 13.) Erroneously often called A. leucotricha, which is the ± unclarified plant, "Echinocactus leucotrichus Phil." from Chile.

A. soehrensii (Krzgr.) Backbg.
Bo. long-cylindric, resembling A. rettigii; **Rsp.** not fine, but firmer and longer; **Csp.** slightly curving; **Fl.** resembling that of A. rettigii, slender, longer, limb only slightly zygomorphic.—Peru (Tacna). Judging by these characters this is a distinct spec. which has not been re-collected since it was first found by J. Soehrens.

A. spinosissima Ritt.—"Taxon", XIII: 3, 115. 1964.
Bo. spherical to elongated, simple; **Ri.** 20–24, c. 5 mm h.; **Sp.** 50–60, white, 3–5 mm lg., some of them 1–2 cm lg., ivory with a brown or blackish tip; **Fl.** 7–8 cm lg., carmine, nectary absent.—Peru (Dept. Arequipa, Quicacha) (FR 196).

Arequipa variicolor (Backbg.) Backbg.: **Oreocereus variicolor** Backbg.

A. weingartiana Backbg.
Bo. spherical at first, eventually elongated, stout and less cereoid than the preceding spec., up to 40 cm h., ashen-grey to green; **Ri.** c. 16; **Ar.** 7 mm lg.; **Rsp.** c. 12 or more, to 15 mm lg.; **Csp.** c. 4, arranged in a cross, thickened at the base, much stouter, to 5 cm lg., at first yellowish and dark-tipped, eventually blackish above, becoming grey below; **Fl.** 5.5 cm lg., 2.5 cm Ø, very zygomorphic, light brick-

red, with a broad **Tu.**; **Fr.** small, spherical.—N. Chile, 3500m (to S. Peru?).
v. **carminanthema** Backbg. has a dark carmine Fl.

Ariocarpus Scheidw. (225)

Plants mostly broadly rounded, ± greyish-green, with stout carrot-like roots. The ribs are replaced by rather long or acuminate, deltoid tubercles arranged in spirals. As in Mammillaria, the flowers are borne around the apex, not in it, sometimes several together in a coronet (!), arising from the axils which have flaky wool. Furrows, or cleft and elongated areoles, as in Roseocactus, are not present. In habitat the plants are mostly sunk in the soil and therefore often difficult to find.— Distribution: Mexico (more towards the E., from the N. frontier to San Luis Potosí). (O. (G.), better in a mainly mineral compost.)
(See under Roseocactus Berg. for the following spec., formerly attributed to Ariocarpus: A. kotschoubeyanus (Lem.) K.Sch., A. fissuratus (Eng.) K. Sch. and A. lloydii Rose.)
Anderson (Am. Journ. Bot., 49: 6, 615–622. 1962) also refers Neogomesia Castañ. and Roseocactus Berg. to Ariocarpus. The supporting morphological and cytological researches are interesting, but the unification is ill-considered. If one unites species where the flowers appear in a coronet from the axils (Ariocarpus) with those where the flowers are borne centrally from the newest areoles (Neogomesia), and others which flower apically and have woolly cleft tubercles, then logic demands that Mammillaria and Coryphantha should no longer be segregated. Has the author overlooked this, in his concern purely with his own very narrow specialism? The remarks under Rebutia are just as applicable here. While a unified classification of the family is made increasingly necessary by the constantly increasing number of new admissions, it also becomes increasingly difficult; and combinations of this kind, without any reference to the overall situation, endanger the comprehensive systematic arrangement of the Cactaceae which constitutes the most vital task of our times. Otherwise the process is bound to be extended, and not just restricted to these three genera. I have to reject this, since the consequences would produce the utmost confusion, particularly as there is no need for amendments of this type which make it more difficult, not easier, to distinguish between species.

Ariocarpus agavioides (Castañ.) And.: **Neogomesia agavioides** Castañ.

A. elongatus (S.D.) M.H. Lee
This spec., or variety of A. trigonus, is disputed. **Tub.** are longer and narrower than in A. trigonus; **Fl.** said to be white as in A. retusus, whereas A. trigonus flowers yellow. 3 different natural forms have been observed (acc. Voldan, Prague).—Mexico (Tamaulipas), Jaumave, San Vicente.

A. furfuraceus (Wats.) Thomps.
Bo. broadly rounded, light grey, to c. 10 cm $\emptyset$, **Tub.** ± broadly compressed, the upper surface calloused and the tip elongated; **Ar.** apical, minute, glabrous; **Fl.** 2.5–3 cm lg., 4–5 cm $\emptyset$, white (to pink?); **Pet.** 6–10 mm br.—Mexico (Coahuila).
v. **rostratus** Berg.: with a woolly Ar. below the tip.

A. retusus Scheidw. (T.)
Bo. rounded, blue or olive or grey-green, to 10–12 cm br., with wool in the crown; **Tub.** acutely trigonous, broad at the base, tapering, smooth, convex and keeled on the underside; **Ar.** minute, below the tip, or absent, otherwise glabrous; **Fl.** 4 cm lg., pale pink; **Sti.** white.—Mexico (San Luis Potosi).

A. scapharostrus Böd.
Bo. broadly rounded, to 9 cm $\emptyset$, dark leaf-green; **Tub.** directed obliquely upwards, prismatically elongated, to 5 cm lg., trigonous, flat and smooth above, curving up at the tip, keeled below; **Ax.** (acc. Böd.) glabrous, but just below it there is a woolly depression, making the **Ax.** appear woolly (does this apply to other spec.?); **Fl.** to 4 cm $\emptyset$, violet-pink; **S.** dull black.—Mexico (Nuevo León).

A. trigonus (Web.) K. Sch.
Bo. broadly rounded, to over 10 cm $\emptyset$; **Tub.** elongated, tapering, curving ± upwards, ± glossy, brownish to greyish-green, numerous, 3.5 cm lg., weakly trigonous, keeled below; **Fl.** often numerous, c. 5 cm $\emptyset$, yellowish; **Sti.** 8–10.—Mexico (Nuevo León). (Fig. 14.)
v. **elongatus** (SD.) Backbg.: **Tub.** to 5 cm lg., evenly tapering, with a broader pruinose band.—Mexico (near Jaumave).

Armatocereus Backbg. (59)

Larger, shrubby or tree-like Cerei with fairly stiffly ascending stems showing a conspicuous constriction at the end of the annual growth; true green to whitish grey-green, poorly or strongly spined; the flowers have a proportionately long tube which, like the ovary, is ± spiny; the perianth is white or in one instance red. The fruits are mostly quite strongly spiny, and fairly large; seeds fairly large.—

Distribution: from Colombia, through Ecuador to Peru, or S. to the valley of the Rio Pisco and Rio Majes. (Some species grow very strongly, others much more slowly. [(R). O.]

A. arboreus Rauh & Backbg.
Bo. broadly tree-shaped, grey-green, with a thick trunk, to 6 m h. or more; **shoots** ascending, numerous, to 60 cm lg., 15 cm $\emptyset$; **Ri.** (5–)6; **Rsp.** mostly not long; **Csp.** 1–3, to 15 cm lg.; **Fl.** white; **Fr.** apparently not very strongly spined.—Central Peru (around the upper Eulalia valley).

A. arduus Ritt. (FR 1060): no description available.

A. cartwrightianus (Br. & R.) Backbg.
Bo. tree-like, fresh green, over 5 m h., with a stout trunk, very strong-growing, even in cultivation; **shoots** to 60 cm lg., 8–15 cm $\emptyset$, **Ri.** 7–8; **Ar.** large, brown; **Sp.** reddish-brown at first, soon becoming whitish with a dark tip; **Rsp.** and **Csp.** scarcely distinguishable, to 20 or even more in age, at first to 2 cm lg., some to 12 cm lg. or more, all eventually dark, brown or grey-white; **Fl.** 7–9 cm lg.; **Tu.** slender, Sp. more distant, few or only short; **Ov.** more densely spiny; **Pet.** white; **Fr.** 9 cm lg., with weak Sp.—S. Ecuador to N. eru. (Fig. 15.)
v. **longispinus** Backbg. has particularly long **Sp.**

A. churinensis Rauh & Backbg.
Bo. only 2 m h., dull green; **Ri.** 5, thin; **Fl.** white; **Fr.** dark green, with dense brown Sp.—Central Peru (Churin valley).

A. confusus Ritt.: Sp. moderately lg., dark at first otherwise identical with A. laetus.—N. Peru. Acc. Backeberg the name-transfer has not been validated.

A. ghiesbreghtii (K.Sch.) is probably identical with A. laetus; the new combination is therefore not completely valid.

A. godingianus (Br. & R.) Backbg.
Bo. tree-like, shoots with longer Seg., light to greyish green, robust, broader towards the base; **trunk** to 50 cm $\emptyset$; **Ri.** 7–11; **Sp.** acicular, robust, 2–4 cm lg., brownish at first; **Fl.** to 11 cm lg., white; **Tu.** only 2 cm lg., thick-walled, it and the **Ov.** with brown wool and yellow bristly Sp.; **Fr.** 10 cm lg., with yellow Sp.; **S.** large, black.—Ecuador (Chanchan valley, around Huigra). Rarely imported.

A. humilis (Br. & R.) Backbg.
Bo. forming broad bushes, to 4 m h.; **shoots** dark green, to 4 cm $\emptyset$, constricted, ± tapering above;

Ri. 3–4(–6); **Ar.** large, white; **Sp.** 5–8, brown at first, later white, acicular, 1–2 cm lg.; **Fl.** greenish-white, 6 cm lg.; **Ov.** spineless at first; **Tu.** with scattered tufts of fine short Sp.; **Fr.** spherical, 4 cm ∅, very spiny.—Colombia (Dagua valley, Venticas del Dagua).

A. laetus (HBK.) Backbg. (T.)
Bo. tall-shrubby, erectly branching, to 6 m h., pale greyish-green; **Ri.** mostly 7, low, acute, becoming flattened; **Sp.** to 12, brown at first, becoming whitish, 1–2 centrals to 8 cm lg.; **Fl.** c. 6.5 cm lg., 5 cm ∅, white; **Tu.** c. 5 cm lg., 2.2 cm ∅, with dark felt and blackish Sp. directed upwards; **Ov.** c. 1.2 cm lg., broadly spherical; **Fr.** with dense reddish-brown Sp.—N. Peru (Rio Huancabamba).

A. mataranus Ritt.
Spec. resembling A. laetus, but growing taller and broader.—Peru.

A. matucanensis Backbg.
Bo. moderately tall, with a broad crown, the trunk only short or absent; **shoots** mostly darker green; **Ri.** 4–5(–8); **Sp.** 8 or more, 1–2 of these longer, one often to 10 cm lg.; **Fl.** white; **Fr.** large, green, densely spiny.—Central Peru (around Matucana). (Fig. 16.)

A. oligogonus Rauh & Backbg.
Bo. leaden-grey, to 3 m h.; **Ri.** mostly 4–5, narrow, prominent; **Sp.** grey, dark-tipped; **Rsp.** 8–12, to 1.5 cm lg.; **Csp.** 1–2, to 10 cm lg.; **Fl.** white; **Fr.** with long brownish Sp.—N. Peru (Huancabamba valley).

A. procerus Rauh & Backbg.
Bo. to 7 m. h., green, without a distinct trunk; **shoots** stiffly erect, strongly articulated; **Ri.** 8–10; **Rsp.** 15–20, to 2 cm lg., whitish; **Csp.** to 4, to 12 cm lg., honey-yellow below, leather-coloured above; **Sp.** numerous from old Ar., radiating, unequal; **Fl.** 10 cm lg., 5 cm ∅, white; **Fr.** 7 cm long, green, with white Sp.—Peru (Rio Casma to Rio Nazca).

A. rauhii Backbg.
Bo. 4–6 m h., bluish to greyish-green, the **trunk** 1 m. h., the **crown** consisting of rigidly ascending branches, these only somewhat re-branching; **Ar.** 3 mm long, white; **Rsp.** 6–7(–10), only 1–2 mm lg.; **Csp.** sometimes present, 6 mm–1–3 cm lg., grey below, black above, other **Sp.** blackish-brown; **Fl.** carmine; **Tu.** with distant Ar. with black to red Sp.; **Fr.** 3–5 cm lg., dark green, with red to black Sp.—N. Peru (Huancabamba valley). (Fig. 17.)

A. riomajensis Rauh & Backbg.
Bo. only 2m h.; **branches** leaden-grey to green; **Ri.**
7–9, narrow, 2 cm h.; **Ar.** blackish, circular; **Rsp.** 10–15, to 1 cm lg., light grey; **Csp.** mostly 1–4, in part to 12 cm lg., brown-tipped, in part contorted or angular; **Fl.** white, 8–10 cm lg.; **Fr.** 15 cm lg., 5 cm ∅, with Sp. to 4 cm lg., grey-violet.—S. Peru (Rio Majes valley).

Arrojadoa Br. & R. (186)

Very slender-stemmed, moderately long or in part creeping plants, with an apical, brush-like tuft of bristles from which the red buds and ± reddish nocturnal flowers arise. The berry-like fruits are spherical and bear floral remains.—Distribution: N. Brazil (Bahia, Piauhy, Pernambuco). [(G).]

A. aureispina Buin. & Bred.
Bo. 0.75–1 m h., 5–5.5 cm ∅, offsetting from the base; **Ri.** 14, to 1 cm apart, 6–7 mm h., obtuse; **Ar.** 4 mm br., 3.5 mm lg., 7–8 mm apart; **Sp.** clustered at the apex, golden-yellow, tipped golden-brown, later whitish; **Rsp.** 12–13, straight; **Csp.** c. 9, c. 14 mm lg.; **Fl.** tubular, 31 mm lg., to 10 mm ∅, dark pink, appearing from an apical Ceph. through which the new growth, c. 15 cm lg., develops during the next season and in turn develops a new Ceph.; **style** yellowish-white; **Fr.** cherry-shaped, pinkish-red; **S.** glossy black.— Brazil (Bahia, NW. of Caitité, among Bromeliads on rocks; discovered 1966 by Horst and Buining). (Fig. 460.)

A. canudosensis Buin. & Bred.
Bo. offsetting from the base; **St.** 1–1.25 m h., 5.5–6 cm ∅, green, erect; **R.** branching; **Ceph.** of brown Br. and white H. through which the new season's growth develops to become c. 20–25 cm lg., this in turn with a new Ceph.; **Ri.** 11–13, 14–15 mm h.; **Ar.** oval, 5 mm lg., 3.5 mm br., with white H. at first, later glabrous, 8 mm apart; **Sp.** yellowish-white at first, tipped brown, later concolorous brown or white; **Csp.** 8, stouter than the Rsp., innermost one stoutest, to 30 mm lg., others 15–17 mm lg.; **Fl.** funnelform, 3 cm lg., pink; **Pet.** and **Sep.** rounded; **Fil.** very numerous, white; **An.** yellow; style 20 mm lg.; **Fr.** 15 mm ∅, light pink at first, later dark violet; **S.** black.—Brazil (Bahia, Canudos, in the Caatinga at 400 m).

A. dinae Buin. & Bred. 1973
Bo. consisting of thin, columnar branches from the base, to 30 cm lg., 18–20 mm ∅; **Ceph.** white-woolly, with 15–20 mm lg. brown Br.; **Ri.** 11, narrow, rounded, 4–5 mm br.; **Ar.** round, 5 mm apart, with greyish-white felt at first, later glabrous; **Sp.** white, often tipped light brown, radiating, flexible, c. 12 Rsp. and 8 Csp., these little differentiated, 4–8 mm lg.; **Fl.** tubular, 29 mm lg.,

to 9 mm br., brownish-carmine, yellow inside; **Fil.** white; **Sti.** 5–6, yellowish; **Fr.** berry-like, brownish-red; **S.** glossy black.—Brazil (Bahia, Serra do Espinhaco, SE. of Urandi, at 900 m, in sandy-loamy soil, beneath shrubs and trees). Found in 1972 by Buining and Horst. (Fig. 461.)

A. eriocaulis Buin. & Bred.
Bo. with thin columnar branches 50 cm lg. or more, 1–1.5 cm ∅, green, with white to yellowish-white H., with a tuberous R.; **Ceph.** with long, silky, yellowish-white H.; **Br.** c. 2 cm lg., light brown, flexible; **Ri.** 8–9, c. 3 mm apart, narrow, rounded, thickened at the Ar., to 3 mm br.; **Ar.** rather sunken, oval, 2–2.5 mm lg., 1.5 mm br., 5 mm apart, with silky, woolly, white to yellowish-white H.; **Rsp.** 10–12, radiating, 4–7 mm lg., yellowish-brown, stiff; **Csp.** 8, 6–12 mm lg., dark brown, one of these directed obliquely upwards, c. 12 mm lg.; **Fl.** tubular, 12 mm lg., to 6 mm br., glabrous, carmine, with very small Sc.; **Sep.** 3.5 mm lg., 2 mm br., light violet-pink; **Pet.** denticulate, acute, light violet-pink; **style** white, with 4–5 creamy-white Sti.; **An.** yellow; **Fr.** berry-like, 14 mm lg., brownish-red; **S.** cap-shaped, dull black.—Brazil (Minas Geraes); near Mato Verde, at 950 m, among grass and shrubs. Discovered 1971 by Horst. (Fig. 462.)

A. medinensis (FR 1335): no description available.

A. multiflora Ritt. (FR 1243): no description available.

A. penicillata (Gürke) Br. & R.
Bo. to 2 m h., inclined-shrubby; **St.** segmented, growing on through the bristle-tufts, continuing to flower from some older annular tufts, thickened apically; **Ri.** 10–12, slender; **Rsp.** 8–12, short, appressed, very fine; **Csp.** 1–2, stouter, rigid, 1–3 cm lg.; **Fl.** opening fairly wide, nocturnal, reddish; **S.** very small, semi-glossy, dark brown.—Brazil (Central and S. Bahia). (Fig. 18.)
  v. **decumbens** Backbg. & Voll: prostrate, more stoutly spined.

A. rhodantha (Gürke) Br. & R. (T.)
Bo. to 2 m h., shrubby, erect to prostate, mostly branching from the base; **St.** mostly short-cylindric, 2–5 cm ∅; **Ri.** 10–12, low; **Ar.** 8–12 mm apart; **Rsp.** and **Csp.** scarcely differentiated, c. 20 outer and 5–6 central ones, to 3 cm lg., mostly darker brown; **Fl.** from the apical tuft, to 3.5 cm lg., 1.2 cm ∅, bluish-red; **Fr.** top-shaped, purple.—Brazil (Bahia, Piauhy, Pernambuco). Ritter reports a v. minensis Ritt. (FR 1241A), without any further details, also a sp.n. (FR 1244) "with red Sp.".

A. theunisseniana Buin. & Bred.
Bo. offsetting from the base; **St.** 40–80 cm lg., 3–4 cm thick, green; apical **Ceph.** with brown Br. to 20 mm lg., with white wool at first, later glabrous; **Ri.** 10–12, fairly obtuse, c. 5 mm h. and 10 mm apart; **Ar.** with white felt, later grey, subcircular; **Rsp.** c. 13, radiating, light yellowish-brown; **Csp.** 8, yellowish-brown, darker-tipped, innermost ones to 22 mm lg.; **Fl.** tubular, 34 mm lg., glabrous, pinkish-red; **style** yellowish-white; **Sti.** 5, yellow, tapering.—Brazil (Bahia, in very dry Caatinga, under shrubs; between Macaubas and Botopura, at c. 600 m).

Arthrocereus Berg. (142)

Small cerei with slender stems, in part with a woody root; in one species the stems are divided into spherical segments, otherwise they are cereoid. The fruits are juicy berries. Two Subgenera are distinguished on the basis of flower-size and hair-development, and the number indicating the relevant Subgenus is given in brackets after the specific name; the self-sterile flowers are nocturnal.
  SG.1: Arthrocereus: flowers long, slender, more weakly hairy;
  SG.2: Cutakia Backbg.: flowers shorter, stouter and more strongly hairy.
Setiechinopsis, which is self-fertile and often autogamous, its flower set with bristle-tipped scales, and its fruit fusiform and dry, is not referable here.—Distribution: Central Brazil (Minas Geraes). [(G) (R).]

A. campos-portoi (Werd.) Backbg. (1)
Bo. simple or offsetting, ± prostrate; **St.** to 15 cm lg., to 3 cm ∅, almost glossy light green; **Ri.** c. 12, low; **Ar.** yellowish-grey at first; **Rsp.** 25–35; **Csp.** 1–2, to 4 cm lg.; **Sp.** all ± dark brown; **Fl.** to 8.5 cm lg.; **Sc.** very small; **Tu.** ± hairy; **Pet.** white, narrowly lanceolate, revolute; **Fr.** small, pear-shaped; **S.** black.—Brazil (Minas Geraes, Bello Horizonte, Serra de Curral).

A. mello-barretoi Backbg. & Voll (2)
Bo. somewhat more slender than in the preceding; **Ri.** 16; **Ar.** 4–5 mm apart; **Sp.** c. 35, greenish-yellow, centrals to 2.5 cm lg.; **Fl.** stouter, 7 cm lg., 5 cm ∅; **Tu.** 5.5 cm lg., stout, densely set with reddish-brown H.; **Pet.** white, spreading horizontally.—Brazil (Minas Geraes, Serra de Lenheiro).

A. microsphaericus (K. Sch.) Berg. (1) (T.)
Bo. consisting of spherical Seg.; **St.** to 6.5 cm lg. or more; **Ri.** 7, very low; **Sp.** numerous, very short, fine; **Fl.** white, c. 11 cm lg.; **Tu.** thin, only sparsely

hairy; **Fr.** spherical.—Brazil.

Arthrocereus mirabilis (Speg.) F. Buxb.: **Setiechinopsis mirabilis** (Speg.) de Haas.

A. rondonianus Backbg. & Voll (2)

Bo. as in A. mello-barretoi; **St.** to 50 cm lg., fresh green; **Ar.** 5–10 mm apart, grey; **Sp.** 40–50, very fine, yellowish, some to 2 cm lg., 1–2 centrals to 7 cm lg. (shorter in grafted plants); **Fl.** pale lilac-red; **Sep.** narrow, spreading; **Pet.** ± trumpet-like; **Tu.** only medium-long, with projecting, upwardly directed, ± bristle-like hairs; **Fil.** purple; **style** projecting; **Sti.** white. Grafted plants produce numerous magnificent flowers.—Brazil (near Diamantina). (Fig. 19.)

Astrophytum Lem. (191)

Plants of very diverse habit: spineless, with few ± acute angles (so-called "Bishop's Cap"); or resembling sea-urchins; or in other species with distinctive soft, long spines; in one species the spines are rigid; mostly spherical in shape although two varieties of the type-species become ± elongated, and one species becomes tall-columnar in age. In general all species have the epidermis set with minute flakes, this in part ± strongly reduced and in some sub-varieties (forms) completely suppressed. Flowers mostly larger, attractive, ± yellow, in part red at the centre. Fruits split widely above, or open below; in some species the wall is firm, in others softer. Seeds brown, relatively soft. Two Subgenera are segregated on the basis of type of dehiscence; the relevant figure is shown in brackets after the specific name.

SG.1: Astrophytum: Ripe fruits splitting above and gaping;
SG.2: Neoastrophytum Backbg.: Fruits opening below, in part not opening at all but disintegrating.

Distribution: USA (Texas) to Mexico (from Coahuila, more eastern parts, to San Luis Potosí and Querétaro). [(G) (R).]

A. asterias (Zucc.) Lem. (2)

Bo. flat, to c. 10 cm. br., green to greyish-green or somewhat darker, spineless; **Ri.** (6–)8(–10), flat; **Ar.** centrally on the Ri., circular, fairly broad; **Fl.** 3 cm lg., to 6.5 cm ⌀, yellow (sometimes with a reddish tinge), with a red centre; **Fr.** greyish-red, ± fleshy, opening below or disintegrating. Young seedlings have small spines.—Mexico (Tamaulipas, Nuevo León) to USA (Texas, Rio Grande valley).

A. capricorne (Dietr.) Br. & R. (2)

Bo. spherical to elongated, strong green, variable in flock-development, in age to 25 cm h.; **Ri.** acute, c. 9; **Ar.** 1.5–3 cm apart, greyish-white; **Sp.** to 10, irregular in arrangement, flattened, very flexible, to 7 cm. lg., ± brown, eventually falling; **Fl.** c. 7 cm lg., yellow, with a carmine centre; **Ov.** green; **Fr.** oblong, red, red inside.—(N. Mexico.) (Fig. 20.)

The following varieties have been segregated:
v. **crassispinum** (Möll.) Ok.: with flock sparse or missing, **Sp.** stout, dark, **Fl.** lacking a red centre;
v. **minus** (Rge. & Quehl) Ok.: with a smaller **Bo.**;
v. **niveum** (Kays.) Ok.: overall white, with upcurving blackish ± terete **Sp.**

A. coahuilense (Möll.) Kays. (2)

Bo. becoming elongated, with few angles, with dense white flock; **Ri.** normally 5; **Fl.** large, sulphur-yellow, with an orange to scarlet centre; **Fr.** purplish-red, opening basally.—N. Mexico (Coahuila).

A. myriostigma Lem. (1) (T.)

Bo. spherical to somewhat elongated, rarely higher, greenish to whitish-grey; **Ri.** mostly 5 (rarely 3–4), acute; **Ar.** 10–15 mm apart; **Fl.** yellow, to 6 cm ⌀; **Sep.** black-tipped; **Fr.** splitting and gaping.—Mexico (central to northern Highlands).

v. **columnare** (K.Sch.) Tsuda is oblong, **Fl.** only medium-large, pale yellow; subv. **glabrum** Backbg. is pure green, with acuter **Ri.**; v. **potosinum** (Möll.) Krzgr. has a more greenish **Bo.** and smaller, pale yellow **Fl.**; its subv. **tulense** (Kays.) Backbg. has a whiter **Bo.**, **Fl.** pale yellow, redder towards the centre; v. **quadricostatum** (Möll.) Baum usually has 4 **Ri.**; v. **strongylogonum** Backbg. has more rounded, less acute **Ri.**, and **Fl.** which are large, light yellow; its subv. **nudum** (R. Mey.) Backbg, is concolourous green.

A. ornatum (DC.) Web. (1)

Bo. at first spherical, becoming columnar, to c. 1 m h., 30 cm ⌀, while individual specimens are said to have attained 3 m. in height (Fittkau); **Ri.** 8, flakes forming a curving pattern; **Sp.** 5–11, straight, subulate, sharp, yellowish to dark brown, the longest ones to 3 cm lg.; **Fl.** 7–9 cm ⌀, light yellow; **Fr.** oblong to spherical; **S.** not numerous.—Mexico (Hidalgo to Querétaro).

subv. **glabrescens** (Web.) Backbg. is dark green, with the flock sparse or absent;
v. **mirbelii** (Lem.) Ok. is distinguished by its attractive golden-yellow **Sp.** and generally stronger flock-development.
There are also the forms: nudum and spirale.

A. senile Frič (2)

Bo. at first spherical, eventually elongated, leaf-green, to 35 cm h. and 15 cm ⌀; **Ri.** 8, acute, flock absent; **Ar.** 1–1.2 cm apart, 5 mm long, yellow; **Sp.**

15–20, $\pm$ terete, flexible, contorted, brownish-red to brownish-black, not falling; **Fl., Fr.** and **S.** as in A. capricorne.— Mexico.

v. **aureum** (Möll.) Backbg. has **Sp.** which are gold to straw-coloured at first, and sometimes slight flock development.

Austrocactus Br. & R. (105)

The distinguishing characteristic of all species is the soft-fleshy, columnar body. Some flower while still spherical. The flowers are $\pm$ funnelform; they and the fruits are $\pm$ bristly-spiny. The perianth of the Argentinian species is $\pm$ reddish, and in the Chilean species yellowish-brown. A genus with distinctive characters of body and flower.— Distribution: S. Argentina (Neuquén, Rio Negro, Chubut, Santa Cruz) and S. upper Chile (upper Maule gorge).

A. bertinii (Cels) Br. & R.
Bo. $\pm$ cereoid, fairly soft, to more than 5 cm $\varnothing$, olive-green, to 40 cm h.; **Ri.** 10–12, strongly tuberculate; **Rsp.** c. 15, acicular, to 1 cm lg., light; **Csp.** mostly 4–6, moderately strong, to 6 cm lg., yellowish to brownish, sometimes all hooked, otherwise straight; **Fl.** 6 cm lg., 10 cm $\varnothing$ (?), pinkish-yellow; **Tu.** with wool and stiff Br.; **style** and **Sti.** red; **S.** flattened.—S. Argentina (near Comodoro Rivadavia). (Fig. 21.)

A. coxii (K.Sch.) Backbg.
Bo. cereoid, to 60 cm lg., to 5 cm $\varnothing$; **Ri.** 6–10, tuberculate; **Rsp.** c. 6–10, 1 cm lg., thin, interlacing; **Csp.** 1–4, stouter, to 4 cm lg., straight or $\pm$ hooked, pale to whitish; **Fl.** 3.5 cm lg. and $\varnothing$, pale reddish; **Ov.** without bristles, sparsely hairy; **style** pink; **Sti.** very dark red.—S. Argentina (Chubut; near Chilean frontier).

A. gracilis Backbg.
Bo. slender, thin, to 1.6 cm $\varnothing$, to 35 cm lg., often prostrate; **Ri.** 8–9, low, slender, $\pm$ tuberculate throughout; **Rsp.** to 11 and sometimes with 1–3 additional minute Sp. above, to 5 mm lg., all whitish, yellowish-tipped; **Csp.** 1–3, stouter, some $\pm$ hooked, yellowish, brown-tipped, to 2 cm lg.; **Fl.** ?— S. Argentina (Patagonia).

A. hibernus Ritt.—Sukkde. (SKG) VII–VIII, 34–36. 1963.
Bo. green, prostrate and/or ascending, to 3 cm $\varnothing$, 10 cm lg.; **Ri.** 7–8, to 6 mm h., quite strongly tuberculate; **Ar.** pale yellow; **Rsp.** 5–8, whitish, mostly very thin, 3–10 mm lg., upper ones stronger, to 2 cm lg., yellowish-brown; **Csp.** 1–4, 1–3 cm lg., straight, yellowish-brown; **Fl.** to 5 cm lg.,

yellowish-brown; **Fil.** whitish; **Sti.** reddish above; **Fr.** green, soft; **S.** 2.25 mm long, black, finely tuberculate with a small hilum.—Chile (Maule gorge, Mine Dolomita, c. 2000 m). The flowers are apparently also dioecious.

A. patagonicus (Web.) Backbg.
Bo. columnar, to 8 cm $\varnothing$, offsetting, to 50 cm lg.; **Ri.** 9–12, tuberculate; **Ar.** white; **Rsp.** 6–10, to 1.5 cm lg., light; **Csp.** 1–4, stronger, to 2.5 cm lg., thickened at the base, horn-coloured at first, becoming blackish, sometimes hooked; **Fl.** 4 cm lg., 5 cm $\varnothing$, whitish to pinkish-white; **Tu.** with dirty white wool, with horn-coloured to black Br.; **style** pink; **Sti.** violet; **Fr.** $\pm$ dry, bristly; **S.** dark, compressed.—S. Argentina (Patagonia; along the rivers Chubut and Negro). Judging by the data on habitat and altitude, A. hibernus is without doubt an invader from the principal Argentine distribution. Ritter (l.c.) also refers Erdisia philippii (Reg. & Schmidt) Br. & R. and Erdisia spiniflora (Phil.) Br. & R. to the genus Austrocactus. Quite apart from the fact that there is no justification based on floral studies, E. philippii has never been re-collected, so that any comb. nov. would be hazardous. E. spiniflora, as shown in the illustration of Br. & R., has the subterranean rhizome-like stem which is typical of E. meyenii, and fruits which much more closely resemble those of Erdisia; the American authors themselves stated that the flowers were alike. I am therefore unable to follow them here since the new combination is not well founded.

Austrocephalocereus Backbg. (181)

Cerei, eventually several meters high, with true cephalia situated laterally, and not arising from a groove or cleft; flowers glabrous. They belong to the S. American branch of cephalium-bearing genera, although the cephalia are not as broad, large or strong as in the cephalium-stages of the Mexican Pachycerei. While Pilosocereus Byl. & Rowl. exhibits only cephalium-like development (which in part is absent) even in older plants, this development is *constant* in the truly cephalium-bearing plants, differing only in character. Austrocephalocereus Backbg. is the sole Brazilian genus with glabrous flowers, and a lateral cephalium which does not arise from a groove; in one species the cephalium is interspersed with bristles but these are absent in the other species. The genus should thus by rights be divided into two subgenera, but I have not done this because we have as yet no certain knowledge as to whether a few bristles do, or do not, sometimes appear; or whether cephalia consisting of thick woolly tufts represent only a slight reduction in as much as no brisles are present.—Distribution: NE. Brazil (Bahia). [(G) (R).]

A. albicephalus Buin. & Bred.
Bo. columnar, offsetting from the base; **branches** to 2.5 m lg., to 9 cm ∅, green; **Ceph.** 30–40 cm lg., often more, 8–9 cm br., with dense silky white wool, with golden-yellow Br. to 5 cm lg. only at the apex; **Ri.** to 32, c. 5 mm h., 8–10 mm br. and distant; **Ar.** 3–5 mm apart, oval, 4 mm lg., 3 mm br., those in the flowering zone 5 mm ∅, with light yellow wool and solitary white H.; **Sp.** numerous, straight, thin and sharp, golden-yellow, later brownish, dark brown below, one downwardly directed Sp. to 1.5 cm lg.; **Fl.** nocturnal, cylindric, bellshaped above, 4.5–5 cm lg., 2.6 cm ∅ when expanded, glabrous, white; **Ov.** 9 mm lg. and br., light green, 2.5–7 mm br.; **Sep.** spatulate, mucronate, fleshy, c. 16 mm lg., whitish, with a brownish-pink tip and M.-stripe; **Pet.** similarly, white; **Fil.** numerous, white; **An.** yellow; **style** 32 mm lg., white, light greenish above; **Sti.** thin, radiating, yellowish, 4 mm lg.; **Fr.** spherical, c. 3 cm lg., 3.5 cm ∅, brownish-red, pulp white, translucent; **S.** ovoid matt black.—Brazil (Minas Geraes; near Mato Verde, on and between rocks, at c. 950 m). Found by Horst, 1972.

A. dybowskii (Goss.) Backbg.
Bo. to 4 m h., branching from the base; **St.** directed fairly stiffly upwards, entirely covered by soft white H., to 8 cm ∅; **Ri.** over 20, narrow, low; **Ar.** crowded; **Rsp.** numerous, short, concealed by the H.; **Csp.** 2–3, yellowish to brownish, projecting to spreading, to 3 cm lg., acicular; **Ceph.** to 60 cm lg., white; **Fl.** 4 cm lg., bellshaped, white; **Pet.** short; **Fr.** spherical, naked, pink, c. 2.5 cm ∅; **S.** black, rough.—Brazil (Bahia, Itumirin). (Fig. 22.)

A. lehmannianus (Werd.) Backbg.
Bo. to 2 m h., branching somewhat from the base; **St.** with a bluish tinge, to 8 cm ∅; **Ri.** c. 20, 5–8 mm h.; **Ar.** close-set; **Sp.** to 40, to 2 cm lg., interlacing, interspersed with white H. to 4 cm lg.; **Ceph.** to 4 cm br., dense, white, brownish at the base, to 50 cm lg.; **Fl.** 3.5 cm lg.; **Ov.** and **Tu.** reddish; **Pet.** white; **Fr.** 2.5 cm lg., top-shaped, with a lid, red; **S.** dull to slightly glossy, black.—Brazil (Bahia, Serra d'Espinhaço).

A. purpureus (Gürke) Backbg. (T.)
Bo. to 5 m h., little branching; **St.** to 12 cm ∅; **Ri.** to 25; **Ar.** close-set; **Rsp.** 15–20, to 15 mm lg.; **Csp.** 4–6, some to 5 cm lg., yellowish to darker brown; **Ceph.** to 1 m lg., 12 cm br., with reddish-brown to blackish Br. to 2 cm lg., wool greyish-white; **Fl.** 3.5 cm lg.; **Sep.** pinkish-red; **Pet.** more whitish; **Fr.** as in the preceding; **S.** deep brownish-black.—Brazil (S. Bahia).

All spec. are still rare in cultivation. Ritt. mentions a "Cephalocereus Ritt. (FR 1212), more slender than dybowskii", which is probably referable here. (Fig. 464.)

Austrocylindropuntia Backbg. (6)

Cylindrical species from S. America, variable in size, height and stem-thickness, distinguished from the northern Cylindropuntia by the complete absence of even rudimentary spine-sheaths. Some species have lesser or greater amounts of hair on the stems, in others this is very sparse or minute. The following groups can be distinguished on the basis of growth-form (indicated by the figures after the specific names):

1. Large shrubby species, or those with stout stems having broader tubercles;
2. Similar in habit; with a strong blue tinge, with narrower tubercles;
3. Low, ± dense groups, in part with some hairs;
4. Slender-stemmed, low-growing plants, in the wild in part spherical in shape, with or without some hair-development;
5. Plants forming thin stems of little over pencil-thickness, without hairs;
6. Plants quite short-stemmed, ± clavate, sometimes unusually shaped.

Fruits quite variable: from large, sometimes sterile and hard, to small and soft; seeds light-coloured, larger and extremely hard.—Distribution: from Ecuador through the Peruvian Highlands to the coast of Chile; in Bolivia and N. Argentina, and into Paraguay. [(R), with one exception.]

A. clavarioides (Pfeiff.) Backbg. (6)
Bo. small, branches resembling stag's horns, not very firm, brownish; **Sp.** to 10, minute; **Fl.** yellowish-brownish, to 6.5 cm lg.; **Ov.** cylindric, with Br.; **Fr.** 1.5 cm long, containing only 1 S.—Argentina (Chilean frontier, above Mendoza). [(G)!]. One form has completely cylindric St.
    v. **ruiz-lealii** (Cast.) Backbg. has green **St.**; **Fl.** to 4 cm lg. (Fig. 23.)

A. colubrina (Cast.) Backbg. (5)
The sole dark green representative of its Group; **Fl.** lemon-yellow, 5.5 cm ∅; **Fr.** red.—Argentina (Formosa).

A. cylindrica (Lamarck) Backbg. (1)
Bo. to 4 m h.; **Ar.** white, sunken, in part with some H.; **Sp.** at first 2–3, short, white (often absent on cultivated plants); **Fl.** pink, limb directed more strongly upwards; **Fr.** 5 cm lg., yellowish-green.—S. Ecuador (to N. Peru?).

A. exaltata (Berg.) Backbg.(1) (T.)
Bo. to 6 m h., forming a denser shrub than the preceding; **L.** to c. 7 cm lg.; **Ar.** longer decurrent; **Sp.** few at first, later to 12 or more, eventually in part quite lg., to 12 cm lg., dark yellow to reddish-brown; **Fl.** ($\pm$ brick) red; **Fr.** to 9 cm long, hard, mostly sterile.—Peru (Highlands).

A. haematacantha (Backbg.) Backbg. (4)
St. only to 8 cm lg., 1.5 cm $\varnothing$; **L.** small, red; **Sp.** 5, 10–15 mm lg., central one to 5 cm lg.; **Fr.** red inside.—Bolivia (near Oruro).

A. humahuacana (Backbg.) Backbg. (3)
Bo. to c. 50 cm h.; **St.** to 4 cm $\varnothing$, leaf-green at first, becoming light green; **Ar.** $\pm$ round to oblong, light; **Glo.** light yellow, erect; **L.** to 1.5 cm lg.; **Sp.** few at first, short, light, later increasing in number, acicular, spreading, to over 2 cm lg., pale yellowish; **Fl.** deep purple.—N. Argentina (near Humahuaca).

A. inarmata Backbg. (4)
Bo. small, dark green, becoming olive; **Ar.** wider than long, white; **L.** to 15 mm lg., erect; **Sp.** mostly absent, rarely one, porrect; **Glo.** scarcely distinguishable, hyaline; **Fl.** red with a slight tinge of orange, 4 cm $\varnothing$; **style** dark violet; **Fil.** red; **Sti.** wine-red.—Bolivia. (Fig. 24.)

A. intermedia Rauh & Backbg. (1)
Bo. to 1.5 m h., freely branching; **Seg.** $\pm$ clavate; **Tub.** with rib-like markings; **Sp.** 2–6, yellowish-white, c. 3 cm lg.; **Fl.** scarlet, limb short; **Pet.** $\pm$ erect; **Fr.** subspherical.—N. Peru (Huancabamba).

A. ipatiana (Card.) Backbg. (5)
Bo. to 30 cm h., with a short trunk; **Seg.** 1.5 cm $\varnothing$, green with a purple sheen, weakly tuberculate, 7–8 cm lg. lower down, terminal shoots 3–4 cm lg., 6 mm $\varnothing$; **Ar.** 7 mm apart, white; **Glo.** yellowish; **Sp.** 5–9, to 2 cm lg., brownish, with a reddish tip; **Fl.** 3.5 cm lg., salmon-pink; **Fr.** purple, 2.5 cm lg., proliferating.—Bolivia (Santa Cruz, 800 m).

A. jujuyensis nom,nud. (Cact. y Suc. Mex. X/1): judging from the inadequate illustration, this is A. humahuacana Backbg.

A. miquelii (Monv.) Backbg. (2)
Bo. to 1 m h., forming colonies to 5 m br.; **Seg.** to 20 cm lg., to 6 cm. $\varnothing$, strongly light-bluish; **Tub.** rather narrow and long; **Sp.** few on cultivated plants, in habitat to c. 10, to 10 cm lg., stout, whitish-grey; **Glo.** brownish; **Fl.** 4–8 cm lg., pink to $\pm$ white.—Chile (Atacama, Huasco valley).
v. **jilesii** Backbg. grows to only 80 cm h., forming colonies to 10 m br.; **Sp.** straw-coloured; **Fl.**

yellow; **Fr.** the size of a hen's egg, yellow (near Vallenar).

A. pachypus (K.Sch.) Backbg. (1)
Bo. to 1 m h.; **Seg.** 3–5 cm $\varnothing$, symmetrically tuberculate; **Tub.** very numerous, 4-sided, flat; **Sp.** 20–30, subulate, 5–20 mm lg.; **Glo.** yellow; **Fl.** 7 cm lg., scarlet; **style** very thick; **Fr.** often proliferating in chains, rooting on falling to the ground.—Peru (Chosica valley).

A. salmiana (Parm.) Backbg. (5)
Bo. bushy, to 2 m h. or lg., freely branching in habitat; **Seg.** 1.5 cm $\varnothing$, terete, not tuberculate, often with a reddish tinge; **Sp.** absent or small, to 1.5 cm lg., whitish; **Fl.** to 3.5 cm $\varnothing$, pale yellow; **Fr.** scarlet (acc. Rivière also "mauve-violet").—Brazil, E. Argentina to Bolivia (near Comarapa ?).
v. **albiflora** (K.Sch.) Backbg. has leaf-green **Seg.**; **Fl.** c. 2 cm $\varnothing$, white; **Fr.** green.—N. Argentina to Paraguay. v. **spegazzinii** (Web.) Backbg. has bluish-green **Seg.**; **Fl.** only 2 cm $\varnothing$, yellow; **Fr.** bluish-green.—N. Argentina (Salta).

A. shaferi (Br. & R.) Backbg. (3)
Bo. 30 cm h., with 2–4 Seg. which are very spiny; **Tub.** often indistinct; **Ar.** c. 1 cm apart; **Sp.** c. 6, brownish, to 6 cm lg., interspersed with long white H.; **Fl.** not known; **Fr.** c. 2 cm $\varnothing$, with white felt and white Glo.; **S.** 4 mm. lg.—N. Argentina.

A. steiniana Backbg. (4)
Bo. spherical at first in the wild, later thin-stemmed, $\pm$ prostrate, to 10 cm lg., 1 cm $\varnothing$; **Tub.** indistinct, broadly oval and prominent in cultivated plants; **Sp.** 2–7, to 1.5 cm lg., sharp, projecting, some appressed, in cultivation only c. 5 mm lg.; **Fl.** and **Fr.** not known.—Bolivia.

A. subulata (Mühlpfrdt.) Backbg. (1)
Bo. stiffly and erectly shrubby, to 4 m h., trunk 6–10 cm $\varnothing$; **Br.** directed sideways and upcurving, to 7 cm $\varnothing$; **Tub.** oblong, flat with a darker border; **L.** to over 12(–15) cm lg., semi-cylindric, tapering and $\pm$ curving, persisting for over a year; **Sp.** 1–2 or more, subulate, to 8 cm lg. or more, $\pm$ light yellowish; **Glo.** sparse; **Fl.** sunken in the Ov., to c. 7 cm lg., opening moderately wide, Per. fairly short, reddish to red; **Ov.** with longer upcurving L.: **Fr.** to 10 cm lg., hard, long-persistent, green, proliferating; **S.** to 12 mm long.—S. Peru (at first incorrectly reported from Chile). (Fig. 25.)
There are plants with shorter and less persistent L. (race or variety?), others with long-persistent L. to 15 cm lg. I have not been able to establish whether the latter should be considered a variety or whether it is "Opuntia ellemeetiana Miqu." (Br. & R.: "with very long L."). The original description says:

"L. to more than 8 cm lg., persisting for several years".
In the collections of F. Rivière and J. Marnier-Lapostolle there are living specimens of plants collected by Rauh in Peru, with 3–4(–6) strong or long brown Sp. up to c. 10 cm lg., and the L. (at least in the Marnier material) fairly long; for this reason Marnier held the plants to be a form or var. of A. subulata. Rauh gives no very specific data regarding his discovery; his photo (Plate 3 in "Die Cactaceae", I. 1958) however, shows A. subulata, to judge from the moderately long-decurrent Tub. and the long L. Apart from this spec., brown Sp. are known only in A. exaltata. Since Rauh also gives no data on Fl.-colour (whether pink or brick-red), the only possible conclusion is that A. subulata can also have brown Sp. This, again, connects it with A. exaltata, and thus raises the question whether this plant—which has never been certainly identified growing wild—is perhaps only a mutation, form or variety of A. subulata. The available evidence is insufficient to clarify the position.

A. tephrocactoides Rauh & Backbg. (1)
Bo. to 40 cm h., forming dense and sometimes ± cushion-like colonies; **Tub.** spiralled, ± hexagonal, depressions slight; **Sp.** 2–8, unequal, one to 3 cm lg., yellowish horn-coloured; **L.** c. 1 cm lg.; **Fl.** and **Fr.** not known.—S. Peru (3599 m).

A. teres (Cels) Backbg. (4)
Bo. forming lax clumps to 30 cm br.; **Seg.** readily detached, in nature ovoid-spherical, in cultivation more elongated; **L.** longer; **Ar.** with short felt and sparse longer **H.**; **Sp.** c. 6, 2–2.5 cm lg., thin, brownish; **Fl.** 2 cm ∅, flame to light carmine; **Ov.** hairy, with small **Sp.**; **Fr.** reddish.—Bolivia (around La Paz).

A. verschaffeltii (Cels) Backbg. (4)
Plants with many **St.**, forming low dense clumps; **Seg.** green, spherical if in full sun in the open, in cultivation mostly elongated, indistinctly tuberculate; **Sp.** 1–3, yellowish, ± bristly, to 3 cm lg.; **St.** in cultivation to 20 cm lg., 1.5 cm ∅, often spineless; **L.** longer, thinner; **Fl.** intense red.—Bolivia (La Paz area), N. Argentina.
v. **digitalis** (Web.): probably only a form (Fig. 26);
v. **hypsophila** (Speg.) Backbg.: **Sp.** 7, brownish, short; not in cultivation (N. Argentina);
v. **longispina** Backbg.: **St.** often with a reddish tinge, somewhat more strongly tuberculate; **Sp.** 3–9, to 5 cm lg., whitish to horn-coloured.

A. vestita (SD.) Backbg. (4)
Bo. in nature in part ± spherical, erect, in cultivation cylindric; **St.** to 2 cm ∅, on grafted plants to 40 cm lg. and thicker; **L.** short, projecting little from the **H.**; **Glo.** white; **Sp.** 4–8, mostly only 4 mm lg., bristly but sharp, in part to 15 mm lg.; **Fl.** 3.5 cm lg., 3 cm ∅, violet-red; **H.** white, densely covering the St. but lax.—Bolivia.
v. **chuquisacana** (Card.) Backbg. has **St.** with finer and denser **H.**, and **L.** somewhat longer;
v. **intermedia** Backbg. has stouter **St.**, **Sp.** in part projecting, some rather stiff; **L.** medium-long;
v. **major** (Backbg.) Backbg. has the longest **L.**, to 3 cm lg.

A. weingartiana (Backbg.) Backbg. (3)
Bo. in colonies to 50 cm h.; **St.** to 5 cm ∅, somewhat zoned, dark green; **Sp.** to 15 or more, **centrals** 3–5, stout, very sharp, reddish, red or pale brown; **Glo.** white at first, eventually pale yellowish; **Fl.** probably red; **Fr.** carmine, spineless, with red pulp; **S.** pear-shaped, c. 4 mm lg.—S. Bolivia (near Tupiza), to N. Argentina (Humahuaca, Azul Pampa).

Aylostera Speg. (102)

Small-spherical to ± elongated plants which offset freely or form cushions, the slender ribs resolved into small tubercles. Flowers slender, red, in part with a golden shimmer, orange and ± white, appearing stem-like because the tube is united with the style; tube hairy and bristly. Fruits small, bristly.—Distribution: S. Bolivia to N. Argentina [O. (R) (G).] See also under **Rebutia** for the segregation of the 2 genera.

A. albiareolata Ritt. (FR 761): no description available.

A. albiflora (Ritt. & Buin.) Backbg.—Descr. Cact. Nov. III: 5. 1963 (Rebutia albiflora Ritt. & Buin., "Taxon" XII: 1, 29. 1963).
Bo. ± spherical, offsetting freely, to 2.5 cm ∅; **Ri.** resolved into distant Tub.; **Ar.** distant, yellowish; **Rsp.** c. 15; **Csp.** c. 5, brownish at the base; **Sp.** to 5 mm lg., straight; **Fl.** 2.5 cm ∅, white with a pink M.-line; **Tu.** white-bristly; **Fr.** and **S.** smaller than in A. albipilosa.—Bolivia (NE. Tarija, Rio Pilaya [FR 766a]). (Fig. 27.)

A. albipilosa (Ritt.) Backbg.—Descr. Cact. Nov. III: 5. 1963 (Rebutia albipilosa Ritt., "Taxon", XII: 1, 29. 1963).
Bo. hemispherical, becoming elongated, dark green, to 5 cm ∅ with few offsets; **R.** napiform; **Ri.** divided into Tub. 2–4 mm across, in 21–25 spiralled rows; **Ar.** 1–2 mm br., white; **Sp.** hairlike, 25–35, soft, white, mostly curving, 10–15 mm lg.; **Csp.**

when present to 4 cm lg., tip reddish-brown; **Fl.** to 4.5 cm lg., to 3 cm ∅, orange to red; **style** united for part of the Tu.; **Ov.** oblong, white with white H. and Br.; **Fr.** to 9 mm lg., greenish-red; **S.** matt black, 1.2 mm lg.—Bolivia (Dept. Tarcia, Narvaëz [FR 754]).

| A. buiningiana: see **Rebutia**.

A. deminuta (Web.) Backbg.
Bo. to 6 cm h. and ∅, leaf-green, offsetting freely; **Tub.** in 11–13 rows; **Sp.** to c. 10–12, white, brown-tipped to all-brown, 6 mm lg.; **Fl.** 3 cm lg. and ∅, **Ov.** with white Br.-Sp.; **Fl.** dark orange-red.— N. Argentina (Trancas).

A. fiebrigii (Gürke) Backbg.
Bo. spherical to ± elongated, to 6 cm ∅, glossy green, not offsetting freely; **Tub.** in 18 rows, 5 mm h.; **Ar.** white; **Br.**—**Sp.** 30–40, white, mostly 1 cm lg., inner ones 2–5, to 2 cm lg., with light brown tips; **Fl.** 3.5 cm lg., brilliant flame-colour; **Ov.** with white Br.—Bolivia (Iscayache, 3600 m).
    v. **densiseta** Cullm. has still finer and denser **Br.**

A. fulviseta Rausch
Bo. simple to caespitose, 15 mm h., 10 mm ∅, dark green; **Ri.** to 16, spiralled, Tub. 2–3 mm lg. and br., reddish or violet-brown; **Ar.** round to oval, 1.5 mm ∅, brown-felty; **Rsp.** 10–12, spreading; **Csp.** 1–3, fine-bristly, projecting, 6–10 mm lg., ochreous to reddish-brown, darker-tipped, thickened below; **Fl.** c. 25 mm lg. and ∅; **Ov.** and **Tu.** violet-red with darker Sc., white H. and Br.; throat, **Fil.** and **style** white; **style** united with the Tu.; **Fr.** spherical, c. 4 mm ∅; **S.** 1 mm lg., cap-shaped, testa black, finely tuberculate.—Bolivia (Arce, near Padcaya at 2200m).

A. heliosa Rausch
Bo. simple, later strongly offsetting, 20 mm h., 25 mm ∅, with a taproot; **Ri.** to 38, spiralled, Tub. 1 mm lg.; **Ar.** 0.5 mm br., 1 mm lg., light brown, felty; **Rsp.** 24–26, 1 mm lg., appressed, directed downwards, silvery-white, thickened and dark brown below; **Csp.** absent; **Fl.** borne low on the Bo., 45–55 mm lg., 40 mm ∅; **Ov.** olive-pink with few Sc. and white H.; **Tu.** pinkish-violet, white above, c. 2–3 mm ∅, narrow; **Sep.** c. 15 mm lg., spatulate, tapering, orange with a violet M.-stripe; **Pet.** c. 10 mm lg., spatulate, orange, orange-yellow inside; throat and **Fil.** whitish, **style** united for half the Fl.-length; **Sti.** 5–8, white; **Fr.** spherical, 4 mm ∅, violet, bristly; **S.** spherical, rough, only 10–20 in each Fr.—Bolivia (Tarija, road to Narvaëz, at 2400–2500 m). (Fig. 466.)

A. jujuyana Rausch
Bo. simple, spherical, to 35 mm ∅, light green; **Ri.**

to 18, spiralled, Tub. 3 mm lg.; **Ar.** round, 2 mm ∅, with white to yellow felt, 3–4 mm apart; **Rsp.** c. 18–20, radiating, bristly, to 10 mm lg., yellowish; **Csp.** 5–7, to 15 mm lg., acicular, brittle, yellow with a small brown tip; **Fl.** 35 mm lg. and ∅; **Ov.** spherical, 4 mm ∅, green with green Sc. and a few white H. and Br.; **Tu.** very slender, pink with green Sc.; **Sep.** rounded, violet-pink, bordered orange; **Pet.** spatulate, rounded, orange; throat only 5 mm lg., open, funnelshaped, white; **style** 13 mm lg., with 8 white **Sti.**; **Fr.** 4–5 mm ∅, dark green with light green Sc., yellowish H. and Br.
The spec. belongs within the complex of A. fiebrigii.—Argentina (Prov. Jujuy). (Fig. 467.)

A. kupperiana (Böd.) Backbg.
Bo. ± spherical, to 3 cm ∅, matt dark leaf-green, with few offsets; **Tub.** in c. 15 rows; **Ar.** yellowish; **Rsp.** 13–15, to 5 mm lg., white, brown-tipped; **Csp.** 1–3(–4), stouter, darker brown throughout, to over 1.2 cm lg.; **Fl.** 4 cm lg., 3.5 cm ∅, ± flame-colour, throat pale green; **Fr.** green; **S.** dark brownish-grey.—Bolivia (near Tarija).

Aylostera mamillosa: see **Rebutia mamillosa** Rausch.

A. muscula (Ritt. & Thiele) Backbg.—Descr. Cact. Nov. III: 5. 1963 (Rebutia muscula Ritt. & Thiele, "Taxon", XII: 1, 29. 1963).
Bo. elongated, green, to 4 cm ∅; **Ri.** resolved into distant Tub.; **Ar.** very distant; **Sp.** ± 50, thin, 2.4 mm lg., straight, all similar; **Tu.** white-bristly; **Fl.** orange.—Bolivia (Narvaëz [FR 753]).

A. narvaecensis Card. 1971
Bo. spherical, 30–35 mm h., 25–35 mm ∅, crown slightly sunken; **Ri.** c. 18, low, tuberculate; **Ar.** 3–4 mm apart, round, white-felty, projecting; **Rsp.** and **Csp.** not differentiated, thin, acicular, 10–20 or more, 2.5 mm lg., spreading, whitish; **Fl.** lateral, numerous, 40–42 mm lg., 40 mm br., light pinkish-lilac; **Ov.** spherical with minute Sc., white H. and spreading Br.; **Sep.** light pinkish-lilac; **Pet.** lighter; **Fil.** very thin, white; **An.** yellow; **style** 25 mm lg., white with light yellow **Sti.**—Bolivia (O'Conor, Dept. Tarija; near Narvaëz at 2700 m).

A. padcayensis Rausch
Named for the type-locality. **Bo.** simple to caespitose, broadly spherical, c. 25 mm h. and to 40 mm ∅, fresh green to greyish-green; **Ri.** 14–16, spiralled, divided into flat Tub. 6 mm lg. and br.; **Ar.** round to oval, 1 mm ∅, with white to brown felt; **Rsp.** 12–14, 5–12 mm lg., forming a web around the Bo., bristly, yellowish-white to tipped brown, later greying; **Csp.** absent; **Fl.** 35 mm lg. and ∅; **Ov.** and **Tu.** yellowish-pink, with naked

green Sc., rarely with 1–2 Br.; **Sep.** red with a green M.-stripe; **Pet.** spatulate, mucronate, red, throat white; **Fil.** yellow, white below; **style** united for c. 14 mm with the Tu., white; **Sti.** 4, white; **Fr.** broadly spherical, 4 mm ∅, brown with green Sc.; **S.** with black tuberculate testa, hilum white.—Bolivia (W. of Padcaya, at 2400–2900 m).

A. pseudodeminuta (Backbg.) Backbg.
Bo. elongating to 10 cm lg., leaf-green; **Ar.** brownish; **Rsp.** over 10, 3–7 mm lg.; white, hyaline; **Csp.** 2–3, yellowish at first, then brown-tipped, to 1.5 cm lg.; **Fl.** 3 cm ∅; **bud** such a dark red it appears ± black; **Pet.** red.—N. Argentina (Salta).
  v. **albiseta** Backbg.: **Csp.** almost entirely white;
  v. **grandiflora** Backbg.: **Fl.** 4 cm ∅;
  v. **schneideriana** Backbg.: **Csp.** to 3.5 cm lg., dark-tipped;
  v. **schumanniana** (Backbg.) Backbg.: **Csp.** golden-brown, c. 1.2 cm lg.

A. pseudominuscula (Spec.) Speg. (T.)
Bo. small, 5 cm h., 3.5 cm ∅, glossy dark green; **Tub.** in 13 rows; **Ar.** 7–8 mm apart; **Sp.** 7–14, yellowish or pinkish-brown, becoming white and brown-tipped, 3–5 mm lg.; **Csp.** 1–4, thin-acicular; **Fl.** 2.5 cm lg., ± purplish or dark red.—N. Argentina (Salta).

A. pulchella Rausch
Bo. simple, spherical, to 5 cm ∅; **Ri.** to 23, spiralled, Tub. 4 mm ∅; **Ar.** round, 2 mm ∅, white-felty; **Rsp.** c. 26, to 5 mm lg., spreading, bristly, brittle, white; **Csp.** 4–7, to 10 mm lg., spreading to projecting, acicular, sharp, white, tipped dark brown; **Fl.** 30 mm lg. and ∅; **Ov.** and **Tu.** light green with light green Sc., white H. and Br.; **Sep.** whitish; **Pet.** rounded, serrate, brilliant orange; throat, **Fil.**, **style** and 5–7 **Sti.** white; style and Tu. united for c. 15 mm; **Fr.** onion-shaped, 3 mm ∅; **S.** of Aylostera-type.—Bolivia (N. of Padilla, at 2200 m). Found by W. Rausch. Spination resembles that of A. fiebrigii.

A. pulvinosa (Ritt. & Buin.) Backbg.—Descr. Cact. Nov. III: 5. 1963 (Rebutia pulvinosa Ritt. & Buin., "Taxon", XII: 1, 29. 1963).
Bo. to 3 cm ∅; **Ri.** divided into distant Tub.; **Ar.** to 5 mm long; **Rsp.** 15–22, to 3 mm lg.; **Csp.** 6, stouter, brownish; **Fl.** 1.8 cm lg., 1.5 cm ∅, orange-yellow; **Tu.** white-bristly; **Fr.** and **S.** much smaller than in A. albipilosa.—Bolivia (same locality as A. albipilosa [FR 766]).

A. rubiginosa (Ritt.) Backbg.—Descr. Cact. Nov. III: 5. 1963 (Rebutia rubiginosa Ritt., "Taxon", XII: 1, 29. 1963).

Bo. flatter than in A. tuberosa, scarcely offsetting; **Ar.** brown; **Sp.** reddish, to 6 mm lg.; **Rsp.** 12; **Csp.** 4; **Fl.** 3 cm lg.; **Fil.** carmine; **Ov.** red-bristly.—Bolivia (100 m above the locality of R. tuberosa [FR 767]).

A. spegazziniana (Backbg.) Backbg.
Bo. soon becoming cylindric, yellowish-green to darker; **Tub.** 3–4 mm br.; **Ar.** slightly felty; **Rsp.** appressed, c. 4 mm lg., light; **Csp.** mostly 2, one above the other, 2 mm lg., yellowish, brown-tipped; **Fl.** c. 4 cm ∅, dark red.—N. Argentina (Salta).
  v. **atroviridis** Backbg. is more bluish or greyish-green; **Csp.** lighter and weaker.

A. spinosissima (Backbg.) Backbg.
Bo. offsetting to form cushions, with dense light Sp.; **St.** light green, to 4 cm ∅ and lg.; **Ar.** very closely spaced, whitish; **Rsp.** and **Csp.** bristly, centrals 5–6, rather stouter, horn-coloured, brown-tipped; **Fl.** light brick-red; **Fr.** very small, faintly bristly.—N. Argentina (Salta).

A. steinmannii (Solms-Laub.) Backbg. has never been imported. The dwarf **Bo.** is 2 cm lg., 1.5 cm ∅; **Sp.** 8, acicular, projecting.—Bolivia.

A. tuberosa (Ritt.) Backbg.—Descr. Cact. Nov. III: 5. 1963 (Rebutia tuberosa Ritt., "Taxon", XII: 1, 28–29. 1963).
Bo. hemispherical, green, to 4 cm ∅, freely offsetting; **R.** napiform; **Ri.** broken up into Tub. 2–4 mm h.; **Ar.** to 3 mm lg., to 1.5 mm br., white; **Rsp.** 4–12; **Csp.** 1 or more; **Sp.** thin-acicular, 2–5 mm lg., brown to yellowish-brown, straight; **Fl.** 3.5 cm lg., 2.5 cm ∅, carmine; **Fil.** in 2 series; **Ov.** with white H. and Br.; **Sti.** 6, pale green; **Fr.** ?—Bolivia (S. Cinti, below Challamarca, 2600 m [FR 770]).

Aylostera vallegrandensis; see **Rebutia vallegrandensis** Card.

A. zavaletae Card.: **Sulcorebutia zavaletae** (Card.) Backbg. comb. nov.

Aztekium Böd. (210)

Broadly spherical plants with greyish-green to grey bodies, offsetting fairly freely when older; grafted plants are green and less attractive; conspicuous characters are the subsidiary ribs and the densely folded surface of the principal ribs. The small, white, apical flowers appear to be on a stalk. Fruits berry-like, appearing only when ripe.—Distribution: Mexico (Nuevo Léon). [(R) (G).]

Aztekium ritteri (Böd.) Böd. (T.)

Bo. depressed-spherical; **R.** shortly napiform; **crown** woolly; main **Ri.** 9–11, folded, with subsidiary Ri. in between, these narrower than the former; **Sp.** not numerous, c. 1–3, only 3–4 mm lg., weak, contorted or bent; **Fl.** 8 mm ⌀, white; **Sep.** pink above; **Fr.** berry-like, pink; **S.** black, 0.5 mm lg.—Mexico (Nuevo León). (Fig. 28.) There is a form with larger Fl. having a longer "stalk".

Azureocereus Ak. & Johns. (66)

Mostly very large and tree-like Cerei, in part to 10 m high; branches stiffly erect; spination mostly very strong, spines in the flowering zone being more flexible and denser. Flowers nocturnal, stout-cylindric, with a somewhat oblique limb and a strongly scaly tube. Fruit said to be dry when ripe. 2 species only identified with certainty: one with magnificent blue stems, the other more green. Probably the following is also referable here: Cereus (Azureocereus?) deflexispinus Rauh & Backbg.—Distribution: Central Peruvian Highlands (Mantaro area, Ayacucho). [(R).]
Buxbaum, in a recently published theory, seeks to unite this genus with Browningia from which it differs in its flowers, dry fruits and uniform stem-spination (see also under Gymnocereus). There is no compelling need for this change.

Azureocereus columnaris Ritt. (FR 1294): no description available.

A. hertlingianus (Backbg.) Backbg. (T.)

Bo. to 8 m h., to 30 cm ⌀; **St.** brilliant blue; **Ri.** to 18 or more, thickened around the Ar. or (later) in part clearly tuberculate; juveniles have a lower spine-count, c. 4 **Rsp.** and 1–3 longer ones, up to 8 cm lg., all yellow with a brown tip, the upper part of older **St.** with up to 30 **Sp.**, ± equal, more flexible; **Fl.** with a ± curved **Tu.**, 5 cm ⌀; **Pet.** white, spatulate; **Tu.** dark purplish-brown; **Sc.** ± ciliate, almost black at maturity; **S.** glossy black.—Peru (Mantaro valley).
Plants under other names seen in the collection of Marnier proved to be A. hertlingianus: A. ayacuchensis Johns., A. imperator Johns., A. ciliiisquamus Ritt.; the latter may perhaps be referable to A. viridis.

A. nobilis Akers: **Azureocereus hertlingianus** (Backbg.) Backbg.

A. viridis Rauh & Backbg.

Bo. similar to the preceding, to 10 m h.; **St.** green; **Sp.** shorter than in A. hertlingianus, (10–)±20, some slightly longer.—Peru (Apurimac valley). (Fig. 29.)

Backebergia H. Bravo (166)

Trree-like Cerei with obliquely ascending branches. The flowering zone is characterised by a unique "helmet-crest cephalium" (K.Sch.); this has long strong wool and numerous bristles which envelop the stem-apex giving it the appearance of a crested helmet; this cephalium can run down the stem for as much as 30 cm. Flowers greenish, ± cylindric, bristly. The fruit also has an erect and rather dense covering of bristles.—Distribution: W. Mexico (Guerrero, Michoacan).
While both this genus and Mitrocereus Backbg. have the decurrent cephalium in common, the woolly covering of flower and fruit in the former is much slighter, and the shapes of seed and cephalium are also different. Despite discrepancies between the two generic diagnoses H. Bravo and Buxbaum have sought to transfer Mitrocereus to the present genus, but this is considered unacceptable for several reasons (see also under **Brachycereus** and **Mitrocereus**).

B. militaris (Aud.) H. Bravo (T.)

Bo. to 6 m h., moderately freely branching; **Ri.** at first 5–7, later 9–11, resolved into Tub. below the insertion of the Ceph.; **Ar.** 5–10 mm apart, grey; **Rsp.** 7–13, acicular, 1 cm lg., grey, black-tipped; **Csp.** 1–4, similar to the Rsp. in colour and shape; **Ceph.** of projecting bristles and wool, encircling the St.; **Fl.** 7 cm lg., 4 cm ⌀, with 2–3 Br. to 8 mm lg. in the Tu.-Ar.; **S.** comma-shaped, ± glossy black.—Mexico (Michoacan: District of Huetamo, Rio Balsas; Guerrero: Pico de Colima). (Fig. 30.)

Backebergia chrysomallus (Lem.) H. Bravo was the name of the first combination.

Bartschella Br. & R. (231)

Plants small-spherical, greyish-green, without milky sap; tubercles broadly circular, ± connected at the base; flowers large, red; fruits drying when ripe and splitting below.—Distribution: Mexico (Baja California). [(G).]

B. schumannii (Hildm.) Br. & R. (T.)

Bo. offsetting from the base, up to 40 heads together; individual **St.** to 6 cm h. and br.; **Tub.** spiralled, terete, 4-sided at the base; **Ar.** circular, white-woolly, becoming glabrous; **Ax.** woolly at first; **Rsp.** (9–)12(–15), 6–12 mm lg., straight, white, black-tipped; **Csp.** 1–2(–4), 1–1.5 cm lg., stouter, the lowest one hooked, white, black-tipped; **Fl.** 4 cm ⌀, light purple; **Fr.** scarlet, to 2 cm lg.; **S.** matt black.—Mexico (Baja California, Cape region). (Fig. 31.)

Bergerocactus Br. & R. (145)

Plants with fairly slender stems and yellow spines, forming larger colonies, but remaining under 1 m high. The relatively small yellow diurnal flowers expand fully, the short tube and the ovary are set with felt and spines. The spherical fruit is densely spiny.—Distribution: USA (SW. coast of California) and Mexico (NW. Baja California). [(R).]
Spontaneous hybrids with both Myrtillocactus and Pachycereus have been reported and named × Myrtgerocactus R. Moran and × Pachgerocereus R. Moran respectively.

Bergerocactus emoryi (Eng.) Br. & R. (T.)
Bo. to 1(–2) m lg., 3–6 cm ∅, light green, freely branching; **St.** to 4 cm ∅; **Ri.** 14–20(–25), with indistinct low Tub.; **Ar.** 7–9 mm apart; **Sp.** 10–50, acicular, yellow to yellowish-brown, with 1–4 stouter centrals to 3–4 cm lg.; **Fl.** 2 cm lg. and ∅ (Br. & R.); **Fr.** 3 cm lg.—USA and Mexico (Baja California, in the NW., and on offshore islands). (Fig. 32.) Lindsay reports that the Fl. can be as much as 5.5 cm lg. and 4.5 cm ∅.

Binghamia sensu Backbg.: **Seticereus** Backbg.

Binghamia Br. & R. non Agardh: **Haageocereus** Backbg.

Blossfeldia Werd. (113)

The smallest of the cacti, flowering at under 1 cm ∅; bodies greyish-green to ± glossy deep green, mostly offsetting quite freely to form clumps; shoots (always?) emerging through the epidermis without any articulation; spines or ribs are not present although the latter are in part faintly discernible at the base of the body where they are quite flattened; areolar cushions small to minute, spiralled. Flowers very small, perianth lax to closed, white, with a tiny pedicel or sessile. The finely papillose seeds are glossy brown and have a large, light-coloured hilum.—Distribution: Argentina (Jujuy to Catamarca), Bolivia (Cochabamba, Chuquisaca, Tarata). [(R) (G). O.]

B. atroviridis Ritt.—"Succulenta", 44: 2, 23. 1965.
Bo. dark green, flat above; **Ar.** more strongly sunken; **Pet.** very obtuse, apiculate; **Ov.** spherical, on a short white pedicel; **Fr.** similarly; **S.** brown, with sparser H.—Bolivia (Mizane, Prov. Mizque, Dept. Cochabamba) (FR 748).
The data are said to show characters distinguishing it from B. liliputana; v. intermedia Ritt. is only a name.

B. campaniflora Backbg.
Bo. greyish-green; **Fl.** sessile, bellshaped-funnelform; **Pet.** rounded above, white.—N. Argentina. (Fig. 33, left.)

B. cyathiformis Ritt., only a name (B. campaniflora Backbg. ?)

B. fechseri Backbg.
Bo. ± glossy, intense or darker green; **Fl.** sessile; **Pet.** very delicate, rounded above, white, translucent; **Fr.** ± yellowish-greenish, with the side exposed to the sun ± reddened, as in other spec. of the G.—Argentina (Catamarca).

B. flocculosa (FR 943): no description available.

B. liliputana Werd. (T.)
Bo. greyish-green, not glossy; **Fl.** minutely pedicellate; **Pet.** white, laxly spreading, acuminate.—N. Argentina (Jujuy, near Tumbaya etc.). (Fig. 33, right.)
v. **caineana** Card.—"Cactus" (Paris). 19–82, 53. 1964.
Bo. stouter than in the type-species, broadly spherical, with a thick taproot; **Fl.** creamy-white, scarcely opening, with a brown M.-line outside; **Pet.** narrow, tapering; **Fil.** yellow; **Sti.** cream.—Bolivia (Prov. Tarata, Rio Caine, 2000 m).
The Bolivian locality is surprising. The Pet. of the var. are narrow and pointed like those of the type-species, while the Fl. has erect Pet. as in B. campaniflora. Differences within this very small-stemmed G. can only be limited. However close investigations such as those of Cardenas show that some of the G. are quite clearly differentiated and they must be segregated carefully to permit more precise knowledge regarding variability.
v. rubrosepala has remained just a name.

B. minima Ritt. (FR 750)
is a name without valid description, given by Ritter to a small-bodied species which I also received from Uebelmann and which probably originated from Fechser who made a speciality of collecting Blossfeldias. Andreae showed this plant in Kakt. u. a. Sukk., 13: 6, 85. 1962; the flower is very lax and spreading, with the petals tapering as in B. liliputana. The stems are smaller than in the type-species and the flower not so bellshaped as the much less widely expanding bloom of Blossfeldia campaniflora Backbg.

B. pedicellata Ritt.—"Succulenta", 44: 2, 23. 1965.
Bo. flattened above; **Ar.** to 1 mm (2 mm) apart; **Fl.** 12–14 mm lg., **Pet.** 5–8 mm (4–5 mm) lg., 2–3 mm (1–1.5 mm) br.; **Ov.** 3–5 mm lg., to 2.5 mm br.

above, narrowing to the base; **Fr.** 5–8 mm (3–4 mm) lg., 3–4 mm br., narrowing to the base, shortly pedicellate; **S.**. less hairy, lighter brown.—Bolivia (Tomina, Dept. Chuquisaca) (FR 749).

The figures in brackets are reputed to show differences between this plant and B. liliputana.

Bolivicereus Card. (70)

Slender, ± erect to prostrate Cerei with relatively short spines. The flowers, borne in profusion, have a slender tube and the limb is bent and oblique; tiny hairs are present at the base of the tube in some species, but these are missing in one species. They do not always constitute a valid diagnostic character, as was proved by Rauh's investigations into the flowers of Loxanthocereus and Haageocereus; but they are helpful in specific determination and guard against confusion, cf. Kimnach (C. & S. J. (USA), p. 94–95. 1960). His photo of "Borzicactus serpens" closely resembles that of B. tenuiserpens ("Die Cact." Vol. II, Fig. 953), of which he says: "with a less well developed ring of hairs, resembles the plants of Aporocactus", whereas of B. serpens he says: "flower with a ring of staminodial hairs". However plants I collected at Humboldt's locality as well as a plant Rauh sent me from there resemble Aporocactus; but in Rauh's flowering material, as I saw for myself, there was a complete absence of hair-development. Because the flowers are shorter than in Loxanthocereus, more strongly zygomorphic, and borne in profusion as in Bolivicereus, in which they have more hairs, extending higher up, I have referred the North Peruvian species to the above genus; Kimnach has already drawn attention to the resemblance between the flowers. The geographical distance is of no special significance since the Colombian species of Frailea and Wigginsia for instance are even further from the main distribution of the respective genera.—Distribution: N. Peru, Bolivia. [(R).]

B. chacoanus Ritt. (FR 841) and
B. margaritanus Ritt. (FR 842)
are two species recently discovered by Ritter, but nothing further is known of them at the moment.

B. croceus Ritt. (FR 1471): no description available.

B. ruficeps (FR 840): no description available.

B. samaipatanus Card. (T.)
Bo. erect, branching from the base, to 1.5 m h., 3.5–4 cm ∅, forming groups; **Ri.** 14–16, low, transversely furrowed; **Ar.** 3–4 mm apart, brown-

ish; **Sp.** 13–22, thin, unequal, 4–30 mm lg., greyish-whitish, yellowish or brownish; **Fl.** 4 cm lg., strongly bent, with **H.** at the base; **Pet.** blood-red, 15 mm lg.; **Fil.** dark purple; **Fr.** spherical, to 11 mm lg., 9 mm ∅, with dense white and brown wool; **S.** minute, blackish-brown or black.—Bolivia (Santa Cruz, near Samaipata, 1890 m). (Fig. 34.)

Acc. a photo of Cullmann, the Pet. are purple, the innermost ones shorter, the Sep. blood-red.

The following varieties grow to only 70 cm h.: v. **divi-miseratus** Card., with 13–18 **Sp.** and **Fl.** 6 cm lg.; v. **multiflorus** Card., with 9–13 **Sp.** and numerous **Fl.** 5 cm lg.

B. serpens (HBK.) Backbg.
Bo. with very slender, ± prostrate **St.**; **R.** large, woody; **St.** to 2 cm ∅; **Ri.** slender, 8–11; **Rsp.** 10–15, very fine, short; **Csp.** 0–1, to 3 cm lg., light yellow to brown; **Fl.** 5 cm lg., flesh-pink or stronger red, without **H.** at the base.—N. Peru (Huancabamba valley, near the place of the same name). (Fig. 35.)

B. tenuiserpens (Rauh & Backbg.) Backbg.
Bo. ± prostrate, freely branching, to 2 m lg., fresh green; **St.** to 1 cm ∅; **Ri.** 9–10, 1 mm h.; **Rsp.** very thin, 2.8 mm lg., pale, pink at first, brown-tipped, all Sp. projecting and spreading, the centrals mostly shorter; **Fl.** not known (possibly floral data by other collectors: "blood-red to crimson" refer to this species).—N. Peru (Huancabamba valley). Johnson, who collected a species which appears very similar to the preceding, describes its flowers as "light scarlet"; perhaps the flower-colour is variable.

Bonifazia Standl. & Steyerm.: **Disocactus** Lindl.

Borzicactella Johns.: an undescribed name for the N. Peruvian species of **Bolivicereus** Card.

Borzicactus Ricc. (71)

Erect Cerei, only moderately stout or rather slender, at most to 1.5 m long, with the ribs rounded, in part transversely notched or ± thickened around the areoles, the flowers obliquely limbed, with a relatively stout tube, with a rather narrow opening. Inside the flower, as far as is known, there are staminodial hairs.* Fruit green,

---

* Probably the "ring of hairs" has no special significance here, or it may not correspond to that of Acanthocalycium. This type of hair-development is sometimes absent, as Rauh has shown in other genera. In Borzicactus it is thus not a diagnostic character of the genus, and other characters are more important for distinguishing it from Seticereus.

subspherical; seeds rather small, black. The species from Ecuador constitute a singularly unified genus, both geographically and in the features of stems and flowers. One American author recently attempted to combine Borzicactus Ricc. (a hybrid genus in Br. & R.) with the various genera listed below, as "Borzicactus sensu Kimn.". Quite apart from newer finds of Peruvian species of "Loxanthocereus" which he included, any study of the strongly differentiated characters of the genera he proposes uniting makes it clear that this is a needless reversion to outdated large genera.— Distribution: Central and S. Ecuador. [(R).]

B. aequatorialis Backbg.
Bo. slender-columnar, to 4 cm ∅; **Ri.** swollen around the Ar.; **Sp.** unequal, spreading in all directions, ± interlacing, to c. 15, centrals not distinct but somewhat stouter, some and especially the lower ones longer, in part recurved and projecting away from the Bo.; **Fl.** red; **Fil.** violet.— Ecuador (on the equator). (Fig. 36.)

Borzicactus calviflorus Ritt.: **Clistanthocereus calviflorus** (Ritt.) Backbg.

Borzicactus cutakii n.prov.: **Fl.** red; **Fil.** violet. Found by L. Cutak in Colombia in 1960, 91 km from Pasto, in the neighbourhood of Pedregal. (Fig. 38.)

Borzicactus madisoniorum Hutch.: **Submatucana madisoniorum** (Hutch.) Backbg.

B. morleyanus Br. & R.
Bo. erect or arching; **St.** to 6 cm ∅; **Ri.** 13–16, low, rounded, with V-shaped notches; **Ar.** circular, fairly large on newer growth, crowded, light; **Sp.** to 20; **Rsp.** bristly, fine, **centrals** longer, flexible, straight, often directed downwards, brown, to over 2.5 cm lg.; **Fl.** to 6 cm lg., carmine, very woolly; **Fil.** violet-carmine.—Ecuador (Chanchan valley near Huigra).

Borzicactus neoroezlii Ritt.: **Seticereus roezlii** (Hge. Jr.) Backbg.

Borzicactus piscoensis Rauh: **Loxanthocereus piscoensis** (Rauh) Rauh & Backbg.

B. pseudothelegonus (Rauh & Backbg.) Rauh & Backbg.—Descr. Cact. Nov. III: 5. 1963 (Cereus pseudothelegonus Rauh & Backbg., Die Cact. II: 1136. 1959).
Bo. semi-prostrate, to 3 m lg.; **St.** to 8 cm ∅, broken up into large, ± hexagonal Tub.; **Ri.** c. 10; **Ar.** oblong, strongly white-felty; **Rsp.** to c. 10; **Csp.** 1, to 2 cm lg.; lateral **Sp.** somewhat shorter; all at first ± blackish; **Fl.** to 8 cm lg., deep red, limb very

zygomorphic; **Tu.** conspicuously S-shaped, red, with white H.; **Fil.** red above, white below, in 2 series, inserted on the inner wall of the Tu. below the base of the Pet.; **An.** dark wine-red; **style** whitish; **Sti.** 10, greenish-yellow; **Ov.** small, with green Sc. and white H.; **Fr.** ?—Ecuador (in the S., Giron Pasaje, 200 m). (Fig. 37.)

Borzicactus samnensis Ritt.: **Clistanthocereus samnensis** (Ritt.) Backbg.

B. sepium (HBK.) Br. & R.
Bo. medium-stout, erect, or prostrate and then curving upwards; **St.** to 1.5 m lg., to 4 cm ∅; **Ri.** 8–11 or somewhat more, with V-shaped notches but no thickening around the Ar., rounded; **Rsp.** 8–10, thin, spreading, to 10 mm lg.; **Csp.** scarcely distinguishable, but 1–3 are longer, one especially lg., directed downwards, darker in part above, to 4 cm lg.; **Fl.** more scarlet; **Fr.** 2 cm ∅.—Ecuador (near Riobamba).

B. ventimigliae Ricc. (T.)

transverse furrow replacing the V-notches, the furrow ± flattened above and below; **Fl.** red, limb moderately oblique, opening narrow; **Pet.** ± laxly erect; **Tu.** cylindric.—Ecuador (precise locality not known).

B. websterianus Backbg.
Bo. erect, forming groups; **St.** to 10 cm ∅, light green; **Ri.** 14, to 1 cm br., ± depressed around the Ar., later with V-furrows above them; **Sp.** golden-yellow, c. 20 **Rsp.** and 4 **Csp.**, one of the latter to 5 cm lg., the others to 12 mm lg.; **Fl.** carmine.— Ecuador (Cuenca).
v. **rufispinus** Backbg.: **St.** darker green, **Sp.** more strongly interlacing, dark to reddish brown.— Ecuador (Cuenca, 3000 m).

Borzicactus sensu Kimm.: Kimnach united the following under this epithet:
Plants without cephalioid development:
Shortly cereoid plants with ± zygomorphic Fl.; ring of wool absent; Fr. dry, opening basally, S. falling out:
Arequipa Br. & R.
Slender Cerei with conspicuously zygomorphic Fl.; ring of wool present; Fr. a berry:
Bolivicereus Card.
Shrubby plants with stout, straight floral tubes, limbs fairly short:
Clistanthocereus Backbg.
Low-growing slender Cerei with ± S-shaped funnelform Fl. and berry-fruits:
Loxanthocereus Backbg.
Plants which are cactoid at first; Fl. glabrous,

zygomorphic; Fr. a dehiscent berry:
>**Matucana** Br. & R.

Stoutly stemmed Cerei with zygomorphic Fl. and large hollow Fr.:
>**Oreocereus** (Berg.) Ricc.

Plants cactoid at first; Fl. ± hairy; Fr. a dehiscent berry:
>**Submatucana** Backbg.

Plants with cephalioid development:
Low-growing Cerei with apical cephalium, zygomorphic Fl. and hollow Fr.:
>**Morawetzia** Backbg.

Low-growing to prostrate Cerei with short-limbed zygomorphic Fl., with compressed Tu. and berry-Fr; flowering zone increasingly to densely set with long Br.:
>**Seticereus** Backbg.

This combination, of distinctive groups of species possessing considerably differing diagnostic characters, has not gained any acceptance up till now.

Brachycalycium Backbg. (117)

This genus was only very recently re-discovered. In habitat the bodies can be to 40 cm tall, to 30 cm br.; the longitudinal furrows are very sinuate and this, together with the depressions between the areoles, produces oblong to subspherical tubercles. The areoles are noticeably oblong, spineless in the upper half, and in part project from a ± discernible shallow depression. The urn-shaped flowers resemble those of Gymnocalycium saglione but have no tube; the style is only 5 mm long.—Distribution: N. Argentina (near Tilcara). [(R.)]

B. tilcarense (Backbg.) Backbg. (T.)
Bo. as described above; **Ri.** spiralled; **Fl.** white, pink at the centre, c. 3 cm lg., almost 5 cm ∅, wide bellshaped; **Pet.** spatulate, ± acuminate; **style** 3 mm thick; **Sti.** capitately closed; **Fil.** very short, throughout the interior of the Fl.; **nectary** not present.—N. Argentina (SE. of Tilcara, c. 2000 m). (Fig. 39, 40.)

Brachycereus Br. & R. (61)

Slender, erect Cerei, forming large colonies. The nocturnal flowers are narrowly funnelform, close to those of the Genus Armatocereus, as is the spiny fruit, which is small in the above genus; but the stems of Brachycereus are not segmented into annual growths, and the spines are relatively flexible.—Distribution: Galapagos Is. (on bare lava). Only recently introduced to cultivation. In Britton & Rose the type-species was given as Cereus thouarsii sensu Br. & R. non Web.

(correctly: Cereus nesioticus K.Sch.). But Cereus thouarsii Web. non sensu Br. & R. is the type of the Genus Jasminocereus, also in Buxbaum's sense. The latter's procedure with Mitrocereus (see under that genus) is shown to be inappropriate because if it were adopted, he would have to rename Jasminocereus as Brachycereus, and replace Brachycereus with a new name "Pseudobrachycereus". His procedure is thus both illogical and unnecessary; in such cases the little phrase "non sensu …" avoids any confusion.

B. nesioticus (K.Sch.) Backbg. (T.)
Bo. slender-columnar, branching from the base, 30–60 cm lg., up to 300 **St.** together; **Ri.** 13–16, scarcely 3 mm h., ± tuberculate; **Ar.** 2.5 mm ∅; **Sp.** over 40, to 3 cm lg., strongly bristly and rigid, straight; **Fl.** 7 cm lg., 2.5–3 cm ∅; **Ov.** with yellow-brown Sp. 5 mm lg.; **Pet.** narrow, white; **Fr.** 2.5 cm lg., 1.3 cm br.; **S.** 1.2 mm lg., reddish-brown.—Galapagos Is. (Albermarle, Narborough, Abingdon, James and Tower). (Fig. 41.)

Brasilicactus Backbg. (107)

One species which is ± cylindric and two species which remain spherical, not producing offsets, with relatively short but fairly stiff spines. Flowers differentiated from those of all other S. American spherical cacti by the usually very short tube which, like the small spherical berry-fruits, has sharp spines. Flowers relatively small, self-fertile, in early spring; petals slender, fairly densely arranged. It is therefore hard to see why the species are sometimes still referred to Notocactus which has quite different characters of flower and fruit. One of the three species seems now to have been lost. It is interesting to note that there is a form of B. haselbergii with broader, zygomorphic flowers having a longer, more slender and spiny tube. This may be avatism, in which case it would also demonstrate that the normal flowers are the product of a reduction-process, this, and other lines of reduction of widely varying kinds elsewhere, providing the most reliable basis for any systematic arrangement because they are based on observation of Nature, and do not rely on hypothetical considerations.—Distribution: N. Uruguay and S. Brazil. [(R). (G).]

B. elachisanthus (Web.) Backbg.
Bo. cylindric, to 25 cm h., 12 cm ∅; **Ri.** 45 or more, divided throughout into Tub.; **Sp.** 12–15, white, to 12 mm lg.; **Fl.** 1.5 cm lg., yellowish-green; **Fr.** greenish, 5–6 mm ∅; **S.** dark brown.—Uruguay (NE. of Maldonado). Probably extinct.

B. graessneri (K.Sch.) Backbg. (T.)

Bo. spherical, to 10 cm h. and mostly rather broader; **Ri.** 50–60, divided entirely into small Tub.; **Sp.** numerous, up to 60 per Ar., to 2 cm lg., 5–6 distinguishable as **centrals**, somewhat stouter and darker, otherwise all are yellow; **Fl.** 1.8 cm lg., greenish.—S. Brazil (Rio Grande do Sul).

v. **albisetus** Cullm.: **Sp.** fine, bristly, **Rsp.** light yellowish-white, **Csp.** more greenish-yellow, also fine white bristly H. up to 3 cm lg.

There is also a variety with pure yellow Fl.:

v. **flaviflorus** Backbg. n.var.

The yellow-colour is the same as in Eriocactus leninghausii.

B. haselbergii (Hge.) Backbg.

Bo. as in the preceding; **Ri.** 30 or more; **Rsp.** 20 or more, yellowish at first, then white, to 1 cm lg.; **Csp.** (3–)4(–5), yellowish; **Fl.** numerous, 1.5 cm lg.; **Pet.** flame-coloured, or with orange margins, to scarlet.—S. Brazil (Rio Grande do Sul). (Fig. 42.)

v. **stellatus** hort.: only a form, with somewhat longer yellowish **Csp.**

Brasilicereus Backbg. (170)

Cerei from NE. Brazil, one species slender and erect, sometimes taller than a man, the second one smaller. The flowers are identical: conspicuously curved, with a bellshaped to funnelform perianth, with more distant, coarser scales, without hairs. The stems are also hairless, and lack any spine-modification in the flowering zone. Despite the differences in height and robustness, the two species show identical floral characters and constitute a completely valid genus.—Distribution: Brazil (Bahia and Minas Geraes). [(G) (R).]

B. markgrafii Backbg. & Voll

Bo. of pencil-thickness in ungrafted plants, to 2.5 cm ⌀, up to 1 m h., rarely branching; grafted plants are longer and stouter; **Ri.** 8–13, flat; **Ar.** 5–10 mm apart, grey; **Rsp.** 12–18, 6–10 mm lg.; **Csp.** 1(–4), to 4 cm lg.; **Fl.** 6 cm lg., 5 cm ⌀; **Tu.** and **Ov.** together 2.5 cm lg., glossy green; **Pet.** c. 12, 3.5 cm lg., light greenish.—Brazil (Minas Geraes). (Fig. 43.)

B. phaeacanthus (Gürke) Backbg. (T.)

Bo. to 4 m h., mostly branching from the base; **St.** to 4–5(–9) cm ⌀; **Ri.** mostly 13, low, narrow; **Rsp.** 10–12, 1–1.5 cm lg.; **Csp.** 1–3, to 3 cm lg.; all **Sp.** yellow-brown at first; **Fl.** 6.5 cm lg., 6 cm ⌀; **Pet.** white, in part with a greenish tinge.—Brazil (central to S. Bahia).

Cereus parvisetus O.: an insufficiently clarified spec. which may be referable here.

Brasiliopuntia (K.Sch.) Berg. (15)

Distinctive opuntia-like plants; tree-like, with a continuous round trunk, the branches with thin leaf-like shoots. The flowers possess staminodes (hair-development). The fruits are yellow or red, variously shaped, some spiny, others not. 4 species, readily distinguished on the basis of shape, colour or spination of the fruits which contain only a few woolly seeds.—Distribution: Brazil, Paraguay, Peru, E. Bolivia, E. Argentina. [(R).]

B. bahiensis (Br. & R.) Berg.

Bo. to 15 m h.; **trunk** to 25 cm ⌀, becoming hollow; **L.** small, 2–3 mm lg.; **Sp.** on terminal shoots, when present, 1–2, thin, red at first, in large groups on the older trunk; **Fl.** not known; **Fr.** oblong (not clavate), red, spineless.—Brazil (Bahia, Toca de Onca).

B. brasiliensis (Willd.) Berg. (T.)

Bo. to 4 m h.; trunk glabrous or spiny; **Seg.** very thin, eventually deciduous, to 15 cm lg., 6 cm br.; **Sp.** 1–2, to 1.5 cm lg.; **Fl.** 5.5 cm lg., yellow; **Fr.** spherical, 2.5–4 cm ⌀, yellow, shortly spined; **S.** often one only, within a yellow pulp.—Central Brazil to E. Peru, E. Argentina, E. Bolivia, Paraguay. (Fig. 44.)

B. neoargentina Backbg.

Bo. several meters h.; **Seg.** more oval, darker green than in the other spec.; **Sp.** red below at first, reddish-brown above, up to 30 together on the trunk, 1–2 on the Seg., oblique, rather lg.; **Fl.** yellow, smaller than in B. brasiliensis; **Fr.** red inside and out, subspherical, with longer projecting Sp.—Origin not known (Paraguay?).

B. schulzii (Cast. & Lelong) Backbg.

Bo. to 15 m h., with branches in whorls; **Seg.** thin, to 13 cm lg., 4 cm br., 2 mm thick; **Sp.** on Seg. to 4 cm lg., subulate, dark brown, and 1–2 thinner Sp. to 1.5 cm lg., those on the trunk in groups of 25–30; **Fl.** greenish-yellow, 4 cm ⌀; **Fr.** clavate, red, 5 cm lg., to 2.75 cm ⌀, spineless; **S.** brownish.—Argentina (galleried forests of Jujuy, Chaco Austral and Boreal).

Brittonia Hought. ex Armstrg.: **Hamatocactus hamatacanthus** v. **davisii** (Hought.) Marsh.

Brittonrosea Speg.: **Echinofossulocactus** Lawr.

Browningia Br. & R. (64)

Tree-like Cerei, occurring as scattered individuals; the primary stem is strongly spined while the branches are completely spineless. The ribs are low and the areoles large. Flowers white, nocturnal, with long thin scales, the oblong fruits similarly but with the large scales drying and persisting. Seeds large, matt black. Remarkable for the variable form of the branches: stiffly erect, bent upwards, in part curving down and then upwards, others are erect, some bend downwards with just the tips bent upwards. No segregation can be made on the basis of habit.—Distribution: the higher-lying arid zones of S. Peru and N. Chile. (Only seedlings known in cultivation; these grow well.)

Buxbaum seeks to unite Gymnocereus and Azureocereus with this polymorphic genus; but this view is based only on theory and phylogenetics, so that it fails to reflect the facts of Nature, and overlooks differential characters.

B. candelaris (Meyen) Br. & R. (T.)

Bo. to 5 m h., **trunk** to 50 cm $\emptyset$; **Ri.** to over 30, only 5 mm h.; **Sp.** only on the trunk, to c. 20, sometimes to 50, 10–15 cm lg., brown at first, becoming grey or black, the Ar. of the flowering zone sometimes with small Br.; **Fl.** unscented, 8–12 cm lg., somewhat curving; **Tu.** 4 cm lg.; **Sc.** fleshy at first; **Pet.** c. 2 cm lg., outer ones brownish to pink, innermost ones white; **Fr.** edible, to 7 cm lg., scented; **S.** 2 mm thick.—S. Peru (near Arequipa) to N. Chile (about 2000 m). (Fig. 45.)

> Ritter's v. chilensis, "with upcurving branches", cannot be justified.

> It is remarkable that fallen shoots never root, i.e. the secondary shoots have obviously lost the ability to root.

B. pileifera (Ritt.) Hutchis. (Gymnanthocereus?)

Bo. 3–4 m h., freely branching; **Ri.** 7–9, acute or rounded; **Ar.** to 1 cm apart, later often confluent, woolly; **Rsp.** 0–3, 1–5 mm lg., soon greying; **Csp.** 0–3, to 5 cm lg.; **Fl.** small, covered with dry brown and white Sc., reminiscent of Escontria.—Peru (Balsas).

Buiningia Buxb. 1971 (Synonym: Coleocephalocereus Backbg. pro parte)

Slender Cerei to only c. 75 cm h., in part prostrate, offsetting from the base, forming groups; juveniles remain hemispherical to spherical for years (to 17 cm $\emptyset$), but eventually become shortly columnar, tapering and conical above; **Ri.** 10–18, straight, $\pm$ notched at the Ar.; **Sp.** dense, long; **Rsp.** to 7–15; **Csp.** 1–4, thin-acicular, flexible; **Fl.** arising from a unilateral Ceph. of dense wool and thin long Br.-Sp. extending over several flattened Ri., 2.5–3.5 cm lg., small, narrowly tubular, only the tips of the Sep. curving somewhat outwards; **style** with 5

stout, papillose, tightly grouped Sti.; **Fr.** a spherical red berry with white pulp; **S.** black, glossy.—Brazil (NE. of Minas Geraes; on rocks, in humus-filled depressions).

Named for the Dutch collector, the late A. F. H. Buining, who made many outstanding contributions to our knowledge of the Cactaceae, especially among the Brazilian species.

B. aurea (Ritt.) Buxb.

Described by Ritter, 1968, as Coleocephalocereus aureus, but then referred to the newly erected Genus Buiningia, on account of various conspicuous divergences.

Bo. offsetting freely from the base, becoming only 40 cm h., 6–7 cm $\emptyset$, green; **Ri.** 10–16, triangular in section, with flanks 7–10 mm br., little tuberculate, obtuse; **Ar.** in the notches, 3–5 mm $\emptyset$, with white felt, 2–5 mm apart; **Sp.** golden-yellow, glossy, flexible, straight or little curving, those of young seedlings brown at first and in part hooked; **Rsp.** 10–15, 5–15 mm lg.; **Csp.** 1–4, lowest one 2–5 cm lg., projecting, stoutly acicular, others shorter; **Ceph.** lateral, present on plants 15 cm h. and more, broad, extending over a larger number of Ri., of dense skeins of white wool 1–2 cm lg., overtopped by acicular, slender, bent, golden-yellow Br.; **Fl.** nocturnal, 30–37 mm lg., greenish-yellow, with pale green Sc. 2–3 mm lg.; **Fil.** white; **style** white, with 5–7 connivent whitish Sti. 2 mm lg.; **Fr.** blood-red, resembling the Fr. of Melocactus, smooth, glossy, 16–22 mm lg.; **S.** black, glossy, 1.5 mm lg.—Brazil (NE. of Minas Geraes, near Agua Vermelha). First discovered by Ritter in 1965. (Fig. 468.)

B. brevicylindrica Buin. 1971

Bo. spherical at first, later shortly cylindric, to 30 cm h. and 17 cm $\emptyset$, fresh green, offsetting from the base, conical at the apex; **Ri.** to 18, vertical, with a protuberance over the Ar.; **Ar.** rather oblong, those in the crown to 6 mm br. and 8 mm lg., with short whitish to $\pm$ yellowish wool, soon becoming glabrous; **Rsp.** c. 7, the lowest one directed downwards, to 2 cm lg., 2 laterals to 3 cm lg., upper ones to 1.5 cm lg., with 3–4 smaller Ssp.; **Csp.** mostly cruciform, bottom one to 6 cm lg., laterals to 3 cm, upper one to 2.5 cm lg., all Sp. noticeably shorter once the Ceph. has developed; lateral **Ceph.** developing on plants while still spherical and 8 cm h., of white wool interspersed with golden-yellow, mostly straight, bristly Sp., Ceph. eventually to 7 cm br. and c. 20 cm lg.; **Fl.** tubular, 15 mm $\emptyset$, to 32 mm lg., glabrous, light yellowish-green; **Sep.** curving strongly outwards; **Pet.** scarcely opening; **style** whitish, with 4–5 Sti. c. 1 mm lg.; **Fr.** spherical, glossy, red, glabrous, 17 mm $\emptyset$; **S.** ovate, with a glossy black testa.—Brazil (Minas

Geraes, N. of the Rio Jequitinhonha among bromeliads and terrestrial orchids). (Fig. 469.)

v. **elongata** Buin.: **Bo.** more columnar, to 62 cm lg.; **Ceph.** developing only later. Locality c. 100 km further westwards;

v. **longispina** Buin.: **Rsp.** to 7 cm lg., lowest **Csp.** to 13 cm lg. Forming large groups. Locality 30 km further S.

B. purpurea Buin. & Bred. 1973

Bo. shortly to oblong-columnar, offsetting from the base, to 87 cm lg., to 10 cm Ø, green to dark green; lateral **Ceph.** to 50 cm lg., with grey wool interspersed with yellow, reddish or grey **Br.**; **Ar.** ± round, 7 mm lg., 6 mm Ø, with grey felt, 7 mm apart; **Ri.** 13, to 23 mm br. and to 15 mm h.; **Sp.** reddish-brown, red or yellowish-brown above at first, later greying, sometimes tipped reddish, often ± curving; **Rsp.** c. 12, radiating, 12–25 mm lg.; **Csp.** c. 4, one directed obliquely downwards, c. 70 mm lg., others directed laterally and upwards, 30–35 mm lg.; **Fl.** tubular, 30 mm lg., to 12 mm br., purplish-red, glabrous; **Tu.** cylindric, with small Sc. 1–2 mm lg., these passing over above into the Pet.; **Sep.** spatulate, to 13 mm lg., to 3 mm br., violet-carmine, curving strongly outwards; **Pet.** to 8 mm lg., to 2.5 mm br., reversed spatulate, erect, narrowly enclosing the uppermost Fil., purplish-red; primary **Fil.** 10–13 mm lg., white, distinctly separated, secondary ones to 5 mm lg., still shorter above, white; **An.** yellow; **style** white below, pink above, with 4–5 white Sti.; **Fr.** spherical, 17 mm Ø, glossy, red; **S.** cap-shaped, testa glossy, black.—Brazil (NE. of Minas Geraes; on the Rio Jequintinhonha, in eroded mineral-rich soil at 350–400 m, on bare ground or together with bromeliads. First discovered by Horst in 1971). (Fig. 470.)

Cactus L.: **Melocactus** Lk. & O. (Linnaeus's name, which was briefly introduced by Br. and R., is still sometimes used in the USA, but it has now been rejected.)

Calymmanthium Ritt. (60)

A treelike or shrubby plant, densely branching, with only 3–4 ribs; the flowers are unique and the angular, slender-clavate fruits, up to 15 cm long, are sometimes minutely spiny. The flower-bud has two stages: at first it is clavate and appears normal, with its felt-cushions and tiny spines. As it increases in length and the tip opens, the true perianth emerges from it at the level of the constriction above the nectary, and then opens normally, with the filaments inserted throughout the entire inner wall. In longitudinal section and at the height of the constriction surmounting the ovary, the first stage

appears to be made up of greatly elongated and united scales; Ritter terms this the "protective cap", but this is only for explanatory purposes. The flower is of great interest to the morphologist. If a flower is regarded as a modified short-lived shoot, then the somewhat angular first stage clearly has the character of a shoot which is retained in the slender fruit; from this "short shoot" there then appears the true perianth, ± tubular in shape, with the inner perianth segments rather longer united. Ritter refers to this upper section of the flower as the "tube", but a longitudinal section reveals that half of the lower section should also be included in the term, since the elongated nectary is situated within it. There is thus a kind of two-stage development of the true flower.—Distribution: N. Peru (Jaén, lower Huancabamba gorge). [(R).]

C. fertile Ritt. (1966)

Distinguished from C. substerile as follows: **Ri.** 3–5, 2–3 cm h.; **Ar.** brownish-red; **Sp.** yellowish, often absent; **Fl.** 8 cm lg., with a ± trumpet-shaped Cor. c. 2 cm lg., whitish-pink; **An.** golden-yellow; **style** pale yellow, reddish above, with mid-yellow Sti.; **Pet.** 20 mm lg., dark carmine; **Fr.** 7–11 cm lg., spineless, pulp hard; **S.** small, 2 mm lg.—Peru (E. of Balsas).

C. substerile Ritt. (Kakt. u. a. sukk. Pflz. 13: 2, 24–28. 1962). (T.)

Bo. treelike, with a dense shrubby crown, to 8 m h.; **branches** light green, to over 1 m lg., 4–8 cm Ø; **Ri.** 3–4, to 4 cm h.; **Ar.** white, fairly plump on the upper shoots; **Rsp.** 3–8, to 1 cm lg., projecting radially; **Csp.** to 6, 1–5 cm lg.; **Sp.** whitish; **Fl.** nocturnal, 9.5–11 cm lg., 3–5 cm Ø when expanded; **Ov.** to 3 cm lg., 17 mm br., with small Sp. to spineless; **Tu.** to 2.5 cm lg. above the elongated nectary, white; **Pet.** to 2.5 cm lg., inner ones white to reddish-brown, outer ones reddish-brown with a green margin; **Fil.** white; **style** red, to 8 cm lg.; **Sti.** whitish; **Fr.** light green, 4–5-angled, to 15 cm lg., 6 cm thick, ± glabrous to completely so, sometimes with minute Sp.; **S.** 2.5 mm lg., greyish-black, matt.—N. Peru (see above). (Fig. 46, 47.)

Carnegiea Br. & R. (154)

Gigantic tree-like columnar cacti with relatively few, very erect branches; the primary stem does not branch below a certain height and its lower portion thus constitutes a trunk; until the branching stage is reached, the plants are solitary columns like Browningia. The flowers are borne in clusters at the shoot-tips, opening slowly at night and remaining open the next day; they have only sparse white felt, the fruit similarly; the latter sometimes bears 1–3 short acicular spines. A bizarre fasciation is fairly commonly seen.—Distribution: USA (Arizona, SE. California), Mexico (Sonora). [(R).]

C. gigantea (Eng.) Br. & R. (T.)
Bo. to more than 12 m h., to 30–65 cm $\emptyset$; **Ri.** 12–24, obtuse; **Ar.** 2–2.5 cm apart, brown; **Rsp.** radiating, c. 12 and more, 1–2 cm lg.; **Csp.** 3–6, stouter, to 7 cm lg.; **Sp.** in the flowering zone shorter and finer; **Fl.** c. 12 cm lg. and $\emptyset$; **Tu.** green; **Sc.** distant; **Ov.** oblong; **Pet.** spreading, obtuse, white; **Fr.** 6–9 cm lg., red inside and out when fully ripe, dehiscent.—USA towards the W. end of the S. border), Mexico (Sonora, near the frontier). (Fig. 48, 49.)

Castellanosia Card. (173)

Large shrubs, in part also inclined, with relatively few ribs. The normal rigid spines are modified in the flowering region into clusters of bristly spines. The flowers are borne towards the apex, nocturnal but remaining open the next day, $\pm$ bellshaped to funnelform, with the limb projecting. The scales are arranged almost imbricately, with white felt, the ovary and the fruit similarly. The latter, very much an exceptional case, is said to be poisonous. The seeds are only 1 mm long and reddish-brown. Only one species certainly identified; a similar but undescribed plant from Peru may possibly be referable here.—Distribution: Bolivia (Dept. Santa Cruz, Cochabamba) and S. Peru? (Rare in cultivation.)

C. caineana Card. (T.)
Bo. erect, to 6 m h.; **branches** greyish-green, $\pm$ flexible, long; **Ri.** 9, rounded, to 3.5 cm br.; **Rsp.** 15–16, 0.8–4 cm lg.; **Csp.** 3–4, 4–7 cm lg., brown to greyish-black; flowering **Ar.** with c. 25 **Br.** 1–4 cm lg., white, grey or dark brown, in stiff clusters; **Fl.** 3–5 cm lg.; **Pet.** purple; **Sti.** pinkish-white; **Fr.** yellowish-green, 3 cm lg., with dark yellow pulp.— E. Bolivia (700–1600 m). (Fig. 50.)

Cephalocereus Pfeiff. (165)

The name was erected by Pfeiffer for a genus whose type-species had white hairs and a broad cephalium, at first on one side only of the stem, but later sometimes enveloping the entire apex. The flowers and fruit were hairy; the latter (becoming glabrous finally?) had a lid, and the fairly large seeds were black and glossy. Later this became a comprehensive genus to which plants with different characters of flower and cephalioid development were referred, so that it covered not only plants

with true cephalia but also species having only tufts of hair or bristle; this was in itself misleading since in some species even these "false" cephalia might be absent. At that time our present knowledge of the different kinds of tuft-development and floral structure was not available. If the type-species is not to be an irrelevance, the species of any one genus must resemble the type in their diagnostic characters; but this cannot be said of the other species earlier placed in the collective genus and sometimes still retained there. Consequently only one species now remains; the other species must be put into more appropriate genera: Austrocephalocereus, Backebergia, Coleocephalocereus, Espostoa, Haseltonia, Micranthocereus, Mitrocereus, Neodawsonia, Pilosocereus.—Distribution: Mexico (Hidalgo). [(R). O.; tolerates small amounts of lime.]

Cephalocereus hoppenstedtii (Web.) K. Sch.: **Haseltonia columna-trajani** (Karw.) Backbg.

C. senilis (Haw.) Pfeiff. (T.)
Bo. to 15 m h., normally branching only rarely; **Ri.** 20–30, low, light green, becoming grey; **Ar.** proximate; **Sp.** 3–5, yellowish or grey, to 4 cm lg., also 20–30 white or rather greyish, long and tangled H., mostly directed downwards; **Ceph.** from c. 6 m h., with whitish wool, at first on one side only, then wider to encircling the entire St.; **Fl.** to 9.5 cm lg., pale yellowish-white, 7.5 cm $\emptyset$; **Tu.** 5 cm lg., $\pm$ pink, it and the **Ov.** hairy; **Sti.** cream; **Fr.** red, with sparse yellowish H., pulp red.—Mexico (Hidalgo; Guanajuato [?]). (Fig. 51.)

Cephalocleistocactus Ritt. (76)

Slender, mostly erect Cerei, quite similar to Cleistocactus in growth-form, floral structure and spination. It is differentiated from the latter by the development in the flowering zone of flexible to bristly or even fine hair-like spines—at first on one side only and later tending to encircle the stem— which are appreciably longer than the others and thus produce a conspicuous bristly tuft which is similar to that in the flowering zone of Seticereus. 4 species identified, but there are probably others.— Distribution: E. Bolivia. [(R).]

C. chrysocephalus Ritt. (T.)
Bo. to 5 m h., offsetting from the base; **St.** 3–5 cm $\emptyset$, later sometimes bending over; **Ri.** 11–14, 4–5 mm h., with V-shaped furrows; **Ar.** 2–3 mm br., larger in the flowering zone, **Sp.** there increasing to c. 30, 3–4 cm lg., golden-yellow to yellowish-brown; **Ceph.** to 1 m lg.; **Fl.** c. 5 cm lg., expanding only slightly, red; **Sti.** green; **Fr.** 2 cm lg., reddish;

S. small, glossy black.—Bolivia (near Inquisivi).

C. pallidus Backbg. n.sp.
Bo. with St. to c. 3.5 cm thick; **Ri.** c. 16; **Ar.** dark at first; **Sp.** ± equal, radials and centrals not distinguishable, c. 25 in all, to c. 5(–6) mm lg., greyish-white, at first also very pale yellowish; **Ceph.** of yellowish Br. to 3 cm lg.; **Fl.** cylindric, yellow.—Bolivia (Consata basin, Palhuaya gorge, acc. Ritter). (FR 324). (Fig. 52.) Somewhat resembles Cephalocleistocactus ritteri Backbg. but the new Sp. in the apex are pale yellowish, while the Br. of the flowering zone are later yellowish, more laxly arranged and stiffer.

C. ritteri Backbg.
Bo. slender, erect, to more than 1 m lg., c. 3 cm ∅, branching from the base; **Ri.** to 12–14 or more; **Ar.** dark brown, becoming whitish; **Rsp.** to 30, fine, short and white; **Csp.** 5, yellowish, to 1 cm lg.; **Ceph.** of ± hairlike, fine, projecting, white Br. to 3 cm lg.; **Fl.** lemon-yellow, c. 4 cm lg., thin-cylindric, slightly bent; **Sti.** green.—Bolivia (Yungas). (Fig. 53.)

C. schattatianus Backbg.—Descr. Cact. Nov. III: 5. 1963.
Bo. erect, or prostrate and then curving upwards, forming denser colonies; **St.** to over 60 cm lg., to c. 5 cm ∅; **Ri.** c. 16–17, low, narrow, slightly tuberculate; **Sp.** to over 30, short, pale yellowish to ± whitish, centrals indistinct, some rather longer, to 1.3 cm lg., porrect; **Ceph.** at first on one side only, widening, of golden-brown Br. of increasing length, to 3 cm lg.; **Fl.** c. 4 cm lg., tubular, scarcely opening; **Tu.** red; **Sep.** and **Pet.** pale yellowish above, tipped with a greenish-yellowish zone; **Fr.** ? (Pollination with the pollen of Cleistocactus has not hitherto succeeded!)—Bolivia. (Fig. 54.)

Cereus Mill. (172)

This genus includes the earliest known columnar cacti. Some of these are great trees, in part with very large crowns and stout trunks, sometimes they are not so large; some species are only shrubby and more slender, while others are only low-growing and freely branching shrubs. In most species the ribs are quite large, set well apart and therefore relatively few in number (often only 4); other species have less prominent ribs while in C. insularis they are especially low and close together by reason of the small diameter of the shoots; this species, with its numerous longer spines, bears little resemblance to others of the genus. The flowers have longer tubes; the scales are rather distant; the axils are glabrous, also on the ovary and fruit. The

petals are mostly white, but sometimes more conspicuously reddish. All species have the following diagnostic character in common (which separates them, for instance, from Monvillea): after the flower has faded or the perianth dropped, the style persists for a time, even for a time on the fruit. The latter is mostly oblong, yellow to red but sometimes greenish. The seeds are quite large and usually dull black, more rarely glossy. Some species of Cereus make good grafting stocks. They are divided into the two subgenera below:

SG.1: Cereus: Fruits dehiscent.
SG.2: Neocereus Backbg.: Fruits indehiscent (only 1 spec.: C. huntingtonianus Wgt.).
Distribution: W. Indies through northern S. America to E. Argentina and Fernando de Noronha Is. (Brazil). [(R).]

C. aethiops Haw.
Bo. to 2 m h., ± bluish, erect, later branching; **St.** 3–4 cm ∅; **Ri.** 8, tuberculate; **Rsp.** 9–12, 5–12 mm lg., black, white below; **Csp.** (2–)4, over 2 cm lg., stouter; **Fl.** 16–20 cm lg., bluish-green or bluish-purple outside; **Pet.** white to ± pink; **Fr.** to 8 cm lg., brownish.—Argentina (Mendoza to Rio Negro).
v. **landbeckii** (Phil.) Backbg. has white **Rsp.** In v. **melanacanthus** (K.Sch.) Backbg. the **St.** are often reddish, with the **Csp.** much longer, directed obliquely upwards and glossy black.

C. alacriportanus Pfeiff.
Bo. to 2 m (?) h., new growth bluish-green but not pruinose; **Ri.** mostly (4–)5; **Sp.** 6–9, light yellow with a red base, or reddish-brownish, to 2.5 cm lg. and more; **Fl.** to 22 cm lg.; **Sep.** reddish; **Pet.** very pale yellowish-pink, bluntly tapering, denticulate.—S. Brazil, Uruguay, Paraguay.

C. argentinensis Br. & R.
Bo. to 12 m h., with a trunk; **branches** numerous, to 15 cm ∅, mid-green; **Ri.** 4–5, thin, to 5 cm h.; **Rsp.** 5–8, 3–5 cm lg., brownish; **Csp.** 1–2, to 10 cm lg.; **Fl.** 17–22 cm lg.; **Sep.** green; **Pet.** white.—Argentina (Chaco).

C. azureus Parm.
Bo. to 3 m h.; **St.** erect, to c. 4 cm ∅, blue-pruinose; **Ri.** 6–7, somewhat sinuate; **Ar.** with brown felt and grey wool; **Rsp.** 8, white; **Csp.** 1–3, dark brown to black, stouter.—Brazil.
There appear to be varieties of this, or possibly further similar species:
K. Schumann described the spec. as "fresh green, somewhat blue, eventually dark green; **Sp.** 10–18, to 9 mm lg., **Csp.** 2–4; **Sp.** all black; **Fl.** 20–30 cm lg.; **Pet.** white with a green dorsal M.-line, spatulate".—S. Brazil. This must be another and

hitherto undescribed spec., in view of the discrepancies by comparison with the above data taken from the original description, although this latter contains nothing regarding the flower or its length. Spegazzini, under the same name, described a plant "up to 1.5 m h., in part curving over, remaining blue even in age, but not initially pruinose; **Ri.** 5; **Ar.** at first with pink felt; **Sp.** brown at first, then reddish-brown, eventually grey, typically 6; **Rsp.** 5, to 2 cm lg.; **Csp.** 1, to 5 cm lg.; **Fl.** 10 cm lg.; **Sep.** olive; **Pet.** white, finely ciliate; **Fr.** ellipsoid, 4.5 cm lg., pink to purplish-pink, ± pruinose.—N. Argentina (between Rio Bermejo and Rio Pilcomayo)." This, likewise, cannot be the plant of the original description, and must therefore remain nameless.

C. braunii Card.
Bo. to 3 m h., green; **Ri.** 4–5, ± swollen around the Ar., to 6 cm h.; **Sp.** 5–6, whitish, with a brownish tip, to 4 cm lg.; **Fl.** 28 cm lg., white.—Bolivia (Prov. Ballivian, near Reyes, 280 m). Probably not in cultivation.

C. caesius SD. ex Pfeiff.
Bo. branching, but not forming a trunk, robust; **branches** 12–16 cm ∅; **Ri.** 5–6, tall, winged, pruinose, sometimes sinuate, slightly notched; **Ar.** 4–6 cm apart; **Rsp.** 7 or more; **Csp.** 4–7, stouter, ± light to dark brown; **Sp.** much more numerous on old growth, sometimes to 10 cm lg. New growth is conspicuously bluish, the bloom gradually disappearing from the green shoots.—Brazil (?).

C. chacoanus Vpl.: obviously is not referable here because the more freely scaly, not very broad-limbed Fl. correspond more closely to those of Monvillea campinensis. Both these plants are insufficiently clarified. The above spec. forms **Bo.** up to 4 m h., with a **trunk** 6 cm ∅; **Sp.** 9–10, subulate, grey; **Csp.** 1, 6 cm lg., stouter than the others; **Fl.** 15 cm lg., pink outside, white inside; **Tu.** with more distant Sc.; **Ov.** with c. 25 Sc.; **Fr.** subspherical, 3 cm lg.; **S.** small, black.—Paraguay (Gran Chaco).

C. chalybaeus O.
Bo. to 3 m h., ± erect, little branching; **shoots** to 10 cm ∅, ± bluish-pruinose, also reddish; **Ri.** 6, narrow, high, weakly notched; **Rsp.** at first c. 7, also several longer **Csp.**, all eventually more numerous, black; **Fl.** c. 20 cm lg.; **Tu.** purple; **Sep.** pink; **Pet.** white; **Fr.** yellow, spherical.—N. Argentina (near Córdoba, formerly also to Santa Fé and Buenos Aires, but probably now lost from those areas). Br. & R. describe under the above name a similar plant with dark brown **Sp.** and

yellow **Fr.** Rare, unnamed.—Origin: as the above spec.

C. childsii Blanc
Bo. erect, bushy; **branches** to 15 cm ∅; **Ri.** 4–5, compressed, obtuse; **Ar.** 5 cm apart; **Sp.** 6–7, 6 mm to 1.5 cm lg.; **Csp.** 1, 7 mm lg.; all at first light brown, becoming blackish-brown; **Fl.** to 24 cm ∅ (?), deep pink, with a sickly-sweet scent.—Brazil (Colonia Roman). One of the few spec. with pink Fl. and every effort should be made to re-collect and distribute it.

C. cochabambensis Card.
Bo. tree-like, 3–4 m h.; **Ar.** 4–5 mm ∅, 1–2.2 cm apart, felt whitish-brown at first, becoming blackish; **Rsp.** 3–4, spreading, 5–25 mm lg., sharp, thin, later subulate; **Fl.** 2–4 on one Ri., nocturnal, 11–12 cm lg., funnelform, curving into an S-shape; **Ov.** 3 cm lg., dark green; **Tu.** 6 cm lg., dark green with a few light green Sc.; **Sep.** light green; **Pet.** spatulate, white, pink-tipped; **style** 5 cm lg., white to light greenish, with 14 light yellow Sti.; **Fr.** 3–5 cm lg., orange-yellow, splitting at maturity, pulp dark magenta, sweet.—Bolivia (El Cercado, Cochabamba, Caico, 2560 m). This spec. resembles C. hankeanus but the latter grows at only 500 m in the Argentinian Chaco, and shows divergences of Sp. and Fl.
   v. **longicarpa** Card.: differs in some of its dimensions; **Fr.** ellipsoid, 8–10 cm lg.—Bolivia (near Alba Rancho at 2565 m).

C. comarapanus Card.
Bo. to 4 m h., with a **trunk** 1.5 m h.; **shoots** bluish-green, with constrictions 20–80 cm apart; **Ri.** 6, high; **Sp.** 3–4 from the lower part of the Ar., acicular, directed downwards, 5–20 mm lg.; **Fl.** 13 cm lg.; **Tu.** 4 cm lg.; **Pet.** spatulate, white; **Fr.** 9 cm lg., dark bluish-purple.—Bolivia (Vallegrande, near Comarapa). Probably not in cultivation.

C. crassisepalus Buin. & Bred.
Bo. tree-like, branching, to 2 m h., dark green, with segmented branches; c. 6 cm ∅ **Ri.** 4–5(–6), obtuse, thickened around the Ar.; **Ar.** ± round, 8–12 mm ∅, with dense reddish-brown wool and bristly H., later greying and then becoming glabrous; **Sp.** spreading in all directions, glossy reddish-brown when new, becoming grey, with black tips, to 2.5 cm lg.; **Csp.** 1–2, upwardly directed, to 3 cm lg.; **Fl.** 7.5 cm lg., white, greenish-violet outside; **style** with 6 long Sti., each with a distinct dorsal stripe; **Fr.** pear-shaped, chrome-green with a violet sheen, pulp white; **S.** cap-shaped, ochre-coloured, testa matt black.—Brazil (Minas Geraes, near Diamantina, 500–1000 m).

C. dayamii Speg.
Bo. to 25 m h., with a **trunk**; **shoots** pale green; **Ri.** 5–6, 3 cm h.; **Sp.** missing or few, 4–12 mm lg., brown, yellowish at the base; **Fl.** to 25 cm lg., white; **Fr.** red, 6–8 cm lg., pulp white(!).—Argentina (Chaco, Colonia Resistencia).

C. fernambucensis Lem.: more usually given as **C. pernambucensis** Lem. (description under the latter).

C. forbesii O.
Bo. to 7 m h.; **shoots** light bluish-green, to 12 cm ∅, becoming greyish-green; **Ri.** 4–7, becoming flatter; **Ar.** with short white felt; **Rsp.** 5, to 2 cm lg., stoutly subulate, thickened at the base, light horn-coloured with a brown base, or black; **Csp.** 1, stouter, to 4.5 cm lg., darker; **Fl.** 25 cm lg., white; **Fr.** plum-sized, with red pulp(!).—Argentina (Catamarca, Tucuman, Jujuy, Córdoba).

C. glaucus SD.
Bo. to 6 m h. or more, **trunk** 40 cm ∅; **shoots** at first 8–18 cm ∅, then 18–30 cm ∅, dull bluish-green to brilliant light blue at first, then greener; **Ri.** 7(6–8), 5–10 cm h.; **Ar.** light grey; **Sp.** at first 5–15, to 2 cm lg., **centrals** to 3 cm lg., **Sp.** eventually to 20; **Fl.** 28 cm lg.; **Sep.** light green; **Pet.** pure white; **Fr.** 11 cm lg., slightly glossy, dark carmine.—Origin not known.

C. grandicostatus Werd.
Bo. to 3.5 m h., at first azure-blue, eventually more yellowish-green; **Ri.** 5–6, to 9 cm h.; **Sp.** 13–19, pale yellowish to brownish; **Rsp.** 7–9, to 1 cm lg.; **Csp.** 2.5 cm lg.; **Fl.** to 26 cm lg., white; **Fr.** unknown.—Origin unknown. Rare in cultivation.

C. hankeanus Web.
Bo. ± tree-like, erect; **Ri.** 4–5, acute, with lines along the flanks, 3 cm h., notched; **Ar.** brown, with sparse felt; **Rsp.** (3–)4, subulate, stout, 8–12 mm lg. amber-coloured to brown; **Csp.** 1, porrect, straight, 16 mm lg., horn-coloured; **Fl.** to 12 cm lg., white, sometimes pink-tipped; **Fr.** cylindric, greenish-yellow with red pulp (Cardenas).—E. Bolivia.

C. hertrichianus Werd.
Bo. more broadly shrubby; **branches** at first greyish-blue, ± pruinose; **Ri.** 5–6, to 2 cm h.; **Rsp.** 4–5 and **Csp.** 1, all straw-coloured at first, becoming brownish, to over 3 cm lg.; **Fl.** to 11 cm lg., scented, white; **Fr.** only 3 cm lg., ± spherical, golden-yellow, eventually more reddish, with white pulp.—Origin not known. Probably rare in cultivation.

C. hexagonus (L.) Mill. (T.)
Bo. tree-like, fairly freely branching; **branches**
rather light green or bluish, suberect; **Ri.** 4 (eventually to 6–7), thin, to 5 cm h.; **Ar.** small; **Sp.** at first missing or small, then up to 8–10, short, to 6 cm lg., all brown at first; **Fl.** to 25 cm lg., white; **Fr.** ± obliquely ovoid, 6–13 cm lg., light red, ± pruinose, pulp white to soft pink.—Surinam to N. Venezuela, and Tobago.

C. hildmannianus K. Sch.
Bo. tree-like, to 5 m h. (and more ?), often freely branching; **branches** finally to 15 cm ∅, blue-pruinose at first, eventually greyish-green; **Ri.** 6, thin, to 6 cm h., crenate, with furrowed flanks; **Ar.** brownish; **Sp.** missing or only 1, but Sp. longer on older growth; **Fl.** over 20 cm lg., white; **Sti.** 12, spreading; **Fr.** ?.—Brazil (Rio de Janeiro).

C. horridus O. & Dietr.
Bo. tree-like, trunk up to 30 cm ∅; **branches** suberect, not pruinose, green; **Ri.** 6 at first, eventually 7–9, with decurrent depressions; **Rsp.** mostly 5; **Csp.** mostly 3, the lowest one dark brown, upper ones yellowish, dark-tipped, old growth with up to 20 centrals, 10 cm lg., yellowish; **Fl.** c. 21 cm lg.; **Pet.** white, with a hairlike tip; **Fr.** spherical to ovoid, brilliant carmine to crimson, pulp white.—Origin unknown.

v. **alatosquamatus** Werd.: **Bo.** lower-growing; **branches** curving more downwards, more pruinose; with cordate Sc. on the **Tu.** and at the point of transition to the Sep.; **Fr.** with deep longitudinal furrows.—Origin?

C. huilunchu Card.
Bo. tree-like, to 4 m h., **trunk** 80 cm lg.; **branches** greyish-green, 6–7 cm ∅; **Ri.** 5, to 3 cm h.; **Ar.** ash-grey; **Sp.** 4–6, grey, to 3 cm lg., centrals not clearly differentiated; **Fl.** 13 cm lg.; **Sep.** dark green; **Pet.** white; **Fr.** cylindric(!), to 7 cm lg., red, pulp white.—Bolivia (Ayopaya, near Bajios de Yagani).

C. huntingtonianus Wgt. (SG. Neocereus Backbg. because of the fruits which, in this one species, are indehiscent.)
Bo. to 3 m h., 4 m br., bushy, branching from the base; **branches** at first bluish-grey and 10 cm ∅, becoming greyish-green, to 25 cm ∅, constricted at intervals of c. 16 cm; **Ri.** (6–)7(–8), 3 cm h., slightly notched; **Rsp.** 1–4, 3–15 mm lg., grey and black, eventually 3–4, to 15 mm lg.; **Csp.** 0–1, 4–10 cm lg., spotted yellowish or reddish-brown; **Fl.** 18 cm lg., pink, bordered white; **Fr.** 7 cm lg., 4.5 cm ∅, red inside and out, the skin becoming leathery, not splitting.—Origin unknown.

C. insularis Hemsl.
Bo. bushy, low, densely branching; **branches** to only 3 cm ∅; **Ri.** to 8; **Sp.** c. 15, unequal, acicular,

centrals scarcely distinguishable, all Sp. yellowish; **Fl.** 12.5 cm lg., yellowish-white; **Fr.** oblong.— Fernando do Noronha. Rare in cultivation (Fig. 55.)

C. jamacaru DC. non SD.
Bo. tree-like, **trunk** to 35 cm ∅ and more; **crown** very large; **branches** light sap-green, mostly not pruinose; **Ri.** 7–8, later to 10, at first 3.5 cm h., eventually higher; **Ar.** yellowish to brownish; **Sp.** often 15–20 at first, 7–9 of these **Rsp.**, the others **centrals**, all yellowish to brownish at first, eventually to 10 cm lg., much stouter; **Fl.** 25 cm lg.; **Sep.** light green; **Pet.** pure white; **Fr.** ovoid to pear-shaped, carmine to coral-red, not pruinose, with white pulp.—Brazil.

C. jugatiflorus Werd.
Bo. with a short trunk, to 3 m h.; **Ri.** to 8, to 4 cm h.; **Rsp.** to 2.5 cm lg.; **Csp.** to 5 cm lg.; **Ar.** brown at first; **Fl.** 16–22 cm lg., whitish; **Fr.** golden-yellow, 7 cm lg., 5 cm ∅, with tiny **Sc.** above; **S.** matt black.—Origin unknown. Rare in cultivation.

C. lamprospermus K. Sch.
Bo. tree-like, to 8 m h., with a **trunk** to 40 cm ∅; **branches** to 50 cm lg., 15 cm ∅; **Ri.** 6–8, 5 cm h.; **Sp.** 8–11, subulate, centrals scarcely differentiated, 1–4 cm lg.; **Fl.** to 16 cm lg., white with a red line; **Fr.** to 6 cm lg., 3.5 cm ∅ (colour ?): **S.** glossy black.— Paraguay (on the Rio Paraguay, Fuerte Olympo and near the Estancia Tagatiya).

C. lindbergianus Web.: see under Mediocactus.

C. llanosii n.nud. was at first my undescribed name for a Cereus spec. from the llanos of N. Colombia; it was later also used by others. I saw a specimen in the Marnier collection under this name: its Fr. was 10 cm lg., 6–7 cm ∅, pink to orange.

C. milesimus Rost
Bo. with erect **branches**; **Ri.** more deeply transversely divided and at times ± monstrose, (9–)10(–12), to 1.5 cm h.; **Fl.** c. 19 cm lg., white, or somewhat reddish at the tip; **Fr.** 7 cm lg., ovoid, orange to pinkish-red. The branches, from near the base and sometimes several meters h., are to 20 cm thick. Probably a hybrid of C. peruvianus f. monstrosus DC.

C. neotetragonus Backbg.
Another of the rare pink-flowering species: **Bo.** to 2 m h., with a dense crown, green; **Ri.** 4(–5), compressed; **Ar.** white; **Sp.** brown to almost black, slender-subulate; **Rsp.** 5–6, to 8 mm lg.; **Csp.** 1 or more, stouter; **Fl.** 13 cm lg.—Brazil.

C. obtusus Haw.: An insufficiently known spec. from E. Brazil; erect or inclined, dark green, with 3–5 **Ri.**, yellowish **Sp.**, 4–7 radials, 1 central, to 5 cm lg.; **Fl.** large, white.

C. pachyrhizus K. Sch.: probably not in cultivation; it grows to 3 m h. and has tuberously swollen **R.**; **branches** to 10 cm ∅, yellowish-green; **Ri.** 6; **Sp.** (10–)13, one of them to 3 cm lg.; **Fl.** ?; **Fr.** ellipsoid, 5 cm lg.—Paraguay (Cerro Noaga).

C. parviflorus K. Sch.: **Cleistocactus parviflorus** (K. Sch.) Goss.

C. parvisetus O.: see under Brasilicereus Backbg.

C. perlucens K. Sch. has probably disappeared from our collections. Only moderately h., with **branches** only 2 cm ∅, oily green, with a bluish-violet sheen; **Ri.** 5–6; **Rsp.** 8–10; **Csp.** 1–2, all brown at first (sometimes white), eventually blackish; **Fl.** and **Fr.** unknown.—Brazil (Manaos). May not be referable to this G.

C. pernambucensis Lem. (see C. fernambucensis)
Bo. low-growing, bushy; **Fl.** 12–16 cm lg. [in C. variabilis Pfeiff. the Fl. are 20 cm lg. or more]; one of a number of rather similar spec. of the E. coast of Brazil which are low-growing and branching from the base; **Sp.** 4–11, ± yellowish; **Ri.** only (3–)4(–5) [whereas C. variabilis Pfeiff. non Eng. has 7(–8) Ri., up to 8 yellowish Sp. to 5.5 cm lg., and Fl. more than 20 cm lg., both a lighter green].—Brazil to Uruguay.

C. peruvianus (L.) Mill.
Bo. branching from the base to form bushes, to more than 3 m h. and 5 m br.; **branches** of 2 types: erect and closer together, or laxer and more spreading, light green at first, bluish-green in the 2nd year, finally greyish-green, to 10–20 cm ∅; **Ri.** flat, mostly 7 (6–8), to 2.5 cm h. but eventually to 5 cm; **Ar.** brown at first; **Sp.** c. 5–6, 1 of these usually a central, to 2 cm lg., light to reddish-brown; **Fl.** 16 cm lg., fully expanding, white; **Fr.** spherical, 6.5 cm lg., light yellow to orange.—Origin remains unknown.
  v. **ovicarpus** Hertr. has **Fl.** more bellshaped or funnelform; **Fr.** ovoid, pale yellow, greenish above;
  v. **persicinus** Werd. has **Fl.** to 20 cm lg., **Pet.** peach-coloured above;
  v. **proferrens** Werd. is distinguished by having the **epidermis** grey and scaberulous;
  v. **reclinatus** Werd. has strongly recurved **Pet.**;
  v. **tortuosus** SD. is a form with noticeably spiralled **Ri.**;
  v. **monstrosus** DC. is now applied to a form with

the **Ri.** more strongly monstrose and broken than in C. milesimus; **Fl.** 15 cm lg., **Fr.** $\pm$ pruinose and tuberculate, the old **epidermis** $\pm$ scaberulous.

C. pseudocaesius Werd.
Bo. several m h., not producing a trunk, branching freely from the base; **branches** at first to 6–11 cm $\emptyset$, later more strongly segmented, light blue at first, pruinose; **Ar.** yellowish-white; **Ri.** 7 (6–8), to 2.5 cm h.; **Sp.** c. 14, fine, often $\pm$ bristly, yellowish to golden brown, 2 **Csp.** somewhat stouter, to 1.5 cm lg.; **Fl.** 26–27 cm lg., pure white; **Fr.** 9 cm lg., olive to brownish or reddish-brownish, without any bloom, pulp white.—Origin unknown.

C. pseudothelegonus Rauh & Backbg.: **Borzicactus pseudothelegonus** (Rauh & Backbg.) Rauh & Backbg.

C. ridleii Dard. de A. Lima
A recently described and previously unknown tree-like Cereus spec. from Fernando Noronha; **branches** somewhat obliquely ascending; **Ri.** 4–5, **Sp.** inconspicuous; **Fl.** ?

C. roseiflorus Speg.
Bo. to 5 m h.; **Ri.** 6; **Sp.** mostly 3, to 1 cm lg.; **Fl.** 20 cm lg., delicate pink; **Fr.** ovoid, violet-red.—Argentina (Misiones, near Fracrán). Probably not found in cultivation.

C. seidelii Lehm., otherwise somewhat similar to C. azureus Lehm., is distinguished by the **Fl.** which are to 30 cm lg., and the **Sp.** which are pitch-black above.—Origin?

C. smithii Pfeiff. (Heliaporus) is a cross between Aporocactus and Heliocereus speciosus, with stouter, 6-angled **St.**, which grows vigorously and has a fine red **Fl.**.

C. stenogonus K. Sch.
Bo. to 8 m h., bluish to yellowish-green; **Ri.** 4–5, thin, prominent; **Sp.** 2–3, conical, to 7 mm lg.; **Fl.** 20–22 cm lg., $\pm$ pink; **Fr.** 10 cm lg., dark red, pulp carmine.—E. Bolivia to Paraguay (Ipacary) and N. Argentina. Probably not found in cultivation.

C. tacuaralensis Card.—"Cactus", 19: 80–81, 19. 1964.
Bo. columnar, branching, to 5 m h.; **St.** to c. 12 cm $\emptyset$; **Ri.** 4, acute, 4–5 cm h., 1.8 cm br.; **Ar.** c. 3.5 cm apart, grey, 1 cm $\emptyset$; **Rsp.** 4, 1.5–3.5 cm lg.; **Csp.** 2, 3–6 cm lg., directed downwards; **Sp.** all subulate, pale brown; **Fl.** numerous on the upper St., to 22 cm lg.; **Sep.** greenish-red, brown above; **Pet.** spatulate, to 10 cm lg., whitish below, reddish

above; **Tu.** 9 cm lg.; **Ov.** ellipsoid, 3 cm lg.; **Fil.** pale green; **An.** brown; **style** 17 cm lg., it and the 14 **Sti.** pale green; **Fr.** ovoid, 8 × 5 cm, dark purple, pulp white; **S.** black.—Bolivia (Prov. Chiquitos, Dept. Santa Cruz, near Tacuaral, 200 m). Probably the Bolivian form or var. of C. stenogonus, with somewhat more numerous Sp. and white pulp (there are other plants in which the pulp-colour is known to vary!)

C. torulosus Werd., also probably not in cultivation; branching from the base; **St.** to 70 cm lg., deep to greyish-green, to 18 cm $\emptyset$; **Ar.** brown; **Ri.** 6; **Rsp.** 5–7, to 2.5 cm lg.; **Csp.** 3(–5), to 3 cm lg.; **Fl.** 23 cm lg., pure white; **Fr.** ovoid, $\pm$ carmine, $\pm$ pruinose, pulp white.—Origin unknown. Among the plants described by Werdermann, which were in the Huntington Garden and whose origin was unknown; some may have resulted from hybridisation.

C. trigonodendron K. Sch.: "To 15 m h., simple or little branching; **Ri.** 3; **Rsp.** 6; **Csp.** 1, c. 6 mm lg.; **Fl.** red, c. 10 cm lg.—NE. Peru (Loreto)." In this plant the **Ri.** have regularly sunken flanks, and the large dark **Ar.** at first produce longer, laxly floccose H. Acc. to its known characters, the spec. may well not be referable to Cereus Mill. The surprising thing is that none of the many collectors have found this spec. again or re-collected it.

C. validus Haw.
Bo. bushy, to 2 m h. or more; **St.** 5–8, bluish-green at first; **Ri.** 4–8, compressed; **Rsp.** 5, to 2 cm lg.; **Csp.** 1 (–2–3), some eventually to 16 cm lg., all horn-coloured; **Fl.** white to reddish; **Fr.** red, pulp red(!)—E. Bolivia to Argentina.

C. vargasianus Card.
Bo. tree-like, with a short **trunk**, to 8 m h.; **branches** $\pm$ suberect, bluish-green, constricted at intervals of c. 50 cm; **Ri.** 4–5, compressed, 5 cm h., somewhat sinuate; **Ar.** grey; **Sp.** c. 9–10, scarcely differentiated; 3–4 centrals sometimes discernible, to 7–15 mm lg., brownish, darker and thickened at the base; **Fl.** only 8–10 cm lg., white; **Sep.** pink; **Fil.** green; **Fr.** to 8 cm lg., ellipsoid, yellow, pulp white.—Peru (Cuzco).

C. variabilis Pfeiff. (only in Brazil): see under C. pernambucensis Lem.

C. xanthocarpus K. Sch.
Bo. to 7 m h., branching freely from the base, bluish light green, not pruinose; **branches** suberect, to 11 cm $\emptyset$; **Ri.** 5, c. 2 cm h. at first, eventually to 6 cm h., somewhat notched; **Ar.** more distant as the plant ages; **Sp.** short at first; **Rsp.** 3–5

and **Csp.** 1, all at first yellowish-brownish, becoming blackish-brown throughout or only below, to c. 2 cm lg.; **Fl.** 17–20 cm lg., pure white; **Fr.** subspherical, c. 9 cm lg., coppery-brownish before dehiscence, then orange to yellowish-red (to carmine ?), pulp white.—Paraguay (Calle Manora).

Chamaecereus Br. & R. (96)

Fairly soft-stemmed, dwarf-cereoid plants which offset freely, the stems readily detached; flowers red, fruits small, spherical, ± dry, seeds matt black. It is unfortunate that the stems drop so easily, and that the plant is susceptible to attack by red-spider mite. Crossing, particularly with Lobivia famatimensis, has produced cultivars with firmer and rather robuster stems and a very wide range of flower-colour.—Distribution: N. Argentina (on the mountains of Tucuman and Salta). [(G). (R), fairly hardy.]

Chamaecereus silvestrii (Speg.) Br. & R. (T.)
Bo. forming small groups to c. 6 cm h., light green; **Ri.** 6–9, slender, low; **Sp.** very short, white, weak; **Fl.** scarlet to mid-red, c. 4 cm lg., with black and white H., ± with some Br.—Argentina (see above).
   f. **crassicaulis** crist. Backbg.: **St.** stouter, less readily detached, with fasciated St.-tips. (Fig. 56.)

Chamaelobivia Y. Ito: Plants under this name in Japan are probably hybrids similar to the crosses mentioned under Chamaecereus.

Chiapasia Br. & R. (39)

Epiphytes with flat, notched stems and small slender, terete, stalk-like trunks. Flowers funnel-form to open bellshaped and thus distinguished from Disocactus, where all 3 species have a much narrower flower which is never bellshaped; in Chiapasia the petals are also more closed. Flowers last for several days. Fruit small, ± broadly spherical, smooth.—Distribution: Mexico (Chiapas). [(R).] Referred by Kimnach to Disocactus, despite the differences of floral structure (see under Disocactus).

C. nelsonii (Br. & R.) Br. & R. (T.)
Bo. freely branching, main St. more so in the upper part; **St.** to 1.6 m lg., 3–4 cm br., slightly notched; **Sp.** absent; **Fl.** c. 5 cm lg., bellshaped, lilac-pink; **Ov.** with minute Sc.; **style** and **An.** projecting; **Sti.** rather lg.; **Fr.** small, broadly spherical, with persistent Fl.-remains; **S.** glossy to matt, brownish-black.—Mexico (Chiapas, near Chicharras). (Fig. 57.)
   v. **hondurensis** (Kimn.) Backbg. n. comb. (Disocactus nelsonii v. hondurensis Kimn., C. & S. J. (US), XXXVII: 2, 33. 1965).
Bo. with main St. only to 50 cm lg., branching more from near the base; **St.** 5–6 cm br.; **Sep.** yellowish-purple (greenish-yellow in v. nelsonii); **Pet.** to 2.4 cm br. (to 2 cm br. in v. nelsonii); **Sti.** and **An.** purple (yellow in v. nelsonii).—Honduras (Comayagua, E. of Siguatepeque, 4 miles SW. of El Rincon).

Chilenia Backbg.: a name at first given to a complex within Neoporteria Br. & R. (1935, 1938), and then to **Neochilenia** Backbg. (1939); not valid.

Chileorebutia Ritt.: **Neochilenia** Backbg. Ritter based his genus on the following characters: "Dwarf habit with thick taproot; tubercles replacing ribs; flowers more strongly furnished with hairs and bristles". In this case none of these characters is diagnostically valid at generic level, since they are all found equally in other Chilean genera: Copiapoa, Neochilenia, Neoporteria, Pyrrhocactus sensu Ritt. in Chile. His genus must therefore be referred to Neochilenia (see also under Neochilenia).

Chileorebutia odieri sensu Ritt.: **Neochilenia imitans** Backbg.

Chilita Orc. or Orc. emend. F. Buxb.: **Mammillaria** Haw.—Species with black seeds.

Chrysocactus Y. Ito: **Eriocactus** Backbg.

Cleistocactus Lem. (75)

Slender-stemmed shrubs, mostly of moderate height, branching from the base or the sides. Spines predominantly fine, in part ± hairlike, interspersed with rather firmer spines. Some species also have longer and stouter spines. More rarely the plants form more freely branching shrubs resembling small trees (C. morawetzianus); sometimes they are ± prostrate (C. smaragdiflorus). Most species grow well, some quite quickly producing longer stems (C. buchtienii); in general they are not at all difficult. Since a whole series of previously unknown species have been found recently, offering great variety of habit, the species of this genus should be of especial interest to the professional grower. Additional interest is provided by the range of flower-colours: white, yellow, red, red with green, orange with red, etc., while others are very free-flowering when mature (C. strausii, C.

94

jujuyensis), so that the genus deserves much more attention than it has hitherto received. The slightly hairy flowers are predominantly ± cylindric with a narrow opening, sometimes ± zygomorphic, with the tube ± bent at the ovary, or forming an angle, or straight. Fruits densely and finely scaly, not large; seeds mostly numerous.—Distribution: from Central Peru through E. Bolivia to N. Argentina, Paraguay and Uruguay. [(R).]

C. albisetus (FR 820): Origin: ? Bolivia.

C. angosturensis Card.
Bo. medium-tall, erect, quite freely branching, to 2 m h.; **St.** to 3.5 cm ∅; **Ri.** c. 15; **Rsp.** 10–13, 3–15 mm lg.; **Csp.** 2–4, 1.5–4 cm lg.; **Sp.** all acicular, yellow; **Fl.** c. 7 cm lg., green; **Fr.** 2 cm ∅, dark red; **S.** dark brown or black, small, glossy.—Bolivia (Cochabamba, Angostura, 2550 m).

C. anguinus (Gürke) Br. & R.
Bo. soon arching over, inclined or creeping; **St.** to 2 cm ∅; **Ri.** 10–11, indistinct; **Rsp.** to 22, **Csp.** to 2, all ± brownish, centrals more yellowish; **Fl.** 7.5 cm lg., S-shaped, orange-red.—Paraguay.

C. apurimacensis Johns. n. nud.
Bo. erect, at first (always ?) branching from the base; **St.** 3.5 cm ∅; **Ar.** c. 10–12 mm apart, soon white, surmounted by a broad S-shaped furrow; **Sp.** amber-coloured; **Rsp.** c. 10, acicular, to 10 mm lg.; **Csp.** to 4, rather stouter, to 2 cm lg., dark and slightly thickened at the base; **Fl.** ?—Peru (vicinity of the Rio Apurimac). Without doubt close to C. morawetzianus.

C. areolatus (Muehlpfrdt.) Ricc.: This species, described without any floral data, was recognised correctly by Ritter as an uncertain spec.; it may have been a Peruvian Loxanthocereus. Since Riccobono, the name has been applied to C. parviflorus.

C. ayopayanus Card.
Bo. 1–1.5 m h.; **St.** to 3.5 cm ∅, pale green; **Ri.** to 15, 4 mm h., transversely furrowed; **Sp.** 13–16, thin, yellow, 1.2–4 cm lg.; **Fl.** 4 cm lg., dark green above; **Fr.** 1 cm ∅, pale green.—Bolivia (Prov. Ayopaya, Morochata-Independencia, 2300 m).

C. azerensis Card.—C. & S. J. (US), XXXIII: 3, 74–75. 1961.
Bo. erect, branching from the base; **St.** greyish-green, to 4 cm ∅; **Ri.** c. 23; **Ar.** brownish; **Sp.** 16–24, scarcely differentiated, to 5 mm lg., white to pale yellow; **Fl.** numerous, to 5 cm lg., 7 mm ∅; **Tu.** slightly curving, bluish-red; **Sep.** pale violet-pink below, greenish above; **Pet.** violet-pink; **Fr.**

spherical, 8 mm ∅; **S.** 1 mm lg., glossy black.—Bolivia (Dept. Chuquisaca, Puente Pacheco, 1100 m). (Fig. 58, left.)

C. baumannii (Lem.) Lem. (T.)
Bo. at first erect, then hanging over; **St.** more than 2.5 cm ∅, deep green; **Ri.** to 16; **Rsp.** 15–20, to 1.5 cm lg.; **Csp.** 1, to 2.5 cm lg., yellowish to dark brown, with a lighter tip; **Fl.** to 7 cm lg., more weakly bent, flame-coloured, lighter inside; **Fr.** to 1.5 cm ∅, red, pulp white.—NE. Argentina, Paraguay, Uruguay.
    v. **flavispinus** (SD.) Ricc.: differs in having golden-yellow **Sp.**
Ritter distinguished also the following Sp.-colours: FR 19b: red; FR 19c: white; FR 19d: black. However the colours are not always constant, and may sometimes vary, even on one and the same plant, e.g. red to white.

C. brookei Card.
Bo. to 50 cm h.; **St.** to 4.5 cm ∅, light green; **Ri.** c. 24, to 3 mm h., with transverse furrows; **Ar.** grey above, brown below; **Sp.** to c. 30, 4–10 mm lg., bristly, yellowish, brownish in the crown; **Fl.** S-shaped, 5 cm lg., dark red; **Ov.** not sharply bent; **Fr.** 1 cm ∅, purple; **S.** dark brown.—Bolivia (Santa Cruz, near Pozo No. 4, Camiri). (Fig. 58, right.)

C. bruneispinus Backbg. resembles C. baumannii, but is more robust; **Sp.** dark reddish-brown; **Fl.** stouter, more S-shaped and curving. Origin unknown.

C. buchtienii Backbg.
Bo. forming a tall shrub, fast-growing; **St.** to 5 cm ∅; **Ri.** c. 18, low, with V-notches; **Ar.** brown; **Sp.** c. 12, acicular, all reddish-brown, including c. 4 scarcely differentiated **Csp.** to 3 cm lg.; **Fl.** 6 cm lg., scarcely opening, wine-red.—Bolivia (Arque-Cochabamba).
    v. (?) **flavispinus** Card. has straw-coloured **Sp.** and only 1 rather longer Csp.; **Ov.** purplish-pink; **Sep.** green.—Bolivia (Prov. Tarata, La Angostura, 2570 m).

C. candelilla Card.
Bo. prostrate to erect, 1 m h.; **St.** 3 cm ∅; **Ri.** 11–12, 3 mm h., transversely furrowed; **Rsp.** 13–15, 5 mm lg.; **Csp.** 3–4, slightly flattened; **Fl.** 3.5 cm lg.; **Sep.** projecting, yellow, brown-tipped; **Pet.** forming a tube, purple with a white border; **Fr.** 1 cm ∅, salmon-red.—Bolivia (Prov. Florida, Pampa Grande, 1400 m).

C. chacoanus Ritt. n.nud. (FR 841)
From the C. baumannii complex: **Ri.** c. 8; **Ar.**

small, brown; **Sp.** brown to black, light-tipped; **Rsp.** c. 12–15, to 3–4 mm lg.; **Csp.** 1(–2), to almost 3 cm lg.; **Fl.** strongly zygomorphic.—Bolivia (Chaco).

C. chotaensis Web.: spec. as yet unclarified, possibly not referable to this genus: **Bo.** to 2 m h.; **Fl.** 5 cm lg., orange, limb 2.5 cm br.; **Ov.** with black hairs.—Peru (Rio Chota). See under Seticereus Backbg.

C. clavicaulis Card.—"Cactus", 19: 80–81, 20. 1964.
Bo. columnar, thickened above, to 60 cm h., 40 cm $\varnothing$; **Ri.** c. 10, rather distant, 5 mm h., 1.2 cm br.; **Ar.** to 8 mm apart, grey, circular; **Rsp.** 5–7, radiating, 5–17 mm lg.; **Csp.** 1, 2.5–3 cm lg., directed downwards; **Sp.** all pale grey, brown-tipped, stoutly acicular; **Fl.** cyclindric, 3.5 cm lg., 8 mm br.; **Sep.** pink below, green above; **Pet.** dark purple below, greenish above; **Tu.** 2 cm lg., red; **Ov.** pale green, spherical, 6 mm lg.; **Fil.** white; **An.** pale purple to yellowish; **style** 3 cm lg., white; **Sti.** 8, green; **Fr.** spherical to oblong, 1–2 cm lg., lilac-purple, Sc. whitish, with sparse white H.—Bolivia (Prov. Gran Chaco, Dept. Tarija, near Angosto de Villa Montes, 460 m).

C. compactus Backbg.
Bo. branching densely from the base, to c. 40 cm h.; **St.** to 3 cm $\varnothing$; **Ri.** 12–14; **Rsp.** to 20; **Csp.** 0–1, light yellowish-brown, darker in the crown; **Fl.** straight, carmine below, light brownish above; **Pet.** reddish in the middle, projecting.—Origin unknown.

C. crassicaulis Card.—C. & S. J. (US), XXXIII: 3, 77–78. 1961.
Bo. slender-columnar, to 60 cm h.; **St.** pale green, to 7 cm $\varnothing$; **Ri.** c. 14; **Ar.** dark grey; **Rsp.** 8–10, radiating, to 5 mm lg.; **Csp.** 1–3, directed downwards, 7–20 mm lg.; **Sp.** all grey, thickened at the base; **Fl.** to 3.5 cm lg., 9 mm $\varnothing$; **Sep.** emerald-green; **Pet.** greenish above, whitish below; **Fr.** spherical, to 1.3 cm lg., reddish; **S.** dark brownish.—Bolivia (Entre Rios, Angosto de Villa Montes).

C. dependens Card.: **Seticleistocactus dependens** (Card.) Backbg. (Fig. 59, left.)

C. flavescens hort. Hge Jr.: **Cleistocactus wendlandiorum** Backbg.

C. flavispinus (K.Sch. non SD.) Backbg.
Bo. erect, light green; **St.** to 3·cm $\varnothing$; **Ri.** to 16; **Ar.** brown above, grey below; **Rsp.** to c. 18, in the lower half of the Ar., thin; **Csp.** c. 3, the longest one to 2

cm lg. or somewhat more; **Sp.** pale yellow; **Fl.** gently curving; **Sep.** orange; **Pet.** in part golden-yellow, to scarlet, ageing to blood-red.—Paraguay?

C. fusiflorus Card.
Bo. erect, branching from the base; **St.** to 2.4 cm $\varnothing$, fresh green; **Ri.** 13–14, 4 mm h.; **Ar.** grey; **Rsp.** 8–9, 3–5 mm lg., some of them 7 mm lg.; **Csp.** 1, 1–2 cm lg.; **Sp.** all thin, light grey, brown-tipped; **Fl.** straight, 3.5 cm lg.; **Tu.** light yellow; **Sep.** pink below, greenish-brownish above; **Pet.** magenta, with a transparent border; **Fr.** 1.5 cm $\varnothing$, yellow.—Bolivia (Valle Grande, Saipina, 1900 m).

C. glaucus Ritt.—"Taxon", XIII: 3, 114. 1964.
Bo. to 2 m lg., branching from the base, greyish-green; **St.** to 4 cm $\varnothing$; **Ri.** (12–)13–17(–18), obtuse, notched, to 5 mm h.; **Ar.** 4–6 mm apart, white or brownish; **Sp.** chestnut-brown; **Rsp.** 7–9, 4–7 mm lg., acicular, the lowest ones longest, none in the upper part of the Ar.; **Csp.** 1–3, straight, stiffer, sometimes only little longer, but 1(–2) much stouter, to 5 cm lg.; **Fl.** straight-limbed, to 4.2 cm lg.; **Pet.** crimson or orange, tipped greenish to greenish-brown; **Tu.** carmine, curving slightly downwards; **Fil.** in 2 series, white; **style** white; **Sti.** greenish; **Fr.** to 1.5 cm lg., reddish; **S.** 1.25 mm lg.—Bolivia (Dept. La Paz, Prov. Murillo, Tirata) (FR 112).
v. **plurispinus** Ritt.—l.c.:
Bo. somewhat taller; **Ri.** 15–20; **Sp.** somewhat thinner; **Rsp.** 10–15; **Csp.** all long; **Pet.** shorter, rounded or acuminate.—Bolivia (Dept. La Paz, border between Prov. Murillo and Loayza) (FR 112a).

C. grossei (Wgt.) Backbg.
Bo. erect, inclined; **St.** c. 2.5 cm $\varnothing$ or somewhat more; **Ri.** to 17, with a slight V-furrow; **Rsp.** c. 17–18, very thin, white; **Csp.** c. 4, 2 longer ones directed upwards and downwards, acicular, amber to light yellow; **Fl.** red, c. 5 cm lg., 1.6 cm $\varnothing$, **buds** white-woolly at first, from brown and white **Ar.**—Paraguay. One of the spec. with a more widely expanded Per.

C. hildegardia and v. **flavirufus** (FR 1126): **C. hildewinterae** v. **flavirufus** Ritt.: "only spec. with more widely opening Fl." (Ritt.); perhaps therefore identical with the preceding spec.?

C. hyalacanthus (K.Sch.) Goss.
A spec. which does not appear to have been re-collected since the description: **St.** thin, only 1.5 cm $\varnothing$; **Ri.** 20; **Sp.** bristly, fine, over 20, white; **Ar.** grey;

Fl. 3.5 cm lg., light red.—Argentina (Jujuy, Rosario de Lerma).

C. ianthinus Card.
Bo. erect, to 70 cm h.; **St.** pale green, to 3 cm ∅; **Ri.** c. 10, 4 mm h.; **Rsp.** 10–14, to 8 mm lg.; **Sp.** at first white or pale pink, becoming grey; **Fl.** 3 cm lg.; **Tu.** lilac-pink; **Sep.** bluish-pink, whitish above; **Pet.** darker; **Fr.** 1 cm ∅, dark bluish-pink.—Bolivia (Prov. Charcas, near Calahuta, 2000 m).

C. jugatiflorus Backbg.
Bo. to 55 cm lg.; **St.** mid-green, to 3 cm ∅; **Ri.** 11; **Ar.** ± greyish-brownish; **Rsp.** c. 12, 4–6 mm lg., thin, glassy; **Csp.** mostly 3–4, to 2.2 cm lg., light horn-coloured, reddish at the base, the longest one eventually to 4.2 cm lg.; **Fl.** 6 cm lg., ± straight, slender; **Pet.** yellowish-red below, passing over to deeper red at the tip.—Origin unknown.

C. jujuyensis (Backbg.) Backbg.
Bo. erect, over 1m h.; **St.** 4–6 cm ∅; **Ri.** c. 20, narrow, low; **Ar.** brownish at first; **Rsp.** c. 25–30; **Csp.** clearly distinguished from the fine Rsp. by both length and colour, ± brownish to yellowish, over 3 cm lg.; **Fl.** 4 cm lg.; **Tu.** light red; **Pet.** ± spreading, ± bluish-carmine; **Fr.** small.—Argentina (Jujuy).
Very vigorous-growing and free-flowering: the "false C. straussii".

C. laniceps (K.Sch.) Goss.
Bo. 4 m h.; **St.** to 5 cm ∅; **Ri.** 9, transversely notched; **Sp.** mostly only 3, grey, to 1.5 cm lg.; **Fl.** 3.5 cm lg.; **Sep.** and **Pet.** probably red; **Fr.** 1 cm ∅; **S.** glossy black.—Bolivia (Cordillera of Tunari, 1300 m).

C. luminosus Johns.
A new species, apparently not described, but interesting:
Bo. to rather more than 1 m h.; **St.** to c. 5 cm ∅, mid to dark green; **Ri.** c. 10–12, tuberculate at first, with a V-furrow; **Sp.** mostly all rather stiff, pungent; **Rsp.** to 13, 2–4 mm lg.; **Csp.** mostly 4, cruciform, 5–8 mm lg., brownish, or reddish-brown at the tip and the base, some of the Rsp. similarly, sometimes light at first; **Fl.** ?—Origin unknown.

C. luribayensis Card.
Bo. columnar to tree-like, 2–3 m h.; **St.** to 4 cm ∅, light green; **Ri.** 13–15, low, with a V-notch; **Ar.** light brown; **Sp.** 8–12, 1–3 of these ± distinguishable as centrals and to 3 cm lg., others to 1 cm lg., all of them thin, acicular, greenish-yellow to honey-coloured or yellowish-brown; **Fl.** to 4.3 cm lg., carmine, limb erect.—Bolivia.

C. mendozae Card.—C. & S. J. (US), XXXV: 6, 202. 1963.
Bo. to 2 m h.; **St.** 4.5 cm ∅, rounded above; **Ri.** c. 25, rather obtuse, 4 mm h., 5 mm br.; **Ar.** elliptical, 2 mm lg., 4 mm apart, ash-grey; **Sp.** yellow, radials and centrals not differentiated, 16–20, 3–12 mm lg.; **Fl.** numerous, tubular, curving near the base, 3.5 cm lg., 8 mm ∅; **Tu.** pale pink, 2 cm lg., with greenish-white Sc., and white as well as black H.; **Sep.** green; **Pet.** 3 mm lg., purple; **Fil.** pale purple; **An.** dark purple; **style** 2.5 cm lg., white below, pink above; **Sti.** 8, pale green; **Fr.** 1.5 cm ∅, pink, with transparent Sc. and white H.; **S.** 1 mm lg., dark brown.—Bolivia (Prov. Tomina, Dept. Chuquisaca, on the road Padilla–Tomina, 2200 m).

C. micropetalus Ritt. n.nud. (FR 830)
St. c. 3 cm ∅, green; **Ri.** 11; **Ar.** brown; **Sp.** more than 20, fine, interlacing, yellow; **Csp.** to over 5, yellow, thin, sometimes to 3 cm lg.—Origin ?

C. monvilleanus (Web.) Web.: an uncertain spec., possibly referable to Seticereus.

C. morawetzianus Backbg.
Bo. shrubby or resembling small trees, to 2 m h.; **St.** greyish-green; **Ri.** to c. 14, with a V-notch; **Sp.** to 14, ± thickened at the base, c. 3 centrals discernible, subulate, golden-yellow at first, soon becoming whitish-grey with tips straw-coloured or darker; **Fl.** c. 5.5 cm lg., ± straight, or ± bent above the Ov., then directed downwards; **Pet.** slightly spreading, white, with a greenish or faintly pink sheen.—Central Peru (Huancavo-Ayacucho).
v. **arboreus** Ak. [C. & S. J. (US), XX: 9, 129. 1948, Fig. 96, flower only] is obviously the form having stouter, bluish-green **St.**; **Rsp.** c. 10; **Csp.** c. 4, all ± equal, c. 5–6 mm lg., directed sideways or downwards, all yellow;
v. pycnacanthus Rauh & Backbg.: see C. pycnacanthus.

C. muyurinensis Ritt.—"Taxon", XIII: 3, 114. 1964.
Bo. branching from the base, to 1.5 m h.; **St.** 2–3 cm ∅; **Ri.** 10–13, notched, to 5 mm h.; **Ar.** to 4 mm apart, dark brown; **Rsp.** 3–5, white, hairlike, 3–5 mm lg., centrals somewhat stouter, upper ones resembling the centrals; **Csp.** 1–2, 2–4 cm lg., yellowish-brown; **Fl.** 3.5 cm lg., limb straight; **Tu.** straight, ± purple; **Ov.** brownish-red to brownish-carmine, it and the Tu. with white H.; **Pet.** violet-purple, bordered violet, rounded to ± acuminate above; **Fil.** white or pale pink, purple above; **style** and 7 **Sti.** reddish-brown; **Fr.** 1.5 cm ∅, brownish-red, weakly white-haired; **S.** 0.75 mm lg., dark.—Bolivia (Dept. Santa Cruz, Prov. Valle Grande, Muyurina) (FR 821).

C. orthogonus Card.
Bo. erect, to 80 cm h., pale green; **St.** 4–5 cm ⌀; **Ri.** 15–17, to 3 mm h.; **Ar.** grey; **Sp.** c. 10, centrals not distinguishable, 5–30 mm lg., yellow; **Fl.** 4.5–5 cm lg.; **Tu.** magenta to red; **Pet.** light magenta to pinkish-red; **Sep.** greenish-purple; **Fr.** 1.5 cm ⌀, with red Sc. and salmon-coloured H.—Bolivia (Dept. Potosi, Chaqui-Betanzos, 2800 m).

C. parapetiensis Card.
Bo. erect, to 60 cm h.; **St.** to 4 cm ⌀, fresh green; **Ri.** 19; **Ar.** greyish-brown; **Sp.** c. 20, 3–6 mm lg., the longer centrals to 10 mm lg., dissimilar, from hairlike to acicular, or somewhat stouter, white or brown; **Fl.** borne quite low on the St., 3–3.5 cm lg.; **Tu.** reddish; **Pet.** greenish-yellow, outer ones pink at the base; **Fr.** 1 cm ⌀, purple.—Bolivia (Prov. Cordillera, Rio Parapeti).

C. parviflorus (K.Sch.) Goss.
Bo. erect, to 3 m h.; **St.** to 4 cm ⌀, green; **Ri.** 12–15, with V-notches; **Sp.** dark yellow, but also greenish or honey-coloured to brownish; **Rsp.** 5–7(–9), to c. 4 mm lg.; **Csp.** 1(–3) to 2.5 cm lg., the others to 4 mm lg.; **Fl.** red, to 3–4 cm lg., straight; **Fr.** yellow, c. 1 cm ⌀.—Bolivia (Pairotani, 2400 m).
Ritter correctly established that C. areolatus Ricc. was identical with C. parviflorus, and that Cereus areolatus Muehlpfrdt. was a nomen dubium; possibly it was a Peruvian Loxanthocereus. But in his article in Kakt. u. a. Sukk., 6: 102–104. 1963, Ritter gave too little weight to the question of spination. Old and almost tree-like specimens in the Marnier collection constantly showed fairly crowded Csp. c. 1.5–2.5(!) cm lg. However other specimens have Csp. only half that length, all ± equal, similar to those of the red-spined plants of the following variety:
v. **aiquilensis** Ritt. l.c.: **Ri.** 14–19; **Sp.** yellow to reddish-brown (and also red!); **Fl.** to 4.5 cm lg., red.—Bolivia (Dept. Cochabamba, Prov. Campero, Aiquile to Chuquisaca, Yotala) (FR 539). I agree with Ritter that the stem of "C. herzogianus" I show in BfK. 1934–6 in fact belongs to C. parviflorus, but even as a fully mature St. it only shows centrals here and there, and overall has shorter and less regular Sp. than the type-species. Even large plants of that spec. have ± equal Sp., longer centrals being the exception, so that I retain for it the name:
v. **herzogianus** (Backbg.) Backbg.—Descr. Cact. Nov. III: 5, 1963, since the **Fr.** was pinkish-orange instead of yellow, and the **Sp.** dull yellowish to reddish, sometimes on one and the same plant. This is the only means of representing correctly the differences of spination. Old specimens of v. aiquilensis Ritt. in Marnier's

collection showed red Sp., without longer centrals, all Sp. being ± equal.
C. piraymirensis Card.: **Seticleistocactus piraymirensis** (Card.) Backbg.

C. pojoensis Card.
Bo. erect, to 3 m h.; **St.** 4–5 cm ⌀; **Ri.** 13–17, 3 mm h.; **Ar.** brown; **Rsp.** 8–12, to 8 mm lg.; **Csp.** 1, 2–3 cm lg.; **Sp.** grey, brown-tipped; **Fl.** tubular, 4 cm lg., yellowish-green below, orange at midway, wine-red above; **Fr.** 1.2 cm ⌀, dark wine-red.—Bolivia (Prov. Carrasco, Hacienda La Habana etc.).

C. pseudostrausii (FR 1145): no description available.

C. pungens Ritt.—"Taxon", XIII: 3, 115. 1964.
Bo. distinguished from that of C. morawetzianus by its offsetting from the base, to 1.5 m h.; **Ri.** c. 13, to 8 mm h.; **Ar.** to 7 mm apart; **Sp.** chestnut-brown, becoming grey, reddish-brown at the tips; **Rsp.** 8–12, to 1 cm lg.; **Csp.** 2–5, mostly somewhat stouter and longer, 1–2 of them still longer, 2–5 cm lg.; **Fl.** 7.5 cm lg., carmine; (**Fr.** ? and) **Ov.** greenish or brownish-red, with some white H.; **Pet.** faintly greenish at the tip, with a blood-red M.-line; **Fr.** 2 cm lg., pale red; **S.** 1.3 mm lg., dark.—Peru (Dept. Ayacucho and Apurimac, frontier-zone on the Rio Pampas) (FR 664). Identical with the following spec.?

C. pycnacanthus (Rauh & Backbg.) Backbg. n.comb. (Cleistocactus morawetzianus v. pycnacanthus Rauh & Backbg., Descr. Cact. Nov. I, 17. 1956).
Bo. erect, over 1.5 m h.; **St.** to 5 cm ⌀; **Ri.** at first 8–10, later more numerous, c. 6 mm br.; **Ar.** circular, c. 5 mm ⌀; **Rsp.** to c. 12, subulate or thinner, scarcely thickened at the base; **Csp.** scarcely recognizable, somewhat stouter, 4(–5), the longest upper one to 3.5 cm lg. or somewhat more; **Sp.** at first reddish-brownish or somewhat lighter; **Fl.** 8.5 cm lg., straight, deep carmine; **Tu.** with greenish Sc. and short brown H.; **Sep.** thin, greenish, narrow; **Pet.** deep purple; **Fil.** and **An.** purple; **style** white; **Sti.** pinkish-white.—Peru (dry region around Ayacucho, 2700 m). Close to C. morawetzianus, but better considered as a distinct spec. because of the spination and flower; the latter only recently became known.

C. reae Card.
Bo. erect, to 2 m h.; **St.** dark green, 3–4.5 cm ⌀; **Ri.** 19, 7 mm h.; **Ar.** grey; **Sp.** 16–20, yellowish, thin, 5–25 mm lg.; **Fl.** 5–7 cm lg., cylindric; **Sep.** purple with dark green tips; **Pet.** pink with white borders;

Fr. 2.5 cm ⌀, red; **S.** 1.5 mm lg., glossy dark brown.—Bolivia (Prov. Inquisivi, Quima, 3000 m). Ritter's No. FR 113.

C. ressinianus Card.

Bo. erect, to 2 m h., branching from the base; **St.** 4 cm ⌀; **Ri.** to c. 22, transversely furrowed, 4 mm h.; **Sp.** 8–15, to 1.5 cm lg., centrals sometimes more clearly distinguishable, to 3.5 cm lg., reddish-brown, spreading; **Fl.** 7–8 cm lg., limb zygomorphic, 1 cm ⌀; **Sep.** dark bluish-pink; **Pet.** 18 mm lg., bluish-pink; **Fr.** spherical, to 3 cm ⌀; **S.** glossy black.—Bolivia (Prov. Oropeza, Sucre-Tarabuco, 2700 m).

C. rojoi Card.

Bo. erect, 60 cm h.; **St.** dark green, to only 2.5 cm ⌀; **Ri.** 17, 4 mm h.; **Sp.** to 25, thin, 3–20 mm lg., whitish or brown; **Csp.** mostly not differentiated, sometimes 3–4, to 2 cm lg., pointing downwards; **Fl.** narrow, 6 cm lg.; **Sep.** dark red, yellow above; **Pet.** salmon-pink; **Fr.** ovoid, 18 mm lg., pink or pale purple; **S.** glossy dark brown.—Bolivia (Prov. Entrerios, Entrerios-Villamontes, 600 m).

C. santacruzensis Backbg. n.sp.

Bo. bluish-green; **St.** to c. 3 cm ⌀; **Ri.** 15–17; **Ar.** dark brown at first, becoming whitish-grey; **Sp.** pale yellow or pinkish-grey at first, becoming whitish-grey; **Rsp.** c. 10, 2–6 mm long; **Csp.** 1(–2–3), one to over 2 cm lg., any others directed upwards and downwards; **Fl.** c. 5 cm lg., red, curving and S-shaped, with distant dark red Sc., somewhat hairy, **limb** oblique, **style** projecting.—Bolivia (Santa Cruz) (FR 356); belongs to the C. baumannii complex but has different spination; **Fl.** shorter. (Fig. 60.)

C. smaragdiflorus (Web.) Br. & R.

Bo. erect to prostrate; **St.** to over 3.5 cm ⌀; **Ri.** 12–14, low; **Sp.** numerous, acicular; **Csp.** several, projecting, rigid, sharp, ± yellowish-brown; **Fl.** 5 cm lg., narrow; **Tu.** and **Ov.** red, **limb** green; **Fr.** 1.5 cm ⌀, spherical.—Paraguay, N. Argentina.

v. **gracilior** Backbg. n.v.: **Bo.** darker green and more slender than in the type; **Ar.** dark reddish-brown, 5 mm apart; **Sp.** reddish-brown, especially above, finer, all shorter. **Csp.** 1, longer, 1–2.5 cm lg.; **Fl.** similar.—Origin? (obtained from Hutchison).

C. strausii (Heese) Backbg.

Bo. erect, 1 m h., grafted plants to several meters h.; **St.** c. 4 (– c. 8) cm ⌀; **Ri.** 25, fresh green; **Ar.** white; **Rsp.** 30–40, to 17 mm lg., hairlike, white; **Csp.** c. 4, light yellow, to 2 cm lg.; **Fl.** 8–9 cm lg., straight, narrow, wine-red, with reddish-brown H.; **Fr.** ±

tapered-spherical, red, woolly; **S.** small, black.—Bolivia (Tarija, 1750 m).

v. **fricii** (Dörfl.) Backbg. has **H.** to 5 cm lg., and the **Fr.** is said to be green. **Fl.** as in the type.

C. sucrensis Card.: listed here as var. of C. tupizensis (Vpl.) Backbg.; also regarded as a valid species.

C. tarijensis Card.

Bo. erect, to 70 cm h.; **St.** to 5 cm ⌀; **Ri.** c. 20, 3 mm h.; **Sp.** c. 20, thin, hyaline to yellowish; **Csp.** sometimes 3–4 are distinguishable, to 2.5 cm lg.; **Fl.** tubular, 4 cm lg.; **Sep.** red, yellow-tipped; **Pet.** bluish-pink, white at the base; **Fr.** 1.5 cm ⌀, spherical, reddish to greenish-red; **S.** glossy, dark brown.—Bolivia (Prov. Cercado, near Tarija, 1900 m).

C. tominensis (Wgt.) Backbg.

Bo. erect, to 2 m h., not branching till much older; **St.** to 5 cm ⌀; **Ri.** 18–22, low, transversely notched; **Sp.** 8–9, at first thin, then stouter, yellowish at the apex, then grey; **Rsp.** scarcely over 1 cm lg., those ± distinguishable as centrals to 2 cm lg., projecting, sometimes reddish-brown or pink-tipped in seedlings; **Fl.** only 2.6 cm lg., narrow, green, yellowish to red, or green below and red above; **Fr.** c. 1.8 cm ⌀, spherical, pale pink, pulp white; **S.** c. 1 mm lg., glossy black.—Bolivia (E. of Sucre, Tomina valley, 1800–2000 m).

C. tupizensis (Vpl.) Backbg.

Bo. erect, branching from the base, c. 1.5 m h. (to 3 m in cultivation); **St.** to c. 6 cm ⌀; **Ri.** 14–24, low; **Sp.** c. 15–20, glassy, brittle, unequal, also 2 **Csp.**, one above the other, to c. 4.5 cm lg., whitish to brilliant reddish-brown, centrals later scarcely distinguishable, all Sp. rather crowded; **Fl.** only slightly curving, 8 cm lg., wine-red, limb ± oblique; **Pet.** red to whitish.—Bolivia (Tupiza).

v. **sucrensis** (Card.) Backbg.: **Sp.** to 6 cm lg., projecting, at first ± straw-coloured; **Fl.** 6.5–8 cm lg.; **Sep.** dark salmon-red; **Pet.** wine-red.—Bolivia (Prov. Oropeza, Sucre-Tarabuco).

C. vallegrandensis Card.—C. & S. J. (US), XXXIII: 3, 75–76, 1961.

Bo. columnar, branching, to 60 cm h.; **St.** dark green, to 2.5 cm ⌀; **Ri.** 12–13; **Ar.** dark brown or black; **Rsp.** 15–18, 5–20 mm lg.; **Csp.** 1, 2–3 cm lg.; **Sp.** crowded, all thin-acicular, ± yellowish; **Fl.** numerous, tubular, to 3.5 cm lg., dark (bluish-)red.— Bolivia (Vallegrande). (Fig. 59, right.)

C. variispinus Ritt.—"Taxon", XIII: 3, 114. 1964.

Bo. branching from about midway up the St.; **Ri.**

14–18, indistinctly notched; **Ar.** white, to 4 mm apart; **Sp.** 30–40, pale yellow, golden or brownish-yellow, the upper ones to 1 cm lg., 1–2 to 2–4 cm lg.; **Fl.** straight-limbed, to 4.8 cm lg., white; **Tu.** carmine or orange; **Ov.** reddish, it and the **Tu.** with some white H.; **Pet.** tipped pale greenish; **Fr.** to 2 cm lg., violet-red; **S.** 1.2 mm lg., glossy black.—Bolivia (Dept. La Paz, Prov. Lareca, Mine Cascabel, 2000 m) (FR 108).

C. villamontesii Card.—C. & S. J. (US), XXXIII: 3, 76–77. 1961.
Bo. erect, offsetting from the base, to c. 40 cm h.; **St.** to c. 3 cm ⌀, tapering at the tip; **Ri.** c. 15; **Ar.** brown; **Sp.** scarcely differentiated, 2–6 mm lg., c. 20, sometimes 1–3 Csp. more discernible, to 1 cm lg., pale brownish, the others whitish; **Fl.** numerous, zygomorphic, c. 5 cm lg.; **Tu.** dark purple, H. white; **Sep.** white below, greenish above; **Pet.** similarly coloured; **An.** deep purple, projecting; **Sti.** emerald-green; **Fr.** spherical, 1.2 cm lg.—Bolivia (Entre Rios, Angosto de Villamontes). Fl. somewhat variable.

v. **longiflorior** Backbg. n.v.:
Separable from the type by c. 14 **Sp.**, the radials light, centrals c.4, brownish, to 2 cm lg.; **Fl.** to c. 7 cm lg.; **Tu.** and **Ov.** with brownish H.; **Sti.** light green.
The **Tu.** is lighter purple towards the upper part, otherwise the colours are as in the type; the **An.** are also deep purple.

| C. villazuensis (FR 1296): no description available.

C. viridialabastri Card.—C. & S. J. (US). XXXV: 6, 201. 1963.
Bo. to 60 cm h.; **St.** to 4.5 cm ⌀, pale green; **Ri.** c. 19, 4 mm h., 5 mm br., furrowed; **Ar.** 6 mm apart, elliptical, 4 mm lg., brownish-grey; **Rsp.** 8–9, 2–10 mm lg.; **Csp.** 1, pointing downwards, 1.5 cm lg.; **Sp.** all acicular, yellow, becoming greyish-white; **buds** pale green, with white H.; **Fl.** 4 cm lg., tapering conically above, pale green below, pink at midway and green above; **Tu.** purplish-pink, with pale green Sc. and soft white H.; **Ov.** with pale green Sc. and short white H.; **Sep.** emerald-green; **Pet.** emerald-green; **Fil.** white; **An.** brown; **style** white below, greenish above; **Sti.** green; **Fr.** 2 cm ⌀, reddish, with pale yellowish-green Sc. and white H.; **S.** 1.2 mm lg., dark brown.—Bolivia (Gran Chaco, Dept. Tarija, on the road Villamontes–Palos Blancos, 600 m).

C. viridiflorus Backbg.—Descr. Cact. Nov. III: 5. 1963.
Bo. to 1.6 m h.; **St.** c. 2.2 cm ⌀; **Ri.** c. 12; **Ar.** brownish; **Sp.** yellowish; **Rsp.** c. 15–18, to 1 cm lg., thin; **Csp.** scarcely recognisable, to 2.2 cm lg.; **Fl.** c.

3.5 cm lg., uniformly green, the Sc. similarly, with brown woolly H.—Bolivia (Ayata) (FR 323). (Fig. 61, left.)

C. vulpis-cauda Ritt. & Cullm.—Kakt. u. a. sukk. Pfl., 13: 3, 38–40. 1962.
Bo. to 2 m lg., pendant, branching from the base; **St.** 2–5 cm ⌀, green; **Ri.** 18–22, weakly transversely notched; **Ar.** yellow to dark brown; **Sp.** replaced by H., to c. 50, flexible, 1–2 cm lg., whitish to reddish-brown, centrals not distinguishable; **Fl.** 6 cm lg., scarcely curving; **Ov.** bent at a right-angle, red; **Tu.** light blood-red, very sparsely white-haired; **Sep.** dark red; **Pet.** light red, limb oblique; **Fr.** red, becoming brown, tessellate, 9 mm lg.; **S.** faintly glossy, black.—Bolivia (Prov. Tomina) (FR 847). The H., from a photo of Cullmann's, can also be bristly, erect in the St.-apex, otherwise projecting. (Fig. 61, right.)

C. wendlandiorum Backbg.
Bo. erect, branching from the base; **St.** to 3.5 cm ⌀ (to 4.5 cm in grafted plants); **Ri.** c. 22, 2 mm h.; **Ar.** ± oblong; **Sp.** c. 40, bristly-fine, short, yellowish at first, soon becoming greyish-white, to c. 1 cm lg., crowded; **Csp.** scarcely distinguishable; **Fl.** 5 cm lg., limb oblique; **Ov.** 3–4 mm lg., bent at a right-angle; **Tu.** slightly curving, light orange; **Sep.** carmine to orange; **Pet.** somewhat darker; **nectary** closed, as by a membrane, by the basal union of the filaments.—Bolivia (in the S. ?). Further spec. of Cleistocactus found by Ritter, some named, some only with numbers: previous experience has shown that these new introductions merit the attention of collectors:
C. albisetus Ritt. (FR 820): "with white Br. **Sp.**";
C. ipotanus Ritt. (FR 829): **Fl.** green;
C. margaritanus Ritt. (FR 842): **Fl.** less zygomorphic than C. chacoanus;
C. otuyensis Ritt. (FR 1002): resembles C. buchtienii, but has dense, long, yellow **Sp.**;
C. pilcomayoensis Ritt. (FR 825): nothing further known;
C. sotomayorensis Ritt. (FR 824): "**Sp.** dense, yellow to red";
C. spec. (FR 358): **St.** c. 4–5.5 cm ⌀; **Ri.** c. 16; **Ar.** brownish-grey at first; **Sp.** 9–11, 3–6 mm lg.; **Csp.** 1, to 1.6 cm lg., all dull yellowish-brown to reddish; **Fl.** carmine (Ritter).—Bolivia (Mataral).

Clistanthocereus Backbg. (67)

Tree-like Cerei, or shrubby and forming dense thickets; ribs very tuberculate, flowers stout, straight, hairy, with fairly straight limbs. Among the genera of Loxanthocerei, this genus includes the tallest-growing plants and the largest flowers. The perianth is not funnelform. The fruits are considerably larger than in Cleistocactus and Loxanthocereus (here "relatively small", Rauh).— Distribution: Northern part of Central Peru. [(R).]

C. calviflorus (Ritt.) Backbg. n.comb. (Borzicactus calviflorus Ritt., "Taxon", XIII: 3, 118. 1964).
Bo. shrubby, resembling C. fieldianus; **St.** somewhat more slender, to 6 cm $\emptyset$; **Ri.** 6–10, rarely to 16; **Sp.** yellowish to reddish-brown; **Rsp.** 10–12, more slender; **Csp.** 1, rather stout, sometimes also 2–3 shorter and thinner Sp.; **Fl.** only 1.5 cm when fully expanded; **Pet.** with a carmine centre and a yellow border, sometimes crimson; **Tu.** weakly white-haired or glabrous; **Ov.** similarly; **Fr.** to 3.5 cm lg., orange or reddish, sparsely white-haired to glabrous; **S.** 2 mm lg., black, slightly glossy.—Peru (Dept. Ancash, Chavin) (FR 1068). The nectary has a ring of dense wool. On the basis of Ritter's comparative data with C. fieldianus, and the flower with its clearly straight limb and rather narrow opening, the spec. should be referred to this genus (rather than Borzicactus).

C. fieldianus (Br. & R.) Backbg. (T.)
Bo. shrubby to $\pm$ tree-like; **St.** to 6 m lg., erect, pendant or even prostrate, to 8 cm $\emptyset$; **Ri.** to 6, with large oblong Tub.; **Ar.** large; **Sp.** at first only c. 5, grey, brownish-tipped, c. 1 cm lg.; **Csp.** eventually 2–3, stout, to 4 cm lg. (on old St. possibly up to 11 whitish Rsp., and 1–3 Csp. to 4 cm lg.); **Fl.** crimson, with the limb projecting horizontally; **Tu.** 1.8 cm $\emptyset$, with brown H.; **Ov.** hairy, red; **Fr.** spherical, 4 cm $\emptyset$.—Northern Central Peru (E. of Huaraz).

C. samnensis (Ritt.) Backbg. n.comb. (Borzicactus samnensis Ritt., "Taxon", XIII: 3, 118. 1964).
Bo. $\pm$ as C. fieldianus; **St.** somewhat more slender, c. 5–7 cm $\emptyset$; **Ri.** 6–9; **Sp.** yellowish to reddish-brown, with 1 Csp. to 8 cm lg., sometimes also 1–3 shorter subsidiary Sp.; **Fl.** straight-limbed, to only 7 mm $\emptyset$, violet-purple; **Tu.** with black H.; **Fr.** to 3.5 cm lg., yellow or yellowish-green; **S.** 1.8 mm lg., dark.—Peru (Dept. Cajamarca [Zangal] to Dept. Ancash [Pariacoto]); type-locality: Samne (Dept. La Libertad) (FR 304). The nectary lacks any hair-development. This spec., for the same reasons as C. calviflorus, must be referred to this genus, whose name clearly speaks for itself. It is interesting to note the variability of the flower's indumentum, or the marked degree of reduction in the previously mentioned spec.

C. tessellatus (Akers & Buin.) Backbg.
Bo. tree-like, to 1.8 m h.; **St.** robust; **Ri.** 5–6, with elongated 6-sided Tub. and transverse furrows;

Rsp. c. 10, 7–15 mm lg., with reddish-brown flecks; **Csp.** mostly 1, subulate; **Fl.** red, Sc. fleshy; **Tu.** stout, it and the limb straight; **Fr.** yellow, with scutate Sc., pulp drying up.—Northern Central Peru (Churin-Oyon, on the Rio Huaura). (Fig. 62.)

Cochemiea (K. Brand.) Walt. (233)

Plants with cylindric stems, forming dense colonies, sometimes of great size. Without milky sap, without furrows on the tubercles. Flowers borne towards the apex, zygomorphic, with a fairly long tube. Except for one species, all have hooked spines. All grow well although sometimes only slowly (C. halei); flowers only borne on rather older stems. Fruits clavate or spherical berries, red, inside similarly as far as is known; seeds matt black, finely pitted.—Distribution: Mexico (Baja California and some of the offshore islands). [(R).]

C. halei (K. Brand.) Walt. (T.)
Bo. to 50 cm h., forming groups; **St.** to 7.5 cm $\emptyset$, fairly firm; **Tub.** short; **Ax.** woolly at first; **Rsp.** 10–20, straight, stiff, to 1.5 cm lg.; **Csp.** 3–4 (–6), to 3.5 cm lg., straight, very stiff, stout; **Sp.** reddish-brown at first, then yellowish, finally grey; **Fl.** 4–5 cm lg., scarlet; **Fr.** 1.2 cm lg.—Mexico (Baja California, Magdalena Is. etc.).

C. maritima Linds.
Bo. 50 cm h., forming colonies to 1 m br.; **R.** thickened; **St.** erect, prostrate or sometimes curving upwards, 3–7 cm $\emptyset$, pruinose, bluish-green; **Tub.** $\pm$ conical; **Ar.** grey; **Rsp.** 10–15, acicular, 1 cm lg.; **Csp.** 4, acicular, the lowest one hooked, to 5 cm lg.; **Sp.** all reddish-brown; **Fl.** 3 cm lg., scarlet, Pet. revolute; **Fr.** spherical, red.— Mexico (Baja California, Punta Blanca).

C. pondii (Greene) Walt.
Bo. to 7 cm h., 3 cm $\emptyset$, little branching; **Ax.** bristly; **Rsp.** 15–25; **Csp.** 8–11, to 3 cm lg., 1–2 of these hooked; **Sp.** crowded, the radials whitish or brownish, the centrals darker; **Fl.** 5 cm lg., light scarlet; **Fr.** thick-clavate, purplish-red, 1.8 cm lg.— Mexico (Baja California, Cedros Is. etc.)

C. poselgeri (Hildm.) Br. & R.
Bo. to 2 m lg., erect at first, later prostrate or pendant, forming large colonies; **St.** bluish-green, becoming greyish-green, to 4 cm $\emptyset$; **Ax.** with white wool and sometimes Br.; **Ar.** at first quite strongly woolly; **Rsp.** 7–9, stiff, to 1.5 cm lg., at first straw-coloured, dark yellow or red; **Csp.** 1, to 3 cm lg., stouter, dark to blackish, $\pm$ hooked; **Fl.** 3 cm lg., glossy, scarlet; **Fr.** spherical, 6–8 mm $\emptyset$.—Mexico

(Baja California, Cape region). (Fig. 63.)

C. setispina (Coult.) Walt.
Bo. to 30 cm h., forming dense groups; **St.** to 4 cm ∅, light greyish-green; **Tub.** somewhat conical; **Ar.** white; **Ax.** with white wool; **Rsp.** 9–12, acicular, milky-white, ± dark-tipped, to 2 cm lg.; **Csp.** 1–3, colour similar to Rsp., the one hooked Sp. longest; **Fl.** 5.4 cm lg., brilliant crimson; **Fr.** clavate, dark red, to 1.7 cm lg.—Mexico (Baja California, San Borgia).

Coleocephalocereus Backbg. (184)

Only moderately tall Cerei, growing in part on steep hillsides. The most distinctive character lies in the cephalium, its dense wool interspersed with longer bristles, which is sunk in a kind of groove and later ± depressed. The flowers, borne in the uppermost section of the cephalium, are naked, with the outer perianth segments recurved and the inner ones more erect and only slightly recurved; the red lidded fruits are smooth and top-shaped, the seeds black.—Distribution: Brazil (near Rio de Janeiro, and in Bahia). [(R) (G), cold-sensitive.]

C. aureus Ritt. (FR 1341) is a still undescribed spec. of Ritter's: "**Bo.** 40 cm h.; **Sp.** long, weak, contorted, brown at first, soon becoming golden-yellow."

C. brevicylindricus: on the basis of data from W. Andreae this is **Buiningia brevicylindrica.**

C. decumbens Ritt. (FR 1340)
Bo. forming bushes with the main St. long, in part erect, 1–3 m lg., 3.5–7 cm thick, soft, greyish-green, with prostrate and creeping branches; **Ri.** 5–13, obtuse, ± tuberculate; **Ar.** round, c. 3 mm ∅, white-felty, 6–12 mm apart; **Sp.** 3–8, 1–4 cm lg., black, greying; **Ceph.** lateral, consisting of skeins of dense white wool and black-brown Br.; **Fl.** nocturnal, 40–45 mm lg., c. 3 cm ∅, opening widely; **Fil.** pale yellow, **An.** cream, **style** whitish with pale yellow Sti.; **Fr.** scarlet; **S.** black, matt, finely tuberculate.—Brazil (in the NE. of Minas Geraes, near Agua Vermelha; found by Ritter in 1965).

C. flavisetus (FR 1339): no description available.

C. fluminensis (Miqu.) Backbg. (T.)
Bo. to 2 m lg., to 10 cm ∅; **St.** dark green, curving upwards and then erect; **Ri.** 10–17, eventually to 1.5 cm h.; **Ar.** white; **Rsp.** 2–3 at first, later 4–7; **Csp.** 1; flowering St. have 2–10 stouter Sp., with 2–4 small Sp. in the upper part of the Ar., all light to greyish-yellow, finally to 3 cm lg., flexible; **Ceph.** eventually longer-decurrent, wool whitish; **Fl.** 5.5–7 cm lg., smooth, ± longitudinally grooved; **Sep.** pale pink; **Pet.** whitish; **Fr.** 2–3 cm lg.—Brazil (Rio de Janeiro, Niteroy). (Fig. 64.)

C. goebelianus (Vpl.) Ritt. n.comb. (Kakt, u. a. Sukk., 16: 3, 61. 1965, Winter's plant-list).
Bo. to 2 m h., c. 6 cm ∅; **Ri.** 10; **Ar.** shortly felty, soon glabrous; **Sp.** 10–12, acicular, thin, brown, to 1 cm lg.; **Ceph.** on one side, extending to 20 cm downwards, 1.5 cm h., densely woolly, with projecting Br.; **Fl.** c. 5 cm lg., bellshaped; **Ov.** c. 1 cm br., 0.4 cm h., thick-walled; **Pet.** short.—Brazil (Central Bahia, Serra das Almas, Rio de Contas area). Since this spec. has not yet been definitely classified, I will here accept Ritter's name-change. While it is not, acc. Werdermann, differentiated from A. purpureus, I have already stated the differences in "Die Cact." IV, 2497. 1960. Possibly A. purpureus will also have to be referred to this genus, but at the present time too little is known as to whether or not the cephalium is sunken. In C. goebelianus, acc. to Ritter's name-change, this character should be present. (See next spec.)

C. pachystele Ritt. 1968 (FR 1234) (synonymous with C. goebelianus Gürke; incorrectly named Austrocephalocereus purpureus by Werdermann).
Bo. columnar, to 6 m h., sometimes branching, 7–12 cm thick, green; **Ri.** 14–27, 8–13 mm h., notched above the Ar.; **Ar.** 2.5–5 mm ∅, 4–10 mm apart, weakly white-felty; **Sp.** flexible, yellowish, reddish-brown below, **Csp.** brown-tipped; **Ceph.** very extensive, of dense white wool; **Fl.** 40–55 mm lg., 25–28 mm ∅, nocturnal, white, with pink Sc. outside; **Fil.** and **style** white; **Fr.** 14–20 mm lg. and ∅, purplish-red, white below; **S.** 1.5 mm lg., black, matt.—Brazil (Bahia, Urandi and other localities in S. Bahia).

C. paulensis Ritt. 1968 (FR 1352)
Bo. to 1 m h., offsetting from the base, **St.** to c. 2 m lg., older parts prostrate, 5–9 cm thick, grass-green; **Ri.** 9–13, obtuse, scarcely tuberculate; **Ar.** round, 1–2 mm ∅, white-woolly, 5–7 mm apart; **Sp.** pale golden-yellow, straight, c. 6, the stoutest one directed downwards, 10–25 mm lg.; **Ceph.** lateral, consisting of skeins of dense white wool interspersed with light golden-yellow straight Br.; **Fl.** nocturnal, scented, 6 cm lg., c. 4 cm ∅; **Sep.** c. 20 mm lg., obtuse above, notched at midway, purplish-pink, bordered paler; **Pet.** 15 mm lg., 6 mm br., tapering above, white; **Fr.** purple, top-shaped, smooth, glossy; **S.** 1.5 mm lg., black, matt, finely tuberculate.—Brazil (Sao Paulo, Ilhabela Island).

C. pleurocarpus (FR 1227): no description available. Acc. Buining = **Cipocereus pleurocarpus**.

C. pluricostatus Buin. & Bred.
Bo. erect, offsetting from the base, to 3.5 m lg., to 9 cm $\emptyset$; **Ri.** 20–25, more at the Ceph., c. 5 mm h., 1 cm apart, with a furrow over the Ar.; **Ceph.** very long, 6 cm br. and extending over c. 7 Ri., with yellow, brown or blackish-brown, dense Br.; **Ar.** round, 2 mm $\emptyset$, grey-felty, becoming glabrous; **Sp.** thin, straight, yellowish; **Rsp.** 5, one directed downwards, c. 11 mm lg., upper ones shorter; **Csp.** 1, c. 6 mm lg.; **Fl.** funnelform-bellshaped, c. 26 mm lg. and 15 mm $\emptyset$; **Ov.** covered with white, reddish-tipped Sc.; **Sep.** coloured similarly; **Pet.** white, apiculate; **Fil.** white; **An.** cream; **style** white, with 6 cream Sti.; **Fr.** glossy, reddish, glabrous; **S.** with a yellow-ochre hilum and black testa.—Brazil (Minas Geraes, on bare mountain-slopes at c. 300 m). Found by A. F. H. Buining and L. Horst.

Coloradoa Boiss. & Davids. (198)

Spherical plants, mostly solitary, rarely offsetting. Ribs tuberculate. Flowers bellshaped to funnel-form, rather short, relatively small, borne around the crown; they and the fruit are glabrous; the fruit, with persistent floral remains, splits open irregularly. The plants are rare; in habitat they are often eaten by maggots, and they are susceptible to dry-rot, while few survive for long in cultivation. 1 species, first described in 1940.—Distribution: USA (SW. Colorado; New Mexico). [(G), ✳.]

C. mesae-verdae Boiss. & Davids. (T.)
Bo. spherical to oblong, to 8 cm h., 6 cm $\emptyset$; **Ri.** 13–17; **Ar.** brownish; **Rsp.** 8–10, c. 1 cm lg., cream-coloured, reddish or brown at the base; **Csp.** mostly absent or 1, 1 cm lg., subulate, grey, dark-tipped, $\pm$ straight; **Fl.** 3.5 cm lg. and br.; **Sep.** brownish-purple, with a white border; **Pet.** cream-coloured to yellowish, with a brownish M.-stripe, throat green; **S.** 4 mm lg.—USA (SW. Colorado, Mesa-Verde Plateau; New Mexico, Shiprock). (Fig. 65.)

Consolea Lem. (16)

Tree-like plants, sometimes with several main stems which are continuous, mostly not completely terete as in Brasiliopuntia, which it somewhat resembles in habit, but at least $\pm$ flattened in the upper part. Trunk-like and continuous primary growths are unique to these two genera, and are thus a diagnostic character. However while the terminal shoots of Brasiliopuntia differ from Opuntia in their blade-like form, and the flowers have hair-development of staminodial type, in Consolea the latter is missing and the terminal shoots resemble the thicker flat-shoots of the Opuntias, but they are oblong, irregular in outline, with one margin more curving than the other; these terminal shoots are mostly arranged with the margins to top and bottom, the upper one being straighter. Between these terminal shoots and the trunk-like growths there are other longer-continuous, and mostly narrower, intermediate shoots which are sometimes more strongly spined. Spination is very variable, in part absent on the terminal shoots, or more numerous and very sharp. The flowers are relatively small but have a longer and sometimes $\pm$ flat ovary into which the perianth is recessed while the seed-cavity is sometimes at midway, sometimes a little higher. Seeds appear always to be few in number or sometimes even missing. Since the ovaries root on falling, propagation is quicker than when the plants develop from seeds. In some plants the ovary is bent in the same way as the terminal shoots. Some species can be seen as quite mature specimens in S. Europe.—Distribution: Antilles, Keys of Florida. [(R).]

C. corallicola Small
Bo. to 2 m h.; **trunk** terete; **shoots** to 30 cm lg.; **Ar.** crowded; **L.** $\pm$ completely reduced; **Sp.** 5–9, bristly, thin, one much longer, to 12 cm lg., all salmon-coloured at first, soon becoming grey; **Fl.** numerous, red; **Ov.** rather flattened.—USA (Keys of Florida).

C. falcata (Ekm. & Werd.) Knuth
Bo. to 1.5 m h.; **shoots** to 35 cm lg., 9 cm br., $\pm$ sickle-shaped; **Sp.** 2–8, 1–4 cm lg., acicular, rough; **Fl.** reddish; **Ov.** 2.5–3 cm lg., to 1.8 cm $\emptyset$; **Fr.** and S. unknown.—Haiti (NW. peninsula).

C. macracantha (Griseb.) Britt.
Bo. over 3 m h., strongly branching; **trunk** to 15 cm $\emptyset$; **shoots** oblong, slightly glossy, green; **Glo.** brown; **Sp.** on the trunk to 15 cm lg., those on the shoots 1–4, $\pm$ white, stiff, subulate, but sometimes completely absent; **Fl.** orange-yellow; **Ov.** to 3 cm lg.—Cuba (predominant among the trees of S. and E. coastal plains).

C. millspaughii (Britt.) Britt.
Bo. to 60 cm h.; **trunk** 7 cm $\emptyset$ below; **shoots** narrow-oblong, to 40 cm lg., to 10 cm br., light green, terminal shoots shorter; **Glo.** yellowish-brown; **Sp.** on the trunk to 15 cm lg., very dense, otherwise fewer and shorter, or only on the margin of the terminal shoots, purple at first; **Fl.** carmine, limb 1 cm br.; **Pet.** erect; **Fr.** compressed-ovoid, 2 cm lg., 1.5 cm $\emptyset$, bearing Ar. with 1–2 yellowish-brown Sp.; **Fr.** ?—Cuba; Bahamas.

C. moniliformis (L.) Britt.
Bo. to 6 m h.; **trunk** becoming thick, densely set with Sp. to 12 cm lg.; **shoots** to 30 cm lg., to 13 cm br.; **Sp.** at first 3–6, 1–2.5 cm lg., eventually 5–8, young growth with 1–3 or none, all yellowish; **Glo.** to 8 mm lg., brownish; **Fl.** 2.5 cm br., yellow to orange, to 5 cm lg.—Hispaniola and Desecheo Is.

C. nashii (Britt.) Britt.
Bo. to 4 m h., with several main trunks; **trunk** to 12 cm ∅; **shoots** to over 1 m lg., 6 cm br., terminal shoots to 30 cm lg., to 8 cm br., matt green; **Sp.** (2–)5, to 6 cm lg., spreading, thin, straight, sharp, light grey; **Glo.** brownish, very small; **Fl.** c. 4 cm lg., 1.5 cm br., red; **Ov.** 3 cm lg., ± clavate, spiny; **Fr.** ?—Bahamas.

C. rubescens (SD.) Lem.
Bo. to 6 m h.; **trunk** to 15 cm ∅, Sp. absent or numerous, to 8 cm lg.; **shoots** to 25 cm lg., terminal shoots thin, flat, mostly dark green, also red (or reddish-green) (ecotypes); **Sp.** missing, or several to 6 cm lg., almost white; **Fl.** over 5 cm lg., c. 2 cm br., yellow, orange or red (also changing colour during anthesis); **Ov.** tuberculate, variable in length; **Fr.** reddish, ovoid to spherical, to 8 cm ∅, those without S. remaining ± flat and similar to the Ov. in shape; **S.** ± round, 6–8 mm lg., hairy;—W. Indies (Fig. 66.) The ± red-colour of some plants sometimes changes to green in cultivation in Europe.

C. spinosissima (Mill.) Lem.
Bo. to 5 m h.; **trunk** to 20 cm ∅; **shoots** 2–4 times as lg. as br., dull to light green; **Glo.** brownish; **Sp.** dense on the trunk, to 8 cm lg. and stouter, 1–3 on the shoots, straw-coloured to whitish, to 8 cm lg., red at the base, sometimes missing; **Fl.** yellow, turning red; **Ov.** to 8 cm lg.—Jamaica.

Copiapoa Br. & R. (129)

One of the most interesting genera of spherical cacti, with two different growth-forms: some species spherical, offsetting or forming cushions, others becoming cereoid when old, to over 1 m high, also offsetting. Whereas the latter only flower after attaining a considerable size, the smaller spherical species bear flowers when still quite small, some of these flowers quite large. Some species are relatively dwarf, some have considerably thickened roots. The colouring of spination and body shows wide differences. Plants may be floury-white, oil-green, grey, or green of different tints, ± flushed brownish or entirely brown(-grey). The spines may be of any colour from black through brown to white, while within individual species there are sometimes variations in number, length and position of the spines. It would seem that within the relatively restricted area of Chile there must once have been quite a small number of ancestral species which, in the course of time, hybridised and gave rise to transitional forms, thus making the de-limitation of species an often difficult task. In some cases (e.g. C. krainziana) widely differing forms occur in any sowing from seed, even the spine-characters varying widely, while even in the wild those species with more conspicuously grey bodies produce seedlings where the bodies are true green. It is therefore not possible to indicate more than the principal forms in the following descriptions. It seems likely that all the known species have not yet been described, including a number of Ritter's plants, since he has been responsible for most of the new species. In some instances they are already in cultivation as larger plants, but not all have flowered; others have proved to be very floriferous once a certain size has been reached. Other known plants show a very different habit when raised from seed, and this adds to the problems of identification. The flowers are fairly large to conspicuous, more or less yellow, apart from one species with reputedly ± red flowers; in a number of cases the flowers are perfumed; all have a very short tube. The fruits mostly split open above, leaving a gaping tear, so that ants are able to carry off the seeds and their fleshy funicles. One example of the difficulties of classification is that species which become columnar with age may sometimes have varieties which form clumps; these different forms must therefore result from only minor modifications of hereditary factors. The genus well deserves a place in collections on account of the wide range of variation as well as the beauty of body and spination, added to which all the known species grow very well; they may indeed be faster-growing when grafted, but do no less well on their own roots.—Distribution: N. to Central Chile. [(R) (G).]

C. alticostata Ritt.—"Taxon", XII: 1, 29. 1963; distinguished from C. cuprea as follows:
Bo. 20–40 cm h., green, forming clusters to 1 m br.; **Ri.** prominent; **Ar.** 8–13 mm ∅; **Sp.** similar to C. cuprea but brown; **Csp.** present even at first, later up to 4; **Fr.** green.—Chile (Freirina, N. of Nicolasa) (FR 717).

C. applanata Backbg.
Bo. broadly spherical, light green, to 10 cm ∅, offsetting; cranial **wool** creamy-white, to 3.5 cm br.; **Ri.** to 21; **Rsp.** 7–8, 1–1.5 cm lg.; **Csp.** 0–1, to 1.75 cm lg.; **Sp.** all whitish-grey, dark-tipped at first; **Fl.** ?—Chile. May vary in having a smaller number of Ri. and individual longer Csp.

C. barquitensis Ritt. (undescribed)
Similar to C. hypogea with tuberculate **Ri.**; somewhat variable in epidermis-colour, offsetting; **Sp.** thin; **Ar.** less sunken.—Chile (found further S. than C. hypogea, Chañaral?).

C. bridgesii (Pfeiff.) Backbg.
Bo. becoming oblong; **Ri.** 10, broad, obtuse; **Ar.** crowded, large, oval, brownish-white; **Rsp.** 7, radiating; **Csp.** 1, longer, to over 3 cm lg.; **Fl.** smaller; **Sep.** greenish-yellow; **Pet.** sulphur-yellow; **Fil.** and **An.** yellow; **Tu.** woolly(?).—Chile. Unless there has been some rather unlikely error, Rümpler's statement that the "tube is woolly" may mean that this plant belonged to Pilocopiapoa, in which the flower-colour (P. solaris) is variable. All the other characters given above would be appropriate, with the exception of the solitary Csp. (2–5 in Pilocopiapoa). However, the variable number of centrals in Pilocopiapoa leads one to assume that cultivated plants perhaps only produce one central. The identity of P. solaris and C. bridgesii could only be established by comparing a population of P. solaris raised from seed with Rümpler's above description of C. bridgesii.

C. brunnescens Backbg. (described without Latin diagnosis).
Bo. broadly spherical, brown; **crown** densely woolly; **Ri.** divided into ± circular Tub.; **Sp.** mostly 6, spreading, stoutly subulate, dark to blackish above, yellow at first below.—Chile.

C. calderana Ritt.
Bo. solitary, hemispherical, later elongated, to 10 cm ∅, greyish-green, not pruinose; **Ri.** 10–17; **Ar.** grey, later black, 5 mm ∅; **Rsp.** 5–7, to 15 mm lg.; **Csp.** 1(–2), to 3 cm lg.; **Sp.** brown to black, becoming grey; **Fl.** 3–3.5 cm lg., 3 cm br., scented; **Fr.** pale green, reddish above, to 15 mm lg.; **S.** glossy black.—Chile (coast of Caldera). Appears to be very variable.

C. carrizalensis Ritt.
Bo. becoming oblong, offsetting, forming groups to 1 m h., individual **St.** to 12 cm ∅; apical **wool** brown to orange; **R.** not napiform; **Ri.** 15–24, to 10 mm h.; **Ar.** brownish-orange at first; **Rsp.** 4–7, to 3 cm lg., fairly straight; **Csp.** 0–1, to 4 cm lg.; **Sp.** black or brown; **Fl.** 2.7 cm lg., 3 cm br., not scented; **Pet.** sometimes golden-yellow, otherwise lighter; **Fr.** 1.5 cm lg., green to brownish-red; **S.** glossy black.—Chile (Carrizal Bajo, coast). Perhaps referable to C. malletiana.
  v. **gigantea** Ritt.: **Bo.** forming large colonies to 1 m h., 2 m across; **Rsp.** 3–6, mostly 4, 2.5 cm lg., more projecting; **Csp.** absent or 1, similar to Rsp.—N. Chile, N. of Carrizal Bajo (FR 508a).

C. castanea Ritt. (not described)
Bo. broadly spherical; **Ri.** numerous, tuberculate near the Ar.; **Rsp.** 8; **Csp.** 1, porrect; **Sp.** chestnut-brown above at first, lighter at the base, becoming whitish.—Chile. The Bo.-colour is more dirty-brown than chestnut-coloured.

C. chanaralensis Ritt. (not described)
Bo. broadly spherical, olive-greenish; **Ri.** numerous, less tuberculate than the preceding; apical **wool** white (in seedlings); **Rsp.** 8; **Csp.** 1; **Sp.** brownish at first, then lightening, brown-tipped; **Fl.** ?—Chile (Chañaral). (Fig. 67.)

C. cinerascens (SD.) Br. & R.
Bo. "spherical" (?becoming elongated), individual **St.** to 8 cm ∅, green; apical **wool** greyish-white; **Ri.** 20–21, swollen around the Ar.; **Rsp.** 8, mostly to 1.2 cm lg.; **Csp.** 1(–2), to 2.5 cm lg., stouter; **Sp.** stiff, yellowish to chestnut-brown, becoming grey; **Sep.** often recurved; **Pet.** yellow, lanceolate, ± denticulate.—Chile (coast of Copiapo).

C. cinerea (Phil.) Br. & R. (T.)
Bo. at first spherical, becoming elongated and columnar, to 1.3 m h., single heads to over 10 cm ∅; apical **wool** whitish-grey; **St.** chalky white; **Ri.** 14–30, transversely indented, scarcely thickened around the Ar.; **Sp.** variable, one in the type, to several, subulate to stoutly subulate, black, sometimes 1–7 Rsp. to 2 cm lg., 1–2 Csp. to 3.5 cm lg.; **Fl.** to 3.5 cm lg. and br., pure yellow, more reddish-yellow outside; **style** cream, tinged pink; **S.** glossy black.—Chile (Paposo, Taltal to Cobre).
  v. **albispina** Ritt.—"Taxon", XII: 1, 30. 1963: **Bo.** smaller than in the T., brownish as far as I could observe; **Ri.** 12–21; **Rsp.** 0–6, pale brownish or white, 2–5 cm lg., straight or slightly curving.—Chile, N. of Taltal (FR 207a).
  v. **columna-alba** (Ritt.) Backbg.: **Bo.** simple, columnar, to 75 cm h., to 20 cm ∅, chalky-white; apex flat, with grey to orange felt, without Sp.; **Ri.** 27–47, obtuse, 1 cm br., thickened below the Ar.; **Ar.** sunken, 2–5 mm thick, 4–8 mm apart, with orange wool which is later grey; **Sp.** yellowish-brown to black; **Rsp.** 4–5, thin, 5–8 mm lg., curving; **Csp.** 1–3, straight, 1–2 cm lg.; **Fl.** funnelform, 2–3 cm lg.; **Tu.** pale yellow with red-tipped Sc.; **style** pale yellow, 2 cm lg., with 10 deep yellow Sti.; **Pet.** pale yellow; **Fr.** spherical to ovoid; **S.** glossy black.—Chile (coastal zone about lat. 26° S.
  v. **dealbata** (Ritt.) Backbg.: **Bo.** forming hemispherical clumps, single heads 6–12 cm ∅; crown with greyish-white felt; **Ri.** 21–33, weakly tuberculate; **Ar.** 5–7 mm lg., 10–15 mm apart, sunken, grey-felty; **Sp.** mostly 1, straight, stiff, 2–5 cm lg., sometimes with 1–3 smaller Sp..; **Fl.**

funnelform, 3.5 cm lg. and $\emptyset$; **style** pale yellow, to 3 mm lg.; **Pet.** pale yellow, weakly acute; **Sep.** brown-reddish in the middle outside; **Fr.** spherical, greenish-white, suffused reddish; **S.** black, tuberculate.—Chile (coastal zone c. lat. 28° S.). The above varieties are also chalky white.
v. flavescens Backbg.: v. **columna-alba** (Ritt.) Backbg.

C. coquimbana (Karw.) Br. & R.
Bo. spherical, offsetting to form large groups to 1 m across, single heads to 10 cm $\emptyset$; **R.** fibrous; **Ri.** 10–17, distinctly tuberculate; **Rsp.** 8–10, rather thin; **Csp.** 1–2, stouter; **Sp.** black to grey; **Fl.** bellshaped, to 3 cm lg.; **Pet.** yellow, obtuse to rounded.—Chile (Coquimbo, La Serena etc.).
    v. **wagenknechtii** Ritt.—"Taxon", XII: 1, 30. 1963: **R.** shortly cylindric; **Ri.** sap-green, resolved into narrowly connected, stout, $\pm$ circular Tub.; **Sp.** 6–7(–8), to 4 cm lg., black, lighter at the foot, thick-subulate, stouter than in the T.; **Csp.** sometimes 1, curving upwards; **Fl.** larger, 4–5.5 cm $\emptyset$.—Chile (El Tambo, Elqui valley) (FR 718, at first accorded specific rank). Description completed by me, from seed-grown plants. (Fig. 72.)

C. cuprea Ritt.
Bo. mostly simple, sometimes offsetting, green or tinged brown, to 20 cm h., to 18 cm $\emptyset$; apical **wool** grey;**Ri.** 11–17, to 2 cm h., 2–3 cm br.; **Ar.** to 1 cm $\emptyset$, brown; **Rsp.** 6–10, to 2.5 cm lg.; **Csp.** 0–1, very stout, to 5 cm lg.; **Sp.** stiff, rough, black, becoming grey; **Fl.** to 4 cm lg., to 3 cm $\emptyset$, scented, pale yellow; **Sep.** with a carmine M.-stripe; **Fr.** 1.5 cm lg., carmine, with red Sc.; **S.** $\pm$ matt black.—Chile (northern coastal Cordillera, 28°25′ lat. S.).

C. cupreata (Pos.) Backbg.
Bo. spherical, dark brown; **Ri.** divided into rhombic Tub. 5 mm h., the angles somewhat rounded, with a nose-like projection; **Ar.** whitish-grey, depressed; **Sp.** (5–)6, 1–2 cm lg., upper ones shorter, curving, brownish-black above, yellowish below; **Fl.** ?—Chile.

C. desertorum Ritt. (not described)
Bo. broadly spherical, at first quite strongly sunken in the soil, dark in colour as are the 4–5 relatively short **Sp.** which are thickened at the base, and lighten in colour from blackish to brownish-grey.—Chile.

C. dura Ritt.—"Taxon", XII: 1, 31. 1963.
Bo. oblong, to 12 cm lg., green, also brownish; **Ri.** 11–15, to 15 mm h., rather obtuse, scarcely tuberculate; **Ar.** round, to 10 mm $\emptyset$, brown to

white; **Rsp.** 7–9, straight or slightly curving; **Csp.** mostly 3, more rarely 1–2, straight, 1–3 cm lg., to 2 mm thick below; **Fl.** 4 cm lg., sulphur-yellow, scented; **Ov.** whitish, with reddish Sc.; **Fr.** pale green, slightly brownish above; **S.** 2 mm lg., minutely tuberculate, with a large white hilum.—N. Chile (E. of Totoral) (FR 546). Seedling plants have shown that the original description is not always applicable; their Ri. are often very tuberculate, at least initially, the epidermis has light spots, the Bo. is also subspherical, the large Ar. are white; the Sp. are stoutly acicular, yellow at the base, then at first with an orange zone, and black towards the tip.

C. echinata Ritt.
Bo. flattened-hemispherical, scarcely offsetting, to 10 cm $\emptyset$, greyish-green, with dense Sp.; **R.** with a neck-like constriction, hard, napiform; **Ri.** 13–21, $\pm$ obtuse, thickened over the Ar.; **Rsp.** 7–12, 5–15 mm lg.; **Csp.** 4–10, 1.5–4 cm lg.; **Sp.** black at first, then grey, straight; **Fl.** to 2.75 cm lg., 3 cm $\emptyset$, yellow; **Fr.** pale green, 1 cm $\emptyset$, with brownish-green Sc.; **S.** glossy black.—Chile (Carrizal Bajo, on coastal cliffs).
    v. **borealis** Ritt. has stouter **Sp.**; **Rsp.** only 6–9, 1–2 cm lg.; **Csp.** only 3–6.—Chile (S. of Monte Amargo).

C. echinoides (Lem.) Br. & R.
Bo. more broadly spherical at first, greyish-green; **Ri.** c. 13–14, somewhat thickened around the Ar., becoming flatter; **Rsp.** 5–7, $\pm$ straight; **Csp.** 1, 3 cm lg.; **Sp.** dark at first, soon becoming grey; **Fl.** pale yellow; **Sep.** reddish; **Pet.** broadly oblong, with a red dorsal M.-stripe.—Chile (Antofagasta).

C. eremophila Ritt., not described; at the seedling-stage it resembles C. gigantea; **Bo.** olive-green, with the **Rsp.** and **Csp.** more horn-coloured; **Ri.**-count similar. Perhaps a form?

C. esmeraldana Ritt. (FR 1457): no description available.

C. ferox Lembcke & Backbg.
Bo. spherical at first, then elongated, pale greyish-green, offsetting, single heads to 15 cm h., to 10 cm $\emptyset$, later with a grey coating; **R.** stout; **Ri.** 8, c. 2 cm h.; **Ar.** large, pale grey; **Rsp.** c. 10, to 3.2 cm lg., stout; **Csp.** to 3, to 5 cm lg., rigid, even stouter; **Sp.** at first pale horn-coloured, later dirty greyish-black to yellowish-grey, sometimes with reddish marks; **Fl.** ?—Chile (Blanco Encalado, S. of Antofagasta).

C. fiedleriana (K.Sch.) Backbg.: **Copiapoa pepiniana** v. **fiedleriana** (K.Sch.) Backbg.

C. gigantea Backbg.
Bo. to 1 m h., offsetting, individual heads to 20 cm ⌀, oil-green, fairly pruinose, not chalky-white; apical **wool** reddish to yellowish-brown; **Ri.** 14–22; **Ar.** larger, becoming dark; **Rsp.** c. 7; **Csp.** 1–2; **Sp.** ± equal, slightly curving, stout, horn-coloured at first, dark-tipped; **Fl.** yellow.—Chile (Pampa de Antofagasta, above Paposo).
Incorrectly regarded by Ritter as identical with C. haseltoniana Backbg.

C. grandiflora Ritt.—"Taxon", XIII: 1, 30. 1963.
Bo. larger than in C. mollicula, later offsetting very freely; **Ri.** more numerous, higher; **Ar.** more distant; **Sp.** longer, stouter, the centrals brownish to black, the radials grey and more appressed; **Fl.** larger, c. 3 cm lg., 5.5 cm ⌀, pale yellow, red outside; **Fr.** larger, stouter, scalier, Sc. more obtuse.—N. Chile (Esmeralda) (FR 523). (Fig. 68.)
The comparative data are by Ritter. Because of the variability of the plants referred to, both these two species and C. montana (which also has large Fl., more reddish on the outside) are not readily distinguished, although in C. montana the apical wool, which is brownish in habitat, can be white in cultivated plants; this is fairly common in Copiapoa.

C. haseltoniana Backbg.
Bo. greyish-greenish to light grey, not pruinose, branching from the base and the flanks; apical **wool** brownish; **Ar.** large, to 9 mm ⌀; **Sp.** increasing in number, to c. 9, eventually pointing ± downwards; **Csp.** 0–1; **Sp.** yellowish, to 3 cm lg., sometimes darker-tipped; **Fl.** yellow. The **Ri.** sometimes eventually become quite flat.—Chile (N. of Taltal). There are spontaneous hybrids with C. cinerea which are somewhat pruinose.

C. humilis (Phil.) Hutch.
Text of first description: "Very small, depressed, ± spherical, 2.5 cm br., 2 cm h.; **Ri.** 10–12, tuberculate; **Rsp.** 10–12, bristly, spreading; **Csp.** 1, 2.2 cm lg.; **Fl.** yellow, 2 cm lg.—Chile (Antofagasta, Paposo)." (Fig. 69.)
Nowadays 3 plants go under this name: Fig. 3465 in "Die Cact." Vol. VI: olive-greenish, sometimes slightly reddish, Sp. bristly, fine (plant collected by Schäfer, Antofagasta, with a stout taproot); Fig. 3466, l.c.: a plant collected by Ritter, dark green or deep green; Fig. 1845, "Die Cact." Vol. III: plant collected by Hutchison which, in the light of material seen in Buining's collection (Hutchison PH 405), is the darkest plant, with a ± reddish overlay, apparently also the smallest, with a large taproot, with the Ri. more, or sometimes less, tuberculate.
The spine-count in each case is approximately the same, and all Sp. are thin, with one central (this being the longest, acc. my Fig. 3465), bristly, white, **Csp.** flexible, c. 2 cm lg.; it therefore most closely corresponds to the original description.
It is still not clear which plant should be considered as the type for the spec. (since Philippi provided neither an illustration nor a type-specimen), and which are to be regarded as a var. or a closely related spec.

C. hypogaea Ritt.
Bo. simple or branching dichotomously, small, to 4 cm ⌀, brownish-grey; **R.** thick, napiform; **Ri.** 10–14, completely resolved into Tub.; **Ar.** sunken; **Sp.** 1–6 at first, 2–4 mm lg., later falling, blackish to ash-grey; **Fl.** 2.2 cm lg., to 4 cm ⌀, pale yellow; **Fr.** small, whitish; **S.** glossy black.—Chile (coast, Prov. Antofagasta).

C. intermedia Ritt. (not described)
Bo. broadly spherical, leaf-green to bluish-green; **Ri.** divided into obtusely conical, spiralled Tub.; **Rsp.** fairly stout, radiating to projecting, c. 10; **Csp.** in the bluish-green plants to c. 4, darker brown, reddish below, and in the leaf-green plants c. 1–2, yellowish-brown at first, soon becoming whitish, all **Csp.** only slightly stouter and longer; **Fl.** ?—Chile.

C. krainziana Ritt.—"Taxon", XII: 1, 30. 1963.
Bo. greyish-green, to 12 cm ⌀, forming clumps to 1 m br.; apical **wool** grey; **Ri.** 13–24, to 1.5 cm h., slightly notched; **Ar.** grey, to 6 mm ⌀; **Sp.** porrect, thin, white to grey, ± bristly-fine, mostly curving; **Rsp.** 10–12, 1–2 cm lg.; **Csp.** 14–20, 2–3 cm lg.; **Fl.** to 3.5 cm lg., yellow; **Fr.** yellow or red; **S.** 1.6 mm lg., hilum brown.—N. Chile (Dept. Taltal, coastal mountains) (FR 210).
   v. **scopulina** Ritt.—l.c. 31. 1963: **Bo.** little offsetting, to 20 cm ⌀; **Sp.** stiff, brown or black; **Rsp.** acicular; **Csp.** subulate.—N. Chile, same locality (FR 209).
The name: "bearing a small broom", is little suited to the stiff Sp. which, in any event, are only sometimes present. The plant initially distributed as C. scopulina, sometimes as seed, had rigid white Br.; it is a form of the type-species, the name being more appropriate to the latter.

C. lembckei Backbg.
Bo. spherical at first, becoming oblong, whitish to greyish-green, to 15 cm lg. (and more?), to 10 cm ⌀; **R.** stout; **Ri.** 11, rounded; **Ar.** greyish-black (blackish when moist); **Rsp.** c. 7, to 13 mm lg.; **Csp.** 1, to 2.2 cm lg., ± porrect; **Sp.** all blackish to black at first, becoming grey to dirty yellowish and ± grey-pruinose; **Fl.** ?—Chile (N. of Caldera). May be identical with C. marginata sensu Ritt.

C. longispina Ritt.—"Taxon", XII: 1, 31. 1963. **Bo.** spherical, simple, greyish-green to blackish; **Ri.** 13–16, 1 cm h.; **Rsp.** 6–10, 1.5–5 cm lg.; **Csp.** 1–2, 2.5–6 cm lg.; **Fl.** 2.5–3.5 cm lg., pale yellow; **Fr.** spherical.—N. Chile (Sierra Hornillos, S. of Copiapo) (FR 505). (Fig. 70.) The description reputedly states the characters distinguishing it from C. humilis, but is too brief to make the plant recognisable, or to determine how far the spec. differs from C. humilis and C. taltalensis of my Fig. 3466 and 3467 in "Die Cact.", Vol. VI.

C. longistaminea Ritt.—"Taxon", XII: 1, 31. 1963. **Bo.** to 50 cm h., to 11(–15) cm ∅, greyish-green, rarely white; **R.** shortly napiform; **Ri.** 15–21; **Ar.** orange-yellow, to 6 mm apart; **Sp.** dark chestnut to ± black; **Rsp.** 4–6, somewhat projecting, 1–3 cm lg.; **Csp.** 0–1; **Fl.** to 2.5 cm lg., pale yellow, often brownish above; **Fr.** pale green; **S.** 1.2 mm lg.—N. Chile (near Esmeralda) (FR 531).

C. malletiana (Lem.) Backbg. **Bo.** simple to offsetting from lower down, grey-green, pruinose, becoming elongated, slow-growing; **Ri.** c. 15–17 (with sinuate longitudinal furrows), thickened around the Ar.; **Ar.** ± sunken; **Sp.** 2–3, pointing ± downwards, to 3 cm lg., later more numerous, all blackish at first; **Fl.** ?—Chile. Description taken from mature plants in cultivation in Europe. The spec. appears to be as variable as C. cinerea (is C. carrizalensis Ritt. referable here?); doubtless the Sp.-count, as is usual, increases with age in this spec. also; the longest Sp. can also be regarded as a Csp.

C. marginata (SD.) Br. & R. **Bo.** becoming cylindric, to 60 cm lg., with several heads, to 12 cm ∅, in part curving over and then ascending, dirty grey (to lighter green in cultivated plants); **Ri.** 8–12; **Ar.** large, circular, later blackish, crowded to confluent; **Sp.** brown at first, 5–10, unequal, subulate, straight, one **Csp.** longer, to over 3 cm lg., darker brown at the tip; **Fl.** c. 2.5 cm lg., yellow; **Fr.** 8 mm lg.; **S.** glossy black.—Chile (coast of Prov. Antofagasta). (Fig. 71.) C. streptocaulon sensu Ritt. must be identical spec.

C. marginata sensu Ritt.: **C. lembckei** Backbg. (?)

C. megarhiza Br. & R. **Bo.** broadly spherical, solitary or in groups of at most 2–3 heads, 8–26 cm lg., 4–9 cm ∅, dark green to ± white; apical **wool** white; **Ri.** mostly 13; **Sp.** c. 12, to 1.5 cm lg., fairly stout, yellow at first, then grey; **Fl.** 2.5 cm lg., yellow; **Fr.** green, to 8 mm lg.; **S.** black.—Chile (near Copiapo, on dry hills).

C. mollicula Ritt.—"Taxon", XII: 1, 30. 1963.

Bo. flat to hemispherical, soft, greyish-green, solitary, to 7 cm ∅; **R.** napiform, long, narrowing above; apical **wool** white; **Ri.** 10–14, rather obtuse, scarcely tuberculate, c. 1 cm br.; **Ar.** to 4 mm ∅, white; **Rsp.** 5–9, acicular, straight, grey, 5–15 mm lg.; **Csp.** 1–3, stouter, 1–3 cm lg., brownish to black; **Fl.** to 3 cm lg., pale yellow; **S.** 1.2 mm lg., hilum white.—N. Chile (N. of Chañaral airstrip) (FR 525).

C. montana Ritt. **Bo.** ± broadly spherical, quite freely offsetting, greyish-green, single heads to 20 cm h., 5–10 cm ∅; **Ri.** 10–17, to 8 mm h., tuberculately thickened around the Ar.; **Ar.** to 1 cm ∅, brown to white (seedling-plants), crowded; **Sp.** equal, straight or ± slightly curving, brownish-red to black; **Rsp.** 4–7; **Csp.** 1–3, to double the length of the Rsp.; **Fl.** fairly large, 4 cm lg., to 5.5 cm ∅, scented; **Tu.** 1.5 cm lg.; **Pet.** pale yellow; **Fr.** to 1.2 cm ∅, pale green to red or brownish-red; **S.** glossy black.—Chile (Taltal area) (FR 522).

C. multicolor hort.: said to orginate with Ritter but not in Winter's catalogues: Plant broadly spherical, darker leaden-green; **Ri.** 11, tuberculate, with a flattened transverse furrow above the Ar.; **Sp.** black at first, lighter at the base, soon concolorous white, but faintly horn-coloured during the transition; **Rsp.** to c. 10; **Csp.** to 3, somewhat stouter, little longer, they and the Rsp. fairly short; **Fl.** ? An interesting plant which I saw in the collection of van Marle, Netherlands.

C. olivana Ritt. (FR 1443): no description available.

C. pendulina Ritt. **Bo.** becoming cylindric, to 2 m lg., offsetting, single heads to 14 cm ∅, dark green; **R.** napiform; apical **wool** brownish-grey, spiny; **Ri.** 22–19, rather obtuse, thickened around the Ar.; **Ar.** light greyish-brown; **Rsp.** 6–8, 1.5–2.5 cm lg., straight to somewhat curving; **Csp.** 1(–2), similarly, stouter, to 4 cm lg.; **Sp.** all brownish-black to black at first; **Fl.** 3.5 cm lg., 3.5–4 cm ∅, somewhat scented; **Fr.** spherical, 1 cm ∅, light green, brownish above; **S.** glossy black.—Chile (near the coast, Frai Jorge). Plants from Ritter's seed included some pure green individuals tending to a cylindric habit, which were perhaps Pfeiffer's "Echinocactus columnaris"; here the Sp. are brown.

C. pepiniana (K.Sch. non Lem.) Backbg. **Bo.** simple(?), elongating(?), soon matt greyish-green, lighter at first, to 20 cm h., to 10 cm ∅; apical **wool** yellowish-white, with Sp.; **Ri.** 12, straight, ± tuberculate, with chin-like projections;

Ar. fairly large, white; **Rsp.** 7, stiff, to 2 cm lg.; **Csp.** 1, larger, stouter; **Sp.** all dark honey-coloured at first.—Chile.

In cultivation there are more spherical plants, as well as cultivated plants of v. **fiedleriana** (K.Sch.) Backbg. which resemble them and form compact clumps; **R.** a thick taproot; colour of **Bo.** and apical **wool** resembling the type, but conspicuously grey on old plants; **Ri.** 13; **Rsp.** 4–6, to 3 cm lg.; **Fl.** pure yellow.—Chile (N. coastal zone). As far as is known, the **Csp.** is absent in the var.

C. pseudocoquimbana Ritt.—"Taxon", XII: 1, 30, 1963.
Bo. to 30 cm h., to 10 cm ∅, green, forming large clusters; apical **wool** grey; **R.** long, thick, napiform, narrowed above; **Ri.** 10–18, to 15 mm br., scarcely notched; **Ar.** round, grey; **Sp.** pale brown at first, soon greying, mostly straight; **Rsp.** 8–12, acicular, to 2 cm lg.; **Csp.** 3–7, stouter, to 4.5 cm lg.; **Fl.** to 4.5 cm lg., pale sulphur, with red Sc.; **Ov.** pale green; **Fr.** reddish-brown outside, pale green inside; **S.** 1.5 mm lg., with a large hilum.—Chile (N. of Choros Bajos, Dept. La Serena) (FR 1086).
v. **vulgata** Ritt.—l.c.: **Ar.** 8–10 mm ∅ (5–8 mm ∅ in the type); **Rsp.** 7–9; **Csp.** 1–3; **Pet.** 1.7 cm lg. (1.8–3 cm lg. in the type).—Chile (near Coquimbo, on the coast) (FR 230).

C. rarissima Ritt. (FR 1452): no description available.

C. rubriflora Ritt.—"Taxon" XII: 1, 31. 1963.
Bo. to 30 cm lg., to 12 cm ∅, green; **R.** napiform, thick, narrowed above; **Ri.** scarcely notched; **Ar.** to 8 mm ∅; **Sp.** brown, strongly curving; **Rsp.** 2–4 cm lg.; **Csp.** 1(–2–3), 2.5–5 cm lg.; **Fl.** c. 3.5–5.5 cm lg.; **Pet.** carmine in the middle, bordered pale pink or pale yellowish; **style** pale yellow or pale carmine; **Sti.** yellow to orange-yellow; **Fr.** carmine; **S.** 1.4 mm lg., hilum brownish.—N. Chile (S. of Taltal, on sterile coastal lands) (FR 211).

C. rupestris Ritt.—"Taxon" XII: 1, 31. 1963.
Bo. to 40 cm lg., 11 cm ∅, firm, green; **R.** napiform; **Ri.** 13–15, rather obtuse, slightly tuberculate; **Ar.** round, pale brown, to 10 mm ∅; **Sp.** subulate, mostly ± recurved, dark brown at first, becoming grey; **Rsp.** 6–8, 1–2 cm lg.; **Csp.** 1–3, 2–4 cm lg.; **Fl.** 2.5 cm lg., pale yellow; **Fr.** 1.5 cm lg., yellow or reddish-green; **S.** 1 mm lg., hilum white.—N. Chile (Cifunchos, on coastal cliffs) (FR 528).

C. scopulina Ritt.: **C. krainziana v. scopulina** Ritt.

C. serpentisulcata Ritt.
Bo. becoming oblong, offsetting, forming clumps

to 60 cm h., to 1 m ∅, single heads to 15 cm ∅, greyish-green, often washed reddish, seedlings also greyish to dark greyish-green; apical **wool** yellowish-brown; **Ri.** 20–38, ± tuberculate; **Ar.** brownish (white in cultivation); **Rsp.** 6–10, to 2 cm lg.; **Csp.** 1–4, to 3 cm lg., ± stouter; **Sp.** all yellowish-brown to black (variable); **Fl.** to 3 cm lg., scented; **Tu.** with brown or red Sc.; **Pet.** pale yellow; **Fr.** spherical 1.5 cm ∅, reddish-green, orange or red; **S.** glossy black.—Chile (Chañaral). An attractive spec.

C. streptocaulon sensu Ritt.: **C. marginata** (SD.) Br. & R.

C. taltalensis (Werd.) Loos.
Bo. mostly simple, spherical to elongated, to 15 cm h., to 10 cm ∅; apical **wool** light brown; **Ri.** 15–16, ± tuberculate; **Ar.** brownish, soon grey; **Sp.** thin-subulate, spreading, often ± curving, to 4 cm lg., the **Csp.** to 5 cm lg.; **Fl.** c. 2.5 cm lg., yellow.—Chile (Antofagasta). Close to C. humilis, acc. Hutchison; the latter has dark bluish-green plants like the above, but are they the same, or a distinct spec. or var.? I saw such divergent plants which still bore a confusing resemblance, and appeared to be referable to C. taltalensis; these had ± brownish apical wool, the Pet. were lanceolate (not rounded above, as in C. humilis), and the Tub. were more distant. Placed alongside one another, they were readily distinguishable.

C. tenuissima Ritt.—"Taxon" XII: 1, 31. 1963.
Bo. flat or hemispherical, blackish-green to black; **Ri.** 13–16, to 4 mm h.; **Ar.** white; **Sp.** thin-acicular, mostly straight, somewhat finely hairlike; **Rsp.** 8–14, 3–6 mm lg.; **Csp.** 0–1(–2), 4–10 mm lg.; **Fl.** fairly large, numerous, pale yellow, c. 2–2.6 cm lg.; **Ov.** reddish; **Fr.** spherical.—N. Chile (coastal mountains near Antofagasta) (FR 539, 540). The Ov. and Fr. are said to have somewhat hairy axils; separation from Pilocopiapoa would then be disputable. However it appears that in the above Copiapoa spec. these are only rudimentary and a proof of reduction, such as also occurs in Rebutia. Stronger hair-development would require segregation, as for instance in the case of Submatucana. Ritter's treatment is not consistent throughout.

C. tocopillana Ritt. (FR 1057): no description available.

C. totoralensis Ritt.
Bo. flattened-spherical to hemispherical, to 10 cm ∅, offsetting; apical **wool** weak, grey, with Sp.; **R.** large, napiform; **Ri.** 10–15, to 1 cm h., thickened around the Ar., transversely furrowed, with longitudinal furrows which are sinuous in seed-

lings, or straight in habitat plants; **Rsp.** 6–10, to 3 cm lg.; **Csp.** 1–4, 2.5–4 cm lg., straight, stout, scarcely thicker than the Rsp.; **Sp.** dark to deep brown or black; **Fl.** to 4 cm lg.; **Pet.** pale yellow, shortly tapering; **Fr.** subspherical, pale green to reddish-brown; **S.** glossy black.—Chile (Totoral).

C. vallenarensis Ritt.: no description available.

C. variispina Ritt. (FR 1447): no description available.

C. wagenknechtii Ritt. n.nud.: **C. coquimbana v. wagenknechtii** Ritt. (Fig. 72.)

C. wagenknechtii v. armata Ritt. (FR 1461): no description available.

C. wageringeliana hort.: no description available. Bo. flat-spherical, freely offsetting, almost black, with white areolar wool. This is presumed to be a monstrose form of Copiapoa tenuissima Ritt.

Corryocactus Br. & R. (53)

A genus closely related to Erdisia, but the plants are much larger, predominantly shrubs branching from near the base, sometimes with fairly stout and mostly stiffly erect stems, some with conspicuously long spines, the ribs usually more strongly swollen around the areoles to tuberculate, tubercles mostly present. In one species the spines are up to 25 cm long, making them (with the exception of some Neoraimondia species) probably the longest in the Cactaceae. A distinguishing character is the size of the flowers—larger to quite large; in the Peruvian species these are yellow to orange, and in the more slender Bolivian species mostly reddish (salmon-red to purplish-red), sometimes orange-red. The ovary is clearly offset, subspherical or oblong, the flower ± beaker to bellshaped, with the petals expanding ± horizontal. Little is known about the seeds; those of the Peruvian species appear to be blackish, and those of the Bolivian species sometimes black, sometimes dark brown. The fruits are variable in size: in the large Peruvian species sometimes almost the size of an apple, mostly subspherical and spiny, although the spines vary greatly in strength and length: in some species they are fairly short, thin and flexible (in C. tarijensis Card. even bristly and thin); in the larger species they are mostly longer. All the species are hardy and quite vigorous-growing, only a few appearing to be slow-growing.—Distribution: most come from higher altitudes, from Central Peru to S. Bolivia; 2 spec. from lower altitudes in N. Chile. [(R).]

C. apurimacensis (FR 1298): no description available.

C. ayacuchoensis Rauh & Backbg.
Bo. to 1 m h., to 10 cm $\emptyset$, fresh green; **Ri.** 6; **Rsp.** 9–10; **Csp.** 3, to 3.5 cm lg.; **Sp.** reddish-brown, the radials mostly lighter; **Fl.** ?—Peru (dry region near Ayacucho, 2700 m).
v. **leucacanthus** Rauh & Backbg. has **shoots** to only 8 cm $\emptyset$; **Sp.** whitish or light-coloured, at first often flecked; **Rsp.** and **Csp.** to 18, scarcely differentiated, to 2.5 cm lg.

C. ayopayanus Card.
Bo. branching from the base, to 1.5 m h., dark green; **St.** to 3.5 cm $\emptyset$; **Ri.** 4–5, tuberculate, 1 cm h.; **Ar.** grey; **Sp.** 10–13, 0.5–5 cm lg., centrals scarcely distinguishable, the longest subulate, to 5 cm lg.; **Fl.** broadly funnelform, 6 cm lg., 7 cm $\emptyset$, salmon-red; **style** pink; **Fr.** soft, 3 cm $\emptyset$, with thin, brownish to white Sp.; **S.** dark brown.—Bolivia (Prov. Ayopaya, Tiquirpaya, 2760 m).

C. brachypetalus (Vpl.) Br. & R.
Bo. to 4 m h., green, branches ascending; **Ri.** 7–8, ± tuberculately swollen; **Sp.** black at first, reddish or brown below, to 20, unequal, mostly under 1 cm lg., the longest 10–16 cm lg., sometimes contorted and compressed; **Fl.** to 6 cm $\emptyset$, deep orange; **Fr.** to 7 cm $\emptyset$, green, juicy, edible, with longer Sp.—Peru (near Mollendo). (Fig. 73.)

C. brevispinus Rauh & Backbg.
Bo. ascending; **Ri.** c. 7, strongly tuberculate, transversely notched; **Sp.** mostly pointing downwards, ± subulate, to c. 3 cm lg., some quite short; **Fl.** yellowish-orange; **Fr.** quite large, spherical, with many relatively shortly spined Ar., green, pulp white; **S.** numerous, black.—Peru (volcano of Coropuna).

C. brevistylus (K.Sch.) Br. & R. (T.)
Bo. robust, to 3 m h., branching from the base; **St.** thick, to 15 cm $\emptyset$; **Ri.** 6–7, quite high and broad at the base; **Ar.** large, round, shortly woolly; **Sp.** c. 15, some under 1 cm lg., others 3 cm lg., still others over 24 cm lg.; **Fl.** yellow, to 10 cm br.; **Ov.** with brown wool, white Br and short Sp.; **Fr.** spherical, juicy, spiny.—Peru (in the S., 2000 m).

C. chachapoyensis Ochoa & Backbg.
Bo. forming a lax shrub to 80 cm lg.; **branches** to 2 cm $\emptyset$; **Ri.** c. 12; **Sp.** several, yellowish, 1 central stouter and longer; **Fl.** yellow, only 2 cm lg. and br.—N. Peru (Amazonas, Chachapoyas-Conila).

C. charazanensis Card.
Bo. to 2 m h., green; **Ri.** 4–5, 1 cm h.; **Ar.** grey; **Sp.**

c. 11, the shortest 5 mm lg., the medium-long ones 1.5 cm lg., the longest 2.5 cm lg., subulate, whitish; **Fl.** few, 6 cm lg., salmon-pink; **Ov.** bristly, with dark felt; **Fr.** 3–5 cm $\emptyset$, with thin Sp. and dark brown felt; **S.** dark brown, 1–2 mm lg.—Bolivia (Dept. La Paz, Charazani, 3000m).

C. heteracanthus Backbg.
Bo. to 2 m h., branching from the base; **branches** to 20 cm $\emptyset$; **Ri.** 8–9, only slightly tuberculate; **Sp.** to c. 10, centrals scarcely distinguishable, often fewer, sometimes fairly short, 2(–3) much longer, to 5 cm lg., pointing upwards or downwards; **Fl.** ?—Peru (Ayacucho).

C. krausii Backbg.
Bo. tree-like, dense and broad; **branches** erect; **Ri.** 8–10, rounded, not tuberculate; **Sp.** unequal, c. 4 shorter, 1–2 longer, scarcely distinguishable as centrals, the longest one to over 8 cm lg.; **Fl.** 5–6 cm lg., perianth funnelform, yellow; **Pet.** crowded; **Ov.** oblong, with short Sp. and crinkly H.—Chile (Mamina).

C. melanotrichus (K.Sch.) Br. & R.
Bo. forming dense shrubs, to over 1.2 m h.; **branches** yellowish-green, to 6 cm $\emptyset$; **Ri.** 7–9, rounded; **Ar.** 3 mm br.; **Sp.** 10–11, unequal, 7 mm–2 cm lg., 1–3 centrals, scarcely differentiated, one longest Sp. to 3 cm lg., the upper ones light brown with dark annular stripes, the lower ones $\pm$ grey; **Fl.** 5 cm lg., 6 cm br., not very numerous, with short brown H.; **Ov.** with whitish Sp. 3 mm lg.; **Pet.** purplish-red; **Fr.** spherical, 4–8 cm $\emptyset$, with Sp. 1 cm lg.; **S.** black.—Bolivia (La Paz, Miraflores, 3300 m). Britton & Rose erroneously state the petal-colour to be "yellow" (based on K. Schumann's dried specimens).
   v. **caulescens** Card. grows to 1.5 m h.; **Sp.** 15–16, pale yellowish, 1–7 cm lg.; **Csp.** mostly only 1(–3), all Sp. $\pm$ thickened below, dark; **Fl.** to 6 cm lg. and br., salmon-red. **Ri.** somewhat more tuberculate than in the type.—Bolivia (La Paz to Cochabamba, Cerro de Arani).

C. otuyensis Card.—"Cactus", 18: 78, 87–88. 1963.
Bo. to 2 m lg., 5 cm $\emptyset$, dark green; **Ri.** 8, 1 cm h.; **Ar.** 2 cm apart; **Sp.** 15–18, acicular or stouter, to 4 cm lg., white or pale brown; **Fl.** bellshaped, subapical, purple, with white H. and brown Br., c. 5.5 cm $\emptyset$; **Fil.** dark purple; **Ov.** with grey felt and white Br.; **Fr.** spherical, light green, 3–5 cm $\emptyset$, with grey and brown H., brownish Br. and fine, yellow and brown Sp.; **pulp** green; **S.** 1.5 mm lg., pitted, glossy black.—Bolivia (Dept. Potosi, near Otuyo, 3600 m).

C. pachycladus Rauh & Backbg.
Bo. to 1.5 m h.; **branches** thick, erect; **Ri.** 6, light green; **Sp.** to 20 cm lg., the longest ones pointing downwards, sometimes only 2–3 longer ones and several which are rather short, all reddish-brown at first.—Peru (Puquio valley, 3500 m). Lower-growing than C. brevistylus, with fewer spines.

C. perezianus Card.
Bo. to 1.2 m h., green; **branches** to only 7 cm $\emptyset$; **Ri.** 8–9; **Ar.** brown or grey; **Sp.** 16–18, 1–6 cm lg., $\pm$ interlacing, yellowish; **Fl.** urn-shaped to fun-nelform, 5–6 cm lg., lilac-pink; **Fil.** purple; **style** whitish-yellow; **Fr.** spherical, 4 cm $\emptyset$; **S.** 1.2 mm lg., matt black.—Bolivia (Prov. Loaiza, Summitas Luribay, 2800 m).

C. pulquinensis Card.
Bo. to 4 m h., sometimes clambering, little branching; **St.** glossy dark green, to 4 cm $\emptyset$; **Ri.** 4–5, to 1.5 cm h., rather obtuse, notched; **Ar.** grey or black; **Sp.** 3–7, centrals scarcely differentiated, sometimes one more distinctly so, acicular to $\pm$ subulate, 5 mm–2 cm lg., $\pm$ compressed, $\pm$ recurved, whitish; **Fl.** to 7.5 cm lg., reddish-orange, more dark orange or golden-yellow inside.—Bolivia (Dept. Santa Cruz, Pulquina-Saipina, 1500 m).

C. puquiensis Rauh & Backbg.
Bo. to 5 m h.; **branches** vivid green, to 20 cm $\emptyset$, erect; **Ri.** mostly 8; **Rsp.** to 15, to 3 cm lg.; **Csp.** mostly 1, to 20 cm lg., grey; **Fl.** 6 cm $\emptyset$, yellow, expanding widely; **Fr.** yellowish-green, to 10 cm $\emptyset$, with short Sp.—Peru (volcano Chachani, 3000 m).

C. tarijensis Card.
Bo. to 60 cm h.; **branches** $\pm$ curving, greyish-green, to 4.5 cm $\emptyset$; **Ri.** 7, 1.5 cm h.; **Ar.** grey; **Sp.** 13, stout, $\pm$ interlacing, 1–5 cm lg., grey, brown-tipped, thickened at the base; **Fl.** 3–4 cm lg., 4 cm $\emptyset$, orange-red; **Ov.** spherical, with brown-felted Ar., several Br. and white H.; **Fr.** spherical, to 2 cm $\emptyset$, with dark brown Sp. and Br.; **S.** brown.—Bolivia (Tarija, near Agua de Toro, 2800 m).

Corynopuntia Knuth (13)

The species of this genus made up Britton & Rose's Series "Clavatae". They are to be regarded as an extreme stage of reduction of Cylindropuntia, the shoots mostly clavate, rather small, rarely short-cylindric, i.e. somewhat more elongated or not conspicuously clavate, but all forming $\pm$ dense groups or clumps; in the more elongated species the shoots may be to c. 20–30 cm long but slender, the exception being the more stoutly-stemmed C. invicta. Fruits said to be dry. In Corynopuntia, as in Cylindropuntia, there is a reduction in the sheaths, but here it is more striking; sometimes they are absent, in other cases rudiments can be seen at the spine-tips, or they are visible only under a lens. Differentiation is based principally on the form of the stem-segments, and whether the central spines are flattened, or thickened at the base. Not very floriferous in cultivation. Micropuntia Dast. is probably better referred elsewhere.—Distribution: From USA to Baja California and N. Mexico (to Zacatecas). [(R).]

C. agglomerata (Berg.) Knuth
Bo. forming dense groups; **R.** spindle-shaped and tuberous; **St.** ovoid or obovoid, to 4 cm lg., greyish-green; **Ar.** whitish-grey, somewhat floccose; **Glo.** yellowish-white; **Rsp.** 6–7, erect, 1–4 mm lg., whitish; **Csp.** 4–5, thickened at the base and yellowish there, all terete, whitish-grey, the 2 lower ones sharply recurved, 1–1.5 cm lg., upper Ar. with one acicular yellowish Csp. c. 3 cm lg.; **Fl.** purple; **Ov.** spiny.—Mexico (Coahuila).

C. bulbispina (Eng.) Knuth
Bo. forming low, broad mats to 1.2 m br.; **St.** laxer in cultivation, ovoid, to 2.5 cm lg., to 1.2 cm $\varnothing$; **Rsp.** 8–12, 3–6 mm lg.; **Csp.** 4, stouter, 8–12 mm lg., terete, thickened at the base, brown; **Fl.** yellow; **Sep.** sometimes reddish-tipped; **Fil.** brownish; **style** and **Sti.** cream.—Mexico (Coahuila to (?) Durango).

C. clavata (Eng.) Knuth (T.)
Bo. forming mats to 2 m br., 15 cm h.; **St.** 3–7 cm lg., greyish to darker green, clavate or obovoid; **Glo.** yellow, numerous; **Rsp.** c. 10 at first, later more numerous; **Csp.** 4–8, the longest one to to c. 3 cm lg., dagger-shaped, flattened, not thickened at the base; **Sp.** pale, ± rough; **Fl.** to 4 cm lg., yellow; **Fr.** to 5 cm lg.—USA (New Mexico).

C. clavigera Y. Ito: **C. clavata** (Eng.) Knuth.

C. dumetorum (Berg.) Knuth
Bo. in groups to 50 cm h.; **St.** cylindric, little tuberculate, ± greyish-green, with fine velvety H. (unique to this spec.!); **Ar.** white, with several H.; **Sp.** unequal, 1 to 1.5 cm lg., the remainder shorter, yellowish-brown, often with darker bands; **Glo.** whitish.—Mexico (Tamaulipas, 700 m).

C. grahamii (Eng.) Knuth
Bo. forming mats, in part very low-growing; **St.** clavate, light green, to 5 cm lg.; **Tub.** large, oblong; **Glo.** numerous, white, later brown; **Sp.** 8–15, ± rough, the more central ones ± flattened, ± 4-angled, not thickened at the base, at most becoming broader there, white at first, then reddish; **Fl.** 5 cm

br., yellow; **bud** with dense, longer, erect Glo.; **Fr.** with densely bristly Ar. and several Sp.; **S.** to 5.5 mm $\varnothing$.—USA (W. Texas, New Mexico) to neighbouring N. Mexico. Flowers have also been seen to develop from old Fr.

C. invicta (Brand.) Knuth
Bo. forming colonies to 2 m br. and 50 cm h.; **St.** dark green, long and stout for the G.; **Tub.** to 4 cm lg.; **Ar.** white; **Glo.** white, sparse; **Rsp.** 6–10; **Csp.** 10–12, strongly 4-sided, not thickened at the base, to 3.5 cm lg., carmine at the base, brown-tipped, later grey; **Fl.** 5 cm $\varnothing$; **Ov.** with reddish Sp.—Mexico (Central Baja California, near S. Juanico).

C. moelleri (Berg.) Knuth
Bo. forming mats; **St.** resembling those of C. clavata but shorter and thinner; **Tub.** more projecting, more oblong, to 1.5 cm lg., c. 1 cm br.; **Rsp.** 7–8, stiffer, also others more like Glo., 3 curving strongly downwards; **Csp.** 1 ± porrect, more brownish, also several whitish ones, 3 of them mostly erect, the lower ones pointing downwards, the longest one to 1.6 cm lg.; **Sp.** all thickened at the base; **Fl.** yellow; **Fil.** yellow; **style** and **Sti.** cream.—Mexico (Coahuila).

C. planibulbispina Backbg.
Bo. forming denser groups; **St.** deep green, to c. 5 cm lg., 2.5 cm $\varnothing$, later to c. 7 cm lg. and over 3 cm $\varnothing$, becoming greyish-green; **Tub.** plump, to 1.5 cm lg.; **L.** reddish, 5 mm lg.; **Glo.** later light straw-coloured; **Sp.** pink at first, then reddish-brown, darker above, finally grey; **Rsp.** to c. 12, thin, light; **Csp.** mostly to c. 6, one porrect, all ± compressed, the longest one more flattened, somewhat rough, later dirty greyish-brown, thickened at the base; **Fl.** c. 8 cm $\varnothing$, yellow, throat greenish; **buds** lacking long Glo-Br.; **Fil.** emerald-green below, yellowish above; **Fr.** to c. 3.5 cm lg., dry, ± conical, with distant, short, whitish tufts of Glo.—Origin not known. (Fig. 74.) Plants have been observed with 2–3 Fl. simultaneously from one Ar. (Schattat).

C. pulchella (Eng.) Knuth
Bo. forming mats to 60 cm br., to 20 cm h.; **St.** to 6 cm lg., slender-cylindric to clavate, tuberculate, reddish; **Glo.** yellow, later numerous, to 1.2 cm lg.; **Sp.** 10–16, thin, reddish, to 6 cm lg., ± flattened, not thickened at the base; **Fl.** 5 cm lg., purple; **Fr.** 2.5 cm lg., with white-woolly Ar. and red Glo., to 1.2 cm lg.; **S.** 4 mm lg.—USA (Nevada, Arizona).

C. reflexispina (I. L. Wigg. & Roll.) Backbg.
Bo. forming low colonies; said to resemble C. bulbispina and C. grahamii, but differentiated by its strongly spiny **Fr.** No further data available.—Mexico (Sonora, W. of Arrieros).

C. schottii (Eng.) Knuth
Bo. forming low mats to 3 m br.; **St.** ascending, clavate, readily detached, to 7 cm lg., to 2 cm ∅, strongly tuberculate; **Rsp.** 6–8; **Csp.** 4 or more, to 6 cm lg., white at first, flattened, not angular, rough, not thickened at the base, sheath present; **Fl.** 4 cm lg., yellow.—USA (S. and W. Texas), N. Mexico.

C. stanlyi (Engl.) Knuth
Bo. forming mats to 3 m br., to 30 cm h.; **St.** erect, clavate, to 15 cm lg.; **Tub.** prominent, laterally compressed, to 4 cm lg.; **Ar.** white; **Sp.** numerous, 3.5–6 cm lg., whitish to reddish-brown, the larger ones strongly flattened, not angular, not thickened at the base; **Fl.** 6 cm br., light yellow; **style** and **Fil.** cream; **Fr.** yellow, to 6 cm lg., very spiny; **S.** to 6.5 mm lg.—USA (SW. New Mexico to E. Arizona), N. Mexico.
   v. **kunzei** (Rose) Backbg.: **Tub.** to only 2.5 cm lg.; **Fr.** somewhat shorter;
   v. **parishii** (Orc.) Backbg.: **St.** small-clavate, to 7.5 cm lg.; **Csp.** 1, acutely angled; **Fr.** with long yellow Glo.;
   v. **wrightiana** (Baxt.) Backbg.: **St.** cylindric, to 20 cm lg.; **Tub.** to 2.5 cm lg.; **Sp.** 14–20, one dagger-like **Csp.** to 3 cm lg. as well as 5–6 ± central Sp. to 2.8 cm lg.

C. stellata hort.
Bo. resembling C. planibulbispina, greyish-green; **Tub.** fairly plump and rounded; **L.** reddish; **Sp.** grey, 9–10, mostly ± flattened (compressed); 1–2 **Csp.** longest, blackish; **Glo.** pale yellow; **Fl.** rather large, light yellow; **Sep.** ± reddish dorsally above.—Origin? (Collection Rivière No. 7953).

C. vilis (Rose) Knuth
Bo. forming mats to 20 cm h.; **St.** rounded, 4–5 cm lg., bluish-green, tuberculate, to c. 1.5 cm ∅; **Rsp.** spreading, thin, whitish, to 12 mm lg., the upper ones interspersed with similar Glo.; **Csp.** to 4, 2.5–3 cm lg., reddish-brown, white-tipped, terete, ± rough, with short sheath-remains; **Fl.** 4 cm lg., glossy purple; **Fil.** light yellow, green below; **style** white; **Sti.** yellow; **Fr.** pale green, becoming black, to 3 cm lg., somewhat dry; **S.** white, large.—Mexico (Zacatecas).
   v. **bernhardinii** (Hildm.) Backbg.: **Rsp.** only 3–4, whitish; **Csp.** 1, subulate, brownish above, white below.
   Grown in less intense light, the St. become thin, with very fine Sp. and crowded, conspicuously white Ar.; L. minute, reddish.

Coryphantha (Eng.) Lem. (219)

The most important diagnostic characters of the genus are the following: flowers borne centrally; tubercles furrowed throughout their length; fruits ± greenish, with watery sap; seeds ± brownish, rather soft. Flower and fruit glabrous. All hitherto known species are alike in possessing these characters. It is therefore inappropriate to segregate species with ciliate outer perianth segments and include them as a Subgenus of Escobaria, where the fruits are ± red and the seeds black; in any event, ciliate features do not constitute a valid diagnostic character. However these species can well be included in the first of the two Subgenera, based on the degree of reduction of fruit-scales:

SG.1: Neocoryphantha Backbg.: Ovary and fruit ± with some scales, either above or laterally; with or without glands;

SG.2: Coryphantha: Ovary and fruit always naked.

SG.1 includes species with entire petals, and others where they are ciliate.
In SG.2, two Series can be distinguished:
Series 1: Sulcolanatae Br. & R. (Aulacothelae Lem.): With no glands in the furrow or axil;
Series 2: Recurvatae Br. & R. (Glanduliferae SD.): With glands in the furrow or axil.

The figures following the specific name indicate the appropriate Subgenus and, in the case of SG.2, the Series as well. Plants of the genus are, in general, not at all difficult but if grafted they look much better, grow faster and flower more freely. The genus deserves to be much better represented in collections than it is now, given the flowers which can be white or yellow or red, some of them very large, sometimes with a red centre, while the spination is noticeable and often attractive; many of the attractive species are suitable for raising commercially.—Distribution: from British Columbia and S. Canada, throughout USA, to S. Mexico (Oaxaca); only one species has been found up to now in Baja California. [(R). (G).]

C. aggregata (Eng.) Br. & R.: **C. vivipara** v. **aggregata** (Eng.) Marsh.

C. albicolumnaris (Herst.) D. Zimmerm. (Escobaria Hest.)
Bo. shortly columnar, similar to C. orcuttii; **Sp.** numerous, white, brittle; **Fl.** faded reddish-white with a pink M.-line, scarcely opening; **Fr.** green; **S.** fairly large, reddish-brown.—USA (Texas, Big Bend Region, NW. of Terlingua).

C. altamiranoi Frič: probably a form of **C. radians** (DC.) Br. & R.

C. alversonii (Coult.) Orc. (1)
Bo. elongated, to 20 cm h., to 10 cm ∅, laxly

branching, up to 12 heads; **Sp.** crowded, light, the centrals blackish above or to midway; **Rsp.** to 35, longer than the Csp.; **Csp.** to 14, white below, subulate; **Fl.** 3 cm lg., purplish-pink.—USA (SE. California).

v. **exaltissima** Wieg. & Backbg. forms compacter groups to over 30 cm br.; individual **St.** more spherical, sometimes to 20 cm ⌀; **Tub.** longer (short and thick in the type), lax, ± cylindric; **Sp.** more densely interlacing, the centrals brown in the upper half; **Fl.** purple.

C. andreae J. A. Purp. & Böd. (2:1)
Bo. compressed-spherical, solitary, to 9 cm ⌀, deep green; **crown** strongly woolly; **Tub.** in Isp. 5:8, to 2.5 cm br., 2 cm h.; **Ar.** elliptic; **Rsp.** to c. 10, to 1.2 cm lg., stoutly acicular, matt greyish-yellow, brown-tipped; **Csp.** 5–7, strongly curving, greyish-yellow, brownish-tipped, the one downwardly directed Sp. to 2.5 cm lg.; **Fl.** 5–6 cm ⌀; **Pet.** narrow-lanceolate, light yellow; **Fr.** 1.5 cm lg.— Mexico (Veracruz, Perote).

C. arizonica (Eng.) Br. & R.: **C. vivipara v. arizonica** (Eng.) Marsh.

C. asterias (Cels) Böd. (2:2)
Bo. solitary, spherical to cylindric, dark green; **Tub.** plump, tip oblique; **Gl.** red with a white ring; **Rsp.** 9, radiating, projecting; **Csp.** 1(–2), stout, hooked at the tip, thickened at the base, pale brown or yellowish; **Fl.** light pink.—Mexico (Guanajuato).

C. aulacothele Lem.: probably only a form of **C. octacantha** (DC.) Br. & R.

C. bergeriana Böd. (2:2)
Bo. solitary, ± clavate, to 12 cm h., 6 cm ⌀, dark leaf-green; **Tub.** in Isp. 8:13, conical, to 1.4 cm lg.; **Gl.** 1–2, red, surrounded by white wool; **Ar.** slightly woolly; **Rsp.** 18–20, lower ones to 1 cm lg., upper ones 6–8, to 1.5 cm lg., greyish-whitish, dark-tipped; **Csp.** 4, thin-subulate, yellowish to horn-coloured, upper ones 1.2 cm lg., lower ones to 2 cm lg.; **Fl.** 4 cm lg., 7 cm ⌀, yellow; **Fr.** large, oblong, light green.—Mexico (Nuevo León).

C. borwigii J. A. Purp. (2:1)
Bo. to 10 cm h., 5–7 cm ⌀, greyish-green; **Tub.** ± rhombic; **Sp.** over 10, upper Rsp. in erect groups; **Csp.** 3, light brownish-grey, somewhat stouter; **Fl.** 6 cm lg., yellow, throat red.—Mexico (Coahuila and/or Tamaulipas).

C. bumamma (Ehrenbg.) Br. & R. (2:1)
Bo. spherical to depressed; **Tub.** very large, rounded above, bluish-green; **Ax.** strongly woolly at first; **Sp.** 5–8, subulate, greyish-brown, ±

recurved, 2 cm lg. or more; **Csp.** 0; **Fl.** yellow, 5–6 cm ⌀; **Pet.** narrowly oblong, rather obtuse.— Mexico (Morelos, Guerrero).

C. calipensis H. Bravo—Cactac. y Suc. Mex., IX: 4, 79–80. 1964 (2:1).
Bo. rounded, offsetting, greyish to olive-green, with a woolly crown; **Tub.** imbricate, Isp. 5:8, large, curved upwards, 3 cm lg. and br., rhombic at the base; **Ax.** woolly; **Ar.** white, 2 mm br., circular; **Rsp.** 10–16, 1–1.5 cm lg., 5–7 of these forming an upwardly directed cluster above, the remainder radiating around the Ar.; **Csp.** 1, rather stouter, 1.5 cm lg., somewhat curving, yellow below, blackish-brown above, later grey with a yellowish tip bent somewhat outwards; **Fl.** 5.5 cm lg., c. 6 cm ⌀; outer **Sep.** brownish-green, inner ones yellowish with a reddish-brown M.-line; **Pet.** narrow, margins entire but denticulate above, yellow; **Fil.** reddish; **style** creamy yellow; **Sti.** 8, light yellowish-green; **Fr.** ?—Mexico (Puebla, Calipan near Tehuacan, at 2000 m). Resembles C. cornifera.

C. calochlora Böd. (2:1)
Bo. offsetting from the base, depressed, blackish-green; **Tub.** conical-ovoid; **Ar.** woolly at first, **Ax.** glabrous; **Sp.** 12–15, very thin, straight, pure white, 1.5 cm lg., 3–5 of these often flattened above; **Fl.** whitish-cream; **Pet.** narrow.—Mexico.

C. chlorantha Eng. (1)
Bo. cylindric, to 25 cm h., to 8 cm ⌀; **Tub.** crowded, concealed by the Sp.; **Rsp.** grey; **Csp.** 4–9, thin, to 2.5 cm lg., pink at first, or tipped red or brown; **Fl.** c. 3.5 cm ⌀, yellowish or greenish-yellow; **Pet.** slender, acute; **Fr.** 2.5 cm lg., green, with 5–6 small Sc. above.—USA (S. Utah, W. Arizona and Central Nevada to SE. California).

v. **deserti** (Eng.) Backbg.: distinguished mainly by having only 3–5 **Csp.** which are white, brown-tipped; **Fl.** 2.5 cm ⌀, straw-coloured. This plant forms dense clusters, individual heads to 12.5 cm h. and to 7.5 cm ⌀. Some specimens have reddish-tipped Sp. This var. somewhat resembles C. alversonii and like the latter it is one of the finest of the G., particularly because of the dense spination.

C. clava (Pfeiff.) Lem. (2:2)
Bo. eventually offsetting; **St.** columnar to ± clavate, to over 30 cm h. and to 10 cm ⌀, bluish or greyish-green; **Tub.** in Isp. 8:13, 1.5 cm h., conical, obliquely truncated; **Gl.** red; **Rsp.** (7–)8–10 or more, thin-subulate, pungent, the longest lower one to 1.4 cm lg.; **Csp.** (1–)3–4, to 2 cm lg.; **Sp.** chestnut, later honey-coloured, darker at the base; **Fl.** 5 cm lg., 4 cm ⌀, glossy, yellow.—Mexico (Hidalgo).

114

v. **schlechtendalii** (Ehrenbg.) Heinr.: distinguished by the weaker **Sp.** and yellow **Gl.**

C. clavata (Scheidw.) Backbg. (1)
Bo. cylindric to clavate, **crown** very woolly; **R.** napiform, whitish; **St.** dark leek-green, sometimes flushed reddish, to 7 cm $\emptyset$; **Tub.** in Isp. 5:8, 8:13, ± oblique-conical, to 2 cm lg.; **Gl.** 1–2, red; **Ar.** and **Ax.** white; **Rsp.** to c. 9, subulate, brownish at first, red (always?) at the base, 8–15 mm lg.; **Csp.** 0–1, yellowish to brown, often dark-banded above; **Fl.** to 5 cm lg., 4 cm $\emptyset$; **Pet.** to 7 mm br.; **Ov.** 1.5 cm lg.; **S.** mahogony-brown, curving pear-shaped, distinctly tessellate.—Mexico (Hidalgo and adjacent areas of the States Querétaro and Mexico). Sep. only rarely ± ciliate.

v. **ancistracantha** (Lem.) Heinr. has a hooked **Csp.**;

v. **radicantissima** (Quehl) Heinr.: **Bo.** more spherical, more rarely elongated, little offsetting; **R.** carrot-like, to 1 cm lg., yellowish(!); **Tub.** in Isp. 8:13, ascending, conical; **Ar.** and **crown** weakly woolly; **Fl.** 2–2.5 cm lg., 1.8–2.5 cm $\emptyset$; **Pet.** fewer than in the type, yellow, they and the Sep. sometimes with a reddish M.-line; **Sep.** entire; **S..** lighter brown than in v. clavata, indistinctly tessellate.—Mexico (State Guanajuato and SW. San Luis Potosi).
Earlier descriptions have no data on locality. Even Quehl could give no origin for v. radicantissima, but with its small flowers and yellowish roots the habitats can be identified in the light of present knowledge.
Acc. Buchenau, who made a close study of the group, the type-species does not come from S. Luis Potosi; in his view, Schumann's stated locality under "Mam. raphidacantha"—near Jaral—is incorrect, and it should be Guanajuato. Schumann may have been thinking of v. radicantissima. Accordingly the plants with whitish roots and mostly elongated bodies must be regarded as the type, with larger flowers and longer tubercles. Taller plants from S. Luis Potosi, with longer Csp., appear to be intermediate between v. radicantissima and v. clavata; accordingly I could not accept any segregation.
Acc. Buchenau, the glands of C. clavata are whitish-yellow in juveniles (seen in Hidalgo). C. exsudans (Zucc.) Lem. may therefore be identical with v. clavata.

C. columnaris Lahm. (1?)
Bo. solitary, columnar, to 17 cm h., to 6 cm $\emptyset$; **Tub.** slender, to 1.2 cm lg.; **Rsp.** 10–18, 5–12 mm lg., white, brown-tipped; **Csp.** 4, light brown, one projecting, longer; **Fl.** 6.5 cm lg., purple; **Fr.** pale green.—USA (Oklahoma, near Altus; rare).

C. compacta compacta (Eng.) Br. & R. (2:1)
Bo. solitary, depressed-spherical, to 6 cm h., to 5–8 cm $\emptyset$; **Tub.** in Isp. 13:21; **Rsp.** 14–16, stiff, appressed, 1–2 cm lg., whitish; **Csp.** mostly absent; **Fl.** only 2 cm lg. and br., yellow.—Mexico (Chihuahua, Cosihuiriachi).

C. conimamma (Lke.) Berg. (2:1)
Bo. spherical to ellipsoid, to 10 cm $\emptyset$, glossy dark green; **crown** very woolly; **Tub.** in Isp. 5:8, to 1.5 cm lg., stout-conical; **Rsp.** 6–9, subulate, to 12 mm lg.; **Csp.** 3–4, bent, to 2.2 cm lg.; **Fl.** 5 cm lg., greenish-yellow, shortly and broadly funnelform.—Mexico.

C. connivens Br. & R. (2:1)
Bo. spherical to depressed-spherical, to 10 cm $\emptyset$; **crown** weakly woolly; **Rsp.** 8–10, thin, in the upper part of the Ar., clustered, upwardly directed, horn-coloured and black-tipped, 5–6 subulate Sp. pointing down or sideways, ± horn-coloured or somewhat darker; **Fl.** yellow, to 7 cm $\emptyset$.—Mexico (near the capital city).

C. cornifera (DC.) Lem. (2:1)
Bo. mostly solitary, to 12 cm h., spherical to short-cylindric, pale to greyish-green; **Tub.** in Isp. 5:8, to 2.5 cm lg., ± rhombic; **Ax.** white; **Ar.** more strongly white-woolly at first, elliptic; **Rsp.** 7–9, to 9 mm lg., waxy yellow; **Csp.** 0–1, stout, to 15 mm lg., ± curving, blackish above, brown below; **Fl.** to 6 cm lg., to 5 cm $\emptyset$, lemon-yellow; **Fil.** pinkish-red, yellow above.—Mexico (Hidalgo, around Ixmiquilpan). Description taken from K. Schumann; his Fig. 81 (Gesamtbschrbg.) shows no tufted Rsp. Rümpler's description is at variance: he gives 20 **Rsp.**, upper ones clustered, **Csp.** to 3; while acc. Britton & Rose there are 16–17 **Rsp.** and the **Fl.** is 7 cm $\emptyset$, reddish. It appears probable that this is a complex in which a further 1–2 var. should be segregated.
Buchenau found, near Oaxaca, a plant with c. 12 **Rsp.**, the upper ones tufted, finer; **Csp.** 1, 1 cm lg.; **Fl.** c. 3.5 cm lg., to 6 cm $\emptyset$; **Sep.** yellow with a brown M.-line; **Pet.** narrow-lanceolate, fringed above, acuminate, yellow; **Fil.** deep red; **Sti.** pale green. This appears to be the plant described by H. Bravo as C. calipensis, a spec. which may be close to that of Rümpler's description ("upper Rsp. clustered"). It is not clear to which of the older descriptions De Candolle's name applies. C. pseudoradians H. Bravo clearly belongs to this complex, but the **Tub.** are in 13 spirals.

C. cornuta (Hildm.) Berg. (2:1)
Bo. solitary, depressed-spherical to hemispherical, to 5 cm h., to 8 cm $\emptyset$; **crown** freely woolly; **Tub.** greyish-green, in Isp. 5:8, ± imbricate, to 1.7 cm lg.

and br.; **Ar.** dirty yellowish-white; **Rsp.** 5–7, radiating, compressed, the upper ones 4–6 mm lg., the lower ones 6–8 mm lg., whitish, often horn-coloured, tips brownish-black; **Csp.** 1, stouter, to 8 mm lg., bent downwards; **Fl.** yellow, fading to pink.—Mexico.

C. daimonoceras (Lem.) Lem.(2:1)
Bo. broadly spherical, greyish-green; **Tub.** curved above, stout; **Rsp.** to 10 and more, grey, sometimes yellow at the base, upper ones clustered; **Csp.** to 3–5, sometimes 4, cruciform, c. 1 cm lg., dirty horn-coloured, dark above, ± curving; **Fl.** ?—Mexico (Sierra de la Paila).

C. delaetiana (Quehl) Berg. (2:1)
Bo. eventually forming mats, single heads to 8 cm h., to 5 cm ∅, fresh green, becoming leek-green; **Tub.** 1 cm lg., ± rhombic; **Ar.** circular, woolly only at first; **Rsp.** to c. 15, thin; **Csp.** 1, slightly curving, rather stouter, to 2 cm lg., black, light at the base, the Rsp. only ± dark-tipped; **Fl.** yellow.—Mexico (Coahuila).

C. densispina Werd. (2:1)
Bo. ovoid; **Tub.** thick-conical at first, later rhombic below; **Ax.** glabrous; **Rsp.** to 25 in a circle, stout-acicular, to 2 cm lg., greyish-white; **Csp.** 4, more stoutly subulate, darker, slightly curving, to c. 2 cm lg.; **Fl.** pure yellow, 5 cm ∅.—Mexico (Coahuila, San Pedro).

C. deserti (Eng.) Br. & R.: **C. chlorantha** v. **deserti** (Eng.) Backbg.

C. difficilis (Quehl) Berg. (2:1)
Bo. solitary, flat-spherical, greyish-green to bluish-greyish-green, to 6 cm h., to 8 cm ∅; **crown** weakly woolly; **Tub.** rhombic, 2.5 cm br., imbricate; **Ax.** weakly woolly, they and the **Ar.** soon glabrous; **Rsp.** 12–14, upper ones to 2 cm lg., lower ones to 1 cm lg., hyaline, sometimes brown-tipped; **Csp.** 4, 3 of these stouter than the Rsp., reddish to horn-coloured, darker or black, to c. 2 cm lg., 3 bent downwards; **Fl.** 4–5 cm ∅, pure yellow.—Mexico (Coahuila).
Similar but stouter-stemmed plants, without conspicuous axillary wool at the St.-apex (un-named?) also go under this name.

C. durangensis (Rge.) Br. & R. (2:1)
Bo. solitary or forming small groups, short-cylindric, single heads to c. 10 cm lg., greyish-green; **Tub.** in Isp. 5:8, imbricate; **Ax.** very woolly at first; **Rsp.** 6–8, acicular, light, spreading, to 1 cm lg.; **Csp.** 1, black at first; all **Sp.** later light grey; **Fl.** 2 cm lg., to 4 cm ∅, cream to pale lemon-yellow.—Mexico (Durango).

C. echinoidea (Quehl) Br. & R. (2:2)
Bo. solitary, spherical or ± broadly spherical, to 6 cm ∅, dark greyish-green, entirely enveloped by the Sp.; **Tub.** 1.5 cm h.; **Gl.** 1–3, grey (or red?); **Ar.** woolly at first; **Rsp.** 20–25, in 2 R., one above the other, to 1.5 cm lg., white, dark-tipped; **Csp.** (1–)2(–3), stouter, to 1.5 cm lg., one porrect, horn-coloured; **Fl.** 6–8 cm br., yellow (fading to yellowish-pink?); **Fil.** yellow, sometimes red.—Mexico (Durango).

C. echinus (Eng.) Br. & R. (2:1)
Bo. solitary, spherical or ± conical, 3–5 cm ∅, almost concealed by Sp.; **Tub.** plump, elongated ovoid; **Rsp.** numerous, 16–30, 10–16 mm lg.; **Csp.** 3–4, upper 3 erect, individuals porrect and stouter, to 2.5 cm lg., thickened at the base, often blackish; **Fl.** 2.5–5 cm lg., yellow.—USA (W. Texas), N. Mexico (Coahuila). (Fig. 75.)

C. elephantidens (Lem.) Lem. (2:1)
Bo. solitary, depressed-spherical, to 14 cm h., to 19 cm ∅; **Tub.** very large, ± flattened, to 4 cm lg., sometimes to 6 cm br. at the base; **Ax.** densely woolly; **Ar.** woolly only at first; **Sp.** 8 subulate radials to 2 cm lg., at first yellowish or brownish with a yellow base, later brownish; **Fl.** to 10 cm br., deep pink to white, throat red.—Mexico (Mich-oacan).

C. erecta (Lem.) Lem. (2:2)
Bo. cylindric, offsetting, erect at first, later pro-strate, forming large colonies, yellowish-green, single **St.** to 8 cm ∅; **crown** white-woolly; **Tub.** in Isp. 5:8, conical, to 8 mm lg.; **Ar.** woolly at first; **Ax.** strongly woolly, with **Gl.** yellow at first, then brown; **Rsp.** 8–14 (–18), to 1.2 cm lg.; **Csp.** 2(–4), to 2 cm lg.; **Sp.** all amber-coloured, becoming yellowish-brown, subulate, sharp, becoming dar-ker; **Fl.** (5.5–)7(–7.5) cm ∅, light yellow.—Mexico (Hidalgo).

C. exsudans (Zucc.) Lem. (2:2)
Bo. ± cylindric; **Tub.** plump, dark green; **Ax.** ± glabrous; **Gl.** yellow; **Ar.** slightly woolly at first, soon glabrous; **Rsp.** 6–7, thin, straight, yellowish, ± equal; **Csp.** 1, scarcely differentiated, straight, yellow, brown-tipped; **Sp.** 6 mm–1.1 cm lg.; **Fl.** yellow.—Mexico (Hidalgo). Probably identical with C. clavata.

C. georgii (Böd.) (2:2)
Bo. depressed-spherical, to c. 7 cm h., 4 cm ∅, dark leaf-green; **crown** woolly; **Tub.** in Isp. 8:13, 1.2 cm lg.; **Ax.** woolly to glabrous; **Gl.** red; **Ar.** woolly at first; **Rsp.** 8–9, acicular, to 1.2 cm lg., matt horn-coloured to whitish, dark-tipped; **Csp.** 1, to 2 cm lg., stouter, later to 3, ± brown, darker and

thickened at the base; **Fl.** c. 2 cm lg., 3.5 cm ∅, glossy, light cream to whitish; **Sep.** carmine, with light borders.—Mexico (San Luis Potosí, near Alvarez).

C. gladiispina (Böd.) Berg. (2:1)
Bo. ± ovoid, to 10 cm h., 6 cm ∅, glossy dark green; **R.** napiform; **crown** spiny, little woolly; **Tub.** in Isp. 8:13, conical, later imbricate; **Ar.** glabrous; **Rsp.** 10–12, to 1.5 cm lg., glassy-grey, dark-tipped, yellowish at the base and thickened, to 2 cm lg., the upper **Sp.** tufted; **Csp.** 4, to 2.5 cm lg., whitish-grey, with a long brownish-black tip, thickened below; **Fl.** pure yellow.—Mexico (Coahuila, Parras).

C. greenwoodii H. Bravo
Bo. flat-spherical, simple, 9 cm ∅, 5–6 cm h., fresh olive-green, crown woolly; **Tub.** thick, 20 mm lg., 14–15 mm br. below; **Rsp.** 7–8, straight or curving, 1–3 in the upper part of the Ar.; **Csp.** 0; **Fl.** 5 cm ∅; **Pet.** yellow with a fine purplish-brown stripe, light green outside, lanceolate; **Fil.** red, **An.** yellow; **style** red with yellowish-green Sti.; **Fr.** clavate, 3.3 cm lg., 12 mm br.; **S.** pear-shaped, 2 mm lg., light brown.—Mexico (Vera Cruz, valley of Acultzingo, on humus-rich soil, at 1600 m). Close to C. connivens but with fewer Sp.; also resembles C. elephantidens.
Named for Edward Greenwood, an outstanding photographer and collector of Mexican cacti.

C. guerkeana (Böd.) Br. & R. (2:2)
Bo. flat-spherical, to 6 cm h., 8 cm ∅, lighter to darker leek-green; **crown** strongly woolly; **Tub.** plump, 1.5 cm lg.; **Ax.** woolly; **Gl.** red; **Ar.** woolly at first; **Rsp.** 7, to 1.5 cm lg., light horn-coloured, also 3–4 thinner group Ssp. above; **Csp.** 2–3, spreading, projecting, stout, often 6-angled, thickened below, 1.5–2 cm lg., whitish-horn-coloured, yellow-ochre to orange-brown above; **Fl.** yellow.—Mexico (Durango, near Durango).

C. hesteri Y. Wright: see **Escobaria hesteri** (Wright) F. Buxb.

C. impexicoma Lem. differs from C. radians (acc. K. Schumann) only by having the Rsp. more numerous and interlacing, and the Csp. absent. Only a form?

C. jalpanensis Buchenau—Cact. y. Suc. Mex., X: 2, 36–39. 1965.
Bo. to 15 cm h., 6 cm ∅, offsetting from the base, forming groups to 25 cm ∅; **R.** fibrous; **St.** leaf-green; **Tub.** in Isp. 8:13, crowded, erect, ± spiralled; **Ax.** white-woolly; **Gl.** 1, ochre-yellow, sometimes reddish; **Ar.** 2 mm ∅, with yellowish-grey wool at first, this soon greyish-black; **Rsp.**

10–13, 6–10 mm lg., acicular, spreading, chalky-white, frosted, brown below and slightly thickened, tipped brown; **Csp.** 3–4, 0.6–1.2 cm lg., subulate, thickened below; **Sp.** all stiff, sharp, centrals cinnamon-brown at first, later horn-coloured; **Fl.** to 4 cm lg., 4.5 cm ∅, yellow, throat pale green; **Pet.** broadly lanceolate, tapering; **Fil.** purple below; **An.** chrome-yellow; **Fr.** and **Sti.** yellowish; **Fr.** 2 cm lg., to 1.2 cm ∅, pale green; **S.** 1.7 mm lg., brown, surface reticulate.—Mexico (Querétaro, hills around Jalpan, c. 1350 m). Description acc. text received from Buchenau. Spec. belongs to the C. clavata complex, but is a characteristic and distinct spec., from a habitat cut off by ranges of mountains.

C. kieferiana Berg. (acc. Bödeker) is only an ecotype of C. poselgeriana; illustrations show the former as lacking the grouped upper Sp., or with fewer and stouter Rsp. flattened on the underside; otherwise indistinguishable from v. poselgeriana.

C. longicornis Böd. (2:1)
Bo. broadly spherical to spherical, to 10 cm ∅, eventually to 20 cm h., slightly glossy, leaf-green to greyish-green; **crown** scarcely woolly; **Tub.** in Isp. 8:13; **Ar.** woolly at first; **Rsp.** 12, light horn-coloured, thin-subulate, dark-tipped; **Csp.** 3, the 2 upper ones to 1 cm lg., the lower to 2.5 cm lg., all stouter, brownish to horn-coloured, dark-tipped; **Fl.** silky, pure yellow; **Fr.** to 15 mm lg.—Mexico (N. Durango).

C. maiz-tablasensis Backbg. (2:1)
Bo. subspherical at first, to 3 cm h., 5.5 cm ∅, offsetting, bluish-green; **Tub.** c. 1 cm lg.; **Rsp.** 6–7, radiating, firm, greyish-white, to 1.2 cm lg., black-tipped at first; **Csp.** 0; **Fl.** yellowish.—Mexico (San Luis Potosí, Ciudad Maíz).

C. marstonii Elz. U. Clov. (2:1)
Rare cushion-forming spec. with small **Fl.**, 4–5 white bristly **Rsp.** and 2–3 brown **Csp.** to 1 cm lg.; **Pet.** yellow.—USA (Utah, near Boulder).

C. melleospina H. Bravo (2:1)
Bo. spherical; **Tub.** in Isp. 8:13; **Rsp.** 17–19, subulate, stout, to 12 mm lg., pectinate, recurved, reddish or yellowish-brown, ± interlacing; **Csp.** 0 or occasionally one; **Fl.** and **Fr.** unknown.—Mexico (Oaxaca, near Huajuapan de León).

C. minima Baird
Bo. minute, to 4.5 cm lg., offsetting; **Sp.** small, thick, ash-grey to yellowish and reddish; **Fl.** only to 1.5 cm ∅, pinkish-purple with ciliate Pet.—USA (Texas, S. of Marathon, 1200 m). The later name—Escobaria nellieae—is a synonym.

C. neoscheeri Backbg. (2:2)

Bo. spherical, offsetting, greyish-green; **Tub.** blunt-conical, plump, almost twice as lg. as br.; **Ax.** broad; **Gl.** small; **Rsp.** 8–9(–10), to 1.9 cm lg.; **Csp.** 1, 3 cm lg., straight; **Sp.** yellow, often whitish, yellow, red, brown or black-tipped, stout to ± subulate; **Fl.** 5 cm ⌀, straw-coloured, with a reddish M.-stripe outside; **Fil.** pinkish-red; style pale green.—Mexico (Hidalgo, Mineral del Monte).

C. nickelsae K. Brand. (2:2)

Bo. spherical, with crowded offsets, pale green, 7 cm h., sometimes pruinose or reddish; **Tub.** low; **Gl.** sometimes present on the upper Ar.; **Rsp.** 14–16, upper ones somewhat flat, spreading at first, then recurved, 8–10 mm lg., yellowish below, black-tipped, becoming lighter; **Csp.** mostly 0, sometimes later one; **Fl.** light yellow, 5–7 cm br., with a red centre; **Fr.** subspherical, to 7 mm lg.—USA (Texas, Laredo) to N. Mexico (N. Nuevo León).

C. obscura Böd. (2:1)

Bo. solitary, oblong-ovoid, to 11 cm h., to 9 cm ⌀, slightly glossy, blackish-green; **crown** little woolly; **Tub.** in Isp. 8:13, ± imbricate, c. 2 cm lg.; **Ar.** woolly at first; **Rsp.** c. 10, light horn-coloured, straight, stiff, thin-subulate, sometimes ± black-tipped; **Csp.** 4, similar to the Rsp., pitch-black above, thickened at the base; **Fl.** 5 cm ⌀, orange-yellow, with a red throat; **Fr.** pale green, large.—Mexico (Nuevo León in the N., and near Lampazos).

C. octacantha (DC.) Br. & R. (2:2)

Bo. solitary to grouping, cylindric, to 50 cm h., to 4–6 cm ⌀; **Tub.** in Isp. 5:8, conical, to 2.5 cm lg.; **Gl.** in the Ax., 1(–2), red; **Ar.** at first with yellow to white felt; **Rsp.** 6–8, to 1.5 cm lg., honey-coloured to lighter at first, sometimes black-tipped; **Csp.** 1–2, larger, stouter, to 2.5 cm lg., brownish; **Fl.** 3 cm lg., to 6 cm br., straw-coloured; **style** yellow or red.—Mexico (Hidalgo, near Pachuca, and to Quebrada Venados).

C. orcuttii (Rose ex Orcutt) D. Zimmerm. (Neolloydia Rose 1926, Escobaria Bödeker 1933)

Bo. cylindric, to 15 cm h., c. 6 cm ⌀; **Tub.** ± conical, firm, 4–8 mm lg., white-woolly at first; **Sp.** very numerous, concealing the Bo. so that the plant appears white; **Rsp.** 30–41, thin, to 8 mm lg., white; **Csp.** 15–18, very rarely fewer, stiff, white, tipped reddish or brownish; **Fl.** c. 8–12 mm br., not opening fully, faded pink; **Sep.** greenish; **Pet.** faded reddish-white, with a greenish-pink M.-line; **style** white or a very delicate pink; **Fr.** greenish-yellow or green at maturity; **S.** reddish-brown.—USA (New Mexico).

C. organensis D. Zimmerm.

Bo. forming groups; **St.** cylindric, ± soft-fleshed, dark yellowish-green, to 12 cm h., to 3 cm ⌀, crown appearing yellow; **Ax.** glabrous; **Ar.** round, 3 cm ⌀; **Rsp.** 33–35, stiff, white, 6–11 mm lg., straight; **Csp.** 9–12, yellowish, 9–19 mm lg., often tipped reddish-brown; **Fl.** 15–16 mm ⌀ when fully open; **Pet.** lanceolate, pale yellow with a pink M.-line; **Sep.** with a brownish M.-stripe; **style** c. 9 mm lg., with 5–6 Sti.; **Fil.** purplish-pink with yellow An.; **Fr.** yellowish-green, 6–14 mm lg.; **S.** reddish-brown.—USA (New Mexico, Organ Mountains, 2400 m, in a gravelly soil, pH 7.5; partly in the shade of trees).

C. ottonis (Pfeiff.) Lem. (2:2)

Bo. spherical to cylindric, to 12 cm h., to 8 cm ⌀, dark greyish-green; **Tub.** plump, furrow woolly; **Ax.** white-felty; **Gl.** red; **Ar.** white-felty at first; **Rsp.** 8–12, ± equal, stiff, yellowish, brown-tipped; **Csp.** 3(–4), ± cruciform, stiffer, stouter, ± yellowish, becoming brown and whitish above midway, to 1.8 cm lg., the longest one very bent; **Fl.** over 5 cm br., white.—Mexico (Hidalgo, Mineral del Monte).

C. pallida Br. & R. (2:1)

Bo. solitary or to 10 heads, sometimes to 12 cm ⌀, bluish-green; **Tub.** in 13 spirals, short, plump, crowded; **Rsp.** 20 or more, white, appressed; **Csp.** to 3 or more, the lowest one porrect or pointing downwards, black or black-tipped; **Fl.** light yellow, 5–7 cm ⌀; **Fil.** red; **Fr.** greenish-brown, 2 cm lg.—Mexico (Tehuacan).

C. palmeri Br. & R. (2:1)

Bo. spherical, pale green; **Tub.** in 13 spirals, crowded; **Rsp.** 11–14, radiating, stouter, yellowish, often black-tipped; **Csp.** 1, stout, terete, porrect, hooked; **Fl.** 3 cm lg., yellow to lighter.—Mexico (Durango, Zacatecas, Coahuila).

C. pectinata (Eng.) Br. & R. (2:1)

Bo. spherical, mostly solitary, 3–6 cm ⌀; **Tub.** to 1.2 cm lg., in 13 spirals; **Sp.** 16–24, ± appressed to recurved, 1.2–1.8 cm lg., yellowish-white, black-tipped; **Fl.** 5 cm lg., yellow, throat (always?) green; **Pet.** awn-tipped.—USA (W. Texas, along the Rio Pecos) to N. Mexico.

C. pirtlei Werd. (2:1)

A rare, subspherical, small spec. to 7 cm h., the **crown** with yellow wool; **Rsp.** 8–11, to 8 mm lg., **Csp.** 1–3, yellow, black-tipped, thickened at the base; **Fl.** 3.5 cm lg., pink.—USA (Texas, Starr County).

C. poselgeriana (Dietr.) Br. & R. (2:2)

Bo. hemispherical, ± bluish-grey to green, becoming fairly large; **Tub.** large, hemispherical, to 2.5 cm br. below; **Ax.** felted at first; **Ar.** rather small, almost glabrous; **Rsp.** 5–7, to 2 cm lg., two-edged, reddish-brown, stout; **Csp.** 1, 4 cm lg., reddish-brown below, whitish above, stout-subulate; **Fl.** to 6 cm lg., often yellowish at first, with a red throat, becoming pink about the second day.—Mexico (Coahuila, near Saltillo). Gl. said to be light red.

v. **valida** (J. A. Purp.) Heinr.: **Tub.** more broadly conical; **Bo.** to 22 cm h., to 14 cm ∅; **Gl.** 3–4; **Rsp.** 5–6 with other thinner Sp. in the upper part of the Ar., erect, almost completely black (above); **Csp.** 1, to 5 cm lg., terete, yellowish to horn-coloured at first, all Sp. thickened below; **Fl.** to 6 cm lg., silky, light to dark pink (see also C. kieferiana).

C. pseudechinus Böd. (2:2)
Bo. ± ovoid, sometimes offsetting, to 9 cm h., to 5 cm ∅, leaf-green to greyish-green; **crown** slightly woolly; **Tub.** in Isp. 5:8 and 8:13, c. 1 cm lg.; **Ax.** woolly; **Gl.** 2–3, yellowish; **Ar.** slightly woolly at first; **Rsp.** 18–25, thin-subulate, to 1.5 cm lg., greyish-white to brown or almost black; **Csp.** 1, porrect, somewhat longer, coloured similarly; **Ssp.** 2–3, in the upper part of the Ar.; **Fl.** 2 cm lg., 3 cm ∅, violet-pink, border lighter; **Fr.** yellowish-green, 1.5 cm lg.—Mexico (Sierra de la Paila).

C. pseudonickelsae Backbg. (2:2?)
Bo. offsetting, single heads to 5 cm h., 6 cm ∅; **Tub.** prominent, 1 cm lg.; **Ax.** woolly only in the crown; **Rsp.** 15–18, greyish-white, to 1.6 cm lg.; **Csp.** 1, black at first, soon whitish-grey, flecked, black-tipped; **Fl.** pale yellowish, 3.5 cm ∅.—Mexico (Durango).

C. pseudoradians H. Bravo (2:1)
Bo. spherical, solitary, greyish-green; **Tub.** in 13 spirals, ± rhombic below; **Ar.** oval; **Rsp.** 13–15, 3–5 erect, grouped; **Csp.** 0(–1–2), in the upper part of the Ar. if present; **Fl.** 3 cm lg., 7 cm ∅, dull yellowish.—Mexico (Oaxaca, Tejupan-Suchixtlahuaca).

C. pycnacantha (Mart.) Lem. (2:1)
Bo. ovoid to short-cylindric, to 10 cm h., 5–7 cm ∅, bluish-green; **Ax.** very woolly; **Tub.** rhombic below, almost 2.5 cm br., to 1.5 cm lg., obtuse; **Ar.** woolly at first; **Rsp.** 10–12, slender, to 1.6 cm lg., slightly curving, yellowish, dark-tipped; **Csp.** 4, stout, more curving, to 2.5 cm lg.; **Fl.** 4–5 cm lg. and ∅, lemon-yellow.—Mexico (Oaxaca).

C. radians (DC.) Br. & R. (2:1)
Bo. spherical to slightly elongated, solitary, green, 5–7 cm ∅, **crown** with Sp. and felt; **Rsp.**

(12–)16–18(–20), to 1.2 cm lg., pectinate and appressed, to 1.2 cm lg., stiff, rough at first, white, yellowish, or brown-tipped; **Csp.** mostly 0; **Fl.** lemon-yellow, to over 7 cm ∅.—Central Mexico (Hidalgo etc.).

C. r(h)aphidacantha Lem.: C. clavata (Scheidw.) Backbg.

C. ramillosa Cut. (2:1)
Bo. mostly solitary, depressed-spherical, greyish-green, to 8 cm h., 6–9 cm ∅; **Tub.** 2 cm lg., 2.5 cm br. below, appressed upwards; **Rsp.** 14–20, 1–3.5 cm lg., projecting, greyish-white; **Csp.** 4, somewhat stouter and longer, the lowest one curving downwards, brown at first, then grey and dark-tipped; **Fl.** 6.5 cm lg., fairly broad, ± pink, lighter towards the centre.—USA (Texas).

C. recurvata (Eng.) Br. & R. (2:2)
Bo. depressed-spherical, to 20 cm ∅, often forming cushions to 60 cm br., with up to 50 heads; **Tub.** low; **Gl.** ?; **Rsp.** 20–30, pectinate, yellow to grey, dark-tipped; **Csp.** 1(–2), darker, recurved, to 2 cm lg.; **Fl.** to 3.5 cm lg., lemon-yellow, brownish outside; **Fr.** green, spherical, c. 7.5 mm ∅.—USA (Arizona), Mexico (N. Sonora).

C. reduncuspina Böd. (2:1)
Bo. solitary, spherical to oblong, to 10 cm ∅, glossy, yellowish to leaf-green; **crown** laxly spiny; **Tub.** in Isp. 13:21, ovoid-conical, erect, to 1 cm lg.; **Ax.** woolly; **Ar.** slightly woolly at first; **Rsp.** 15–20, stiffly acicular, interlacing, to 1.2 cm lg., whitish to straw-coloured, often brownish-tipped; **Csp.** 2–3, stout, porrect and curving downwards, to 2.5 cm lg., blackish-brown at first, then lighter to yellowish-horn-coloured; **Fl.** 4–5 cm ∅, pure yellow; **Fil.** and **throat** red.—Mexico (Tamaulipas to [?] Coahuila).

C. retusa (Pfeiff.) Br. & R. (2:1)
Bo. depressed-spherical, to 10 cm ∅; **crown** very woolly; **Tub.** rather large; **Ar.** elliptic; **Sp.** 6–12, radials only, appressed, subulate, the upper 2–3 acicular, all yellowish to brownish; **Fl.** c. 3 cm lg., 4 cm ∅, yellow.—Mexico (Oaxaca).

v. **pallidispina** Backbg. differs in having mostly 15 **Rsp.**, 3 of these thinner, erect, all pale grey; the **Tub.**, in Isp. 13:21, are more crowded than in the type.

C. robustispina (Schott) Br. & R. (2:1)
Bo. spherical or oblong, solitary or offsetting, single heads to 15 cm lg., densely spiny; **Tub.** large, to 2.8 cm lg., in 13 spirals, densely crowded, pale greyish-green; **Rsp.** 12–15, the lowest 3 very stout, brownish, upper ones weaker, the top 2–3 tufted,

rather weak and pale; **Csp.** 1, very stout, erect, $\pm$ bent to $\pm$ hooked, yellow, to 3.5 cm lg., all stouter Sp. thickened below; **Fl.** 3.75 cm $\varnothing$, yellow (to?) salmon-coloured or even white.—USA (S. Arizona) to N. Mexico (N. Sonora).

C. roederiana Böd. (2:1)
Bo. oblong to elliptic, to 11 cm h., 7 cm $\varnothing$, little offsetting, glossy, dark leaf-green; **crown** fairly woolly; **Tub.** in Isp. 8:13, lax, conical, erect, c. 16 mm lg.; **Ax.** and **Ar.** very woolly at first; **Rsp.** 10–12, stiffly acicular, to 1.8 cm lg., greyish-white, the upper ones dark-tipped; **Csp.** 1, to 1.5 cm lg., thicker, curving, pruinose, light to dark brown; eventually 3 additional upper thin **Sp.**; **Fl.** 5 cm $\varnothing$, yellow.—Mexico (S. Coahuila).

C. salm-dyckiana (Scheer) Br. & R. (2:1)
Bo. mostly solitary, 10–15 cm $\varnothing$, broadly spherical, light green; **crown** spiny, with white wool; **Tub.** $\pm$ rhombic, 1 cm lg., $\pm$ imbricate; **Ar.** with sparse felt at first; **Rsp.** 7–15, to 1.5 cm lg., grey or whitish, several erect, clustered; **Csp.** 1–4, to 2.5 cm lg., reddish to black, the lowest one the stoutest, to 2.5 cm lg., slightly curving; **Fl.** 4 cm lg., pale yellow; **Fil.** greenish.—Mexico (Chihuahua).

C. schwarziana Böd. (2:2)
Bo. simple, oblong-ovoid; **Tub.** shortly conical, c. 8 mm thick below; **Ax.** slightly woolly at first; **Ar.** oval; **Rsp.** to 20, acicular, often slightly curving, to 9 mm lg., whitish-grey; **Csp.** 0–1, thin-subulate, straight, projecting, somewhat longer, yellowish to horn-coloured, dark-tipped; **Fl.** pale yellow(?).—Mexico (Guanajuato). Gl.-colour not stated.

C. scolymoides (Scheidw.) Berg. (2:1)
Bo. pale green, spherical, becoming ovoid; **Tub.** imbricate, appressed; **Ax.** woolly; **Ar.** woolly at first; **Rsp.** (12–)14–20, fewer at first, light, $\pm$ dark-tipped, to 2 cm lg.; **Csp.** (1–)3(–4), to over 3.5 cm lg., $\pm$ bent, darker; **Fl.** over 5 cm $\varnothing$, yellow with a red throat; **Pet.** denticulate.—Mexico (in the N.).

C. speciosa Böd. (2:1)
Bo. solitary, spherical to shortly ovoid, glossy, dark leaf-green to bluish-green, to 9 cm h., 8 cm $\varnothing$; **crown** woolly; **Tub.** in Isp. 8:13, $\pm$ slender-conical, 2.5 cm lg.; **Ar.** very woolly at first; **Rsp.** 7–9, $\pm$ subulate, the upper ones more crowded and somewhat thinner, 1.5–1.7 cm lg., greyish-white, black-tipped, the upper ones pitch-black on the underside; **Csp.** 4, the lowest one pointing downwards, black on the underside; **Fl.** 6 cm $\varnothing$, golden-yellow with a dark centre.—Mexico (Coahuila, W. of Monclova).

C. sulcata (Eng.) Br. & R. (2:1)

Bo. offsetting, single heads to 12 cm $\varnothing$; **Tub.** large, to 1.2 cm lg., lax, weak, not curving outwards; **Rsp.** 12–14, acicular and thin, straight, white; **Csp.** 0 at first, then several, $\pm$ appressed, 1 stouter, curving outwards; **Fl.** to over 5 cm $\varnothing$, yellow with a red centre.—USA (S. Texas).

C. sulcolanata (Lem.) Lem. (2:1) (T.)
Bo. depressed-spherical, offsetting, to 5 cm h., 6 cm $\varnothing$ or more; **Tub.** $\pm$ 5-angled below, conical above; **Ax.** very woolly at first; **Rsp.** 9–10, unequal, to 1.6 cm lg., brownish, black-tipped, whitish-yellow at first, purple-tipped; **Csp.** 0; **Fl.** large, yellow.—Mexico (Hidalgo, Mineral del Monte).

C. unicornis Böd. (2:2)
Bo. solitary at first, later offsetting to form groups, glossy, light bluish-green, single heads to 8 cm $\varnothing$, spherical; **crown** spiny, moderately woolly; **Tub.** in Isp. 5:8, lax, conical, to 1.5 cm lg.; **Ax.** slightly woolly; **Gl.** red; **Ar.** woolly at first; **Rsp.** 7–8(–9), to 1.5 cm lg., light yellowish to brownish-grey; **Csp.** 1, somewhat thicker, to 2 cm lg., nodose below, dark reddish-brown, red at first; **Fl.** yellow(?).—Mexico (Coahuila, Viesca).

C. vaupeliana Böd. (2:2)
Bo. solitary, spherical to shortly ovoid, to 7 cm $\varnothing$, matt bluish-green; **crown** spiny; **Tub.** in Isp. 8:13, thick, 3-angled to $\pm$ conical, c. 2 cm lg., somewhat keeled; **Ax.** faintly woolly; **Gl.** red; **Ar.** woolly at first; **Rsp.** c. 15, upper ones clustered, thinner, to 1.5 cm lg., pruinose, dirty white, brown-tipped, the others subulate, 8–9, c. 1.2 cm lg., thickened below; **Csp.** 4, thicker and stouter, to 2 cm lg., nodose below, matt greyish-yellow, brown-tipped; **Fl.** large, yellow.—Mexico (Tamaulipas, Jaumave).

C. villarensis Backbg. (2:2)
Bo. solitary, spherical at first, becoming elongated, to 15 cm h., to 13 cm $\varnothing$, almost blackish-green; **Tub.** large, 3 cm lg.; **Ax.** very woolly at first; **Gl.** yellow; **Rsp.** 9–11, 5–15 mm lg., yellowish at first with the base and tip dark or reddish-brown or flecked, finally flecked and tipped black; **Csp.** 1, to 3 cm lg., yellowish, dark-tipped, then white with a black tip, finally dirty yellow; **Fl.** 4 cm lg., 5 cm $\varnothing$, light yellow.—Mexico (San Luis Potosí, Villar).

C. vivipara (Nutt.) Eng. (2:1)
Bo. subspherical, solitary, later offsetting, to 5 cm $\varnothing$, 3 cm h., eventually forming small groups; **Rsp.** (14–)16(–22), white or brown; **Csp.** 1–4, to 2 cm lg., brown or flecked; **Fl.** 3.5 cm lg. and br., purplish-pink; **Fil.** purple or pink; style white or pink; **Sti.** pale yellow or pink; **Fr.** 2 cm lg., 1 cm $\varnothing$, greenish to brownish.—Canada (in the S.), USA (from Kansas to N. Texas).

v. **aggregata** (Eng.) Marsh.: later forming larger groups; **Csp.** 5–6, white, brown-tipped; **Fl.** 5–7 cm $\varnothing$;

v. **arizonica** (Eng.) Marsh.: also forming larger groups than the type; **Fl.** only 3.75 cm $\varnothing$;

v. **neomexicana** (Eng.) Backbg.: little offsetting; **Csp.** several, white, with black or brown tips; **Fl.** 4–5 cm $\varnothing$;

v. **radiosa** (Eng.) Backbg.: also little offsetting; single heads more ovoid; **Csp.** 5–6(–8); **Fl.** 3.5 cm $\varnothing$.

C. voghtherriana Werd. & Böd. (2:2)
Bo. solitary, flattened-spherical, to 4.5 cm h., 8 cm $\varnothing$, glossy, bluish-green; **R.** stout; **crown** with some white wool; **Tub.** in Isp. 5:8, flattened or shortly conical, to 1.2 cm lg.; **Ax.** very woolly; **Gl.** red, mostly concealed; **Ar.** more strongly woolly at first; **Rsp.** 5–6, to 8 mm lg., thin, rough, mostly whitish, several upper ones with brown or blackish tips, slightly thickened below; **Csp.** at first 0, later 1, curving downwards, to 1.5 cm lg., slightly stouter; **Fl.** 3 cm $\varnothing$, light yellow.—Mexico (San Luis Potosi).

C. werdermannii Böd. (2:1)
Bo. simple, depressed-spherical at first, then more ovoid, to 8 cm h., 6 cm $\varnothing$, old plants $\pm$ columnar and offsetting from the sides, light greyish-green; **Tub.** in Isp. 21:34, pyramidal, 5 mm lg.; **Ax.** glabrous; **Ar.** glabrous; **Rsp.** 15–20, stiffly acicular, appressed, to 6 mm lg., light greyish-white; **Csp.** appearing only later, higher up the Bo., to 4, to 2.2 cm lg., one slightly curving and porrect, $\pm$ brownish, darker above; **Fl.** 6 cm lg., often yellowish at first, becoming pink about the 2nd day, throat red; **Sep.** reddish above, with a reddish dorsal stripe.—Mexico (Sierra de la Paila).

Coryphantha Lem.: for further names see also **Escobaria** Br. & R. (e.g. C. tuberculosa), **Neobesseya** Br. & R. (C. wissmannii), **Neolloydia** Br. & R. (C. ceratites) and **Lepidocoryphantha** Backbg. (C. macromeris).

Cryptocereus Alex. (32)

Bushy epiphyllum-like plants with notched, dentate or lobed flat shoots; flowers funnelform to $\pm$ bellshaped-funnelform, with spines on the ovary and to some extent on the tube. Fruits, as far as known, also spiny. The genus is thus placed at the beginning of the reduction-line of the "leaf-cacti". Kimnach has referred two species to Eccremocactus although the generic diagnosis here speaks only of traces of felt on the ovary, and glabrous fruits; the unreliability of his classification is shown

by the fact that he at first referred C. imitans to the cereoid genus Werckleocereus Br. & R. If it is argued that the type of the Genus Cryptocereus Alex. is more clambering than E. imitans and E. rosei, and has lobed shoots as well as differently coloured fruits and larger flowers, these are still insignificant points since identical differences occur, for instance, in Epiphyllum; in Echinopsis, the fruits vary even more widely in colour.—Distribution: Mexico, Costa Rica, Ecuador. [Vigorous-growing.]

C. anthonyanus Alex. (T.)
Bo. branching freely; **St.** 7–15 cm br., leaf-green, the blades arising opposite the notches, 2.5–4.5 m lg.; **Ar.** small, with short Sp.; **Fl.** c. 12 cm lg., creamy-white; **Tu.** 3 cm lg., robust, with Sc. to 6 mm lg., with felt and Br. in the Ax.; **Ov.** with denser dirty grey felt and greyish-brown Br. as well as stiff brown Sp. to 3 mm lg.—Mexico (Chiapas, Pico Carrizal). (Fig. 76.)

C. imitans (Kimn. & Hutch.) Backbg. (Kimnach: Eccremocactus)
Bo. as in the preceding; **Ar.** with 1–2 tiny Sp.; **Fl.** only 6–7 cm lg., white; **Tu.** $\pm$ curving above the Ov., **Sc.** woolly; **Ov.** densely areolate, with Sp. to 4 mm lg.; **Fr.** ovoid, spiny.—Costa Rica (El General Valley, near Cañas).

C. rosei (Kimn.) Backbg. n.comb.
(Eccremocactus rosei Kimn., C. & S. J. (US), XXXIV: 3, 80. 1962).
Bo. bushy, pendant; **St.** $\pm$ terete below, the wider part to 90 cm lg., 4–8 cm br., with a stout M.-rib, the margin with rounded notches; **Ar.** white-felty, with 1–4 small Sp.; **Fl.** to 7 cm lg., funnelform; **Sep.** reddish-yellow to light purple; **Pet.** greenish-cream; **Tu.** and **Ov.** with crowded fine Sp. to 1 cm lg.; **Fr.** oblong, 4.5 cm lg., red, with numerous Sp. 1 cm lg., Per.-remains persisting.—Ecuador (valleys of the Rio Cañar and Rio Chanchan).

Cullmannia Dist.: **Wilcoxia** Br. & R.

Cumarinia (Knuth) Buxb.: **Neolloydia** Br. & R., SG. **Cumarinia** (Knuth) Backbg. (earlier known as Coryphantha Lem., SG. Cumarinia Knuth).

Cylindropuntia (Eng.) Knuth emend. Backbg. (8)

The genus belongs to the northern branch of the cylindric Opuntias, most of them larger than the Austrocylindropuntia species of S. America. While the latter have no sheath-development of the

spines, this character is present in Cylindropuntia, even if only as rudiments, so that it is easy to establish whether any particular plant belongs to the northern or the southern group. The following Series are distinguished, the appropriate figure being given in brackets after the specific name:
Mostly with only 1 principal spine:
Series 1: Ramosissimae Br. & R.: terminal shoots very thin, to 1 cm ∅; shoots with flat lozenge-shaped tubercles;
Series 2: Leptocaules Br. & R.: terminal shoots seldom more than 1 cm ∅; shoots without lozenge-shaped tubercles, these missing or ± oblong.
With several spines:
Series 3: Thurberianae Br. & R.: terminal shoots not over 2 cm ∅;
Series 4: Echinocarpae Br. & R.: terminal shoots 2 cm thick and more; fruit dry;
Series 5: Bigelowianae Br. & R.: terminal shoots 2 cm thick and more; tubercles at first scarcely longer than broad; fruit fleshy;
Series 6: Imbricatae Br. & R.: terminal shoots 2 cm thick and more; tubercles distinctly longer than broad, narrow, prominent, laterally compressed; fruit fleshy;
Series 7: Fulgidae Br. & R.: terminal shoots 2 cm thick and more; tubercles broad, low; fruit fleshy.
Many of the species are characterised by conspicuous spination, with sheaths which are sometimes brightly coloured; the spines are very sharp in some species, in others the flowers are variously coloured (e.g. C. versicolor). Proliferating fruits occur, these sometimes appearing chain-like and giving rise to clumps of plants. Habit can be either little or freely branching, erect or sometimes even ± prostrate.—Distribution: from the more S. parts of USA to Central Mexico and Baja California. [(R). O.]

C. abyssi (J. P. Hest.) Backbg. (4)
Bo. bushy, to 40 cm h.; **St.** to 30 cm lg., c. 2 cm ∅, strongly tuberculate; **Tub.** to 1.5 cm lg.; **Ar.** light brown; **Glo.** yellow; **Sp.** c. 10, dark brown, to 3 cm lg.; **Sh.** loose; **Fl.** 4 cm lg., terminal, yellowish-green; **Fr.** ovoid, 2 cm lg., umbilicate, often spiny above.—USA (S. California).

C. acanthocarpa (Eng. & Big.) Knuth (4)
Bo. much branching, to 2 m h.; **branches** at an acute angle to the **trunk**, becoming woody, terminal **shoots** to 8 cm lg., very tuberculate; **Tub.** laterally flattened; **Sp.** 8–25, to 3 cm lg., dark brown; **Sh.** light-coloured; **Glo.** yellow; **Fl.** 5 cm lg. and ∅, red to yellow; **Fr.** c. 3 cm lg., stoutly spiny, apical depression weak, broad.—USA (Arizona, Cactus Pass).

v. **ramosa** (Peebl.) Backbg.: distinguished by somewhat more slender, crowded **Br.**; **Fr.** also dry;
v. **thornberi** (Thornb. & Bonk.) Backbg.: lower-growing, at most to 1.50 m h., **Sp.** to 10; **Fl.** bronze-yellow, deep red and yellow; **Fr.** more shortly spined.

C. alamosensis (Br. & R.) Backbg. (3)
Bo. shrubby, to 3 m h., mostly forming a **trunk** to 12 cm ∅; **branches** long, to 1.5 cm ∅, tuberculate at first, becoming terete; **Tub.** elongated; **Ar.** brown; **Glo.** numerous, brown; **Sp.** 4, the central one brown below, yellow above, to 2 cm lg.; **Fl.** lemon-yellow; **Fr.** to 3 cm lg., yellow or reddish.—Mexico (Sonora, Alamos to Sinaloa).

C. alcahes (Web.) Knuth (7)
Bo. strongly branching, very spiny, to 1 m h.; **branches** terete; **Tub.** ± lozenge-shaped, prominent; **Sp.** to 12 at first; **Sh.** pale to white; **Fl.** moderately large, greenish-yellow; **Fr.** spherical, small, plump, yellow.—Mexico (Baja California).

C. arbuscula (Eng.) Knuth (2)
Bo. bushy, to 3 m h., with a many-branched crown; **trunk** short, woody, to 12 cm ∅; **terminal shoots** to 7.5 cm lg., 8 mm ∅; **Tub.** low, indistinct; **Sp.** mostly 1, to 4 cm lg.; **Sh.** straw-coloured; **Fl.** 3.5 cm lg., yellowish-green to brownish or yellowish-white; **Fr.** to 3.5 cm lg., red, often proliferating; **S.** often only 1.—USA (Arizona), N. Mexico (Sonora).
v. **congesta** (Griff.) Backbg.: distinguished by the more clavate, more noticeably tuberculate **Fr.**

C. bigelowii (Eng.) Knuth (5)
Bo. shrubby, to 1 m h., with short laterals; **branches** to 15 cm lg., plump; **Tub.** not very prominent, ± 4-sided, as long as br., 1 cm lg.; **Sp.** and **Sh.** yellowish-white; **Fl.** subapical, 4 cm lg., violet-carmine, yellow or greenish-yellow with a purple spot; **Fr.** mostly naked, strongly tuberculate.—USA (S. Nevada to California and Arizona), Mexico (N. Baja California). Proctor ("Arizona Highways") illustrates the Fl. with white Pet. and a greenish throat.
v. x **hoffmannii** (C. B. Wolf) Backbg. n.comb. (Opuntia bigelowii v. hoffmannii C. B. Wolf, Occ. Papers Rancho St. Ana Bot. Gard., 1:2, 79, 1938): **Fl.** light carmine; a lax spontaneous hybrid with long dense Sp., resembling C. munzii (see also under the latter).

C. brevispina (H. E. Gat.) Backbg. (7)
Bo. bushy, to 1 m h. and br., bluish-green to brown; **branches** to 4 cm ∅, to 25 cm lg.; **Tub.** ± lozenge-shaped, 2.5 cm lg., 5 mm br.; **Glo.** missing (?); **Rsp.**

5, from the lower part of the Ar., to 5 mm lg., recurved; **Csp.** 1, to 2 cm lg., dark brown; **Sh.** only on the upper part of the Sp.; **Fl.** rotate, 3 cm lg. and ∅. bronze to reddish-purple; **Fr.** 1.8 cm lg., spherical, yellow.—USA (Gulf of California, Ballena Is.).

C. brittonii (G. Ort.) Backbg. (2)
Bo. scrubby, to 5 m br., 1 m h.; **branches** 5–20 mm ∅, becoming woody; **Ar.** white; **Sp.** 1, white; **Sh.** transparent; **Glo.** numerous, red, yellow-tipped; **Fl.** 2 cm ∅, greenish-white; **Fr.** 2 cm lg., ovoid, smooth, red.—Mexico (Sinaloa, Angostura).

C. burrageana (Br. & R.) Backbg. (4?)
Bo. bushy, to 1 m h.; **trunk** thin, to 2 cm ∅, spiny; **branches** cylindric to slender-clavate, to 15 cm lg.; **Ar.** brown, crowded; **Sp.** numerous, rarely to 2 cm lg.; **Sh.** thin, light yellow; **Glo.** light yellow when present; **Fl.** to 4 cm ∅, brownish-red, greenish below; **Fr.** 2 cm ∅, spherical, ± tuberculate, dry (?).—Mexico (Baja California).

C. californica (Torr. & Gray) Knuth (4)
Bo. ascending or prostrate; **branches** slender, to 2.5 cm ∅, bluish-green, strongly tuberculate; **Tub.** to 1.5 cm lg., flattened laterally; **Sp.** 7–20, brown; **Sh.** yellowish-brown, c. 1 cm lg.; **Glo.** light brown; **Fl.** terminal, 4 cm ∅, greenish-yellow, red outside; **Fr.** very spiny.—USA (S. California) and Mexico (northern Baja California).

C. calmalliana (Coult.) Knuth (3)
Bo. not described; **branches** bluish-green; **Tub.** narrow, long, to 2.5 cm lg.; **Ar.** yellow; **Glo.** white; **Sp.** mostly 4, the upper one stout, erect, reddish, yellow-tipped, to 2.5 cm lg., lower ones thinner, recurved, to 1.5 cm lg.; **Fl.** purple (?); **Ov.** spiny; **Fr.** smooth, ovoid, juicy.—Mexico (Baja California, Calmalli).

C. caribaea (Br. & R.) Knuth (2)
Bo. shrubby, to 3 m h., forming thickets; **branches** eventually horizontal, to 10 cm lg., robust for this Series; **Tub.** ± prominent, short; **Ar.** large, white, with several H.; **Sp.** 1(–3), to 3 cm lg.; **Sh.** brown; **Glo.** dark brown; **Fl.** light yellow; **Fr.** red, to 2 cm lg., glabrous or at most with a few Sp. above, sterile.—W. Indies (Hispaniola).

C. cholla (Web.) Knuth (6)
Bo. tree-like, to 3 m h.; **trunk** 15 cm ∅, increasingly spiny; **crown** dense, broad; **branches** often in whorls, horizontal, pale; **Tub.** large, compressed; **Sp.** often numerous; **Sh.** loose, brownish; **Glo.** numerous, yellow; **Fl.** rather small, 3 cm ∅, deep purple; **Fr.** to 5 cm lg., proliferating and forming clumps.—Mexico (Baja California).

C. ciribe (Eng.) Knuth (5)
Bo. bushy, densely branching, to 1 m h.; **end-shoots** to 5 cm ∅; **Tub.** stout, regularly arranged, 5–7 mm br. and lg.; **Sp.** 4–6, very sharp, to 3 cm lg., some Br. or H. present; **Sh.** yellowish; **Glo.** numerous; **Fl.** yellow; **Fr.** very tuberculate, to 4 cm lg., spineless.—Mexico (Central Baja California).

C. clavellina (Eng.) Knuth (3)
Bo. laxly branching, to 1 m h.; **terminal shoots** thin, spreading, ascending, ± clavate, to 10 cm lg., rather over 1 cm ∅; **Tub.** oblong, to 8 mm lg.; **Sp.** 3–6, the central one very long; **Sh.** straw-coloured or brown; **Fl.** yellow; **Fr.** clavate, short, tuberculate.—Mexico (Baja California).

C. davisii (Eng. & Big.) Knuth (3)
Bo. low-shrubby, to 50 cm h., much branching, with dense yellow Sp.; **terminal branches** 8 cm lg., c. 1 cm ∅, very tuberculate; **Sp.** 6–12, the longest ones to 5 cm lg.; **Sh.** thin; **Glo.** numberous, yellow; **Fl.** 3.5 cm lg. and br., olive-green to yellow; **Ov.** with several Sp.; **Fr.** 3 cm lg., ± tuberculate, glabrous.—USA (W. Texas, E. New Mexico). R. widely branching and tuberously thickened.

C. densiaculeata Backbg. (4)
Bo. with a short trunk and squarrose branches; **shoots** ± whorled, to 50 cm lg., ± curving upwards, densely spiny; **Tub.** short, ± merging into ribs, spiralled; **Sp.** whitish, with a ± reddish sheen, 20 or more, ± projecting, interlaced; **Fl.** deep purple, to 6 cm ∅; **Ov.** with pink Sp.; **Fil.** dark lilac-red; **style** light red; **Sti.** yellow; **Fr.** to 5 cm ∅, deeply umbilicate, green.—Origin?

C. echinocarpa (Eng. & Big.) Knuth (4)
Bo. shrubby, to 1.5 m h., freely branching, **trunk** woody, to 3 cm ∅, becoming smooth; **shoots** short, very tuberculate; **Sp.** numerous, yellow at first, then brownish, finally grey; **Sh.** sometimes present; **Fl.** yellowish, red-tipped outside; **Ov.** short, top-shaped, densely spiny above; **Fr.** very spiny.—USA (S. States), Mexico.

C. fulgida (Eng.) Knuth (7)
Bo. tree-like, to 3 m h., sometimes lower, in the S. part of its distribution also forms low bushes; **trunk** to 20 cm ∅; **end-shoots** to 20 cm lg., to 5 cm ∅, sappy, tuberculate, readily detached; **Sp.** to 12, yellowish to brownish, to 3.5 cm lg.; **Sh.** loose; **Glo.** whitish to light yellow; **Fl.** to 3.5 cm ∅, light red; **Pet.** few, truncate; **Fr.** tuberculate at first, becoming smooth, to 5 cm lg., freely proliferating, green.—USA (Arizona), Mexico (Sonora, Sinaloa). (Fig. 77:6.)

v. **mamillata** (Schott) Backbg.: **Sp.** shorter, inconspicuous; **shoots** more sappy; **Tub.** more prominent.

C. heteracantha Ritt. (undescribed) is probably **Austrocylindropuntia humahuacana** Backbg.

C. hualpaensis (J. P. Hest.) Backbg. (3)
Bo. bushy, to 1.5 m h., fairly densely branching; **Tub.** 4–6 mm br. and h., to 1.5 cm lg., spiralled; **Ar.** yellow; **Glo.** yellowish; **Sp.** 2–4, to 3 cm lg., brownish to ash-grey, also 3–6 Sp. only 5–8 mm lg.; **Fl.** funnelform, c. 2 cm lg., 4 cm ∅, greenish-yellow; **Ov.** green, tuberculate, with ash-grey Sp.; **Fr.** 3.5 cm ∅, fleshy, to 4 cm lg.—USA (Arizona, in the NW.).

C. imbricata (Haw.) Knuth (6) (T.)
Bo. tree-like, to over 3 m h., with a woody **trunk**; **branches** obliquely ascending, **terminal shoots** to 3 cm ∅, very tuberculate; **Tub.** to 2.5 cm lg., flattened laterally; **Sp.** 8–30, to 3 cm lg., brown; **Sh.** thin; **Fl.** terminal, 4–6 cm lg., to 9 cm br., purple; **Ov.** tuberculate, with a few Br.; **Fr.** glabrous, yellow, to 3 cm lg.—USA (southern States) to Central Mexico.
    v. **argentea** (Anth.) Backbg.: differs in having silvery **Sp.** with a red base; **Tub.** shorter (to 2 cm lg.)

C. kleiniae (DC.) Knuth (2)
Bo. shrubby, to 2.5 m h., woody at the base; **Tub.** long; **Ar.** white-woolly, large, longer than br.; **Sp.** mostly 1, sometimes several, to 5 cm lg., yellowish or brownish; **Sh.** yellow; **Ar.** later also with some Br.; **Glo.** yellow to brown; **Fl.** 3 cm lg., purple; **Pet.** broad, rounded above; **Fr.** 2.5 cm lg., red, long-persisting.—USA (Texas) to Central Mexico.

C. leptocaulis (DC.) Knuth (2) v. **leptocaulis**
Bo. bushy, sometimes with a short **trunk**, to 2 m h.; **branches** fresh green, fairly dense, scarcely tuberculate, very thin; **Sp.** often missing, mostly 1, light, sometimes 2–3 on older shoots, to 5 cm lg.; **Sh.** loose or firm, variously coloured; **Ar.** with short white felt; **Fl.** to 2 cm lg., greenish-yellow; **Ov.** ± conical, with many small brown Ar. and Glo.; **Fr.** small, ± subspherical to clavate (also in the type?), red or yellow, (var.?), 10–18 mm lg.—USA (in SW.), Mexico. In habitat a very sharply spined, extremely troublesome weed.
    v. **badia** (Berg.) Knuth: **Sp.** long, stout; **Sh.** chestnut-coloured. A form of this name (Rivière No. 8096) has constantly yellow **Sp.** with light brown **Sh.**; **Fl.** light greenish-yellow, to 17 mm ∅; **Fr.** oblong to pear-shaped, red;
    v. **brevispina** (Eng.) Knuth: **new shoots** mostly 2 from an Ar., one pointing upwards, the other downwards; **Sp.** either white, over 1 cm lg., or very short, yellowish, dark-tipped; **Fl.** 2 cm ∅, whitish to yellowish-green; **Fr.** 1.4 cm lg., oblong, red, yellowish-orange inside; **S.** 3 mm lg.;

v. **glauca** Backbg.: **shoots** dull bluish-green; **Sp.** 1, to 4.5 cm lg., white below, brown at midway, lighter above; **Sh.** 2 mm br., brilliant glossy brown, lighter below; **Fl.** light greenish-yellow, 2 cm ∅; **Ov.** naked; **Fr.** spherical, dark scarlet, 1.5 cm lg., **pulp** glassy whitish-green;
v. **longispina** (Eng.) Knuth: **Sp.** (and **Sh.**) coffee-coloured, to 4 cm lg.; **Fl.** brownish to greenish-yellow, c. 2 cm ∅; **Glo.** light brown;
v. **pluriseta** (Berg.) Knuth: dark green; **Sp.** short; **Sh.** indistinct; **Ar.** with several H., but no flecks below;
v. **robustior** (Berg.) Knuth: lateral **shoots** short, light green; **Sp.** long, light yellow; **Sh.** light;
v. **tenuispina** Backbg.: **shoots** thin, leaf-green; **Sp.** 1, light greyish-brownish, with darker zones; **Sh.** yellowish; **Fl.** light yellowish-green, c. 2 cm ∅; **Ov.** with small Sp.; **Fr.** oblong (not clavate), sterile, 1.8 cm lg., greenish at the base, **pulp** colourless, glassy;
v. **vaginata** (Eng.) Knuth: **Fl.** 2 cm ∅, light yellowish-green; **Ov.** spiny; **Sp.** to 4 cm lg., with broad straw-coloured **Sh.**; **Glo.** brown.

C. lloydii (Rose) Knuth (3)
Bo. tall-shrubby, to 3 m h. and br.; **shoots** ± terete, c. 2 cm ∅; **Tub.** prominent, oblong; **Sp.** few, 3 on previous year's growth, 1.5 cm lg., reddish; **Fl.** 3 cm lg., opening in the afternoon, dark purple; **Fr.** 3 cm lg., weakly tuberculate, yellow to orange.—Central Mexico.

C. metuenda (Pitt.) Backbg. (2): **shoots** thinner than in C. caribaea, and **Fl.** smaller; but probably at most a var. of the latter.

C. molesta (Brand.) Knuth (6–7)
Bo. tall-shrubby, to 2 m h., lower in cultivation; **branches** squarrose, ± cylindric, sometimes ± clavate, to 40 cm lg., sometimes to 4 cm ∅, pale green; **Tub.** low, broad, to over 4 cm lg.; **Sp.** 6–10, unequal, to 5 cm lg., straw-coloured; **Sh.** thin, loose; **Fl.** 5 cm ∅, purple; **Fr.** ovoid, 2.5 cm lg., glabrous or somewhat spiny.—Mexico (Baja California, San Ignacio).

C. mortolensis (Br. & R.) Knuth (2)
Bo. small-shrubby, to 60 cm h., dark green; **shoots** with ± reddish or dark marks below the Ar., sometimes only 2 cm lg., 4–5 mm ∅; **Tub.** indistinct; **L.** to 4 mm lg., bronze at the tips; **Ar.** with some deciduous H.: **Glo.** few, brown; **Sp.** on old Ar. 1, 3–5 cm lg.; **Sh.** brownish; **Fl.** and **Fr.** ?—Mexico.

C. multigeniculata (Clok.) Backbg. (3)
Bo. bushy, to 50 cm h.; **shoots** numerous, to 2 cm ∅; **Tub.** low, 4–6 mm lg., to 3 mm br.; **Sp.** c. 12,

acicular, 2–4 centrals to 18 mm lg.; **Sh.** white; **Fl.** 2.5 cm lg. and br.—Origin?

C. × munzii (C. B. Wolf) Backbg. n.comb. (Opuntia × munzii C. B. Wolf, Occ. Papers Rancho Sta. Ana Bot. Gard., 1 : 2, 79. 1938): a spontaneous hybrid of C. bigelowii, with dull yellowish-white **Sp.** and a laxer habit than C. bigelowii v. × hoffmannii; **Fl.** brownish- to greyish-pink.

C. parryi (Eng.) Knuth (4)
Bo. low-bushy, to 40 cm h.; **branches** cylindric, to 30 cm lg., to 2 cm ∅, very tuberculate; **Tub.** to 1.5 cm lg.; **Ar.** light brown; **Glo.** yellow; **Sp.** c. 10, to 3 cm lg., dark brown; **Fl.** apical, 4 cm lg., yellow; **Fr.** ovoid, 2 cm lg., deeply umbilicate, often spiny above, full and spherical at maturity.—USA (S. California).

C. prolifera (Eng.) Knuth (7)
Bo. shrubby, to 2 m h.; **trunk** woody; **terminal shoots** to 12 cm lg., 3–5 cm ∅, easily detached, fleshy; **Tub.** short, plump; **Sp.** 6–12, to 12 mm lg., brown; **Glo.** pale; **Fl.** red, rather small; **Ov.** with reddish Sp.; **Fr.** proliferating, to 3.5 cm lg., often sterile.—USA (S. California).

C. ramosissima (Eng.) Knuth (1)
Bo. bushy, sometimes to 2 m h.; **shoots** grey, broadly spreading, to 9 cm lg., c. 6 mm ∅; **Tub.** flat, lozenge-shaped, 4–6-sided; **Ar.** brownish at first; **Sp.** (0–)1, to 6 cm lg., reddish at first; **Sh.** loose, yellow; **Fl.** 4 cm lg., greenish-yellow; **Fr.** dry, weakly spiny.—USA (S. States), Mexico (Baja California, Sonora).

C. recondita (Griff.) Knuth (3)
Bo. low-growing and densely bushy, to rather taller and shrubby, to 1.5 m h.; **trunk** cylindric, to 7 cm ∅; **shoots** readily detached, to 10 cm lg., older ones to 30 cm lg., to 2 cm ∅, very spiny; **Tub.** 5 cm lg., 6 mm br., becoming flatter; **Ar.** broadly oval, to 6 mm br.; **Glo.** yellow; **Sp.** 2–4 at first, later 6–8(–10), spreading, to 5 cm lg., brown above; **Sh.** rather glossy; **Br.** between the Sp., to 6 mm lg., sheathless, dirty black; **Fl.** 2.5 cm ∅, purple; **Fr.** greenish-yellow, with a red overlay, to 3.5 cm lg., Glo. brown.—Mexico (La Perla).
  v. **perrita** (Griff.) Backbg.: **shoots** somewhat longer and more squarrose; **Sp.** with pale yellowish **Sh.**

C. rosarica (Linds.) Backbg. (4)
Bo. low-shrubby, spreading, to 1 m h., mostly without a trunk; **Br.** to 20 cm lg., 2–5 cm ∅, bluish to olive-green, becoming brownish; **Tub.** to 3 cm lg., 1 cm br., almost forming ribs; **Glo.** numerous, golden-yellow, to 4 mm lg.; **Sp.** 4–7, to 3.5 cm lg.,

with some **Br.**; **Sh.** reddish-brown; **Fl.** subapical, 3.5 cm ∅, light yellow, bordered reddish; **Fr.** proliferating, often sterile, tuberculate, with Sp. and Br.—Mexico (Baja California, around San Telmo).

C. rosea (DC.) Backbg. (6)
Bo. to 1 m h., with a **trunk** to 5 cm ∅, very spiny; **branches** dense and projecting above; **Sp.** few at first, later to 20 or more, 3–4 cm lg.; **Sh.** white; **Ov.** glabrous or bristly; **Fl.** pink; **Fil.** and **style** pink; **Fr.** ovoid, tuberculate, to 2.5 cm lg., yellowish-brownish, with fine Sp. to 2.5 cm lg.—Mexico (Hidalgo, Tula).
  v. **atrorosea** Backbg.—Descr. Cact. Nov. III: 5. 1963: **Fl.** deep carmine-pink, noticeably darker than the type; **Fr.** 4 cm lg., green inside, with Sp. to 3 cm lg. (Fig. 78.)

C. spinosior (Eng.) Knuth (6)
Bo. tree-like, to 4 m h., ± with a **trunk**; **crown** lax; **terminal shoots** to 30 cm lg., to 2.5 cm ∅, often purplish, very tuberculate; **Tub.** to 12 mm lg. and more, narrower, rather crowded; **Sp.** 6–12, later to 25, to 15 mm lg., spreading, grey to brownish; **Sh.** thin; **Glo.** yellowish-white; **Fl.** to 6 cm br., pink, purple, yellow or white; **style** cream or pink; **Fr.** spherical to oblong, very tuberculate, spineless, yellow, to 4 cm lg.—USA (Arizona, New Mexico), N. Mexico.

C. tesajo (Eng.) Knuth (2)
Bo. bushy, to 30 cm h. and br.; **branches** of pencil-thickness, scarcely tuberculate, to 5 cm lg.; **Ar.** 5–6 mm apart; **Sp.** 2 at first, to 8 mm lg., small, dark coffee-coloured, later one main Sp. to 5 cm lg., tipped yellow; **Fl.** to 1.8 cm lg., yellow.—Mexico (Central Baja California).
  v. **cineracea** (I. L. Wigg.) Backbg.: taller-growing; **epidermis** ash-grey.

C. tetracantha (Toumey) Knuth (3)
Bo. low-shrubby, to 1.5 m h.; **trunk** woody, to 8 cm ∅; **branches** to 30 cm lg., 1.5 cm ∅, reddish; **Tub.** prominent at first, to 2.2 cm lg.; **Glo.** brown; **Sp.** 3–6, mostly 4, thin, somewhat downcurving; **Fl.** to 2 cm br., orange to scarlet; **Fr.** coloured similarly, to 2.5 cm lg., deeply umbilicate.—USA (Arizona, Tucson). (Fig. 77:1.) This spec. is regarded by many authors as a form of C. arbuscula; but the branches are longer, the Sp. more numerous and the Fl.-colour is different.

C. thurberi (Eng.) Knuth (3)
Bo. tall-shrubby, to 4 m h.; **branches** slender, to 25 cm lg., 1–1.2 cm ∅; **Tub.** to 2 cm lg., compressed laterally; **Sp.** 3–5, to 12 mm lg., spreading; **Sh.** thin, brown; **Fl.** 3.5 cm ∅, brownish; **Fr.** to 3 cm ∅.—

Mexico (Sonora, Bacuachic; W. coast).

C. tunicata (Lehm.) Knuth (6)
Bo. low-bushy (also described as forming a trunk; perhaps confused here with C. rosea?); **branches** readily detached, short or to 15 cm lg., very tuberculate; **Sp.** reddish at first, mostly 6–10, to 5 cm lg.; **Sh.** white, thin; **Fl.** 3 cm lg. and br., yellow; **Ov.** spiny or glabrous.—Mexico (a troublesome weed of the Highlands); carried by man as far as S. America.
In cultivation this yellow-flowered plant and the very similar but pink-flowered C. rosea are very popular; however, if given insufficient light, the papery-sheathed Sp. become weak.

C. versicolor (Eng.) Knuth (6)
Bo. bushy to tree-like, crown open, broad, sometimes to 4 m br.; **trunk** and larger branches becoming woody; **terminal shoots** to 20 cm lg., c. 2.5 cm $\emptyset$, rather variable in epidermis-colour, not very tuberculate; **Tub.** 1.5 cm lg.; **Sp.** 5–11, to 2.5 cm lg., dark; **Sh.** narrow; **Glo.** reddish-brown; **Fl.** 3–5.5 cm br., yellow, green, red or brown; **Ov.** tuberculate, with felt, Glo. and long deciduous Br.; **Fr.** long-persisting, to 4 cm lg., spherical to pear-shaped, sometimes proliferating, ± tuberculate at first.—USA (Arizona), N. Mexico (Fig. 77: 2–5.)

C. viridiflora (Br. & R.) Knuth (3)
Bo. shrubby, to 60 cm h.; **terminal shoots** to 7 cm lg., 1.5–2 cm $\emptyset$, often brittle; **Ar.** grey or yellow; **Sp.** 5–7, to c. 2 cm lg., dark brown; **Glo.** numerous, yellow, short; **Fl.** subapical, to 4.5 cm lg., green with a reddish tinge; **Fr.** very tuberculate, with long deciduous Br.—USA (New Mexico, Santa Fé and Fort Marcy).

C. vivipara (Rose) Knuth (3)
Bo. to 3.5 m h., strongly branching; **trunk** to 10 cm $\emptyset$; **branches** bluish-green, readily detached, 1–2 cm $\emptyset$; **Tub.** oblong, low, to 2 cm lg.; **Ar.** yellow; **Glo.** few or missing; **Sp.** 1–4, to 2 cm lg.; **Sh.** straw-coloured; **Fl.** subapical, purple; **Ov.** very tuberculate, with white deciduous Br.; **Fr.** oblong, to 6 cm lg., yellowish-green, weakly umbilicate.—USA (Arizona, near Tucson).

C. whipplei (Eng. & Big.) Knuth (3)
Bo. low, freely branching; **terminal shoots** 1–2 cm $\emptyset$; **Ar.** oblong, light brown; **Glo.** pale yellow; **Sp.** c. 12, to 2 cm lg., dark brown; **Sh.** light brown; **Fl.** 2 cm br., yellow; **Fr.** very tuberculate, spineless, to 4 cm lg., deeply umbilicate.—USA (N. Arizona, New Mexico).
> v. **enodis** (Peebl.) Backbg.: differs in that the **Fr.** is not tuberculate and the apical depression is slight.—USA (Arizona, Hualpai Mts).

Cylindropuntia: see also **Austrocylindropuntia** Backbg. (S. American spec.).

Cylindrorebutia Frič & Krzgr.: **Mediolobivia** Backbg., SG.2 **Pygmaeolobivia** Backbg., Series 1: Conoideae Backbg.

Dactylanthocactus Y. Ito: **Brasilicactus** Backbg.

Deamia Br. & R. (43)

Distinctive tree-climbing epiphytes; stems mostly 3-winged with thin ribs but sometimes with 5–8 ribs or wings, clambering by means of aerial roots. Areoles mostly with short thin spines. In the flowering season the plants produce numerous large, creamy-white blooms with laxly spreading, narrower outer perianth-segments, and more crowded inner ones which are pointed. Styles with almost 20 thin long stigma-lobes spreading horizontally. These plants are far too seldom seen in our collections since they grow well, although they do require greenhouse conditions.—Distribution: S. Mexico to Colombia [◗, ///.]

D. diabolica Clov.
Bo. with stout, segmented, 3–5-angled **St.**; **Ri.** thin, to 4 cm h., somewhat notched; **Ar.** to 2 cm apart; **Sp.** acicular, 0.5–5.2 cm lg., brown, becoming grey, thickened below, one often much longer than the others; **Fl.** to 24 cm lg., white; **Tu.** with brownish felt and brown to yellowish H.; **Ov.** with dense golden-brown Sp.; **Fr.** small, laxly spiny.—British Honduras (Corozal).

D. testudo (Karw.) Br. & R. (T.)
Bo. ± tree-like or shrub-like, clambering up trees or over rocks, to 3 m lg.; **branches** to 15 cm lg., 8 cm br., light to emerald green; **Ri.** 3–5–8; **Ar.** to 2.5 cm apart; **Sp.** 3–4 at first, later to over 10, to 2 cm lg., rather stiff, yellowish at first, then brown; **Fl.** to 28 cm lg., to 20 cm $\emptyset$, numerous on older plants, white to creamy-white; **Fr.** spiny, red.—Mexico to Colombia. (Fig. 79.)

Delaetia Backbg. (123)

A hitherto monotypic genus. Bodies ± spherical, with conspicuous chin-like tubercles and mostly only 4 spines (more at first on cuttings). The relatively small flowers remain open for up to 14 days; they have extremely narrow petals and are obviously unisexual. The genus is named for the Belgian, De Laet, whose imported plants drew many people to the cactus-hobby.—Distribution: Chile. [(G)?]

D. woutersiana Backbg. (T.)
Bo. subspherical, greyish-green; **Ri.** 13, with pronounced chin-like projections; **Ar.** large, ± round to oblong, white; **Sp.** mostly 4, 1–2.5 cm lg., black to greyish-black, sometimes with annular markings; **Fl.** 2 cm lg. and about as br.; **Pet.** light brownish to orange-yellow, only to 1.8 mm br., bent outwards; **Fr.** opening basally.—Chile (origin not known). (Fig. 80.)

Dendrocereus Br. & R. (132)

A monotypic genus with a tree-like habit similar to that of the Genus Neoabbottia Br. & R., but with flowers which are longer and broadly funnelform (not cylindric), and fruits which are fairly large; old plants have a stout trunk to 60 cm thick; flowers only occasionally show tiny spines.—Distribution: only in Cuba. [(R).]

D. nudiflorus (Eng.) Br. & R. (T.)
Bo. tree-like, to 10 m h., with a **trunk** to over 1 m lg.; **branches** dark green, to 12 cm thick, 3–5-winged; **Ri.** sinuate to notched, to 7 cm h.; **Ar.** to 5 cm apart; **Sp.** missing or acicular, 2–15, to 4 cm lg.; **Fl.** to 14 cm lg., the corolla expanding widely; **Tu.** with the upper Sc. united, those below sometimes with a small Sp., **Ov.** similarly; **Pet.** to 4 cm lg.; **Fr.** to 12 cm lg., thick-walled, smooth, green, naked.—Cuba (Havana to the E. Provinces). (Fig. 81.)

Denmoza Br. & R. (79)

One species is ± spherical; the second ultimately becomes columnar, eventually with longer hair-like spines mingling with the normal ones; the flowers have extremely short petals and scarcely expand, with the clustered anthers projecting; the fruit is spherical and dry, and dehisces laterally.—Distribution: NW. Argentina. [(R).] (Fig. 82.)

D. erythrocephala (K.Sch.) Berg.
Bo. eventually columnar, to 1.5 m h., to 30 cm ⌀; **Ri.** 20–30; **Sp.** numerous, over 30, the inner ones to 6 cm lg., fairly stiff, chestnut-coloured, the outer ones bristly, thin, eventually interspersed with H.; **Fl.** 7.5 cm lg.; **Pet.** 1 cm lg., connivent.—Argentina (Mendoza, La Rioja, San Juan and reputedly also in Salta). The crown in very old specimens is sometimes near-vertical (Fechser).

D. rhodacantha (SD.) Br. & R. (T.)
Bo. spherical, eventually only moderately elongated, to 16 cm br. has been reported; **Ri.** c. 15, straight; **Ar.** to 2.5 cm apart; **Rsp.** 8–10, radiating, recurved, red, to 3 cm lg.; **Csp.** 0–1, somewhat

stouter; **Fl.** 7 cm lg., limb slightly oblique; **Pet.** red.—Argentina (Tucuman, reputedly also in Mendoza).

Digitorebutia Frič & Krzgr. is a name for species of the Genus **Mediolobivia** Backbg. (SG. Pygmaeolobivia Backbg.), with an elongated habit, and the style ± united at the base.

Diploperianthium Ritt.: an early n.nud. for the Genus **Calymmanthium** Ritt.

Discocactus Pfeiff. (188)

Spherical Cacti, with some resemblance in habit to the Melocactus species, but the apical cephalium is smaller, remains low, and is ± interspersed with bristles. Flowers nocturnal, white, elongated and slender funnelform, perfumed; fruit berry-like. Older imported plants are difficult to keep on their own roots. Seedling plants present fewer difficulties.—Distribution: Brazil, Paraguay, Bolivia. [(G).]

D. alteolens Lem.
Bo. broadly spherical, deep dull green, to 22 cm ⌀, to 11 cm h.; **Ceph.** to 2.5 cm h., to 5 cm ⌀, with bristly Sp. 1 cm lg., black; **Ri.** to c. 10, divided into ± oblique oval Tub.; **Rsp.** c. 5, horn-coloured, sometimes an additional Sp. above, rather weaker than in D. tricornis, to 2 cm lg., recurved; **Fl.** to 7 cm lg., 5 cm ⌀, with longer Sc. on the Tu.; **Pet.** more broadly rounded, shortly tapering, ± linear, the outer ones spreading, the inner ones curving ± upwards; **Fr.** white to pink.—Brazil (W. Matto Grosso). (Fig. 83 left.)

D. bahiensis Br. & R.
Bo. small, to 6 cm ⌀; **Ceph.** with a few Br.; **Ri.** c. 10, ± concealed by the Sp.; **Sp.** 7–9, flattened, pink, robust, recurved, 1–3 cm lg.; **Fl.** 4–5 cm lg., with a slender Tu.; **Pet.** oblong, yellowish-white.—Brazil (Bahia).

D. boliviensis Backbg.—Descr. Cact. Nov. III: 5. 1963.
Bo. broadly spherical, bluish-green, to over 15 cm ⌀, to c. 7 cm h.; **Ri.** c. 13, not tuberculate to more strongly so, to 4 cm br. below; **Ar.** only 2 on each Ri., dirty brownish; **Rsp.** 5, 2 uppers to 12 mm lg., terete, pressed closely against the Bo. above, light brownish to horn-coloured, subulate, sometimes ± flecked, 3 lower Sp. much stouter, to 3 cm lg., 2 mm br., not thickened below, stout-subulate, ± projecting, especially the bottom central one, all dirty horn-coloured, often fissured lengthwise, the bottom one sometimes ± compressed but not

flattened; **Ceph.** to 4 cm $\varnothing$, dirty brownish-felted, lacking Br. and Sp.; **Fl.** 5 cm lg.; **Sep.** tinged pale pinkish-brick; **Pet.** white; **Fr.** white; **S.** black, finely tuberculate.—Bolivia (plateáu of La Cruz, 10 km from San Cyrilo, among rocks). (Fig. 84.) Distinguished from the other spec. by the absence of Br. in the Ceph. The only species known to occur in Bolivia.

D. boomianus Buin. & Bred.
Bo. flat-spherical, offsetting from the base, to 10 cm $\varnothing$, 6 cm h., green to dark green; **R.** branching; **Ri.** 16–20, spiralled, almost completely resolved into Tub.; **Ar.** with creamy-white wool at first, later glabrous, c. 3 mm lg.; **Sp.** 12–13, upper part yellow to light brown, darker-tipped, later greyish-white; **Rsp.** 5 on either side, bent to the Bo. and $\pm$ pectinate, also 1 pointing obliquely upwards and another obliquely downwards, these 3 cm lg., sometimes with a **Csp.** 3.5 cm lg.; **Ceph.** 4.5 cm $\varnothing$ and h., especially large; **Fl.** 9 cm $\varnothing$, nocturnal, strongly scented, with a small round pericarpel.—Brazil (Bahia, Serra de Espinhaco, c. 900 m).

D. hartmannii (K.Sch.) Br. & R.
Bo. broadly spherical, glossy; **Ceph.** with many Br.; **Ri.** 12–16, transversely divided into large Tub.; **Sp.** subulate, yellow; **Rsp.** 6–12, recurved to appressed; **Csp.** 1; **Fl.** with a few spreading Sc.; **Sep.** green; **Pet.** lanceolate to oblong, white; **Fr.** yellow; **S.** 2 mm lg., glossy black.—Paraguay (on the Rio Capivary).

D. heptacanthus (Rodr.) Br. & R.
Bo. to 16 cm $\varnothing$, 6 cm h.; **Sp.** uniformly 7; **Ceph.** to 5 cm $\varnothing$, 3.5 cm h.—Brazil (Matto Grosso, near Cuyabá).

D. horstii Buin. & Bred.
Bo. flat-spherical, 4.5 cm $\varnothing$, to 2 cm h.; **Ri.** 17–18, with flat sides, 3 mm br., 7 mm deep, greyish-green, tinged violet; **Ar.** small, 6 mm apart; **Sp.** 9–10, bent towards the Bo. and clawlike, grey, tipped black, appressed; **Fl.** pure white, to 60 mm lg. and $\varnothing$, opening in the evening, strongly perfumed; **An.** whitish-yellowish; **Sti.** concealed at the base of the Tu. (Fl. develop only in quite hot weather); **Ceph.** 2 cm br., over-topped by brown Br. 2 cm lg. A dwarf spec. of this unusual genus, with an extremely unusual appearance and quite distinct spination; it flowered in 1972 in the collections of several collectors.—Brazil (Mato Grosso, c. 1200 m, in pure quartz sand.*

* Translator's note: for articles with further information as well as photos, see the following: Nat. Cact. & Suc. J. (GB): 1972 XXVII, 4, p. 94 and 1975 XXX, 1, p. 16–7; also Kakt.u.a.Suk. 1975, XXVI, 3, p. 64–5. Most

growers seem to have found imported plants difficult, and many of these have been lost; I myself have not found the spec. easy from seed, even when these are available. One nursery advises a minimum of 20°C for establishing imports; the soil must be open and mostly mineral, with watering only from below, and the atmosphere should preferably be moist during rooting. Plants which have thoroughly dried out are difficult to bring into growth again, and like all species of the genus they need higher temperatures than most greenhouses here can provide in winter, so special arrangements are called for—perhaps in the propagator. Interesting SEM photographs from Heidelberg have shown that the spines are openly cellular in structure, and it is believed this is a device for water-absorption.

D. paranaensis Backbg.: **Ceph.** small, with few Br.; **Ri.** c. 20, the largest known number.—Brazil (Paraná acc. Voll (or Serra Paraná, N. of Brasilia?)).

D. placentiformis (Lehm.) K.Sch. (T.)
Bo. broad, low, bluish-green; **Ri.** 10–14, broad, low; **Ar.** c. 6–7 on each Ri.; **Rsp.** dark, stout, 6–7, $\pm$ recurved; **Csp.** mostly 0(–1); **Fl.** large, with several R. of shorter inner Pet.; **Sep.** pinkish-red; **Pet.** white; **Fr.** white.—Brazil (locality?). Ceph. (acc. Pfeiffer) smaller, with Br.

D. subnudus Br. & R.: spec. which has not been re-collected; **Ceph.** small, $\pm$ spineless.—Brazil (Bahia).

D. tricornis Monv.
Bo. depressed-spherical; **Ri.** 10 or more, tuber-culate, broad, not prominent; **Ceph.** 5 cm $\varnothing$; 3 main **Sp.** (and 3 thinner uppers) brown, directed downwards, $\pm$ twisted; **Csp.** 0; **Fl.** slender, 8 cm lg., Pet. radiating laxly upwards and downwards, the lower **Pet.** recurved at anthesis; **Fr.** top-shaped, white or pale pink.—Brazil (near Diamantina). (Fig. 83 right.)

D. zehntneri Br. & R.
Bo. small-spherical, entirely covered by the **Sp.** which are almost white, thin-acicular, to 2.5 cm lg.; **Csp.** 1; **Ceph.** of long soft wool with some Br., these in part absent; **Fl.** only 3 cm lg.; **Fr.** small, spherical, red.—Brazil (Bahia, near Sentocé).

Disocactus Lindl. (40)

Epiphytic plants, with the main stems $\pm$ terete, and terminal shoots broad and leaf-like. If one follows Britton & Rose in restricting the Genus to the 3 species given below (i.e. excluding Chiapasia as well as the species recently referred thereto by Kimnach), they have complete uniformity of floral characters: shape ± tubular; tube slender, terete, ± curving; perianth segments narrow, curving ± outwards. The flowers of each species are red, they and the small white to red fruits being glabrous. The species are therefore readily identifiable in both the Classification and the Key. The position is different if, following Kimnach, one includes Chiapasia as well as Pseudorhipsalis and Rhipsalis ramulosa (see under the latter); he also refers the following to his "Disocactus ramulosus (SD.) Kimn.": Rh. coriacea, angustissima, jamaicensis, purpusii and leiophloea. If one considers the form and size of the flowers in the species Kimnach gathers under Disocactus: Chiapasia with its large bellshaped flowers; the uniformly slender shape of the three species given hereunder; the flowers of Pseudorhipsalis, and finally the minute, strongly rhipsalis-like forms of "Disocactus ramosus", then it is difficult to foresee all the consequences of his procedure, particularly when practical requirements are taken into account. Previous classifications of all species worked reasonably well, whereas a very drastic combination of this kind can scarcely be reflected in either Classification or Keys, and diagnosis then becomes more difficult. Again, if one considers Kimnach's changing treatment of "Werckleocereus imitans" for instance, together with similar changes in Buxbaum's treatments, the system of combinations may perhaps be justified on grounds of phylogenetic theory, but can certainly not be upheld on the basis of phytographic practice, where the tasks are of a different order. In a comprehensive work like the present one there must of course be uniformity, ignoring any narrow specialisms, so that within the present framework it is not possible to accept this kind of deviation from previous classificatory methods.—Distribution (of the 3 species hitherto referred to Disocactus): Guatemala to Honduras. [(R).]

D. biformis (Lindl.) Lindl. (T.)
Bo. bushy; **shoots** narrow, long, with only slight step-like notches; **Fl.** 5–6 cm lg.; **An.** little projecting; **Pet.** more strongly spreading-recurving.—Honduras and Guatemala (Alotenango).

D. eichlamii (Wgt.) Br. & R.
Bo. bushy, branching from near the base; **shoots** to 22 cm lg., 4.5 cm br., broader than the preceding, dentately notched; **Fl.** 6–7 cm lg.; **An.** further projecting; **Pet.** less spreading.—Guatemala (near Sta. Lucia). (Fig. 85.)

D. quezaltecus (Standl. & Steyerm.) Kimn.
Bo. bushy; **Fl.** 8.5–9 cm lg., whitish-purple; **Fr.** 18 mm lg., yellowish-red. Fl. last 4 days.—Guatemala.

This spec. was first described as belonging to the Genus Bonifazia; it has the lightest-coloured Fl. and Fr.

D. ramulosus (SD.) Kimn.: **Rhipsalis ramulosa** (SD.) Pfeiff.

Dolicothele (K.Sch.) Br. & R. emend. Backbg. (230)

This Genus has received widely different treatment: it is not recognised by some authors, while others see the small-flowered species as a valid Genus by themselves (Buxbaum), or as a Subsection of Mammillaria. A character common to both the large and the small flowering groups are the usually more flexible spines, together with tubercles which are mostly softer and frequently unusually long, especially in the small-flowered species, but also in the large-flowered ones and in part also in those with hooked spines. If the various species are placed side by side, they are seen to constitute a quite separate and distinctive group, as Vaupel recognised; the seeds of the large-flowered species are larger and black, and those of the small-flowered ones small and brown.—Distribution: USA (Texas) to Mexico (from the NE. States to Oaxaca). [(R).]
The figure in brackets after the specific name refers to the appropriate Series: 1. Macrofloridae Tieg. (large-flowered); 2. Microfloridae Tieg. (small-flowered).

D. albescens (Tieg.) Backbg. (2)
Bo. offsetting, individual **St.** spherical; **Tub.** longer and soft, green, to 2 cm lg.; **Ax.** with 2–4 yellowish **Br.**; **Rsp.** 4–5(–6), 8–15 mm lg.; **Csp.** mostly 0 (sometimes 1, to 1.5 cm lg.); all **Sp.** yellowish at first, then white; **Fl.** 2 cm lg., 1.8 cm br.; **Sep.** pale greenish-white; **Pet.** similarly or white; **Fr.** 2.5 cm lg., green to reddish.—Mexico (Querétaro).

D. balsasoides (Craig) Backbg. (1)
Bo. solitary or offsetting, single heads to 7 cm ∅; **Ax.** with 2–6 Br. the same length as the Tub.; **Rsp.** 10–11, to 6 mm lg., white, spreading; **Csp.** 4, to 9 mm lg., the lowest one hooked; **Fl.** bellshaped, 4 cm br.; **Sep.** light green; **Pet.** orange, acute, 3 mm br.; **Fr.** and **S.** ?—Mexico (Guerrero).

D. baumii (Böd.) Werd. & F. Buxb. (1)
Bo. ± ovoid, to 8 cm h., 6 cm ∅, offsetting; **Tub.** glossy, green, to 1 cm lg.; **Ax.** woolly at first; **Rsp.** 30–35, to 1 cm lg., thin, hair-like, white; **Csp.** 5–6, to 1.8 cm lg., thin-acicular, pale yellow; **Fl.** 3 cm lg. and br., strongly perfumed; **Sep.** greenish-yellow; **Pet.** sulphur-yellow; **Fr.** greyish-green, broadly

ovoid, 1.5 cm lg.—Mexico (Tamaulipas, near San Vicente).

D. beneckei (Ehrenbg.) Backbg. (1)
Bo. oblong, offsetting, darker to lighter to yellowish-green; **Tub.** cylindric; **Ax.** woolly; **Rsp.** 12–15, radiating, appressed, whitish to brown-tipped; **Csp.** 2–6, stouter, 1–2 of these twice as long as the others, hooked, brown, black-tipped; **Fl.** to 4 cm br.; **Sep.** greenish, bordered yellow; **Pet.** to 1.7 cm lg., to 4 mm br., a milky buttercup-yellow; **Fr.** deep dull reddish-green.—Mexico (Guerrero, lower Rio Balsas).

D. camptotricha (Dams) Tieg. (2)
Bo. forming groups, single heads to 7 cm br.; **Tub.** deep to light green, long and slender conical, to 2 cm lg.; **Ax.** somewhat woolly, with 2–5 yellowish Br. to 15 mm lg.; **Rsp.** 4–6(–8), to 3 cm lg., thin, ± contorted, greenish-white at first, soon becoming yellow; **Csp.** 0; **Fl.** 1.3 cm lg., scarcely 1 cm $\emptyset$, perfumed; **Pet.** white with a greenish M.-stripe; **Fr.** 2 cm lg., slender, pale green, sometimes tinged reddish.—Mexico (Querétaro). There is a form with more appressed, shorter, stouter, bent, yellow Sp.

D. decipiens (Scheidw.) Tieg. (2)
Bo. forming groups, single heads ± spherical; **Tub.** soft, to 11 mm lg., cylindric; **Ax.** weakly woolly, with 4 white to pink Br.; **Rsp.** 7–8, to 1 cm lg., fine-acicular, yellowish-white; **Csp.** 1(–2), to 1.8 cm lg., thin-acicular, straight, stiffer, yellowish below, reddish-brown above, porrect; **Fl.** to 2 cm lg.; **Pet.** white, M.-line pink; **Fr.** green, washed reddish, to 2 cm lg., 4 cm thick.—Mexico (San Luis Potosí).

D. longimamma (DC.) Br. & R. (1) (T.)
Bo. solitary or offsetting; **Tub.** laxly arranged, rather soft, 3–7 cm lg.; **Ax.** felty to glabrous; **Rsp.** 9–10, to 2 cm lg., white to pale yellow, thin and flexible; **Csp.** 0–1(–3), to 2.5 cm lg., acicular, light brown, dark-tipped; **Fl.** to 6 cm $\emptyset$; **Sep.** greenish-yellow or darker; **Pet.** light yellow; **Fr.** thick-clavate, yellowish-green.—Mexico (Hidalgo). (Fig. 86.)
    v. **gigantothele** (Berg) Craig: probably only a form;
    v. **globosa** (Lk.) Craig: **Per.** more closed; **Bo.** more spherical, dark green, with up to 12 Sp.

D. melaleuca (Karw.) Craig (1)
Bo. solitary to offsetting, glossy, green; **Tub.** conical to cylindric, to 2.5 cm lg.; **Ax.** often woolly, sometimes with Br.; **Rsp.** 6–7(–9), radiating, to 1.4 cm lg., acicular, upper ones blackish-red, others chalky horn-coloured; **Csp.** 0–1, 1 cm lg., similarly

coloured, stiffly acicular, rough; **Fl.** yellow, fairly large.—Mexico (Oaxaca).

D. nelsonii (Br. & R.) Backbg. (1)
Bo. solitary or offsetting; **Tub.** dark green, often reddish, shortly and broadly conical, to 7 mm lg.; **Ax.** somewhat woolly; **Rsp.** 13–15, to 8 mm lg., finely acicular, white, brownish-tipped; **Csp.** (2–)4(–6), the lowest one to 1 cm lg., hooked; **Fl.** yellow, fairly large; **Fr.** reddish.—Mexico (Michoacan, Guerrero).

D. sphaerica (Dietr.) Br. & R. (1)
Bo. offsetting to form mats to 50 cm br.; **Tub.** rather soft, pale to darker green, conical-cylindric, to 1.6 cm lg.; **Ax.** weakly woolly; **Rsp.** 12–15, to 9 mm lg., white to pale yellow, darker below, spreading sideways; **Csp.** 1, to 4 mm lg., thin-subulate, smooth, chalky-yellowish; **Fl.** to 7 cm $\emptyset$, light yellow; **Fr.** greenish-white, sometimes tinged purple, to 1.5 cm lg.—USA (Texas) to N. Mexico (Nuevo León, Tamaulipas).

D. surculosa (Böd.) F. Buxb. (2)
Bo. offsetting to form mats, single heads rather small, to 3 cm $\emptyset$; **Tub.** soft, dark green; **Ax.** glabrous; **Rsp.** to 15, to 1 cm lg., white to pale yellow; **Csp.** 1–2, to 2 cm lg., smooth, one sharply hooked; **Fl.** funnelform, to 1.8 cm br.; **Sep.** chrome-yellow with a pink dorsal stripe; **Pet.** sulphur-yellow with a tiny red tip and an orange stripe on the underside, 3 mm br.; **Fr.** clavate, green, sometimes reddish or darker.—Mexico (Tamaulipas).

D. uberiformis (Zucc.) Br. & R. (1)
Bo. offsetting, single heads depressed-spherical, to 10 cm $\emptyset$; **Tub.** to only 3.5 cm lg., conical-cylindric; **Ax.** glabrous; **Rsp.** only (3–)4–5(–6), to 1.6 cm lg., reddish-brown at the base, straight or rather contorted, rough, horn-coloured; **Fl.** 3.5 cm $\emptyset$; **Sep.** reddish; **Pet.** in 2 series, yellow, serrate.—Mexico (Hidalgo).

D. zephyranthoides (Scheidw.) Backbg. (1)
Bo. solitary, depressed-spherical, rarely elongated, to 8 cm h., 10 cm $\emptyset$, carrot-like below; **Tub.** soft, especially during dormancy, dark bluish-green, conical, to 2.5 cm lg.; **Ax.** naked; **Rsp.** 12–18, to 1.2 cm lg., ± hairlike, rough, white; **Csp.** 1(–2), short, to 1.4 cm lg., one always hooked, at first also reddish, then yellowish to reddish-brown, rough; **Fl.** 4 cm lg. and br.; **Sep.** greenish to brown; **Pet.** white to yellow; **Fr.** ovoid, stout, reddish. There appear to be two forms, differing in Tub.-size; the Fl.-colour therefore also perhaps different?—Mexico (Querétaro, Oaxaca).

Dracocactus Y. Ito is a name for **Horridocactus** Backbg.

Ebnerella F. Buxb. was a synonym for the later Genus Chilita (Orc.) F. Buxb., which the author eventually referred to **Mammillaria** Haw.

Ebneria Backbg. is a Subgenus of **Monvillea** Br. & R.

Eccremocactus Br. & R. (36)

Plants similar in habit to Epiphyllum, but the flowers have a rather short tube and a bellshaped perianth; the ovary is set with some short felt (rarely with minute bristles); the oblong fruit is somewhat angular and the numerous small seeds are black. Only 1 species.—Kimnach (USA) referred to this Genus two species with spiny ovaries, whereas the generic diagnosis specifies for Eccremocactus only "traces of felt". For this reason those species must both be referred to Cryptocereus.—Distribution: only in Costa Rica. [(R).]

E. bradei Br. & R. (T.)
Bo. bushy, pendulous, epiphytic; **shoots** to 30 cm lg., to 10 cm br., light matt green, margins not deeply notched; **Ar.** with 1–3 small Sp. to 6 mm lg., or these absent; **Fl.** to 7 cm lg., bellshaped-funnelform; **Sep.** thick, glossy, pink to whitish-pink; **Pet.** waxy, white; **Ov.** ± angular.—Costa Rica (Cerro Turiwares). (Fig. 87.)

Eccremocactus imitans (Kimn. & Hutch.) Kimn.: **Cryptocereus imitans** (Kimn. & Hutch.) Backbg.

Eccremocactus rosei Kimn.: **Cryptocereus rosei** (Kimn.) Backbg.

Echinocactus Lk. & O. (189)

Small to very large plants, some of the latter the largest of all the spherical Cacti; all have yellow flowers, with one pink-flowered exception; the large species mostly bear numerous flowers. The crown is woolly, the tube similarly; hooked spines are never present. The ± oblong woolly fruit is virtually dry and dehisces basally; the relatively large seeds are dull or glossy, brownish-black and black. the flesh of some species is candied as sweetmeats.—Distribution: USA (Southern States) to Mexico (from the N., to S. Puebla). [Seedlings: (G).]

E. amazonicus Witt: possibly a Melocactus species.

E. californicus Monv.: not clarified, probably a Ferocactus.

E. glaucus K.Sch.: see under **Sclerocactus** Br. & R.

E. grandis Rose
Bo. stoutly cylindric, to 2 m h., to 1 m ∅, dull green; young plants with red transverse bands; **Ri.** numerous but at first only c. 8; **Ar.** eventually confluent; **Sp.** stout, subulate, yellowish at first, then reddish-brown, sometimes banded; **Rsp.** 5–6, 3–4 cm lg.; **Csp.** 1, 4–5 cm lg.; **Fl.** 4–5 cm lg.; **Fr.** to 5 cm lg.—Mexico (Puebla). The correct (and earliest) name is probably: E. minax Lem.

E. grusonii Hildm.
Bo. large, spherical, either broadly so or tall, to 1.3 m h. and 80 cm ∅, light green; **Ri.** to over 30; crown with thick white wool; **Ar.** later confluent above; **Rsp.** 8–10, to 3 cm lg.; **Csp.** mostly 4, cruciform, to c. 5 cm lg.; **Sp.** all yellow; **Fl.** bellshaped, to 6 cm lg., 5 cm ∅; **Sep.** brownish outside; **Pet.** cadmium-yellow, narrowly lanceolate; **Fr.** c. 2 cm lg., densely white-woolly; **S.** 1.5 mm lg.—Mexico (San Luis Potosí to Hidalgo). (Fig. 88.)

E. horizonthalonius Lem.
Bo. flattened-spherical to elongated, to 25 cm h., pruinose-grey; **Ri.** mostly 8(–13), straight or spiralled; **Sp.** 6–9, to 4 cm lg., terete to ± flattened or claw-like, mostly only 1 ± central, variable in colour from dark reddish at first, or above and at the base, otherwise amber-coloured; **Fl.** pale to pinkish-red, to 3 cm lg.; **Fr.** to 3 cm lg., oblong, red, very woolly; **S.** 3 mm lg., papillose, brownish-black.—USA (S. States) to Mexico (from the N. to the Federal District).

E. ingens Zucc.
Bo. stoutly cylindric, to 1.5 m h. and 1.25 m ∅, greyish-green; **crown** white-woolly; **Ri.** to over 50; **Ar.** yellowish-woolly; **Rsp.** c. 8; **Csp.** 1; all **Sp.** brown at first, 2–3 cm lg.; **Fl.** 2 cm lg., 3 cm ∅; **Pet.** ± obtuse, yellow; **Fr.** 3 cm lg., very woolly.—Mexico (Hidalgo).

E. krausei Hildm., although not completely clarified, probably belongs to the Genus **Echinomastus** Br. & R. The species is said to have a spiny Fl., which is unusual for the whole of the Northern Group (anomalous?)

E. leucotrichus Phil.: **Arequipa leucotricha** (Phil.) Br. & R.

E. minax Lem. is probably the correct name for **E. grandis** Rose

131

E. palmeri Rose

Bo. stout-cylindric, to 2 m h., to 50 cm ∅; **Ri.** 12–26 or more; **Rsp.** 5–8, shorter, lighter and weaker than the 4 **Csp.** which are robust, banded, to 8 cm lg., yellow above, brown below; **Fl.** relatively small, yellow; **Pet.** 2 cm lg.; **Fr.** 3 cm lg., densely white-woolly.—Mexico (S. Coahuila to Zacatecas).

E. parryi Eng.

Bo. subspherical at first, becoming cylindric, bluish-grey, to 30 cm h. or more, to 35 cm ∅, always solitary; **Ri.** c. 13, tuberculate, spiralled; **Sp.** to 15, white, rigid, straight; **Rsp.** to 11; **Csp.** 4, to 5 cm lg.; **Fl.** very woolly; **Pet.** brilliant yellow; **Fr.** oblong.—USA (El Paso) to N. Mexico (Chihuahua, near the frontier).

E. platyacanthus Lk. & O. (T.)

Bo. broadly spherical (always?), to 50 cm ∅, fresh green; **Ri.** 21–24; **Rsp.** smaller, 4; **Csp.** 3–4, the larger ones flattened, transversely banded; **Fl.** 3.75 cm lg., yellow.—Mexico. E. palmeri may be a form of, or even identical with, E. platyacanthus, since the latter has never been rediscovered, and the former shows only insignificant differences.

E. polycephalus Eng. & Big.

Bo. spherical to cylindric, freely offsetting to form large groups, single heads to 70 cm lg. have been noted; **Ri.** 13–21, ± sinuate; **Rsp.** to c. 10, to 5 cm lg.; **Csp.** 4, stouter, 3–9 cm lg., ± banded; **Sp.** downy at first, then smooth, subulate, reddish; **Fl.** to 6 cm lg., yellowish; **Fr.** 2.5 cm lg., densely woolly; **S.** papillose, angular, dull black.—USA (Utah and more southern States) to Mexico (Baja California, N. Sonora).

E. visnaga Hook.

Bo. stoutly cylindric, to 3 m h., to 1 m ∅; **crown** brownish to light; **Ri.** to 40, with a longitudinal furrow along the crest; **Ar.** ± confluent above; **Sp.** only 4, cruciform, stout, to 5 cm lg., pale brown; **Fl.** to 8 cm ∅, yellow; **Pet.** to 3.5 cm lg.; **Fr.** cylindric, very woolly.—Mexico (San Luis Potosí).

E. xeranthemoides (Coult.) Eng.

Bo. forming groups, single heads to 18 cm h., light green; **Ri.** 13, slightly tuberculate; **Sp.** 10–15, whitish-pink at first, thin, stiff, banded; **Rsp.** 3–4 cm lg., ± recurved; **Csp.** 4, 3–6 cm lg., one longer than the others, stiff, somewhat curving; **Fl.** 5 cm lg., light yellow; **Fr.** 3 cm lg., densely woolly; **S.** 2.5 mm lg., glossy, brownish-black.—USA (Utah –Arizona border).

Echinocereus Eng. (137)

The species of this Genus were for some time referred to Cereus, the large collective Genus of this name, on account of their predominantly cylindric form. However, as ± shortly cereoid plants with soft flesh and ± acicularly spiny flowers and fruits, they constitute a very characteristic and diverse group of species—i.e. predominantly cereoid in form, reducing to small-spherical—for which I have therefore segregated their own Group, Echinocerei; Engelmann gave expression to this special position in the generic name. The Genus is particularly difficult to classify since many species are very variable, and there are transitional forms between similar species. The older authors followed the same principle as I have done: to record clearly the natural swarms of species and forms by dividing also into varieties. Some recent authors, particularly those in America, have objected to this and have in fact grouped the species into larger genera, although no two opinions agree. This can only be damaging to our knowledge of the astonishing natural variability which is so prominent a feature of Echinocereus; precise recording is therefore of greater importance than subjective groupings, and we must apply Spegazzini's phrase: "melius abundare quam deficere", so that accurately recorded data can provide the tool for further investigations.

Most of the species tend to offset, some very much so; and many—particularly the "Pectinati", those with a ± comb-like arrangement of the spines—have conspicuously colourful spination; in many species the flowers last for quite a long time, while the size varies from relatively large funnelform, to fairly small. The fruits of some species are used for making jam (even nowadays?).—Distribution: USA (from roughly the central W. States to the S. frontier), Mexico (Baja California, W. coast, and from the N. to the Central Highlands). [(R.), (G); the green, freely offsetting species grow well on their own roots.]

For the sake of clarity, the species have been grouped in the following Series, and the appropriate figure is shown in brackets after the specific name:

Flowers slender, fairly
  long .... 1. Scheeriani Backbg.
Flowers small to larger
  funnelform, or without
  a long tube:
Spines inconspicuous
  or missing .... 2. Subinermes K. Sch.
Spines more
  conspicuous
  Body (eventually)
    prostrate .... 3. Prostrati K. Sch.
  Body erect
    (including the
    pectinate species) . 4. Erecti K. Sch.

E. acifer (O.) Lem. (4)
Bo. offsetting; **Ri.** c. 7, very tuberculate; **Rsp.** 7–8, radiating and projecting, thin; **Csp.** 1–4; all **Sp.** brown, the centrals somewhat stouter; **Fl.** red.—N. Mexico(?). A little understood species which can still be found in older collections.
    v. durangensis (Pos.) K. Sch. is better accorded specific rank, as was earlier the case: **E. durangensis** Pos.;
    v. **trichacanthus** Hildm. is doubtfully referable here; it has whitish **Rsp.**, 1 dirty brown **Csp.**, and the **Fl.** and **An.** are garnet-red.

E. adustus Eng. (4)
Bo. solitary, shortly cylindric, to 6 cm h.; **Ri.** 13–15; **Ar.** elliptic; **Rsp.** 16–20, ± appressed; **Csp.** 0–1, often elongated and projecting; all **Sp.** with brown or dark tips; **Fl.** to 4 cm lg., purple, with longer **H.** and short brown **Sp.**—Mexico (Chihuahua).

E. albatus Backbg. (4)
Bo. short-cylindric, somewhat branching, to c. 4 cm ∅; **Ri.** c. 12, low, with small Tub.; **Rsp.** c. 40; **Csp.** c. 10, scarcely differentiated; all **Sp.** stiff, white, dense, brittle; **Fl.** light red with a darker M.-stripe, c. 10 cm ∅.—Mexico.

E. amoenus (Dietr.) K.Sch. (2)
Bo. low-growing, thickened below; **Ri.** 13, sometimes weakly tuberculate; **Sp.** at first only 6–8, short, eventually dropping; **Fl.** 5 cm lg., light purplish-red, green-striped on the outside; **Tu.** and **Ov.** with shorter brown **H.** and **Br.**—Mexico (San Luis Potosí; Hidalgo).

E. arizonicus Orc. (4)
Bo. forming groups; **Ri.** 10, ± tuberculate; **Ar.** white; **Rsp.** 10, unequal, white; **Csp.** 1–4, stout, the lowest one longest, to 2.5 cm lg., weakly angular below, purple; **Fl.** carmine.—USA (Arizona). Sometimes referred to E. fendleri and E. triglochidiatus; therefore better regarded as distinct spec.

E. armatus (Pos.) Knuth (4)
Bo. cylindric; **Ri.** c. 20; **Rsp.** dull olive to brownish; **Csp.** 1 at first, later 2, somewhat longer than the Rsp., projecting, blackish.—Origin? Formerly referred to E. pectinatus, but quite clearly differentiated from the latter.

E. baileyi Rose (4)
Bo. cylindric, to over 10 cm h., 5 cm ∅; **Ri.** 15, ± spiralled; **Rsp.** c. 16, white at first, later yellowish, or brownish tinged pink; **Csp.** 0; **Fl.** 6 cm ∅, light purple; **Ov.** shortly hairy, with 10–12 thin whitish or brownish **Sp.**; **Fr.** green, ovoid, c. 1 cm ∅.—USA (Oklahoma, Wichita Mts.). The following

varieties are distinguished:
    v. **albispinus** (Lahm.) Backbg.: **Sp.** white, longer;
    v. **brunispinus** Backbg.: **Sp.** long, all brown;
    v. **caespiticus** Backbg.: forming cushions; **Sp.** short, white;
    v. **flavispinus** Backbg.: **Sp.** long, weak, yellowish-white;
    v. **roseispinus** Backbg.: **Sp.** long, weak, pink above.

E. barthelowanus Br. & R. (4)
Bo. forming groups; **St.** cylindric, to 20 cm lg., 4–5 cm ∅; **Ri.** c. 10, ± tuberculate; **Sp.** ± interlacing, more numerous, to 7 cm lg., pink at first, becoming white or yellow, tipped brown or black; **Csp.** c. 6, thickened below, one of these longer; **Fl.** purple, very short; **Pet.** only 3–4 mm lg.; **Ov.** very spiny, with white, pink-tipped Sp.—Mexico (Baja California, Sta. Maria Bay).

E. blanckii (Pos.) Palm. (3)
Bo. freely offsetting; **St.** dark green, 5–6-angled, to 2.5 cm ∅, tuberculate; **Rsp.** 8, white, one of them mostly red at first above; **Csp.** 1–2, to 3 cm lg. or more, mostly brown or black; **Fl.** large, ± fluttering, violet-red.—Mexico (Tamaulipas). The following varieties are distinguished, all previously regarded as having specific rank:
    v. **berlandieri** (Pos.) Backbg.: darker green; **Csp.** 1, yellowish-brown; **Fl.** not fluttering, carmine-pink;
    v. **leonensis** (Matths.) Backbg.: light green; **Ri.** 6–7; **Rsp.** entirely white; **Csp.** only 1, to 3 cm lg.; **Fl.** purplish-violet, dark-striped;
    v. **poselgerianus** (Lke.) Backbg.: light green; **Ri.** 6–7; **Csp.** 1–3, with brown bands; **Rsp.** white, yellow-tipped; **Fl.** carmine-violet.

E. bonkerae Thornb. & Bonk.: see **E. fendleri** (Eng.) Rümpl.

E. boyce-thompsonii Orc.: see **E. fendleri** (Eng.) Rümpl.

E. brandegeei (Coult.) K.Sch. (4)
Bo. forming groups; **St.** long-cylindric; **Ri.** tuberculate; **Ar.** 1–1.5 cm apart; **Sp.** 12–16, 5–15 mm lg., reddish-yellow to grey, mostly thickened and light brown below; **Csp.** 4, cruciform, flattened and dagger-like, 3-angled, base as for Rsp., the lowest one to 8 cm lg., all very robust; **Fl.** to 5 cm lg., rather more across; **Sep.** violet-red, M.-stripe olive-coloured; **Pet.** to 4.5 cm lg., reddish-violet; **Fr.** spherical, 3 cm ∅.—Mexico (Baja California and neighbouring islands).

E. bristolii Marsh. (4)
Bo. offsetting; **St.** to 20 cm lg., 4 cm ∅, whitish-

133

green; **Ri.** 15–16, tuberculate; **Rsp.** 20, thin, white; **Csp.** 3, the lowest one curved downwards, white below, red-tipped; **Fl.** 9 cm lg., purple; **Fr.** very spiny.—[Distribution, amended by W. Haage] Mexico (Sonora, W. of Moctezuma).

E. caespitosus Eng. (4)
Bo. fairly slender; **St.** rather elongated, especially in cultivated plants; **Ri.** 12–18; **Ar.** ± woolly at first; **Rsp.** 20–30, mostly whitish to ± pink; **Csp.** absent or very rarely 1–2, short; **Fl.** to 8 cm lg. and br., brilliant pink.—USA to N. Mexico (Saltillo). Obviously a rather variable spec. I have a specimen which corresponds fairly closely with the Fig. of Boissevain & Davidson ("Colorado Cacti", 46. 1940, Fig. 32) and is very slender, with only 11 Ri.; Sp. brownish-white at first, soon all white; most Ar. lack any Csp., but sometimes one finer, shorter, dark Sp. is present; Fl. c. 7.5 cm $\emptyset$, as in the above description, but the throat, Fil. and style are greenish. The Sp. are "not interlocking" (Boiss. & Davids.).
Britton & Rose referred the spec. to E. reichenbachii and said: "spines interlocking". Thus the 2 spec. are *not* identical; however E. caespitosus is probably somewhat variable, like some other spec. In their description, Boiss. & Davids. give the Fil. as brownish-purple and the style as yellowish.

The form with pure white Sp. is sometimes known as **E. caespitosus** v. **tamaulipensis** (Frič) Borg; it also offsets from the flanks.

E. canyonensis Clov. & Jott.: probably only an ecotype of **E. roemeri.**

E. castaneus hort.: see **E. pectinatus** v. **castaneus** (Eng.) Maths.

E. chisoensis Marsh. (4)
Bo. solitary, cylindric; **Ri.** 15–16, spiralled, tuberculate; **Rsp.** 11–14, bristly, brown, white below; **Csp.** bristly, 1–4, dark; **Fl.** 6 cm lg., with wool and bristly Sp.; **Sep.** pink; **Pet.** pink; **Fr.** clavate, 3.5 cm lg., red.—USA (Texas, Chisos Mts.).

E. chloranthus (Eng.) Rümpl.: **E. viridiflorus** v. **chloranthus** (Eng.) Backbg.

E. chlorophthalmus (Hook.) Br. & R. (4)
Bo. offsetting; **St.** ± spherical, bluish-green; **Ri.** 10–12, ± tuberculate; **Rsp.** 7–10, thin-acicular, to 18 mm lg.; **Csp.** 1, stouter; **Fl.** purple, throat white; **Ov.** very tuberculate.—Mexico (Real del Monte).

E. cinerascens (DC.) Rümpl. (3)
Bo. forming mats to 1.2 m br. and 30 cm h.; **St.** 4–5 cm $\emptyset$; **Ri.** mostly (5–)6–8(–12), broad, rather

obtuse; **Rsp.** 8–10, to 2 cm lg.; **Csp.** 1–4, to 2(–3) cm lg., ruby-red below at first (Schumann); **Sp.** all whitish; **Fl.** 6–8 cm lg., to 6 cm $\emptyset$; **Tu.** short, with white wool and Br.; **Pet.** purple, throat lighter; **Fr.** violet-pink, to 3 cm $\emptyset$.—Central Mexico. Rather variable, acc. Berger.

E. coccineus Eng. (4)
Bo. spherical-ovoid, 3–5 cm $\emptyset$, eventually elongated and offsetting to form groups to 1 m br., to 20 cm h., sometimes in colonies of to 200 St.; **Ri.** 8–11, tuberculate; **Rsp.** acicular, 8–12, to 2 cm lg., mostly white; **Csp.** several, longer and rather stouter, yellowish, whitish or even reddish or blackish; **Fl.** 5–7 cm lg., scarlet (to carmine).—USA (S. States to Colorado).
v. **kunzei** (Gürke) Backbg.: differentiated by 1–3 **Csp.**, purplish-red at first above, becoming white, thickened below; **Fl.** to 8 cm $\emptyset$, scarlet with a broad carmine stripe.—USA (Arizona, Phoenix; rare).

E. conglomeratus Först. (4)
Bo. forming groups; **St.** 10–20 cm lg.; **Ri.** 11–13, slightly sinuate; **Rsp.** 9–10, to 1.6 cm lg., glassy, yellow below; **Csp.** several, to 7 cm lg., flexible; **Fl.** 6–7 cm lg., widely expanding, purple, with white Sp.; **Pet.** 2 cm lg.; **Fr.** 3 cm $\emptyset$.—Mexico (Coahuila, Nuevo León, Zacatecas). Sp.-colour said to vary from white to brownish (Knuth).

E. cucumis Werd.: **E. gentryi** Clov.

E. dasyacanthus Eng. (4)
Bo. mostly solitary, cylindric, to 30 cm lg., to 10 cm $\emptyset$, densely spiny; **Ri.** 15–21, low; **Rsp.** 16–24, pink at first, fine; **Csp.** 3–8, somewhat stouter; **Fl.** to 10 cm lg., c. 7.5 cm $\emptyset$, opening only around midday, yellowish; **Ov.** very spiny; **Fr.** spherical, purple, to 3.5 cm $\emptyset$.—USA (W. Texas, S. New Mexico), Mexico (Chihuahua). Sp.-tips vary from reddish through brownish to blackish.
v. **ctenoides** (Eng.) Backbg.: **Ri.** only to 17; **Sp.** more distinctly thickened below; **Csp.** mostly only 2–3; **Fl.** rather shorter;
v. **steereae** (Clov.) Marsh.: similar to the type but the **Fl.** is red.

E. davisii A. D. Houghton: **E. viridiflorus** v. **davisii** (A. D. Houghton) Marsh. (also regarded as a distinct spec.). (Fig. 89.)

E. decumbens Clov. & Jott. (3)
Bo. offsetting; **St.** to over 50, to 60 cm lg., to 5 cm $\emptyset$; **Sp.** yellow to white or pink; **Csp.** 3–4, the lowest one longest, to 3.5 cm lg., the others and the **Rsp.** to 2.2 cm lg., weak, flexible; **Fl.** ?—USA (Arizona).

E. delaetii Gürke (4)
Bo. offsetting; **St.** erect, laxly branching, to 30 cm lg.; **Rsp.** 18–36, (yellowish-)white, 8–10 mm lg., sharp; **Csp.** 4–5, bristly, yellowish, reddish-tipped, 2–3 cm lg., straight or contorted, to 3 cm lg., also several ± contorted stout **H.** 6–10 cm lg., white or grey; **Fl.** 6–7 cm lg., 6 cm ∅, light purplish-pink.—Mexico (Coahuila).

E. dubius (Eng.) Rümpl. (4)
Bo. offsetting, forming dense groups; **St.** to 20 cm lg., lighter green, to 20 cm lg.; **Ri.** c. 6–7, swollen around the Ar.; **Rsp.** 5–8, 12–30 mm lg.; **Csp.** 1–4, 3.7 to c. 7 cm lg.; **Fl.** 6 cm lg., pale purple, with white **Br.**; **Fr.** very spiny, to 3 cm lg.—USA (SE. Texas).

E. durangensis Pos. (4)
Bo. cylindric, offsetting; **Ri.** 10, transversely divided and ± tuberculate above; **Rsp.** 8–9, to 12 mm lg., light horn-coloured, darker above and below; **Csp.** 1(–3–4), porrect, dark brown or horn-coloured, dark-tipped; **Fl.** 7 cm lg., 5 cm ∅, with white flock and dark-tipped **Sp.**; **Pet.** blood-red, lighter at the base.—Mexico (Durango). Because of a misinterpretation, earlier referred to E. acifer as a var.; better regarded as a distinct spec.

E. engelmannii (Parry) Rümpl. (4)
Bo. forming lax groups; **St.** cylindric, to 45 cm lg., to 6 cm ∅; **Ri.** 10–13(–14), low, indistinctly tuberculate; **Rsp.** stiff, c. 10; **Fl.** 5–8 cm lg., to 7.5 cm ∅; **Fr.** 3 cm lg., spherical to ovoid.—USA (S. States) to N. Mexico. So variable in Sp.-colour that v. albispinus Cels, v. fulvispinus Cels, etc., can really only be regarded as forms.
    v. **nicholii** L. Bens. forms large groups; **St.** to c. 60 cm lg., to 7.5 cm ∅; **Sp.** all yellow.—USA (Arizona).

E. enneacanthus Eng. (3)
Bo. offsetting to form groups up to 1 m br.; **St.** 5–7 cm ∅, weak, ± decumbent; **Ri.** 7–8(–12), unequal, mostly under 1.2 cm lg., acicular, yellowish then brownish; **Csp.** mostly 1, 3–5 cm lg., terete; **Fl.** 5–6 cm lg., 7.5 cm ∅, light purple; **Fr.** 2 cm lg., spherical, reddish.—USA (New Mexico, S. Texas), Mexico (in the N., e.g. Chihuahua).
    v. **carnosus** (Rümpl.) Quehl: dark sap-green; **Sp.** stouter, whitish-grey; **Fl.** larger, to 10 cm lg., 9 cm ∅.

E. fendleri (Eng.) Rümpl. (4)
Bo. offsetting, erect; **St.** to 15 cm lg., 6–10 cm ∅, ± limp; **Ri.** 9–10(–12), indistinctly tuberculate; **Rsp.** 9–11, shorter than the centrals, white to pale grey; **Csp.** 1, curving upwards, to 3.7 cm lg., pale grey; **Fl.** light to deep purple, to 6.75 cm ∅; **Fr.** c. 3 cm lg.—

USA (New Mexico, Arizona), N. Mexico (Sonora, Chihuahua). Spec. varies; some specimens resemble E. triglochidiatus, but latter has scarlet **Fl.**
    v. **albiflorus** (Wgt.) Backbg.: differs in having **Fl.** white to pale pink;
    v. **bonkerae** (Thornb. & Bonk.) L. Bens.: **Bo.** forming groups of up to 15 **St.**, to 20 cm lg., c. 6.25 cm ∅; **Ri.** 11–16; **Csp.** 1(–3) to 0.8 cm lg., projecting, white or pale grey, brown-tipped; **Fl.** to 6.25 cm ∅; **Fr.** to 2.5 cm lg.—USA (Arizona). This has been accorded different status by 3 American authors, including specific rank, which demonstrates how the views of the specialists are at variance, and how impossible it is to follow any one of them unquestioningly; in any event the "var." is noticeably differentiated by its short appressed spination. However, transitional forms have been observed;
    v. **boyce-thompsonii** (Orc.) L. Bens.; **Ri.** 12–14(–18); **Sp.** differing in colour, from straw to reddish or brownish, or white with a light brown base.—USA (Arizona); a variant with more brightly coloured Sp. and numerous Ri. which is accorded specific status by many authors;
    v. **rectispinus** (Peebl.) L. Bens.: **Csp.** to only 2.5 cm lg., dark-tipped;
    v. **robustus** (Peebl.) L. Bens.: **Csp.** over 2.5–7.5 cm lg.

E. ferreirianus Gat. (4)
Bo. erect, offsetting; **St.** to 30 cm h., to 8 cm ∅; **Ri.** 9–13, somewhat tuberculate; **Rsp.** c. 9–13, to 2 cm lg., grey to brown; **Csp.** several, mostly 3–5 cm lg., the longest one porrect to down-curving, all thickened below, brown, more reddish below at first; **Fl.** to 6 cm lg., 4 cm ∅; **Pet.** pink, more orange below.—Mexico (Baja California, Los Angeles Bay and islands).

E. fitchii Br. & R. (4)
Bo. short-cylindric, somewhat offsetting; **St.** 8–10 cm lg., 4–5 cm ∅, concealed by Sp.; **Ri.** 10–12, low, rounded; **Rsp.** c. 20, white; **Csp.** 4–6, acicular, variable in colour, mostly brownish, also white below; **Fl.** 6–7 cm lg., pink to purplish-pink, mostly darker at the centre; **Ov.** delicately hairy, densely spiny.— USA (Texas, Laredo). Very free-flowering. [(G).]

E. floresii Backbg. (4)
Bo. slender-cylindric, to c. 10 cm h., 3 cm ∅, sometimes offsetting, with a thick taproot; **Ri.** 14, low; **Rsp.** acicular, interlacing, c. 16 mm lg., whitish, brownish above; **Csp.** 0–1–2, where present one is longer, eventually mostly pointing downwards, brown; **Tu.** and **Ov.** with dense Sp. 1.5 cm lg.; **Fl.** 4.5 cm lg., 7 cm ∅, red.— Mexico (Sinaloa, Topolabampo).

E. fobeanus Oehme (4)
Bo. cylindric, offsetting; **St.** glossy green, to c. 9 cm h., 5 cm ⌀; **Ri.** 10, spiralled, tuberculate; **Sp.** finely acicular, brittle, projecting; **Rsp.** 12–14, to 1 cm lg., white, pink or dark-tipped; **Csp.** 2, 1.5 cm lg., red; **Fl.** 9 cm lg., 12 cm ⌀, pink, throat white, woolly, with brown, pink-tipped Sp.; **Pet.** fimbriate.— Origin?

E. gentryi Clov. (1)
Bo. prostrate or decumbent, offsetting, with few St.; **St.** to 15 cm lg., 2.5 cm ⌀; **Rsp.** 8–12, 1–2 mm lg., brownish; **Csp.** mostly 1, similar to the Rsp.; **Fl.** slender-funnelform, to 8 cm lg., 5–6 cm ⌀, pink, open mainly at night.— Mexico (Sonora). Better known under the name E. cucumis Werd. (E. nocturniflorus hort. or E. noctiflorus hort.)

E. glycimorphus Rümpl.: **E. cinerascens** (DC.) Rümpl. (form).

E. gonacanthus Rümpl.: **E. triglochidiatus** v. **gonacanthus** (Eng. & Big.) Boiss.

E. grandis Br. & R. (4)
Bo. solitary to group-forming, thick-cylindric, eventually to 40 cm h., to 12 cm ⌀; **Ri.** 21–25; **Rsp.** 15–25; **Csp.** 8–12; **Sp.** whitish to cream; **Fl.** 5–6 cm lg., not expanding widely, with white H. and straw-coloured Sp.; **Sep.** white with a green M.-line; **Pet.** 1.5 cm lg., white, green below; **Fr.** densely spiny.— Mexico (S. Esteban Is. and others).

E. hancockii Daws. (4)
Bo. offsetting, forming groups of to 30 St., 35 cm h., 1.1 m br.; **St.** mostly to 12 cm lg., 5.5–7 cm ⌀; **Ri.** low; **Sp.** pink at first, later dark straw-coloured, subulate, stiff, straight; **Rsp.** 10–12, to 2.5 cm lg.; **Csp.** 7–8, to 6 cm lg., 2 mm thick below; **Fl.** 6 cm lg., yellow, fading to salmon-pink.—Mexico (Baja California, Bahia San Hipolito).

E. hempelii Fobe (4)
Bo. dark green, erect; **St.** to 15 cm lg., to 7 cm ⌀; **Ri.** tuberculate; **Rsp.** (4–)6, spreading, white, brown-tipped, to 1 cm lg.; **Csp.** 0; **Fl.** to 8 cm br., funnelform; **Pet.** lax, 3 cm lg., light lilac-pink.— Mexico (acc. Br. & R.).

E. huitcholensis (Web.) Gürke (1)
Bo. freely offsetting; **St.** to c. 6 cm lg., 2 cm (?) ⌀; **Ri.** 12, rounded, low; **Rsp.** 2–5 mm lg.; **Csp.** 1, to 1 cm lg.; **Fl.** very slender, 11 cm lg., delicately hairy, with white Sp.; **Pet.** orange (?).—Mexico (Sierra de Nayarit).

E. knippelianus Liebn. (2)
Bo. solitary, the subterranean portion napiform,

the visible portion spherical to somewhat elongated, to 10 cm h.; **St.** deep green, sappy and soft; **Ri.** c. 5 at first, rounded; **Sp.** short, yellowish, soon dropping; **Fl.** medium-large, pink, to 3 cm lg.— Mexico (Coahuila).

E. kunzei Gürke 1907
Bo. cylindric, greyish-green, to 24 cm h., to 8 cm ⌀, crown not depressed, overtopped by the Sp.; **Ri.** 13, vertical, separated by deep furrows, dived into Tub. by shallow indentations; **Ar.** ± round, 1 cm apart, with short, greyish-white woolly felt, soon becoming glabrous; **Rsp.** 15–17, white, radiating, tipped brownish, lower ones 8–10 mm lg., upper ones mostly only 3–5 mm lg.; **Csp.** mostly 1, white, dark purplish-red above midway, pointing obliquely downwards, 10–12 mm lg., often also 2–3 shorter Csp.; **Fl.** lateral, 9 cm lg.; **Ov.** 15 mm lg., dark green, with triangular Sc.; **Sep.** lanceolate, olive with a dull red M.-line; **Pet.** spatulate, salmon to scarlet, with a carmine M.-stripe; **style** white with 12 dark emerald Sti.; **Fr.** green or greenish-yellow.—USA (Arizona). Spec. appears to have been exterminated or to have disappeared. (Collected by Dr. R. E. Kunze).

E. ledingii Peebl. (4)
Bo. forming fairly dense groups; **St.** cylindric, to 50 cm lg., to 10 cm ⌀; **Ri.** 12–14, indistinctly tuberculate; **Rsp.** 10–12, straight, to almost 2 cm lg.; **Csp.** (main Sp.) 1, robust, stiff, down-curving, often with 2 Ssp.; all **Sp.** yellow; **Fl.** 5 cm ⌀, purple; **Fr.** pale green, almost 2.5 cm lg.—USA (Arizona).

E. leeanus (Hook.) Lem. (4)
Bo. forming mats; **St.** erect, vivid green, to 30 cm h., to 9 cm ⌀; **Ri.** 12–14, ± transversely furrowed; **Rsp.** 10–13, thin-subulate, reddish-brown at first, straight, 5–12 mm lg.; **Csp.** 2–3, to 2.5 cm lg., reddish-brown, becoming grey; **Fl.** 7 cm lg., brick-red to carmine; **Pet.** broadly spatulate, ± rounded above.—Mexico.
   v. **multicostatus** (Cels) K.Sch.: **Csp.** darker red, not soon becoming grey, the entire spination thus appearing more reddish. E. durangensis Pos. may be a related spec.

E. longisetus (Eng.) Rümpl. (4)
Bo. erect, offsetting quite freely; **St.** to 20 cm lg., to 4.5 cm ⌀, at first dark then lighter green; **Ri.** 11–14; **Rsp.** 15–25, to 1.5 cm lg.; **Csp.** 5–7, to 4 cm lg., white, dark-tipped, thickened and brownish below; **Sp.** all bristly and thin, dense, not interlacing; **Fl.** 6 cm lg. and br., light purple; **Pet.** lanceolate, 3 cm lg.—Mexico (Coahuila, Sierra de la Paila). This spec., with its projecting Sp., is attractive but rather rare.

E. luteus Br. & R. = Echinocereus subinermis v. luteus (Br. & R.) Backbg.
Differentiated from E. subinermis by shorter white **Sp.**—Sonora, near Alamos. The widely separated origin of this variety justifies classification as an independent spec.

E. mamillatus (Eng.) Br. & R. (4)
Bo. offsetting; **St.** ascending, 20–30 cm lg., 3.5–6 cm ∅; **Ri.** 20–25, very tuberculate; **Rsp.** 10–25, acicular, 3–12 mm lg.; **Csp.** 3–4, much stouter, to 2.5 cm lg.; **Sp.** reddish at first, then white; **Fl.** purple.—Mexico (Baja California, Mulegé).

E. mariae Backbg.—Nat. Cact. & Succ. Journ. (Gr. Brit.), 20: 2, 19, 1965 (4)
Bo. slender-columnar, erect, tapering towards the apex, densely covered with short Sp. and white felt, the latter eventually loosening and disappearing from the lower Bo.; **St.** to c. 15 cm lg., 1.5–2.3 cm ∅, branching from the base; **Ri.** c. 14, narrow, low, c. 4 mm br., tuberculate above, distinctly spiralled; **Ar.** c. 3 mm ∅, with white hairy felt; **Sp.** 15–20, very thin, to c. 4–5 mm lg., white, radiating, the centrals light brown and somewhat thickened below, the longer ones sometimes directed ± downwards; **Fl.** apical, c. 7–7.5 cm ∅, purple; **Pet.** noticeably narrowing to the base; **Fr.** green, laxly floccose.—USA (Oklahoma, Wichita Mts., the extreme W. margin of the Headquarter Mts., c. 3 miles W. of Granite, or 3 miles N.). A·rare and unusual spec.; named for its finder, Mrs. Mary Polaski.

E. maritimus (Jon.) K.Sch. (4)
Bo. forming groups or mounds to 30 cm h., to 90 cm br., of up to 200 heads; **St.** spherical to cylindric, 5–15 cm lg.; **Ri.** 8–10; **Rsp.** 9(–10), spreading; **Csp.** 1(–3–4), ± subulate, the uppermost one also angular, to over 3 cm lg.; **Fl.** small, to 3–4 cm lg.; **Pet.** ± lanceolate, rounded above, glossy greenish-yellow.—Mexico (Baja California, W. coast).

E. marksianus F. Schwarz n.sp. (4)
Bo. eventually ± arching over, offsetting freely from the base, bluish-green, later lighter green; **St.** to 40 cm lg., to 6.5 cm ∅; **Ri.** 10; **Sp.** dark brown to black at first, reddish in the lowest third; **Rsp.** 10–11, 3–10 mm lg., becoming greyish-white; **Csp.** 1(–4), cruciform, the longest one to 3.5 cm lg.; **Fl.** more funnelform and open, light crimson to true red, c. 8 cm lg., 7 cm ∅; **Tu.** reddish; **Ov.** grass-green, spiny; **throat** yellow; **Fil.** and **style** yellowish below, red above; **Fr.** with dense black Sp.—N. Mexico. Has been in collections for quite a long time, but not hitherto described. Close to E. leeanus, but with a more open perianth. Found and

named by F. Schwarz, so that I now provide the missing Latin diagnosis (omitted in translated text).

E. matthesianus Backbg.—Descr. Cact. Nov. III: 6. 1963 (1)
Bo. columnar, erect, green; **St.** to c. 4.8 cm ∅; **Ri.** c. 12, c. 11 mm br., rounded, rather flat; **Ar.** white, c. 2 mm ∅; **Rsp.** mostly 9, to 8 mm lg., the upper ones shortest, pale reddish-grey; **Csp.** mostly 4, 5–11 mm lg., thickened below, somewhat darker; **Fl.** c. 10 cm lg., 4.5 cm ∅, fiery red; **Tu.** with white flock and brown to white Br. to c. 1.5 cm lg.; **style** pale green; **Fil.** pale green below, white above.—Mexico (?). (Fig. 90.)

E. melanocentrus Lowry (4)
Bo. short-cylindric; **St.** to 3.5 cm ∅; **Ri.** c. 12, low, tuberculate; **Sp.** not interlacing; **Rsp.** c. 17, brownish, blackish at first; **Csp.** sometimes present, short; **Fl.** rotate, purple, darker at the centre.—USA (Texas, near Alice).

E. merkeri Hildm. (4)
Bo. offsetting to form groups; **St.** erect, 12–15 cm ∅, light green; **Ri.** 8–9, sinuate; **Rsp.** 6–9, white, glossy; **Csp.** 1(–2), to 5 cm lg., white, thickened and with a red spot below; **Fl.** 6 cm lg.; **Pet.** shortly oblong, 3 cm lg., purple; **Ov.** with long Br.-Sp.—N. to Central Mexico. Br. and R. state only that the St. are "erect", without any indication of length; Schumann described the spec. as follows: "St. columnar, erect at first, then prostrate, creeping, then offsetting, to 2 m lg. and 15 cm ∅". In this case the spec. is better referred to Series 3: Prostrati.

E. mojavensis (Eng. & Big.) Rümpl. (4)
Bo. freely branching, forming groups of up to 800 heads; **St.** pale green, 5–20 cm lg.; **Ri.** 8–12, very tuberculate; **Rsp.** to 10, acicular, 1–2.5 cm lg.; **Csp.** (?0–)1, subulate, porrect, often weak, also contorted, to over 5 cm lg.; **Sp.** all white to grey; **Fl.** rather narrow, 5–7 cm lg., carmine to pale scarlet with a "nopal-red" tinge; **Pet.** broad, ± truncate; **Fr.** 3 cm lg.—USA (SW. States to Nevada and Utah).

E. neo-mexicanus Standl. (4)
Bo. forming groups; **St.** to 25 cm lg., to 7 cm ∅, bluish-green; **Ri.** 11–12, obtuse, low, ± tuberculate; **Rsp.** 13–16, to 1.5 cm lg., white; **Csp.** 6, the lowest one yellowish to white, others reddish, to 4 cm lg.; **Sp.** all slender-subulate; **Fl.** 5 cm lg., narrow, not expanding widely, light scarlet.—USA (New Mexico, W. of the Organ Mts.)

E. noctiflorus hort. or E. nocturniflorus hort.: **E. gentryi** Clov.

E. ochoterenae G. Ort. (4)
Bo. forming groups; **St.** 10 cm lg., 4–7 cm ∅, green, spotted red; **Ri.** (8–10–)11; **Rsp.** 9, to 1 cm lg., slender-subulate; **Csp.** 4, to 1.2 cm lg., (in one form with darker Sp. the Csp. are to 2 cm lg.); **Sp.** all reddish-yellow at first, soon white, then grey; **Fl.** 7 cm lg., reddish outside; **Pet.** canary-yellow.—Mexico (Concordia, Cerro de la Cobriza).

E. octacanthus (Mühlpfrdt.) Br. & R. (4)
Bo. offsetting to form groups of many heads; **St.** ovoid, yellowish-green, to 10 cm lg., 5–7 cm ∅; **Ri.** 7–9, obtuse, ± tuberculate; **Rsp.** 7–8, 1–2.4 cm lg.; **Csp.** 1, stouter, 2–3 cm lg.; **Sp.** all stiff, greyish-brown at first; **Fl.** 5 cm lg., open for several days, purple-reddish.—USA (Texas and New Mexico to Utah and Colorado). Often seen in collections, incorrectly, as E. labouretianus hort.

E. oklahomensis Lahm. was only a name for **E. baileyi** v. **brunispinus** Backbg.

E. ortegae Rose (4)
Bo. forming groups, dark green; **Ri.** 7–8, low; **Rsp.** 0; **Csp.** 3–4, acicular, under 1 cm lg., yellowish at first, flecked brown, soon whitish; **Fl.** 7 cm lg., 6 cm ∅, scarlet; **Pet.** numerous, oblong or spatulate; **Ov.** with short felt and dense Sp.—Mexico (Rio Tamazula).

E. pacificus (Eng.) Br. & R. (4)
Bo. forming groups of up to 100 heads, to 60 cm br.; **St.** 15–25 cm lg., 5–6 cm ∅; **Ri.** 10–12, obtuse; **Rsp.** 10–12, 5–10 mm lg.; **Csp.** 4–5, to 2.5 cm lg.; **Sp.** all grey, tinged reddish; **Fl.** fairly small, c. 3 cm lg., deep red, with long brownish-yellow wool and reddish-brown Br.—Mexico (Baja California, Bahia de Todos Santos).

E. palmeri Br. & R. (4)
Bo. small, to 8 cm h.; **St.** only 2–3 cm ∅; **Ri.** 9–10; **Rsp.** 12–15, thin, brown-tipped; **Csp.** 1, porrect, to 2 cm lg., brown to blackish; **Fl.** 3.5 cm lg., purple; **Ov.** with white wool and brown Sp.—Mexico (near Chihuahua).

E. papillosus Lke. (3)
Bo. rather freely offsetting, dark green, decumbent; **St.** to 30 cm lg., 2–4 cm ∅; **Ri.** 6–10, very tuberculate; **Rsp.** acicular, c. 7, white to yellow, to 1 cm lg.; **Csp.** 1, porrect, to over 1.2 cm lg., yellowish-white; **Fl.** to 12 cm ∅, yellow, with a red centre; **Pet.** 6 cm lg.—USA (W. Texas).
　v. **angusticeps** (Clov.) Marsh.: more densely branching, **St.** to 8 cm lg., to 3 cm ∅ (Texas, Linn).

E. pectinatus (Scheidw.) Eng. (4)

Bo. erect, stoutly cylindric, to 15 cm lg., to 6 cm ∅, ± concealed by the Sp.; **Ri.** 20–22; **Rsp.** c. 30, mostly under 1 cm lg., pectinate, white or pink, the colours often changing in zones; **Csp.** several, short; **Fl.** 6–8 cm lg.; **Tu.** and **Ov.** only felty and spiny; **Fr.** to 3 cm ∅.—Mexico (from Chihuahua to Guanajuato).
　v. **castaneus** (Eng.) Maths.: mostly with more slender **St.**, **Sp.** brown; **Rsp.** c. 20; **Fl.** over 8 cm br.; **Pet.** linear, not very br. There are other colour-variants: v. chrysacanthus K.Sch. with greenish-yellow Sp., and others where the Sp. are blackish; all are probably only forms of v. castaneus; there is also a reddish-brown form known as v. rubescens hort.;
　v. **rigidissimus** (Eng.) Rümpl.: mostly robuster, the colour-zones similarly; **Rsp.** c. 16; **Csp.** 0; **Fl.** to 7 cm lg.—USA (SE. Arizona) to N. Mexico (Sonora). (Fig. 91.)

E. pensilis (K. Brand.) J. A. Purp. (3)
Bo. ± offsetting; **St.** to 4 cm ∅; **Ri.** low; **Rsp.** 8; **Csp.** 1; **Sp.** not over 2 cm lg., yellow at first, then reddish-grey; **Fl.** slender, 5–6 cm lg., with short yellow or white wool and brown Br.-Sp.; **Fr.** 2 cm ∅.—Mexico (Baja California, Cape region, on mountain-sides).

E. pentalophus (DC.) Rümpl. (3)
Bo. forming mats, offsetting very freely; **St.** fresh green; **Rsp.** 3–5(–6), very short, white, brown-tipped; **Csp.** mostly absent, darker, to 1.5 cm lg.; **Fl.** large, 7–12 cm lg. and br., lilac to carmine, **throat** white; **Fil.** greenish.—USA (S. Texas) to N. Mexico (in the E.).
　v. **ehrenbergii** (Pfeiff.) Backbg.: **St.** to 20 cm lg., to 2.5 cm ∅, pale green, prostate; **Ri.** (5–)6, tuberculate, rather obtuse; **Rsp.** white; **Csp.** yellowish below; **Fl.** 6 cm lg., 4.5 cm ∅, light purple.—Central Mexico. This var. is seen by many authors, primarily because of the smaller Fl., as a valid spec.: E. ehrenbergii Pfeiff.
　v. **procumbens** (Eng.) Krainz can be distinguished as follows: **Rsp.** 4–6, brownish at first; **Csp.** mostly 1, darker; **Fl.** to 8 cm br., carmine-violet, white or yellowish below.

E. perbellus Br. & R. (4)
Bo. solitary or offsetting, slender-cylindric; **St.** to over 10 cm lg.; **Ri.** 15, low; **Rsp.** 12–15, 5–7 mm lg., somewhat spreading, white below, pale brown to reddish above; **Fl.** 4–6 cm lg., purple; **Pet.** broad, ± lanceolate.—USA (Texas, Big Springs).

E. phoeniceus Rümpl.: **E. coccineus** Eng.

E. pleiogonus (Lab.) Crouch. (4)
Bo. cylindric; **St.** greyish-olive; **Ri.** 13, tuberculate,

very low; **Rsp.** 9, spreading, thin, 4–11 mm lg.; **Csp.** 4, equalling the Rsp.; all **Sp.** reddish-brown at first, then dirty grey; **Fl.** ?—Mexico. A very distinctive spec. which was later regarded as E. leeanus; but it is clearly distinguishable from this.

E. polyacanthus Eng. (4)
Bo. forming mats of up to 50 heads; **St.** pale green, often reddish; **Ri.** 9–13, with flat transverse furrows; **Rsp.** 8–12, 1.4–2.3 cm lg., stout, subulate, terete, whitish or reddish-grey, dark-tipped; **Csp.** 2–4, thickened below, sometimes to 5 cm lg., often horn-coloured and flecked brown at first; **Fl.** 4.5–6 cm lg., ± funnelform, scarlet to carmine; **Pet.** horizontal at anthesis, some inner ones also blood-red.—Mexico (Chihuahua, Durango). Distinguished from similar spec. by the marked development of floral hair.

E. poselgeri Lem.: **Wilcoxia poselgeri** (Lem.) Br. & R.

E. poselgerianus Lke: **E. blanckii** v. **poselgerianus** (Lke.) Backbg.

E. primolanatus Schwarz (4)
Bo. cylindric, erect; **St.** to c. 10 cm lg., 4.5 cm ∅; **Ri.** 21–22, low; **Rsp.** c. 20, finely subulate, pectinate, c. 2 mm lg., one rather more central upper Sp. 1 mm lg., pointing upwards; **Sp.** all pinkish-white; young Ar. with solitary Br. to 7 mm lg. or longer; **Fl.** and **Fr.** ?—Mexico (in the N.?).

E. procumbens Eng.: **E. pentalophus** v. **procumbens** (Eng.) Krainz.

E. pulchellus (Mart.) K.Sch. (2)
Bo. offsetting, low, later elongated; **St.** to 10 cm lg., 4 cm ∅, bluish-green, then grey; **Ri.** finely tuberculate, to c. 12; **Sp.** few, short, yellowish, dropping; **Fl.** 4 cm lg., moderately large, whitish to light pink.—Mexico (Pachuca). Differentiated from E. amoenus (which has a more purple Fl. without longer H.) by having only 3–4(–5) Sp., and longer H. and Br. on Tu. and Ov.

E. purpureus Lahm. (4)
Bo. solitary to somewhat offsetting; **St.** slender-cylindric, to c. 12 cm h., 2–3 cm ∅; **Ri.** c. 12–14; **Rsp.** 14–18, pectinate, white, purplish-brown above; **Csp.** 0; **Fl.** to 10 cm lg., 7.5 cm ∅, brownish-purple, rather darker inside.—USA (Oklahoma, Wichita Res.).

E. radians Eng. (4)
Bo. stoutly cylindric; upper **Rsp.** 2–4 mm lg., laterals to 1 cm lg., lower ones to 6 mm lg.; **Csp.** 1, much stouter, porrect(!), brown to black, 2.5 cm

lg.—Mexico (Chihuahua, Cosihuiriachi). The first description is short and inadequate; on the basis of these data or the dark projecting Csp., this would appear to have been E. schwarzii hort. which had these characters; **Fl.** light purple, funnelform, c. 5 cm ∅.

E. reichenbachii (Tersch.) Hge. Jr. (4)
Bo. cylindric, solitary or somewhat offsetting; **St.** to 20 cm lg., 9 cm ∅; **Ri.** to 19; **Sp.** to 30, white to reddish or brownish, always of one colour only, dense and ± pectinate, somewhat spreading, or recurved, to 8 mm lg.; **Csp.** 0–1(–2?), like the Rsp.; **Fl.** to 7 cm lg. and br., with floccose H.—USA (Texas) to N. Mexico).

E. roemeri (Mühlpfrdt.) Rydb. non Eng. (4)
Bo. cylindric, forming groups; **St.** to 15 cm lg., to 6 cm ∅, **Ri.** (8–) 9–10; **Rsp.** (9–)10, grey or yellow, stout, almost 2 cm lg.; **Csp.** (1–)4, 3–5 cm lg., often angular and down-curving, also straight or flattened, ± keel-like, dark yellow to dark brown; **Fl.** 5 cm ∅, orange-red; **Fr.** red, 2 cm ∅.—USA (Texas to New Mexico and Colorado).

E. roetteri (Eng.) Rümpl. (4)
Bo. ± cylindric; **St.** to c. 15 cm h., 6.5 cm ∅; **Ri.** 10–13, tuberculate; **Rsp.** 8–15, to 16 mm lg.; **Csp.** 1–5, 8–12 mm lg., thickened below, stouter than the Rsp.; **Sp.** reddish, subulate; **Fl.** to 7.5 cm lg., light purple; **Fr.** to 2 cm lg.—USA (border, Texas and New Mexico), Mexico (Chihuahua).

> v. **lloydii** (Br. & R.) Backbg.: in groups of up to 6 very stout **St.**, to 25 cm h., to 10 cm ∅, light green; **Ri.** 11, ± straight; **Sp.** wine-red, c. 1 cm lg., paler below; **Rsp.** c. 14; **Csp.** 4–6, porrect; **Fl.** 8 cm lg.; **Ov.** with reddish Sp.—USA (Texas, Tuna Springs).

E. rosei Woot. & Standl. (4)
Bo. forming groups of up to 40 **St.** to 20 cm lg., 5–8 cm ∅; **Ri.** 8–11, obtuse; **Rsp.** c. 10, spreading; **Csp.** 4, 4–6 mm lg.; **Sp.** all pink to brownish-grey; **Fl.** 4–6 cm lg., scarlet; **Pet.** broad, rounded; **Tu.** and **Ov.** shortly hairy, with brownish to yellowish Sp.—USA (border, Texas and New Mexico), Mexico (adjacent region).

E. rufispinus Eng. (4)
Bo. cylindric; **St.** greyish-greenish; **Ri.** c. 11; **Rsp.** 16–18, appressed, interlacing, 9–20(?) mm lg., the laterals longest, dark brown, recurved; **Csp.** 1, stout, reddish-brown, porrect, to 2.5 cm lg.; **Fl.** large, funnelform, purple.—Mexico (W. of Chihuahua). The low rib-count may have been based on immature plants. In the Dahlem Bot. Gard. I saw under this name a plant which corresponded to the principal characters above: "Csp. reddish-brown,

porrect, longer"; it did not match the description of any other plant.

E. russanthus Weniger
Bo. later offsetting, c. 8 cm h.; **Ri.** 13–14; **Sp.** 15–18, c. 8 mm lg., densely tangled; **Fl.** at midway on the flank or lower, reddish, with a greenish M.-stripe. Clearly differentiated from E. chloranthus.— Mexico.

E. salm-dyckianus Scheer (1)
Bo. offsetting to form groups; **St.** decumbent, yellowish-green; **Ri.** 7–9, ± weakly sinuate; **Rsp.** 8–9, c. 1 cm lg.; **Csp.** 1, often ± thickened below, porrect, somewhat longer; **Fl.** to 10 cm lg., with a long, slender **Tu.**, slightly hairy, white-bristly, carroty-red.—Mexico (Chihuahua, Durango).

E. salmianus Rümpl. 1885
Bo. dark green, creeping, freely branching, to 15 cm lg., 3 cm ∅; **Ri.** 7–8, rounded, only 1 cm apart; **Ar.** small, round, crowded, grey-felty; **Rsp.** 8, straight; **Csp.** 1, straight, porrect, rather longer, brown, greying; **Fl.** with a rather stout greenish Tu., like E. scheeri opening completely only in the evening; **Pet.** very numerous, salmon to carrot-colour.— Mexico (Chihuahua; sent to Kew by Potts, 1847; nowadays regarded as a synonym or form of E. scheeri).

E. sanborgianus (Coult.) K.Sch. (4)
Mostly regarded as a synonym of E. brandegeei ("with Ar. to 1.5 cm apart"), but described as having "Ar. proximate"; acc. Coulter the Sp. are also lighter than in E. brandegeei ("with reddish Sp."); **Fl.** large, pure purple. A clarification based on living material is needed.—Mexico (Baja California). I have seen a plant with yellowish Sp.

E. sarissophorus Br. & R. (4)
Bo. forming groups; **St.** short, thick, pale green, c. 10 cm ∅; **Ri.** 9; **Rsp.** 7–10, thin; **Csp.** several, somewhat angular, often bluish, the longer ones ± interlacing; **Fl.** 7–8 cm lg., purple; **Pet.** broad; **Tu.** and **Ov.** with short white wool and 3–5 pale Br.-Sp.; **Fr.** spherical, to 3 cm ∅.—N. Mexico (Coahuila, Durango). All the cultivated plants I have seen have had white Sp.; all the Csp. were thickened below while the longest ones were directed upwards or downwards.

E. scheeri (SD.) Rümpl. (1)
Bo. forming groups; **St.** decumbent, yellowish-green; **Ri.** 8–10, low, spiralled, indistinctly sinuate; **Rsp.** 7–12, thin, projecting, ray-like, to 3 mm lg.; **Csp.** 1, stouter, porrect, over 1 cm lg., tipped brown or black, also yellowish-white; **Fl.** pinkish-red, long and slender funnelform.—Mexico (Chihuahua).

E. schwarzii hort.: see **E. radians** Eng.

E. sciurus (K. Brand.) Br. & R. (4)
Bo. offsetting freely to form groups to 60 cm br.; **St.** slender, to 20 cm lg., often entirely concealed by the Sp.; **Ri.** 12–17, low, tuberculate; **Rsp.** 15–18, thin, to 1.5 cm lg.; **Csp.** several, shorter than the Rsp., brown-tipped: **Fl.** 7 cm lg., to 9 cm ∅, pinkish-purple.—Mexico (Baja California, San José del Cabo).

E. scopulorum Br. & R. (4)
Bo. solitary, cylindric, to 40 cm lg., almost covered by the Sp.; **Ri.** 13 or more, low, somewhat tuberculate; **Rsp.** somewhat spreading, more numerous; **Csp.** 3–6, like the Rsp.; **Sp.** colourful, pink or brownish, black-tipped, also whitish at first; **Fl.** 9 cm ∅. rose-scented; **Pet.** 4 cm lg., pinkish-purple to ± white, in 2 series.—Mexico (Sonora and Sinaloa).

E. spinibarbis Hge. Jr. non K.Sch. (4)
Bo. offsetting fairly freely; **St.** light green, to 6 cm lg., 3.5–4 cm thick; **Ri.** mostly 5, 1 cm h., with stout subcircular Tub., transversely indented above the Ar.; **Rsp.** mostly 8, to 3.3 cm lg., straight or ± curving; **Csp.** 1–2(–3), to 4.2 cm lg., thickened below, stouter than the Rsp.; **Sp.** all white, glassy, at first pale yellow below, here soon reddish, sometimes with transverse banding; **Fl.** probably purple (acc. Haage).—Mexico.

E. standleyi Br. & R. (4)
Bo. spherical to shortly cylindric, 4–5 cm ∅; **Ri.** 12; **Rsp.** c. 16, stout, white, yellow below, quite early pectinate and ± strongly interlacing; **Csp.** 1, much longer and stouter than the Rsp., 2–2.5 cm lg., porrect; **Fl.** ?—USA (New Mexico, Sacramento Mts.)

E. steereae Clov. resembles E. dasyacanthus but has red **Fl.**; generally held to be a variety: **E. dasyacanthus** v. **steereae** (Clov.) Marsh.

E. stoloniferus Marsh. (4)
Bo. solitary, but new St. rise from stolons so that colonies to 30 cm br. are formed; **St.** cylindric, greyish-green; **Ri.** 14–16, indistinctly tuberculate; **Rsp.** 10–12, bristly, spreading, interlacing, white, tipped black or red at first; **Csp.** 3–4, to 6 mm lg., brown, one of these more readily distinguishable, down-curving, to 2.5 cm lg., later white; **Fl.** yellow; **Tu.** and **Ov.** very spiny.—Mexico (Sonora, Rancho Guirocoba). The spec. appears to be variable. Some plants have large white Ar., rather stouter Rsp. and 4(–5) robuster, projecting, golden-brown Csp. to 1.2 cm lg., the Rsp. sometimes brown-tipped and to 8 mm lg.; **Fl.** yellow, c. 6 cm ∅. I have

seen flowering-sized plants which were c. 10 cm lg., 5.5 cm $\emptyset$, under the name "E. subterraneus"; but they were not the more slender and brittle spec. which I have described under this name. The type of the spec. has denser and more interlacing Sp., but both it and these other plants produce new plants by means of stolons. Since it is possible that transitional forms occur, no variety can yet be described.

E. stramineus (Eng.) Rümpl. (4)
Bo. offsetting to form colonies to 2 m $\emptyset$ and 30 cm–1 m h.; **St.** 12–25 cm lg., 3–5 cm $\emptyset$; **Ri.** c. 13; **Rsp.** 7–14, to 3 cm lg., spreading; **Csp.** 3–4, 5–9 cm lg.; **Sp.** fairly densely interlacing, brown to straw-coloured at first, soon becoming white; **Fl.** 8–12 cm lg., purple; **Tu.** and **Ov.** with short white Sp.; **Fr.** spherical, 3–4 cm $\emptyset$, red, edible.—USA (border, Texas and New Mexico), N. Mexico (Chihuahua).

E. subinermis SD. (2)
Bo. at first depressed-spherical, then considerably elongated, later sometimes offsetting; **Rsp.** to 8 at first, with 1 **Csp.**, 2–4 mm lg., later only 3–4 stouter little Sp. scarcely 1 mm lg. (or these missing), yellowish to blackish, or white and dark-tipped; **Fl.** yellow, to 8.5 cm lg., 9 cm $\emptyset$, the **Per.** broadly spreading, the **Tu.** slender; **Fr.** 2 cm lg., 1.3 cm $\emptyset$, dark green.—Mexico (Chihuahua).
v. **luteus** (Br. & R.) Backbg.: **Fl.** c. 7 cm lg., 5.5 cm $\emptyset$, **Per.** funnelform.—Mexico (Sonora, above Alamos).

E. subterraneus Backbg. (4)
Bo. mostly offsetting from fairly low down; **St.** slender-cylindric, fresh green, to c. 5 cm lg., c. 3 cm $\emptyset$, cultivated plants stouter, with soft flesh, brittle; **Ri.** narrow, low, finely tuberculate, c. 15; **Rsp.** c. 15, the upper ones very short; **Csp.** of the same length, clustered, projecting; **Fl.** c. 3 cm lg., 4 cm $\emptyset$, pinkish-purple; **Tu.** and **Ov.** with felt only, densely spiny.—Mexico. This name is also erroneously used for a var. or form of E. stoloniferus with more open spination and golden-brown Csp.

E. tayopensis Marsh. (4)
Bo. solitary or sprouting from stolons to form groups of up to 12 heads; **St.** to 15 cm lg., 7.5 cm $\emptyset$; **Ri.** mostly 12; **Rsp.** 3–4 mm lg. (upper ones), or c. 1 cm lg. (the others), grey, dark-tipped; **Csp.** much stouter, 1–2 ascending and 5 mm lg., the others down-curving, 15–20 mm lg., black at first, then grey, dark-tipped; **Fl.** 7 cm lg., 6 cm $\emptyset$, light yellow; **Pet.** 4.5 cm lg., 1 cm br.—Mexico (Sonora, Rancho Saucito).

E. triglochidiatus Eng. (4)
Bo. forming large mats; **St.** cylindric, dark-green, to 15 cm lg., to 6 cm $\emptyset$; **Ri.** (6–)7(–10); **Rsp.** (3–)5(–8); **Csp.** 0–1–5; **Sp.** all angular or ribbed; **Fl.** 7.5 cm lg., 5 cm $\emptyset$, scarlet; **Fr.** red, edible, 3 cm $\emptyset$.—USA (Arizona, W. Texas to S. Colorado). Descriptions vary for the Arizona plants, e.g.: "St. to 60 cm h., in colonies of the same width; **Ri.** mostly 5–8; **Sp.** 3–16, to c. 3 cm lg.; **Csp.** 0–16, somewhat longer than the Rsp. which can number 3–10; **Sp.** only described as grey; **Fr.** 2.5 cm lg., $\pm$ cylindric".
v. **gonacanthus** (Eng. & Big.) Boiss.: **Rsp.** 8; **Csp.** 1, to over 6 cm lg.; all **Sp.** very angular, in part contorted or curving, yellow, with a dark tip;
v. **hexaedrus** (Eng. & Big.) Boiss.: **Rsp.** 5–7, straight; **Csp.** 0–1; **Sp.** angular, short, reddish-yellow; **Ri.** 6;
v. **paucispinus** (Eng.) Marsh.: only the **Csp.** are angular; **St.** $\pm$ spherical at first; **Ri.** 5–7; **Rsp.** brown or reddish; **Csp.** brownish-black, 0–1; **Fl.** deep scarlet, more yellowish inside.

E. tuberosus Rümpl.: **Wilcoxia poselgeri** Lem.

E. uehrii Hge. Jr.: probably identical with **E. cinerascens** (DC.) Rümpl. Haage adds:
This is a now-forgotten but quite valid spec., described around 1900, well differentiated from E. cinerascens as follows:
Bo. larger, spination more robust.

E. uspenskii Hge. Jr. (4)
Bo. offsetting; **St.** erect, to c. 15 cm lg., to 7 cm $\emptyset$, sometimes $\pm$ spherical; **Ri.** 6–7, tuberculate; **Rsp.** to 8, to 2 cm lg.; **Csp.** to 4, thickened below, to 3.5 cm lg.; **Sp.** all hyaline to white, reddish below; **Fl.** 7.5 cm lg., c. 6 cm $\emptyset$; **Pet.** deep purple, more brownish outside below; **Tu.** and **Ov.** only felty, with stout Sp.; **Fil.** violet; **Sti.** 9, emerald.—Mexico.

E. viereckii Werd. (4)
Bo. offsetting freely; **St.** erect, to 20 cm lg. and more; **Ri.** 8–9, to 8 mm h., tuberculate; **Rsp.** 7–9, 3–9 mm lg., $\pm$ straw-coloured, later whitish; **Csp.** 4, the bottom one longest, c. 2 cm lg., thickened below; **Fl.** violet-pink, to 11 cm $\emptyset$; **Tu.** and **Ov.** with hyaline and light golden-brown Sp.—Mexico (Tamaulipas).

E. viridiflorus Eng. (4) (T.) v. **viridiflorus**:
Bo. offsetting, variable in size, from rather small to stouter and longer, 2.5–7.5 cm lg., 2.5–5 cm $\emptyset$; **Ri.** 13; **Sp.** 13–15, 0.5 cm lg., white, red, or both colours present; **Csp.** similarly, sometimes missing; **Fl.** borne on the flanks or lower, to 3 × 3 cm in size, yellowish-green, with a greenish M.-stripe inside and a brownish one outside; **Fr.** 1 cm lg., ellipsoid, greenish.—USA (New Mexico to Colorado).

141

v. **chloranthus** (Eng.) Backbg.: **Bo.** cylindric, to 30 cm h., 4–7 cm $\emptyset$; **Ri.** 13–18; **Rsp.** 12–20, radiating or appressed, bristly, white, often purple-tipped, also 5–10 bristly Ssp. above; **Csp.** (2–)3–5, mostly purple, the upper ones shorter, $\pm$ thickened below; **Fl.** brownish-green, funnelform, not expanding widely, 2.5 cm lg. Csp. are often absent at first, later to 3 cm lg.; Sp-colour very variable: from whitish to yellowish or reddish, also in zones, with or without a more distinctly projecting or longer Csp.; **Bo.** later cylindric, but the Csp. are unlike those of Engelmann's illustration of v. cylindricus.

Engelmann distinguished (as Cereus viridiflorus cylindricus Eng.) a v. **cylindricus** Eng., and obviously this is the variety to which Rümpler referred: almost always solitary, mostly cylindric; **Ri.** c. 13; Sp. 12–18, short, stiff, pectinate, with 2–6 additional bristly Sp. above, the lower ones (rarely all of them) purple, soon becoming brown, the upper ones white; **Csp.** 0, rarely 1, porrect, stouter, purple, sometimes surmounted by an additional thinner one; **Fl.** subapical, yellowish-greenish.—USA (Texas, Limpia to El Paso);

v. **davisii** (A. D. Houghton) Marsh.: **Bo.** very small, to 1.5 cm h., solitary or offsetting; **Ri.** 6–7, $\pm$ tuberculate, dark green; **Rsp.** 9–12(–14), the upper ones (up to 7) reddish-black at first, the lower ones whitish or sometimes dark-tipped, pectinate, spreading, to c. 17 mm lg., the upper Sp. shorter, mostly straight, the others sometimes $\pm$ curving; **Fl.** 2.5 cm lg., 2 cm $\emptyset$, dirty greenish-yellow; **Fr.** 1 cm lg.—USA (Texas, 4 miles S. of Marathon). Grafting recommended! (Fig. 89.) The small plants are so very different in overall habit that they can well be regarded as a valid spec.: **E. davisii** A. D. Houghton;

v. **intermedius** Backbg.: solitary; **Ri.** 12; **Rsp.** white, to 8 mm lg.; **Csp.** (2–)4(–5), stouter, purple, to 7 mm lg., thickened below; **Fl.** borne lower on the Bo., pure green, to 3 cm lg.—USA (Texas).

E. websterianus G. Linds. (4)
Bo. offsetting to form dense groups; **St.** to 60 cm h., to 8 cm $\emptyset$; **Ri.** 18–24, somewhat tuberculate; **Rsp.** 14–18, c. 1 cm lg., golden-yellow to brownish; **Csp.** 6–8, acicular, 1 cm lg., golden-yellow, eventually brown; **Fl.** 6 cm lg., lavender-pink; **Pet.** passing over to white or glossy green at the margin.—Mexico (Sonora, S. Pedro Nolasco. [Origin acc. W. Haage].)

E. weinbergii Wgt. (4)
Bo. flattened-spherical at first, later spherical, to 13 cm h. and $\emptyset$; **Ri.** 15, tuberculate, transversely furrowed, greyish-green; **Rsp.** 9–12, white or pink, later yellowish, 3–11 mm lg.; **Csp.** 0; **Fl.** 3.6 cm $\emptyset$, pink with white floccose H., with yellow Br.-Sp.; **Pet.** with a greenish M.-stripe outside and a carmine one inside.—Origin? The plant usually seen under this name is a hybrid, probably of E. pulchellus; it is elongated, with spiralled Ri., and usually with 8 radiating Sp.

Echinofossulocactus Lawr. (197)

This genus is very homogeneous, all the bodies (with one exception) having numerous ribs. The glabrous flowers are mostly fairly small, often tinged $\pm$ violet or striped, sometimes appearing several together, mostly quite early in Spring. The deep green bodies, with their distinctive and quite often conspicuously flattened spines, form an attractive contrast to the flowers; the latter and the spines are rather longer in only a few species. But the widely differing types of spination are not constant, and show a wealth of transitional forms—from robust in character to dense—which complicates any classification based on the main diagnostic features and thereby also the delimitation of their species; this fact demonstrates how necessary it is to take into account the individual conditions within any one genus. To ignore this would be to regard most species of this genus as mere varieties of a single species, which does not advance our knowledge of these plants, or reflect the great range of natural variation which is so conspicuous here. To assist the finding of any given species, a figure will be found in brackets after each specific name, to indicate the principal characters according to the groups listed below. Where a plant does not fully conform to any description of this most variable genus, it must be regarded as transitional to the most closely related described species.—Distribution; Mexico (from N. to approximately Central Mexico). [$\bigcirc$, (R), ///. (G).] (Fig. 92.)

1: Bodies lacking wavy ribs; these broader, angular above;
2: Bodies with over 100 blade-like ribs;
3: Bodies with fewer but very narrow ribs:
   a: Glassy, light radial spines and sometimes darker centrals; spination fairly dense;
   b: Spination laxer; the upper or main spines often flattened and blade-like, but sometimes terete.

E. albatus (Dietr.) Br. & R. (3a)
Bo. mostly spherical, bluish-green; **Ri.** c. 35; **Rsp.** c. 10, bristly, to 13 mm lg., 1–3 often missing in the upper Ar.; **Csp.** 4, much stouter, dark-coloured, the top one usually the longest, slightly com-

pressed, to 5 cm lg., others more terete, one sometimes missing; **Sp.** whitish-yellow apart from the centrals; **Fl.** 2 cm lg., white.—Mexico.

E. anfractuosus (Mart.) Lawr. (3b)
Bo. eventually somewhat elongated-spherical, dull green; **Ri.** to c. 30; **Rsp.** 7, the 4 lower ones thin, the 3 upper ones (sometimes 2) to 3 cm lg., terete or (the middle one) broad; **Csp.** 1, c. 2.5 cm lg., brownish; **Fl.** white, M.-stripe carmine(?).—Mexico (Hidalgo). Rsp. variable in shape and number.

E. arrigens (Lk.) Br. & R. (3b)
Bo. elongated-spherical, to 13 cm h., c. 12 cm $\emptyset$; **crown** with yellowish-white flaky felt; **Ri.** matt to bluish-green, 50–60, very narrow; **Rsp.** 4–7, acicular, hyaline to yellowish, to c. 1 cm lg.; **Csp.** to 3 in the centre of the Ar., ± erect, yellowish to paler, subterete, the lower part of the Ar. also often with 2–3 additional thinner Sp., also 1 compressed and keeled **upper Sp.** to 4 cm lg. (acc. Br. & R., 8–11 Sp. in all; acc. Werdermann, seldom more than 8 in all); **Fl.** 3 cm lg., 2.5 cm $\emptyset$; **Pet.** purple-violet with a light border. Apparently very variable.—Mexico.

E. boedekerianus (Berg.) Croiz. (3a)
Bo. flat-spherical, to 7 cm br., matt dark green; **crown** with white wool and Sp.; **Ri.** c. 40; **Rsp.** c. 20, to c. 1.2 cm lg., acicular, white; **Csp.** mostly 9, 8 forming an outer circle, the innermost one flattened, all thickened below, brownish, yellowish above, brownish-red at the tip; **Fl.** ?—Mexico (Zacatecas, near Concepción).

E. bravoae Whitm.: only a name.

E. bustamantei (H. Bravo) Croiz. (3b)
Bo. spherical, to c. 10 cm $\emptyset$; **Ri.** c. 35; **Rsp.** 8–9, 10–15 mm lg., radiating, interlacing, whitish; **Csp.** 3, the uppermost and longest one 3–5 cm lg., broad, much flattened, banded, the side ones darker-tipped, rather stouter than the radials; **Fl.** 2–2.5 cm lg., dark violet-purple, with a white border or M.-line.—Mexico (Hidalgo).

E. cadaroyi hort.: just a name for a plant with thin wavy Ri., with up to 6 thin white lower Rsp. and 3 dark upper ones, and one flattened but not broad ± central Sp.; Fl. ?

E. caespitosus Backbg. (3b)
Bo. apparently remaining smaller, subspherical, soon offsetting; **Ri.** c. 27; **upper Sp.** 3, 2 of these terete and upcurving, one flattened middle one to 21 mm lg., yellowish, to 2 mm br.; **Rsp.** 4, small, whitish; **Csp.** 1, ± compressed, directed outwards to downwards or curving, equal in length to the

middle upper Sp.; **Fl.** c. 11 mm lg., white, greenish in the middle.—Mexico.

E. carneus Whitm.: only a catalogue-name.

E. confusus Br. & R. (3b)
Bo. solitary, columnar to short-clavate, pale green, to 15 cm h., 6–8 cm $\emptyset$; **Ri.** 26–30, thin, low; **Sp.** all yellow, subulate; **Rsp.** 4–5 (at most ± compressed), 7–10 mm lg.; **Csp.** 1, to 4 cm lg., usually porrect; **Fl.** 4 cm $\emptyset$, purple.—Mexico.

E. coptonogonus (Lem.) Lawr. (1) (T.)
Bo. solitary to offsetting, up to 8 heads, spherical, to 10 cm h., greyish or bluish-green; **Ar.** very white-felty at first; **Sp.** mostly 5, stout, banded, ± curving, all horn-coloured; the stoutest and longest **upper Sp.** to 4 cm lg.; **Fl.** to 3 cm lg., whitish, light purple to carmine in the middle.—Mexico (San Luis Potosí, Pachuca).

E. crispatus (DC.) Lawr. (3b)
First description insufficient. Acc. Berger: **Bo.** resembles that of E. arrigens; **Ar.** 3–4 cm apart; **Sp.** brightly coloured at first; **Csp.** 1, terete, stiff, straight, c. 2 cm lg.; **Rsp.** 7–8, the uppermost one flattened, of equal length; **Fl.** to 3.5 cm lg. (purple, acc. Br. & R.).—Mexico (Hidalgo).

E. densispinus (Tieg.) Schmoll:
Only the name, with an illustration, has been published; close to E. boedekerianus (Berg.) Croiz.

E. dichroacanthus (Mart.) Br. & R. (3b)
Bo. ovoid, to 15 cm h., 10 cm $\emptyset$; **Ri.** 32, thin, acute, wavy; **Ar.** only few on one Ri.; **Rsp.** 4–6, white, the central of the 3 upper ones flat, keeled at midway, dagger-like, 2 cm lg.; **Csp.** 0–1, ± 4-angled, curving downwards, scarcely longer than the upper Sp.; the 3 **upper Sp.** and the **Csp.** banded, ruby-red at first, tipped blackish-red, the **Rsp.** 7–8 mm lg.; **Fl.** pinkish-violet.—Mexico (Hidalgo).

E. erectocentrus Backbg. (3b)
Bo. broadly spherical, to c. 8 cm br., 5 cm h.; **Ri.** c. 50 or more, thin, very wavy; **Ar.** over 2 cm apart; **Rsp.** glassy, 5–6(–9) in a semi-circle below, mostly thin, to 1 cm lg.; 1 **upper Sp.** directed towards the crown, to over 5 cm lg., flattened, thin at the edge, thickened in the centre, brownish to horn-coloured, striped, ± dark-tipped; **Csp.** 2, terete, c. 2 cm lg., lying alongside one another, banded, slightly thickened below; **Fl.** under 2 cm lg., whitish.—Mexico.

E. gladiatus (Lk. & O.) Lawr. (3b)
Bo. ovoid to oblong, to c. 12 cm h., 10 cm $\emptyset$, light bluish-green; **crown** spiny; **Ri.** 14–22 (or more: to

27?); **upper Sp.** 3, the middle of these flattened, to 3 cm lg., the flanking ones more terete and shorter; **Csp.** 1, to 4 cm lg., porrect, many-angled or ± terete; all **Sp.** reddish horn-coloured, dark-tipped; lower **Rsp.** 4–6, white, glassy, 8 mm lg.—Mexico. Description more or less from Tiegel-Oehme; Fl.-colour given in part as yellow, in part as reddish-violet. An insufficiently clarified spec.

v. **carneus** Schmoll: published only with illustration, and included by me, with brief data, in "Die Cact.", p. 2779. E. carneus Whitm., not validly published, is probably the same plant.

E. grandicornis (Lem.) Br. & R. (3b)
Bo. solitary, spherical to elongated, to c. 10 cm h., to 6 cm ∅, bluish-green; **crown** with yellow felt and Sp.; **Ri.** to 35, thin, acute; mostly with 3 **upper Sp.**, the middle one very stiff, stout, flattened, banded and keeled, to over 5 cm lg., the flanking ones terete, to 3 cm lg.; **Rsp.** several, the upper ones often missing or thin, 4–5 mm lg., the lower ones more subulate, 4, to 1.2 cm lg.; all **Sp.** ± yellowish; **Fl.** c. 3 cm lg., whitish (to light purple?).—Mexico.

E. guerraianus Backbg. (3b)
Bo. solitary, hemispherical, to 20 cm br., dark green; **crown** spiny; **Ri.** to 35; **Ar.** to 4 cm apart; **Sp.** mostly 8, yellowish, brown above; **upper Sp.** 3, to 1.8 cm lg., ± flattened; **Rsp.** 2–4 bottom ones thin, to 1 cm lg., 2 flanking ones subterete, to 2.8 cm lg.; **Csp.** 1, subulate, terete, to 4 cm lg.; **Fl.** 3 cm ∅, violet with a white margin.—Mexico (Hidalgo).

E. hastatus (Hopff.) Br. & R. (3b)
Bo. depressed-spherical, to 10 cm h., to 12 cm ∅, light green; **Ri.** to 35, somewhat notched; **Rsp.** 5–6, short, the 2 upper ones stouter, sometimes also 2–3 additional ones below, as well as 2 bristly ones behind the upper ones; **upper Sp.** 3 cm lg., flattened; **Csp.** 1, 4 cm lg., porrect, terete; **Fl.** whitish, light to darker purple (carmine) in the middle.—Mexico (Hidalgo, Metztitlan).

E. heteracanthus (Muehlpfrdt.) Br. & R. (3b)
Bo. spherical to elongated, matt light green, c. 8 cm ∅; **Ri.** 30–40 or more; **Ar.** 2 cm apart; **Rsp.** 11–13, white, finely acicular, to 7 mm lg., yellowish below; **Csp.** (main Sp.) 4, the uppermost one flattened, dagger-like, straight or recurved, to 1.5 cm lg., 1.5 mm br.; all **Sp.** ± brownish to lighter (also ruby-red at first?), also dark-tipped; **Fl.** greenish-yellow.—Mexico (Coahuila, Durango).

E. kellerianus Krainz (3b)
Bo. flattened-spherical, c. 7 cm br., 4 cm h.; **crown** densely woolly; **Ri.** c. 60, fairly robust; **Rsp.** 2–4, to c. 5 mm lg., light brown; **upper Sp.** 1, 1 cm lg., c. 1.5 mm br., the upperside black, the underside whitish-

grey; **Csp.** 0; **Fl.** 2.5 cm br.; inner **Pet.** pure white, outer ones with a violet M.-stripe.—Mexico.

E. lamellosus (Dietr.) Br. & R. (3b)
Bo. spherical to elongated, bluish-green, to c. 10 cm h., 8 cm ∅; **Ri.** 30–35, irregularly wavy; **Ar.** few, white; **Rsp.** 4, white, the 2 upper ones pointing ± upwards, 2 pointing obliquely downwards, finer than the slender upper ones and only half as long; **upper Sp.** 1, to 3 cm lg., flattened, curved inwards, with longitudinal channels and transverse bands, brown-tipped; **Csp.** 1, ± triangular, to 4 cm lg., tipped light or dark; **Fl.** to 4 cm lg., flesh-coloured, carmine inside.—Mexico (Hidalgo).

E. lancifer (Dietr. non Reichb.) Br. & R. (3b)
Bo. broadly spherical (acc. the first description); **Sp.** 8, white, or brown-tipped, some broad and flat; **Fl.** pink, quite large; **Pet.** linear-oblong, widely spreading.—Mexico. Description taken from Br. & R.; acc. Pfeiffer's illustration, there are 3 flattened upper Sp., and one down-curving central; it is not possible to see whether this is flat or terete. Regarded by many authors as identical with E. obvallatus or E. hastatus. The specific name is dubious and the description inadequate.

E. lexarzai (H. Bravo) Croiz. (3b)
Bo. broadly spherical, to 10 cm h., to 12 cm ∅; concealed by the Sp.; **Ri.** 40–50, somewhat wavy, thin; **Rsp.** mostly 8(–10), interlacing, 8–13 mm lg., acicular, white; **upper Sp.** 3, the middle one to 6.5 cm lg., broad and flattened, banded, whitish, curving over the crown above, the 2 flanking upper ones whitish, darker-tipped, to 2 cm lg.; **Csp.** 1, flattened, shorter and narrower than the middle upper Sp.; **Fl.** 3 cm lg., pale light pink with a reddish or violet M.-stripe.—Mexico (Hidalgo, Real del Monte).

E. lloydii Br. & R. (3b)
Bo. ± spherical, to c. 12 cm h. and br., overtopped by the Sp.; **Ri.** very numerous, thin, wavy; **Ar.** brownish at first; **Rsp.** white, acicular, 10–15, 2–8 mm lg. (not 2.8 mm, as in "Die Cact." p. 2771), spreading; **upper Sp.** (main Sp.) 3, light brown, much elongated, connivent, the middle one very thin, 4–8 cm lg., banded, the two flanking ones similar, not so papery-thin; **Fl.** small, almost white.—Mexico (Zacatecas).

E. multicostatus (Hildm.) Br. & R. (3b)
Bo. depressed-spherical to spherical, fresh green, to 10 cm ∅; **Ri.** extremely thin, to over 100, with few Ar.; **Rsp.** mostly 4, terete, hyaline; **upper Sp.** 3, angular, white, ascending, not broad, often curving like horns, yellowish to brownish, rather thin, approximately equal, to 3 cm lg.; **Fl.** 2.5 cm lg.,

white, purple-violet in the middle.—Mexico (Coahuila, Saltillo; Durango, Cerro del Risco).

E. obvallatus (DC.) Lawr. (3b)
Bo. spherical to elongated; **Ri.** c. 25, thin, wavy; **Sp.** c. 7–8, the larger ones red at first, then brown above and below; **Rsp.** c. 4, white, scarcely 8 mm lg., subulate; **upper Sp.** 3, flattened, the middle one broader, c. 2.5 cm lg.; **Csp.** 1, subterete, porrect, over 2.5 cm lg., indistinctly banded; **Fl.** to c. 2.4 cm lg., purplish-red; **Pet.** bordered white.—Mexico (Hidalgo). The above description refers to the plant to which the name is applied nowadays. The original illustration is not very informative.

E. ochoterenaus Tieg. (3a)
Bo. spherical, bluish-green, to c. 7 cm h., 10 cm ⌀; **Ri.** c. 30, thin, wavy; **Ar.** at first with yellowish felt; **Rsp.** acicular, thin, spreading, 12 mm lg., hyaline; **Csp.** 4, flattened, the upper one 2 mm br., to 6 cm lg., the lowest one mostly somewhat longer but sometimes narrower, the side ones shorter, weaker, often one small Ssp. behind the upper one, all **Sp.** golden-yellow at first, banded, later straw-yellow; **Fl.** whitish, longer, with a dark M.-line outside.—Mexico (Guanajuato; Querétaro). (Fig. 93.) To this complex we must refer the following (not validly published) names for similarly spined plants with generally purple-reddish flowers although in some cases these are somewhat longer:
E. densispinus (Tieg.) Schmoll: Sp. fine, densely interlacing, light-coloured; Csp. long, projecting;
E. parksianus Schmoll: crown with light wool; with dark, longer, projecting Csp.;
E. rosasianus Whitm.: Ar. fairly large, light-felty; Csp. light, longer;
E. sphacelatus Whitm.: Csp. finer, only medium-long, projecting, darker at first.

E. parksianus Schmoll: see under preceding spec.

E. pentacanthus (Lem.) Br. & R. (3b)
Bo. compressed-spherical to elongated, bluish-green; **Ri.** c. 25 or more (to 50?); **Ar.** few to a Ri.; **upper Sp.** 3, the middle one blade-like, mostly curving upwards to the Bo., the others ± flattened, thinner and shorter than the middle one; **Rsp.** 2, pointing downwards, thin, shortest; **Fl.** deep violet, not long but quite large; **Pet.** bordered white.—Central Mexico.

E. phyllacanthus (Mart.) Lawr. (3b)
Bo. depressed-spherical to elongated, to 15 cm h., to 10 cm ⌀, dark green; **Ri.** 30–35, thin; **crown** concealed by the Sp.; **upper Sp.** 3, 4–8 cm lg., the middle one much elongated, all flat, keeled and banded (or perhaps only the middle one), rosy-red to ruby-red at first, finally brownish; **Rsp.** mostly c.

5, spreading, thinner, weaker; **Fl.** to 2 cm lg., yellowish-whitish, reddish in the middle.—Central Mexico.

E. rectospinus Schmoll: a name which has not been validly published; perhaps belongs to the complex of E. ochoterenaus Tieg.

E. rosasianus Whitm.: see E. ochoterenaus Tieg.

E. sphacelatus Whitm.: see E. ochoterenaus Tieg.

E. tetraxiphus (Otto) Oehme (3b)
Bo. eventually elongated, light green, to 15 cm h., to 10 cm ⌀, densely spiny; **crown** white-woolly, spiny; **Ri.** 30 or more, thin; **Rsp.** 16–18, light-coloured or white, acicular, the lower ones to 15 mm lg.; **Csp.** 4, flattened, the upper one to 4 cm lg., ± bent, dark yellow to brown, banded; **Fl.** 3.5 cm ⌀, white; **Pet.** with a red M.-stripe, **throat** red.—Mexico (Hidalgo). (Description acc. Berger.)

E. tricuspidatus (Scheidw.) Br. & R. (3b)
Bo. spherical to elongated, 5–8 cm br., light green; **Ri.** 30–55, thin, wavy; **Rsp.** 5 or more, radiating, hyaline, terete, c. 5–7 mm lg., pointing sideways and downwards, sometimes also 2 subsidiary upper Sp., curving upwards and somewhat stouter; **upper Sp.** 1, blade-like, thin, ± curving or ± straight, 0.8–3.3 cm lg., reddish at first, with the black tip sometimes slit or dentate; **Fl.** 1.5 cm lg., greenish-yellow.—Mexico (San Luis Potosí).

E. vaupelianus (Werd.) Tieg. & Oehme (3a)
Bo. hemispherical, matt green; **Ri.** 30–40; **Rsp.** radiating, hyaline, sometimes darker-tipped, thin-acicular, mostly straight, interlacing laterally, 1–1.5 cm lg.; **Csp.** 1–2, one over the other, to c. 7 cm lg., subulate, sharp, often ± flat, porrect, one sometimes curving upwards, brownish-black at first, then reddish-brown, frosted; **Fl.** cream, with a dark stripe on the outside.—Mexico.

E. violaciflorus (Quehl) Br. & R. (3b)
Bo. spherical to elongated, to 10 cm ⌀, bluish-green; **crown** spiny; **Ri.** c. 35, thin, deeply notched; **Ar.** grey-felty at first; **Rsp.** 4, hyaline, terete, the upper pair 7–9 mm lg., the lower pair c. 12 mm lg.; **upper Sp.** 3, the middle one to 3(–6?) cm lg., resembling a wood-shaving, keeled and banded, ± appressed, honey-coloured at first, brown-tipped, the 2 flanking Sp. less broad, somewhat thicker, sometimes with a further glassy, thin Ssp. behind the middle Sp.; **Fl.** 2.5 cm lg., white, purple-violet in the middle.—Mexico (Zacatecas; Aguascalientes).

E. wippermannii (Muehlpfrdt.) Br. & R. (3a)
Bo. spherical to elongated, to 15 cm h., dark green;

Ri. (25–)35(–40), slightly wavy; **Rsp.** 18–22, bristly, white, the lowest ones to 1.5 cm lg.; **Csp.** erect, subulate, 2–6 cm lg., the 3 uppermost ones ± flattened, faintly banded, the bottom one straight, porrect, subterete, thickened below, all ± blackish-brown; **Fl.** 1.5 cm lg., yellow with a brownish M.-stripe.—Mexico (Hidalgo).

E. zacatecasensis Br. & R. (3b)
Bo. solitary, spherical, to 10 cm ∅, pale green; **Ri.** c. 55, very thin; **Rsp.** 10–12, thin-acicular, 8–10 mm lg., radiating; **Csp.**: 1 as an **upper Sp.**, directed upwards towards the Bo., flattened, to 4 cm lg., never banded, also 2 recurved flanking Csp., longer, but shorter than the upper Sp., all 3 Sp. brownish; **Fl.** 3–4 cm ∅, white with a pale violet-pink tint.—Mexico (N. Zacatecas).

Echinomastus Br. & R. (200)

Diagnostic characters of the Genus as follows: ribs fairly strongly divided into tuberculate protuberances but still fairly clearly distinguishable; spine-clusters arise from the end of furrow-like long areoles, felted in flowering plants, although this felt is sometimes absent at first; flowers ± bellshaped, sometimes quite small, sometimes medium-sized; the ovaries and the dry, variously dehiscent fruits are scaly.
The species have been referred by some authors to Thelocactus, as did Schumann with his Subgenus of the same name. However, closer study of all the species shows them to be a closely related and distinctive group, with conspicuously attractive spination, the flowers being mostly bellshaped, and smaller than in Thelocactus. The spines are ± interlacing throughout. It is also worth noting that unlike Thelocactus, where the plants mostly grow well, the species of this Genus are sometimes difficult on their own roots with the possible exception of E. macdowellii. They have such unmistakable similarities of habit that it is best to preserve their distinct generic status. The seeds, as far as known, are dull or glossy, black, finely reticulate or tuberculate.—Distribution: USA (S. States including W. Utah), Mexico (the N., and to Zacatecas). [(G) ✳.]

E. acunensis Marsh.
Bo. flattened-spherical, to 17.5 cm h., to 10 cm ∅; **R.** fusiform; **Ri.** c. 18, laterally compressed, with confluent Tub.; **Ar.** white-woolly at first, with the Fl.-furrow extending to the depression of the Tub.; **Rsp.** 12, spreading, acicular, white below, reddish above; **Csp.** 3–4, developing later, upper ones connivent, to c. 2.5 cm lg., acicular, reddish, brown-tipped, white in the lowest third; **Fl.** c. 2.5

cm lg. and br., intense red; **Fr.** 1.5 cm lg., pale green, with thin Sc.; **S.** black, wrinkled.—USA (Arizona, Acuna Valley).

E. carrizalensis Kuenzl.: an undescribed name. (Fig. 95?)

E. dasyacanthus (Eng.) Br. & R.: **E. intertextus** v. **dasyacanthus** (Eng.) Backbg.

E. durangensis (Rge.) Br. & R.
Bo. hemispherical or ovoid, described as to 8 cm h., to c. 7 cm ∅, but in fact to 25 cm lg. and 10 cm ∅; **crown** spiny; **Ri.** 18, with fairly deep transverse indentations; **Tub.** 8 mm h.; **Ar.** white; **Rsp.** over 30, the lower ones to 1.5 cm, the upper ones to 3 cm lg., stiff, white, little curving; **Csp.** (3–)4, curving ± upwards, blackish; **Fl.** bellshaped-funnelform, rather small (brownish-reddish?).—Mexico (Durango, Rio Nazas).

E. erectocentrus (Coult.) Br. & R. (T.)
Bo. ovoid to short-cylindric, to 20 cm lg., to 10 cm ∅, pale bluish-green; **Ri.** 15–20(–21), tuberculate; **Tub.** crowded; **Rsp.** c. 14, straight, pale, c. 1.25 cm lg.; **Csp.** reddish or purple, ± projecting to erect, to 2.5 cm lg., slightly thickened below, sometimes with 1 additional very short Csp.; **Fl.** c. 2 cm ∅, c. 3(–5? Br. & R.) cm lg., pink-madder, darker at the centre, tipped brownish-pink; **Fr.** pale green, cylindric, c. 1.5 cm lg., splitting laterally; **S.** matt black, finely tuberculate.—USA (SE. Arizona). Acc. L. Benson, the Fl. also opens to 3–4 cm ∅.

E. intertextus (Eng.) Br. & R.
Bo. ovoid-spherical to cylindric, to 12.5 cm h., 5–7 cm ∅; **Ri.** 13; **Rsp.** 16–25, appressed, interlacing, the upper 5–9 also in part bristly (in cultivated plants all the Rsp. are ± alike); **Csp.** (3–)4, one being shorter, more central and projecting, the others pointing straight upwards; all **Sp.** light to reddish; **Fl.** 2.5 cm lg., light purple, bordered white; **Fr.** spherical, dry, splitting all round below and opening; **S.** glossy.—USA (W. Texas), Mexico (Chihuahua).

> v. **dasyacanthus** (Eng.) Backbg.: **Csp.** and **Rsp.** alike, bluish-purple (the bristly upper Sp. white), acicular, thin, sometimes missing at first, one Sp. curving ± upwards; **Fl.** white to purple.—USA (Texas (near El Paso)).

E. johnsonii (Parry) Baxt.
Bo. becoming cylindric, to c. 25 cm h., to c. 12 cm ∅, solitary; **Ri.** mostly 18–20, broken into low Tub.; **Rsp.** 8–15 (Hester), to 2 cm lg.; **Csp.** 6–13, to 4 cm lg.; all **Sp.** red to reddish-grey; **Fl.** flesh-coloured to purplish-pink to white, to 6.5 cm lg. and ∅; **Fr.** oblong, to 1.5 cm lg., ± naked,

dehiscing laterally.—USA (S. States, from Utah and Nevada southwards).

v. **lutescens** (Parrish) Marsh.: to 40 cm lg., to 15 cm ∅; **Rsp.** 10–14; **Csp.** 4(–7); **Fl.** c. 6 cm lg., 5 cm ∅, pale to deep yellow, brownish-red in the centre, remaining open up to 7 days. Sp. vary from pale yellow to pink or brownish-red (Arizona).

E. kakui Backbg.—Descr. Cact. Nov. III: 6, 1963. **Bo.** subspherical to elongated, c. 8 cm h. and 5.5 cm br. has been noted, pale greyish-green; **Ri.** 13, tuberculate but continuous; **Tub.** to 1 cm lg.; **Ar.** oval, with dirty greyish-brown felt, to 2 mm lg., becoming glabrous; **Rsp.** 10–14, 1–2.5 cm lg., stoutly acicular, horn-coloured, violet-grey above, sometimes with a Ssp. in the upper margin of the Ar.; **Csp.** 1, strongly erect, c. 1.5 cm lg., violet-grey in the lower part; all **Sp.** interlacing over the crown; **Fl.** ?—USA (Arizona?). (Fig. 94.) An earlier proposed name was E. pallidus.

E. krausei (Hildm.) Borg **Bo.** cylindric-ellipsoid, to 15 cm lg., 12 cm ∅, ± bluish-green; **crown** woolly; **Ri.** 21–23, notched, 1 cm h., obtuse; **Ar.** white at first; **Rsp.** 14–20, white, dark above and below; **Csp.** 2–4, to 4 cm lg., brown, lighter below; **Fl.** to 4 cm lg., white, pinkish-red above and outside, to 2.5 cm ∅; **Sti.** purple; **Fr.** ?—USA (Arizona, Dragoon Summit). Acc. Schumann, the Fl. is set with sparse felt and a few white or red Sp.; this latter is very unusual in the northern group. Perhaps an anomaly? Unfortunately the spec. has not been re-collected in the type-locality, and botanists studying the cacti of Arizona would perform a useful task by clarifying this interesting spec. In the light of the above unusual characters, Borg's inclusion in Echinomastus can only be justified if these represent atavistic phenomena.

E. macdowellii (Reb.) Br. & R. **Bo.** broadly spherical, to over 10 cm ∅; **crown** with yellowish felt; **Ri.** to 30 or more, tuberculate; **Rsp.** 20–27, thin, to 3 cm lg., white, almost concealing the Bo.; **Csp.** 3–4, stouter, thickened below, 2.5–4.5 cm lg., dark below, transparent and straw-coloured above; **Fl.** funnelform, red, 4 cm lg.—Mexico (Nuevo León, Coahuila).

E. mapimiensis Backbg. **Bo.** to 10 cm h., to 8 cm ∅; **Ri.** c. 13, greyish-green, tuberculate; **Rsp.** c. 22, white, to 2 cm lg., appressed, interlacing; **Csp.** mostly 4, fairly stout, projecting or ± down-curving, whitish, tipped brownish, the projecting Sp. ± bent at the tip, shorter than the others which are to 3 cm lg., and directed strongly towards the apex; **Fl.** c. 3 cm lg., 2

cm ∅, dirty white, with a dull reddish centre.—Mexico (Sierra Mapimi). **Sp.** not as stout as in E. unguispinus, the **Fl.** larger and somewhat differently coloured.

E. mariposensis J. P. Hest. **Bo.** solitary, spherical to elongated, to 9 cm h., 6 cm ∅; **R.** stalk-like, bearing fibrous R.; **Ri.** 21, indistinctly tuberculate; **Rsp.** 25–35, acicular, the shortest ones 4 mm lg.; **Csp.** 4(–6), 0.5–1.5 cm lg., the upper ones directed towards the apex, the lowest one porrect to bending somewhat downwards, stiffer than the Rsp.; all **Sp.** white, with a small brown tip; **Fl.** 2.5 cm lg., 2 cm ∅, pink; **Fr.** ± spherical, disintegrating horizontally at one side; **S.** black, finely tuberculate.—USA (Texas, not far from the Mariposa Mine).

E. unguispinus (Eng.) Br. & R. **Bo.** solitary, spherical to ± tapering above, to 10 cm h., 7 cm ∅; **crown** woolly, spiny; **Ri.** c. 21, strongly tuberculate; **Ar.** round, to 5 mm ∅; **Rsp.** c. 21, thin-subulate, sharp, 1.2–2 cm lg., the upper ones to 3 cm lg., white, interlacing; **Csp.** 4–8, much stouter, one of them very robust, bent downwards and clawlike, to 4 cm lg., brown to blackish, the remainder directed strongly upwards, bluish, tending to horn-coloured, 2.4–3.5 cm lg.; **Fl.** 2(–2.5) cm lg., 2 cm ∅, greenish, with a greenish-brown to reddish-brown centre.—Mexico (Chihuahua, Zacatecas).

Echinopsis Zucc. (93)

The genus was erected as early as 1837 and disputes have raged for a long time as to the species it should include, and those which should be excluded; Hooker, for instance, saw it as a group of forms belonging to Cereus. If this reasoning is followed, then it would be impossible to segregate Trichocereus Br. & R. from Echinopsis, since there are low-growing species in the former, and cereoid species of Echinopsis as well as the cactoid ones. The relatively insignificant differences of floral structure—in a concept such as Hooker's—would likewise fail to justify any separation. Other authors (e.g. Castellanos) have united Lobivia Br. & R. with Echinopsis; since the former genus includes species with flowers opening in the evening, and remaining open throughout the first night and also the following day (a phenomenon also known in Echinopsis, however), it really is not possible to draw any distinction between these last two genera on the basis of night- or day-flowering, or the bright flower-colours of Lobivia. For this reason I have erected the Genus Pseudolobivia for plants which are broadly spherical, with ±

hatchet-shaped, tuberculate ribs, with the flowers short (as in Lobivia) to longer and in part long and slender, but then less stout than in Echinopsis, in colours of yellow, red and white. The founding of Pseudolovia proved necessary because this genus clearly stands halfway between Echinopsis and Lobivia and is an essential justification for the existence of the latter; in other words if Pseudolobivia is not accepted, then Lobivia as a valid genus would also disappear, and Trichocereus likewise. In this event, all the species of these genera would revert to the earliest name: Echinopsis. But this, in view of the great number of species now known, would give rise to an outsize genus and consequent difficulties of understanding and elucidation. Smaller genera also have the virtue of representing essentially homogeneous groups of species. These conventional genera thus reflect, at least to a certain extent, the facts of Nature's creations and are also far more comprehensible than large and amorphous genera. Trichocereus and Lobivia are now generally accepted and logically, therefore, the same should apply to Pseudolobivia whose species vary in character from near-Echinopsis to near-Lobivia. Small genera such as these have the additional requirement of demanding preciser determination of the differential characters and are thus more significant to any phytographic work—and for practical applications—than any theoretical combinations. The phylogeneticist may see everything in terms of ± connected evolutionary lines, but other points of view carry greater weight with the phytographer.

Diagnostic characters of Echinopsis: plants spherical to more strongly elongated in age, or sometimes cereoid; flowers hairy, stouter and longer funnelform, varying in colour from white to ± purplish-pink; in general, however, the plant-bodies show greater degrees of body-reduction than occurs in the species of Trichocereus; by comparison with the latter, the fruits of Echinopsis are also smaller, subspherical to elongated and ± strongly hairy, lacking bristles or extended bristly or spiny scale-tips, coloured green or ± reddish to dirty purple or brick-red, the seeds rather small and black, but not described for most species.—Distribution: from N. Bolivia to S. Argentina, Paraguay, Uruguay and S. Brazil. [(R).]

E. albispinosa K.Sch.
Bo. spherical, eventually elongated, somewhat offsetting; **Ri.** 10–11; **Sp.** 11–14, thin, to c. 10, the upper pairs longest, interlacing laterally; **Csp.** 2 differentiated; **Sp.** more strongly spreading, the central(s) dark reddish-brown at first, all later becoming white; **Fl.** to 19.5 cm lg., white.—Origin ?

    v. **fuauxiana** Backbg.: **Ri.** c. 12; **Sp.** equal in

number to those of the type but stouter, the upper 1–3 sometimes darker, the lower central one to 2.5 cm lg. or rather more; **Pet.** c. 2 cm br., ± fimbriate, with a slender tip.

E. ancistrophora Speg.: **Pseudolobivia ancistrophora** (Speg.) Backbg.

E. arebaloi Card.
Bo. spherical, more freely offsetting, to 10 cm h. and ∅, dark green; **Ri.** c. 11, rounded, 1 cm h.; **Rsp.** and **Csp.** scarcely differentiated, 12–15, 5–20 mm lg., grey, brownish-tipped; **Fl.** 16 cm lg.; **Tu.** 10 cm lg., thus scarcely greater than the Fl.-∅; **Pet.** white.—Bolivia (Comarapa).

E. baldiana Speg.
Bo. solitary, elliptic-cylindric, to 30 cm h., 15 cm ∅, rarely offsetting; **Ri.** 13–14, not notched; **Ar.** 8 mm ∅, grey; **Rsp.** 9–11, to 15 mm lg.; **Csp.** 3–4, to 5 cm lg.; all **Sp.** dark chestnut at first, rather redder below, becoming pinkish-grey and then grey, dark-tipped; **Fl.** very large, scented.—Argentina (Catamarca).

E. boyuibensis Ritt.: **Pseudolobivia boyuibensis** (Ritt.) Backbg.

E. brasiliensis Frič ex Pažout—Fričiana Řada 1: 7, 3. 1962.
Bo. fairly small, glossy greyish-green; **Ri.** 9, acute; **Ar.** small, 1 cm apart, with some greyish-white felt; **Sp.** 7–9, subulate, yellowish-white, 1 cm lg., radiating, dark-tipped; **Fl.** to 10 cm br., agreeably scented; **Tu.** 12 cm lg., hairy; **Pet.** broad, light red; **Fil.** and **Sti.** yellowish-white.—Brazil (in the S.)

E. bridgesii SD.
Bo. eventually oblong, offsetting; **St.** to 10 cm ∅; **Ri.** to 10–12, prominent; **Ar.** large, brown-felty; **Sp.** (**Rsp.**) 8–10, brown at first, noticeably unequal, sometimes more numerous, in part as long as the longest Csp.; **Csp.** (0–)several, often one only, thickened below, becoming light grey with a dark tip; **Fl.** 15–18 cm lg., white; **Tu.** with grey and black H.—Bolivia (Highlands around La Paz).

E. calliantholilacina Card.
Bo. spherical, greyish-green, to 4 cm h., to 9 cm ∅; **Ri.** acute, 10–12, divided into hatchet-shaped Tub.; **Rsp.** 7–9, ± curving, pectinate and appressed, thin-subulate, 8–15 mm lg.; **Csp.** 1, directed upwards, 1.5–2 cm lg.; all **Sp.** grey, tipped brownish; **Fl.** 15 cm lg., light magenta-lilac, almost white; **Sep.** lanceolate, magenta-lilac; **Pet.** spatulate, 6 cm lg.; lower **Fil.** pale green, upper ones white; **style** green; **Sti.** greenish. The **Tu.** is curving, 8 cm lg., brownish-green.—Bolivia (Prov. Oropeza, Dept.

Chuquisaca, near Sucre, 2700 m).

E. calochlora K.Sch.
Bo. rather small, spherical, light green, 6–9 cm $\emptyset$; **Ri.** 13, broad, notched; **Ar.** 15 mm apart; **Rsp.** ascending, 14–20, 0.5–1 cm lg.; **Csp.** 3–4, somewhat longer than the Rsp.; all **Sp.** yellow, the centrals either darker or darker-tipped; **Fl.** 16 cm lg.—Brazil (Corumba).

v. **albispina** Backbg.: bluish-green, moderately glossy; **Sp.** to c. 22, several centrals distinguishable, all pale brownish at first, later below only, otherwise white, especially on the offsets at first; **Fl.** pinkish-red.—S. Brazil.

Echinopsis calochrysea Ritt. (FR 985): no description available.

E. calorubra Card.: referred to Pseudolobivia because of the compressed-spherical Bo., the hatchet-shaped Ri., and the Fl., which is orange-red to bluish-pink (inside). See **Pseudolobivia calorubra** (Card.) Backbg.

E. campylacantha Pfeiff. non R. Mey.: **Echinopsis leucantha** (Gill.) Walp.

E. cerdana Card.
Bo. greyish-green, 8–10 cm h., 10–20 cm $\emptyset$; **Ri.** 11–16, acute, notched; **Rsp.** 8–12, 1–3 cm lg.; **Csp.** 1, 3–6 cm lg.; **Sp.** all very stout, grey, brownish-tipped, subulate, compressed-terete, thickened below; **Fl.** 14 cm lg.; **Sep.** light lilac-purple; **Pet.** 4 cm lg., white.—Bolivia (near Cerda). Perhaps belongs to Pseudolobivia, similar to Ps. wilkeae?

E. chacoana Schütz
Bo. spherical, eventually shortly cylindric, light green; **Ri.** 12–18, straight, not tuberculate; **Ar.** grey, 2 cm apart; **Csp.** 1, porrect, to over 7 cm lg.; **Rsp.** 7–8, to 2 cm lg.; all **Sp.** fairly robustly subulate, ± brown at first, then grey; **Fl.** white; **Tu.** with white and brown H.; **Fr.** brown.—Paraguay (Chaco Boreal).
Ritter distinguishes v. spinosior Ritt. (Succulenta, 44: 2, 26. 1965); Ri. 10–15; Rsp. 8–9, 2–4 cm lg.; Csp. 3–4, 3–8 cm lg.—Bolivia (Prov. Gran Chaco, Taringuiti: FR 783a). Since the data are not significantly different, either the spec. (with the description based on a single plant) is more variable than suggested, or Ritter's details merely amplify the original description, and this is not a good variety. The spec. may even be identical with E. meyeri.

E. cochabambensis Backbg.
Bo. soon oblong, freely offsetting, glossy oil-green; **Ri.** c. 10, rounded and tuberculately notched; **Ar.** depressed, 1 cm apart, more strongly felty at first; **Rsp.** 5–9, somewhat projecting; **Csp.** mostly 1, all **Sp.** deep brown at first, c. 1 cm lg. or rather more, very sharp; **Fl.** white.—Bolivia (Cochabamba).

E. comarapana Card.
Bo. shortly cylindric, offsetting, forming groups to 40 cm br., single heads to 15 cm h., 8 cm $\emptyset$; **Ri.** 10–12, 1 cm h.; **Rsp.** 9–11, 5–11 mm lg., grey; **Csp.** 1, pointing downwards, 1.5–2 cm lg.; **Sp.** all thin-acicular, thickened below, grey; **Fl.** 15 cm lg., 6 cm $\emptyset$, white, washed pink at the tips; **Fr.** 3 cm $\emptyset$, dark green.—Bolivia (Comarapa, S. Isidro).

E. cordobensis Speg.
Bo. solitary, eventually thick-cylindric, to 50 cm h., 35 cm $\emptyset$, dull green, somewhat pruinose; **Ri.** 13, acute; **Rsp.** 8–10, 1–2 cm lg.; **Csp.** 1–3, longest one 3–5 cm lg., all thickened below; all **Sp.** straight, dark at first, then grey; **Fl.** erect, 20–22 cm lg., white; **Fr.** spherical, 2.5 cm $\emptyset$, yellowish-red.—Argentina (Córdoba, Villa Mercedes).

E. coronata Card.
Bo. solitary, spherical, to 15 cm h., to 17 cm $\emptyset$, greyish-green; **Ri.** 13, acute, notched; **Rsp.** 8–10, 1–2 cm lg.; **Csp.** 1, 1.2–3 cm lg.; all **Sp.** subulate, grey; **Fl.** to c. 18 cm lg.; **Pet.** pure white; **Sep.** greenish in the middle; **Fr.** 3 cm lg., dehiscing longitudinally.—Bolivia (near Valle Abajo, Dept. Santa Cruz).

E. cotacajesi Card.
Bo. spherical, 4–6 cm h., 7–8 cm $\emptyset$, dark green; **Ri.** 8–10, obtuse, 1–1.5 cm h., 2–2.5 cm br. at the base; **Ar.** 12–15 mm apart, round, 4–6 mm $\emptyset$; **Rsp.** 6–10, 5–8 mm lg.; **Csp.** 1, 16–18 mm lg., directed upwards; all **Sp.** sharp, acicular, dark ash-grey; **Fl.** apical, 11 cm lg., 5 cm br.; **Ov.** green, spherical, with pink Sc. and white H.; **Tu.** 6.5 cm lg., 12 mm br., green, with Sc. and H.; **Sep.** recurved, lanceolate, 30 × 7 mm, greenish outside, white inside; **Pet.** 30 × 10 mm, white; **style** 7.5 cm lg., green with 11 yellow Sti.; **Fr.** spherical, 2–2.5 cm $\emptyset$.—Bolivia (Prov. Ayopaya, Dept. Cochabamba, near Cotacajes, 2700 m).

E. cylindrica (FR 1094): no description available.

E. dehrenbergii Frič
Bo. spherical; **Ri.** acute; **Ar.** round, c. 1.5 cm apart; **Sp.** increasing in number with age, 5–20, sometimes only 3–4 or somewhat more towards the apex; **Csp.** 1, to 1.5 cm lg.; **Fl.** ?—Paraguay. Belongs to the complex of E. paraguayensis (still undescribed).

v. **blossfeldii** Backbg.: **Bo.** broadly spherical; **Ri.** to 16, lower than in the type, becoming flatter below; **Sp.** very variable in number, often to 30 on older growth, subulate, fewer above; **Csp.** 1, straight or ± curving, dark brown.—Paraguay.

E. eyriesii (Turp.) Zucc. (T.)
Bo. solitary at first, eventually more freely offsetting, spherical to short-columnar; **Ri.** 11–18, not tuberculate; **Ar.** round, white or pale brownish; **Sp.** very short, often scarcely visible through the wool, dark brown; **Rsp.** to 10, c. 5 mm lg.; **Csp.** 4–8, to 5 mm lg.; **Fl.** 17–25 cm lg., white.—S. Brazil to Argentina (Entre Rios).
    v. **grandiflora** R. Mey. non Lke.: **Rsp.** bristly, to 6, scarcely visible; **Csp.** 5, 3 directed upwards, 2 downwards, to 3 mm lg., brownish; **Fl.** large, pink; **Sep.** strongly recurved.—Brazil (Rio Grande do Sul). Attribution to this spec. is dubious.

E. fiebrigii Gürke: **Pseudolobivia obrepanda** v. **fiebrigii** (Gürke) Backbg. [Note by W. Haage: Dr. H. Friedrich's studies have shown this should be known as E. obrepanda (K.Sch.) v. fiebrigii.]

E. forbesii (Lehm.) Dietr. was possibly the first name for E. rhodotricha K.Sch.

E. formosa Jac.: **Soehrensia formosa** (Pfeiff.) Backbg.

E. gemmata K.Sch.: see **Echinopsis turbinata** (Pfeiff.) Zucc.

E. grandiflora Link 1857
Bo. 6 cm h., 4 cm ∅, dark green; **Ri.** 12, vertical, scarcely wavy, with deep furrows; **Ar.** 0.5–1 inch apart, light grey on new growth, becoming glabrous; **Rsp.** 5–13; **Csp.** 1; all **Sp.** straight, subulate, reddish-brown at first, later black; **Fl.** trumpet-shaped, 4.5 inches ∅, white, agreeably perfumed, remaining open for 3–5 days; **Tu.** slender, green; **Ov.** oblong, with tufted H.; **Sep.** lanceolate; **Pet.** in 2 Ser., pure white; **Fil.** white with yellow An.; **style** yellowish-white with 12 yellowish Sti.—S. Brazil.

Echinopsis 'Haku-jo' hort. (Haku-jomaru)
A monstrose Echinopsis form from Japan, more recently distributed also in USA; the name translates roughly as: "Ball with stripes of grey felt".
Bo. dark green, offsetting to form groups; **Ri.** acute; **Ar.** connected by broad ribbons of grey wool; **Rsp.** c. 8; **Csp.** 1. Presumably a hybrid.*

---

* Translator's note: While the grey-felty appearance gives the Bo. an interestingly "different" look, the only Fl. I have seen were very small, orange-yellow and so distorted-crumpled that the plant seems more of a monstrosity than a hybrid as suggested by Haage.

E. hamatacantha Backbg.: **Pseudolobivia hamatacantha** (Backbg.) Backbg.

E. hamatispina Werd.: **Pseudolobivia kratochviliana** (Backbg.) Backbg.

E. hammerschmidii Card.
Bo. short-cylindric, solitary or offsetting, to 10 cm h., to 9 cm ∅; **Ri.** 15, acute, notched, dark green, sometimes ± reddish above, c. 1.5 cm h.; **Ar.** grey; **Rsp.** 8–9, 6–8 mm lg.; **Csp.** 1, 15–18 mm lg.; all **Sp.** grey, swollen below; **Fl.** white; **Fr.** spherical or elliptic, 2.5 cm lg., dark green; **S.** spherical, black.—Bolivia (Las Lajas, Dept. Santa Cruz).

E. herbasii Card.
Bo. offsetting, to 6 cm h., to 10 cm ∅, faded green; **Ri.** 20–23, notched, acute; **Rsp.** and **Csp.** not differentiated, 20–25, one of these to 1.4 cm lg., brown-tipped; **Fl.** 14 cm lg., white.—Bolivia (Dept. Chuquisaca). (FR 643, 1089.)

E. huotii (Cels) Lab.
Bo. solitary, columnar, to 35 cm h., to 8 cm ∅, glossy dark green, later offsetting from the base; **Ri.** 11, to 1.2 cm h.; **Ar.** yellowish-white; **Rsp.** 9–11, subulate, to 2.2 cm lg.; **Csp.** usually 4, the longest one porrect, to 4 cm lg. or more; **Fl.** 17–20 cm lg., to 13 cm ∅, white.—Bolivia.

E. ibicuatensis Card.
Bo. solitary, spherical, to 9 cm h., to 14 cm ∅, pale green; **Ri.** later to 13, acute, 2.5 cm h.; **Rsp.** c. 10, to 1.2 cm lg.; **Csp.** 1, to 1.2 cm lg.; all **Sp.** ash-grey; **Fl.** 18 cm lg., white; **Fr.** oblong, 3 cm lg., with white H. and pink Sc.—Bolivia (Dept. Santa Cruz).

E. imperialis hort. (Hummel): a hybrid between a Trichocereus and an Echinopsis. This imposing plant, already over 2 m h., is in the Jardin Exotique, Monaco; it offsets strongly and produces huge white Fl. It is very vigorous-growing. Since it has already been widely distributed, it should be named as an intergeneric hybrid: × Trichoechinopsis (see also the introductory text on the subject of intergeneric hybrids).

E. intricatissima Speg.
Bo. solitary, ± ovoid, to 20 cm h.; **Ri.** 16; **Rsp.** 8–13, to 1.5 cm lg.; **Csp.** 4–6, the 1–2 longest to 10 cm lg., ± upcurving; **Sp.** mostly 3–6 cm lg. (centrals), all strongly interlacing, at first reddish to ashy (to blackish?); **Fl.** to 22 cm lg., faintly perfumed; **Fr.** to 3 cm lg., green at first, then yellowish.—Argentina (Mendoza).

E. kladiwaiana Rausch 1972
Bo. cylindric, forming groups, fresh green, to 20 cm

h. and 6 cm ∅; **Ri.** 11–13, straight, c. 7 mm h., ±
tuberculate; **Ar.** c. 16 mm apart, 2 mm ∅, white-
felty; **Rsp.** 12–14, radiating, to 15 mm lg.; **Csp.** 1–3,
directed upwards, to 10 cm lg.; all **Sp.** thin, flexible,
brown, lighter below; **Fl.** subapical, to 22 cm lg.
and 12 cm ∅; **Ov.** with tuberculate Sc.; **Tu.** with
fleshy Sc. and long black H.; **Sep.** lanceolate, green
with a long brownish tip; **Pet.** spatulate, 80 mm lg.
and to 20 mm br., white, throat white; **Fil.** greenish-
white; **style** 14 cm lg., light green with 10 greenish-
yellow **Sti.**; **Fr.** c. 30 mm ∅, with Sc. and greyish-
black H.—Bolivia (near Inquisivi, 2800–3100 m).
Related to E. ayopayana Ritt. & Rausch, but
distinguished by the lighter green Bo., more
crowded Ar. and long flexible Sp.

E. klimpeliana Weidl. & Werd.: **Acanthocalycium
klimpelianum** (Weidl. & Werd.) Backbg.

E. klingleriana Card.
Bo. simple, 12–14 cm h., 13 cm ∅, light green; **Ri.**
13, acute, notched, 2 cm h., 3 cm br.; **Ar.** 2.5–3 cm
apart, round, prominent, with dark grey wool, 1 cm
∅; **Rsp.** 5–6, 2–3 cm lg., thin-subulate, whitish or
yellow, 1 **Csp.** sometimes present; **Fl.** lateral,
funnelform, 12 cm lg., white; **Ov.** spherical, 12 mm
lg., with acute pink Sc. and brown H.; **Sep.**
lanceolate, 2 cm lg., brownish-lilac; **Pet.** lan-
ceolate, 2.5 cm lg., white; **Fil.** thin, white, 3–4 cm lg.;
An. yellow; **style** 7 cm lg., greenish, white above;
Sti. 15, 12 mm lg.; **Fr.** elliptic, 2–3 cm lg., with
Sc. and white and brownish wool.—Bolivia
(Chiquitos, Santa Cruz, near the Salinas de San
José, in part on very salt-impregnated soil). Acc.
Markus, this spec. is identical with E. chacoana;
specimens are known to reach a height of 50 cm.
Named for Father E. Klingler, San José.

E. korethroides Werd.: **Soehrensia korethroides**
(Werd.) Backbg.

E. kratochviliana Backbg.: **Pseudolobivia kratochviliana** (Backbg.) Backbg.

E. lecoriensis Card.: **Pseudolobivia lecoriensis**
(Card.) Backbg.

E. leucantha (Gill.) Walp.
Bo. spherical to ellipsoid, never columnar, green,
sometimes ± frosted, to c. 15 cm ∅; **Ri.** 14–16, to
1.5 cm h.; **Ar.** yellowish-felty; **Rsp.** 9–10, yellowish-
brown, to 2.5 cm lg.; **Csp.** 1, over 5 cm lg., brown,
darker-tipped; **Fl.** to 17 cm lg., white; **Fr.** dark
red.—Argentina (NW. Provinces).
v. **brasiliensis** Speg.: cylindric, to 15 cm h., 10 cm
∅; **Ri.** 13; **Ar.** with ash-grey felt; **Sp.** 7, robust;
Csp. 1, to 7 cm lg., black to ash-grey; **Fl.** 16 cm
lg.—Brazil (Santos). Appears to have died out,
and was probably a valid spec.;

v. **volliana** Backbg.: broadly spherical; **Ri.**
10–11, acute; **Rsp.** to c. 7; **Csp.** 1, long, thickened
below; **Sp.** all projecting; **Fl.** white, shorter than
in the type.—Origin?

E. leucorhodantha Backbg.: **Pseudolobivia
leucorhodantha** (Backbg.) Backbg.

E. lobivioides Backbg.: **Pseudolobivia pelecyrhachis** v. **lobivioides** (Backbg.) Backbg.

E. mamillosa Gürke
Bo. solitary, broadly spherical, to c. 12 cm h., 10 cm
∅, glossy green; **Ri.** to over 30, with ± chin-like
Tub.; **Rsp.** 8–10(–12), 5–10 mm lg.; **Csp.** 1–4, to 1
cm lg., yellowish, brown above; **Fl.** 13–18 cm lg., 8
cm ∅, white, sometimes washed ± pink above; **Fr.**
spherical, with grey H.; **S.** matt black.—Bolivia
(Tarija).
I have seen some plants which were larger. Ritter
also distinguishes the following variety of which at
least the first description is only supplementary to
that of Gürke, who based his on a single specimen,
as did Bödeker: v. ritteri (Böd.) Ritt.: Bo. 10–25 cm
∅; Ri. 18–32; Rsp. 12–15, 1–2.5 cm lg.; Csp. 3–8;
Sp. somewhat stouter.—Bolivia (Tarija; FR 79).
The identical locality is an additional reason for
treating the above details as no more than an
amplification of the original description.
v. orozasana Ritt.: **Pseudolob. orozasana** (Ritt.)
Backbg.;
v. **tamboensis** Ritt.—Succulenta, 44: 2, 25. 1965:
distinguishable by more numerous Sp.; **Rsp.**
12–18; **Csp.** 3–12.—Bolivia (Prov. O'Connor,
Tambo; FR 780).

E. mataranensis Card. 1969
Bo. spherical, 12–13 cm h., 18–20 cm thick, bluish-
green, crown sunken; **Ri.** 8–10, acute, tuberculate;
Ar. 2–3 cm apart, 5–15 mm lg., obliquely sunken in
the Tub., with light brown felt; **Sp.** 11–13, ±
pectinate, 1–5 cm lg., spreading or appressed,
curving, horny-grey, thickened below; **Fl.** lateral,
funnelform, 16–18 cm lg., 8 cm ∅; **Ov.** 2 cm lg.; **Sc.**
6 mm lg., brownish, with black, brown and white
H.; **Tu.** 8–9 cm lg., with Sc. 1 cm lg., greenish-
brown, mostly with black H.; **Sep.** lanceolate,
brownish or greenish-white, 40 × 5 mm; **Pet.**
lanceolate, 50 × 10 mm, white; **style** 11 cm lg.,
greenish-yellow, with 12 yellow **Sti.** 1 cm lg.—
Bolivia (Tarata, Cochabamba, near Matarani).
Conspicuous by reason of the long Sp. and the
dense black H. of the Sc. on the Tu.

E. melanopotamica Speg.
Bo. cylindric in age, to 50 cm h., 15 cm ∅, offsetting
only when older, dark green, then ± frosted, finally
grey; **Ri.** 14, notched; **Rsp.** 5–9, tipped reddish to

ash-coloured, straight at first, then somewhat curving; **Csp.** 1, to 4 cm lg., ash-grey, reddish-tipped; **Fl.** unscented, 22 cm lg.; **Fr.** 3.5 cm lg., dirty red.—Argentina (Rio Negro, Rio Colorado).

E. meyeri Heese
Bo. spherical, c. 10 cm $\emptyset$, pale green; **Ri.** 14–16, acute; **Rsp.** 7–8; **Csp.** 1(–3?); **Sp.** (acc. Borg) 2–3 cm lg., yellowish-grey at midway, reddish-brown above; **Fl.** to 20 cm lg., 12 cm br.; **Pet.** all extremely narrow-linear.—Paraguay. Possibly the first name for E. chacoana Schütz, with abnormally narrow Pet.; the spec.—with Fl. as described—has not been re-collected.

E. minuana Speg.
Bo. solitary, rarely offsetting, to 80 cm h., to 15 cm $\emptyset$; **Ri.** to 12, acute; **Rsp.** 4–7, 2–3 cm lg., somewhat projecting; **Csp.** 1, 5–6 cm lg., thickened below; all **Sp.** straight, dark brown; **Fl.** unscented, 20 cm lg., white(?); **Fr.** 4.5 cm lg., greenish-red.—Argentina (Entre Rios).

E. mirabilis Speg.: **Setiechinopsis mirabilis** (Speg.) De Haas.

E. molesta Speg.
Bo. solitary, spherical, to 20 cm $\emptyset$, pale green, not glossy; **Ri.** 13, fairly prominent, acute, somewhat wavy; **Ar.** large; **Rsp.** 6–8, to 15 mm lg., not interlacing; **Csp.** 4, to 3 cm lg., thickened below, only slightly curving; all **Sp.** grey; **Fl.** faintly perfumed, 22–24 cm lg.—Argentina (Córdoba).

E. multiplex (Pfeiff.) Zucc.
Bo. solitary or freely offsetting, to 30 cm h., spherical to somewhat clavate; **Ri.** 13–15, broad below, acute above; **Ar.** large, white; **Rsp.** 5–15, mostly to 10, to 2 cm lg., yellowish-brownish; **Csp.** (2–)4, to 4 cm lg.; **Sp.** fairly subulate; **Fl.** 15–20 cm lg., pink.—S. Brazil.

E. nigra Backbg.: **Pseudolobivia longispina** v. **nigra** (Backbg.) Backbg. [Note by W. Haage: = Lobivia ferox Br. & R. v. nigra Backbg.]

E. obrepanda (SD.) K.Sch.: **Pseudolobivia obrepanda** (SD.) Backbg.

E. oreopogon (Speg.) Werd.: **Soehrensia oreopogon** (Speg.) Backbg.

E. orozasana Ritt. n.nud.: **Pseudolobivia orozasana** (Ritt.) Backbg. (held by Ritter to be a variety of E. mamillosa.)

E. oxygona (Lk.) Zucc.
Bo. subspherical, solitary or offsetting, c. 25 cm $\emptyset$,

$\pm$ frosted; **Ri.** 14, rounded above; **Rsp.** 5–15, unequal, to 1.5 cm lg.; **Csp.** 2–5, somewhat longer; all **Sp.** horn-coloured, black-tipped; **Fl.** c. 22 cm lg., pale red.—S. Brazil, Uruguay, to NE. Argentina.

E. pamparuizii Card. 1968
Bo. spherical to shortly cylindric, 7 cm h., 8–9 cm thick, light green, crown sunken; **Ri.** c. 11, 1.5 cm h., acute, 2 cm br.; **Ar.** 15–18 mm apart, round, 4 mm $\emptyset$, grey-felty; **Rsp.** 6–8, very thin, 4–20 mm lg., curving sideways towards the Bo.; **Csp.** 1, straight, 15–25 mm lg.; all **Sp.** horn-grey; **Fl.** lateral, 14–15 cm lg., 4–5 cm br.; **Ov.** 15 mm lg., green; **Tu.** very slender, only 4 mm thick at midway, with dark brown and grey H.; **Sep.** few, lanceolate, light green, recurved; **Pet.** spatulate, pure white; **style** 9.5 cm lg., very light green, yellowish below, whitish above; **Sti.** 8, light yellow, 10 mm lg.— Bolivia (Prov. Boeto, Chuquisaca, Pampa Ruiz (hence the specific name), on the road to Rio Grande at 1400 m). A similar spec. is E. semidenudata Card.

E. paraguayensis Knebel: an undescribed name for the complex: **E. dehrenbergii** Frič, **E. schwantesii** Frič and **E. werdermannii** Frič, which has not been validly described.

E. pelecyrhachis Backbg.: **Pseudolobivia pelecyrhachis** (Backbg.) Backbg.

E. pereziensis Card.—"Cactus", 18: 88–90, 1963.
Bo. to 15 cm h., 8 cm $\emptyset$, dark green; **Ri.** c. 12, to 1 cm h.; **Sp.** not differentiated, not very projecting, 18–20, acicular, 6–10 mm lg., light grey, brown-tipped, thickened below, individual centrals to 1.5 cm lg.; **Fl.** 15 cm lg., 11 cm $\emptyset$, white; **Tu.** with white and brown H.; **style** long-projecting.—Bolivia (Santa Cruz, near Perez, 1900 m).

E. pojoensis Card.
Bo. solitary, spherical to short-cylindric, to 10 cm h. and br., bluish-green; **Ri.** 10, rather obtuse, 1.5 cm h.; **Ar.** grey; **Sp.** 7–10, 5–25 mm lg., radiating, grey, red-tipped; **Fl.** 17 cm lg., 7 cm $\emptyset$, white, greenish above.—Bolivia (Dept. Cochabamba, Puente Pojo).

E. polyancistra Backbg.: **Pseudolobivia polyancistra** (Backbg.) Backbg.

E. potosina (Werd.) Backbg.: **Pseudolobivia potosina** (Werd.) Backbg.

E. pseudomamillosa Card.
Bo. solitary, spherical or broadly so, to 8 cm h., to 12 cm $\emptyset$; **Ri.** c. 18, somewhat obliquely notched; **Sp.** pectinate, 4 lateral ones, 2 directed upwards

and 1 downwards, the shortest ones 5 mm lg., the medium-long ones c. 12 mm lg., the longest 3–4 cm lg., all acicular, grey, brown-tipped, thickened below; **Fl.** 18 cm lg., 8 cm $\emptyset$, white.—Bolivia (Dept. Cochabamba, Cerro de San Pedro).

E. pudantii Pfersd.
Bo. elongated-spherical, eventually probably more strongly elongated; **Ri.** c. 16, moderately prominent; **Rsp.** c. 14, white; **Csp.** 4–8, blackish-brown, thin; **Fl.** 17 cm lg., 9 cm $\emptyset$, white with a faint greenish sheen.—Origin? (perhaps S. Brazil).

E. rhodotricha K. Sch.
Bo. becoming cylindric, offsetting (dull greyish-green: Br. & R.; probably only v. argentiniensis R. Mey.), leaf-green, to 80 cm h., to 9 cm $\emptyset$; **Ri.** 8–13, low, faintly sinuate; **Rsp.** 4–7, somewhat curving, to 2 cm lg.; **Csp.** 1, to 2.5 cm lg.; all **Sp.** yellowish-brown at first, darker-tipped, eventually light horn-coloured; **Fl.** 15 cm lg., white.—Paraguay and NE. Argentina.

v. **argentiniensis** R. Mey. is said to be distinguished as follows:
Bo. more spherical; **Rsp.** 7, **Csp.** similar in appearance;

v. **robusta** R. Mey. is said to have larger **Fl.** and up to 3 **Csp.**

E. ritteri Böd.: **Echinopsis mamillosa** Gürke (held by Ritter to be a variety of E. mamillosa).

E. riviere de caraltii Card.
Named for Sr. Fernando Rivière de Caralt, the celebrated cactophile who has developed what is probably the world's most complete collection of Opuntias, at Blanes near Barcelona, Spain. No description is available.

E. robinsoniana Werd.
Bo. columnar, to 1.2 m h., to 20 cm $\emptyset$, dull light green to darker greyish-green; **crown** with yellowish-grey felt; **Ri.** 19, 1.5 cm h.; **Sp.** 10–12 (later sometimes several more, thin), 1–3 distinguishable as centrals, to 2.5 cm lg., light to dark brown, straight to $\pm$ curving; **Fl.** 16 cm lg.; **Tu.** reddish-brown; **Pet.** white; **Sep.** sometimes reddish above.—Origin?

E. rojasii Card.: **Pseudolobivia rojasii** (Card.) Backbg.

E. roseo-lilacina Card.
Bo. spherical, solitary or offsetting, to 7 cm h., to 13 cm $\emptyset$, greyish-green; **Ri.** 14–20, acute above, 8 mm h.; **Ar.** grey; **Rsp.** 6–7; **Csp.** 1 sometimes present, to 2 cm lg.; all **Sp.** whitish, brown-tipped; **Fl.** 14 cm lg.; **Sep.** purplish-brown; **Pet.** white below, rose-

lilac above, spatulate; **Fr.** spherical, to 5 cm $\emptyset$, purple.—Bolivia (on the road Cochabamba—San Isidro).

E. salmiana Web.: **Echinopsis bridgesii** SD.

E. salpi(n)gophora Preinr.: **Echinopsis spegazziniana** Br. & R.

E. schwantesii Frič
Bo. broadly spherical; **Sp.** radiating sideways, c. 9, thin; **Csp.** similar, when present; **Fl.** greenish-white; **Tu.** brown.—Paraguay. From the complex of E. paraguayensis and, like it, not validly described.

E. semidenudata Card.
Fl. with a very narrow Tu.; resembles E. pamparuizii Card.—Bolivia (Tarija, Villa Montes, 600 m).

E. shaferi Br. & R.
Bo. solitary to somewhat offsetting, to 1.5 m h., to 18 cm $\emptyset$, dark green; **Ri.** 10–12, 2 cm h.; **Ar.** to 1 cm apart; **Rsp.** 6–9, 1.5–3.5 cm lg., straight, brownish at first, later grey, thin-subulate; **Csp.** 1, to 10 cm lg., $\pm$ decurved, often dark below, lighter above; **Fl.** slender, 20 cm lg., white; **style** and **Fil.** pale green; **Fr.** 3 cm lg., ovoid, brick-red.—N. Argentina (Tucuman, Trancas). The tallest known species of this genus, later resembling a Trichocereus. Young growth densely spiny.

E. silvatica Ritt.—"Succulenta", 44: 2, 24. 1965 (Details in brackets refer to E. mamillosa).
Bo. apparently similar to E. mamillosa, to 1 m lg., to 20(–15) cm $\emptyset$; **Ri.** 13–16(–24), 1.5–3 cm h., slightly notched (or more so ?); **Ar.** 10–15 mm apart, 4–8 mm $\emptyset$; **Sp.** straight to slightly curving; **Rsp.** (0.5–1.2)–4.5 cm lg., stouter; **Csp.** like the Rsp., number not stated; **Pet.** to 6.5 cm lg., to 2.7(–4) cm br.—Bolivia (Prov. O'Connor, Dept. Tarija, Tacuarandi; FR 782). Since Ritter does not specify any differences for the Fl., when compared with E. mamillosa, presumably Fl.-length and $\emptyset$ are the same.

E. silvestrii Speg.
Bo. spherical at first, eventually elongated, little offsetting, to over 10 cm h., 8 cm $\emptyset$; **Ri.** 12–14; **Rsp.** and **Csp.** (1 erect) all fairly short, stiff, to 1.2 cm lg., yellow at first, later dirty grey; **Fl.** 20 cm lg., white, not perfumed.—Argentina (borders of Prov. Tucuman and Salta). (Fig. 96.)

E. smrziana Backbg.: **Trichocereus smrzianus** (Backbg.) Backbg.

E. spegazziniana Br. & R.
Bo. eventually cylindric, to 30 cm h., to 9 cm ⌀, dark green; **Ri.** 12–14, to 1.2 cm h., scarcely notched; **Ar.** yellowish-white; **Rsp.** 7–8, short, subulate, straight, brown; **Csp.** 1, to c. 2 cm lg., moderately curving, brown; **Fl.** 15–17 cm lg., 6 cm ⌀, white, washed pink towards the margin.—Argentina (in the NW.).
E. campylacantha R. Mey. non Pfeiff. was a synonym for this spec.

E. spiniflora (K. Sch.) Berg.: **Acanthocalycium spiniflorum** (K. Sch.) Backbg.

E. subdenudata Card.
Bo. solitary, to 8 cm h., to 12 cm ⌀, greyish-green; **Ri.** 10–12, straight, acute; **Rsp.** 3–5, ashy brown, to 1.5 cm lg., thickened below; **Csp.** 1, ashy brown, 2 mm lg.; **Fl.** narrow-funnelform, to 20 cm lg., white.—Bolivia (Angosto de Villamontes).

E. sucrensis Card.—C. & S. J. (US), XXXV: 6, 200–201, 1963.
Bo. spherical to short-cylindric, forming groups; **St.** to 7 cm ⌀, greyish-green; **Ri.** c. 12, narrow above; **Ar.** to 1 cm apart, grey; **Rsp.** 14–16, laterally appressed, acicular, 8–15 mm lg.; **Csp.** 1, pointing downwards, subulate, 15–20 mm lg.; **Sp.** all light grey, thickened below; **Fl.** 21 cm lg., 10 cm ⌀; **Tu.** with white and brown H., light purple, 10 cm lg.; **Sep.** narrow, white below, green above; **Pet.** spatulate, snow-white; **Fil.** green below, white above; **style** green below, yellow above; **Sti.** light yellow; **throat** emerald.—Bolivia (Prov. Oropeza, Dept. Chuquisaca, Sucre, 2750 m).

E. tamboensis Ritt. (Bolivia): not described.

E. tapecuana Ritt.—"Succulenta", 44: 2, 24. 1965. (Data in brackets refer to E. obrepanda.)
Bo. 5–12 cm ⌀ (–18 cm); **Ri.** 12–16(–28), less notched than in E. obrepanda; **Ar.** round or broadly oval, 2–4 mm ⌀, 1–2 cm apart; **Sp.** thin-subulate; **Rsp.** 0.5–2(–6) cm lg., often shorter or missing in age; **Fl.** apparently resembles that of E. obrepanda.—Bolivia (Prov. O'Connor, Tapecua; FR 777).
Since I have referred E. obrepanda to Pseudo-lobivia, and in view of the notched Ar. and of his comparison with the latter spec., Ritter's spec. is probably better referred to Pseudolobivia if my separation of the genus is accepted.

E. torrecillasensis Card.: **Pseudolobivia torrecillasensis** (Card.) Backbg. Described by Cardenas as having a flattened-spherical Bo. and a thick taproot, with a Fl. to 8 cm lg., red to salmon-red. May be identical, as a ± red-flowering variety, with Lob. arachnacantha Ritt. & Buin. (see this latter).

E. tubiflora (Pfeiff.) Zucc.
Bo. solitary or offsetting, ± spherical, dark green, to c. 12 cm ⌀; **Ri.** c. 12; **Ar.** white; **Rsp.** to 20, yellowish-white, dark-tipped; **Csp.** 3–5, to 1.5 cm lg., black; all **Sp.** subulate; **Fl.** 20 cm lg., white.—Argentina (Tucuman, Catamarca, Salta).

E. turbinata (Pfeiff.) Zucc.
Bo. spherical, simple or offsetting; **Ri.** 13–14, broad below; **Rsp.** later to 10–14, fewer at first, to 5 mm lg., yellowish-brown; **Csp.** 1–2 at first, later more numerous, to 7 mm lg., stiff, black; **Sp.** subulate; **Fl.** 15–17 cm lg., strongly perfumed, white. Britton and Rose regard E. gemmata as synonymous with this spec., but this seems somewhat dubious.—Argentina (Entre Rios).

E. valida Monv.: **Trichocereus validus** (Monv.) Backbg.

E. vellegradensis Card.
Bo. solitary, spherical, 5–7 cm h., 8–9 cm ⌀, pale green; **Ri.** c. 12, straight, obtuse, 1 cm h.; **Ar.** grey or brownish; **Rsp.** 7–11, 8–15 mm lg., somewhat compressed, greyish-white; **Csp.** 1, directed upwards, 2–3 cm lg., ashen; **Fl.** borne high on the flank, 20 cm lg., white.—Bolivia (Prov. Valle Grande). The name is presumably the result of a typographical error, and should correctly be **E. vallegrandensis.**

E. werdermanii Frič ex Fleischer: (Fričiana Řada 1:7, 4. 1962): (E. backebergii Frič, nomen nudum 1926)
This spec. has now been described and closely resembles E. subdenudata Card.: the **Ri.**-count is ± identical, as are also the extremely short **Sp.** and the acute **Ri.**; **Sp.** blackish, 3–8 (3–5 in E. subdenudata); **Fl.** of similar length but light pink (white in E. subdenudata).—Paraguay. The Tu. of E. werdermannii appears to be somewhat stouter. In view of the general characters and the geographical distribution, this spec. is probably only a variety of E. subdenudata. More conspicuous colour-differences are found in the flowers of Gymnocalycium mihanovichii, for instance, and others also.

E. zuccarinii (zuccariniana) Pfeiff.: **Echinopsis tubiflora (Pfeiff.) Zucc.**

Echinorebutia Frič was an undescribed name for **Aylostera** Speg.

Encephalocarpus Berg. (221)

Small spherical plants with flat imbricate tubercles bearing a furrow on the upperside; axils very woolly. Small spines are found only on the youngest areoles and are ± pectinate. The flowers arise from the very youngest tubercles in the crown, and have a short, narrow tube. The fruit ripens within the apical wool and there dries up; seeds c. 1 mm long, dark grey, ± bent-clavate. 1 species only.—Distribution: Mexico (Tamaulipas). [(G).]

E. strobiliformis (Werd.) Berg. (T.)
Bo. spherical, with a compressed **taproot**; **crown** with grey felt; **Tub.** in distinctly oblique R., appressed, convex and keeled outside; **Ar.** persist only on younger Tub.; **Sp.** present on the Tub. only in newer growth, c. 12, c. 5 mm lg., white, feathery at first, then bristly, they and the Ar. dropping; **Fl.** to 3 cm lg., brilliant violet-red.—Mexico (Nuevo León, Doctor Arroyo. Amended by W. Haage). (Fig. 98.)

Eomatucana Ritt.
A new genus erected by Ritter for plants with actinomorphic flowers and some hairiness of the ovary. It remains to be seen whether the only species—Eomatucana oreodoxa Ritt.—should be referred to Submatucana. Actinomorphic flower-forms also sometimes occur in Matucana (C. Backeberg).

Epiphyllanthus Berg. (27)

A group of species differing in habit from all other Brazilian small-stemmed epiphytes: the branches are subspherical to cylindric or dwarf-"opuntioid"; the apical flowers are c. 4 cm long, very zygomorphic, the outer or lower petals are more strongly directed upwards, or extend higher, than in Zygocactus; in the latter, "some of the stamens are united into a short tube around the base of the style" (K. Schumann), but in Epiphyllanthus they are only situated on the margin* (Vaupel, Drawing 24E, "Die Kakteen" 1926). A nectar-protecting annular membrane is present. Opinions differ as to the delimitation of species with regard to E. candidus and E. obovatus; the former is regarded by some authors as an ecotype of the latter from shady localities. However the fruit of E. candidus was described as "spherical", and that of E. obtusangulus as "more or less pear-shaped, obtusely angled, broadly umbilicate". One can thus assume that both are valid species and that the "E. obtusangulus with shorter cylindric

---

* Perhaps a misprint for "wandständig" = situated on the wall. Translator's note.

shoots" shown in "Die Cact." (Fig. 657) is actually E. candidus from a sunnier locality, with correspondingly shorter stems, since its berries are completely spherical. The three species must therefore be segregated here. The seeds, as far as is known, are glossy dark brown.—Distribution: Brazil (along the borders of the states: Rio de Janeiro, Minas Geraes and São Paulo). [(G).]

E. candidus (Löfgr.) Br. & R.
Bo. shrubby, pendant; **St.** ± longer-cylindric, also ± clavate to slightly angular, younger ones somewhat more slender, 0.7–2 cm ∅, 3–5–6 cm lg.; **Sp.** 6–30, sharp, bristly, more numerous on the St. from older and larger Ar.; **Fl.** 3.5 cm lg., white; **Fr.** spherical, smooth, red.—Brazil (Itatiaya Mts.)

E. obovatus (Eng.) Br. & R.
Bo. shrubby, pendant; **St.** segmented or subterete, to 40 cm lg.; **branches** 2–6 cm lg., to 3 cm ∅, terminal Seg., in 2's, 3's or 4's, flat, obovate, dwarf-"opuntioid", dark green; **Ar.** laterally and on the Seg., with white felt; **Sp.** very fine, to 5 mm lg., to 30 on old Seg.; **Fl.** c. 4.5 cm lg., scarlet; **Fr.** top-shaped, to c. 8 mm lg., to 1.2 cm ∅, glossy reddish.—Brazil (various mountains between Rio de Janeiro, Minas Geraes and São Paulo).

E. obtusangulus (Lindb.) Berg. (T.)
Bo. shrubby, epiphytic or semi-epiphytic, between rocks, in part erect; **branches** mostly dividing in 2's or 3's, Seg. ± spherical to somewhat elongated and ± angular, sometimes almost disc-shaped, to 2.5 cm lg. (possibly somewhat more in the case of elongated shoots), to 6 mm ∅; **Ar.** scaly; **Sp.** bristly, scarcely sharp, to 6 mm lg.; **Fl.** 4–4.5 cm lg., ± purplish-pink; **Ov.** top-shaped, 5–6-angled; **Fr.** ± pear-shaped, obtusely angled, 7 mm ∅.—Brazil (Itatiaya Mts.). (Fig. 99.)

Epiphyllopsis Berg. (29)

Plants resembling Zygocactus, but the individual segments are longer, with shallow notches, the small marginal areoles with occasional bristles, and the apical flowering areoles ± bearded to virtually glabrous. The flowers are regular in structure, up to 6 appearing at one time, the tube is short and the filaments are in one group. The ovary is 5-angled, the stigma-lobes spreading, and the fruit a berry with 5 acute angles, c. 1.5 cm long. The seeds taper to both ends, scarcely exceed 1 mm long, and are very glossy, brown and smooth. 1 species only.—Distribution: Brazil (Santa Catharina). [(R).] Very free-flowering, especially if given a suitable cactus-fertiliser and—if at all possible—kept in the open air during the summer. Lindinger (1942) and Reid

Moran (1953) referred the genus to Rhipsalidopsis. At first sight this is quite understandable since Berger (Entwcklgsl., 28–29, 1926) states that seedlings have 6-angled stemlets with white bristles, these becoming 3–4-angled, and only eventually becoming flat. This penomenon is common, however, to many epiphytes of the Hylocereeae. Rhipsalidopsis Br. and R., however, is a dimorphic plant, its var. remanens always appearing many-angled and bristly, while the type-species is only occasionally so. In addition Epiphyllopsis has a minute nectary, with the filaments inserted above it within the interior of the tube; in Rhipsalidopsis, on the other hand, they crowd round the base of style, no nectary is present, and the ovary and the slightly compressed fruit are 4-angled; in Epiphyllopsis the ovary is 5-angled. The separation of the genera attempted by Britton & Rose and Berger has been of greater service in showing the differential diagnostic characters more accurately than could have been achieved by any combination; the former procedure is better adapted to the special conditions of this complex of genera, while within my classification no combination is possible; I regard it moreover as far from essential to change old-established names only in restricted areas. My reasons for this have been stated repeatedly in the present work.

E. gaertneri (Reg.) Berg. (T.)
Bo. branching freely to form hanging bushes, the **St.** later becoming hard; **branches** eventually becoming woody at the base, thick, subterete to ± angular, the Seg. flat, mostly ± reddish at first, with shallow notches along the margins; **Br.** replace Sp., occasionally present along the margins, beard-like at the apex; **Fl.** c. 4 cm lg., scarlet.—Brazil (Santa Catharina). (Fig. 100.)
   v. **serrata** (Lindgr.) Backbg.: shoot-tip somewhat more rounded, ± beardless, the epidermis darker green;
   v. **tiburtii** Backbg. & Voll: somewhat smaller in overall habit, shoot-length and flower-size; **Fl.** crimson to darker; **Ov.** 5-winged.—Brazil (Paraná).

Epiphyllum Haw. (35)

Bushy, vigorous-growing epiphytes with stem-segments which are slender, long and rather thin, hence the names of "leaf-cactus" and "Phyllocactus". However, Haworth's first name is the valid one. Zygocactus, Schlumbergera and Epiphyllanthus were also later known for a time as Epiphyllum. The true Epiphyllum species have nocturnal glabrous flowers, with the tube either very thin and very long, when the perianth is smaller; or ± shorter, with a larger perianth. The fruits can be subspherical, oblong, scaly or even angular. In 2 species the shoots have serrate lobes, the projecting teeth being fairly long. "Epiphyllum grandilobum (Web.) Br. & R." (on which no reliable floral data are available) may in fact be a species of Marniera with a bristly hairy ovary, since the lobes are here extremely long, rather resembling Marniera chrysocardium (Alex.) Backbg. Epiphyllum crenatum (Lindl.) G. Don has often been used for hybridising on account of its large and scented blossoms; it is usually said to be diurnal, but in my view no-one has satisfactorily established whether in fact it has not opened during the first night, like the hybrid Seleniphyllum cooperi Rowl., whose flowers sometimes stay open for 2 days. Spines are virtually always absent although they can be observed on seedlings. The flesh of the red fruit is white or red, the seeds are glossy black.—Distribution: From Mexico to S. America (northern coastal zones; S. Ecuador near the coast, to Peru, Bolivia, Paraguay [Chaco], Brazil); in the W. Indies, only on Trinidad and Tobago. [(R.]

E. anguliger (Lem.) G. Don
Bo. bushy, **St.** terete, branches flattened; **shoots** fairly fleshy, deeply dentate; **Ar.** sometimes with 1–2 Br.; **Fl.** over 8 cm lg., white; **Tu.** with triangular-lanceolate Sc.; **Sep.** yellowish flesh-coloured; **Pet.** c. 5 cm lg.; **Fr.** to 4 cm ∅—Mexico (Nayarit, Jalisco).

E. cartagense (Web.) Br. & R.
Bo. shrubby, to 3 m lg.; **branches** 4–5 cm br., often weakly incised; **Fl.** c. 20 cm lg., little fleshy, white; **Sep.** pink to yellowish; **style** pink to white; **Fr.** 8 cm lg., oblong, red outside, white inside; **Ov.** with very small Sc.—Costa Rica (Cartago).

E. caudatum Br. & R.
Bo. bushy, **St.** terete, thin; **branches** to 4 cm br., long-lanceolate, terete below, to 20 cm lg., margin wavy, terminal shoots tapering above; **Fl.** white; **Tu.** 7 cm lg.; **Pet.** c. 6 cm lg.—Mexico (Oaxaca).

E. caulorhizum (Lem.) G. Don
Bo. bushy; **branches** lanceolate, brownish-green, notched; **Ar.** with a few Br.; **Fl.** to 25 cm lg.; **Tu.** angular, with projecting Sc. thickened below; **Sep.** yellow; **Pet.** white, tips light yellow.—Honduras (?)

E. costaricense (Web.) Br. & R.
Bo. robust, bushy; **branches** to 30 cm lg., to 7 cm br., margins ± straight; **Ov.** not scaly; **Fl.** ?; **Fr.** 9 cm lg., to 7 cm ∅, with a tough red naked skin and weak longitudinal Ri., Sc. absent.—Costa Rica (San José; La Urnia).

E. crenatum (Lindl.) G. Don

Bo. bushy, old **St.** woody, terete; **branches** bluish-green, rather stiff, to 3 cm br., erect at first, with thick Ri., rounded between the areolar notches; **Ar.** with Br. and H.; **Fl.** to 12 cm ∅, cream to greenish-yellowish, strongly perfumed; **Tu.** to 12 cm lg., thin, with linear Sc. to 3 cm lg.; **Ov.** with Sc. to 2 cm lg.; **style** white.—Honduras, Guatemala (Sacobaja).

The Br. occasionally observed on the Ov. must be regarded as a reversion to earlier stages of reduction.

E. crenatum v. **kimnachii** H. Bravo

Bo. bushy; **St.** to 50 cm lg., 7–15 cm br., tapering to ribbed below, rather obtuse above, with ± flat notches, green, sometimes at first ± reddish; **Sp.** to 10, c. 7–12 mm lg., more numerous in the lower part of the shoot; **Fl.** (16–)22–29 cm lg., 14–20 cm external ∅, 10–12 cm inner ∅; **Tu.** curving, to 18 cm lg., Sc. to 1 cm lg., with plentiful yellowish wool and 6(–20) Br., these fairly stiff, 6–12 mm lg.; **Sep.** brownish-yellow; **Pet.** yellowish-cream; **Ov.** ± tuberculate, with ± stiff Br. (acc. illustration); **Fil.** yellowish, greenish below; **Fr.** spherical to oblong, to 7 cm lg., with up to 10 stiff bristly Sp., pulp white; **S.** to 2 mm lg., glossy black.—Mexico (Oaxaca, Chiapas; several localities known).

Quite unrelated to E. crenatum, which occurs further S., and has glabrous Fl. In "Gesamtbeschrbg.", p. 203, K. Schumann said of this complex: "Ov. never with tufts of wool, bristles or spines". If the plant is regarded as a variety of any spec., then it must be Marniera macroptera, so that it must be listed here as **Marniera macroptera** v. **kimnachii** (H. Bravo) Backbg. n.comb. (basionym as above). Since Britton & Rose, differentiation of floral indumentum has not been regarded as having major significance. The important factor is that Marniera now claims 2 species and 1 variety, all having bristly Sp. on Fl., Ov. or Fr. (acc. Backeberg).

E. darrahii (K. Sch.) Br. & R.

Bo. freely branching, **St.** terete, woody; **branches** to 30 cm lg., rather thick, to 5 cm br., serrate-incised, the teeth rounded or pointed; **Fl.** 18 cm lg., white; **Sep.** yellow; **Pet.** somewhat yellowish above; **Tu.** 11 cm lg.; **Ov.** somewhat angular, tuberculate, with subulate Sc. 3 mm lg.; **style** white.—Mexico.

E. gigas Woods. & Schery

Spec. with an enormous **Fl.**—Panama (Cerro Trinidad). See also under the following spec.

E. grandilobum (Web.) Br. & R.

Description acc. Br. & R., amended from that of Weber:

Branches light green, very large, to 25 cm br., the margin deeply lobed, with a thick M.-nerve, the apex obtuse or rounded, the lobe-projections rounded, 3–5 cm lg.; **Fl.** said to be very large, white, nocturnal; **Fr.** red outside. (Weber gives no details as to the size of the lobes, saying merely that they are rounded (cf. Schumann's details in his Key), and that the Fr. is red inside; he questioned whether it was also red outside).

Kimnach (C. & S. J. (US), XXXVII: 1, 15–20. 1965) discusses a plant he held to be E. grandilobum and with which he also assumed E. gigas to be identical. The most significant characters as follows:

Bo. clambering, to over 100 m lg., at first 3–5 cm br., later widening to 15–25 cm, terete below, with a stout M.-Ri.; **branches** ± notched, the intervening margin ± projecting, rounded, often slightly oblique or wavy, 1.5–5 cm lg. and c. (4–)6(–9) cm br. between the Ar., margin brown; **Fl.** tubular-funnelform, 32–38 cm lg., 18 cm br.; **Tu.** 22–27 cm lg.; **Pet.** (inner Per.-segments) creamy-white, with a hair-like tip; **Sep.** (outer Per.-segments) greenish-yellow; **nectary** 13 cm lg., finely papillose in the upper half; **Sc.** few, c. 2 cm lg., projecting (acc. drawing); **Ov.** without Br., with few and shorter Sc.—Costa Rica (several stations) and Panama (Cerro Trinidad). The largest known Epiphyllum and Fl. Material collected by Wercklé was regarded as the lectotype: the margin between the Ar. projected ± strongly or had a large, variously prominent margin. The indentations shown in the drawing vary even more strongly; these are weak at first in the case of Californian cultivated material. In the light of this and the fact that Britton & Rose illustrated a similar plant as E. macropterum (although the Fig. does not represent this spec. since the Ov. lacks Br.), and that the true spec. also originates in Costa Rica, one may well ask if the Paris herbarium-material was not in fact Marniera macroptera, which also has horny and brownish stem-margins. Weber's description is insufficient, lacking details of the floral characters. There appears to have been confusion about the dried material in Weber's time, since K. Schumann's Key gives the following data for Phyllocactus grandilobus: "St. extremely long and broad, divided into long linear (!) lobes". Kimnach had clearly overlooked this information. Schumann cannot have obtained it for himself, but must have received it from Weber. The question is, in my view, insufficiently clarified, and may in fact never be satisfactorily settled. If Weber's description refers to material of M. macroptera, his name becomes a synonym of this species, and the correct name for Kimnach's species would be E. gigas; the data in

Schumann's Key can only refer to the earliest known material of Marniera chrysocardium since at that time no other species was known to which these characters were applicable. Further investigations seem to be necessary.

E. guatemalense Br. & R.
Bo. bushy, rather lg.; **branches** 1 m lg. and more, green, 4–8 cm br., ± terete below, the margin extensively notched, the apex somewhat rounded; **Fl.** c. 28 cm lg., white; **Tu.** c. 15 cm lg., hairy inside; **Pet.** narrow, to 9 cm lg.; **style** orange; **Fr.** wine-red, 8 cm lg., slender, angular.—Guatemala.

E. hookeri (Lk. & O.) Haw.
Bo. forming a fairly large bush, mostly to 3 m lg., sometimes to 7 m; **branches** light green, c. 9 cm br., with ladder-like incisions at the margin, tapering to the base; **Ri.** not very br.; **Fl.** to 20 cm lg., white, unscented; **Tu.** to 13 cm lg.; **Pet.** narrow, 5 cm lg.; **style** carmine; **Fr.** oblong, red, somewhat scaly; **S.** numerous, glossy black.—Northern S. America (Guayana, Venezuela), Trinidad and Tobago. (Fig. 101.)

E. lepidocarpum (Web.) Br. & R.
Bo. shrubby, old **St.** cylindric; **branches** to 3 cm br., not very stiff, in part 3-winged below, the margin with ladder-like notches; **Ar.** with some felt and small Br.; **Fl.** 20 cm lg., white; **Fr.** with conspicuous, ± projecting Sc.; **pulp** white or red.—Costa Rica (near Cartago).

E. macrocarpum (Web.) Backbg.
Bo. forming a large shrub; **Fl.** very large, white; **Fr.** to 15 cm(?) lg., 5 cm ∅, carmine-pink, with numerous low irregular Ri.; **pulp** white.—Costa Rica (Piedras Negras).

E. macropterum (Lem.) Br. & R.: **Marniera macroptera** (Lem.) Backbg.

E. oxypetalum (DC.) Haw.
Bo. freely branching; **branches** fairly long, to 3 m, to 12 cm br., flat and thin, long-tapering, deeply notched, matt green; **Fl.** 25–30 cm lg., to 12 cm ∅; **Sep.** reddish-yellowish, to 10 cm lg.; **Pet.** white, oblong; **perfume** disagreeable.—Mexico to Guatemala, Venezuela to Brazil.
   v. **purpusii** (Wgt.) Backbg.: distinguished by its smooth **epidermis**; **Sep.** purple to carmine; **perfume** agreeable.—Mexico (Orizaba).

E. phyllanthus (L.) Haw. (T.)
Bo. forming long and large shrubs, main **St.** slender, terete, sometimes 3–4-angled; **branches** mostly flat and thin, light green, sometimes bordered purple, to 7 cm br., extensively notched,

teeth rounded; **Fl.** 5–6 cm ∅, to 30 cm lg., white; **Tu.** thin, very long; **Per.** relatively small, ± greenish outside; **Pet.** to 2.5 cm lg., narrow; **style** reddish; **Fr.** oblong, 7–9 cm lg., faintly 8-ribbed, light red.—Panama to Guayana, Peru, Bolivia, Brazil, Paraguay.
   v. **boliviense** (Web.) Backbg.: **Fl.** only 3 cm ∅, laxly rotate, **style** vivid red;
   v. **columbiense** (Web.) Backbg.: **Tu.** only 6 cm lg., **style** red;
   v. **paraguayense** (Web.) Backbg.: **style** pale red to ± white; **Fr.** carmine.
The type of the spec. came from Brazil. I showed Voll's photo of the unusually long flower with its small limb in "Die Cact.", II: Fig. 678. The Fl. of v. columbiense is similar but much shorter. In both, the Tu. has "minute Sc." (Br. & R.). Of Weber's other names, the plant with a Fl. only 3 cm ∅ must undoubtedly be referred to v. boliviense; v. paraguayense is insufficiently clarified. Kimnach gave an excellent paper (C. & S. J. (US), XXXVI: 4, 105–115, 1964) on the above varieties and associated species. From Kimnach's Table I, the plant with a Pet.-length of 1.5–3 cm must be attributed to this spec. since it has the typical small flower with "minute scales". The plants Kimnach includes, although with varietal status—E. guatemalense, hookeri and pittieri, with Pet. to 5–7–11 cm lg.—are better segregated for the sake of clarity, likewise the spec. which Br. & R. separated: E. stenopetalum and strictum (acc. Br. & R.'s Key). All these species come from Central America. They are without any doubt quite closely related, and E. pumilum could also be added. The flower illustrated by Kimnach which he regarded as being that of v. phyllanthus, from a plant collected by Horich in Ecuador, is distinct from that of the type in having more numerous and clearly projecting scales; it appears to be transitional to:
   v. **rubrocoronatum** Kimn. l. c.: **Bo.** with stiff **St.**; **branches** terete to 3-angled below, then flattened and to 9 cm br.; **Fl.** to 29 cm lg., to 11 cm br.; **Fil.** (a principal diagnostic character in additition to that of Fl.-size) yellowish-orange below, purple-reddish above.—Panama, W. Colombia, Ecuador. If the species are separated, this variety must be given specific status.

E. pittieri (Web.) Br. & R.
Bo. freely branching, to 3 m lg., **St.** terete below; **branches** thin, flat, mostly to 5 cm br., margin extensively incised, ± ladder-like; **Fl.** rather small, white to greenish-white, with some red Sc.; **Sep.** yellowish-green; **Pet.** shorter than the Sep.; **style** white above, red below; **Fr.** dark red.—Costa Rica.

E. pumilum Br. & R.
Bo. shrubby, to 5 m lg., main **St.** terete, often

pendant; **branches** to 1.5 m lg., uniformly flat, or only above, terete below, with **terminal shoots** rarely 3-winged, the flat shoots mostly only to 60 cm lg., 8.5 cm br.; **Fl.** small, white; **Tu.** to only 6 cm lg., greenish-white to reddish; **Sep.** similarly coloured; **Pet.** 4 cm lg., lanceolate; **style** to 7 cm lg., thin, white; **Fr.** glossy cherry-red, 5–7-angled, with several small Sc.; **pulp** white; **S.** very small, black.—Guatemala (in the lowlands).

E. ruestii (Wgt.) Backbg.
Bo. erect-shrubby, **St.** round, above that irregularly 1–3-angled; **branches** dark green, rising from the St., lanceolate, notched; **Ar.** with 1 Br.-Sp.; **Fl.** long-funnelform, 25–30 cm lg., white; **Tu.** thin, long, yellow, somewhat angular, with small Sc.; **Sep.** yellow, narrow-lanceolate; **Fil.** yellow; **style** white, with 10 yellow **Sti.**—Honduras.

E. stenopetalum (Först.) Br. & R.
Bo. forming a broad bush; **shoots** light green, large, broad, firm, ± wavy, the margin fairly deeply notched, lobes rounded; **Fl.** c. 25 cm lg., agreeably scented, white; **Tu.** to 15 cm lg., with small spreading pink Sc.; **Sep.** pink to reddish-green; **Pet.** to 8 cm lg., only 4–7 mm br.; **style** pink or purple.—Mexico (Oaxaca).

E. strictum (Lem.) Br. & R.
Bo. laxly shrubby, ± erect, to 3 m h.; **shoots** and **St.-Seg.** subterete below, sometimes also rather higher and then expanding above, or broadly linear, stiff, the stout M.-nerve with visible branching, the margin incised, like well-spaced rungs on a ladder; **Fl.** to 25 cm lg., white; **Tu.** to 15 cm lg., thin, green, with distant Sc.; **Sep.** pink; **Pet.** narrow, to 8 cm lg.; **style** pink or red; **Fr.** spherical, to 5 cm ∅.—S. Mexico to Panama.

E. thomasianum (K. Sch.) Br. & R.
Bo. bushy, ascending, to 3 m h.; **shoots** terete below, widening above, the flattened sections to 40 cm lg., to 8 cm br., vivid green, with small notches, with a M.-nerve; **Ar.** minute; **Fl.** to 30 cm lg., bellshaped to funnelform, pure white, at most with a yellowish tinge; outer **Sep.** red, inner ones yellowish with a reddish M.-stripe; **Pet.** to 2.5 cm br.; **Fil.** yellowish; **style** white, with 14 yellow **Sti.**—Origin ?
Ov. ± cylindric, glabrous, Tu. extensively set with red Sc.; for this reason the identification with E. macropterum (Marniera) which prevailed for some time was erroneous because Marniera has a bristly Ov. This demonstrates the importance of observing the stages of reduction in the indumentum which are often ignored by some authors.

E. sp. 'Chichicastenango': **shoots** also ± subterete at first, then with one side of the shoot often missing, the other fairly broad, with irregular, deep and rounded lobes, often continuing over to the other side; **Fl.** large, creamy-white; **Sep.** yellow; **Tu.** and long Sc. green.
A plant of remarkable habit. It is also regarded as a hybrid of E. crenatum. No further data available.

E. sp. 'Kinchinjunga': **shoots** lacking deeper notches; **Fl.** c. 12 cm lg., 8 cm ∅; **buds** and **Sep.** brownish-red; **Pet.** broad below, long-tapering above, yellowish-cream; **Tu.** green, with reddish Sc. 1.5 cm lg. A plant apparently never described, bearing magnificent Fl. with dark, stellately projecting Sep.

Epithelantha (Web.) Br. & R. (212)

Broadly spherical to spherical or elongated plants, sometimes forming groups of small heads, the taproot sometimes with a neck-like constriction above, their small tubercles giving a resemblance to Mammillaria, and therefore for a long time held to be species of the latter genus. However the flowers do not arise in a coronet from the axils, but from the newest areoles in the crown; but the fruits resemble those of Mammillaria. The spination, according to species or variety, is appressed or somewhat projecting, sometimes with stouter central spines, the apical indumentum varying from weakly to strongly woolly.—Distribution: From the USA (W. Texas) to N. Mexico. [(G): if grown on their own roots, they should (acc. Marshall) be given 20% lime in the compost.]

E. bokei Benson
Bo. simple or with a few offsets, 2.5–5 cm lg. and ∅; **Tub.** 1.5 mm lg. and br.; **Ar.** 1 mm ∅, 2 mm apart; **Sp.** very dense, concealing the Bo., c. 35–38, white; **Fl.** 10–12 mm ∅ and lg.; **Sep.** pink, bordered lighter; **Pet.** to 9 mm lg. and 3 mm br.; **style** with 3 Sti., yellowish; **Fr.** red, with only few S. 0.7 mm lg., black.—Mexico (Chihuahua), USA (Texas, Rio Grande in the Big Bend region and W. Brewster County, on mountain-ridges and rocks at 750–1200 m). Named for Norman H. Boke.

E. densispina H. Bravo: **Epithelantha micromeris** v. **densispina** (H. Bravo) Backbg.

E. micromeris (Eng.) Web. (T.)
Bo. spherical, mostly simple, sometimes offsetting; **R.** more fibrous; **crown** ± depressed, sometimes very woolly; **St.** 1.5–4 cm ∅; **Tub.** very small, 1 mm lg.; **Sp.** numerous, white, to c. 2 mm lg., the upper ones in the newest Ar. to 4 times as long, later

breaking and equal to the others, centrals not clearly distinguishable; **Fl.** whitish to pinkish-red, to 6 mm ∅; **Fr.** an oblong red berry.—USA (W. Texas) to N. Mexico. (Fig. 102).

v. **densispina** (H. Bravo) Backbg.: **Sp.** rather longer, more densely interlacing and spreading, to 1 cm lg. in the crown, yellowish below.—Mexico (Coahuila);

v. **greggii** (Eng.) Borg: robuster; **Tub.** 2 mm lg.; upper **Rsp.** to 8 mm lg.; **Csp.** 5–7, stouter, mostly pointing obliquely downwards, ± equal in length to the Rsp.—Mexico (Coahuila);

v. **rufispina** (H. Bravo) Backbg.: (upper) **Sp.** brownish to reddish-brown.—Mexico (Coahuila);

v. **unguispina** (Böd.) Backbg.: the projecting **Sp.** longer, fairly stout, curving or erect, brownish to blackish.—Mexico (Nuevo León).

E. pachyrhiza (Marsh.) Backbg.
Bo. elongated, cylindric or with a taproot, sometimes with a constriction above, the base of the plant slender, often appearing stalk-like; **Sp.** white, fairly long in the crown and forming an erect cluster.—Mexico (Coahuila).

v. **elongata** Backbg.: **Bo.** cylindric, never constricted above the stouter R., but elongated below.—Mexico (Coahuila).
There are also plants ± forming cushions (? v. neomexicana—only a name) as well as a cylindric form with cranial wool, with many cylindric offsets towards the base, sometimes ± yellowish.

E. polycephala Backbg.
Bo. branching to form several heads; **St.** small, lax, subspherical; **Sp.** spreading, ± projecting and interlacing, mostly greyish-white, usually brownish to rust-coloured near the apex.—Mexico (Coahuila, Ramos Arispe).

E. rufispina H. Bravo: **Epithelantha micromeris** v. **rufispina** (H. Bravo) Backbg.

E. spinosior Schmoll: **Epithelantha micromeris** v. **unguispina** (Böd.) Backbg.

× Epixochia Rowl.: a hybrid genus: Epiphyllum × Nopalxochia.

Erdisia Br. & R. (54)

Cerei with slender stems, erect or ± prostrate, the spination fairly long, sometimes denser and finer or even quite robust. The tallest species grows only c. 2 m tall. Two of the southerly Pacific species show a remarkable form of reproduction, by ascending, ± clavate to cylindric shoots arising from a branching underground rhizome. The flower is always funnelform. The ovary, and the relatively short tube, which continues above it without any visible constriction, are set with dense and fairly long spines; the fairly large, ± green, rather thin-skinned fruit is similarly spiny. In some species there is a tendency—as in Wilcoxia albiflora—to form the flower from the apex without any differentiation, but this is not constant throughout those species.—Distribution: Southern Peru to Chile. [(R).]

E. apiciflora (Vpl.) Werd.
Bo. prostrate or ascending; **St.** to 50 cm lg., to 2.5 cm ∅; **Ri.** low and narrow, c. 8; **Rsp.** c. 10, to 1 cm lg., thin; **Csp.** 1, acicular, to 2 cm lg.; **Sp.** all fairly light-coloured; **Fl.** 4 cm lg., scarlet, sometimes from the St.-tip.—Peru (Prov. Huari).

E. aureispina Backbg. & Jacobs.
Bo. slender-columnar, semi-prostrate, to 1(–2) m lg., to 3 cm ∅; **Ri.** 6–9, narrow, low; **Ar.** dark; **Rsp.** (lower Sp.) 6–10, thin, some directed upwards, some downwards, the lowest ones very fine, to 1 cm lg.; **Csp.** (upper Sp.) 8(–10), spreading in all directions, c. 6 more stellately or sometimes almost vertically upwards, blackish-brown below, golden-yellow at the tip; **Fl.** 2.5–4 cm lg., to 5 cm ∅, light red; **Fr.** to 2 cm ∅.—Peru (Ollantaitambo).

E. erecta Backbg.
Bo. slender-columnar, erect, to 1 m h.; **St.** ascending from below, little branching, to c. 3 cm ∅; **Ri.** 5–6, narrow, not prominent; **Sp.** c. 10(–18), unequal, spreading in all directions, light with a dark base, some short, sometimes 1–2 projecting and directed upwards and downwards, thickened below; **Fl.** scarlet-carmine or flame; **Fr.** c. 2 cm ∅.—S. Peru (Urcos).

E. fortalezensis Ritt.—"Taxon", XIII: 3, 116. 1964.
Bo. semi-prostrate, little branching, to 1 m lg., green; **St.** 2.5–4 cm ∅; **Ri.** 10, to 7 mm h., notched; **Ar.** 6–10 mm apart, black; lower **Sp.** black, upper ones white; **Rsp.** 10–15, 4–15 mm lg., very thin, appressed; **Csp.** 6–10, 7–30 mm lg., thin; **Fl.** borne on the flanks, 3.5 cm lg., brownish-yellow; **Tu.** spiny; **Ov.** with black Ar. and brown Sp.; **Pet.** rather obtuse above, spatulate; **Fil.** yellow, in 2 series; **style** and 15 **Sti.** white; **Fr.** 2.5 cm lg., spherical, green, spiny; **S.** 2 mm lg., with a white hilum.—Peru (Dept. Ancash, Valle Fortaleza, c. 3500 m) (FR 1058).

I E. gracilis (FR 1299): description not available.

E. maxima Backbg.
Bo. shrubby, erect to inclined, forming larger

colonies; **St.** to 2 m lg., fresh green; **Ri.** c. 6, rounded, rather low; **Ar.** white at first, then brownish; **Rsp.** c. 10, to 2 cm lg., unequal; **Csp.** 1, to 3 cm lg., variously directed, sometimes also 2 longer ones; **Sp.** hyaline at first, becoming yellowish, sharp; **Fl.** to 5 cm lg. and br., orange-red.—Peru (Mariscal Caceres and its vicinity).

|E. melaleuca (FR 687): description not available.

E. meyenii Br. & R.
Bo. erect, ± clavate, arising from a branching rhizome, also cylindric; **St.** mostly ± strongly tapering below, to 20 cm lg. (to 50 cm sometimes in cultivation), 3–5 cm $\emptyset$; **Ri.** 5–8, 1 cm h. and more; **Rsp.** 9 11, unequal, usually one which is longer; **Csp.** 1(–2), longest, to 6 cm lg.; all **Sp.** brownish to blackish, or lighter with a dark tip, sometimes thickened below; **Fl.** c. 4 cm lg., orange-yellow to orange-red; **Fr.** c. 2 cm $\emptyset$, reddish(-green?).—S. Peru (Arequipa) to N. Chile (Tacna).

E. philippii (Reg. & Schm.) Br. & R.
Bo. erect, thin-columnar, bluish-green; **St.** c. 3 cm $\emptyset$; **Ri.** 8–10, obtuse, with ellipsoidal Tub.; **Rsp.** 8, to 12 mm lg.; **Csp.** 4–5, the upper one longest, to 2.5 cm lg., colour ?; **Fl.** c. 4 cm lg., bellshaped to funnelform, yellowish below, reddish above; **style** purple.—Chile.
Ritter considered the spec. belonged to Austrocactus and referred it there; however it has never been re-collected. Regel stated: "branching above", and the body has not been described as soft. In the absence of living material, any such referral appears hasty, to say the least. The description could equally apply to Erdisia.

E. quadrangularis Rauh & Backbg.
Bo. shrubby, squarrosely branching, in part pendant, to 1.5 m h.; **branches** 4(–5)-angled; **Rsp.** 4–8, pale yellow, 1–2 cm lg.; **Csp.** to 5 cm lg., porrect, sometimes an additional lower, more radial Sp. which is sometimes longer; **Sp.** very stiff, pale yellow, the longest ones being very robust; **Fl.** brilliant crimson; **Fr.** 3 cm $\emptyset$, reddish-green.—Peru (Puquio valley). (Fig. 103.)

|E. quivillana (FR 688): no description available.

E. ruthae Johns.: not validly described; **Ri.** only c. 5, narrow, relatively prominent, with long notches to appear ladder-like; **Rsp.** to c. 7; **Csp.** 1–2, scarcely differentiated, thickened and dark below; **Sp.** light to dark, 1–2 sometimes much thinner than the others, one longest porrect Sp. is usually stoutest.—Peru.

E. spiniflora (Phil.) Br. & R.

Bo. clavate, arising from a branching rhizome; **St.** to 20 cm lg., bluish-green, to 4.5 cm $\emptyset$; **Ri.** 8, 5–10 mm h., obtuse, shallowly indented; **Rsp.** mostly 2–5, subulate, straight, spreading; **Csp.** 1, to 2.5 cm lg., blackish below, brown above; **Fl.** 4 cm $\emptyset$, pale purplish-red, yellowish below; **Fr.** ellipsoidal to clavate, to 5 cm lg., 2.5–3 cm $\emptyset$, yellowish.—Chile (Aranas).
Ritter held the spec. to be an Austrocactus and referred it thereto. However the original illustration shows the same habit as E. meyenii, with an underground rhizome and the fruit and the branching habit are much closer to Erdisia. Ritter provides no further details to support the suggested "similarity of the flower to Austrocactus"; in any event this should not, by itself, be decisive (see also Austrocactus).

E. squarrosa (Vpl.) Br. & R. (T.)
Bo. with a stout taproot, squarrosely branching, prostrate to ascending; **St.** to 25 cm lg., 2–2.5 cm $\emptyset$, green, often reddish; **Ri.** 7–8, 8 mm h., obtuse, notched; **Rsp.** 9(–10) (or if 11, the 2 shortest ones point downwards), to c. 12 mm lg.; **Csp.** mostly 1 more conspicuous and projecting, c. 3 cm lg., together with 1 shorter Sp., but sometimes 4, cruciform, the stouter ones thickened and dark below; all **Sp.** yellowish-horn-coloured, then paler, yellow-tipped, or the centrals dark-tipped; **Fl.** to 4.5 cm lg., yellowish to reddish; **Fr.** 2.5 cm lg., 1.7 cm $\emptyset$; **S.** (as in all spec.) numerous, black.—Central Peru (Tarma).

E. tarijensis (Card.) Ritt.: **Corryocactus tarijensis** Card.

E. tenuicula Backbg.
Bo. squarrose, ± prostrate to ascending, with a stout woody **R.**; **St.** 1.5–3 cm $\emptyset$; **Ri.** 8(–10), slender, low; **Rsp.** or scarcely distinguishable Csp. all ± hyaline, to 5 mm lg., thin; **Csp.** 1 ± distinguishable, only slightly longer and stouter; **Fl.** c. 2.6 cm lg., 3.6 cm $\emptyset$; **Tu.** short; **Pet.** orange-red, fairly br.—Peru (Tarma).

Eriocactus Backbg. (110)

Very uniform and clearly characterised species, becoming columnar when older, the crown ± oblique and woolly, the flowers relatively large, broadly funnelform, with a short tube covered with brown wool. The fruits are spherical berries dehiscing basally, containing numerous loose seeds, these rather small and brown. The hilum is never red; this feature, together with the relatively great body-size when older, the fruits and seeds, and the strong apical wool differentiate the genus from Notocactus.—Distribution: Paraguay, S. Brazil. [(R).] Eriocephalus Backbg. was an earlier name for it as a SG.; but the term Eriocephala (Backbg.) Backbg. was abandoned on account of the similarity between it and Eriocephalus L. (Compositae).

E. grossei (K. Sch.) Backbg.: **Eriocactus schumannianus** (Nic.) Backbg. Only a form of the type of the G., together with its earlier varietal name under Echinocactus: v. longispinus Hge. Jr. and—under Notocactus—v. nigrispinus (Hge. Jr.) Berg.

E. leninghausii (Hge Jr.) Backbg.
Bo. broadly spherical to spherical at first, becoming columnar, to c. 1 m h., to c. 10 cm $\emptyset$, offsetting freely from the base and somewhat higher up, to form groups, sometimes curving at the base; **crown** oblique in older plants; **Ri.** to over 30, low; **Ar.** white at first; **Rsp.** to 15, thin, bristly, whitish-yellow; **Csp.** 3–4, eventually to 4 cm lg., $\pm$ golden-yellow, bristly, $\pm$ curving; **Fl.** 4 cm lg., 5 cm $\emptyset$; **Sep.** greenish; **Pet.** yellow.—S. Brazil. (Fig. 104.)
    f. **apelii** W. Heinr.: an interesting juvenile form; low-growing, offsetting freely;
    v. longispinus Ritt.: only a name.

E. magnificus Ritt. 1964
Bo. spherical, later elongated, sometimes offsetting, mature plants with a blue-frosted epidermis; apex oblique towards the light, $\pm$ sunken, later entirely covered with white felt; **Ri.** 11–15, narrow, with thickened white-felty Ar.; **Ar.** 1–3 mm apart, 3–5 mm lg. on flowering plants and connected by felt; **Sp.** 12–15, hair-like, yellow, 5–6 mm lg.; **Csp.** 8–12, weak, acicular, brown; **H.** numerous, white, c. 8 mm lg.; **Fl.** apical, diurnal, 4–5.5 cm lg., funnelform, sulphur-yellow, rounded-spatulate; **Tu.** densely set with fleshy triangular little Sc. tipped with a white to brown Br.-Sp. c. 10 mm lg.; **Fil.** and **Sti.** light yellow; **Fr.** spherical, c. 1 cm thick; **S.** c. 1 mm lg., reddish-brown, glossy.— Brazil (Rio Grande do Sul, Serra Geral, Julio de Castilho, 2200 m). This spec. was discovered by Leopold Horst, who sent the first specimens of this magnificent plant to Kakteen-Haage, in 1962, with the brief note: " Bo. blue, with yellow Sp." He re-collected it in 1964, with F. Ritter. This is one of the finest discoveries of recent decades.

E. schumannianus (Nic.) Backbg. (T.)
Bo. broadly spherical at first, later $\pm$ clavate-columnar, to over 1 m h.; **crown** becoming $\pm$ oblique; **Ri.** more numerous with age, to over 30, narrow, acute; **Ar.** soon glabrous; **Sp.** 4–7(–10), centrals not clearly differentiated, straight or contorted, somewhat thickened or darker below, otherwise later yellowish to brownish or darker,

also banded; **Fl.** c. 3.5 cm lg., 4 cm $\emptyset$, expanding fully; **Fr.** firm, at first appearing fleshy; **S.** small, brown, under 1 mm lg.—Paraguay (Paraguari).

Eriocephala (Backbg.) Backbg. and Eriocephalus Backbg.: see **Eriocactus** Backbg.

Eriocereus (Berg.) Ricc. (140)

Prostrate, leaning or climbing Cerei, sometimes shrubby and arching, the shoots $\pm$ terete or $\pm$ angular, with several ribs. The flowers are nocturnal, fairly large, funnelform, the tube $\pm$ stout, the petals white to pink; the tube and ovary are $\pm$ hairy, the dehiscent red fruit similarly, although the spines, in all species except two, are completely reduced. The plants resemble Harrisia, which grows much further north and has indehiscent fruits.—Distribution: Brazil, Paraguay, Uruguay, E. Argentina to Buenos Aires State. [(R).]

E. adscendens (Gürke) Berg.
Bo. shrubby, arching; **shoots** to 5 cm $\emptyset$; **Ri.** 7–10, rounded, broken up into oblong Tub.; **Ar.** with small Sc.; **Sp.** 10, robust, the outer ones appressed, 2–3 cm lg., thickened below, yellow or brown, darker-tipped; **Fl.** 25 cm lg., white, with brownish-yellow H.; **Fr.** $\pm$ ovoid, to fist-sized, light red, tuberculate, brown-felty.—Brazil (Bahia; Pernambuco).

E. bonplandii (Parm.) Ricc.
Bo. prostrate to clambering, to 3 m lg. and more; **shoots** 3–8 cm $\emptyset$, bluish-green, becoming greyish-green; **Ri.** 4–6, sometimes 4-angled, furrows flat; **Sp.** 6–8(–10), red at first, then grey; **Fl.** to 25 cm lg., white; **Tu.** scaly, Sc. often recurved; **Pet.** to 12 cm lg.; **Fr.** 4–6 cm $\emptyset$, tuberculate, with longer Sc. and hairy felt, carmine; **S.** to 3 mm lg., glossy black.— Brazil to Argentina. (Fig. 105.)

E. crucicentrus Ritt.: an undescribed name; Csp. cruciform.

E. guelichii (Speg.) Berg.
Bo. clambering; **shoots** to 5 cm $\emptyset$, 3–4-angled, the sides flat, the angles acute and $\pm$ sinuate; **Ar.** white at first, then grey; **Rsp.** 4–5, eventually falling, 4–5 mm lg., the upper ones longest; **Csp.** 1, robust, to 2.5 cm lg.; **Fl.** 20–25 cm lg., white, green outside, with large Sc., almost without wool; **Fr.** red, with long narrow Sc.—Argentina (Chaco).

E. jusbertii (Reb.) Ricc.
Bo. dark green, little branching; **shoots** 4–6 cm $\emptyset$; **Ri.** 5(–6), furrows flat; **Ar.** yellow at first, then grey; **Rsp.** 7, conical, 4 mm lg., the upper ones longer;

Csp. 1, stouter, red, becoming brown to blackish, also to 4 and then cruciform; **Fl.** 18 cm lg., brownish-green outside, white inside; **Fr.** flattened-spherical, red, to 6 cm ⌀.—Regarded as a hybrid; a good stock for grafting plants of smaller ⌀.

E. martinii (Lab.) Ricc.
Bo. leaning, to over 2 m lg.; **shoots** 2–2.5 cm ⌀, green to greyish-green; **Ri.** 4–5, broad, often indistinctly tuberculate; **Rsp.** mostly 5–7, short; **Csp.** 1, light brown, darker above and below, 2–3 cm lg.; **Fl.** 20 cm lg., white, light green outside; **Fr.** red, with prominent spiny Tub.—Argentina (Chaco).

E. platygonus (O.) Ricc.
Bo. branching, leaning; **shoots** slender, 2 cm ⌀; **Ri.** 6–8, flat, rounded, furrows shallow; **Ar.** raised, small; **Sp.** 12–15, yellowish-brown at first, then grey, spreading, bristly and thin, to 12 mm lg.; **Csp.** 1, somewhat stouter; **Fl.** 12 cm lg., white, light green outside; **Sep.** brownish above.—S. America.

E. pomanensis (Web.) Berg.
Bo. fairly erect, bluish or greyish-green; **Ri.** 4–6, obtuse, not sinuate; **Rsp.** 6–7, radiating, 1 cm lg.; **Csp.** 1, 1–2 cm lg., subulate, red or white at first, then grey and black-tipped; **Fl.** 15 cm lg., white; **Tu.** with ovate Sc.; **Fr.** evenly spherical, weakly tuberculate, scaly, spineless.—N.W. Argentina.
v. **uruguayensis** (v. Ost.) Backbg.: differentiated by the more numerous Ri. (6–8) with more distinct Tub.; **Fl.** to 20 cm lg.—Uruguay.

E. regelii (Wgt.) Backbg.
Bo. shrubby; **shoots** 1.2–2 cm ⌀; **Ri.** 4–5(–7), low, obtuse; **Rsp.** c. 5, to 3 mm lg., white with brown tips, sharp, at first directed upwards, but later downwards; **Csp.** 1(–2), to 1.5 cm lg., stiff; **Fl.** 22 cm lg., purple outside; **Pet.** white, pink-tipped, greenish below.—Origin ?

E. tarijensis Ritt.: an undescribed spec. from Tarija, Bolivia. (FR 850, 619.)

E. tephracanthus boliviensis (Web.) Marsh.:
Roseocereus tephracanthus (Lab.) Backbg.

E. tortuosus (Forb.) Ricc. (T.)
Bo. arching over and down, branching; **shoots** to 1 m lg., 2–4 cm ⌀, dark green; **Ri.** (5–)7, rounded, slightly indented, furrows sinuate, acute; **Sp.** 6–10, spreading, to 2 cm lg.; **Csp.** 1–3 distinguishable, stouter, 3–4 cm lg., reddish-brown at first; **Fl.** 16 cm lg., white; **Tu.** with short Sp. and white wool; **Ov.** with similar indumentum, tuberculate, with reddish triangular Sc.; **Sep.** brownish-green; **Fr.** spherical, tuberculate, spiny.—Argentina (Prov.

Buenos Aires). Has recently become a serious nuisance in Australia.

Eriosyce Phil. (126)

Genus of large spherical Cacti from Chile, very variable in habit. The distribution extends from only 200 m above sea-level up to over 2000 m; this is reflected in the differences of growth-forms, although these can still vary within quite a narrow area, in features such as spine-colour. While the spination is relatively uniform in number and arrangement in immature plants, older specimens vary more strongly in habit (spherical or elongated), in spine-colour (from blackish through yellow to grey) and in the apical indumentum (only spiny and with the areoles moderately woolly, to a ± wide and densely woolly zone); the flower-colour, where known, is also variable—from pink to dull red. A comparison of the fruits reveals similar differences: from spherical to elongated, the bristles above ranging from fine and short to almost as long as the fruit itself, and from quite thin to somewhat stouter. Small differences are even observable in seed-shape: in v. jorgensis, for instance, the prominence above the hilum scarcely curves inwards on its lower edge, while in v. zorillaensis the seed is more cap-shaped. A constant character is the noticeably longer and dense indumentum of the bellshaped to tubular flowers, which is overtopped by stiffer bristles of variable length (similar to that of the bristles on the fruits). The petals are fairly strongly erect, the style and anthers are at approximately the same level above, and the stigma-lobes are yellowish as far as is known. The petals extend very slightly beyond these other parts. In one and the same variety, the number and length of the bristles on the fruit can vary. Taken all round, and within the limits of present knowledge of the characters, there is no justification for any segregation into different species, and for the present I regard the forms deviating from the originally described type-species as being no more than varieties, even although Ritter gives several specific names (still undescribed). The characters listed below must be understood to refer to younger plants; more information as well as some colour-photographs will be found in my Handbook, "Die Cactaceae", Vols. III and VI. As regards Ritter's nomina nuda, it is not even possible to say with any certainty which of his plants are referable to the varieties I describe. Further study of this genus of large spherical Cacti (which can sometimes reach 1 m in height and ½ m in diameter) will be required in order to clarify the differential characters of all the members of the genus. In addition to v. ceratistes, 6 varieties have been described, and probably at least a further 2 should be added: E. lapampaensis Ritt. n.nud., and an as yet unnamed plant which is broadly spherical, with dense, long, grey spines (Fig. 3455, "Die Cact.", VI).—Distribution: Chile, from the S. Province of Atacama, to the Santiago area. [(R), (G): the plants grow vigorously but grafting speeds growth; however stouter stocks will later be required when re-grafting.]

E. aurata (Pfeiff.) Backbg.: since there are several forms with yellowish Sp., it is impossible to determine from Pfeiffer's description to which variety his name should be ascribed.

E. ausseliana Ritt.: a name without description for a plant with somewhat finer brown spines.

E. ceratistes (O.) Br. & R. (T.) v. **ceratistes**
Bo. spherical, to 50 cm $\varnothing$; **Ri.** over 20–30 (when old); **crown** soon becoming woolly; **Sp.** more numerous on older plants, c. 8 at first and 1 **Csp.**, later to c. 20, fairly straight to $\pm$ curving, to over 3 cm lg., subulate, thick, black, sometimes lighter on new growth; **Fl.** to c. 3.5 cm lg., red; **Pet.** c. 1.5 cm lg.; **Fr.** to 4 cm lg.; **S.** black, ovoid, c. 3 mm lg.—Chile (above Santiago de Chile). (Fig. 106.) The following varieties are differentiated from v. ceratistes with its $\pm$ blackish Sp.:

v. **combarbalensis** Backbg.: **Bo.** spherical to barrel-shaped; **Sp.** dirty yellowish-grey, none of them straightly erect, to c. 3.6 cm lg.; **Fr.** with Br. c. 11 mm lg., brownish-grey.—Chile (Manquehua, near Combarbalá);

v. **coquimbensis** Backbg.: **Bo.** spherical; **crown** not woolly when flowering stage is reached; **Sp.** deep brown; **Fl.** pink; **Fr.** with Br. c. 13 mm lg., rust-brown.—Chile (Prov. Coquimbo, Frai Jorge);

v. **jorgensis** Backbg.: **Bo.** compressed-spherical; **Sp.** dirty to yellowish-grey, 1 Sp. longer, straight, porrect, compressed, to 4.5 cm lg.; **Fr.** with dirty-grey Br. 13–15 mm lg.—Chile (Frai Jorge);

v. **mollesensis** Backbg.: **Bo.** spherical; **Sp.** yellowish to amber-coloured, more brownish in the crown, to 5.5 cm lg., almost all of them slightly curving, none longer and projecting; **Fr.** with thin, dark brown Br. c. 7 mm lg.—Chile (Prov. Coquimbo, Rio Molles);

v. tranquillaensis (Ritt.): not described; **Sp.** brownish (Ritter gave his name specific rank);

v. **vallenarensis** Backbg.: **Bo.** $\pm$ barrel-shaped; **Sp.** fairly light-coloured, longer, very erect and interlacing; **Fl.** dull red.—Chile (Prov. Atacama, Vallenar);

v. **zorillaensis** Backbg.: **Bo.** depressed-spherical; **Sp.** pale brown; **crown** with much white wool; **Fr.** with Br. 17 mm lg.; **Fl.** intense red.—Chile (Dept. Ovalle, Zorilla).

E. ihotzkyanae Ritt.: not described; Sp. darker brown, much bent.

E. lapampaensis Ritt.: not described; **Sp.** longer, $\pm$ curving, laterally strongly interlacing, light brownish at first, soon becoming whitish and brown-tipped, one Sp. longer, projecting.

E. sandillon Remy: a synonym for the type-species of the G.; the specific name is the one given to the plant by the natives.

Erythrorhipsalis Berg. (25)

Pendant epiphytes, later branching, with numerous cylindric stems covered with appressed bristles; flowers apical, small, similarly bristly, followed by small-spherical, red, bristly fruits.—Distribution: Brazil. (Must be allowed to hang down when cultivated.)

E. pilocarpa (Löfgr.) Berg. (T.)
Bo. forming large hanging bushes, branching verticillately; **St.** 3–6, weakly ribbed, to 12 cm lg., to 6 mm $\varnothing$, dirty greyish-green; **Ri.** 8–10, indistinct; **Ar.** with 3–10 Br. instead of Sp.; **Fl.** solitary or paired, scented, to 2.5 cm br., pale yellow, also with a slight greenish tinge; **Fr.** 12 mm lg. and $\varnothing$, with yellowish Br.; **S.** fairly large, black.—Brazil (São Paulo; Rio de Janeiro). (Fig. 107.)

Escobaria Br. & R. (217)

Small or very small, $\pm$ spherical to cylindric plants becoming more strongly elongated in age, usually quite freely offsetting, sometimes forming larger groups. The small apical flowers are white to purple, also pink to greenish-white, in one instance yellowish. The berries resemble those of Mammillaria and are red, the seeds are black. The genus is distinguished from Coryphantha by the fruit-colour and the hard seeds, but the latter genus and Escobaria have in common the furrowed tubercle which is also found in the relatively large-flowering Genus Neobesseya; the latter also has red fruits but the seeds have a larger aril and the flowers are subapical, whereas in Escobaria they arise in the crown. The fruits of both genera have a watery sap, but those of Neolloydia, which also mostly have cylindric bodies with furrowed tubercles and apical flowers, are not watery and are dull in colour and desiccate.—Distribution: USA (W. Texas; S. New Mexico), Mexico (Chihuahua to Tamaulipas and Zacatecas). [(R), (G).]
Some species have been attributed to Coryph-

antha, others to Neobesseya and Neolloydia, two to Escobesseya Hest., and one even to Thelocactus.

E. albicolumnaria Hest.: **Escobaria tuberculosa** (Eng.) Br. & R.

E. arizonica (Eng.) F. Buxb.: **Coryphantha vivipara** v. **arizonica** (Eng.) Marsh.

E. bella Br. & R.
Bo. small-cylindric, offsetting; **St.** 6–8 cm lg.; **Tub.** rounded, with a white furrow set with a narrow brownish Gl. (peculiar to this spec.?); **Rsp.** several, whitish, to 1 cm lg.; **Csp.** 3–5, brown, to over 2 cm lg., ascending, brown; **Fl.** almost 2 cm ∅, pink; **Sep.** ciliate; **Pet.** with a pale border.—USA (Texas, Devil's River).

E. bisbeeana (Orc.) Marsh.: spec. from Bisbee (USA: Arizona); not validly described.

E. boregui Schmoll: only a catalogue-name. Said to be: "small, only 2.5 cm ∅, ± columnar; **Tub.** small, round; **Rsp.** 23; **Csp.** 4; all **Sp.** white, Csp. thickened below".

E. chaffeyi Br. & R.
Bo. columnar, to 12 cm lg.; **St.** 5–6 cm ∅, almost completely concealed by the Sp.; **Tub.** very short, light green, furrow narrow; **Rsp.** bristly; white; **Csp.** 1(?) to several, shorter than the Rsp., tipped brown or black; **Fl.** 1.5 cm lg., creamy-pink with a brownish M.-stripe; **Fr.** carmine, c. 2 cm lg.—Mexico (Zacatecas, Cedros).

E. chihuahuensis Br. & R.
Bo. solitary to forming groups; **St.** spherical to short-cylindric, to 12 cm lg., to 6 cm ∅, densely spiny; **Tub.** short, concealed by the Sp.; **Rsp.** numerous, spreading; **Csp.** several; all **Sp.** brownish, centrals sometimes black; **Fl.** to 1.5 cm lg., purple; **Sep.** ciliate.—Mexico (near Chihuahua).

E. chlorantha (Eng.) F. Buxb.: **Coryphantha chlorantha** Eng.

E. dasyacantha (Eng.) Br. & R.
Bo. spherical to oblong, to 20 cm lg.; **St.** to 7 cm ∅; **Rsp.** to over 20, white, bristly; **Csp.** c. 9, stouter, rather longer, reddish or brownish above, often to 2 cm lg.; **Fl.** pink; **Sep.** ciliate; **Fr.** clavate, scarlet, to 2 cm lg.; **S.** 1 mm lg., black.—USA (W. Texas; S. New Mexico); Mexico (Chihuahua).

E. deserti (Eng.) F. Buxb.: **Coryphantha chlorantha** v. **deserti** (Eng.) Backbg.

E. duncanii (Hest.) Backbg.

Bo. 6 cm lg., with a tapering taproot, also offsetting; **St.** to 3.4 cm ∅; **Tub.** small, short; **Rsp.** 24–36, ± appressed, radiating, white, to 1.2 cm lg.; **Csp.** mostly 3–8(–16), to 1.2 cm lg., colour as for the Rsp.; **Fl.** pink, 1.5 cm lg. and ∅; **Sep.** ciliate; **Fr.** scarlet, 2 cm lg.; **S.** matt black.—USA (Texas, near Hot Springs).

E. emskoetteriana (Quehl) Backbg.
Bo. forming mats; **St.** to 5 cm h., to 4 cm ∅, dark green; **Tub.** conical, 1 cm lg.; **Rsp.** over 20, stoutly acicular, brown-tipped, to 2 cm lg.; **Csp.** 6–8, to 2 cm lg., some of them thickened below, white, reddish-brown above; **Fl.** 3 cm lg., dirty white, greenish-red at the centre; **Sep.** ciliate; **Pet.** to over 2 cm lg.—Mexico (San Luis Potosí?).

E. fobei Frič: **Escobaria lloydii** Br. & R. ?

E. hesteri (Wright) F. Buxb.
Bo. small, forming groups; **St.** to 2.5–4 cm h., colonies to 30 cm ∅; **crown** covered by Sp.; **Tub.** conical, to 12 mm lg.; **Rsp.** 14–16, not always in one plane, also several finer ones (mostly above) to 15 mm lg., hyaline; **Csp.** 0; **Fl.** light purple, 2.3 cm lg., 2.5 cm ∅; **Sep.** ciliate; **Pet.** 1 cm lg.—USA (Texas, Mt. Ord). (Fig. 108.)

E. leei Böd.
Bo. offsetting; **St.** 1.5 cm h., 5 mm ∅; **Sp.** numerous, white, to 3 mm lg. (Description inadequate).—USA (New Mexico).

E. lloydii Br. & R.
Bo. forming groups; **Rsp.** c. 20, later dropping, spreading, thin, white; **Csp.** several, robust, tipped brownish or blackish, 2 cm lg.; **Fl.** greenish, 2.5 cm lg., with a brownish dorsal stripe; **Fr.** spherical to oblong, 6–12 mm lg., red; **S.** black, 1 mm lg.—Mexico (Zacatecas, Sierra Zuluaga).

E. muehlbaueriana (Böd.) Knuth
Bo. offsetting; **St.** ovoid-cylindric, to 5 cm h., 3 cm ∅, glossy dark leaf-green; **Tub.** ± conical, 8 mm lg.; **Rsp.** 15–20, upper ones very fine, others thin, stiffly acicular, whitish, brown-tipped, c. 8 mm lg.; **Csp.** mostly 6, directed upwards or projecting, 1.5 cm lg.; **Fl.** 1.5 cm lg., 2.5 cm ∅, greenish-yellow with a reddish-brown dorsal stripe (Sep.); **Fr.** 5 mm ∅, red; **S.** glossy, dark reddish-brown.—Mexico (Tamaulipas).

E. nellieae (Croiz.) Backbg.
Bo. quite freely offsetting; **St.** to 4.5 cm lg., oblong; **Ri.** 8–14, tuberculate; **Tub.** only 2 mm lg.; **Rsp.** c. 18, thin-subulate, radiating, the longer ones above sometimes 1 cm lg., erect, flanked by fine Ssp.; **Csp.** 0; all **Sp.** honey-yellow or somewhat darker, also

white or reddish above; **Fl.** to only 1.5 cm $\emptyset$, purple.—USA (Texas, S. of Marathon). (Fig. 109.)

E. neomexicana (Eng.) F. Buxb.: **Coryphantha vivipara** v. **neomexicana** (Eng.) Backbg.

E. oklahomensis (Lahm.) F. Buxb.: an intermediate between **Coryphantha vivipara** and v. **radiosa** (Eng.) Backbg.

E. orcuttii Böd.
Bo. ovoid, to 6 cm h.; **Rsp.** thin, numerous, white, to 8 mm lg.; **Csp.** to 15, 1–2 in the middle, these stouter and somewhat longer, slightly darker-tipped; **Fl.** pink, 1.5 cm $\emptyset$.—USA (?, Texas ?).

E. peloncillensis Kuenzl. n.prov.: **Escobaria tuberculosa** v. **caespititia** (Quehl) Borg.

E. radiosa (Eng.) Frank: **Coryphantha vivipara** v. **radiosa** (Eng.) Backbg.

E. rigida Backbg.
Bo. solitary or offsetting, spherical to cylindric, bluish-green; **Tub.** slender; **Rsp.** fairly numerous, densely interlacing laterally, more erect in the crown and concealing this; **Csp.** several, rather stouter, $\pm$ projecting to $\pm$ porrect, to 1.5 cm lg.; **Sp.** all white at first, then more greyish-white; **Fl.** 1.5 cm lg., violet; **Fr.** oblong, red.—Mexico (?).

E. roseana (Böd.) Backbg.
Bo. later offsetting; **St.** ovoid, to 4 cm h., to over 3 cm $\emptyset$, matt yellowish or leaf-green; **Tub.** 8 mm h. and br.; **Ar.** yellow; **Rsp.** c. 15, smooth, thinly acicular, interlacing, the lower ones to 10 mm lg., the uppers to 15 mm lg.; **Csp.** 4–6, spreading slightly upwards; all **Sp.** sulphur-yellow, lighter at first; **Fl.** reddish-white, small; **Fr.** 15 mm lg., green; **S.** dark brown, 1 mm lg.—Mexico (Coahuila, Saltillo).

E. runyonii Br. & R.
Bo. freely offsetting to form colonies of over 100 heads; **St.** spherical to shortly oblong, greyish-green, 3–5 cm lg.; **Tub.** 5 mm lg.; **Rsp.** numerous, white, acicular, 4–5 mm lg.; **Csp.** stouter, 5–7, slightly spreading, tipped brown or black, 6–8 mm lg.; **Fl.** 1.5 cm lg., pale purple, darker in the centre, margins paler; **Fr.** scarlet, to 9 mm lg.—USA (Texas, Brownsville), N. Mexico (N. Tamaulipas).

E, sneedii Br. & R.
Bo. offsetting to form colonies of up to 50 heads; **St.** cylindric, to 6 cm lg., 1–2 cm $\emptyset$; **Tub.** to 3 mm lg., rounded; **Sp.** to 20, appressed, densely interlacing, to 6 mm lg., brown-tipped, concealing the crown; **Fr.** 7 mm lg.; **S.** brown.—USA (W. Texas).

E. strobiliformis sensu Böd.: **Escobaria tuberculosa** (Eng.) Br. & R.

E. tuberculosa (Eng.) Br. & R. (T)
Bo. offsetting; **St.** cylindric, to 18 cm h., to 6 cm $\emptyset$, greyish to bluish-green; **Tub.** 6 mm lg.; **Rsp.** 20–30, acicular, 4–15 mm lg.; **Csp.** 5–9, somewhat stouter and longer, brown or blackish towards the tip, otherwise white like the Rsp.; **Fl.** 2.5 cm $\emptyset$, pink; **Sep.** violet-pink; **Fr.** oblong, to 2 cm lg., carmine.—USA (W. Texas, S. New Mexico) to N. Mexico.
A very variable spec. Of the varieties which have been named, the following are more strongly differentiated:
v. **caespititia** (Quehl) Borg: **Bo.** more spherical, densely offsetting; **Rsp.** 20, milky-white; **Csp.** 3–5, brown-tipped; **Sep.** pink, with white cilia; **Pet.** pale pink, bordered white. This densely spined plant was also sold in the USA as E. peloncillensis Kuenzl. nom. prov.;
v. **durispina** (Quehl) Borg: **Bo.** stoutly cylindric; **Sp.** hard, brittle, white; **Csp.** stouter, tipped reddish or brown; the most attractive of the varieties;
v. **gracilispina** (Quehl) Borg and v. **pubescens** (Quehl) Borg both have thin **Sp.**; in the latter they are red-tipped at first, as also in v. **rufispina** (Quehl) Borg, but this has only 15–20 **Rsp.**.

E. varicolor Tieg.
Bo. solitary, conical-spherical, to c. 6 cm h. and $\emptyset$, light green; **Tub.** 7 mm lg.; **Rsp.** 15–18, thin-acicular, 6 mm lg., appressed, radiating, glassy, dirty white; **Csp.** 4, 3 appressed upwards, the other one projecting, 1 cm lg., subulate but thin, honey-coloured to reddish or horn-coloured; **Fl.** whitish to carmine-pink, c. 3 cm lg.; **Sep.** ciliate.—USA (W. Texas).

E. vivipara (Nutt.) F. Buxb.: **Coryphantha vivipara** (Nutt.) Eng.

E. zilziana (Böd.) Backbg.
Bo. becoming cylindric, offsetting both from the base and higher up; **St.** to over 10 cm lg., light bluish-green; **Ax.** quite woolly towards the crown in older plants; **Rsp.** 12–15, to 1.5 cm lg., whitish, brown-tipped, also c. 4–7 shorter, thinner, upper Ssp.; **Csp.** 0–1, not longer; **Fl.** c. 2.5 cm lg., 1.5 cm $\emptyset$, yellow to olive; **Fr.** clavate, 2 cm lg., crimson.—Mexico (Coahuila, N. of the Sierra Paila).

Escobesseya Hest. (E. dasyacantha and duncanii): **Escobaria** Br. & R.

Escontria Rose (161)

Larger much-branching trees with smaller, glabrous, shortly bell-shaped flowers, they, the ovary and the fleshy fruit with larger, dry and parchmenty, triangular scales which are dense and imbricate. Fruit-colour is variously reported as greyish-green (probably when unripe), brownish-red (ripening?) and purple. The fruits have an aroma of gooseberries, and are on sale in the local markets.—Distribution: Mexico (S. Puebla to Oaxaca). [(R).]

E. chiotilla (Web.) Rose (T.)
Bo. tree-like, to 7 m h., developing a shorter, robust **trunk**; **branches** weak, readily detached, light green; **Ri.** 7–8; **Ar.** very crowded and later confluent; **Rsp.** to 10–15, fairly short, recurved; **Csp.** several, 1 main Sp. to 7 cm lg., sometimes ± flattened; all **Sp.** light-coloured; **Fl.** 3 cm lg., yellow; **Fr.** c. 5 cm ∅.—S. Mexico (S. Puebla). (Fig. 110.)

Espostoa Br. & R. emend. Werd. (183)

Peruvian Cerei, from tall and shrub-like to ± tree-like, almost all set with dense white hairs; the radial spines are mostly shorter, fine, white, yellowish or red, the centrals sometimes longer to quite long, horn-coloured, or even ± red-flecked to reddish-coloured. The hair-development where present is ± dense and web-like, silky; unlike the more Central Peruvian genus, Pseudoespostoa, the apical hair is not conspicuously soft and dense or like cotton-wool. In his amendment (1931) Werdermann restricted Espostoa to the more northern and predominantly E. Andean species which branch from the sides and have a grooved cephalium and matt seeds; however he (still) placed the plants of my genus Pseudoespostoa in Cephalocereus on account of the superficial cephalium; moreover these latter plants, which are never so tall-growing, branch from the base and have glossy seeds. In Espostoa the cephalium is whitish to yellowish or brownish, according to the species; it develops from a seam-like depression running down from the apex, quite shallow at first but becoming wider and deeper, with flat and broader areoles, so that it can be described as a grooved cephalium. The nocturnal flowers are borne mostly in the upper part, but also quite low on the flanks; they are spreading at anthesis, and of varying length. The berry-fruits are red when ripe and they, like the flowers, are laxly hairy. Species sometimes rather variable, especially in hair-development, but the latter never resembles cotton-wool.—Distribution: S. Ecuador to N. Peru. [(R).]
I have followed Werdermann's amendment, i.e. I have retained his segregation of Espostoa and Pseudoespostoa, for the following reasons: habit,

branching, hair-development, cephalium-arrangement and seed-testa are all different, so that they should be seen as two distinct genera. Even in young plants it is possible to foresee the development of these differential characters, whereas in a plant said to be "Espostoa nana Ritt." (Pseudoespostoa), this does not apply. If a cross-section shows that the cephalium does not arise from close to the axis (F. Buxbaum in Kakt.u.a.Sukk., 15: 3, 45. 1964), the plant when adult still shows a juvenile, incompletely sunken cephalium. Any arguments against this segregation ignore the fact that where the characters of a complex of species are so distinct, and yet so uniform within the group, this represents a natural generic classification; any larger grouping is more artificial and overlooks the differences; this in turn has produced the fairly frequent confusions of the past. It may be objected that the two distributions are geographically close, but this is not unusual and was already known from Weberbauer's work on the Andean flora. Humboldt had observed the cleft character of the Espostoa cephalium, with its conspicuously seam-like subapical depression (see also Pseudoespostoa).

E. blossfeldiorum (Werd.) F. Buxb.: **Thrixanthocereus blossfeldiorum** (Werd.) Backbg.

E. calva (FR 1314): no description available.

E. dautwitzii (Hge. Jr.) Borg: clarification is lacking as to whether this spec. belonged to Pseudoespostoa or Espostoa.

E. dybowskii (Goss.) Frič: **Austrocephalocereus dybowskii** (Goss.) Backbg.

E. huanucensis Ritt.
A spec. with finer and also ± projecting H.; possibly only a variety.

E. hylaea Ritt.—"Taxon" XIII: 4, 143. 1964.
Bo. branching from the base to midway; **St.** ascending, to 5 cm ∅; **Ri.** 21–28, with H. to 1 cm lg.; **Rsp.** 30–40, 5 mm lg., yellow or reddish-brown; **Csp.** scarcely distinguishable, sometimes 1 rather stouter Sp. to 1 cm lg.; **Ceph.** light brown; **Fl.** to 5 cm lg., to 6 cm ∅, with white floccose H., colour? (probably white); **S.** 1.4 mm lg., matt.—Peru (Prov. Bagna, Dept. Amazonas, Rio Marañon, Magdalena). (FR 668.)

E. lanata (HBK.) Br. & R. (T.)
Bo. tree-like and trunk-forming, to 4 m h.; **Br.** erect; **Ri.** 20–30, low; **Ar.** crowded; **Rsp.** numerous, yellowish, short, sharp, sometimes ± reddish-tipped; **Csp.** mostly 2, very robust, projecting,

several cm lg., yellowish to horn-coloured, red-tipped; **Ceph.** whitish; **Fl.** c. 5 cm lg.—N. Peru. (Fig. 111.)
> v. **sericata** (Backbg.) Backbg.: lacks the longer **Csp.** of v. lanata. (Fig. 112.)

E. lanianuligera Ritt. (FR 660): "with greyish-white H. and ivory Sp."; still not described.

E. laticornua Rauh & Backbg.
Bo. forming wide-crowned trees, to only 2 m h., with a **trunk** to 50 cm lg., to 30 cm $\varnothing$; **branches** $\pm$ erect; **Sp.** mostly at first with longer Csp. which may later disappear, Sp. in the type are lighter in colour; **Ceph.** yellowish-green; **Fl.** 6 cm lg.; **Fr.** 4 cm lg.—S. Ecuador to N. Peru. Br. & R. depicted this spec., which they erroneously believed to be identical with E. lanata.
> v. **atroviolacea** Rauh & Backbg.: **Rsp.** purplish-violet; **Csp.** 1(–2), those in the crown dark brownish-red to $\pm$ black; **Ceph.** pure white to greenish-white; **Fl.** c. 5 cm lg.;
> v. **rubens** Rauh & Backbg.: **Rsp.** reddish; **Csp.** 1–2, to 8 cm lg., amber-coloured or sometimes with lengthwise lines; **Ar.** yellowish-brown; **Ceph.** pure white to yellowish-white.

E. melanostele (Vpl.) Borg: **Pseudoespostoa melanostele** (Vpl.) Backbg.

E. mirabilis Ritt.—"Taxon", XIII: 4, 143. 1964.
Bo. probably shrubby to tree-like; **St.** to 9 cm $\varnothing$; **Sp.** bristly-thin on immature plants, interlacing and projecting, some longer and hair-like, especially towards the base; **Csp.** erect in the crown, acicular and thin in young plants, white below, reddish above, older plants have several stouter, longer and projecting Csp.; **crown** with quite dense white wool, Ar. rather large; **Ceph.** golden-brown to reddish-brown; **Fl.** as in other Espostoas, 5.5 cm lg.—N. Peru (middle Marañon Gorge). (FR 670.)
> v. **primigena** Ritt., l.c.: **St.** only 4–8 cm $\varnothing$; **Ceph.** mostly reddish-brown to yellowish; **Fl.** 4–5 cm lg.—Same locality as the type (FR 1061).

E. mocupensis Johns. and E. lanata mocupensis Ritt.: undescribed names.

E. nana Ritt.: **Pseudoespostoa nana** (Ritt.) Backbg.

E. procera Rauh & Backbg.
Bo. tree-like, to 7 m h.; **branches** to 15 cm $\varnothing$, not very numerous, squarrose; **crown** with dense white wool; **Csp.** to 2 cm lg. on Ceph.-bearing plants, yellowish towards the base, red above; **Ceph.** over 2 m lg., with yellowish wool; **Fl.** 4.5 cm lg.—N. Peru (Olmos Valley).

E. ritteri Buin.
Bo. tree-like, branching, to 4m h., broader than high; **branches** to 7 cm $\varnothing$, dark green; **Ri.** 18–22, transversely furrowed; **Ar.** white; **H.** white, fine, sometimes $\pm$ projecting, 2–3 cm lg.; **Rsp.** c. 25, thin, reddish-brownish, yellowish or whitish; **Csp.** 1, 7–20 mm lg., said to be black, also reddish-brown in seedling plants, thin; **Ceph.** yellowish; **Fl.** to 8 cm lg., white.—N. Peru (banks of the River Marañon).

E. ruficeps Ritt. (FR 573A), not described: plant with longer, $\pm$ projecting H. and fine short reddish Sp. Since no data are given as to habit and cephalium, it is impossible to say whether it should be attributed to any of the known spec. (Fig. 3512, "Die Cact.", Vol. VI.)

E. sericata (Backbg.) Backbg.: **Espostoa lanata** v. **sericata** (Backbg.) Backbg.

E. ulei (Gürke) F. Buxb.: **Facheiroa ulei** (Gürke) Werd.

Eulychnia Phil. (88)

Mostly tree-like Cerei, mostly freely branching, the branches fairly erect, sometimes with fairly long central spines. In some species even very young plants develop white or grey, $\pm$ long areolar felt, or this may be hair-like, dense and long, so that the crown is concealed by floccose felt or hairs. The flowers are bellshaped to funnelform, or almost rounded-bellshaped below, variously long, set fairly densely with felty or (shortly) hairy areoles; the thick-walled fruits sometimes have dense appressed hairs, or felt, and are sometimes scented. The seeds, as far as known, are rather small, dark brown or black. At least one species differs by its dwarf or even semi-prostrate habit, its spination with a conspicuous resemblance to that of Trichocereus skottsbergii (SG. Medioeulychnia), but clearly distinguishable from this by the woolly and bellshaped flowers. A similar low-growing plant with conspicuously spiny(!) flowers must be regarded as an earlier stage in the evolutionary line and referred to its own genus, Philippicereus Backbg. 7 species have been described: Ritter distinguishes a further 2 (undescribed) species, so that some 9 recognisable species are known.—Distribution: Chile (N. coastal regions). [(R).]

E. acida Phil.
Bo. tree-like, to 7 m h., with a trunk to 1 m lg.; **Ri.** 11–12, broad, low; **Sp.** scarcely differentiated unequal, brownish at first, becoming grey, to 20 cm lg.; **Fl.** 5 cm lg., top-shaped, densely set with Sc. and distinct cushions of very short felt, not H.; **Pet.**

pink, later also white; **Fr.** fleshy.—Chile (Choapa to Coquimbo). Ritter distinguishes a v. **procumbens**. The plant I list as E. procumbens is also a semi-prostrate and low-growing plant but has densely hairy and stoutly bellshaped Fl. I have no information as to whether Ritter's variety has the same Fl. as the type.

E. aricensis Ritt.—"Taxon", XIII: 3, 115. 1964.
Bo. as for E. iquiquensis: **Ri.** more numerous, 14–17; **Ar.** larger, to 1 cm ∅, with short, pale grey felt; **Sp.** weaker, the longest 2–4 cm lg.; **Fl.** shorter, 4.5–5.2 cm lg., with yellowish-brown, white, grey or brownish felty H., these becoming paler; **Pet.** smaller, to 1.8 cm lg., 0.4–0.5 cm br.; **Fil.** inserted below, crowded around the opening; **Fr.** smaller, 4–5 cm lg. and br.; **S.** fewer.—Chile (S. of Arica, on coastal cliffs). (FR 197.)

E. breviflora Phil.: **Eulychnia spinibarbis** (O.) Br. & R.

E. floresiana Ritt., not described; said to resemble E. saint-pieana Ritt. (FR 202A.)

E. iquiquensis (K. Sch.) Br. & R.
Bo. tree-like, to 7 m h., virtually spineless below; **trunk** short, to 25 cm ∅; **branches** arising from near the base; **Ri.** 12–15, ± tuberculate; **Ar.** crowded, white, to 1 cm ∅; **Sp.** on sterile shoots c. 12–15, mostly c. 1 cm lg., 1–2 fairly stout, to 12 cm lg., the Sp. from flowering Ar. are often bristly and numerous; **Fl.** 6–7 cm lg., with silky white H.; **Pet.** short, white; **Fr.** 5–6 cm ∅, fleshy, with dense silky white H.—Chile (Prov. Atacama, Antofagasta, Tarapacá, near the sea). (Fig. 113.)

E. longispina Ritt: not described. Said to have Fl. with long golden-yellow H. (FR 214A).
v. lanuginosior Ritt.; only a name (FR 215), likewise v. tenuis Ritt. (FR 215A).

E. procumbens Backbg.—Descr. Cact. Nov. III: 6. 1963.
Bo. erect to semi-prostrate, low-growing; **St.** often slightly curving, often glabrous below; **Ri.** c. 9–11, obtuse, ± tuberculate; **Ar.** plump, grey; **Sp.** varying in number and length, but mostly fairly to very long, sometimes slightly curving to directed downwards, several of them of a length greater than the St.-∅, those at the apex ± erect; **Fl.** stoutly and broadly bellshaped, white, with dense soft H. as far as the limb, the Tu. thus remaining concealed; **Pet.** fairly short.—Chile (S. of Los Viles). (Fig. 114.)

E. ritteri Cullm.
Bo. tree-like or shrubby, to 3 m h., freely branching

from near the base; **branches** 6–8 cm ∅; **Ar.** very crowded, to 7.5 mm across, with tufted, longer, greyish-white felt; **Rsp.** to 12, 1–2 cm lg., brownish, thin; **Csp.** 1–4, black, 3–6 cm lg., the longest ones pointing downwards; **Fl.** c. 2 cm lg., 1.5 cm ∅, with white wool and green Sc.; **Pet.** pink, to 1 cm lg., rounded; **Fr.** greenish-orange, to 3 cm ∅, spherical; **pulp** colourless, slimy, acid.—Peru (coast near Chala).

E. saint-pieana Ritt.—"Taxon", XIII: 3, 115. 1964.
Bo. resembling that of E. spinibarbis but the **Ar.** are circular, to 8 mm ∅, 3–8 mm apart, with pale grey felt 5–10 mm lg., appearing as lax white flock on mature plants; **Fl.** 6–7.5 cm lg., 5–7.5 cm ∅; **Pet.** to 3 cm lg. and 0.8 cm br., white, spatulate, sometimes with a pink M.-stripe, narrower at the base, rounded or acuminate above, with a tiny brownish point; **Fr.** ± pear-shaped, c. 8 mm lg.; **pulp** brownish-yellow, virtually sapless.—N. Chile (Atacama) (FR 479A). No mention is made of the Sp. which are yellow in seedlings; the latter also have a covering of dense white H.

E. spinibarbis (O.) Br. & R. (T.)
Bo. tree-like, to 4 m h., branching; **branches** to 7.5 cm ∅; **Ri.** 12–13; **Sp.** c. 20, scarcely differentiated centrals to 15 cm lg., others mostly to c. 18 mm lg.; **Fl.** 3–6 cm lg., with light yellowish-brown H.; **Pet.** white or pink, 2 cm lg., acuminate; **Fr.** c. 7 cm lg., 4.5 cm ∅, with long light brown H.—Chile (Prov. Coquimbo, coast).
v. taltalensis Ritt. (FR 214): only a name.

Facheiroa Br. & R. (177)

Tree-like plants with a short trunk and numerous ribs. Flowering shoots bear a lateral superficial cephalium consisting of a compact mass of brownish-reddish woolly hairs. The nocturnal flowers are rather short, cylindric to bellshaped, with a short limb, with brownish hair. The fruit is pear-shaped, hairy at first but the hairs dropping at maturity.—Distribution: Brazil (Bahia). [(R.)]

F. pubiflora Br. & R.: **Facheiroa ulei** (Gürke) Werd.

F. ulei (Gürke) Werd. (T.)
Bo. to 5 m h., **trunk** to 12 cm ∅; **branches** slender, numerous to 7 cm ∅, light green to greyish-green; **Ri.** 15–20; **Ar.** greyish-brown; **Rsp.** 10–15, 1–1.5 cm lg.; **Csp.** 3–4, c. 1–2.5 cm lg.; all **Sp.** brown, not very sharp; **Ceph.** to 20 cm lg., to 4 cm br., brownish-reddish, H. to 4.5 cm lg., Br. absent; **Fl.** to 4.5 cm lg., to 2 cm ∅; **Tu.** and **Ov.** with dense small Sc. and brownish H. 1 cm lg.; **Pet.** white; **Fr.**

6 cm lg., 4 cm $\varnothing$; **S.** 1.5 mm lg., matt black (Werd.) or glossy (Gürke).—Brazil (Bahia, Serra do S. Ignacio). (Fig. 115.)

Ferocactus Br. & R. (195)

Plants of quite widely varying habit: flattened-spherical, low-spherical, fairly tall and elongated, or forming cushion-like groups of hundreds of heads, thick-columnar, solitary or offsetting, sometimes to 4 m h., and thus the tallest of the cactoid forms. The spination shows comparable variability: subulate to flattened, the central spines straight to curving or even sharply hooked, often brilliantly coloured and sometimes accompanied by hair-like subsidiary spines. Common to all are the relatively short, glabrous, densely scaly flowers, yellow or red, as far as known, or in intermediate tones, and the basally dehiscent fruits which are similarly scaly. In a number of species no information is available about the seeds, otherwise they are mostly black, sometimes brown, matt or $\pm$ glossy. Most plants grow relatively slowly when cultivated in pots.—Distribution: USA (S. States from Utah and Nevada to the S. frontier), Mexico (Baja California and states s. to Oaxaca). [(R).]

F. acanthodes (Lem.) Br. & R.
Bo. stout-columnar, to 3 m h., mostly solitary; **Ri.** to c. 27, to 2 cm h.; **Ar.** brown, often very crowded; **Rsp.** to c. 13, thin-acicular to bristly; **Csp.** subulate, never hooked, at most $\pm$ bent, thin, $\pm$ flattened or $\pm$ contorted, to 12 cm lg.; **Sp.** whitish, pink, light red or yellowish; **Fl.** bellshaped, yellow to orange, 4–6 cm lg., with purple Sc.; **Fr.** 3 cm lg.—USA (S. Nevada) to Mexico (Baja California). (Fig. 116.)
v. **lecontei** (Eng.) Linds.: to only 2 m h., considerably more slender; **Ri.** to 30.—USA (SW.) to Mexico (Sonora, Baja California).

F. alamosanus Br. & R.
Bo. spherical, to 25 cm h., to 30 cm $\varnothing$, sometimes forming groups; **Ri.** c. 20; **Rsp.** mostly 8, 3–4 cm lg., $\pm$ spreading; **Csp.** 1, porrect, to 6 cm lg., somewhat flattened laterally; **Sp.** yellowish; **Fl.** yellow.—Mexico (Sonora).
v. **platygonus** Linds.: eventually $\pm$ cylindric, to 1 m h. and 40 cm $\varnothing$; **Ri.** to 13 (occasionally to 20), to 4 cm h. and br.; **Sp.** amber-coloured, later red below; **Fl.** to 4.5 cm lg., 3.5 cm $\varnothing$, greenish-yellow; **Fr.** 4 cm lg., 3 cm $\varnothing$; **S.** intense dark brown to black.—Mexico (Sonora; SW. Chihuahua).

F. chrysacanthus (Orc.) Br. & R.
Bo. spherical to $\pm$ cylindric; **Ri.** c. 18, tuberculate; **Ar.** with nectar-glands; **Rsp.** 4 to numerous, thin,

white; **Csp.** to 10, to 5 cm lg., yellow or red, curving; **Fl.** 5 cm $\varnothing$, yellow.—Mexico (Baja California).

F. coloratus Gat.
Bo. cylindric, to 1 m h., to 30 cm $\varnothing$; **Ri.** 13–20; **Ar.** large, elongated; **Rsp.** 10–14, bristle-like, matt white, spreading, slightly sinuate; **Csp.** 9(–11), stiff, stout, banded, straight, to 5 cm lg., the lowest central one broadest, light brownish-red, one of these hooked; **Fl.** $\pm$ straw-coloured, appearing orange or red because of the red M.-stripe; **Fr.** yellow; **S.** black, rather matt.—Mexico (Baja California, Aguaje San Andreas).

F. cornigerus and var. (names of Schmoll): **Ferocactus latispinus** (Haw.) Br. & R.

F. covillei (Br. & R.) Berg.: **Ferocactus emoryi** (Eng.) Backbg.

F. diguetii (Web.) Br. & R.
Bo. cylindric, to 4 m h., to 80 cm $\varnothing$; **Ri.** to c. 40; **Ar.** eventually very crowded; **Sp.** 6–8, 3–4 cm lg., slightly curving, somewhat spreading, subulate, terete; **Fl.** 3.5 cm lg.,; **Pet.** red, bordered yellow, 2 cm lg.—Mexico (islands of the Gulf of California, e.g. Santa Catalina Is.).
v. **carmenensis** Linds.: to only 1 m h., to 40 cm $\varnothing$; **Sp.** stouter than in the type.—Mexico (Gulf of California, Carmen Is.).

F. echidne (DC.) Br. & R.
Bo. broadly subspherical, to 12.5 cm h., to 18 cm $\varnothing$, green, later offsetting(?); **Ri.** 13, acute; **Ar.** oval; **Rsp.** c. 7, stiff, c. 2 cm lg., yellow; **Csp.** 1, porrect, to over 3 cm lg.; **Fl.** 3 cm lg., lemon-yellow to sulphur-yellow.—Mexico (Hidalgo).

F. emoryi (Eng.) Backbg.
Bo. solitary, spherical to cylindric, to 2.4 m h.; **Ri.** 22–32, to 4 cm h., rather thin, $\pm$ tuberculate at first; **Ar.** distant, brown at first, glandular; **Rsp.** 5–8, subulate, somewhat spreading, to 6 cm lg.; **Csp.** 1, straight, bent or very hooked, banded, round to flattened or triangular, 3–8 cm lg.; **Sp.** red to white; **Fl.** to over 6 cm lg., yellow to red with yellow flecks; **Fr.** 5 cm lg.—USA (S. Arizona) to Mexico (Sonora, Guaymas). Probably represents more than a single spec.

F. flavovirens (Scheidw.) Br. & R.
Bo. $\pm$ elongated-spherical, offsetting to form colonies, dull pale green; **St.** to 20 cm $\varnothing$, to 40 cm h.; **Ri.** (11–)13, to 2 cm h.; **Ar.** grey; **Rsp.** 14, projecting, to 2 cm lg.; **Csp.** 4, the lowest one 5–8 cm lg.; all **Sp.** red to brown, then grey, stout, subulate, banded; **Fl.** yellow.—Mexico (Puebla,

Tehuacan).

F. fordii (Orc.) Br. & R.
Bo. spherical to short-cylindric, greyish green, to 12 cm ∅; **Ri.** mostly 21, 1 cm h.; **Ar.** 2 cm apart; **Rsp.** c. 15, acicular, spreading, whitish; **Csp.** mostly 4, 1 flattened, to 4 cm lg., bent to hooked, the others subulate, somewhat angular; **Fl.** 4 cm lg., light purple.—Mexico (Baja California, W. coast).
v. **grandiflorus** Linds.: somewhat taller, to 1 m; **Fl.** 6 cm lg., yellowish-red; **Pet.** 4 cm lg.—Baja California (Cap San Eugenio to Abreojos Point).

F. gatesii Linds.
Bo. spherical to cylindric, to 1.5 m h., to 30 cm ∅; **Ri.** 30–32; **Ar.** light brown; **Rsp.** c. 16, radiating, terete; **Csp.** 4, cruciform, flattened laterally, to 3 mm br., the lowest one longest, to 7 cm lg., never hooked; **Csp.** and some lateral Sp. banded, others bristly, fine; **Fl.** to 6 cm br. and lg., red; **Fr.** to 7.5 cm lg., 2.5 cm ∅.—Mexico (Baja California, islands of Los Angeles Bay).

F. glaucescens (DC.) Br. & R.
Bo. spherical, later slightly elongated, bluish-green; **Ri.** 11–13; **Sp.** yellow; **Rsp.** 6–7; **Csp.** 1; all ± equal, to 3 cm lg.; **Fl.** 2 cm lg., yellow; **Pet.** oblong.—Eastern Central Mexico.
F. pfeifferi (Zucc.) distinguished from the preceding as follows: **Bo.** more elongated; **Sp.** 6, ± equal, pale yellowish, brown below, banded, only rarely 1 **Csp.**—Mexico (Toliman).

F. gracilis Gat.
Bo. spherical to cylindric, to 3 m h., to 30 cm ∅; **Ri.** 24, tuberculate; **Ar.** narrowly elliptic; **Rsp.** 5 on each side, 2.5–4 cm lg., later spreading, acicular, whitish; **Csp.** 7–13, subulate, except for the central upper one which is flattened on both sides, and the central lower one which is subterete below, concave above, sometimes hooked at first; **Sp.** banded, sharp, dull dark red, sometimes light-tipped, all becoming black; **Fl.** 4 cm lg., straw-coloured with a reddish-brown M.-stripe; **Fr.** oblong, yellow; **S.** glossy black.—Mexico (Baja California, Misión San Fernando).

F. (S.D.) haematacanthus Borg
Bo. simple, spherical, later cylindric, 30–120 cm h., 20–26 cm ∅, green, with a white-woolly crown; **Ri.** 13–27, narrow, slightly wavy; **Ar.** 16–23 mm apart, silky-yellow at first, later greying; **Rsp.** 6, upper 2 flattened, 25–35 mm lg., deep red below, tipped yellow; **Csp.** 4, directed downwards, similarly coloured, straight or slightly curving, 40–80 mm lg.; **Fl.** in a ring around the crown, 60–70 mm lg., 25–30 mm br., purplish-red; **Fr.** ovoid, deep purple, 22–35 mm lg., 14–27 mm ∅; **S.** 1.8 mm lg.,

black.—Mexico (Pueblá, on limestone mountains between Esperanza and Cumbres de Acultzingo at 2700–2900 m).
Not a variety of F. stainesii.

F. hamatacanthus (Mühlpfrdt.) Br. & R.: **Hamatocactus hamatacanthus** (Mühlpfrdt.) Knuth.

F. herrerae G. Ort.
Bo. spherical, eventually cylindric, to 2 m h.; **Ri.** 13–14, tuberculate at first; **Ar.** 2 cm lg., white or light grey; **Rsp.** 8, 2 of these white, the others flecked red; **Csp.** 1, hooked at first, becoming straight; **Br.** to 8, contorted, to 3 cm lg.; **Fl.** funnelform, 7 cm ∅, 7 cm lg.; **Pet.** reddish, bordered yellow; **Fr.** 4 cm lg., 3 cm ∅.—Mexico (Mazatlan, Durango).

F. hertrichii Weing.: an insufficiently clarified spec.: **Bo.** to 1.5 m h., to 60 cm ∅; **Ri.** 12–24; **Rsp.** 17–19, mostly bristly, to 4 cm lg.; **Csp.** 4, 4–6 cm lg., the lowest one hooked; **Fl.** 6 cm lg., reddish-brown with a darker centre.—USA (Arizona, Tortilla and Gila Mts.).

F. histrix (DC.) Linds.
Bo. eventually large-spherical with an oblique crown, to 70 cm h., olive to bluish green, solitary; **Ri.** c. 24, many more in old plants; **Rsp.** 7–12; **Csp.** 3–4, one of these porrect, to 6 cm lg.; all **Sp.** amber-coloured; **Fl.** numerous, with the buds arising from a ring of thick wool, to 3.5 cm lg., light yellow, broadly funnelform; **Pet.** linear-oblong, ± pointed; **Fr.** 2 cm lg.; **S.** minute, brown.—Central Mexico.

F. horridus Br. & R.
Bo. spherical, becoming elongated, to 1 m h., to 30 cm ∅; **Ri.** 13, 2 cm h.; **Ar.** large; **Rsp.** 8–12, 3–4 cm lg., acicular, white; **Csp.** 6–8, spreading or porrect, reddish, one longest projecting hooked Sp. to 12 cm lg.; **Fl.** ?—Mexico (Baja California, S. Francisquito Bay).

F. johnsonii (Parry) Br. & R.: **Echinomastus johnsonii** (Parry) Baxt.

F. johnstonianus Br. & R.
Bo. shortly cylindric, to 60 cm h., to 35 cm ∅; **Ri.** 24–31, wavy; **Ar.** crowded, elliptic; **Sp.** 20 or more, subulate, all alike, never hooked, slightly projecting, banded, to 7 cm lg., brownish-yellow to yellow; **Fl.** 5 cm lg., yellow, reddish outside; **Fr.** 2.5 cm ∅.—Mexico (Baja California, Angel de la Guardia island).

F. latispinus (Haw.) Br. & R.
Bo. spherical to compressed-spherical, to 40 cm ∅

and h., rarely elongated; **Ri.** 15–23; **Ar.** large; **Rsp.** 6–10, thin, banded, white to pink, 2–2.5 cm lg.; **Csp.** 4 or more, stouter, more intensely coloured, one of them much flattened and hooked, directed downwards; Sp.-colour varies from red to yellow; **Fl.** bellshaped, whitish to pink or purple; **Pet.** narrowly oblong; **Fr.** 4 cm lg.—Central Mexico to Durango. Because of habit, flower and kidney-shaped seed this plant is perhaps better referred to Glandulicactus Backbg.

F. lecontei Br. & R.: **Ferocactus acanthodes** v. **lecontei** (Eng.) Linds.

F. lindsayi H. Bravo
Bo. simple, spherical, eventually cylindric, 60 cm h., 40 cm ∅, greyish-green; **Ri.** 13–18, 4 cm h., acute; **Ar.** 6–10 mm apart, elliptic, c. 3 cm lg., grey-felty, flowering Ar. yellow-woolly, with 7–9 red Gl.; **Rsp.** 5–6, round or ± flattened, 2.5–3 cm lg.; **Csp.** 1, straight, 4.5 cm lg., grey, tipped black; **Fl.** subapical, bellshaped, 3–4 cm br., glossy yellow, c. 4 cm lg.; **Fr.** ovoid, 1.5 cm lg. and ∅, purplish-red; **S.** small, black.—Mexico (Michoacan, lower course of the Rio Balsas). Named for Dr. G. Lindsay.

F. macrodiscus (Mart.) Br. & R.
Bo. compressed-spherical, sometimes slightly elongated, to 45 cm ∅, light green; **Ri.** 16–21, acute; **Ar.** light yellow, distant; **Rsp.** 6–8, ± compressed, to 2 cm lg.; **Csp.** 4, stouter, more compressed, the lowest one to 2 cm lg., pointing downwards; **Sp.** yellow, reddish-yellow or blood-red; **Fl.** 5 cm lg., funnelform; **Pet.** linear-oblong, dark red to purple or carmine, with a darker M.-stripe.—Mexico (San Luis Potosí to Oaxaca).
　v. **multiflorus** (R. Mey.) Berg.: said to flower more readily than the type; **Sp.** purple below at first, soon becoming dull yellow; **Fl.** 3–4 cm lg. and br.; **Pet.** pale pink with a purple M.-stripe.

F. melocactiformis sensu Br. & R. (Echus. electracanthus Lem.): **Ferocactus histrix** (DC.) Linds.

F. nobilis (L.) Br. & Br.: **Ferocactus recurvus** (Mill.) Berg.

F. orcuttii (Eng.) Br. & R.
Bo. spherical to oblong, offsetting, to 20 heads, to 1.3 m h., to 45 cm ∅, dark green; **crown** with white felt; **Ri.** 13–30, rather obtuse, to c. 1.5 cm h.; **Ar.** crowded; **Rsp.** 9–13(–15), subulate, radiating, sometimes bent and banded, to c. 2 cm lg.; **Csp.** 4(–7), banded, stouter, angular or flat, 1 bottom Sp. to 3 cm lg., keeled, not hooked; **Fl.** 3–5 cm lg., carmine to wine-red; **Pet.** rounded; **Fr.** carmine; **S.** black.—Mexico (Baja California, near Tia Juana).

F. peninsulae (Web.) Br. & R.
Bo. spherical at first, then columnar, to 2.5 m h.; **Ri.** 13–21; **Ar.** distant; **Rsp.** c. 11, upper 6 thin-subulate, white, straight, to 2.5 cm lg., lower ones stouter, angular, ± bent, banded, red then becoming grey, to 3 cm lg.; **Csp.** 6, ruby-red, 4 cruciform, the lowest one hooked, angular, to 6 cm lg.; **Fl.** 4–4.5 cm lg., 5.5 cm ∅, purple with a carmine M.-stripe.—Mexico (S. Baja California).
　v. **viscainensis** (Gat.) Linds.: **Bo.** to only 1.5 m h.; **Csp.** 5–9, one of them to 13 cm lg., to 6 mm br., ± concave above; **Sp.** greyish-brown; **Fl.** 4.5 cm lg., straw-coloured with a purple dorsal stripe.—Mexico (Baja California, near Mesquital).

F. pfeifferi (Zucc.): see under F. glaucescens. The very similar plant found by H. Sanchez Mejorada in Hidalgo (Quebrada de Venados) may also be referable here: **Rsp.** 6–8 cm lg., yellow; **Csp.** 0; **Fl.** yellow.

F. pottsii (SD.) Backbg.
Bo. spherical to elongated, glossy, greyish-green, sometimes flushed reddish; **Ri.** 12–13, with tuberculate prominences; **Tub.** rather pointed; crown with yellowish-grey felt; **Ar.** distant; **Rsp.** mostly 6(–7), reddish at first, later yellowish, 1–2 cm lg.; **Csp.** 1, to 3 cm lg., purple at first, then light red; **Fl.** straw-coloured, red inside.—Mexico (Chihuahua).

F. pringlei (Coult.) Br. & R.: **Ferocactus stainesii** v. **pringlei** (Coult.) Backbg.

F. rafaelensis (J. A. Purp.) Borg: **Ri.** to 20, Gl. present; **Csp.** 1, to 6 cm lg.; **S.** small, 1 mm lg., glossy, deep black.—Mexico (Minas de San Rafael). Possibly only a form of F. echidne (DC.) Br. & R.

F. rectispinus (Eng.) Br. & R.
Bo. becoming cylindric, to 2 m h.; **Rsp.** 8–12, the upper ones stouter; **Csp.** 1, 9–13 cm lg., never hooked, sometimes curving; all **Sp.** reddish(?); **Fl.** 6 cm lg., yellow; **Pet.** 5 cm lg., lanceolate.—Mexico (Central Baja California).

F. recurvus (Mill.) Berg.
Bo. oblong, to c. 25 cm h., 20 cm ∅; **Ri.** spiralled, 13–15, 3 cm h.; **Ar.** distant, dark grey; **Rsp.** subulate, 8, 2 of these ± compressed, banded, to 2.5 cm lg.; **Csp.** 1, very stout, to 7 cm lg., bent or hooked; **Sp.** dark red to dark greyish-red, the weaker ones also yellowish; **Fl.** 2.5–4 cm lg. (–5 cm lg.?), red, bordered white or pink; **Fr.** 2 cm lg.; **S.** slightly glossy, brownish-black.—Mexico (Puebla; Oaxaca).

F. rhodanthus Schwarz, not described.

Younger plants have 12 Ri., the Bo.-colour is bluish-green, somewhat glossy; apical felt brownish-white; Ar. with white felt, cushions rather large and oblong; Rsp. c. 8, spreading to projecting, the upper one shortest; Csp. sometimes 1, ± twice the length of the Rsp.; all Sp. reddish-brownish at first, later brownish to horn-coloured, ± banded with darker zones; Fl. not known, but from Schwarz's specific name can be presumed to be red.

Seedling plants are difficult. The spec. perhaps belongs within the complex of F. emoryi, which shows great variability of spination, flower-colour and seed, with the Csp. varying from terete and straight, to flattened and hooked; this is why it has long been suspected that several species were involved, rather than one only.

F. robustus (Lk. & O.) Br. & R.
Bo. large, forming heap-like colonies to over 1 m h. and to 3 m ⌀, with hundreds of heads to 20 cm br., fresh green; **Ri.** 8; **Ar.** brown at first; **Sp.** variable in number and length, in part also in thickness, from stouter and lax, to finer and ± interlacing (Rsp.); **Rsp.** to c. 14, the upper ones thin to bristle-like, 3 lower ones directed downwards, acicular to subulate, light-coloured; **Csp.** 4(–6), to 6 cm lg., sometimes flattened, brown or red at first, darker below; **Fl.** to 4 cm lg. and ⌀, yellow; **Fr.** c. 2.5 cm lg.; **S.** black.—Mexico (Puebla, Tehuacan).

F. rostii Br. & R.
Bo. to 3 m h., offsetting; **Ar.** white; **Rsp.** bristly, 2–8 or missing, white to yellowish; true **Sp.** c. 12 or fewer; **Csp.** 3–4, banded, flattened, sometimes one above which is ± curving; **Sp.** yellow, also reddish at first on newer growth, none of them hooked; **Fl.** dark yellow; **Fr.** red.—USA (S. California) to Mexico (N. Baja California). Also regarded as a variety of F. acanthodes, but it is more slender and more freely offsetting than the latter.

F. santamaria Br. & R.: **Ferocactus townsendianus** v. **santamaria** (Br. & R.) Linds.

F. schwarzii Linds.
Bo. solitary, ± spherical, to 80 cm h., to 50 cm ⌀; **Ri.** 13–19, acute, to 5.5 cm h., pale green; **Ar.** light brownish at first, with pale orange Gl.; **Sp.** scarcely differentiated, at first 3–4–5, later mostly 1–3, 1.5–5.5 cm lg., only slightly curving, yellow at first, then horn-coloured, slightly banded, ± terete; **Fl.** 5 cm lg., 4 cm ⌀, yellow; **Fr.** reddish, not opening below.—Mexico (N. Sinaloa).

F. stainesii (Hook.) Br. & R.
Bo. soon becoming cylindric, offsetting; **St.** to 1.5–3 m h., to 60 cm ⌀; **Ri.** c. 18; **Rsp.** c. 5 or more, projecting; **Csp.** 4, cruciform, ± banded, ± flattened, the longest upper one curving, not hooked; **H.** missing in the Ar., or only slight; **Sp.** red to yellow; **Fl.** orange.—Mexico (San Luis Potosí).

v. **haematacanthus** (SD.) Backbg.: **Bo.** to 50 cm h.; **Ri.** 12–20; **Sp.** reddish, yellowish-tipped; **Rsp.** 6; **Csp.** 4, 3–6 cm lg., the bottom one rather broad below; **Fl.** 6 cm lg., purple or flame-coloured.—Origin?(See also F. haematicanthus.)

v. **pilosus** (Gal.) Backbg.: with more H. in the Ar., especially towards the crown, and more interlacing sideways; **Ri.** to 20; **Csp.** to 4 cm lg.; **Fl.** reddish-orange, yellowish inside.—Origin?

v. **pringlei** (Coult.) Backbg.: **Rsp.** 7–9, the upper ones flexible; **Csp.** 6–7; **Fl.** 3.5–4 cm lg., brownish-red.—Mexico (Coahuila).

F. tiburonensis (Linds.) Backbg.
Bo. cylindric, to 1 m h., 35 cm ⌀; **Ri.** c. 21, slightly tuberculate, to 3 cm h.; **Sp.** scarcely differentiated, noticeably banded, the Rsp. weaker, never bristly, the central 4 terete apart from the bottom one which is somewhat flattened, to 9 cm lg., all Sp. reddish(?); **Fl.** 6 cm lg., 5 cm ⌀, yellow; **Fr.** to 3 cm lg., yellow; **S.** black.—Mexico (Baja California, Tiburon Is.). Also regarded as a variety of F. wislizenii, but distinguished from this by the lower habit, Rsp. which are not bristly-fine, and Csp. not so distinctly hooked.

F. tortulospinus Gat.
Bo. simple, to 60 cm h., to 40 m ⌀; **Ri.** 20, not broad; **Tub.** indistinct; **Ar.** fairly close-set at first; **Rsp.** 6–8 on each side, acicular, greyish-white; **Csp.** 11, stiff, thin, spreading or appressed, banded, dull greyish-red, yellow-tipped, straight except for the much longer lowest one which is to 13 cm lg., contorted and hooked; **Fl.** 4–6 cm lg., yellow to orange.—Mexico (Baja California, N. of Laguna Seca Chapala).

F. townsendianus Br. & R.
Bo. shortly cylindric, to 40 cm h.; **Ri.** c. 16, often spiralled or wavy; **Ar.** large, distant; **Rsp.** 14–16, spreading, 3–4 cm lg., mostly bristle-like except sometimes 2, more subulate; **Csp.** all subulate, banded, grey, one bent or hooked; **Fl.** c. 6 cm lg., pink in the middle, with a greenish-yellow border.—Mexico (Gulf of California, San José Is.).

v. **santamaria** (Br. & R.) Linds.: **Bo.** to 60 cm h.; **Ri.** c. 14; **Rsp.** only threadlike; **Csp.** in 2 Ser., 1 main Sp. flatter, ascending, curving above, all grey, banded, subulate; **Fl.** 7 cm lg., yellow; **Fr.** to 4 cm lg.—Mexico (Baja California, shores of Santa Maria Bay).

F. uncinatus (Gal.) Br. & R.: **Glandulicactus uncinatus** (Gal.) Backbg.

F. victoriensis (Rose) Backbg.
Bo. divergent from that of F. echidne by its eventually more cylindric and more freely offsetting habit; **Sp.** longer, more brittle; flowering Ar. oblong; **Csp.** to 9 cm lg.; **Fl.** yellow; **Fr.** with ciliate Sc. (margins entire in F. echidne).—Mexico (near Ciudad Victoria).

F. viridescens (Torr. & Gray) Br. & R.
Bo. spherical to stoutly cylindric, to 45 cm h., to 35 cm ⌀, simple or offsetting, deep green, ± glossy; **Ri.** 13–21, ± wavy, to 2 cm h.; flowering **Ar.** with red Gl.; **Rsp.** 9–20, to 2 cm lg., ± spreading; **Csp.** 4, flattened below, sometimes ± curving, to 3.5 cm lg.; **Fl.** 4 cm lg., yellowish-green; **Fr.** 2 cm lg., reddish.—USA (California), Mexico (N. Baja California).
  v. **littoralis** G. Linds.—C. & S.J. (US), XXXVI: 1, 8–11. 1964. **Bo.** eventually elongated-spherical, to 30 cm h., 18 cm ⌀, mostly simple; **Ri.** c. 21–34; **Sp.** 22–33, terete, banded, somewhat curving, straw to ± flesh-coloured; **Fl.** greenish-yellow, funnelform, c. 3 cm lg., 2.5 cm ⌀; **Fr.** reddish to yellowish, spherical, c. 15 mm ⌀; **S.** 1.5 mm lg., black.—Mexico (Baja California, coastal zone N. of Enseñada to Misión Santo Domingo. Found by H. E. Gates in 1930). An interesting and fairly densely spined variety.

F. viscainensis Gat.: **Ferocactus peninsulae** v. **viscainensis** (Gat.) Linds.

F. wislizenii (Eng.) Br. & R. (T.)
Bo. spherical at first, becoming cylindric, to 2 m h., simple; **Ri.** to 25, 3 cm h.; **Ar.** brown, distant; **Rsp.** bristly or finely acicular, to 5 cm lg.; **Csp.** several, white to red, subulate, banded, one of these much stouter, flattened, strongly hooked, to 15 cm lg.; **Fl.** to 6 cm lg., yellow to reddish; **Fr.** to 5 cm lg., yellow; **S.** matt black.—USA (Texas to Arizona), Mexico (in the N., to Baja California).

F. wislizenii v. tiburonensis Linds.: **Ferocactus tiburonensis** (Linds.) Backbg.

Floresia Ritt.: an undescribed name for **Weberbauerocereus** Backbg.

Frailea Br. & R. (112)

Rather small plants, spherical to oblong, with rows of fine tubercles or low ribs, the epidermis light green to brown. Flowers differing in size, usually moderately large, always yellow, mostly not opening at all, i.e. they set seeds cleistogamously. Kilian investigated a number of species and found most of them distinct, even where the seed-shape

was typical (see descriptions as well as line-drawings of seeds). Almost all the species offset when older.
Until quite recently the genus received little attention and the question of species-delimitation is therefore insufficiently clarified. It is therefore necessary to start from the basis of the original descriptions, the principal features of which I have reproduced below. The divergent forms of F. castanea (the type-species), together with the names F. pseudograhliana and F. pseudopulcherrima, are proof enough of the inadequate data available as to the variability of some species. We are also still lacking information on the typical shape and colour of the seeds in some species, although hat and cap shapes can be distinguished. Fruit-development from the bud-stage has also not been clarified. Perhaps the seed-colour changes or darkens in some species after the opening of the fruit. Studies are still continuing in some cases on the extent of variability of shape.—Distribution: From S. Brazil and Uruguay through N. and SE. Argentina and Paraguay, to Bolivia and into Colombia from which Werdermann gave a reliable report of a wild population. [(R).]

F. alacriportana Backbg. & Voll
Bo. cylindric, offsetting freely, green; **St.** to 6 cm h., 2 cm ⌀; **Tub.** in c. 18 R.; **Rsp.** bristly fine, 1–5 mm lg., grey; **Csp.** 2, one above the other, ochre or chocolate-colour, 1–7 mm lg.; **Fl.** light yellow.—Brazil (Rio Grande do Sul). (Fig. 123: 10, 12, 19.) Krainz regarded the spec. as identical with F. gracillima which has Fl. red inside, and an ashen greyish-green Bo.; moreover F. gracillima mostly remains simple and has amber-coloured Sp.

F. albiareolata Buin. & Bred.
Bo. simple, to 3.5 cm ⌀ and 2 cm h., dark green; **Ri.** vertical, c. 20, 4–5 mm apart, tuberculate; **Ar.** 1.5–2 mm lg., densely white-woolly, later glabrous; **Sp.** glassy, somewhat reddish-brown, later light brown, stiff; **Rsp.** 15–16, radiating; **Csp.** 1–4, dark brown; **Fl.** funnelform, 25 mm lg., yellow; **style** white, with 7 very papillose white Sti.; **Fr.** with Ar., greyish-white H. and light brown Br.; **S.** cap-shaped, with a semi-glossy chestnut-brown testa.—Uruguay (W. of Tacuarembo towards Paysandu, among sparse grass on scree).

F. albicolumnaris Ritt.
Bo. columnar, 4–6 cm h., 20–26 mm br.; **Ri.** 21–24, divided into Tub. c. 1 mm h.; **Ar.** brown, 1–1.5 mm lg., 1.5 mm apart; **Sp.** white, reddish-brown below, sharp, curving downwards; **Rsp.** 14–18, 3–5 mm lg.; **Csp.** 2–4, 4.4 mm lg., yellow; **Fl.** with the Fil. inserted c. 2 mm above the base; **Pet.** 25 mm lg., 5–7 mm br., long-tapering, sulphur-yellow; **S.** dark

blackish-brown, smooth, glossy, 2 mm lg., 2.5 mm br.—Brazil (Rio Grande do Sul, Livramento). (White columnar F.)

F. albifusca Ritt. (FR 1392)
Differentiated from F. gracillima by the twisted Sp.; **Rsp.** 8–11, 3–4 mm lg.; **Csp.** 2–5, 5–10 mm lg.; **Fl.** c. 35 mm lg., and $\varnothing$; **Tu.** mid-green inside for 3 mm below, then sulphur-yellow for 4 mm, with **Fil.** inserted only in the green section of the Tu.; **An.** golden-yellow; **S.** brown.—Uruguay. (White to reddish-brown F.)

F. asperispina Ritt. (FR 1368)
Bo. simple, cylindric, 2–5 cm. h., 10–25 mm $\varnothing$, green; **Ri.** 14–19, tuberculate, 0.5–1 mm h.; **Ar.** 0.6–1 mm lg., 1–2 mm apart; **Rsp.** white, sharp, scabrous, 8–13, 1.5–3 mm lg.; **Csp.** 0; **Fl.** 40 mm lg., 35 mm $\varnothing$; **Ov.** with dense red Sc., with dense white wool and brown Br.; **Tu.** 7 mm lg., light yellow inside, greenish below, yellow and brown outside; **Fil.** light yellow; **An.** pale golden-yellow; **Sti.** 7–9, pale yellow; **Pet.** lanceolate, 25 mm lg., 5–6 mm br., sulphur-yellow; **Fr.** green, spherical; **S.** blackish-brown, smooth, glossy,—Brazil (Rio Grande do Sul, Sao Pedro). (Rough-spined F.)

F. asterioides Werd.: **Frailea castanea** Backbg.

F. aurea Backbg.: **Frailea pygmaea** v. **aurea** (Backbg.) Backbg.

F. aureispina Ritt. (FR 1386)
Bo. cylindric, light green 15–25 mm br., simple; **Ri.** 13–18, 0.5–1 mm h., tuberculate; **Ar.** 0.8 mm lg., 0,5 mm br., brownish-red, 1–1.5 mm apart; **Sp.** light yellow; **Rsp.** 10–13, 3–4 mm lg., sharp, acicular, straight; **Csp.** absent or 1–2; **Fl.** 4 cm lg.; **Ov.** covered with grey wool and brown H.; **Tu.** pale yellow inside, yellowish-green outside; **S.** almost black.—Brazil (Rio Grande do Sul, Quarai and northwards). (Golden-spined F.)
v. **pallidior** Ritt.: distinguished by the **Ar.** being rather longer and grey-felty; **Sp.** paler; **Pet.** sulphur-yellow.—Brazil (Rio Grande do Sul, Livramento and eastwards).

F. carminifilamentosa Kilian—Descr. Cact. Nov. III: 6. 1963.
Bo. spherical, green to violet-brown, c. 3.5 cm $\varnothing$; **Ri.** with 6-sided flat Tub. in c. 17 R.; **Ar.** white to yellowish; **Rsp.** 12, clustered; **Csp.** 2; all **Sp.** 4 mm lg., ochre-brownish at first, later projecting and interlacing, straight, wavy or $\pm$ bent; **Fl.** 1.8 cm lg., 2 cm $\varnothing$; **Sep.** reddish-brownish; **Pet.** light yellow, striped carmine at the sides below; **Tu.** green with reddish Sc., ochre to light yellow Br. and white wool; **Fil.** carmine below, yellow above; **style**

yellow; **Sti.** 11, creamy-yellowish; **Fr.** yellowish-green at maturity, spindle-shaped, 6 mm $\varnothing$; **S.** 2 mm $\varnothing$, brown, spherical or cap-shaped.—Origin ? (Fig. 117, 123: 5.)
v. **winkelmanniana** Kilian n.v.: Differentiated from the type as follows: **Fl.** longer, broader, c. 2.5 cm lg., c. 3.5 cm $\varnothing$, the slender lanceolate Pet. being 3 mm br.; **Tu.** 1 cm longer than the type, Br. fewer, the white H. similarly; **Ov.** red; **Fr.** dark green, $\pm$ glabrous.

F. castanea Backbg.
Bo. flattened-spherical and vivid brown in plants on their own roots, grafted plants are more spherical and also $\pm$ brownish-green; **Ri.** 10–15, flat, not tuberculate; **Ar.** with scarcely visible felt, not white; **Sp.** mostly (7–)8 (–11), minute, reddish at first, then black, mostly appressed downwards; **Fl.** c. 4 cm lg. and $\varnothing$, yellow, with brownish wool and Br.; **Fil.** red below; **S.** glossy brownish-black, compressed hat-shape.—S. Brazil to N. Uruguay. (Fig. 118, 123: 2.)
My name is older than that of Werdermann (F. asterioides); later endeavours to reverse this cannot be justified, but it probably shows that this is a rather variable species. Plants have been found more recently with more distinctly white Ar., with clusters of Sp. pressed downwards or sometimes slightly projecting, while the body-colour varies from pure bluish-green to a reddish-brown tinge. Other plants have clusters of Sp. as wide as the Ri., the latter also being slightly tuberculate. There is even a form in which the Fl. is said to have a red throat. We now know, through the Bolivian spec. F. uhligiana, that colour may be inconstant. It has first to be established with F. castanea whether any further subdivision is practicable. In the Marnier collection I saw seedlings grafted on Peireskiopsis which had a constantly brown coloration!

F. cataphracta (Dams) Br. & R. (T.)
Bo. depressed-spherical, to 4 cm $\varnothing$, simple at first, later offsetting, fresh green; **Tub.** in 15 R., flat, with a crescent-shaped, red or brown or violet mark under the Ar.; **Rsp.** 5, directed downwards, thin, appressed, acicular at first, to 2 mm lg.; **Csp.** 0; **Fl.** 3.8 cm lg. and br., the breadth apparently variable, with light grey wool; **Sep.** greenish-yellow; **Pet.** light yellow; **Fr.** 4 mm $\varnothing$, with light brown H.; **S.** 2 mm lg., glossy, blackish-brown.—Paraguay. (Fig. 123: 1.)

F. cataphractoides Backbg. n.sp.
Bo. small-spherical (offsetting?), leaf-green, to c. 2.5 cm $\varnothing$; **Ri.** completely resolved into minute Tub., with a violet-red tint below the Ar. or in the lower half of the Tub., but not crescent-shaped; **Sp.** to c. 10, thin, somewhat curving, to 4 mm lg., $\pm$

appressed or somewhat projecting, scaberulous, pale brown at first, then grey or darker, or hyaline and brown-tipped.—Bolivia (salt-dunes near San José, on the Paraguayan frontier) (Coll. Uhlig, U 2181; found by Father Hammerschmid).

F. chiquitana Card.
Bo. solitary or forming flat cushions, with a large **R.**, yellowish-green; **St.** to c. 3 cm $\varnothing$, sometimes elongated; **Ri.** c. 24, made up of connected small Tub.; **Ar.** dark brown, with several white H.; **Rsp.** pectinate, in 4–5 pairs, bristly, hyaline, to 3 mm lg.; **Csp.** 1–3, 3 mm lg., thickened below, dark brown; **Fl.** to 2 cm lg. and $\varnothing$, light yellow; **Tu.** with white H. and brown Br.; **S.** 2 mm lg., glossy, dark brown, a rimless cap-shape.—E. Bolivia (Montana Divi Miserato). (Fig. 119, 123: 3.) [Haage adds: Probably identical with F. pullispina (Lau).]

F. colombiana (Werd.) Backbg.
Bo. simple, to offsetting and forming cushions, leaf-green; **St.** spherical to ± ovoid, to 4 cm $\varnothing$; **Tub.** in 17–18 R.; **Ar.** to 5 mm apart, with whitish or brownish felt; **Rsp.** 15–20, bristly, to 4 mm lg.; **Csp.** 2–5, one of these to 6 mm lg., scarcely distinguishable from the **Rsp.**; all **Sp.** yellowish, darker-tipped; **Fl.** 2.5 cm lg., pure yellow or greenish-yellow; **Pet.** lanceolate, tapering, revolute; **Tu.** with whitish-grey wool and brown Br.—Colombia (Dagua). (Fig. 123: 6.)

F. concepcionensis Buin. & Moser
Bo. forming groups, 2.5–8 cm $\varnothing$, to 1.75 cm h., green; **Ri.** to 13, divided into small round reddish Tub.; **Ar.** oval, to 2 mm lg., with a little white to yellowish felt; **Sp.** 8–10, spreading, projecting, 3–5 mm. lg., light yellowish; **Csp.** rarely 1; **Fl.** funnelform, 24 mm lg. and br., light lemon-yellow; **Sep.** 5–11 mm lg., spatulate, mucronate; **Pet.** 13–15 mm lg., spatulate, with an acicular tip, with a finely notched margin; **style** yellowish-white, with 8 light yellow **Sti.**; **Fr.** green, with fleshy reddish little Sc. and white woolly H. and Br.; **S.** cap-shaped, with a light brown glossy testa.—Paraguay (near the airstrip at Concepción, along the Rio Paraguay, among grass and shrubs). Found 1966 by A. M. Friedrich of Asunción.

F. curvispina Buin. & Bred.
Bo. simple, cylindric, to 5 cm h. and 3 cm br., ± greyish-green; **Ri.** c. 32, vertical, c. 2 mm apart, divided into small round Tub. 1 mm h. and 2 mm br.; **Ar.** oval, with some yellow felt, soon glabrous; **Sp.** in a dense web around the Bo., brush-like in the crown, ± bent and tangled, white to yellowish, hyaline, greyish-brown below; **Rsp.** c. 14, 4–6 mm lg.; **Csp.** 1, of the same length; **Fl.** 30 mm lg., 26 mm br., yellow; **Ov.** bristly above, glabrous below; **Sep.**

and **Pet.** lanceolate; **An.** yellow; **style** and **Sti.** cream; **Fr.** 18 mm lg., 12 mm br., with greyish-white H. and long brown Br.; **S.** boat-shaped, chestnut-brown.—Brazil (Rio Grande do Sul, N. of Santiago, on flat rocks).

F. dadakii Frič: **Frailea pygmaea** v. **dadakii** (Frič) Backbg.

F. deminuta Buin. & Bred. 1973
Bo. simple, flat, to 1 cm h., 2.5 cm $\varnothing$, dark green; **Ri.** 17–20, vertical, in Tub. 3 mm $\varnothing$; **Ar.** 1.5 mm lg., 1 mm br., 1.5 mm apart, with light brown felt, later glabrous; **Sp.** thin, amber-coloured; **Rsp.** c. 15, 3.5–4 mm lg., radiating, pectinate; **Csp.** to 2, often missing, projecting, ± curving, darker than the Rsp.; **Fl.** funnelform, lemon-yellow, 18 mm lg., 20 mm br., with Br. and H. outside; **Sep.** and **Pet.** spatulate, mucronate; **style** 9 mm lg., white with 4 cream Sti.; **Fr.** 13 mm lg., with light brown Br. and H.; **S.** cap-shaped, 1.5–1.7 mm lg., with a glossy brownish-black testa.—Brazil (Rio Grande do Sul, N. of Livramento, at c. 340 m on stony hills, among grass).

F. friedrichii Buin. & Moser
Bo. mostly solitary, to 3 × 3 cm, dark green to coppery-red; **Ri.** to 19, divided into Tub. 4 mm $\varnothing$; **Ar.** oval, with some light brown felt; **Sp.** ± distant, sometimes curving and pectinate, 6 on each side, with a smaller **Csp.** above and below, all 3 mm lg., reddish to horn-coloured; **Fl.** funnelform, 23 mm lg. and br., yellow; **Ov.** 4 mm lg. and br., with Br. and white H.; **Rec.** c. 3–4 mm lg., with Br. and white H.; **Sep.** spatulate, pointed above, with a golden-yellow stripe; **Pet.** spatulate, yellow; **style** yellowish-white, with 8 similarly coloured Sti.; **Fr.** 6–8 mm $\varnothing$, with Br. and woolly H.; **S.** cap-shaped, black, slightly glossy, 1.5 × 1.2 mm.—E. Paraguay (near Chololó-i).
Named for A. M. Friedrich, discoverer of a number of these Fraileas as well as new spec. of Gymnocalycium.

F. fulviseta Buin. & Bred.
Bo. dark green, simple, 7 cm lg., or 11 cm lg. down to the neck-like R.-constriction, 2.2–3 cm $\varnothing$; **R.** napiform; **Ri.** to 20, 2–3 mm apart, divided into round Tub. to 2 mm h., 2–3 mm $\varnothing$; **Ar.** 2–3 mm apart at first, later to 1 mm, oval, with woolly, golden-yellow hairlets at first, becoming glabrous; **Sp.** golden-brown, 1.5–2 mm lg., thin, radiating to pectinate, mostly downwardly directed; **Rsp.** 6–7(–8) on each side, thickened below; **Csp.** 2, one pointing upwards, the other downwards, c. 1.5 mm lg., thickened below; **Fl.** funnelform, 34 mm lg., 38 mm br., yellow; **Tu.** scaly, with yellowish-brown Br. and H.; **Sep.** pointed-spatulate, margin

smooth; **Pet.** spatulate, pointed, 5.5 mm br., margin denticulate; **style** 15 mm lg., white; **Sti.** 9, white, papillose, 4 mm lg.; **Fil.** whitish; **An.** yellow; **Fr.** oval with light brown bristly Ar. and H.; **S.** cap-shaped, with a glossy blackish-brown testa.—Brazil (Rio Grande do Sul, near Sao Francisco de Assis, at 100–200 m, in humous-rich soil between broken rocks. Discovered by Horst in 1969).

F. gracillima (Monv. ex Lem.) Br. & R.
Bo. slender-cylindric, ashen grey to green, to 10 cm h., to 2.5 cm ∅; **Tub.** in c. 13 R., round, 2 mm h.; **Ar.** white at first; **Rsp.** to 16, light, to 1.5 mm lg., thin, ± appressed; **Csp.** mostly 2, darker, projecting, to 5mm lg.; **Fl.** 3 cm lg., yellow; **Pet.** carmine at the base; **Tu.** with white wool and brown Br.; **Fr.** 6 mm ∅, greenish; **S.** glossy, yellowish-brown.—Paraguay. (Fig. 123: 10.)

F. grahliana (Hge. Jr.) Br. & R.
Bo. flattened-spherical, quite freely offsetting, to 4 cm br., brownish-green; **Tub.** in 13 R., scarcely 2 mm h., round; **Ar.** elliptic; **Sp.** 9–11, not appressed, yellow at first, to 3.5 mm lg.; **Fl.** 4 cm br., yellow; **Fr.** yellowish, with yellowish wool and yellow Sp.; **S.** glossy chestnut-brown, cap-shaped.—Paraguay (Rio Paraguari) and Argentina (Misiones, Santa Ana). (Fig. 123: 8.)
This spec. is said to produce smaller Fr. from the bud-stage, these containing fewer S., without any An. being present. Further investigation required.
    v. **rubrispina** Y. Ito: reputedly a form with brownish-red Sp.

F. horstii Ritt. (FR 1353)
Bo. longer than in F. gracillima; **Ri.** 20–33; **Rsp.** 15–20; **Csp.** 3–6, brown; **Fl.** 4 cm lg., 5 cm ∅ when open; **Tu.** 4–5 mm lg.; **Pet.** 27 mm lg., 2.5–4 mm br., ± linear.—Brazil (Rio Grande do Sul, Cacapava).

F. ignacionensis Buin. & Moser
Bo. simple, 2.5–3 cm h., 4–4.5 cm br., green; **Ri.** to 18, divided into flat Tub. 6 mm ∅; **Ar.** oval, with brown felt; **Sp.** ± pectinate, 5 on each side, one shorter Sp. below and one or several small Ssp. above, to 5 mm lg., light to reddish-brown; **Csp.** mostly 1, to 4 mm lg., darker reddish-brown; **Fl.** funnelform, 24–30 mm lg., 20–45 mm br., sulphur-yellow; pericarpel 5.5 mm lg., 4 mm br., with light brown Br. and white H., the 3 mm lg. Rec. similarly; **Sep.** spatulate, pointed above, whitish to pale yellow; **Pet.** similarly but longer and broader, sulphur-yellow; **style** 10 mm lg., yellowish-white; **Sti.** 5, 2 mm lg., yellowish-white; **Fil.** yellowish-white; **An.** yellow; **Fr.** spherical, 5–6 mm ∅, with light brown Br. and grey H.; **S.** cap-shaped,

brownish-black, slightly glossy.—Paraguay (near San Ignacio).

F. knippeliana (Quehl) Br. & R.
Bo. cylindric, simple, 4 cm lg., 2 cm ∅, bright grass-green (Quehl), glossy; **Tub.** in c. 15 R., flat, 3 mm br.; **Ar.** yellowish, with white H. projecting through the felt but soon dropping; **Rsp.** 14, ± appressed; **Csp.** 2, indistinguishable at first, 3–5 mm lg.; **Sp.** amber-coloured at first, the Csp. becoming darker; **Fl.** to 2.5 cm lg., with a red stripe outside; **Pet.** light yellow; **S.** 1–2 mm lg., chestnut-brown.—Paraguay. (Fig. 123: 9.)*

F. lepida Buin. & Bred. 1973
Bo. simple, cylindric, to 5 cm lg., 1–1.5 cm ∅, dark to blackish-green; **Ri.** to 18, vertical, divided into round Tub.; **Ar.** at the tip of the Tub., 1 mm lg., c. 2 mm apart, white-woolly, becoming glabrous; **Rsp.** 18–20, radiating, 1.5–2 mm lg., thin, white; **Csp.** 2–4, directed vertically upwards, 2.5–3 mm lg., brown, stouter than the Rsp.; **Fl.** funnelform, 19 mm lg., 22 mm br., yellow, with light brown Br. and greyish-white H. outside; **Sep.** spatulate, 9–10 mm lg., lemon-yellow; **Pet.** pointed, glossy, lemon-yellow; **Fil.** light yellow; **An.** yellow; **style** light yellow, with 5–6 yellowish-white Sti.; **Fr.** 8 mm ∅; **S.** cap-shaped, testa glossy, brownish-black.—Brazil (Rio Grande do Sul, W. of Dom Pedrito, E. of Livramento, c. 200 m, among dense pampa grass on broken rocks). Found by L. Horst.

F. mammifera Buin. & Bred.
Bo. simple, rarely offsetting, c. 3 cm h., to 2.5 cm br., glossy dark green; **Ri.** to 17, c. 3 mm br., divided conspicuously into round or broad, sometimes ± tapering Tub. 2–3 mm h., to 2.5 mm br. below, blackish-green on the underside; **Ar.** on the upper side of the Tub., oval, 1.25–1.50 mm lg., 1 mm br., with golden-brown felt at first, later glabrous; **Sp.** spreading to directed sideways or ± pectinate, 3 on either side, sometimes 1–2 directed downwards, with fine golden-yellow H., later dirty white, 2.5–3 mm lg.; **Csp.** absent; **Fl.** funnelform, light yellow, 25 mm lg. and ∅; **Pet.** light yellow, with a red fleck below; **Fr.** 17 mm lg., 10 mm br., spherical; **S.** boat-shaped, glossy, chestnut-brown.—Brazil (Rio Grande do Sul, N. of Pedrito, c. 250 m, on grassy, rather rocky, sites). Discovered by L. Horst.

---

* G. Moser, Austria (Nat. Cact. & Suc. J., G.B., 1977) reports: Spec. re-collected by A. M. Friedrich of Paraguay, after apparently being lost, and he sent it to Moser for study. Plant offsets freely, but only when older; simple plants produce large Fl., while those of caespitose specimens are smaller and slender.—This tallies with the first description of the Fl. (Quehl. MfK. 1926). [Translator.]

F. matoana Buin. & Bred.
Bo. simple, depressed-spherical, to 11 mm h., 25 mm ∅, red to dark brown; **Ri.** c. 15, divided into small, ± square Tub.; **Ar.** oval, to 2 mm lg., 1 mm br., with greyish-white felt, c. 2 mm apart; **Sp.** radiating, ± pectinate, 4 to either side, 1–2 directed downwards, sometimes with 1–2 smaller upwardly directed Sp.; **Csp.** sometimes 1, shorter, straight; all **Sp.** rust-coloured; **Fl.** funnelform, 21 mm lg., 20 mm ∅, yellow; **Tu.** with white H., and light brown Br. 11 mm lg.; **Sep.** spatulate, 6–13 mm lg.; **style** 12 mm lg., yellowish-white, with 8 Sti.; **Fil.** yellow; **Fr.** 5–6 mm lg., 6–7 mm br.; **S.** chestnut-brown.— Brazil (Mato Grosso (hence the specific name), Serra de Maracaju, at 270–300 m, on sandy soil among grass and small shrubs). Found by W. Uebelmann and L. Horst, 1967.

F. moseriana Buin. & Bred.
Bo. forming groups, single heads to 3.5 cm ∅ and to 2.5 cm h., green; **Ri.** to 15, divided into round Tub., each with a lunate fleck beneath it; **Ar.** round, with dirty yellow felt, soon becoming glabrous; **Sp.** concealing the crown, radiating, curving somewhat to the Bo., ± pectinate, 5 to each side, to 5 mm lg., lowest one shorter; **Csp.** sometimes 1, to 4 mm lg., projecting upwards; **Fl.** 24 mm lg., light yellow; **S.** cap-shaped, glossy, chestnut-brown.—E. Paraguay (near Ytá-Ybaté, on the high plateau). Discovered by A. M. Friedrich of Asunción.

F. perumbilicata Ritt. (FR 1385)
Bo. spherical, simple, 2–3 cm ∅; **Ri.** 16–19, tuberculate, ± flat; **Ar.** brownish, 0.7 mm lg., 2–3 mm apart; **Sp.** brown, sharply acicular, twisted, ± spreading; **Rsp.** 6–10, 2–3 mm lg.; **Csp.** mostly absent, occasionally 1; **Fl.** 34–40 mm lg.; **Ov.** covered with white wool and dark red Br.; **Tu.** green below, yellow above, 7 mm lg.; **Fil.** mid-yellow, lower ones 12 mm lg., upper ones 6 mm; **style** yellow.—Brazil (Rio Grande do Sul, between Livramento and Passo da Garda).
v. **spinosior** Ritt.: distinguished by its 14–18 **Ri.**, with the **Ar.** 1.5–2 mm apart; **Rsp.** 8–11, paler, with a further 1–3 Ssp.—Brazil (Rio Grande do Sul, Livramento and northwards).

F. phaeodisca Spec.: **Frailea pygmaea** var. **phaeodisca** (Speg.) Y. Ito.

F. pseudograhliana Frič & Krzgr.: not validly described. The plant cultivated under this name is light green, with lanceolate Ar., blackish-brown Sp. and a similarity to F. schilinzkyana (Hge. Jr.) Br. & R.

F. pseudopulcherrima (hort.) Borg (1951), validly described by Y. Ito (1957).

Bo. mostly depressed-spherical, offsetting later, deep green; **Tub.** in c. 15 R., round, flat; **Sp.** c. 10, thin, 3 mm lg., spreading and sometimes recurved, brown at first, then more greyish; **Fl.** funnelform, c. 2 cm lg., 3 cm ∅, with grey wool and brown Sp.— Uruguay. (Fig. 123: 4, 18.)
In "Die Cact.", Vol. III, I showed in Fig. 1593 a plant which may be this spec.: Sp. sometimes fewer than 10, Fl. somewhat smaller; but variable Fl.-size has already been remarked in Frailea by other authors.

F. pulcherrima (Ar.) Backbg.
Bo. to 5 cm h., to 2 cm ∅, dark green; **Ri.** 19–21, low, with flat Tub.; **Rsp.** 10–12, white, 1–2 mm lg.; **Csp.** 0–1, somewhat stouter; **Fl.** to 2 cm lg., to 3 cm ∅, yellow; **Fr.** 1 cm lg.—Uruguay (Paso de los Toros). (Fig. 123: 13?)
The Rsp. may also vary to light brownish.

F. pullispina Backbg.—Descr. Cact. Nov. III: 6. 1963
Bo. simple, subspherical, bluish-green, to c. 3.5 cm ∅, c. 2.5 cm h.; **Ri.** c. 22, to 4 mm br., divided by acute transverse notches into oval Tub.; **Ar.** with dirty white felt, somewhat elongated, c. 2 mm apart; **Rsp.** to c. 12, appressed, recurved, dark brown, somewhat lighter above; **Csp.** 0; bud with light greyish-white wool and reddish-brown Br.; **Fl.** c. 3 cm ∅, yellow; **S.** glossy blackish, rimless capshaped.—Bolivia (Roboré). (Fig. 120 above.)
v. **atrispina** Backbg., l.c.: Distinguished as follows: more frequently has 4 instead of 5(–6) pairs of **Rsp.**, these blackish-brown, sometimes with a very fine upper one, predominantly thickened below.—Bolivia (San Juan). (Fig. 120 below);
v. **centrispina** Backbg., l.c.: Differs as follows: epidermis darker bluish-green; **Ar.** with more white wool persisting longer; later often 1 Csp. in the upper part of the Ar., sometimes even a second one which is fine; **Sp.** all dark brown, not blackish.—Bolivia (Roboré-Santiago). (Fig. 121.) [Haage adds: Acc. Lau, identical with F. chiquitana.]

F. pumila (Lem.) Br. & R.
Bo. spherical, offsetting freely, deep green, sometimes reddish; **Ri.** 13–15, ± finely tuberculate; **Ar.** small; **Rsp.** (9–)12–14, to 5 mm lg., bristly, mostly bent; **Csp.** 1–2(–3), scarcely distinguishable; **Fl.** 2 cm lg., with white wool and brown Br.; **Pet.** yellow, ± spatulate, sometimes rounded above, little recurving; **Fr.** pea-sized, green, with red Sc.; **S.** black (?blackish-brown), cap-shaped.—Paraguay and adjacent areas of Argentina. (Fig. 123: 7.)

F. pygmaea (Speg.) Br. & R.
Bo. simple to offsetting, spherical to slightly elongated, to c. 3 cm lg. and ⌀, dirty to light greyish-green; **Ri.** 13–21, with minute Tub.; **Ar.** grey; **Sp.** 6–9, bristly, 1–4 mm lg., appressed, white; **Fl.** to 2.5 cm lg., 3 cm ⌀; **Pet.** yellow, lanceolate; **Tu.** with reddish felt and Br.; **Fr.** spherical; **S.** cap-shaped.—Uruguay, Argentina (Entre Rios). (Fig. 123: 16.)

v. **atrofusca** Backbg.: **Sp.** dark reddish-brown at first;

v. **aurea** (Backbg.) Backbg.: **Ar.** brown(!); **Sp.** golden-yellow;

v. **dadakii** (Frič) Backbg.: **Sp.** brownish at first, becoming whitish, fairly strongly appressed (Fig. 123: 16);

v. **phaeodisca** (Speg.) Y. Ito: **Ar.** brown(!); **Sp.** hyaline.—Uruguay (Tacuarembó).

The first 3 of these varieties have only been reported from Uruguay (Montevideo area). An interesting and attractively variable spec.

F. schilinzkyana (Hge. Jr.) Br. & R.
Bo. broadly spherical, offsetting to form mats, single heads to c. 4 cm ⌀, light green; **Tub.** in 10–13 R., 6-sided to ± round, c. 1.5 mm h.; **Ar.** lanceolate; **Sp.** (10–)12–14, appressed to ± projecting, 2–3 mm lg., thin, blackish; **Fl.** to 3.5 cm lg., rarely opening, but then fairly large; **Tu.** and **Ov.** green with white wool, brown Br. and brownish Sc.; **Sep.** reddish outside; **Pet.** sulphur-yellow; **Fr.** 5 mm ⌀; **S.** chestnut-brown, cap-shaped.—Argentina (Misiones), Paraguay (Rio Paraguari). (Fig. 123: 17.)

F. uhligiana Backbg.—Descr. Cact. Nov. III: 6. 1963.
Bo. simple, plants cultivated in the open reddish-brown to suffused red, gradually becoming greener when in a glasshouse, to c. 3.5 cm ⌀, 2.5 cm h.; **Ri.** to c. 25, to 5 mm br., not really tuberculate but appearing slightly so at first because of weak horizontal furrows which eventually become flatter, leaving only slight protuberances; **Ar.** ± glabrous, with very little brown felt; **Rsp.** 4–5 pairs, very fine, c. 2 mm lg., light brown at first, darker below; **Csp.** 0; buds with light brownish wool; **Fl.** yellow, 3 cm ⌀; **S.** blackish, rounded cap-shaped, with a rim.—Bolivia (San José). (Fig. 122.)

F. ybatense Buin. & Moser 1971
Bo. simple, flattened-rounded, to 4 cm ⌀, to 2.5 cm h., mid to dark green; **Ri.** to 24, divided into Tub. 6 mm ⌀, mostly reddish to violet; **Ar.** oval, with ivory felt; **Sp.** ± curving, pectinate, radiating, 5 on either side, directed laterally, 1 each directed up and down; **Csp.** rarely 1; all **Sp.** scaberulous,

hyaline; **Fl.** funnelform, 30 mm lg. and ⌀, lemon-yellow; **pericarpel** 8 mm lg., 5 mm br., glabrous below, with brown Br. and white H. in the upper part; **Rec.** 5 mm lg., with similar indumentum; **Sep.** spatulate, mucronate, dirty yellow with a green stripe; **Pet.** spatulate, pointed, finely ciliate, light lemon-yellow; **style** 10 mm lg., light yellow; **Sti.** 5, 3 mm lg., yellowish-white; **Fil.** light yellow; **An.** 1 mm lg., yellow; **Fr.** spherical, 7 mm ⌀, with light brown Br. and white H.; **S.** cap-shaped, dark brown, semi-glossy, testa with flat Tub.—Paraguay (near Ytá-Ybaté, SE. of Asunción, in red sandy soil among stones).

Glandulicactus Backbg. (213)

A group of species with distinctive characters, regarded by Britton & Rose and also by Hester as an independent genus: ribs very tuberculate, with elongated areoles, flower-insertion close to the body, glands nearer the spine-clusters. The main spines are relatively long and brightly coloured, the flowers fairly small and semi-funnelform with a very short tube and the petals erect; the black seeds are laterally compressed and curved to ± kidney-shaped; the fleshy fruit is edible.—Distribution: USA (W. Texas) to Central Mexico. [(G).]

G. crassihamatus (Web.) Backbg.
Bo. ± subspherical, bluish-green, simple; **Ri.** c. 13, ± deeply tuberculate; **Ar.** to 1 cm lg., 8 mm br., very felty, with Gl. close to the Sp.-cluster; **Rsp.** 8, to 2 cm lg.; **Csp.** 1 at first, later to 5, stoutly subulate, one main Sp. to 3 cm lg., porrect, hooked; **Sp.** ± red, lighter or flecked above; **Fl.** only half-open, 2 cm lg., purple, bordered lighter.—Mexico (Querétaro).

G. uncinatus (Gal.) Backbg. (T.)
Bo. oblong, with spindle-shaped R., to c. 20 cm h.; **Ri.** mostly c. 13, deeply indented; **Ar.** with the typical Gl., large, flat, yellow, with a ring of yellow H.; **Rsp.** 7–8, 2.5–5 cm lg., the upper ones flattened, straw to yellow, the lower ones terete, hooked, red; **Csp.** to 4, the 3 upper ones to 2.5 cm lg., robust, the lowest one very long, to over 9 cm lg., flattened, mostly straw-coloured below, reddish above, hooked; **Fl.** to 2.5 cm lg., half-open, brownish-purple; **Fr.** ovoid, to 2.5 cm lg.; **S.** compressed, bent, glossy, to 1.4 mm lg.—Mexico (Chihuahua to San Luis Potosí).

v. **wrightii** (Eng.) Backbg.: main **Sp.** longer, to 15 cm lg., **Csp.** only 1; **Fl.** to 3.5 cm lg., dark purple.—USA (Texas) to N. Mexico (Chihuahua). (Fig. 124.)

Grusonia F. Reichb. (9)

This genus is regarded as including only plants resembling Cylindropuntia which, like the type of the genus, have continuous ribs, spines with reduced sheaths, and glochids present only in the newest areoles and on the fruit; the flowers must be genuinely terminal, at least where solitary; in the type-species they are borne on the axis, and only from shortly below that if the stem-tip is already bearing another flower. No investigations have yet been made to show whether all the species named below should in fact be regarded as belonging to Grusonia. G. hamiltonii Gates has not yet been completely validly described, and since its flowers arise more around than at the apex, it is possible that this plant is better referred to Cylindropuntia even although the ribs, which are somewhat tuberculate, are continuous. 3 spec. have been referred to this genus.—Distribution: Mexico (Coahuila and Baja California). (Vigorous-growing.)

G. bradtiana (Coult.) Br. & R. (T.)
Bo. cylindric, forming large colonies to 2 m br.; **St.** light green, segmented, to 7 cm $\emptyset$; **Ri.** 8–10, low, slightly tuberculate; **Ar.** to 1.5 cm apart; **Glo.** present only in flowering Ar.; **L.** 8 mm lg.; **Sp.** 15–25, yellowish-brown, soon white, to 3 cm lg., Sh. missing; **Fl.** to 4 cm $\emptyset$, yellow; **Ov.** with bristle-like Sp., white wool and Glo.; **Fr.** ellipsoid, deeply umbilicate.—Mexico (Coahuila). (Fig. 125.)

G. (?) hamiltonii Gates (as yet without a Latin diagnosis)
Bo. laxly branching, often prostrate; **Ri.** continuous, slightly tuberculate, c. 8; **Sp.** 2–3 at first, short, later c. 12, thin, 1–2 Csp. to 1.5 cm lg., directed downwards, $\pm$ compressed, pink below; **Fl.** around the apex, yellow to white; **Pet.** tapering; **Fr.** ?—Mexico (Baja California, Hamilton Ranch).

G. (?) santamaria Baxt.
Bo. cylindric, to 60 cm h.; **St.** to 3.75 cm $\emptyset$; **Ri.** 8–9, slightly spiralled; **Sp.** c. 20, 8–12 cm lg., purple-reddish, occasionally with a short Sh.; **Fl.** white inside, with a pinkish-red M.-vein, on the 2nd day uniformly light pink; **Fil.** green; **style** white; **Ov.** with spiny Br., wool and Glo., 2.5 cm lg., 1.2 cm $\emptyset$.—Mexico (Baja California, Magdalena Is., S. part of Santa Maria Bay).

Gymnantha Y. Ito (1957): **Weingartia** Werd. (1937).

Gymnanthocereus Backbg.: **Seticereus** Backbg.

Gymnocactus Backbg. (203)

A group of species with very uniform characters: the spination is mostly finer and predominantly lighter, the tubercles are fairly slender so that the ribs remain clearly recognisable, and the apex has conspicuous light-coloured wool. The medium-sized flowers are mostly purple, otherwise pink or white. The diagnostic characters are the naked ovary and fruit. The seeds are probably always matt black. Another typical feature is the $\pm$ well-developed elongated areole, which sometimes appears like a short furrow, from which the flowers arise. F. Buxbaum separated the species with a neck-like root-constriction, and put them into his genus Rapicactus F. Buxb. & Oehme; but this segregation cannot be justified since roots of this type are well known in other genera, e.g. Weingartia, Neochilenia or Neoporteria; and there are no diagnostic differences in the floral characters. The Genus Turbinicarpus, with similarly naked flowers and fruits, is closely related to Gymnocactus but the bodies are considerably smaller throughout, the spination is softer, with the spines mostly early deciduous, and the fruits have a minute lid.—Distribution: From NE. Mexico to Zacatecas and Hidalgo. [(R): taprooted spec. are better grafted.]

G. aguirreanus Glass & Foster
Bo. mostly simple, 5 cm h., 7 cm $\emptyset$, frosted; **Ri.** often divided into thick lax Tub. 1 cm lg., 15 mm br., turning coppery or purplish-red in the sun, epidermis rough, granular; **Sp.** orange-brown, dense at the apex, upper ones brownish, orange-yellow below, becoming greyish-white with black tips; **Csp.** 2 or more, like the Rsp., 12–15 mm lg.; **Fl.** small, 18 mm lg., yellowish or reddish-yellow; **Sep.** and **Pet.** with a broad reddish M.-stripe and tip; **Fr.** a naked berry, bronze to greenish-purple, c. 12 mm lg.; **S.** 1.5 mm lg., testa dark purplish-red to black, with small Tub.—Mexico (S. Coahuila, Sierra de la Paila, Cañon Verde, also in the mountains of Cuatrocienegas).

G. beguinii (Web.) Backbg.
Bo. simple, becoming oblong, bluish-green, to 15 cm h., to c. 8 cm $\emptyset$; **Ri.** tuberculate, in **Isp.** 13 : 21; **Ar.** quite strongly white-woolly at first; **Rsp.** mostly 12, to 17 mm lg. or shorter; **Csp.** 1, to c. 3 cm lg.; **Sp.** hyaline, Csp. lighter below and above midway dark brown to black and relatively stout; **Fl.** to 3.5 cm lg., $\pm$ violet, to brownish inside.—Mexico (Coahuila, Zacatecas).
  v. **senilis** (hort.): **Rsp.** and **Csp.** longer, finer, the darker colour of the latter extending less far down the Sp.; sometimes to 3 Csp.;
  v. **smithii** (Mühlpfrdt.) Backbg.: **Csp.** 4, stouter, mostly rather shorter than in the type; **Rsp.** to c.

25.—Mexico (San Luis Potosí).

G. conothelos (Reg. & Klein) Backbg.: **Thelocactus conothelos** (Reg. & Klein) Knuth.

G. gielsdorfianus (Werd.) Backbg.
Bo. spherical, simple or rarely offsetting, matt yellowish to bluish-green; **Tub.** conical to pyramidal, spiralled; **Ar.** with only a short furrow-extension; **Rsp.** 6–8, thin-subulate, ± curving, to c. 2 cm lg., dark brown and blackish-tipped at first, becoming chalky; **Csp.** mostly 0; **Fl.** to c. 2.5 cm lg., white.—Mexico (Tamaulipas, Jaumave).

G. horripilus (Lem.) Backbg.
Bo. offsetting quite freely to form groups, single heads subspherical, ± bluish-green, to 9 cm h. and ∅; **Tub.** ± pyramidal, in **Isp.** 8:13, scarcely 1 cm h.; **Rsp.** 9–12(–16), to 15 mm lg. or a little more; **Csp.** 1, sometimes missing, somewhat longer; **Sp.** all yellowish-white at first, reddish-brown above, becoming white with a dark tip; **Fl.** to 3 cm lg., purple.—Mexico (Hidalgo, Barranca Meztitlan).

G. knuthianus (Böd.) Backbg.
Bo. small, subspherical, sometimes offsetting, single heads to 6 cm ∅, glossy, dark leaf-green; **Tub.** in 20 or more spiralled R.; flowering **Ar.** more woolly; **Rsp.** 18–20, 8 mm lg., white, thin, with a yellowish base at first; **Csp.** 1, to 1 cm lg., little stouter, sometimes dark-tipped; **Fl.** 2.5 cm lg., light lilac-pink; **Fr.** ovoid, glossy green to brown.—Mexico (San Luis Potosí, Villar).

G. mandragora (Frič) Backbg.
Bo. simple, spherical, to c. 6 cm ∅, greyish-green, **R.** with a constricted neck; **Tub.** crowded, ± 4-sided; **Ar.** white at first; **Rsp.** c. 12, radiating, subulate, white; **Csp.** mostly 2, hyaline, brown-tipped, c. 2 cm lg., often also 2 thinner **Ssp.**; **Fl.** 2 cm lg., 2.5 cm ∅, white, with a slender pink dorsal stripe.—Mexico.

G. saueri (Böd.) Backbg. (T.)
Bo. simple, compressed-spherical, to 4 cm h., to c. 6 cm ∅, bluish-green; crown with much white wool; **Tub.** in 13 R., flattened-conical, c. 5 mm h.; **Rsp.** 12–14, to 1.5 cm lg., acicular, hyaline, the upper ones dark-tipped; **Csp.** 1, curving upwards, to 2 cm lg., blackish-brown, lighter below; **Fl.** 1.5 cm lg., 2 cm ∅, white, sometimes a delicate pink in the centre.—Mexico (Tamaulipas, near S. Vicente).

G. saussieri (Web.) Backbg.: **Thelocactus saussieri** (Web.) Berg.

G. subterraneus (Backbg.) Backbg.

Bo. rather oblong, the taproot having a long neck, single heads ± clavate, to c. 5 cm lg. (or longer if grafted), to c. 3 cm ∅, leaf-green; **Ar.** very white-woolly at first; **Rsp.** c. 16, to 6 mm lg., white, radiating; **Csp.** 2, one of them directed upwards, to 2 cm lg., blackish-grey, also several Br.-Sp. over 3 cm lg., white, ± appressed; **Fl.** c. 3 cm ∅, pinkish-violet.—Mexico (Nuevo León, Tamaulipas). [Locality amended by Haage.]

G. valdezianus (Möll.) Backbg. ("Die Cact." V: 2863. 1961)
Bo. dwarf, with a taproot, rarely offsetting, single heads to c. 2.5 cm ∅; **crown** with white wool; **Tub.** in 13 spiralled R., slightly glossy, bluish-green, minute; **Sp.** c. 30, to 2 mm lg., ± hairlike and feathery, appressed; **Fl.** to 2 cm lg., violet-pink.—Mexico (Coahuila, near Saltillo).
I refer the spec. to this genus since it lacks the hatchet-shaped Tub. characteristic of Pelecyphora.
    v. **albiflorus** (Paz.) Backbg. n.comb. (Pelecyphora valdeziana v. albiflora Paz., Kaktusy 129. 1960) has white Fl.

G. viereckii (Werd.) Backbg.
Bo. simple or offsetting, to 7 cm ∅, bluish-green, matt, subspherical; **crown** with dense white wool; **Tub.** in c. 15–18 ± continuous R., c. 6 mm h.; **Rsp.** c. 20, 1 cm lg., radiating, acicular, white; **Csp.** 4, cruciform, eventually over 2 cm lg., brown above midway, black-tipped, white below, sometimes also 1–3 rather shorter, finer Ssp.; **Fl.** c. 2 cm lg., delicate violet-pink.—Mexico (Tamaulipas). (Fig. 126.)

G. ysabelae (K. Schlange) Backbg.
Bo. depressed-spherical, to c. 6 cm h., 7–9 cm ∅; **crown** woolly; **Tub.** in c. 20 R., 5 mm h., 4-angled below; **Rsp.** 16–20, to 7 mm lg., white, tipped yellowish-brown, yellowish below; **Csp.** 1, stouter, curving upwards, to 9 mm lg., bluish to brownish-black above, white below, or dark ± throughout; **Fl.** 1 cm lg., 0.75 cm ∅, ivory, greenish below.—Mexico (San Luis Potosí, Rancho El Vergel).
    v. **brevispinus** (K. Schlange) Backbg.: **Tub.** shorter, slighter; **Sp.** shorter, scarcely interlacing.

Gymnocalycium Pfeiff. (116)

Recognised as early as 1845 as a separate genus, and separated from the collective concept of "Echinocactus"; during the period of omnibus genera it once again lost its identity, and was only recognised again by Britton & Rose. It is one of the largest genera of S. American spherical cacti and the species vary greatly in size, some being minute, others quite large, and the ribs are mostly ± tuberculate. Flower-size is equally variable, ranging from quite small and more bellshaped to funnelform, to quite large and funnelform. Vaupel (Zeitschr.f.Sukkde, 116. 1923) has a longitudinal section which shows quite clearly the unique arrangement of tube and ovary in G. damsii, which justifies the expression "ovary-tube". However this is not uniformly long and can even be quite short, so that a clear line of reduction is recognisable. The uniform diagnostic character of the entire genus lies in the glabrous flowers with distinct scales. The fruits are similarly scaly, ± elongated to quite long —correspondingly shorter in the more strongly reduced flower-form of the "Lafaldensia"— and while they often show an attractive blue bloom, the colouring varies widely. The seeds show marked differences of shape and colour: smaller or larger, ± matt black or brown, with or without a conspicuous hilum-margin, while one species even has a corky testa.

B. Schütz of Brünn ("Fričiana Řada I"—Zpráv. C. 1, 3. 1962) attempted to classify the seeds according to Frič's "Subgroups according to Seed-Type" (Kreuzinger, "Verzeichnis", 13. 1935): Ovatisemineae, Macrosemineae, Trichosemineae, Microsemineae and Muscosemineae. Failing any German version of the text one can only say that this would be an aid to identification if ... seeds were available; but that is all, unless of course any firm concepts for classification are offered, and this I am unable to gather from the Czech-language text.

But if this is so, it should be pursued throughout the entire family: in Thrixanthocereus, for instance, the 3 species should be divided into 2 groups: 2 of them with seeds very closely resembling Astrophytum, and the third having hard, black, round seeds. In other words, a classification on this basis must not be taken too far. It has already become apparent that seed-typing is not the complete answer for systematic evaluation. I have therefore based my classification on the characters of the plants themselves: they are always more readily available than seeds, and are of greater importance for unravelling problems and making a diagnosis, because they are uniform. The following arrangement in Series thus seems preferable. Many of these plants grow well on their own roots but in general grafting leads to more rapid growth and a greater wealth of flowers. The genus has one of the largest distributions of all the genera of spherical cacti, especially in its North–South axis— Distribution: Bolivia, Paraguay, S. Brazil, Uruguay and Argentina (from its N. frontier and thence far southwards). [(R), (G).]

Many species are rather variable or extremely so. G. Frank showed variability of this kind (Kakt. u. a. Sukk. 15: 6, 116–117. 1964) with his illustrations of

G. spegazzinii; but in this case there is at least some uniformity of rib-shape and spine-curvature although spine-length varies strongly. The problems of description are far greater with species showing as great a variability as G. hybopleurum, ochotenai, mazanense, etc., as is demonstrated by illustrations of the first two named species. In cases like this, it is essential to see a whole shipment of plants of a species before any judgment can be made as to the range of variability, the principal variants then being described as varieties, with transitional forms perhaps connecting them. This is the only way to build up an approximately accurate picture of the variability occurring in natural populations. The validity of these remarks is most apparent if one thinks of Tephrocactus articulatus where the varietal names fully reflect the range of different forms; and yet the American method, suppressing all varietal names, permits only a single name (in this case an incorrect one: Opuntia glomerata), thus failing either to convey any impression of the possible variability, or to assist our understanding of the individual stages. Even Spegazzini in his day recognised this with certain Argentinian species, correctly pointing out that too much was better than too little, since the whole purpose of a description is to convey a picture of Nature, within the limits of our knowledge. Unfortunately quite extraordinary variations sometimes occur in flower-colour, not only in Gymnocalycium (e.g. G. baldianum, oenanthemum, mihanovichii, etc.) but even more so in certain other S. American species such as Lobivia famatimensis. Because of this, even a colour-scale is of little help, even if available; and what is needed is a carefully formulated and fully comprehensible statement of the facts. Here the basic requirement is first that one should know the range of variability in colour, not only of flowers but also (as in Copiapoa) of spines, cephalium, etc. More important than any standardized information regarding colour, with the obvious difficulties this involves, is at least a brief indication of the range of variability; otherwise unjustifiable "novelties" are the result. But there may well be no completely satisfactory solution to these particular difficulties.

The following Series (indicated by the number in brackets after the specific name) will make it easier for the user to find any species he is seeking:

1. Lafaldensia Backbg.: small-stemmed plants, offsetting freely; flowers subapical, smaller;

2. Hybogona Backbg.: larger to medium-sized plants; flowers ± subapical, funnelform;

3. Schickendantziana Backbg.: larger to medium-sized plants; flowers with the ovary-tube more slender and often curving,

often appearing lower on the body; fruit ± spindle-shaped.

G. albispinum Backbg. (1)
Bo. small, offsetting, single heads spherical to ± oblong; **Ri.** c. 14, only 4 mm br.; **Ar.** crowded; **Sp.** bristly, fine, white, c. 25, to 1 cm lg., centrals scarcely differentiated, brownish below; **Fl.** to 3 cm ∅, delicate lilac-pink, rotate; **Fr.** oblong-spherical.—N. Argentina (Córdoba).

G. andreae (Böd.) Backbg. (2)
Bo. spherical, fairly large, offsetting, dark bluish-green, often suffused bronze-colour, to c. 5 cm ∅; **Ri.** 8, flattened-rounded, to 1.5 cm br.; **Rsp.** (5–)7, appressed, matt white, brownish below; **Csp.** 1–3, as long or somewhat shorter, rough, blackish-brownish at first; **Fl.** to 4.5 cm ∅, sulphur-yellow; **Fr.** little elongated, bluish-green.—Argentina (Córdoba).
  v. **grandiflorum** Krainz & Andreae: **Bo.** stouter; **Ri.** 11; **Sp.** longer, mostly bent; **bud** rounded (cylindric in the type); **Fl.** opening in the morning (afternoon, in the type), larger;
  v. **svecianum** Pazout: **Sp.** short; **Fl.** smaller than in the type, brownish outside, glossy white inside; **Tu.** short. Is it really a variety of this spec.?

G. anisitsii (K. Sch.) Br. & R. (3)
Bo. becoming quite elongated, to over 10 cm lg., leaf-green; **Ri.** 11, with chin-like protuberances; **Ar.** elliptic; **Sp.** 5–7(–9), not clearly differentiated, matt whitish, somewhat angular, darker above; **Fl.** to 4 cm lg., numerous on larger plants, white; **Fr.** 2.5 cm lg., 1 cm ∅, red.—Paraguay (Rio Tigatiyami).

| G. antherosacos Ritt. (FR 964): not yet described.

G. antherostele Ritt.: an undescribed name.

G. artigas Hert. (2)
Bo. mostly ± spherical, flat at first, to 8 cm ∅, to 3 cm h., dark green; **Ri.** 6–8–10; **Tub.** 6-sided; **Sp.** 3–5(–6), to 2 cm lg.; **Fl.** 5 cm lg. and br., unisexual, lemon-yellow.—Uruguay (Blanquillo). Similar in habit to G. uruguayense (Ar.) Br. & R.

G. asterium Y. Ito (2)
Bo. flattened-spherical, sometimes raised in the centre, to c. 10 cm ∅, greyish or brownish-green; **Ri.** 7–11, little prominent; **Tub.** ± chin-like; **Sp.** 3–5, ± projecting, dark at first; **Fl.** 6–6.5 cm lg., fairly broadly funnelform, white; **Fr.** cylindric, ± pruinose.—Argentina (Córdoba). The first name, based on a homonym, was G. stellatum (Speg.) Speg.
  v. **minimum** (Paz) Paz. (G. stellatum minimum

Paz, Kaktusy, 132. 1960): smaller, to 6 cm ∅;
v. **paucispinum** Backbg. n.v.: **Bo.** very flat, tapering conically towards the base, as in the type, but even flatter; **Ri.** 10–11, very flat, only faintly tuberculate, with a shallow short transverse furrow; **Sp.** regularly 3, dark to blackish when young or moist; **Fl.** 2 cm lg., 3.2 cm ∅, whitish, with a wine-red throat; **Fil.** cream; **Fr.** greyish-olive, to 3.5 cm lg., with broad, light-bordered Sc.; **S.** glossy brown, the narrow oblong hilum having a prominent margin (Coll. Uhlig and Backeberg, U 2171; collected by Fechser). (Fig. 127.)

G. baldianum (Speg.) Speg. (2)
Bo. depressed-spherical, to 7 cm ∅, dark greyish to bluish-green, with a stout R.-section; **Ri.** 9–11, fewer at first, becoming more distinctly tuberculate; **Sp.** all radial, 5–7, pinkish-grey to horn-grey or ash-grey, ± appressed or directed laterally, somewhat darker below at first; **Fl.** lighter or darker red to ± blood-red, variable.—Argentina (Catamarca).

G. bayrianum Till 1967
Bo. depressed-hemispherical, bluish-green; **R.** shortly napiform; **Ri.** 6–10, broad and flat below, slightly angular in the crown, with a short transverse notch over the Ar.; **Ar.** c. 2 cm apart, with yellowish felt at first, this greying later; **Rsp.** 5, 25–30 mm lg., mostly terete, curving towards the Bo., light brown at first, sometimes dark-tipped; **Csp.** sometimes present, 35–45 mm lg.; **Fl.** subapical, funnelform, c. 62 mm lg., 40 mm ∅, creamy-white, glossy, throat pink; **Tu.** and **Ov.** short, greyish-green, with lilac-pink Sc.; **Sep.** spatulate, c. 22 mm lg., 8 mm br., creamy-white with a metallic glossy M.-stripe; **Pet.** broadly lanceolate, c. 27 mm lg., 6 mm br., creamy-white, glossy, reddish below; **Fil.** long, white, lower ones pressed against the style, others successively up the Tu.-wall, far overtopping the style; **An.** light yellow; **style** with Sti. 16 mm lg., 1.6 mm ∅, greenish-yellow; **Sti.** 11, greenish-yellow; **Fr.** ovoid, ± angular, greyish-green, blue-frosted, with lilac-pink Sc., dehiscing by a longitudinal tear; **S.** small, oblong, slightly bent, testa matt, reddish-brown, finely tuberculate, hilum oval, without a raised border.—Argentina (Tucuman near Medina, c. 1000–1500 m). Close to G. cardenasium and G. spegazzinii, but clearly differentiated by the lighter Bo.-colour, fewer broader Ri., shorter Fl. and oblong S., etc. Named in honour of Alfred Bayr, for many years President of the Austrian Cactus Society.

G. bicolor Schütz—Fričiana Řada 1: 7, 2–3. 1962 (2)
Bo. spherical, dark green, to 15 cm ∅; **Ri.** to c. 17,

with a marked horizontal indentation above the Ar.; **Tub.** nose-like and prominent; **Ar.** c. 2 cm apart, 6 mm lg., more woolly at first; **Rsp.** 11, to 2.5 cm lg., somewhat recurved; **Csp.** 1, scarcely longer; **Sp.** hoary, brownish when damp, upper radials white, lower ones and the Csp. bluish-grey; **Fl.** 4 cm lg., 4.5 cm ∅, white; **S.** matt black, 5 mm lg.—Argentina (Córdoba).

G. bodenbenderianum (Hoss.) Berg. (2)
Bo. closely resembling that of G. asterium, flat and ± disc-like, to c. 8 cm ∅, brownish or greyish-green; **Ri.** 11–14, low, broad, rounded; **Tub.** projecting above a fairly acute transverse furrow, not prominent; **Sp.** 3–5, stout, at first blackish and then greyish-brown, c. 1 cm lg., ± recurved; **Fl.** c. 3.5 cm lg., faded pink, opening only moderately wide; **Fr.** rather short.—Argentina (Córdoba; La Rioja).

G. brachyanthum (Gürke) Br. & R. may be a form of G. monvillei (Lem.) Br. & R.; it has never been re-collected. **Bo.** to 18 cm ∅, to 7 cm h.; **Sp.** to 7, yellowish, to 2.5 cm lg., **Csp.** missing; **Fl.** to 5 cm lg., bellshaped, white to pink.—N. Argentina (Paraguay?).

G. brachypetalum Speg. (2)
Bo. to 10 cm lg., 7 cm ∅, bluish to dark green; **Ri.** 13, with chin-like Tub.; **Ar.** elliptic; **Sp.** 5–7, to 2.5 cm lg., stiffly subulate, yellowish at first; **Csp.** 0; **Fl.** 5.5 cm lg., white; **Tu.** bluish-green.—Argentina (Rio Negro, near Carmen de Patagones). Differentiated from G. gibbosum and G. chubutense by the Pet. being only 2 cm lg.

G. brevistylum Ritt. (FR 1133): no description available.

G. bruchii (Speg.) Hoss. (1)
Bo. small, to 3.5 cm h., to 6 cm ∅, green, very freely offsetting to form cushions, very variable; **Ri.** c. 12; **Tub.** small, not chin-like; **Sp.** thin, bristly-fine, sometimes more brownish below, to c. 10; **Csp.** 0–3, sometimes brownish; **Fl.** slender to ± bellshaped-funnelform or somewhat broader, 3.5(–5) cm lg., delicate to deeper pink, sometimes with a darker M.-stripe; **Fr.** ± spherical.—Argentina (Córdoba). Extremely variable. It is not possible to say whether several forms (described under "G. lafaldense" and rather variable in body-size and spination, sometimes with a darker throat to the flower) can be justified since there is inadequate data on transitional forms.
    v. (f.) **enorme** (Oehme); **Bo.** later forming large cushions, single heads to c. 5 cm ∅ (or rather more?); **Csp.** sometimes 1; **Fl.** to 5.5 cm lg. and br.

A similarly large form Oehme called f. **evolvens**: **Csp.** developing later, to 3, ivory, brownish below; **Fl.** to 4 cm lg. and br.
Fl. can also be suffused ± light pink outside. I have seen large groups, somewhat over 20 cm ∅ and with larger heads, which appeared to be hybrids. The following is more clearly differentiated by the unusual Fl.-form:
    v. **hossei** Backbg.: **Bo.** small, **Pet.** fluttering, the tip sometimes longer or rather elongated.

G. calochlorum (Böd.) Y. Ito (2)
Bo. forming cushions, single heads depressed-spherical, to c. 6 cm ∅, to 4 cm h.; **Ri.** c. 11, tuberculate; **Rsp.** to 9, to 9 mm lg., rough, appressed, ± curving; **Csp.** 0; **Fl.** to 6 cm lg., pale pink, only moderately opening, **Pet.** not revolute; **Tu.** lighter green.—Argentina.
    v. **proliferum** (Backbg.) Backbg.: differentiated by the rather larger, darker, and blue-pruinose **Bo.**; **Fl.** opening fully, brownish-white to pink to pure white, often with a pink throat; **Pet.** much longer, recurved;
    v. **roseiacanthum** hort.: **Bo.** flattened-spherical, c. 35 mm ∅, 25 mm h., bluish-green; **Ri.** 11; **Ar.** round, yellowish; **Sp.** 9, all appressed, twisted, pink; **Fl.** white, large, throat red.—Argentina (Sierra de Córdoba). A dwarf variety from the complex of G. sigelianum.

G. capillaense (Schick) Backbg. (2)
Bo. broadly spherical, offsetting, to c. 9 cm h. and ∅, bluish-green; **Ri.** to c. 13, flat; **Tub.** moderately chin-shaped; **Rsp.** 5, to 1.2 cm lg., yellowish-white; **Csp.** 0; **Fl.** to 7 cm lg., to 6 cm ∅, delicate pinkish-white; **Fr.** frosted light blue, ± clavate.—Argentina (Córdoba).

G. cardenasianum Ritt.—"Taxon", XIII: 4, 144. 1964 (2)
Bo. spherical, greyish or bluish-green; **Ri.** c. 8; **Sp.** 3–5 at first, **Csp.** absent at first, very variable in colour, blackish to light brown, horn-coloured or even lighter, becoming rather long; **Rsp.** 3–6, to 6 cm lg.; **Csp.** later mostly 1–2, to 8 cm lg.; **Fl.** pink to white (with a greenish throat), 5 cm lg., to 8–9 cm ∅; **Tu.** only 1 cm lg.; **Fr.** light brown, c. 8 mm lg., rather dry.—Bolivia (Prov. Mendez, Dept., Tarija, Carrizal) (FR 88).

G. castellanosii Backbg. (2)
Bo. simple, velvety matt bluish-green, to 15 cm h., 10 cm ∅; **Ri.** 10–12, rather broad, with rounded Tub.; **Ar.** with dense felt, yellowish at first, then white; **Rsp.** 5–7, projecting, ± curving; **Csp.** (0–)1; all **Sp.** robust, to 2.5 cm lg., white, dark-tipped; **Fl.** 4.5 cm ∅, bellshaped to funnelform, white suffused pink.—Argentina (Córdoba).

G. centeterium sensu Hoss.: an erroneous name for **G. valnicekianum** Jajó.

G. chiquitanum Card.—"Cactus", 18: 78, 95–96. 1963 (2)
Bo. flattened-spherical, 2–4 cm h., 6–9 cm ∅, greyish-green, also washed reddish; **Ri.** 6–7, 5 mm h., 2.5 cm br., tuberculate; **Ar.** to 2 cm apart, grey, elliptic; **Rsp.** to 6, appressed, ± curving, 1.5–2.3 cm lg.; **Csp.** 0–1, 1.8 cm lg., stoutly acicular, grey, brown-tipped; **Fl.** to 6 cm lg., funnelform; **Tu.** 2.5 cm lg., light purplish-lilac, Sc. white-bordered (also on the Ov.); **Ov.** dark purple; **Sep.** pinkish-brown; **Pet.** lilac-pink, 2.5 cm lg., 6 mm br.; **Fil.** purple; **An.** yellow; **style** 2.2 cm lg., purple; **Sti.** 8, yellow; **throat** light magenta; **Fr.** ellipsoid, 2 cm lg., bluish, later purple; **S.** 1 mm lg., light brown, testa granular.—Bolivia (Santa Cruz, San José, 600 m). (Fig. 128.) [Haage adds: Acc. Lau, identical with G. hammerschmidii.]

G. chubutense (Speg.) Speg. (2)
Bo. simple, broadly spherical, to 15 cm br., to 10 cm h., ashy or greyish-green; **Ri.** c. 15, broad; **Ar.** oblong, with a rounded tubercular swelling underneath; **Rsp.** 5–7, thick, stiff, projecting, to 4 cm lg., chalky blackish-grey, sometimes ± compressed, not thickened below; **Fl.** to 8.5 cm lg., c. 4 cm br. or more, pure white.—Argentina (Chubut).

G. chuquisacanum Card.
Bo. flattened-spherical, 5–6 cm h., 12 cm br., greyish-green; **Ri.** 13, Tub. 1 cm h.; **Ar.** 1.5 cm apart, rounded-elliptic, 7 mm ∅, with greyish to blackish felt; all **Sp.** horn-grey, tipped brownish; **Rsp.** 7–10, spreading, curving towards the Bo., 2–3 cm lg.; **Csp.** 1, curving upwards, 2.5–3 cm lg.; **Fl.** few, apical, beaker-shaped, 6.5 cm lg., 5 cm br., white, widely opening; **Tu.** terete, 12 mm ∅, light green, with green Sc. 5 mm br. and bordered white; **Sep.** lanceolate, greenish outside, pink inside, **Pet.** lanceolate, salmon pink; **Fl.** magenta; **An.** brownish; **style** 11 mm lg., light magenta with 22 yellow **Sti.** 5 mm lg.—Bolivia (Prov. Azero, Chuquisaca, near Boyuibe, 700 m). May also have been described by Ritter, and belongs to the G. zegarrae-G. lagunillasense group. The **Fl.**, 6.5 cm lg., are conspicuous.

G. comarapense Backbg. (not described): **Bo.** large, spherical, with numerous **Ri.**; **Rsp.** 8–9, longer, interlacing; **Csp.** 1, still longer, projecting; **Ar.** rather felty; **Fl.** bellshaped, white, **throat** pink.—Bolivia (Comarapa). Regarded by Cardenas as a form of G. zegarrae.

G. damsii (K. Sch.) Br. & R. (3)
Bo. simple, light to dark green, flat-spherical; **Ri.** to c. 10, fairly broad, with short acute transverse

notches; **Tub.** prominent; **Sp.** scarcely differentiated, 2–8, to 1.2 cm lg., whitish, darker brown above and below, soon becoming grey; **Fl.** to 6.5 cm lg., 5 cm ∅, white, wine-red in the centre, with crowded, oblong, imbricate Sc.; **An.** grey; **Fr.** slender-cylindric, red, 2.5 cm lg.—N. Paraguay. As a result of newer discoveries and observations, the spec. is seen to be as variable as G. mihanovichii. Seeds are just 1 mm lg.

v. **centrispinum** Backbg.—Descr. Cact. Nov. III: 6. 1963: **Ri.** with chin-prominences weaker than in the type, lacking the distinct transverse swelling of the next variety, the furrows over the Ar. acute, flattened above and below; **Rsp.** almost always 7, 0.6–2 cm lg., the upper ones longest; **Csp.** 1, to c. 2 cm lg.; all **Sp.** ± horn-coloured to brownish; **Fl.** white, also in the centre; **Sep.** narrow, long, tapering, green, they and the oblong Sc. with a red dot above; **Tu.** 2.5 cm lg., very thin.—Bolivia (Roboré area). (Fig. 129 above);

v. **rotundulum** Backbg.—l.c.: **Ri.** flat, broad, rounded, with swellings but without distinct transverse thickening, increasingly reddish towards the base, transverse notches moderately flattened, shallow, without distinct Tub. or chin-like protuberances; **Rsp.** c. 7, 6–12 mm lg.; **Csp.** 0; **Fl.** c. 3.2 cm lg., 3 cm ∅, white; **Sep.** green, broadly linear; **Tu.** 2 cm lg., 4 mm ∅, with oblong Sc.; **throat** white; **style** projecting; **Sti.** long, white.—Bolivia (Roboré). (Fig. 129 below);

v. **torulosum** Backbg.—l.c.: **Ri.** fairly acute, without rounded chins but with tuberculate projections, the transverse notching shallow, not flattened, with distinct but not very prominent transverse thickening; **Rsp.** mostly 5; **Csp.** 0(–1), brownish if present; **Fl.** white, also in the throat, 3 cm lg., 3.5 cm ∅; **Sep.** rounded and broader above, olive-reddish, light-bordered; **Tu.** 1.7 cm lg., c. 5 mm ∅, Sc. transversely oval; **style** rather short; **S.** round, yellowish-brown, with irregular black Tub., 0.8 mm lg., testa corky.—Bolivia (San José). (Fig. 130.)
This very unusual testa-type (presumably constant in the type and all varieties) demonstrates the unsuitability of seeds for purposes of classification (see also Parodia and Thrixanthocereus);

v. **tucavocense** Backbg.—l.c.: **Bo.** differentiated by being flatter, deep green, offsetting freely from the Ar.; **Ri.** ± tuberculate; **Sp.** 5, stouter, appressed; **Fl.** 5 cm lg., 4 cm ∅, pale pink; **Tu.** 1.5 cm lg., with broad Sc.—Bolivia (San José). (Fig. 131.)
These represent the clearly differentiated variants; there are probably intermediate forms of lesser importance.

G. deeszianum Dölz (2)
Bo. depressed-spherical to elongated, glossy, light olive-green, becoming more deep green, to c. 6.5 cm ∅; **Ri.** 7–8; **Tub.** with a rather pointed chin; **Sp.** c. 7, appressed or slightly spreading, curving, to c. 2.5 cm lg., dirty pale yellow, brownish below; **Fl.** to 5 cm lg., creamy-white, delicate pink in the centre.—Argentina (Córdoba?).

G. denudatum (Lk. & O.) Pfeiff. (2) (T.)
Bo. flattened-spherical at first, glossy dark green, to c. 8 cm br. (much larger if grafted); **Ri.** 5–8, broad below, flattened-rounded, without Tub.; **Rsp.** 5, to c. 1.5 cm lg., ± contorted, directed sideways and downwards; **Fl.** with a slender Tu., to 5 cm lg., 7 cm ∅, glossy white; **Pet.** in several R., slender-tapering; **Fr.** oblong-clavate; **S.** large, black.—S. Brazil to Argentina (Misiones).
　　v. **backebergii** Paž. (Fričiana Řada, 3: 15, 6. 1963): not a true variety, but a juvenile form of the spec., with still flatter Ri.; in age they too become ± rounded-tuberculate.
There are numerous hybrids, mostly with ± tuberculate Ri.

G. euchlorum Backbg.: **Gymnocalycium hybopleurum** v. **euchlorum** Backbg.

G. eurypleurum Ritt. (FR 1178)
Bo. simple, subspherical, to 7 cm ∅, fairly glossy; **Ri.** 8, straight, flat, obtuse, broken between the Ar. by a transverse furrow; **Ar.** 15–20 mm apart, oval, at first with yellowish-white H., later glabrous; **Rsp.** 5–6, one of these pointing downwards; **Csp.** 0–1; all **Sp.** sharply acicular, 25–30 mm lg., little recurved, dark yellowish at first, later greying, apical Sp. deep brown; **Fl.** 45–50 mm ∅; **Tu.** with pale, white-bordered Sc. tipped with a crimson fleck; **Pet.** lanceolate, pinkish-violet, with a pale pink M.-line, tipped reddish-brown; **Fil.** white; **An.** yellow; **style** white, with 12 light yellow Sti.; **Fr.** spherical, 20 mm ∅; **S.** brown.—Paraguay (Cerro León, collected at considerable personal risk by Ritter, in the territory of the savage Moro Indians).

G. eytianum Card. (2)
Bo. depressed-spherical, to 15 cm h., to 30 cm ∅, bluish-green; **Ri.** c. 18, 4 cm br. below, transversely furrowed; **Tub.** 4 cm br.; **Sp.** scarcely differentiated, c. 4–5, appressed, to 2.5 cm lg., subulate, brownish-yellow to whitish-yellow, brown-tipped, yellowish-green below; **Fl.** bell to beaker-shaped, to 4.5 cm lg., pure white.—Bolivia (Eyti).

G. fleischerianum Backbg. (2)
Bo. spherical to elongated, sometimes offsetting, glossy, light green; **Ri.** c. 8, fairly broad below; **Tub.** rounded, without a transverse furrow; **Sp.** c.

20, bristly, flexible, radiating, yellowish-white and brown at first, to 2.5 cm lg.; **Csp.** scarcely differentiated; **Fl.** to 4 cm lg., 3.5 cm ∅, white; **throat** pink.—Paraguay.

G. fričianum Plesnik—Kakt. u. a. Sukk., 15: 6, 110. 1964 (3)
Bo. simple, greyish-green, broadly spherical, to 9 cm ∅, 6 cm h.; **Ri.** 11, acute, with chin-like projections; **Ar.** beige-coloured at first; **Rsp.** 2–3 at first, later 7; **Csp.** 0; **Fl.** 5 cm lg., 3 cm ∅, bellshaped, white inside; **Tu.** 3 cm lg., slender; **Fil.** white; **An.** greyish-greenish; **style** yellow; **Fr.** carmine, with pink Sc.; **S.** brownish.—Paraguay.
The spec. belongs to the Series "Schickendantziana", and thus doubtless to the complex of G. marsoneri (Frič) Y. Ito. which is rather variable, also to some extent in flower-size, as I was able to see from Uhlig's abundant material. Maybe that is why Frič did not originally describe the above form. This shows once again the perils of describing from single specimens, without some knowledge of all the forms in a possible swarm. Much of the above description applies equally well to G. marsoneri.

G. gibbosum (Haw.) Pfeiff. (2)
Bo. spherical to long-elongated, rarely offsetting, to 60 cm h., to c. 15 cm ∅, bluish to dirty green; **Ri.** 12–19, to 1.5 cm h., with acute transverse furrows; **Ar.** grey; **Rsp.** 7–10(–14), ± projecting, medium-stout, ± slightly curving, mostly reddish below; **Csp.** 1–3(–5), coloured like the Rsp., variously long; **Fl.** to 6.5 cm lg., fairly broad, ± whitish; **Fr.** ± clavate.—S. Argentina (Rio Chubut, Rio Negro, etc.).
　　v. **leucodictyon** (K. Sch.) Y. Ito: **Bo.** more bluish-green, smaller, more freely offsetting;
　　v. **nigrum** Backbg.: **Bo.** blackish-green; **Sp.** blackish; **Csp.** 0–1;
　　v. **nobile** (Haw.) Y. Ito: **Bo.** becoming large-spherical; **Sp.** more numerous, to c. 15, longer, to 3.5 cm lg., whitish, red below, often quite strongly interlacing; **Csp.** to 6.

G. glaucum Ritt.—Sukkde. (SKG.), VII–VIII, 37. 1963 (2)
Bo. ashen to greyish-green, hemispherical, to 12 cm ∅; **R.** long, napiform, hard, white; **Ri.** 10–16, obtuse, broad, to 1.5 cm h., faintly tuberculate, transversely furrowed; **Ar.** white, to 1.5 cm lg., 5–7.5 mm br., white; **Sp.** faintly curving, reddish-brown at first, then grey, with 2–3(–4) pairs on each side, 2–4 cm lg., the middle one to 7 cm lg., sometimes with 1 Ssp. above; **Csp.** 0; **Fl.** 3.5–5.5 cm lg., 2.5–4.5 cm ∅, opening towards noon, white; **Pet.** with a thin purple stripe above, broader towards the base, **throat** coloured similarly; **style**

pale green, reddish below; **Fr.** 3 cm lg., reddish below, greyish or brownish-green above; **S.** black, 1 mm lg.—N. Argentina (SE. of Tinogasta in Prov. Catamarca) (FR 961).

G. grandiflorum Backbg. (2)
Bo. flattened-spherical, green; **Ri.** c. 8, with marked transverse furrows; **Tub.** chin-like; **Rsp.** 5, somewhat appressed, pinkish or whitish-grey; **Fl.** to 7 cm ∅, medium-long, pure white.—NW. Argentina.

G. griseo-pallidum Backbg. n.sp. (3?)
Bo. flattened-spherical, whitish-grey, c. 6.5 cm ∅ and 3 cm h. has been observed, forming some offsets; **Ri.** 7, with transverse furrows on the flanks or between the Ar. (so far, unique to this spec.), c. 1.5 cm br. at midway and 7 mm h.; **Sp.** 4–5(–6), to 1.5 cm lg., black, the lower ones ± appressed or ± bent, the middle ones projecting, all eventually grey; **Fl.** ?—Bolivia (salt-dunes near San José, close to the Paraguayan frontier). The weak Tub. formed by the transverse furrows become suffused pale reddish during the dry season. Distinguishable from all other spec. of the genus by its light, almost chalky, colour (Coll. Uhlig, U 2179; found by Father Hammerschmid). (Fig. 132.)

G. guanchinense Schütz: belongs to the complex of G. mazanense Backbg.; v. robustius Ritt. is only a name.

G. guerkeanum (Heese) Br. & R. (2)
Bo. flattened-spherical; **Ri.** 9, rather flat and broad; **Tub.** faintly chin-shaped; **Ar.** yellowish; **Sp.** always 5, to 12 mm lg., rough, yellowish, brownish-red below; **Fl.** to 5 cm lg., almost 4 cm ∅, glossy, light yellow.—Bolivia.

G. hamatum Ritt. (2)
Bo. subspherical; **Ri.** 9, rounded, transversely indented; **Rsp.** 6, projecting and radiating, to 1.5 cm lg., the bottom one longest, whitish-yellow at first, brown above, then horn-grey; **Csp.** 0; **Fl.**?— Origin? (Fig. 133.) Presumably never described; the plants I have seen had no hooked Sp., although some of the lower radials were ± slightly bent at the tip.

G. hammerschmidii Backbg. (2)—Descr. Cact. Nov. III: 7. 1963.
Bo. broadly spherical, to 15 cm ∅, slightly glossy, leaf-green; **Ri.** c. 7, prominent, rounded, to 3 cm br. below; **Tub.** swollen, rounded, with an acute transverse furrow to c. 1.5 cm br.; **Rsp.** 5, subulate, directed laterally and downwards, to c. 2 cm lg., ± recurved, often also 2 upper thin-subulate Sp. to 6 mm lg.; **Csp.** (0–)1, c. 1.5 cm lg.; all **Sp.** light horn-

coloured, ± flecked, light greenish-yellow below at first, dark-tipped; **Fl.** 4–6.5 cm lg., 3.5–6 cm ∅, the larger dimensions applying to solitary Fl., pale salmon-pink to white; **Tu.** reddish or bluish; **Sep.** olive outside; **Pet.** narrow below; **Fr.** blackish-bluish; **S.** medium-sized.—Bolivia (San José: found by Father Hammerschmid). (Fig. 134.) Flowers open only for a short time, in full sun; Fl.-colour varies from white to reddish. [Haage adds: Acc. Lau, identical with G. chiquitanum.]

G. horridispinum Frank (2)—Kakt. u. a. Sukk., 14: 1, 8–10. 1963.
Bo. to 8 cm ∅, dark leaf-green; **Ri.** 10–13, with strong chin-Tub. and acute longitudinal furrows; **Rsp.** 10–12, stout, subulate, 2–2.5 cm lg., grey, brown-tipped, curving towards the Bo.; **Csp.** coloured similarly, 4, cruciform, still stouter, projecting, thickened below, 3–4 cm lg.; **bud** purplish-red, plump, tapering; **Fl.** white with a violet-pink border or uniformly purplish-pink, 6 cm lg., 6 cm ∅, with a darker M.-stripe; **throat** white; **Sep.** violet-pink.—N. Argentina (Córdoba, SW. of Salsacate). (Fig. 135.)
The Fl. can remain open for about a week.
There is a similar plant with less fierce and also shorter Sp., the Bo. being more broadly-spherical and more bluish-green; possibly a variety (Coll. Uhlig and Backeberg, U 2177).

G. horstii Buin.
Bo. to 11 cm ∅, to 7 cm h., fresh glossy green, with fibrous R.; **Ri.** 5–6, sometimes weakly tuberculate; **Ar.** 3 on each Ri., ± felty, oval, 5 mm lg., 4 mm br., 3 cm apart; **Sp.** 5, straight, obliquely projecting, not appressed, 1 of them pointing downwards, light yellow, to 3 cm lg.; **Csp.** 0; **Fl.** to 11 cm lg. and br., opening widely in full sunshine, from morning to evening; **Tu.** set with small pink Sc.; **Pet.** lilac-pink to creamy-white, pointed, with a pink M.-stripe, outer ones dark pink; **Fil.** and **An.** light yellow; **style** light yellow, with 9 Sti.; **Fr.** ovoid, green with a blue tinge, ripening very slowly, dehiscing laterally; **S.** cap-shaped, small.—Brazil (Rio Grande do Sul, near Cacapava). Named for its discoverer, Leopold Horst.
v. **buenekeri** Buin.: distinguished by the dark green epidermis, robuster **Sp.** and dark pink **Fl.**

G. hossei (Hge. Jr.) Berg. (2)
Bo. ± flat-spherical to elongated, dark brownish-green; **Ri.** 13, fairly broad; **Tub.** chin-like, with a transverse notch; **Ar.** greyish-whitish; **Sp.** mostly 7, somewhat spreading and recurved, to 15 mm lg., subulate; **Csp.** one sometimes present later; all **Sp.** brown at first, then grey, dark-tipped; **Fl.** with a short Tu., deep pink.—Argentina (Córdoba?; La Rioja). (Fig. 136.)

v. longispinum (Hge Jr.) hort. is an unclarified variety.

G. hybopleurum (K. Sch.) Backbg. (2)
Bo. broadly spherical, dull to greyish-green; **crown** sunken; **Ri.** c. 13, broad, hemispherical; **Tub.** sharply chin-shaped; **Ar.** light brownish at first; **Sp.** mostly 9, one directed downwards, the others interlocking, recurved, to 3 cm lg., brown at first, then dull white; **Csp.** 0; **Fl.** to c. 4 cm lg., white to greenish-white; **throat** greenish-pink; **Fr.** green.—Argentina (Córdoba).
Probably offsets later; often erroneously named as G. mostii.
v. **breviflorum** Backbg. n.v.: Differs in having much shorter **Fl.**, to c. 2.5 cm lg. and br.; **Csp.** 1 sometimes present, bent towards the crown, to c. 2.8 cm lg. (Fig. 137 above);
v. **centrispinum** Backbg. n.v.:
Differs in having 2–3 **Csp.** which are bent upwards; **Sp.** not stouter than in the type (Coll. Uhlig and Backeberg, U 2146; collected by Fechser);
v. **euchlorum** Backbg.: **Bo.** lighter greyish-green; **Sp.** shorter, fewer;
v. **ferocius** Backbg. n.v.: **Sp.** much stouter, ash-grey when dry, chestnut-brown when wet; **Rsp.** c. 7–9, similar to those of the type; **Csp.** (1–)2, porrect or curving upwards, to 3.5 cm lg., they and the Rsp. ± compressed and/or ± angular (Coll. Uhlig and Backeberg, U 2167; collected by Fechser). (Fig. 137 centre);
v. **ferox** Backbg. n.v.: Differentiated by the **Rsp.** which are very stout-subulate, ± compressed, **Csp.** missing; **Fl.** very stout, c. 3.5 cm lg., 4.5 cm ∅; **Tu.** c. 1.2 cm br.; **Sep.** to 1 cm br., green, broadly rounded above, with a light border; **Pet.** very pale olive to whitish; **throat** red; **Fil.** carmine. (Fig. 137 below.)

G. hyptiacanthum (Lem.) Br. & R. (2)
Bo. depressed-spherical at first, elongating, to 10 cm ∅, dark green; **Ri.** 9–11; **Tub.** 5 mm h., conical; **Rsp.** 5–8, to 1 cm lg.; **Csp.** 0–1; **Sp.** ± subulate, sharp, somewhat recurved, whitish, brownish below; **Fl.** 5 cm lg., yellowish-white.—Uruguay.
v. **citriflorum** (Frič) Schütz: **Fl.** lemon-yellow; perhaps a hybrid.

G. immemoratum Cast. & Lelong: **Gymnocalycium valnicekianum** Jajó.

G. intertextum Backbg. n.sp. (2)
Bo. simple, hemispherical, to 11 cm ∅ has been noted, greyish-green; **Ri.** c. 13–15, c. 1.5–2 cm br., transversely furrowed; **Tub.** chin-like often extending over the furrow; **Sp.** tangled, irregularly bent, sometimes curving and ± claw-like, in part

compressed, when dry pinkish-grey, dirty grey or horn-coloured, rather stout, not thickened below; **Rsp.** 5–7, to 2.5 cm lg.; **Csp.** mostly 0, sometimes 1 curving towards the apex, not stouter than the Rsp.; **Sp.** sometimes to c. 2 mm thick below; **Fl.** ?—N. Argentina (Coll. Uhlig and Backeberg, U 2176; collected by Fechser). (Fig. 138.) When wet, the Sp. are reddish-brownish.

G. izozogsii Card.
Bo. simple, spherical, 4–5 cm h., 9–12 cm ∅, greyish-green, suffused reddish; **Ri.** 9–10, tuberculate; **Ar.** 1.5–2.5 cm apart, round, 6–8 mm ∅, grey-felty; **Rsp.** 10–11, radiating or weakly appressed, 10–25 mm lg., grey or horn-coloured; **Csp.** 15 mm lg.; **Fl.** funnelform or urn-shaped, 4 cm lg., 3 cm ∅; **Ov.** spherical, 7 mm lg., brownish with pink Sc.; **Tu.** short, brownish, with brownish pink-bordered Sc. 6 mm lg.; **Sep.** spatulate, 8–16 mm lg., salmon-pink, light brown outside; **Pet.** spatulate, 20 × 7 mm, light salmon, magenta below; **Fil.** magenta, **An.** yellowish-brownish; **style** pink, with 18 Sti.; **Tu.** red inside. Close to G. pflanzii, but the Sp. are shorter and appressed, the Fl. is differently coloured and the locality is also different.—Bolivia (Prov. Cordillera, Santa Cruz, Izozog Basin near El Atajado, in loose sandy soil, among thorn scrub, at 400 m).

G. joossensianum (Böd.) Br. & R. (3)
Bo. simple, depressed-spherical; **Ri.** c. 6–9, somewhat tuberculate; **Sp.** 6–9, the lowest ones longest; **Fl.** wine-red; **Tu.** moderately long; **Fr.** spindle-shaped, with a few red Sc.—Paraguay or N. Argentina.

G. knebelii Frič (G. knebelianum) (3): not described. The plant was ± brownish-green; Tub. not very broad; epidermis distinctly spotted.—Paraguay.

G. kozelskyanum Schütz
Bo. depressed-spherical, bronze-coloured, 6 cm h., 10 cm ∅, crown slightly sunken; **Ri.** c. 14, low, Tub. scarcely developed; **Ar.** c. 20 mm apart; **Rsp.** 3, straight or curving slightly upwards, stiff, 20 mm lg., dark brown, later ash-grey; **Fl.** subapical, c. 6 cm lg.; **Ov.** and pericarpel dark bluish-green with semicircular Sc.; **Sep.** spatulate, 10 mm br., pink to dark greyish-green; **Pet.** lanceolate, intense pink, purple below; **Fil.** and **style** white; **Sti.** 8; **Fr.** dark bluish-green, scaly; **S.** dark brown, glossy.—Argentina (Córdoba). Also distributed as G. vatteri.

G. kurtzianum (Gürke) Br. & R.: **Gymnocalycium mostii** v. **kurtzianum** (Gürke) Backbg.

G. lafaldense Vpl.: **Gymnocalycium bruchii** (Speg.) Hoss.

G. lagunillasense Card. (2)
Bo. simple, broadly spherical, to 4 cm h., to 14 cm ⌀, greyish-green; **Ri.** c. 13, low; **Tub.** ± 4-sided; **Ar.** grey; **Rsp.** c. 7, subulate, curving, whitish below, pink at midway, brown above, 1–3 cm lg.; **Fl.** c. 5 cm lg., funnelform, cream-coloured above, white below; **throat** bluish-red; **Fr.** spherical, 2 cm ⌀, red.—Bolivia (Lagunillas).

G. leeanum (Hook.) Br. & R. (2)
Bo. depressed to spherical, bluish-green; **Ri.** to over 15; **Tub.** hemispherical, ± 6-sided below; **Sp.** c. 11, thin, **radials** to 12 mm lg., ± appressed and curving, **Csp.** 1, porrect, straight; **Fl.** large, pale yellow, unisexual; **S.** large, black.—Uruguay, adjacent areas of Argentina.
v. **brevispinum** Backbg.: **Sp.** much shorter, straighter, very short in the crown.—Uruguay (Maldonado);
v. **netrelianum** (Monv.) Backbg.: **Sp.** 5–8, **Csp.** mostly absent; **Fl.** pale lemon-yellow.—Uruguay.

G. leptanthum (Speg.) Speg. (2)
Bo. broadly spherical, to c. 7 cm ⌀; **Ri.** 8 or more, low, broad below; **Tub.** rounded, not prominent, transversely indented below; **Sp.** typically 7, appressed; **Fl.** with a conspicuously long Tu., to 6.5 cm lg., white; **throat** reddish; **Tu.** very slender, densely scaly.—Argentina (Córdoba).

G. loricatum Speg.: **Gymnocalycium spegazzinii** Br. & R.

G. lumbarasense Ritt.: an undescribed name.

G. marquezii Card. (2)
Bo. broadly spherical, dull bluish-green, to 4 cm h., to 10 cm ⌀; **Ri.** c. 8, low; **Tub.** 2 cm h., 3 cm br.; **Ar.** white; **Sp.** 6–7, thin-subulate, appressed, grey below, pinkish-brown above, 1–2.5 cm lg.; **Csp.** only sometimes present; all **Sp.** thickened below; **Fl.** broadly beaker-shaped, 4 cm lg., pink with a brown M.-stripe.—Bolivia (Angosto de Villa Montes).
v. **argentinense** Backbg. n.v.**Bo.** deep leaf-green, epidermis finely granular and pitted; **Ri.** 8(–10), to over 3.5 cm br. below; **Sp.** ash-grey when dry, dirty chestnut-brown when damp, or darker above at first, reddish below; **Rsp.** (7–)9(–12), curving sideways, to 2.5 cm lg.; **Csp.** 1–2(–4), more projecting, not longer than the Rsp.; **Fl.** to 5 cm lg., 5.5 cm ⌀, white; **throat** light red; **Fil.** red; **Sti.** long, spreading, crimson.—N. Argentina (Coll. Uhlig and Backeberg, U 2166);

collected by Fechser between Tucuman and Salta, with no further habitat data). (Fig. 139.) Old Ar. can be to 11 mm lg. and 9 mm br., the felt soon becoming blackish-grey.

G. marsoneri (Frič) Y. Ito (3)
Bo. simple, flat-spherical, matt greyish-green; **Ri.** c. 15, conspicuously oblique and divided into low, larger Tub.; **Ar.** yellowish-brownish; **Rsp.** 7, to 3 cm lg.; **Csp.** 0; **Fl.** funnelform to bellshaped, to 3.5 cm lg., 3–4.5 cm ⌀, pale yellowish-white to white.—Paraguay (?). A somewhat variable spec. with a shorter, rather slender Tu., and the Pet. in several Ser. (Fig. 140.)

G. mazanense Backbg. (2)
Bo. large, broadly spherical, brownish to greyish or dull green; **Ri.** 10–12, low, rounded; **Tub.** rounded, chin-shaped, stout, transversely furrowed; **Ar.** white; **Rsp.** c. 7 or more, to 3 cm lg., ± interlacing, ± pinkish-brown, becoming grey; **Csp.** 0 or one occasionally present; **Fl.** stoutly funnelform, **Pet.** fairly crowded, whitish to pink; **throat** darker.—N. Argentina (Mazan).
v. **breviflorum** Backbg.: **Fl.** still shorter, olive to pinkish-white;
v. **ferox** Backbg.: **Csp.** and **Rsp.** fairly thick, large, crowded and projecting.

G. megalothelos (Sencke) Br. & R. (2)
Bo. depressed-spherical, to c. 16 cm ⌀ and h., light to darker green; **Ri.** 10–12; **Tub.** plump and chin-like, transversely indented; **Ar.** large; **Rsp.** 7–8, subulate, to 1.5 cm lg., first yellow then dirty brownish-yellow, finally horn-coloured; **Csp.** 1, porrect; **Fl.** large, pinkish-white.—Paraguay. Probably belongs to the complex of G. monvillei (Lem.) Br. & R.

G. megatae Y. Ito (3)
Bo. flat-spherical, c. 6 cm h., to 20 cm ⌀, light green; **Ri.** 9–13, acute; **Rsp.** to 5, thin, 2 cm lg., brown at first, then darker; **Fl.** 5 cm lg. and br., white.—Paraguay.

G. melanocarpum (Ar.) Br. & R. (2)
Bo. simple, hemispherical, to c. 9 cm ⌀; **Ri.** 15, broad, rounded; **Tub.** stout; **Rsp.** 10–12, to 2.5 cm lg., subulate, yellow at first, then grey, appressed; **Csp.** 0; **Fl.** ?; **Fr.** spherical, 2 cm ⌀, glossy, dark olive-green.—Uruguay (Paysandú).

G. michoga (Frič) Y. Ito (3)
Bo. simple, spherical, greyish-green to reddish; **Ri.** c. 11, acute, tuberculate; **Rsp.** c. 7, sharp, 2 cm lg., dark brown at first, then black; **Fl.** bellshaped to funnelform, to 5 cm lg., 4 cm ⌀, white, with a

brownish-green stripe; **Tu.** deep green.—Argentina (Paraguay?).

G. mihanovichii (Frič & Gürke) Br. & R. (3)
Bo. broadly spherical to ± elongated, to c. 6 cm ∅, greyish-green or ± reddish-brown; **Ri.** narrow, acute, with transverse prominences or with lighter and darker cross-banding; **Rsp.** usually 5(–6), sometimes dropping, to 1 cm lg.; **Fl.** bellshaped to funnelform; **Sep.** yellowish-green, ± reddish at the tip; **Pet.** revolute at anthesis, greenish-yellow or paler to white, sometimes narrow.—Paraguay (Bahia Negra). Like G. damsii, an extremely variable spec. More clearly differentiated varieties include that with ± pink Fl., and v. filadelfiense with large Fl. coloured brown above, which do not open wide and last a long time.
There are, as Werdermann showed, transitional forms to all the other varieties.
v. **albiflorum** Paz.—Fričiana Řada, 3: 17, 5–7. 1963:
Sp. 8, stouter; **Fl.** pure white; no further data available;
v. **angusto-striatum** Paz.—Fričiana Řada 1: 7, 3. 1962:
Ri. c. 12, with close-set narrow transverse stripes; **Sp.** missing or sparse, short; **Fl.** as in v. friedrichii;
v. **filadelfiense** Backbg. n.v.: **Bo.** later elongated, to c. 10 cm h. has been noted, brownish, mostly with dark spots, transverse banding sometimes absent or indistinct; **Ri.** acute, straight, or made ± tuberculate by low transverse depressions, the edge of the Tub. mostly darker, the depressions directed slightly downwards; **Sp.** blackish and usually longer persisting; **Fl.** to c. 5 cm lg., not opening widely, the Tu. either slender or stouter, the bud spherical; **Per.** brownish to olive-green, darker than in the type, slightly reddish towards the base.—Paraguay (near Filadelfia) (Coll. Uhlig and Backeberg, U 2125; found by Unger). (Fig. 141.) The Fl.-colour is very uniform;
v. **fleischerianum** Paz.—Kaktusarské Listy, 1948–51: **Bo.** broadly spherical, light green, with dark dots; **Ri.** c. 12, acute; **Sp.** 4–6, yellow; **Fl.** to 8 cm lg., white, scarcely opening.—Paraguay (Chaco Boreal);
v. **friedrichii** Werd.: banding distinct, in thin stripes; **Bo.** under 10 cm ∅; **Fl.** deep pink, somewhat smaller than the type;
v. **melocactiforme** Paz.: banding virtually absent; **Bo.** can be over 10 cm ∅; **Fl.** with conspicuously narrow Pet.;
v. **pirarettaense** Paz.: **Bo.** under 10 cm ∅; banding present or missing or indistinct; **Fl.** variable, from deep pink to white.
f. **rubrum**: a red form without chlorophyll which is also known under other names;

v. **stenogonum** Frič & Paz.: **Bo.** to 15 cm ∅, with narrow Ri. and close-set banding: **Fl.** yellowish to greenish-white;
v. **stenostriatum** Paz.—Fričiana Řada, 1: 7. 1962 (illustration).
Bo. rather elongated; **Ri.** with close-set transverse markings; **Sp.** mostly absent, sometimes one, curving slightly downwards.

G. millaresii Card.
Bo. simple, spherical, weakly compressed, bluish-green, 6–8 cm h., 12–14 cm ∅; **Ri.** 16–19, straight, divided into Tub. 6–8 mm h., 2–2.5 cm ∅; **Ar.** 3 cm apart, elliptic, 1 cm lg., with blackish felt; **Sp.** 7–9, pectinate, bent; **Csp.** 1–2, directed upwards; all **Sp.** grey, tipped brownish, 2–4 cm lg.; **Fl.** borne in the crown, funnelform, 4 cm lg., 4 cm ∅; **Ov.** spherical, light green to lilac; **Sc.** broadly rounded, light-bordered; **Tu.** 2 cm ∅, with lilac-bordered, light green Sc.; **Sep.** broadly spatulate, 1 cm lg., pink, greenish outside; **Pet.** lanceolate, salmon-pink, magenta below; **An.** 5 mm lg., yellow; **style** 17 mm lg., magenta; **Sti.** 13.—Bolivia (Saavedra, Potosí, near Millares, at 2600 m, in quartite rocks).
Differentiated from G. zegarrae by its unusual Sp. as well as the Fl.-colour and habitat.

G. monvillei (Lem.) Br. & R. (2)
Bo. simple, large, spherical, to c. 22 cm ∅, glossy, light green, varying to lighter or darker; **Ri.** 13–17; **Tub.** large, 5–6-sided; **Ar.** yellowish at first; **Rsp.** 7–13, subulate, curving, ascending, compressed, to 4 cm lg., horn-yellow, greenish-yellow or darker; **Csp.** 0; **Fl.** to 8 cm lg., broad, white with a pinkish-red tinge.—Paraguay. Very variable in the colour of Bo. and Sp.

G. moserianum Schütz
Bo. depressed-spherical, dark green, to 15 cm br., 10 cm h.; **Ri.** c. 10, little tuberculate, with flat transverse furrows; **Ar.** 20 mm apart, with thick white felt at first, later glabrous; **Rsp.** 3–5, to 25 mm lg., dark brown below, lighter above; **Fl.** subapical, pure white, centre red; **Fil.** wine-red below, yellow above; **S.** brown, glossy, 0.6 mm lg.—Argentina (N. Córdoba, near Serrazuela). Introduced by H. Fechser. Named for the well-known Gymnocalycium specialist, Günther Moser of Kufstein.

G. mostii (Gürke) Br. & R. (2)
Bo. simple, dark to bluish-green, to c. 7 cm h., 13 cm ∅; **Ri.** 11–14, broad, obtuse, fewer at first; **Tub.** with a projecting rounded chin, strongly transversely indented; **Rsp.** 7, 6–22 cm lg.*, stoutly

---

* Translator's note: I suspect these figures are corrupt; my own cultivated plants, of 2 forms, have very few Sp. exceeding 3 cm.

subulate, recurved or bent; **Csp.** 1, ± straight; all **Sp.** light horn-coloured, tipped glossy brown; **Fl.** large, beaker-shaped to rotate, to 8 cm br., light salmon to pinkish-red.—Argentina (Córdoba).

v. **kurtzianum** (Gürke) Backbg.: **Ri.** to 18; **Rsp.** 8; **Csp.** 1, bent strongly upwards, horn-coloured, mostly brownish-tipped; **Fl.** 7–8 cm lg., white, throat red.—Argentina (Córdoba).

G. mucidum Oehme: at most a form of G. mazanense Backbg.

G. multiflorum (Hook.) Br. & R. (2)
Bo. solitary at first, then offsetting and forming groups, single heads to over 9 cm h., to 12 cm ∅, green; **Ri.** 10–15, swollen-tuberculate, ± acute; **Sp.** 7–10, all radials, to 3 cm lg., somewhat flattened, yellowish; **Fl.** to 4 cm lg., shortly bellshaped, pink to almost white.—Argentina (Córdoba).

v. **albispinum** (K. Sch.) Backbg.: **Sp.** whitish-grey; **Tub.** chin-like below; **Csp.** 1; **Sp.** in part darker below, the Csp. shorter and more slender than the stoutly subulate Rsp.;

v. **parisiense** (K. Sch.) Backbg.: **Sp.** stouter, interlacing, red below; **Fl.** with a red throat.

G. netrelianum (Monv.) Br. & R.
Bo. simple, occasionally offsetting, spherical or broadly spherical, crown glabrous; **Ri.** 14, broad, rounded, tuberculate, ± bluish; **Rsp.** 5–8, brownish, bristly, flexible, less than 1 cm lg.; **Csp.** absent; **Fl.** pale lemon-yellow, 5 cm lg., said to be unisexual; inner **Pet.** broadly oblong, pointed; **Fil.** and **style** white.—Uruguay or Argentina. This spec. is regarded as synonymous with G. guerkeanum and G. uruguayense. Acc. to Dr. Weber it closely resembles G. hyptiacanthum but is much smaller and has not the white Fl. of the latter spec.

G. nidulans Backbg. (2)
Bo. solitary, tapering-spherical, to 10 cm h. and br., matt brownish-green; **Ri.** to 17; **Tub.** broader than high, divided by acute transverse notches, chin-projection small; **Ar.** tufted, yellowish-grey; **Rsp.** c. 6, curving upwards, more strongly projecting, tips interlacing; **Csp.** sometimes 1; **Fl.** ± bellshaped to funnelform, **Pet.** pinkish-white, in several Ser., **throat** darker.—Argentina (Mazan).

G. nigriareolatum Backbg. (2)
Bo. broadly spherical, simple, velvety bluish-green, to c. 15 cm ∅; **Ri.** 10, medium-broad; **Tub.** elongated, swollen, acute above, with a smallish chin; **Ar.** at first with somewhat tufted yellowish-brown felt, soon becoming black, large, oblong; **Rsp.** 7–8, pinkish-grey, to 3 cm lg., sometimes ± curving; **Csp.** rather longer; all **Sp.** dark-tipped at first; **Fl.** porcelain-white, slightly bellshaped; **Sep.**

greenish.—Argentina (Catamarca).

v. **densispinum** Backbg.: **Ri.** to 15; **Sp.** denser, thinner, longer.

G. occultum Frič ex Schütz (Fričiana Řada 1: 7, 4. 1962) (2). In the absence of any description, I merely noted this spec. in "Die Cact." III. p. 1725, under G. bodenbenderianum; I did not refer it to the latter. In the light of the present description it must be regarded as only one of the numerous forms of G. quehlianum, and not as a distinct spec.; it has the typical 5 Rsp. and only indistinct tuberculation of the Ri., which are given in the original description.—Argentina (Córdoba, habitat of G. quehlianum).

G. ochoterenai Backbg. (2)
Bo. flat-spherical, olive-green; **Ri.** c. 16, becoming broad and flat; **Tub.** suffused brownish, hump-like; **Ar.** white to yellowish; **Sp.** 3–5 radials, mostly bent towards the Bo., horn-coloured to whitish-yellow, dark-tipped; **Fl.** 3.5 cm lg., white, throat pale pink.—Argentina (La Rioja?).
An extremely variable spec., as can be seen from any larger-sized consignment of imported plants. The more extreme variants—if seen by themselves—would be regarded as belonging to different spec. In order to show the complex adequately, the following principal varieties have been established; between these there are always intermediates which, depending on their habit, are referable to one or other variety. At the present time no further subdivision is possible:

v. **cinereum** Backbg.: **Bo.** more ashen to greyish-green; **Ri.** and **Tub.** with broader humps; **Sp.** shorter, ± blackish at first; **Fl.** shorter;

v. **polygonum** Backbg. n.v.: **Bo.** olive-grey to suffused reddish-brownish; **Ri.** to ± 2 cm br. below, (12–)18–26; **Ar.** to 5 mm lg.; **Rsp.** ash-grey to blackish at first, or when moist; **Fl.** somewhat longer; **Fr.** to 4 cm lg., 1.9 cm ∅, dirty red, with pink Sc. (Coll. Uhlig and Backeberg, U 2169; collected by Fechser). (Fig. 142 above);

v. **tenuispinum** Backbg. n.v.: **Bo.** fairly uniformly flat-spherical, ± greyish-olive or suffused brownish; **Ri.** c. 10–12, with a more conspicuous chin-like protuberance; **Sp.** 3–5, shorter than in the type, light grey, horn-coloured at first or when wet, reddish below; **S.** glossy, black, 0.75 mm lg., ± cap-shaped, with a narrow oblong hilum having a swollen and protruding rim. (Coll. Uhlig and Backeberg, U 2170; collected by Fechser). (Fig. 142, centre);

v. **variispinum** Backbg. n.v.: **Bo.** flat-spherical, olive-green to ashen-olive or slightly brownish-green; **Ri.** c. 12, with acute transverse furrows and fairly prominent chins; **Sp.** very variable in colour and more strongly projecting: yellowish, pinkish-brown, to black or bi-coloured (lighter, with a ± reddish-brownish base), also variable in length but longer than in the type, sometimes to 4 cm lg. (Coll. Uhlig and Backeberg, U 2168; collected by Fechser). (Fig. 142 below.)

If the photos of the type-species are compared with those of the varieties, considerable differences will be noted. Only by showing the more widely diverging forms can one give any idea of the degree of variability of this spec., which proves yet again that specific descriptions based on single specimens are often incomplete, i.e. they fail to give any idea of the possible range of variation.

G. oenanthemum Backbg. (2)
Bo. fairly depressed-spherical, becoming subspherical, matt greyish to bluish-green, to c. 10 cm ∅; **Ri.** c. 10–11, to 2 cm br. below; **Tub.** widening below, swollen, with a short sharp chin; **Sp.** typically 5, light grey, stout, sometimes reddish-translucent; **Csp.** 0; **Fl.** to c. 5 cm lg., wine-red to salmon-coloured; **Fr.** ovoid, green.—Argentina.

G. onychacanthum Y. Ito (3)
Bo. flattened-spherical, simple, to 20 cm ∅; **Ri.** divided into oblique Tub.; **Sp.** 9, stoutly subulate, to 3 cm lg., pectinate, greyish-brown; **Fl.** 2.5 cm lg., bellshaped to funnelform, to 3 cm br., dirty white; **Tu.** bluish.—Uruguay (?).

G. parvulum (Speg.) Speg. (2)
Bo. small-spherical, to 3 cm br. and h., dirty ashen-green; **Ri.** mostly 13, with many Tub.; **Sp.** 5–7, fine, often curving and appressed, to 4 mm lg., greyish-white; **Csp.** 0; **Fl.** 4.5–6 cm lg., white.—NW. Argentina (San Luis).

G. paediophilum Ritt. (Not yet described)
Bo. simple, subspherical, reaching flowering size when 55 mm h. and c. 60 mm ∅; **Ri.** 7, vertical, with a tubercular prominence around the Ar.; **Ar.** round, ± white-woolly, 5 mm ∅, 20 mm apart; **Rsp.** 9–12, to 20 mm lg., greyish-pink; **Csp.** 3, 2 of these smaller, directed upwards, other one longer, to 25 mm lg., projecting; **Fl.** c. 53 mm lg., 54 mm ∅ when open, creamy-yellowish at first, later white; **Sep.** with a broad grey M.-stripe, broad above, rounded, narrower below; **Pet.** similarly shaped but mucronate; **throat** red; **Ov.** bluish, with broad white-bordered Sc.; **Fil.** reddish; **An.** whitish-ivory; **style** white; **Sti.** white; **Fr.** only 2 cm lg., subspherical, bluish, with pink Sc.; **S.** blackish-brown, pitted.—Paraguay (Cerro León). (FR1177.)

G. pflanzii (Vpl.) Werd. (2)
Bo. broadly spherical, sometimes offsetting, to 50 cm ∅, velvety, matt to yellowish-green; **Ri.** c. 7

(certainly more in larger plants), rounded, made tuberculate by the broad, acute, down-curved, transverse notches over the Ar.; **Ar.** large, oblong, thickly white-woolly; **Rsp.** 6–9, ± curving, to 2.5 cm lg.; **Csp.** 1, mostly shorter than the longest Rsp.; all **Sp.** whitish, tinged pink, dark-tipped, reddish-brown at first below, becoming rough; **Fl.** to 5 cm lg. and ∅, beaker-shaped to funnelform, white to salmon-pink, faintly violet at the base.—Bolivia (Rio Pilcomayo) to N. Argentina (collected there by Fechser).

G. platense (Speg.) Br. & R. (2)
Bo. ± broadly spherical, green to darker bluish-green; **Ri.** 8–14; **Tub.** broadly rounded because of the shallow transverse indentations; **Sp.** typically 7, soon becoming whitish, reddish below; **Fl.** with a slender Tu. (only two-thirds as long as in G. leptanthum), white, **throat** reddish.—Argentina (Prov. Buenos Aires).

G. proliferum Backbg.: **Gymnocalycium calochlorum** v. **proliferum** (Bckbg.) Backbg.

G. pseudomalacocarpus Backbg. n.sp. (3)
Bo. flattened-spherical, 7 cm ∅ and 3 cm h. has been noted, resembling Malacocarpus (Wigginsia), dirty greenish-olive, the bleached flanks of the Ri. suffused somewhat reddish during dormancy; **Ri.** c. 11, acute, transversely furrowed, with narrow Tub., thickened around the Ar.; **Ar.** c. 1.5 cm apart, ± sunken; **Sp.** 3–5, directed sideways and downwards, to 1.7 cm lg., slightly curving, the lowest one stoutest, thickened below, sometimes an upper pair which is very thin and light-coloured, all Sp. otherwise dull brown; **Csp.** 0; **Bl.** ? Bud-development marked by the development of tufts of white H. in the Ar., suggesting the plant is referable to Ser. "Schickendantziana".—Bolivia (salt-dunes near San José, close to the Paraguayan frontier) (Coll. Uhlig, U 2180; found by Father Hammerschmid). (Fig. 143.) [Haage adds: Bolivia: discovered SE. of Taperas near Lourdes, by Father Klingler.]

This spec. is unusual because of its resemblance to Malacocarpus (Wigginsia), with its narrow flanks and acute Tub.; like G. griseo-pallidum, it had to be described before anything was known of the Fl. so that the data about these unusual and outlying species should not be lost.

G. pugionacanthum Backbg. n.sp. (2)
Bo. simple, hemispherical, 10 cm ∅ has been noted, deep bluish-green; **Ri.** c. 10, with a thin transverse furrow, to 2.5 cm br., 8 mm h.; **Rsp.** very stout, ± appressed, 4 pairs directed laterally, one Sp. pointing downwards, all 10–20 mm lg., somewhat compressed, black at first, then ash-grey or still

blackish above; **Csp.** 0; **Fl.** 4 cm lg., 4.5 cm $\varnothing$; **Tu.** only 1.5 cm lg.; **Sep.** olive-green, with a white border and red tip; **Pet.** creamy-white suffused light grey, brownish-pink at the base, more pink outside; **Fil.** cream; **An.** pink, with or without pollen. Flowers in Europe end April.—N. Argentina (Córdoba?) (Coll. Uhlig and Backeberg, U 2148; gathered by Fechser; no further data available re locality.) (Fig. 144.)

G. pulquinense (Card.) Hutch.: **Weingartia pulquinensis** Card. and its v. **corroana** Card.

G. pungens Fleischer—Fričiana Řada 1: 7, 4. 1962 (2)
Bo. simple, spherical, to 10 cm h., 8 cm $\varnothing$, dark green; **Ri.** 13, divided into $\pm$ oblique Tub.; **Ar.** 5 mm lg., 2 mm br.; **Rsp.** 7; **Csp.** rarely 1–2; all Sp. rather thin, 4–4.5 cm lg., pale grey, darker-tipped; **Fl.** 4 cm lg., white; **Ov.** 1.2 cm lg., with hemispherical Sc.; **Fr.** spherical, light red.—Origin?

G. quehlianum (Hge. Jr.) Berg. (2)
Bo. broad to flat-spherical or subspherical, reddish to greenish-grey, mostly to c. 7 cm $\varnothing$ and more; **R.** thick, napiform; **Ri.** c. 11, made up entirely of **Tub.** to 12×15 mm, rounded or chin-shaped and projecting; **Rsp.** 5, appressed, spreading, to 5 mm lg., translucent, horn-coloured, reddish below; **Csp.** 0; **Fl.** with a slender Tu., to 6 cm lg., pure white inside, **throat** reddish; **S.** brown(!).—Argentina (Córdoba).
v. **albispinum** Bozs.: **Sp.** chalky-white, red below; **Fl.** larger;
v. **flavispinum** Bozs.: **Sp.** concolorous yellow, not red below;
v. **rolfianum** Schick: **Ri.** to 10, broader, more obtuse; **Sp.** stouter, ivory above, reddish-brown below;
v. **zantnerianum** Schick: **Ri.** to 15; **Sp.** pungent, to 4 mm lg.; **Fl.** lilac-pink outside; **Fil.** concolorous white or yellowish-white.

G. ragonesii Cast. (2)
Bo. small, flat to hemispherical, smoky grey; **Ri.** 10, very flat, only slightly transversely notched; **Sp.** 6, appressed and spider-like, to 3 mm lg., bristly fine, whitish; **Csp.** 0; **Fl.** to 4 cm lg; **Fl.** creamy-white, throat dull red; **bud** slender, smoky grey outside; **Pet.** ?—Argentina (Catamarca).

G. rhodantherum Böd.: **Gymnocalycium mazanense** var. **breviflorum** Backbg.

G. riograndense Card. (2)
Bo. simple, broadly spherical, to 6 cm h., to 20 cm $\varnothing$, glossy, dark green; **Ri.** c. 13, to 3 cm br.; **Tub.** obtusely conical; **Rsp.** 8(–9), to 2.5 cm lg., slightly

curving, thin-subulate, stiff, grey, black-tipped, brownish below; **Csp.** 0; **Fl.** beaker-shaped, white; **throat** bluish-red.—Bolivia (Rio Grande).

G. riojense Frič ex Paz (2)
Bo. simple, dark green at first, then brownish-green to brownish, to 10 cm $\varnothing$, 8 cm h.; **Ri.** c. 15, 1 cm br. below; **Ar.** 12 mm apart; **Sp.** mostly 5, appressed, pale brownish, brown above, 2 cm lg.; **Fl.** 3.5 cm $\varnothing$; **Sep.** rather obtuse, with a reddish or brownish M.-line; **Pet.** paler, with a reddish M.-line; **throat** carmine.—Argentina (La Rioja).

G. ritterianum Rausch
Bo. simple or forming small groups, flattened-spherical, as in G. megalothelos offsets often develop in upper half of the Bo., light green or tinged brownish, 3–4 cm h., to 11 cm $\varnothing$, with a long taproot; **Ri.** 10–12, vertical, divided into Tub. by transverse furrows; **Ar.** sunken, in upper half of the Tub., 5 mm lg., white-felty; **Rsp.** 7–9, spreading, curving to the Bo., to 25 mm lg., one Sp. directed downwards; **Csp.** rarely 1, curving upwards, to 30 mm lg.; all **Sp.** pinkish-brown; **Fl.** apical, 65 mm lg. and 75 mm $\varnothing$; **Tu.** dark green, with rounded Sc.; **Sep.** spatulate, pinkish-white with a greenish M.-stripe; **Pet.** spatulate, very br. white, glossy; **throat** light violet-pink; **style** thick, 20 mm lg., with 10 yellowish Sti.; **Fr.** pear-shaped, bluish with whitish-pink Sc.; **S.** 1 mm $\varnothing$, blackish-brown.—Argentina (La Rioja, near Famatina, at 3000–3500 m). Named for Friedrich Ritter.

G. roseiacanthum hort. = G. calochlorum v. roseiacanthum: resembles G. sigelianum.

G. saglione (Cels) Br. & R. (2)
Bo. simple, spherical, bluish-green, to 30 cm $\varnothing$; **Ri.** 13–32; **Tub.** low, broadly swelling, to 4 cm lg., with an acute transverse furrow; **Rsp.** 8–10 at first, later to 15 or more, to 4 cm lg.; **Csp.** 1 or several; **Sp.** reddish-brown to black, $\pm$ curving; **Fl.** 3.5 cm lg., white or faintly pink; **Fr.** reddish, 2 cm $\varnothing$.—N. Argentina (Salta, Tucuman, Catamarca). Very variable.
v. **rubrispinum** n.nud.: **Sp.** concolorous reddish; probably a good variety.

G. sanguiniflorum (Werd.) Werd.: a form of **Gymnocalycium baldianum** (Speg.) Speg.

G. schickendantzii (Web.) Br. & R. (3)
Bo. simple, often broadly spherical, to c. 10 cm $\varnothing$, dark green; **Ri.** 7–14 or more; **Tub.** obtuse, 5-sided, connected basally; **Ar.** oblong; **Rsp.** 6–7, to 3 cm lg., $\pm$ flattened and recurved, projecting, reddish-grey to horn-coloured; **Csp.** 0; **Fl.** to 5 cm lg., white to somewhat reddish, pink inside, bellshaped to

funnelform; **bud** greenish-white; **Tu.** with somewhat acute light-bordered Sc.—NW. Argentina (Córdoba to Tucuman).

Sometimes in a single plant simultaneously there is a continuous transverse division of the Tub., or the furrow is absent, or only short and inconspicuous. It is therefore only possible to segregate and name a variety where both bud-colour and rib-form deviate from the description. In v. delaetii, for instance, it is only new tubercles that are sometimes discontinuous, while they are later marked with only a short transverse furrow.

v. **delaetii** (K. Sch.) Backbg.: **Bo.** lighter green; **Tub.** rounded, not connected at the base (or with an acute transverse furrow); **buds** reddish; **Tu.** with rounded Sc. bordered pink to violet; **Fl.** deeper pink, particularly inside.

G. schroederianum v. Osten (2)
Bo. broadly spherical; **Ri.** 24, tuberculate; **Ar.** 2 cm apart; **Rsp.** 7, yellow, red below; **Csp.** 0; **Fl.** c. 7 cm lg., greenish-white.—Uruguay.

G. sigelianum (Schick) Berg. (2)
Bo. flat-spherical, to 7 cm br., brownish-grey or dark brownish-green; **Ri.** 10, low, slightly tuberculate, distinctly transversely furrowed; **Ar.** white at first; **Sp.** 3(–5), to 12 mm lg., stout, scaberulous, whitish-grey, dark-tipped; **Tu.** fairly stout; **Fl.** pink.—Argentina (Córdoba).

G. spegazzinii Br. & R. (2)
Bo. simple, depressed-spherical at first, later sometimes ± oblong, to 20 cm h., 18 cm ∅, bluish or greyish-green to brownish; **Ri.** 10–15 or more, broadly rounded, divided into Tub. by ± distinct transverse furrows, to 4 cm br.; **Ar.** yellowish-grey, later grey; **Rsp.** 5–7, to 5.5 cm lg., pale reddish-brown, pruinose, rough, at first dark brown to blackish or reddish-brown, or bi-coloured, pale pink below, dark above, stoutly subulate, appressed and ± curving, ± thickened below; **Csp.** mostly 0, sometimes 1 ± porrect and slightly down-curving, more strongly thickened below; **Fl.** to 7 cm lg., 5 cm ∅, whitish to faintly pink, **throat** purple, **Pet.** sometimes with a broader red central zone; **Fr.** spherical-oblong, ± pruinose; **S.** 1 mm lg., dark brownish-red to black.—Argentina (Salta, Cafayate, Valle de Lerma). (Fig. 145.) A magnificent and very variable spec. The following have been segregated:

v. **horizonthalonium** (Frič), not described: **Bo.** flat-spherical; **Sp.** 5–7, greyish-black, light below. Only one of several forms;

v. **major** Backbg.: **Bo.** brilliant bluish-green; **Sp.** 7–9, rusty to blackish-brown, clawlike; **Ri.** c. 20.

G. stellatum (Speg.) Speg. and v. minimum Paz.:

Gymnocalycium asterium Y. Ito and v. **minimum** (Paž.) Backbg. (FR 1176.)

G. stenopleurum Ritt.: Paraguay (Cerro León): not yet fully described. (FR 1176.)

G. striglianum Jeggle 1973
Bo. simple, 30–50 mm h., 40–80 mm br., epidermis bluish-grey to brown; **Ri.** 8–12, notches rather wavy; **Ar.** ± oblong, to 5 mm lg., 2–3 mm br., with greyish-brown felt, 10–15 mm apart; **Sp.** 3–5, to 15 mm lg., blackish, not becoming grey; **Fl.** 40 mm ∅, 50 mm lg., creamy-white, suffused pink; **Tu.** long, with round, white-bordered Sc.; **style** with 10 yellowish Sti.; **Fr.** greyish-green, dehiscing laterally; **S.** black, rough. Juvenile plants resemble G. asterium and G. bodenbenderianum.—Argentina (Mendoza).

G. stuckertii (Speg.) Br. & R. (2)
Bo. subspherical, to 4 cm h., 6.5 cm ∅, dark green; **Ri.** 9–11, later flattened; **Tub.** medium-sized, rounded, chin not prominent; **Rsp.** 7–9, to 2.4 cm lg., pink to brown, scaly-pruinose; **Fl.** 4 cm ∅, whitish to pink; **Pet.** ± fleshy.—Argentina (Salta to Córdoba).

G. sutterianum (Schick) Berg. (2)
Bo. flat-spherical; **Ri.** 10; **Tub.** oblong, transverse furrows short, deep; **Ar.** whitish; **Sp.** mostly 5, appressed, to 15 mm lg., whitish-grey; **Fl.** large, whitish-pink.—Argentina (Córdoba). Possibly only a form or variety of G. sigelianum (Schick) Berg.

G. tillianum Rausch 1970
Bo. simple, broadly spherical, to 10 cm h., to 15 cm ∅, bluish-grey to green; **Ri.** to 15, straight, 15–20 mm br., divided by transverse notches into angular Tub. 15–20 mm lg.; **Ar.** c. 8 mm lg., 5 mm br., felty; **Rsp.** in 3 pairs and 1 directed downwards, spreading, curving to the Bo.; **Csp.** 0–1, projecting, curving somewhat upwards; all **Sp.** to 30 mm lg., subulate, thickened below, black to brown, later greying; **Fl.** 30 mm lg. and 25 mm ∅; **Ov.** short; **Tu.** green with pink Sc.; **Pet.** rounded, dark red; **throat** and **Fil.** carmine-pink; **style** and **Sti.** (8–9) orange-yellow; **Fr.** broadly spherical; **S.** scarcely 1 mm lg., cap-shaped, testa brown.—Argentina (Sierra Ambato, 3500 m).

Spec. resembles G. oenanthemum but is distinguished by the longer Sp., the presence at times of a Csp., by the smaller darker Fl. and different S.-shape.

G. tortuga hort. (3), collected by Blossfeld and never described: **Bo.** to c. 10 cm ∅; **Tub.** sharply chin-shaped; **Sp.** reddish-black at first, c. 7, to 1.5

cm lg., becoming pinkish-grey, some Sp. ±
compressed; **Csp.** 0. May be variable: I saw plants
with a reddish chin and more yellowish Sp. (G.
tudae Y. Ito?).—Paraguay (?).

G. triacanthum Backbg. (2)
Bo. spherical, sometimes projecting somewhat over
the base, brownish to ashy-green; **Ri.** to c. 12,
flattened to rounded; **Tub.** indistinct, transverse
notches short, acute; **Rsp.** almost always 3 (rarely
to 5), appressed, horn-grey, ± gently curving; **Fl.**
3.5 cm lg., white, **throat** darker.—Argentina.

G. tudae Y. Ito (3)
Bo. flat-spherical, 6 cm h., to 17 cm ∅, bluish-
green, ± velvety; **Rsp.** to 7, light yellow, darker-
tipped; **Csp.** 0; **Fl.** 4 cm lg. and ∅, white.—
Paraguay.

G. uebelmannianum Rausch
Bo. simple, flattened-spherical, 1 cm h., to 7 cm ∅,
greyish-green, with a taproot; **Ri.** 8–12, straight,
divided by transverse furrows into Tub. 5–8 mm
lg.; **Rsp.** 5–7, chalky-white, 5–15 mm lg., curving
downwards; **Csp.** 0; **Fl.** 35 mm lg. and ∅, white;
throat pink; **style** thick, yellow, with 10 **Sti.**; **Fr.**
spherical, 6 mm ∅, green with ochre-coloured Sc.;
S. 1 mm lg., matt black, with a basal hilum.—
Argentina (Sierra de Velasco, 2200–2800 m).
Differentiated from G. andreae and G. baldianum
above all by the white Sp. and the greyish
epidermis.

G. uruguayense (Ar.) Br. & R. (2)
Bo. flat-spherical, dark green; **Ri.** 12–13, with very
hump-like **Tub.**; **Ar.** grey at first; **Sp.** 3, radial, to 2
cm lg., white; **Fl.** c. 4 cm lg., broadly funnelform;
Sep. pale greenish-yellow, whitish inside; **Pet.** light
lilac-coloured to (sometimes, when fading?) white,
linear-lanceolate; **S.** semi-matt, greyish-black.—
Uruguay (Paso de los Toros).
The ± lilac-flowered form is also known as v.
roseiflorum (Frič) Y. Ito, but in my view it should
not be segregated. G. artigas Hert., which is very
similar in habit, is distinctive in having the Fl.
lemon-yellow inside.

G. valnicekianum Jajó (2)
Bo. broadly spherical at first, later spherical to
elongated, to 30 cm h., to 18 cm ∅, sometimes
offsetting to form groups, smooth, dark grass-
green; **Ri.** c. 10(–13); **Tub.** swollen, rounded, chin-
like; **Ar.** light grey; **Sp.** variable in number, 7–15 or
more whitish-grey to dirty white, thickened below;
Csp. 1–6; **Fl.** 5 cm ∅, white; **throat** reddish; **S.** matt
black.—Argentina (Córdoba).
Schütz also distinguishes v. centrispinum.

G. vatteri Buin. (2)
Bo. hemispherical at first, to 4 cm h., to 9 cm ∅,
matt, olive-green; **Ri.** (8–)11(–16), 2.5 cm br.
below, to 12 mm h.; **Tub.** swollen and humped,
with an acute transverse notch below; **Ar.** grey; **Sp.**
1–3(–5), radial, ± appressed or projecting, horn-
coloured or a dirty darker colour, lower Sp.
variable in length and curvature but these also
sometimes projecting and fairly stout, other Sp.
bent and closely appressed; **Fl.** 5 cm lg., 4 cm ∅,
white, **throat** reddish; **S.** 1 mm lg., glossy, light
brown.—Argentina (Córdoba, Sierra Grande, near
Nono). (Fig. 146.) In the form with more conspicuously claw-like Sp., these can also be irregularly interlacing.

G. venturianum Frič: **Gymnocalycium baldianum**
(Speg.) Speg.

G. villa-mercadense (FR 6): no description available.

G. weissianum Backbg. (2)
Bo. broadly spherical, to 9 cm h., to 14 cm ∅, dull
greyish-green; **Ri.** to 19, almost 2 cm br. below,
greatly swollen around the Ar.; **Tub.** with a chin-
like protuberance; **Ar.** moderately felty; **Rsp.** 6–8,
with laterally directed pairs, also one pointing
downwards, to 3 cm lg., light-coloured; **Csp.** 1,
pointing upwards; **Sp.** dark at first; **Fl.** ±
bellshaped to funnelform, brownish or whitish-
pink, **throat** darker.—Argentina (Mazán).
  v. **atroroseum** Backbg.: differs in having longer,
stouter, interlacing **Sp.** and deep pink **Fl.**;
  v. **cinerascens** Backbg.: more depressed-
spherical; **Sp.** ± black at first, then silver-grey,
straighter, but the **Csp.** curving upwards.

G. westii Hutch.: **Weingartia westii** (Hutch.)
Backbg.

G. zegarrae Card. (2)
Bo. simple, spherical, bluish-green, to 10 cm h., to
18 cm ∅; **Ri.** 13; **Tub.** 5–6-sided, 2 × 3 cm; **Ar.**
elliptic, light grey; **Rsp.** 8, ± pectinate, to 2.5 cm
lg.; **Csp.** 1, somewhat longer; all **Sp.** greyish-white,
tipped brownish or blackish, stoutly subulate,
projecting and ± curving; **Fl.** beaker-shaped,
3.5–4.5 cm lg., 4 cm ∅, white or delicate pink,
throat red; **style** short; **Sti.** reddish, long; **S.** 0.5 mm
lg., glossy, brown.—Bolivia (Perez–Mairana road).

The following are, till now, only names by Ritter:
G. brevistylum (FR 1133); G. eurypleurum (FR
1178); G. paediophilum (FR 1177); G. stenopleurum (FR 1176). The 3 last-named are from
Paraguay.

Gymnocereus Backbg. (65)

Tree-like Cerei with erect, deep green branches, with numerous finely tuberculate ribs and the areoles rather crowded, especially in the flowering zone. They are characterised by the spines which are not stout, but longer, very flexible, pointing downwards, or interlacing with those above and below, later dropping, and the branches are then subterete. The nocturnal flowers are funnelform and glabrous, opening very widely and densely set with large scales which become black as the flower fades. Seeds small, ± glossy black. Flowering areoles are larger or more strongly felty. A group of species of very uniform character.—Distribution: N. Peru (Canchaque on the W. Andean slopes, to the tropical valleys on the E. side, on the rivers Marañon and Paucartambo). [(R).]

Buxbaum (Kakt. u. a. sukk. Pflz., 14: 10, 185. 1963) states incorrectly that the name Gymnocereus is illegitimate, since the group of species had already been validly published by me as Gymnanthocereus Backbg., with his illustration, and with G. chlorocarpus as the type-species. He refers this plant (l.c.) to Browningia Br. & R. As I had suggested in 1937 (BfK.), Cactus chlorocarpus HBK. later proved to belong to Seticereus. Since the type-species has to retain the generic name, Gymnanthocereus is a synonym of Seticereus; and it became necessary to find a new name for the genuinely glabrous-flowered plants: Gymnocereus Backbg., with his illustration, and with G. "Browningia chlorocarpa" shows yet again how essential it is to have adequate knowledge of the living material. It is also reasonable to ask what benefit can come from his combination with the conspicuously dimorphic genus Browningia, in addition to the inclusion of Azureocereus (see these genera also). The erection of Gymnanthocereus in 1937 was due to the use of inadequate dry material and to the incomplete understanding at that time of the Peruvian cerei. (See also Seticereus.)

G. altissimus (Ritt.) Backbg.
Bo. tree-like, to 5 m h. (dry areas) to 10 m h. (wetter zones), with a stout **trunk**; **Ri.** 7–8; **Ar.** with brown felt, becoming grey, also with white H. at first; **Rsp.** 5–6, 5–10 mm lg., ± projecting; **Csp.** mostly 1(–2–4), 2–6 cm lg., projecting or directed downwards; **Fl.** 5–6 cm lg., slightly perfumed, with crowded broad Sc.; **Pet.** greenish-white, strongly recurved.—Peru (Marañon, Bellavista).

G. amstutziae Rauh & Backbg.
Bo. tree-like, 5 m h.; **branches** 5–6 cm ⌀ at first, stouter later, greyish to dirty green; **Ri.** 11 at first; **Ar.** brownish, crowded; **Sp.** to c. 15, ± bristle-like, ± brittle, brownish at first, soon dark grey to

blackish, c. 6 scarcely distinguishable as centrals, to 4.5 cm lg., directed downwards; **Fl.** 4.5 cm lg. and ⌀, opening widely, cream to white inside.—N. Peru (Rio Paucartambo, Jaupi Bajo).

G. microspermus (Werd. & Backbg.) Backbg. (T.)
Bo. tree-like, to 6 m h., with a smooth terete **trunk** to 30 cm ⌀, spineless below; **Ri.** to over 20; **Ar.** white; **Sp.** thin, ± bristle-like and flexible, ± chestnut-coloured, sometimes lighter, pointing downwards, 12–16 on new growth, to over 30 on older branches; **Fl.** 6 cm lg. and ⌀, white, with fleshy Sc.; **S.** 1 mm lg., slightly glossy, brownish-black or completely black.—N. Peru (Canchaque and Olmos valleys). (Fig. 147.)

Haagea schwartzii Frič (Porfiria coahuilensis Böd.): **Porfiria schwartzii** Böd.

Haageocereus Backbg. (90)

A genus with relatively numerous species; plants erect or prostrate, spines robust or finer, in some cases interspersed with hairs, the central spines in part shorter, sometimes much longer. The flowers are funnelform, with the limb varying from narrow to wide, and coloured green to greenish-white to white, or ± pink to dark red, but never yellow. The fruits are mostly fairly large, weakly hairy, subspherical berries. The genus occurs only in Peru, and only on the Pacific slopes, but with marked differences in altitude, from near sea-level up to 2400 m. The flowers are always nocturnal, opening at different times during the afternoon and sometimes still remaining ± open for a time the following morning. 48 species, nearly all of them vigorous-growing and thus welcome additions to our collections, especially on account of their bright spine-colours, running from pure white to yellow and red to dark brown and blackish. The descriptions given refer almost exclusively to plants grown in habitat, since material from other sources would probably not be identifiable: it is a characteristic of Haageocereus that plants grown in more northerly latitudes or in a glasshouse have weaker spination, the central spines being conspicuously shorter; the colouring however is retained for a long time, so that the plants for the most part become even more attractive. Unless dual descriptions could be provided to reflect these differences, other characters would have to be employed for a diagnosis. Imported plants grown in sunnier and warmer climates usually retain their natural character, so that the latter has to be taken as the basis for any descriptions. In some species it has been necessary to introduce varieties because, although there is a natural variability, new growth—and all Haageocereus species offset from low on the body or from the base—may be different in colour from older stems.—Distribution: throughout the Pacific region of Peru, mostly below 1000 m altitude. [(R).] 5 Series have been distinguished, and these are reproduced below in order to simplify identification:

Plants erect (or at
least predominantly
so)
 Spines stout
  Stems stouter,
  sometimes with api-
  cal bristles........ 1. Acranthi Backbg.
 Spines finer
  Stems more slen-
  der, without bristles 2. Versicolores Backbg.
  Stems stouter
   Without hairs bet-
   ween the spines... 3. Asetosi Backbg.
   With hairs (bris-
   tles) between the
   spines........... 4. Setosi Backbg.
Plants prostrate...... 5. Decumbentes Backbg.

The appropriate Series is indicated by the figure in brackets after the specific name.

H. acanthocladus Rauh & Backbg. (3)
Bo. branching and bushy, to 70 cm h.; **branches** 6 cm $\emptyset$; **Ri.** 18; **Rsp.** numerous, stout, to 1.5 cm lg.; **main Sp.** 1–2, fairly stout, to 5 cm lg., projecting upwards and downwards and interlacing, yellow below, brown-tipped; **Fl.** c. 10 cm lg., greenish-white; **Fr.** 2 cm $\emptyset$, wine-red.—Central Peru (Rio Huaura [Churin valley]; Sayan, 900 m).

H. achaetus Rauh & Backbg. (1)
Bo. little branching, to 1.2 m h.; **shoots** to 15(–20) cm $\emptyset$; **Ri.** 13; **Ar.** ochreous-brown at first; **Rsp.** numerous, to 1.5 cm lg., yellow-ochre; **Csp.** mostly 1, longer, to 5 cm lg., very stout, ochreous-brown with lighter zones; **Fl.** c. 5 cm lg., white.—Central Peru (Churin valley, 1200 m, rare).

H. acranthus (Vpl.) Backbg. (1)
Bo. erect, or prostrate and then ascending, to 3 m lg. if prostrate; **shoots** to 8 cm $\emptyset$; **Ri.** 12–14, more tuberculate at first; **Ar.** yellow to dark brown; **Rsp.** c. 20–30, yellow, to 1 cm lg.; **Csp.** set in transitional Sp., several stouter, one longest Sp. to 4 cm lg.; **Fl.** 6–8 cm lg., ± greenish-white; **Fr.** broadly spherical, green at first.—Central Peru (type locality: Rimac valley, Santa Clara, 400–600 m; from the valley of the Rio Fortaleza to that of the Rio Pisco, at 400–2400 m).
  v. **crassispinus** Rauh & Backbg.: **Bo.** more strongly branching; **Csp.** sometimes absent,

otherwise conspicuously thick (Cañete and Pisco valleys);
  v. **fortalezensis** Rauh & Backbg.: **Ar.** with persistent woolly flock; habit later more decumbent; **Csp.** not very long, light brown (Rio Fortaleza);
  v. **metachrous** Rauh & Backbg.: **Sp.** light brown to coffee-coloured, at first interspersed with fine **Br.-Sp.** (Pisco valley, 2000 m).

H. akersii Backbg. (4)
Bo. robust, erect, to 1 m h.; **St.** 10–15, to 7 cm $\emptyset$; **Ri.** 17–18; **Rsp.** c. 23, to 1 cm lg., fine, pale yellow; **Br.-H.** to 25, silky, to 4 cm lg., white; **main Sp.** 1–2, flexible, to 4.5 cm lg., yellowish, brown-tipped; **Fl.** 7 cm lg., 5 cm $\emptyset$, deep purplish-pink; **Fr.** 4 cm lg., ovoid, bluish-red.—Central Peru (Cajamarquilla).

H. albidus Ritt.: an undescribed name.

H. albisetatus (Akers) Backbg. (4)
Bo. erect, to 2 m h.; **St.** to 6 cm $\emptyset$; **Ri.** 25–26; **Rsp.** c. 25, short, bristly, to 13 mm lg., yellowish at first, then whitish; **Br.** white, short, to 1 mm lg.; **Csp.** 0, or 1 thin-acicular, to 1.5 cm lg., coloured like the Rsp.; **Fl.** greenish-white, to 4.5 cm $\emptyset$; **Fr.** 4.5 cm lg., yellowish-red.—Central Peru (Eulalia valley, 1000 m).
  v. **robustus** Akers: **Fl.** reddish; only a form?

H. albispinus (Akers) Backbg. (4)
Bo. erect, to 1 m h., to 15 St., 7–9 cm $\emptyset$; **Ri.** 25–26; **Rsp.** 20–25, to 5 mm lg., pale yellow; **Br.** 30–35, white, to 7 mm lg.; **Csp.** 1, to 1.2 cm lg., yellowish; **Fl.** 4 cm br., deep red with a bluish or orange tinge; **Fr.** 6 cm $\emptyset$.—Central Peru (Eulalia valley). (Fig. 148.)
  v. **floribundus** (Akers) Backbg.: **St.** somewhat more slender; **Sp.** yellower, somewhat longer; **Fl.** more numerous;
  v. **roseospinus** (Akers) Backbg.: **St.** to only 7 cm $\emptyset$; **Csp.** more distinctly projecting, pink.

H. ambiguus Rauh & Backbg. (5)
Bo. prostrate, branching from the base; **St.** to 80 cm lg., 4 cm $\emptyset$; **Ri.** 15–16; **Rsp.** numerous, to 1 cm lg., brownish to later greyish-violet; **main Sp.** 1–2(–3), mostly 1, to 5 cm lg., directed downwards, appearing reddish-brown against the light, pruinose below at first, and later throughout.—S. Peru (Atico).
  v. **reductus** Rauh & Backbg.: **Ri.** 17–18; **Rsp.** only 5–7 mm lg.; **main Sp.** only 2.5 cm lg., one shorter and thinner, leather-brown, tipped violet-brown.

H. aureispinus Rauh & Backbg. (3)
Bo. erect, to 80 cm h.; **St.** 6–8 cm $\emptyset$; **Ri.** 18–20,

fresh green; **Ar.** crowded, whitish-yellow; **Rsp.** 30–40, to 1 cm lg., brilliant yellow, without Br.; **Csp.** 1(–2), to 4 cm lg., light yellow at first, dark-tipped, later reddish to blackish-violet, pruinose; **Fl.** 6–7 cm lg., to 3 cm $\emptyset$, pure white; **Fr.** $\pm$ spherical, wine-red.—Peru (Canta valley, Rio Chillon, 800–1200 m).

v. **fuscispinus** Rauh & Backbg.: **Sp.** reddish-brown at first; **Csp.** 1–2, light brown below, tipped dark brown, later black;

v. **rigidispinus** (Rauh & Backbg.) Rauh & Backbg.: **Rsp.** 40–50, 8 mm lg., amber-coloured at first, often tipped reddish-brown; **Csp.** 1–2, one to 4 cm lg., much thickened below, one Sp. somewhat shorter, appressed downwards, coloured like the Csp. of the preceding variety; **Fl.** 5–6 cm lg., greenish outside, white inside.

H. australis Backbg. (5)
Bo. prostrate, to 1 m lg., **R.** napiform and branching; **St.** to over 25 cm lg., 4–6 cm $\emptyset$, darker green to greyish-green; **Ri.** c. 14 or rather more; **Ar.** light brownish at first; **Rsp.** c. 20, hyaline, fine, to 8 mm lg.; **Csp.** more numerous, sometimes scarcely differentiated, stouter; **main Sp.** 1(–2), pale horn-coloured, brownish above at first, thickened below, to 4.5 cm lg.; **Fl.** white, more strongly hairy, c. 7 cm lg., 3.5 cm $\emptyset$; **Fr.** eventually pink, c. 4 cm lg.—S. Peru (from Atico southwards, in the coastal zone) and neighbouring N. Chile.

v. **acinacispinus** Rauh & Backbg.: **St.** to 50 cm lg., prostrate, 4–5 cm $\emptyset$; **R.** napiform; **Rsp.** thin, reddish-violet at first; **Csp.** 2–3, to 3 cm lg., thickened below, $\pm$ angular, curving upwards and sabre-like, colour as for the Rsp., later silvery-grey, black-tipped; **Fl.** to 10 cm lg., less hairy than the type, but somewhat more so than H. decumbens, white (?).—S. Peru (coast, near Atico, Panamericana Km 697).

H. bicolor Ritt., undescribed: Haageocereus dichromus Rauh & Backbg.?

H. chalaensis Ritt.: undescribed.

H. chosicensis (Werd. & Backbg.) Backbg. (4)
Bo. erect, to 1.5 m h., forming groups; **Ri.** c. 19; **Ar.** yellowish-white; **Rsp.** radiating, 30 or more, sometimes bristly, fine; **Br.-H.** fine; **Csp.** 3–4, 1–2 more conspicuous in addition to the transitional Sp., $\pm$ subulate, to 2 cm lg.; **Sp.** varying in colour from whitish to rusty-yellow or brownish; **Fl.** with a slender tube, lilac-red to carmine-violet; **Fr.** spherical, green to pink.—Central Peru (Chosica and the Eulalia valley).

v. **rubrospinus** (Akers) Backbg.: main **Sp.** reddish-brown.

H. chrysacanthus (Akers) Backbg. (4)
Bo. erect, to 1 m h.; **St.** to 25 together, to 7.5 cm $\emptyset$; **Ri.** 17–18; **Sp.** to c. 65, dissimilar, to 12 mm lg., yellowish with brownish flecks; **main Sp.** 2–3, thin, sharp, to 4.5 cm lg.; **Br.-H.** c. 15, yellowish-white, to 17 mm lg.; **Fl.** 5 cm $\emptyset$, greenish-white; **Fr.** 4 cm lg., green to reddish-green.—Central Peru (Panamericana Km 226, N. of Lima).

H. chryseus Ritt.: undescribed: **Haageocereus chrysacanthus** (Akers) Backbg.

H. clavatus (Akers) Cullm.: **Haageocereus pseudomelanostele** v. **clavatus** (Akers) Backbg.

H. clavispinus Rauh & Backbg. (1)
Bo. mostly directed upwards, to 1 m h.; **St.** to 10 cm $\emptyset$; **Ri.** 13; **Ar.** large, grey; **Rsp.** numerous, stout, c. 25; **transitional Sp.** thicker, to 12, to 1 cm lg.; **main Sp.** 1, thick and nail-like, to 3 cm lg.; all **Sp.** violet-grey at first, then grey, granular and rough; **Fl.** to 6.5 cm lg., white, reddish outside; **Fr.** 2.5 cm lg., dark green.—Peru (Ataconga Desert, 200 m). (Fig. 149.)

H. comosus Rauh & Backbg. (3)
Bo. erect, to 1.3 m h.; **St.** to 10 cm $\emptyset$; **Ri.** c. 20; **Ar.** white; **Rsp.** numerous, thin, yellow; **Br.-H.** erect, to 3.5 cm lg., white; **main Sp.** yellow, thin, flexible, to 3 cm lg., later directed $\pm$ downwards; **Fl.** red, chocolate-coloured outside; **Fr.** 4 cm $\emptyset$, yellowish-green with a pink tinge.—Central Peru (Eulalia valley, 1000 m).

H. convergens Ritt.: undescribed (? Loxanthocereus).

H. crassiareolatus Rauh & Backbg. (4)
Bo. erect, to 1 m h.; **St.** to c. 6 cm $\emptyset$ or rather more; **Ri.** 18; **Ar.** whitish-yellow at first; **Rsp.** numerous, to 8 mm lg., bristly, fine; **transitional Sp.** similarly; **Br.-H.** to 1.3 cm lg.; **main Sp.** to 2 cm lg.; outer **Sp.** pale yellowish, inner ones greyish-yellow; **Fl.** 8 cm lg., whitish-green, outer Pet. grey; **Fr.** 5 cm lg., red.—Peru (Churin valley, Rio Huaura, 1200 m).

v. **smaragdisepalus** Rauh & Backbg.: **Bo.** thicker, to 8 cm $\emptyset$; **Ri.** c. 20; **Rsp.** to 1.8 cm lg.; **Csp.** 1, to 3.5 cm lg., often flecked; **Tu.** and **Fl.** vivid emerald-green outside; **Pet.** pale green.—Peru (Churin valley, 1400 m).

H. decumbens (Vpl.) Backbg. (5)
Bo. decumbent, often in colonies; **St.** to 5 cm $\emptyset$; **Ri.** c. 20; **Rsp.** numerous, to 30 or more, to 5 mm lg., light-coloured; **Csp.** 1–2 as main Sp., to 5 cm lg., often directed downwards, light to dark brown; **Fl.** c. 8 cm lg., c. 4.5 cm $\emptyset$, white, brownish-green outside, only slightly hairy.—S. Peru (neigh-

bourhood of Chala and Mollendo).

    v. **multicolorispinus** Buin.: occurs between Nazca and Lomas, on sandy dunes, almost without water, coming into growth whenever moisture is available. Also found in Dept. Arequipa and Ica;

    v. **spinosior** Backbg.: **Csp.** confused and interlacing, to 10 cm lg., silvery-grey.

H. deflexispinus Rauh & Backbg. (1)
Bo. erect; **St.** to 1.5 m h., to 12 cm $\emptyset$; **Ri.** 12, with V-furrows; **Ar.** light brown; **Rsp.** stout, to 1 cm lg., amber-coloured at first; main **Sp.** 1, to 8 cm lg., amber-coloured, very stout, directed downwards; **Fl.** ?—Peru (Churin valley, Rio Huaura, 1200 m).

H. dichromus Rauh & Backbg. (4)
Bo. erect, to 1 m h.; **St.** to 8 cm $\emptyset$; **Ri.** 20; **Ar.** yellowish; **Rsp.** numerous, fine, 8 mm lg., reddish-brown at first; **Br.** sparse; main **Sp.** pungent, to 2 cm lg., mid to lemon-yellow or intermediate colours to garnet-red, sometimes banded; **Fl.** white, wine-red outside; **Tu.** green.—Peru (Churin valley, Rio Huaura, 1200 m).

    v. **pallidior** Rauh & Backbg.: **St.** to 5 cm $\emptyset$; **Ri.** c. 18; **Sp.** shorter, equal, to c. 5 mm lg., $\pm$ whitish or yellowish or pale reddish below, tipped coppery or greyish-reddish; **Br.** sparse; main **Sp.** mostly missing, or to 2 cm lg. (Churin valley, 1700 m).

H. divaricatispinus Rauh & Backbg. (4)
Bo. erect, freely offsetting, to 1.2 m h.; **St.** to 10–15 cm $\emptyset$; **Ri.** 18–19; **Ar.** whitish; **Rsp.** projecting, yellow to purplish-reddish; **Br.-H.** erect; main **Sp.** mostly 1, to 4 cm lg., directed upwards, outwards or downwards, also 3–6 shorter **Sp.**, greyish-yellow below, brownish above; **Fl.** 10 cm lg., with staminodial **H.** inside, **Pet.** and **Tu.** dark purple; **Fr.** ovoid, to 6 cm lg., 4 cm $\emptyset$, pale wine-red.—Central Peru (Lurin valley, frequently seen at 800–1200 m).

H. elegans and v. heteracanthus Ritt.: undescribed, probably identical with H. versicolor (Werd. & Backbg.) Backbg.

H. fulvus Ritt.: v. gautanensis Ritt. (FR 1067): description not available.

H. horrens Rauh & Backbg. (3)
Bo. erect, to 1 m h., more freely branching; **St.** to 5.5 cm $\emptyset$; **Ri.** c. 18, pure green; **Rsp.** over 60, stiffly acicular, projecting, to 1 cm lg.; **Csp.** several, indistinctly differentiated, stouter to subulate, mostly 2 longer ones, pointing upwards and downwards, to 4 cm lg., horn-coloured to grey, dark above or flecked; **Sp.** dense, projecting stiffly, the radials horn-coloured, indistinctly flecked, yellowish below; **Fl.** greenish-white, greenish-red

outside; **Fr.** wine-red, 4 cm lg.—Peru (Trujillo, Panamericana Km 720). (Fig. 150 left.)

    v. **sphaerocarpus** Rauh & Backbg.: to 1.3 m h.; **St.** to 10 cm $\emptyset$; **Ri.** c. 22; **Rsp.** strongly interlacing; main **Sp.** 1–2, to 9 cm lg., yellowish below, brownish above; **Fl.** to 7 cm lg., white, greenish-red outside; **Fr.** spherical, c. 2–3 cm $\emptyset$, wine-red.—Peru (Rio Fortaleza, Km 230).

H. icensis hort.: a spec. collected by Ritter: Bo. slender, Sp. dense, mostly alike, stout, reddish-brown.

H. icosagonoides Rauh & Backbg. (2)
Bo. erect, branching and bushy, to 1.5 m h.; **shoots** to 5 cm $\emptyset$; **Ri.** c. 20; **Ar.** brownish; **Sp.** fine, dense, amber-coloured, reddish in the crown, to 1 cm lg.; **Csp.** not distinguishable; flowering region with persistent flock; **Fl.** 6 cm lg., white.—Peru (Rio Saña valley).

H. lachayensis Rauh & Backbg. (1)
Bo. erect; **St.** to c. 8 cm $\emptyset$; **Ri.** c. 12 or more; **Ar.** very felty; **Rsp.** to 50, acicular, radiating; **Csp.** somewhat stouter, several still more robust, 1–2 longest, to c. 3 cm lg., mostly pointing upwards and downwards, chestnut-brown, yellowish at first below; **Fl.** ?—Peru (Chanchay, Lomas de Lachay, 500 m).

H. laredensis (Backbg.) Backbg. (3)
Bo. erect; **St.** to c. 7 cm $\emptyset$; **Ri.** c. 18; **Sp.** 40–45, golden-yellow, brownish in the crown, to 12 mm lg.; **Csp.** one, longer, directed upwards; **Fl.** white.—N. Peru (Laredo).

    v. **longispinus** Rauh & Backbg.: **Bo.** to 1 m h.; **St.** to 5 cm $\emptyset$; **Rsp.** densely interlacing, amber-coloured; main **Sp.** 1–3 distinguishable, to 6 cm lg., flexible.—Peru (Rio Fortaleza valley).

H. limensis (SD.) Ritt. irecombined from Cereus limensis SD., an old name which can no longer be identified with certainty.

H. litoralis Rauh & Backbg. (5)
Bo. decumbent, to 80 cm lg.; **St.** c. 8 cm $\emptyset$; **Ri.** 16; **Rsp.** numerous, 8–10 mm lg.; main **Sp.** 1–2, to 2 cm lg.; **Sp.** yellowish at first below, darker towards the tip; **Fl.** white, greenish outside.—S. Peru (coast near Atico).

H. longiareolatus Rauh & Backbg. (4)
Bo. erect, to 1 m h.; **St.** to 6.5 cm $\emptyset$; **Ri.** 20; **Ar.** white, to 6 mm lg.; **Rsp.** c. 30–50, to 4 mm lg., yellowish; **Br.-H.** in the crown; main **Sp.** 1–2(–4), to 2.5 cm lg., reddish-yellow at first; **Sp.** fairly rigid, scarcely interlacing; **Fl.** ?; **Fr.** ?—Central Peru (Eulalia valley, 1000 m).

H. mamillatus Rauh & Backbg. (5)
Bo. prostrate; **St.** to 50 cm lg., to 3.75 cm ∅; **Ri.** c. 16–17; **Rsp.** 20–30, to 5 mm lg.; **main Sp.** 1–2, to 3(–5) cm lg.; all **Sp.** brownish to darker, or darker-tipped; **Fl.** ? (white?).—S. Peru (road Camana–Arequipa, Km 165, 400 m).
 v. **brevior** Rauh & Backbg.: **St.** to 20 cm lg., 4–5 cm ∅; **Ri.** 17–18; **Rsp.** very thin, to 5 mm lg., greyish-white; **main Sp.** 2–3, to 4 cm lg., light brown at first, dark-tipped, later pruinose; **intermediate Sp.** (between radials and main Sp.) obliquely projecting; **Fl.** ?—S. Peru (desert between Ocona and Camana, 500 m). Cultivated form with white Sp., Csp. shorter, dark-tipped.

H. **marksianus** Ritt.: **Haageocereus dichromus** Rauh & Backbg. (?)

H. **multangularis** (Willd.) Ritt.: Cactus multangularis Willd. is a name which, acc. Werdermann, cannot now be clarified because of both the richness of forms in Haageocereus, and the number of species; any combination with Haageocereus would therefore be dubious.

H. multicolorispinus Buin.—Sukkde. (SKG), VII/VIII: 41. 1963 (3 or [?] 5).
Bo. slender-columnar, ± erect, branching from the base; **St.** to 1 m lg., 3.5 cm ∅; **Ri.** c. 15; **Rsp.** c. 30, bristly, fine, white, to 5 mm lg.; **Csp.** 4–8, white, black-tipped, darker at the base; most **Sp.** light yellowish-red, later greyish-white, to 5 mm lg., one of them to 2.5 cm lg., thickened below; **Fl.** 8 cm lg., 6.5 cm ∅; **Tu.** reddish-brown; **Sep.** reddish-brown; **Pet.** white; **Fr.** oval, carmine to purple; **S.** cap-shaped.—Peru (between Nazca and the sea, on sandy dunes).
In the wild probably not completely erect; close to H. australis which has a Csp. thickened below, but differing in the number and the three colour-zones of the Sp. as well as the rotate Fl. with crowded Pet., and the sparse H. of the Tu.

H. **ocona-camanensis** Rauh & Backbg. is probably a Loxanthocereus with lighter Rsp.; Fl. not known.

H. olowinskianus Backbg. (1)
Bo. erect, slender, branching quite freely from the base, to 1 m h., leaf-green; **St.** to 7 cm ∅; **Ri.** c. 13; **Ar.** yellowish-white, surmounted by a V-furrow; **Rsp.** over 30, firm, to over 1 cm lg.; **Csp.** 10–12, scarcely differentiated, 1–2(–3) as stouter **main Sp.** to 6 cm lg.; **Sp.** on plants in the wild stouter than in cultivated plants, reddish or rusty-brown; **Fl.** c. 8 cm lg., white.—Central Peru (50 km S. of Lima, close to the sea, in a restricted area).
 v. **repandus** Rauh & Backbg.: **St.** to 10 cm ∅; **Ri.**

to 16; **Fl.** 8 cm lg., white;
 sv. **erythranthus** Rauh & Backbg.: same characters; **Fl.** red (Fig. 150 right);
 v. **rubriflorior** Rauh & Backbg.: **St.** to only 6 cm ∅; **Ri.** 13; **Fl.** vivid red, to 8 cm lg.;
 v. **subintertextus** Rauh & Backbg.: **St.** to 10 cm ∅; **Ri.** 14; **Rsp.** bristly, interlacing; **main Sp.** mostly 1(–3), to 3 cm lg.; **Fl.** 5–6 cm lg., greenish-white. Differentiated by shorter Fl. and denser Sp.
In cultivation the type also has denser and thin-acicular, chestnut-brown Sp.; the varieties differ in the softer, dense, violet-brown Sp., the colour being most intense in the apical region.

H. pacalaensis Backbg. (3)
Bo. erect, yellowish-green, to 1.7 m h.; **St.** 10–12 cm ∅; **Ri.** 17–20; **Ar.** brownish; **Rsp.** to c. 25, to 1 cm lg., fine, radiating; **Csp.** stouter, c. 4, to 1 cm lg., sometimes also 1–2 to 7 cm lg., flexible, directed downwards; all **Sp.** yellow; **Fl.** c. 10 cm lg., white; **Fr.** 8 cm across, broadly spherical, reddish-green.—N. Peru (close to the coast, Dept. Libertad).

H. **pacalaensis** v. **laredensis** (Backbg.) Krainz: **Haageocereus laredensis** (Backbg.) Backbg.

H. **pacalaensis** v. **longispinus** (Rauh & Backbg.) Krainz: **Haageocereus laredensis** v. **longispinus** Rauh & Backbg.

H. **pacalaensis** v. **repens** (Rauh & Backbg.) Krainz: **Haageocereus repens** Rauh & Backbg.

H. **pacaranensis** and v. **tenuispinus** Ritt.: not described: to 50 cm h., with fine yellow or brown-tipped Sp.; no further clarification.

H. pachystele Rauh & Backbg. (4)
Bo. erect, branching from the base, to 80 cm h.; **St.** 10–15 cm ∅; **Ri.** 16–20; **Ar.** yellow-ochre; **Rsp.** numerous, ± subulate, to 1 cm lg., c. 17–20 which are stiffer, also to 40 which are bristly, thin, white, to 1.5 cm lg.; **Br.-H.** sparse, to 1.5 cm lg.; **main Sp.** 1(–3), to 3 cm lg., erect or porrect, amber-coloured, brown-tipped; **Fl.** white, greenish outside; **Fr.** 4 cm ∅, pale wine-red.—Central Peru (Churin valley, Sayan, 900 m).

H. paradoxus Rauh & Backbg. (3)
Bo. low-growing, to 25 cm h.; **St.** 4 cm ∅; **Ri.** c. 17; **Br.** absent; **Rsp.** bristly, fine, to over 1 cm lg., reddish at first, becoming whitish with a coloured tip; **main Sp.** firmer but very flexible, to 6 cm lg., mostly solitary, scarcely pungent, reddish to red at first, eventually black; **Fl.** ?—Central Peru (Eulalia valley, 1000 m [No. K 42]).

H. peculiaris Ritt.: Loxanthocereus peculiaris Rauh & Backbg.?

H. peniculatus Rauh & Backbg. (4)
Bo. to 50 cm h.; **St.** to (over?) 4 cm ∅; **Ri.** c. 15; all **Sp.** densely projecting, ± equal, brush-like, fine, flexible, whitish below, reddish above, especially at the apex; **Br.** only sparse; **Csp.** scarcely distinguishable, but sometimes longer-projecting; **Fl.** ?— Central Peru (Eulalia valley, 1000 m [No. K 40]).

H. piliger Rauh & Backbg. (4)
Bo. fairly stout, to 70 cm h.; **St.** to almost 20 cm ∅ but mostly 10 cm; **Ri.** to 17; **Ar.** whitish; **Rsp.** very finely acicular, pale yellowish, rather stiff; **Br.-H.** to 2.5 cm lg., white, erect, closely covering the Bo.; **main Sp.** 0–1(–2), to only 2 cm lg., yellowish; **Fl.** white(?), to 5 cm lg.—Central Peru (Pachacamac). Cultivated form with all H. and Br. white.

H. platinospinus (Werd. & Backbg.) Backbg. (5)
Bo. decumbent; **St.** to 5 cm ∅ and more; **Ri.** 13–15; **Ar.** oblong, yellowish-brown, later grey and fairly large; **Rsp.** c. 10–13, to 1.5 cm lg.; **Csp.** 1–4, stoutly subulate, to 7 cm lg.; all **Sp.** lighter to darker brown (to almost black) at first, later silvery-white, especially the Csp., all dirty dark brown when moist; **Fl.** white, c. 7 cm lg.; **Tu.** brownish-red.—S. Peru (near Arequipa, 2200–2400 m).

H. pluriflorus Rauh & Backbg. (1)
Bo. erect, strongly branching from the base, to 80 cm h., light greyish-green; **St.** to 10 cm ∅; **Ri.** c. 11; **Rsp.** to 15, to c. 8 mm lg., pruinose, light grey, tipped brownish; **Csp.** 1(–2) to 6 cm lg., directed obliquely downwards, violet-brownish at first, later light grey; all **Sp.** yellowish at first below, tipped blackish-brown; **Fl.** numerous, to 12 cm lg., to 4.5 cm ∅; **Tu.** brownish; **Pet.** creamy-white; **Fr.** ?—S. Peru (Rio Majes, Hacienda Ongoro, 800–1200 m).

H. pseudoacranthus Rauh & Backbg. (1)
Bo. erect, branching from the base; **Ri.** c. 13; **Ar.** brownish, surmounted by a V-furrow; **Sp.** 3-seriate: the lowest ones to 20, thin, acicular, **transitional Sp.** 6 or more, ± subulate, **main Sp.** 1–2(–4), subulate, porrect, brownish; **Fl.** ?— Central Peru (Lurin valley(?); Churin valley, 1000 m).

H. pseudomelanostele (Werd. & Backbg.) Backbg. (4) (T.)
Bo. erect, branching from the base, to 1 m h.; **St.** to 10 cm ∅; **Ri.** to over 18–22; **Ar.** moderately felty; **Rsp.** numerous, golden-yellow; **Br.-H.** fine, under 2 cm lg., later dropping; **main Sp.** 1 or more, stouter, distinctly longer, some to 8 cm lg.; **Fl.** to 5 cm lg., 3 cm ∅, greenish-white.—Central Peru (Cajamarquilla, 500 m).

v. **carminiflorus** Rauh & Backbg.: **Bo.** to 1.2 m h.; **St.** to 10 cm ∅; **Ar.** whitish; **main Sp.** 1–2, to 3 cm lg.; **Fl.** 8 cm lg., carmine.—Central Peru (Eulalia valley, 1000 m);

v. **clavatus** (Akers) Backbg.: **Bo.** to 1 m h.; **St.** to 10 cm ∅; **Ri.** 18–20; **Rsp.** c. 30, yellow, flecked brown; **Br.-H.** 30–35, yellowish; **main Sp.** 2, yellow, brown-tipped, to 4 cm lg.; **Fl.** 6.5 cm lg., 5 cm ∅, deep pink.—Peru (N. of the Lurin valley, in the canyons of the coastal mountains).

H. pseudoversicolor Rauh & Backbg. (2)
Bo. erect, branching from the base and bushy, to 1.2 m h.; **branches** 8–10 cm ∅; **Ri.** c. 18; **Ar.** brownish, the wool from the Fl.-bud sometimes persisting; **Rsp.** numerous, to 1 cm lg., yellowish-brown; **Csp.** 1(–2), to 3 cm lg., pale brown to darker, directed ± downwards; **Fl.** to 5.5 cm lg., white; **Fr.** to 3 cm ∅, greenish-red.—N. Peru (Rio Saña valley, 100–200 m).

H. repens Rauh & Backbg. (5)
Bo. prostrate, often very sinuate; **St.** decumbent, to 2 m lg., to·8 cm ∅; **Ri.** 19; **Ar.** yellow-ochre; **Br.** absent; **Rsp.** c. 40, ± erect, to 10 mm lg., very thin, ± yellow-ochre at first; **main Sp.** 1(–2), less stout, to 1.5 cm lg.; **Sp.** amber-coloured at first; **Fl.** to 7 cm lg., to 3.5 cm ∅, opening widely, pure white.— N. Peru (S. of Trujillo, coastal sandy desert, Km 535). (Fig. 151.)

H. rubrospinus (Akers) Backbg.
Bo. to 1.5 m h. and 6 cm thick; **Sp.** dense, fine, yellowish and reddish, with fine white bristly H.; **Fl.** to 6 cm br., carmine-pink, opening widely.— Peru.

H. salmonoideus (Akers) Backbg. (4)
Bo. erect, to 1 m h.; **St.** to 10 cm ∅; **Ri.** c. 22; **Br.** short, white; **Rsp.** c. 60–80, 30% of these being Br. to 8 mm lg., yellow at first; **main Sp.** 1–2, stouter, to 2 cm lg., light yellow, shorter in cultivation; **Fl.** 6 cm lg., pink; **Fr.** 6.5 cm ∅, green, pink above.— Central Peru (Rimac valley above Chosica).

v. **rubrispinus** Rauh: **Sp.** brown to reddish-brown (Lurin valley, 1000–1200 m).

H. seticeps Rauh & Backbg. (4)
Bo. to 1 m h.; **St.** to 5 cm ∅; **Ri.** 19; **Ar.** strongly felty; **Rsp.** c. 50, 5 mm lg., thin; apical **Br.** short; **Csp.** 1–4, to 4 cm lg., bristly, thin, sometimes stouter or contorted, projecting above, yellowish at first; **Fl.** red(?); **Fr.** wine-red, to 2.5 cm ∅.— Central Peru (Eulalia valley, 1000 m).

v. **robustispinus** Rauh & Backbg.: **Ri.** fewer, c. 17; **Csp.** to 2.2 cm lg., ± reddish-brown at first;

Br. 1.5 cm lg., white; **Fl.** wine-red; **Fr.** as in the type.

H. setosus (Akers) Backbg. (4)
Bo. columnar, 1–3 m h., to 25 **St.** together, to 6 cm ⌀; **Ri.** 20–21; **Ar.** circular; **Sp.** numerous, to 100 including Br., one-third of these acicular, yellow; **Br.** 70 % over 2 cm lg., yellow, red or silvery-grey, the fine Rsp. at the apex forming a tuft; **main Sp.** 1–2, to 2 cm lg., brownish; **Fl.** 5 cm lg., red or scarlet-pink; **Fr.** 4 cm ⌀, green, pink above.—Central Peru (Caracoles Hills, S. of Lima, close to the coast).
  v. **longicomus** (Akers) Backbg.: **Bo.** to only 30 cm h., little branching; **St.** 6 cm ⌀; **Rsp.** c. 20, fine, yellow; **Br.** c. 50, to 4.5 cm lg.; **main Sp.** 1–2, to 3.5 cm lg., stoutly acicular, reddish.
Hoffmann reports a form(?) to only 1.2 m h., with **Fl.** 7.5 cm lg., carmine inside.

H. smaragdiflorus Rauh & Backbg. (4)
Bo. erect, to c. 50 cm h.; **St.** to c. 5 cm ⌀; **Ri.** c. 20; **Sp.** white, bristly, thin, interlacing, numerous, 0.5–1 cm lg.; **Csp.** occasionally 1, thin, to 2 cm lg.; **Fl.** 5 cm lg., emerald-green, with H. to 1 cm lg. at the base of the Fil.; **style** with green **Sti.**—Central Peru (Eulalia valley, 1300 m).

H. superbus Cullm.: only a name.

H. symmetros Rauh & Backbg. (4)
Bo. erect, to 1.2 m h.; **St.** 8–10 cm ⌀; **Ri.** 21; **Ar.** fairly crowded, arranged in symmetrical Isp., with light and fairly dense felt; **Rsp.** short, fine, radiating, numerous, 5 mm lg., amber-coloured; **Br.** very short at the apex, amber-coloured; **Csp.** 1–2, short, to 2 cm lg., brownish-yellow, lighter-zoned; **Sp.** all thin at first, only c. 5 mm lg.; **Fl.** c. 5 cm lg., white.—Central Peru (Churin valley, Rio Huaura, 1200 m).

H. tenuispinus Rauh & Backbg. (3)
Bo. erect, branching from the base, to 60 cm h.; **St.** 8 cm ⌀; **Ri.** to c. 28; **Ar.** yellowish-white; **Rsp.** c. 30, radiating, 1 cm lg., yellowish; **main Sp.** mostly 1, thin-acicular, flexible, bristly-fine at first, pale yellow, later to 5 cm lg.; **Fl.** ?—N. Peru (Panamericana, Km 465, between Trujillo and Chimbote).

H. turbidus Rauh & Backbg. (4)
Bo. erect, to 1.2 m h., branching from the base and bushy; **branches** 5–8 cm ⌀; **Ri.** c. 19; **Rsp.** very thin, numerous, ± projecting, yellow to reddish-brown at first; **Br.** curly, lax; **main Sp.** 1–2, to 8 (–10) cm lg., yellow below, yellowish to reddish above, later pruinose, grey, projecting; **Fl.** 5(–6) cm lg., white.—Peru (Nazca valley, 600–800 m).

v. **maculatus** Rauh & Backbg.: **Sp.** somewhat shorter; **main Sp.** directed more strongly downwards, amber-coloured to flecked reddish-yellow; **Fl.** 8 cm lg., white; **Fr.** to 2 cm ⌀, light wine-red.—Peru (Nazca valley, 1200 m).

H. variabilis Ritt. (syn. H. ferrugineus Ritt.): only names, referable to Loxanthocereus (Rauh; L. ferrugineus?).

H. versicolor (Werd. & Backbg.) Backbg. (2)
Bo. erect, slender-columnar, to 1.5 m h., forming colonies; **St.** to 5 cm ⌀; **Ri.** 16–22; **Rsp.** 25–30, finely acicular, to 5 mm lg.; **Csp.** 1–2 more clearly distinguishable, to 4 cm lg.; **Sp.** zoned in different colours, Csp. yellowish below at first, reddish-brown or lighter above; **Fl.** c. 8 cm lg., to c. 6 cm ⌀, opening widely, white.—N. Peru (E. desert zone, 100–500 m).
  v. **aureispinus** Backbg.: **Sp.** golden-yellow; **Csp.** often missing;
  v. **catacanthus** Rauh & Backbg.: **Csp.** directed ± downwards, stout, light brown; **Rsp.** dark reddish-brown;
  v. **fuscus** Backbg.: **Sp.** fine, dense, deep reddish-brown; **Csp.** ± distinctly longer than the others;
  v. **humifusus** (Werd. & Backbg.) Backbg.: **Rsp.** 10–15, very fine, to 3 cm lg.; **Csp.** thin, pale brown; **Sp.** yellowish at first;
  v. **lasiacanthus** (Werd. & Backbg.) Backbg.: **Sp.** more bristle-like; no longer **Csp.** present;
  v. **xanthacanthus** (Werd. & Backbg.) Backbg.: **Ri.** mostly 10–12(–14); **Csp.** fairly robust, considerably longer, to over 2.5 cm lg. or more, pale yellowish.

H. viridiflorus (Akers) Backbg. (3)
Bo. erect, to c. 1 m h.; **St.** to 20 together, to 7 cm ⌀; **Ri.** 19–20; **Rsp.** to c. 60, very fine, 5 mm lg., pungent, interspersed with Br.; **Csp.** several, to 2.5 cm lg., ± subulate, directed ± downwards; all **Sp.** (pale) yellow; **Fl.** almost 7 cm lg., 4.5 cm ⌀, greenish-white with a green centre; **style** creamy-white with longer **Sti.**; **Fr.** spherical to top-shaped, over 4 cm ⌀, plum-coloured.—Peru (canyon of the Rio Chillon). Distinguished from H. smaragdiflorus by the yellowish Sp., longer Fl., and the absence of H. at the base of the Fil.

H. zehnderi Rauh & Backbg. (4)
Bo. erect, branching from the base to form groups; **St.** at first 4.5 cm ⌀, later to 8 cm ⌀, dirty green; **Ri.** c. 18; **Ar.** dirty white; **Rsp.** numerous, very thin, dense, sometimes interspersed with stouter Sp., to 3 cm lg.; **main Sp.** scarcely distinguishable, sometimes to 5 cm lg., pointing ± downwards; **Br.** to 3.5 cm lg.; **Sp.** and **Br.** yellow; **Fl.** greenish(?)-white.—Peru (Santa valley, Huallanca, 1300m).

H. zonatus Rauh & Backbg. (1)
Bo. erect, branching from the base to form groups; **St.** to 1.5 m h., to 7(–10) cm ∅; **Ri.** 13–14; **Ar.** yellowish-brown; **Rsp.** 15–25(–40), radiating, to 5 mm lg., pale yellow; **H.** in the flowering zone silky, white, 2.5–3 cm lg., persisting as tufts; **main Sp.** 1–2(–4), stout, 2–2.5 cm lg., porrect or directed downwards, ochreous-brown, ± zoned; **Fl.** 7 cm lg., white.—Peru (Churin valley, 2000 m).

Hamatocactus Br. & R. (196)

Plants with the ribs continuous, ± swollen around the areoles or ± indented below them, but not distinctly tuberculate. The central spines are ± strongly elongated, flexible and in all areoles some are hooked. The flowers are more funnelform, the tubes being more slender and less densely scaly than in Ferocactus; they are yellow, sometimes all-yellow, sometimes red at the centre. The fruit, which can be relatively small or to 5 cm long, has few scales and dehisces basally. The seeds are black. These plants are very popular because they are so easy to grow, with flowers appearing even on quite small plants.—Distribution: USA (Texas, New Mexico) to N. Mexico. [(R.)]

H. crassihamatus (Web.) F. Buxb.: **Glandulicactus crassihamatus** (Web.) Backbg.

H. davisii (Hought.) Y. Ito: **Hamatocactus hamatacanthus** v. **davisii** (Hought.) Marsh.

H. hamatacanthus (Mühlpfrdt.) Knuth
Bo. spherical at first, then elongated, to 60 cm h. when it may have several heads (or only if the growing tip has been damaged?), dark green; **Ri.** mostly 13, to 5 cm h.; **Ar.** to 3 cm apart, with nectar thorns; **Rsp.** 8–12, terete to flattened, 1–7 cm lg., sometimes ringed; **Csp.** 1–3(–4), the upper 3 straight, the bottom one to 12 cm lg., porrect, ± straight, angular to flattened; **Sp.** often red or flecked at first, later horn-coloured, then grey; **Fl.** to 7 cm lg., yellow, throat red; **Fr.** 2–5 cm lg., green; **S.** 1.5 mm lg.—USA (Texas, New Mexico) to N. Mexico.
　v. **davisii** (Hought.) Marsh.: distinguished by the more strongly indented **Ri.**, denser and somewhat finer **Sp.**, more numerous **centrals**, and the concolorous yellow **Fl.**—USA (Texas).

H. setispinus (Eng.) Br. & R. (T.)
Bo. to only c. 15 cm h., 8–12 cm ∅, more subspherical, fresh green; **Ri.** c. 13, the crest rather narrow, often ± sinuate; **Ar.** white; **Rsp.** 12–15, radiating, thin-subulate, not very sharp, 0.5–4 cm lg., the upper ones brown, the lower ones white;

Csp. 1(–3), mostly hooked, dark brown, lighter-tipped, somewhat longer than the Rsp.; **Fl.** to 7 cm lg., yellow with a red centre; **Fr.** only 6–18 mm ∅, reddish-brown to coral-coloured.—USA (Texas) to N. Mexico. (Fig. 152.)
　v. **cachetianus** (Monv.) Knuth: **Bo.** eventually cylindric; **Csp.** brown, moderately lg.;
　v. **orcuttii** (K. Sch.) Borg; **Bo.** eventually cylindric; **Csp.** yellow, fairly lg.

H. sinuatus (Dietr.) Orc.: **Bo.** smaller; **Rsp.** 8–12, thin, often bent; **Csp.** 4, the lowest one very lg., angular; **Fl.** 6.5 cm lg., concolorous yellow; **Fr.** green, ovoid (Eng.).—USA (Texas).
The position of this name has not been clarified; if v. davisii above is the only other plant with a concolorous yellow flower, this plant may be a further variety of H. hamatacanthus.

H. uncinatus (Gal.) F. Buxb.: **Glandulicactus uncinatus** (Gal.) Backbg.

Hariota DC. non Adans.: **Hatiora** Br. & R.

Harrisia Britt. (141)

Night-flowering Cerei from the West Indies which, with one exception, are erect, shrubby to tree-like, i.e. they often form a trunk, this being the main character differentiating the genus from Eriocereus or, in the case of H. earlei which is prostrate, it is distinguished by the indehiscent fruits, this as well as the yellow to orange colour of the fruits being a constant character throughout the genus, whereas in Eriocereus the fruits are never of these colours and they split open.—Distribution: USA (Florida) and Antilles. [(R.)]

H. aboriginum Small
Bo. to 6 m h.; **Ri.** 9–11, rounded; **Ar.** brown; **Sp.** 7–9, acicular, mostly only to 1 cm lg., rarely more, pink at first, later grey, brown-tipped; **buds** with dense brown **H.**; **Fl.** c. 15 cm lg., faintly perfumed, white with brown **H.**; **Fr.** spherical, yellow, 6–7.5 cm ∅.—USA (Florida).

H. adscendens (Gürke) Br. & R.: **Eriocereus adscendens** (Gürke) Berg.

H. bonplandii (Parm.) Br. & R.: **Eriocereus bonplandii** (Parm.) Ricc.

H. brookii Britt.
Bo. to 5 m h., freely branching, light green; **branches** 3–4 cm ∅; **Ri.** c. 10; **Ar.** white; **Sp.** 9–12, the longest ones to 2.5 cm lg., upper ones brown at first, lower ones white; **buds** with a few lax white

203

H.; **Fl.** white?: **Fr.** ± spherical, c. 8 cm ∅, yellowish.—Bahamas (Long Island).

H. deeringii Backbg. nom. prop., still undescribed: **Bo.** like that of H. simpsonii Small, only 2 m h.; (6 m in H. simpsonii); floral limb as long as the Tu.—Florida (Pumpkin Key).

H. divaricata (Lam.) Backbg.
Bo. erect, freely branching; **Ri.** 9, obtuse; **Ar.** proximate, little felty; **Rsp.** 8–10, white; **Csp.** 4, brownish, 2–2.5 cm lg.; **Fl.** white, **Tu.** lg.; **Fr.** spherical, yellow, **pulp** white.—Santo Domingo (Pfeiffer) and Haiti (Port-de-Paix). ("Fr. flattened-spherical, tuberculate, yellow": Ekman).

H. earlei Br. & R.
Bo. prostrate, to 3 m lg., dark green, **trunk** ± terete; **branches** to 6 cm ∅; **Ri.** 5–7; **Ar.** white; **Sp.** 5–8, to 5 cm lg., grey, acicular; **Fl.** to 20 cm lg., white; **Tu.** white-hairy; **Ov.** with short Br. and short white H.; **Fr.** depressed-spherical, to 7 cm ∅, yellow.—Cuba (Pinar del Rio).

H. eriophora (Pfeiff.) Britt.
Bo. light green, to 3.5 m h.; **trunk and branches** 4 cm ∅; **Ri.** 8–9; **Ar.** white; **H.** in the flowering zone to 1.5 cm lg.; **Sp.** 6–9, to 4 cm lg., light brown, black-tipped; **buds** with white H. 1.5 cm lg.; **Fl.** 12–18 cm lg., white; **Fr.** subspherical, c. 6 cm ∅, yellow.—Cuba (central to western regions and Pinos Island).

H. fernowii Britt.
Bo. to 3 m h.; **branches** light green, to 2.5 cm ∅; **Ri.** 9; **Ar.** brownish-yellow in the flowering zone; **Sp.** 8–11, light brown, black-tipped, the longest ones to 6 cm lg.; **buds** with light brown H. to 1 cm lg.; **Fl.** c. 20 cm lg., white.—Cuba (Prov. Oriente).

H. fimbriata sensu Knuth non Cactus fimbriatus Lam.: **Harrisia nashii** Britt.

H. fimbriata sensu Knuth v. straminia Marsh.: **Harrisia nashii** v. **straminia** (Marsh.) Backbg.

H. fragrans Small
Bo. erect and arching over, to 5 m h.; **Ri.** 10–12; **Sp.** 9–13, acicular, grey, yellowish-tipped, one longest Sp. 2–4 cm lg.; **buds** with dense white H.; **Fl.** 12–20 cm lg., pink or white; **Ov.** with long white H.; **Fr.** spherical to ± ovoid, faintly reddish, white-hairy.—USA (Florida, Fort Pierce).

H. gracilis (Mill.) Britt. (T.)
Bo. erect, to 7 m h.; **branches** fairly slender; **Ri.** 9–11; **Sp.** 10–16, 2–2.5 cm lg., black-tipped; **buds** white-hairy; **Fl.** 20 cm lg., white; **Fr.** yellow, depressed-spherical, c. 5 cm lg., to 7 cm ∅.—Jamaica. (Fig. 153.)

H. guelichii (Speg.) Br. & R.: **Eriocereus guelichii** (Speg.) Berg.

H. hurstii Marsh.
Bo. erect, with a **trunk**; **branches** greyish-green; **Ri.** 10–12, very low; **Ar.** white, even in age; **Rsp.** 9, acicular, straw-coloured; **Csp.** 4, cruciform, 5–7.5 cm lg., the lowest one to 2.5 cm lg., all straw-coloured, tipped ± dark brown; **Fl.** c. 20 cm lg., white; **Fr.** ovoid, 5 cm lg., 2.5 cm ∅, lemon-yellow.—Hispaniola.

H. jusbertii (Reb.) Borg: **Eriocereus jusbertii** (Reb.) Ricc.

H. martinii (Lab.) Br. & R.: **Eriocereus martinii** (Lab.) Ricc.

H. nashii Britt.
Bo. erect, with a trunk; **branches** 3–4 cm ∅; **Ri.** 9–11; **Sp.** 3–6, grey, to 1.5 cm lg.; **bud** with long white H.; **Fl.** 16–20 cm lg., white.—Hispaniola.
v. **straminia** (Marsh.) Backbg.: distinguished by 7 **Rsp.**, 4 **Csp.**, all straw-coloured; branches more spreading.

H. platygona (O.) Br. & R.: **Eriocereus platygonus** (O.) Ricc.

H. pomanensis (Web.) Br. & R.: **Eriocereus pomanensis** (Web.) Berg.

H. portoricensis Britt.
Bo. erect, to 3 m h., little branching; **branches** to 4 cm ∅; **Ri.** to 11; **Sp.** 13–17, greyish-white to brown, dark-tipped, the longest ones 2.5–3 cm lg.; **buds** with many white **H.**; **Fl.** c. 15 cm lg., white; **Fr.** spherical to ovoid, yellow, 4–6 cm ∅. Puerto Rico (Ponce), islands of Mona and Desecheo.

H. regelii (Wgt.) Borg: **Eriocereus regelii** (Wgt.) Backbg.

H. simpsonii Small
Bo. erect and arching over, to 6 m h., simple or somewhat branching; **Ri.** 8–10; **Sp.** 7–14, later grey, to 2.5 cm lg.; **buds** with white H.; **Fl.** 12–17 cm lg., white (?), with sparse white H.; **Fr.** orange-red, depressed-spherical, 4–6 cm ∅.—USA (Florida, Hammocks, Keys and coast).

H. taylori Britt.
Bo. to 2 m h., light green; **branches** 4–5 cm ∅, ascending, fairly stout; **Ri.** 9; **Sp.** 9–12, longer ones 3–5 cm lg.; **bud** with sparse grey wool.—Cuba (Prov. Oriente, coast).

H. tortuosa (Forb.) Br. & R.: **Eriocereus tortuosus** (Forb.) Ricc.

H. undata Britt.: **Harrisia gracilis** (Mill.) Britt.

Haseltonia Backbg. (167)

Gigantic unbranched columns, with more than one stem probably only as a result of damage, with flexible, light-coloured and rather long spines. As flowering is reached, a fairly broad, one-sided cephalium of woolly hairs develops while at the same time the surrounding spines are longer and interspersed with bristles; in older cephalia the individual areolar tufts are clearly distinguishable. As the length of the cephalium increases the columns, which taper towards the apex, begin to bend over towards the cephalium-bearing side, this direction being constant in any population, giving the impression that the cephalia always develop at the same point of the compass. The flowers are nocturnal, shortly bellshaped and glabrous, the fruit probably also glabrous.—Distribution: Mexico (Puebla-Oaxaca). [(R).]

H. columna-trajani (Karw.) Backbg. (T.)
Bo. erect columnar, simple, to over 10 m h. and to over 20 cm $\varnothing$, soon becoming greyish-green, $\pm$ ventricosely thickened below; **Ri.** to over 16, $\pm$ tuberculate; **Ar.** small, soon becoming glabrous; **Sp.** scarcely differentiated; **Rsp.** 14–18, to 1 cm lg., whitish, **Csp.** 5–8, to 8 cm lg., thickened below, yellowish at first, later white, often dropping; all **Sp.** flexible, the longer ones directed $\pm$ strongly downwards; **Fl.** 4–5 cm lg., pale sulphur-yellow, glabrous; **Sep.** white, tipped pink; **Fr.** to 3 cm $\varnothing$, $\pm$ ovoid, yellowish to greenish-white, with a lid, with traces of distant **Sc.**; **S.** glossy black.—Mexico (S. Puebla to NE. Oaxaca). (Fig. 154).
Later names, better known than that of Karwinksi, were: Pilocereus or Cephalocereus hoppenstedtii (Web.) K. Sch.

Hatiora Br. & R. (24)

Bushy, erect or $\pm$ pendant epiphytes, densely branching, the individual segments branching from the apical areoles, $\pm$ cylindric to $\pm$ clavate, the clavate section almost spherical to oblong, the basal section of the shoot of varying thickness, sometimes fairly thin. The small flowers are bellshaped to funnelform, borne in the apical areoles, often several at a time, coloured yellow to orange-red and pink; the berries are probably mostly white, sometimes flecked; the seeds are black. The stems are either glabrous or they have short, $\pm$ bristle-like spines; older stem-segments become woody.—Distribution: Brazil (region of Rio de Janeiro, Ilha Grande, Minas Geraes, São Paulo). (In cultivation, best grown in a hanging basket.)

H. bambusoides (Web.) Br. & R.
Bo. erect, shrubby, very freely branching; **shoots** in 2's or 3's from the apical areoles, to 5 cm lg., slender-clavate but not stalk-like, the nodose, $\pm$ thickened tip to 4 mm $\varnothing$; **Fl.** orange-red; **Pet.** mostly erect.—Brazil (Rio de Janeiro).

H. clavata (Web.) Moran: **Rhipsalis clavata** Web.

H. cylindrica Br. & R.
Bo. erect, bushy and branching, to 1 m $\varnothing$; **shoots** branching dichotomously or in 3's in a whorl, to 3 cm lg., cylindric, light green, sometimes red or flecked red; **Fl.** solitary, 12 mm lg., orange-yellow; **Fr.** white, slightly purple-spotted, translucent.—Brazil (Rio de Janeiro). (Fig. 155.)

H. herminiae (C.-Porto & Cast.) Backbg.
Bo. forming erect shrubs, sometimes arching over; **shoots** branching dichotomously or verticillately, cylindric, only slightly thickened above, matt dark green; **Ar.** with 1–2 minute **Br.**; **Fl.** mostly solitary, rarely paired, 2 cm lg., to 2.5 cm $\varnothing$, dark pink; **Fr.** olive-green, to 8 mm lg,; **S.** chestnut-brown.—Brazil (Campos do Jordão).

H. salicornioides (Haw.) Br. & R. (T.)
Bo. forming erect shrubs, freely branching, to 40 cm h.; **shoots** paired or 3–5 in a whorl, cylindric or barrel-shaped at first, later appearing to have a distinct stalk, to 3 cm lg.; **Ar.** sparsely felty, sometimes bristly, glabrous in cultivation; **Fl.** 1–2(–3), bellshaped, to 13 mm lg., 10 mm $\varnothing$, yellow; **Fr.** top-shaped, whitish, translucent, reddish-tipped; **S.** black.—Brazil (Rio de Janeiro, Minas Geraes).
  v. **gracilis** (Web.) Backbg.: **Seg.** thin or slender; **Fl.** light yellow;
  v. **stricta** (Web.) Backbg.: **Seg.** shorter, stiffer;
  v. **villigera** (K. Sch.) Backbg.: more conspicuously hairy at the shoot-tip.

Heliabravoa Backbg. (150)

Tree-like and very freely branching cerei, with an indistinct trunk. The buds and the shortly tubed flowers are hairy and also set with fairly dense, long bristles, the fruits similarly; the perianth is rotate, the upper series of anthers rises erect above it, surrounding the moderately exserted style. When ripe the fruit is purple, hairy and bristly and the seeds are black. The genus is presumably night-flowering, the blooms remaining in part open until noon the next day, and hence erroneously described as diurnal (Buxbaum?). The opening of the flowers requires careful verification.—Distributuin: Mexico (Puebla to Oaxaca). [(R).]

H. chende (Goss.) Backbg. (T.)
Bo. tree-like, to 7 m h., forming a wide crown; **branches** dense, erect, sometimes slightly curving and re-branching; **Ri.** 7–9, fairly acute, slightly thickened or raised below the Ar.; **Ar.** ± felty only at the apex; **Rsp.** (2–)4–5, 1–2.5 cm lg., thin, yellow to brown; **Csp.** when present only slightly longer; **Fl.** to 5 cm lg., more or less the same $\varnothing$, white (to delicate pink?): **Fr.** 4 mm $\varnothing$, it and the **Tu.** with beige-coloured H., Br.-Sp. darker.—Mexico (Puebla, Tehuacan; Oaxaca, Oaxaca de Juarez). (Fig. 156, 157.)

Helianthocereus Backbg. (95)

A genus of cerei, divided into 2 subgenera or groups of species (see below), each of which is very uniform: one consists of low-growing shrubs, branching ± from the base, while the plants of the second are erect, sometimes simple and columnar at first, and robust or even very robust. One species within the latter group sometimes grows in large stands along the N. Argentine frontier, presenting a unique sight*; similar species are also found in the Bolivian altiplano. Here also, branching is mostly ± from the base, relatively little and usually only on older plants. The low-growing group is mostly widely branching. In all the species the flowers are diurnal, funnelform and white, red or ± yellow. The tube and ovary, or fruit, are hairy. The extent of the genus, or even the genus to which some of the species were referable, long remained unclarified; in the case of some of the especially low-growing species, some were described as Lobivia; other plants were attributed to Trichocereus, including the gigantic members from the high plateaux which have apical or subapical flowers, whereas the lower-growing species bear their flowers subapically or rather lower down the body. A diagnostic character common to both groups is the funnelform, hairy, diurnal flower, mostly brilliantly coloured; in a few only of the species from high altitudes, the flower is rather longer and bears a considerable resemblance, with its funnel-shape, to the nocturnal flowers of Trichocereus. A comparison of juvenile plants is sufficient to show how closely related the two subgenera are to one another: younger seedlings of the robust and tall-growing Helianthocereus orurensis bear a remarkable resemblance, in spination also, to those of the low-growing and relatively slender Helianthocereus huascha which has stouter central spines. In age, some of the high-altitude species develop a dense covering of longer and almost bristle-like spines.—Distribution: N. Argentina (from Catamarca northwards) to Bolivia. [(R).]

The figure in brackets after each specific name refers to the subgenera below:

SG. 1: Helianthocereus: plants with robust stems, or stoutly columnar, high-altitude species, mostly branching from or near the base; flowers ± apical;

SG 2: Neohelianthocereus Backbg.: more slender-stemmed, low-growing species, always branching from the base; flowers ± lateral.

H. andalgalensis (Web.) Backbg.: **Helianthocereus huascha** v. **rubriflorus** (Web.) Backbg.

H. antezanae (Card.) Backbg. (1)
Bo. to 2.5 m h.; **St.** to 25 cm $\varnothing$; **Ri.** 21; **Ar.** grey; **Sp.** c. 27, thin-acicular, to c. 10 cm lg., pale yellow, those in the apex reddish-yellow, ± interlacing, the longest ones directed downwards; **Fl.** 11 cm lg., light yellow, with brown and white H.; **Fr.** yellowish-green, 2.5 cm $\varnothing$; **S.** glossy black.—Bolivia (Oruro, near La Joya).

H. atacamensis (Phil.) Backbg. (1)
Bo. mostly unbranched, to 6 m h. or more, to 70 cm $\varnothing$; **Ri.** numerous; **Ar.** brown; **Sp.** numerous, to c. 40, often very thin, to c. 10 cm lg.; **Fl.** to 14 cm lg., white (acc. Cardenas).—Chile (Atacama: San Bartolo mine).

H. bertramianus (Backbg.) Backbg. (1)
Bo. branching from the base or from a short trunk, erect; **St.** to 2 m lg., to 25 cm $\varnothing$; **Ri.** c. 20, acute, to 3 cm h.; **Ar.** light brown at first; **Sp.** numerous, to c. 30, ± whitish at first, then hyaline to pale yellow, sometimes bristly, the shortest ones 5 mm lg., the longest ones to 8 cm lg., acicular, pointing downwards; **Fl.** yellowish to creamy white; **S.** glossy black.—Bolivia (La Paz: Comanche mine). (Fig. 158.)

H. conaconensis (Card.) Backbg. (1)
Bo. simple or branching from the base, to 2 m h.; **St.** to 15 cm $\varnothing$; **Ri.** c. 17; **Ar.** blackish-grey, with sparse white H.; **Sp.** c. 18, acicular-bristly, pungent, hyaline, to 15 cm lg.; **Fl.** 11–15 cm lg., to 12 cm $\varnothing$, deep cream-colour.—Bolivia (Cochabamba: Cona-Cona).

---

* See the photograph opposite the title-page.

H. crassicaulis Backbg. n.sp. (2)
Bo. spherical at first, soon elongating and to 16 cm h. has been noted, leaf-green, offsetting from the base, sometimes slightly tapering above, reaching flowering-size at c. 15 cm lg., to 11.5 cm $\emptyset$; **Ri.** (9–)11–14, c. 2 cm br. at midway, rounded; **Ar.** pale brownish, c. 1.5 cm apart, ± circular at first, later often shield-shaped; **Sp.** brown at first above, pale yellow below, ageing to more brownish; **Rsp.** c. 7–12, to 3 cm lg., later fairly stout; **Csp.** 1–4(–5), subulate, c. 3.3–3.7 cm lg.; **Fl.** c. 8 cm lg., 9 cm br. (Uhlig), flame-coloured; **Tu.** with acuminate green Sc. and dark brown H.; **Ov.** green.—N. Argentina (Catamarca, La Estancia; found by Fechser). (Fig. 159.)
Very vigorous-growing; all the characters mark it out as a typical robust or low-growing member of the SG. Neohelianthocereus.

H. escayachensis (Card.) Backbg. n.comb. (Trichocereus escayachensis Card., C. & S. J. [US], XXXV: 5, 157. 1963) (1)
Bo. to 4 m h., with a stout, broad crown; **branches** to 40 cm $\emptyset$; **Ri.** 14–16, 2 cm h., 3 cm br.; **Rsp.** 9–12, 2–4 cm lg.; **Csp.** 1, 4–6 cm lg.; all **Sp.** subulate, grey; **Fl.** numerous, apical, funnelform, 15–17 cm lg., white; **Sep.** tipped purple-brown; **style** green below, yellow above; **Sti.** 15, light yellow; **Fr.** 5 cm $\emptyset$, dark green, with brown H. and white pulp; **S.** 1.5 mm lg., black, spotted.—Bolivia (Prov. Mendez, Dept. Tarija, between Las Carreras and Escayache, 2300 m).
Despite the relatively long Fl., this spec. is a typical Helianthocereus of the arid high plateaux of Bolivia, with its robust habit and very stout shoots.

H. grandiflorus (Br. & R.) Backbg. (2)
Bo. shortly columnar, to 35 cm h., deep green, branching from the base; **St.** to 6 cm $\emptyset$; **Ri.** c. 14; **Ar.** yellow at first; **Rsp.** mostly 8–9(–12), finely acicular, whitish-yellowish, tipped brownish; **Csp.** mostly 1, c. 1 cm lg., somewhat stouter than the Rsp., later also up to 4 weaker Sp.; **Fl.** borne high on the sides, c. 8 cm lg., brilliant red, rather variable in colour.—Argentina (Catamarca: between Andalgalá and Concepción). (Fig. 160.)

H. herzogianus (Card.) Backbg. (1)
Bo. erect-columnar, simple or branching from the base, to 2.2 m h.; **St.** ± clavate, intense green, to 20 cm $\emptyset$; **Ri.** c. 21, acute; **Ar.** grey; **Rsp.** 10–14, acicular, to 4 cm lg., white, brownish above, appressed; **Csp.** 1, pale yellow, brownish above, directed downwards; **Fl.** creamy-white; **Fr.** 7 cm lg., dark green, with white and brownish H.—Bolivia (La Paz: Tirco).
v. **totorensis** (Card.) Backbg.: differentiated by

having 3–4 brownish-yellow **Csp.**, 10–12 straw-coloured **Rsp.**, and **St.** ± clavate, to 15 cm $\emptyset$.—Bolivia (Cochabamba: road to Totora).

H. huascha (Web.) Backbg. (2)
Bo. fairly stout, branching from the base; **St.** cylindric, ± curving upwards, to c. 5 cm $\emptyset$ and more, fresh green; **Ri.** c. 17; **Rsp.** mostly 9–11 or rather more; **Csp.** 1–2, yellowish to brownish, variable in length, usually longer and stouter than the Rsp.; **Fl.** to 10 cm lg., to c. 7 cm $\emptyset$, broadly funnelform, golden-yellow; **Fr.** spherical, green, fairly hairy.—Argentina (Catamarca). Description acc. Schumann, and Fl.-$\emptyset$ acc. Werdermann: "Blüh. Kakt. u.a. sukk. Pflz.", Plate 67.
The type of the spec. is thus lighter green, with Sp. ± amber-coloured and the Fl. only 7 cm $\emptyset$; Werdermann recorded a similar plant in the Huntington Botanical Garden, USA. The following varieties are distinguished:
v. **auricolor** (Backbg.) Backbg.: **Fl.** with more strongly recurved **Sep.**; **Pet.** red with a bluish sheen; **Sp.** evenly dark amber-coloured;
v. **macranthus** Backbg. n.v.:
Distinguished by the darker green **Bo.**; **Fl.** golden-yellow, 12 cm $\emptyset$(!). (Fig. 161.);
v. **rosiflorus** (Y. Ito) Backbg. n.comb. (Soehrensia rosiflora Y. Ito, 1962): **Fl.** pinkish-red;
v. **rubriflorus** (Web.) Backbg.: **Fl.** more true red; **Csp.** c. 6. Vatter reports having seen this plant also with Fl. of other colours.

H. hyalacanthus (Speg.) Backbg. (2)
Bo. erect, cylindric, greyish-green, to 35 cm h., to 10 cm $\emptyset$; **Ri.** 12–16; **Ar.** ashen-grey; **Sp.** 12–20, 1–4 of these longer, scarcely distinguishable as centrals, all bristle-like, yellowish at first, then hyaline, the longest ones mostly directed downwards; **Fl.** 10–12 cm lg., to 8 cm $\emptyset$.—Argentina (Catamarca, valley of Piedra Blanca).

H. narvaecensis (Card.) Backbg. (1)
Bo. columnar, to 1 m h., branching from the base; **branches** to 20 cm $\emptyset$, glossy, dark green; **Ri.** 18; **Ar.** light grey; **Rsp.** c. 12, to 2 cm lg., whitish-grey; **Csp.** 3, to 3 cm lg.; **Fl.** c. 12 cm lg., white; **Fr.** 5 cm br., ovoid, with brown or white H.; **S.** glossy black.—Bolivia (Narvaez).

H. orurensis (Card.) Backbg. (1)
Bo. columnar, to 1.8 m h. or more; **St.** to 25 cm $\emptyset$; **Ri.** to c. 21; **Ar.** greyish-brown; **Sp.** 25–35, acicular to moderately thick, 1.3–8–9 cm lg., brownish-yellow; **Fl.** to 13 cm lg., 10 cm $\emptyset$, light purple or purplish-pink. Bolivia (Oruro, near La Joya).
v. **albiflorus** (Card.) Backbg.: to 2.8 m h.; **Sp.** c.

16, acicular, thin, light yellow, to 10 cm lg*, the longest ones brownish, darker below, to 4 cm* lg.; **Fl.** to 13 cm lg., white.—Same locality.

H. pasacana (Web.) Backbg. (1)
Bo. stoutly columnar, later branching, to 10 m h.; **St.** to over 30 cm $\varnothing$; **Ri.** over 20, later more numerous; **Sp.** numerous, **Csp.** scarcely distinguishable, yellow, unequal, the longest sometimes to 14 cm lg., very stiff at first, later more flexible, and finally $\pm$ stiff and bristly, lighter and sometimes almost white; **Fl.** to 12 cm lg., white; **Fr.** spherical to elongated, green.—Argentina (high valleys from Catamarca to the N. frontier), S. Bolivia.

H. pecheretianus Backbg. (2)
Bo. fairly erect, branching from the base, leaf-green; **St.** to 11 cm $\varnothing$, to 45 cm lg.; **Ri.** 15–20; **Rsp.** 8–10 or rather more, to 1.2 cm lg., thin; **Csp.** 1, to 2.5 cm lg.; all **Sp.** light brown or dark-tipped; **Fl.** to 9 cm lg., 8 cm $\varnothing$, blood-red; **Fr.** spherical, green; **S.** slightly glossy.—Argentina (Catamarca). (Fig. 162.) Ritter recently re-collected this spec. and gave it his number FR 426 (Form 1).
Just as with H. huascha, this stouter-stemmed spec. has a darker green form with somewhat smaller Fl.:
    v. **viridior** Backbg. n.v.: Distinguished from the type by the darker green **Bo.**; **Sp.** brownish; **Csp.** 1, only c. 11 mm lg.; **Fl.** brilliant deep red, c. 8 cm lg. and 6.5 cm $\varnothing$.—N. Argentina (Famatina, acc. Ritter; Form 1 similarly). FR 426A (Form 2).
A speciment of the type (and of H. huascha v. macranthus) is in the Botanical Garden "Les Cèdres", St. Jean-Cap Ferrat). (Fig. 163.)

H. poco (Backbg.) Backbg. (1) (T.)
Bo. stoutly columnar, simple at first, then branching sparingly from the side, 1.5–4.5 m h.; **St.** to 35 cm $\varnothing$; **Ri.** c. 25, later more; **Ar.** grey; **Sp.** scarcely differentiated, c. 50, dissimilar, stiff-bristly or acicular, stouter at first, also $\pm$ curving, light to brownish, sometimes with dark stripes, 1–8 cm lg.; **Fl.** to 12 cm lg., light purple to purplish-pink; **Fr.** 5 cm lg., light green; **S.** glossy, black.—Bolivia (more widely distributed in the S.).
    v. **albiflorus** (Card.) Backbg.: to 6 m h.; **St.** to 20 cm $\varnothing$; **Sp.** c. 20, bristle-like, flexible, glossy white, tipped reddish-brown, to 8 cm lg.; **Fl.** 14 cm lg., creamy-white.—Bolivia (Cuchu Ingenio);
    v. **fricianus** (Card.) Backbg.: distinguished by the lighter to white **Sp.** which are dense, projecting, bristle-like, glossy, to 13 cm lg.; **Fl.** to 13 cm lg., purplish-red.—Bolivia (Potosí, Cuchu Ingenio);

---

* Obviously one of these figures is corrupt! Translator.

v. **sanguiniflorus** Backbg. n.v.: **Fl.** differs by its brilliant blood-red colour.—N. Argentina. (Fig. 165.)

H. pseudocandicans Backbg. n.sp. (2)
Bo. similar to T. candicans, light green, sometimes $\pm$ curving; **St.** to almost 10 cm $\varnothing$; **Ri.** 11–14, to 2 cm br., rounded above; **Ar.** c. 2 cm apart, oblong, densely woolly, to 1.5 cm lg., 1 cm br.; **Sp.** 13–16, horn-coloured, soon becoming grey, some thin, others stouter, scarcely distinguishable as Rsp. and Csp.; **Rsp.** thinner; **Csp.** stouter, longer, sometimes to 8 cm lg.; **Fl.** brilliant red (Fechser), funnelform.—NE. Argentina (Catamarca). Reported many years ago by Vatter; re-collected by Fechser who informed me of the main flower-colours, which must certainly show intermediate shades. I studied living material at "Les Cèdres" which first enabled me to place this plant correctly, despite its resemblance to T. candicans; the brightly coloured diurnal flowers show it belongs to this genus.
    v. **flaviflorus** Backbg. n.v.: **Fl.** yellow;
    v. **roseoflorus** (Backbg.) Backbg. n.comb.—Descr. Cact. Nov. III: 15. 1963 (as Trichoc. candicans var.)
Sp. $\pm$ yellowish, sometimes reddish below, **Csp.** sometimes also brownish; **Fl.** lilac-pink. (Fig. 164.)
Remaining characters of both varieties as in the type.

H. randallii (Card.) Backbg. n.comb. (Trichocereus randallii Card., C. & S. J. [US], XXXV: 5, 158. (1963) (1)
Bo. short, thick, fresh green, only to 1 m h. and to 30 cm $\varnothing$; **Ri.** 20, 2 cm h., 4 cm br., transversely furrowed; **Ar.** only 5–7 mm apart, grey, prominent; **Sp.** not separable into Rsp. and Csp. 25–32, acicular, stiff, 1.5–5 cm lg., somewhat compressed, reddish-brown; **Fl.** numerous, apical, funnelform to urn-shaped, 8 cm lg., 7 cm $\varnothing$; **Tu.** with white and some brown H.; **Sep.** deep purple; **Pet.**, **Fil.** and **style** coloured similarly; **Sti.** light yellow.—Bolivia (Prov. Mendez, Dept. Tarija, valley of Paicho, 2300 m).
This low-growing and cylindric Helianthocereus spec., with short deep purple flowers, demonstrates more clearly than most that these high-altitude cerei form a coherent and distinctive group of species, and that they are not members of Trichocereus.

H. tarijensis (Vpl.) Backbg. (1)
Bo. stoutly columnar, to 1.5 m h., dark green; **St.** to 25 cm $\varnothing$; **Ri.** c. 15; **Ar.** yellowish-brown at first, then grey; **Sp.** 10–17, more subulate at first, rigid, pungent, yellowish to reddish-brown, thickened

and reddish-brown at the base, with similar transverse banding, 3–4 **Csp.** more prominent, to 4(–7) cm lg., **Sp.** later more acicular to bristle-like; **Fl.** only 10 cm lg., light wine-red; **Fr.** 3.5 cm ⌀, salmon-red; **S.** slightly glossy, black.—Bolivia (Escayachi).

× Heliaporus Rowl.: a hybrid genus (Heliocereus × Aporocactus).

Heliocereus (Berg.) Br. & R. (144)

Day-flowering plants; stems not very stiff, ± prostrate to clambering, often bushy and erect in cultivation. The shoots have few ribs, and the spines are rather thin and inconspicuous. However the flowers are large and usually red although this varies somewhat from species to species. Little is known of fruits and seeds; the former are probably always ± spiny, the ovary similarly, these spines variable in thickness. The genus has played an important role as one of the parents of the hybrid genera: Heliochia, Heliaporus, Heliphyllum and Helioselenius. 3(–4) species have been described; according to some authors, the varieties of H. speciosus are to be considered as independent species, but this is still in dispute.—Distribution: Mexico, Guatemala. [(R).]

H. **amecamensis** (Heese) Br. & R. is a white-flowering variety of H. speciosus: **Heliocereus speciosus** v. **amecamensis** (Heese) Wgt.

H. **cinnabarinus** (Eichl.) Br. & R.
Bo. erect or creeping; **St.** to only 1.5 cm ⌀, or to 3 cm ⌀ in age, 3(–4)-angled; **Sp.** c. 10, bristly, yellowish-brownish, mostly 5(–8) mm lg., the lower ones only half as long; **Fl.** c. 15 cm lg., not opening very widely, light crimson, yellowish inside.—Guatemala (volcanoes of Agua and Santa Maria).

H. **heterodoxus** Standl. & Steyerm.
Bo. bushy, epiphytic; **St.** flat or 3-winged; **Sp.** 4–8, to 8 mm lg.; **Fl.** 8–11 cm lg., colour ?—Guatemala (Rio Vega, near San Rafael), Mexico (Tacaná volcano).

H. **schrankii** (Zucc.) Br. & R.
Bo. matt green, sometimes also suffused reddish at first; **St.** with 3–4 angles or wings, 2.3 cm ⌀; **Sp.** 7–10, scarcely 1 cm lg., white, eventually light yellow, 3 upper ones more robust, 3 lower ones longer; **Fl.** 14 cm lg., scarlet to blood-red, with a brilliant carmine-red spot.—Mexico (Zimapan). Possibly only another variety of H. speciosus.

H. **serratus** (Wgt.) Borg: **Heliocereus speciosus** v. **serratus** (Wgt.)

H. **speciosus** (Cavan.) Br. & R. (T.)
Bo. bushy, erect, clambering or pendant, also epiphytic; **St.** to over 1 m lg., reddish-green at first, becoming darker green; **Ri.** 3–5; **Ar.** large; **Sp.** 5–8, later more numerous, to 1.5 cm lg., thin-subulate, yellow to brownish; **Fl.** 12–15 cm lg., brilliant carmine; **Fr.** 3–5 cm lg., ovoid, red, spiny.—Central Mexico (vicinity of Mexico City). (Fig. 167.)
  v. **amecamensis** (Heese) Wgt.: **St.** light green; **Sp.** yellow to brownish; **Fl.** white;
  v. **elegantissimus** (Br. & R.) Backbg.: **Ri.** more winged; **Sp.** only 2–6 mm lg.; **Fl.** scarlet with a faint carmine sheen; **Pet.** sometimes long-tapering;
  v. **serratus** (Wgt.): **St.** with 3–4 **Ri.**; **Sp.** yellowish, 8 mm lg.; **Fl.** mid-purple, without any blue sheen;
  v. **superbus** (Ehrenbg.): **St.** with up to 7 **Ri.**; **Sp.** yellowish, 8 mm lg.; **Fl.** dark crimson-red.

H. superbus (Ehrenbg.) Berg.: **Heliocereus speciosus** v. **superbus** (Ehrenbg.).

The following are further hybrid genera:
× Heliochia Rowl.: (Heliocereus × Nopalxochia);
× Helioselenius Rowl.:
(Heliocereus × Selenicereus);
× Heliphyllum Rowl.:
(Heliocereus × Epiphyllum).

Hertrichocereus Backbg. (162)

The genus is monotypic, the only ± prostrate plant among its Group, and close to Ritterocereus in the characters of flower and fruit; however the flowers open early in the morning, the ovary only occasionally has prickles, and the fruit is spiny; it alone of its Group shows basal dehiscence ("like Oreocereus": Werdermann); the fairly large seeds are glossy black. The ribs are raised into tubercles, but this character, as well as the spination and flower-colour, vary within the species.—Distribution: Mexico (Guerrero). [(R).] Will not tolerate too cool a position in winter.

H. **beneckei** (Ehrenbg.) Backbg. (T.)
Bo. mostly arching over, to semi-prostrate and then ascending, sparingly or freely branching and then somewhat more erect, white-pruinose from the apex to far down the St. (cultivated plants should only be watered from below in order not to damage this lovely coating); **St.** to 7 cm ⌀, the flesh inside yellowish and hard; **Ri.** 7–9, with rather oblong Tub.; **Ar.** brown, later darker; **Rsp.** to c. 5, sometimes dropping, to 1.5 cm lg.; **main Sp.** 1, to 5 cm lg., directed ± downwards, pungent, stiff; **Sp.**

sometimes missing at first or few, light brown, later dark brown or grey, ± reddish above; **Fl.** to c. 7.5 cm lg., 6 cm ⌀, ivory-white to ± reddish; **Fr.** tuberculate, white-pruinose, later reddish, spiny, splitting basally, pulp disappearing; **S.** loose.—Mexico (Guerrero: Canyon de la Mano and Canyon del Zopilote). (Fig. 168.)

Earlier often known, on account of its beautiful mealy coating, as Cereus farinosus Hge.

Hickenia Br. & R.: **Parodia** Speg.

[Hildewintera Ritt. 1966: synonymous with Winteria Ritt. (1962) and Winterocereus Backbg. (1966). There are no valid grounds for segregating this genus from **Borzicactus** sensu Kimnach (Rowl., I.O.S. Repertorium XXIV 1975).

H. aureispina (Ritt.) Backbg. should accordingly now be known as **Borzicactus aureispinus** (Ritt.) Rowl. Description will be found here under **Winterocereus**. Translator.]

Homalocephala Br. & R. (190)

A monotypic genus. The plants, which become quite large, are depressed and broadly spherical, fairly hard, and have robust spines. The subapical flowers are variable in colour; the fruits are red and spineless, with felty flock, and eventually become dry; they may split open irregularly or not at all. The seeds are glossy black. In some parts of their range the plants have been completely eradicated in the interests of agriculture.—Distribution: USA to N. Mexico [(R).]

H. texensis (Hopff.) Br. & R. (T.)
Bo. simple, depressed-spherical, to 30 cm ⌀, 15 cm h.; **Ri.** 13–27, acute, broad; **Ar.** white; **Rsp.** mostly 6(–7), spreading and recurved, unequal, ± flattened, 1.2–4(–5) cm lg., reddish at first, becoming yellow, sometimes banded; **Csp.** 1, ± flat and broader, bent downwards, to 6.5 cm lg., 8 mm br.; **Fl.** broadly bellshaped, to 6 cm lg. and ⌀, scarlet and orange, pink above, to almost white, also with a pink centre; **Fr.** to 4 cm ⌀, juicy at first; **S.** 2.5 mm lg.—USA (Texas, SE. New Mexico) to N. Mexico (in the NE.). (Fig. 169.)

Horridocactus Backbg. (122)

Plants mostly simple, sometimes becoming quite large; flowers differentiated from those of other similar Chilean genera by the absence of hairs; instead they are only sparsely felty-floccose, bristles being present only on the tube above, and sometimes considerably reduced. The hollow fruit is basally dehiscent, with very slight felt or almost glabrous. The seeds are probably always black.—Distribution: N. to Central Chile. [(R).]

Ritter at first placed a number of his newly discovered Chilean globular cacti in Horridocactus—which would imply that their flowers and fruits were only very weakly felty-floccose. He later referred them all to Pyrrhocactus. This is understandable in the case of those species which I had to regroup in Neochilenia; however the species I have left in Horridocactus clearly show the above generic characteristic of ± glabrous flowers and fruits, which distinguishes them from Pyrrhocactus. They must stay there for the present since a precise survey of the individual complexes of species of "Pyrrhocactus Berg. sensu Ritt." only becomes possible if the groups of E. Andean species are kept separate from those of the W. Andes, the W. Andean (Pacific) species being restored to the genera Horridocactus Backbg. and Neochilenia Backbg., which represent different stages of shoot-reduction in the flower. In that case Chileorebutia Ritt. will also have to be included in Neochilenia because Ritter's whole argument for his segregation of Chileorebutia loses its validity. Another important reason for keeping Pyrrhocactus (E. Andean) separate from Horridocactus and Neochilenia (Pacific or W. Andean) is that the high mountain-wall of the Andes has been a barrier for countless ages, and this has given rise to separate lines of development. It is of no significance that there are certain similarities between Pyrrhocactus and Neochilenia, for instance, and it does not necessarily follow that they are one and the same genus. As an example, Rowley has shown that "synthetic species" (i.e. crosses) can show exactly the same characters as certain true species. In the same way similarities may have arisen in the course of evolution in two separate areas of distribution, as a result of processes which have not yet been given sufficient consideration. Precisely for this reason it is important to keep the individual groups of species clearly separate, so that the problem can be studied further.

Since individual names sometimes appear in different guises in the literature, the trade and in collections, I have given these specific names below, together with the appropriate reference. My partial re-naming was based on the original descriptions, in some cases with reservations because of insufficient data regarding floral indumentum.

H. aconcaguensis (Ritt.) Backbg.
Bo. simple, hemispherical, later elongated, to 12 cm ⌀; **Ri.** to c. 21; **Ar.** grey; **Rsp.** c. 9–11, 1–2 cm lg.; **Csp.** mostly 4–6(–9), ± curving, to 2.5 cm lg.; **Sp.** brown to black at first; **Fl.** to 5 cm lg. and ⌀, yellowish-red; **Fr.** red.—Central Chile (Chacres).

v. **orientalis** (Ritt.) Backbg.: **Ri.** fewer, **Sp.** somewhat longer, **S.** smaller, 1.25 mm lg. (1.75 mm lg. in the type).

H. andicolus Ritt.
Bo. hemispherical, simple, later elongated, to 20 cm h., to 16 cm ⌀; **Ri.** 16–24; **Ar.** white to grey; **Rsp.** 10–14, 2–3 cm lg.; **Csp.** stouter, 4–7, 3–4 cm lg.; all **Sp.** whitish below, reddish to blackish above; **Fl.** c. 5.5 cm lg., 5 cm ⌀, reddish-yellow; **Fr.** 1.5 cm lg., greenish-red to carmine.—Chile (between Santiago and Los Andes).
v. **descendens** Ritt.: **Bo.** smaller; **Rsp.** 10–20; **Csp.** 2–6; **Fl.** smaller, **S.** similarly.—Chile (33°S.);
v. **mollensis** Ritt.: **Bo.** stouter, to 20 cm ⌀; **Sp.** mostly longer; **Fl.** with the M.-stripe yellow rather than red.—Chile (Molles);
v. **robustus** Ritt.: **Bo.** as for the preceding variety; **Sp.** more yellowish; **Fl.** with a more blood-red M.-stripe.—Chile (above Tilama).

H. armatus (Ritt.) Backbg.
Bo. hemispherical, dark green, to 25 cm h., to 18 cm ⌀; **Ri.** 15–21; **Ar.** brown; **Rsp.** 8–12, 1.5–4 cm lg.; **Csp.** 2–8, of equal length but stouter; all **Sp.** conspicuously robust, brown to black; **Fl.** to 4.5 cm lg., to 4.8 cm ⌀, yellowish, tinged brownish, with a broad carmine M.-stripe; **style** and **Fil.** pink above, white below; **Fr.** red.—Chile (SW. of Santiago).

H. atroviridis (Ritt.) Backbg.
Bo. hemispherical, simple, later to 10 cm lg., dark greyish-green; **Ri.** 13–16, slightly tuberculate; **Rsp.** c. 10, 2–4 cm lg.; **Csp.** 4–5, 3–5 cm lg.; **Sp.** greyish-black, new **Ar.** with only 1 Csp.; **Fl.** c. 4–5 cm lg. and ⌀, carmine with a light border; **S.** brownish-black.—Chile (Vallenar).

H. calderanus Ritt.: **Neochilenia calderana** (Ritt.) Backbg.

H. carrizalensis (Ritt.) Backbg.—Descr. Cact. Nov. III: 7. 1963 (Pyrrhocactus carrizalensis Ritt., "Taxon", XII: 1, 33. 1963)
Bo. 5–7 cm ⌀; **R.** napiform, yellowish; **Ri.** 13, narrower than in H. atroviridis, with short, rather pointed Tub.; **Ar.** white; **Sp.** black or greyish-brown, straight; **Rsp.** 12–18, 10–25 mm lg.; **Csp.** 4–8, stouter, 2–4 cm lg., curving inwards; **Fl.** to 5.5 cm lg., 4.5–7 cm ⌀, white or yellow, with a red stripe; **Fil.** greenish or reddish; **S.** 0.8 mm lg., near-black, hilum minute.—N. Chile, Prov. Atacama, W. of Carrizal Alto (FR 493).
Since no details of any Br. or wool on the Fl. are given, but the spec. is compared with H. atroviridis, it can only be a member of Horridocactus.

H. centeterius sensu Ritt.: an unclarified spec.

H. chilensis albidiflorus Ritt.: undescribed; a form of **Neochilenia chilensis** (Hildm.) Backbg.

H. choapensis (Ritt.) Backbg.
Bo. flattened-spherical to spherical, to 10 cm ⌀, dark green, sometimes with a brown tinge; **Ri.** 14–22; **Ar.** brownish at first, later white (white in seedlings); **Rsp.** 8–10, 1–2 cm lg.; **Csp.** 4–7(–9), ± slightly curving; **Sp.** mostly greyish-brown or darker; **Fl.** to 4.5 cm lg., 3–5 cm ⌀, light to olive-yellow; **Fr.** to 1.5 cm lg., reddish.—Central Chile (Illapel).

H. confinis Ritt.: **Neochilenia confinis** (Ritt.) Backbg.

H. copiapensis Ritt. (rejected): **Neochilenia kunzei** (Först.) Backbg.

H. crispus (Ritt.) Backbg.
Bo. hemispherical, simple, blackish to greyish-green, to 7 cm ⌀; **R.** napiform; **Ri.** 13–16; **Ar.** white; **Rsp.** 6–10, 2–5 cm lg.; **Csp.** 2–4, 4–8 cm lg.; **Sp.** black, becoming grey, very thin; **Fl.** 3.5 cm lg. and ⌀, outer **Pet.** more red, inner ones whitish with a reddish M.-stripe.—Chile (Freirina). Perhaps referable to Neochilenia?

H. curvispinus (Bert.) Backbg.
Bo. spherical, to over 15 cm ⌀; **Ri.** 16, to 3 cm h., transversely indented; **Ar.** to 15 mm lg.; **Rsp.** mostly 6–10; **Csp.** 2–4, rather stouter; all **Sp.** fairly stout, yellowish at first, darker above, especially in the crown, all ± curving upwards, especially the Csp.; **Fl.** 3.5 cm lg., straw-coloured; **Fr.** almost glabrous.—Chile (vicinity of Santiago). Ritter distinguishes several varieties, but these are probably only forms.

H. dimorphus Ritt.: **Neochilenia dimorpha** (Ritt.) Backbg.

H. echinus (Ritt.) Backbg.—Descr. Cact. Nov. III: 7. 1963 (Pyrrhocactus echinus Ritt., "Taxon", XII: 1, 33. 1963).
Bo. to 9 cm ⌀, pale greyish-green; **R.** napiform, thick, short; **Ri.** c. 13, with chin-like Tub.; **Ar.** to 14 mm lg., brownish; **Sp.** greyish-black or pale greyish-brown, black-tipped, stiff, subulate; **Rsp.** 10–14, 2–3(–4) cm lg.; **Csp.** stouter, 4–8, 2–5 cm lg.; **Fl.** pale yellow, no data regarding size but probably c. 3 cm lg.; **style** pale reddish; **Sti.** 9, pale yellow; **Fr.** 1.5 cm lg.; **S.** 1.4 mm lg.—N. Chile (Cerro Coloso near Antofagasta) (FR 537).
Ov. and Tu. without Br., no data on woolly indumentum; all the above is compatible with Horridocactus.

v. **minor** (Ritt.) Backbg. n.comb. (Pyrrohocactus var., l.c.)
Bo. only half as large; **Ar.** smaller; **Sp.** equal (FR 537a).

H. engleri Ritt.
Bo. hemispherical, later elongated, to 18 cm ∅, to 30 cm h., densely spiny; **Ri.** 16–20; **Rsp.** 12–20, length as for the Csp.; **Csp.** 5–8, 4–7 cm lg., lower ones white or yellowish, upper ones brown and mostly black-tipped; **Fl.** 5–6 cm lg., to 4.5 cm ∅, yellow and red or light lemon-yellow with a pink or red M.-line, outer **Pet.** more olive; **Fr.** reddish.—Chile (Cordillera between Santiago and Valparaiso). Seedlings can also have Sp. concolorous white.
v. **krausii** Backbg.: differentiated by the bluish-green **Bo.**, greenish-yellow **Fl.** and green **Fr.**

H. eriosyzoides Ritt.: **Neochilenia eriosyzoides** (Ritt.) Backbg.

H. froehlichianus (K. Sch.) Backbg.
Bo. spherical to slightly elongated, to 17 cm ∅, light green at first; **Ri.** 16, to 3 cm h.; **Rsp.** and **Csp.** scarcely differentiated, to c. 17, straight or slightly curving, acicular, to 3 cm lg., greyish-yellow at first, with darker bands, smaller Sp. light yellow; **Fl.** to 6.5 cm lg., 6 cm ∅, glossy yellow, brownish outside.—Chile (vicinity of Santiago).
v. vegasanus Ritt.: see H. robustus.

H. fuscus Ritt., not described: **Neochilenia neofusca** Backbg.

H. garaventai Ritt.
Bo. spherical, later elongated, simple, grass-green to bluish-green; **Ri.** 11–16, slightly tuberculate; **Ar.** grey; **Rsp.** c. 12; **Csp.** 1–6, 2.5–4.5 cm lg.; all **Sp.** ± alike in length and thickness, light yellow to yellowish-brown; **Fl.** 5 cm lg., c. 4 cm ∅, light yellow, reddish below; **Fr.** light yellowish-green, to 2 cm lg.—Central Chile (Cerro de la Campana).

H. geissei (Pos.) Dölz
Bo. spherical, simple, bronze-coloured; **Ri.** 18–20, obtuse, scarcely tuberculate; **Ar.** sparsely white-felty; **Rsp.** 14–16, radiating, subulate, sometimes thinner, yellowish at first; **Csp.** 4, cruciform, bent, the lowest one to 2.5 cm lg.; **Fl.** 5.5 cm lg., buff with the centre of the Pet. reddish.—Chile. Spec. only recollected recently.

H. grandiflorus (Ritt.) Backbg.
Bo. hemispherical, simple, green to greyish-green, to 15 cm ∅; **Ri.** 21–23; **Ar.** white; **Rsp.** c. 9–12, 1.5–3 cm lg., curving ± upwards; **Csp.** 1 at first, later 4–7, stouter, curving upwards, 2–4 cm lg.; **Sp.**

moderately robust, black to brown; **Fl.** to 7 cm lg. and ∅, white to light yellowish, with the red M.-stripe half the width of the Pet.; **S.** blackish-brown to black.—Chile (E. of Santiago, Cerro Ramón).

H. heinrichianus Backbg.
Bo. depressed-spherical, to over 9 cm ∅, c. 5 cm h.; **R.** napiform; **Ri.** c. 22, thickened around the Ar.; **Rsp.** c. 5–6, stiff, to 2.6 cm lg.; **Csp.** 1, to 3 cm lg., sometimes 1 additional Sp., appressed downwards; all **Sp.** black, becoming grey; **Fl.** c. 3 cm lg. and ∅, pale light yellow, with a dark stripe.—Chile (Huasco).

H. horridus (Colla) Backbg.: **Horridocactus tuberisulcatus** (Jac.) Y. Ito.

H. kesselringianus Dölz
Bo. depressed-spherical, dark olive-green to dark violet-brown, to c. 7 cm ∅; **Ri.** 16–20, acute, tuberculate; **Ar.** dirty white; **Rsp.** c. 10, radiating, projecting; **Csp.** 1(–2), to 2 cm lg., darker to blackish; all **Sp.** thickened below, only slightly curving, dirty brownish at first, rigid, all soon becoming light grey; **Fl.** 4.5 cm lg., red below, then yellowish-brownish, with a broad red central zone, the reddish-brownish colour predominant; **Fr.** 1.7 cm lg.—Chile.
v. **subaequalis** Backbg.: **Rsp.** 12–14, **Csp.** 4, to 3 cm lg.; **Sp.** rather longer, thinner, more interlacing; **Fl.** somewhat larger.

H. kunzei (Först.) Ritt.: only a name.

H. lissocarpus (Ritt.) Backbg.
Bo. simple, hemispherical, greyish-green, to 20 cm ∅; **Ri.** 17–21, little tuberculate, obtuse; **Ar.** grey; **Rsp.** 8–12; **Csp.** 1–6, subulate, curving upwards, 1.5–5 cm lg.; **Sp.** greyish-yellowish or brownish to ± black; **Fl.** 3–4–5 cm lg. and ∅, perfumed; **Fr.** over 2 cm lg. and ∅, red.—Chile (near Caugenes).
v. **gracilis** (Ritt.) Backbg.: **Sp.** finer, light brownish to reddish-brown, **Ar.** more crowded, **S.** larger.—Chile (W. of S. Francisco de Mostazal, at high altitudes).

H. marksianus (Ritt.) Backbg.
Bo. hemispherical, greyish-green, to 24 cm ∅; **Ri.** 16–28, tuberculate; **Ar.** white; **Rsp.** 8–12, 1.5–2.5 cm lg.; **Csp.** 1–6, stouter, longer, curving strongly upwards, subulate; **Sp.** stout, greyish-brown, darker-tipped; **Fl.** to 4 cm lg. and ∅, lemon or reddish-yellow; **Fr.** 1.5 cm lg., light reddish-brownish; **S.** brownish-black.—Chile (Villa Prat).
v. **tunensis** (Ritt.) Backbg.: smaller, with fewer **Ri.**; **Rsp.** 6–10, **Csp.** 1–4; **Fl.** larger; **Fr.** red.

H. nigricans (Dietr.) Backbg. & Dölz

Bo. broadly spherical, soon becoming greyish, to c. 10 cm $\emptyset$; **Ri.** c. 15, with slight transverse indentations, rounded or acute; **Ar.** white; **Rsp.** 8–9, to 7 mm lg. or more, at most slightly curving; **Csp.** 1–2, somewhat stouter, curving upwards or erect, thickened below; all **Sp.** glossy black at first; **Fl.** to c. 4.5 cm lg., pale and dull to dirty yellowish, with a darker centre outside; **Fr.** clavate, pale red; **S.** small, scarcely 1 mm lg.—Chile. Not re-collected for a long time.

H. nigricans sensu Ritt. and v. grandiflorus Ritt.: predominantly green as seedling-plants at most suffused reddish near the Tub.; appears to be a different spec. or a form; it is not unusual for Chilean spec. raised from seed to look unlike their wild counterparts.

H. paucicostatus Ritt. and v. viridis Ritt.: **Neochilenia pauciocostata** (Ritt.) Backbg. and v. **viridis** (Ritt.) Backbg.

H. pulchellus Ritt.: probably only a form of Neochilenia pygmaea (Ritt.) Backbg.

H. robustus Ritt.: a catalogue-name of Ritter's, at first undescribed; Pyrrhocactus robustus Ritt., Succ., 6: 65. 1960—Neochilenia robusta (Ritt.) Backbg., Die Cact., VI: 3781. 1962).
Bo. mostly simple, to 20 cm $\emptyset$, hemispherical; **Ri.** 16–22, with chin-like Tub.; **Ar.** grey-felty; **Rsp.** 10–12, 1–1.5 cm lg.; **Csp.** 4–7, 2–3.5 cm lg.; **Sp.** very robust, especially the Csp., straight or curving, dirty grey; **Fl.** 4.5–5.5 cm lg., to 3.5 cm $\emptyset$, yellowish to brownish-red with a greenish sheen, border lighter, with traces of felt and fine white Br.; **Fr.** to 2 cm lg., blackish to reddish-green.—Chile (Ocoa) (FR 239a).
    v. **vegasanus** Ritt. (originally held by Ritter to be H. froehlichianus) (Pyrrhocactus robustus v. vegasanus Ritt. l.c.—Neochilenia robusta v. vegasana [Ritt.] Backbg., l.c.).
Bo. smaller; **Ar.** closer; **Fl.** shorter (I have seen some of a brownish colour, with the pink centre of the Pet. becoming wider below, c. 5.3 cm $\emptyset$).—Chile (near Las Vegas).
I have referred both the spec. and the variety (l.c.) to Neochilenia since the Dutch description has insufficient data regarding floral indumentum, as was often the case with Ritter's diagnoses; this makes the classification difficult.

H. rupicolus and v. intermedius Ritt.: **Neochilenia rupicola** (Ritt.) Backbg.

H. scoparius Ritt. (FR 1085): no description available.

H. setosiflorus Ritt.: **Neochilenia setosiflora** (Ritt.) Backbg. and v. **intermedia** (Ritt.) Backbg.

H. simulans Ritt.: **Neochilenia simulans** (Ritt.) Backbg.

H. taltalensis (and v. densispinus?) Ritt. (FR 212): **Bo.** brown; **Fl.** whitish: **Neochilenia fusca** (Mühlpfrdt.) Backbg.

H. trapichensis Ritt.: later regarded as a Pyrrhocactus spec. and not described; probably referable to Neochilenia.

H. tuberisulcatus (Jac.) Y. Ito (T.)
Bo. simple or offsetting, dark green to bluish-green; **Ri.** 14–20, thickened and strongly tuberculate around the Ar.; **Ar.** white, to 1.5 cm lg.; **Rsp.** 10–12, subulate, additional Sp. appearing later; **Csp.** 4–5, very stoutly subulate, to 2.5 cm lg., sometimes $\pm$ curving, brownish at first, zoned darker, yellow below at first; **Fl.** to over 4.5 cm lg., 3.8 cm $\emptyset$, stoutly funnelform, pale brownish or dirty yellow, sometimes with a red M.-stripe below; **Fr.** virtually glabrous.—Chile (vicinity of Santiago). (Fig. 170 left, 171.)
    Ritter lists also v. **minor**, undescribed: **Sp.** shorter, finer; **Fl.** pure yellow inside **Pet.** narrower. (Fig. 170 right.)

H. vallenarensis (Ritt.) Backbg.
Bo. simple, greyish-green, hemispherical, to 10 cm $\emptyset$; **Ri.** 13–25, with $\pm$ chin-like Tub.; **Ar.** white; **Rsp.** 10–14, to 2.5 cm lg.; **Csp.** 2–6, 2–5 cm lg., curving strongly upwards; **Sp.** light brown to greyish-black at first; **Fl.** 5 cm lg. and $\emptyset$, glossy brownish-yellow, with a light carmine M.-stripe; **Fr.** greenish to reddish; **S.** brownish-black to black.—Chile (S. of Vicuña.)

H. wagenknechtii Ritt.: **Neochilenia wagenknechtii** (Ritt.) Backbg.

Hylocereus Br. & R. (49)

Climbing or clambering epiphytes, sometimes with climbing spines, 3-angled or 3-winged, developing aerial roots. Spines are mostly short or absent; at first or in seedlings they are often bristly. The nocturnal flowers are very large, noticeably scaly and glabrous, the scaly ovary and the fruit are glabrous. The seeds are fairly large and black, and the cotyledon-leaves rather large. Some of the species are popular ornamental plants in warmer countries; some are used as grafting stocks for epiphytic cacti.—Distribution: from Mexico, through Central America and the Antilles, to northern S. America and Peru. [(R).]

H. antiguensis Br. & R.
Bo. climbing up tall trees, and forming large colonies in their crowns; **St.** 2–4 cm ∅, 3(–4)-angled, angles not horny, scarcely sinuate; **Sp.** 2–4, c. 6 mm lg., Ssp. or Br. 2–5; **Fl.** 14 cm lg., yellow, at least when fading; **Tu.** with linear acute Sc.; **stigma** not divided.—Antigua.

H. bronxensis Br. & R.
Bo. with the St. acutely 3-angled, dark greyish-green, to 4 cm ∅; **Ri.** brown, horny, strongly sinuate; **Sp.** c. 10, acicular, c. 6 mm lg., becoming brown; **Fl.** 25 cm lg., probably white; **Ov.** with broad Sc.; **stigma** probably divided.—Origin?

H. calcaratus (Web.) Br. & R.
Bo. strongly 3-winged; **St.** 4–6 cm ∅; **Ri.** with tongue-like protuberances; **Ar.** lacking Sp. but with 2–4 small white Br.; **Fl.** white, **Per.** funnelform; **Sep.** revolute.—Costa Rica.

H. costaricensis (Web.) Br. & R.
Bo. probably the stoutest of the genus; **St.** sometimes to 10 cm ∅, greenish at first, or reddish, soon becoming whitish and finally green or grey, mostly 3-angled; **Ri.**-flanks mostly thin, later rather plumper, angles straight or ± sinuate, never horny; **Sp.** 2–4, short, stout, brownish, mostly with 2 H. or Br., soon dropping; **Fl.** to over 30 cm lg., white; **stigma** not divided; **Fr.** scarlet, oblong, 10 cm lg.—Costa Rica.

H. cubensis Br. & R.
Bo. strongly rooting; **St.** long, 2–4 cm ∅, 3-angled; **Ri.** scarcely sinuate, becoming horny; **Sp.** 3–5, 2–3 mm lg., black; **Fl.** to 20 cm lg., white; **Fr.** 10 cm lg., reddish.—Cuba and Pinos island.

H. estebanensis Backbg.
Bo. with long St., sometimes subterete, mostly soon whitish or greyish-green, mostly 3-angled; **Ri.** fairly straight, with recurved tuberculate protuberances (climbing Tub.); **Sp.** 2–4, short, stout, brown; **Fl.** to 25 cm lg., white.—Venezuela (N. coast, San Esteban).

H. extensus (SD.) Br. & R.
Bo. fairly slender, creeping and clambering, green; **Ri.** quite straight, rounded; **Ar.** small, felty, also bristly; **Sp.** 2–3(–4), short, stout, 1–2 mm lg., dark brown; **Fl.** large, pink; **stigma** not divided.—Trinidad.

H. guatemalensis (Eichl.) Br. & R.
Bo. climbing high up trees; **St.** often narrow and terete below, to 5 m lg., mostly 3-angled, 2–7 cm ∅,

pruinose, becoming greener, angles horny; **Sp.** 2–4, conical, dark, 2–3 mm lg., bristly in seedlings; **Fl.** 30 cm lg., white; **Fr.** to 7 cm ∅, with large Sc.—Guatemala.

H. lemairei (Hook.) Br. & R.
Bo. fairly slender, climbing high up trees, green; **St.** 3-angled, to 3 cm ∅, strongly rooting on one side; **Sp.** mostly 2, very short, thickened below, brownish; **Fl.** c. 27 cm lg., whitish, pink below; outer **Sep.** green, inner ones more reddish; **Sti.** deeply divided; **Fr.** purple, to 7 cm lg., pulp white.—Tobago; Trinidad (?).

H. microcladus Backbg.
Bo. freely branching, **Seg.** fairly short, clinging by putting out many R.; **St.** 3(–5)-angled, fresh green, to 15 cm lg., to 2 cm ∅; **Ar.** crowded; **Sp.** bristle-like, small, few to several, often falling; **Fl.** not known.—Colombia to N. Peru.

H. minutiflorus Br. & R.: **Wilmattea minutiflora** (Br. & R.) Br. & R.

H. monacanthus (Lem.) Br. & R.
Bo. green; **St.** 3-angled; **Ri.** sinuate; **Sp.** mostly solitary, sometimes paired, strongly thickened below; **Fl.** 28 cm lg., 17 cm ∅, white, pink below; **Fil.** similarly; **Sti.** not always divided.—Colombia, Panama.

H. napoleonis (Grah.) Br. & R.
Bo. light green, strongly branching; **St.** 3-angled; **Ri.** acute, tuberculate, not horny, flanks concave; **Sp.** 4–5, c. 9 mm lg., thickened below; **Fl.** 20 cm lg. and ∅, white; **stigma** not divided.—Origin?

H. ocamponis (SD.) Br. & R.
Bo. light green, soon becoming pruinose, later dark bluish-green; **St.** acutely 3-angled; **Ri.** sinuate, brown, horny; **Sp.** 5–8, acicular, 5–12 mm lg.; **Fl.** to 30 cm lg. and almost as wide, white; **stigma** not divided, green.—Mexico.

H. peruvianus Backbg.
Bo. vivid green, somewhat pruinose at first; **St.** often ± contorted, to 80 cm lg. and more, 4–6 cm ∅; **Sp.** to 4, short, stout; **Fl.** ?—Peru (dry woodlands of the Sechura to the Rio Saña valley).

H. polyrhizus (Web.) Br. & R.
Bo. strongly branching, clinging to tree-trunks by means of many aerial R.; **St.** mostly to 4 cm ∅, often reddish at first, soon whitish-pruinose, eventually green; **Ri.** more winged at first, later plumper, slightly sinuate, not horny; **Sp.** 4–5, 2–3 mm lg., fairly robust, brownish, sometimes also 2(–4) deciduous Br.; **Fl.** to almost 40 cm lg., with

broad Sc. elongated above and then imbricate, projecting above; **Pet.** white; **Sti.** (always?) divided; **Fr.** scarlet, oblong, 10 cm lg., with large Sc.—Colombia, Panama. (Fig. 172.)

H. purpusii (Wgt.) Br. & R.
Bo. clambering, dark green, bluish-pruinose; **St.** over 3 cm ⌀; **Ri.** 3–4, acute, slightly sinuate, horny; **Sp.** 3–6, short, scarcely 1 mm lg., one of these sometimes more central; **Fl.** 25 cm lg. and ⌀, reddish to fiery carmine outside, intermediate Pet. golden-yellow tipped dark carmine, inner ones white, tipped yellow (Wgt.), or golden-yellow at midway with a slightly carmine tip (Berger).—Mexico (Tuxpan, W. lowlands). Probably the most attractive Fl. of any Hylocereus spec.

H. scandens (SD.) Backbg.
Bo. bluish-green; **St.** narrow, long, 3-angled, tapering to both ends; **Ri.** sinuate; **Sp.** 4–6, stout but minute, recurved, reddish at first, then greyish-brown, thickened below; **Fl.** ?—Guayana.

H. schomburgkii (O.) Backbg.
Bo. clambering, very freely branching, intense green, sometimes slightly pruinose; **St.** slightly curving, tapering to both ends, c. 2 cm ⌀, 3-angled, sometimes also 2-angled (flat) at first; **Ri.** long-sinuate, with small protuberances, **Ar.** to 5 cm apart; **Sp.** 0; **Fl.** large, white, very numerous.—Guayana. A few short bristly prickles are sometimes present.

H. stenopterus (Web.) Br. & R.
Bo. only weakly rooting, light green; **St.** 4 cm ⌀, not pruinose; **Ri.** 3, thin; **Sp.** 1–3, small, yellow; **Fl.** to only 12 cm lg.; **Tu.** only 2 cm lg., with relatively large imbricate Sc.; **Sep.** and **Pet.** linear, c. 7 cm lg., purple; **stigma** not divided.—Costa Rica (Valle Tuís).
Doubtless transitional to Wilmattea Br. & R., because of the smaller and rather short Fl. with purple Pet.

H. triangularis (L.) Br. & R. (T.)
Bo. climbing high up trees, also creeping; **St.** to 4 cm ⌀, producing numerous **R.**; **Ri.** 3, acute, rather straight, not horny; **Sp.** mostly 6–8, acicular, thickened below, short, spreading; **Fl.** 20 cm lg. and more, white; **stigma** not divided; **Fr.** red.—Jamaica (coastal zone).

H. tricostatus Br. & R.: **Hylocereus undatus** (Haw.) Br. & R.

H. trigonus (Haw.) Saff.
Bo. to 10 m lg., climbing; **St.** slender, to 3 cm ⌀, deep green; **Ri.** 3, very sinuate, not horny; **Sp.**

mostly 8, 4–7 mm lg., stiff, greenish at first, soon becoming dark brown, mostly also 2 Br. or Ssp.; **Fl.** large, white; **Sc.** large, thin; **Fr.** oblong, 10 cm lg., red.—Antilles.

H. trinitatensis (Lem.) Berg.
Bo. with broad 3-winged **St.** and thus diverging from H. lemairei (Hook.) Br. & R., to which Britton and Rose had referred it as a synonym; the **Sp.** are also different. No further data available.—Trinidad.

H. undatus (Haw.) Br. & R.
Bo. branching to form creeping, pendant or ascending masses, dark green; **St.** to c. 7 cm ⌀; **Ri.** mostly 3, prominent, thin, mostly ± stepped and ladder-like, horny in age; **Sp.** 1–3, small, 2–4 mm lg.; **Fl.** to 29 cm lg. and more, white, yellowish-green outside; **stigma** not divided; **Fr.** oblong, to 12 cm ⌀, red.—Origin?
Much planted in the Tropics as an ornamental plant; can be grown in the open on the Riviera.

H. venezuelensis Br. & R.
Bo. with **St.** fairly slender, 3–4 cm ⌀, bluish and strongly whitish; **Ri.** 3, not horny; **Sp.** 2–3, short, stout, brown to black; **Fl.** 25 cm lg., strongly perfumed, white, pink towards the base; **Sc.** bordered red; **Sti.** deeply divided.—Venezuela to N. Peru.

Hymenolobivia Frič & Kreuzgr. is a name without description for species of **Lobivia** Br. & R. developing a rather conspicuous hymen.

Hymenorebulobivia Frič: **Lobivia** Br. & R.

Hymenorebutia Frič ex Buin.: no adequate diagnostic differences have been put forward for the segregation of this genus.

Islaya Backbg. (127)

Plants spherical to oblong, in most cases probably remaining simple unless damaged, the dense apical felt varying in extent, the flowers yellow except in one species where they are partly reddish. The fruits are red, with floccose hairs, the floral remains persisting together with the upper radial bristles; at maturity the fruits are elongated and hollow, and open basally to reveal the seeds which may or may not be contained within a carpel-sac; the seeds are matt black. A very unified group of species.—Distribution: Pacific S. Peru, from the coast to approximately 1000 m altitude; N. Chile. [(R), (G): imported plants are sometimes difficult to grow.]
The discrepancies between my diagnoses in Descr.

Cact. Nov. I, and those of Rauh in his work on Peru, reflect the differences between his field-notes which he sent me, and his later treatment. The definitive data are given here. The same remarks apply to other genera also, e.g. Oroya etc. These circumstances appear to have been unknown to Krainz who, for obvious reasons, reproduces both texts.

I. bicolor Akers & Buin.
Bo. later becoming elongated, to c. 20 cm h., 10 cm ∅, sometimes suffused purple; **crown** with white woolly felt; **Rsp.** 12–14, stout, projecting, 3–10 mm lg.; **Csp.** 4, stouter, to 1.25 cm lg.; **Sp.** grey, brown-tipped; **Fl.** 2 cm lg., 2 cm br., not opening fully, yellow tipped reddish-brown; **Sep.** ± reddish.—S. Peru (high plateau of Nazca).

I. brevicylindrica Rauh & Backbg.
Bo. spherical at first, then shortly cylindric, greyish or bluish-green; **Ri.** 19–22; **Rsp.** to c. 20, those above sometimes fairly short, (3–)7–10 mm lg.; **Csp.** scarcely differentiated, 1–3, to 2 cm lg., directed strongly downwards; **Sp.** whitish, reddish-tipped at first; tuft of **apical wool** to 2.5 cm ∅, light brownish-white; **Fl.** light golden-yellow; **Sep.** orange-reddish; **Fr.** 4 cm lg., pale carmine; **S.** without seed-pocket.—S. Peru (near Camaná).

I. chalaensis Ritt.: **Islaya grandiflorens** Rauh & Backbg.

I. copiapoides Rauh & Backbg.
Bo. flattened-spherical to spherical, then to 10 cm h., 8 cm ∅, greyish-green, offsetting; **Ri.** 17–22; **Rsp.** 8–13, 5–7 mm lg., thin-subulate; **Csp.** 1–2, one above the other, to 1.5 cm lg., more stoutly subulate; **Sp.** at first reddish below, black to violet above; tuft of **apical wool** to 2 cm ∅, light brownish; **Fl.** small, to 1.5 cm lg., 1.2 cm ∅; **Fr.** to 3 cm lg., carmine.—S. Peru (Ocoña-Camaná desert).

I. divaricatiflora Ritt.—"Taxon", XIII: 4, 144. 1964.
Bo. flatter to hemispherical, to 7 cm ∅; **Ri.** 16–25, to 8 mm h., notched; **Ar.** to 5 mm apart, elliptic, grey; **Sp.** brown; **Rsp.** 12–16, 3–7 mm lg., thin; **Csp.** 4–8, stouter, 4–10 mm lg.; **Fl.** 2–3 cm lg., the **Ov.** sometimes without Br.; **Tu.** with minute Sc., white H. and several white Br.; **Pet.** greenish-yellow or reddish; **styles** yellow in the green Fl., reddish in the red Fl.; **Fr.** to 2 cm lg., red; **S.** 1.2 mm lg., black, smooth.—Peru (Dept. Arequipa, Camaná: in the main mist-zone of the mountains) (FR 588). (Fig. 174.)

I. flavida Ritt., undescribed: Sp. light yellow with dark brown tips (I. grandiflorens in part?)

I. grandiflorens Rauh & Backbg.
Bo. very sunken, greyish-green to green, 10 cm h. and br.; **Ri.** (16–)20–21; **Rsp.** thin, 10–12(–15), to 1 cm lg., sometimes pectinate; **Csp.** 2–3, to 2.5 cm lg.; **Sp.** blackish at first, red or yellowish below, soon becoming horn-coloured, finally ash-grey and black-tipped; **apical wool** not extensive, yellowish; **Fl.** c. 4 cm ∅; **Sep.** greenish; **Fr.** carmine, to 3 cm lg.—S. Peru (Panamericana Km 697).
    v. **spinosior** Rauh & Backbg.: **Rsp.** 20–25, not pectinate; **Csp.** to 8, to 2 cm lg., stout;
    v. tenuispina Rauh & Backbg.: identical with the type.

I. grandis Rauh & Backbg.
Bo. relatively large-spherical eventually, to 30(–50) cm h., 20 cm ∅, greyish or bluish-green; **Ri.** to 17; **Rsp.** and **Csp.** virtually indistinguishable, ± uniform, 9–20, 1–3 cm lg., pruinose and horn-coloured at first, dark-tipped; **apical wool** very restricted, whitish-grey; **Fl.** 1.5 cm lg.; **Fr.** 2(–4) cm lg., pale carmine; **S.** without seed-pocket.—S. Peru (valley of the Rio Majes).
    v. **brevispina** Rauh & Backbg.: **Rsp.** and **Csp.** fewer, lighter, shorter; **apical wool** rather more rather more extensive. Same locality.

I grandis v. neglecta Simo: **Islaya grandis** v. **brevispina** Rauh & Backbg.

I. islayensis (Först.) Backbg.
Bo. simple, 5–7 cm ∅; **Ri.** 19–25, low, obtuse; **Rsp.** 8–22, 1–10 mm lg.; **Csp.** 4–7, stouter, straight, 12–16 mm lg., grey to horn-coloured; **Fl.** small, 1.5–2 cm lg., yellow; **Sep.** reddish.—S. Peru (Islay).

I. krainziana Ritt.—Sukkde. (SKG) VII/VIII: 31–33. 1963.
Bo. prostrate, always away from the prevailing wind, to 75 cm lg., greyish-green, hard, expanding above in age to ± clavate, little branching, to 12 cm ∅, apex flat, grey; **R.** fibrous; **Ri.** 16–23, made ± tuberculate by transverse notches, to 1.2 cm h.; **Ar.** 1–3 mm apart, later to 1.5 cm lg., 1 cm br.; **Sp.** stout, subulate, mostly light yellow, sometimes brownish, mostly directed downwards, rather short; **Rsp.** c. 8–12, 5–10 mm lg.; **Csp.** 4–8, to 1.5 cm lg.; **Fl.** 3.25 cm lg., to 3 cm ∅, scented; **Tu.** green to reddish, with white H. and yellow Br.; **style** and **Sti.** white; **Sep.** red or with a red M.-stripe; **Pet.** golden to lemon-yellow; **Fr.** to 3 cm lg., purple, with white H., with brownish-yellow to white Br. (except in the lower part); **S.** 1.5 mm lg., black, finely tuberculate, hilum white.—Extreme N. of Chile (near Poconchile, close to the Peruvian frontier). (Fig. 173.)
The longest and most southerly spec. of a genus previously known only with a Peruvian distribution.

I. maritima Ritt. (FR 590): described by Rauh as **I. grandiflorens**.

I. minor Backbg. (T.)
Bo. simple, dark green, to c. 13 cm h., 7 cm ∅; **Ri.** to c. 17, 6 mm h.; **Ar.** with much whitish-grey felt at first; **Rsp.** 20–24, to 6 mm lg., thin, pungent; **Csp.** 4, usually cruciform, to 18 mm lg., stouter, thickened below; all **Sp.** black at first, later light grey; **apical wool** light grey; **Fl.** 2.2 cm ∅, golden-yellow to light greenish-yellow; **Fr.** carmine; **S.** in a sac.—S. Peru (above Mollendo).

I. minuscula Ritt. (FR 1462): at present only a name.

I. mollendensis (Vpl.) Backbg.
Bo. simple, shortly columnar, to 20 cm h., 10 cm ∅; **crown** becoming oblique; **Ri.** to c. 19, not prominent, swollen around the Ar.; **Ar.** brownish-white at first; **Rsp.** to c. 10, c. 1 cm lg.; **Csp.** later 3–4, little longer or stouter; **Sp.** dark brownish-red at first, becoming blackish-grey to grey, rigid, pungent; **apical wool** brownish-white; **Fl.** 2 cm lg., dull yellow; **Fr.** reddish.—S. Peru (Mollendo).

I. paucispina Rauh & Backbg.
Bo. simple or a few heads together, green to greyish-green, spherical, to 8 cm ∅; **Ri.** 12–16; **Rsp.** 5–8, 8–15 mm lg., pale reddish below at first, tipped blackish-brown; **Csp.** absent or 1, to 3 cm lg., brownish-red below, blackish-brown above; **apical wool** yellowish; **Fl.** 1.5 cm lg., vivid yellow; **Fr.** to 3.5 cm lg., pale carmine; **S.** without any sac.—S. Peru (coastal terraces near Chala).
v. **curvispina** Rauh & Backbg.: distinguished by the **Rsp.** which are very short, appressed, noticeably bent; **Csp.** mostly 1, bent strongly downwards. It is possible that both this spec, and its variety may have to be united with Islaya paucispinosa Rauh & Backbg.

I. paucispinosa Rauh & Backbg.
Bo. probably always simple, low in the soil; **Ri.** 11; **Rsp.** 6–10; **Csp.** mostly 1; **Sp.** strongly subulate, ash-grey; **apical wool** not extensive; **Fl.** with Pet. broader and shorter than in I. mollendensis; **Fr.** 2 cm lg., red.—S. Peru (near Chala, Km 528).

I. roseiflora Hoffm.: **I. divaricatiflora** Ritt. (Fig. 174.)

Isolatocereus (Backbg.) Backbg. (159)

The plants of this monotypic genus eventually develop a trunk and become tree-like. The flowers are nocturnal, ± tubular-funnelform, numerous, borne on older plants almost in a chain, one below the other down from the apex. The floral-tube lacks bristles, the ovary is bristly, the fruit occasionally has a few bristles.—Distribution: Central Mexico. [(R).]

I. dumortieri (Scheidw.) Backbg. (T.)
Bo. to 15 m h.; **trunk** to 1 m h., to 30 cm ∅; **branches** numerous, ascending, light to bluish-green; **Ri.** (5–)6–7, to 2 cm h., acute; **Ar.** yellowish; **Rsp.** 9–11, radiating, thin, to 12 mm lg.; **Csp.** 1–4, to 3 cm lg.; all **Sp.** acicular, yellowish-white, the stoutest ones thickened below; **Fl.** 5 cm lg., 2.5 cm ∅, white, brownish-red outside; **Ov.** with felt, or this virtually absent, with or without Br.; **Fr.** to 4 cm lg., ovoid, spineless, sometimes with a few small Br.; **pulp** red.—Central Mexico (Hidalgo to Oaxaca). (Fig. 175.)
The Ri. are sometimes strongly spiralled. The earliest and thus the valid name appears to have been "Cereus anisacanthus DC." which thus covers also its varieties: v. ortholophus DC. and v. subspiralis DC.

Jasminocereus Br. & R. (62)

A genus of larger cerei from the Galapagos Islands on which adequate information has only recently become available; the stems are mostly robust and, like the Genus Armatocereus Backbg. from the nearest part of the S. American mainland, they have constrictions marking annual growth. The nocturnal flowers are funnelform, the relatively slender tubes are extensively scaly, the scales on the ovary being fairly dense and very small, at most with traces of felt. The fruits are rather variable, ovoid at maturity, bearing the floral remains and minute scales. The seeds are small and black. At first only one species was known, or rather, recognised. I then established that at least two species were distinguishable, and recent, more thorough investigation of the islands by Y. Dawson has revealed three species in all, two of them with a variety, the new spec.—J. howellii Daws.—having flowers only half as long as those of the type-species. The interesting point is that J. thouarsii (Web.) Backbg. has crowded, longer spines only on the trunk or towards the base, those on the upper branches being short, whereas J. howellii v. delicatus Y. Daws. has longer and denser spination in the flowering zone as well.— Distribution: Galapagos Islands [probably (R), but there is little experience by which to judge]. See also Brachycereus Br. & R.

J. galapagensis (Web.) Br. & R. was based on a name published elsewhere and on insufficiently clarified material.

J. howellii Y. Daws.—C. & S. J. [US], XXXIV: 3, 71–72. 1962.
Bo. tree-like, to 5 m h. or more; **Ri.** 18–19, to 2 cm h.; **Rsp.** 8–14, 1–2 cm lg.; **Csp.** 2–4, 4–9 cm lg.; **Sp.** alike on old and new growth, brownish at first, then grey-flecked; **Fl.** reddish, only 5(–6) cm lg., remaining open during the earlier part of the morning; **Tu.** to 6 mm ∅; **Fr.** ovoid to spherical, indehiscent, 2–4.4 cm lg., reddish; **pulp** white, viscous.—Galapagos Is. (Indefatigable Is., also known as Isla Santa Cruz: on lava in Academy Bay).
    v. **delicatus** Y. Daws. (l.c.): **Fl.** larger, to 6.5 cm lg.; **Tu.** more slender, c. 3.5 mm ∅; **St.** with longer Sp. throughout their length.— Bartholomé and Santiago (James) Is. (Fig. 177 right.)

J. sclerocarpus (K. Sch.) Backbg.
Bo. tree-like, to 6 m h.; **branches** 15–22 cm ∅, ascending, ± parallel; **Ri.** low, 1 cm h.; **Sp.** not differentiated, 20–25, to 4.5 cm lg., straight, subulate, pungent, shorter on the upper branches; **Fl.** reddish (Weber says; acc. Naundorff white, or else his plant is a form, variety or another spec.?), noticeably waxy, to 11 cm lg.; **Per.** funnelform; **Pet.** truncate-rounded; **Ov.** oblong; **Fr.** spindle-shaped when unripe, becoming ovoid at maturity, c. 7 cm lg.—Galapagos Is. (several islands). (Fig. 176.)

J. thouarsii (Web.) Backbg. (T.)
Bo. to 8 m h. or more; **trunk** to 30 cm ∅; **branches** robust, the constricted parts more stoutly ovoid, to 14 cm ∅; **Ri.** to 22, 1 cm h.; **Ar.** brown; **Sp.** dense and longer on the trunk (acc. Dawson's photo), to 10 per Ar., to 8 cm lg., fewer above, 1.3–5 cm lg., one Csp. 3–5 cm lg., the lower ones longest, ± bristle-like and flexible; **Fl.** to 11 cm lg., less waxy than in the preceding, "brown with yellow stripes" (Br. & R.; Dawson says nothing of the colour, which is unusual here; perhaps based on herbarium-material?); **Per.** broader; **Tu.** slender, 6–6.5 mm ∅; **Ov.** rather oblong; **Fr.** ovoid to spherical, reddish; **pulp** white.—Galapagos Is. (Charles Is.)
    v. **chathamensis** Y. Daws.—C. & S. J. [US], XXXIV: 3, 73. 1962.
Bo. branching from nearer the base; **Ri.** 19–21 on young plants, 12–13 on older ones; **Fl.** to 11 cm lg., colour? (not stated by Dawson); **Tu.** stouter, 9–10 mm ∅; **Ov.** more spherical, stouter, 14 mm ∅; **Pet.** more spatulate.—Galapagos Is. (Chatham Is.). (Fig. 177 left.)

Krainzia Backbg. (228)

Mammillaria-like spherical plants with quite large

flowers, their tubes fairly long and styles free, the seeds lacking a large corky hilum. Flower-colour red or purple, although a white-flowering mutation has been observed in the type-species; K. guelzowiana also has fruits dehiscing laterally at maturity. Both species have hooked spines.— Distribution: Mexico (Durango). [(R), (G).]

K. guelzowiana (Werd.) Backbg.
Bo. sometimes offsetting later, single heads to 7 cm h., to 6 cm ∅; **sap** watery; **Ax.** glabrous; **Ar.** yellow; **Rsp.** numerous, to 80, hair-like and bristly, to 1.5 cm lg.; **Csp.** 1, to 1 cm lg., hooked, yellowish to reddish-brown; **Fl.** 5 cm lg., to 6 cm ∅, remaining open 4–5 days; **Fr.** light red, ovoid; **S.** ± black, with a small white aril.—Mexico (Durango).

K. longiflora (Br. & R.) Backbg. (T.)
Bo. spherical, sometimes caespitose; single head to 6 cm h., 5 cm ∅; **sap** watery; **Tub.** to 7 mm lg.; **Ar.** glabrous or weakly felty; **Rsp.** c. 30, white, thin, to 1.3 cm lg.; **Csp.** 4, one of these hooked, light yellow to reddish-brown, stouter, to 13 mm lg.; **Fl.** to 4.5 cm lg., 4 cm ∅, pink; **Fr.** ovoid, drying at maturity; **S.** as in the preceding spec.—Mexico (Durango, Santiago, Papasquiaro). (Fig. 178.)

Lasiocereus Ritt. (58)

A hitherto undescribed genus of tree-like plants, densely spiny, with "pseudocephalia" (Ritter), from which arise the "black and white, tubular flowers, densely covered with wool and bristles". "Fruit dry, unusual in structure".—Distribution: Peru [(R).]

L. fulvus Ritt.
Bo. shrubby, to 3 m h., offsetting from the base, branches 3–7 cm ∅; **Ri.** 10–14, obtuse, 7–10 mm h., scarcely notched; **Ar.** 4–6 mm ∅, 4–7 mm apart, rust-coloured; **Sp.** brownish-red, tipped yellow, straight; **Rsp.** 8–12, acicular, 5–10 mm lg.; **Csp.** 3–6, subulate, longest ones 2–5 cm lg.; **Fl.** apical, nocturnal, 6 cm lg.; **Ov.** densely covered with greyish-brown wool, with many Sc. 5–10 mm lg., reddish, nectary 7 mm lg.; **style** c. 3 cm lg., with 16 yellow Sti.; **Fr.** spherical; **S.** black, 1 mm lg., 0.7 mm br.—Peru (E. of Balsas). (FR 1303.)

L. rupicola Ritt.
Shoots with fairly numerous **Ri.**, resembling a yellow-spined Haageocereus.—Peru (where?) (FR 661). (Fig. 179.)

Lemaireocereus Br. & R. emend. Backbg. (148)

Formerly a widely-embracing genus of disparate species, now a genus with only one (or two?) species.
Larger columnar cacti from Mexico, the shoots readily detached; flowers numerous, subapical, open (only?) during the day, stoutly cylindric to bellshaped, the tube densely covered with white hairs or bristles. The edible fruit is spiny and does not become dry.—Distribution: Mexico (Puebla, Tehuacan). [(R).]

L. hollianus (Web.) Br. & R. (T.)

Bo. simple or little branching from the base, to 5 m h.; **branches** $\pm$ erect, to 6 cm $\varnothing$, dark green; **Ri.** 8–14, acute; **Rsp.** 8–14, to 3.5 cm lg., thin, grey; **Csp.** 3–5, thickened below, to 10 cm lg.; **Fl.** to 10 cm lg., to 3.5 cm $\varnothing$; **Tu.** greenish, with long Br. and H., and Sc. with white felt; **Sep.** brownish-green, ciliate; **Pet.** ivory-white, ciliate and apiculate, obliquely projecting; **Fr.** ovoid, 6–8 cm lg., pulp purple; **S.** 2–3 mm lg., glossy black.—Mexico (Puebla, near Tehuacan). (Fig. 180.)
A second spec., reported from the neighbourhood of Zapotitlán, is clearly referable here but has not been described: **Bo.** to 10 m h.; **trunk** to 1.5 m lg., 30 cm $\varnothing$; **Sp.** to 20 cm lg.; **Fl.** large, white to pink; **Fr.** large, dark purple.—Mexico (Puebla, Zapotitlán de las Salinas).

The following species have hitherto been ascribed to **Lemaireocereus** in the absence of sufficient information; all(?) have nocturnal flowers, and most are probably referable to Marshallocereus or Ritterocereus:

L. longispinus Br. & R.

Bo. erect, stout; **branches** light green, $\pm$ pruinose at first; **Ri.** 6, prominent and $\pm$ tuberculate; **Rsp.** c. 10, spreading to recurved, acicular; **Csp.** sometimes present, porrect, to 8 cm lg., grey; **Fl.** ?; **Fr.** ?—Guatemala.

L. martinezii G. Ortega

Bo. tree-like, to 5 m h.; **branches** cylindric, yellowish-green; **Ri.** 9; **Ar.** reddish-brown; **Rsp.** 7–11; **Csp.** 3, one of them much thickened below; **Sp.** black, red below; **Fl.** ?; **Fr.** ?—Mexico (Sinaloa, Mazatlan).

L. montanus Br. & R.

Bo. tree-like, to 7 m h., with a distinct **trunk**; **Ri.** mostly 8; **Ar.** brown, large; **Sp.** to 6, 1–3 cm lg., pale; **Fl.** 6–7 cm lg., slightly curving, **Per.** strongly revolute; **Sep.** reddish; **Pet.** white; statements differ as to the Sp. on the **Ov.**; **Fr.** to 7.5 cm lg.,

fleshy, $\pm$ spineless; **S.** reddish-black, numerous.—Mexico.

L. quevedonis G. Ortega

Bo. tree-like, to 5 m h.; **branches** dark green; **Ri.** 7–9, transversely furrowed; **Ar.** brown; **Rsp.** 12, to 1 cm lg.; **Csp.** 7, 1 more central, 4 cm lg.; **Sp.** white and brown; **Fl.** 6 cm lg., nocturnal; **Sep.** reddish outside, greenish-white inside; **Pet.** white and pink; **Fr.** spherical; **S.** dark brown.—Mexico (Sinaloa, Guamuchil; Guerrero).

L. schumannii (Maths.) Br. & R.

Bo. to 15 m h., robust, with few **branches**; **Ri.** 8, very rounded, $\pm$ pruinose; **Rsp.** 6–7; **Csp.** 1, white, brown-tipped;—Honduras. (The older name for Ritterocereus eichlamii?)

See also the remarks at the end of Ritterocereus.

Lemaireocereus sens. lat. Br. & R.: For species where the diagnostic characters of flower and fruit do not accord with the type of Lemaireocereus, see the specific name under the following genera: Armatocereus, Isolatocereus, Marginatocereus, Marshallocereus, Ritterocereus, Stenocereus.

Leocereus Br. & R. (135)

Shrubby, thin-stemmed, erect to prostrate plants, with numerous fine ribs with crowded areoles. The short-limbed, relatively small flowers are rather narrowly funnelform, the scales on the tube are almost hidden under wool interspersed with bristly spines, and the fruit is small, spherical. Seeds dark brown to black.—Distribution: S. to NE. Brazil. [(G).]

L. bahiensis Br. & R. (T.)

Bo. erect, sometimes inclined, to 2 m lg.; **Ri.** c. 12–14, low, very narrow; **Ar.** $\pm$ brownish; **Sp.** acicular, yellow; **Rsp.** c. 10; **Csp.** 1(–2), one mostly longer, porrect, to 3 cm lg., stouter; **Fl.** 4 cm lg.; **Pet.** white; **Fr.** c. 1 cm $\varnothing$; **S.** c. 1.5 mm lg.—Brazil (Bahia, near Barrinha). (Fig. 181.)

L. glaziovii (K. Sch.) Br. & R.

Bo. erect; **branches** somewhat spreading, 1.5–2 cm $\varnothing$; **Ri.** 12, low; **Sp.** 20–30, unequal, 0.4–2.3 cm lg., brown to ash-grey; **Fl.** weakly bent, 6 cm lg.; **Fr.** 2 cm lg., umbilicate; **S.** 1.5 mm lg., black.—Brazil (Minas Geraes, on the Pico d'Itabira do Campo). Flowering Ar. show stronger lighter woolly felt.

L. melanurus (K. Sch.) Br. & R.

Bo. erect or inclined, to c. 1 m lg.; **branches** to 3 cm $\varnothing$; **Ri.** 12–16, very low; **Sp.** 20–50 and more, bristly to thin-acicular to stouter, overtopping the crown, **Csp.** to 5 cm lg., brown to blackish; **Fl.** to 7 cm lg., colour ?; **Fr.** spherical, with brown wool and Fl.-remains; **S. c.** 5 mm lg., dark brown. — Brazil (Minas Geraes, Serra de S. João del Ray).

L. paulensis Speg.
Bo. mostly simple, erect, to 1 m h.; **branches** many stouter; **Sp.** only c. 12, bristly, one longest **Csp.** often curving slightly upwards; **Pet.** purple-violet. — Brazil (State São Paulo). Never re-collected.

Lepidocoryphantha Backbg. (218)

A genus related to Coryphantha, but with the furrows extending over only half the tubercle; shoots arise from here so that ± large and taprooted cushions are formed. The flowers of this genus, unlike the naked ones of Coryphantha, have ± felty axils, the ovary is sometimes scaly, also the watery fruit which contains moderately soft seeds. The flowers are quite large, ± light purple. — Distribution: S. States of the USA to N. Mexico. [(R): imported plants should be given a chemical fertilizer.]

L. macromeris (Eng.) Backbg. (T.)
Bo. broadly spherical, mid-green, forming cushions; **Tub.** furrowed for ± half their length; **Ar.** felty at first; **Rsp.** 10–17, stiff, angular, pungent, white; **Csp.** stouter, to 4, to 5 cm lg., pink at first, then brown to black, straight or curving to contorted; **Fl.** 5–6.5 cm lg., 6–8 cm ∅, from the base of the furrow, funnelform; **Sep.** lanceolate, fimbriate, green with a reddish tinge; **Pet.** narrow, deep pink to purplish-pink, with a darker stripe; **Fr.** ellipsoidal, green, to 2.5 cm lg.; **S.** to 1.5 mm lg. — USA (W. Texas to New Mexico), Mexico (Chihuahua to Zacatecas).

L. runyonii (Br. & R.) Backbg.
Bo. greyish-green, forming clumps to 50 cm ∅; **R.** thick, napiform, elongated; **Tub.** terete to flattened, furrowed through only half the length; **Rsp.** c. 6, spreading, acicular, to c. 3 cm lg., light-coloured to reddish-orange, dark-tipped; **Csp.** to 3, reddish-orange below, dark-tipped; **Fl.** to 5 cm ∅, purplish-pink; **Sep.** ciliate; **Pet.** ± denticulate; **Fr.** green; **S.** brown. — USA (Texas, Rio Grande). (Fig. 182.)

Lepismium Pfeiff. (21)

[Buxbaum reports that all Lepismium spec. (except L. cruciforme with its different flower-structure) should now be referred back to Rhipsalis.]

Predominantly pendant epiphytes with slender segments which can be terete, flat or angular. The conspicuous diagnostic character of the genus is in the ovary, which is sunken in the areole so that a large scar sometimes remains after flowering. Even the buds are ± sunken. The flowers are mostly small, only occasionally relatively large, and are white (or yellowish) to pink. The fruit is a ± spherical berry, white to red. 19 species. — Distribution: Brazil, Argentina, Venezuela, Paraguay (E. Bolivia?). [(R),///].
The genus has been split into 5 subgenera, based on stem-shape and areolar bristles. In the following descriptions, the figure after the specific name refers to the subgenus, as given in the systematic survey at the beginning of the work.

L. chrysanthum (Löfgr.) Backbg. (2)
Bo. ± erect, rigid; **St.** branching dichotomously or in whorls, **Seg.** 3–8 cm lg., to 12 mm ∅, greyish-green; **Ar.** with ± woolly felt and Br. (these later disappearing); **Sc.** vivid red; **Fl.** ± terminal, relatively large, opening widely; **Fr.** small, red. — Brazil (Parana, coast).

L. commune Pfeiff.: **Lepismium cruciforme** (Vell.) Miqu.

L. cruciforme (Vell.) Miqu. (1) (T.)
Bo. bushy, to 60 cm lg., green, sometimes suffused red; **Seg.** 3-winged; **Ar.** crowded, greyish-white to brownish; **Fl.** ± bellshaped, ± whitish, ± reddish outside; **Fr.** ± spherical, violet; **S.** dark brown. — Brazil, Argentina, Paraguay.
    v. **anceps** (Web.) Backbg.: **shoots** flat; **Fl.** lilac-white, bellshaped, **Pet.** strongly revolute;
    v. **cavernosum** (Lindbg.) Backbg. is moderately branching; the **Ar.** are deeply sunken, with much reddish-brown to grey wool;
    v. **knightii** (Preiff.) Boom: **Fl.** translucent white;
    v. **myosurus** (SD.) Backbg.: moderately branching; **Fl.** pinkish-red; sv. **vollii** (Backbg.) Backbg. is distinguished by short shoots to 3 cm lg.

L. dissimile Lindbg. (2)
Bo. strongly branching, main **St.** ribbed or cylindric, to 1 cm ∅; **shoots** slender, ribbed, ± terete, bristly at first; **Fl.** 6 mm br., borne laterally, white with a pink centre; **Fr.** purple, compressed. — Brazil.

L. epiphyllanthoides (Backbg.) Backbg. (2)
Bo. erect; **shoots** 2–4 cm lg., shortly overlapping; **Ar.** on a reddish prominence, with white felt, bristly at first; **Fl.** to 3 cm ∅, yellowish-white; **Sep.** darker-tipped; **Fr.** unknown. — Brazil (in the S., in depressions in tufa-rock).

L. floccosum (SD.) Backbg. (2)
Bo. shrubby, erect, then pendant; **shoots** mostly offset to one another, cylindric, dull greyish-green; **Ar.** with much woolly felt, not set on a reddish prominence; **Fl.** enveloped in yellowish-white wool, lateral, to 1.4 cm ∅, rotate, greenish-white; **Fr.** white.—Brazil (Minas Geraes; São Paulo, Serra da Cantareira).

L. gibberulum (Web.) Backbg. (2)
Bo. shrubby, little branching; **branches** dividing dichotomously or in whorls, to 20 cm lg., 3–4 mm ∅, greenish-yellow; **Ar.** rarely woolly, without Br.; **Sc.** minute; **Fl.** numerous, lateral, to 1.4 cm ∅, slightly incurving at the tip, white; **Fr.** white, flat.— Brazil (São Paulo, Serra da Cantareira).

L. grandiflorum (Haw.) Backbg. (2)
Bo. shrubby, pendant; **branches** forking or in whorls, to 1 cm ∅, cylindric, reddish-brown at first, eventually ± vivid green; **Ar.** little felty; **Fl.** lateral, to 2.5 cm ∅, rotate, whitish, striped green; **Fr.** reddish.—Brazil (Rio de Janeiro; Minas Geraes; São Paulo).

L. knightii Pfeiff.: **Lepismium cruciforme** v. **knightii** (Pfeiff.) Boom.

L. marnieranum Backbg. (5)—Descr. Cact. Nov. III: 7. 1963.
Bo. laxly branching, erect at first, later ± arching; **shoots** dimorphic, in juvenile plants c. 5–6 mm ∅, with 5 low slender angles, the crowded Ar. with several erect to appressed white Br. to 1 cm lg.; later shoots c. 1–2 cm ∅, subterete at first, then 3–4-angled, these angles sometimes slightly offset and somewhat prominent towards the Ar.; young shoots more bluish-green, older ones more dirty olive-green; Ar. on young shoots short and weakly felty, with small red Sc., those on older shoots stout, with dense projecting tufts of wool to over 1 cm lg., at most with solitary Br.; **Fl.** concolorous white, 1(–1.75) cm ∅, often paired or ternate, with the **Ov.** sunken; **Pet.** crowded, obtuse, c. 5 mm br.; **Fr.** carmine-pink, subspherical, with dried floral remains; **S.** 1 mm lg., glossy, black, boat-shaped.—Origin? (Fig. 183, above and below.)
A very characteristic species of which the origin remains unknown. It has been shown by experiments with seed-sowing at the Botanical Garden "Les Cèdres" that the plants come true from seed.

L. megalanthum (Löfgr.) Backbg. (2)
Bo. shrubby; **branches** ± in whorls but sometimes ± forking, to 1.2 cm ∅; **Ar.** often reddish, flowering Ar. expanded, with floccose felt; **Fl.** to 4 cm ∅, yellowish-white, rotate; **Fil.** pink towards

the base; **Sti.** c. 7, to 5 mm lg., white; **Fr.** white to pink.—Brazil (São Paulo, island of São Sebastião). (Fig. 184.)
The Fl. arise from the axis and thus leave deep cavity-like scars. I have studied various "short flowering shoots": these were to c. 2 cm lg., with distinct Sc. to over 2 mm lg., but the Fl. itself never developed fully, although it was still recognisable as such, sometimes at the shoot-apex. This demonstrates that the lengths of Tu. and Fl. are simply a process of reduction, or stages thereof.

L. neves-armondii (K. Sch.) Backbg. (2)
Bo. shrubby, ± erect; **shoots** always in whorls, to 10 cm lg., to 5 mm ∅; **Ar.** spiralled, with short Br.; **Fl.** borne subapically, rotate, to 2 cm ∅, yellowish-white; **Fr.** white to yellowish-white.—Brazil (Rio de Janeiro, Tijuca and near Petropolis).

L. pacheco-leonii (Löfgr.) Backbg. (2)
Bo. creeping to pendant, branching irregularly, never whorled; **shoots** variable in shape and colour; terete to angular to ± cylindric; **Ar.** with felt and Br., these later disappearing; **Fl.** lateral, rotate, small, ± light pinkish-red; **Fr.** spherical, red.— Brazil (Rio de Janeiro: Cabo Frio).

L. paradoxum SD. (3)
Bo. shrubby, to 5 m lg., pendant; **shoots** short, 3-angled, the angles and faces offset in successive Seg., these to 5 cm lg.; **Ar.** without Br.; **Fl.** solitary, subapical, to 2 cm lg., white; **Fr.** reddish.—Brazil (São Paulo, common near the city). Flowers only rarely in cultivation.

L. pittieri (Br. & R.) Backbg. (2)
Bo. shrubby, freely branching, pendant; **shoots** terete, to 6 mm ∅, branches ± forking; **Ar.** without a reddish zone; **Fl.** greenish-yellow; **Fr.** white. Habit similar to that of Rhipsalis cassutha.—Venezuela (near Puerto Cabello).

L. pulvinigerum (Lindbg.) Backbg. (2)
Bo. shrubby, branching; **shoots** in whorls, cylindric, spreading, to 60 cm lg., to 4 mm ∅, glossy, green; **Ar.** spiralled, set on a reddish zone, with short wool and Br. only at flowering; **Fl.** solitary, 2.2 cm ∅, rotate, delicate greenish-white; **Fr.** purple.—Brazil (São Paulo; Minas Geraes), NE. Paraguay.

L. puniceo-discus (Lindbg.) Backbg. (2)
Bo. shrubby, little branching; **shoots** in whorls, to 40 cm lg., to 6 mm ∅, ± dark green; **Ar.** weakly felty, **Br.** absent; **Fl.** solitary, ± funnelform, to only 1.5 cm ∅, white; **Fr.** spherical, blackish, becoming yellowish.—Brazil (Minas Geraes).
 v. **chrysocarpum** (Löfgr.) Backbg.: differentiated

by the ± disc-shaped, light orange **Fr.**; the **style** is concolorous white, unlike the type where it is pink below.

L. rigidum (Löfgr.) Backbg. (2)
Bo. unusually rigid, ± erect, little branching; **shoots** arranged irregularly, never in whorls, to 60 cm lg., to 1.5 cm ∅, dark green; **Ar.** scarcely felty; **Br.** to 15, white, fairly rigid; **Fl.** lateral, ± rotate, straw-coloured; **Fr.** disc-shaped at first, shape and colour at maturity not known.—Brazil (São Paulo: Serra da Cantareira).

L. saxatile Friedr. & Red. (2)—mentioned but not named in Mitt. Württ. Kakteenfreunde, Aug. 1963(4)—The Nat. Cact. & Succ. Journ. (Gr. Brit.), 4: Dec. 1965, with illustration.
Bo. shrubby or pendant; **shoots** glabrous or bristly, c. 1.5 cm ∅; **Ri.** c. 6, straight or contorted; **Ar.** c. 12 mm apart, with white wool when ready to flower; **Br.** light to yellowish, to 15, to 7 mm lg., later black; **Fl.** to 1.5 cm ∅, white, yellow in dried material; **Fr.** flesh-coloured; **S.** black.—Brazil. Prostrate plants can be to 2 m lg.
An interesting new spec. Type-material (holotype) is in the Herbarium at Kew Gardens.
Dr. Friedrich states the following: "Occurs in hilly terrain, in the middle course of the Tiefê,where several hundred groups were found in an area of c. 2 hectares (approximately 4½–5 acres). **Fl.**, when fading, canary-yellow; **Fr.** a fleshy berry 8–10 mm ∅; **S.** black. Plants grow to 50 cm lg. with the **Fl.** borne subapically."

L. trigonum (Pfeiff.) Backbg. (4)
Bo. shrubby, pendant, over 2 m lg.; **shoots** with 3 continuous angles, to 10 cm lg., to 1.5 mm ∅, ± contorted; **Ar.** strongly woolly at flowering and then also with 1 Br.-Sp.; **buds** brownish to reddish-yellowish; **Fl.** solitary, rotate, whitish or reddish; **Fr.** spherical, red.—Brazil (São Paulo; (?) Rio de Janeiro).

L. tucumanense (Web.) Backbg. (2)
Bo. shrubby, ± branching; **shoots** ± whorled, to 1 cm ∅; **Ar.** set on a reddish zone, bristly at first; **Fl.** lateral, to 1.8 cm ∅, white; **Fr.** flattened-spherical, ± pinkish-white.—N. Argentina.

Leptocereus (Berg.) Br. & R. (134)

An interesting genus which, when compared with genera shown by the flower-morphology to be closely related (i.e. Acanthocereus), exhibits progressive spine-reduction. In some species the flowers are relatively spiny, but in Leptocereus grantianus there are only traces of bristles. A diagnostic character of the genus is also the ± bellshaped-cylindric flower-form, with mostly relatively short petals, giving a certain resemblance to the flowers of Neoabbottia which has a partly overlapping distribution. It is also worth noting that some Leptocereus species, like Neoabbottia and the Cuban genus Dendrocereus, possess a tree-like habit with a distinct trunk. The flowers of each genus are, however, quite distinctive. This shows moreover that their evolutionary significance within so narrow an area is extremely difficult or impossible to assess for the present, and demarcation has to be based on the stages of reduction and the additional characters of the flowering region. The flowers of Leptocereus are reputedly open during the daytime although some (like L. grantianus) are nocturnal, so that it is clearly possible all the species open first at night, and remain open the next day; closer investigations have yet to be made. The fruits are ± spiny and contain, as far as is known, numerous black seeds. An important factor in determinining the individual species is the diameter of the terminal shoots. —Distribution: Cuba, Haiti, Santo Domingo, Puerto Rico. [(R), ✳.] *

L. arboreus Br. & R.
Bo. tree-like, to 6 m h., freely branching; **Ri.** 4, narrow; **Ar.** 2.5–4 cm apart; **terminal shoots** to 6 cm ∅; **Sp.** c. 10, to 5 cm lg., ± yellowish; **Fl.** bellshaped, to 3 cm lg., ± whitish; **Tu.** and **Ov.** very spiny; **Fr.** ellipsoidal, to 10 cm lg., to 6 cm ∅, with dense long Sp.—E. Cuba. [Haage adds: Sp. c. 12–20, 1–3 cm lg.—Cuba S. coasts of Prov. Las Villas, also near Yaguanabo and eastwards, on dry scarps towards Trinidad).]

L. assurgens (C. Wright) Br. & R. (T.)
Bo. shrubby, to 3 m h., **trunk** short, to 6 cm ∅; **Ri.** to 9; **Ar.** at first white-felty; **terminal shoots** to 3 cm ∅; **Rsp.** to 16; **Csp.** 4; all **Sp.** yellowish-white; **Fl.** to 15 together, apical, c. 4 cm lg., light yellow; **Tu.** with reddish Sp.; **Fr.** with dense long Sp.—Cuba. [Haage adds: to 1 m h.—Cuba (Pinar del Rio, on limestone cliffs; Ensenada de Valle, 2 km from Vinales).]

L. ekmanii (Werd.) Knuth
Bo. prostrate to semi-erect; **Ri.** to 7, clearly notched; **Ar.** with short brown felt; **terminal shoots** to 2 cm ∅; **Rsp.** c. 10, acicular, to 4 cm lg.; **Csp.** 1, longer and stouter; all **Sp.** thickened below, ± brownish; **Fl.** to 2 cm lg., ± funnelform; **Pet.** 4 mm

* Haage reports: 2 interesting new spec. of Leptocereus were collected by Dr. A. Areces Mallea in Prov. Camagüey, Sierra de Najana, and in the north coastal plains of Prov. Oriente, Cuba.

lg., yellow; **Tu.** with yellowish-brown Sp.; **Fr.** not known.—Cuba.
[Haage adds: Dr. A. Areces Mallea, Bot. Gard. Havana, was unable to re-collect it in 1974 in Somorrostro and the Anafe Mts., Cuba.]

L. grantianus N. L. Britt.
Bo. erectly shrubby, to 1.5 m h.; **Ri.** low, notched; **Ar.** with black Sp. to only 1 mm lg., these later disappearing; **terminal shoots** 3–5-ribbed; **Fl.** solitary, nocturnal, to 6 cm lg.; **Tu.** with blackish Ar. and few Sp. c. 1 mm lg.; **Sep.** greenish; **Pet.** cream-coloured, c. 8 mm lg.; **Fr.** spherical, c. 4 cm ⌀.—Puerto Rico. (Fig. 185.)

L. leonii Br. & R.
Bo. tree-like or shrubby, to 5 m h.; **trunk** to 30 cm ⌀ below; **Ri.** to 8, notched; **terminal shoots** to 2 cm ⌀; **Sp.** 6–12, 9 cm lg., yellowish; **Fl.** bellshaped, 3.5 cm lg., ± pink; **Tu.** with 1–4 short Sp.; **Fr.** spherical to ovoid, 2 cm ⌀, sparsely spiny; **S.** black.—Cuba.
[Haage adds: not found again in 1974 by Dr. A. Areces Mallea.]

L. maxonii Br. & R.
Bo. bushy, to 1.5 m h., ± branching; **Ri.** 5–7, sinuate; **Ar.** circular; **terminal shoots** c. 3 cm ⌀; **Sp.** c. 20, acicular, yellow to dark brown, to 3 cm lg.; **Fl.** to 6 cm lg., ± yellowish-green; **Pet.** numerous, spreading horizontally; **Tu.** and **Ov.** with dense yellow Sp.; **Fr.** with dense, ± yellowish-brownish Sp.—Cuba.
[Haage adds: up to 1 m h.; Ri. (5–)6–7; Ar. 1–2 cm apart.—Cuba (Oriente, E. of Daiquiri and in Maisi).]

L. prostratus Br. & R.
Bo. prostrate to creeping; **Ri.** 7, scarcely notched; **Ar.** prominent; **terminal shoots** to 2 cm ⌀; **Sp.** to 20, to 2 cm lg., ± yellow; **Ov.** with dense yellow Sp.; **Pet.** 1.5 cm lg.; **Fr.** c. 1.5 cm ⌀.—Cuba.

L. quadricostatus (Bello) Br. & R.
Bo. erectly shrubby or arching to bent, often forming thickets; **Ri.** thin, low; **terminal shoots** mostly 4-ribbed; **Sp.** to 4 cm lg., acicular; **Fl.** 4 cm lg., 2 cm ⌀; **Sep.** green; **Pet.** ± yellowish to greenish-white; **Tu.** and **Ov.** with short Sp.; **Fr.** ± spherical, red, weakly spiny.—Puerto Rico (in the SW.).

L. sylvestris Br. & R.
Bo. tree-like, to 5 m h.; **Ri.** to 7, strongly notched; **terminal shoots** to 3 cm ⌀; **Sp.** to 9 cm lg., light brown; **Fl.** not known; **Fr.** ± spherical, to c. 8 cm lg., the short Sp.-cushions soon dropping.—Cuba.
[Haage adds: Acc. Mallea, recently common in

Cuba, in Prov. Oriente, W. of Pilón, on dry coastal plains, Las Puercas River].

L. weingartianus (Hartm.) Br. & R.
Bo. clambering, sometimes creeping; **Ri.** to 7; **Ar.** with short white wool at first; **terminal shoots** 1 cm ⌀; **Sp.** yellow to reddish-brown; **Rsp.** to 12; **Csp.** to 6, to 1.5 cm lg., stouter; **Fl.** c. 4 cm lg.; **Fr.** c. 2 cm lg., Sp.-clusters later dropping.—Hispaniola.

L. wrightii León
Bo. tree-like, to 3 m h., freely branching when older; **trunk** to 20 cm ⌀; **Ri.** 4(–5); **Ar.** with grey to brownish felt; **terminal shoots** to 5 cm ⌀; **Sp.** to 14, to 4 cm lg., to 8 cm on the terminal shoots, grey to brownish; **Fl.** 2–4, apical, to 6.5 cm lg., 3.5 cm ⌀; **Tu.** with reddish Sp.; **Sep.** red, recurved; **Pet.** pink, whitish-yellow below; **Fr.** to 10 cm lg., 7.5 cm ⌀.—Cuba.
[Haage adds: Cuba (between Havana del Este and Cojimar, on limestone cliffs).]

Leptocladodia F. Buxb. (Leptocladia F. Buxb.): Mammillaria Haw.—SSer. Leptocladodae K. Sch.

Leuchtenbergia Hook. (193)

Monotypic genus. Above a stout taproot, passing over in age into a trunk-like body, the plant develops long triangular tubercles which project obliquely upwards in all directions, and are tipped with raffia-like spines; it may then offset, and old plants sometimes form groups. The yellow flowers are borne in the centre of the plant, on the newest areoles, and have a tube with fairly dense, large scales. The fruit is spindle-shaped, dry, scaly. The seeds are dark brown.—Distribution: Central to N. Mexico. [(R); grafted seedlings grow more rapidly.]

L. principis Hook. (T.)
Bo. simple or eventually offsetting, to 70 cm h.; **Tub.** ± truncate at the tip, later dying back from above and finally disappearing; **Ar.** densely grey-felty; **Sp.** thin, paper-like; **Rsp.** to 14, c. 5 cm lg.; **Csp.** 1–2, sometimes 10 cm lg.; **Fl.** to 8 c, lg., ± funnelform; **Sep.** green with a reddish centre; **Pet.** yellow with a silken sheen.—Central to N. Mexico. (Fig. 186.)

Leucostele Backbg. (94)

Large, robust, columnar Cerei, simple at first, later somewhat branching, with numerous rounded and not very prominent ribs. The body is fairly densely clad with soft white flexible bristles instead of spines. The flowers are ± bellshaped to funnelform and subapical; they are very hairy and have firmly appressed triangular scales, while the ovary is set with erect to appressed or sometimes contorted bristles to 1 cm long. The fruits too have contorted bristles, which constitute the principal diagnostic character separating Leucostele from Helianthocereus.—Distribution: probably S. Bolivia. [(R).]

L. rivierei Backbg. (T.)
Bo. to over 5 m h.; **Ri.** c. 25 or more; **Ar.** grey-felty; **Rsp.** and **Csp.** not differentiated, to 4 cm lg., bristly, weak, white; **Fl.** 10 cm lg., bellshaped to funnelform, pure white, diurnal; **Fil.** in 2 Ser.; **Fr.** with ± contorted Br.—S. Bolivia (?). (Fig. 187, 188.) Quite fast-growing.

Lobeira Alex. (34)

This genus was one of the first of the newer discoveries which—together with Cryptocereus, Marniera and Pseudonopalxochia—revealed the unbroken line of reduction in floral indumentum among the epiphylloid genera. Lobeira represents the final stage in this series before the glabrous state is reached: the ovaries and fruits still have felty cushions. The shoots are robust but not broad, the step-like notches on one side are opposite lobes on the other margin; the areoles are prominent and felty. The funnelform flowers arise towards the apex of the shoot; they are c. 8 cm long, with a tube c. 3.5 cm long. The fruit is green and the numerous seeds are black.—Distribution: Mexico (Chiapas). [(R).]

L. macdougallii Alex. (T.)
Bo. erect at first, then hanging down; **shoots** to 25 cm lg., to 5 cm br., tapering towards the apex; **Ar.** with very short felt; **Sep.** recurved; **Pet.** curving slightly outwards, expanded, often apiculate, purplish-pink; **Fr.** 2.8 cm ∅, felt-cushions pale brown.—Mexico (Chiapas, near San Cristobal Las Casas, at c. 2400 m). (Fig. 189.)

Lobivia Br. & R. (100)*

The plants of this genus are mostly relatively small-bodied, either single or caespitose, sometimes

---

* "Lobivia: the day-flowering Echinopsidinae", by Walter Rausch: German language, also in English translation by John Donald; descriptions, synonymies, many colour photographs, maps and botanical drawings. Published in 3 parts by Rudolf Herzig, Vienna. [Translator's note.]

forming cushions, some becoming cylindric in age. The spination is very variable. The ± funnel-shaped flowers come in colours of white to yellow to red, with every intermediate shade; they and the relatively small fruits are hairy. Many species have a conspicuously coloured hymen (a membranous process on the inner wall of the flower) from which the filaments arise; these flowers are among the most attractive of all. Differences in flower-form are the basis for a division into two subgenera:

SG. 1: Lobivia: inner petals ± erect to sometimes bending inwards;
SG. 2: Neolobivia Backbg.: inner petals never bending inwards, flower ± broadly funnelform.
SG. 1 contains only a single series:
Series 1: Pentlandianae Backbg.: floral characters as for the subgenus above.
SG. 2 has been subdivided into the following 14 series, the principal diagnostic characters being given with each:
Series 2: Mistienses Backbg.: Plants forming groups; flowers fairly large, petals lax, narrow-tipped;
Series 3: Bolivienses Backbg.: sometimes forming large groups, bodies ± broadly-spherical; flowers funnelform, petals crowded;
Series 4: Hertrichianae Backbg.: forming slender groups, more freely offsetting; flowers funnelform, petals delicate, red to bluish-red, mostly with a silky sheen;
Series 5: Haageanae Backbg.: groups of cylindric, ± stoutly-spined stems; flowers varying considerably in colour;
Series 6: Shaferae Backbg.: smaller, ± cylindric plants, with quite large flowers;
Series 7: Pseudocachenses Backbg.: smaller, ± cushion-forming plants, individual bodies ± flattened-spherical; free-flowering;
Series 8: Pugionacanthae Backbg.: small plants, with a taproot and dagger-like spines;
Series 9: Breviflorae Backbg.: ± broadly spherical, medium-sized plants; no hooked spines present; flowers fairly short;
Series 10: Caineanae Backbg.: robust, cylindric, ± cereoid plants; flowers borne close to the apex;
Series 11: Famatimenses Backbg.: plants forming cushions or groups, single bodies relatively small, spines fine, short or longer, to ± interlacing; flowers funnelform, variable in size, of widely different colours;
Series 12: Wrightianae Backbg.: taprooted, ± slender, caespitose plants; flowers very slender-funnelform;

Series 13: Jajoianae Backbg.: moderately off-setting plants, single heads ± spherical to oblong, later quite large; with solitary ± hooked spines; flowers bellshaped to funnelform, with a hymen (union of the filament-bases), mostly in a fairly strongly contrasting colour;

Series 14: Sanguiniflorae Backbg.: ± broadly spherical bodies, sometimes later oblong, ± cushion-forming, with solitary hooked spines; flowers funnelform, medium-sized;

Series 15: Tiegelianae Backbg.: bodies mostly simple, ± depressed-spherical, spines very fine; flowers funnelform with slender tubes (free-flowering).

The Lobivias are exceedingly floriferous, and their flowers are particularly attractive. They thus deserve more attention from professional growers. Grafted plants, which flower even more profusely, are recommended.—Distribution: from Central Peru to N. Argentina. [(R); grafting gives more rapid growth and freer flowering.]

The first figure after each specific name indicates the appropriate subgenus; the second figure shows the series.*

L. abrantha Y. Ito (1962); **Lobivia caineana** Card.

L. acanthoplegma (Backbg.) Backbg. n.comb. (Pseudolobivia acanthoplegma Backbg., "Die Cact.", VI: 3726. 1962) (2:9)
Bo. broadly flattened-spherical, to c. 11 cm ∅, leaf-green, with some grey felt in the crown; **Ri.** low, wider below, c. 26, acute, Tub. offset; **Rsp.** 9–11, interlacing sideways, to 2 cm lg., subulate, horn-coloured; **Csp.** 0; **Fl.** c. 5 cm lg., 4 cm ∅; **Tu.** only c. 1 cm lg., green, scaly, with some brown H.; **Sep.** narrow, long, olive-green; **Pet.** flame-colour, 11 mm br., obtusely rounded above; **Fil.** in 2 Ser., the lower one light red, the upper darker red; **style** green below, ± reddish-green above; **Sti.** light green.—Bolivia (near Ansaldo, road to the Rio Caine, 2050 m?). (Fig. 190.)

L. achacana Wessn.: an undescribed name.

L. aculeata Buin. (2:3 [?])
Bo. depressed-spherical, 5 cm h., 7 cm ∅, glossy

---

* While only naturally occurring species can be dealt with in this work, attention must be drawn to the often very beautiful Lobivia-hybrids raised in Japan, as shown by Yoshio Ito in the many fine colour-photos of his cactus-books in the series "Hoikuscha Color Books" (1962) and "The Charming of Flowers-Cacti" (1963). Both works are of great importance because of the insight they provide into the breeding potential of Lobivias (see illustration in the Introduction).

fresh green; **Ri.** 16; **Sp.** acicular, brownish at first; **Rsp.** to 12, to 3.5 cm lg.; **Csp.** 1–3, the longest one 4.5 cm lg.; **Fl.** 6.3 cm lg., 5 cm ∅, ± golden-yellow, purple-bordered, scented; **hymen** white.—Bolivia (Potosí, Huari-Huari).

L. adpressispina Ritt. (FR 977): no description available.

L. aguilari Vasquez 1973
Bo. simple, spherical, 9 cm h., to 17 cm ∅, green; **Ri.** c. 17, spiralled, tuberculate; **Sp.** 11–18, erect, slightly bent above, shortest one 1 cm, longest one to 8 cm lg., older Sp. grey, newer ones white; **Fl.** near the apex, bellshaped, 8.5 cm lg.; **Ov.** spherical, 1 cm ∅, whitish-green with pink Sc. and dense white H. in their axils; **Tu.** short, bellshaped, with pink Sc., with white and black H. in the axils; **Sep.** linear, 3.5 × 1 cm, light magenta outside, magenta-red inside; **Pet.** oblong, 4 × 1.3 cm, red; **style** and **Sti.** light green; **Fil.** magenta-red; **An.** yellow; **Fr.** subspherical, 17 × 15 mm, green; **S.** 1 mm lg., black.—Bolivia (Dept. Cochabamba, Prov. Mizque, close to Molinero, at 2500 m). Spec. discovered by Edgar Aguilar.

L. akersii Rausch
Bo. simple, flattened-spherical, 20 mm h. and to 70 mm ∅, dark green to violet-brown; **Ri.** to 18, broken up into acutely-angled Tub. tipped with the Ar.; **Ar.** round, white-felty; **Rsp.** 4–5, 7–12 mm lg., curving to the Bo., sometimes appressed; **Csp.** 0–1, to 25 mm lg., strongly curving to curling inwards, brown; all **Sp.** soft, flexible; **Fl.** 40 mm lg., 20 mm ∅; **Ov.** ovoid; **Tu.** narrow, violet-red with dark brown Sc. and white and brown H.; **Sep.** lanceolate, violet-pink; **Pet.** only 12–14 mm lg.; **throat** narrowly funnelform, pink, white inside; inner **Fil.** white, outer ones orange; **style** 22 mm lg., white with yellow Sti.; **Fr.** spherical, 2–3 cm ∅; **S.** small, as in L. tegeleriana (Acantholobivia!).—Peru (near Oyon, at 3700 m). Self-fertile.
The segregation of Acantholobivia as a distinct genus is scarcely justified. Acc. Rausch, he has found both spiny and spineless Fr. within many spec. of Lobivia.
L. akersii was earlier distributed as Lobivia churinensis.

L. albolanata (Buin.) Krainz: **Lobivia famatimensis** v. **famatimensis**.

L. allegraiana Backbg. (2:4)
Bo. simple to caespitose, to 8 cm h. and ∅, dark bluish-green; **Ri.** spiralled, Tub. ± square; **Sp.** to 12, to 3 cm lg., ± curving, yellowish at first; **Rsp.** and **Csp.** scarcely differentiated; **Fl.** 5 cm lg., 4 cm

$\varnothing$, silky, blood-red; **Fr.** c. 1.5 cm lg., green.—SE. Peru.

L. amblayensis Rausch
Bo. simple, to 2 cm h., 3 cm $\varnothing$, dark to brownish-green, with a taproot; **Ri.** 11–17, straight, vertical; **Ar.** round, 2 mm $\varnothing$, 1–2 mm apart, with whitish to light brown felt; **Rsp.** 14–16, 3–6 mm lg., spreading to pectinate, bristly, brittle, white, reddish-brown below, later brown; **Csp.** 2–3, to 8 mm lg., arranged in a vertical line, projecting, stouter, brownish-black on new growth, later black; **Fl.** lateral, 8 cm lg., 6 cm $\varnothing$; **Ov.** long-elliptic; **Ov.** and **Tu.** pinkish brown with brown Sc. and brownish-grey H.; **Sep.** violet-pink or reddish, with a brown M.-stripe; **Pet.** spatulate, to 15 mm br., serrate, mucronate above, orange-yellow, bordered red; **hymen** white, throat and inner **Fil.** carmine, outer ones yellow; **style** green or dark red, 11 **Sti.** similarly; **Fr.** ellipsoid, blackish-brown with pink Sc. and whitish-grey wool; **S.** spherical, testa black, finely tuberculate.—Argentina (Salta, E. of Amblayo, at 2800 m). (Fig. 471). (= Echinopsis amblayensis [Rausch] H. Friedr.)

v. **albispina** Rausch: distinguished from the type by its white **Sp.**—Argentina (Salta, S. of Amblayo, at 2300 m). (= Echinopsis amblayensis [Rausch] H. Friedr. v. albispina Rausch.)
While this complex resembles L. densispina, the habitats are widely separated; moreover it is distinguished by its generally reddish-brown appearance, dark green to brownish epidermis, Sp. which are red, becoming brown to blackish, Ov. more than twice as long as broad, the mostly orange-red border to the Pet.; 15 km further S. there is also a population with entirely white-spined plants, with orange Fl.

L. andalgalensis Br. & R. (2:3)
Bo. forming cushions, individual heads to 10 cm $\varnothing$; **Ri.** c. 13, scarcely notched; **Sp.** straight, subulate, white; **Rsp.** to 10, to 7 mm lg.; **Csp.** 1, to 2.5 cm lg., stouter; **Fl.** c. 6 cm lg., red; **Fil.** $\pm$ purple; **style** reddish or yellow.—W. Argentina (Catamarca: Ancasti, Andalgalá).

L. arachnacantha Buin. & Ritt. (2:7)
Bo. flattened-spherical, to 2 cm h., to 4 cm $\varnothing$, dark green; **Ri.** 14, weakly notched; **Sp.** appearing spider-like; **Rsp.** to 15, to 5 mm lg., pale brown at first, then whitish; **Csp.** 1, 5 mm lg., black, curving upwards; **Fl.** with a slender Tu., yellow to orange; **Fr.** reddish-green.—Bolivia (Samaipata).
This name is applied also to Cardenas's material, known as "Echinopsis torrecillasensis", but not possessing the stoutly napiform lower part shown in the drawing of Cardenas. Plants from the seeds he sent, with the above name, gave plants which

were undoubtedly attributable to Lob. arachnacantha, published somewhat earlier. The flower-description most closely matching "Echps. torrecillasensis" is the form with green Tu. and Sc., hymen inconspicuous, Pet. true red, slender, acute; **Sti'** green [Haage adds: = Echinopsis arachnacantha (Buin. et Ritt.) H. Friedr.]
Kilian has observed the following variants:
1. var.?: (Cardenas material): Bo. green, bluish-green, olive or brownish-green; Sep. light olive; Pet. orange, spatulate; Fil. orange above, lilac-carmine below; style green; Sti. light green; Tu. light olive-brownish with whitish-grey H.
2. var.?: Bo. green; Sep. and Pet. red-madder, spatulate, acute; Fil. lilac-carmine; style green; Sti. light green to yellowish; Tu. green with carmine Sc.
3. var.?: Bo. green; Pet. obtuse, spatulate; Sep. light olive-yellow tinged pink; Pet. carmine; Fil. lilac-carmine; style olive; Sti. green; Tu. pinkish-olive, Sc. pink, H. black.
4. var.?: Bo. green; Pet. acute, spatulate; Sep. light yellowish-olive; Pet. red; Fil. carmine; style green; Sti. white; Tu. light green, Sc. similarly, H. white, interspersed with short black ones; hymen distinct, pinkish-carmine.
The best solution would appear to be to subdivide the spec. into var. arachnacantha with yellow Fl., and var. torrecillasensis with red Fl., providing the latter with a type, and either describing it as rather variable, or listing the variants as sv. The hymen appears to be inconspicuous in Nos. 1 and 2, i.e. not so markedly carmine as in Nos. 3 and 4. However, in the absence of information as to the possible range of variability, accurate naming presents serious problems; as an instance, there are so many variants of Lob. famatimensis that individual names for all of them are scarcely thinkable.

v. **torrecillasensis** hort. europ. (Card.?): diverges in having the **Ri.** either fewer or more numerous; **Rsp.** 9–12; **Csp.** (0–)1(–2); **Sp.** reddish-brown at first; **Fl.** $\pm$ carmine. [Haage adds: = Echinopsis arachnacantha (Buin. et Ritt.) H. Friedr. v. torrecillasensis Card.]

L. argentea Backbg. (2:3)
Bo. forming groups, single heads to 10 cm h., to 15 cm $\varnothing$, glossy, greyish-green; **Ri.** 24, Tub. sharply angular; **Rsp.** to 14, to 2 cm lg.; **Csp.** to 8 cm lg., dark at first, red below, becoming pinkish-grey; **Fl.** delicate silvery to lilac-white; **Pet.** lax, narrow, tapering.—Bolivia (Prov. Oruro).

L. aurantiaca Backbg. (2:3)
Bo. $\pm$ oblong, offsetting from the base, dull

brownish-green; **crown** with few Sp. but with fine Br.; **Ri.** 21, $\pm$ reddish, divided into oblique Tub.; **Sp.** tangled, $\pm$ contorted, to c. 8 cm lg., light grey, brownish-tipped; **Fl.** c. 5 cm lg.; **Sep.** bronze-coloured; **Pet.** broadly truncate to rounded, $\pm$ denticulate, orange-yellow; **style** pale greenish.—Origin?

L. aurea (Br. & R.) Backbg. and variety: **Pseudolobivia aurea** (Br. & R.) Backbg. and variety.

L. aureolilacina Card. (2:3)—C. & S. J. [US], XXXIII: 4, 110–111. 1961.
Bo. simple, spherical, 7–8 cm h., 13–14 cm $\varnothing$, greyish-green; **Ri.** c. 18; **Rsp.** 8, pectinate, 1.5–3.5 cm lg.; **Csp.** 1.3–7 cm lg.; **Sp.** subulate, horn-coloured, curving and whitish-grey at the tip, thickened below; **Fl.** 7 cm lg.; outer **Pet.** yellowish to lilac, inner ones light yellow.—Bolivia (Chuquisaca, Impora).

L. aureosenilis Kniže 1969
Bo. spherical at first, later elongated, forming large groups, light green; **R.** thread-like at first; **Ri.** 12–13, straight, obtuse, broader below; **Ar.** small, with grey wool; **Sp.** dissimilar, $\pm$ straight, flexible; **Rsp.** 8–10, 1 cm lg., radiating; **Csp.** 3–5, golden-yellow, to 7 cm lg., directed towards the crown, often cruciform; **Fl.** pinkish-red, 3.5–4.5 cm $\varnothing$, 3.5 cm lg.; **Fr.** brown, naked or with small violet Sc.; **S.** black, matt, 0.2–3 mm (?) $\varnothing$.—Peru (Arequipa, near Tarucani, at 4000 m).

L. backebergiana Y. Ito (2:3)—The Full Bloom of Cact. Flow., 50. 1962.
Bo. spherical to elongated; **Ri.** acute, 17–20; **Rsp.** 10–12, 1–2.5 cm lg., whitish-brown; **Csp.** 1, to 3 cm lg., whitish to reddish-brown; **Fl.** to 7 cm lg., fairly large funnelform, light yellow; **Pet.** apiculate.—Argentina. In the colour-photo the Sp. are shown as grey, dark-tipped.

L. backebergii (Werd.) Backbg. (2:12)
Bo. simple or offsetting, spherical to oblong, 4.5 cm $\varnothing$, light green; **Ri.** c. 15, with somewhat oblique furrows; **Sp.** all radials (3–)5(–7), unequal, projecting $\pm$ obliquely, 0.5–5 cm lg., $\pm$ brownish to grey, individual Sp. hooked; **Fl.** c. 4.5 cm lg., light carmine, with a bluish sheen; **Pet.** oblong; **throat** white.—Bolivia (near La Paz, at c. 3600 m).

L. binghamiana Backbg. (2:4)
Bo. later offsetting freely, rich glossy light green, spotted white; single heads to 8 cm h. and $\varnothing$; **crown** sunken; **Ri.** c. 22; **Sp.** light golden-yellow, acicular, sharp, to 12, scarcely differentiated; **Csp.** later mostly 3, longer, to 1.5 cm lg., thickened below, darker; **Fl.** c. 5 cm lg. and $\varnothing$, brilliant silky

red-madder, with a bluish sheen; **Fr.** green, subspherical.—SE. Peru (near Cuzco).

L. boedekeriana Hard.: **Lobivia rossii** v. **boedekeriana** (Hard.) Backbg.

L. boliviensis Br. & R. (2:3)
Bo. forming groups, single St. $\pm$ spherical, to 10 cm $\varnothing$, often hidden by the thin dense Sp.; **Ri.** to 20, shortly tuberculate; **Sp.** 6–8, $\pm$ flexible, to 9 cm lg., brownish; **centrals** scarcely distinguishable; **Fl.** $\pm$ aniline-red.—Bolivia (near Oruro).
Many of the varieties formerly listed under "Lobivia pentlandii", assuming they are not hybrids, are doubtless referable here, or to other Bolivian spec. with widely funnelform flowers.

L. breviflora Backbg. (2:9)
Bo. depressed-spherical, glossy, dark green; **crown** sunken; **Ri.** c. 25, $\pm$ rounded, becoming flatter, obliquely tuberculate; **Sp.** to 25, pectinate, $\pm$ curving; **Rsp.** and **Csp.** scarcely differentiated, to 13 mm lg., brownish, later whitish; **Fl.** c. 3 cm lg., brilliant light blood-red, with a very short Tu.; **Sep.** lighter.—Argentina (Salta). This spec. has the shortest Fl. of any known Lobivia.

L. bruchii Br. & R.: **Soehrensia bruchii** (Br. & R.) Backbg.

L. brunneo-rosea Backbg. (2:3)
Bo. later offsetting, single heads to 10 cm $\varnothing$; **Ri.** c. 18, slightly spiralled, obliquely notched; **Rsp.** c. 10, c. 2 cm lg., acicular, curving; **Csp.** 1(–2), to 6 cm lg.; **Sp.** interlacing, light, darker-tipped; **Fl.** opening widely, strongly revolute, brownish old-rose; **hymen** light-coloured.—Bolivia (Oruro—La Paz).

L. buiningiana (FR 55): no description available.

L. cabradai Frič nom.nud.
Description by K. Wilhelm, Mainz:
Bo. oblong-spherical, green to bluish-green, 6–10 cm h., 5–7 cm $\varnothing$; **Ri.** c. 12, unbroken; **Rsp.** c. 10–15, to 10 mm lg., straight, reddish-brown, later horn-coloured; **Csp.** 1–3, to 10 mm lg., brown; **Fl.** red, to 6 cm lg. and 3–5 cm $\varnothing$.—Peru (no locality stated; found by Frič.).

L. cachensis (Speg.) Br. & R. (2:14)
Bo. simple or caespitose, c. 9 cm h., 6.5 cm $\varnothing$; **Ri.** c. 19, transversely notched; **Rsp.** 7–20, 4–5 mm lg., straight; **Csp.** 4, 1–2 longer, hooked; **Sp.** weak, grey, tipped yellowish; **Fl.** c. 7 cm lg., red.—N. Argentina (Salta, near Cachi, 2500 m).

L. caespitosa (J. A. Purp.) Br. & R. (2:2)
Bo. forming groups; **St.** cylindric, mid-green; **Ri.** c.

12, rounded, slightly wavy; **Rsp.** 12, 2 cm lg., acicular; **Csp.** 1, to 5 cm lg., ± curving; **Sp.**-colour variable, brownish to amber; **Fl.** to 8 cm lg., yellowish-red.—Bolivia (N. of La Paz).

L. caineana Card. (2:10)
Bo. simple, cylindric to cereoid, to 20 cm h., 9 cm ∅, vivid green; **Ri.** 9, broad; **Sp.** to 18, to 7 cm lg., subulate, older Sp. bent, whitish-grey; **Fl.** subapical, funnelform, to 7 cm lg., pinkish-violet.—Bolivia (Calahuta, Rio Caine).
The habit of this little known spec. and its Fl. are so remarkable that acc. Ritter they merit independent generic status.

L. camataquiensis Card. (2:9)—"Cactus", 18: 90–91. 1963.
Bo. to 10 cm h., to 11 cm ∅, greyish-green; **Ri.** c. 23, 1 cm h., notched, Tub. hatchet-shaped; **Ar.** to 1.2 cm apart; **Sp.** not differentiated, 15–17, acicular, 5–35 mm lg., upper ones at first stiffer, brown; **Fl.** numerous, in a subapical coronet, broadly funnelform, 4.5 cm lg., 4 cm ∅; **Pet.** crimson, apiculate; **Fil.** in 2 Ser., lower Ser. dark red, upper Ser. crimson; **Sti.** light green; **Tu.** with white H. and purple Sc., widely opening; **style** green.—Bolivia (S. Cinti, between Camataqui [Abecia] and Carreras, 2300 m). Resembles L. cintiensis Card., from which it is distinguished by the erect, longer Sp.; the ring of Fl. is similar to L. neocinnabarina Backbg.

L. cariquinensis Card.: **Lobivia pentlandii** (Hook.) Br. & R.: type or a form only?

L. cardenasiana Rausch 1972
Bo. simple, flattened-spherical, to 8 cm h., 10 cm ∅; **Ri.** to 18, vertical, c. 12 mm br., flat; **Ar.** 16–18 mm apart, round to oval, 4–6 mm lg., white-felty; **Rsp.** 12, in 5 pairs and one each directed upwards and downwards, 10–12 mm lg., appressed; **Csp.** 1–3 arranged vertically, projecting, 15–30 mm lg.; all **Sp.** subulate, white to yellowish, with brown or black tips, later greying; **Fl.** lateral, 8–10 cm lg., 6–7 cm ∅; **Ov.** and **Tu.** green, with brownish-pink Sc. and black H.; **Sep.** lanceolate, pink; **Pet.** spatulate, rounded, magenta; **throat** greenish-white; **Fil.** violet-pink, lighter below; **style** somewhat united, green; **Sti.** 10, green; **Fr.** ovoid, 20 mm lg., brownish-green; **S.** spherical, testa black, glossy.—Bolivia (E. of Tarija, 2300–2400 m). Named for Prof. Dr. M. Cardenas who has made such notable discoveries among the Bolivian cacti. (Fig. 472.) (= Echinopsis cardenasiana [Rausch] H. Friedr.)

L. carminantha Backbg. (2:3)
Probably quite closely related to L. leucorhodon, but differs in having a dull greyish-green epidermis and a carmine Fl.—N. Bolivia (highlands).

L. cerasiflora Frič nom.nud.
Description by K. Wilhelm, Mainz:
Bo. spherical to oblong, to 10 cm lg., 7–10 cm ∅, green; **Ri.** c. 15, small, straight, unbroken; **Rsp.** to 15, only a few mm lg., grey to whitish-grey, flexible, bristly, concealing the Bo.; **Csp.** 1–3 at maturity, rather longer than the Rsp.; **Fl.** flesh-coloured, to 6 cm lg., 3–5 cm ∅; throat red to lighter.—Bolivia (no exact locality known).

L. charazanensis Card. (2:3)
Bo. grouping, single heads to 4 cm h., 5 cm ∅, light green; **Ri.** 13–15, acute, Tub. ± offset; **Rsp.** c. 12, 0.5–5 cm lg., thin-acicular, spreading; **Csp.** 1, c. 6 cm lg.; all **Sp.** golden-yellow; **Fl.** stoutly funnelform, 5 cm lg., 4 cm ∅, sulphur-yellow; **Sep.** reddish above.—Bolivia (Charazani, 3000 m).

L. charcasina Card. (2:3)—"Cactus", 19: 82, 42–43. 1964.
Bo. simple, 4 cm h., 9 cm ∅; **Ri.** c. 19, Tub. hatchet-shaped; **Ar.** 1.5 cm apart, grey; **Sp.** 14–16, pectinate, to 1 cm lg., subulate, grey to white, thickened below; **Fl.** to 6 cm lg., shortly funnelform; **Pet.** spatulate, red; **Tu.** only 2 cm lg., green, with white and black H.; **Ov.** with many white H.; **Fil.** purple; **style** green.—Bolivia (Chuquisaca, near Sucre, Charcas).

L. chereauniana (Schlumb.) Backbg. (2:9)
Bo. elongated-spherical, dark green; **Ri.** very narrow at first, very obliquely notched; **Rsp.** to 10, ± subulate, light yellow, reddish below; **Csp.** sometimes 1, rather stouter; **Fl.** glossy, scarlet-carmine.—Origin unknown, probably Bolivia.

L. chionantha (Speg.) Br. & R.: **Acanthocalycium chionanthum** (Speg.) Backbg.

L. chiquitana hort.: syn. L. rigidispina Backbg. No description available.

L. chlorogona Wessn.: **Lobivia rebutioides** v. **chlorogona** (Wessn.) Backbg. Commercial growers also use Wessner's name for ± long-spined forms of L. famatimensis.

L. chrysantha (Werd.) Backbg. (2:5)
Bo. depressed-spherical, 4.5 cm h., to 7 cm ∅, becoming oblong, dull greyish-green; **Ri.** 5–13, narrow above; **Rsp.** 3–7, to 2 cm lg., straight, subulate, pungent, blackish above, reddish below, sometimes pale; **Csp.** absent; **Fl.** c. 5 cm lg., broadly funnelform, golden to orange-yellow; **throat** greenish, dark purple below.—Argentina (Salta).

v. **hossei** (Werd.) Backbg.: **Csp.** 1–3, to 3 cm lg.; **Fl.** yellowish-orange, often suffused reddish;

v. **janseniana** (Backbg.) Backbg.: **Rsp.** c. 10–14, concolorous black, thickened below, c. 1 cm lg.; **Fl.** bellshaped to funnelform, golden-yellow;

v. **leucacantha** (Backbg.) Backbg.: **Bo.** light green; **Fl.** yellowish, almost white.

It is clear from the records of the late Mr. Schelle, including photographs by both Frič and Kreuzinger, for all of which I am indebted to Mr. G. Redecker of Tübingen, that L. staffenii Frič (without description) is a synonym of the above spec. Frič's original photograph shows that the spec. is variable: the Tu. can be more slender or stouter, Fl. yellow or reddish, and Pet. apiculate or obtuse. Two further photos (Frič and Kreuzinger) provide no further help on identification. Because of the variability of the spec., no further varieties can be segregated. The varietal names cover only the more conspicuous or most widely divergent variants. L. staffenii v. lagunilla Frič (undescribed) has finer, more numerous Sp. and is a form of L. polaskiana, which also belongs to this complex of species.

L. chrysochete Werd. (2:3)

Bo. simple or offsetting from the base, subspherical, c. 8 cm ⌀, fresh green; **Ri.** c. 20, obliquely transversely notched; **Sp.** eventually to 30, long, yellow to brownish-yellow, ± bristly and thin, centrals to 8 cm lg.; **Fl.** widely erect-funnelform, c. 4 cm ⌀, glossy, orange to brick-red; **throat** white.—Argentina (Prov. Jujuy).

L. cinnabarina (Hook.) Br. & R. (2:9)

The following is taken from Hooker's original description (Curtis' Bot. Mag., 73, pl. 4326. 1847): **Bo.** broadly spherical, to 15 cm ⌀; **Fl.** carmine, c. 8 cm ⌀; **Rsp.** several in a circle, 12, $\frac{1}{4}$–$\frac{1}{2}$ inch lg., pale brown, stoutly acicular; **Csp.** 1, longer, stouter, somewhat curving; **Pet.** obtuse, numerous; **Fil.** red; **An.** yellow; **Sti.** erect.—Bolivia (Fig. 191.) The diagnosis of Britton & Rose does not tally with the original description, and perhaps refers to the plants Cardenas held to be the above spec. The latter illustrated this spec. in "Cactus", 18: 78, 93. 1963, and added: "discovered by Bridges in 1846, and since then completely lost; I rediscovered it again at Colomi (Cochabamba). It is frequent on the slopes of the Provinces Chapare and Punata, at c. 3400 m". This view is erroneous, and the plant he had in mind is my L. neocinnabarina with smaller Fl., which comes from the same locality as Cardenas has given. Rausch of Vienna established that L. cinnabarina was a different plant, which he also re-collected.

v. **spinosior** (SD.) Y. Ito: Salm-Dyck's brief description reads: "Bo. somewhat more robust; Sp. stiffer, 1.5–2 cm lg.; Csp. always present". It is probable that Salm-Dyck understood some other plant under this name, since he mentions "1–3 Csp., sometimes missing", and refers to a description by C. Morren, but fails to mention the conspicuously large flower of the original description, or to give the spine-count for v. spinosior. In view of the confusing similarities of plants in the L. cinnabarina complex of species, or the variability of its different species (except those where the flower has a white throat, like L. neocinnabarina, and is easily recognisable) it cannot be excluded that v. spinosior is identical with a plant Hoffmann found in E. Bolivia, with the following characters: Bo. glossy green, Ri. narrow at first; Sp. few at first, brownish, soon more numerous, to c. 20, stiff and pungent, Csp. and upper Rsp. soon becoming blackish and ± thickened below, Csp. to 4 or rather more; Fl. medium-sized, scarlet-carmine, with a red throat; Tu. with very little hair.

In the light of the foregoing I have not yet felt able to ascribe specific rank to Hoffmann's plant.

L. cintiensis Card. (2:9)

Bo. spherical to cylindric, to 50 cm lg., to 10 cm ⌀, greyish-green; **Ri.** c. 20, low; **Rsp.** to 17, 0.5–1.5 cm lg., ± pectinate, acicular; **Csp.** to 3, to 2.5 cm lg.; **Sp.** white; **Fl.** funnelform, 5 cm lg., crimson; **Tu.** only 1 cm lg.—Bolivia (S. Cinti, near Impora, 3000 m).

v. **elongata** Ritt.—"Taxon", XII: 3, 124. 1963
Bo. to 60 cm h., to 8 cm ⌀; **Ri.** 4–7 mm h., narrower; **Ar.** 3–4 mm ⌀, 0.5–1 cm apart; **Fl.** 3.5 cm lg., golden-yellow or paler.—Bolivia (Prov. Mendez, Dept. Tarija, El Puente) (FR 82).

L. claeysiana Backbg. (2:9)

Bo. simple, to 12 cm h., greyish-green; **Ri.** 16, compressed at first; **Rsp.** 7, to 2.2 cm lg., radiating, stiff, horn-coloured, ± dark-tipped, red below at first; **Csp.** 1, to 5 cm lg., ± bent, horn-coloured; **Fl.** 4.5 cm lg., 5.5 cm ⌀, light yellow, darker outside; **throat** greenish.—S. Bolivia (near Tupiza).

L. corbula (Herrera) Br. & R.: **Lobivia pentlandii** (Hook.) Br. & R.

L. coriquinensis nom. prov. Wilhelm

Bo. oblong-rounded, caespitose, to 8 cm h., 6 cm ⌀, green; **Ri.** c. 13, divided into obliquely arranged, hatchet-shaped Tub.; **Rsp.** 6–8(–10), unequal, to 3.5 cm lg., ± straight, directed towards the Bo., horn to yellow, brown above and below; **Csp.** 0 at first, later 1, coloured as the Rsp. but longer, curving slightly to the crown; **Fl.** yellowish-red, 7 cm lg., to 6 cm ⌀; **Pet.** yellowish-red above, whitish below; **Sep.** violet-red; **style** and **Sti.** light green.—Bolivia (Camacho, Dept. La Paz, near Coriquina, at c. 3000 m).

L. cornuta Rausch
Bo. simple, to 5 cm h. and 6 cm $\emptyset$, greyish-green, with a long taproot; **Ri.** c. 12, broken into flat Tub. 12 mm lg., 10 mm br., imbricate; **Ar.** white-felty, set on the uppermost part of the Tub.; **Sp.** 2 longer ones c. 4 cm lg., curving upwards, spreading, and 2 smaller thinner ones, also directed upwards, and 1 small Sp. pointing downwards, all brownish-red at first, thickened and black below, later greying; **Fl.** lateral, 5 cm lg., 4 cm $\emptyset$, hairy below, greenish; **Sep.** very acute, brown; **Pet., style** and **Sti.** yellow; **Fr.** spherical, c. 8 mm $\emptyset$, blackish-brown with dense light brown wool; **S.** oblong-ovoid, 2 mm lg., 1.2 mm br.—Bolivia (Tarija, near Yunchara, at 3900 m). Seed-structure closely resembles that of L. pugionacantha. Discovered by W. Rausch. (Fig. 473.)
Acc. "Stachelpost", May 1972, this spec. was to be found quite a long time ago in collections; however Wessner's description was lost in the confusions of wartime.

L. cruciaureispina Kniže 1968
Bo. dark green, c. 20 cm h., to 8 cm $\emptyset$, forming groups; **R.** much branching, thread-like; **Ri.** 15–20, rounded, 1 cm h., thickened around the Ar.; **Ar.** without any wool, 3–4 mm $\emptyset$; **Sp.** golden-yellow; **Csp.** 1–2, bent or hooked, to 10 cm lg.; **Rsp.** 7–9, straight, c. 2.5 cm lg.; **Fl.** orange-yellow, 8–9 cm lg., c. 6 cm $\emptyset$; **Tu.** with fine whitish-brown H.; **Fr.** violet-brown, 1.5 cm $\emptyset$; **S.** black, matt, 0.2–3 mm lg.—Peru (Dept. Apurimac near Andahuaylas, 2500–2800 m).

L. culpinensis Ritt. (FR 797)
Bo. green, 5–15 cm $\emptyset$; **Ri.** 15–30, narrow, 4–8 mm h., $\pm$ notched; **Ar.** 5–8 mm lg., 4–5 mm br., 8–20 mm apart; **Sp.** straight, black to yellow; **Rsp.** 8–12, directed sideways, sometimes white, 1–5 cm lg., lower ones thin, upper ones stout; **Csp.** 1–6, subulate, 2–6 cm lg.; **Fl.** 5–6 cm lg., nectary 1–4 mm lg., **Pet.** 20–26 mm lg., 7–13 mm br., spatulate, yellow or red; **Fil.** brownish-red below, or green, red to reddish-lilac above; **style** and **Sti.** green; **S.** dark brown, $\pm$ ribbed.—Bolivia (S. Chichas, Mal Paso).

L. cumingii (SD. non Hopff.) Br. & R.: **Weingartia neocumingii** Backbg.

L. cylindrica Backbg. (2:5)
Bo. simple, to 12 cm lg., 6 cm $\emptyset$, dull leaf-green; **Ri.** c. 11, unbroken; **Rsp.** c. 7, to 8 mm lg., radiating, subulate, pinkish-grey, darker to black below; **Csp.** 1, 1–3 cm lg., stiffer; **Fl.** to 5.5 cm lg., broadly funnelform, golden-yellow.—N. Argentina (Sierra Chica).

L. cylindracea Backbg. (2:6)
Bo. slender-cylindric, to 7 cm h., 4 cm $\emptyset$; **Ri.** c. 13, low, straight; **Rsp.** c. 15, short, thin, $\pm$ interlacing sideways, whitish; **Csp.** c. 6, to 1.2 cm lg., thin, darker; **Fl.** 5.5 cm lg. and $\emptyset$, opening widely, yellow.—N. Argentina. [Haage adds: = Echinopsis c. (Backbg.) H. Friedr.]

I L. divaricata (FR 696): no description available.

L. dobeana Dölz: **Lobivia andalgalensis** Br. & R.

L. dragai (Frič): see **Lobivia polaskiana** Backbg.

L. draxleriana Rausch: named for the collector, Paul Draxler, of Wiener Neustadt.
Bo. simple, to 6 cm h., 14 cm $\emptyset$, bluish to greyish-green, mostly with a taproot; **Ri.** to 25, divided into Tub. c. 15 mm lg.; **Ar.** oval, 5–7 mm lg., white-felty, later glabrous; **Rsp.** 9–12, 8–15 mm lg., spreading towards the Bo., whitish, tipped brown; **Csp.** 2–5, 20–30 mm lg., upper ones overtopping the crown, later projecting, curving, red, black-tipped, later greying; **Fl.** c. 75 mm lg., 65 mm $\emptyset$; **Sep.** narrowly lanceolate, green, bordered pink; **Pet.** spatulate, red with a bluish sheen, **hymen** violet-pink, **throat** violet; **An.** brownish; **style** green with 6–8 green Sti.; **Fr.** spherical; **S.** brownish-black.—Bolivia (near Aiquile, 2500 m). Related to L. cinnabarina but distinguished by the more bluish epidermis and Fl., red Csp. in the new growth, brown An. and larger S. (Fig. 474.)

L. drijveriana Backbg. (2:7)
Bo. simple or caespitose, low, small, 3–8 cm $\emptyset$, greyish-green, with a long taproot; **Ri.** c. 12, spiralled, low, tuberculate; **Rsp.** to 12, appressed, whitish; **Csp.** eventually to 4, sometimes bent, from a few mm to 6 cm lg., light yellow to black if longer, to stoutly subulate; **Fl.** concolorous yellow, varying to $\pm$ orange tints; **Pet.** in 3 Ser., $\pm$ lax, **throat** green; **style** and **Sti.** mostly purple.—Argentina (Cachipampa). (Fig. 192).
v. **astranthema** Backbg.: **Fl.** brilliant yellow, **Pet.** narrower, laxer;
v. **aurantiaca** Backbg.: **Fl.** old-gold;
v. **nobilis** Backbg.: **Fl.** dark reddish-orange.

L. ducis pauli Frič non Först.: **Pseudolobivia longispina** (Br. & R.) Backbg.

L. durispina Backbg. is a n.prop. for a new hard-spined spec. found by Frau Muhr (Argentina, 20 km W. of La Quiaca); Uhlig No. U 2133; Fl. unknown.

L. duursmaiana Backbg. (2:14)
Bo. caespitose, single heads to c. 4 cm $\emptyset$, grafted

plants become elongated; **Ri.** to 14, divided into ± angular Tub.; **Rsp.** 10–14, to 10 mm lg., radiating, ± curving, brownish to pinkish-grey; **Csp.** 1, directed upwards; **Fl.** ? (said to be red).—N. Argentina.

L. echinata Rausch 1973
Bo. simple to caespitose, to 15 cm h. and c. 5 cm ∅, light green; **Ri.** 15–18, straight, rounded, ± tuberculate; **Ar.** round, 2–4 mm ∅, white-felty, 6–7 mm apart; **Rsp.** 8–10, radiating, interlacing, 15–20 mm lg.; **Csp.** 1–2, to 60 mm lg., projecting; all **Sp.** acicular, brown, yellow below, later greying; **Fl.** 50 mm lg. and ∅; **Tu.** slender, ochreous green with reddish Sc. and white H.; **Sep.** lanceolate, brownish; **Pet.** lanceolate to spatulate, red, throat white to pink; **Fil.** red, white below; **style** with 5–7 green or reddish Sti.; **Fr.** spherical, c. 10 mm ∅, reddish-brown.—Peru (near Ollantaitambo, 2900 m). Discovered by W. Rausch. Related to L. minuta, but Sp. larger, acicular.

L. elongata Backbg. (2:5)
Bo. cylindric to cereoid, to 20 cm lg., 6 cm ∅; **Ri.** to 14, low, narrow; **Rsp.** c. 8, thin-acicular, to 1.2 cm lg., laxly interlacing; **Csp.** scarcely differentiated, several, 1(–2) longer ones to 3.75 cm lg., stouter, darker below; all **Sp.** dark brownish at first, ± zoned; **Fl.** stout, yellow (also red?).—N. Argentina (Salta, Cachi). [Haage adds: = Echinopsis e. (Backbg.) H. Friedr.]

L. emmae Backbg. (2:7)
Bo. simple, later caespitose, to 10 cm h., 5 cm ∅, olive to brownish-green; **Ri.** c. 16, narrow, low; **Rsp.** 12, c. 1 cm lg., spreading laterally, ± bent, chestnut-brown at first; **Csp.** 2, to 2.5 cm lg., ± contorted, almost hooked at the tip; **Fl.** 3 cm lg., 4 cm ∅, funnelform, carmine, ± crimson below; **throat** scarlet.—Argentina (Salta).
v. **brevispina** Backbg.: **Bo.** light green; **Ri.** c. 13, broader; **Csp.** only c. 1 cm lg., sometimes absent.

L. famatimensis (Speg.) Br. & R. (2:11)
Bo. simple to caespitose, shortly cylindric, to 3.5 cm h., to 2.8 cm ∅, greyish to dark green, grafted plants becoming long-cylindric; **Ri.** (18–)24, narrow, low, ± tuberculate; **Ar.** crowded; **Sp.** small, appressed, whitish; **Fl.** 3 cm lg. (yellowish, according to the photo) (description taken from Br. & R.).—Argentina (La Rioja, Famatina, 2000–3000 m [to Jujuy]).
v. **famatimensis** is the plant described by Buining as Hymenorebutia, with closely spaced Ar. and a yellow Fl. only 4 cm ∅; the Tu. tallies with Spegazzini's photo as to length and H. (Fig. 366.)
I also distinguish the following:
v. **albiflora** (Wessn.) Krainz: **Bo.** reddish to dark

green; **Fl.** ± white; **throat** green; **hymen** glossy, white;
v. **aurantiaca** (Backbg. ex Wessn.) Backbg.: **Bo.** dark bronze-green; **Fl.** orange-yellow to deep golden-yellow;
v. **densispina** (Werd.) Backbg.: **Bo.** dark green; **Rsp.** bristly, soft; **Csp.** to 7, brown, acicular, stouter; **Fl.** satiny, pale to golden-yellow; **throat** green; **hymen** white;
v. **haematantha** (Backbg. ex Wessn.) Backbg.: **Bo.** light to dark green; **Fl.** ± blood-red; **Fil.** very variable, from whitish-yellow to pale pink to blood-red;
v. **leucomalla** (Wessn.) Backbg.: "white, close-cropped bristly coating" (Wessner); **Fl.** with a ± slender Tu., lemon-yellow; **throat** white;
v. **setosa** Backbg.: **Bo.** more elongated; **Br.** ± longer, white; **Csp.** missing; **Fl.** yellow, also red.
The above represent only the principal variants; within these the Fl. can vary in size and colour. There are a number of further specific and varietal names which are referable to this very variable spec., under Hymenorebulobivia Frič & Krzgr. or Buining, as well as Lobivia pectinifera Wessn., and L. famatimensis Y. Ito.
From the plants listed as varieties, mostly from the above-named authors, the following are considered to be subvarieties:
v. **albiflora** sv. **eburnea** (Wessn.): **Fl.** ivory-white, **throat** green;
v. **albiflora** sv. **sufflava** (Wessn.): **Fl.** pale yellowish, **throat** green;
v. **densispina** sv. **blossfeldii** (Wessn.): **Fl.** large, deep yellow, **throat** purple;
v. **densispina** sv. **sanguinea** (Wessn.): **Fl.** light blood-red;
v. **famatimensis** sv. **citriflora** (Frič): **Fl.** lemon-yellow;
v. **famatimensis** sv. **kreuzingeri** (Frič ex Buin.): **Fl.** golden-yellow with pink; **throat** carmine;
v. **haematantha** sv. **cinnabarina** (Backbg. ex Wessn.): **Fl.** carmine, **throat** green;
v. **haematantha** sv. **subcarnea** (Wessn.): **Fl.** light flesh-coloured; **throat** green;
v. **leucomalla** sv. **rubispina** (Wessn.): **Br.** (centrals) sometimes reddish-brown;
v. **setosa** sv. **longiseta** Backbg.: **Br.** almost pure white, to 4 cm lg.
In several of the varieties, the Bo.-colour can vary from dark to blackish-green, or it varies with the variety. The Fl. are sometimes quite large. Further names of Frič & Krzgr., unsupported by descriptions, cannot be given here as they have not been grown from seed to check whether the characters are constant.
As explained above, v. famatimensis can only be the plant found by Blossfeld in the Sierra Famatina, Buining's "Hymenorebutia albolanata".

Blossfeld himself held this view, which was accepted by Krainz in "Sukkde." III: 44. 1949 in connection with his new combination "Lob. albolanata (Buin.) Krainz". There are thus no grounds for the continued use of L. pectinifera as a specific epithet, or 'generic names such as "Hymenorebutia"; equally, Britton & Rose's proposed referral of Spegazzini's plant to Lobivia can be accepted. In the face of the confusing duplication of names for the representatives of this, in my view, very polymorphic species, I have listed all the preceding, even those previously accorded specific rank. Geographical distance and diverging root-forms are here of little consequence; the former must be seen in the light of the much greater distances involved in the range of Weingartia vorwerkii, for instance. This seems to me to be both the simplest and the most logical solution in the interests of clarifying any general survey, and of finalising nomenclature. In this instance I consider the process of "lumping" can advantageously be applied.

Ritter's plant (FR 459), sometimes known as "L. famatimensis sensu Ritt.", does not belong here, but is referable to Reicheocactus (see Reicheocactus). In Winter's list of 1965 it was simply offered as "genus?", with no name given.

The following names of Y. Ito are clearly referable to the above extremely variable spec.: Lobivia albicentra Y. Ito, L. kreuzigeri Y. Ito, L. nigra Y. Ito, L. pectinifera v. oligacantha Y. Ito, L. purpurea Y. Ito and L. ruberrima Y. Ito—all in "The Charming of Flowers-Cacti" (1963).

L. ferox Br. & R.: **Pseudolobivia ferox** (Br. & R.) Backbg.

L. formosa (Pfeiff.) Marsh.: **Soehrensia formosa** (Pfeiff.) Backbg.

L. fričii Rausch 1973

Bo. mostly simple, flattened-spherical, 30 mm h. and to 70 mm $\emptyset$, light to greyish-green; **R.** napiform; **Ri.** to 20, straight, rounded, $\pm$ tuberculate; **Ar.** round to oval, 2 mm $\emptyset$, white-felty, c. 7 mm apart; **Rsp.** 9–11, to 7 mm lg., curving, appressed, thin, white to yellowish; **Csp.** 0–1, to 8 mm lg., rolled in and upwards, brownish, tipped black; **Fl.** 25 mm lg., 35 mm $\emptyset$; **Tu.** short, green with lighter Sc. and white and brown H.; **Sep.** narrowly lanceolate, recurved, greenish to pinkish-grey; **Pet.** spatulate, rounded, mucronate, dirty violet, throat violet-pink; **Fil.** in 2 Ser.; **style** green with 6 green Sti.; **Fr.** spherical, 7 mm $\emptyset$, blackish-brown with brown H.; **S.** long-spherical, testa black.—Argentina (Salta, near Rhodeo, at 2800 to 3300 m). Rediscovered by Rausch. Frič had regarded it as a red-flowering form of his Pseudol-obivia graulichii but never provided a valid description. (Fig. 475.) (= Echinopsis fričii [Rausch] H. Friedr., acc. Haage.)

L. glauca Rausch 1971

Bo. simple, c. 10 mm h. and 40 mm $\emptyset$, growing almost entirely below the soil, light greyish-green; **Ri.** 10–13, Tub. c. 10 mm lg., acute, obliquely arranged; **Ar.** oval, with white felt; **Rsp.** 6–7, in 3 pairs, also 1 directed downwards, curving towards the Bo., 6–8 mm lg., brown to black; **Csp.** directed upwards, to 30 mm lg., black, red below, later grey; **Fl., Fr.** and **S.** as in L. jajoiana, **Fl.** orange to red, with a black throat.—Argentina (Jujuy, W. of Purmamarca at 3500 m). (Fig. 476.)

v. **paucicostata** Rausch: with only 7–9 **Ri.**; **Rsp.** only 4–5, 6–15 mm lg., 1 **Csp.** to 50 mm lg. Grows S. of Purmamarca at 2500 m. Both spec. and variety have a light greyish-green epidermis and bluish-black Sp.

L. grandiflora Br. & R.: **Helianthocereus grandiflorus** (Br. & R.) Backbg.

L. grandis Br. & R.: **Soehrensia grandis** (Br. & R.) Backbg.

L. graulichii Frič: see **Pseudolobivia ancistrophora** (Speg.) Backbg.

L. haageana Backbg. (2:5)

Bo. simple at first, later also caespitose, to 30 cm h., 8 cm $\emptyset$, bluish to dark green; **Ri.** c. 22, $\pm$ oblique, obliquely notched; **Rsp.** c. 10, to 2 cm lg., interlacing sideways, straw-coloured; **Csp.** to 4, to 7 cm lg., blackish-brown at first but variable; **Fl.** to 7 cm lg., bellshaped to funnelform, light yellow; **throat** red.—N. Argentina (near Humahuaca).

v. **albihepatica** Backbg.: **Fl.** whitish-beige to dark beige;

v. **bicolor** Backbg.: **Fl.** pink above, yellow to pink inside (**throat** red; also vice-versa);

v. **chrysantha** Backbg.: **Fl.** deep golden-yellow; **throat** green or reddish;

v. **cinnabarina** Backbg.; **Sp.** lighter to whitish; **Fl.** crimson or carmine;

v. **croceantha** Backbg.: **Fl.** saffron-yellow;

v. **durispina** Backbg.: **Sp.** stouter than in the type and the varieties, subulate; **Csp.** long-projecting;

v. **grandiflora-stellata** Backbg.: **Fl.** conspicuously large, true red; **Pet.** laxly radiating;

v. **leucoerythrantha** Backbg.: **Sp.** often very light to white; **Fl.** light blood-red.

L. haematantha (Speg.) Br. & R. (2:7)

Bo. $\pm$ depressed-spherical, 5 cm h., 6 cm $\emptyset$; **Ri.** 11, rounded, broad, $\pm$ tuberculate; **Rsp.** 6–8, to 1 cm lg., thin, $\pm$ appressed; **Csp.** 3, one to 5 cm lg., projecting, stouter, pale grey, tipped yellowish; **Fl.** 3–4 cm $\emptyset$, purple (throat white?).—Argentina (Salta, Amblayo).

L. hastifera Werd. (2:3)
Bo. ± spherical, caespitose, dark green; **Ri.** c. 16 or more, narrow, ± straight; **Rsp.** 5–7, c. 1 cm lg.; **Csp.** 4, cruciform, oblique or spreading upwards, to 10 cm lg., yellowish to horn-coloured; **Sp.** rigid, pungent; **Fl.** c. 8 cm lg., expanding to funnelform, intense pinkish-red.—N. Argentina.

L. hermanniana Backbg. (2:2)
Bo. forming large groups, single heads later cylindric, to 20 cm lg., 5 cm $\emptyset$, fresh green; **Ri.** c. 13, straight; **Sp.** indistinctly differentiated, 3 sometimes discernible as Csp., 1.5 cm lg., later to 6 cm lg., eventually densely interlacing, golden-brown at first; **Fl.** c. 6.5 cm lg., to 6 cm $\emptyset$; **Sep.** violet-pink; **Pet.** light crimson, all narrow, tapering, lax, revolute.—Bolivia (Yungasrand, Pongo, c. 2500 m).
   v. **breviflorior** Backbg. n.v.: **Bo.** similar to that of v. hermanniana, **Sp.** also; **Fl.** only 4 cm lg., ± light salmon to pinkish-red, ± whitish towards the throat; **Fil.** cream; **Sti.** greenish-cream; **Pet.** rounded, fairly crowded, inner ones somewhat shorter. Found by W. Rausch.

L. hertrichiana Backbg. (2:4)
Bo. simple, soon offsetting freely; single heads to 10 cm $\emptyset$, light green; **Ri.** 11, acute, with deep transverse furrows; **Rsp.** c. 7, to 1.5 cm lg., somewhat spreading, brownish-yellow; **Csp.** 1, to 2.5 cm lg., curving upwards, straw-coloured to light brownish; **Fl.** opening fairly widely, to 6 cm $\emptyset$, flame to dark flesh-coloured; **throat** pale.—SE. Peru (at c. 3000 m).

L. higginsiana Backbg. (2:3)
Bo. flattened-spherical, caespitose, greyish to olive-green; **Ri.** c. 17, with hatchet-shaped Tub.; **Rsp.** c. 10, 6 mm lg., curving downwards, 2 uppers to 4.5 cm lg.; **Csp.** 1, to 7.5 cm lg., curving upwards; **Sp.** variously directed; ± interlacing, pink to reddish-grey at first; **Fl.** c. 6 cm lg., wine-red, yellowish inside.—Bolivia (near N. frontier).

L. hoffmanniana Backbg.
Bo. simple, 2.5–3 cm h., to 4.5 cm $\emptyset$, becoming cylindric in cultivation and offsetting freely from the base; **Ri.** c. 24, very acute, low, entirely divided into small, erect, narrow Tub.; **Ar.** linear; **Rsp.** 11, later also more, pectinate, lowest ones shorter, the shortest one only 3 mm lg. at first, later somewhat longer, very fine, brownish, finally reddish-brown below; **Csp.** later to 2, to 8 mm lg., one of these at the upper Ar.-margin and appressed ± upwards,

the lower one ± projecting, subulate, stout, sometimes appearing pruinose; **Fl.** not known.—Bolivia (Oruro).
See also **Sulcorebutia hoffmanniana** (Backbg.) Backbg.

L. horrida Ritt. (2:9)—"Taxon", XII: 3, 124. 1963. Acc. Ritter, distinguishable from L. kupperiana as follows:
Bo. 2–3 times as lg., 6–9 cm $\emptyset$; **Ri.** 16–18, to 1.5 cm h.; **Ar.** 1.2–2 cm apart, to 12 mm lg.; **Sp.** dark brown; **Rsp.** 12–14, lower ones 1–3 cm lg., upper ones 2–6 cm lg.; **Csp.** 4–6, straight, 3–8 cm lg. or more; **Fl.** brownish golden-yellow; **Fil.** similarly coloured above, flesh-coloured below.—Bolivia (S. of El Puente, 3000 m) (FR 974).

L. hossei (Werd.) Backbg.: **Lobivia chrysantha** v. **hossei** (Werd.) Backbg.

L. hualfinensis Rausch
Bo. simple, 6 cm h., 7 cm $\emptyset$, greyish-green to brownish-violet; **R.** napiform; **Ri.** 10–13, straight, tuberculate; **Ar.** c. 2 cm apart, white-felty, later glabrous; **Rsp.** 6–8, to 5 cm lg., spreading, curving; **Csp.** 1–3, upper ones curving downwards, often twisted, to 6 cm lg., brown, black-tipped; **Fl.** lateral, c. 55 mm lg. and br.; **Tu.** brownish-green with dark Sc. with a fine reddish tip, with brown H.; **Sep.** violet with an olive-brown M.-stripe; **Pet.** spatulate, orange-red with dark red borders, throat white; **Fil.** pink, yellowish or greenish; **style** green; **Sti.** 8–10, green; **Fr.** brown with grey wool; **S.** 1.5 mm lg., testa black, glossy, tuberculate.—Argentina (Catamarca, on mountain-peaks near Hualfin, at 2600 m). Spec. belongs to the L. haematantha complex.
   v. **fechseri** Rausch: **Bo.** simple, c. 4 cm h. and $\emptyset$, bluish-green; **Ri.** 10–12, straight, divided by transverse notches into round Tub. 12 mm lg. and 5 mm h.; **Ar.** oval, 5 mm lg., white-felty; **Rsp.** 12–16, to 10 mm lg., spreading, curving to the Bo.; **Csp.** 0–1 to 2 cm lg., slightly curving; **Sp.** all white, tipped black; **Fl.** c. 5 cm lg. and $\emptyset$; **Tu.** olive to brownish-red, Sc. greenish with white and brownish-red H.; **Sep.** lanceolate, yellow with a brownish-red M.-stripe; **Pet.** spatulate, more acute, pale yellow, bordered golden-yellow; **throat, Fil.** and **style** white; **Sti.** 6–8, yellowish-green; **Fr.** spherical, c. 8 mm $\emptyset$; **S.** 1 mm lg., 0.8 mm br.—Argentina (Catamarca, near Nacamientos at 2500 m). Named for H. Fechser.

L. huascha (Web.) Marsh.: **Helianthocereus huascha** (Web.) Backbg.

L. huilcanota Rauh & Backbg. (2:4)
Bo. forming cushions, single heads to 15 cm $\emptyset$,

flattened-spherical, ± bluish-green; **Ri.** c. 13, narrow, ± straight, little tuberculate, fairly acute, with weak oblique notching; **Rsp.** to 12, unequal, to 2 cm lg., the bottom ones mostly shortest, appressed, brownish-black at first; **Csp.** to 4, sometimes slightly longer than the Rsp., projecting to porrect, subulate, much thickened below, becoming whitish-grey, tipped brown; **Fl.** to 4 cm lg., 3 cm ∅; **Tu.** very narrow; **Sep.** narrow, lanceolate, pale brownish-red; **Pet.** red (?); **Fil.** carmine; **An.** white.—S. Peru (Huilcanota valley, 3200 m).

L. hyalacantha Speg.: **Helianthocereus hyalacanthus** (Speg.) Backbg.

L. hystrichacantha Y. Ito (2:3)—"The Full Bloom of Cact. Flow.", 47. 1963: description only in Japanese.
Bo. oblong; **Ri.** to c. 20, not broad, rounded above; **Sp.** finely acicular, fairly long and dense, golden-yellow, **Csp.** scarcely differentiated, or 0; **Fl.** fairly large funnelform, yellow.—Bolivia (?). Closely resembles L. charazanensis Card., but the Fl. appears to be larger or broader.

L. hystrix Ritt. (FR 975)
Bo. hemispherical, to 18 cm ∅, ± bluish-green; **Ri.** 16–24, 8–15 mm h., Tub. hatchet-shaped; **Ar.** grey, 8–15 mm lg., 3–5 mm br., 12–20 mm apart; **Sp.** yellowish-brownish, few at first, later more numerous; **Rsp.** 15–20, straight, directed obliquely downwards, 1–3 cm lg.; **Csp.** 5–12, bent upwards, 1.5–5 cm lg.; **Fl.** c. 45 mm lg., nectary virtually absent, Tu. 20 mm lg., funnelform, carmine inside; **Pet.** 16–20 mm lg., 5–7 mm br., spatulate, reddish-lilac below, crimson to blood-red above; **Fil.** reddish-lilac below and above, green at midway; **style** and **Sti.** green; **Fr.** subspherical, green with very small reddish Sc., covered with white or brown wool; **S.** black, ± umbilicate.—Bolivia (S. of Mendez).

L. imporana Ritt.: later described by Cardenas as **Lobivia cintiensis**.

L. incaica Backbg. (2:4)
Bo. eventually freely offsetting, single heads at first spherical, later ± cylindric, to 15 cm h., 7.5 cm ∅, leaf-green; **Ri.** c. 15, ± straight, acute, with conspicuously oblique notches; **Sp.** scarcely differentiated, c. 14–20 (sometimes to 7 stouter Csp. recognisable), subulate, one upper Sp. very stiff, very pungent, light brown, reddish below; **Fl.** rather short, c. 4 cm ∅, blood-red.—S. Peru (near Inca solar observatory at Intihuatana).

L. intermedia Rausch 1972
Bo. to 20 cm h., 8 cm ∅, dark greyish-green, forming groups; **Ri.** c. 17, Tub. c. 15 mm lg., acute, offset; **Ar.** round to oval, 3 mm ∅, white-felty; **Rsp.** 8–10, in 3–4 pairs and 1 each directed up and down, interlacing around the Bo., often ± curving; **Csp.** 1–3, to 7 cm lg.; all **Sp.** yellow to brown, acicular to flexible; **Fl.** 65–75 mm lg., 30–40 mm ∅; **Tu.** narrow, pink to greenish, with fleshy pink Sc., ± channelled; **Ov.** broadly spherical, with dense white down and brown H.; **Sep.** lanceolate, recurved, red with a violet-pink M.-stripe; **Pet.** spatulate, c. 20 mm lg., serrate, mucronate, suberect, red, orange inside, throat c. 45 mm lg., very narrow, little expanded, white; **Fil.** white, outer ones yellow; **style** 45 mm lg., white, with 8 thin white **Sti.**; **S.** spherical to ovoid, 1.3 mm lg., testa black, glossy, hilum small, oblique, pit-like.—Peru (near Challuanca, at 3000 m). While the spec. recalls L. pentlandii in general appearance, the Fl. are rather smaller but more numerous, acc. Rausch.

L. iridescens Backbg. (2:12)
Bo. forming groups, single heads to 5 cm lg. and ∅, with a large **taproot**; **Ri.** very narrow at first, acutely notched; **Rsp.** 7–9, to 5 mm lg., appressed, radiating regularly; **Csp.** 1, to c. 7 mm lg., ± hooked; **Sp.** whitish, Csp. dark-tipped; **Fl.** c. 4 cm ∅, uniquely coloured, with a whitish shimmer, bluish to brownish-pink.—Bolivian-Argentine frontier.

L. jajoiana Backbg. (2:13)
Bo. mostly solitary, later elongated, sap-green; **Ri.** c. 14, Tub. slightly oblique; **Rsp.** 8–10, to c. 1 cm lg., slightly reddish-white; **Csp.** 1, over 2.5 cm lg., directed upwards, to blackish; **Sp.** sometimes bent; **Fl.** expanding to beaker-shaped, wine-red to pink; hymen blackish.—N. Argentina.
v. **fleischeriana** Backbg. (syn.: v. longispina Y. Ito): **Sp.** longer; **Rsp.** sometimes stouter, one sometimes hooked; **Csp.** thin, to 5 cm lg.; **Fl.** tomato-red;
v. **nigrostoma** (Krzgr. & Buin.) Backbg.: **Fl.** yellow, sometimes bordered violet; **hymen** violet-black, lower **Fil.** similarly. There are intermediates with ± orange Pet.

L. johnsoniana Backbg. (2:3)
Bo. caespitose, **R.** stoutly napiform; single heads 3 cm h., c. 6 cm ∅, ± ovoid, light leaf-green; **Ri.** c. 16, very narrow at first, with oblique transverse notches; **Rsp.** 1–7(–10), 0.8–1 cm lg., one upper Sp. to 3 cm lg., curving sideways, light-coloured, subulate; **Csp.** mostly absent; **Fl.** c. 4.5 cm ∅, delicate lilac.—Bolivia.

L. jujuiensis (FR 54, not yet described): named for its place of origin, Prov. Jujuy in Argentina.
Bo. c. 7 cm h., 5 cm ∅, grass-green, with Sp. in the crown; **Ri.** 15 or more, Tub. hatchet-shaped, ± offset; **Ar.** surmounted by a deep notch; **Rsp.** 13, to 6 mm lg., straight to slightly curving, those on new growth red below and dark-tipped, later greying; **Csp.** 1 with 2 upper Ssp., to 10 mm lg.; **Fl.** yellow suffused ± orange-yellow, 6 cm lg., 5.5 cm ∅, **throat** dark wine-red to black; **Fil.** wine-red; **An.** light yellow; **style** and **Sti.** light green.—N. Argentina (Prov. Jujuy).

L. katagirii Y. Ito and variety: cannot be described here as they are probably crosses.

L. klusacekii Frič, not described: judging by Kreuzinger's original photo, certainly referable to **L. polaskiana**; this spec., like L. chrysantha, varies towards orange-red.
v. roseiflora Subik: Fl. pink. This Fl.-colour is unusual, so perhaps this is a hybrid? In the records left by Frič and Schelle there was no written or photographic note of a variant of this kind.

L. korethroides Werd.: **Soehrensia korethroides** (Werd.) Backbg.

L. kuehnrichii Frič (2:7)
Bo. simple, spherical to shortly cylindric, greyish-green, taprooted; **Ri.** to 11(–14), broad with flat Tub.; **Rsp.** 9–11, brown; **Csp.** 1, to 1.5 cm lg., stouter, curving downwards or S-shaped, black; **Fl.** orange to light ochre, **Tu.** fairly short and broad, throat white.—N. Argentina (Salta).

L. kupperiana Backbg. (2:9)
Bo. simple, to 10 cm h., 8 cm ∅, greyish-green, crown bluish-green; **Ri.** c. 20, acute, eventually flatter, very oblique, obliquely notched; **Rsp.** 10 or more, c. 2.5 cm lg., light, darker-tipped; **Csp.** 1–2, to 4 cm lg., stiff, subulate, pungent, ± curving, dark; **Fl.** c. 4.5 cm lg.; **Sep.** dirty reddish-green; **Pet.** faded yellow, also ± whitish (Wilke).—Bolivia (Tupiza).
v. **rubriflora** Backbg.: **Sp.** light to whitish; **Sep.** projecting, lanceolate; **Pet.** slightly wavy, true red; **throat** deeper red.

L. larabei Johns.: a newer spec., found by Johnson, which is quite frequently seen in European collections; **Fl.** red; **Bo.** light green, with fine Sp., caespitose; probably referable to the "Hertrichianae". Colour-photo: "Die Cact." Vol. VI, Fig. 3388. See also L. minuta. Not yet described.

L. larae Card. (2:3)—C. & S. J. (US), XXXVI: 1, 24. 1964.
Bo. depressed-spherical, to 4 cm h., 12 cm ∅; **Ri.** 11–12, acute; **Ar.** 1.5 cm apart, creamy-white; **Rsp.** pectinate, 9–12, ± curving, 6–25 mm lg., acicular, pale grey to whitish, thickened below; **Fl.** to 6 cm lg., funnelform; **Tu.** pale green; **Ov.** with pink Sc.; **Sep.** pinkish-lilac; **Pet.** 3 cm lg., dark violet; **Fil.** white; **style** green below, yellow above; **Sti.** pale yellow, 11, 1 cm lg.—Bolivia (Prov. Tarato, Dept. Cochabamba, on the road Tarato-Rio Caine, 2500 m).

L. lateritia (Gürke) Br. & R. (2:6)
Bo. simple, short-cylindric, to c. 7 cm h., 6 cm ∅, greyish-green; **Ri.** 16, weakly notched; **Rsp.** mostly 10, to 1 cm lg., side ones to 2 cm lg.; **Csp.** to 2, to 2.5 cm lg., curving upwards, stouter; **Sp.** thickened below, brilliant brown at first, with dark banding; **Fl.** 4.5 cm lg., 4 cm ∅, funnelform, dirty crimson, tips tinged bluish.—Bolivia.

L. laui Donald 1974
Bo. short, cylindric, offsetting freely from the base to form many-headed groups, single heads c. 10 cm h., 5 cm br., bluish-green, varying also from yellowish-green to dark green; **Ri.** 10–11 or even more, straight, little tuberculate, 10 mm h., 10 mm br. below; **Ar.** offset in oblique notches, 3–4 mm ∅, with dense light wool, 10 mm apart; **Sp.** straight, acicular, thickened below, mostly reddish-brown but also varying from light yellow through brown to black; **Rsp.** 8, 10–20 mm lg.; **Csp.** mostly only 1, to 30 mm lg.; **Fl.** variable in form and colour, 40–50 mm lg., 40–65 mm br., scarlet to crimson or magenta to pinkish-red; **Tu.** deep olive-green, 6 mm ∅, with hairy Sc., throat green, Sep. light green; **style** 30 mm lg., with 5–6 **Sti.**; **Fr.** to 10 mm ∅, spherical; **S.** black.—Peru (Cuzco, near the village Urubamba, at 3000 m). Named for Alfred Lau who first discovered this plant in 1969.

L. lauramarca Rauh & Backbg. (2:2)
Bo. caespitose; single heads 5.5 cm ∅, low-spherical, pale green; **Ri.** 12–15, tuberculate; **Rsp.** 6, to 1.5 cm lg., very thin to flexible or stiff, upper one bent ± upwards, pale brown; **Csp.** missing; **Fl.** 6 cm lg., 3.5 cm ∅, ± erectly funnelform; **Sep.** pale wine-red; **Pet.** brick-red above, white towards the throat.—S. Peru (Hacienda Lauramarca).

L. leptacantha Rausch
Bo. simple to offsetting, to 15 cm h. and 7 cm ∅, fresh green; **Ri.** c. 15, Tub. long, angular, little offset; **Ar.** oval, 3 mm lg., white-felty; **Rsp.** 10–12, 2–3 cm lg.; **Csp.** 1–2, to 7 cm lg., thin, flexible, yellowish to brownish; **Fl.** 65 mm lg., 55 mm br.; **Ov.** spherical, green with small Sc., white felt and

brown H. to 7 mm lg.; **Tu.** green, with pink fleshy Sc. and brown H.; **Sep.** red to yellowish; **Pet.** red, also orange-yellow to violet-red, orange to yellow inside, **hymen** and **throat** white; **Fil.** yellow, white below; **style** green, reddish above, with 6–9 green or yellow Sti.; **Fr.** spherical, reddish-brown with small Sc. and white wool; **S.** 1.2 mm lg., testa black, glossy, finely tuberculate.—Peru (near Paucartambo, at 3000–3100 m). Spec. readily distinguishable by the thin, flexible Sp. and magnificent Fl. of yellow, orange, red, to red with a bluish sheen. Related to L. quiabayensis Rausch. (Fig. 477.)

L. leucomalla Wessn.: **Lobivia famatimensis** v. **leucomalla** (Wessn.) Backbg. [Haage adds: = Echinopsis 1. (Wessn.) H. Friedr.]

L. leucorhodon Backbg. (2:3)
Bo. to 10 cm h., 7 cm ⌀, leaf-green; **Ri.** c. 18–21, fairly straight, narrow, obliquely tuberculate; **Rsp.** c. 7, ± irregularly bent; **Csp.** sometimes 1(–2), bent towards the crown, 2–4 cm lg.; **Sp.** yellowish; **Fl.** c. 4 cm lg., 3.5 cm ⌀, light lilac-pink, **Tu.** stout.—Bolivia (near La Paz).

L. leucoviolacea Backbg. (2:3)
Bo. somewhat elongated, light greyish-green; **Ri.** acute; **Sp.** scarcely differentiated, to 14, to 9 cm lg., very thin, flexible, interlacing over the entire Bo., whitish to pinkish-white; **Fl.** c. 5 cm lg., light pinkish-lilac.—Bolivia (E. of Oruro).

L. longispina Br. & R.: **Pseudolobivia longispina** (Br. & R.) Backbg.

L. marsoneri (Werd.) Backbg. (2:3)
Bo. c. 8 cm h. and ⌀, light greyish-green; **Ri.** c. 20, strongly compressed; **Rsp.** 8–12, to 3 cm lg.; **Csp.** 2–5, projecting obliquely, ± hooked, thickened below; **Sp.** whitish-grey to yellowish, brownish below; **Fl.** c. 5.5 cm lg., c. 6 cm ⌀, yellow, **throat** purplish-red.—N. Argentina (Los Andes).

L. matuzawae Y. Ito (Hybrid?)
Bo. spherical to cylindric, 5–8 cm lg., 5–6 cm ⌀; **Rsp.** c. 10, to 3.5 mm lg.; **Csp.** 1, to 1 cm lg., stouter, white at first, brown-tipped, later reddish-brown; **Fl.** mid-red or crimson, light red outside.—Origin?

L. maximiliana (Heyd.) Backbg.: **Lobivia pentlandii** (Hook.) Br. & R.

L. megacarpa Ritt.: not described; presumably not referable to Lobivia. See remarks at the end of **Lobivia**.

L. megatae Y. Ito (Hybrid?)
Bo. 3–5 cm ⌀, later to 10 cm h., rich green; **Ri.**

11–16; **Rsp.** 10–15, to 1 cm lg.; **Csp.** (0–)1, to 1 cm lg., brown; **Fl.** 6–7 cm lg., 5.5–7 cm ⌀, red to carmine.—Origin?

L. miniatiflora Ritt. (2:2)—"Taxon", XII: 3, 124. 1963
Acc. Ritter, distinguished from L. caespitosa as follows:
Bo. 2–4 cm ⌀, 3–6 cm lg.; **Ri.** 10–13, obtuse; **Sp.** much thinner; **Rsp.** 3–10 mm lg.; **Csp.** 4–8, 1–5 cm lg.; **Fl.** 5–6 cm lg.; **Pet.** to 2.5 cm lg., 4–6 mm br., tapering, crimson, outer (?) lower Pet. carmine.—Bolivia (above Inquisivi, Dept. La Paz, 3300 m) (FR 330).

L. minuta Ritt. (2:4)—"Taxon", XII: 3, 124. 1963.
Acc. Ritter, distinguished from L. hertrichiana as follows:
Bo. to 4 cm ⌀, pale green; **Ri.** 9–15, not notched; **Sp.** light brown, soon grey, dark-tipped, straight or slightly curving; **Rsp.** 8–11, 4–8 mm lg.; **Csp.** 1–2 cm lg., darker and somewhat stouter, mostly only 1, porrect; **Fl.** to 4.5 cm lg., to 4 cm ⌀; **Pet.** scarlet, outer lower ones paler; **Fil.** pale red above, greenish below.—Peru (Ollantaitambo, Prov. Urubamba, Dept. Cuzco) (FR 695). Acc. Ritter, "probably identical" with L. larabei Johns. (not described). My colour-photos in "Die Cact." Vol. VI, p. 3736, 1962, Fig. 3388–3389, show however that these are two different spec.

L. mirabunda Backbg. (2:7)
Bo. 2.5 cm h., 4 cm ⌀; **Ri.** c. 16; **Rsp.** 6–9, to 6 mm lg., ± brownish at first; **Csp.** mostly absent, occasionally 1, c. 5 mm lg., curving slightly upwards; **Sp.** interlacing laterally; **Fl.** 5 cm lg., 4.5 cm ⌀; **Sep.** pale yellow, M.-line green; **Pet.** concolorous yellow, broad, truncate, apiculate; **Fil.** yellowish above in the upper Ser. and wine-red below, lower Ser. wine-red. Fl. disproportionately large for the small Bo.—N. Argentina (Salta?).

L. mistiensis (Werd. & Backbg.) Backbg. (2:2)
Bo. ± flattened-spherical, dark bluish-green, **R.** large-napiform; **Ri.** c. 25–30, obliquely notched; **Sp.** scarcely differentiated, 9 or more, to 5 cm lg., brown to ruby-red or blackish at first, later whitish-grey; **Fl.** to 8 cm lg., slightly reddish-brown, yellowish to red inside; **Pet.** narrow, apiculate.—S. Peru (Misti volcano).
Some plants have a paler Fl.-colour (v. leucantha n. nud.), others have noticeably short Sp. (v. brevispina n. nud.).

L. mizquensis Rausch
Bo. simple, flattened-spherical, to 10 cm h., 14 cm ⌀; **Ri.** to 24, Tub. c. 20 mm lg., acute, offset; **Ar.** c. 7 mm lg., oval, white-felty; **Rsp.** mostly 10, in 4

pairs, spreading and ± curving, 20 mm lg., also 1 each directed downwards and upwards, the latter the longest, to 50 mm lg., curving, often hooked; **Csp.** 1, rather shorter than the upper Rsp.; all **Sp.** brown, thickened and ± yellowish-green below, later greying; **Fl.** appearing on quite young plants, 65–75 mm lg., 60 mm ∅; **Tu.** and **Ov.** greenish with green or pink Sc. and long H.; **Sep.** long-lanceolate, green, bordered pink; **Pet.** rather shorter, spatulate, mucronate, red, throat pink or whitish, greenish inside; **Fil.** violet-pink, green inside; **style** very short, green; **Sti.** 7–11, green; **Fr.** brown; **S.** with a black glossy testa.—Bolivia (between Vila-Vila and Rio Caine at 3200 m). In habit resembles Echinopsis obrepanda but, surprisingly, plants only 3 cm ∅ produce red Fl. c. 7 cm lg. (Fig. 478.)

L. muhriae Backbg. (2:3)—Descr. Cact. Nov. III: 7. 1963.
Bo. spherical but the part visible above ground is ± flattened-spherical, to c. 7 cm ∅, 3 cm h., greyish-green, darker towards the crown; **Ri.** c. 18, acute; **Ar.** slightly offset, c. 1.5 cm apart, brownish-white at first, dirty white later; **Rsp.** c. 8, thin, flexible, lower ones weaker than the uppers, to 1.2–2 cm lg., pale horn-coloured at first; **Csp.** (1–)2(–3), to 3.5 cm lg., curving towards the crown, rather stouter but flexible, blackish first, becoming lighter, thickened below and red there at first; **Fl.** reddish-orange, c. 6 cm lg., 5 cm ∅, throat reddish-brown; **Sep.** lilac to light red; **Tu.** orange-red; **Ov.** reddish to dark green, it and the Tu. strongly dark grey-haired; **style** and **Sti.** greenish.—N. Argentina (Jujuy, near El Aguilar). (Fig. 193.)
v. **flaviflora** Backbg.—l.c.: Fl. yellow, c. 5 cm lg. and ∅, throat reddish-brown; Sep. light pink; Tu. yellow, with some whitish H.; Ov. light green; style and Sti. greenish.—(El Aguilar).

L. multicostata Backbg. (2:3)—Descr. Cact. Nov. III: 7, 1963.
Bo. simple, broadly spherical, bluish-green; **Ri.** 18, fairly acute; **Ar.** brownish-white, not large; **Rsp.** to 10, extending sideways in pairs, the smallest Sp. directed ± downwards, the upper 2 appearing to be Csp., longest, directed laterally, unequal, irregularly curving or recurved, later somewhat darker than the lower ones; **Csp.** 1–2, more central, one of these longest and stoutest, porrect, to c. 4 cm lg., the 2 upper Rsp. sometimes similar and almost as long; all **Sp.** blackish at first, reddish below, then flecked greyish-white, finally paler; **Fl.** c. 4–4.5 cm ∅; **Sep.** light brownish-yellow; **Pet.** yellow; **Tu.** green, moderately long, with dark H.—Origin? (Fig. 194.)
Seen in the collection of van Urk, Holland. Like L. vanurkiana and L. rigidispina, this is a true spec. and not a hybrid, but it is no longer possible to

establish their locality; probably collected by Ritter.

L. napina Pažout (2:11)
Bo. spherical, to 5 cm ∅, greyish-green with a brownish to violet or black shimmer, soft, **R.** napiform; **Ri.** 14–17; **Rsp.** 12, 6 on either side; **Csp.** 3, c. 3 mm lg., thickened below, brown to black; **Fl.** 3 cm ∅, flesh-coloured, **throat** green.—Origin?
Transferred by Pažout (Kakt. u.a. Sukkk., 15: 7, 125, 1964) to the genus Hymenorebutia Frič ex Buin., as H. napina (Paž.) Paž.; this generic name is misleading, and the genus cannot be segregated. These plants are said to have been raised from seed collected in 1935 by Blossfeld in N. Argentina (Sierra de Famatina).

L. nealeana Backbg. (2:7)
Bo. rarely offsetting, to 7 cm h., 3 cm ∅, pale leaf-green; **Ri.** 14; **Rsp.** c. 8, 4 mm lg., very fine; **Csp.** 0; **Fl.** to 5 cm lg., 6 cm ∅, rotate, brilliant red with a satiny sheen.—N. Argentina (Salta). [Haage adds: = Echinopsis n. (Backbg.) H. Friedr.]
v. **grandiflora** Y. Ito: said to have Fl. 8–10 cm ∅;
v. **purpureiflora** Y. Ito: Fl. with a deep purple stripe inside.

L. neo-haageana Backbg. and v. flavovirens Backbg.: **Mediolobivia pygmaea** (R. E. Fries) Backbg. and v. **flavovirens** (Backbg.) Backbg.

L. nigricans Wessn.: **Mediolobivia nigricans** (Wessn.) Krainz.

L. neocinnabarina Backbg. (2:9)—Descr. Cact. Nov. III: 7. 1963.
Bo. simple, spherical, later elongated, to c. 12 cm lg., 6–7 cm ∅, vivid green; **crown** with white felt; **Ri.** c. 18, divided into acute, obliquely arranged Tub. c. 1.6 cm lg.; **Ar.** c. 1.5–1.7 cm apart; **Rsp.** c. 10–14, ± dark at first, to brownish or lighter, to 1 cm lg.; **Csp.** similarly coloured, to 3–5, stouter, to c. 1.7 cm lg., thickened below; **Fl.** carmine, c. 2.5–3 cm lg., to 3.5 cm ∅, **throat** white; **Tu.** short, green, with red Sc.-tips; **Fil.** carmine, the upper Ser. united below with the white **hymen**, lower ones greenish below; **buds** very numerous, similarly red.—Bolivia (Prov. Chapare and Punata or near Colomi, at c. 3400 m). (Fig. 195.)
This is the spec. collected by Cardenas which he believed was a re-collection of Lobivia cinnabarina; but latter had a much larger Fl., 8 cm ∅.

L. nigrispina Backbg. (2:14)
Bo. caespitose, with a stout taproot, single heads to 4 cm h., c. 3 cm ∅, glossy, dark green, becoming pale green; **Ri.** c. 15, obliquely notched; **Rsp.** c. 10,

to 1 cm lg., thin, radiating, white; **Csp.** mostly 4, stouter, only 1 clearly recognisable, mostly blackish, projecting, hooked, c. 1 cm lg.; **Fl.** yellow, with a short **Tu.** and opening widely, **throat** light green.—N. Argentina (Salta).

v. **rubriflora** Backbg.: differentiated by the red, mostly larger **Fl.**

L. nigrostoma Krzgr. & Buin.: **Lobivia jajoiana** v. **nigrostoma** (Krzgr. & Buin.) Backbg.

L. oculata (Werd.) Wessn.: **Mediolobivia euanthema** v. **oculata** (Werd.) Krainz.

L. oligotricha Card. (2:9)—"Cactus", 18: 91–92. 1963.
Bo. simple, to 8 cm h. and ∅, light green; **Ri.** c. 18, spiralled, with hatchet-like Tub. to 4 mm h., 7 mm br.; **Ar.** c. 8 mm apart; **Sp.** not differentiated, c. 15, acicular, sometimes very thin, whitish, thickened below, to 1.5 cm lg., interlacing over the crown; **Fl.** numerous, borne around the crown, 3 cm lg., 2.5 cm ∅, light red; **Tu.** only 4 mm lg., with a few white H. and reddish Sc.; **Pet.** spatulate; **Fil.** in 2 Ser., purplish-red, lower ones green below; **Sti.** 5, green.—Bolivia (Cochabamba, Cuchu Punata, 2568 m).

L. omasuyana Card. (2:3)—Kakt. u.a. Sukk., 16: 2, 22. 1965
Bo. spherical, 3–5 cm h., to 6 cm ∅, greyish-green, caespitose, forming cushions to 30 cm br.; **Ri.** 14–17, Tub. acute, hatchet-shaped; **Ar.** white-felty; **Sp.** 7–8, 1–7 cm lg., directed upwards, or horizontally, then interlacing, reddish-brown above, thickened below; **Fl.** c. 6 cm lg., 3–5 cm ∅; **Tu.** 3 cm lg.; **Sep.** spatulate; **Pet.** broadly spatulate, salmon to purplish, yellowish below.—Bolivia (Prov. Omasuyo, Dept. La Paz, near Lake Titicaca, 3800 m).

L. orurensis Backbg.: **Mediolobivia pectinata** v. orurensis (Backbg.) Backbg.

L. otukae and var. Y. Ito: appear to belong to the swarm of forms around **Lobivia famatimensis**.

L. pachyacantha Y. Ito (2:3)—The Full Bloom of Cact. Flow., 50. 1963.
Bo. mostly simple, depressed-spherical, dark green; **Ri.** c. 15, notched into hatchet-shaped Tub.; **Rsp.** to 7, 2–3 cm lg.; **Csp.** 1, to c. 5 cm lg., curving and interlacing over the crown, brownish in the upper half, light below that, some of the longer upper **Rsp.** similarly coloured; **Fl.** 5.5–6 cm lg. and ∅, dark red to dark pink.—Bolivia.

L. pampana Br. & R. (2:2) (Lob. scheeri S.D.?)
Bo. spherical, 5–7 cm ∅, caespitose; **Ri.** 17–21, ±

wavy; **Sp.** 5–20, to 5 cm lg., pubescent, acicular, ± curving, brownish; **Fl.** to 6 cm lg., red, sometimes with a yellowish tinge; **Pet.** apiculate.—S. Peru (Pampa de Arrieros, c. 4000 m).

L. peclardiana Krainz (2:15)
Bo. broadly spherical, to 5 cm h. and 6 cm ∅, dark green; **Ri.** 16; **Rsp.** 14–16, to 12 mm lg., acicular, white to honey-coloured at first, becoming reddish-brown; **Csp.** 3–5, to 15 mm lg., hooked; **Fl.** 6.5 cm lg., 6 cm ∅, violet-pink.—Origin? Without doubt a hybrid between L. tiegeliana and a Pseudolobivia. There is thus a white-flowering v. **albiflora** Krainz, and a lilac-flowering v. **winteriae** Krainz.

L. pectinata Backbg. non Frič: **Mediolobivia pectinata** (Backbg. non Frič) Backbg.

L. pectinifera Wessn. and var.: **Lobivia famatimensis** (Speg.) Br. & R. and var.

L. pentlandii (Hook.) Br. & R. (1:1) (T.)
Bo. caespitose; **Ri.** c. 15, obliquely notched; **Rsp.** 7–12, unequal, to 3 cm lg., yellowish to brownish; **Csp.** (0–)1 (to several), to c. 3 cm lg.; **Fl.** c. 5 cm lg., orange-reddish above, lighter inside. Colour and length of both Bo. and Sp. are variable.—S. Peru, N. Bolivia. (Fig. 196.)
3 varieties can be distinguished:
v. **albiflora** (Weidl.) H. Neum.: **Fl.** white, suffused pink;
v. **forbesii** (A. Dietr.) Y. Ito: **Fl.** ± dark pinkish-red;
v. **ochroleuca** (R. Mey.) Borg: **Fl.** pale yellow.

L. peterseimii (Frič) hort.: **Mediolobivia nigricans** (Wessn.) Krainz.

L. pilifera (Frič) hort.: **Mediolobivia ritteri** v. **pilifera** (Frič) Backbg.

L. pictiflora Ritt. (FR 1137) (Pseudolobivia Backbg.)
(Figures in brackets are those of L. ferox, for comparison.)
Bo. spherical, to 16 cm h. and ∅; **Ri.** 1–2 cm h. (2–3 cm), Tub. hatchet-shaped, 15–25 mm h. (25–35 mm), 6–10 mm lg., 5–7 mm br. (10–15, and 5–10 mm); **Ar.** less oblique, 1–2 cm apart (2–3 cm); **Sp.** not banded, less curving; **Rsp.** 8–14 (7–12), 1–5 cm lg. (3–8 cm), less projecting; **Csp.** 4–10 cm lg. (6–19 cm); **Fl.** 6–8 cm lg. (10–13 cm), agreeable scented (unperfumed), nectary 3–6 mm lg. (8–15 mm), Tu. funnelform (tubular below), 22–36 mm lg. (40–50 mm); **Pet.** 20–35 mm lg. (30–50 mm), mostly white, rarely pink, reddish-lilac, yellow or of 2–3 colours (always white, pink outside); **Fil.** 5–15 mm lg.

(15–20 mm); **Sti.** 7–12 mm lg. (10–20 mm); **S.** brown (black).—Bolivia.

L. planiceps Backbg. (2:4)
Bo. flat above, to 8 cm $\emptyset$, $\pm$ leaf-green; **Ri.** c. 15, acute, made wavy by the oblique notches; **Sp.** c. 10, scarcely differentiated (Csp. thickened below), to 2.5 cm lg., horn-coloured at first; **Fl.** 4 cm $\emptyset$, broadly funnelform, dark flame-colour.—SE. Peru.

L. pojoensis Rausch
Bo. simple, 15 cm h., to 10 cm $\emptyset$, grass-green; **Ri.** 13–16, straight, tuberculate; **Ar.** 2 cm apart, white-felty, becoming glabrous; **Rsp.** 6–10, 10–15 mm lg., 1 stouter Sp. directed upwards and 1 smaller one curving down to the Bo.; **Csp.** 1(–3), to 2 cm lg., curving at the tip, yellow or brown; **Fl.** lateral, 6 cm lg., 5 cm $\emptyset$; **Sep.** acute, pink with a green M.-stripe; **Pet.** rounded-spatulate, orange-red, bordered red, **hymen** and **throat** pink; inner **Fil.** carmine, outer ones orange-red; **style** short, green; **Sti.** 5–6, green; **Fr.** brownish-green; **S.** black, rough.—Bolivia (Cochabamba, E. of Pojo, 3000 m).
　v. **grandiflora**: **Fl.** 10 cm lg., 8 cm $\emptyset$, dark red with a bluish gloss; **style** purple or green; **Sti.** 10, green.—Near Mizque, 2600 m.

L. polaskiana Backbg. (2:5)
Bo. cylindric, simple at first, later offsetting, to 20 cm h., 5 cm $\emptyset$, matt greyish-green; **Ri.** 15; **Rsp.** 8–10, to 1 cm lg., appressed, whitish; **Csp.** 3, 1 porrect, to 1.2 cm lg., darker; **Fl.** 5.5 cm lg., 5 cm $\emptyset$; **Pet.** in 3 Ser., buttercup-yellow, mottled red below, wavy, lax.—N. Argentina.
Lobivia dragai Frič (with still finer and more whitish Sp.) and Lobivia klusacekii Frič (with Pet. neither in 3 Ser. nor mottled red) belong, at most with varietal status, to the above variable spec., and this in turn is part of the complex of spec. around Lobivia chrysantha. Some plants have whitish-golden Pet., in others they are reddish.

L. polyantha Y. Ito (Hybrid?)
Bo. simple, cylindric, to 20 cm lg., to 5 cm $\emptyset$, light green; **Ri.** 12–15; **Rsp.** 16–20, 5 mm lg., bristle-like; **Csp.** 1–3, stouter, longer; **Sp.** white at first, later grey, brown-tipped; **Fl.** 5–6 cm lg., to 7 cm $\emptyset$, red.—Origin?

L. polycephala Backbg. (2:14)
Bo. offsetting freely to form cushions, single heads flattened-spherical, c. 4 cm $\emptyset$ and more; **R.** thick-napiform; **Ri.** c. 16; **Rsp.** c. 10, c. 1 cm lg., the uppermost one sometimes longer; **Csp.** 3–4, longer, thickened below, sometimes $\pm$ strongly bent above; **Sp.** dark brown at first, reddish below, later

grey; **Fl.** c. 3 cm lg., 4 cm $\emptyset$, brilliant crimson-carmine, glossy.—Argentina (Salta).

L. prestoana Card. 1969
Bo. broadly spherical, 3 cm h., 6–7 cm $\emptyset$, greyish-green; **Ri.** c. 12, acute, Tub. 5 mm h.; **Ar.** 12 mm apart, elliptic, 8 mm lg., grey-felty; those in the crown spineless, round, white-felty; **Rsp.** 9–10, appressed, 7–15 mm lg., horn-grey to brownish, thickened below; **Csp.** mostly absent, sometimes 1–2; **Fl.** lateral, funnelform, 5.5 cm lg., 4.5 cm br.; **Ov.** 7 mm lg., with green, white-haired Sc.; **Tu.** 2 cm lg., with green Sc. 5 mm lg., these with Br. and white H.; **Sep.** lanceolate, 30 × 9 mm, crimson to purplish-red; **Pet.** spatulate, 30 × 10 mm, red to crimson; **style** 15 mm lg., dark green, with 7 lighter Sti.—Bolivia (Zudañez, Chuquisaca, near Presto, 2400 m). Noticeably divergent from other Lobivias of the region because of the Br. on the Tu.

L. pseudocachensis Backbg. (2:7)
Bo. flattened-spherical, 3 cm h., c. 4 cm $\emptyset$, leaf-green, passing over into a long taproot below, forming groups; **Ri.** c. 14; **Rsp.** c. 10, thin, laterally appressed, yellowish-brown; **Csp.** (scarcely recognisable) 1, longer, curving upwards, blackish-brown; **Fl.** c. 6 cm lg. and $\emptyset$, funnelform, brilliant dark red.—N. Argentina. [Haage adds: = Echinopsis p. (Backbg.) H. Friedr.]
　v. **cinnabarina** Backbg.: **Fl.** glossy, crimson-carmine with a bluish sheen;
　v. **sanguinea** Backbg.: **Fl.** light blood-red.

L. pseudocariquinensis Card. (2:3)—C. & S. J. (US.), XXXIII: 4, 111–112. 1961.
Bo. caespitose, St. spherical to conical, 6–7 cm h., 7 cm $\emptyset$, light green; **Ri.** c. 20; **Ar.** cream-coloured; **Sp.** scarcely differentiated, c. 8, 5–20 mm lg., spreading, subulate, yellowish; **Fl.** 3–3.5 cm lg., to 3 cm $\emptyset$, not opening widely; **Sep.** magenta; **Pet.** light red above, yellowish-orange below.—Bolivia (La Paz, Charazani).

L. pseudocinnabarina Backbg. (2:9)—Descr. Cact. Nov. III: 7. 1963.
Bo. $\pm$ broadly spherical, simple, c. 6.5 cm $\emptyset$, 5 cm h., green; **crown** with light brownish felt; **Ri.** c. 21, slightly spiralled and divided into $\pm$ obliquely arranged Tub.; **Ar.** c. 1 cm apart; **Rsp.** c. 14, rather thin, 7–8 mm lg., horn-coloured to brownish at first, darker above and below; **Csp.** to c. 7, similarly coloured, rather stouter, to 1.3 cm lg., thickened below; **Fl.** c. 3 cm lg., 3.5 cm $\emptyset$, carmine, throat carmine; **buds** green; **Tu.** slender, 1.5 cm lg., carmine, only slightly felty; **Sti.** green.—E. Bolivia (found by Cardenas). (Fig. 197.) Rather variable in length and density of the Sp.

239

L. pugionacantha (Rose & Böd.) Backbg. (2:8)
Bo. simple or caespitose, **R.** a long, conical taproot, upper part of the Bo. only c. 4.5 cm ∅ (more elongated if grafted), matt greyish-green; **Ri.** c. 17; **Sp.** 4–5–7, the stoutest ones dagger-like, directed sideways, to over 2.5 cm lg., light yellow, 1 smaller lower Sp., often missing; **Fl.** c. 4.5 cm lg. and br., reddish-yellow.—Bolivia (near Villazon, 3400 m).
  v. **flaviflora** Backbg.: **Sp.** brownish; **Fl.** light yellow.

L. purpureominitata Ritt. (FR 997): no description available.

L. pusilla Ritt.
(Data in brackets show differences from L. tiegeliana, which it resembles.)
Bo. simple or more usually caespitose (simple, rarely offsetting); crown spiny (± spineless), 15–40 mm ∅ (25–70 mm); **Ri.** 11–17 (15–30), not or scarcely notched (deeply notched), with or without scarcely developed Tub. (Tub. well developed); **Ar.** 1.5–3 × 1–1.5 mm (3–6 × 1.5–2 mm), 1–4 mm apart (8–10 mm), straight, rarely ± oblique (more obliquely set); **Rsp.** 11–21 (8–13), directed ± laterally, 1–5 mm lg. (5–10 mm), rarely with 1 projecting Csp. 5 mm lg. (sometimes 1); **Fl.** smaller, 36–40 mm lg., Pet. 15–16 × 6–8 mm (18–28 × 4–7 mm), intense reddish-lilac to violet-red, as in L. tiegeliana; **Ov.** 8 × 5 mm, narrower below (± spherical); **Fr.** ± spindle-shaped (spherical or slightly longer than broad), obtuse below, narrower near apex; **S.** as in L. tiegeliana.—Bolivia (Dept. Tarija, in the N. of Prov. Arce). (Fig. 479.) From the same locality there is also a form—f. flaviflora—with yellow Pet. (Fig. 480.)

L. quiabayensis Rausch
Bo. simple to grouping, 3 cm h., 7 cm ∅, grass-green; **Ri.** 15–20, Tub. long; **Ar.** white-felty, oval, to 5 mm lg., 2 mm br.; **Rsp.** 10–14; **Csp.** 0(–3); all 30–50 mm lg., yellowish-brown, tipped dark brown, tangled around the Bo.; **Fl.** lateral, 4.5 cm lg., 3.5 cm ∅; **Tu.** olive-green with brown or black H.; **Sep.** lanceolate, orange or violet; **Pet.** carmine, orange inside, throat white; **Fil.** carmine-pink, white below; **style** green or pink; **Sti.** 4–6, yellow; **S.** black, glossy, pitted.—Bolivia (La Paz, near Quiabaya—hence the specific name; at 3500 m).

L. raphidacantha Backbg. (2:3)
Bo. caespitose, flat, becoming oblong, glossy, dark green; **Ri.** c. 16, slightly spiralled; **Sp.** not distinguishable as centrals·and radials, one sometimes recognisable as a Csp. and to 7 cm lg., all Sp. acicular, pungent, ± bent, chocolate-brown, reddish below, ± tangled, interlacing; **Fl.** light red.—Bolivia (between Oruro and Tolapampa).

L. rebutioides Backbg. (2:11)
Bo. forming cushions, with small heads (to 2 cm ∅), ± bluish-green (but never reddish or blackish), **R.** napiform; **Ri.** (10–)12(–14), very low and narrow, weakly tuberculate; **Rsp.** 8–9 (and more), very fine, very short, whitish; **Csp.** mostly 1–2, often rather longer, stouter and darker, slightly thickened below; **Fl.** c. 4 cm lg. and ∅, flame-coloured, **hymen** ± red to whitish, **throat** green.—N. Argentina. [Haage adds: = Echinopsis r. (Backbg.) H. Friedr.]
  v. **chlorogona** (Wessn.) Backbg.: **Fl.** deep golden-yellow, limb coppery, throat green;
  v. **citriniflora** Backbg.: **Fl.** lemon to buttercup-yellow, throat green;
  v. **kraussiana** Backbg.: **Fl.** opening to quite flat, to 10 cm ∅, Pet. in several Ser., brilliant yellowish;
  v. **sublimiflora** (Backbg. ex Wessn.) Backbg.: **Fl.** rotate, c. 6 cm lg. and ∅, salmon-pink with a carmine shimmer, throat brilliant pink-madder. The Fl. of v. kraussiana and v. sublimiflora are among the most lovely within Lobivia. There are also variants in which the colour and shape of the Pet. and throat are different (sv. cupreoviridis, purpureostoma, rubroviridis, versicolor).

L. rigidispina Backbg. (2:3)—Descr. Cact. Nov., III: 7. 1963.
Bo. broadly spherical, bluish-green, can flower at 5–6 cm ∅; **Ri.** 13, acute; **Ar.** oblong, dirty white; **Rsp.** 7–9, directed sideways, thin-subulate to stouter, the laterals mostly longest, to over 2 cm lg.; **Csp.** 1–3, very stoutly subulate, ± irregularly curving, much more thickened at the dark base; **Sp.** dark at first, the upper Rsp. and the Csp. mostly dark in bands, or above or below, all later pale horn-coloured, sometimes still dark-tipped, to c. 5 cm lg., rigid; **Fl.** funnelform, c. 5 cm ∅, dark flesh-coloured, lighter outside; **Tu.** dark, with greyish-white H.; **Fil.** pink.—Origin? (Fig. 198.) (Collection of van Urk, Holland.)

L. ritteri Wessn.: **Mediolobivia ritteri** (Wessn.) Krainz.

L. rossii Böd. (2:3)
Bo. spherical or elongated, to over 7 cm ∅, later offsetting; **Ri.** 18, Tub. oblique, hatchet-shaped; **Rsp.** 4–6, to 6 cm lg., lower ones to only 1.2 cm lg., subulate, stiff, pungent, reddish horn-coloured to grey, dark-tipped; **Csp.** absent; **Fl.** c. 4 cm lg., mid-orange, **throat** green.—Bolivia.
A very variable spec. The following varieties can be distinguished:
  Sp. ± stiff, pungent, reddish horn-coloured to grey, dark-tipped:
    v. **boedekeriana** (Hard.) Backbg.: **Fl.** flame to

orange, centre light yellow;
v. **hardeniana** (Böd.) Backbg.: **Fl.** orange-yellow, **throat** green;
v. **stollenwerkiana** (Böd.) Backbg.: **Fl.** golden-yellow, bordered orange;
Sp. stiff, pungent, yellowish or light grey to brown:
v. **walterspielii** (Böd.) Backbg.: **Fl.** carmine, **Pet.** broader, ± truncate;
Sp. more flexible:
v. **carminata** Backbg.: **Fl.** carmine, **Sp.** ± interlacing;
v. **salmonea** Backbg.: **Fl.** salmon-coloured to delicate wine-pink;
v. **sanguinea** Backbg.: **Fl.** blood-red.

L. rowleyi and its varieties v. longispina and rubroaurantiaca, described by Y. Ito, are known only in Japan and may be hybrids.

L. rubescens Backbg. (2:14)
Bo. simple, sometimes forming groups, **R.** stoutly napiform, single heads to 10 cm ∅, greyish-green, suffused ± reddish below; **Ri.** c. 12; **Rsp.** c. 7, upper ones 2–3 cm lg., lower ones sometimes 5–7 mm lg., horn-coloured on new growth; **Csp.** 1–2 to 5 cm lg., sometimes hooked, ± black on new growth, reddish below; **Fl.** to 6 cm ∅; **Pet.** in 2 Ser., golden-yellow, bordered reddish; **hymen** bluish-red.—N. Argentina.
v. **tenuispina** Backbg.: distinguished from the type by thinner **Csp.** and smaller, almost orange-yellow **Fl.**

L. saltensis (Speg.) Br. & R. (2:6?)
Bo. simple, later densely caespitose; **Ri.** 17–18; **Rsp.** 12–14, 4–6 mm lg.; **Csp.** 1–4, longer and stouter; **Fl.** red, glabrous (!—acc. Speg.); **Pet.** short.—Argentina.
Perhaps this is not a Lobivia after all, or it is weakly hairy; a little known spec.

L. sanguiniflora Backbg. (2:14)
Bo. mostly simple, with a thick taproot and variable Bo.-colour, to 10 cm h. and ∅; **R.** 18, obliquely notched; **Rsp.** c. 10, 8–15 mm lg., radiating, sometimes appressed; **Csp.** several, often cruciform, one Sp. eventually to 8 cm lg., very hooked; all **Sp.** dark at first, red below, sometimes lighter, upper ones becoming grey less quickly than the rest; **Fl.** c. 5 cm lg., ± blood-red.—N. Argentina.
v. **pseudolateritia** Backbg. (perhaps a valid spec.?): **Rsp.** mostly more numerous; **Fl.** ± carmine, Per. closed-funnelform, Pet. then recurving.—N. Argentina? Often known, incorrectly, as L. lateritia, but latter has

no hooked Sp.

L. scheeri S.D. is probably the first name for L. pampana Br. & R.

L. schieliana Backbg. (2:15)
Bo. ± elongated-spherical, slender, offsetting from below, c. 4.5 cm lg., c. 3.5 cm ∅; **Ri.** c. 14; **Rsp.** c. 14, pectinate to radiating, interlacing; **Csp.** often absent at first, later 1 longer Sp. c. 5–6 mm lg., bent towards the crown; **Sp.** light brown; **Fl.** with a slender Tu., brilliant light red.—S. Bolivia (?).
v. **albescens** Backbg.: differentiated by the mostly less interlacing, whitish **Sp.**; **Fl.** 3 cm lg., 3 cm ∅, light carmine; **throat** and **Fil.** carmine; **style** pink; **Sti.** white. (Fig. 199.)—There is another form or variety with hooked Sp. Grafted plants become cylindric.

L. schmiedcheniana Köhl.: **Mediolobivia schmiedcheniana** (Köhl.) Krainz.

L. schneideriana Backbg. (2:3)
Bo. simple or caespitose, shortly cylindric, ± bluish-green; **Ri.** c. 14–18; **Sp.** scarcely differentiated, c. 4–12 mm lg., radiating and projecting, 1 longer Sp. to 4 cm lg., ± bent towards the crown; **Sp.** horn-coloured; **Fl.** broadly funnelform; **Pet.** revolute, beige-coloured.—Bolivia (La Paz).
This spec. is variable as to Fl.-colour; the following varieties have been described:
v. **carnea** Backbg.: **Fl.** old-rose (Csp. mostly missing);
v. **cuprea** Backbg.: **Fl.** copper-coloured.

L. schreiteri Cast. (2:14)
Bo. forming mats to 30 cm broad, single heads only 1.5–3 cm ∅; **Ri.** 9–14; **Rsp.** 6–8, ± whitish, very fine, curving, one upper Sp. longer, darker; **Csp.** mostly missing, or 1 to 2 cm lg.; **Fl.** c. 3 cm lg. and ∅, purplish-red, **throat** blackish.—N. Argentina (Tucuman).

L. scoparia Werd. (2:11)
Bo. simple or caespitose, ± spherical; **Ri.** c. 13; **Rsp.** c. 20–30, unequal, bristly, ± bent, whitish; **Csp.** 3–6, to 1.5 cm lg., acicular, pungent, straight, ± brownish to brown; **Fl.** c. 6 cm lg., orange-yellow, bordered copper, **throat** white, greenish below.—Argentina.

L. scopulina Backbg. (a separate Ser.?)
Bo. simple, cylindric, to over 20 cm h., 8.5 cm ∅, dull pale greyish-green; **Ri.** c. 18, divided at first into almost cylindric Tub., these later separated by only a transverse depression; **Ar.** fairly broad, white; **Rsp.** c. 9–10, c. 1–2.5 cm lg., ± spreading sideways; **Csp.** mostly 2, to 2.5 cm lg., thickened

below; **Sp.** later all curving upwards, golden-brown at first, becoming grey; **Fl.** yellow, no further data available.—Bolivia (Fig. 200). Diverges by the unusual habit from all other known Lobivias from Bolivia.

L. shaferi Br. & R. (2:6)
Bo. laxly branching, slender-cylindric, 7–15 cm h., 2.5–4 cm ∅; **Ri.** c. 10; spination dense; **Rsp.** 10–15, to 1 cm lg., acicular, white or brown; **Csp.** several, to 3 cm lg., stout, 1 often much stouter; **Fl.** 4–6 cm lg., 3–4 cm ∅, yellow.—Argentina (Catamarca: Andalgalá).

L. sicuaniensis Rausch
Bo. simple, c. 10 cm h. and ∅, dark greyish-green, with a taproot; **Ri.** to 19, spiralled, with acute Tub. 2 cm lg. and 5–7 mm br.; **Ar.** round to oval, c. 5–7 mm lg., with white felt; **Rsp.** mostly 6, 4–6 cm lg., one smaller one directed downwards, brown, lighter and thickened below, ± curving; **Csp.** 0; **Fl.** c. 4 cm lg. and br.; **Ov.** and **Rec.** greenish, also yellowish or pink, with dark green or wine-red Sc. and white H.; **Sep.** orange, pink, red to violet, with a brownish-green M.-stripe; **Pet.** ± connivent, orange-red or yellow to red, orange inside, **throat** white; **Fil.** yellow or orange to red, white towards the centre; **style** and 5–7 **Sti.** green; **Fr.** spherical, c. 8 mm ∅, dark brownish-red, with pink to brown Sc. and white woolly H.; **S.** oblong-ovoid, laterally compressed, 1.5 mm lg. and 1 mm br., finely tuberculate, residual membranes cover testa.— Peru (near Sicuani—thus specific name; 3500–3600 m). Differentiated from L. maximiliana (otherwise similar) by more bluish-green Bo. and lighter Fl.-colours as well as the S.-shape. (Fig. 481.)

L. simplex Rausch
Bo. simple, to 20 cm h. and 10 cm ∅, dark green to brownish-red; **Ri.** 18–20, divided into acute Tub. to 22 mm lg.; **Ar.** oval, to 6 mm lg. and 3 mm br., white-felty; **Rsp.** 10, 2–3.5 cm lg., one smaller Sp. directed downwards; **Csp.** 1–2, to 8 cm lg.; all **Sp.** stout, sharp, thickened below, reddish-brown, tipped darker; **Fl.** lateral, c. 5 cm lg. and 4.5 cm br.; **Tu.** orange to brownish-red, with brownish-red, thick, woolly-hairy Sc.; **Pet.** spatulate, red, white inside; **throat, style** and 7 **Sti.** white; **Fr.** spherical, 8 mm ∅, rust-coloured, covered with brown H.; **S.** 1.5 mm lg., 1 mm br., testa tuberculate.—Peru (near Huambutio, 3200 m).

L. spinosissima Backbg. (name-proposal): spec. with long, erect, flexible Sp., found by Frau Muhr (Argentina, W. of La Quiaca); Uhlig No. U 2143.

L. staffenii Frič, not described; see **Lobivia chrysantha** (Werd.) Backbg.

L. staffenii v. lagunilla Frič, not described: belongs to **Lobivia polaskiana** Backbg.

L. steinmannii sensu Backbg. 1934: **Mediolobivia pectinata** v. **neosteinmannii** Backbg.

L. stilowiana Backbg. (2:14)
Bo. mostly simple, c. 6 cm h., 5 cm ∅, dark green; **Ri.** c. 23, Tub. sharply offset; **Rsp.** 5–7, 5–14 mm lg.; **Csp.** 1, to 1.7 cm lg., irregularly projecting; **Sp.** at first deep red below, blackish above, soon whitish-grey; **Fl.** c. 4 cm lg., 3.8 cm ∅, crimson to carmine, **throat** whitish-red.—N. Argentina.

L. taratensis Card. 1966
Bo. simple or caespitose, flattened-spherical, very variable in shape and size, 1–7 cm h., 7–12 cm ∅, fresh to greyish-green; **Ri.** 15–30, divided into hatchet-shaped Tub. 5–10 mm h. and 7–15 mm br.; **Ar.** 10–15 mm apart, narrowly elliptic, 6–8 mm lg., grey-felty; **Sp.** 10–14, appressed at first, later radiating and projecting, acicular, sometimes interlacing, 4–30 mm lg., light yellow or grey, thickened below; **Fl.** lateral, encircling the Bo., funnelform, 3–3.5 cm lg., 2.5–3 cm ∅; **Ov.** spherical, 5 mm ∅, scaly and hairy; **Tu.** 6 mm lg., with pink Sc. 3 mm lg. and dense white and dark brown H.; **Sep.** lanceolate, 1 cm lg., light red, greenish outside; **Pet.** spatulate, 1.5 cm lg., crimson, magenta or orange-red, whitish below; lower **An.** 5–7 mm lg., with golden-yellow Fil., upper An. 7 mm lg., Fil. golden-yellow, red above; **style** 1 cm lg., greenish, with c. 6 greenish Sti. 5 mm lg.—Bolivia (Tarata [hence the specific name], Cochabamba, on the road from Tarata to Isata, among rocks or in grass, at 3000 m).
This spec., one of the short-flowered Lobivias, is extremely variable in habit and flower-colour. It is possibly a form of this spec. which Bridges collected in 1865 at Tarata, and which was the old L. cinnabarina (Hook.) Br. & R.
    v. **leucosiphus** Card. 1966: clearly differentiated from the type by its shorter, fewer Sp., and the floral tube which is white inside. Occurs near Tarata at 3000 m.

L. tegeleriana Backbg. and var.: **Acantholobivia tegeleriana** (Backbg.) Backbg. and var.

L. tenuispina Ritt.
Resembles L. pictiflora, but distinguished as follows: **Bo.** flatter; **Ar.** more oblique, narrower; **Sp.** thinner; **Fl.** with nectary 1.5–4 mm lg., Tu. light yellow inside, **Pet.** always brightly coloured, golden-yellow or orange; **Sti.** shorter, 6 mm; **S.** black.—Bolivia (Prov. Mendez, San Antonio).

L. thionantha (Speg.) Br. & R.: **Acanthocalycium thionanthum** (Speg.) Backbg.

L. tiegeliana Wessn. (2:15)
Bo. depressed-spherical, to 6 cm ∅, glossy green; **Ri.** 18; **Rsp.** in 4–6 pairs to 1 cm lg., ± pectinate, later interlacing, acicular, pale honey-coloured at first, with a reddish-brown tip; **Csp.** 1–3, one above, slightly curving, acicular, brown, lighter below; **Fl.** 2.5 cm lg., c. 4.2 cm ∅, brilliant violet-pink, **hymen** paler.—S. Bolivia (Tarija). (Fig. 482.)
    v. **distefanoiana** Cullm. & Ritt.—Kakt.u.a.Sukk., 1: 7–8. 1961. (FR 620): **Bo.** dark green, weakly glossy; **Ar.** more elongated; **Rsp.** 12–14, clearly pectinate, 3–4 mm lg., white, tipped red or brown; **Csp.** 0–1, if present curving upwards, black, mostly thinner and shorter than the stoutest Rsp.—Bolivia (E. of Tarija).
For hybrids—mostly known as "forms"—see L. peclardiana.

L. titicacensis Card. (2:3)
Bo. caespitose, single heads 5–8 cm lg., 4–8 cm ∅, glossy, dark green; **Ri.** 14–18; **Sp.** radials only, 9–15, 0.5–8 cm lg., recurved, ± straw-coloured; **Fl.** 5 cm lg., 3.5 cm ∅; outer **Pet.** light purplish-reddish, whitish below, inner ones orange, pale yellow below.—Bolivia (Lake Titicaca, "Island of the Sun"). Probably only a form of L. higginsiana.

L. torrecillasensis hort. europ.: **Lobivia arachnacantha** v. **torrecillasensis** hort. europ. (Card. ?)

L. uitewaaleana Buin. (2:13)
Bo. to 7 cm h., 6 cm ∅, greyish-green; **Ri.** 13, with hatchet-shaped Tub.; **Rsp.** 6–8, the upper pair to 12 mm lg., slightly curving; **Csp.** 3–4, to 15 mm lg., cruciform, sometimes ± hooked; **Sp.** brown, radials tipped black; **Fl.** yellow-ochre, **hymen** violet, **throat** brownish-violet.—N. Argentina. Closely related to Lob. jajoiana.

L. urubambae (FR 698): no description available.

L. vanurkiana Backbg. (2:3)
Bo. offsetting, dull bluish-green; **St.** 4–5 cm ∅; **Ri.** c. 10, acute; **Ar.** white; **Rsp.** 5–7, ± recurved, the bottom one longest, c. 2–3 cm lg.; **Csp.** 0–1, bent irregularly upwards; all **Sp.** grey, ± thickened and dark below; **Fl.** 8 cm lg., c. 7 cm ∅; **Sep.** brownish in the centre; **Pet.** concolorous yellow; **Tu.** with rather dense dark H.; **Fil.** in 2 Ser.; **throat** greenish; **Sti.** greenish.—Origin? (Fig. 201.)
Remarkable for the relatively large Fl. on the groups of quite small Bo. Named for the Dutch collector, van Urk.

L. varians Backbg. (2:3)

Bo. caespitose, single heads to 8 cm h. and 11 cm ∅, light greyish-green; **R.** rather long; **Ri.** 21; **Sp.** to 10, scarcely differentiated, to 10 cm lg., ± confused and interlacing, brown at first, later pinkish-grey; **Fl.** c. 5–6 cm lg., to 4 cm ∅, light orange-red, **throat** lighter.—Bolivia (E. of Oruro).
    v. **croceantha** Backbg.: distinguished by the saffron to light orange-yellow **Fl.**;
    v. **rubroalba** Backbg.: **Fl.** light blood-red, throat white.

L. vatteri Krainz (2:13)
Bo. spherical, later elongated, c. 6 cm h. and 5 cm ∅, dark green; **R.** napiform; **Ri.** 14–16; **Rsp.** 10(–12), ± curving, light brown, darker-tipped; **Csp.** 2,4–8 cm lg., mostly erect and slightly curving, black at first, later brown, tipped brownish-red, Sp. on new growth ruby-red below; **Fl.** c. 6 cm lg., to 7 cm ∅, white, **throat** or **hymen** black.—Argentina (Jujuy, c. 3000 m).
    v. **robusta** Backbg.: to c. 10 cm h., broader than the type, with over 20 **Ri.**; **Fl.** only c. 4.8 cm lg. and ∅, **throat** and **hymen** burgundy-red.
One of the spec. in the complex around L. jajoiana, and clearly rather variable in Fl.-colour; Rausch, for example, found specimens with the Fl. orange and the throat black.

L. vilcabambae Ritt. (2:4)—"Taxon", XII: 3, 124. 1963.
Acc. Ritter, distinguished from L. hertrichiana as follows:
Bo. mostly simple, hemispherical, to 7 cm ∅; **Ri.** 12–18, divided into hatchet-shaped Tub.; **Ar.** to 5 mm lg.; **Sp.** pale brown, bent, interlacing, mostly dark above; **Rsp.** 6–11, 1–3 cm lg.; **Csp.** mostly 0, sometimes 1, 3–4 cm lg.; **Fl.** 5 cm lg., 4–5 cm ∅, closing at night; **Pet.** red, orange below, tipped crimson; **Fil.** orange, white below.—Peru (Vilcabamba mountains, Prov. Urubamba, Dept. Cuzco, 3500 m and higher). (FR 697.)

L. watadae Y. Ito (? Hybrid)
Bo. mostly simple, to 8 cm ∅, light green; **Ri.** 13–15; **Rsp.** 8–10, 5–7 mm lg.; **Csp.** 1, 1–1.2 cm lg., salmon-coloured at first, then whitish-brown to grey; **Sp.** acicular, pungent, centrals stouter; **Fl.** to 8 cm lg., 8.5–10 cm ∅, yellow; **Pet.** darker-striped.—Origin ?
    v. **salmonea** Y. Ito: **Fl.** somewhat smaller; **Pet.** salmon-coloured, with a darker stripe; **Sep.** light to dark pink.

L. wegheiana Backbg. (2:3)
Bo. eventually forming cushions, with a very long **R.**; **Ri.** to 20; **Rsp.** 7–8, radiating to both sides, dark at first, rather stiff; **Csp.** 1, c. 4 cm lg., directed upwards; **Sp.** later light-coloured, Rsp. sometimes

longer; **Fl.** c. 6 cm lg., light lilac-colour, agreeably scented.—Bolivia (Oruro area).

v. **leucantha** Backbg. n.nud.: **Sp.** whitish to amber-coloured, mostly longer and ± strongly interlacing laterally; **Csp.** darker, to 6 cm lg.; **Fl.** differentiated by the narrower, longer, more recurved Sep.

L. wegneriana Grun. & Kluegl.
Bo. spherical, caespitose, 8–10 cm h., 6–7 cm ⌀, dark green; **Ri.** 18–20, obtuse, tuberculate; **Ar.** matt yellowish, later white-felty, 20 mm apart; **Rsp.** 10–12, spreading, straight, 8–10 mm lg.; **Csp.** 3–5, straight, directed obliquely upwards, 12 mm lg., slightly twisted, also 1 upper **Sp.** to 20 mm lg., dark brown, later greying, acicular, thickened below; **Fl.** lateral and low on the Bo., to 3.5 cm lg., 7 cm ⌀, rotate, carmine, silky and glossy, throat whitish; **Pet.** entire; buds with greyish-brown H.; **Ov.** pinkish-lilac with acute Sc.; **Tu.** with brown and white H.; **Sep.** pink with brownish-olive M.-stripes; lower **Fil.** whitish below, yellow above, upper ones whitish below, light carmine above; **An.** light yellow; **style** yellowish-olive with 6 similarly coloured **Sti.**—Bolivia (exact locality not known).

L. wessneriana Fritz.: **Lobivia rebutioides** v. **sublimiflora** (Backbg. ex Wessn.) Backbg.

L. westii P. C. Hutch. (1:1)
Bo. caespitose, single heads to 20 cm lg., 6 cm ⌀, dark green; **Ri.** 16–18, narrow, acute; **Rsp.** c. 8, to 9 mm lg.; **Csp.** 1, to 2.5 cm lg., later to 4 cm lg. and curving; **Sp.** straw-coloured, tipped brown, or brown to grey; **Fl.** to 7 cm lg., 4 cm ⌀, slender, bellshaped to funnelform; **Tu.** relatively lg.; **Sep.** orange-pink to golden-orange; **Pet.** light golden-orange.—Peru (Dept. Apurimac).

L. winteriana Ritt. (FR 1213)
Bo. spherical, later elongated, 4–7 cm ⌀, greyish-green, soft-fleshed, **R.** ± napiform; **Ri.** 13–19, 4–7 mm h.; **Ar.** white-felty, oval, 2–3 mm lg., 2–5 mm apart; **Sp.** light brown, greying; **Rsp.** 6–14, bent towards the Bo., acicular, ± subulate. c. 4–7 mm lg.; **Csp.** 1(–3), often absent, bent inwards, 1–3 cm lg., rarely to 6 cm, tipped black; **Fl.** diurnal, closed at night, lateral, 6–9 cm lg., 7–9 cm ⌀; **Ov.** brownish, with reddish-brown, whitish-tipped Sc.; **Tu.** funnelform, white inside; **Pet.** ruby-red, linear, acutely tapering; **Sep.** rather narrow, with a green M.-stripe; **Fr.** 12–18 mm lg., 8–15 mm br., dark green to reddish-brown, soft-fleshed, juicy; **S.** purse-shaped, acutely keeled, testa matt, black.—Peru (Huancavelica; discovered by Ritter in 1964, and named for his sister, Frau Hildegard Winter). Has some resemblance to L. wrightiana but the Fl. are much larger.

L. wrightiana Backbg. (2:12)
Bo. later sometimes offsetting, single heads spherical at first, becoming ± cylindric, dark greyish-green; with a longer **taproot**; **Ri.** c. 17; **Rsp.** c. 10, c. 5–7 mm lg., weak, spreading, appressed; **Csp.** 1, contorted to curving, pointing like a feeler, variously directed, to 7 cm lg.; **Fl.** c. 6 cm lg., slender-funnelform, delicate lilac-pink.—Central Peru (Mantaro valley). Pet.-shape somewhat variable.

v. **brevispina** Backbg.: differentiated by shorter Sp. and paler Fl.
The following of Ritter's undescribed plants also belong here:
Lobivia imporana Ritt.: "related to L. lateritia": light Sp., Fl. large, colourful.—Bolivia (Chuquisaca). (FR 82B.)

v. elongata Ritt. (FR 82) and v. brevispina Ritt. (FR 82C).
Lobivia megacarpa Ritt. (FR 809): "related to L. caespitosa", apparently with especially large Fr. (see also in the preceding).

L. zecheri Rausch
Bo. simple, rarely offsetting, to 7 cm h. and br., frosted light bluish-grey; **Ri.** 12–18, spiralled, tuberculate; **Ar.** oval, to 6 mm lg., with white wool; **Rsp.** 7–11, spreading, 3–5 cm lg., mostly 6–8 and 1 smaller **Sp.** pointing downwards; **Csp.** 0–1, 6 cm lg.; all **Sp.** stiff, brown, thickened and light yellow below, there with a black spot, otherwise white; **Fl.** c. 3 cm lg. and br., yellowish-brown with orange-yellow Sc., with white to brown wool; **Pet.** dark red to violet-red; **Sep.** greyish-brown, bordered pink; **style** red with 5 pink Sti.; **Fr.** spherical, c. 12 mm ⌀, reddish-brown with pink Sc. and white wool; **S.** 2 mm lg. and 1.2 mm ⌀, bent strongly to one side, black, finely tuberculate.—Peru (along the road from Ayacucho to Huanta, at 2400 m). (Fig. 483). Named for the collector, Ernst Zecher, who accompanied W. Rausch on some of his expeditions.

L. zudañensis Card.
Bo. spherical, flattened, 4–5 cm h., 10–15 cm ⌀, greyish-green, crown depressed; **Ri.** c. 22, acute, Tub. hatchet-shaped; **Ar.** 1.5 cm apart, elliptic, grey-felty; **Rsp.** 6–7, spreading, 1.3 cm lg.; **Csp.** directed upwards, 3, 5–8 cm lg.; all **Sp.** grey, thickened below; **Fl.** lateral, funnelform, 5 cm lg., 4 cm ⌀; **Ov.** spherical, 6 mm lg., brown, with Sc. and long black H.; **Sep.** broadly lanceolate, 2 cm lg., red; **Pet.** spatulate, 2.5 × 1 cm, rounded above, light blood-red; **Fil.** dark magenta; **An.** light yellow; **style** light green with 10 light green Sti.—Bolivia (Prov. Zudañez, Dept. Chuquisaca, on the road Zudáñez-Tarabuco, 2400 m).

Lobiviopsis Frič: only a name for the genus **Pseudolobivia**.

Lophocereus (Berg.) Br. & R. (169)

Erect columnar cacti, branching from below, rarely with a short trunk, with nocturnal flowers. Juvenile plants of one species appear monstrose. Flowering areoles are large and felty, sometimes with much modified spines, so that the shoot-tips, enveloped in long bristles, have a brush-like appearance. The flowers are relatively small and funnelform, several sometimes appearing at once from the same areole. Tube and ovary are slightly scaly. The fruit is a rather small red spherical berry, mostly glabrous but occasionally somewhat prickly; in general the pricles are completely reduced. The seeds are rather small, glossy black.—Distribution: USA (S. Arizona) to Mexico (Baja California, Sonora and Sinaloa). [(R).]

L. australis (K. Brand.) Br. & R. is regarded as a variety of L. schottii, with a short trunk and thinner, longer shoots.

L. gatesii M. E. Jon.
Bo. branching freely from the base to form groups to 3 m across; **branches** to 3 m h., c. 9 cm $\varnothing$, pale olive-green; **Ri.** 10–15; **Rsp.** 8–10, stoutly acicular, very light grey; **Csp.** 2, later to 5, 1.5 cm lg. and more, subulate; **Sp.** with a bulbous thickening below; **flowering shoots** have woollier Ar. and to 20 Sp., to 6 cm lg., light grey; **Fl.** 3 cm lg. and $\varnothing$, dark coral-red; **Fr.** ?—Mexico (Baja California).

L. mieckleyanus (Wgt.) Backbg.
Bo. with the pseudo-monstrose juvenile stage $\pm$ long-persistent or even permanent; **branches** sap-green to light green, matt, sometimes weakly pruinose; **Ri.** few, variable in shape, interrupted or offset, but narrow and prominent on normal growth; **Ar.** irregularly distributed, shortly felty, later glabrous; **Sp.** mostly absent, sometimes a few as in L. schottii, these bristly above, c. 1–3 cm lg., sometimes only a few small Br. are present, without the conspicuous modification seen in L. schottii; **Fl.** pink, scattered or more numerous.—Mexico (Baja California). (Fig. 203.)
The anomalous rib-form is very variable. Lindsay added 2 forms to the type-species (see below). Gates regarded it not as a single species, but a whole genus, under the name Weinbergia cereiformis hort. (C. & S. J. [US], III: 137. 1932). The remarkable thing about Lindsay's two "forms" is that both can be seen NE. of El Arco, in a relatively small area, sometimes forming a single large population!

L. sargentianus (Orc.) Br. & R.
Bo. forming groups of 8 or more St.; **Ri.** 5–6; **sterile shoots** to 1.5 m h., **Sp.** 10 or more, to 1.8 cm lg.; **fertile shoots** to 4.5 m h., **Sp.** more strongly modified, long, flexible, stiffly bristly, to 50 from one Ar.; **Fl.** 2.5 cm lg., pink.—Mexico (Baja California). (Fig. 202, left.) The Fl. is noticeably smaller than in L. schottii. For a comparison of the Fl., see "Die Cact." IV: 2282, Fig. 2185–86. 1960.

L. schottii (Eng.) Br. & R. (T.)
Bo. with no trunk, with numerous St. to 3(–7) m h., $\pm$ yellowish-green, $\pm$ pruinose; **Ri.** 5–7(–9); **Sp.** on sterile shoots c. 5 or more at first, 6–8 mm lg., subulate, with a strongly bulbous thickening below, dark reddish at first, later with 1 **Csp.**; **Sp.** on fertile shoots thinner, longer, to c. 25 (or more?); **Fl.** c. 4 cm lg., 3 cm $\varnothing$, white to (?) reddish.—Mexico (Baja California, Sonora, Sinaloa) to USA (S. Arizona). (Fig. 202, right.)
v. **australis** (K. Brand.) Borg: **Bo.** with a short **trunk** to 50 cm $\varnothing$, and the **crown** to 8 m h. and 5 m br.; **branches** yellowish-green, to 6 m lg', to 10 cm $\varnothing$; **Ri.** 6–9, but increasing to 9–11 on fertile shoots, acute, rounded above; **Ar.** 1–2 cm apart below, to 1 cm thick above; **sterile shoots** with 7 Rsp., mostly 1–2 centrals; **fertile shoots** with up to 40 grey Br.-Sp., to 7 cm lg.; **Fl.** as in the type. Distinguished by its greater height and the presence of a trunk.
v. **tenuis** Linds.—C. & S. J. (US), XXXV: 6, 187. 1963.
Bo. with the St. more spreading and little branching, greyish-green to yellowish-green, mostly under 2 m lg., sometimes to 5 m h., the stoutest 7 cm $\varnothing$ below, 3 cm $\varnothing$ above; **Ar.** densely tomentose when capable of flowering; **Sp.** on sterile sections 6–8, short, grey, thickened below, 1 **Csp.** to 1 cm lg.; fertile sections have 15–25 contorted bristly Sp. 2–5 cm lg.; **Fl.** to 3 cm lg. and $\varnothing$, pale pink.—Mexico (Sonora, 44 miles SE. of Guaymas).
The inclusion of other species as varieties, together with the recombination and segregation of the monstrous spec. in L. schotti f. mieckleyanus Linds. and f. monstrosus Linds. (l.c.), cannot be followed here, for the reasons set out in my Handbook, and also because of the great variability in the development of such abnormal juvenile rib-development, as observed in the Marnier collection; this applies particularly to the referral of L. sargentianus to the type-species. L. gatesii, which has been left as a valid species, could equally well have been given varietal status under that species. Any kind of grouping tends to reflect individual opinions rather than natural phenomena.

Lophophora Coult. (211)

Simple or sometimes ± freely offsetting soft-fleshed plants with a stout taproot; bodies bluish to yellowish-green, and spineless; minute spines are present only in the early seedling stage. The ribs are broad and rounded, with ± distinct tubercles. The tufts of felt which develop in the areoles are denser in the crown, and the small white, pink or yellow flowers emerge through this. The elongated, berry-like fruits mostly ripen in the same year and then protrude through the wool; they are naked, red to pink. The seeds are black, minutely tuberculate and rough. Acc. L. Croizat, who has made the closest study of the genus, 3 species and the following varieties can be distinguished.—Distribution: Central Mexico to USA (S. Texas). [(R).]
To the Mexican Indians the plants were the god, Peyotl, who was deemed to have magic powers—which is hardly surprising since they contain 9 different alkaloids, one of which (mescalin) produces an extraordinary state of intoxication. A great deal has been written on this subject. The genus was known for a time as Anhalonium.

L. echinata Croiz.
Bo. simple, to 13 cm ∅, bluish-green (mid-green has also been observed); **Ri.** c. 10 or more, divided into 5–6-sided **Tub.**; **Ar.** with thick tufts of H.; **Fl.** to 2.5 cm lg. and ∅, white; **Fr.** ± pale pink.—USA (Texas). (Fig. 204.)
v. **diffusa** Croiz.: distinguished by broadly rounded **Tub.** which seldom merge.

L. jourdaniana (Reb.) Krzgr.: only a name for a violet-pink flowered form of L. williamsii (Lem. ex SD.) Coult.

L. lewinii (Henn.) Rusby, acc. Croizat, is **Epithelantha micromeris** v. **greggii** (Eng.) Borg.

L. lutea (Rouh.) Backbg.
Bo. simple, faded green; **Ri.** with sinuous longitudinal furrows, only weakly tuberculate; **Fl.** larger, yellowish-white.—Type-locality not stated.

L. williamsii (Lem. ex SD.) Coult. (T.)
Bo. bluish to greyish-green; **Ri.** 8(–10), Tub. only indistinctly merging, with tufts of stiff H.; **Fl.** small short, c. 1.25 cm ∅, pink; **Pet.** few; **Fr.** reddish.—USA (SE. States) to Mexico (N. States, to Querétaro).
v. **caespitosa** hort. appears to be no more than a local form; it offsets freely, eventually forming large cushions; individual heads smaller;
v. **decipiens** Croiz.: smaller than the type, to c. 6 cm ∅; **Ri.** c. 11 at first, then divided into conical Tub.; **Fl.** pink, with a longer Tu.;

v. **pentagona** Croiz.: distinguished by having only 5 broader and indistinctly tuberculate **Ri.**; **Fl.** also larger;
v. **pluricostata** Croiz.: more commonly offsetting; **Ri.** 10–13; **Tub.** indistinctly merging; **Fl.** small, pink; **Tu.** short;
v. **texana** (Frič ex Krzgr.) Backbg.: distinguished from the type by having up to 14 ± straight, scarcely tuberculate **Ri.**

L. ziegleri (or ziegleriana) Schmoll: **Lophophora lutea** (Rouh.) Backbg.

Loxanthocereus Backbg. (68)

Erect to decumbent and mostly relatively slender columnar cacti. In some species there is weak hair-development at the apex. The ribs are slender to tuberculate. The flowers are of slightly varying shades of red, predominantly ± oblique-limbed, rarely ± radial, the opening is funnelform, not constricted, the tube ± bent; although there is some slight hair-development in the tube in some members of the genus, this is not a diagnostic character as it is absent in other species.
The fruits are relatively small and the seeds probably always ± black.—Distribution: only in Peru (from close to the coast, up to 3300 m). [(R).]
In cultivated plants the spination is quite often finer, while the central spines are also shorter; in some cases the difference is conspicuous, and as with Haageocereus could give rise to a misleading duplication of descriptions unless there is an awareness of the likely differences of habit. In the following, the descriptions refer to wild populations.

L. acanthurus (Vpl.) Backbg. (T.)
Bo. prostrate, sometimes ascending, often hanging down over cliffs; **St.** to 50 cm lg., to 5 cm ∅; apical H. grey, felty; **Ri.** to 18, with acute transverse furrows; **Ar.** small, crowded; **Rsp.** c. 20; **Csp.** to 5, scarcely differentiated; **Sp.** c. 1 cm lg. (1 Csp. sometimes longer, to 1.5 cm), ochre-coloured on new growth; **Fl.** to 5 cm lg., scarlet to carmine (Rauh); **Tu.** little bent; **Fr.** to 2.5 cm ∅.—Peru (near Matucana). In very hot weather the Pet. are strongly recurved.
v. **ferox** (Backbg.) Backbg.: **Rsp.** 25–28; **Csp.** 1, to 2 cm lg., stouter, brownish to horn-coloured. (Fig. 205.)

L. aticensis Rauh & Backbg.
Bo. in part prostrate, to 50 cm lg.; **St.** to 5 cm ∅; **Ri.** c. 12; **Ar.** small, round, set on a tuberculate prominence; **Rsp.** c. 15, 1–1.5 cm lg., greyish-brown at first; **Csp.** (1–)2(–4), to 2.5 cm lg., greyish-

brown, pruinose, tipped dark violet; **Fl.** red (only seen in the bud-stage); **Fr.** not known.—S. Peru (near Atico).

L. (?) brevispinus Rauh & Backbg.
Bo. erect, to 30 cm h.; **St.** to 6 cm $\emptyset$; **Ri.** c. 14, with a shallow V-notch; **Ar.** elongated; **Rsp.** to 25, only 3–4 mm lg., those on the new growth yellowish, tipped ± black; **Csp.** 1–3, 1.5–2 cm lg., very stout, mostly directed obliquely upwards, greyish-brown to violet at first; **Fl.** and **Fr.** not known.—Peru (Pisco valley).

L. camanaensis Rauh & Backbg.
Bo. prostrate, to only 20 cm lg.; **St.** 4 cm $\emptyset$; **Ri.** c. 13(–14), made tuberculate by the acute transverse furrows; **Ar.** round, c. 1 cm apart; **Rsp.** c. 6–10, to 5 mm lg., radiating, stoutly acicular; **Csp.** 1–2(–3), to 3 cm lg., stoutly acicular, rigid, greyish-brown at first; **Fl.** subapical, c. 8 cm lg., ± zygomorphic, ± orange-red; **Fr.** c. 2 cm lg., 2.2 cm $\emptyset$, greenish; **S.** glossy, black.—S. Peru (Loma Desert). (FR 1025).

L. canetensis Rauh & Backbg.
Bo. prostrate, to 80 cm lg.; **St.** to 8 cm $\emptyset$; **Ri.** 21, transversely furrowed; **Rsp.** 20–30, 5 mm lg., ± bristle-like, brownish, becoming grey; **Csp.** 0–1(–3), sometimes 1 to 1.5 cm lg.; **Fl.** to 10 cm lg., ± zygomorphic, vivid crimson; **Fr.** dark wine-red, c. 1.5 cm lg.—Peru (Cañete valley, Imperial).

L. cantaensis Rauh & Backbg.
Bo. erect to ± prostrate, with a **taproot**; **St.** to 60 cm lg., to 5 cm $\emptyset$; **Ri.** 18; **Ar.** very small; **Rsp.** very numerous, c. 5 mm lg., thin, bristle-like, leather-brown at first; **Csp.** mostly 1, to 2.5 cm lg., dark brown at first; **Fl.** to 8(–10) cm lg., c. 3 cm $\emptyset$, weakly zygomorphic, vivid carmine; **Fr.** ?—Peru (Canta valley).

L. clavispinus Rauh & Backbg.
Bo. erect, branching from the base, with thick **R.**; **St.** 20–50 cm h., 8–10 cm $\emptyset$; **Ri.** 14; **Ar.** crowded; **Rsp.** to 30, c. 1.5 cm lg., very stout, brownish; **Csp.** 2–3, to 3 cm lg., stiff and nail-shaped, light grey-pruinose at first below, tipped chocolate-brown; **Fl.** red, **Tu.** to 8 cm lg., strongly bent; **Fr.** ?—Peru (Nazca valley).

L. crassiserpens (Rauh & Backbg.) Rauh & Backbg.
Bo. prostrate, moderately branching; **St.** to 2 m lg., 3–4 cm $\emptyset$; **Ri.** c. 12; **Ar.** ± elongated, small, set on somewhat tuberculate prominences; **Rsp.** c. 20, c. 5–7 mm lg., radiating, thin, yellowish-brownish; **Csp.** scarcely differentiated, 1–2 longer ones, or in the crown 1 upper Rsp. which is bristly, elongated, to 2 cm lg., brownish, darker below; **Fl.** moderately curving, red.—N. Peru (Olmos: eastwards).

L. cullmannianus Backbg.
Bo. erect, later probably branching from the base; **St.** to c. 60 cm lg., c. 6.5 cm $\emptyset$, matt green; **Ar.** c. 5 mm lg., 4 mm $\emptyset$; **Rsp.** c. 32, to 9 mm lg., radiating in all directions, fine, yellowish; **Csp.** 2, to 2 cm lg., one directed upwards, the other downwards, stout, acicular, brownish, soon becoming paler; **Fl.** zygomorphic, even in the bud-stage, 9 cm lg., 4.5 cm $\emptyset$, salmon-red; **Sep.** light salmon-orange; **Fr.** c. 4 cm lg., slightly yellowish-greenish.—Peru.

L. erectispinus Rauh & Backbg.
Bo. prostrate and then curving upwards; **St.** to 60 cm lg., to 3 cm $\emptyset$; **Ri.** 16; **Ar.** fairly large, elongated, crowded; **Rsp.** very numerous, to 1.5 cm lg., quite strongly projecting, very thin; **Csp.** (scarcely differentiated) 2–4, to c. 3 cm lg., thin, brittle, directed obliquely upwards, sometimes light golden-yellow; **bud-wool** persisting; **Fl.** (seen only in the bud-stage) crimson; **Fr.** ?—Central Peru (Churin valley). Recognizable by the dense, almost bristly spination (FR 1075).

L. erigens Rauh & Backbg.
Bo. erect, branching from the base, to 1.5 m h., **St.** to 10 cm $\emptyset$; **Ri.** 14; **Ar.** crowded; **Rsp.** numerous, 1 cm lg., bristly fine, yellowish-brown, becoming grey; **Csp.** 1–3, 2(–2.5) cm lg., stoutly acicular, leather-coloured, eventually grey; **Fl.** c. 8 cm lg., mostly borne on one side only, crimson; **Fr.** c. 2 cm $\emptyset$, wine-red when unripe.—Central Peru (Cañete valley).

L. eriotrichus (Werd. & Backbg.) Backbg.
Bo. branching, semi-prostrate; **St.** to 40 cm lg., to 3.5 cm $\emptyset$; **Ri.** c. 16; **Ar.** strongly yellow-felty at first, later with longer woolly **H.**, denser in the apex; **Rsp.** to 15, to 8 mm lg.; **Csp.** 3–6, equal, scarcely distinguishable; **Sp.** yellowish-white at first, later grey, sometimes dark-tipped; **Fl.** flame-colour; **Fr.** cherry-sized, yellowish-green.—Peru (Rimac valley).

L. eulalianus Rauh & Backbg.
Bo. prostrate to semi-erect; **St.** to 30 cm lg., 3–5 cm $\emptyset$; **Ri.** c. 19, not transversely furrowed; **Rsp.** c. 30, thin, sometimes 1 longer stouter upper one to 2 cm lg., yellow, the others golden-brown at first; **Csp.** scarcely differentiated, to 10; **Fl.** and **Fr.** unknown.—Central Peru (Eulalia valley). Rauh later wrote the name as L. eulaliensis.

L. faustianus (Backbg.) Backbg.
Bo. prostrate to ascending; **St.** to 40 cm lg., to 5 cm $\emptyset$; **Ri.** c. 18; **Ar.** fairly crowded; **Rsp.** 35–40, to 1 cm lg., fine, bristly; **Csp.** hardly differentiated, to 6, 1–3 of these longer, c. 3 cm lg., very stout; **Sp.** yellow at first below, brown above, later becoming

black, rather tangled; **Fl.** c. 6 cm lg., funnelform, obliquely expanding, flame-coloured; **Fr.** small, spherical.—Peru (Rimac and Eulalia valleys).

L. ferrugineus Rauh & Backbg.
Bo. erect, branching from the base; **St.** to 80 cm h., 4–5 cm ∅; **Ri.** 20; **Rsp.** numerous, thin, ± interlacing; **Csp.** 1–4, sometimes 2 longer ones, the longest one to 2 cm lg., those at the apex erect, later porrect or directed downwards, stout, rusty brown, later grey; **Fl.** 10 cm lg., crimson; **Fr.** to 4 cm ∅, pale wine-red.—Peru (Nazca valley).

L. gracilis (Akers & Buin.) Backbg.
Bo. prostrate, with a woody underground rootstock; **St.** 10–20, c. 5 cm ∅; **Ri.** 11, tuberculate; **Rsp.** 8, c. 1 cm lg., radiating, stiff, yellow; **Csp.** 1–3, c. 2 cm lg., stiff, yellow; **Fl.** zygomorphic, orange-scarlet; **Tu.** bent, S-shaped; **Fr.** tuberculate, yellowish-green.—S. Peru (near Chavina).

L. gracilispinus Rauh & Backbg.
Bo. prostrate, branching from below; **St.** to 60 cm lg., to c. 10 cm ∅; **Ri.** 18, very narrow; **Ar.** very small; **Rsp.** very numerous, to 5 mm lg., thin, mingled near the crown with fine white woolly H., forming an erect tuft in the crown itself; **Csp.** to over 10, the principal one to 2 cm lg., dark brown at first, yellowish below, fine-acicular; **Fl.** to c. 12 cm lg., 2 cm ∅, crimson, almost rotate, arising from dense areolar wool, old bud-wool persisting; **Fr.** greenish.—Central Peru (Loma Desert near Pachacamac).

L. granditessellatus Rauh & Backbg.
Bo. prostrate; **St.** to 2 m lg., 5 cm ∅; **Ri.** 6–7, noticeably tessellate because of the transverse furrows, tessellae acutely angled, borders appearing ± pruinose; **Rsp.** 8–10, unequal, to 1 cm lg., stout, brownish, tipped purplish-brown; **Csp.** 1–2, to 5 cm lg., very stout, purplish-brown at first; **Fl.** to 10 cm (?) lg., red; **Tu.** slender, ± bent, with dense tufts of curly woolly H.; **Fr.** spherical, to 3 cm ∅, green.—Central Peru (Santa valley).

L. hystrix Rauh & Backbg.
Bo. prostrate and then arching upwards, to 1.5 m lg., to 10 cm ∅, fiercely spined; **Ri.** to 15(–16); **Rsp.** numerous, to 2.5 cm lg., stout, spreading in all directions, olive-brownish at first, then becoming grey, tipped dark brown; **Csp.** 6–8, to 2.5 cm lg., 1 main Sp. to 10 cm lg., very stout, often contorted; **Sp.** ± brown, later pruinose; **Fl.** (seen only in the bud-stage) 5 cm lg., later probably more, red.—Peru (Nazca-Lucanas).
  v. **brunnescens** Rauh: stouter; **Ri.** to 19, constricted; **Rsp.** mostly to 1 cm lg., mingled with others which are stouter, leather-coloured and to

1.5 cm lg.; **Csp.** mostly 1, to 5 cm lg., dull leathercolour, neither pruinose nor contorted.

L. jajoianus (Backbg.) Backbg.
Bo. forming groups; **St.** erect to curving, to 60 cm lg., to 6 cm ∅; **Ri.** c. 12; **Rsp.** c. 20, to 6 mm lg.; **Csp.** 1–4, to 6 cm lg., thickened below, stout; **Sp.** straw-coloured; **Fl.** salmon-orange, c. 7 cm lg.; **Fr.** spherical, c. 1.3 cm ∅, yellowish-green, with short white woolly flock; **S.** matt black, 1.25 mm lg.—S. Peru (Uyupampa).

L. keller-badensis Backbg. & Krainz
Bo. branching from the base, to 65 cm h.; **St.** to 5.5 cm ∅; **Ri.** c. 15; **Ar.** crowded, yellow-felted, becoming white; **Rsp.** 25–30, to 8 mm lg., light brownish-yellow, eventually whitish-grey; **Csp.** 1–3, the middle one porrect, 1.6 cm lg., others shorter, yellow, becoming blackish; **Fl.** to 8 cm lg., opening fairly wide, to funnelform, bluish-carmine; **Fr.** c. 1.2 cm ∅, spherical, green.—Peru (Rimac, side-valleys).

L. multifloccosus Rauh & Backbg.
Bo. prostrate, branching from the base; **St.** to 40 cm lg., 5(–8) cm ∅; **Ri.** 17–18; **Rsp.** numerous, to 1 cm lg., radiating, interlacing, snow-white on new growth; **Csp.** scarcely distinguishable, 1(–2), to 2 cm lg., somewhat stouter, brown; **Br.-H.** in the apex, but no soft H.; **Ar.** eventually forming a dense tuft of white wool, this sometimes persisting along the entire length of the St.; **Fl.** crimson; **Tu.** ± straight.—Peru (Loma Desert, near Pachacamac).

L. nanus (Akers) Backbg.
Bo. offsetting freely; **St.** to only 10 cm lg.; **Ri.** 12–14; **Rsp.** and **Csp.** variable in number and length, hardly distinguishable, projecting, brown on new growth; **Fl.** crimson, faintly zygomorphic.—S. Peru (near Chala-Atico).

L. neglectus Ritt.—"Taxon", XIII: 3, 116. 1964.
Bo. resembling L. faustianus, but shorter and more slender; **St.** only 2.3 cm ∅, prostrate; **Sp.** more numerous; **Rsp.** 20–30, 3–8 mm lg., pale yellow or brownish-yellow; **Csp.** 15–20; **Fl.** less zygomorphic, 5–7 cm lg.; **Tu.** less funnelform; **Pet.** only half as long, 1.7–2 cm lg.; **Fil.** ± the same length; **Sti.** shorter, pale yellow.—Peru (E. of Lima, near Santa Clara) (FR 135).
  v. **chimbotensis** Ritt. l. c.: **Ar.** 3–5 mm apart; **Sp.** somewhat fewer, young Sp. very variable: brownish-red or pale yellow; **Csp.** always a deeper dark brown; **S.** smaller, slightly glossy (matt in the type).—Peru (coastal mountains, near Chimbote) (FR 277A).

L. otuscensis Ritt., not described: probably identical with L. sulcifer Rauh & Backbg.

L. pachycladus Rauh & Backbg.
Bo. sometimes prostrate, St.-tips directed upwards; **St.** 2(–2.5) m lg., to 10 cm ⌀; **Ri.** 10(–12), constricted between the Ar., with a V-notch; **Rsp.** 8–12, to c. 1.5 cm lg., very stout, at first yellowish-brown and darker below, later grey-pruinose, brown-tipped; **Csp.** 1, to 7 cm lg., very stout, leather-coloured at first, transversely ribbed, becoming grey; **Fl.** and **Fr.** not known.—Central Peru (Cañete valley).

L. parvitessellatus Ritt., not described: appears to be close to L. sulcifer Rauh & Backbg., or its v. longispinus.

L. peculiaris Rauh & Backbg.
Bo. sometimes prostrate; **St.** to 80 cm lg., to 5 cm ⌀; **Ri.** 17(–18); **Ar.** very small; **Rsp.** numerous, to 5 mm lg., bristly fine, yellowish-brown at first, interlacing; **Csp.** 1–2(–4), c. 2 cm lg., (longest one to 3.5 cm lg.), yellowish-brown at first, directed obliquely downwards or upwards; **Fl.** to 8 cm lg., c. 2 cm ⌀, ± rotate, crimson to carmine; **Tu.** only 5 mm ⌀, crimson.—S. Peru (Pisco valley).

L. piscoensis Rauh & Backbg.
Bo. sometimes prostrate, branching from the base; **St.** to 1 m lg., to 8 cm ⌀; **Ri.** 10–12, transversely furrowed; **Rsp.** to c. 15, 1–1.5 cm lg., sometimes very stout, they and the Csp. yellowish-brown above at first, pale yellow below, becoming yellowish-brownish; **Csp.** mostly 1(–4), very stout, to 5 cm lg., later directed downwards; **Ar.** light brown at first, 1–1.2 cm apart, then grey, fairly large, the upper (flower-bearing) part brown; **Fl.** strongly zygomorphic, to 9.5 cm lg., 3.5 cm ⌀; **Ov.** and lower **Tu.** green with white H., H. brown in the upper part of the Tu.; **Pet.** and recurved **Sep.** apiculate, light yellowish to pure red, especially on the underside, or as a M.-line with a crimson tint; **An.** and **Fil.** carmine-violet, the latter with short H. below; **style** pale pink, projecting for 2 cm; **Sti.** capitately united, red; **Fr.** ?—Peru (Pisco and Cañete valleys). (Fig. 206.)
Rauh did not see the Fl. when fully expanded, hence his length of 6 cm; he referred the spec. to Borzicactus because of the short H. at the base of the Fil.; but this feature has also been observed in several spec. of Haageocereus. The diagnostic feature here is the open funnel-shape of the Per.

L. pullatus Rauh & Backbg.
Bo. ± decumbent; **St.** to 50 cm lg., 3–5 cm ⌀; **Ri.** c. 18; **Rsp.** c. 20, to 7(–10) mm lg., thin, horn-coloured, interlacing; **Csp.** 1–4, 1–2 longest ones to 2.5 cm lg., directed upwards, brownish, ± interlacing in the crown, ± mingled with H., dark brown, soon becoming black, lighter below; **Fl.** crimson; **Tu.** 4 cm lg.—Peru (desert, N. of Lima).
　v. **brevispinus** Rauh & Backbg.: **Csp.** shorter, less interlacing in the crown, sometimes absent (Rauh);
　v. **fulviceps** Rauh & Backbg.: **Csp.** longer, ± greenish-yellow; crown more strongly ochre-coloured.

L. rhodoflorus Akers(?), n.nud., is possibly identical with L. gracilispinus Rauh & Backbg.

L.(?) riomajensis Rauh & Backbg.
Bo. little branching; **St.** to 50 cm lg., to 3(–5) cm ⌀, with noticeably dense rigid Sp.; **Ri.** to 17; **Rsp.** numerous, very stiff, pungent, to 1 cm lg.; **Csp.** **(main Sp.)** only to 1.5 cm lg., directed obliquely downwards; **Sp.** floury greyish-yellow to reddish-grey, tipped violet-black; **Fl.** not known.—S. Peru (Rio Majes valley).

L. sextonianus (Backbg.) Backbg.
Bo. prostrate, with a woody underground section; **St.** (in cultivation) to 1.5 m lg., to 3 cm ⌀, branching from low on the sides; **Ri.** c. 13; **Ar.** very small, crowded; **Rsp.** to 30, 0.5 cm lg., very thin, radiating, pinkish to yellowish, grey or brown; **Csp.** scarcely differentiated, 1–2, to 3 cm lg., the longest ones always on the outside of the St.-curvature, directed obliquely downwards, grey, dark brown in the crown; **Fl.** c. 5–6 cm lg., red; **Tu.** very slender; **Fr.** green.—Peru (above Mollendo).

L. splendens (Akers) Backbg.
Bo. erect to prostrate; **St.** c. 3 cm ⌀; **Ri.** c. 12–14; **Rsp.** to c. 14, thin; **Csp.** 1–4, stouter, 1 longer Sp. brownish, porrect, erect in the crown; **Fl.** red; **Tu.** stouter.—Peru (locality not known).

L. sulcifer Rauh & Backbg.
Bo. prostrate and arching upwards; **St.** 1–2 m lg., to 8 cm ⌀; **Ri.** c. 8, broken into elongated hexagonal Tub.; **Ar.** surmounted by a longitudinal furrow, gradually becoming larger, with thicker yellowish-brown felt when flowering is reached; **Rsp.** to 10, 5–9 mm lg., light to dark brown; **Csp.** 1–4 (cruciform if 4), 2.5–4 cm lg., stout, yellowish to darker; **Fl.** zygomorphic, 4 cm ⌀, vivid crimson to carmine; (unripe) **Fr.** c. 1 cm lg.—Peru (Rio Fortaleza).
　v. **longispinus** Rauh & Backbg.: differentiated from the variable type by the **Tub.** having equal sides (not oblong): **Csp.** mostly longer.

Machaerocereus Br. & R. (143)

Cerei of creeping habit, to densely shrubby and squarrose, the spination in part very fierce, the central spine ± dagger-like, as indicated by the generic name. The pink to white flowers have a slender tube and are believed to be nocturnal but they remain open throughout part of the following day. The tube and ovary show felt in the scale-axils and later develop spines in the lower part. The spherical edible fruit is also at first covered with spines but these drop at maturity. Seeds black.— Distribution: Mexico (Baja California and some of the offshore islands; Sonora?).

M. eruca (Brand.) Br. & R. (T.)
Bo. prostrate and rooting, with the tip ascending, **St.** thick, densely spiny, little branching, 1–3 m lg., 4–8 cm ∅; **Ri.** c. 12; **Ar.** large; **Sp.** c. 20, unequal, pale grey to white, outer ones subulate, inner ones stouter, flat, especially the one dagger-like backwardly directed Csp. 3 cm lg. which is keeled below; **Fl.** 10–14 cm lg., 4–6 cm ∅, white, delicate pink below; **Ov.** very spiny; **Fr.** 4 cm lg., scarlet.— Mexico (Baja California, Magdalena Is.). (Fig. 207.) [Must be grown prostrate in cultivation.]

M. gummosus (Eng.) Br. & R.
Bo. branching squarrosely from the base, or ± erect and bushy; **St.** to 1 m lg., 4–6 cm ∅; **Ri.** 8(–9); **Rsp.** 8–12, to 1 cm lg.; **Csp.** 3–6, flattened, one lower Sp. backwardly directed, to 4 cm lg., but not as stoutly dagger-like as in M. eruca; **Sp.** eventually black; **Fl.** 10–14 cm lg., purple outside (acc. Diguet, white to pink inside); **Fr.** 6–8 cm lg., ± reddish-green.

Maihuenia Phil. (3)

The species of this genus form rounded cushions, these flatter in one species only, the ± cylindric shoots bearing longer-persisting small leaves which are cylindric or ± ovoid; the flowers are fairly large, white to ± yellow or red; floral insertion remains to be clarified in some species. The seeds, as far as known, are black and glossy.— Distribution: Cordilleras of more S. Chile at higher altitudes, and the SW. Andean regions of Argentina. [Slow-growing.]

M. albolanata Ritt. and v. viridulispina Ritt.: not described, or only names.

M. brachydelphys (K. Sch.) K. Sch.
Bo. forming mats; **St.-Seg.** very short, rarely over 2 cm lg., to 1 cm ∅, cylindric; **L.** 2–3 cm lg., acute; **Sp.** mostly only 1, 3 cm lg. and more, terete, stiff,

pungent, yellow, brownish below; **Fl.** to 3.5 cm lg., 5 cm ∅, red, from ± terminal **Ar.**, with woolly felt; **Fr.** not known.—Frontier, Chile and Argentina (Paso Cruz).

M. patagonica (Phil.) Speg. non sensu Br. & R.
Bo. forming cushions, **St.** 20–30 cm h., densely branching; **Seg.** c. 2.8 cm lg., to c. 1.2 cm ∅, ± cylindric; **L.** 2–4 mm lg., ovoid; **Sp.** 3, to 1 cm lg., the middle one to 4 cm lg., all Sp. light flesh-coloured, becoming grey; **Fl.** 3.5–4 cm ∅, yellowish-white, "at the branch-tip"; **Fr.** c. 2 cm ∅, spherical.—Patagonia.

M. patagonica sensu Br. & R.: **Maihuenia philippii** (Web.) Web.

M. phillippii (Web.) Web.
Bo. forming very flat groups; **Seg.** to 1.5 cm ∅, ± spherical; **L.** subulate; young **Ar.** with white H.; longest **Sp.** 1–1.5 cm lg., flexible, white; **Fl.** c. 3 cm lg., white, terminal; **Fr.** c. 1 cm lg.—Chile (Cordillera of Linares).

M. poeppigii (Otto) Web. non Speg. (T.)
Bo. forming broad dense colonies to 1 m across; **Seg.** 6 cm lg., 1.5 cm ∅, cylindric; **L.** 4–6 mm lg., cylindric; **Sp.** 3, 2 of these very short, 1 to 2 cm lg., yellowish; **Fl.** yellow, terminal (Br. & R.), sessile to pedunculate (Vaupel); **Fr.** 4–5 cm lg., 2–3 cm ∅.— Chile (Chillan, Cordillera of Talca).

M. poeppigii Speg. non (Otto) Web.: **Maihuenia valentinii** Speg.

M. tehuelches Speg.: **Maihuenia patagonica** (Phil.) Speg. non sensu Br. & R.

M. valentinii Speg.
Bo. forming dense colonies 10–25 cm h.; **Seg.** 1–3.5 cm lg., ± clavate; **L.** ovoid, small; **Sp.** 3, creamy at first, then reddish-grey; **Csp.** 1, longest, 2–6 cm lg.; **Fl.** 2 cm ∅, white to light yellow, subapical; **Fr.** ?—Argentina (Chubut). (Fig. 208.)

Maihueniopsis Speg. (12)

Plants resembling Tephrocactus, not since recollected, with the reputedly unique character of the shoots being united at the base. One species only.—Distribution: N. Argentina (Jujuy, puna near Santa Catalina) (?).

M. leptoclada Ritt. (FR 1050): no description available.

M. molfinoi Speg. (T.)

Bo. forming dense groups; **Seg.** ovoid to spherical, c. 1–1.5 cm lg. and ∅, light green, united at the base; **Ar.** 5–6 on the free part of the St., white-felty; **Glo.** in the lower Ar.; **Sp.** only in the 2 upper Ar., one, stiffer and curving slightly outwards, 1.5–2.5 cm lg., ashy-brown, dark-tipped; **Fl.** c. 3 cm lg., sulphur-yellow with a satiny sheen; **Fr.** not known.—For distribution, see above. (Fig. 209.)

Malacocarpus SD. (109) = **Wigginsia** D. M. Port.* (see also under the latter)

Plants mostly solitary, broadly spherical at first, later spherical but rarely elongated, with a woolly crown. The flowers are short, in various shades of yellow, and their tubes are strongly woolly. The styles or stigmas are red. The soft berry-like fruits push through the apical wool at maturity.— Distribution: Brazil, Uruguay, Argentina, with an isolated distribution in Colombia. [(R).; since the seedlings grow slowly, it is advantageous to graft them.]
Since Malacocarpus sensu Br. & R. was a collective genus, combinations had been made under that generic name; but since the restoration of the genus to its original narrower sense, the specific names affected will now be found under the following genera: Austrocactus, Brasilicactus, Eriocactus, Frailea, Horridocactus, Islaya, Neochilenia, Noto-cactus, Parodia, Pyrrhocactus.
Details cannot be given here of the name-changes within these genera. Where necessary, the specific name must be looked up under these genera. The species given below are those where the essential characters conform to those of the generic de-scription or, in the case of undescribed plants, where they are clearly referable here.

M. aciculatus SD.: **Wigginsia erinacea** (Haw.) D. M. Port.

M. acuatus SD.: **Wigginsia tephracantha** (Lk. & O.) D. M. Port.

---

* In "Taxon" XIII: 210, 1964 Salm-Dyck's name, which had been in use for 115 years, was rejected (as being a homonym of Malacocarpus Fisch. & Mey. [1843], a genus within Zygophyllaceae) as also was Byles's proposal that the earlier and commonly used name should be retained as a nom. cons. (Dict. of Gen. & Subg. Cactac., 19. 1957). D. M. Porter replaced it (l. c.) by the name Wigginsia. In the present work no re-arrangement of the text could be made at that stage; in any case Malacocarpus is still the name most widely used. All that could be done here was to insert the valid names, and it is hoped this will be a useful guide for most users of the Lexicon.

M. arechavaletai (K. Sch. ex Speg.) Berg.— **Wigginsia arechavaletai** (K. Sch. ex Speg.) D. M. Port., l. c., 211
Bo. ± spherical, dark green; **Ri.** 13–21, tuber-culate; **Rsp.** c. 9 (or more), to 2 cm lg., spreading, light-coloured, red below, tipped black; **Csp.** 1(–4), c. 2 cm lg., stout, straight, pointing downwards, dark brown to black; **Fl.** 3–4 cm lg., to 5 cm ∅, golden-yellow; **Fr.** to 2 cm lg., 5 mm ∅, white.— Uruguay (near Maldonado); acc. Spegazzini, also in adjacent parts of Argentina.

M. bezrucii Frič: only a name.

M. callispinus Y. Ito: **Wigginsia arechavaletai** (K. Sch. ex Speg.) D. M. Port.

M. corynodes (O. ex Pfeiff.) SD. (T)—**Wigginsia corynodes** (O. ex Pfeiff.) D. M. Port., l. c. 211.
Bo. spherical to cylindric, to 20 cm h., 10 cm ∅ (acc. K. Sch., to 60 cm h., 30 cm ∅!), dark green; **Ri.** 13–16, with shallow transverse indentations; **Rsp.** 7–12, bottom 3 to 2 cm lg., dull yellowish, sometimes ringed; **Csp.** 0–1, rather longer; **Fl.** to 5 cm lg. and ∅, canary-yellow; **Fr.** oblong, dirty red.—S. Brazil, Uruguay, Argentina.

M. corynodes v. erinaceus SD.: **Wigginsia erinacea** (Haw.) D. M. Port.

M. courantii SD.: **Wigginsia tephracantha** (Lk. & O.) D. M. Port.

M. erinaceus (Haw.) Lem. ex Först.—**Wigginsia erinacea** (Haw.) D. M. Port., l. c., 210.
Bo. ± spherical, c. 15 cm h. and ∅, dark green; **Ri.** 15–20, spiralled, weakly transversely indented; **Tub.** compressed above and below; **Rsp.** 6–8, 1 cm lg., upper ones shorter, lower ones twice as long; **Csp.** 1, rather longer, ± pressed downwards, brown; **Fl.** to 5 cm lg., to 7 cm ∅, canary-yellow.— S. Brazil, Uruguay, Argentina.
M. erinaceus v. elatior (Monv.) Y. Ito: a name referable here.

M. fricii (Ar.) Berg.—**Wigginsia fricii** (Ar.) D. M. Port., l. c. 210.
Bo. depressed-spherical, c. 4 cm h., 6 cm ∅, glossy, light green; **Ri.** c. 20, somewhat wavy; **Rsp.** 6–7, unequal, bent, appressed, flexible, likewise the minute **Csp.** if present; **Fl.** c. 3 cm lg., yellowish.— Uruguay.

M. hennisii hort. referable, as a name, to **Wigginsia vorwerkiana** (Werd.) D. M. Port.

M. kovaricii (Frič) Berg.—**Wigginsia kovaricii**

(Frič) Backbg. n.comb. (Malacocarpus kovaricii Frič in Berger, Kākteen, 206. 1929).
Bo. flattened-spherical, dark green; **Ri.** 16, acute; **Ar.** with white wool; **Sp.** c. 10, reddish-brown; **Csp.** 1, somewhat longer.—Uruguay?

M. langsdorfii (Lehm.) Br. & R.—**Wigginsia langsdorfii** (Lehm.) D. M. Port., l. c., 211.
Bo. elongated-spherical, c. 10 cm h. and ∅ (to 40 cm h.?) leaden-grey; **crown** strongly white-woolly; **Ri.** 17, very tuberculate; **Rsp.** c. 6; **Csp.** 1(–4), erect at first, later directed obliquely downwards; **Sp.** thin but stiff, horn-coloured; **Fl.** c. 5 cm lg., only c. 1.5–2 cm ∅, yellow; **Sti.** purple.—Central and S. Brazil.

M. leucocarpus (Ar.) Backbg.—**Wigginsia leucocarpa** (Ar.) D. M. Port., l.c., 211.
Bo. eventually ± elongated-spherical, leaden-grey; **Ri.** c. 20; **Sp.** c. 5, ± equal, spreading; **Fl.** not very large; **Fr.** white.—Uruguay.

M. macrocanthus (Ar.) Hert.—**Wigginsia macrocantha** (Ar.) D. M. Port., l. c., 210.
Bo. ± hemispherical to spherical, light green; **Ri.** 12–14; **Rsp.** 7, 3 lower ones to 3 cm lg., upper ones shorter; **Csp.** 1, curving ± upwards; **Fl.** relatively large, pale yellow; **Sti.** blackish-red.—Uruguay. (Fig. 210.)

M. macrogonus (Ar.) Hert.—**Wigginsia macrogona** (Ar.) D. M. Port., l. c., 210.
Bo. broader than high, 15(–20) cm ∅, dark green; **Ri.** 12–21, fairly prominent and broad; **Rsp.** 9, the 3 lower ones longer; **Csp.** 0; **Fl.** medium-sized.—Uruguay.

M. martinii Lab. ex Rümpl.: **Wigginsia sessiliflora** v. **martinii** (Lab. ex Rümpl.) D. M. Port.

M. orthacanthus (Lk. & O.) Hert.—**Wigginsia orthacantha** (Lk. & O.) Backbg. n.comb. (Malacocarpus orthacanthus (Lk. & O.) Hert., Cactus, 92. 1954).
Bo. spherical, c. 7 cm h. and ∅, bluish-green; **Ri.** 18, laterally compressed, with distinct prominences; **Rsp.** 7, c. 1.2 cm lg., 1 longest Sp. c. 2 cm lg.; **Csp.** 1, straight, stout.—Uruguay.
Perhaps a variety of the variable Wigginsia tephracantha (Lk. & O.) D. M. Port.?

M. pauciareolatus (Ar.) Berg.: **Wigginsia sessiliflora** v. **pauciareolata** (Ar.) Backbg.

M. polyacanthus SD.: **Wigginsia langsdorfii** (Lehm.) D. M. Port.

M. rubricostatus Frič, not described:

Ri. somewhat wavy; **Rsp.** c. 5 (and more); **Csp.** 1, projecting; **Fl.** medium-sized, intense yellow; **Sti.** brownish-red.
More likely a form (or variety?) of Malacocarpus tephracanthus (Lk. & O.) K. Sch.

M. sellowii K. Sch. (sellowianus SD.): Malacocarpus tephracanthus (Lk. & O.) K. Sch.—**Wigginsia tephracantha** (Lk. & O.) D. M. Port., l. c., 210.

M. sessiliflorus (Mackie) Backbg.—**Wigginsia sessiliflora** (Mackie) D. M. Port., l. c., 210. (Porter wrote it as "sessiflora").
Bo. flattened-spherical, 20 cm ∅, dark to greyish-green; **Ri.** fewer at first, later to 30, thickened around the Ar.; **Sp.** only (2–)3–4 at first, later to 5, to 2 cm lg., 3 lower ones often ± bent, horn-coloured to white; **Csp.** mostly 0, rarely 1; **Fl.** relatively small.—Uruguay, Argentina.
v. **martinii** (Lab. ex Rümpl.) D. M. Port., l. c. 210: **Bo.** small, greyish-green; **Ri.** only 12; **Rsp.** 4–5, 3 lower ones longer; **Csp.** 0; **Fl.** only c. 2 cm ∅, sulphur-yellow, early;
v. **pauciareolata** (Ar.) Backbg. n.comb. (Malacocarpus pauciareolatus (Ar.) Berger, Kakteen, 207. 1929): **Ri.** 15–21; **Ar.** only 2 per Ri.; **Sp.** 4, 3 directed downwards, 1 upwards, subulate, pungent; **Fl.** golden-yellow.—Uruguay.

M. stegmannii Backbg.—**Wigginsia stegmannii** (Backbg.) D. M. Port., l. c., 211.
Bo. flattened-spherical, then hemispherical, greyish-green; **Ri.** 17, spiralled; **Rsp.** c. 9, the lowest ones longest, c. 1 cm lg., upper ones thin, bent; **Csp.** 0–1, shorter; **Fl.** only c. 1.5 cm ∅, yellow; **Tu.** with darker wool and Br.—Argentina (Sierra Lihuel Calel).

M. tephracanthus (Lk. & O.) K. Sch.—**Wigginsia tephracantha** (Lk. & O.) D. M. Port., l. c., 210.
Bo. ± hemispherical, to 15 cm h. and ∅, ± greyish-green; **crown** with much woolly felt; **Ri.** 16–18(–20 and more), acute, somewhat wider above the Ar.; **Rsp.** 5–7, the 2–4 uppers to 1.5 cm lg., the 3 lower ones to 2.5 cm lg., stouter; **Csp.** often only later, 1, straight or bent downwards, to 2 cm lg.; **Sp.** all horn-coloured; **Fl.** c. 4.5 cm lg., often rather broader, canary-yellow. A very variable spec.—S. Brazil, Uruguay, Argentina.
v. **courantii** (SD.) Backbg. n.comb. (Malacocarpus tephracanthus v. courantii (SD.) Backbg., Die Cact. III: 1619. 1959): **Bo.** glossy, dark green; **Ri.** 19–21; **Rsp.** 7–9; **Csp.** 1; **Fl.** larger, pale yellow; **Sti.** blackish-red;
v. **depressa** (Speg.) D. M. Port.: lower, to 5 cm h., to 7 cm ∅, ± top-shaped, matt green; **Ri.** 9–17; **Rsp.** often only 3, only to 5 mm lg., stouter, pale.

252

Some of the varieties placed here are in fact other spec.; or else their names, where considered valid, must be sought under the other spec. There is a seedling-form which is suffused ± deep red.

M. tetracanthus R. Mey.: **Wigginsia sessiliflora** (Mackie) D. M. Port.

M. turbinatus (Ar.) Hert.—**Wigginsia turbinata** (Ar.) D. M. Port., l. c., 211.
Bo. flat, ± disc-shaped or passing over into the taproot to form ± a top-shape, dark green; **Ri.** 12–20 (or more), low; **Rsp.** 5–10; **Csp.** 0–1; **Sp.** only moderately lg.; **Fl.** over 3 cm ⌀, opening widely.—Uruguay.

M. vorwerkianus (Werd.) Backbg.—**Wigginsia vorwerkiana** (Werd.) D. M. Port., l. c., 210.
Bo. flattened-spherical, to 5 cm h., to 9 cm ⌀, slightly glossy, vivid green; **Ri.** c. 20, ± wavy, somewhat spiralled; **Rsp.** 5–6, projecting ± horizontally, subulate, dirty yellowish-white; **Csp.** 0–1, same length as the Rsp., later mostly curving upwards, bent, stouter; **Fl.** c. 2 cm ⌀ (and more), yellow.—Colombia (near Sogamoso).

Mamillopsis (Morr.) Web. (232)
See page 299.

Mammillaria Haw. (226)

Plants which may be spherical to elongated, simple or caespitose, with or without milky sap; those with milky sap either visibly milky externally if damaged during the growing period, or only inside and less strongly so. Instead of ribs the plants have tubercles which are variable in form, and arranged in intersecting spirals which are, in general, a diagnostic character of the relative species. The flowers are never apical, but appear in a ring from the axils of the previous year's growth. The axils (depressions between the tubercles) can be completely glabrous, or they can have wool of variable length, sometimes also bristles or ± long hairs; the areoles (seat of the spine-clusters on the tubercles) usually have visible felt or ± wool, at least at first, but mostly later become glabrous. In these cases the crown is ± woolly as a result of the felt or wool in axils and areoles; in a number of species the axillary wool develops more strongly in the flowering zone, so that rings of wool appear. The flowers are variable in size but mostly small, colours ranging from white to yellowish to red, and in some species, particularly among those with hooked spines, the flowers are quite large. In plants with hooked spines where the flesh is ± soft (these plants often being ± hairy), the flowers are normally small. In other hook-spined species there occur flowers more bellshaped to funnelform, which are variable in size. Hooked spines occur in each of the three Sections, irrespective of sap-type. The tube and ovary are glabrous and virtually lacking in scales. When the flower has faded the fruit is not initially visible, but it appears from the axil at maturity, i.e. it is pushed outwards. In colour, the fruits can be green to red or even a ± reddish-green, or sometimes ± coral-red. The seed-testa is smooth to pitted or minutely tuberculate, ± dull to glossy, yellowish to black, while size and shape are equally variable. The spines also exhibit a wide range of variation in number and type: they may be straight, ± curving or sometimes hooked, very fine to stout, smooth, rough or finely hairy, sometimes they are bristly and soft, or hair-like and even feathery. In the species here regarded as referable to this genus, the tubercles are never basally connected; the flowers never have a longer tube, and the berry-fruits do not split or dehisce basally. The genus is thus restricted here to species showing the above very uniform characters; any other species belong to other genera, in accordance with proposals already made by various authors at different times. Failing segregation of this type Mammillaria would lose any cohesion, because now—even restricting the genus to the uniform diagnostic characters described—over 350 known and distinguishable species have been described, with 98 varieties; in addition to these there are more than 80 plants which are inadequately described and therefore not listed here, since they can no longer be clarified or identified with any known species. Even with a limitation of this kind, Mammillaria remains by far the largest genus of the Cactaceae. According to the Code of Nomenclature, the generic name should be written as "Mammillaria".* As Salm-Dyck and Schumann have already shown, this spelling is incorrect—i.e. there is no basis for altering the spelling, since the Latin diminutive of "mamma" should correctly be "mamilla", and the genus Mamillopsis follows this, as does the Subcategory "Mamillariae". The Code gives Mammillaria mamillaris as a synonym of the type-species Mamillaria simplex with duality of spelling. It is high time that uniformity was insisted on, as is done here and by the majority of German authors.

---

* Translator's note: Backeberg himself always uses "Mamillaria"—but while his usage is common in the German-speaking countries, American and British practice requires "Mammillaria", as Haworth wrote it.

As a guide to the characters of the different groups, the figures after the specific names refer to the following Key. The first figure is that of the Section; after that, and separated by a colon, there is the Subsection, where appropriate; the third figure indicates the Series, and separated from that by a colon is the Subseries. The following example illustrates the procedure:—

$(3:1, 1:2)$ Section 3—Watery sap (Sect. Hydrochylus K. Sch.)
Subsection 1: Parviflorae Backbg. (small-flowered)
Series 1: Rectispinae Backbg. (straight-spined)
Subseries 2: Candidae K. Sch. (whitish species)

Summary of the Groups of Species:—

With milky sap
  Milking immediately upon injury . . . . Sect. 1: Galactochylus K. Sch.
    Plants ± spherical
      Spines all straight
        Spines white or noticeably light (tips sometimes
            coloured)
          Axils with or without bristles, with wool. . . . Ser. 1: **Leucocephalae** Lem.
        Spines not all white or light
          Axils without bristles, with or without wool
            Tubercles often larger, sometimes ± angular Ser. 2: **Macrothelae** SD.
          Axils with bristles, sometimes sparse
            Tubercles ± angular to ± conical . . . . Ser. 3: **Polyedrae** Pfeiff.
      Spines: 1 central hooked
        Axils only woolly
          Tubercles ± angular . . . . Ser. 4: **Uncinatae** Vpl.
    Plants cylindric
      Spines: 1 central straight to hooked, sometimes
          bristly, not hooked . . . . Ser. 5: **Rossianae** Backbg.
  Not immediately clearly milking upon injury   . . . . Sect. 2: Subhydrochylus Backbg.
    Plants not long-cylindric
      Spines all straight, white, centrals in part yellow or
          brownish . . . . Ser. 1: **Elegantes** K. Sch.
      Spines (centrals) bent or (mostly) hooked . . . . Ser. 2: **Ancistrophorae** Backbg.
    Plants long-cylindric in age
      Spines (centrals) straight or hooked . . . . . . Ser. 3: **Guerrerones** Backbg.
With watery sap . . . . Sect. 3: Hydrochylus K. Sch.
  Flowers small, short . . . . Ssect. 1: Parviflorae Backbg.
    Spines all straight . . . . Ser. 1: **Rectispinae** Backbg.
      Plants very slender-cylindric   . . . . Sser. 1: **Leptocladodae** (Lem.)
      Plants not very slender-cylindric
        Spines (radials) white or yellowish, sometimes
            hair-like, feathery or fibrous, very fine . . . Sser. 2: **Candidae** K. Sch.
        Spines not (all) white or light
          Axils without bristles
            Radial spines to max. 25   . . . . Sser. 3: **Amoenae** Backbg.
            Radial spines fine, c. 30   . . . . Sser. 4: **Polyacanthae** (SD.)
          Axils with bristles, at least in age
            Radial spines few to more numerous (to 30),
              spines variously coloured acc. to species
                Bodies sometimes eventually stoutly
                    cylindric . . . . Sser. 5: **Heterochlorae** (SD.)
      Spines with a greater or lesser tendency for a central to
          be bent or hooked, but possibly also
          straight, even on the same plant Ser. 2: **Subcurvispinae** Backbg.
      Spines light, mostly with coloured tips, acicular to

finer, 1 central also stouter, straight to
   hooked . . . .   Sser. 6: **Wuthenauianae** Backbg.
Spines always with 1 hooked central . . . . . .   Ser. 3: **Curvispinae** Backbg.
   Radials usually thin to hair-like
     Bodies rather soft-fleshed . . . .   Sser. 7: **Hamatispinae** Backbg.
Flowers larger or ± bellshaped, or more widely opening   Ssect. 2.: Grandiflorae Backbg.
   Spines straight, none of them hooked . . . . .   Ser. 4: **Rectispinosae** Backbg.
     Bodies with a longer root-section
     Flowers large, opening widely . . . .   Sser. 8: **Napinae** Backbg.
     Spines with at least 1 ± hooked central (this
       sometimes appearing only later) . . .   Ser. 5: **Curvispinosae** Backbg.
       Flowers ± bellshaped to funnelform, in part .
       quite large: fruit sometimes stoutly clavate   Sser. 9: **Ancistracanthae** (K. Sch.)

Distribution: From the S. States of the USA, through Mexico to Guatemala and Honduras, through the West Indies (missing from Guadeloupe southwards) to Venezuela and northern Colombia, also Curaçao. [Most spec. (R), the exceptions being shown individually as (G).— ○. / / /.]

Catalogue of the species

which can now rank as being diagnosed with certainty, i.e. those which have been studied from living material in collections in both the Old World and the New, by the Mexican author, Helia Bravo, the Mammillaria specialists Craig, Shurly and Heinrich, as well as by myself. Those plants which were listed in "Die Cact." Vol. V pp. 3462–91 as "little known species", sometimes with short descriptions, have now been omitted since Craig says that with few exceptions they can probably never now be identified. In a small number of cases this has now been possible. Further, no mention is made here either of those plants which (l. c., pp. 3492–97) were merely listed as "species known only as names", or plants sometimes named as Mammillaria which are now referred to other genera.
The first figure in the brackets after the specific name shows the sap-character. The abbreviation "Isp". (intersecting spirals) explains the arrangement of the ± spiralled rows of tubercles, which intersect as expressed by the figures: 3:5, 5:8, 8:13, 13:21, 21:34, 34:55; it will be noted that apart from 5:8, which is the initial figure, each difference is the sum of the 2 corresponding preceding differences. Anomalous arrangements do sometimes occur. There is also an occasional doubling of the above figures (e.g. in Mammillaria wiesingeri): 6:10, 16:26, where the second set of figures results from the sum of the two previous ones.

M. acanthoplegma Lehm. (2:1)
Bo. spherical to elongated, to 20 cm h., 6 cm ⌀, greyish-green, little offsetting; **Tub.** conical, with light spots; **Isp.** 13:21; **Ax.** moderately woolly, later glabrous; **Rsp.** c. 20(–24), acicular, to thinner, 2–5 mm lg.; **Csp.** 2, directed upwards and downwards, 6–9 mm lg., ± thin-subulate, stiff,

white below, tipped reddish-brown to black; **Fl.** 1.3 cm ⌀, bluish to purplish-red; **Sti.** yellow.—USA (S. Texas, where it was collected by Edelmann).

M. alamensis Craig (3:2, 5:9)
Bo. ± conically tapering, to 4.5 cm h., 4 cm br., dark greyish-green; **Tub.** truncated conical, 5 mm lg. and br.; **Isp.** 5:8; **Ar.** circular, glabrous; **Ax.** naked; **Rsp.** 9, 6 mm lg., fine, smooth, stiff, white, brown-tipped; **Csp.** 1, 9 mm lg., somewhat stouter, hooked, purplish-brown to black; **Fl.** ?; **S.** black, glossy.—Mexico (Sonora, near Alamos).

M. albiarmata Böd. (1:1)
Bo. flattened-spherical, taprooted below, upper part green, to 4 cm ⌀, 1.5 cm h.; **Tub.** pyramidal; **Isp.** 13:21; **Ar.** white to cream; **Ax.** without Br.; **Rsp.** 20–25, 2–5 mm lg., white with a coloured tip; **Csp.** 0; **Fl.** 2 cm lg. and ⌀, creamy-white; **Fr.** pink, 1 cm lg.; **S.** brown.—Mexico (Coahuila, Saltillo). Bödeker at first called this spec. Porfiria coahuilensis v. albiflora Böd., but this was only a provisional name.

M. albicans Berg. (3:1, 1:2)
Bo. becoming elongated, to 20 cm lg., 6 cm ⌀, caespitose; **Ax.** woolly; **Sp.** dense, ± white; **Rsp.** numerous; **Csp.** several, straight, stiff, dark-tipped; **Fl.** ?; **Fr.** clavate, red, to 1.8 cm lg.; **S.** black.— Mexico (Baja California, islands of Sta. Cruz and S. Dieguito).

M. albicoma Böd. (3:1, 1:2)
Bo. caespitose, fairly small, to 5 cm h., 3 cm ⌀, leaf-green; **Tub.** conical; **Isp.** 8:13; **Ax.** white-woolly; **Rsp.** 30–40, to 10 mm lg., hair-like; **Csp.** 1–4, often missing, very short or 4–10 mm lg., white, tipped reddish-brown; **Fl.** 1.5 cm lg., pale greenish-yellow

to white; **Sti.** light greenish-yellow; **Fr.** small, red; **S.** ± darker grey.—Mexico (Tamaulipas).

M. albidula Backbg. (3:1, 1:2)
Bo. oblong, 11 cm h., 6 cm ⌀, greyish-green; **Tub.** 5 mm lg.; **Isp.** 21:34; **Ax.** weakly felty; **Rsp.** c. 16, 3–6 mm lg., white; **Csp.** 0–1, 7 mm lg., yellowish below, brownish above; **Fl.** carmine, bordered whitish; **Pet.** with borders entire; **Fr.** ?—Mexico.

M. albiflora (Werd.) Backbg. (3:2, 4:8) [G.]
Bo. delicate, slender-cylindric, much more robust when grafted, taprooted; **Tub.** very small; **Sp.** very short, over 30, white, very fine, interlacing in all directions; **Fl.** to 3.5 cm ⌀, white; **Pet.** ± revolute; **Sti.** greenish; **Fr.** not known.—Mexico (San Luis Potosi, Querétaro).

M. albilanata Backbg. (3:1, 1:2)
Bo. eventually stoutly cylindric, over 15 cm h., c. 8 cm ⌀, greyish-green, hidden by the Sp.; **Tub.** cylindric-conical above; **Isp.** 13:21; **Ax.** white-haired; **Rsp.** 15–20, 2–4 mm lg., stiff, smooth, chalky-white, ± brownish below; **Csp.** 2(–4), 2–3 mm lg., slender-subulate, white to cream, ± dark-tipped; **Fl.** deep carmine, 7 mm lg.; **Fr.** ± light red; **S.** pale brown.—Mexico (Guerrero, Chilpanzingo).

M. alpina: provisional name for the plant eventually described as **M. kraehenbuehlii**.

M. amoena Hopff. (3:1, 1:3)
Bo. spherical to elongated, to 20 cm h., 12 cm ⌀, bluish milky green; **Tub.** conical-ovoid; **Isp.** 8:12; **Ax.** weakly woolly; **Rsp.** 16–20, 2–5 mm lg., bristly, white; **Csp.** 2, 8–15 mm lg., acicular, at most slightly curving, stiff, yellowish-brown to red; **Fl.** opening widely, 2 cm lg., 1.5 cm ⌀; **Pet.** reddish-brown in the middle, bordered white; **Fr.** red; **S.** brown.—Mexico (Morelos, Cuernavaca; Hidalgo, Pachuca).

M. ancistroides Lem. non Lehm. (3:1, 3:7)
An insufficiently clarified spec.; **Bo.** yellowish-green; **Ax.** naked or weakly woolly; **Rsp.** 30–40, thin, hyaline; **Csp.** 5, the bottom one to 1.4 cm lg., stouter, hooked, the others to 6 mm lg., straight; all **Sp.** stiff, reddish-yellow below, tipped dark violet; **Fl.** not opening widely; **Pet.** with an intenser pink M.-line; **Sti.** white.—Origin? If Lehmann's spec. (1832: Ax. bristly; Rsp. 6–8; the hooked Csp. brown-tipped) proves to have been adequately described, then the plant later described by Lemaire (1839) would have to be renamed.

M. angelensis Craig (3:2, 5:9)
Bo. oblong, 15 cm h., 6 cm ⌀, yellowish to olive-green; **Tub.** conical; **Isp.** 8:13; **Ax.** with wool and Br.; **Rsp.** 16, to 10 mm lg., acicular, white, in part brown-tipped; **Csp.** 3–4, to 14 mm lg., the bottom one hooked, dark purplish-brown, lighter below; **Fl.** ± bellshaped, 2 cm lg., 3 cm ⌀, white; **Fr.** reddish, clavate; **S.** black.—Mexico (Baja California, Los Angeles Bay and Angel de la Guardia Island).

M. applanata Eng. (1:2)
Bo. simple, flattened-spherical, to 5 cm h., 11 cm ⌀, matt green; **Tub.** almost 4-sided; **Isp.** 13:21; **Ax.** glabrous; **Rsp.** 15–20, 5–12 mm lg., whitish, or the lower ones light brown; **Csp.** 1, to 5 mm lg., stiffly acicular, dark brown at first, soon becoming yellowish-brown; **Fl.** to 2.5 cm lg., to 3.5 cm ⌀; **Fr.** to 3.5 cm lg., scarlet; **S.** reddish-brown.—USA (Central and S. Texas).

M. arida Rose (1:2)
Bo. simple, spherical, to 6 cm ⌀, matt greyish-green; **Tub.** rounded, keeled; **Isp.** 8:13(?); **Ax.** weakly woolly; **Rsp.** 15, 6–10 mm lg., thin, stiff, somewhat yellowish, dark-tipped; **Csp.** 4–7, 12–16 mm lg., stiffly acicular, dark brown; **Fl.** 1 cm lg., 2.5 cm ⌀, cream to light greenish-yellow; **Fr.** red, clavate, 1.5 cm lg.; **S.** brown.—Mexico (Baja California, La Paz).

M. armatissima Craig (1:2)
Bo. simple, to 15 cm h., 12 cm ⌀, light green; **Tub.** pyramidal; **Isp.** ?; **Ax.** glabrous; outer 6 **Rsp.** to 2 cm lg., inner 4–6 to 5 mm lg., acicular; **Csp.** 0–1, 1.4 cm lg., stoutly subulate, straight to contorted; **Sp.** cream below, tipped reddish-brown to brown or black; **Fl.** ?; **Fr.** ?—Mexico.

M. armillata K. Brand. (3:2, 5:9)
Bo. cylindric, simple or caespitose, to 30 c h., 5 cm ⌀, bluish-green; **Tub.** conical to cylindric above; **Isp.** 5:8; **Ax.** weakly woolly, with up to 3 Br.; **Rsp.** 9–15, 7–12 mm lg., thin, white to yellowish, tipped dark brown; **Csp.** 1–4, to 2 cm lg., bottom one(s) hooked, yellowish-grey to brown; **Fl.** to 2 cm lg. and ⌀, white to pink; **Fr.** red, clavate, to 3 cm lg.; **S.** black.—Mexico (Baja California, San José del Cabo).

M. atroflorens Backbg. (1:3)
Bo. simple to branching; **St.** to 10 cm lg., 7.5 cm ⌀, dark green; **Tub.** four-sided; **Isp.** 13:21; **Ax.** rather felty, with several Br.; **Rsp.** 8–9, to 5 mm lg., whitish, concolorous or tipped reddish-brown; **Csp.** 4, to 6 mm lg., reddish-brown; **Fl.** small, dark carmine; **Fr.** red, 2 cm lg.; **S.** yellowish.—Mexico.

M. aureiceps Lem. (3:1, 1:5)
Bo. simple, rarely branching, spherical, dark green;

Tub. conical; **Isp.** ?; **Ax.** with white wool and yellow Br.; **Rsp.** to 30 or more, golden-yellow, acicular; **Csp.** 6(–7), to 1.8 cm lg., dark golden-yellow, slender-subulate; **Fl.** dark red(?) or greenish to creamy-white(?); **Fr.** green; **S.** ?—Mexico (Querétaro).

M. aureilanata Backbg. (3:1, 1:2) [grafting recommended]
Bo. simple, dark green, to 7.5 cm h.; **Tub.** cylindric; **Isp.** 8:13; **Ax.** glabrous; **Rsp.** 25–30, hair-like, in several Ser., to 15 mm lg., ± golden-yellow; **Csp.** 0; **Fl.** 3 cm lg., to 1.8 cm ∅, white to pale pink; **Fr.** light pink; **S.** black.—Mexico (San Luis Potosí).
   v. **alba** Backbg.: H. pure white; **Fl.** pink.

M. aureoviridis W. Heinr. (3:1, 3:7)
Bo. caespitose, single heads spherical to oblong, to 7 cm h., 4.5 cm ∅; **R.** fleshy; **Tub.** shortly cylindric; **Isp.** 8:13; **Ax.** somewhat woolly, with occasional yellowish Br.; **Rsp.** c. 20–25, ± yellow, to 8 mm lg., bristly; **Csp.** (3–)4, 9–10 mm lg., the longest one hooked, to 1.3 cm lg., golden-yellow to golden-brown; **Fl.** 2 cm lg., 1.4 cm ∅, glossy, creamy-white; **Fr.** deep pink, clavate, 2.5 cm lg.; **S.** black.—Mexico.

M. auriareolis Tieg. (3:1, 1:5)
Bo. flattened-spherical, dividing dichotomously to form groups, bluish-green, single heads to 6.5 cm h., 8 cm ∅; **Tub.** conical-cylindric above; **Isp.** 13:21; **Ax.** woolly, with long Br.; **Rsp.** 25–40, 3–5 mm lg., white, bristly; **Csp.** 4, 3–6 mm lg., stiffly acicular, straight, golden-yellow below, then white, tipped reddish-brown; **Fl.** ?; **Fr.** light carmine, clavate, 2 cm lg.; **S.** dark yellowish-brown.—Mexico (border between Guanajuato and Querétaro).

M. auricantha Craig (3:1, 1:5)
Bo. simple, cylindric, light green, to 6 cm h., 4 cm ∅; **Tub.** conical-cylindric; **Isp.** 8:13; **Ax.** weakly woolly, with a few Br.; **Rsp.** 12–15, 3–7 mm lg., finely acicular, white to pale yellow; **Csp.** 2(–4), 5–14 mm lg., acicular, the bottom one longest, golden-yellow; **Fl.** ?; **Fr.** ?—Mexico (Chihuahua-Sonora).

M. aurihamata Böd. (3:1, 3:7)
Bo. simple or caespitose, single heads spherical to ovoid, to 6 cm h., 4 cm ∅, leaf-green; **Tub.** shortly cylindric, keeled; **Isp.** 8:13; **Ax.** glabrous, with c. 8 Br. as long as the Tub.; **Rsp.** 15–20, 8 mm lg., ± hair-like, yellowish-white; **Csp.** 4, 1–1.5–2.5 cm lg., the bottom one longest, hooked, whitish-yellow at first, then golden to brownish-yellow; **Fl.** 1.5 cm lg., 1.2 cm ∅, light sulphur-yellow; **Fr.** small, clavate,

red; **S.** dark brown, almost black.—Mexico (San Luis Potosí; Guanajuato).

M. aurisaeta Backbg. (3:1, 1:5)
Bo. simple, c. 3 cm ∅, dull green; **Tub.** slender-conical; **Isp.** 8:13; **Ax.** shortly woolly, with long white hair-like Br.; **Rsp.** c. 8, to 12 mm lg. thickened below, also to 5 hair-fine Br. to 7 mm lg., on the lower Ar.-margin; **Csp.** mostly 0, otherwise 1, 1 cm lg.; all **Sp.** yellow or brown, thickened below, bristly and flexible; **Fl.** 1.4 cm ∅, white, M.-stripe reddish; **Fr.** 2 cm lg., coral-red.—Mexico (Zacatecas).

M. auritricha Craig (1:3)
Bo. simple, ovoid, to 7 cm lg., 5 cm ∅, light green; **Tub.** cylindric; **Isp.** 13:21; **Ax.** with white H. and Br.; **Rsp.** 25, 1–7 mm lg., fine-acicular; **Csp.** 5–7, to 1.2 cm lg., thin-acicular, straight, golden-yellow; **Fl.** ?; **Fr.** ?—Mexico (Chihuahua-Sonora).

M. autlanensis Schwarz is only a name (M. scrippsiana v. autlanensis Craig & Daws.?)

M. avila-camachoi Shurly (1:1)
Bo. simple, depressed-spherical, to 4.5 cm h., 8 cm ∅; **Tub.** 4-sided; **Isp.** 13:21; **Ax.** weakly woolly, with 8–10 white longer Br.; **Rsp.** 30–35, 3–4 mm lg., white, yellowish below; **Csp.** 4, 3–5 mm lg., mostly white, red-tipped, or reddish at first, dark-tipped; **Fl.** ?; **Fr.** ?—Mexico.

M. aylostera Werd.: **Dolicothele beneckei** (Ehrenbg.) Backbg.

M. bachmannii Böd. (1:2)
Bo. spherical, to 18 cm ∅, dark green; **Tub.** conical to hemispherical; **Isp.** 8:13; **Ax.** strongly white-woolly; **Rsp.** 6–10, 2–5 mm lg., hair-like, light brownish, dark-tipped; **Csp.** 4, 3 of these 6 mm lg., the bottom one longest, to 2 cm lg., stoutly acicular, black; **Fl.** 1.7 cm lg., 2 cm ∅, Pet. deep pink, with a lighter border, M.-stripe purplish-pink; **Fr.** carmine above, almost white below, stoutly clavate; **S.** brown.—Mexico.

M. backebergiana Buchenau
Bo. spherical to oblong, intense green, c. 5–6 cm ∅, soon offsetting; **Tub.** slender-cylindric, in Isp. 8:13; **Ax.** weakly white-woolly at first; **Rsp.** 8–10, 1 mm lg., thin, light; **Csp.** 1–2, 1 cm lg., acicular, yellowish-brown, dark-tipped; **Fl.** 1.8 cm lg., to 1.5 cm ∅, carmine.—Mexico. Named for Curt Backeberg.

M. balsasensis Böd.: **Dolicothele nelsonii** (Br. & R.) Backbg.?

M. balsasoides Craig: **Dolicothele balsasoides** (Craig) Backbg.

M. barbata Eng. (3:1, 3:7)
Bo. caespitose, subspherical, single heads 3–5 cm ∅; **Tub.** hemispherical to cylindric; **Isp.** 8:13; **Ax.** naked; **Rsp.** 50–60, 6–8 mm lg., acicular, outer ones white, inner ones yellowish-brown, dark-tipped; **Csp.** 1(–2), to 15 mm lg., stoutly acicular, hairy at first, brownish, hooked; **Fl.** to 2 cm lg. and ∅, pinkish-red, M.-stripe darker; **Fr.** 1.2 cm lg., red; **S.** black.—Mexico (Chihuahua, Cosihui-riachi).

M. barkeri Shurly (3:2, 5:9?)
Bo. simple, somewhat elongated, c. 6 cm h., 5 cm ∅, green; **Tub.** rounded; **Isp.** 8:13; **Ax.** ± glabrous; **Rsp.** 8–10, 5–8 mm lg., white, tipped red or black, then yellowish; **Csp.** 3(–4), the longest one hooked, 1.5 cm lg., the others c. 6 mm lg., thickened below, blackish in the upper half, yellowish-brownish below; **Fl.** ?—Mexico.

M. baumii Böd.: **Dolicothele baumii** (Böd.) Werd & F. Buxb.

M. baxteriana (Gat.) Böd. (1:1)
Bo. simple, flattened-spherical, yellowish-green, to 10 cm ∅; **Tub.** conical; **Isp.** 13:21; **Ax.** shortly woolly; **Rsp.** 8–10, acicular, spreading, white, 1–1.5 cm lg.; **Csp.** mostly 1, 1.5–2 cm lg., acicular, white; all Sp. brown-tipped; **Fl.** yellow; **Fr.** purple, clavate, 2 cm lg.; **S.** brown.—Mexico (Baja California, SE. of La Paz).

M. bella Backbg. (3:1, 2:6)
Bo. simple, later offsetting, to 15 cm lg., 9 cm ∅, deep green; **Tub.** conical; **Ax.** with Br.; **Rsp.** very thin, c. 20, to 8 mm lg.; **Csp.** 4(–6), somewhat stouter, to 2 cm lg., the lowest one longest, to 3 cm lg., sometimes hooked, thickened below; all Sp. hyaline.—Mexico (Guerrero, near Taxco).

M. bellacantha (Craig (1:3)
Bo. depressed-spherical, dark greyish-green, to 8 cm h., 10 cm ∅; **Tub.** 4-sided; **Isp.** 8:13; **Ax.** woolly, with Br. as long as the Tub.; **Rsp.** 15, 3–8 mm lg., bristly, white, dark-tipped; **Csp.** 4, 5–7 mm lg., thinly acicular, straight, stiff, light reddish-brown, darker-tipped, soon horn-coloured; **Fl.** ?; **Fr.** ?—Mexico (Chihuahua-Sonora).

M. bellisiana Craig (1:2)
Bo. simple, sometimes caespitose, light green; **Tub.** rounded-conical; **Isp.** 13:21; **Ax.** woolly at first; **Rsp.** 6–9, the upper ones 3–5 mm lg., acicular, the lower ones 9–15 mm lg., stouter; **Csp.** 1, 1.5 cm lg., stout, straight, thickened below; **Sp.** brownish-

pink, the centrals sometimes also purplish-brown at first, then horn-coloured, dark-tipped; **Fl.** carmine; **Sep.** ciliate; **Fr.** ?—Mexico (Chihuahua-Sonora).

M. beneckei Ehrenbg.: **Dolicothele beneckei** (Ehrenbg.) Backbg.

M. bergii Miqu.: first name for Mamillaria ortegae (Br. & R.) Orc.?

M. blossfeldiana Böd. (3:2, 5:9) [Grafting recommended.]
Bo. mostly simple, rounded, to c. 4 cm ∅, matt leaf-green; **Tub.** shortly conical; **Isp.** 5:8; **Ax.** only weakly woolly; **Rsp.** c. 20, 5–7 mm lg., stiffly acicular, yellowish at first below, dark brown to blackish above; **Csp.** (3–)4, the bottom one longest, to 10 mm lg., hooked, dark brown to black; **Fl.** c. 2 cm ∅, ± bellshaped, Pet. pinkish-carmine, with a darker middle; **Fr.** orange, clavate; **S.** black.—Mexico (Baja California).
v. **grandiflora** hort.: a form with **Fl.** more than twice as large.

M. blossfeldiana v. shurliana Gat.: **Mammillaria shurliana** (Gat.) Gat.

M. bocasana Pos. (3:1, 3:7)
Bo. spherical, offsetting, single heads 4–5 cm ∅, light to dark bluish-green; **Tub.** soft, ± conical; **Isp.** 8:13; **Ax.** naked (or with Br.?); **Rsp.** 25–30, 8–20 mm lg., hair-like; **Csp.** 1(–3), 5–8 mm lg., thin-acicular, hairy, the bottom one hooked, more porrect, yellow to yellowish-brown; **Fl.** 1.6 cm lg., 1.2 cm ∅, Pet. yellowish with a reddish-brown M.-line; **Fr.** slender, red; **S.** dark brown or (?) black.—Mexico (San Luis Potosí).
v. **splendens** Reb.: only a name for a conspicuously white and finely haired form, usually with yellowish hooked **Sp.** There are also forms without any hooked Sp., and others which are strongly caespitose.
The seeds, as far as I know, are brown.

M. bocensis Craig (1:2–3)
Bo. flattened-spherical to elongated, to 8.5 cm ∅, 9 cm h., dark green; **Tub.** pyramidal; **Isp.** 8:13, 13:21; **Ax.** somewhat woolly, occasionally with 1–2 very short Br.; **Rsp.** 6–8, 5–14 mm lg., stoutly acicular, upper ones white, lower ones reddish, dark-tipped; **Csp.** 1, 8–12 mm lg., fairly robust, slightly thickened below, reddish-brown, dark-tipped; **Fl.** 2 cm lg., Pet. greenish-cream, sometimes bordered slightly pink; **Fr.** 2.5 cm lg., red, clavate; **S.** light brown.—Mexico (Sonora, Las Bocas).

M. boedekeriana Quehl (3:1, 3:7)

Bo. spherical to elongated, to 7 cm h. (more if grafted), 4 cm $\emptyset$, dark green; **Tub.** $\pm$ cylindric; **Isp.** 8:13; **Ax.** naked; **Rsp.** 20 and more, 1 cm lg., white (sometimes with a yellowish gloss); **Csp.** 3–4, 8–13 mm lg., acicular, light brown, dark-tipped, the lowest one hooked; **Fl.** to 3 cm lg.; **Pet.** pinkish-brownish in the middle, bordered brownish-yellow; **Fr.** red; **S.** black.—Mexico (San Luis Potosí).

M. bogotensis Werd.: **Mammillaria columbiana** v. **bogotensis** (Werd.) Backbg.

M. bombycina Quehl (3:1, 3:7)
Bo. simple or more strongly caespitose, elongated, light green, to 20 cm h., 6 cm $\emptyset$; **Tub.** conical to cylindric; **Isp.** 11(?):18; **Ax.** very woolly, sometimes with 1 Br.: **Rsp.** 30–40, 2–10 mm lg., white; **Csp.** 2–4, the lower one hooked, 2 cm lg., the other(s) 0.7–1 cm lg., rather thin, white to yellow, tipped $\pm$ brownish-red; **Fl.** 1.5 cm lg. and $\emptyset$, Pet. light carmine, with a darker middle; **Fr.** whitish, clavate; **S.** black, small.—Mexico (Coahuila; San Luis Potosí).

M. bonavitii Schmoll: not validly described; **Bo.** hemispherical, to 6 cm h., 8 cm $\emptyset$; **Tub.** rounded; **Isp.** ?; **sap.** ?; **Ar.** more strongly woolly at first; **Rsp.** c. 16; **Csp.** to 6, longer and stouter; **Fl.** ?; **Fr.** 18 mm lg., white below, greenish above; **S.** light brown.—Mexico (locality?). (Fig., "Die Cact." V, Plate 251, below).

M. boolii Linds. (3:2, 5:9)
Bo. $\pm$ spherical, to 3.5 cm h., 3 cm $\emptyset$, also caespitose; **Tub.** rounded; **Isp.** 5:8; **Ax.** woolly at first, then glabrous; **Rsp.** c. 20, acicular, white, 1.5 cm lg.; **Csp.** 1, subulate, 1.5–2 cm lg., very hooked, yellowish, with a darker tip; **Fr.** to 3 cm lg., orange; **S.** black.—Mexico (Sonora, San Pedro Bay).

M. brandegeei (Coult.) Brand. (1:3)
Bo. spherical to cylindric, dark green, to 9 cm $\emptyset$, later also caespitose; **Tub.** acutely 4-angled, conical above; **Isp.** 13:21; **Ax.** woolly, with occasional white Br.; **Rsp.** 8–10 and more, 7–10 mm lg., thin-acicular, whitish, tipped yellowish-brown or darker; **Csp.** 2–3–4, to 2 cm lg., stiff, $\pm$ straight, reddish-brown below, darker above; **Fl.** 8 mm lg., greenish-yellow, M.-line red; **Fr.** light red; **S.** brown.—Mexico (Baja California, San Jorge).

v. **gabbii** (Coult.) Craig: **Tub.** cylindric; **Isp.** 8:13; **Rsp.** to 16, shorter; **Csp.** mostly 1; **Fl.** small, yellowish-red.—Mexico (Baja California, San Ignacio);

v. **magdalenensis** Schwarz: not validly described; reputedly distinguished by **Csp.** 1–2, to 2.4 cm

lg., lighter below; **Fl.** to 11 mm lg., 1.5 cm br. (Baja California, Magdalena).

M. brauneana Böd. (1:3)
Bo. mostly simple, later stoutly clavate, greyish-green, to 8 cm $\emptyset$; **Tub.** broadly pyramidal; **Isp.** 21:34; **Ax.** white-woolly, with contorted white Br.; **Rsp.** 25–30, c. 5 mm lg., white, hair-like; **Csp.** 2–4, 5–7 mm lg., $\pm$ subulate, reddish, black-tipped, later horn-coloured; **Fl.** 1.3 cm lg., violet-red; **Fr.** c. 1.2 cm lg., carmine; **S.** dark brown.—Mexico (Tamaulipas, Jaumave).

M. bravoae Craig (1:3)
Bo. spherical, mostly simple, glossy, light grass-green, to 6.5 cm h. and $\emptyset$; **Tub.** conical, keeled below; **Isp.** 13:21; **Ax.** with wool and Br.; **Rsp.** 28–30, 4–7 mm lg., acicular, white; **Csp.** 2, 6–8 mm lg., thin-subulate, straight, cream to light brownish-pink, blackish above; **Fl.** 1 cm lg. and $\emptyset$, Pet. deep pink, M.-stripe darker; **Fr.** carmine, 1.5 cm lg.; **S.** light brown.—Mexico (Guanajuato, Rio Blanco).

M. bucareliensis Craig (1:2)
Bo. flattened-spherical, bluish to greyish-green, 5 cm h., 9 cm $\emptyset$; **Tub.** acutely 4-sided; **Isp.** 8:13, 13:21; **Ax.** white-woolly; **Rsp.** 3–5 (also 0), under 1 mm or to 5 mm lg., thin, whitish, brown-tipped; **Csp.** 2–4, 0.5–4 cm lg., acicular to subulate, stiff, light brown, black-tipped; **Fl.** 1.5 cm lg., 1.8 cm $\emptyset$, deep pink to purple; **Fr.** carmine, 1.5 cm lg.; **S.** light brown.—Mexico (Guanajuato, Bucarel).

v. **bicornuta** Schmoll: **Fl.** pale cream inside, M.-stripe pale green; **Sep.** entire (type: serriculate).—Mexico (Bucarel.)

M. buchenauii Backbg. (3:1, 1:3)—Descr. Cact. Nov. III:8, 1963.
Bo. spherical to oblong, branching freely, dichotomously, to over 30 heads, single heads to 5 cm $\emptyset$, groups to c. 22 cm $\emptyset$, leaf-green; **Tub.** slender, conical, 2–4 mm h., sap watery; **Isp.** 13:21; **Ax.** woolly, weak at first, flowering zone with dense white wool; **Ar.** glabrous; **Rsp.** to c. 30, to little over 1 mm lg.; **Csp.** (2–4–)5–6, scarcely longer than the Rsp.; all **Sp.** hyaline, minute but $\pm$ subulate, especially the Csp., these in particular being brown below; **Fl.** small, light reddish, 3–4 mm $\emptyset$; **Fr.** carmine, slender-clavate, c. 11 mm lg., to 3 mm $\emptyset$, with Fl. remains; **S.** light brown, spherical, only 0.5 mm lg.—Mexico (borders Puebla-Oaxaca, road Tehuacan-Oaxaca, in the upper part of W. cliff-faces). Craig's type-locality for M. crucigera may refer to the above spec.
In "Die Cact.", VI:3895 I gave the provisional name: M. falsicrucigera ("false M. crucigera") as well as the diagnostic characters. In the meantime I

have learnt the identity of the discoverer, for whom I have now been able to name the spec. (Fig. 211.) [Haage adds: Dr. Lau considers this name (M. buchenauii) cannot be upheld since the plant is indistinguishable from M. crucigera.]

M. bullardiana (Gat.) Böd. (3:2, 5:9)
Bo. cylindric, to c. 12 cm lg., 4 cm ∅, quite freely offsetting, bluish to greyish-green; **Tub.** conical; **Isp.** ?; **Ax.** weakly woolly; **Rsp.** 20–30, 5–10 mm lg., acicular, white; **Csp.** 1, 1 cm lg., hooked, brown, or white and brown-tipped; **Fl.** 2 cm lg., 2.5 cm ∅, pale pink; **Fr.** 1.2 cm lg., scarlet; **S.** black.—Mexico (Baja California, near La Paz).

M. cadereytana n.nud. (name by F. Schmoll, Cadereyta) (3:1, 3:7)
Bo. elongated-spherical, dark green; **R.** fibrous; **Ax.** with long Br.; **Tub.** in Isp. 13:21, cylindric, soft; **sap** watery; **Rsp.** (15–)18(–22), hair-like, forming a web concealing the Bo., to somewhat over 1 cm lg.; **Csp.** 4, reddish-brown, projecting, ± erect, or only 2, 1 of them basally thickened, hooked, c. 1.5 cm lg. or more; **Fl.** small, white, margins entire; **Sep.** with a reddish centre; **Fr.** ?— Mexico (Cadereyta). The Csp. are minutely rough. Clearly a valid spec., closely related to M. pygmaea but with white Pet., Csp. brownish-red and Rsp. usually more numerous.

M. cadereytensis Craig (1:1 or 1:3)
Bo. spherical, simple, branching dichotomously, also elongated, to 11 cm h., 8.5 cm ∅, dark greyish-green; **Tub.** pyramidal, keeled below; **Isp.** 13:21; **Ax.** weakly woolly, with up to 10 Br.; **Rsp.** c. 30, 3–5 mm lg., white; **Csp.** to 6, 4–10 mm lg., subulate, chalky-white, black-tipped; **Fl.** ? **Fr.** scarlet, 1.5 cm lg.; **S.** reddish-brown.—Mexico (Querétaro, Cadereyta; Guanajuato).
v. **quadrispina** Craig: **Csp.** only 4, thinner; **Tub.** more slender and Sp. thus appearing denser.

M. caerulea Craig (1:3)
Bo. spherical, simple, dark bluish-green, to 12 cm h., 6 cm ∅; **Tub.** 4-sided below, pyramidal and rounded above; **Isp.** 13:21; **Ax.** woolly at first, with occasional Br.; **Rsp.** 18–20, 1–5 mm lg., ± bristly, thin, white; **Csp.** (3–)4(–6), 8–10 mm lg., acicular, thickened below, dark brown, later more chalky reddish-brown; **Fl.** and **Fr.** ?—Mexico (Coahuila, Saltillo).

M. calacantha Tieg. (1:2)
Bo. spherical, eventually rather stoutly cylindric, light green, grafted plants to 30 cm h., 10 cm ∅; **Tub.** ± 4-sided; **Isp.** 13:21; **Ax.** woolly at first; **Ar.** more strongly woolly at first; **Rsp.** 25–35, 5–7 mm lg., thin, pale yellow; **Csp.** 2–4, 1–1.5 cm lg., stiffly

acicular, light brown or reddish(-brown), variable; **Fl.** 8 mm lg., to 1.4 cm br., Pet. carmine-pink, greenish-white below; **Fr.** pink, c. 2 cm lg.; **S.** light yellowish-brown.—Mexico (Querétaro, Guanajuato).

M. calleana Backbg. (3:1, 3:7)
Bo. depressed-spherical, to c. 2.5 cm h., 6.5 cm ∅, dark green; **Tub.** cylindric; **Isp.** ?; **Ax.** weakly woolly at first; **Rsp.** 22, light yellow, to 6 mm 1 g.; **Csp.** 1, honey-coloured, to 1 cm lg., hooked; **Fl.** white; **Fr.** and **S.** ?—Mexico (Hidalgo).

M. candida Scheidw. (3:1, 1:2)
Bo. spherical at first, then elongated, pale bluish-green, to c. 14 cm ∅, also offsetting; **Tub.** cylindric; **Isp.** 13:21; **Ax.** with to 7 Br. as long as the Tub.; **Rsp.** over 50, to 9 mm lg., thin, white; **Csp.** 8–12, 4–7 mm lg., acicular, white, tipped brownish; **Fl.** 2 cm lg., 1.5 cm ∅, dirty pink, borders white, serrate; **S.** black.—Mexico (San Luis Potosí).
v. **rosea** (SD.) K. Sch.: **Csp.** thinner, twice as long, pink at first; **S.** glossy, black, not wrinkled (Shurly) as in the type.

M. canelensis Craig (1:3)
Bo. spherical, simple, yellowish-green; **Tub.** rounded; **Isp.** 13:21; **Ax.** quite strongly white-woolly, with long white Br.; **Rsp.** 22–25, 5–15 mm lg., thin-acicular, white; **Csp.** 2–4, to 3 cm lg., stoutly acicular, ± straight, orange-yellow; **Fl.** 1.8 cm lg., 1.5 cm ∅, light greenish-yellow; **Fr.** ?—Mexico (Chihuahua-Sonora). For the so-called "red-flowered M. canelensis" (Schwarz) see under M. floresii v. hexacentra.

M. capensis (Gat.) Craig (3:2, 5:9)
Bo. cylindric, later offsetting from the base, to 25 cm lg., olive-green, 3–5 cm ∅; **Tub.** ovoid-cylindric; **Isp.** 5:8; **Ax.** glabrous, but sometimes with 1–3 Br.; **Rsp.** 13(–16), 8–15mm lg., acicular; **Csp.** 1, 1.5–2 cm lg., porrect, hooked, stoutly acicular; **Sp.** varying from white to darker, tipped reddish-brown or blackish, sometimes thickened below; **Fl.** bellshaped to funnelform, c. 2.5 cm ∅, pale pink, Pet. also with a darker M.-stripe; **Fr.** scarlet-orange, 2 cm lg.; **S.** black.—Mexico (Baja California, Puerto de Bahia de los Muertos).

M. caput-medusae O.: **Mammillaria sempervivi** v. **caput-medusae** (O.) Backbg.

M. carmenae Castañ. & Nuñ. de Cac. (3:1, 1:2)
Bo. spherical to ovoid and elongated, 5–8 cm lg., also caespitose; **Tub.** conical, whitish-green below; **Isp.** ?; **Ax.** with white wool and white Br.; **Rsp.** over 100, 5 mm lg., white or light yellow; **Csp.** 0,

replaced by fine hairlets; **Fl.** 1.1 cm lg. and ∅, white, tinged delicate pink; **Fr.** 6 mm lg., greenish-white; **S.** black.—Mexico (Tamaulipas, Jaumave).

M. carnea Zucc. (1:2)
Bo. spherical to cylindric, to 10 cm h., light to dark green, also caespitose; **Tub.** pyramidal, angular; **Isp.** 8:13; **Ax.** yellow-woolly; **Rsp.** 0 or 1–2 Br.; **Csp.** 4(–5), unequal, the bottom one 1.5–4 cm lg., the others 0.6–2 cm lg., flesh-coloured, black-tipped; **Fl.** pink, dark-tipped, throat pale green; **Fr.** red, 2.5 cm lg.; **S.** light brown.—Mexico (Hidalgo; Guerrero; Puebla; Oaxaca).
v. **aeruginosa** (Scheidw.) Gürke: 3 upper **Sp.** equal, the bottom one much longer, straight or recurved;
v. **cirrosa** (SD.) Gürke: the top **Sp.** and the bottom one more strongly twisted (tendril-like), purple at first, later flesh-coloured;
v. **subtetragona** (Dietr.) Backbg.: **Tub.** indistinctly angular; **Sp.** (2–3–) 4(–6), concolorous blackish-brown, or whitish with only the tip and base blackish-brown; **Sti.** light pink (green to pale yellow in the type).

M. carretii Reb. (3:2, 5:9)
Bo. spherical to elongated, dark green, to 6 cm ∅, later offsetting; **Tub.** cylindric, firm; **Isp.** 8:13; **Ax.** glabrous; **Rsp.** c. 14, to 13 mm lg., yellow, brown above; **Csp.** 1, porrect, hooked, to 16 mm lg., chestnut-brown; **Fl.** 2.5 cm lg., 1.5 cm ∅ or somewhat more, perfumed, Pet. whitish with a pink M.-stripe; **Fr.** slender, green, reddish above; **S.** brown.—Mexico (Nuevo León).

M. casoi H. Bravo (1:3)
Bo. spherical; **Tub.** 4-sided; **Isp.** 13:21; **Ax.** woolly, with Br.; **Rsp.** 5–8, shortly subulate, white; **Csp.** 3–4(–5), subulate, variable, short to very long, mostly ± curving, to 6 cm lg., the shortest ones 4–10 mm lg., reddish-brownish, later ± white; **Fl.** purple; **S.** brownish.—Mexico (Oaxaca, Suchixtlahuaca).

M. celsiana Lem. (2:1)
Bo. spherical to cylindric, to 12 cm h., 8 cm ∅, bluish-green, also offsetting from the base; **Tub.** conical; **Isp.** 13:21; **Ax.** white-woolly at first; **Rsp.** 24–30, 6–8 mm lg., thin-acicular; **Csp.** 4–6, 8–14 mm lg., the lowest one to 3 cm lg., pale to dark yellow, brown-tipped; **Fl.** 11 mm lg., pink to flame or carmine; **Fr.** red; **S.** light brownish.—Mexico (from San Luis Potosí to Oaxaca).

M. centraliplumosa Fittk.
Bo. cylindric, simple or offsetting from the base, to 15 cm h., 4.4 cm ∅, dark green, crown rounded; **Tub.** cylindric-conic, 6–9 mm lg., 7–8 mm br. below,

crowded; **Ax.** with sparse white wool; **Ar.** oval, 2.5 × 1.5 mm; **Rsp.** 20–25, hyaline or yellowish, tipped brown, radiating; **Csp.** 4–9, to 12 mm lg., lower ones 6–10 mm, straight, sometimes 3 lower ones hooked, red, tipped brown to black; Csp. always feathery; **Fl.** borne in coronets from February to May, 1.7–1.9 cm lg., bellshaped, not scented, yellowish-green below, pink above; **style** white, passing over to pinkish-violet above; **Fr.** pale pink below, brown to olive-green above; **S.** brown.—Mexico (State Mexico, near Calderon, at 1700–1900m).

M. centricirrha Lem. (1:2)
Bo. spherical, more broadly-spherical at first, of various shades of green, mostly to 12(–20) cm ∅, later offsetting; **Tub.** 4-angled, broadly based: **Ax.** woolly; **Isp.** 5:8 (always?); **Rsp.** mostly 4–6; **Csp.** 1(–2); **Sp.** very variable in number and length, similarly the wool in the Ar. and Ax.; **Fl.** 2.5 cm lg., deep carmine, sometimes with a darker centre; **Fr.** carmine, clavate, 1.5 cm lg.; **S.** yellow to brown.—Mexico. Because of the extreme variability, this plant appears under many names in the literature, most being scarcely identifiable nowadays. The following can be distinguished:
v. **bockii** K. Sch.: **Tub.** smaller, greyish-green, clearly angular; **Rsp.** mostly 4; **Csp.** 1–2, robust, 1 fairly long, ± curving, blackish-brown at first, later lighter;
v. **glauca** (Dietr.) Schelle: **Rsp.** more strongly curving; **Fl.** lighter;
v. **neumanniana** (Lem.) Schelle: **Csp.** fine, short, acicular to subulate, straight;
v. **versicolor** (Scheidw.) Schelle: **Sp.** very robust, mostly bent downwards (transitional to M. gladiata Mart.).
Often erroneously combined with the creamy-white flowering M. magnimamma Haw. non O., which is rather variable but not so conspicuously so as M. centricirrha, the latter being readily differentiated by the ± carmine Fl.

M. cerralboa (Br. & R.) Orc. (3:1, 2:6)
Bo. elongated, to 15 cm h., 6 cm ∅, simple, yellowish-green; **Tub.** conical; **Isp.** ?; **Ax.** glabrous; **Rsp.** 10, 1 cm lg., thin-acicular, yellowish; **Csp.** 1, c. 2 cm lg., porrect, acicular, straight or hooked; **Fl.** 1 cm lg.; colour?—Mexico (Cerralbo Is., Gulf of California).

M. chapinensis Eichl. & Quehl: **Mammillaria woburnensis** Scheer.

M. chavezii Cowper 1963 (syn. M. orestera)
Bo. spherical, 2–3 cm h., 3–4 cm ∅, simple or caespitose; **Tub.** bluish-green, conic, not angular, c. 7 mm lg., obtuse, not slack or soft, in Isp. 8:13; **Ar.**

5–7 mm apart, round, cream or orange, with a little white wool only in the crown, later glabrous; **Ax.** sometimes with fine white Br., otherwise glabrous; **sap** watery; **flesh** pale pink at the base of the plant, **R.** deeper pink; **Sp.** not concealing the Bo.; **Rsp.** 20–22, thin, straight, stiff, silvery-white, sometimes tinged reddish-brown, covered with a fine white down, this here more clearly visible than on the Csp., spreading fairly evenly, those in the crown erect, later projecting, c. 5–7 mm lg., lower ones mostly weaker and rather shorter than the upper ones, lower ones never coloured, mostly bristly; **Csp.** 1, 1–1.25cm lg., stiffly acicular, erect, strongly hooked when young, those in the crown white below, to light reddish-brown at the tip, later concolorous matt reddish or greyish-brown, covered with fine white down which is scarcely visible to the naked eye; **Fl.** around the crown, bellshaped, 1.5 cm lg. and ∅; **Sep.** 5–6 mm lg., lanceolate, light green, with a narrow white ciliate border, strongly recurved; **Pet.** pale pink or cream, with a pale carmine M.-stripe, this broader and olive-green on the underside, linear-lanceolate, borders densely ciliate, Pet. c. 1 cm lg., 1.5–2.5 mm br., larger ones with 2 separate, light red longitudinal stripes instead of a M.-stripe; **Ov.** smooth, glabrous, vivid green; **Fil.** c. 4–5 mm lg., densely swirling, light pink; **An.** light orange; **style** c. 1 cm lg., stout, light green; **Sti.** 5, 1–2 mm lg., deeper in colour than the style.—USA (New Mexico, among grass in a rocky valley near Tyrone). Named for Don Epifanio Chavez, discoverer of the plant.

M. chionocephala J. A. Purp. (1:1 or 1:3)
Bo. spherical, bluish-green, to 12 cm h. and ∅, rarely offsetting; **Tub.** pyramidal, 4-angled, white-spotted; **Isp.** 13:21; **Ax.** with much white wool and numerous H. 2 mm lg. (reduced Br.-H.?); **Rsp.** 22–24, to 8 mm lg., bristly, white; **Csp.** 2–6, 4–6 mm lg., subulate, thickened below, dirty white to brownish, tipped blackish; **Fl.** to 22 mm lg., white to flesh-coloured; **Fr.** dark carmine, to 2.2 cm lg.; **S.** light brown.—Mexico (Coahuila, Sierra de Parras; Monterrey; Durango).

M. coahuilensis (Böd.) Moran: **Mammillaria schwartzii** (Frič) Backbg.

M. coahuilensis v. albiflora (Böd.) Moran: **Mammillaria albiarmata** Böd.

M. collina J. A. Purp. (3:1, 1:2)
Bo. spherical to oblong, greyish-green, mostly simple; **Tub.** cylindric; **Isp.** 13:21; **Ax.** woolly at first; **Rsp.** 16–18, 1–5 mm lg., thin, white; **Csp.** 1(–2), 5–8 mm lg., rather stiffly acicular, thickened below, greyish brown, lighter below, darker-

tipped; **Fl.** to 2 cm lg., pinkish-red, M.-stripe darker; **Fr.** carmine, to 2.5 cm lg.; **S.** brown.—Mexico (Puebla, Esperanza).

M. collinsii (Br. & R.) Orc. (1:3)
Bo. spherical, to over 6 cm ∅, often suffused reddish, offsetting and sometimes forming mats: **Tub.** conical-cylindric; **Isp.** 8:13; **Ax.** white-woolly, with Br. often longer than the Tub.; **Rsp.** 7, 5–7 mm lg., acicular, yellow below, dark above; **Csp.** 1, to 8 mm lg., porrect, dark brown; **Fl.** 1.5 cm lg., pink, **Pet.** bordered yellowish; **Fr.** deep red, 2 cm lg.: **S.** light brown.—Mexico (Oaxaca, San Jeronimo).

M. colonensis Craig (3:1, 2:6)
Bo. broadly spherical, 6–7 cm ∅, c. 5 cm h., greyish-green, sometimes offsetting; **Tub.** conical; **Isp.** 8:13; **Ax.** glabrous, but with 8–10 white Br.; **Rsp.** c. 15, 6–7 mm lg., thin, white, orange below; **Csp.** 1–4 (only 1 at first), 1–3 mm lg., the bottom one to 7 mm lg. and often hooked, or all straight; **Fl.** 2.3 cm lg., cream, M.-stripe narrow, pink; **Fr.** and **S.** ?—Mexico (Guerrero, Colonia).

M. columbiana SD. (3:1, 1:3)
Bo. cylindric, caespitose; **Ax.** woolly (especially in the flowering zone); **Isp.** ?; **Rsp.** 18–20(–24), white; **Csp.** 4–5, golden-brown, thickened below; **Fl.** red.—Colombia (probably Candellaria Desert, 1200 m).
v. **albescens** W. Haage & Backbg. n.v.:
To 22 cm lg., later developing a whitish crown (wool and lighter Sp.); **Rsp.** 20–25; **Csp.** 4; all **Sp.** whitish to white, sometimes slightly brownish in the crown at first.—Colombia (Villa de Leiva, 2200 m);
v. **bogotensis** (Werd.) Dugand ("Mutisia", 9. 1954: **Bo.** to 20 cm lg.; **Rsp.** to 27–30, whitish; **Csp.** almost always 6, yellowish, tipped brownish, or concolorous yellow; **Fl.** red.—Colombia (Sogamoso, 1200 m).—See also M. soehlemannii.

M. compressa DC. (1:3)
Bo. spherical, later freely offsetting to form hemispherical cushions, light bluish to greyish-green, individual heads later elongated, to 20 cm lg., 5–8 cm ∅; **Tub.** obtusely angled; **Isp.** 8:13; **Ax.** white-woolly, with stout white Br.; **Rsp.** (2–)4–6, 2–7 cm lg., acicular to subulate, often angular, sometimes contorted, varying from white to reddish, later grey, brown-tipped; sometimes also 1–3 very short Ssp.; **Csp.** 0; **Fl.** to 1.5 cm lg., deep purple, border lighter; **Fr.** light red, 2 cm lg.; **S.** light brown.—Mexico (San Luis Potosí to Querétaro).

Very variable, hence the names v. brevispina, fulvispina, longiseta, rubrispina, triacantha. But there are also intermediates.

M. confusa (Br. & R.) Orc. (1:3)
Bo. broadly spherical, light greyish to olive-green, simple or branching dichotomously, heads to 15 cm h., 10 cm ∅; **Tub.** dark green at first, ± 4-sided, keeled below; **Isp.** 8:13; **Ax.** white-woolly, with 10–12 Br. which are longer than the Tub.; **Rsp.** 4–6, 5–30 mm lg., acicular to stouter, black at first, then light brownish and dark-tipped; **Csp.** mostly 0 (–1–2, and then robust); **Fl.** to 2 cm lg., pale greenish-white to greenish-yellow; **Fr.** red, 2 cm lg.; **S.** light brown.—Mexico (Oaxaca).
v. **centrispina** Craig: **Rsp.** 4–6, to 1.5 cm lg., straight or curving; **Csp.** 1–2, strongly subulate, to 2.5 cm lg., sometimes bent;
v. **conzattii** (Br. & R.) Craig: **Rsp.** only, 4–5, to 9 mm lg., not stout;
v. **longispina** (only a name?): **Csp.** 1, ± curving, very long;
v. **robustispina** Craig: **Rsp.** only, 4–5, stoutly acicular to stoutly subulate.
M. confusa and varieties may all be referable, as additional varieties, to Mammillaria collinsii (Br. & R.) Orc.

M. conspicua J. A. Purp. (3:1, 1:5)
Bo. spherical to cylindric, greyish-green, simple, to 14 cm lg., 10 cm ∅; **Tub.** conical to obtusely 4-angled; **Isp.** ?; **Ax.** with wool or curly H.; **Rsp.** 16–25, to 6 mm lg., bristly, thin, white; **Csp.** 2, c. 1 cm lg., stoutly acicular, straight to ± curving, white, tipped brown, reddish-brown at first; **Fl.** pink, with a darker centre; **Fr.** carmine; **S.** light brown.—Mexico (Puebla, Zapotitlán). Craig's report: "Br. in the Ax." is incorrect, and contradicts the description of Purpus.

M. cowperae Shurly (3:1, 3:7)
Bo. spherical to elongated, simple, deep green, then greyish-green, to 10 cm ∅, c. 11 cm h.; **Tub.** rounded; **Isp.** 13:21; **Ax.** weakly felty at first, then glabrous; **Rsp.** 40–50, 7–9 mm lg., acicular, white; **Csp.** 8–10, thickened below, central one to 2 cm lg. or more, hooked, one lower Sp. similarly, somewhat shorter, the remainder straight, cream to yellow to reddish-brown; **Fl.** bellshaped, 2 cm lg., 1.5 cm ∅, **Pet.** white with a pale pink M.-stripe; **Fr.** whitish to pale green; **S.** black.—Mexico (Zacatecas).

M. craigii Linds. (1:2)
Bo. simple or branching dichotomously, light yellowish to greyish-green; **Tub.** 4-sided, angular above; **Isp.** 13:21; **Ax.** somewhat white-woolly;

Rsp. 7–8, 4–12 mm lg., stiff to flexible, somewhat thickened below, golden-brown; **Csp.** (1–)2(–3), 1–2 cm lg., thin-acicular, stiff, thickened below, golden-brown; **Fl.** bellshaped, to 2 cm lg., to 1.5 cm ∅, deep pink, M.-line dark; **Fr.** red, 1.2 cm lg.; **S.** light brown.—Mexico (Chihuahua-Sonora).

M. criniformis DC. (3:1, 1:3)
Bo. offsetting from below, light green; **Tub.** soft, ovoid to oblong; **Isp.** ?; **Ax.** ± glabrous; **Rsp.** 8–10, 8 mm lg., bristly, thin, hairy, white; **Csp.** 1, hooked, stiff, yellow to pink, porrect; **Fl.** to 1.6 cm lg.; **Fil.** and **style** pink; **Fr.** ?; **S.** black(?).—Mexico (Hidalgo).

M. crinita DC. (3:1, 3:7)
Bo. spherical, to 4 cm ∅, sometimes offsetting, dull greyish-green; **Tub.** soft, ovoid to oblong, circular; **Isp.** 8:13; **Ax.** naked; **Rsp.** 15–20, 16–18 mm lg., bristle-like, hairy, white; **Csp.** 4–5, 12–15 mm lg., thin-acicular, hairy, yellow, ± hooked; **Fl.** 1.6 cm lg., white to yellowish or creamy-pink, M.-line pink; **Fr.** reddish, 1.4 cm lg.; **S.** black.—Mexico (Hidalgo, Zimapan).

M. crispiseta Craig (1:3)
Bo. flattened-spherical, simple, dark green, to 8.5 cm ∅; **Tub.** pyramidal, angular above; **Isp.** 13:21; **Ax.** with long contorted Br.; **Rsp.** 8, 4–7 mm lg., thin-acicular, white, brown-tipped; **Csp.** 4–5, 7–18 mm lg., acicular, pink to brown or black, dark-tipped; **Fl.** ?; **Fr.** carmine, 1.5 cm lg.; **S.** light brown.—Mexico (Querétaro?).

M. crocidata Lem. (1:2)
Bo. spherical to oblong, dark bluish-green, to 10 cm h., 7–8 cm ∅, sometimes caespitose; **Tub.** pyramidal, 4-sided at first, then rounded; **Isp.** 13:21; **Ax.** only woolly; **Rsp.** 2–4, 8–17 mm lg., stoutly acicular to slender-subulate, pinkish-white, tipped dark purple to black, sometimes with additional hair-like Sp.; **Csp.** 0; **Fl.** bellshaped, 1.5 cm lg., carmine, M.-line purple; **Fr.** light pink, to 1.8 cm lg.; **S.** light brown.—Mexico (Hidalgo, Querétaro).

M. crucigera Mart. (2:1)
Bo. cylindric or obovoid, offsetting; **Tub.** light green, conical, 5 mm lg.; **Ax.** woolly; **Csp.** 4(–6) at first, yellowish, surrounded by a crown of **Br.**; **Fl.** (acc. Martius) as large as that of M. sphacelata (1.5 cm lg.); **Sti.** purple.—Mexico (no locality given). Taken from the original description of Martius.
The radial Br. are c. 3.7 mm lg., the Csp. at first cruciform. Acc. Pfeiffer, the spec. belongs within the complex of M. elegans. Little more can be gleaned from the original etching. The inadequacy of the description has led to confusion (viz.

Bödeker, whose M. crucigera he later called M. pseudocrucigera Böd. non Craig, which I in turn had to re-name M. neocrucigera Backbg., since Craig's name was a valid one). An unclarified spec., and it is not certain that later supplementary descriptions in fact refer to it.

M. dawsonii (Hought.) Craig: **Mammillaria glareosa** Böd.

M. dealbata Dietr. (2:1)
Bo. spherical to shortly cylindric, bluish-green, densely spiny; **Tub.** slender; **Isp.** ?; **Ax.** densely woolly at first; **Rsp.** c. 20(–26), white short, appressed; **Csp.** 2, stouter, to 1 cm lg., white, dark-tipped; **Fl.** small, carmine; **Fr.** red; **S.** brown.—Mexico.

M. deherdtiana Farwig
Bo. depressed-spherical, 4.5 cm ⌀, 2.5 cm h., simple, with watery sap; **R.** thick-fibrous; **Tub.** in Isp. 8:13, conical, to 10 mm lg., mid-green; **Ax.** with little wool, sometimes naked; **Ar.** oval, 4 mm lg., 2 mm br., white-felty; **Rsp.** 33–36, acicular, 3–6 mm lg., lower ones longer, stouter; **Sp.** light yellow at first, later white, sometimes tipped ± reddish-brown; **Csp.** 1–6, sometimes absent, variable, 3–5 mm lg., light to dark reddish-brown; **Fl.** funnelform, to 5 cm ⌀; **Tu.** to 20 mm lg., flesh-coloured, with small olive-green Sc.; **Sep.** to 10 mm lg., lanceolate, bordered flesh-colour, greenish in the centre; **Pet.** to 23 mm lg., 4 mm br., lanceolate, light pinkish-violet, with a dark M.-stripe and tip; **style** white, with 4 Sti., white passing over to light violet; **Fr.** spherical, 3–4 mm ⌀, light green; **S.** dark brownish-black, 2 mm lg., 1 mm br., pitted.—Mexico (Oaxaca, on the road between Nejapa, Inquila Mixes and Lachiguiri). Closely related to the Sect. Phellosperma. First discovered by Fr. Schwarz, and named for Cyriel de Herdt, the well-known Belgian nurseryman.

M. deliusiana Shurly: **Mammillaria bella** Backbg.

M. densispina (Coult.) Vpl. (3:1, 1:3)
Bo. spherical to elongated, to 10 cm ⌀ and h.; **Tub.** conical; **Isp.** 8:13; **Ax.** woolly at first; **Rsp.** 20–25, 8–13 mm lg., thin, white to yellow, later darker; **Csp.** 5–6, 10–20 mm lg., stiffly acicular, white below, rarely dark with a lighter zone above, usually yellow to brownish-red above, sometimes tipped blackish; **Fl.** 2 cm lg., 1 cm ⌀, sulphur-yellow; **Fr.** red; **S.** reddish-brown.—Mexico (San Luis Potosí, Querétaro; Guanajuato). Quehl's name, M. pseudofuscata, referred to material from San Luis Potosí, where Coulter's material also originated; the names are thus synonyms. There is also a very similar but slower-growing plant which

is not identical with M. densipina. This may be M. eschanzieri Orc., non (Coult.) Vpl., incorrectly written as "Chilita eschauzieri Orc.", named M. esshausieri by Frič, but not from the hook-spined "Cactus eschanzieri Coult." At any rate, Frič's plant also resembled M. densispina. There is no valid description of this second spec.

M. denudata (Eng.) Berg. (3:1, 1:2)
Bo. spherical, to 4 cm ⌀ and h., hidden beneath the Sp.; **Tub.** in Isp. 13:21; **Sp.** 50–80, 3–5 mm lg., hairless, white; **Fl.** white, to 1.2 cm lg., c. 1.5 cm ⌀; **Fil.** white (in M. lasiacantha: yellow to pale lavender, Sti. yellowish-green); **Sti.** white.—USA (Texas), N. Mexico (Coahuila).

M. diacentra Jac. (1:2)
Bo. spherical, dark green, to 8.5 cm ⌀; **Tub.** ovoid or pyramidal; **Isp.** 13 Ser.; **Ax.** woolly at first; **Rsp.** (3–)5(–6), 5–10 mm lg., stout, ± yellowish-white with a reddish or brown tip; **Csp.** 2, subulate, one c. 12 mm lg., the other to 3 cm lg., both reddish-brown, tipped black; **Fl.** 1 cm lg., 1.7 cm ⌀, pinkish-white, M.-line reddish; **Fr.** purple, 2 cm lg.; **S.** light brown.—Mexico.

M. dioica K. Brand. (3:2, 5:9)
Bo. cylindric, bluish-green, to 33 cm h., 10 cm ⌀, offsetting from the base; **Tub.** shortly cylindric, firm; **Isp.** 8:13; **Ax.** ± woolly, with 5–15 Br. almost as long as the Tub.; **Rsp.** 11–22, 5–7 mm lg., acicular, white to pink, dark-tipped; **Csp.** 1–4, 8–15 mm lg., the bottom one longest, hooked, all brownish to brownish-black; **Fl.** bellshaped to funnelform, to 3 cm lg., incompletely dioecious, cream, M.-line purple; **Fr.** scarlet, to 2.5 cm lg.; **S.** black.—USA (S. California) to Mexico (Baja California, S. tip and several islands). Variable, also in St.-length, and Fr. size; Fl. frequently not dioecious.

M. discolor Haw. (3:1, 1:3)
Bo. broadly subspherical, to 18 cm h., 13 cm ⌀ (Rümpler); **Tub.** ovoid to conical; **Isp.** 8:13; **Ax.** weakly woolly to glabrous; **Rsp.** 16–20, to 1 cm lg., thin, white; **Csp.** 6(–8), 1 cm lg., and more, colour variable, from light to yellow to black, or dark-tipped, ± curving; **Fl.** 2 cm lg., 1.6 cm ⌀, white with a pink M.-line; **Fr.** reddish-brownish, 2.5 cm lg.; **S.** brown.—Mexico (Puebla).

M. dixanthocentron Backbg. (1:2)—Descr. Cact. Nov. III: 8. 1963.
Bo. columnar, simple, green, to 20 cm h., c. 7(–8) cm ⌀; **Tub.** conical, c. 6 mm lg., sap semi-milky; **Isp.** 13:21; **Ax.** with curly grey wool; **Ar.** with weak brownish to white felt at first; **Rsp.** c. 19–20, thin-

subulate, 2–4 mm lg., white; **Csp.** 2(–4), one above the other or cruciform, the top one erect, c. 5 mm lg., the lower one projecting to directed downwards, to c. 1.5 cm lg., both light at first, becoming horn-coloured or whitish tipped horn-colour; **Fl.** light red; **Fr.** 2 cm lg., slender, yellow below, orange above.—Mexico (Arroyo Verde, c. 30 km S. of the type-locality of M. buchenauii). (Fig. 212, left). The semi-milky sap is under considerable pressure and if the epidermis is pierced it rapidly appears in considerable quantities; I have indeed seen it spurt out in a jet c. 3 cm lg. The sap is slightly sticky and hardens only slowly.

M. dodsonii H. Bravo
Bo. depressed-spherical, simple, to 4 cm br. and 3 cm h., sap watery; **Tub.** in 5–8 spiralled R., conical, 5 mm lg.; **Ax.** glabrous; **Ar.** round, 1 mm lg., with white wool at first; **Rsp.** 20–21, hyaline, upper ones c. 1 cm lg., lower ones to 18 mm, sharp, $\pm$ appressed, twisted inwards; **Csp.** (3–)4–5, cruciform, stouter than the Rsp., upper ones 1 cm lg., lower ones to 2 cm; **Fl.** c. 4 cm $\varnothing$ when open; **Pet.** acute, purple; **Sep.** lanceolate; **style** pale purple, with 4 Sti., overtopping the white Fil.; **An.** yellow; **Ov.** concealed within the Bo.; **S.** black, 1.5 mm lg., with a corky basal hilum.—Mexico (N. of Oaxaca, Cerro de San Felipe del Agua, among moss and ferns in clefts in the rocks, at 3000 m). Belongs to the SG. Phellosperma, Section Krainzia; very close to M. deherdtiana. but distinguished by the smaller number of spirals, fewer Rsp., more numerous Csp. and the round Ar. Named for J. W. Dodson, Curator of the Cactus and Succulent Botanical Garden, Berkeley, Calif.

M. dolichocentra Lem.: **Mammillaria obconella** Scheidw.

M. donatii Berge (3:1, 1:3)
Bo. spherical, light bluish-green, to 9 cm $\varnothing$, sometimes offsetting; **Tub.** conical; **Isp.** 13:21; **Ax.** glabrous; **Rsp.** 16–18, 6–8 mm lg., thin, white; **Csp.** 2, to 1 cm lg., stiffly acicular, dark brown; **Fl.** to 1.5 cm lg. and $\varnothing$, flame to carmine; **Fr.** red, to 1.5 cm lg.; **S.** brown.—Mexico (Puebla, Boca del Monte).

M. droegeana (Reb.) Hildm. (3:1, 1:4)
Bo. eventually columnar, to 8 cm lg., 4 cm $\varnothing$, dark greyish-green, sometimes offsetting; **Tub.** moderately firm, carinate below; **Isp.** 8:13; **Ax.** glabrous; **Rsp.** 30, to 6 mm lg., pale yellow, darker below; **Csp.** 8–11, to 1 cm lg., stiffly acicular, dark reddish-brown; **Fl.** 1 cm lg., 1.5 cm $\varnothing$, white flushed pink, M.-line pink; **Fr.** light yellowish-brownish, 2 cm lg.; **S.** light brown.—Mexico (Querétaro, Sierra de San Moran).

M. dumetorum J. A. Purp. (3:1, 1:2)
Bo. spherical, greyish-green, to 2.5 cm $\varnothing$, caespitose, taprooted; **Tub.** cylindric; **Isp.** 8:13; **Ax.** glabrous; **Rsp.** 40–60, to 4 mm lg., appressed, white, bristly, hairy; **Csp.** 0; **Fl.** 1.2 cm lg. and $\varnothing$, white, M.-line reddish; **Fr.** scarlet, to 2 cm lg., spherical to clavate; **S.** black.—USA (Texas; SE. New Mexico (N. Chihuahua). Often incorrectly called M. schiedeana.

M. duoformis Craig & Daws. (2:3)
Bo. cylindric, dark bluish-green, to 9 cm h., 3.5 cm $\varnothing$, sometimes caespitose; **Tub.** conical; **Isp.** 13:21; **Ax.** bristly; **Rsp.** 18–20, to 7 mm lg., pale yellow, soon becoming chalky; **Csp.** 4, to 12 mm lg., slightly thickened and brownish-pink below, tipped black, the bottom Sp. longest and darker, straight or hooked; **Fl.** bellshaped, 1.5 cm lg., 1.2 cm $\varnothing$, light carmine; **Fr.** brownish-pink, 1.8 cm lg.; **S.** brown.—Mexico (Puebla; Guerrero).
v. **rectiformis** Craig & Daws.: differentiated by the **Sp.** all being straight, never hooked.—Mexico (Puebla, Tehuitzingo).
Possibly belongs to the complex around M. hamata.

M. durispina Böd. (3:1, 1:3)
Bo. simple, spherical to elongated, dark green, to 20 cm h., 11 cm $\varnothing$; **Tub.** conical; **Isp.** 8:13, 21:34; **Ax.** woolly at first; **Rsp.** 6–9, the upper one to 15 mm lg., the others to 8 mm lg., rather stout; **Csp.** seldom present; **Sp.** dark reddish-brown to black or horn-coloured at first, or flecked, or tipped golden-brown; **Fl.** 1.5 cm lg. and $\varnothing$, Pet. purplish-pink, pale greenish-white below, with a dark M.-line; **Fr.** carmine, 2 cm lg.; **S.** pale yellow.—Mexico (Guanajuato; Querétaro, near San Moran).

M. dyckiana Zucc. (2:1)
Bo. mostly simple, to c. 6.5 cm h., 5 cm $\varnothing$, greyish-green to bluish-green; **Tub.** conical; **Isp.** ?; **Ax.** woolly; **Rsp.** 16–18, stiff, white; **Csp.** 2, one directed upwards, the other downwards, stouter, horn-coloured, tipped reddish, to 1.5 cm lg.—Mexico. Fl. believed to be light carmine.

M. ebenacantha Shurly (without Latin diagnosis): **Bo.** broadly spherical; **Tub.** 4-angled; **Rsp.** only 4, black, subulate; **Csp.** 0; **Fl.** and **Fr.** ?—Mexico. (No further data available.)

M. egregia Backbg. (3:1, 1:2)
Bo. spherical to elongated, to 5 cm h. and $\varnothing$; **Tub.** conical; **Isp.** 13:21; **Ax.** woolly; **Rsp.** to c. 50, interlacing, white, sometimes pink at first, in several Ser.; **Csp.** 0; **Fl.** 11 mm lg., to 9 mm $\varnothing$, olive-brownish to whitish; **Fr.** ?—Mexico.

M. eichlamii Quehl (1:3)
Bo. spherical, yellowish-green, to 25 cm lg., to 6 cm ∅, mat-forming; **Tub.** conical; **Isp.** 8:13; **Ax.** and **Ar.** with yellow wool, later also with Br.; **Rsp.** 6, to 7 mm lg., yellowish-white, dark-tipped; **Csp.** 1, 1 cm lg., brownish-red above; **Fl.** 2 cm lg., cream to yellow; **Fr.** red; **S.** light brown.—Guatemala (Sabanetas), Honduras.

M. ekmanii Werd. (1:2)
Bo. spherical to elongated, to 8 cm h., 6 cm ∅; **Tub.** conical; **Isp.** 13:21; **Ax.** with much white wool; **Rsp.** mostly 15, 7–10 mm lg., snow-white; **Csp.** (3–)4(–5), to 1.4 cm lg., whitish-yellow, tipped brownish-red, brownish and thickened below; **Fl.** and **Fr.** ?—W. Indies (Haiti, La Navasse Island).

M. elegans DC. (2:1)
Bo. simple, rather small, spherical, little over 5 cm ∅; **Tub.** ovoid; **Isp.** ?; **Ax.** glabrous; **Rsp.** 25–30, to 6 mm lg., white, appressed and interlacing; **Csp.** mostly 2, to 1 cm lg., stiff, white, tipped brown; **Fl.** carmine; **Fr.** carmine, 2 cm lg.—Mexico (Federal District).
The following, which are often erroneously combined with the preceding, will here be treated separately: M. acanthoplegma, dealbata, dyckiana, haageana, meissneri and supertexta.

M. elongata DC. (3:1, 1:1)
Bo. cylindric, offsetting from the base to form colonies, leaf-green, heads to 3.75 cm ∅, later sometimes prostrate; **Tub.** slender-conical; **Isp.** 3:5, 5:8; **Ax.** weakly woolly to glabrous; **Rsp.** c. 20, to 8 mm lg., appressed, yellow; **Csp.** 0, rarely 1, scarcely longer; **Fl.** to 1.5 cm lg., whitish to yellowish; **Fr.** dirty red; **S.** light brown.—Mexico (Hidalgo).
v. **anguinea** (O.) K. Sch.: **Bo.** long, stout; **Rsp.** to 20, yellow, brown-tipped; **Csp.** always 1, darker (close to v. echinaria);
v. **densa** (Lk. & O.) Backbg.: **Rsp.** crowded, clearly projecting; **Csp.** 0–3–4, brilliant yellow (M. mieheana Böd.?);
v. **echinaria** (DC.) Backbg.: **Bo.** and **Csp.** stouter, latter fairly long, to 3, brownish above, heads to 2.8 cm ∅;
v. **echinata** (DC.) Backbg.: **Csp.** only 1, rarely 2, to 1 cm lg., thin, brown-tipped; heads to only 2 cm ∅;
v. **intertexta** (DC.) SD: **Rsp.** ± projecting, interlacing, yellowish; **Csp.** rarely present; heads to 2–2.5 cm ∅;
v. **obscurior** W. Heinr. n.v.:
Bo. light green, slender-cylindric, c. 1.8 cm ∅; **Tub.** shortly conical; **Isp.** 5:8; **Ar.** very small, elliptic, scarcely 1 mm br., 1.5 mm lg., with slight

yellow felt; **Rsp.** c. 23, pectinate, directed sideways, slightly recurved, the bases forming a light brownish ring around the Ar., c. 8 uppers blackish-red at first, 3 mm–6 mm lg., later all alike; **Csp.** 0; **Fl.** small, **Pet.** broadly spatulate, yellowish-white, irregularly laciniate, opening widely; **Fil., style** and **Sti.** creamy-white; **Fr.** and **S.** ? Acc. W. Heinrich, the darkest variety known to date, and thus clearly differentiated;
v. **rufocrocea** (SD.) K. Sch.: **Rsp.** more shaggily projecting, yellowish, tipped orange-brown; **Csp.** mostly 0, sometimes 1 (rarely 2); heads 2–3 cm ∅;
v. **stella-aurata** (Mart.) K. Sch.: **Csp.** only 1, thinner, mostly over 1 cm lg., **Rsp.** and **Csp.** yellow, brown-tipped;
v. **straminea** hort.: **Sp.** straw-coloured to brilliant yellow; **Csp.** absent; heads to 2.2 cm ∅;
v. **subcrocea** (DC.) SD.: **Sp.** whitish-yellow, tipped brown to flame, **Csp.** mostly absent; heads 1.5–1.8 cm ∅;
v. **tenuis** (DC.) K. Sch.: **St.** thin but erect, to 1.25 cm ∅; only **Rsp.** present, closely appressed;
v. **viperina** Backbg. non Marsh.: **Sp.** and St.-thickness as in the preceding, but St. much elongated and later prostrate.

M. erectohamata Böd. (3:1, 3:7)
Bo. ± conical, leaf-green, to 6 cm ∅, offsetting from below; **Tub.** cylindric; **Isp.** 13:21; **Ax.** glabrous, bristly; **Rsp.** to 25, 7 mm lg., fine, white; **Csp.** 2(–3), to 17 mm lg., stiffly acicular, nut-coloured to blackish-brown, later yellowish, golden-yellow below; **Fl.** 1.8 cm ∅, pure white inside; **Fr.** red, 1.2 cm lg.; **S.** dark brown.—Mexico (San Luis Potosí).

M. eriacantha Lk. & O. (3:1, 1:3)
Bo. cylindric, to 15 cm h., 5 cm ∅, light emerald-green, sometimes caespitose; **Tub.** conical; **Isp.** 8:13; **Ax.** woolly; **Rsp.** 20–25, 3–6 mm lg., finely acicular, golden-yellow, hairy; **Csp.** 2, 8–10 mm lg., golden-brown at first, hairy, stoutly acicular; **Fl.** 1.5 cm lg. and ∅, straw to canary-yellow; **Fr.** greenish-white, orange or reddish, 1 cm lg.; **S.** ± light yellow.—Mexico (Vera Cruz, Jalapa).

M. ernestii Fittk. 1971
Bo. simple, sometimes offsetting from the base, ± cylindric, to 45 cm lg. and 6 cm ∅, taller plants prostrate, rounded at the apex, dark green; **Tub.** conical, c. 9–11 mm lg., 6–9 mm thick below; **Ax.** and **Ar.** with sparse white wool, later glabrous; **Rsp.** 5–11, 4–10 mm lg., straight or slightly curving, yellowish, tipped brown; **Csp.** 1, pointing obliquely upwards, later ± appressed, 8–12 mm lg., straight or slightly curving; **Fl.** in a coronet, c. 22 mm lg.

and 24 mm $\emptyset$; **Sep.** yellowish-green; **Pet.** reddish; **style** white, with 4–6 yellowish-green **Sti.**; **Fr.** olive-green above, salmon-coloured below, 13–25 mm lg.; **S.** light brown.—Mexico (La Puerta, 1200–1800 m). Related to M. matudae and M. backebergiana.

M. erythrocalyx Buchenau
Bo. caespitose, forming groups, single heads 2–10 cm lg., 2.5 cm $\emptyset$; **R.** fibrous; **Tub.** soft, hemispherical, acute; **Isp.** 5:8 and 8:13; **Ax.** with 1–5 white Br. and a little wool; **Ar.** white-woolly, later glabrous; **Rsp.** 16–20, 3–6 mm lg., white, ochre below; **Csp.** 4–7, 5–8 mm lg., straight, yellowish-white, tipped red, bottom one sometimes hooked; **Fl.** in a coronet, 18–20 mm lg., bellshaped, red to reddish-brown; **Fr.** 18 mm lg., reddish-brown; **S.** 1.2 mm lg., cinnamon-coloured.—Mexico (Pueblo, S. of Chiautla at 1300 m, on black rocky ground, under bushes and trees; soil with pH 6). Specific name means "red-flowered".

M. erythrosperma Böd. (3:1, 3:7)
Bo. spherical to somewhat elongated, to 5 cm h., 4 cm $\emptyset$, dark green, quite freely offsetting; **Tub.** cylindric; **Isp.** 8:13; **Ax.** glabrous, with thin Br.; **Rsp.** 15–20, 8–10 mm lg., very thin, hairy at first, white, yellowish below; **Csp.** 1–3(–4), 1 cm lg., bottom one hooked, yellow, tipped reddish-brown; **Fl.** 1.5 cm lg., carmine, border lighter; **Fr.** carmine, 2 cm lg.; **S.** blackish-red.—Mexico (San Luis Potosí, Alvarez).
v. **similis** De Laet: **Bo.** smaller; **Csp.** often yellow; **Rsp.** shorter, hairy; **Fl.** lighter.

M. eschanzieri (Coult.) Vpl. non Orc., non Frič (3:1, 3:7)
Bo. depressed-spherical, 3 cm h. or $\emptyset$, simple; **Ax.** glabrous; **Rsp.** 15–20, 10–12 mm lg., dark-tipped; **Csp.** 1, 15–20 mm lg., thin, mostly hooked; all **Sp.** hairy; **Fl.** red(?) **Fr.** reddish; **S.** reddish (-brown?).—Mexico (San Luis Potosí).
This spec. has never been re-collected, but the description resembles that of M. monancistracantha Backbg.; however the latter always has over 20 **Rsp.**, 2 **Csp.** develop later, one of these straight, the other hooked, all **Sp.** hairy; **Fl.** pale yellowish!

M. esperanzaensis Böd. (3:1, 1:3)
Bo. spherical, to 8 cm $\emptyset$, deep green, offsetting basally; **Tub.** cylindric to conical; **Isp.** 13:21(?); **Ax.** glabrous; **Sp.** "all hard, with a metallic shimmer" (Böd.); **Rsp.** to 20, thin, light yellow; **Csp.** 4–7, the longest one pointing downwards, amber-coloured, darker at first; **Fl.** 2.5 cm $\emptyset$, white with a pink dorsal stripe.—Mexico (Puebla).
In his Comparative Key to the Mammillarias, Bödeker also gives the name M. fuscata-esperanza

(a n.nud. of J. A. Purpus, 1914); Schmoll held the view that it was identical with M. ochoterenae, which would be possible on the basis of Sp.-characters. Perhaps only a form?

M. esseriana Böd. (1:3)
Bo. spherical at first, later columnar, offsetting from the flanks, to over 9 cm $\emptyset$, over 20 cm h., greyish-green, sometimes branching dichotomously; **Tub.** large, indistinctly polygonal; **Isp.** 13:21; **Ax.** with white wool and Br.; **Rsp.** to 10, thin-acicular, white; **Csp.** 6, $\pm$ stoutly acicular, 0.7–1.5 cm lg., translucent, amber-coloured, tipped $\pm$ dark reddish-brownish; **Fl.** c. 1.2 cm $\emptyset$, carmine; **Fr.** and **S.** ?—Mexico (Chiapas) to Guatemala (?).

M. estanzuelensis Möll. (3:1, 1:3)
Bo. subspherical or elongated, to 8 cm h. or more, to c. 6 cm $\emptyset$, light green, sometimes caespitose; **Tub.** conical; **Isp.** ?; **Ax.** $\pm$ glabrous; **Rsp.** numerous (pectinate, acc. Böd.), in several Ser., to 6 mm lg., acicular, glossy white; **Csp.** 0 (but apparently present in some specimens); **Fl.** small, whitish.—Mexico (Durango?).

M. estebanensis Linds. 1967
Bo. cylindric, forming groups; **sap** watery; **Ax.** with wool and Br.; **Isp.** 13:21; **Csp.** 1, straight or hooked, 4–15 mm lg., chestnut-brown, tipped chocolate-colour; **Rsp.** 15–22, straight, to 10 mm lg., chestnut-brown or golden, fading to white; **Fl.** c. 20 mm $\emptyset$, white; **style** with 5–6 light green Sti., not spreading; **Fr.** clavate, 15–20 mm lg., red; **S.** black, pitted.—Mexico (Baja California, Isla San Esteban, in a broad inlet on the SE. side of the island). Belongs to the group around M. dioica, but this spec. is more robust than any others. Named for the type-locality; collected by George E. Lindsay in 1961.

M. evermanniana (Br. & R.) Orc. (1:1)
Bo. spherical to oblong, light green, to c. 5–7 cm $\emptyset$, sometimes off-setting; **Tub.** conical; **Isp.** 13:21; **Ax.** woolly, with contorted Br.; **Rsp.** 12–15, 5–8 mm lg., thin-acicular, white; **Csp.** 2–4, 1.2–1.5 cm lg., stoutly acicular, reddish-brown at first, later white, brown-tipped; **Fl.** 1.5 cm lg., pinkish to purplish-red in the middle, bordered greenish-cream; **Fr.** red, 1 cm lg.; **S.** light brown.—Mexico (Baja California and islands, Cerralbo Is.).

M. falsicrucigera Backbg.: provisional name, "Die Cact." VI, p. 3895: **Mammillaria buchenauii** Backbg.

M. fasciculata Eng. (3:1, 5:9)
Bo. soon becoming columnar, to 8 cm $\emptyset$, offsetting

to form colonies to 30 cm br.; **Tub.** cylindric to conical; **Isp.** 5:8; **Ax.** glabrous; **Rsp.** 13–20, 5–7 mm lg., finely acicular, white, dark-tipped; **Csp.** 1(–3), to 1.8 cm lg., stiff, thin-acicular, hooked, brownish to black; **Fl.** 3 cm lg., 2 cm ∅, white, M.-stripe carmine or purple; **Fr.** scarlet, 8 mm lg.; **S.** black.—USA (S. Arizona), Mexico (N. Sonora).

M. felicis Schreier n. prov.
Bo. c. 20 cm h., 5 cm br.; **Ri.** notched, resembling M. polyedra; **Rsp.** 5–6, snow-white, tipped delicate brown, 3 cm lg.; **bud** pink; **Fl.** resembling M. nejapensis, creamy-white with a pink M.-stripe.— Mexico (Gulf of Tehuantepec). Named for its discoverer, Felix Krähenbühl.

M. fera-rubra Schmoll (3:1, 1:3)
Bo. simple, later elongated, to 10 cm h., 9 cm ∅, yellowish to greyish-green; **Tub.** 4-sided; **Isp.** 13:21; **Ax.** shortly woolly; **Rsp.** 15–18, to 7 mm lg., thin-acicular, white; **Csp.** 6(–7), 1.2 cm lg., stoutly acicular, orange-brown, yellowish-brownish below; **Fl.** ?; **Fr.** scarlet, 2 cm lg.; **S.** brown.— Mexico (Querétaro, San Lazaro).

M. fertilis Hildm. (3:1, 1:3)
Bo. spherical to elongated, deep green, c. 5–6 cm ∅, soon offsetting freely; **Tub.** slender-cylindric; **Isp.** 8:13; **Ax.** at first with laxly curly white wool; **Rsp.** 8–10, 6 mm lg., thin, pale; **Csp.** 1–2, 1 cm lg., acicular, yellowish-brown, dark-tipped; **Fl.** 1.8 cm lg., to 1.5 cm ∅, carmine; **Fr.** ?—Mexico.

M. fischeri Pfeiff. (1:3)
Bo. subspherical, very little offsetting, dark green, to 12.5 cm ∅; **Tub.** several-sided; **Isp.** ?; **Ax.** bristly; **Rsp.** 5–6, white, black-tipped, top and bottom Sp. elongated, bent, 1.25 cm and to 3.75 cm lg., the others to 1 cm lg.; **Csp.** 0; **Fl.** ?—Mexico (border, Puebla-Oaxaca).

M. fittkaui Glass & Foster
Bo. cylindric, caespitose, c. 10 cm h., 4–5 cm ∅, light to dark yellowish-green, crown slightly sunken; **Tub.** variable, round, 7 mm br. below, 5 mm br. above, to 10 mm lg., with watery sap, epidermis thin, with glittering stomata; **Ar.** slightly sunken, scarcely white-woolly, later glabrous, 1–2 mm ∅; **Ax.** naked; **Rsp.** 7–9, projecting irregularly, white, weak, 5.5–7 mm lg.; **Csp.** 4, reddish-brown, the 3 upper ones projecting, scarcely distinguishable from the Rsp. except that they are a little stouter, darker and longer, the other Sp. hooked, erect, 8–10 mm lg., dark brown, lighter below; **Fl.** 1 cm∅, 1.5 cm lg.; **Tu.** 2.5 mm ∅, light green; **Pet.** whitish, bordered pink, with a darker M.-stripe, the outer ones deeper pink, with a broader M.-stripe; **style** and **Sti.** white; **Fr.** 7 mm

lg. and 5 mm ∅, brown, light pink below; **S.** large, few, 1 mm ∅, testa very dark brown.—Mexico (Jalisco, Lake Chapala: on rocks). Resembles M. monancistria Berg., but distinguished from this by the naked Ax., the Sp. which are not hairy and differ in number, and the colour of the style. Named for Hans Fittkau.

M. flavescens (DC.) Haw. non Zucc. non Hitch. (1:2)
Bo. spherical at first, then columnar, dark greenish, offsetting freely from the base; **Tub.** pyramidal; **Isp.** 8:13, 13:21; **Ax.** woolly; **Ar.** with much white, long-persisting, wool, crown completely woolly; **Rsp.** 8–10; **Csp.** 4(–5); **Sp.**, especially the centrals, rather long, thin-acicular, light to sulphur-yellow; **Fl.** pale sulphur-yellow; **Fr.** red.—W. Indies.
　　v. **nivosa** (Lk.) Backbg.: **Bo.** more spherical, olive-green, little offsetting; **Fr.** spherical to clavate, bearing Fl.-remains.

M. flavicentra Backbg. (3:1, 1:2–1:3)—Descr. Cact. Nov. III: 8. 1963.
Bo. simple, ± clavate to cylindric-columnar, greyish-green, to c. 18 cm h., c. 9–10 cm ∅; crown flat, with white wool; **Tub.** pyramidal, c. 7 mm h., c. 6 mm br. below, **sap** watery; **Isp.** 21:34; **Ax.** with curly wool, Br. absent; **Ar.** glabrous; **Rsp.** c. 22–24, thin-acicular, c. 2–4 mm lg., hyaline; **Csp.** 4–6, thin-subulate, thickened below, c. 5–6 mm lg., yellowish; **Sp.**, especially the centrals, brown below; **Fl.** red, c. 3–4 mm ∅; **Fr.** c. 1.5 cm lg., whitish-greenish below, passing over into pink above, thick-clavate; **S.** brown.—Mexico (on higher W. slopes, above the locality of M. buchenauii). (Fig. 212, right.)

M. flavihamata Backbg. (3:1, 3:7)
Bo. hemispherical, simple, to 4.5 cm ∅; **Tub.** conical; **Isp.** 8:13; **Ax.** glabrous; **Rsp.** to 35, to 5 mm lg., very thin, yellowish; **Csp.** c. 6(–7), to 9 mm lg., yellowish, thickened below, one Sp. hooked; **Fl.** 1.5 cm lg., 1.1 cm ∅, white; **Fr.** ?—Mexico (Aguascalientes).

M. flavovirens SD. (1:2)
Bo. subspherical to elongated, to 8 cm h., sometimes caespitose; **Tub.** pyramidal, 4-sided; **Isp.** 8:13; **Ax.** woolly in the flowering zone; **Rsp.** 4–5, to 6 mm lg., ± subulate, reddish-brown, sometimes with small Ssp.; **Csp.** 1(–2), to 1.5 cm lg., subulate, dark at first; **Fl.** 2 cm lg., 1.2 cm ∅, white to cream; **Fr.** carmine, 1.7 cm lg.; **S.** light brown.—Mexico (Guanajuato, Hacienda de la Barrancas).

M. floresii Backbg. (1:2)
Bo. spherical, light green, to 16 cm h., 12 cm ∅;

Tub. thick-conical, rather short; **Isp.** 8:13; **Ax.** quite strongly woolly; **Rsp.** 11–12, thin, brown; **Csp.** 4, to 2 cm lg., the longest one somewhat down-curving, darker brown at first; **Fl.** c. 1.5 cm lg., 2 cm ∅, light carmine; **Fr.** ?—Mexico (Sonora, foothills of the Sierra Canelo).

v. **hexacentra** Backbg. n.v.:
Distinguished as follows from the type: **Rsp.** to 14, the upper ones thinner, whitish, the lower ones rather stouter, yellowish; **Csp.** to 6, stouter, projecting, horn-coloured or brownish, darker and somewhat thickened below.—Mexico (Sonora).
F. Schwarz listed this plant as a "red-flowering M. canelensis"; but this latter has more numerous Rsp. (to 25) which are concolorous white, quite apart from its greenish-white Fl.-colour.

M. formosa Gal. (1:1)
Bo. spherical to elongated, light green, to 8 cm ∅, later sometimes off-setting; **Tub.** slender-pyramidal; **Isp.** 13:21; **Ax.** woolly; **Rsp.** 20–25, 3–6 mm lg., thin, white; **Csp.** 4–6, to 8 mm lg., stoutly acicular, flesh-coloured, black-tipped; **Fl.** to 1.5 cm lg., and ∅, purplish-pink with a light border; **Fr.** light carmine, 1.5 cm lg.; **S.** light brown.—Mexico (San Luis Potosí, San Felipe).

M. fraileana (Br. & R.) Böd. (3:2, 5:9)
Bo. cylindric, later offsetting from the base; **Tub.** shortly conical; **Isp.** 5:8; **Ax.** with a few Br.; **Rsp.** 11–12, 8–10 mm lg., thin-acicular, reddish-brown at first, then white; **Csp.** 3(–4), c. 1 cm lg., somewhat stouter, dark brown at first, the longest one porrect, hooked; **Fl.** over 3 cm ∅, pink, darker at the throat; **Fr.** lilac-pink; **S.** black.—Mexico (Baja California, islands of Pichilinque, Cerralbo, Catalina).

M. fuauxiana Backbg. (3:1, 1:2)
Bo. eventually columnar, to 30 cm h., 8 cm ∅, light green; **Tub.** conical, small; **Isp.** ?; **Ax.** felty, woolly in the flowering zone; **Rsp.** 20–22, 2.5 mm lg., very thin, white; **Csp.** 2, one directed upwards, one downwards, 5 mm lg., white, reddish-brown at the tips; **Fl.** 7 mm lg. and ∅, dark wine-red; **Fr.** orange-red; **S.** light brown.—Mexico (Guerrero, Puente Mescala).

M. fuliginosa SD. (3:1, 1:3)
Bo. spherical, dark green, to 8 cm ∅; **Tub.** conical; **Isp.** 21:34; **Ax.** weakly woolly; **Rsp.** 16, 1–2 mm lg., bristly, white; **Csp.** 4, 8–10 mm lg., stiffly acicular, white, black-tipped; **Fl.** 1.5 cm lg., 1 cm ∅, deep pink; **Fr.** carmine, 2 cm lg.; **S.** light brown.—Mexico (?).

M. fuscata Pfeiff. (3:1, 1:3)
Bo. eventually oblong, sometimes branching dichotomously, pale bluish-green; **Tub.** conical to 4-sided; **Isp.** 13:21(?); **Ax.** ± white-woolly; **Rsp.** 25–28, 6–8 mm lg., thin, whitish to golden-yellow; **Csp.** 4–6, 10–30 mm lg., stiffly acicular, varying from yellowish-brown to reddish-brown; **Fl.** 1.6 cm ∅, purple; **Fr.** purplish-red, 2 cm lg.; **S.** light brown.—Mexico (Central Highlands).

v. **russea** (Dietr.) Backbg.: **Bo.** conical, light green; **Ax.** at first with thread-like wool but no Br.; **Rsp.** 16–20, 6.5 mm lg., bristly, thin, white, tipped ± brownish; **Csp.** 4(–6), slender-subulate, to 1.2 cm lg., brownish-red;

v. **sulphurea** (Sencke) Backbg.: **Bo.** more yellowish-green; **Tub.** rounded to conical; **Ax.** woolly at first; **Sp.** vivid sulphur-yellow at first, later dark yellow; **Rsp.** lighter, 16–24, bristly, thin; **Csp.** 6(–8); **Fl.** 2.5 cm lg., dark pinkish-red.
The type and its varieties are differentiated from M. rhodantha and varieties by the absence of axillary Br.

M. fuscata-esperanza Böd.: **M. esperanzaensis** Böd.

M. fuscohamata Backbg. (3:1, 3:7)
Bo. spherical, c. 6 cm h. and ∅, green; **Tub.** conical; **Isp.** 13:21; **Ax.** glabrous; **Rsp.** to 23, thin, white, yellowish below, 8 mm lg.; **Csp.** 3(–4), to 12 mm lg., one of these hooked, reddish-brown, also 2(–3) more erect brownish-white Sp., to c. 8 mm lg.; **Fl.** bellshaped, limb whitish-pink, white below; **Fr.** green, ± whitish below, 1.9 cm lg.; **S.** black.—Mexico (Jalisco). (Fig. 213.)

M. garessii Cowper
Bo. small-spherical to spherical, forming groups, single heads to 8 cm h., to 5 cm ∅; **Tub.** dark to greyish-green, shortly cylindric; **Isp.** 8:13; **Ax.** mostly naked, rarely with wool or Br.; **Ar.** round, with short brown wool in Ar. close to the crown, later orange and greyish-brown below; **Csp.** 1(–2), stout, stiff, acicular, light reddish-brown to dark red, hooked, smooth; **Rsp.** 16–22, translucent white or light pink, with tiny black dots, yet the plant (apart from the crown) gives a uniformly white appearance, to 1.5 cm lg., smooth; **Fl.** bellshaped, 1.5 cm br., 2.5 cm lg., not curving; **Pet.** lanceolate, acute, creamy-white or light pink; **Sep.** rather shorter, green on the underside, with ciliate borders; **style** and **Fil.** white; **An.** yellow; **Fr.** shortly clavate, firm, fleshy, green to red; **S.** reddish-brown, darker at maturity.—Mexico (Chihuahua, S.W. of Mtachio, on a bush-covered mountain-slope, in semi-shade, in cracks in rocks).

269

First collected by Elmer Garess and John Green in 1962, and by Cowper in 1965; belongs to the complex M. wilcoxii-wrightii-viridiflora, and the "Sonoran flora". Readily distinguished by the flame-red appearance of the crown, the characteristically tapering Csp., and the caespitose habit. [Very sensitive to moisture, so that cultivated plants require a dry atmosphere, and careful watering, only when the weather is warm; keep completely dry in winter. Seedlings should be grafted as early as possible.]

M. gasseriana Böd. (3:1, 1:3)
Bo. subspherical, ± tapering above, 3–4 cm ∅, greyish-green; **Tub.** shortly ovoid; **Isp.** 8:13; **Ax.** naked; **Rsp.** 40–50, in several Ser., 5–8 mm lg., fine-acicular, roughly hairy, white, sometimes red-tipped at first; **Csp.** 1–2(–3), 8 mm lg., stiffly acicular, hooked, one of these more porrect, white below, tipped reddish to brownish; **Fl.** to 8 mm ∅, creamy-white, throat greenish; **Fr.** brownish-red, small; **S.** ± blackish.—Mexico (Coahuila, Torreón).

M. gatesii Jon. (1:2)
Bo. spherical to elongated, to 20 cm lg., 15 cm ∅, sometimes offsetting; **Tub.** conical; **Isp.** 8:13; **Ax.** white-woolly; **Rsp.** 6–8, 8–13 mm lg., stoutly acicular, yellowish-white, dark-tipped, projecting; **Csp.** 1, 2.5–3 cm lg., acicular to subulate, straight, dark reddish-brown to purple at first, yellowish below, later horn-coloured; **Fl.** bellshaped, 1.6 cm lg., 2 cm ∅, greenish to golden-yellow; **Fr.** red, 1.5 cm lg.; **S.** dark brown.—Mexico (Baja California, SW. tip).

M. gaumeri (Br. & R.) Orc. (1:2)
Bo. spherical to elongated, to 15 cm h., dark green, sometimes offsetting; **Tub.** 4-sided; **Isp.** 8:13; **Ax.** woolly to glabrous; **Rsp.** 12–14, 5–7 mm lg., white, brown-tipped; **Csp.** 1, to 1 cm lg., subulate, purplish-brown, black-tipped; **Fl.** to 1.4 cm lg., creamy-white; **Fr.** carmine, to 2 cm lg.; **S.** brown.—Mexico (Yucatán, Progreso).

M. geminispina Haw. non DC. (1:3)
Bo. spherical, cylindric or clavate, to 18 cm lg., 8 cm ∅, light green, freely offsetting to form cushions to 2 m br.; **Tub.** rounded above; **Isp.** 13:21; **Ax.** with white wool and Br.; **Rsp.** 16–20, to 7 mm lg., thin; **Csp.** 2–4(–6), 7 mm–2 cm lg., stiffly acicular; all **Sp.** white, centrals ± brown-tipped; **Fl.** 1.9 cm lg., **Pet.** cream with a carmine centre; **Fr.** carmine, 1 cm lg.; **S.** brown.—Mexico (Hidalgo, San Luis Potosí, Vera Cruz).

v. **brevispina** (Hildm.) Backbg.: **Csp.** shorter, more numerous, not bent;

v. **nobilis** (Pfeiff.) Backbg.: **Bo.** greyish-green; **Sp.** in 2 Ser., 23–26; **Csp.** 1(–2–3), very long, tipped ± brownish-red.

M. gigantea Hildm. (1:2)
Bo. depressed-spherical, to 10 cm h., to 17 cm ∅, bluish to greyish-green, simple; **Tub.** pyramidal, 4-angled; **Isp.** 13:21; **Ax.** woolly; **Rsp.** 12, to 5 mm lg., thin, ± white; **Csp.** 4–6, 1.5–2 cm lg., stoutly subulate, yellowish to reddish-purple, dark-tipped at first; **Fl.** 1.5 cm lg. and ∅, reddish, bordered green; **Fr.** purplish-pink, 3 cm lg.; **S.** light brown.—Mexico (Guanajuato; Querétaro, Moran).

M. gilensis Böd. (3:1, 3:7)
Bo. spherical to elongated, glossy, light yellowish leaf-green, later caespitose; **Tub.** conical to cylindric; **Isp.** 8:13; **Ax.** glabrous, with white Br.; **Rsp.** 20–25, to 6 mm lg., ± hair-like, yellowish to white; **Csp.** 3(–4), 0.7–1 cm lg., thickened below, brownish-yellow; **Fl.** cream, M.-stripe pink; **Fr.** small; **S.** dark brownish-grey.—Mexico (Aguascalientes, San Gil).
M. aurihamata Böd., with glabrous **Ax.** and white **Br.**, is similar but differentiated by its light sulphur-yellow **Fl.**; M. aureoviridis Heinr., which is also similar, has weakly woolly **Ax.** and yellowish **Br.**, while the **Rsp.** are light to darker yellow.

M. gladiata Mart. (1:2?) has often been referred to M. magnimamma, and was described (without Fl.) by me in "Die Cact.", V, 3135. 1961 (footnote). Since the Fl., acc. Dietrich, is "light straw-coloured", my assumption that this is a valid spec. would appear to be correct: Bo. similar to that of M. centricirrha v. versicolor (crown glabrous), but with white wool in the crown.

M. glareosa Böd. (1:2)
Bo. fairly small, the part above ground flattened-spherical; **Tub.** 4-angled; **Ax.** woolly; **Rsp.** to c. 9, to 6 mm lg., 2–3 upper ones thin and whitish, the remainder and 1 **Csp.** of equal length are stouter, subulate and brown (especially the Csp.); **Fl.** ?—Mexico (Baja California, 28½° N.).
This is the original description of Bödeker (Comparative Key to the Mammillarias, 59. 1933). While it is remarkable enough that the spec. has never again been re-collected despite intensive later searches, it is still more noteworthy that it grows in the same latitude as M. dawsonii (Houghton) Craig, and all its characters (apart from the missing floral data) tally with those of Bödeker's spec. Moreover, the illustration in C. & S.J. (US) XXXII: 6, 171. 1960, and the one in my Handbook, "Die Cact.", V: p. 3472, Fig. 3203, show very similar plants.

I therefore consider the two spec. to be identical, and would add the following additional information: main **R.** fleshy; **Tub.** 6 mm lg.; **sap** milky; **Ar.** weakly woolly at first, soon becoming glabrous; **Fl.** 1.2 cm lg., 6 mm $\emptyset$; **Sep.** brownish-red in the middle, bordered greenish-yellow; **Pet.** pale greenish-yellow, sometimes with a brownish-green M.-line; **style** greenish-yellow; **Sti.** similarly, 4–5; **Fr.** 1.5 cm lg., pink above, creamy-whitish below; **S.** light brown, 0.8 mm lg.—Mexico (Baja California, 28°40′ N., close to the sea, SW. of Punta Prieta).

M. glassii Foster
Bo. spherical, forming groups; **Tub.** with watery sap; **Ax.** with 20–30 white hair-like **Br.**; **Csp.** 1, 4–5 mm lg., porrect, hooked, amber-coloured; 6–8 **Sp.**, placed $\pm$ centrally, scarcely distinguishable from the Rsp.; **Rsp.** 50–60, 10–15 mm lg., hair-like, white, tangled; **Fl.** to 14 mm lg., light pink; **Fr.** spindle-shaped, to 20 mm lg., green, pink on nearing maturity; **S.** black.—Mexico (Nuevo León, near Dieciocho de Marzo, in full shade, on well-drained soil). Closely related to M. albicoma and M. subtilis. Named for Charles Glass, editor of the Cactus & Succulent Journal (US).

M. glochidiata Mart. (3:1, 3:7)
Bo. cylindric, 2–3.5 cm $\emptyset$, glossy, light green, caespitose; **Tub.** soft, cylindric to $\pm$ conical; **Isp.** 5:8; **Ax.** with to 5 fine **Br.**; **Rsp.** over 12, to 1.2 cm lg., bristly, white; **Csp.** 3–4, 6–12 mm lg., one of these hooked, dark yellow to reddish-brown; **Fl.** 1.5 cm lg., 1.2 cm $\emptyset$, **Pet.** brownish to pinkish-red in the middle, bordered white; **Fr.** scarlet, 1.6 cm lg.; **S.** black.—Mexico (Hidalgo: S. Pedro Nolasco, Zimapan, Ixmiquilpan).

M. glomerata (Lam.) DC. 1828 (Cactus glomeratus Lamarck 1783)
Bo. forming groups, single heads ovoid, scarcely larger than a hen's egg, bluish-green, densely woolly; **Sp.** very small; **Fl.** red.—W. Indies (San Domingo). Had been presumed identical with M. prolifera, but in view of the Fl.-colour this supposition has to be rejected.

M. goldii Foster & Glass
Bo. simple or forming some offsets; **St.** small, $\pm$ spherical; **Tub.** 5–7 mm lg., terete, with watery sap; **Ax.** naked; **Rsp.** 35–45, 2–3 mm lg., thin, tangled, hyaline; **Fl.** large funnelform, c. 3.5 cm lg. and $\emptyset$; **Pet.** dark lavender-pink; **An.** orange-yellow; **Sti.** 4, whitish; **Ov.** and **Fr.** embedded in the Bo.; **S.** black, 1.5 mm lg.—Mexico (Sonora, N. of Bacozari at c. 1000 m, on greyish-white volcanic tufa, in full sun, but almost completely covered by grit.

M. goodrichii Scheer (3:2, 5:9) [Grafting recommended]
Bo. spherical to oblong, to 4 cm $\emptyset$, later sometimes offsetting; **Tub.** cylindric above; **Isp.** 3:13; **Ax.** weakly woolly; **Rsp.** 11–15, 4–7 mm lg., white, dark-tipped; **Csp.** 3–4, to 10 mm lg., white, brownish above, the longest one hooked; **Fl.** 1.5 cm lg., 2.5 cm $\emptyset$, deep pink, **Pet.** bordered whitish; **Fr.** scarlet, to 2 cm lg.; **S.** black.—Mexico (Baja California, islands of Cedros and Guadalupe).
   v. **rectispina** Daws.: differs in having all **Sp.** straight, or only occasionally 1 curving Csp.; **Sti.** red (green in the type). Occurs only on Cedros Is.

M. gracilis Pfeiff. (3:1, 1:2–1:3)
Bo. small-cylindric, to 10 cm h., to 4.5 cm $\emptyset$, fresh green, freely offsetting; **Tub.** conical; **Isp.** 5:8 (Craig), 8:13 (K. Sch.); **Ax.** weakly woolly; **Rsp.** 12–14, stoutly bristly, 5–9 mm lg., $\pm$ whitish; **Csp.** 3–5, to 15 mm lg., light to dark brown; **Fl.** 1.7 cm lg., 1.3 cm $\emptyset$, yellowish-white; **Fr.** yellowish-red, 1 cm lg.; **S.** black.—Mexico (Hidalgo).
   v. **fragilis** (SD.) Berg.: **Bo.** somewhat smaller; **Csp.** 2, white, brown-tipped;
   v. **pulchella** SD. non Hopff.: **Bo.** more slender, 2–3 cm $\emptyset$; **Rsp.** weaker, brownish; **Csp.** 0; **Fr.** dark carmine, to 2 cm lg.

M. graessneriana Böd. (3:1, 1:2)
Bo. spherical to ovoid, dark bluish-green, to 8 cm h., 6 cm $\emptyset$, later $\pm$ caespitose; **Tub.** 4-sided, pyramidal; **Isp.** 21:34; **Ax.** with much white wool; **Rsp.** 18–20, to 8 mm lg., glossy, white; **Csp.** 2–4, to 8 mm lg., dull reddish-brown, lighter below; **Fl.** small, red(?); **Fr.** and **S.** ?—Mexico (Central Highlands).
Seldom seen in collections; more frequently encountered is its hybrid, M. schulzeana (see also under M. rutila). (Fig. 214, left.)

M. grusonii Rge. (1:2)
Bo. spherical to elongated, mostly solitary, becoming large, to 25 cm $\emptyset$, light green; **Tub.** 4-angled; **Isp.** ?; **Ax.** weakly woolly to glabrous; **Rsp.** 14, to 6–8 mm lg., reddish at first, then white; **Csp.** 2, 4–6 mm lg., stouter, reddish at first, then snow-white; **Fl.** 2.5 cm lg. and $\emptyset$, yellow; **Fr.** scarlet; **S.** ?—Mexico (Coahuila, Sierra Bola).

M. gueldemanniana Backbg. (3:1, 2:6–3:7)
Bo. eventually cylindric, light greyish-green, to 10 cm lg., 4.8 cm $\emptyset$, later caespitose; **Tub.** 4-sided below, rounded above; **Isp.** 8:13; **Ax.** glabrous; **Rsp.** 20–21, thin, c. 6 mm lg., whitish; **Csp.** 1, short, to 2 mm lg., subulate, $\pm$ dark; **Fl.** $\pm$ campanulate, 1.7 cm lg., 1 cm $\emptyset$, white, Pet. bordered light pink, throat carmine-pink; **Fr.** ?—Mexico (Sonora, near Alamos).

v. **guirocobensis** (Craig) Backbg.: **Csp.** 1–3, to 1 cm lg., reddish-brown, one of these hooked; **Fl.** 2 cm lg., more widely bellshaped; **Fr.** scarlet, 1.2 cm lg.; **S.** black.—Mexico (Sonora, Alamos District; NE. Sinaloa; SW. Chihuahua).

M. guerreronis (H. Bravo) Backbg. (2:3)
Bo. cylindric, to 60 cm lg., 6 cm ∅, light green, caespitose; **Tub.** conical; **Isp.** 8:13; **Ax.** with white wool and to 20 Br.; **Rsp.** 20–30, bristly, fine, white, to 1 cm lg.; **Csp.** (2–)4(–5), to c. 1.5 cm lg., lower ones longer, white, sometimes pink, one of these hooked, either only at first or on individual plants; **Fl.** red; **Fr.** red, to 2 cm lg.; **S.** brown.—Mexico (Guerrero, Canyon del Zopilote).
Acc. to whether all Sp. are straight, or one Csp. sometimes hooked, 2 varieties have been segregated: v. recta Craig, and v. subhamata Craig; v. zopilotensis Craig referred to plants with more numerous hooked Sp.

M. guiengolensis Bravo
Clump-forming, with few orange-yellow Fl. and a short flowering-period (only 2 weeks); difficult in cultivation.
[Translator's note:—I.S.I. (US) distributed this plant in 1972 with the following notes:—
M. guiengolensis Bravo & MacDougall: "This recently published spec. is of a group recognized by Buxbaum as the genus Oehmea, distributed from Sinaloa (Rio Elota) to Oaxaca, with Guerrero the center of distribution. There is considerable doubt that more than one spec. (M. beneckei, the first published) should be recognized for all have similar dark, hooked Sp. and large fragrant Fl. quite untypical of most Mammillarias. M. guiengolensis grows in clumps of 50 to 100 heads in shallow pockets of leafmold among rocks. Type locality: Cerro Guiengola, 4 miles W. of Tehuantepec, Oaxaca".
My own I.S.I. plant is as follows:—Single head spherical, 1.5 cm ∅, epidermis dull greyish-green, purplish in the sun; Tub. conical; Ax. ± glabrous; Ar. with some white wool at first; Rsp. c. 9, white, very sharp, 1 cm lg.; Csp. 2, one of these 1 cm lg., light below, brown above, straight, sharp, ± erect, the other stouter, hooked strongly upwards, brown below, blackish-brown and glossy above midway, 1.5 cm lg. Fl. not seen.
Parent-plant, grown in clay pot and close under roof-glass, offered no problems apart from difficulty of retaining it intact (worse than M. yaquensis); several offsets rooted successfully if slowly, in summer, without bottom heat.]

M. guilluminiana Backbg. (3:1, 3:7)
Bo. spherical, taprooted, to 5.5 cm h. and ∅, light green; **Tub.** conical, sometimes suffused reddish;

Isp. 8:13; **Ax.** glabrous; **Rsp.** c. 30–32, to 7 mm lg., bristly, fine, white; **Csp.** 4–5, to 6 mm lg., the bottom one hooked, tipped brownish, lighter below; **Fl.** 1 cm lg., to 1 cm ∅, Pet. white with a faint pink sheen and a pink M.-line; **Fr.** ?; **S.** black.—Mexico (Durango, 60 km E. of the town).

M. gummifera Eng. (1:2)
Bo. spherical, to 12 cm ∅, 11 cm h., light greyish-green; **Tub.** 4-sided, pyramidal; **Isp.** 13:21; **Ax.** weakly woolly at first; **Rsp.** 10–12, the bristly upper ones 4–6 mm lg., the lower ones 13–15(–25) mm lg., stoutly acicular, ± recurved, white, tipped brownish; **Csp.** 1–2, 4 mm lg., slender-subulate, light brown, black-tipped; **Fl.** 2.5–3 cm lg., 1.5–2.5 cm ∅, bluish-pink, Pet. bordered ± white; **Fr.** scarlet; **S.** dark brown.—Mexico (Chihuahua, Cosihuiriachi).

M. haageana Pfeiff. (2:1)
Bo. oblong, simple, rarely offsetting, bluish-green, to 8 cm h., 5 cm ∅; **Tub.** conical; **Isp.** 13:21; **Ax.** with flocky wool; **Rsp.** 18–20(–25), 3 mm lg., thin, white; **Csp.** 2, 6–8 mm lg., ashen-grey to blackish to reddish-brown or black; **Fl.** 1.2 cm lg., purplish-pink; **Fr.** light red, 1.1 cm lg.; **S.** light brownish-olive.—Mexico (Vera Cruz, Perote).

M. haehneliana Böd. (3:1, 3:7)
Bo. ± spherical, 4–5 cm ∅, simple or caespitose, light leaf-green; **Tub.** cylindrical above; **Isp.** 8:13; **Ax.** with several Br.; **Rsp.** 25, 7 mm lg., thin, white; **Csp.** 5–7, to 8 mm lg., stiffly acicular, light yellow, more whitish-yellow below, brownish-yellow at the base, slightly knotted, lowest one hooked, to 1.2 cm lg., all faintly rough; **Fl.** 1.5 cm lg. and ∅, Pet. cream with a pink middle; **Fr.** red, small; **S.** dark reddish-brown.—Mexico (San Luis Potosi).

M. hahniana Werd. (1:1)
Bo. ± broadly spherical, to 9 cm h., 10 cm ∅, light green, offsetting to form groups; **Tub.** conical; **Isp.** 13:21; **Ax.** shortly white-woolly, with to 20 longer Br.; **Rsp.** 20–30, 5–15 mm lg., hair-like, white, interlacing; **Csp.** 1(–2–5), 4(–5–8) mm lg., soon dropping, whitish, tipped reddish-brown; **Fl.** 1.5–2 cm ∅, purple; **Fr.** purplish-red, 7 mm lg.; **S.** dirty brown.—Mexico (Guanajuato; Querétaro, Sierra de Jalapa).
  v. **giselana** Neale: Ax.-H. to 1.5 cm lg.; **Rsp.** to 40;
  v. **werdermanniana** Schmoll: Ax.-H. to 2.5 cm lg.; **Sti.** brownish-pink (yellowish-white in the type).

M. halbingeri Böd. (3:1, 1:5)
Bo. broadly spherical, light green, simple; **Tub.** conical to ovoid; **Isp.** 13:21; **Ax.** with a few Br.;

Rsp. to 25, 5–7 mm lg., thin-acicular, white; **Csp.** 2, one pointing upwards, the other downwards, 5–6 mm lg., thin-subulate, slightly thickened below, yellowish-white, tipped pale brown; **Fl.** to 1.2 cm lg., sulphur-yellow; **Fr.** small, whitish(?); **S.** light reddish-brown.—Mexico (SE. Oaxaca).

M. hamata Lehm. (3:1, 3:7) or (1:5 or [?] 2:3)
Bo. cylindric, caespitose; **Tub.** conical; **Isp.** ?; **Ax.** weakly woolly at first; **Rsp.** 18–20, white to light cream, rarely with the extreme tip slightly darker; **Csp.** 4–6, brownish, lowest one hooked but occasionally straight; **Fl.** swollen bellshaped, limb bent, red; **Fr.** greenish, light below, later pale reddish; **S.** brown.—Mexico.

M. hamiltonhoytea (H. Bravo) Werd. (1:3)
Bo. depressed-spherical, simple, dark olive-green, to 18 cm ∅; **Tub.** rounded above, keeled on the underside; **Isp.** 13:21; **Ax.** white-woolly, sometimes with 1 Br.; **Rsp.** 5(–8), lowest one to 1.7 cm lg., others 3–5 mm lg.; **Csp.** 2–3, upper ones 1–2 cm lg., lower ones to 3.5 cm lg.; **Sp.** creamy-whitish, dark-tipped, centrals also tipped pinkish-orange or reddish; **Fl.** 2 cm lg., deep purplish-pink, Pet. bordered white to pale pink; **Fr.** purple, 2 cm lg.; **S.** reddish-brown.—Mexico (Querétaro).
v. **fulvaflora** Craig: **Fl.** rather smaller, 1.2–1.5 cm lg.; **Pet.** pale pink above, bordered yellowish-brownish, with an orange-brownish M.-stripe on the underside, margins ± entire. Same locality as the type.

M. hastifera Krainz & Kell. (1:3)
Bo. broadly spherical, c. 8 cm ∅, dark green; **Tub.** 4-sided; **Isp.** ?; **Ar.** with yellow felt; **Ax.** sparsely woolly, with occasional black-tipped Br.; **Rsp.** 6, 3 smaller ones directed upwards, c. 5 mm lg., 3 longer ones pointing downwards, all whitish-yellow, black-tipped; **Csp.** 1, fairly stout, projecting, 1.5–2 cm lg., brown, black-tipped; **Fl.** cream, 2 cm lg., 1.5 cm ∅, M.-stripe brown; **Fr.** ?—Mexico.

M. heeriana Backbg. n.nud. (Catalogue F. Schwarz): regarded by some authors as synonymous with M. hamata Lehm., and by others as a synonym of M. duoformis Craig & Daws. The latter may also belong to the complex of spec. around M. hamata.

M. hemisphaerica Eng. (1:2)
Bo. subspherical to elongated, dark bluish-green, to 12 cm ∅; **Tub.** rounded above, keeled on the underside; **Isp.** 8:13, 13:21; **Ax.** ± glabrous; **Rsp.** 9–13, 2–8 mm lg., thin, cream to brownish, dark-tipped; **Csp.** 1, 3–4(–8) mm lg., thin-subulate, dark brown to black, sometimes lighter; **Fl.** opening widely, to 1.5 cm lg., pink, M.-line darker; **Fr.** red,

1.5 cm lg.; **S.** reddish-brown.—USA (SE. Texas), N. Mexico.
v. **waltheri** (Böd.) Craig: **Csp.** mostly 2, 7–8 mm lg., amber to deep brownish-violet; inner **Pet.** shorter, centre slightly brownish-olive; **Fr.** red, small; **S.** light reddish-brown.—Mexico (Coahuila, Viesca).

M. hennisii Böd. (3:1, 1:3)
Bo. eventually elongated, c. 4 cm ∅, light leaf-green; **Tub.** shortly conical; **Isp.** 13:21; **Ax.** white-woolly; **Rsp.** c. 20, hyaline, yellowish below, 5–6 mm lg.; **Csp.** 3–4, stoutly acicular, brownish at first, then brownish-red, 8–12 mm lg.—Venezuela (Maracay area).

M. herrerae Werd. (3:2, 4:8)
Bo. cylindric, simple, little offsetting, to 3.5 cm ∅; **Tub.** cylindric; **Isp.** 8:13 (Craig) and 13:21; **Ax.** glabrous; **Rsp.** c. 100, appressed, white, very fine, 1–5 mm lg., in several Ser.; **Csp.** 0; **Fl.** 2–3 cm ∅, pale pink to violet; **Fr.** carmine, subspherical; **S.** matt black.—Mexico (Querétaro, Cadereyta).

M. hertrichiana Craig (1:3)
Bo. flattened-spherical, deep green, later offsetting to form groups to 1 m across; **Tub.** irregularly angular above; **Isp.** 13:21; **Ax.** with wool as long as the Tub., sometimes with Br.; **Rsp.** 12–15, 3–10 mm lg., thin-acicular, white to pale brownish, tipped brown; **Csp.** 4–5, 5–10 mm lg., lower ones to 2.5 cm lg., acicular, slightly thickened below, walnut-coloured; **Fl.** 1.8 cm ∅, 1 cm lg., deep pink to purplish-pink, centre darker; **Fr.** scarlet, 3 cm lg.; **S.** light brown.—Mexico (Sonora, E. of Tesopaco).
v. **robustior** Craig: **Csp.** to 3.5 cm lg., much stouter.

M. heyderi Mühlpfrdt. (1:2)
Bo. depressed-spherical, light to dark green; **Tub.** elongated-pyramidal; **Isp.** 13:21; **Ax.** woolly at first; **Rsp.** 20–22, upper ones 4–6 mm lg., lower ones 7–8(–12) mm lg., all bristly, creamy to pure white; **Csp.** 1, 4–8 mm lg., stoutly acicular, yellowish-grey to brown, darker below, tipped reddish-brown; **Fl.** 2–2.5 cm lg., brownish-pink; **Pet.** bordered cream; **Fr.** carmine, 3.7 cm lg.; **S.** reddish-brown.—USA (Texas; New Mexico), N. Mexico.

M. hidalgensis J. A. Purp. (3:1, 1:3)
Bo. eventually columnar, sometimes branching dichotomously, dark green, to 30 cm h., 13 cm ∅; **Tub.** conical; **Isp.** 8:13; **Ax.** with dirty white wool; **Rsp.** usually 0, or to 6–8 and bristly, fine, soon dropping; **Csp.** 2–4, 1 cm lg., acicular, greyish-white to yellowish-brown, tipped reddish-brown, directed upwards and downwards; **Fl.** 1.8 cm lg.,

6–7 mm ⌀, light carmine; **Fr.** purplish-red, to 2 cm lg.; **S.** light brown.—Mexico (Hidalgo).

M. hirsuta Böd. (3:1, 3:7)
Bo. ± spherical, greyish-green, to 6 cm ⌀, later caespitose; **Tub.** cylindric, spotted; **Isp.** 8:13; **Ax.** glabrous, with few Br.; **Rsp.** to over 20, thin, hyaline, 10–15 mm lg.; **Csp.** 3–4, upper ones whitish, bottom one projecting, hooked, whitish below, dark reddish-brown above, rough, knotted below; **Fl.** 1 cm lg., bellshaped, light yellow, suffused pink; **Fr.** greenish; **S.** black.—Mexico (Guerrero).

M. hoffmanniana (Tieg.) H. Bravo (3:1, 1:3)
Bo. spherical, later columnar, to 30 cm h., 12 cm ⌀, light green, simple; **Tub.** with 4 rounded sides to cylindric; **Isp.** 13:21; **Ax.** woolly, later rather more so; **Rsp.** 18–20, 1–3 mm lg., fine, white; **Csp.** (2–)4, sometimes more, to 2.5 cm lg., shorter, white to cream, tipped brownish; **Fl.** purple; **Fr.** carmine, 2 cm lg.; **S.** light brown.—Mexico (Querétaro, La Templadora; Guanajuato).

M. huajuapensis H. Bravo (1:3)
Bo. spherical, simple; **Tub.** conical to angular; **Isp.** 21:34; **Ax.** woolly, with many white Br.; **Rsp.** 6–8, subulate, white; **Csp.** 2(–3), subulate, reddish-yellow, darker at first above; **Fl.** purplet(?); **S.** light brown. —Mexico (Oaxaca, E. of Huajuapán de León).

M. humboldtii Ehrenb. (3:1, 1:2)
Bo. spherical to elongated, light green, sometimes caespitose; **Tub.** cylindric; **Isp.** 13:21; **Ax.** with white wool and 7–8 Br.; **Rsp.** 80 and more, in several Ser., 2–8 mm lg., thin-acicular, snow-white; **Csp.** 0; **Fl.** 1.5 cm ⌀, light red; **Fr.** reddish; **S.** black.—Mexico (Hidalgo, Ixmiquilpan, Meztitlán).

M. hutchisoniana (Gat.) Böd. (3:2, 5:9) [Grafting recommended.]
Bo. cylindric, to 15 cm lg., 4–6 cm ⌀, olive-green, sometimes tinged red, later caespitose; **Tub.** broadly rounded; **Isp.** 8:13; **Ax.** glabrous; **Rsp.** 15–20, 5–8 mm lg., purple to black at first; **Csp.** mostly 3, 2 of these 8 mm lg., one longer, shortly hooked, white below, purple above; **Fr.** scarlet, 2 cm lg.; **S.** black.—Mexico (Baja California, W. of Calmalli).

M. icamolensis Böd. (3:1, 3:7)
Bo. shortly cylindric, 6 cm h., 4 cm ⌀, leaf-green, simple; **Tub.** cylindric; **Isp.** 13:21; **Ax.** shortly hairy; **Rsp.** 16–20, 5–7 mm lg., almost hair-like, white, appressed; **Csp.** 4, 7 mm lg., the lowest one hooked, ± brown; **Fl.** 1.2 cm ⌀, pale pinkish-white, M.-stripe somewhat darker; **Fr.** small; **S.**

olive-grey(?).—Mexico (Nuevo León, Icamol and Monterrey).

M. inaiae Craig (3:2, 5:9; Sp. only ± curving above)
Bo. cylindric, to 20 cm h., 6 cm ⌀, light green, sometimes caespitose; **Tub.** rounded-pyramidal; **Isp.** 13:21; **Ax.** woolly at first, sometimes with a few Br.; **Rsp.** 17–24 (mostly c. 20), 4–6 mm lg., acicular, white; **Csp.** 2(–3), thin-subulate, at most curving at the tip, reddish-brown to ± black, one Sp. porrect; **Fl.** 1.8 cm lg., c. 2 cm ⌀, white to cream, pink inside, M.-line pinkish-brown; **Fr.** scarlet, 11 mm lg.; **S.** black.—Mexico (Sonora, San Carlos Bay).

M. infernillensis Craig (1:1–1:2)
Bo. broadly spherical, to c. 9 cm ⌀, greyish-green, simple; **Tub.** 4-sided, spotted white; **Isp.** 13:21; **Ax.** white-woolly; **Rsp.** 25–30, 2–10 mm lg., bristly, thin, white; **Csp.** 1–2(–4), 4–10 mm lg., stoutly acicular, white to chalky lavender, dark-tipped; **Fl.** deep purplish-pink, darker in the middle; **Fr.** light pink, 1.2 cm lg.; **S.** light brown.—Mexico (Querétaro, Infernillo).

M. ingens Backbg. (3:1, 1:3)
Bo. columnar in age, to 40 cm h., 15 cm ⌀, lighter to leaf-green, simple; **Tub.** conical above; **Isp.** 13:21; **Ax.** ± woolly; **Sp.** mostly only 2(–3), pointing upwards and downwards, wavy, 2(–3) cm lg., yellowish below midway, light to coffee-brown above; **Fl.** only 1 cm lg., light mid-red; **Fr.** red.—Mexico (Hidalgo, upper Barranca Grande).

M. insularis Gat. (3:2, 5:9) [Grafting recommended.]
Bo. ± broadly spherical, c. 6 cm h. and ⌀, sometimes caespitose, bluish-green, **R.** stoutly napiform; **Tub.** conical, sap sticky; **Isp.** 5:8; **Rsp.** 20–30, 5 mm lg., thin-acicular, white; **Csp.** 1, 1 cm lg., acicular, hooked, light below, passing over above from brown to black; **Fl.** bellshaped, to 2.5 cm lg., fairly wide, white with a light pink M.-stripe; **Fr.** orange-red, 1 cm lg.; **S.** black.—Mexico (Baja California, Los Angeles Bay).

M. jaliscana (Br. & R.) Böd. (3:1, 3:7) [Grafting recommended.]
Bo. spherical to oblong, c. 5 cm ⌀, light green, sometimes caespitose; **Tub.** cylindric; **Isp.** 13:21; **Ax.** naked; **Rsp.** 30 or more, 8 mm lg., acicular, white; **Csp.** 4–8, upper ones 7–9 mm lg., one more central, the bottom one longest, hooked, more strongly porrect, subulate, lighter to darker reddish-brown; **Fl.** 1 cm ⌀, scented, purplish-pink; **Fr.** whitish to pink, 8 mm lg.; **S.** black.—Mexico (Jalisco, Rio Blanco near Guadalajara).

M. johnstonii (Br. & R.) Orc. (1:2)
Bo. ± spherical, to 20 cm h., dull bluish to greyish-green, rarely off-setting; **Tub.** 4-angled; **Isp.** 13:21; **Ax.** ± woolly; **Rsp.** 10–15, 6–9 mm lg., acicular, white to horny-brown, tipped reddish-brown or darker; **Csp.** (1–)2, 1 cm lg., subulate, light purple to black at first; **Fl.** 1.5–2 cm lg., pink, M.-line brownish; **Fr.** red to scarlet, 2.5 cm lg.; **S.** light brown.—Mexico (Sonora, San Carlos Bay).
   v. **guaymensis** Craig: **Csp.** 4–6, to 1.8 cm lg.; **Rsp.** c. 18;
   v. **sancarlensis** Craig: **Csp.** 2, to 2.5 cm lg., somewhat flexible, ± contorted; **Rsp.** 15–18.

M. jozef-bergeri: Resembles M. collinsii. Named by Dr. W. Wojnowski for the Warsaw cactophile Jozef Berger (c. 1880).

M. karwinskiana Mart. (1:3)
Bo. spherical to ovoid-cylindric, light bluish-green to dark green, simple, offsetting or branching dichotomously; **Tub.** pyramidal; **Isp.** 13:21; **Ax.** woolly, with whitish, brown-tipped Br. as long as the Tub.; **Rsp.** 4–6, lateral ones 4–16 mm lg., upper and lower ones 10–30 mm lg., red at first, then white below, tipped dark brown to black; **Csp.** 0 (–1, to 2.5 cm lg.); **Fl.** 2 cm lg., 1.5 cm ∅, whitish, with a red M.-line above; **Fr.** red, to 2 cm lg.; **S.** light brown.—Mexico (Puebla).
   v. **centrispina** (Pfeiff.) SD.: more stoutly spined; **Csp.** mostly present, variable in colour, sometimes darker.

M. kelleriana Schmoll (3:1, 1:3)
Bo. spherical to elongated, to 12 cm h., 8 cm ∅, dark green, simple; **Tub.** cylindric to conical; **Isp.** 13:21; **Ax.** white-woolly at first; **Rsp.** 6, 9–20 mm lg., the lowest ones longest, purplish-brownish, tipped darker; **Csp.** 0–1, 1.5 cm lg., stoutly acicular, coloured like the Rsp.; **Fl.** 1 cm lg., 8 mm ∅, bluish-reddish, darker at the centre; **Fr.** scarlet, 2 cm lg.; **S.** light brown.—Mexico (Querétaro, San Moran).

M. kewensis SD. (1:2)
Bo. subspherical, later elongated, bluish to greyish-green, to 12 cm h., 9 cm ∅, simple or caespitose; **Tub.** broadly conical; **Isp.** 8:13; **Ax.** persistently white-woolly; **Rsp.** 6, upper ones 6–12 mm lg., the bottom one to 3 cm lg., stoutly acicular, reddish-brown to black at first, then lighter; **Csp.** 0; **Fl.** to 1.5 cm ∅, deep purplish-pink; **Fr.** greenish to ± pink, to 2 cm lg.; **S.** light brown.—Mexico (Central Highlands to Guanajuato).
   v. **craigiana** Schmoll: **Tub.** more slender; **Sp.** shorter, more projecting.—Mexico (Guanajuato; Querétaro, San Juan del Rio).

M. klissingiana Böd. (1:1)
Bo. spherical at first, then elongated, to 16 cm h., 9 cm ∅, simple or offsetting from the base; **Tub.** pyramidal to conical; **Isp.** 13:21; **Ax.** more woolly in the flowering zone, with numerous Br. 1 cm lg.; **Rsp.** 30–35, 3–7 mm lg., fine, white, yellowish below; **Csp.** 2–4(–5), 2 mm lg., acicular, sometimes rather stouter, white, tipped dark brown; **Fl.** 1 cm lg., 8 mm ∅, delicate pink, throat greenish; **S.** dark reddish-brown.—Mexico (Tamaulipas, near Ciudad Victoria or Calabazos).

M. knebeliana Böd. (3:1, 3:7)
Bo. oblong, leaf-green, later sometimes offsetting; **Tub.** cylindric; **Isp.** 13:21; **Ax.** with 5–8 white Br.; **Rsp.** 20–25, 5–7 mm lg., thin, bristly, white; **Csp.** 4(–5–7), the lower one longest, hooked, to 1.5 cm lg., others to 8 mm lg., all reddish-brown, yellowish below; **Fl.** 1.5 cm ∅, light yellow; **Fr.** red; **S.** reddish-brown.—Mexico (Guanajuato, Sierra de San Luis Potosi).

M. knippeliana Quehl (1:3)
Bo. subspherical, deep green, to 6 cm h., 4–5 cm ∅, later offsetting; **Tub.** pyramidal; **Isp.** 13:21; **Ax.** white-woolly, with contorted Br.; **Rsp.** (4–)6, to 3 cm lg., acicular, white, tipped red or brown; **Csp.** 0; **Fl.** 1.5 cm lg., 1 cm ∅, straw-coloured, tipped red; **Fr.** red, 9 mm lg.; **S.** dark yellowish-brown.—Mexico (Morelos, near Cuernavaca).

M. kraehenbuehlii Krainz (also written as "krähnbühlii"; provisionally named M. alpina.)
Bo. cylindric, 3–12 cm lg., 3.5 cm ∅, forming large cushions; **R.** a thin taproot; **Tub.** 5–10 mm lg., 5–6 mm ∅, soft-fleshy, with watery sap; **Isp.** 8:13; **Ar.** c. 2 mm ∅; **Ax.** glabrous; **Rsp.** 18–24, very thin, white, sometimes brown-tipped, 3–8 mm lg.; **Csp.** absent or 1, longer than the Rsp.; **Fl.** funnelform-bellshaped, c. 18 mm lg.; **Sep.** spatulate to lanceolate, white to bordered ± carmine, with a broad carmine-lilac M.-stripe; **Pet.** 18 mm lg., carmine-lilac, bordered lighter; **Fil.** white, with yellow **An.**; **style** and 5 **Sti.** yellowish-white; **Fr.** dark carmine; **S.** glossy, black.—Mexico (Oaxaca, near Tamazulapan, on rocky peaks or among grass and shrubs). Named for Felix Krähenbühl of Basel, who discovered it in 1968.

M. kuentziana P. & B. Fearn—Nat. C. & S.J., 18:3, 33. 1963 (3:1, 1:2)
Bo. later freely branching; **St.** ± clavate, to 6 cm h., 3 cm ∅; **Tub.** pale green, conical to cylindric, not angular, 1 cm h., 0.7 cm ∅; **Isp.** 5:8; **Ax.** glabrous; **Rsp.** 18–20, 4–8 mm lg., laterals longest, straight, fine-acicular, pubescent, later chalky white; **Csp.** 4, cruciform, only 2 at first, rather stouter, all pubescent, upper one to 8 mm lg., lower one to 1 cm

lg., laterals to 7 mm lg., reddish-brown at first, later darker, lower Sp. porrect, others spreading; **Fl.** c. 1 cm br.; **Sep.** greenish, bordered cream, pale red in the middle, margins entire; **Pet.** linear-lanceolate, c. 3 mm br., sometimes pale pink in the middle, margins entire; **Fr.** green to reddish, slender-clavate, with Fl.-remains; **S.** spherical, black, pitted, 1.5 mm lg.—Mexico (locality? From F. Schmoll, Cadereyta).

M. kunthii Ehrenbg. (3:1, 1:2)
Bo. spherical, later elongated, simple; **Tub.** pyramidal; **Isp.** ?; **Ax.** woolly, bristly; **Rsp.** 20, short, whitish; **Csp.** 4, stouter, dirty white, tipped brown or black; **Fl.** dark pink, Pet. with a lighter border.—Mexico (Fig. 3208, "Die Cact.", p. 3478.)

M. kunzeana Böd. & Quehl (3:1, 3:7)
Bo. spherical to elongated, to 9 cm h., 5–6 cm ∅, glossy, light green, later offsetting; **Tub.** ± cylindric, soft; **Isp.** 8:13; **Ax.** without wool, with numerous contorted thin Br.; **Rsp.** 20–25, 4–10 mm lg., bristle-like, snow-white; **Csp.** 3–4, 1–2 cm lg., thin-acicular, hairy, the lower one longest, hooked, white below, then amber, tipped orange to purplish-brown; **Fl.** to 2 cm lg., 1.5 cm ∅, cream to white; **Fr.** red, spherical, 1.5 cm lg.; **S.** black.—Mexico (Zacatecas; Querétaro, Ocotillo).

M. lanata (Br. & R.) Orc. (3:1, 1:2)
Bo. simple or offsetting basally, light green; **Tub.** in **Isp.** 13:21, 21:34; **Ax.** more woolly in the flowering zone; **Rsp.** 12-20, 1–2 mm lg., white, brownish below; **Csp.** 0; **Fl.** 1 cm ∅; **Pet.** light pink, with a wide, paler to whitish border, entire; **Sep.** serrate; **style** deep pink above; **Sti.** purplish-pink; **Fr.** scarlet; **S.** olive-greenish to brown.—Mexico (Puebla, Oaxaca).
Br. & R. state "small", and Craig says "single heads 2.5–3 cm ∅"; but these data do not tally either with the original photo, or the plant we know nowadays under this name, which eventually becomes larger and ± cylindric.

M. laneosumma Craig (1:3)
Bo. broadly spherical, c. 8 cm ∅, light green, simple; **Tub.** shortly conical; **Isp.** 13:21; **Ax.** white-woolly, especially in the flowering-zone, with white Br. overtopping the Tub.; **Rsp.** 13–15, 5–15 mm lg., fine-acicular, white; **Csp.** 2(–3), 1–1.2 cm lg., acicular, stiff, brownish-orange, projecting; **Fl.** ? **Fr.** ?—Mexico (SW. Chihuahua, SE. Sonora, Sierra Canelo).

M. lanifera: acc. to D. R. Hunt this name (derived from the woolly Ar.) is the older name by 6 years for M. rhodantha.

M. lasiacantha Eng. (3:1, 1:2)
Bo. spherical to ovoid, to c. 4 cm h. and ∅, greyish-green, simple or offsetting; **Tub.** cylindric; **Isp.** 8:13; **Ax.** glabrous; **Rsp.** in Ser., 40–60, white, 3–4 mm lg., bristle-like, pubescent; **Csp.** 0; **Fl.** 1.2 cm lg. and ∅, white, M.-stripe purplish-reddish; **Fr.** scarlet, to 2 cm lg.; **S.** black.—USA (W. Texas, SE. New Mexico), Mexico (N. Chihuahua).

M. lengdobleriana Böd. (3:1, 1:2)
Bo. cylindric, to c. 9 cm lg., 3 cm ∅, leaf-green, simple; **Tub.** shortly cylindric; **Isp.** 8:13; **Ax.** naked; **Rsp.** in 2 Ser., to over 40, c. 5 mm lg., very thin, white, pale yellowish below; **Csp.** 0; **Fl.** 1.2 cm lg., and ∅, straw-coloured; **Fr.** and **S.** ?—Mexico (NE. Durango).

M. lenta Brand. (3:1, 1:2)
Bo. spherical to elongated, 3–5 cm ∅, light green to yellowish-green, off-setting and also dividing dichotomously; **Tub.** slender-conical; **Isp.** 13:21; **Ax.** shortly woolly, sometimes 1 Br. present; **Rsp.** 30–40, in several Ser., bristly, to 5 mm lg., weak, interlacing, some ± projecting, yellowish to hyaline; **Csp.** 0; **Fl.** 2 cm lg., 2.5 cm ∅, whitish; **Fr.** red, 1 cm lg.; **S.** black.—Mexico (Coahuila, Viesca and Torreón).

M. leona Pos. (3:1, 1:1–2)
Bo. cylindric, to 15 cm h., 4 cm ∅, bluish-green, offsetting to form groups; **Tub.** conical; **Isp.** 8:13; **Ax.** ± woolly; **Rsp.** to 35, to 5 mm lg., fine-acicular, white, interlacing; **Csp.** 7–8, 4–10 mm lg., stiffly acicular, thickened below, yellowish to chalky-purple or ± slate-coloured, tipped brown; **Fl.** 1 cm lg.; **Pet.** pinkish-red bordered orange-pink; **Fr.** red; **S.** dark brown.—USA (Texas, Big Bend), Mexico (N. States to S. Zacatecas).

M. lesaunieri (Reb.) K. Sch. (3:1, 1:3)
Bo. ± spherical to oblong, dark green, simple; **Tub.** slender-conical; **Isp.** 13:21; **Ax.** weakly woolly; **Rsp.** 11–13, 4–8 mm lg., thin-acicular, white; **Csp.** 1–4, 5–8 mm lg., acicular, purplish-brown; **Fl.** 2.5 cm lg., 1.5 cm ∅, flame to carmine; **Fr.** red, 1.5 cm lg.; **S.** light brown.—Mexico (Vera Cruz, near Gozatlán, Cerro Gordo).

M. leucantha Böd. (3:1, 3:7)
Bo. spherical to oblong, dark leaf-green, 3.5 cm ∅, rarely caespitose; **Tub.** cylindric; **Isp.** 8:13; **Ax.** woolly at first, with white Br. 5 mm lg.; **Rsp.** c. 18, 5–6 mm lg., very softly hairy, white with a tiny brownish tip; **Csp.** 3–4, 5–6 mm lg., 3 of these hooked, 1 straight, all dark amber; **Fl.** 1.5 cm lg., white, M.-line greenish; **Fr.** ?; **S.** dark greyish-brown.—Mexico (San Luis Potosí, Soledad Diez Gutierrez).

M. lewisiana Gat. (1:2) [Grafting recommended.]
Bo. spherical, with a stout taproot, simple, to 7 cm
h., 11 cm ∅, bluish-green; **Tub.** ± 4-sided,
pyramidal; **Isp.** 8:13; **Ax.** sparsely woolly; **Rsp.** c.
10–13, acicular, tipped brown, or the laterals
whitish, the lower ones brownish; **Csp.** 1(–3),
stoutly acicular, ± blackish-purple, to over 2 cm
lg., often very strongly curving above or contorted;
Fl. 2 cm lg., 1 cm ∅, yellowish-green; **Sep.** reddish;
Fr. white or red, to 1.5 cm lg.; **S.** pinkish-brown.—
Mexico (Baja California, N. Viscaino Desert). (Fig.
214, right.)

M. lindsayi Craig (1:3)
Bo. spherical, to 15 cm h. and ∅, dark greyish-
green, offsetting freely to form groups to 1 m br.;
Tub. conical to 4-sided, with the angles indistinct,
keeled on the underside; **Isp.** 13:21; **Ax.** strongly
white-woolly, with white Br.; **Rsp.** 10–14, 2–8 mm
lg., upper ones thin, white, lower ones stouter,
brownish to golden-yellow; **Csp.** 2–4, mostly 4–12
mm lg., acicular, light golden-brown to reddish; **Fl.**
to 2 cm lg., greenish-yellow; **Fr.** scarlet, 2 cm lg.; **S.**
light brown.—Mexico (SW. Chihuahua, Molinas
to Sierra Colorada).
　v. **robustior** Craig: **Tub.** to 1.3 cm br. below; **Sp.**
　stouter; **Rsp.** to 1.3 cm lg.—Mexico (apparently
　only near Molinas).

M. lloydii (Br. & R.) Orc. (1:2)
Bo. broadly spherical to elongated, to 7 cm ∅,
simple, dark green; **Tub.** 4-angled above; **Isp.** 8:13;
Ax. woolly at first; **Rsp.** 3–4, to 6 mm lg., subulate,
reddish to dark brown; **Csp.** 0; **Fl.** 1.5 cm ∅, white,
suffused pink, M.-line darker; **Fr.** pink, 8 mm lg.;
S. light brown.—Mexico (Zacatecas).

M. longicoma (Br. & R.) Berg. (3:1, 3:7)
Bo. spherical to oblong, dark green, 3–5 cm ∅,
offsetting; **Tub.** conical; **Isp.** 13:21; **Ax.** with long
woolly hairs; **Rsp.** to over 25, 6–8 mm lg., hairy,
white, interlacing; **Csp.** 4, to 1.2 cm lg., thin-
acicular, 1–2 hooked, all hairy, lighter brown,
below; **Fl.** ± white to creamy-pink; **Fr.** red, 1.5 cm
lg.; **S.** black.—Mexico (San Luis Potosi, near the
State capital).

M. loricata Mart. (1:2?)
Bo. spherical, bluish-green; **Ax.** woolly; **Rsp.** 12, to
12 mm lg.; **Csp.** 2, to 10 mm lg., stouter, tipped
black; **Fl.** 2.5 cm lg., yellow; **Fil.** purple; **style** and
Sti. yellow.—Mexico (acc. Dietrich). Perhaps a
Coryphantha? (Shurly).

M. louisae Linds.—C. & S. J. (US), XXXII: 6, 169.
1960. (3:2, 5:9)
Bo. subspherical, to c. 3 cm h., scarcely offsetting;
R. fibrous; **Ar.** ± white-woolly at first, soon

glabrous; **Ax.** ? **Rsp.** c. 11, 5–7 mm lg., light brown,
tips darker; **Csp.** 4, cruciform, to 1 cm lg., brown,
dark-tipped, lower one hooked; **Fl.** to 3.5 cm lg., 4
cm ∅; **Sep.** olive to brownish-green, bordered
pink; **Pet.** entire, lavender, bordered light pink or
white; **Fil.** white, light pink above; **style** similarly;
Sti. olive-green; **Fr.** 2 cm lg., red; **S.** 1.1 mm lg.,
black.—Mexico (Baja California, 1 mile S. of
Socorro).
Close to M. blossfeldiana, but has fewer Rsp.

M. macdougalii Rose (1:2)
Bo. broadly spherical, deep green, to 15 cm ∅,
simple or offsetting; **Tub.** ± rounded above; **Isp.**
21:34; **Ax.** often with long white wool; **Rsp.** 10–12,
to 2 cm lg., acicular, white to yellowish, dark-
tipped; **Csp.** 1–2, to 1 cm lg., acicular, yellowish,
dark-tipped; **Fl.** 3.5 cm lg., 4 cm ∅, pale greenish-
cream, M.-line pale brownish; **Fr.** green, pink
above; **S.** dark brown.—USA (SE. Arizona),
Mexico (N. Sonora).

M. macracantha DC. (1:2)
Bo. broadly spherical, to 5 cm h., to 15 cm ∅,
simple(?); **Tub.** oval to ± 4-sided; **Isp.** 13:21(?);
Ax. woolly; **Rsp.** 0; **Csp.** 1–2, to 5 cm lg., ±
angular, white to brownish, rarely 3, sometimes
with a few Ssp., more radially placed; **Fl.** red(?).—
Mexico (Central Highlands).
　v. **retrocurva** Kell.: **Bo.** more spherical, **Csp.**
　curving upwards.

M. magallanii Schmoll (3:1, 1:2) (3:1, 3:7)
[Grafting recommended.]
Bo. spherical, simple, light greyish-green, 4–5 cm
∅; **Tub.** cylindric; **Isp.** 13:21; **Ax.** ± woolly; **Rsp.**
70–75, 2–5 mm lg., thin-acicular, orange-brownish
below, soon chalky-white, brown-tipped, strongly
interlacing; **Csp.** 0–1, 1–3 mm lg., coloured as for
the Rsp., occasionally hooked (a variety?); **Fl.** 1 cm
lg., 6 mm ∅, cream, M.-line pinkish-brownish;
Fr. light carmine, 3 cm lg., **S.** black.—Mexico
(Coahuila).
　v. **hamatispina** Backbg. (3:1, 3:7): **Bo.** simple or
　somewhat offsetting; **Rsp.** only 40–45, interlac-
　ing, radiating regularly; **Csp.** 1, hooked, to 8 mm
　lg.—Mexico (Coahuila).

M. magneticola Meyran: **Mammillaria vetula**
Mart.

M. magnifica Buchenau
Bo. cylindric, to 40 cm h., 7–9 cm ∅, forming
groups, with milky sap; crown depressed, woolly,
covered with Sp.; **R.** fibrous; **Tub.** pyramidal to
conical, 8–9 mm h., with watery sap; **Isp.** 13:18;
Ax. with white wool and Br.; **Ar.** oval, 2.5 mm lg., 2
mm br., with yellow wool, eventually white, or the

Ar. is glabrous; **Rsp.** 18–24, radiating, 3–8 mm lg., straight, translucent white; **Csp.** 4–6, cruciform, the bottom one 35–55 mm lg., almost always hooked, the others 9–16 mm lg., straight, brown below, then yellowish, brown-tipped; **Fl.** in a coronet, bellshaped, 20 mm lg., 11–12 mm $\emptyset$ when open; **Sep.** dark purple, bordered yellowish, lanceolate; **Pet.** white below, pink to flesh-coloured above, bordered brownish; **Fil.** white; **An.** cream; **style** 13 mm lg., white; **Fr.** pink below, red-violet above, 15–22 mm lg.; **S.** dark brown.—Mexico (Puebla, near San Juan Baptista, at 1500 m, on rocks, in black humus-rich soil, pH 4–5).

v. **minor**: **Bo.** only 25 cm h. and 6 cm $\emptyset$; **Tub.** lower but broader; **Isp.** 8:13; **Csp.** 4–8, bottom one 15–25 mm lg., mostly hooked, others 6–15 mm lg., light golden-yellow; **Fl.** 17–18 mm lg.; **Pet.** with flesh-coloured M.-stripe, bordered brownish-white; **Fr.** dirty red, 9–15 mm lg.; **S.** rather smaller.—Mexico (Puebla, Cerro de la Cruz, at 1500 m, on rocks in brown loamy soil, pH 5–6). Variety closely resembling M. tomentosa and M. flava, but in the case of these latter 2 plants no data are available regarding Fl., Fr. and S.

M. magnimamma Haw. non 0. (1:2)
Bo. broadly spherical, greyish to dark bluish-green, offsetting to form cushions; **Tub.** 4-sided, angles not acute; **Isp.** 8:13; **Ax.** with white wool, especially in the flowering zone; **Rsp.** 3–5, 1.5–2.5 cm lg., $\pm$ curving, subulate, horn-coloured, black-tipped; **Csp.** 0, or sometimes 1 Rsp. more centrally placed; **Fl.** to 2.5 cm lg. and $\emptyset$, Pet. dirty cream with a fine reddish M.-line; **Fr.** carmine, 2 cm lg.; **S.** dark brown.—Mexico (Central Highlands to San Luis Potosí).

v. **divergens** (DC.) Borg: **Rsp.** mostly 4, lower one longest, often angular, it and the other long Sp. regularly twisted in the same direction, all yellow at first, then horn-coloured; **Fl.** with the M.-line more reddish(?).

M. mainae K. Brand. (3:1, 3:7)
Bo. hemispherical to $\pm$ tapering above, pale to bluish or greyish-green, to 10 cm h., sometimes caespitose; **Tub.** cylindric to conical; **Isp.** 8:13; **Ax.** glabrous; **Rsp.** 10–15, 6–10 mm lg., stiff, thin-acicular; **Csp.** 1–2(–3), 1.5–2 cm lg., hooked, stouter; **Sp.** yellowish, tips darker, sometimes pubescent when young; **Fl.** to 2 cm lg., to 2.5 cm $\emptyset$, white with a red M.-stripe; **Fr.** red, spherical to ovoid, to 2 cm lg.; **S.** black.—USA (Arizona, Sells), Mexico (Sonora, Hermosillo; Sinaloa, Fuerte).

M. mamillaris (Mor.) Karst.: **Mammillaria simplex** Haw.

M. marksiana Krainz (1:2)
Bo. broadly spherical, simple, light green, 4.5 cm h., 8 cm $\emptyset$; **Tub.** faintly 4-sided, pyramidal; **Isp.** 13:21; **Ax.** woolly, later glabrous; **Rsp.** 8–10, thin, stiff, 5–8 mm lg.; **Csp.** 1, c. 8 mm lg., scarcely stouter; all **Sp.** $\pm$ golden-yellow; **Fl.** c. 1.5 cm lg., greenish-yellow; **Fr.** ?; **S.** light to dark brown.—Mexico (Sinaloa, Sierra Madre).

M. marnierana Backbg. (3:2, 4:8)
Bo. shortly cylindric, simple or caespitose, to 10 cm h., 6.5 cm $\emptyset$, crown flat; **Tub.** conical; **Isp.** 13:21; **Ax.** glabrous; **Rsp.** to c. 30, to 8 mm lg.; **Csp.** 1, $\pm$ subulate and stout, only 2 mm lg.; all **Sp.** white, faintly brownish below; **Fl.** 1.5 cm lg., 3.5 cm $\emptyset$, Pet. revolute, purplish-carmine to pink; **Fr.** ?—Mexico (Sonora, Santana and San Bernardo).

M. marshalliana (Gat.) Böd. (1:2)
Bo. broadly spherical, very low-growing, to 12 cm $\emptyset$, bluish-green; **Tub.** and **Isp.** ?; **Ax.** weakly woolly; **Rsp.** 8–13, irregularly to 1 cm lg., spreading, white, dark-tipped, later all white; **Csp.** 1, to 1 cm lg., white, dark-tipped; **Fl.** 1.5 cm lg., 2 cm $\emptyset$, light greenish-yellow; **Fr.** ?—Mexico (Baja California, canyons around San Bartolo).

M. martinezii Backbg. (3:1, 1:2)
Bo. elongated, to 14 cm h., 7.5 cm $\emptyset$, bluish-green, simple; **Tub.** slender; **Isp.** ?; **Ax.** woolly; **Rsp.** c. 20, very thin, to 13 mm lg.; **Csp.** 2, not stouter or longer, directed up and down; all **Sp.** hyaline, yellowish below; **Fl.** 1.1 cm $\emptyset$, carmine; **Fr.** ?—Mexico (Oaxaca, near Mixteca).

M. mathildae Krähenb. & Krainz 1973
Bo. caespitose, flowering at 5–6 cm h., 5 cm $\emptyset$, glossy, dark to lavender-green, densely set with glittering epidermal cells, crown $\pm$ sunken; **Tub.** oblong-rhomboid to cylindric, 8–10 mm lg., rounded above, flatter below, with watery sap; **Isp.** 8:13; **Ar.** directed obliquely downwards, 2 mm $\emptyset$, $\pm$ round, shortly white-woolly at first; **Ax.** $\pm$ naked, rarely somewhat woolly; **Rsp.** 12–13, thin-acicular to bristly and flexible, 5–14 mm lg., snow-white, also 3–4 stouter, rather darker Sp. brownish at midway, brownish-red above, ciliate; **Csp.** 1, stout, stiff, 6–10 mm lg., reddish-brown, brilliant red at first; **Fl.** several at once, subapical, bellshaped-funnelform, 20 mm lg., 15–17 mm $\emptyset$, white; **Sep.** with a greenish-pink M.-stripe; **style** cream, greenish below, with 4–5 yellowish **Sti.**; **Fil.** carmine-pink below; **An.** light yellow; **Fr.** 6–7 mm lg., 4–5 mm $\emptyset$, carmine; **S.** rounded, cap- to helmet-shaped, matt black.—Mexico (Querétaro, SE. of the town of that name, near La Cañada, among low bushes and stones, in company with Ferocactus latispinus. Found in 1968 by Frau

Mathilde Wagner of Cadereyta de Montes, and introduced to Europe by Felix Krähenbühl. Spec. related to M. zeilmanniana, M. nana and M. rowlii.

M. matudae H. Bravo (2:3)
Bo. slender-cylindric, to 20 cm lg., to 3 cm ∅, sometimes caespitose; **Tub.** ± conical; **Isp.** 13:21; **Ax.** naked; **Rsp.** 18–20, acicular, 2–3 mm lg., yellowish below; **Csp.** 1, acicular, 4.5 mm lg.; all **Sp.** white, at least later, Csp. at first tinted or tipped pink, others brown; **Fl.** 1.2 cm lg., light purple; **S.** light brown.—Mexico (borders of Michoacán, near La Junta).

M. mayensis Craig (1:3)
Bo. oblong, light olive to greyish-green, to 19 cm h., 15 cm ∅, simple; **Tub.** 4-sided; **Isp.** 13:21; **Ax.** strongly white-woolly, with Br.; **Rsp.** 25–30, 2–6 mm lg., thin-acicular, white, tipped yellowish or brownish; **Csp.** 5, c. 5 mm lg., thin-subulate, brownish at first, then horn-coloured; **Fl.** 1.2 cm lg., 1.5 cm ∅, deep pink; **Fr.** ?; **S.** ?—Mexico (SW. Chihuahua; SE. Sonora, Rio Mayo).

M. mazatlanensis (Reb.) K. Sch. & Gürke (3:2, 5:9)
Bo. shortly columnar, freely offsetting, single heads to 12 cm lg., to 4 cm ∅, greyish-green; **Tub.** shortly and broadly conical; **Isp.** 5:8; **Ax.** weakly woolly, (any Br. being perhaps only young Sp. on new growth); **Rsp.** 13–15, 6–10 mm lg., white, acicular, rigid; **Csp.** 3–4, 8–15 mm lg., light brown, somewhat more robust, pungent; **Fl.** 4 cm lg., carmine; **Fr.** brown to reddish-yellow below, 2 cm lg.; **S.** black.—Mexico (Sinaloa, Mazatlán).

M. meiacantha Eng. (1:2)
Bo. broadly subspherical, to 11 cm ∅, dark to bluish-green, simple; **R.** napiform; **Tub.** angular, pyramidal; **Isp.** 8:13; **Ax.** woolly in the flowering zone, otherwise glabrous; **Rsp.** 5–9, c. 5.5 mm lg. or more; **Csp.** 1(–2), 6–7 mm lg., rather stouter; **Sp.** ± horn-coloured, dark-tipped; **Fl.** 2.5–3.2 cm lg., 2 cm ∅, white, M.-stripe wide, light red; **Fr.** carmine, to 2.2 cm lg.; **S.** yellowish-brown.—USA (Texas; New Mexico), N. Mexico.

M. meissneri Ehrenbg. (2:1)
Bo. oblong to cylindric, to 12.5 cm h., 2.5–7 cm ∅, offsetting from the sides, ± light green; **Tub.** pyramidal; **Isp.** ?; **Rsp.** 16–22, bristly fine, whitish; **Csp.** 2, rather stouter, directed up and down, light brown, dark-tipped; **Fl.** red.—Mexico (Puebla, San Andreas).

M. melanocentra Pos. (1:2)
Bo. depressed-spherical to spherical, to 16 cm h., 11 cm ∅, bluish-green, simple; **Tub.** acutely 4-angled; **Isp.** 8:13; **Ax.** white-woolly at first; **Rsp.** 7–9, upper

ones 4–6 mm lg., the lower one to 2.5 cm lg., sometimes ± curving, black, becoming grey; **Csp.** 1–2, to 5.5 cm lg., ± subulate, black, soon brownish; **Fl.** 1.8 cm lg., 2.5 cm ∅, Pet. deep pink, darker in the middle; **Fr.** pink to scarlet, 3 cm lg.; **S.** reddish-brown.—USA (Texas; New Mexico), Mexico (Nuevo León; Coahuila).

M. melispina Werd. (1:2)
Bo. somewhat elongated, simple, to c. 8 cm h., 6 cm ∅, glossy, green, later bluish-green, rarely off-setting; **Tub.** 3–4-sided; **Isp.** ?; **Ax.** white-woolly at first; **Rsp.** 0; **Csp.** (1–)2(–4), 8–12 mm lg., acicular, thickened below, lighter yellow, becoming darker yellow; **Fl.** 3 cm lg., lemon-yellow; **Fr.** ?; **S.** brown.—Mexico (Tamaulipas, Jaumave).

M. mendeliana (H. Bravo) Werd. (1:3)
Bo. spherical to oblong, simple, to 9 cm ∅, dark olive-green; **Tub.** rounded above; **Isp.** 13:21; **Ax.** very white-woolly, with Br. (often disappearing in cultivation?); **Rsp.** only present as short, white, bristly H.; **Csp.** 2–4, 1.5–2 cm lg., pruinose-rough, brownish-red, black-tipped; **Fl.** with deep pink Pet., bordered lighter pink; **Fr.** ± purple, 2 cm lg.; **S.** light brown.—Mexico (Guanajuato; Querétaro, Tarajeas).

M. mercadensis Pat. (3:2, 5:9)
Bo. spherical, c. 5 cm ∅, olive to dark green, sometimes caespitose; **Tub.** ± conical; **Isp.** 8:13; **Ax.** naked; **Rsp.** 25–30, 5–8 mm lg., thin-acicular, pubescent at first; **Csp.** 4–7, 1.5–2.5 cm lg., stiffly acicular, white below, brown to red or yellow above, the lower Sp. longest, hooked; **Fl.** 3 cm ∅ (? or sometimes less), pale pink.—Mexico (Durango, Cerro de Mercado).

M. mexicensis Craig (1:2)
Bo. spherical, simple, to 6 cm h. and ∅, light greyish-green; **Tub.** pyramidal; **Isp.** 8:13; **Ax.** ± woolly at first; **Rsp.** 15–16, 8–12 mm lg., acicular, creamy-white; **Csp.** 2–8, 8–11 mm lg., acicular, creamy-white, brown-tipped; **Fl.** and **Fr.** ?—Mexico.

M. meyranii H. Bravo (2:3)
Bo. eventually long-cylindric, to 55 cm lg., to 5 cm ∅, yellowish-green, offsetting; **Tub.** small; **Isp.** 13:21; **Ax.** white-woolly at first; **Rsp.** 17–19, 3–6 mm lg., acicular, yellowish-red at first, tipped brown, then white, yellow below; **Csp.** 2, to 1 cm lg., acicular, orange-yellow at first, brown-tipped, then dirty white; **Fl.** 1.8 cm lg., purple; **Fr.** 2 cm lg., light greenish-purple; **S.** light brown.—Mexico (Mexico State, near Santa Barbara).

v. **michoacana** Buchenau: **Bo.** to 15 cm lg., 7 cm

∅, dark green, forming groups, crown covered with Sp. and wool; **Tub.** 7 mm lg.; **Isp.** 13:21; **Ar.** oval, 1.2 mm lg., yellowish-brown; **Ax.** woolly in the crown only; **Rsp.** 16–18, 5–8 mm lg., lower ones longest, yellowish, dark-tipped; **Csp.** 4, cruciform, 8–10 mm lg., straight; **Fl.** in a coronet, 16–17 mm lg., 11–12 mm ∅, yellowish-brownish; **Pet.** lanceolate; **Fr.** red, 13–15 mm lg., 8 mm ∅; **S.** brown.—Mexico (Michoacan, near San José Purna, growing in full sun or under bushes). Named for Jorge Meyran.

M. microcarpa Eng. (3:2, 5:9) [Grafting recommended.]
Bo. spherical to cylindric, dark greyish-green, to 16 cm lg., to 6 cm ∅, ± tapering above, offsetting; **Tub.** conical; **Isp.** 13:21; **Ax.** naked; **Rsp.** 20–30, 6–12 mm lg., thin, white to dark yellow, brown-tipped; **Csp.** 1–3(–4), 3 upper ones appressed, to 1.8 cm lg., lower one hooked, little thickened below, colour varying from light brownish to black; **Fl.** to 2.5 cm lg., 4 cm ∅, pink, M.-stripe darker; **Sti.** light green; **Fr.** dimorphic, scarlet, to 2.5 cm lg., or green, spherical, small; **S.** black.—S. USA to Mexico (Sonora, Chihuahua).
v. **auricarpa** Marsh.: **Csp.** golden-yellow, 1 sharply hooked; **Fr.** golden-yellow;
v. **grahamii** (Eng.): **Sp.** denser, white; **Sti.** yellowish;
v. **milleri** (Br. & R.) Marsh.: **Bo.** later cylindric, over 20 cm lg., 8 cm ∅; **Csp.** 2–4, hooked, brown; **Fl.** 2.5 cm ∅, pink to purple; **Sti.** yellow to cream.—These varieties occur only in USA (Arizona).

M. microhelia Werd. (3:1, 1:1)
Bo. eventually cylindric, over 15 cm lg., 3.5–4.5 cm ∅, mid-green, sometimes offsetting from below; **Tub.** shortly conical; **Isp.** 8:13(?); **Ax.** weakly woolly at first; **Rsp.** to c. 50, 4–6 mm lg., thin, stiff, white above, colour variable, golden-yellow to reddish-brown or red below; **Csp.** (0–)1–2(–4), usually appearing only later, increasing in number, to 11 mm lg., red to dark brown, subulate, ± curving; **Fl.** 1.6 cm lg. and ∅, white to yellowish-greenish, sometimes verging on pink; **Fr.** whitish to pink, 1.1 cm lg.; **S.** golden-brown.— Mexico (Querétaro, Sierra San Moran). With intermediate stages to:
v. **microheliopsis** (Werd.) Backbg.: **Rsp.** and **Csp.** more numerous. **Csp.** 6–8, to 9 mm lg., very variable in colour, from light grey to flesh-coloured, reddish-brown and blackish-brown; **Fl.** purplish-red, also lighter, sometimes even greenish; **Fr.** only pale green. Little more than a form.

M. microthele Mühlpfrdt. non Monv. (1:1)

Bo. spherical, greyish-green, to c. 8 cm ∅, sometimes old plants have several heads; **Tub.** slender, crowded, cylindric-conical; **Isp.** ?; **Ax.** weakly woolly, woollier in the flowering zone; **Rsp.** over 20(–24), bristly, white, appressed, ± interlacing; **Csp.** rather stouter, 2, one above the other, c. 2 mm lg., brown at first above, then grey; **Fl.** 1.2 cm ∅, 1.5 cm lg., pure white; **Sep.** with a red dorsal stripe; **Fr.** c. 8 mm lg., red; **S.** light brown.—Mexico (Coahuila, Parras).

M. mitlensis H. Bravo (3:1, 1:5)
Bo. spherical to cylindric, to 12 cm lg., 5–6 cm ∅, to 55 cm lg. in age; **Tub.** conical; **Isp.** 13:21; **Ax.** with a few Br.; **Rsp.** 20–25, 6–10 mm lg., acicular, white; **Csp.** 6, to 2.5 cm lg., reddish-brown to black, one hooked; **Fl.** 2 cm lg., purple; **Fr.** greenish-red, 3 cm lg.; **S.** light brown.—Mexico (Oaxaca, near Mitla).

M. mixtecensis H. Bravo (1:3)
Bo. spherical, simple; **Tub.** 4-sided; **Isp.** ?; **Ax.** with white Br.; **Rsp.** 8–9, subulate, white; **Csp.** 6–7, 1 of these more central, subulate, greyish-reddish, middle and lowest ones longest; **Fl.** purple.— Mexico (Oaxaca, between Tejupán and Suchixtlahuaca).

M. moelleriana Böd. (3:1, 3:7)
Bo. becoming oblong-clavate, glossy, leaf-green, simple, c. 6 cm ∅; **Tub.** cylindric-ovoid; **Isp.** 8:13; **Ax.** naked; **Rsp.** 35–40, 7–9 mm lg., acicular, white; **Csp.** to 8–9(–10), to c. 2 cm lg., stoutly acicular except for the one longer, stouter, hooked Sp., all Cs. light honey-coloured, darker above, to golden or reddish-brown; **Fl.** 1.5 cm lg. and ∅, yellowish-cream, M.-stripe pink; **Fr.** greenish-white, 1.5 cm lg.; **S.** black.—Mexico (Durango, Sierra Santa Maria).

M. mollendorffiana Shurly (3:1, 1:5)
Bo. spherical to oblong, dark green; **Tub.** ± cylindric; **Isp.** 13:21; **Ax.** very white-woolly, later with Br.; **Rsp.** 24–28, white, to 5 mm lg.; **Csp.** (4–)6, stiffly acicular, 1.4 cm lg., light yellowish-brown, red-tipped, the extreme tip black, thickened and yellowish-brown below; **Fl.** 1 cm lg., 8 mm ∅, purple above, yellowish-white below; **Fr.** 1.4 cm lg., purple; **S.** yellowish-brown.—Mexico (Hidalgo).

M. mollihamata Shurly (3:1, 3:7)
Bo. subspherical to ± oblong, dark green, somewhat reddish, to 11 cm h., 9.5 cm ∅, sometimes caespitose; **Tub.** conical, soft(?); **Isp.** 21:34 (anomalous: 19:30); **Ax.** glabrous; **Rsp.** 28, very thin, ± contorted, 1 cm lg., white; **Csp.** 4, to 1 cm lg., lower one hooked, 0.8 cm lg., all yellowish-brown; **Fl.** white; **Fr.** red, 1 cm lg.; **S.** black.—Mexico.

Variable; Fl. sometimes white, or with a red M.-stripe; Sp. golden-brown or yellow.

M. monancistracantha Backbg. (3:1, 3:7)
Bo. simple, to c. 3.7 cm ∅, 4.5 cm h., darker green, subspherical at first, then ± tapering above; **Tub.** slender-conical; **Isp.** 8:13; **Ax.** with felt and Br.; **Rsp.** c. 23, thin, white, interlacing; **Csp.** 1(–2), hooked (or only one hooked, if 2 are present); reddish-brown, to 8 mm lg., in the centre of the Ar.; **Fl.** 1.8 cm lg., 1.5 cm ∅, pale yellowish; **Sp.** all pubescent; **Fr.** and **S.** ?—Mexico (San Luis Potosí).

M. monancistria Berg.: **Mammillaria scheidweileriana** O.

M. monocentra Jac. (1:2)
Bo. broadly spherical, dark green, to 8.5 cm ∅, later elongated, to 12.5 cm h.; **Tub.** pyramidal; **Isp.** ?; **Ax.** white-woolly in the flowering zone; **Rsp.** 6, 2–5 mm lg., sometimes stouter, all projecting; **Csp.** 1, to 2.5 cm lg., stoutly acicular, ± recurved, yellowish-brown, black-tipped; **Fl.** small, pink; **Sti.** reddish-yellow; **Fr.** ?—Mexico.

M. montensis Craig (1:3)
Bo. flattened-spherical, dark green, simple, 3 cm h., 5 cm ∅; **Tub.** conical; **Isp.** 8:13; **Ax.** sparsely woolly, with white Br.; **Rsp.** 20, 3–7 mm lg., stiff, white, sometimes brown-tipped; **Csp.** 2(–3), to 1.5 cm lg., acicular, stiff, dark purplish-brown, projecting obliquely up and down; **Fl.** ?; **Fr.** ?—Mexico (SW. Chihuahua; SE. Sonora, Sierra Cajurichi).
v. **monocentra** Craig: **Rsp.** 20, 3 mm lg.; **Csp.** 1, 4 mm lg.—Mexico (Sonora, Sierra Charuco);
v. **quadricentra** Craig: **Rsp.** to 22, 5–8 mm lg.; **Csp.** 4–5, to 2.5 cm lg.—Mexico (Sonora, Sierra Canelo).

M. morganiana Tieg. (1:1)
Bo. spherical to clavate, light bluish-green, to 8 cm ∅, simple or branching dichotomously; **Tub.** pyramidal, weakly angular; **Isp.** variable: 8:13, 13:21, 21:34; **Ax.** with numerous H. as long as the Tub.; **Rsp.** 40–50, to 1.2 cm lg., very fine to hair-like, contorted, interlacing; **Csp.** 4–6, 1 cm lg., stiffly acicular, white, brown-tipped; **Fl.**, **Fr.**, **S.** ?—Mexico (Guanajuato, Bucareli; Querétaro).

M. morricalii Cowper 1969
Bo. simple, sometimes in small groups of 2–5 heads 5–13 cm h., 1.5–8 cm ∅, ovoid to shortly cylindric, noticeably yellowish-green; **Tub.** cylindric, green; **Isp.** 13:21; **Ax.** with short white wool; **Ar.** with short yellowish wool, round, 8 mm apart; **Sp.** concealing the Bo., lending it a yellowish appearance; **Rsp.** c. 22, straight, regularly spreading, 5–8 mm lg., light yellowish, ± erect; **Csp.** 1,

hooked, yellowish below, otherwise orange with a dark tip; **Fl.** small, shortly bellshaped, 2 cm ∅ when fully expanded; **Sep.** greenish, shorter than the Pet.; **Pet.** under 1 cm lg., oblong-lanceolate, not recurved, pink to yellowish-orange with a darker M.-stripe; **style** pale green with 5–6 light green **Sti.**; **Fr.** green to purplish-red, 8–15 mm lg., shortly clavate; **S.** dark reddish-brown, 1–1.25 mm lg.—Mexico (Chihuahua, Majalca, on fairly steep rocky slopes among grass, particularly under oaks; rare). Belongs to the complex M. wrightii-wilcoxii-viridiflora. Named for its discoverer, D. Morrical of Las Cruces, New Mexico.

M. movensis Craig (1:3)
Bo. flattened-spherical, yellowish to greyish-green, 5 cm h., to 10 cm ∅, simple; **Tub.** ovoid-conical above; **Isp.** 13:21; **Ax.** with 4–8 white Br., some as long as the Tub.; **Rsp.** 10–13, 3–15 mm lg., fine-acicular, upper ones shortest, white, laterals tipped brownish, lower ones reddish-brown, black-tipped; **Csp.** (1–)4, 5–20 mm lg., stouter, reddish-brown, thickened below; **Fl.** ?; **Fr.** red, 2 cm lg.; **S.** light brown.—Mexico (SE. Sonora, Movas).

M. muehlenpfordtii Först. (1:3)
Bo. spherical to oblong, to c. 10 cm h., 8 cm ∅, dark green; **Tub.** pyramidal; **Isp.** 13:21; **Ax.** white-woolly at first, sometimes with Br. overtopping the Tub.; **Rsp.** 40–50, 2–6 mm lg., bristly-fine, white; **Csp.** 4, upper ones 4–12 mm lg., lower ones 5–35 mm lg., acicular, stiff, yellow, brown-tipped; **Fl.** 1.5 cm lg., 1 cm ∅, purplish-red, M.-line dark; **Fr.** red, to 2 cm lg.; **S.** light brown.—Mexico (Querétaro; Guanajuato).
v. **brevispina** (Craig): **Csp.** only 5–6 mm lg.;
v. **hexispina** (Schmoll): **Csp.** 6, to 3.5 cm lg.; **Fl.** more tubular, smaller, to 9 mm lg.;
v. **longispina** (Craig): **Csp.** 4, to 2.5 cm lg. and more;
v. **nealeana** (Tieg.): **Ax.** with many long-projecting Br.-H.; **Rsp.** very fine; **Csp.** 4, cruciform, dark; plants attaining over 10 cm ∅; **Fl.** fairly deep red.
There is a much stouter and dichotomously branching form which Frau Schmoll called M. potosina v. gigantea.

M. multicentralis Craig (3:1, 3:7)
Bo. subspherical, dark green, to 2 cm ∅, offsetting to form low mats; **Tub.** soft, cylindric; **Isp.** ?; **Ax.** glabrous; **Rsp.** 30–40, to 1.2 cm lg., hair-like, white; **Csp.** 12–15, 4 mm lg., one stouter, acicular, hooked, yellowish to brownish, the others very fine-acicular, white, tipped light brownish; **Fl.** 8 mm lg., 6 mm ∅, pale pink; **Fr.** reddish, ovoid, 1.3 cm lg.; **S.** dark reddish-brown.—Mexico (Querétaro, Tarajeas?). The turnip-like R. is rather limp.

M. multiceps SD. (3:1, 1:5)
Bo. spherical to shortly-cylindric, to 2 cm ∅, to over 10 cm lg., darker greyish-green, freely offsetting to form larger groups; **Tub.** slender, rather soft; **Isp.** 8:13; **Ax.** with longer hairlike contorted Br.; **Rsp.** 30–50, 2–5 mm lg., hair-fine, pubescent, white; **Csp.** 6–8(–12), 6–8 mm lg., spreading, thin-acicular, hairy, thickened and whitish below, otherwise reddish-yellow to reddish-brown; **Fl.** to 2 cm lg.; **Pet.** brownish, bordered pale greenish-yellow; **Fr.** scarlet, 8–12 mm lg.; **S.** black.—USA (Texas, Eagle Pass and Rio Grande), Mexico (Coahuila; Tamaulipas; Nuevo León).
> v. **perpusilla** Meinshsn.: **Bo.** very small; **Sp.** paler; **Csp.** yellowish, ± appressed; general appearance is whitish.

M. multidigitata Linds. (3:1, 2:6) (also 3:1, 1:1)
Bo. cylindric, to 20 cm lg., 2–5 cm ∅, green, with up to 100 heads together; **Tub.** conical; **Isp.** 13:21(?); **Ax.** weakly woolly; **Rsp.** 15–25, 6–8 mm lg., white, thin-acicular; **Csp.** (1–)4, to c. 8 mm lg., brown at first, reddish below, then darker above, white below midway, straight or one Sp. sometimes hooked; **Fl.** 15 mm lg., white, Pet. sometimes with a yellowish stripe; **Fr.** clavate, red, 15 mm lg.; **S.** black.—Mexico (Baja California, San Pedro Nolasco island).

M. multiformis (Br. & R.) Böd. (3:1, 3:7)
Bo. spherical to more strongly clavate or oblong, several times as long as broad, greyish-green, offsetting; **Tub.** conical, soft, sometimes cylindric; **Isp.** 8:13(?); **Ax.** with white wool and long white Br.; **Rsp.** c. 30, thin-acicular, yellow, projecting; **Csp.** 4, 8–10 mm lg., stiffly acicular, lower one porrect, hooked, all reddish above; **Fl.** to 1 cm ∅, deep purple; **Fr.** ± spherical; **S.** black.—Mexico (San Luis Potosí, Alvarez).

M. multihamata Böd. (3:1, 3:7)
Bo. spherical to shortly cylindric, dark leaf-green, to 5 cm ∅; **Tub.** cylindric; **Isp.** 8:13; **Ax.** glabrous, but with hair-like Br.; **Rsp.** c. 25, 8 mm lg., bristly, hairy, white; **Csp.** 7–9, 1 cm lg., 2–3 straight, others hooked, dark red to reddish-brown; **Fl.** 1.5 cm lg., 1.2 cm ∅, white (to pink, acc. Böd.), M.-stripe pink or darker; **Fr.** ?; **S.** brownish-black.—Mexico (Guanajuato).

M. multiseta Ehrenbg. (1:3)
Bo. spherical to cylindric, mostly simple, light green, to 12.5 cm h., to 7.5 cm ∅; **Tub.** 4-sided, pyramidal; **Isp.** ?; **Ax.** white-woolly, with to c. 30 white Br. to 16 mm lg.; **Rsp.** 4–6, 8–10 mm lg., 1 darker, more central, others to 7 mm lg., acicular, white, tipped dark-brown; **Fl.** ?; **Fr.** 2 cm lg.,

purple; **S.** coffee-coloured.—Mexico (Puebla, Petlalzingo-Acatlán).

M. mundtii K. Sch. (3:1, 1:3)
Bo. spherical to elongated, leaf-green, to 7 cm ∅; **Tub.** conical; **Isp.** 8:13; **Ax.** naked; **Rsp.** 10–12, thin-subulate, white, to 5 mm lg.; **Csp.** 2(–4), to 10 mm lg., somewhat stouter-aciculate, more brown, lighter below; **Fl.** to 2 cm lg., 1.4 cm ∅, carmine; **Fr.** ?; **S.** brown.—Mexico (Querétaro, La Fosiquín).

M. mystax Mart. (1:3)
Bo. spherical to oblong, dark greyish-green, to 15 cm h., 10 cm ∅, simple or caespitose; **Tub.** 4-angled, pyramidal; **Isp.** 13:21; **Ax.** white-woolly, with contorted Br.; **Rsp.** 5–6(–10), 4–8 mm lg., white, brown-tipped; **Csp.** 3–4, mostly 3, to 2 cm lg., one more central to 7 cm lg., dark purple at first; **Sp.** very variable in length and colour; **Fl.** 2.5 cm lg., 2 cm ∅, purplish-pink, lighter inside; **Fr.** red, 2.5 cm lg.; **S.** dark brown.—Mexico (Hidalgo to Oaxaca).

M. nana Backbg. (3:1, 1:2 or 3:7)—Descr. Cact. Nov. III: 8, 1963.
Bo. spherical, with a taproot, to c. 2.5 cm ∅, mostly less, c. 1.5 cm h., glossy, fresh green; **Tub.** cylindric, to c. 6 mm lg. when turgid; **sap** watery; **Isp.** 5:8; **Ax.** at first with some wool, later also with slender Br.; **Ar.** oblong, c. 2 mm lg., with short white felt virtually only in the middle; **Rsp.** c. 35, very thin, hyaline, radiating, pubescent; **Csp.** 0, then 1 in the upper part of the Ar., later sometimes 2, one above the other, the upper one straight, lower one hooked, both brownish (in 1 Ar. I have also seen 4 Csp. in a vertical R.), directed upwards, pubescent, to c. 5 mm lg., thin; **Fl.** c. 1 cm lg., 1.5 cm ∅, Pet. entire; **Sep.** creamy white, with a red M.-line, c. 2.5 mm br., linear, tapering; Pet. equally narrow, concolorous creamy-white or at most with a faint dorsal M.-line; **Sti.** short, greenish-cream; **Fr.** ?—Mexico (San Luis Potosí, on the road to Balnearios Lourdes). (Fig. 215.) In habitat, this spec. remains smaller and the Csp. are missing. Mammillaria nana hort. was only a name in MfK., 129. 1894.

M. nana nom. prov. Krähenbühl: KuaS Dec. 1968/228: no description available.

M. napina J. A. Purp. (3:2, 4:8) [Grafting recommended.]
Bo. hemispherical, passing over into the turnip-like taproot, light green, c. 4–6 cm ∅; **Tub.** conical; **Isp.** 8:13; **Ax.** weakly woolly or glabrous; **Rsp.** 10–12, 8–9 mm lg., appressed, interlacing, hyaline to light yellow; **Csp.** 0; **Fl.** 4 cm ∅, violet-pink, lighter

towards the centre; **Fr.** ?; **S.** black(?).—Mexico (Puebla, W. of Tehuacan).

    v. **centrispina** Craig: mostly with 1 **Csp.** 5–8 mm lg.

M. nealeana Tieg.: **Mammillaria muehlenpfordtii** v. nealeana (Tieg.) Backbg.

M. nejapensis Craig & Daw. (1:3)
Bo. spherical to ± clavate-elongated, to 15 cm h., 7.5 cm $\varnothing$, offsetting or sometimes branching dichotomously; **Tub.** conical; **Isp.** 13:21; **Ax.** more woolly above, with long ± contorted Br.; **Rsp.** (3–)4(–5), 2–5 mm lg., lower one longest, to 2.5 cm lg., all acicular, white, reddish-brown at the extreme tip; **Csp.** 0; **Fl.** 1.8 cm lg., 1 cm $\varnothing$; **Pet.** pale reddish-brown, bordered whitish, or sometimes with a scarlet M.-stripe; **Fr.** light red, 2 cm lg.; **S.** pale golden-yellow.—Mexico (Oaxaca, NW. of Nejapa).
    v. **brevispina** Craig & Daws.: **Rsp.** only 2–4 mm lg.;
    v. **longispina** Craig & Daws.: upper **Rsp.** 4–5 mm lg., lower ones to 5 cm lg.
The spec. and its varieties can also be considered as more divergent forms of M. praelii Mühlpfrdt. which occurs in the same province.

M. neobertrandiana Backbg. (3:1, 1:2)
Bo. rather oblong, to 6 cm lg., 4 cm $\varnothing$, dark olive-green, caespitose; **Tub.** conical; **Isp.** 13:21; **Ax.** naked; **Rsp.** and **Csp.** not differentiated, similar, to c. 36, 1–5 mm lg., first pinkish, then all white, very fine, appressed; **Fl.** very small, white; **Sep.** with a brown dorsal stripe.—N. Mexico.

M. neocoronaria Knuth (3:1, 1:2)
Bo. spherical at first, then elongated, to c. 15 cm h., to 7 cm $\varnothing$, green, becoming greyish-bluish, caespitose; **Tub.** conical; **Isp.** 8:13; **Ax.** glabrous; **Rsp.** 16–18, whitish, to 8 mm lg.; **Csp.** mostly 6, to c. 1.5 cm lg., varying from yellowish or brown to ruby-red; **Fl.** to 17 mm lg., light carmine.—Mexico (Hidalgo, Real del Monte, Sierra Rosa).

M. neocrucigera Backbg. (2:1)
Bo. depressed-spherical to more oblong, mostly solitary; **Tub.** small, conical; **Ax.** woolly; **Rsp.** ± numerous, short, white; **Csp.** 4, to 6 mm lg., stouter, cruciform, flat against the Bo., greyish-brown to blackish; **Fl.** small, violet-pink; **Sti.**, style and **Fil.** coloured similarly.—Mexico (San Luis Potosí).
This is my new name for a plant Bödeker erroneously first called M. crucigera, and later M. pseudocrucigera; but this was never validly published and was a homonym of Craig's spec. The

description was insufficient for any positive identification.

M. neomystax Backbg. (1:3)
Bo. spherical to elongated, to 10 cm h., 8 cm $\varnothing$; **Tub.** 4-angled; **Isp.** 8:13(?); **Ax.** moderately woolly at first, with longer Br.; **Rsp.** (3–)4(–5), to 6 mm lg., white, tipped dark brown; **Csp.** 0–1, to 2 cm lg., curved upwards, brown; **Fl.** light red, c. 7 mm lg., 1.3 cm $\varnothing$; **Fr.** red; **S.** brown.—Mexico (mountains W. of Rio Grande, in the Tehuacan-Oaxaca area).

M. neopalmeri Craig (3:1, 1:2 or 1:5)
Bo. rather oblong, to 9 cm lg., 5 cm $\varnothing$, caespitose, whitish to greyish-green to bluish-green; **Tub.** truncated-conical; **Isp.** 8:13; **Ax.** white-woolly, with short Br.; **Rsp.** 25–30, 5–6 mm lg., very fine-acicular, white; **Csp.** (3–)4, 7–8 mm lg., thin-acicular, brownish, dark-tipped, lowest Sp. porrect; **Fl.** 1.2 cm lg., 1 cm $\varnothing$, pale greenish-white to light cream, M.-line olive-green; **Fr.** scarlet, 1.3 cm lg.; **S.** black.—Mexico (Baja California, NW. coast, San Benito island).

M. neophaeacantha Backbg. (3:1, 1:3)
Bo. eventually cylindric; **Tub.** conical; **Isp.** 8:13; **Ax.** very woolly; **Rsp.** 0; **Csp.** (2–)4, first blackish, then grey, reddish-brown when wet, to 2.2 cm lg.; **Fl.** 1.8 cm lg., carmine; **Fr.** red, 1.8 cm lg.; **S.** light brown.—Mexico (Guanajuato, Dolores Hidalgo).

M. neoschwarzeana Backbg. (1:2)
Bo. broadly spherical, later caespitose; **Tub.** 4-sided, angles not acute; **Isp.** 8:13(?); **Ax.** woolly; **Rsp.** 7, stoutly acicular, projecting, light; **Csp.** 1, mostly shorter than the Rsp., porrect, less stout, reddish-brownish; **Fl.** 2.3 cm lg., cream to reddish-white, M.-line faintly reddish; **Fr.** carmine; **S.** 1 mm lg., light brown.—Mexico (N. Sinaloa to Sonora).

M. nivosa Lk.: **Mammillaria flavescens** v. nivosa (Lk.) Backbg.

M. nunezii (Br. & R.) Orc. (3:1, 1:5 or 2:6)
Bo. becoming oblong, little offsetting, dull green, to 15 cm h., 8 cm $\varnothing$; **Tub.** conical; **Isp.** 13:21; **Ax.** with 8–10 Br.; **Rsp.** 25–30, 5–7 mm lg., thin-acicular, white; **Csp.** (2–)4(5–6), subulate, reddish-brown above to black-tipped; **Fl.** 15 mm lg., deep pink to purplish-pink; **Fl.** pale greenish-white, pale pink above, 2.3 cm lg.; **S.** brown.—Mexico (Guerrero, Taxco and Iguala, near Buenavista de Cuellar).
    v. **solisii** (Br. & R.) Backbg.: **Rsp.** in part rather longer; **Csp.** 1, hooked. Form with all centrals hooked; there are also plants with mixed Sp.-types.

M. obconella Scheidw. (3:1, 1:3)
Bo. becoming columnar, to 30 cm h., sometimes much taller, to 12 cm ⌀, dark green, caespitose in habitat, forming colonies; **Tub.** with 4 rounded sides, almost conical; **Isp.** 13:21; **Ax.** with much white wool at first; **Rsp.** 0 or few, very thin; **Csp.** 4(–5–6), 1 curving upwards, to 2.5 cm lg., yellowish-brownish to dark honey-coloured at first; **Fl.** 2 cm lg., carmine; **Fr.** dark red, to 2.3 cm lg.; **S.** yellowish-brown.—Mexico (Hidalgo, Barrancas of Meztitlán). Mostly known by the more recent name: M. dolichocentra Lem.; close to M. ingens.

   v. **galeottii** (Scheidw.) Backbg.: **Tub.** conical, light green; **Ax.** always glabrous; lower part of Ar. sometimes with 1–3 short Br., soon falling; **Csp.** 4–5, yellowish, brown-tipped, strongly recurved.—Mexico (Jalapa).

M. obscura Hildm. (1:2)
Bo. ± depressed-spherical, simple, to 8 cm h., 11 cm ⌀, dark green; **Tub.** shortly pyramidal; **Isp.** 13:21; **Ax.** white-woolly at first; **Rsp.** 6–8, 8–14 mm lg., thin-subulate, whitish to horn-coloured, shortly brown-tipped; **Csp.** 2–4, the lowest one longest, to 2 cm lg., upper ones shorter, thin-subulate, rough, reddish to horn-coloured, tipped dark brown to black; **Fl.** 1.5 cm ⌀, dirty whitish-yellow, M.-line pink; **Fr.** red; **S.** dark brown.—Mexico (Querétaro, near Toliman; Zacatecas).

   v. **wagneriana-turtulospina** Craig: **Csp.** to 4.5 cm lg., contorted.

M. obvallata O.: possibly the older, and therefore valid, name for M. fuliginosa SD.

M. occidentalis (Br. & R.) Böd. (3:1, 1:5 or 2:6)
Bo. slender-columnar, to 15 cm h., 2–3 cm ⌀; **Tub.** conical; **Isp.** 5:8; **Ax.** not woolly, sometimes with a few Br.; **Rsp.** 12–18, 3–8 mm lg., thin-acicular, white to yellowish, brown-tipped; **Csp.** 4–5, 5–12 mm lg., acicular, stiff, reddish-brown, lowest one hooked or straight; **Fl.** 1 cm lg., pink to deep pink; **Fr.** reddish; **S.** black.—Mexico (Colima, Manzanillo; Nayarit; Sinaloa).

   v. **monocentra** (Craig) Backbg.: **Csp.** 1, 7 mm lg., acicular, reddish-brown, straight to bent, sometimes ± hooked.—Mexico (Sonora, Yaqui valley). There are also forms with very short Csp.

M. ochoterenae (H. Bravo) Werd. (3:1, 1:3)
Bo. depressed-spherical to slightly elongated, simple, light green, to 8 cm ⌀; **Tub.** conical; **Isp.** 13:21; **Ax.** naked; **Rsp.** 17–18, 4–9 mm lg., thin-acicular, white to light amber, interlacing; **Csp.** 5–6, 10–20 mm lg., thin-subulate, sometimes slightly curving, yellowish-grey, tipped red, becoming brown, tipped black; **Fl.** 1 cm lg., pink,

bordered white; **Fr.** red, 2 cm lg.; **S.** light brown.—Mexico (Oaxaca).

M. ocotillensis Craig (1:2)
Bo. flattened-spherical, simple, matt light green, to 6 cm ⌀, 7 cm h.; **Tub.** weakly 4-sided; **Isp.** 13:21; **Ax.** glabrous; **Rsp.** (2–)3(–4), 3–10 mm lg., thin-acicular, chalky-white; **Csp.** 1–2(–3), upper ones 3–15 mm lg., lower ones 12–35 mm lg., stoutly acicular, dark purplish-brown, ± black above; **Fl.** cream-coloured, M.-stripe reddish; **Fr.** carmine, 1.7 cm lg.; **S.** reddish-brown.—Mexico (Querétaro, Ocotillo, Sierra San Moran).

   v. **brevispina** Craig: **Tub.** shorter, 5 mm lg.; **Rsp.** 4–10 mm lg.; upper **Csp.** 3–4 mm lg., lower ones to 1.2 cm lg.;

   v. **longispina** Craig: **Tub.** longer, 8 mm lg.; **Rsp.** 4–10 mm lg.; upper **Csp.** to 15 mm lg., lower ones to 3.5 cm lg.

M. oliviae Orc. often goes under its own name, but is generally held to be only a form of **M. microcarpa** Eng. in which the centrals are not hooked; there are forms intermediate to the latter in which hooked centrals sometimes occur; **Fl.** 3 cm ⌀, purple; **Sti.** green (!).—USA (Arizona, Tucson).

M. orcuttii Böd. (1:2)
Bo. spherical to shortly columnar, glossy, dark bluish-green, 6–7 cm ⌀, simple; **Tub.** ± shortly conical; **Isp.** 13:21; **Ax.** with much white wool at first, becoming glabrous; **Rsp.** 0; **Csp.** 4(–5), spreading outwards, stiff-acicular, pitch-black at first, brownish below, becoming frosted-grey, lowest Sp. to 2 cm lg., others to 1.5 cm lg.; at first also 6–8 hair-like Ssp. 2 mm lg., soon dropping; **Fl.** c. 1.2 cm lg. and ⌀, light carmine, M.-stripe darker; **Fr.** red, to 3 cm lg.; **S.** reddish-brown.—Mexico (Puebla, near Esperanza).
The first name may have been M. bergii Miqu.

M. ortegae (Br. & R.) Orc. (1:2)
Bo. shortly clavate, to 8 cm ⌀, simple; **Tub.** pyramidal; **Isp.** 8:13; **Ax.** woolly; **Rsp.** 3–4 (sometimes with 1–2 Ssp.), 6–10 mm lg., stoutly acicular, yellowish-brown, projecting; **Csp.** 0; **Fl.** reddish (?); **Fr.** reddish, 1 cm lg.; **S.** light brown.—Mexico (Sinaloa).

M. ortiz-rubiona (H. Bravo) Werd. (3:1, 1:2)—(3:2, 4:8)
Bo. depressed-spherical, greyish-green, to 10 cm ⌀, quite freely offsetting; **Tub.** cylindric to clavate; **Isp.** 8:13; **Ax.** with numerous Br.-H. overtopping the Tub.; **Rsp.** 25–30, 4–15 mm lg., ± hair-fine, white, interlacing; **Csp.** 4–6, 1.2–1.5 cm lg., acicular, white, sometimes pink-tipped; **Fl.** 3.5 cm lg., 3 cm ⌀, pale greenish-white to pale pink; **Fr.**

carmine; **S.** black.—Mexico (Guanajuato; Querétaro, on the border between the two States).

M. pachycylindrica Backbg. (1:2)
Bo. simple, stout-cylindric, to 26 cm h., 11.5 cm ∅, greyish-greenish; **Tub.** conical; **Isp.** 13:21; milky **sap** drying to brownish; **Ax.** later weakly felty; **Rsp.** 20–23, 4–8 mm lg., whitish-grey; **Csp.** c. 6, thin; **Sp.** ± pinkish-white at first, centrals dark to blackish above; **Fl.** c. 2 cm lg. and ∅, greenish-pink to dirty pink (inside); **Fr.** 2.5 cm lg., carmine both outside and in; **S.** brown.—Mexico.

M. pachyrhiza Backbg. (1:2)
Bo. simple, to 15 cm ∅, leaf-green, visible part aboveground to 4 cm h., with a stout taproot deep in the soil; **Tub.** ± compressed; **Isp.** 13:21(?): **Rsp.** 15–18, to 1 cm lg., white, interlacing; **Csp.** 4–6, ± thickened below, to 1.2–1.6 cm lg., white, yellowish or reddish; **Fl.** white; **Fr.** dull red; **S.** ?—Mexico (borders of Puebla and Jalapa, Las Derrumbadas, among grasses).

M. pacifica (Gat.) Böd. (1:2)
Bo. spherical, to 15 cm h. and ∅, dark green, caespitose or branching dichotomously; **Tub.** weakly 4-angled; **Isp.** ?; **Ax.** woolly; **Rsp.** 7–12, white, brown-tipped, 5–10 mm lg.; **Csp.** 1, to 1.5 cm lg., stiffly acicular, brown-tipped; **Fl.** greenish-yellow, darker in the middle; **Fr.** ?—Mexico (Baja California, coast near Todos Santos).
Although sometimes referred to both M. baxteriana and M. marshalliana, this spec. diverges in size, dark-green Bo.-colour and more closely-spaced Tub. Possibly only a variety.

M. painteri Rose (3:1, 3:7)
Bo. spherical to oblong, 2 cm ∅; **Tub.** rounded; **Isp.** 8:13; **Ax.** weakly woolly; **Rsp.** 20 or more, 5 mm lg., hair-fine, white; **Csp.** 4–5, 1 cm lg., thin-acicular, lowest one hooked, dark brown above; all **Sp.** hairy; **Fl.** to 1.5 cm lg., greenish-white, pale yellow in the middle; **Fr.** red, 1 cm lg.; **S.** black.—Mexico (Querétaro, San Juan del Rio).

M. palmeri Jac. non Böd. (3:1, 1:3)
Bo. spherical to ± columnar, to 12 cm h., 6–7 cm ∅, simple, dark green; **Tub.** broadly to cylindrically conical, compressed; **Isp.** ?; **Ax.** thickly woolly; **Rsp.** (18–)24–26, 4–7 mm lg., bristle-like, white, dense; **Csp.** 4, 4–6 mm lg., amber below, reddish-brown above; **Fl.** to 17 mm lg., 20 mm ∅, light greenish-yellow, M.-stripe narrow, yellowish-red; **Fr.** ?—Origin?

M. parensis Craig (3:1, 1:5)
Bo. spherical to shortly columnar, very low in the ground, dark greyish-green, branching dicho-

tomously or caespitose; **Tub.** rounded; **Isp.** 8:13; **Ax.** with a few white Br.; **Rsp.** 18–20, 3–4 mm lg., thin, white, yellow below; **Csp.** 4–5, 5–8 mm lg., acicular, orange-yellow, one often projecting; **Fl., Fr.** and **S.** ?—Mexico (Chihuahua, between Parras (Coahuila) and Chihuahua city).

M. parkinsonii Ehrenbg. (1:1 or 1:3)
Bo. (depressed-)spherical to elongated, branching dichotomously to form large groups, bluish-green, single heads to 15 cm h., 8 cm ∅; **Tub.** pyramidal, minutely spotted; **Isp.** 8:13, also 13:21; **Ax.** white-woolly, with white Br.; **Rsp.** 30–35, 3–7 mm lg., white; **Csp.** 2–4(–5), upper ones 6–8 mm lg., lower ones to 3.5 cm lg., mostly shorter, to c. 2 cm lg., ± stoutly subulate, milk-white to reddish, tipped dark brown; **Fl.** 1.5 cm lg.; **Pet.** brownish-pink, bordered cream; **Fr.** scarlet, 1 cm lg.; **S.** light brown.—Mexico (Hidalgo to Querétaro).
   v. **brevispina** Craig: **Tub.** in **Isp.** 13:21; **Rsp.** 35–40, 1–4 mm lg.; **Csp.** 4(–5), 3–5 mm lg.; **Fl.** white below, tipped pale pink;
   v. **dietrichae** (Tieg.) Backbg.: **Csp.** less stoutly subulate, rather long and crowded, whitish to ± blackish-brown above.
A very variable spec. There are also forms with stouter Bo.

M. patonii (H. Bravo) Werd. (3:2, 5:9)
Bo. columnar, olive-green, to 15 cm lg., 4–5 cm ∅, offsetting; **Tub.** ± cylindric; **Isp.** 5:8(?); **Ax.** naked; **Rsp.** 13–15, grey, brown-tipped; **Csp.** 4, stouter, to 1.2 cm lg., one slightly hooked, blackish-red; **Fl.** 3 cm lg., purple; **Fr.** green; **S.** black.—Mexico (Nayarit, Islas Marias).
   v. **sinalensis** (Craig) Backbg.: **Rsp.** only 10–12, 5–7 mm lg.; **Csp.** 1, 8–10 mm lg., strongly hooked; **Ax.** glabrous; **Fl.** 2.5 cm lg., 4 cm ∅, purplish-pink.—Mexico (Sinaloa).

M. pearsonii hort.: only a name; seedlings resemble M. elegans.

M. peninsularis (Br. & R.) Orc. (1:2)
Bo. broadly spherical, sunk low in the ground, to 4 cm ∅, pale bluish-green, sometimes caespitose; **Tub.** acutely 4-angled, rounded above, keeled below; **Isp.** 5:8; **Ax.** long-woolly at first; **Rsp.** 4–8, ± slender-subulate, pale yellow, brown-tipped; **Csp.** 0, or 1 Rsp. placed more centrally; **Fl.** 1.5 cm lg., greenish-yellow, M.-line reddish; **Fr.** and **S.** ?—Mexico (Baja California, Cape San Lucas).

M. pennispinosa Krainz (3:1, 3:7)
Bo. spherical, simple, to c. 3 cm h. and ∅, more elongated when grafted; **R.** napiform; **Tub.** cylindric, minutely floccose; **Isp.** 8:13; **Ax.** shortly felty at first; **Rsp.** 16–20, 5–8 mm lg., thin, greyish-

white; **Csp.** 1(–3), one hooked, projecting, fairly long, yellow below, reddish-brown or lighter above; all **Sp.** hairy*; **Fl.** 1.5 cm lg., 1.2 cm ∅, white, M.-stripe carmine-pink; **Fr.** long-clavate, red; **S.** black.—Mexico (Coahuila).

M. pentacantha Pfeiff. (1:2)
Bo. spherical, intense green, offsetting from the sides, to 12 cm ∅; **Tub.** angular-conical; **Isp.** 5:8, 8:13?; **Ax.** increasingly white-felty; **Rsp.** 4, cruciform; **Csp.** 1, c. 4 cm lg., porrect or pointing downwards; **Sp.** brownish, then ash-grey.— Mexico. Variable spec.

M. perbella Hildm. (2:1)
Bo. broadly spherical, branching dichotomously, bluish to greyish-green, single heads scarcely over 6 cm ∅; **Tub.** slender-conical; **Isp.** 13:21; **Ax.** weakly woolly; **Rsp.** 14–18, 1.5–3 mm lg., bristly, thin; **Csp.** 2, 4–6 mm lg., stouter; **Fl.** to 10 mm lg., carmine-red; **Fr.** ?—Mexico. Variable. One form (v. lanata Schmoll) has a woollier crown and rather longer, whiter Rsp.

M. petrophila Brand. (1:3)
Bo. depressed-spherical to elongated-spherical, to 15 cm ∅, greyish-green, sometimes caespitose; **Tub.** conical, weakly angular; **Isp.** 8:13; **Ax.** with light brownish wool and Br.; **Rsp.** 8–10, 1–1.5 cm lg., thin-acicular; **Csp.** 1–2, to 2 cm lg., acicular, dark nut-brown, later paler; **Fl.** 1.8–2 cm lg., pale greenish-yellow; **Fr.** small, spherical, red; **S.** reddish-brown.—Mexico (Baja California, near the S. cape, Sierra de la Laguna and Francisquito).

M. petterssonii Hildm. (1:2)
Bo. subspherical, dull light green, simple or caespitose; **Tub.** indistinctly 4-angled, keeled below; **Isp.** 13:21; **Ax.** with curly wool; **Rsp.** to 10–12, uppers 3 mm lg., lower ones 10–15 mm lg., thin-acicular, dirty white, dark-tipped; **Csp.** 1–4, uppers to 2 cm lg., lowest one to 4.5 cm lg., stouter, brownish, darker-tipped; **Fl.** 2.4 cm lg., deep purplish-pink; **Fr.** ?—Mexico (Guanajuato).
  v. longispina Schwarz, not described: Rsp. variable in length, mostly less numerous, at first black like the Csp., soon becoming ± horn-coloured; Csp. much longer.

M. phaeacantha Lem. (3:1, 1:5)
Bo. spherical, simple, green; **Tub.** ± cylindric, slightly compressed laterally; **Isp.** 8:13; **Ax.** white-woolly, with contorted Br.; **Rsp.** 16–20, 4–5 mm lg., bristly-fine, white, darker below; **Csp.** 4, laterals

8–9 mm lg., upper one 1.4 cm lg., lower one to 1.2 cm lg., subulate, thickened below, reddish, becoming black; **Fl.** deep red or lighter; **Fr.** pink, 1.5 cm lg.; **S.** light brown.—Mexico (San Toro, Regla).

M. phitauiana Baxt.: **Mammillaria verhaertiana** Böd.

M. phymatothele Berg (1:2)
Bo. spherical to oblong, dark bluish-green, to 9 cm ∅, rarely offsetting; **Tub.** pyramidal, keeled below; **Isp.** 8:13; **Ax.** moderately woolly; **Rsp.** 3–7, upper ones 3–6 mm lg., laterals to 1.7 cm lg., lowest one to 3.5 cm lg., greyish-white, red-tipped, sometimes with 3 short Ssp.; **Csp.** 1(–2), to 2 cm lg., reddish-yellow to darker red, becoming grey, black-tipped; **Fl.** to 1.5 cm lg., flame to carmine; **Fr.** ?—Mexico (Hidalgo).
  v. **trohartii** Craig non Hildm.: **Bo.** more depressed; **Csp.** to 4; **Pet.** deep purplish-pink, border paler; **Fr.** reddish, 2.1 cm lg.; **S.** light brown.— Mexico.

M. picta Meinshsn. (3:1, 1:5)
Bo. spherical to elongated, taprooted, glossy, dark leaf-green, simple, to 4 cm ∅; **Tub.** conical-cylindric; **Isp.** 8:13; **Ax.** glabrous, with a few Br.; **Rsp.** 12–14, 6–8 mm lg., very thin, white, ± dark-tipped at first; **Csp.** 1(–2), to over 1 cm lg., acicular, yellowish below, otherwise white, tipped dark reddish-brown; **Sp.** sometimes ± hairy (acc. Böd.) but this, as with some other spec., is not constant; **Fl.** 9 mm lg., 11 mm ∅, Pet. creamy-white, olive-green in the middle; **Fr.** red, small; **S.** black.— Mexico (Tamaulipas, Rio Blanco).

M. pilensis Shurly (1:1 or 1:2)
Bo. elongated-clavate, to 10 cm h., to 18 cm ∅ (or vice-versa?), light green; **crown** very woolly; **Tub.** short, 4-angled; **Isp.** 13:21; **Ax.** very woolly, becoming glabrous; **Rsp.** 4–6, acicular, white, sometimes tinged pink, tipped reddish-black, lower ones mostly longer; **Csp.** 1–2, the lower one considerably longer, mostly concolorous black, the shorter one white, dark-tipped; **Sp.** variable in length; **Fl.** and **Fr.** ?—Mexico (Querétaro, Rio Infernillo).

M. pilispina J. A. Purp. (3:1, 1:3)
Bo. ± flattened-spherical, dark green, to c. 4 cm ∅, forming small groups; **Tub.** cylindric, papillose; **Isp.** 8:13(?); **Ax.** with curly H.; **Rsp.** with a circle of fine hair-like Sp., white, also 4–5 stouter ones, 6–7 mm lg., thickened below and yellow, white above that, tipped brown; **Csp.** 1, to 7 mm lg., coloured similarly; all **Sp.** shortly hairy; **Fl.** 1.5 cm ∅,

---

* Appearing feathery, giving the plant its characteristic appearance; grafted plants, at least, offset fairly freely when older (Translator).

whitish-yellow.—Mexico (San Luis Potosí, Minas San Rafael).

M. pitcayensis H. Bravo (1:3)
Bo. cylindric, to 24 cm lg., 4 cm ∅; **Tub.** conical-cylindric; **Isp.** 13:21(?); **Ax.** woolly, with up to 10 **Br.**; **Rsp.** and **Csp.** not separable, c. 17 outer ones and c. 14 more central, 5–6 mm lg., acicular, thin, weak, yellowish to dirty white; **Fl.** 2 cm lg., purple; **Fr.** and **S.** ?—Mexico (Guerrero, Barranca de Pitcaya).

M. plumosa Web. (3:1, 1:2) [More attractive on own roots than when grafted.]
Bo. subspherical, to c. 7 cm ∅, light green, offsetting to form cushions; **Tub.** soft, cylindric; **Isp.** 8:13; **Ax.** white-woolly; **Rsp.** to 40, 3–7 mm lg., soft, white, feathery; **Csp.** 0; **Fl.** 1.5 cm lg., 1.4 cm ∅, white, M.-line inconspicuous, throat greenish; **Fr.** reddish; **S.** black.—Mexico (Coahuila, growing on cliffs, from Saltillo to Monterrey).

M. polyedra Mart. (1:2–3)
Bo. spherical to oblong, to c. 10 cm h. and ∅, deep green, simple or caespitose; **Tub.** angular-pyramidal, keeled below; **Isp.** 13:21; **Ax.** woolly, later with **Br.**; **Rsp.** (2–)4(–6), uppers 3–4 mm lg., lower one c. 2.5 cm lg., somewhat stouter, others thin-acicular, black to purplish-brown, becoming lighter, red-tipped; **Csp.** 0; **Fl.** to c. 2.5 cm lg., 2 cm ∅, pale to pinkish-red, M.-line darker; **Fr.** scarlet, 2 cm lg.; **S.** reddish-brown.—Mexico (Oaxaca).

M. polygona SD. (1:3)
Bo. becoming clavate to oblong, to 10 cm h.; **Tub.** 4-angled, pyramidal; **Isp.** ?; **Ax.** with wool and hair-like **Br.**; **Rsp.** 8, 1–4 mm lg., uppers 2–3, minute, whitish, sometimes absent; **Csp.** 2, to 2.5 cm lg., stoutly subulate, flesh-coloured below, reddish-brown above; **Fl.** pale pink; **Fr.** and **S.**?—Mexico (Puebla; Morelos: Böd.). Craig's statement that the base of the Sp. was "carmine" was due to an error in translation ("carneis" = flesh-coloured). Appears to be close to M. phymatothele, but insufficiently known, or rare in cultivation.

M. polythele Mart. (1:2)
Bo. spherical to oblong, to 50 cm h., 10 cm ∅, dark greyish to bluish-green, rarely offsetting; **Tub.** conical; **Isp.** 13:21; **Ax.** woolly, becoming glabrous; **Rsp.** missing, or rare and dropping, thin; **Csp.** mostly 2(–4), yellowish or reddish to dark brown, arranged vertically or cruciform, to 2.5 cm lg.; **Fl.** 2 cm lg., 1 cm ∅, pink to carmine; **Fr.** red; **S.** dark brown.—Mexico (Hidalgo, Ixmiquilpan).
v. **columnaris** SD.: to 1 m h.; **Sp.** 5–6, more projecting, brown, lower ones longer; **Fl.**

carmine.—Mexico (Hidalgo, Actopan, Zimapan);
v. **setosa** SD.: **Bo.** to 30 cm h., dark green; **Rsp.** longer-persisting, 8–14, pendant and beard-like; **Csp.** c. 6, the lowest one longest, blackish-red becoming greyish-whitish; **Fl.** small, dark pinkish-red (locality ?).
Variable, apparently more so with increasing age.

M. posseltiana Böd. (3:1, 3:7)
Bo. spherical to elongated, dark leaf-green, to 5 cm ∅, simple; **Tub.** conical; **Isp.** 8:13; **Ax.** white-woolly; **Rsp.** 20, 9 mm lg., thin-acicular, white; **Csp.** 4, 9 mm lg., stiffly acicular, lower one concolorous brown, ± hooked; **Fl.** 2.5 cm lg., 1.5 cm ∅, white, M.-stripe deep pink; **Fr.** pale green, 1.5 cm lg.; **S.** black.—Mexico (Guanajuato, Sierra de Guanajuato).

M. potosina Reb.: **Mammillaria muehlenpfordtii** Först.

M. praelii Muehlpfrdt. (1:3)
Bo. spherical to oblong, pale to dark bluish-green, to c. 11 cm lg., 8 cm ∅, later offsetting freely; **Tub.** 4–6-angled, keeled below; **Isp.** 13:21; **Ax.** with dense white to brownish wool, with up to 18 **Br.** as long as the **Tub.**; **Rsp.** 4(–5), c. 2.8 mm lg., stoutly acicular, yellowish-cream to brown, becoming white, brown-tipped; **Csp.** 0; **Fl.** to 2 cm lg., 1 cm ∅, greenish to yellowish-white, M.-line reddish; **Fr.** red, 2 cm lg.; **S.** brown.—Mexico (Oaxaca). Variable; M. nejapensis may also be referable here.
v. **viridis** (SD.) Craig: **Rsp.** 5(–6); **Csp.** 1(–2); **Fl.** pale yellow, M.-line red.

M. pringlei (Coult.) Brand. (3:1, 1:3–5)
Bo. spherical to elongated, to c. 16 cm h., 7 cm ∅, yellowish to greyish-green, simple; **Tub.** conical, **sap** semi-milky; **Isp.** 13:21; **Ax.** white-woolly, sometimes with one short **Br.**; **Ar.** at first yellowish (always so?), woolly; **Rsp.** 15–20, 5–8 mm lg., fine-acicular, yellowish; **Csp.** 6(–7), stiffly acicular, ± strongly curving, yellow, to 2.5 cm lg.; **Fl.** c. 1 cm ∅, deep red; **Sti.** brownish (Craig: in M. rhodantha, green to pink); **Fr.** reddish, 1.5 cm lg.; **S.** brown.—Mexico (Mexico State; San Luis Potosí).
v. **longicentra** Backbg.—Descr. Cact. Nov. III: 8. 1963; differs in the **Bo.** being more broadly spherical, green, to 11 cm ∅, 10 cm h.; **Ar.** very white-woolly at first; **milk** produced only within the Bo.; **Ax.** woolly, Br. not perceptible; **Rsp.** c. 20, not in one plane, to 10 mm lg., yellow; **Csp.** 4, cruciform, the lowest one pointing ± downwards, to 4 cm lg., the 3 others projecting, contorted or curving around the Bo., ± equal, light yellow.—Mexico (Hidalgo, Barranca Venados). (Fig. 216, above.)

M. prolifera (Mill.) Haw. (3:1, 1:5)
Bo. spherical to oblong, to 6 cm lg., 4 cm ⌀, dark green, offsetting strongly to form cushions; **Tub.** soft, rounded to conical; **Isp.** 5:8; **Ax.** weakly woolly, with white Br. overtopping the Tub.; **Rsp.** to 40, 6–10 mm lg., bristle-like, white; **Csp.** 5–9(–12), to 8 mm lg., thin-acicular, hairy, thickened below, pale yellow; **Fl.** 1.4 cm lg., creamy-yellow, M.-line reddish-brownish; **Fr.** orange-red, 1 cm lg.; **S.** black.—W. Indies (Cuba; Haiti?).

> v. **haitiensis** (K. Sch.) Borg: **Bo.** somewhat stouter, to 7 cm ⌀ (Borg); **Sp.** more numerous, denser, whiter; **Csp.** yellowish, becoming pure white; less floriferous than the type.—Haiti.

M. pseudoalamensis Backbg. (3:2, 4:8)
Bo. conically elongated, offsetting from the base, ± concealed by the Sp.; **Tub.** shortly conical; **Isp.** 8:13(?); **Ax.** glabrous; **Rsp.** to c. 23, white, interlacing; **Csp.** 1, little longer, projecting; **Fl.** just over 2 cm ⌀, red, light olive below; **style** carmine; **Pet.** funnelform, not revolute.—Mexico (Sonora, near Alamos).

M. pseudocrucigera Craig non Böd. (1:2) or (1:1)
Bo. flattened-spherical, low in the soil, dark grey to olive-green, simple, to 5 cm ⌀; **Tub.** 4-angled, pyramidal, keeled below; **Isp.** 8:13; **Ax.** ± woolly; **Rsp.** 12–13, 1–2 mm lg., fine-acicular, white; **Csp.** 4, 3–4 mm lg., subulate, thickened below, chalky-white, orange-brown below, tip small, dark; **Fl.** 1.2 cm lg., 1.5 cm ⌀, with a pink M.-line and a broader white border; **Fr.** light red, 2 cm lg.; **S.** brown.—Mexico (Querétaro, between Cadereyta and Colón).

M. pseudocrucigera Böd. non Craig: **Mammillaria neocrucigera** Backbg.

M. pseudoperbella Quehl (3:1, 1:3–4)
Bo. flattened-spherical to shortly cylindric, leaf-green, to 15 cm ⌀, simple or branching dichotomously; **Tub.** cylindric; **Isp.** 13:21; **Ax.** ± woolly; **Rsp.** 20–30, to 3 mm lg., bristle-fine, pure white; **Csp.** 2, upper one 5 mm lg., lower one shorter, projecting, subulate, brown, tipped reddish-brown; **Fl.** 1.5 cm lg., Pet. carmine, darker in the middle; **Fr.** light red; **S.** brown.—Mexico (Querétaro, Higuerillas; Central Mexico; Oaxaca).

M. pseudorekoi Böd. (2:3)
Bo. spherical to shortly cylindric, to 12 cm h., 5–6 cm ⌀, green, simple; **Tub.** conical; **Isp.** 8:13; **Rsp.** c. 20, scarcely 6 mm lg.; **Csp.** 4–7, to 1 cm lg., brown to black, straight, or the lowest one hooked; **Fl.** slightly over 1.5 cm lg.; **Fr.** red.—Mexico (Puebla; Morelos).

M. pseudoschiedeana Schmoll (to date without Latin diagnosis) (3:1, 1:2): **Bo.** larger than in M. schiedeana and M. dumetorum, offsetting freely; **Sp.** in several Ser., whitish or light, bristly, fine-acicular, interlacing and ± distinctly projecting.—Mexico.

M. pseudoscrippsiana Backbg. (1:2)
Bo. somewhat oblong, bluish-green, to 10 cm h., 4 cm ⌀, caespitose; **Tub.** broadly rounded; **Isp.** 8:13(?); **Ax.** very woolly; **Rsp.** 7–8, upper one 2 mm lg., others longer, lowest one to 6 mm lg., stoutly acicular, white; **Csp.** 2, one directed upwards, the other projecting, to 9 mm lg., scarcely stouter, reddish, becoming white; **Fl.** to 2 cm lg., glossy, white; **Fr.** red; **S.** brown.—Mexico (Nayarit, near Ahuacatlán).

M. pseudosimplex W. Haage & Backbg. n.sp. (3:1, 1:3)
Bo. broadly spherical to spherical; **Tub.** conical; **Isp.** 13:21(?); **Ax.** weakly woolly; **Rsp.** 12, 4 mm lg., white, red-tipped; **Csp.** (2–)4, 5 mm lg., scarcely stouter, reddish-brownish; **Fl.** small, light yellow; **Fr.** ?—Colombia (Sogamoso).

M. pubispina Böd. (3:1, 3:7)
Bo. spherical, dark leaf-green, to 4 cm ⌀, simple; **Tub.** soft, cylindric; **Isp.** 13:21; **Ax.** weakly woolly, with a few hair-like Br.; **Rsp.** 15, 8–12 mm lg., hair-like, ± contorted, interlacing, white; **Csp.** (3–)4, 9–10 mm lg., thin-acicular, reddish to blackish-brown, the lowest one hooked; all **Sp.** ± hairy; **Fl.** 1.8 cm lg., 1.5 cm ⌀, pure white to cream, M.-stripe pink; **Fr.** ?, **S.** black ?—Mexico (Hidalgo, Ixmiquilpan).

M. pullihamata Backbg. (not yet completely validly described) (3:1, 3:7?)
Bo. (at first?) broadly spherical, (over?) 6 cm ⌀, green; **Tub.** broadly conical; **Isp.** 8:13; **Ax.** weakly woolly, with a few Br.; **Ar.** woolly at first; **Rsp.** 22–26, dull white, those in the upper third thinner than the thin-acicular ones of the lower Ser., not exactly in one plane, to 6 mm lg.; **Csp.** 6, dirty reddish to golden-brown, 3 straight, porrect, lower one hooked, c. 1.5 cm lg.; **Fl.** ?; **Fr.** slender-clavate, dull carmine, 1.5 cm lg., with floral remains; **S.** c. 1 mm lg., yellow, obliquely oval, hilum low on one side.—Mexico (Oaxaca, 2800–3000 m, growing with orchids, on cliffs). Colour-photo in "Die Cact.", VI: 3900, Fig. 3546, 1962.

M. pusilla Sweet: **Mammillaria prolifera** (Mill.) Haw.

M. pygmaea (Br. & R.) Berg. (3:1, 3:7)
Bo. spherical to oblong, dark reddish-green, to over

3 cm ∅, caespitose; **Tub.** soft, cylindric; **Isp.** 13:21; **Ax.** with fine contorted Br.; **Rsp.** to 15, to 1.2 cm lg., hair-like, scarcely pubescent, white; **Csp.** 4, 5–8 mm lg., fine-acicular, smooth, golden-yellow to somewhat brownish-yellow, the lowest one hooked; **Fl.** to 1.2 cm lg., creamy-white, M.-stripe brownish; **Fr.** reddish; **S.** black.—Mexico (Querétaro, Cadereyta).

M. pyrrhocephala Schweidw. (1:3)
Bo. oblong, to 8 cm h., greenish to ± bluish-green, simple or caespitose; **Tub.** 4–5-angled, keeled below; **Isp.** 13:21; **Ax.** with white or brownish wool and long Br.; **Rsp.** 4–6, 2–4 mm lg., subulate, dark reddish-brown, reddish below; **Csp.** 0, rarely 1, to 3 mm lg., black; **Fl.** 2 cm lg., Pet. pink, centre deep pink; **Fr.** pink below, light green above, 2 cm lg.; **S.** light brown.—Mexico (Hidalgo; Oaxaca).

M. queretarica Craig (1:2)
Bo. spherical, to 7 cm ∅, 6 cm h., dark green, simple; **Tub.** 4-sided; **Isp.** 13:21; **Ax.** sparsely woolly; **Rsp.** 30, 3–4 mm lg., bristly, white; **Csp.** 4, 4–7 mm lg., the lowest one longest, stoutly acicular, light brown, tipped dark or black, later chalky-white; **Fl.** and **Fr.** ?—Mexico (Querétaro, Rio Infernillo).

M. quevedoi Schmoll, not described; appears to have been a form of M. bravoae, with darker Csp.

M. radiaissima Linds. (3:1, 1:3)
Bo. subspherical, to 5 cm h. and ∅, offsetting freely to form groups; **Tub.** soft; **Isp.** 8:13(?); **Ax.** glabrous or weakly woolly; **Rsp.** to 50, to 1.8 mm lg., bristle-like, white; **Csp.** 1–8, to 6 mm lg., pale brown; **Fl.** 3 cm lg., 1.5 cm ∅, lemon-yellow; **Fr.** and **S.**. ?—Mexico (Baja California, Puente Escondido, N. of La Paz.) [Haage adds: Lau reports he was unable to find it in this locality.]
Appears to resemble M. vetula, but with more Csp. and rather longer Rsp.; is this the "lemon-yellow flowered M. vetula" mentioned in the literature?

M. rekoi (Br. & R.) Vpl. (2:2)
Bo. subspherical to elongated, green, to 12 cm h., 5–6 cm ∅, simple; **Tub.** conical; **Isp.** 8:13; **Ax.** white-woolly, with up to 8 white Br.; **Rsp.** 20, 4–6 mm lg., thin-acicular, white; **Csp.** 4, 1–1.5 cm lg., stiffly acicular, brown, the lowest one ± curving and hooked; **Fl.** 1.5 cm lg., deep purple; **Fr.** red, 1.2 cm lg.; **S.** brown.—Mexico (Oaxaca).

M. rekoiana Craig (2:1)
Bo. ± clavate, to 12 cm h., simple; **Tub.** conical; **Isp.** 8:13; **Ax.** with tufts of white wool and to 8 Br.; **Rsp.** c. 20, 4–6 mm lg., thin-acicular, white; **Csp.**

4–5, 10–15 mm lg., stoutly acicular, brown, porrect, straight; **Fl.** bellshaped, 15 mm lg., deep purple; **Fr.** red; **S.** brown.—Mexico (Oaxaca).

M. rettigiana Böd. (3:1, 3:7)
Bo. depressed-spherical to oblong, dark leaf-green, to 4 cm ∅, somewhat branching; **Tub.** long-cylindric; **Isp.** 8:13; **Ax.** naked or weakly woolly; **Rsp.** 18–20, to 1 cm lg., very thin, white to yellow, later grey; **Csp.** 3–4, upper ones 1.2 cm lg., lowest one to 1.5 cm lg., hooked, all red to dark brown, lighter below; **Fl.** 1.5 cm ∅, delicate pink, with a lighter border; **Fr.** red, small; **S.** brownish-black.—Mexico (Hidalgo; Guanajuato).

M. rhodantha Lk. & O. (3:1, 1:5)
Bo. spherical to oblong, to 30 cm h., 10 cm ∅, simple, offsetting or branching dichotomously, dark green; **Tub.** cylindric-conical; **Isp.** 13:21; **Ax.** white-woolly, bristly; **Rsp.** 16–20, 6–10 lg., lower ones longest, thin-acicular; **Csp.** 4–7, 10–25 mm lg., ± straight, stoutly acicular, smooth; all **Sp.** whitish to yellowish; **Fl.** 2 cm lg., 1.6 cm ∅, deep purplish-pink; **Fr.** reddish, 2.5 cm lg.; **S.** light brown.—Mexico (valley of Mexico; Hidalgo; Querétaro).
v. **crassispina** K. Sch.: **Sp.** long, stout, dark yellow to brown;
v. **fulvispina** (Haw.) Schelle: **Sp.** light to mid-brown;
v. **rubens** Pfeiff.: **Sp.** ruby-red, becoming dark brown;
v. **rubra** K. Sch. (including v. ruberrima K. Sch.): **Sp.** mid to dark red.

M. ritteriana Böd. (1:3)
Bo. spherical, dark leaf-green, to 6 cm ∅, simple; **Tub.** pyramidal; **Isp.** 13:21; **Ax.** shortly white-woolly, with stout white Br.; **Rsp.** 18–20, 5–7 mm lg., ± hair-like, pure white; **Csp.** 1–2, 1 cm lg., thin-subulate, white to yellowish-brown or ± black; **Fl.** to 1.4 cm lg. and ∅, white with a pink M.-line; **Fr.** red, 1 cm lg.; **S.** pale reddish-brown.—Mexico (Coahuila, between Monterrey and Saltillo, near Higueras).
v. **quadricentralis** Craig: **Csp.** 4, 5–6 mm lg., stiffly acicular, purple, then brownish, black-tipped; **Fl.** pale greenish-white, M.-line greenish.—Origin?

M. rosensis Craig (1:2)
Bo. flattened-spherical, greyish-green, to 10 cm ∅, 4 cm h., simple or branching dichotomously; **R.** napiform; **Tub.** conical; **Isp.** 13:21; **Ax.** densely white-woolly; **Rsp.** c. 25, 3–4 mm lg., thin-acicular, white; **Csp.** 4(–5), ± projecting, top and bottom ones 1.2–1.7 cm lg., stoutly subulate, laterals 4–6 mm lg., stoutly acicular, thickened below, dark

brown to black, becoming chalky, brownish-white, tipped dark brown; **Fl.** ?; **Fr.** carmine; **S.** light brown.—Mexico (Querétaro, San Juan de la Rosas).

M. roseoalba Böd. (1:2)
Bo. broadly spherical, to 18 cm ∅, 6 cm h., dark bluish to greyish-green, simple; **Tub.** pyramidal; **Isp.** 8:13; **Ax.** weakly woolly; **Rsp.** 4–6, to 1.5 cm lg., upper ones smaller, laterals 5–6 mm lg., ± thin-subulate, cream-coloured, black-tipped; **Csp.** 0; **Fl.** 1.5 cm lg., 2.5 cm ∅, bellshaped, white, M.-line light to dark pink; **Fr.** red, 1.5 cm lg.; **S.** brownish-yellow.—Mexico (Tamaulipas, near Victoria).

M. roseocentra Böd. & Ritt. (3:1, 1:3)
Bo. spherical, caespitose and forming mats; **R.** stout; **Tub.** short; **Isp.** ?; **Ax.** naked; **Rsp.** 25, in 2 rows, short, white, inner ones shorter, an attractive pink at first, ± red in the crown; **Fl.** and **Fr.** ?—Mexico (Coahuila, near Viescas).

M. rossiana Heinr. (1:5)
Bo. columnar, to 30 cm h., over 5 cm ∅, greyish-green, caespitose; **Tub.** cylindric-conical, with milky **sap**; **Isp.** 8:13; **Ax.** weakly woolly at first; **Rsp.** c. 20, to 7 mm lg., thin, white or sometimes yellowish; **Csp.** 2–3(–4), the bottom one longest, to 11 mm lg., mostly ± hooked, all brown; **Fl.** to 2.1 cm lg., 8 mm ∅, ± tubular, carmine-pink, throat whitish; **Fr.** ?—Mexico.

M. rubida Backbg. (1:2)
Bo. broadly spherical, to c. 9 cm h., 13 cm ∅, bluish-green, usually suffused reddish all over, but especially where exposed to the sun; **Tub.** pyramidal, flanks ± angular; **Isp.** 8:13(?); **Ax.** woolly; **Rsp.** c. 8, to 1.5 cm lg., acicular; **Csp.** 1, to 2 cm lg., later rather longer, little stouter; all **Sp.** at first reddish to darker; **Fl.** 2.2 cm lg., greenish-white; **Fr.** and **S.**?—Mexico (Sinaloa, Sierra Madre near Bacuribito).

M. ruestii Quehl (3:1, 1:5)
Bo. spherical at first, later oblong, to over 7 cm h., to 5 cm ∅, leaf-green, simple, perhaps later offsetting; **Tub.** conical; **Isp.** 13:21; **Ax.** with white wool and Br.; **Rsp.** 16–22, to 6 mm lg., thin-acicular, glossy, white; **Csp.** 4(–5), cruciform, 7–8 mm lg., acicular-subulate, rather thicker below, light to dark reddish-brown, at first sometimes ± black, becoming lighter below; **Fl.** 2 cm lg. and 1.5–2 cm ∅, carmine, throat white; **Fr.** red; **S.** brown.—Honduras and Guatemala.

M. rutila Zucc. (3:1, 1:3)
Bo. spherical, dark green, to 13 cm h. and ∅; **Tub.** conical; **Isp.** ?; **Ar.** felty at first; **Rsp.** 14–16, white,

upper ones much shorter; **Csp.** 4–6, to 13 mm lg., stiff, spreading, ± bent, brownish-red, horn-coloured below, bottom Sp. very long; **Fl.** almost 1.5 cm lg., vivid purplish-red; **Fil.** and **style** light purplish-red.—Mexico (Hidalgo, Atotonilco el Chico, Sierra Rosa). Craig believes the above name may be the earliest one for M. graessneriana; but whereas the Ax. in M. rutila are described as "felty at first", just as in the M. graessneriana hybrid, M. schulzeana (Fig. 3110, "Die Cact." V, p. 3363), in M. grassneriana the Ax. have plenty of much longer-persisting curly wool. The number of Rsp. can be somewhat higher than that given by Bödeker, and I have counted up to 6 Csp. which were yellow with a reddish-brown tip; acc. to Bödeker the Sp. (which are certainly variable) are reddish-brown, as given for the 4–6 Csp. of M. rutila; and this was probably why Craig gave the two plants as being perhaps identical; but M. rutila has only 14–16 Rsp. Clarification is not possible until these plants are re-collected.

M. saboae Glass
Bo. remaining small, simple or offsetting, 1–2 cm h. and ∅; **Tub.** very small, c. 2.5 mm lg.; **Ar.** with some white wool; **Rsp.** numerous, hyaline, yellow below, 2 mm lg.; **Fl.** 4 cm lg., 4 cm ∅, pink with lighter borders and a dark M.-stripe; **S.** black, glossy.—Mexico (SW. of Chihuahua, at c. 2000 m, on volcanic tufa. Has been described as "the smallest Mammillaria with the largest Fl.". Named for its discoverer, Mrs. Kathryn Sabo of Woodland Hill, Calif.

M. saetigera Böd. & Tieg. (1:3)
Bo. spherical, to 7 cm h. or rather more, dark green, simple; **Tub.** pyramidal; **Isp.** 13:21; **Ax.** white-woolly, with white Br.; **Rsp.** 15–20, to c. 7 mm lg., white; **Csp.** 2, 7–11 mm lg., thin-subulate, white, brown-tipped, projecting; **Fl.** 2 cm lg. and ∅, white with a deep pink M.-stripe; **Fr.** red, 1.8 cm lg.; **S.** yellowish-brown.—Mexico (Querétaro, borders of San Luis Potosí, Hacienda Cenca).
    v. **quadricentralis** Craig: **Bo.** bluish to greyish-green; **Tub.** 4-angled; **Isp.** 13:21; **Ax.** with dirty-white wool and numerous yellow Br.; **Rsp.** 16–18; **Csp.** 4, to 14 mm lg., light purple at first, tipped dark brown; **Fl.** 1.3 cm lg., 1.5 cm ∅, pale pink, M.-stripe darker.

M. saffordii (Br. & R.) H. Bravo (3:2, 5:9)
Bo. spherical to oblong, to 4 cm h., dark green; **Tub.** soft; **Isp.** ?; **Ax.** naked; **Rsp.** 12–14, later bent ± outwards, at first white below, tipped light red, later yellowish below; **Csp.** 1, stout, reddish, 1.5 cm lg., hooked; all **Sp.** hairy on new growth; **Fl.** 2.5 cm lg., pink.—Mexico (Nuevo León, Icamole).

M. saint-pieana Backbg.(1:2)—Descr. Cact. Nov. III: 8. 1963.
Bo. simple, spherical, greyish-green, to c. 7 cm ⌀; **sap** milky; **Isp.** 13:21; **Tub.** pyramidal, ± angular; **Ax.** woolly; **Ar.** glabrous; **Rsp.** 4–6, 2–6 mm lg., horn-coloured to white, 1–2 uppers shorter and thinner; **Csp.** 4, sometimes ± angular, straight or weakly curving, reddish to horn-coloured, 0.5–1.2 cm lg., one directed downwards, to 2.7 cm lg., sometimes thickened below; **Fl.** 1.5 cm lg., 1.2 cm ⌀, whitish; **Sep.** entire, with a reddish M.-line; **style** whitish.—Mexico (no more precise locality given; probably collected by Schwarz). (Fig. 216, below.)

M. sanluisensis Shurly (3:1, 3:7)
Bo. subspherical, dark green, to c. 2.5 cm ⌀ and more, caespitose, forming groups; **Tub.** soft, cylindric; **Isp.** 8:13; **Ax.** glabrous, with to 12 sinuate white Br.; **Rsp.** c. 40, 7 mm lg., white, very thin; **Csp.** 5–8, c. 1 cm lg., ± concolorous reddish-brown at first, later only above, white below; all **Sp.** smooth; **Fl.** 2 cm lg., 1.5 cm ⌀; **Pet.** few, pure white; **Fr.** light red, 5 mm lg.; **S.** black.—Mexico (N. San Luis Potosí).

M. santaclarensis Cowper
Bo. to 16 cm lg., to 5 cm ⌀, with spherical branches; **Tub.** 5–10 mm lg., 3–6 mm ⌀; **Isp.** 8:13; **Ax.** glabrous; **Ar.** round, white or yellowish, glabrous or nearly so; **Rsp.** 30, more on older plants, fewer on juveniles, 5–12 mm lg., white or straw, longer ones reddish-brown; **Csp.** 1–4, 5–18 mm lg., one of these longer, strongly hooked, reddish-brown, yellowish below; **Fl.** long-bellshaped, 2 cm lg., to 1.5 cm ⌀ when fully open, not recurved; **Pet.** pink or light pink with a darker M.-stripe; **style** white or light green, with light green **Sti.**; **An.** yellow; **Fr.** green to red, 8–15 mm lg.; **S.** dark reddish-brown.—Mexico (Chihuahua, in the Santa Clara Canyon [hence the specific name], c. 27 km W. of Ciudad Juarez).

M. sartorii J. A. Purp. (1:2, rarely 1:3)
Bo. spherical to elongated, dark bluish-green, to c. 12 cm ⌀, sometimes caespitose; **Tub.** firm, pyramidal; **Isp.**: 8:13; **Ax.** very white-woolly, sometimes with a small Br.; **Rsp.** 4(–6), 5–8 mm lg., acicular, smooth, dirty to brownish-white below, tipped brown, strongly projecting, often with bristly Ssp.; **Csp.** 0–1 or more, 1–8 mm lg., strongly acicular, tipped white to brownish; **Fl.** to 2 cm lg., yellowish to brilliant carmine, M.-line darker; **Fr.** carmine, 1.6 cm lg.; **S.** reddish-brown.—Mexico (Vera Cruz, Huatusco: Hacienda El Mirador).
v. **brevispina** J. A. Purp.: **Bo.** dark green; **Sp.** 1–2 mm lg., brown;
v. **longispina** J. A. Purp.: **Sp.** to 8 cm lg., curving.

M. scheidweileriana O. (3:1, 3:7)
Historically an insufficiently known spec. The plant usually known nowadays by this name—with axillary Br.—was described by Br. & R.:
Bo. spherical to oblong, light green, offsetting; **Tub.** cylindric; **Isp.** 8:13; **Ax.** bristly; **Rsp.** 9–11, bristly fine, 1 cm lg., white; **Csp.** 1–4, brown, 1–2 of these hooked; all **Sp.** hairy; **Fl.** to 13 mm lg., pinkish-red; **Fil.** and **style** white below, carmine or pink above.—Mexico (no locality stated).
Craig described similar plants under this name: "dark green; **Ax.** only woolly; **Rsp.** 25–30; **Csp.** 1–4, yellowish-white below, purple-tipped; **Fl.** pink, M.-line and tip brownish; **S.** black".—(In the State of Hidalgo, near Zimapán). This may be a still undescribed spec.

M. schelhasei Pfeiff. (3:1, 3:7)
Bo. spherical to oblong, pale green to dark green (above), caespitose; **Tub.** soft, cylindric; **Isp.** 8:13; **Ax.** ± woolly; **Rsp.** 15–20, 8–10 mm lg., bristle-fine, white; **Csp.** 3, 12–18 mm lg., all reddish-brown, uppers bristly, lower ones stout, hooked; **Fl.** to 2.5 cm lg., 1.2 cm ⌀, white, M.-line pink or red; **Fr.** red; **S.** black.—Mexico (Hidalgo, Real del Monte, Ixmiquilpan and Actopan).

M. schiedeana Ehrenbg. (3:1, 1:2)
Bo. broadly subspherical, to 4 cm ⌀, offsetting to form groups; **Tub.** rather soft, cylindric-conical; **Isp.** 13:21; **Ax.** with longer white woolly H.; **Rsp.** to 75, in several Ser., 2–5 mm lg., hair-like, interlacing, whitish below to yellowish above, to golden-yellow in the crown, roughly pubescent; **Csp.** 0; **Fl.** 2 cm lg., 1.5 cm ⌀, white to yellowish-white; **Fr.** light carmine, c. 1.2 cm lg.; **S.** black.—Mexico (Hidalgo, e.g. Puente de Diós in the Barranca of Meztitlán). **R.** often napiform. There are various forms: **Bo.** sometimes dark green, sometimes lighter; **R.** sometimes napiform, elongated; **Sp.** concolorous white, or yellow in the crown, or all yellow.

M. schieliana Schick (3:1, 1:5)
Bo. broadly spherical and tapering, or elongated, to 10 cm h., 7 cm ⌀, sparsely offsetting, dark green; **Tub.** conical; **Isp.** 21:34; **Ax.** white-woolly at first, with longer hair-like Br.; **Rsp.** 25–30, bristly, c. 5 mm lg. white, slightly brownish below; **Csp.** 5–6, rather stouter, c. 5 mm lg., pungent, white, brownish-red above, and initially also further down; **Fl.** perfumed, to 1.3 cm ⌀, ivory-white, M.-line reddish; **Fr.** ?—Mexico.

M. schmollii (H. Bravo) Werd. (3:1, 1:3)
Bo. depressed-spherical, 7 cm ⌀, olive-green, simple; **Tub.** conical; **Isp.** 8:13; **Ax.** naked; **Rsp.** 23–25, 4–5 mm lg., thin-acicular, glossy, white;

Csp. 11–15, 7–10 mm lg., one longer and more central, all honey-coloured; **Fl.** yellow; **Fr.** and **S.** ?—Mexico (Oaxaca, near Mitla, presumably in the mountains).

M. schwartzii (Frič) Backbg. n.comb.—Haagea (Porfiria Böd.) schwartzii Frič, Möllers Dtsch. Gärtn.-Ztg., 219. 1926 (1:1)
For a description, see Porfiria schwartzii (Frič) Böd., since this is the name still more widely used. Bödeker's name was correctly based on Frič's corrected basionym. Moran's M. schwarzii is a homonym of Shurly's name for another spec. Moran's M. coahuilensis v. albiflora (Böd.) Moran, which he named as a variety (fig. in Succulenta, 11: cover, 1963) was originally only provisional; Bödeker later described the plant as M. albiarmata Böd.

M. schwarzii Shurly (3:1, 2:6)
Bo. spherical, becoming ± elongated, to over 3.5 cm ∅, increasingly hidden by the Sp., green, offsetting; **Tub.** soft, ± cylindric; **Isp.** 8:13; **Ax.** with up to 6 Br. to 5 mm lg.; **Ar.** with persistent white wool; **Rsp.** 34–40, c. 8 mm lg., thin, hair-like, straight, ± projecting, interlacing; **Csp.** 8–9, 1 quite central, 5–6 mm lg., glossy, white, mostly light brownish-red above, sometimes entirely so or to midway, one Csp. sometimes hooked; **Fl.** 1.5 cm lg., 1.2 cm ∅, white, M.-line pale green; **Fr.** ?—Mexico (N. Guanajuato).

M. scrippsiana (Br. & R.) Orc. (1:2)
Bo. spherical to elongated, bluish-green, to 6 cm h., simple; **Tub.** oval, rounded; **Isp.** 13:21; **Ax.** very woolly; **Rsp.** 8–10, 6–8 mm lg., thin-acicular, pale reddish above; **Csp.** 2, 8–10 mm lg., stiffly acicular, brown; **Fl.** 1.5 cm ∅, pink, border paler; **Fr.** red; **S.** brown.—Mexico (Jalisco, Barranca de Guadalajara).
v. **autlanensis** Craig & Daws.: **Bo.** forming mats, single heads to 29 cm lg., 8.5 cm ∅; **Isp.** 8:13 and 13:21; **Ax.** very woolly; **Rsp.** 6, to 10 mm lg., stouter, pale straw-coloured; **Csp.** 1, 9–12 mm lg., thin-subulate, yellowish-brown; **Fl.** 1.3 cm ∅; **Pet.** deep pink, bordered pale pink.—Mexico (Jalisco, SW. of Autlán);
v. **rooksbyana** Backbg.: **Bo.** broadly spherical; **Rsp.** 12–14, to 1.7 cm lg.; **Csp.** 4, to 1.8 cm lg.; **Fl.** deep pink; **Sep.** and **Pet.** entire (ciliate or serrate in the preceding variety).—Mexico (Jalisco, locality?).

M. seideliana Quehl (3:1, 3:7)
Bo. spherical to oblong, dark green or reddish, offsetting; **Tub.** soft, slender-cylindric; **Isp.** 8:13; **Ax.** glabrous, occasionally with a few Br.; **Rsp.** 20 or more (–25), 5–8 mm lg., bristly, white; **Csp.** 3–4,

upper ones 5–8 mm lg., lower one to 1.5 cm lg., thin-acicular, hooked, all white, brown-tipped; **Sp.** hairy at first; **Fl.** to 2 cm lg., 1.5 cm ∅, light yellow to white, M.-line brownish-red; **Fr.** scarlet, 2 cm lg.; **S.** black.—Mexico (Zacatecas and Querétaro).

M. seitziana Mart. (1:3)
Bo. spherical to oblong, green, offsetting; **Tub.** pyramidal; **Isp.** 8:13; **Ax.** with wool and Br.; **Rsp.** 4–6, unequal, lower one to 3 cm lg., others 3–4 mm lg., sometimes also 1 Ssp., all straight or ± curving, flesh-coloured to yellowish-brown, black-tipped; **Csp.** 0; **Fl.** 2.5 cm lg., 1.5 cm ∅, pale flesh-pink; **Fr.** ?; **S.** brown.—Mexico (Hidalgo, near Ixmiquilpan and Zimapán).

M. sempervivi DC. (1:2)
Bo. spherical to elongated, to over 7 cm ∅, dark green, sparsely offsetting; **Tub.** slender-pyramidal, angled; **Isp.** 13:21; **Ax.** woolly; **Rsp.** only on new growth, 3–7, short, acicular, to 3 mm lg., pure white; **Csp.** mostly 2, stout, scarcely exceeding 4 mm lg., ± subulate, reddish, then white or horn-coloured; **Fl.** 1 cm lg., Pet. dirty white with a reddish dorsal stripe, or to yellowish and even pink; **Fr.** red, 8 mm lg.; **S.** light brown.—Mexico (Hidalgo to Vera Cruz).
v. **caput-medusae** (O.) Backbg.: **Bo.** bluish to greyish-green; **Tub.** slender-conical, angular below; **Sp.** 3–6, to 5 mm lg., subulate, reddish to ± pinkish-red, tipped brown, becoming grey, rough; **Fl.** 1.6 cm lg., white, dorsal stripe red. (Hidalgo, Barranca Venados, near Meztitlán);
v. **tetracantha** DC.: **Csp.** mostly 4. (Hidalgo, near Ixmiquilpan).

M. senilis SD.: The name is not referable to Mamillopsis, as was long considered to be the case, but was published for a form of M. spinosissima. Acc. Rowley, the name was not given by Loddiges, so that Salm-Dyck is the sole author.

M. sheldonii (Br. & R.) Böd. (3:2, 5:9)
Bo. becoming columnar, green to dark green, to 25 cm lg., 6 cm ∅, caespitose; **Tub.** conical-cylindric; **Isp.** 8:13; **Ax.** naked; **Rsp.** 10–15, 6–9 mm lg., reddish-brown, lighter below, darker-tipped, 3–4 upper Sp. similarly; **Csp.** 1–3, 9–12 mm lg., stoutly acicular, smooth, lower one longer, hooked, all dark reddish-brown; **Fl.** 2 cm lg., 3 cm ∅, Pet. light pink or darker in the centre, border white, broad; **Fr.** pale scarlet, to 3 cm lg.; **S.** black.—Mexico (E. Sonora, Hermosillo, also near Guaymas and in the Yaqui valley).

M. shurliana Gat. (3:2, 5:9)
Bo. becoming columnar, to c. !0 cm h., 3.5 cm ∅,

olive-green, rarely offsetting; **Tub.** rounded; **Isp.** ?; **Ax.** weakly grey-woolly; **Rsp.** 16–20, 5 mm lg., radiating, acicular, brown or grey; **Csp.** 3, 0.6–1 cm lg., acicular, blackish above, brown below, the lowest one longest, thickened below, shortly hooked; **Fl.** 2 cm lg. and ⌀, carmine-pink, bordered whitish; **Fr.** orange, 2 cm lg.; **S.** black.—Mexico (Baja California, W. of Mesquital Ranch, 28°30′ lat. N., 113°55′ long. W.).

M. shurlyi F. Buxb.: invalid name for **Mammillaria schwarzii** Shurly.

M. simplex Haw. non Torr. & Gray (1:2) (T.)
Bo. spherical to oblong, light to dark green, to 20 cm h., caespitose; **Tub.** conical; **Isp.** 8:13; **Ax.** weakly woolly; **Rsp.** 10–16, 5–8 mm lg., acicular, reddish, becoming grey; **Csp.** 3–5, 7–8 mm lg., subulate, ± thickened below, smooth, reddish-brown, darker-tipped, porrect; **Fl.** to 1.2 cm lg., white; **Fr.** carmine, to 2 cm lg.; **S.** brown.—Venezuela (N. coast, Patos and Margarita islands), islands off Curaçao. Fig. of the type-spec. in "Die Cact.", V: p. 3204, Fig. 2971. In VI: p. 3887, Fig. 3534, right below, I showed a colour-photo of a leaf-green plant with Rsp. c. 10, all white, and Csp. 3, pale or light brown; this has not been either named or described in the literature, but I give it below as it is a sufficiently differentiated variety:
v. **albidispina** Backbg. n.v.: Distinguished by the **Sp.** which soon become whitish.

M. sinistrohamata Böd. (3:1, 3:7)
Bo. broadly spherical, glossy, leaf-green, to 5 cm ⌀, simple; **Tub.** shortly cylindric; **Isp.** 13:21; **Ax.** naked; **Rsp.** 20 or more, 8–10 mm lg., very thin, slightly thickened below; **Csp.** 4, 3 upper ones 8–10 mm lg., lower one c. 1.4 cm lg., hooked leftwards, all stoutly acicular, amber-coloured; **Fl.** 1.5 cm lg., 1.2 cm ⌀, greenish-cream to ivory; **Fr.** red, small; **S.** black.—Mexico (Zacatecas; Durango; Coahuila).

M. slevinii (Br. & R.) Böd. (3:1, 1:2)
Bo. oblong, to 10 cm h., 6 cm ⌀, simple, entirely covered by the whitish Sp.; **Tub.** apparently slender; **Isp.** ?; **Ax.** if woolly, then much less so than M. albicans (to which Craig referred this plant), which is moreover caespitose; **Rsp.** numerous, thin, densely interlacing; **Csp.** c. 6, scarcely longer or stouter than the Rsp., ± spreading; **Sp.** pink below, tipped brownish or black, becoming white; **Fl.** ?; **Fr.** 1 cm lg., red; **S.** black.—Mexico (Baja California, San José island).

M. soehlemannii W. Haage & Backbg. n.prov.: either simple or caespitose; **Sp.** reddish-brown; **Ax.**

white-woolly throughout; **Fl.** very numerous, **Fr.** similarly.—Colombia (Candellaria Desert, 2800 m). [Addendum by W. Haage: A definitive description must await the receipt of living material. For another new spec. from Colombia, see under M. pseudosimplex.]

M. solisioides Backbg. (3:1, 1:2)
Bo. broadly subspherical, light green, to 4 cm ⌀, simple, taprooted, the part above ground little over 1 cm h.; **Tub.** shortly conical; **Isp.** 8:13; **Ax.** weakly felty to glabrous; **Rsp.** c. 25, to c. 5 mm lg., pectinate, appressed, white; **Csp.** 0; **Fl.** c. 1.4–2.2 cm lg., 1.5–2.6 cm ⌀, yellowish-white, tubular to funnelform; **Fr.** small, scarcely overtopping the Tub.; **S.** black.—Mexico (Puebla, S. of Petlalzingo). Referred to Solisia by Krainz and Buxbaum, but this spec. is quite unrelated to that genus.

M. sonorensis Craig (1:2, or 1:3)
Bo. spherical, dark bluish-green, to c. 8 cm ⌀, also caespitose; **Tub.** stout, 4-sided but not 4-angled; **Isp.** 5:8, 8:13; **Ax.** white-woolly, hair-like Br. sometimes present; **Rsp.** 8–15, 1–20 mm lg., thin-acicular to rather stouter, whitish to cream, tipped reddish; **Csp.** 1–4, 0.5–4.5 cm lg., acicular to subulate, ± straight, stiff, smooth, thickened below, reddish-brown, ± projecting; **Fl.** 2 cm lg., deep pink, M.-line fine, darker; **Fr.** scarlet, 1.2 cm lg.; **S.** brown.—Mexico (SE. Sonora, Guirocoba; NE. Sinaloa; SW. Chihuahua).
v. **brevispina** Craig: **Rsp.** 8; **Csp.** 1–2, to 8 mm lg., acicular; it is questionable whether this is a good variety;
v. **maccartyi** Craig: **Rsp.** 8–10; **Csp.** 1–3, stoutly acicular, bent strongly upwards, to 2 cm lg.

M. sphacelata Mart. (3:1, 1:1)
Bo. cylindric, to 20 cm lg., to 3 cm ⌀, light green, freely offsetting to form larger cushions; **Tub.** conical; **Isp.** 5:8; **Ax.** woolly, bristly; **Rsp.** 10–15, 5–8 mm lg., stoutly acicular, stiff, white; **Csp.** 1–4, 4–6 mm lg., thin-subulate, 1 porrect, stouter, all Sp. white, tips ruby-red at first, then brown; **Fl.** 1.5 cm lg., 0.8 cm ⌀, dark red; **Fr.** red; **S.** black.—Mexico (Puebla, Tehuacan; Oaxaca).

M. spinosissima Lem. (3:1, 1:4)
Bo. eventually columnar, often curving below, dark bluish-green, to 30 cm lg., 10 cm ⌀, simple (always ?); **Tub.** ovoid-conical; **Isp.** 13:21; **Ax.** woolly, bristly; **Rsp.** 20–30, 4–10 mm lg., bristly, mostly white; **Csp.** 7–15, to 2 cm lg., acicular, flexible, ± thickened below, very variable in colour, white to ruby-red, yellowish-brown, pink or reddish-brown, one Sp. sometimes hooked, or individual plants with hooked Sp., but this is not typical; **Fl.** to 2 cm

lg., 1.5 cm ⌀, reddish-pink to purple; **Fr.** red, 2 cm lg.; **S.** reddish-brown.—Mexico (Morelos, e.g. near Carantla; Hidalgo, Real del Monte; Puebla; Michoacan; Guerrero, near Taxdo).

The variable Sp.-colour has resulted in many synonyms. Red-spined plants mostly become lighter in cultivation. Less common is v. flavida SD., with **Sp.** glossy golden-yellow.—The name M. senilis SD., together with 2 varieties, is referable here as a synonym, and not to Mamillopsis.

M. standleyi (Br. & R.) Orc. (1:3)
Bo. spherical, deep green, to 15 cm ⌀, offsetting to form mats to 1 m br.; **Tub.** conical, keeled below; **Isp.** 13:21; **Ax.** white-woolly, with white Br.; **Rsp.** 16–19, 4–8 mm lg., fine-acicular, white, dark-tipped; **Csp.** 4, 6–8 mm lg., stoutly acicular, reddish-brown; **Fl.** 1.2 cm ⌀, purplish-pink, M.-line darker; **Fr.** scarlet, to 1.6 cm lg.; **S.** brownish.—Mexico (Sonora, Sierra de Alamos, near Alamos).

v. **robustispina** Craig; **Tub.** rather longer; **Rsp.** 20, 4–6 mm lg., white to cream; **Csp.** 5–6, 5–8 mm lg., subulate, dark cream, brown-tipped.

M. stella-de-tacubaya Heese (3:1, 3:7)
Bo. spherical; **Tub.** light green, cylindric; **Isp.** 13:21; **Ax.** weakly woolly; **Rsp.** 35–40, 3–5 mm lg., bristly, white, interlacing; **Csp.** 1, 5–6 mm lg., slender-acicular, hooked, black, porrect; **Fl.** 1.5 cm lg., reddish-white; **Fr.** reddish, 2 cm lg.; **S.** ?—Mexico (Federal District, Rancho de Tacubaya). Not re-collected for a long time.

M. strobilina Tieg. (1:3)
Bo. conical-subspherical, 6 cm ⌀, dark green; **Tub.** pyramidal, upwardly curving; **Isp.** 13:21; **Ax.** white-woolly, sometimes with a few Br.; **Rsp.** 4–5, 6 mm lg., stoutly acicular, ash-grey, tips dark, becoming whitish; **Csp.** 1, 12 mm lg., subulate, often ± bent above, ash-grey; **Fl.** 1.8 cm ⌀, dirty white to pale greenish-yellow, often with a reddish-brown M.-line; **Fr.** carmine, 2 cm lg.; **S.** light brown.—Mexico (Oaxaca). This may perhaps have been an anomalous plant with the Tub. curving upwards (such as has been observed elsewhere) from the complex of M. confusa or M. collinsii. At all events, it has not been re-collected.

M. subdurispina Backbg. (3:1, 1:3)
Bo. spherical to shortly columnar, deep green, simple, to c. 8 cm h., 7 cm ⌀; **Tub.** broadly conical; **Isp.** 13:21; **Ax.** woolly; **Rsp.** mostly 6, radiating evenly, c. 6 mm lg., blackish, becoming grey; **Csp.** 0; **Fl.** purplish-carmine; **Fr.** greenish-pink.—Mexico (Querétaro; Guanajuato).

M. subpolyedra SD.: Acc. Craig, at most a variety of **Mammillaria polyedra** Mart.

M. subtilis Backbg. (3:1, 1:5)
Bo. small-spherical, green, simple; **Tub.** conical, c. 3 mm lg.; **Isp.** ?; **Ax.** with curly Br.; **Rsp.** c. 30, hairlike, curly; **Csp.** 6–7, c. 1–1.2 cm lg., 1–2 of these uppers, brownish or reddish, others white, all ± bristly; **Fl.** c. 1 cm lg., opening widely, white; **Fr.** ?—Mexico (San Luis Potosi, 80 km. N. of the town of the same name). The coloured Csp. project tuft-like above the crown.

M. supertexta Mart. (2:1)
It is not entirely certain to what plant this name was earlier given. It is nowadays usually applied to a plant with the following characters: **Bo.** fairly broadly spherical, to c. 7 cm ⌀, hidden beneath the Sp.; **Tub.** conical; **Isp.** ?; **Ax.** ?; **Rsp.** 16–18 or more, white, tipped blackish; **Csp.** 2, one darker, more erect, longer, c. 6 mm lg., darker above than below; **Fl.** light red; **Fr.** ?—Mexico (Oaxaca?).

v. **leucostoma** Backbg.: **crown** not interspersed with noticeably darker Sp., the 2 **Csp.** being yellowish, darker tips only short; **Fl.** more bellshaped to funnelform, white inside, limb alone more reddish.

M. swinglei (Br. & R.) Böd. (3:2, 5:9)
Bo. oblong, dark green, to 20 cm h., 3–5 cm ⌀, sometimes caespitose; **Tub.** cylindric-conical; **Isp.** 8:13; **Ax.** with or without Br.; **Rsp.** 11–18, (7–)8–9(–14) mm lg., stoutly acicular, straight, matt, white, dark-tipped; **Csp.** 1–4, 8–15 mm lg., the lower ones longest, lowest one hooked or very rarely straighter, all dark brown to black; **Fl.** with the M.-stripe pink, sometimes greenish to brownish, Pet. bordered white or cream, 3 cm ⌀, **Fr.** dark red, to 1.8 cm lg.; **S.** black.—Mexico (Sonora, near Guaymas, on the coast).

M. tegelbergiana Gat.: description incomplete (1:2?) **Bo.** broadly spherical; **Tub.** conical; **Isp.** ?; **Ax.** ± woolly; **Ar.** strongly woolly at first; **Rsp.** 16, white; **Csp.** 2–4, projecting, white, at first yellowish, tipped brownish, not thickened below; **Fl.** red, darker in the centre; **Sep.** and **Pet.** entire.—Mexico (probably Baja California, where Gates and Tegelberg collected together). **Mammillaria vonwyssiana** Krainz ? (see the latter).

M. tenampensis (Br. & R.) Berg. (1:3)
Bo. spherical, to c. 6 cm ⌀, light yellowish-green, simple; **Tub.** 4-angled above; **Isp.** 8:13; **Ax.** with yellowish wool and Br.; **Rsp.** 8–10, small, bristly; **Csp.** 4–6, 1–6 mm lg., acicular, smooth, brownish, dark-tipped; **Fl.** 1.2 cm lg. and 8 mm ⌀, reddish-purple; **Fr.** ?—Mexico (Mexico State, Barranca de Tenampa).

M. tesopacensis Craig (1:2)
Bo. spherical to oblong, to 18 cm h., 13 cm ⌀,

bluish to greyish-green, simple; **Tub.** pyramidal-conical; **Isp.** 13:12; **Ax.** glabrous or ± woolly only in the flowering zone; **Rsp.** 10–15, 4–7 mm lg., thin-acicular; **Csp.** 1(–2), 10–12 mm lg., stoutly acicular, stiff; **Sp.** reddish-brownish below, tipped black, all Sp. later ashy-brown; **Fl.** 2 cm lg. and ∅, cream, M.-line pink; **Fr.** scarlet, 1.8 cm lg.; **S.** light brown.—Mexico (Sonora, Tesopaco).

v. **rubraflora** Craig: **Fl.** deep purplish-pink, M.-line darker.—Mexico (Sonora, Movas, E. of Tesopaco).

M. tetracantha SD. non Hook. (3:1, 1:3)
Bo. ± spherical, simple; **Tub.** angular, pyramidal; **Isp.** ?; **Ax.** ± woolly; **Rsp.** or **Sp.** 4, short, stiff, 4–6 mm lg., the bottom one rather longer, all reddish at first, tipped blackish; **Fl.** small, reddish; **Fr.** ?—Mexico.

M. tetracentra O. (1:2)
Bo. spherical to elongated, to 15 cm ∅, bluish-green to grey, simple; **Tub.** weakly 4-angled; **Isp.** 21:34; **Ax.** glabrous; **Rsp.** (0?–)4, short, soon dropping, 2 mm lg., blackish at first, becoming horn-coloured, dark-tipped, lower ones to 11 mm lg., lighter brown; **Csp.** 2–3(–4), brownish at first, dark-tipped, later white, dark-tipped; **Fl.** brilliant purple; **Fr.** ?—Mexico.

M. theresae Cutak
Bo. conical-cylindric, mostly simple, olive-green, often tinged purple; **Tub.** tiny, slender; **Ar.** woolly, mostly round; **Rsp.** numerous, 2 mm lg., with whitish pinnae; **Csp.** 9; **Fl.** violet-purple, funnelform with a narrow Tu., 35–40 mm lg., 30 mm ∅; **Sep.** greenish-brown, bordered pale pink; **Fil.** white; **An.** yellow; **style** white; **S.** black, very small, deeply embedded in the Bo. This dwarf spec. with its long Fl. was discovered in 1966 by Mrs. Theresa Bock; it grows at 2200 m near the Coneto Pass, Durango, Mexico. [(R); easy from seed. Translator.]

M. tiegeliana Backbg. (1:1)
Bo. spherical, to c. 10 cm ∅, branching dichotomously, greyish-green; **Tub.** with 4 ± rounded angles; **Isp.** 21:34; **Ax.** white-woolly, with short white Br.; **Rsp.** to c. 36, to 7 mm lg., bristly-fine, white; **Csp.** 4, cruciform, projecting, to c. 11 mm lg., white, tipped brown; **Fr.** deep carmine, 3 cm lg.; **S.** ?—Mexico.

M. tobuschii Marsh.: **Ancistrocactus tobuschii** Marsh.

M. tolimensis Craig (1:3)
Bo. broadly spherical, to 10 cm ∅, greyish to yellowish-green, sometimes caespitose; **Tub.** rounded-pyramidal, keeled below; **Isp.** 8:13, 13:21; **Ax.** white-woolly, with stout white contorted Br.; **Rsp.** 5–10, 1–5 mm lg., thin-acicular, chalky-white, lower 3 set ± in a furrow; **Csp.** (5–)6(–7), 5–6.5 cm lg., upper ones thin-subulate, lower ones stouter, chalky-white; **Fl.** red; **Fr.** carmine, 2 cm lg.; **S.** light brown.—Mexico (Querétaro, Toliman).

v. **brevispina** Craig: **Rsp.** to 9, 1–5 mm lg., thin-acicular, contorted; **Csp.** 6, 5–18 mm lg., sometimes curving;

v. **longispina** Craig: **Rsp.** 5, 1–8 mm lg.; **Csp.** 6, upper ones 4–12 mm lg., lowest one to 6.5 cm lg., subulate, ± contorted;

v. **subuncinata** Craig: **Isp.** 13:21; **Rsp.** 5, 1–4 mm lg.; **Csp.** 5, 7–15 mm lg., acicular, ± bent or ± hooked.

M. trichacantha K. Sch. (3:1, 3:7)
Bo. spherical to oblong, to 5 cm ∅, bluish-green, offsetting; **Tub.** clavate; **Isp.** 13:21; **Ax.** with a few Br. (or none?); **Rsp.** 15–18, to 8 mm lg., white below, yellowish above, fine-acicular; **Csp.** 2(–3), the bottom one longest, to 1.2 cm lg., hooked, all acicular, nut-brown, reddish at first, eventually grey, tipped brown; all **Sp.** pubescent; **Fl.** to 1.5 cm lg. and ∅, greenish-cream, M.-line light green; **Fr.** red, 1 cm lg.; **S.** black.—Mexico (San Luis Potosí; Querétaro).

M. trohartii Hildm. (1:2)
Bo. depressed-spherical, dark bluish-green, scarcely exceeding 6 cm ∅, later offsetting freely; **Tub.** slightly angular-conical; **Isp.** 8:13; **Ax.** glabrous; **Rsp.** 5, white, tipped dark brown; **Csp.** 1, subulate, stiff, straight or slightly curving, dark brown; **Fl.** ?—Mexico.

M. umbrina Ehrenbg. (3:1, 2:6?)
Bo. eventually oblong, to 15 cm h., 10 cm ∅, dark bluish-green, caespitose; **Tub.** conical; **Ax.** woolly(?), bristly (always?): **Rsp.** 22–24, upper ones 4 mm lg., lower ones to 12 mm lg., all bristle-like, whitish; **Csp.** (1–)2(–4), upper ones 8–10 mm lg., lower ones longer, bottom one to 2.4 cm lg., stouter, hooked (also reported as "usually" hooked), all red at first, then more brownish, tipped brown; **Fl.** 1.8 cm lg., 1.2 cm ∅, deep pink; **Fr.** ?—Mexico (Hidalgo?). Insufficiently clarified spec., possibly confused in part with M. neocoronaria.

M. uncinata Zucc. (1:2)
Bo. spherical, to 8 cm h., 10 cm ∅, dark bluish-green, simple or (rarely?) branching or offsetting; **Tub.** pyramidal, rounded above; **Isp.** 8:13; **Ax.** white-woolly at first; **Rsp.** 4–7, 5–6 mm lg., the smaller upper ones flesh-coloured, lower ones white, black-tipped; **Csp.** 1(–2–3), to 1.2 cm lg.,

stout to subulate, flesh-coloured, dark-tipped; **Fl.** to 2 cm lg., 1.8 cm ∅, reddish-white, tipped pink, M.-line brownish; **Fr.** red, to 1.8 cm lg.; **S.** light brown.—Mexico (San Luis Potosí; Guanajuato; Hidalgo, Pachuca, Real del Monte).

v. **bihamata** (Pfeiff.) Backbg.: **Isp.** 13:21; **Csp.** 2–4, 8–11 mm lg., strongly subulate, lower ones longer, stouter, only incompletely hooked, ± contorted.—Mexico (Hidalgo, Real del Monte).

M. unihamata Böd. (3:1, 3:7)
Bo. spherical to oblong, to 3.5 cm ∅, leaf-green, rarely caespitose; **Tub.** conical; **Isp.** 8:13; **Ax.** glabrous; **Rsp.** 16–20, 6 mm lg., acicular to thin-subulate, white, ± yellowish below; **Csp.** 1(–2), to 1.2 cm lg., smooth, hooked, reddish-brown to brownish-red, light yellowish below; **Fl.** ?; **S.** black.—Mexico (Nuevo León, near Asunción).

M. vagaspina Craig (1:2)
Bo. depressed-spherical, to 8.5 cm ∅, dark greyish-green, simple; **Tub.** ± angular, keeled below; **Isp.** 8:13; **Ax.** white-woolly; **Rsp.** (2–)3(–5), 1–10 mm lg., stiffly acicular, smooth, chalky brownish-white; **Csp.** 2, unequal, 0.6–6 cm lg., the bottom one longest, all stoutly acicular, very contorted, ± angular, smooth, chalky-brownish; **Fl.** 1 cm ∅, Pet. bordered pink, middle darker; **Fr.** crimson, 1.1 cm lg.; **S.** light brown.—Mexico (Querétaro, near Tierra Blanca).

M. varieaculeata Buchenau 1966
Bo. spherical, later cylindric, caespitose, rarely dividing dichotomously, forming groups, single heads 13 cm h., 9 cm ∅, **R.** fibrous; crown depressed, white-woolly; **sap** milky; **Tub.** pyramidal, slightly angular, 5–6 mm h., in Isp. 13:21; **Ax.** white-woolly; **Ar.** oval, white-woolly, later grey; **Rsp.** 17–20, 4–7 mm lg., tangled, hyaline, light brown below at first, later darker; **Csp.** 3–5 at first, later 1, rarely 2, 4–12 mm lg., occasionally to 45 mm lg., cinnamon-brown, broad below, tipped dark brown, later greying; **Fl.** in a coronet, funnelshaped, 17–18 mm lg., 12–15 mm ∅; **Sep.** chestnut-brown, bordered yellowish; **Pet.** scarlet with a light border, pink below, lanceolate; **Fil.** white; **An.** light yellow; **style** 11 mm lg., pale green below, light red above; **Fr.** scarlet, 15–20 mm lg.; **S.** pale brown, testa reticulate, rough.—Mexico (Puebla, S. of Chilac at 1200 m, between rocks on stony clay). Related to M. huajuapensis, mixtecensis and casoi Bravo.

M. vaupelii Tieg. (2:1)
Bo. ± spherical, c. 6 cm ∅, light bluish-green, simple; **Tub.** rounded, white-pitted; **Isp.** 13:21; **Ax.** with curly wool and Br.; **Rsp.** 16–21, 5–6 mm lg., acicular, glossy, white; **Csp.** 2(–4), upper ones c. 10 mm lg., lower ones to 15 mm lg., all subulate, orange-brown, cream below, pink above with a tiny dark tip, becoming grey; **Fl.** 1.7 cm lg., 1 cm ∅, light purplish-pink, throat white; **Fr.** carmine, 1.5 cm lg.; **S.** yellowish-brown.—Mexico (Oaxaca, Mixteca).

M. verhaertiana Böd. (3:1, 2:6) [Grows more quickly when grafted.]
Bo. oblong, later long-cylindric, green, over 4 cm ∅, to 30 cm lg., later offsetting from the base to produce colonies; **Tub.** shortly conical; **Isp.** 8:13(?); **Ax.** woolly, with numerous white Br.; **Rsp.** over 20, interlacing, thin, white, c. 8–15 mm lg., at first yellowish-white to concolorous white; **Csp.** 4–6, rather stouter, to 1.2 cm lg., creamy-whitish, yellowish-brown to darker above, later sometimes white or coffee-coloured, straight or with an occasional hooked Sp. on mature plants; **Fl.** tube-like, to 2 cm lg.; **Sep.** white, M.-stripe greenish or reddish; **Pet.** ± white; **Fr.** orange to coral-red; **S.** black.—Mexico (Baja California). M. phitauiana Baxt. is a commonly used synonym. More recently, a more laxly spined form (or variety?) has appeared: all Sp. straight, dark brownish at first.

M. vetula Mart. (3:1, 1:3)
Bo. subspherical (elongated at the base), ± glossy, fresh green, to c. 4 cm ∅, offsetting quite freely to form groups; **Tub.** conical; **Isp.** 5:8 (K. Sch.), and later also 8:13 (Craig: anomalously 7:18, 11:29?); **Ax.** glabrous; **Rsp.** c. 30, to 10 mm lg., bristly, white, somewhat unevenly projecting and radiating; **Csp.** few at first, then to 4–7, to c. 1.2 cm lg., brownish above, whitish below, light yellowish-brown below and ± thickened; **Fl.** 1.5 cm lg., 1.2 cm ∅, dirty yellowish-cream, M.-stripe pale reddish-brown (not "yellow"); **Fr.** c. 1.5 cm lg., white below, greenish above, sometimes suffused reddish; **S.** black.—Mexico (Hidalgo, N. of Zimapan, near Encarnación and San José del Oro, 2600–3000 m). (Somewhat variable). A more recent synonym is M. magneticola Meyran.

M. viereckii (Böd.) (3:1, 1:5)
Bo. subspherical to elongated, to c. 4 cm ∅, dark green, caespitose; **Tub.** slender-cylindric; **Isp.** 8:13; **Ax.** white-woolly, with up to 10 longer Br.; **Rsp.** 6–7(–10), 4–5 mm lg., very fine-acicular, white; **Csp.** scarcely differentiated, subcentral, ± projecting, not porrect, 9–11, c. 12 mm lg., thin-acicular, light ochre below and only slightly thickened, amber-yellow to lighter above; **Fl.** 1.2 cm lg., creamy-white, M.-line pale olive-green; **Fr.** reddish-brown; **S.** black.—Mexico (Tamaulipas, near Nogales).

v. **brunispina** Neale: **Csp.** more clearly distinguishable, or 1–2 centrals more clearly projecting, one of these exactly central; **Rsp.** 10–12, firmer and sometimes 4 of these very thin, directed downwards; all **Sp.** light below, brownish above, later only the Csp. so coloured.

M. viescensis (author and description, 1973, still unknown): a small, soft-fleshed spec. with many white **Rsp.** and hooked reddish-brown **Csp.** The name suggests it originates near the town of Viesca, N. Mexico.

M. viperina J. A. Purp. (3:1, 1:1) [✳]
Bo. slender-cylindric, offsetting freely from the base, densely spiny, light green; **St.** 1.5–2 cm $\varnothing$; **Tub.** shortly cylindric; **Isp.** 8:13(?); **Ax.** ± woolly, with H. or Br. often the same length as the Tub.; **Sp.** numerous, fine, rigid, interlacing, c. 5 mm lg., snow-white at first, light brown or to deep brown, all becoming white; **Fl.** light carmine, c. 11 mm lg., not opening very widely; **Fr.** red, 8 mm lg.; **S.** light brown.—Mexico (Puebla, Rio de Zapotitlán, on humus-free limestone, prostrate and rooting). (Fig. 217.)

M. virginis Fittk. & Klad.
Bo. elongated-cylindric, mostly simple, to 25 cm h., 8 cm $\varnothing$, dark green, crown scarcely depressed; **Tub.** 4–5 mm thick below, c. 8–10 mm lg., in **Isp.** 8:13 and 13:21; **Ar.** oval, with sparse white wool; **Ax.** mostly naked; **Rsp.** 15–21, 2–7 mm lg., whitish, tipped red, yellowish below; **Csp.** 2–8, 4–12 mm lg., reddish-brown, darker-tipped, lowest one sometimes hooked; **Fl.** in a coronet around the crown, bellshaped, 12–14 mm lg., 9 mm br.; **Sep.** brownish-red, bordered lighter; **Pet.** pinkish-red with a violet M.-line; **style** with 3–5 green **Sti.**; **Fr.** 20–26 mm lg., salmon-coloured, olive-green above; **S.** light reddish-brown.—Mexico (Guerrero, near Ancón, at 1800–2100 m, on limestone cliffs, also in open oak-woods). Self-sterile. Related to M. umbrina. Named for the Virgin of Guadalupe.

M. viridiflora (Br. & R.) Böd. (3:2, 5:9)
Bo. spherical to elongated, to 10 cm lg., covered by the Sp.; **Tub.** rounded; **Isp.** 8:13(?); **Ax.** glabrous; **Rsp.** 20–30, bristly-fine, to 12 mm lg., white, brown-tipped; **Csp.** scarcely differentiated, to 2 cm lg., one or several hooked; **Fl.** greenish, 1.5 cm lg., narrowly bellshaped; **Fr.** purple, to 15 mm lg.; **S.** black(?).—USA (Arizona, Boundary Monument). Acc. Craig, the Pet. are very narrow; Fl. to 3.5 cm $\varnothing$, reminiscent of Neobesseya, also sometimes verging on reddish. Sometimes regarded as a variety of M. wilcoxii, but it differs appreciably from this.

M. vonwyssiana Krainz (1:2)
Bo. broadly spherical, bluish-green, c. 6 cm h. and

$\varnothing$ (or more?), simple; **Tub.** conical, 4-angled above; **Isp.** 13:21?; **Ax.** glabrous at first, then woolly; **Rsp.** 18–20, 3–6 mm lg., bristly, white; **Csp.** 2(–3), rarely 4, thin-subulate, yellowish, black-tipped, to 5 mm lg.; **Fl.** 2 cm lg., 1.8 cm $\varnothing$, carmine-pink, M.-stripe broad, darker; **Fr.** red, to 2 cm lg.; **S.** light brown.—Mexico.
The earliest name was probably M. tegelbergiana Gat.; insufficiently described (see also there).

M. weingartiana Böd. (3:1, 3:7)
Bo. spherical, dark leaf-green, to over 5 cm $\varnothing$, simple or caespitose; **Tub.** slender-conical; **Isp.** 13:21; **Ax.** glabrous or with traces of wool; **Rsp.** 20–25, 6–8 mm lg., very thin, white; **Csp.** 1–4, to 12 mm lg., stiffly acicular, 1–2 hooked, all smooth, red, becoming brownish-black; **Fl.** 1 cm lg., 1.2 cm $\varnothing$, pale greenish-yellow, M.-line darker; **Fr.** red, small; **S.** black.—Mexico (Nuevo León, near Asunción).

M. wiesingeri Böd. (3:1, 1:3 or 5)
Bo. broadly spherical, leaf-green, 4 cm h., to 8 cm $\varnothing$, simple; **Tub.** soft, slender-pyramidal; **Isp.** 16:26 (twice 8:13); **Ax.** woolly, sometimes with 1–2 thin Br.; **Rsp.** 18–20, 5–6 mm lg., thin-acicular, smooth, white; **Csp.** 4(–5–6), 5–6 mm lg., somewhat stouter-acicular, smooth, slightly thickened below, reddish-brown; **Fl.** bellshaped, 1.2 cm lg. and $\varnothing$, Pet. pink with a darker M.-stripe; **Fr.** carmine, 1 cm lg.; **S.** brown.—Mexico (Hidalgo, near Mezquititlán).

M. wilcoxii Toumey (3:2, 5:9) [G.]
Bo. broadly spherical to elongated, dark green, to 10 cm h., sometimes caespitose; **Tub.** conical-cylindric, rather long, lax, soft during dormancy, firmer in the growing period, to 2 cm lg.; **Isp.** 5:8 and (?) 8:13; **Ax.** naked; **Rsp.** 14–22, 1–1.5 cm lg., bristly to thin-acicular, white, brown-tipped; **Csp.** 1–3(–5–6), 2–3 cm lg., stiffly acicular, 1 or more hooked, dark amber to reddish-brown; **Sp.** either smooth or pubescent, centrals sometimes even feathery; **Fl.** 3.5 cm lg., 4 cm $\varnothing$, cream with a brownish-green M.-stripe, to ± purplish-pink; **Fr.** 2.5 cm lg., pink below, darker above or with a greenish tinge; **S.** black.—USA (Arizona, Nogales and Benson; New Mexico, Silver City). (Fig. 218.)

M. wilcoxii v. viridiflora (Br. & R.) Marsh.:
Mammillaria viridiflora (Br. & R.) Böd.

M. wildii Dietr. (3:1, 3:7)
Bo. subspherical to oblong, dark bluish-green, to 15 cm lg., to 6 cm $\varnothing$, freely offsetting; **Tub.** soft, cylindric to clavate; **Isp.** 13–21, fewer at first; **Ax.** with minute wool-tufts and some Br.; **Rsp.** 8–10, 6–8 mm lg., bristly, white; **Csp.** 3–4, 8–10 mm lg.,

thin-acicular, the lowest one hooked, rough, $\pm$ amber-coloured; **Fl.** 1.2 cm lg. and $\emptyset$, white; **Fr.** brownish-red; **S.** black.—Mexico (Hidalgo, Barranca Venados; Querétaro).

M. winteriae Böd. (1:2)
Bo. broadly spherical, light to bluish-green, simple; **Tub.** with 4 rounded angles above; **1 sp.** 8:13; **Ax.** becoming more woolly; **Rsp.** 4, cruciform, to 3 cm lg., laterals only 1.5 cm lg., stoutly acicular, yellowish-grey to slightly reddish above, tipped brownish; **Csp.** 0; **Fl.** 3 cm lg., 2.5 cm $\emptyset$, Pet. yellowish-white, bordered white, the yellowish M.-stripe with a red M.-line; **Fr.** pink; **S.** light reddish-brown.—Mexico (Nuevo León, near Monterrey).

M. woburnensis Scheer (1:3)
Bo. spherical to more oblong, dark leaf-green, to 20 cm lg., 8 cm $\emptyset$, quite freely offsetting; **Tub.** bluntly conical; **Isp.** 8:13; **Ax.** white-woolly, with to 10 white Br.; **Rsp.** 8–9, 4–5 mm lg., cream, tipped reddish-brown; **Csp.** 1–3, to c. 7 mm lg., dark brown at first, then more yellowish, tipped reddish-brown; **Bl.** 2 cm lg., yellow with a brownish-reddish dorsal stripe; **Fr.** carmine-red, 2.5 cm lg.; **S.** yellowish-brown.—Guatemala (Rancho San Agustín). Spec. which can vary as to colour of Bo. and Sp., position of the offsets, and size of its clumps.

M. woodsii Craig (1:3)
Bo. broadly spherical, matt grass-green, to c. 8 cm $\emptyset$, later $\pm$ elongated; **Tub.** in **Isp.** 13:21; **Ar.** white-woolly at first; **Ax.** with dense white wool, especially in the flowering zone, and Br. to 2.5 cm lg.; **Rsp.** 25–30, 4–8 cm lg., hyaline, fine; **Csp.** 2(–4), the lowest one to 8–16 mm lg., thin-subulate, others thinner, c. 4–5 mm lg., all purplish-pink, black-tipped; **Fl.** to c. 1.5 cm $\emptyset$; **Sep.** serriculate; **Pet.** deep pink in the middle, borders pink, smooth; **style** and **Sti.** $\pm$ strongly pink; **Fr.** deep pink; **S.** matt brownish.—Mexico (Guanajuato, Hacienda Tarajeas).

M. wrightii Eng. (3:2, 5:9)
Bo. simple, dark green, to 8 cm $\emptyset$; **Tub.** in **Isp.** 8:13, fairly soft, to 15 mm lg.; **Ar.** white-woolly at first; **Ax.** naked; **Rsp.** 12–14, 8–12 mm lg., $\pm$ acicular, fine, hairy, white, dark-tipped; **Csp.** mostly 2(–4), to 1.2 cm lg., the bottom one hooked, all stiffly acicular, dark brown or often black, hairy; **Fl.** 2.5 cm lg. and $\emptyset$, purple, borders (mostly) entire; **Fil.** and **style** greenish below, $\pm$ strongly reddish above; **Sti.** yellow; **Fr.** purple, 2.5 cm lg.; **S.** black.—USA (New Mexico and Texas), Mexico (Chihuahua, near Lago Santa Maria).

M. wuthenauiana Backbg. (3:1, 2:6)

Bo. later rather oblong, to c. 12 cm h. or more, to c. 8 cm $\emptyset$, dark green, caespitose and sometimes forming groups; **Tub.** conical; **Isp.** 8:13; **Rsp.** to 28, very thin, hyaline, interlacing; **Csp.** 4, stouter, to 1.8 cm lg., reddish-brown, all straight or one hooked, directed downwards; **Fl.** carmine-red.—Mexico (Morelos to Guerrero [Tixtla, Taxco]).

M. xanthina (Br. & R.) Böd. (1:2)
Bo. depressed-spherical, bluish-green, to 9 cm $\emptyset$; **Tub.** shortly and broadly conical; **Isp.** 13:21; **Ax.** woolly at first; **Rsp.** 10–12, to 4 mm lg., acicular, white; **Csp.** 2, 4–6 mm lg., stoutly acicular, lowest one porrect, brownish; **Fl.** lemon-yellow; **Fr.** and **S.** ?—Mexico (Durango, near Monte Mercado). Spec. has never been re-collected. Acc. Bödeker, the Fl. are 16 mm $\emptyset$ and pale ochreous-yellow.

M. yaquensis Craig (3:2, 5:9) [Grafted plants grow faster, flower better.]
Bo. very small, oblong, to 7 cm lg., 1.5 cm $\emptyset$, reddish-green, offsetting freely from the sides, becoming larger if grafted; **Tub.** shortly conical; **Isp.** 5:8; **Ax.** with only traces of felt; **Rsp.** 18, 5–6 mm lg., finely acicular, cream-coloured, tipped light brown; **Csp.** 1, 7 mm lg., acicular, reddish-brown, strongly hooked; **Fl.** bellshaped, to 2 cm lg. and $\emptyset$, whitish-pink; **Sti.** long, light purple; **Fr.** 9 mm lg., scarlet; **S.** black.—Mexico (Sonora, Fort Pithaya).

M. yucatanensis (Br. & R.) Orc. (3:1, 1:3)
Bo. spherical to oblong, light yellowish-green, to 15 cm h., to 7 cm $\emptyset$, caespitose; **Tub.** shortly conical; **Isp.** 13:21; **Ax.** woolly; **Rsp.** 20–30, 3–5 mm lg., thin-acicular, smooth, cream-coloured; **Csp.** 3–6, 4–8 mm lg., stoutly acicular, smooth, brownish-yellow, brown-tipped; **Fl.** to 1.2 cm lg., Pet. white, with a $\pm$ broad pink M.-line above; **Fr.** orange-red, 1.6 cm lg.; **S.** brown.—Mexico (Yucatán, Progreso).

M. zacatecasensis Shurly (3:1, 3:7) [Grafting recommended.]
Bo. spherical, to c. 7 cm $\emptyset$, 5 cm h., darker green; **Tub.** cylindric; **Isp.** 13:21; **Ax.** glabrous; **Rsp.** 20–24, 7–8 mm lg., pale to deeper yellowish-green, rather darker below; **Csp.** 3–4, c. 1 cm lg., one central c. 1.5 cm lg., all stoutly acicular, yellowish to reddish-brownish, bottom one hooked; **Fl.** 1.4 cm $\emptyset$, Pet. white with a pink M.-line, or delicate pink and darker in the middle; **Fr.** red; **S.** black.—Mexico (Zacatecas).

M. zahniana Böd. & Ritt. (1:2)
Bo. depressed-spherical, dark leaf-green, simple; **Tub.** 4-angled to $\pm$ terete; **Isp.** 8:13; **Ax.** weakly woolly; **Rsp.** 4, 3–8 mm lg., lowest one to 15 mm lg., all subulate, straight, thickened below, whitish to

horn-coloured, with a short blackish tip; **Csp.** 0; **Fl.** 3 cm lg., 2.5 cm ∅, sulphur-yellow, border lighter, tip darker; **Fr.** red; **S.** reddish-brown.—Mexico (Coahuila, Saltillo).

M. zapilotensis Craig: a hook-spined form of **M. guerreronis** H. Bravo, named for the type-locality; no description available.

M. zeilmanniana Böd. (3:1, 3:7)
Bo. becoming oblong, dark leaf-green, sometimes offsetting; **Tub.** soft, ovoid-cylindric; **Isp.** 13:21; **Ax.** naked; **Rsp.** 15–18, 1 cm lg., thin, hairy, white; **Csp.** 4, 8 mm lg., reddish-brown; lowest one hooked; **Fl.** 2 cm ∅, violet-red to purple (anomalously white); **Fr.** green, small; **S.** black.—Mexico (Guanajuato, near San Miguel Allende). Very floriferous.

M. zeyeriana Hge. Jr. (1:2)
Bo. becoming columnar, to 10 cm ∅, pale bluish-green, simple; **Tub.** ovoid; **Isp.** 13:21; **Ax.** glabrous; **Rsp.** c. 10, 3–10 mm lg., upper ones shortest, all fine-acicular, smooth, white; **Csp.** 4, 1.5–2.5 cm lg., acicular, all ruby-red at first, then nut-brown, lastly grey; **Fl.** with Pet. reddish-orange, bordered yellowish; **Fr.** 2.5 cm lg., carmine; **S.** brown.—Mexico (Coahuila; Durango).

M. zuccariniana Mart. (1:2)
Bo. spherical to oblong, to 20 cm h., dark green, simple; **Tub.** conical; **Isp.** 16–26; **Ax.** woolly at first; **Rsp.** 3–4, often missing or dropping, 2–6 mm lg., bristly, white; **Csp.** (1–)2(–4), upper one(s) to 13 mm lg., lower one(s) to 25 mm lg., ± stoutly acicular, stiff, smooth, white with purple tips, later greyish to horn-coloured; **Fl.** 2.5 cm lg., brownish-reddish or more purplish-pink; **Fr.** red, 1 cm lg.; **S.** brownish.—Mexico (San Luis Potosí; Hidalgo, Ixmiquilpan). Close to M. centricirrha.

An interesting plant distributed by Johnson (USA) deserves mention here: **M. spec.**: **Bo.** spherical, offsetting freely from the base, to c. 5 cm h., 4.5 cm ∅, leaf-green; **Tub.** in Isp. 13:21, conical, rather soft; **Ax.** with some Br.; **Rsp.** c. 9–10, thin, to c. 11 mm lg., ± curving, laterally interlacing; **Csp.** 1, slightly thickened below, to 2 cm lg., straight or sometimes hooked; all Sp. smooth, pale yellow; **Fl.** small, c. 1.4 cm lg., 5 mm br., vivid purple, borders entire; **Fil.** and **style** red; **Sti.** greenish-cream; **Fr.** ? The Fl. is ± bellshaped above, and green in the lower part.—Origin ? In the Keys of Craig and myself, the spec. is placed with M. colonensis, but it bears little resemblance to the latter. All Sp., including the Csp., are fairly thin and very flexible; Ar. ± white-felty at first, soon becoming glabrous. This plant cannot be named since it would first

have to be compared with some little-known spec. and in view of our mostly insufficient descriptions of these, clarification appears unlikely. I do not know whether Johnson gave this plant any name.

The following are plants from F. Schmoll, Cadereyta, which are either undescribed, or are sometimes found under these names in collections: Mammillaria atarageaensis, M. haseltonii, M. longispina, M. melaleuca, M. sombreretensis and M. webbiana. No further information available.

Mamillopsis (Morr.) Web. (232)

Spherical to shortly-cylindric and densely spined plants from high altitudes, sometimes covered by snow in winter, forming larger groups; sap not milky. Axils set with hairs and bristles. Flowers large, with a long scaly tube. Fruits indehiscent, containing relatively large black seeds.— Distribution: Mexico (Chihuahua to Oaxaca). [(R), ✳; grafted plants are too lush.]
The type of the genus is held to be the large-flowered plant described by Weber (in D. Bois, Dict. d'Hort., 805. 1898) under the name Mamillopsis senilis Web., and *not* the plant Weber at the same time named Mammillaria senilis (Lodd.) SD., which was a hook-spined form of M. spinosissima; this is clear from the names Salm-Dyck referred to the latter as varieties, and from Rümpler's additional note on flower-size: "Flowers small". Weber's name can thus stand as referable to a Mamillopsis species, but "Lodd.", previously cited as the author in parenthesis, must be omitted.

M. diguetii (Web.) Br. & R.
Bo. forming cushions of up to 35 heads; single heads to 25 cm ∅; **Rsp.** numerous, dark straw-coloured; **Fl.** c. 3 cm lg., 2 cm ∅, deep red; **Ov.** with small Sc.—Mexico (Nayarit to Jalisco).

M. senilis Web. (T.)
Bo. eventually forming mats, individual heads becoming elongated, to 15 cm lg. (and more), to 6 cm ∅, glossy, fresh green; **Tub.** in spirals of 8 and 13; **Rsp.** to 40, to c. 1.4 cm lg., bristle-like, stiff, not pungent, pale yellowish to pure white; **Csp.** 5–6, scarcely differentiated but the lowest one stouter, porrect, hooked, tipped ± brownish-yellow, to 2 cm lg.; **Fl.** to 7 cm lg., to 6 cm ∅, orange-red tinged violet, M.-stripe darker; **Fil.** close to the style, long-projecting; **Fr.** red.—Mexico (Chihuahua; S. Durango; Nayarit; Oaxaca). (Fig. 219.)

Mammilloydia F. Buxb., or M. candida and M. ortiz-rubiona; genus based on incorrectly named seed; these spec. cannot be segregated from Mammillaria.

Marenopuntia Backbg. (10)

Low-growing bushy plants with a thick taproot. Shoots cylindric, with glochids. The flower is terminal, sunken within the ± thickened apex, the fruit similarly; when this is ripe, the swollen stem-tip splits laterally. Seeds fairly large, kidney-shaped. Only one species.—Distribution: Mexico (Sonora). [?]

M. marenae (S. H. Parsons) Backbg. (T.)
Bo. sparsely shrubby. low-growing; **shoots** crowded, more slender below; **Ar.** round, light; **Sp.** few at first, later 8–9 (or more), unequal, all ± appressed at first, later only the outer ones; **Csp.** 1–2, unequal, projecting downwards, sometimes one directed sideways, longest; **Fl.** relatively large, opening wide.—Mexico (Sonora, Kino Bay). (Fig. 220.)

Marginatocereus (Backbg.) Backbg. (157)

Large columnar cacti which, in nature, form a trunk; branches erect; cultivated plants branch from the base. The nocturnal white and pinkish-red flowers which are borne on the sides, sometimes in pairs, are shortly felty, the tubes sometimes with a few soft bristles. The fruits, set with stiff bristles, contain black, ± glossy seeds of medium size.—Distribution: Mexico (Hidalgo, Querétaro, Guanajuato, Oaxaca). [(R).]

M. marginatus (DC.) Backbg. (T.)
Bo. dark greyish-green, trunk to 1.5 m h., 30 cm ∅; **branches** to 7 m lg., to 15 cm ∅; **Ri.** 5–6(–7), acute, becoming broad and rounded; **Ar.** almost confluent, brown-felty or dark; **Sp.** rarely to 9, usually fewer, very short, soon quite inconspicuous or dropping, at first ± conical, stiff, often dark reddish; **Csp.** scarcely differentiated; **Fl.** solitary or paired (also in 3's?), to 5 cm lg., c. 3 cm ∅, stoutly short-cylindric, white, limb slightly revolute at anthesis; **Fr.** c. 4 cm ∅, glossy, spherical, strongly tuberculate; **S.** 4 mm lg.—Mexico (see above). (Fig. 221, left.)
  v. **gemmatus** (Zucc.) Backbg.: differentiated by the initially lighter colour, whitish areolar felt, bristly and flexible **Sp.** which are longer, especially at the apex, up to c. 10, ± erect, light to brownish at first; **Fl.** to only c. 3 cm lg., **Pet.** pink, **Tu.** somewhat bristlier. (Fig. 221, right);
  v. **oaxacensis** Backbg.—Descr. Cact. Nov. III: 8. 1963: distinguishable, even as a seedling, by the

elongated **Ar.** which are discrete, even near the apex, separated by approximately the length of the Ar., while in the type of the genus they are ± confluent at first, and also feltier.—Mexico (Oaxaca). (Fig. in "Die Cact.", VI, p. 3861.)

Maritimocereus Akers & Buin.: **Loxanthocereus** Backbg.

Maritimocereus gracilis Akers & Buin., and M. nana Akers: see **Loxanthocereus**.

Marniera Backbg. (33)

Epiphyllum-like plants; shoots broad, weakly notched, or long-lobed and deeply serrate, with a stout midrib. Flowers large, nocturnal, with a fairly long tube; ovary with stiffer hairs or bristles, a character not present in any of the Epiphyllum species.—Distribution: Costa Rica and S. Mexico (Chiapas). [(R).]

M. chrysocardium (Alex.) Backbg.
Bo. epiphytic, branches strongly spreading; **shoots** serrate, with very broad lobes, to 30 cm br., incised as far as the M.-rib, lobes to 15 cm lg., 4 cm br.; **Ar.** small, sometimes with 2–3 Br.; **Fl.** c. 32 cm lg., the actual Per. c. 12.5 cm lg.; **Ov.** strongly tuberculate, Sc. fairly crowded, with 2–4 stiffer white Br. to 8 mm lg. in the Ax.; **Tu.** 16 cm lg., 1.25 cm ∅, with narrow projecting Sc. c. 1 cm lg.; **Sep.** dirty purplish-pink; **Pet.** broader, white, with a ± oblique apiculus; **style** milky-white; **Sti.** 13; **Fr.** spiny.—Mexico (Chiapas). (Fig. 222, 223.) See also Epiphyllum grandilobum (Web.) Br. & R.

M. macroptera (Lem.) Backbg. (T.)
Bo. epiphytic; **shoots** sometimes to 10 cm br., thin, margin horny, weakly notched, not dentate; **Fl.** very large, curving; **Tu.** to 12 cm lg., fairly robust; **Ov.** with thinner Br.; **Sep.** tipped salmon or yellow, narrow; **Pet.** to 9 cm lg., to 3 cm br., pure white; **style** pure white; **Fr.** ovoid, red.—Costa Rica. (Fig. 224.)
  v. **kimnachii**: see **Epiphyllum crenatum** v. **kimnachii**.

Marshallocereus Backbg. (151)

Large Cerei, with or without a shorter trunk, to strongly tall-shrubby. Flowers nocturnal, funnelform, their tube with felty areoles which are rarely bristly. The ovary (a diagnostic character) is set with felt and is ± stiffly spined. For this reason the genus must be kept distinct. The fruit is ± densely spiny, the seeds black. Two species and one variety have been described; Ritterocereus chacalapensis H. Bravo & Th. MacDoug., which is perhaps referable here, is insufficiently clarified.— Distribution: from USA through W. Mexico to W. Costa Rica. [(R).]

M. aragonii (Web.) Backbg. (T.)
Bo. columnar, to 6 m h., apparently without a trunk; **branches** erect, to 15 cm ∅, with regular constrictions, dark green, with floury markings; **Ri.** 6–8, very broad; **Ar.** brown; **Rsp.** c. 8–10. later more, to c. 1 cm lg.; **Csp.** 2–3 cm lg.; **Sp.** grey; **Fl.** 6–8 cm lg., greenish-brown (K. Sch.; white inside?); **Ov.** tuberculate, with clustered Sp.; **Fr.** rounded-conical,. 3–4 cm ∅; **S.** matt.—W. Costa Rica.

M. thurberi (Eng.) Backbg.
Bo. to 7 m h., usually without a trunk; **branches** numerous, broadly curving and ascending, to 20 cm ∅, not distinctly constricted; **Ri.** 12–17; **Ar.** brown, sometimes with a waxy mass; **Rsp.** 9–10, c. 1 cm lg.; **Csp.** 1–3, the bottom one longest, to c. 5 cm lg.; **Sp.** brownish to blackish at first, or mottled; **Fl.** to c. 7.5 cm lg., ± broadly funnelform, (light) purple; **Fr.** spherical, 4–7.5 cm ∅; **S.** glossy.— USA (S. Arizona), Mexico. (Fig. 225.)
   v. **littoralis** (K. Brand.) Backbg.: **Bo.** to only 90 cm h.; **branches** to 5 cm ∅; **Fl.** c. 2.5 cm lg., deep pink to red; **Fr.** scarcely 2.5 cm ∅.—Mexico (southernmost tip of Baja California).

Possibly referable here:
Ritterocereus (Marshallocereus?) chacalapensis H. Bravo & Th. MacDoug.
Bo. tree-like, to 20 m h.; **trunk** to 3 m h., 50 cm ∅; **branches** erect, c. 15 cm ∅; **Ri.** 7, slightly sinuate and notched; **Ar.** brown, later ± black-felty; **Sp.** 10–14, scarcely differentiated, 0.5 to (centrals) c. 2.8 cm lg., beneath them sometimes one longer Sp., porrect to directed upwards, all blackish, grey or brown, thin-subulate or stoutly acicular; **Fl.** 14 cm lg., 7 cm ∅, ± funnelform, white; **Ov.** with yellow wool and a few short bristle-like Sp.; **Fr.** very bristly-spined.—Mexico (Oaxaca, Chacalapa).

See also notes at the end of Lemaireocereus and Ritterocereus.

Matucana Br. & R. (82)

Flattened-spherical to elongated-cylindric plants, with relatively slender ribs and finer, very variable spination; simple or somewhat offsetting to forming large cushions. The diurnal flowers are in shades of red, yellow only in one known species, stout and of varying length, with the limb ± zygomorphic and the perianth mostly quite strongly recurved. The generic type, in the sense of Britton & Rose, has a glabrous flower, with traces of hair observed only in exceptional cases, vestiges of the process of reduction. Style, filaments and stigma-lobes are usually vividly coloured. The fruit is small and opens by means of longitudinal tears; the seeds, as far as known, are small, matt and greyish-black.—Distribution: Central Peru (Matucana; from the upper Rio Saña valley to S. of the Pisco valley). [(R); (G) recommended.] All descriptions are based on plants in the wild.
Unlike his treatment in segregating Copiapoa and Pilocopiapoa, Ritter here included several species with typically hairy flowers which, on the basis also of differences of rib and spine-character, should be referred to Submatucana (see under this genus), since Britton & Rose's generic diagnosis specifies Matucana flowers as having "tube and ovary naked".

M. aurantiaca (Vpl.) Ritt.: **Submatucana aurantiaca** (Vpl.) Backbg.

M. blancii Backbg.
Bo. mostly forming large cushions, individual heads later oblong, to 30 cm h., 20 cm ∅; **Sp.** numerous, scarcely differentiated, crowded, bristly, silvery-white, sometimes several centrals rather longer and ± darker, especially at the tip; **Fl.** to 6 cm lg., carmine-red (or salmon-coloured: Rauh); **Fil.** carmine; **An.** yellow.—Peru (Cordillera Negra). (Fig. 226.)
   v. **nigriarmata** Backbg.: differentiated by the much longer, stouter and concolorous black **Csp.**

M. breviflora Rauh & Backbg.
Bo. always simple, ± spherical, to 15 cm lg., 15 cm ∅; **Rsp.** numerous, to 2 cm lg., ± pectinate, interlacing; **Csp.** mostly 3–4, to 7 cm lg., very stout; **Sp.** crowded, very variable in colour, light brown to amber or black below, dark brown to deep purple above; **Fl.** only c. 4 cm lg., carmine; **Tu.** ± deep dark carmine.—S. Peru (W. of Incuio, among tola-scrub on bleak uplands).

M. calliantha Lau: no description available.

M. calocephala Skarupke 1973
Bo. to 50 cm h., to 12 cm br., greyish-green, scarcely offsetting; **Ri.** 24–30, vertical, 8–12 mm apart, tuberculate; **Ar.** oblong, 1 cm apart; **Sp.** mostly directed upwards, very dense, enveloping the Bo., interspersed with fine H. especially in the apex, beige to light brown at first, later in part whitish, 1–3 cm lg.; **Csp.** brown-tipped, to 2.5 cm lg.; **Fl.** zygomorphic, to 5 cm lg., 3 cm ∅, pink, with a stout pinkish-violet M.-stripe; **Tu.** with a few Sc.; **Fil.** beige below, pinkish-violet above; **An.** reddish-

violet; **style** intense violet, projecting 1 cm beyond the Fl.; **Sti.** 4, yellowish-violet, closely surrounding the style; **Fr.** 2 cm lg., green, drying to dark brown; **S.** cap-shaped, matt, grey.—Peru (Dept. Ancash near Llamelin).

M. calvescens (Kimn. & Hutch.) Ritt.: **Submatucana calvescens** (Kimn. & Hutch.) Backbg.

M. cereoides Rauh & Backbg.
Bo. cereoid, to 50 cm lg., 10 cm $\emptyset$; **Ri.** 24; **Rsp.** numerous, to 2.5 cm lg., thin, snow-white; **Csp.** (0–)1–4, to 5 cm lg., thin, curving upwards, concolorous white, or white below and light brownish to blackish in the upper third; **Fl.** to 8 cm lg., carmine; **An.** yellow; S. Peru (Pisco valley).

M. coloris-splendida Ritt., v. grandiflora and v. setosa Ritt.: **Matucana yanganucensis** Rauh & Backbg., or v. grandiflora and v. setosa Ritt.; the latter's varieties have not been described.

M. comacephala Ritt.
Bo. eventually columnar, usually 75 cm (–1.2 m) lg., to 8 cm $\emptyset$; **Ri.** c. 25, distinctly tuberculate; **Rsp.** 15–20, 1–5 cm lg., ± hair-like, ± projecting; **Csp.** 5–10, 1–4 cm lg., stouter, directed obliquely upwards, ± curving, sometimes 1 directed downwards; **Sp.** white; **Fl.** to 5.5 cm lg., red; **Fil.** and style carmine; **Fr.** greenish.—Peru (Cordillera Blanca, E. flanks).

M. crinifera Ritt.—"Taxon", XII: 3, 125. 1963.
Bo. to 30 cm h., 7–10 cm $\emptyset$; **Ri.** 22–26, to 6 mm h., strongly notched; **Ar.** pale brown, to 5 mm lg., 3–5 mm br., 3–5 mm apart; **Sp.** 15–25, thin-acicular, yellowish, sometimes black; **Fl.** 6–7 cm lg., weakly zygomorphic; **Tu.** 3–4 cm lg., 5 mm $\emptyset$; **Pet.** orange, white below, tipped crimson; **Fil.** white below, reddish above; **style** orange or golden-yellow; **Sti.** 5, pale green or golden-yellow; **S.** 1.2 mm lg., dark, ± rough.—Peru (Machac, Prov. Huari, Dept. Ancash) (FR 595).

M. currundayensis Ritt.: **Submatucana currundayensis** (Ritt.) Backbg.

M. elongata Rauh & Backbg.
Bo. columnar, to 60 cm lg., 15 cm $\emptyset$, sometimes branching from the tip; **Rsp.** numerous, to 2 cm lg., interlacing, hard, brittle, white; **Csp.** to 3, to 5 cm lg., directed obliquely upwards, brownish, tipped darker, becoming grey; **Fl.** c. 5 cm lg., red; **Fil.** and style carmine; **An.** yellow; **Sti.** green; **Fr.** spherical, reddish-brown.—Central Peru (valley of Rio Fortaleza).

I **M. fruticosa** Ritt. (FR 1307)

Bo. freely branching from the base, shrub-like; **branches** 10–50 cm lg., mostly 3–6 cm $\emptyset$; **Ri.** 10–21, mostly 13–15, 5–7 mm h., notched; **Ar.** 2–3 mm lg., white, 5–10 mm apart; **Sp.** acicular, straight, glossy, yellow or brown; **Rsp.** 13–22, mostly 5–20 mm lg.; **Csp.** 5–10, 0.7–6 cm lg., lower ones shorter; **Fl.** 6–9 cm lg., actinomorphic or weakly zygomorphic; **Ov.** green, with a few small Sc. and flakes of wool, latter sometimes absent; **Tu.** 7–9 mm br., wider below, with small Sc. and white or black flock; **Fil.** white, golden-yellow above, tipped crimson; **style** 6.5–8.5 cm lg.; **Sti.** green; **Pet.** erect, 22–30 mm lg., 5–7 mm br., golden-yellow, tip partly carmine; **Sep.** spreading outwards; **Fr.** 15 mm $\emptyset$, tapering above; **S.** black, 2 mm lg., ribbed and tuberculate.—Peru (San Juán).

M. hastifera (FR 1306): no description available.

M. haynei (O.) Br. & R. (T.)
Bo. mostly simple, spherical at first, later elongated to shortly columnar, to 30 cm h., to c. 10 cm $\emptyset$; **Ri.** 25–30, spiralled, tuberculate; **Sp.** in all over 30, Csp. distinguishable later; **Rsp.** bristly, whitish; **Csp.** brownish, tipped darker to black, stouter, rather longer; **Fl.** 6–7 cm lg., scarlet-carmine; **style** carmine; **Sti.** green; **Fr.** clavate.—Peru (near Matucana).
    v. **erectipetala** Rauh & Backbg.: differentiated by the finer, more numerous **Sp.**, with the **Fl.** only c. 4 cm lg.; unlike the type, in which the **Pet.** are strongly revolute, those of the variety are ± erect.
    v. elongata Ritt. (FR 142 C), v. gigantea Ritt. (FR 142 A) and v. multicolor Ritt. (FR 142 B) are undescribed names.

M. herzogiana Backbg.
Bo. ± elongated, c. 10 cm h., to 7 cm $\emptyset$; **Ri.** with very rounded Tub.; **Sp.** appressed, radiating, ± curving, bristly, only somewhat interlacing; **Csp.** scarcely differentiated, thin; **Fl.** not known.—Peru (Cordillera Negra).
    v. **perplexa** Backbg.: differs in having longer, densely interlacing bristly **Sp.** completely concealing the Bo.

I M. hualgalensis: no description available.

M. hystrix Rauh & Backbg.
Bo. elongated, to 30 cm h., to c. 10 cm $\emptyset$; **Ri.** c. 23; **Rsp.** numerous, to 1.5 cm lg., ± pectinate, ± stiff; **Csp.** to 4, to 5 cm lg. ± subulate, thickened below, dark brown but variable in colour; **Fl.** to 7 cm lg., 2.5 cm $\emptyset$, deep dark carmine; **Fil.** and style brilliant carmine; **An.** yellow; **Sti.** greenish; **Fr.** c. 1 cm lg., greenish-red.—S. Peru (between Nazca and Lucanas).

v. **atrispina** Rauh & Backbg.: **Sp.** stouter, intense black, thickened and ashy-grey at the base;

v. **umadeavoides** Rauh & Backbg.: **Csp.** still stouter, thick-subulate, often bent, ± light horny-grey, appearing frosted, tipped brownish, base slightly thickened.

M. megalantha Ritt.: **Submatucana calvescens** (Kimn. & Hutch.) Backbg.

M. multicolor Rauh & Backbg.

Bo. simple or caespitose, depressed-spherical at first, later to 40 cm lg., to 15 cm ∅; **Ri.** c. 14; **Rsp.** numerous, to 2 cm lg., mostly white, pectinate, stout, interlacing; **Csp.** 2–4, to 7 cm lg., very stout, ± honey-coloured below, tipped brownish-red; **Sp.**-colour very variable, from pure white to grey, Csp. amber to ± blackish-violet above, also variable in length; **Fl.** c. 5(–7) cm lg., carmine; **Fr.** to 1.5 cm lg.—S. Peru (Nazca-Puquio).

M. nigricantha (FR 1305): no description available.

M. pallarensis (not yet described; found by Ritter) **Bo.** flattened-spherical; **Sp.** dense, brownish-yellow, concealing the crown; **Fl.** intense orange; **Fil.** red; **Sti.** green; **Tu.** yellowish-green, throat green.—Peru.

M. paucicostata Ritt.: **Submatucana paucicostata** (Ritt.) Backbg.

M. rarissima Ritt., not described; colour-photo in "Die Cact." VI, Fig. 3361, right above.

M. ritteri Buin.: **Submatucana ritteri** (Buin.) Backbg.

M. robusta Ritt., not described: colour-photo in "Die Cact.", VI, Fig. 3361, right below.

M. supertexta (FR 690): no description available.

M. variabilis Rauh & Backbg.

Bo. oblong, to 15 cm lg., (perhaps more?), to 8 cm ∅; **Ri.** 23; **Rsp.** numerous, to 1.5 cm lg., fine, white, bristly, interlacing; **Csp.** 1–3, scarcely distinguishable, scarcely longer, white, tipped brownish; **Fl.** (dried material) c. 4 cm lg., carmine; **Fr.** c. 1 cm lg.—Central Peru (N. of Churin).

v. **fuscata** Rauh & Backbg.: **Bo.** at first flattened-spherical, later long-cylindric, to 40 cm lg., to 10 cm ∅, spination much denser; **Rsp.** stout, whitish-yellow at the apex; **Csp.** 2–3, to 4 cm lg., brownish-red, becoming blackish-grey; **Fl.** (dried material) c. 5 cm lg., salmon-pink to carmine; **Fr.** c. 1.5 cm lg.

M. weberbaueri (Vpl.) Backbg.

Bo. depressed-spherical, c. 7 cm h., to c. 15 cm ∅; **Ri.** 21, tuberculate; **Sp.** c. 30, to 4 cm lg., radiating in all directions, dark reddish-brown, becoming ± black; **Fl.** 5.5 cm lg., narrow-funnelform, lemon-yellow; **Fr.** c. 1.3 cm lg.—Peru (Chachapoyas).

M. weberbaueri v. blancii Backbg. n.prov.: **Matucana yanganucensis** v. **albispina** Rauh & Backbg.

M. winteriana Ritt., not described; referable to **Matucana yanganucensis** Rauh & Backbg.

M. yanganucensis Rauh & Backbg.

Bo. spherical, to 10 cm ∅ and more, sometimes offsetting freely; **Ri.** 27; **Rsp.** numerous, to c. 1.2 cm lg., stout, yellowish-brown at first, then whitish; **Csp.** 1–2, to 2.5 cm lg., acicular, yellowish-brown; **Fl.** to 6 cm lg., 2–2.5 cm ∅, reddish-violet; **Fil.** violet above; **An.** carmine-violet; **style** violet; **Sti.** yellowish.—N. Peru (Cordillera Blanca).(v. yanganucensis).

v. **albispina** Rauh & Backbg.: **Sp.** concolorous white; **Rsp.** pectinate, interlacing; **Csp.** 2–3, to 2 cm lg., yellowish-tipped; **Ri.** c. 30; **Fl.** light carmine; **style** and **Sti.** violet-carmine.—(Cordillera Blanca);

v. **fuscispina** Rauh & Backbg.: **Bo.** mostly unbranching; **Ri.** c. 25; **Csp.** scarcely distinguishable, to 3 cm lg., darker brown, eventually grey, projecting; **Fl.** 6 cm lg., carmine; **Fil.** and **style** carmine; **An.** and **Sti.** yellow.—(Cordillera Negra);

v. **longistyla** Rauh: **Bo.** spherical, to 15 cm ∅; **Ri.** 23, with warty prominences; **Rsp.** to c. 1.2 cm lg., whitish, blackish-brown below, interlacing; **Csp.** 2–3, to 1.5 cm lg., intense brown, tipped blackish; **Fl.** 4.5 cm lg., 2 cm ∅, crimson to pale carmine; **Fil.**, **style** and **Sti.** violet; **style** conspicuously long.—(Cordillera Blanca);

v. **parviflora** Rauh & Backbg.: **Bo.** spherical to flat and depressed; **Sp.** longer, stouter, erect and tufted in the crown; **Fl.** to only 4 cm lg., 1.5 cm ∅, little zygomorphic, vivid carmine; **Fil.** and **style** pink; **An.** yellow.—(Cordillera Blanca);

v. **salmonea** Rauh & Backbg.: **Bo.** broadly-spherical; **Ri.** c. 30; **Rsp.** brownish at first, later yellowish-white; **Fl.** salmon-coloured; **Fil.** salmon-pink above; **An.** yellowish.—(Cordillera Blanca);

v. **suberecta** Rauh & Backbg.: **Bo.** eventually to 20 cm lg., 10 cm ∅; **Rsp.** more bristly, projecting, to 2 cm lg., whitish; **Csp.** 3–4, whitish, tipped brownish, scarcely differentiated, rather longer; **Fl.** to 5 cm lg., red.—(Santa valley).

At the present time, no further information is available regarding the following undescribed plants: M. celendinensis Ritt. (FR 692), M. fruticosa Ritt. (FR 1307), M. hastifera Ritt. (FR 1306) and M. intertexta Ritt. (FR 693).

Mediocactus Br. & R. (46)

The genus, according to Britton & Rose, is intermediate between Hylocereus (with which it shares, among other characters, shoots which are often 3-angled) and Selenicereus (which mostly has several ribs), with a spiny and quite strongly tuberculate ovary. This genus of ± epiphytic plants shows long pendant stems which are fairly thin and produce aerial roots, while the areoles are only shortly spiny. The large white nocturnal flowers are funnelform, the ± tuberculate ovary and the fruit are spiny. In one species the entire tube and also the ovary have bristly spines.—Distribution: E. Peru, (Colombia?,) Bolivia, Paraguay, Argentina, Brazil, (W. Indies?). [(R)]

M. coccineus (SD. in DC.) Br. & R. (T.)
Bo. pendant; **St.** mostly with 3 (rarely 4–5) winged angles, c. 2 cm br., light green, margins slightly sinuate, ± acute; **Ar.** at first bristly, later also with 2–4 Sp. 1–3 mm lg., conical, reddish, becoming brownish; **Fl.** 25–30 cm lg.; **Fr.** red, ovoid, strongly tuberculate, with Sp. 1–2 cm lg.—Brazil to Argentina. (Fig. 227.)
   v. xanthocarpus Card.: apparently not described; with a yellow fruit, to judge by the varietal name. No other distinguishing characters known.—Bolivia (San Ignacio). Uhlig No. U 272.

M. hahnianus Backbg.
Bo. pendant; **St.** indistinctly 5-angled, with flat Tub. in transverse zones, c. 1.5 cm ∅; **Ar.** scarcely felty; **Sp.** c. 10, ± equal, short, bristly, thin, light-coloured; **Fl.** c. 12–14 cm lg., c. 9 cm ∅, white tinged greenish; **Tu.** and **Fr.** with dense H. and Br.—Paraguay(?).

M. hassleri (K. Sch.) Backbg.
Bo. ± erect; **St.** to 5 cm ∅, mostly with 3 (also 4–5) angles, dark green; **Sp.** not interspersed with Br., 3–7, unequal, 1–6 mm lg., rigid, thickened below, brownish; **Fl.** over 20 (? to 30) cm lg., white suffused yellowish; **Fr.** carmine, to 6 cm lg., c. 3.5 cm ∅.—Paraguay (Cordillera de Altos; Estancia Tagatiya).

M. lindmanii (Web.) Backbg.
Bo. climbing by means of R.; **St.** 3-angled, to 3 cm ∅, green; **Ar.** very short-felty; **Rsp.** 6–10, to 2 mm lg., radiating, ± appressed; **Csp.** 1(–2), clavate, rather longer; all **Sp.** thickened below; sometimes also 3–5 very thin, appressed Ssp.; **Fl.** 20 cm lg.; **Ov.** tuberculate, with clusters of conical pungent Sp. 4–6 mm lg.; **Fl.** 20 cm lg.; **Pet.** green; **Sep.** white.—Paraguay (Chaco, Puerto Casado near Asunción).

M. megalanthus (K. Sch.) Br. & R.
Bo. forming masses of pendant branches, these 3-angled, often only 1.5 cm ∅, margins weakly indented; **Sp.** 0–3, 2–3 mm lg., yellowish, at first mingled with a few white Br.; **Fl.** to 38 cm lg., white; **Ov.** stiffly spiny.—E. Peru (Dept. Loreto).

M. pomifer Wgt.
Bo. climbing(?), to 4(–5) m h. (?); **St.** to 25 cm lg., c. 3 cm ∅, 3-angled, margin rounded; **Ar.** scarcely felty; **Sp.** 3–4, 3–4 mm lg., cruciform, conical, rigid, pungent, blackish-brown, the lower one ± bent; **Fl.** "small"; **Tu.** c. 7 cm lg.; **Per.** c. 3.1 cm lg. (description from herbarium material); **Fr.** c. 3.5 cm lg., 3 cm ∅, stiffly spiny.—W. Indies (Martinique). Relationship to Mediocactus uncertain, in the absence of more adequate floral data.

M. setaceus (SD.) Borg: **Mediocactus coccineus** (SD. in DC.) Br. & R.

Possibly referable to this genus: "Cereus lindbergianus Web.": **St.** creeping, rooting, green, scarcely 1 cm ∅; **Ri.** 4–6, compressed, winged; **Ar.** without felt; **Sp.** at first forming a small bundle of hairy Br., later disappearing; the indentations between the Ri. become completely flat; **Fl.** unknown.—Paraguay.

Mediolobivia Backbg. (101)

Plants spherical to cylindric, always caespitose, with slender tubercles or the ribs strongly divided so as to form these. Flowers funnelform, in tones of yellow and red, sometimes varying greatly in colour, hairy and bristly. In some species the style is somewhat united at the base. The small fruit dries to become thin-membranous. Seeds ± black. Popular, also as nurseryman's plants, because they are so floriferous.—Distribution: Bolivia to N. Argentina. [(R); grafting recommended.]
The genus is divided into the following subgenera and series:
SG.1: **Mediolobivia**
   Plants spherical; ribs broken up into tubercles; style (probably always) free.
SG.2: **Pygmaeolobivia** backbg.
   Plants becoming ± elongated; ribs still ± distinguishable; style in part shortly united with the tube.
      Ser. 1: **Coniodeae** Backbg.

Bodies later cylindric; ribs noticeably tuberculate.

Ser. 2: **Pygmaeae** Backbg.
Bodies later cylindric-elongated; ribs more clearly recognisable.

The numbers of the appropriate SG. and Ser. are given in brackets after each specific name; of these, the first figure indicates the SG.

See under Rebutia regarding recent attempts to unite the species of this genus with Rebutia. If species with hairy, bristly, stalk-like, glabrous and funnelform flowers are all to be gathered together, then the same procedure should logically be adopted throughout the entire family. Unfortunately this does not prevent individual authors from making confusing recombinations of this kind, basing their attempts on their own narrow specialism, without any thought of the logical consequences.

M. albopectinata Rausch 1972 (described as **Rebutia**)
Bo. simple, spherical, to 15 mm $\emptyset$, greyish-green, taprooted; **Ri.** to 16, vertical or $\pm$ spiralled, divided into Tub. 1.5 mm lg.; **Ar.** oval, 1 mm lg., 1 mm apart, with white or light brown felt; **Rsp.** 13, in 6 pairs and one directed downwards, to 3 mm lg., appressed, covering the Bo.; **Csp.** 0–2, to 1 mm lg., projecting; all **Sp.** white, thickened and brown below; **Fl.** lateral, 50 mm lg., 45 mm $\emptyset$; **Ov.** and **Tu.** pink, with brownish-red Sc., white H. and Br.; **Sep.** violet-pink with a green M.-stripe; **Pet.** red, throat pink, white below; **Fil.** pink; **style** united with the Tu., green; **Sti.** 5–7, green; **Fr.** spherical, 5 mm $\emptyset$, with white H. and Br.; **S.** spherical, glossy black, c. 1 mm $\emptyset$.—Bolivia (near Culpina, at 3400 m). Resembles Aylostera heliosa but the Ri. are $\pm$ straight.

M. atrovirens (Backbg.) Backbg.: **Mediolobivia pectinata** v. **atrovirens** (Backbg.) Backbg.

M. auranitida (Wessn.) Krainz (2:2)
Bo. $\pm$ cylindric, little caespitose, matt dark green, suffused bronze; **Ri.** 11, spiralled; **Tub.** with the prominences darker green; **Rsp.** 9, to 7 mm lg., thickened below, 1 directed downwards, glossy reddish-brown to pink at first, soon becoming yellowish-white; **Fl.** 3 cm $\emptyset$, laxly funnelform, golden-bronze.—Bolivia(?).
v. **flaviflora** Backbg.: **Ri.** to 14; **Sp.** in part $\pm$ bent; **Fl.** pure yellow;
v. **gracilis** (Wessn.) Backbg.: **Bo.** much smaller than the type, strongly bronze-coloured; **Sp.** only c. 2 mm lg.; **Fl.** deep golden-yellow.

M. aureiflora (Backbg.) Backbg. (1) (T.)
Bo. forming groups, leaf-green, mostly suffused

reddish; **Tub.** $\pm$ strongly spiralled; **Sp.** c. 15–20, to 6 mm lg., bristly, **centrals** 3–4, the longest ones at first to 1 cm lg., directed upwards, yellowish-brownish, Sp.-count and length increasing with age; **Fl.** c. 4 cm $\emptyset$, orange-yellow, throat white.—N. Argentina (Jujuy; also Salta?). Both the type and its varieties are $\pm$ variable; the following are the only validly published names:
v. **albiseta** Backbg.: Bristly **Sp.** soft, white, 1 cm lg. and more, sometimes much longer;
v. **aureiflora**:
　sv. **leucolutea** (Backbg.) Backbg.: **Fl.** light lemon-yellow or light buttercup-yellow; **throat** white;
　sv. **lilacinostoma** (Backbg.) Backbg.: **Fl.** mostly buttercup-yellow; **throat** delicate lilac;
v. **boedekeriana** (Backbg.) Backbg.: **Bo.** always flattened-spherical, glossy, dark green; **Ri.** still connected at the base, to 20; **Rsp.** c. 12–14; **Csp.** 2–3, rather stiffer, golden-brown, to 2.5 cm lg., projecting vertically;
v. **duursmaiana** (Backbg.) Backbg.: **Bo.** often tapering above, predominantly blackish-violet; **Rsp.** c. 10–12, to c. 5 mm lg., very thin, hyaline; **Csp.** 1, c. 3–4 mm lg.; **Fl.** more slender-funnelform;
v. **rubelliflora** (Backbg.) Backbg.: **Rsp.** over 10; **Csp.** only 1, little longer, mostly rather darker; **Fl.** orange-red;
v. **rubriflora** (Backbg.) Backbg.: **Bo.** deep green; **Br.-Sp.** longer, brownish, sometimes 1 central, rather stiffer or darker; **Fl.** $\pm$ bluish-red, lighter or darker;
v. **sarothroides** (Werd.) Backbg.: **Bo.** light to yellowish-green; **Rsp.** 15–16, hyaline; **Csp.** 3–4, also 2 upper Sp., to over 2 cm lg., $\pm$ bent, reddish-brown; **Fl.** c. 4 cm lg., deep flame-colour or blood-red.

M. blossfeldii (Werd.) Buin.: **Mediolobivia aureiflora** v. **rubriflora** (Backbg.) Backbg.

M. blossfeldii v. compactiflora Wessn.: **Mediolobivia aureiflora** v. **rubelliflora** (Backbg.) Backbg.

Mediolobivia boedekeriana Backbg.: **Mediolobivia aureiflora** v. **boedekeriana** (Backbg.) Backbg.

M. brachyantha (Wessn.) Krainz (2:2)
Bo. shortly cylindric, c. 2 cm $\emptyset$; **Ri.** 12; **Sp.** 7–9(–10), c. 5 mm lg., hyaline, acicular, thickened and brownish below; **Csp.** 0; **Fl.** c. 2 cm lg., slightly bellshaped, light scarlet; **style** somewhat united.—Origin?

M. brunescens Rausch 1972 (described as **Rebutia**)
Bo. simple, spherical, to 50 mm $\emptyset$; **Ri.** 13–14, straight or $\pm$ spiralled, divided by transverse

furrows into round Tub., brown-violet, $\pm$ dark green around the Ar.; **Ar.** oval, 2–3 mm lg., brown-felty; **Rsp.** 11–13, tangled around the Bo.; **Csp.** 0–2, to 10 mm lg.; all **Sp.** brown, darker-tipped, darker and thickened below; **Fl.** lateral, 40 mm lg., 30 mm $\emptyset$; **Ov.** and **Tu.** whitish-pink with green to brown Sc., with white felt and Br.; **Sep.** pink with a green M.-stripe; **Pet.** red, throat whitish; **Fil.** whitish-pink; **style** greenish-white, with 7 yellow **Sti.**; **Fr.** spherical, brown with darker Sc., white felt and Br.; **S.** spherical, testa rough with large Tub.—Bolivia (Tarabuco, at 3500 m). (Fig. 484.)

M. cajasensis Ritt. (FR 1141 + a): no description available.

M. columnaris (Wessn.) Krainz: **Mediolobivia conoidea** v. **columnaris** (Wessn.) Backbg.

M. conoidea (Wessn.) Krainz (2:1)
Bo. very slender-cylindric, tapering above, metallic violet-green; **Ri.** not clearly recognisable; **Tub.** somewhat spiralled; **Rsp.** in 4–6 pairs, 2–3 mm lg., $\pm$ appressed, those in the crown projecting slightly, acicular, whitish-grey to brownish, brown and somewhat thickened below; **Csp.** 0; **Fl.** c. 1.2 cm lg., to 2.8 cm $\emptyset$, pale golden-yellow.—Argentina (Chani Volcano).
   v. **columnaris** (Wessn.) Backbg.: distinguished by the pale greyish-green **Bo.** with a faint violet shimmer; **Pet.** golden-yellow inside.

M. costata (Werd.) Krainz (2:2)
Bo. oblong, deep green, freely offsetting; **Ri.** only 8–9, indistinctly tuberculate; **Sp.** in the crown more strongly projecting; **Rsp.** to 12, 7 cm lg.; **Csp.** 0 (rarely with Rsp. so arranged); **Fl.** to 3.5 cm lg., orange-red; **Pet.** bordered carmine.—Origin ?

M. costata v. brachyantha (Wessn.) Donald: **Mediolobivia brachyantha** (Wessn.) Krainz.

M. costata v. eucaliptana (Backbg.) Donald: **Mediolobivia eucaliptana** (Backbg.) Krainz.

M. digitiformis (Backbg.) (Backbg.) **Mediolobivia pectinata** v. **digitiformis** (Backbg.) Backbg.

M. duursmaiana Backbg.: **Mediolobivia aureiflora** v. **duursmaiana** (Backbg.) Backbg.

M. elegans Backbg. (1)
Bo. spherical, lighter green; **Tub.** slender, flat, spiralled, suffused reddish below: **Ar.** finer, crowded; **Sp.** c. 25 (and more), 2 mm to (later, the longest ones only) 1.2 cm lg., sometimes interlacing, whitish; **Fl.** slender-funnelform. brilliant yellow.—N. Argentina (Salta. Jujuy?).

M. eos Rausch (**Rebutia, Digitorebutia**)
Bo. simple, shortly cylindric, to 25 mm h. and 20 mm $\emptyset$, brownish-green; **R.** napiform; **Ri.** 12–13, straight or slightly spiralled, Tub. 4 mm lg.; **Ar.** oval, 2 mm lg., brown-felty; **Rsp.** 8–10, to 6 mm lg., bristly, brownish-grey, brown below; **Csp.** 1 to 5 mm lg., stouter, brown to black, directed upwards; **Fl.** opening widely, 40 mm lg., 35 mm br.; pericarpel spherical, reddish-brown with dark brown bristly Sc.; **Rec.** pink, glabrous below, with dark green lanceolate Sc. with white H.; **Sep.** whitish, with a brownish M.-stripe; **Pet.** spatulate, whitish-pink; **style** and **Sti.** light green; **Fr.** brown, covered with darker Sc. and white wool.—Argentina (Jujuy, near Tafna, at 3600 m). Spec. resembles M. nigricans but is clearly differentiated by the Fl.-colour which varies on any one plant between whitish-pink and pure white. (Fig. 485.)

M. euanthema (Backbg.) Krainz (2:2)
Bo. elongated, cushion-forming, long-taprooted; single heads elongated, to 5 cm h., c. 3 cm $\emptyset$, dull leaf-green; **Ri.** c. 10, very flat, weakly tuberculate; **Sp.** in the crown more strongly projecting; **Rsp.** c. 12, 2 uppers to 1 cm lg., hyaline, reddish-brown below; **Csp.** 0; **Fl.** 3-coloured, reddish inside below, yellowish-red above that, carmine outside; **Pet.** often faintly striped.—Border-zone between S. Bolivia and N. Argentina.
   v. **fricii** (hort.) Backbg.: **Bo.** greyish to olive-green; **Ri.** c. 14, strongly tuberculate; **Sp.** in part fairly strongly projecting; **Fl.** lacking the yellowish-red middle zone, darker outside, glossy blood-red inside, c. 3 cm $\emptyset$ (Fig. 228);
   v. **oculata** (Werd.) Krainz: Unlike the type, which has the **Tu.** flesh-coloured, that of the variety is slightly glossy and whitish; **Pet.** of only two colours, yellowish to golden-bronze inside, $\pm$ bluish-carmine outside.

M. euanthema v. pygmaea (sensu Backbg.) Donald: **Mediolobivia neopygmaea** Backbg.

M. euanthema v. ritteri (Wessn.) Donald: **Mediolobivia ritteri** (Wessn.) Krainz.

M. eucaliptana (Backbg.) Krainz (2:2)
Bo. oblong, forming smaller groups, light leaf-green; **Ri.** to 9, tuberculate above midway; **Ar.** with a little brownish felt; **Sp.** in the crown more strongly projecting, 9–11, to 1.2 cm lg., bristly, often bent at the tip, yellowish; **Fl.** brilliant light red; **throat** red-madder; **Pet.** fully outspread at anthesis.—Bolivia (near La Paz, close to Eucaliptos).

M. fricii hort.: **Mediolobivia euanthema** v. **fricii** (hort.) Backbg.

M. fuauxiana Backbg. (2:2)
Bo. oblong, forming small groups; **Ri.** c. 13, quite distinct, often acute; **Sp.** in the crown more strongly projecting, c. 7–9, short, less obviously bristly-fine, whitish, later darker; **Fl.** fairly large, rotate, pure orange-red.—Origin?

M. haagei (often incorrectly called M. haageana) (Frič & Schelle) Backbg.: **Mediolobivia pygmaea** (R. E. Fries) Backbg.

M. haefneriana Cullm. (2:2)
Bo. elongated, dark olive-green, c. 8 cm h., 3.5 cm $\emptyset$, taprooted; **Sp.** in the crown projecting, to 12, to c. 5 mm lg., bristly, yellowish, later white; **Fl.** c. 3 cm lg., 3.5 cm $\emptyset$, blood to cherry-red; **Tu.** slender.—Origin?

|**M. hirsutissima** Card. 1971
Bo. freely offsetting, single heads 3 cm lg., 2.5 cm $\emptyset$, grey, with a sunken crown; **R.** napiform, 7–8 cm lg.; **Ri.** c. 13, straight, 2 mm h., 4 mm br.; **Ar.** elliptic, 2–3 mm lg., grey-felty; **Sp.** pectinate, 13 on either side of the Ar., 4 mm lg., flattened sideways, very thin, grey, upper ones yellowish; **Fl.** funnelform, 4 cm lg., 3 cm $\emptyset$, with light brown Sc. and white H. outside, those on the Tu. in part brownish; **Sep.** greenish outside, light purple inside; **Pet.** spatulate; **Fil.** purple; **style** with 5 green **Sti.**—Bolivia (Boeto, Dept. Chuquisaca, near Villa Serrano, at 2000 m).

M. ithyacantha Card. 1969
Bo. flattened-spherical, 1.5–2.5 cm h., 2–4 cm $\emptyset$, light green; **Ri.** 12–18, furrowed, Tub. 3–5 mm lg.; **Ar.** 4–6 mm apart, 3–4 mm $\emptyset$, grey-felty; **Rsp.** 15–17, spreading, 4–15 mm lg.; **Csp.** 1–2, spreading, 10–25 mm lg.; all **Sp.** thin, stiff, brown at first, later greyish-whitish, those in the crown short, brown, interlacing; **Fl.** lateral, funnelform, 3–3.5 cm lg., 2–2.5 cm $\emptyset$; **Ov.** spherical, 4 mm $\emptyset$, light brown to yellowish, with hairy Sc.; **Sep.** spatulate, 14 mm lg., light lilac-red outside, brilliant reddish-orange inside; **Pet.** lanceolate, 16 × 5 mm, acute; **Fil.** white; **An.** yellow; **style** 18 mm lg., white, with 7 yellow **Sti.**; **Fr.** spherical, light red with white-haired Sc.—Bolivia (Vallegrande, Dept. Santa Cruz, near Comarapa, at 2200 m).

M. kesselringiana Cullm.: **Mediolobivia aureiflora** v. **rubriflora** (Backbg.) Backbg.

M. neopygmaea Backbg. (2:2)
Bo. elongated, simple, sometimes offsetting, crown distinctly white-woolly; **Ri.** very low; **Sp.** ± projecting, mostly short, quite fine, hyaline, darker below; **Fl.** to 3 cm lg., light purple.—S. Bolivia.

M. nigricans (Wessn.) Krainz (2:2)
Bo. elongated, brownish-green; **Ri.** c. 11; **Sp.** in the crown more strongly projecting, 8–12, the longest ones 1 cm lg., glossy, bronze-coloured, then whitish-grey; **Fl.** broadly funnelform, 2.5 cm $\emptyset$, glossy, flame-coloured; **style** somewhat united basally.—N. Argentina (?).
In the form known as v. peterseimii (Frič), the **Fl.** are purple, 3.5 cm $\emptyset$.
In Sukkde. (SKG.) VII/VIII, 103. 1963, Buining & Donald mention another f. hahniana (of "Rebutia ritteri"): **Sp.** dark brown; **Fl.** very short, orange-red; **style** united for 3–4 mm; **Tu.** funnel-like. Although the authors refer it to "Reb. ritteri", which is a matter of opinion, the plant may well belong here.

M. orurensis (Backbg.) Backbg.: **Mediolobivia pectinata** v. **orurensis** (Backbg.) Backbg.

M. pectinata (Backbg.) Backbg. non Frič (2:2)
Bo. elongated, light to bluish to leaf-green; **Sp.** in the crown appressed, ± bent, thickened below, darker; **Fl.** fairly stoutly funnelform, red; **Pet.** broader; **Tu.** fairly short.—Bolivia.
v. **atrovirens** (Backbg.) Backbg.: **Bo.** glossy, dark green; **Sp.** whitish, upper ones brown.—N. Argentina;
v. **digitiformis** (Backbg.) Backbg.: **Bo.** more elongated, passing over into a similarly shaped taproot, greyish-green; sometimes with one upper, longer, more central **Rsp.**; **Fl.** flame-coloured.—N. Argentina;
v. **neosteinmannii** Backbg.: **Bo.** more elongated, ± light green; **Fl.** rotate to ± bellshaped, mid-red, lighter in the centre;
v. **orurensis** (Backbg.) Backbg.: **Bo.** forming small cushions of several heads together, dark olive-green; **Sp.** only 1–2 mm lg., yellowish-white; **Fl.** broadly funnelform; **Pet.** narrower, red; **throat** darker(?).

M. pygmaea (R. E. Fries) Backbg. (2:2)
Bo. simple or offsetting, with a longer taproot, greyish to light bluish-green; **Sp.** strongly pectinate and appressed in the crown, to 12, 2–3 mm lg., thin, somewhat thickened and darker below, hyaline above; **Fl.** with a slender Tu., pink to salmon, variable, sometimes striped; **Pet.** fairly broad.—N. Argentina (Prov. Jujuy).
v. **flavovirens** (Backbg.) Backbg.: **Bo.** more yellowish-green; **Sp.** dirty yellowish-white, brownish below, all Sp. in the apex brownish.

M. ritteri (Wessn.) Krainz (2:2)
Bo. ± spherical to elongated, greyish-green; **Ri.** c. 15, more tuberculate, ± completely resolved into Tub.; **Sp.** in the crown projecting, sometimes

erect, 8–10, to 1 cm lg., acicular, whitish-grey, the upper pair brown, darker at the tip and the base; **Fl.** c. 4 cm lg., 4.5 cm $\varnothing$, flame to crimson; **throat** reddish-violet.—Bolivia (near Escayache).
  v. **pilifera** (Frič) Backbg.: differs in having **Sp.** which are concolorous whitish, often longer and $\pm$ interlacing; **Fl.** purplish-red.

M. rubelliflora Backbg. **Mediolobivia aureiflora** v. **rubelliflora** (Backbg.) Backbg.

M. rubriflora Backbg.: **Mediolobivia aureiflora** v. **rubriflora** (Backbg.) Backbg.

M. rutiliflora Ritt. (FR 1113): no description available.

M. sarothroides (Werd.) Buin.: **Mediolobivia aureiflora** v. **sarothroides** (Werd.) Backbg.

M. schmiedcheniana (Köhl.) Krainz (2:1)
Bo. very slender-cylindric, dark brownish-green, quite freely offsetting; **Tub.** in 13–16 fairly straight R.; **Sp.** mostly appressed, those in the crown $\pm$ projecting, to 12, 3–5 mm lg., bristly, grey and brownish; **Fl.** 3 cm lg., 3.5 cm $\varnothing$, deep golden-yellow; **throat** pale yellow.—N. Argentina (Salta, Chani Volcano; the varieties similarly).
  v. **einsteinii** (Frič) Backbg.: **Tub.** spiralled; **Sp.** very short to missing, those in the crown projecting; **buds** bronzy-black; **Fl.** larger;
  v. **karreri** (Frič) Backbg.: **Bo.** more green; **Sp.** spreading and projecting; **Fl.** fairly large, yellow;
  v. **rubriviridis** (Frič) Backbg.: **Bo.** with a strong red tinge; **Sp.** longer, projecting, laterals directed obliquely upwards; **Fl.** yellow, larger;
  v. **steineckei** (Frič) Backbg.: **Bo.** mid-green; **Sp.** somewhat longer, projecting, denser; **Fl.** small, mid-yellow.

M. spiralisepala Jajó (2:2?)
Bo. eventually $\pm$ elongated, dark green; **Tub.** spiralled; **Rsp.** to c. 16, to c. 8 mm lg., rather stiff, irregularly curving; **Csp.** 4, c. 2 cm lg. (or more), more contorted; **Sp.** dark brown, yellowish below, later greyish-brown; **Fl.** c. 3.2 cm lg. and $\varnothing$, orange-red, M.-stripe reddish.—Origin ? (Fig. 229.) The stout and contorted Csp. are a diagnostic character.

M. steinmannii hort. (non Solms-Laub.: Aylostera): **Mediolobivia pectinata** v. **neosteinmannii** Backbg.

M. vulpina (FR 939) (vulpispina?): no description available. Name means "fox-coloured".

Megalobivia bruchii (Br. & R.) Y. Ito, and M.

korethroides (Werd.) Y. Ito: **Soehrensia bruchii** (Br. & R.) Backbg., and **S. korethroides** (Werd.) Backbg.

Melocactus (Tourn.) Lk. & O. (187)

Some of the plants in this genus are among the oldest cacti known in Europe, where they were at one time called "Melonendistel" (melon-thistle). Bodies spherical or elongated, simple or sometimes offsetting, later with a cephalium of felt $\cdot$ $\pm$ interspersed with bristles, which may be flat, hemispherical, spherical to shortly or moderately long-cylindric, from which the small bellshaped to funnelform reddish flowers arise. The spination is very variable, even in one and the same species. The fruit, which is slender-clavate and coloured red or white, is pushed out when ripe and then dries to become thin-membranous; the seeds it contains are black, and either matt or glossy. In some species there may be a divided cephalium, or new shoots may be produced from it, producing new cephalia in their turn. Young plants are usually difficult to identify since they only become recognisable when fully grown and bearing the characteristic cephalium. Flower-size is also an important diagnostic character. The numerous synonyms of some species are attributable to their extensive distribution.—Distribution: From Mexico, Guatemala and Honduras, through the West Indies, to S. America as far as Central Peru and N. Brazil. [Cephalium-bearing plants are difficult in cultivation; grafted seedlings usually grow well.]

M. acuñai León
Bo. eventually cylindric, to 30 cm h., to 9 cm $\varnothing$, sometimes branching above; **Ceph.** eventually elongated, to 10 cm h., 8 cm $\varnothing$, later densely bristly below; **Rsp.** c. 12, to c. 1 cm lg., subulate, $\pm$ curving, light and then dark brown; **Csp.** 3–4, to 5 cm lg., stouter; **Fl.** 3 cm lg., dark red.—Cuba (Maisi, on the coast). [Haage adds: named for the type-locality.]

M. albicephalus Buin. & Bred.
Bo. simple, to 12 cm h. and 15 cm $\varnothing$, green; **Ceph.** c. 4 cm h., to 7.5 cm $\varnothing$, with dense white wool, with red Br. in the lower part; **Ri.** 9–10, fairly acute, to 5 cm br. and 3 cm h., with acutely projecting Tub. between the Ar.; **Ar.** round, c. 7 mm $\varnothing$, depressed, soon glabrous; **Rsp.** mostly 9, one of these directed $\pm$ vertically downwards, 44 mm lg., lower Sp.-pairs the longest, upper ones only 4–7 mm lg.; **Csp.** 1(–2), pointing obliquely downwards, c. 30 mm lg., rather curving, thickened below; all **Sp.** light brown at first, soon becoming light greyish-pink, tipped light

brown, very robust; **Fl.** 23 mm lg., 10 mm ∅, carmine, darker above; **An.** curving towards the style; **Fil.** white; **style** 12 mm lg., light pink; **Fr.** wedge-shaped, 23 mm lg., glossy carmine; **S.** cap-shaped, 1.3 mm lg., 1 mm br., testa glossy black.—Brazil (Central Bahia, on the W. slopes of the Serra do Espinhaco, in crevices among rocks, at c. 900 m). (Fig. 486.)

M. amethystinus Buin. & Bred.
Bo. simple, 12 cm h. including Ceph., to 17 cm ∅, green; **Ceph.** 4 cm h., 8 cm ∅, white-woolly, interspersed with dark red Br. so that the Ceph. later appears reddish; **Ri.** 9, acute, 3 cm h., 5.5 cm apart, with hatchet-shaped Tub. between the Ar.; **Ar.** sunken into the Ri. closely beneath these Tub., round, 7 mm ∅, white-woolly, later glabrous, c. 1 cm apart; **Rsp.** 9, one of these directed downwards, 2.5–3.8 cm lg., 3 pairs on either side, upper ones shortest, also several short Ssp.; **Csp.** pointing downwards, strongly thickened below, to 3 cm lg., 1.5 mm thick; all **Sp.** light reddish-brown, later greyish-brown, straight to slightly curving; **Fl.** 15 mm lg., to 6 mm ∅, tubular, carmine; **Fil.** white; **An.** yellow; **style** pink with 5–6 yellow **Sti.**; **Fr.** red, oblong to pear-shaped; **S.** cap-shaped, testa glossy black, hilum white.—Brazil (Bahia, Brejinho das Ametistas near Caitité at c. 1000 m, under shrubs and small trees. Found in 1968 by Horst and Buining, and recognised as an independent spec.)

M. amoenus (Hoffm.) Pfeiff.
Bo. later tapering-conical, bluish-green; **Ceph.** broad, flat, with much white wool and few Br.; **Ri.** to 12, somewhat compressed, acute; **Rsp.** c. 8, to 1.2 cm lg.; **Csp.** 1, to 1.6 cm lg., erect; **Sp.** subulate, ± straight, reddish or reddish-brownish; **Fl.** 2.5 cm lg., light red, limb outspread.—Coast, Venezuela to Colombia.

M. amstutziae Rauh & Backbg.
Bo. pyramidal, to 11 cm h., c. 13 cm ∅ below, c. 9 cm ∅ above, greyish-green; **Ceph.** tall, rounded, 5–6 cm lg., c. 7 cm ∅, with red Br.; **Ri.** c. 13; **Rsp.** mostly 6–8 pressed sideways, to 2.5 cm lg., stronly flattened on the upperside, ± angular, keeled above, dark brown; **Csp.** 0, sometimes 1 Sp. more centrally placed; **Fl.** carmine.—Peru (Rimac valley).

M. antonii (Britt.) Knuth: **Melocactus intortus** v. **antonii** (Britt.) Backbg.

M. azureus Buin. & Bred.
Bo. simple, to 17 cm h., to 14 cm ∅, frosted, azure-blue; **R.** branching; **Ri.** 9–10, c. 3.5 cm h., acute; **Ar.** oval, 7 × 14 mm, ± sunken; **Rsp.** 7, one pointing downwards, sometimes curving at the tip,

to 4 cm lg., with small Ssp. above; **Csp.** 1(–3), lowest one to 2.5 cm lg., 2 uppers shorter, thinner; all **Sp.** greyish-white, tipped dark brown; **Ceph.** to 3.5 cm h., to 7 cm ∅, wool pure white, interspersed with fine red bristly H.; **Fl.** tubular, carmine, darker above; **style** 8 mm lg., light pink; **Sti.** 4–5, yellow; **S.** cap-shaped, 1.4 mm lg., testa glossy black.—Brazil (Bahia, Serra do Espinhaco, on weathered rocks, on very dry mountain slopes, on the Rio Jacaré at c. 450 m. Found in 1968 by Horst and Buining). (Fig. 487.)

M. bahiensis (Br. & R.) Werd.
Bo. spherical, later sometimes ± elongated, to 10 cm h. and 15 cm ∅, dull green; **Ceph.** low, with many dark brown Br.; **Ri.** 10–12; **Rsp.** 7–10, to 2.5 cm lg.; **Csp.** c. 4, to 3.5 cm lg.; **Sp.** brown, becoming grey; **Fl.** pink, shorter.—Brazil (Bahia, near Machada Portella).

M. bellavistensis Rauh & Backbg.
Bo. becoming pyramidal, to 50 cm lg., to 40 cm ∅, dark to bluish-green; **Ceph.** eventually cylindric, to 30 cm lg., 10 cm ∅, not infrequently forking, the apical white wool overtopped by brilliant red Br.; **Ri.** 12–20, ± acute; **Rsp.** 3 on either side, to 1.2 cm lg., bent, reddish-grey, also 1 shorter upper Sp. and 1 longer lower; **Csp.** 0; **Fl.** 0.5 cm ∅, light carmine.—N. Peru (between Chamaya and Jaën, and near Bellavista).

M. brederooianus Buin.
Bo. simple, 10–11 cm h., 11–12 cm ∅, green; **Ceph.** 2.5 cm h., 5.5 cm ∅, greyish-white with red Br.; **Ri.** 10–14, obtuse, to 4 cm apart below; **Ar.** round, 4 mm ∅, ± sunken, white-felty, later glabrous; **Sp.** reddish, light below, later grey and tipped brown, firm, stiff; **Rsp.** one pointing obliquely downwards, to 25 mm lg., 3 pairs on either side, one lateral pair directed upwards, to 17 mm lg.; **Csp.** 1, pointing downwards, 18–25 mm lg.; **Fl.** tubular, carmine, 18 mm lg., 4.5 mm br.; **Sep.** 6–7 mm br., spatulate, denticulate at the tip; **Pet.** c. 7 mm lg., otherwise as Sep.; **Fil.** white; **An.** yellow, 1 mm lg.; **style** 10 mm lg., white, with c. 4 Sti.; **Fr.** with floral remains, 24 mm lg., glossy carmine; **S.** cap-shaped, testa black, slightly glossy.—Brazil (Bahia, near Andorinha, under acacia-shrubs, at 500 m).

M. broadwayi (Br. & R.) Backbg.
Bo. spherical, eventually ± elongated, to 20 cm h., yellowish-green; **Ceph.** flattened-rounded, only c. 2–3 cm h., with white wool and soft brown Br.; **Rsp.** 8–10, 1–1.5 cm lg., ± incurving, acicular, horn-coloured, ± brown-tipped; **Csp.** 1(–2–3), rather stouter, at first concolorous brown; **Fl.** shorter, purple.—Islands of Tobago and Grenada.

M. caesius Wendl.
Bo. ± spherical, bluish-grey; **Ceph.** tall, rounded, more strongly bristly below; **Ri.** c. 10, broadly rounded; **Rsp.** c. 7, the lowest one usually longest; **Csp.** 1, not longer; **Sp.** moderately robust; **Fl.** small, slightly spreading.—Trinidad (Patos island).

M. communis Lk. & O.
Bo. spherical to ovoid, ± dark green; **Ceph.** flat at first, eventually long-cylindric, interspersed with purplish-brown Br.; **Ri.** 8–14(–20); **Rsp.** mostly 8–9, the top one shortest, the bottom one 2 cm lg. and more; **Csp.** c. 3, to 1.7 cm lg.; **Sp.** stiff, straight, yellowish to light brownish, more rarely whitish; **Fl.** outspread, c. 1.8 cm ∅, deep pinkish-red (K. Sch.: to 3 cm lg.).—W. Indies (Fig. 230.)

M. concinnus Buin. & Bred.
Bo. simple, with Ceph. 8–9 cm h., 10–11 cm ∅, green to weakly bluish-green; **R.** fibrous; **Ceph.** 2.5–3 cm h., 6–7 cm ∅, new growth white-woolly, with fine reddish Br., red coloration predominant in older growth; **Ri.** 10–13, acute, 2–2.5 cm h. below and 4 cm apart; **Ar.** sunken, ± round, white-felty; **Sp.** reddish at first, lighter below, later grey, tipped brown, stout, stiff; **Rsp.** 1, 25 mm lg., projecting downwards, also 4 curving Sp. to 6 mm lg. and 2 short Ssp., all directed upwards; **Csp.** 1, 16 mm lg., pointing downwards, often curving upwards; **Fl.** 18 mm lg., 6.5 mm br., carmine; **style** white, with 4 white **Sti.**; **Fr.** glossy carmine, reversed clavate; **S.** cap-shaped, glossy black.—Brazil (Bahia, W. of Seabra, at 1000 m, on rocky, very dry and sandy soil among scree, under caatinga-type shrubs and bushes. Found early 1968 by Horst and Uebelmann). (Fig. 488.)

M. coronatus (Lam.) Backbg. (T.)
Bo. ± cylindric, to c. 1 m h.; **Ceph.** to 3–5 cm h., 10 cm br., with long brown Br.; **Ri.** 10–15; **Sp.** c. 10–12 (and more), to 5 cm lg., stout, yellowish to brown; **Fl.** to 4 cm lg., narrowly cylindric, carmine; **Fr.** 5–6 cm lg., clavate.—Jamaica (dry S. zones).

M. cremnophilus Buin. & Bred.
Bo. simple, 12 cm h., 14 cm ∅, green to dark green; **Ceph.** to 12 cm h., 6–7 cm ∅, consisting of thin red Br. and grey wool; **Ri.** 11(–13), obtuse, without prominences between the Ar.; **Ar.** rather sunken, 1.5 cm apart, round to ± elliptic, 5–7 mm lg., 5 mm br., with short white felt, this soon disappearing; **Sp.** glassy, horn-coloured below and light reddish-brown above at first, soon greying, tipped dark brown, stout, straight, thickened below; **Rsp.** 8–9, one lower Sp. 6–7 cm lg., 3 on either side of the Ar., lower ones longest (to 4.5 cm); **Csp.** 4, cruciform, bottom one 3.5–4 cm lg.; **Fl.** carmine, 16 mm lg., 3.5 mm ∅; **Fr.** clavate, 22–25 mm lg., 5–6 mm br.,

red; **S.** small, round.—Brazil (Bahia, Serra do Espinhaco, at 850 m). Discovered by Horst and Uebelmann, 1967–68. (Fig. 489.)

M. curvicornis Buin. & Bred.
Bo. simple, 20 cm h. and more, 10–19 cm br., green; **R.** branching; **Ceph.** 30 cm h., 7–8 cm ∅, the white wool interspersed with short red Br., these later more prominent; **Ri.** 13, fairly acute, often ± spiralled, 4–5 cm apart, 4.5 cm h.; **Ar.** sunken, ± oblong, 7 mm lg., 4 mm br., white-felty at first, later glabrous, 15 mm apart, between them hatchet-shaped Tub. to 5 mm h., with a thickening around the Ar.; **Sp.** at first light horn-coloured below, tipped dark brown, curving or often straight, later grey, tipped brown, rough, very robust, thickened below; **Rsp.** 7, one of these curving down over the Tub., 2–2.5 cm lg., 3 pairs directed laterally, the lowest pair curving obliquely downwards, 2–2.5 cm lg., the middle pair curving sideways, 1.5–2 cm lg., the upper pair pointing obliquely upwards, straight, 1.3–1.5 cm lg., often also several thin Ssp.; **Csp.** 1 directed obliquely upwards, 1.7 cm lg.; **Fl.** 15 mm lg., 6–7 mm ∅, naked, carmine; **Sep.** 4 mm lg., 1.3 mm br., spatulate, apiculate, carmine; **Pet.** light carmine; **style** 9 mm lg., white, with 4 **Sti.**; **Fr.** c. 14 mm lg., reversed clavate, very light pink; **S.** ovoid to pear-shaped, glossy black.—Brazil (Bahia, near Macaubas, at 950–1000 m, in rock-crevices, among bromeliads and rough grasses; found February 1966 by Horst and Dr. G. Baumgardt; more closely studied in 1968 by Horst and Buining, who found that the Sp. on immature plants were much stouter and more noticeable than was the case once the Ceph. had developed.

M. curvispinus Pfeiff.
Bo. depressed-spherical; **Ceph.** flattened-hemispherical, with few Br.; **Ri.** 10–12; **Rsp.** 7, to 1.6 cm lg., ± strongly bent, brownish to whitish; **Csp.** (1–)2, to 2.5 cm lg., subulate, darker at first; **Fl.** small.—Mexico.

M. dawsonii H. Bravo 1965
Bo. spherical, simple, to 20 cm h., 15 cm ∅; **Ri.** 14; **Ar.** oval, 4 mm lg.; **Rsp.** 9–11, bent sideways, 3–3.5 cm lg., subulate, whitish to dull yellow; **Csp.** mostly 4; **Ceph.** c. 5 cm h., with white wool and brownish-red Br.; **Fl.** with Ov. 4 cm lg.; **Fr.** clavate, to 5 cm lg.; **S.** 2 mm lg., coffee-coloured.—Mexico (Jalisco, Rancho Cuixmala, near Tenacatita). Differentiated from other Mexican Melocacti by its more numerous Csp. and larger Fl.

M. deinacanthus Buin. & Bred.
Bo. simple, to 35 cm h. and 18 cm ∅, green; **Ceph.** to 20 cm h. and to 9 cm ∅, with white wool and many red Br., giving a generally red appearance;

Ri. 10(–12), c. 4.5 cm br. and apart, fairly acute, with hatchet-shaped prominences between the Ar.; **Ar.** oval, to 17 mm lg. and to 11 mm br., 2–2.5 cm apart, deeply sunken; **Sp.** reddish to flesh-coloured at first, later grey to black, stout, hard, curving, thickened below; **Rsp.** radiating, the bottom one to 5 cm lg., others shorter; **Csp.** 4, cruciform, 3–4 cm lg.; **Fl.** tubular, glabrous, violet, 19 mm lg.; **style** whitish, with 4 cream **Sti.**; **Fr.** clavate, white; **S.** cap-shaped, testa matt black, with prominent rounded Tub.—Brazil (Bahia, NW. of Caitité, at c. 200 m, on and between naked rocks). Discovered in 1971 by Buining and Horst.

M. delessertianus Lem.
Bo. spherical, slightly tapering, to 10 cm h., 9 cm $\emptyset$, greyish-green; **Ceph.** c. 4 cm h., 5 cm $\emptyset$, interspersed with numerous orange-red Br. to 3 cm lg.; **Ri.** 15, ± spiralled; **Rsp.** 9–10, to 2 cm lg., subulate, curving slightly towards the Bo.; **Csp.** 2, one above the other, upper one erect, to 2.5 cm lg., lower one to 2.8 cm lg.; all **Sp.** grey, tinged pink, tipped reddish-brown; **Fl.** 2.5 cm lg., purplish-pink; **Fr.** c. 3 cm lg.—Mexico (Jalapa).

M. depressus Hook.
Bo. depressed-pyramidal, c. 8 cm h., 15 cm $\emptyset$, vivid green; **Ceph.** flat, with short brown Br.; **Ri.** c. 10, broad, obtuse; **Sp.** 5–7, to 2 cm lg., brownish to ash-grey; **Fl.** not known; **Fr.** c. 2.5 cm lg., light carmine to pinkish-red.—Brazil (near Pernambuco).

M. ernestii Vpl.
Bo. later much elongated; **Ceph.** almost the width of the apex, the older part with crowded projecting Br.; **Ri.** 10, acute, slightly spiralled; **Sp.** c. 10 (and more?), 3 later directed distinctly and obliquely downwards, at least 1 sometimes longer than half the plant's height; **Fl.** small, opening widely; colour ?—Brazil (Bahia, Rio da Contas).

M. erythranthus Buin. & Bred.
Bo. simple, spherical to slightly conical, to 11 cm h., to 12 cm $\emptyset$, green; **Ri.** 11–12, fairly acute, to 3 cm apart below, to 1 cm above; **Ar.** round, 6–7 mm $\emptyset$, with short creamy-white felt at first, sunken, to 2 cm apart; **Sp.** yellowish-brown to deep red at first, later grey; **Rsp.** c. 7, one of these 10–13 mm lg., curving, directed downwards, others arranged around the Csp., 1.5–3 cm lg., ± curving; **Csp.** 4, cruciform, bottom one 4.5–5.5 cm lg., others 1.5–2 cm lg.; **Ceph.** to 6 cm h. and $\emptyset$, with snow-white wool interspersed with short red Br. which, as the white wool shrinks, give the Ceph. a deep red appearance; **Fl.** tubular, almost 21 mm lg., to 5 mm br., lilac-red; **Sep.** spatulate; **Pet.** lanceolate; **Fr.** clavate, 22–25 mm lg., 5–7 mm br., glossy wine-red;

S. 1.2 mm lg., 0.8 mm br., black.—Brazil (Bahia, Serra do Espinhaco, among flat hills at c. 900 m). (Fig. 490.)

M. ferreophilus Buin. & Bred.
Bo. simple, to 33 cm h. including Ceph., to 19 cm $\emptyset$, green to greyish-green; **Ceph.** 5 cm h., 9 cm $\emptyset$, with white wool and many red Br.; **Ri.** 10, straight, vertical, acute, with prominences between the Ar.; **Ar.** oval, c. 10 mm lg., with light grey wool at first, later glabrous, 2 cm apart; **Fl.** carmine, 15 mm lg.; **style** white, with 6 white Sti.; **Fr.** pinkish-white to white, to 29 mm lg.; **S.** spherical to cap-shaped.—Brazil (Bahia, near Cameleiros, at c. 840 m, in strongly ferruginous soil, pH 7–8). Found 1967–8 by Horst and Uebelmann. (Fig. 491.)

M. fortalezensis Rauh & Backbg.
Bo. to 20 cm h., 10 cm $\emptyset$, greyish-green; **Ceph.** stout-cylindric, to c. 10 cm lg., 6 cm $\emptyset$, interspersed with red Br.; **Ri.** 9–12, ± obtuse; **Rsp.** to 10, to 4(–6) cm lg., ± curving; **Csp.** 1–3, to 6 cm lg., usually one above the other(s), 1 projecting and bent ± upwards; **Sp.** in newer growth reddish, becoming black, very stout, sometimes ± grooved, ± thickened below; **Fl.** c. 1 cm $\emptyset$, rotate, carmine; **Fr.** carmine. Ceph. also developing from apical shoots, sometimes forking.—Peru (Rio Fortaleza).

M. giganteus Buin. & Bred.
Bo. simple, to 48 cm h. without Ceph., to 20 cm $\emptyset$, green; **Ceph.** to 26 cm lg., to 9 cm $\emptyset$, white-woolly, strongly interspersed with red Br., especially on the sides; **Ri.** to 15, often twisted to the left, 2–2.3 cm apart; **Ar.** round, 6–8 mm $\emptyset$, sunken, grey at first, then glabrous, 2 cm apart; **Sp.** very stout, brownish-pink at first, greyish-brown later, thickened below; **Rsp.** c. 8, spreading around the Csp., 11–18 mm lg., ± curving; **Csp.** 1, 15–17 mm lg., to 4 mm thick below, curving obliquely upwards; **Fl.** tubular, 6–8 mm lg., brilliant lilac; **Fr.** 18 mm lg., to 7 mm $\emptyset$, containing c. 35 cap-shaped **S.**—Brazil (Bahia, Serra San Inacio, on and between naked rocks, sometimes under shrubs, at c. 520 m). Found by Buining and Horst in 1968, and re-collected in 1972.

M. glaucescens Buin. & Bred.
Bo. simple, subspherical, to 14 cm h. and $\emptyset$, greyish-green to bluish-green; **Ri.** 11, 2–3.5 cm br.; **Ar.** round, 4 mm $\emptyset$, white-felty, later glabrous, 10–18 mm apart; **Sp.** c. 8, grey, tipped black, 25 mm lg.; 2 smaller shorter **Rsp.**, only 11 mm lg.; **Csp.** 2, one of these directed obliquely upwards, 14 mm lg., the other slightly hooked at the tip and thickened below, pointing straight downwards, 15 mm lg.; **Fl.** 21 mm lg., 6 mm $\emptyset$, red, arising from a dense **Ceph.** 7 cm $\emptyset$, with ivory-white H. and

311

very few Br.; **Fr.** 12 mm lg., red; **S.** round, 1–1.3 mm lg.—Brazil (Central Bahia, in W. Serro do Espinhaco, at 900 m). (Fig. 492.)

M. guaricensis Croiz.
Bo. truncate-spherical to truncate-conical, to 10 cm h., c. 9 cm ∅, yellowish-green; **Ceph.** broadly hemispherical, to 4 cm h., 8 cm br., Br. reddish; **Ri.** c. 10; **Rsp.** and **Csp.** 7–9, to c. 1.8 cm lg., all slightly curving, later rigid, dark yellow to dark brown, new ones frosted; **Fl.** ?; **Fr.** to 1.5 cm lg.—Venezuela (Guárico, N. of Parmana).

M. guitarti León
Bo. depressed-spherical, to c. 11 cm h., 15 cm ∅; **Ceph.** to c. 3 cm h., 8 cm ∅, scarcely overtopped by reddish-brown Br.; **Ri.** 12; **Rsp.** 9–10, to 2.5 cm lg., spreading horizontally, slightly curving, sometimes reddish, usually yellowish, stiff; **Csp.** 2, to 3.5 cm lg., rather stouter than the Rsp., projecting, yellowish; **Fl.** to 4 cm lg., Pet. spreading to recurved, deep pink; **Fr.** 3–4 cm lg., clavate, glossy, red.—Cuba (Sierra de Jatibonico).

M. harlowii (Br. & R.) Vpl.
Bo. elongated-ovoid, to 25 cm h., light green; **Ceph.** to 7.5 cm h. and ∅; **Ri.** 12; **Rsp.** c. 12, to 3 cm lg., thin, spreading, reddish, later straw-coloured; **Csp.** to 4, to 2 cm lg., rather stouter; **Fl.** c. 2 cm lg., pinkish-red; **Fr.** c. 2 cm lg., red.—E. Cuba (Guantánamo region).

M. havannensis Miqu. is probably identical with Melocactus guitarti León or may be an earlier name for the latter.

M. hispaniolicus Vpl.: regarded as a synonym of M. lemairei (Monv.) Miqu., but differs considerably in having a flat Ceph. ± overtopped by ruby-red and ± spine-like Br., and thus probably constitutes a valid species.—Haiti (Gonaives).

M. horridus Werd.
Bo. to c. 12 cm h., greyish-green, ± pyramidal; **Ceph.** c. 3 cm h., 5–6 cm ∅, with red acicular Sp.; **Ri.** c. 12, ± notched; **Rsp.** 8–10, porrect, 1–5 cm lg., stiff, subulate, thickened below, rusty-red; **Csp.** 3–4, to 3 cm lg., porrect, stout; **Fl.** and **Fr.** unknown.—Brazil (Pernambuco, Villa Bella).

M. huallancaensis (huallancensis) Rauh & Backbg.
Bo. pyramidally tapering, to c. 8 cm h., to 13 cm ∅, bluish to greyish-green; **Ceph.** to 3 cm h. (and more?), c. 6.5 cm ∅, with sparse brownish-red Br.; **Ri.** 14; **Rsp.** 4 on either side, spreading, to 2 cm lg., 1 upper one, more erect, c. 1 cm lg., with 1 thinner Ssp., 1 more central lower one directed downwards, to 1.5 cm lg.; **Csp.** 1, porrect, slightly curving,

somewhat stouter; **Sp.** thin, flexible, whitish or ± pale reddish, often darker above and below, becoming grey; **Fl.** red, long-projecting, scarcely opening, **Pet.** ± erect; **Fr.** red, to 2 cm lg.—N. Peru (Santa valley, near Huallanca).

M. intortus (Mill.) Urb.
Bo. spherical, later cylindric, to 1 m h., ± pale green; **Ceph.** broadly rounded, later short-cylindric, with brown Br.; **Ri.** 14–20, broad, ± spiralled; **Sp.** 7–10–15, 2–7 cm lg., stout, yellow to brown; **Fl.** to 2 cm lg., pink; **Fr.** red.—W. Indies.
　　v. **antonii** (Britt.) Backbg.: more ovoid in shape, **Ri.** conspicuously wider below; **Sp.** thinner, longer; **Fl.** less projecting; **Fr.** red above, white below.—Desecheo Is., near Puerto Rico.

M. jansenianus Backbg.
Bo. spherical, to 20 cm ∅, greyish-green; **Ceph.** eventually long-cylindric, to 20 cm lg., 8 cm ∅, densely set with brownish Br.; **Ri.** c. 10, later flatter; **Rsp.** c. 10, ± curving to the Bo., upper ones shorter, bottom one longest; **Csp.** 1(–3), 2–3 cm lg., ± curving; **Sp.** deep brownish, later black, lower ones thickened below; **Fl.** very small, brilliant red; **Fr.** c. 2.5 cm lg., slender, red.—Peru (Libertad, close to the sea).

M. lemairei (Monv.) Miqu.
Bo. to 30 cm h., to 20 cm ∅, mostly more slender, tapering above; **Ceph.** to 10 cm h., with brown Br.; **Ri.** 9–10; **Rsp.** 8–12, 2–3 cm lg.; **Csp.** 1–2–3; **Sp.** stout, ± flattened, horn to brownish; **Fl.** c. 2 cm lg., pink; **Fr.** slender, pink.—Hispaniola (Santo Domingo).

M. lobelii Sur.
Bo. ± spherical, c. 16 cm h. and br.; **Ceph.** flattened-rounded, c. 2.5 cm h., 7.5 cm ∅, Br. brown; **Ri.** 12–14, ± acute; **Rsp.** 7(–10), 1.5–3 cm lg., radiating, sometimes ± recurved; **Csp.** (1–)2–3, to 4 cm lg., ± curving; **Sp.** acicular, yellowish or light brownish to horn-coloured, tipped dark brown, usually ± frosted; **Fl.** to c. 3.5 cm lg., purple; **Fr.** red.—Venezuela (Margarita Is.).

M. macrocanthos (SD.) Lk. & O.
Bo. spherical, to 30 cm ∅, pale green; **Ceph.** eventually to 20 cm h., to 10 cm ∅, interspersed with, or overtopped by brown Br.; **Ri.** 11–15, rounded; **Sp.** variable in number and length, yellow to brownish; **Rsp.** to 15, 3 cm lg. (and more), acicular, spreading; **Csp.** 4 (and more), unequal, to 7 cm lg., stouter, subulate; **Fl.** c. 2 cm lg.; **Fr.** stout-clavate, to 2 cm lg., glossy, red.—Islands off Curaçao. One of the most variable spec., hence the many synonyms.

M. macrodiscus Werd.
Bo. ± depressed-spherical, to c. 14 cm h., 18 cm ⌀, dull light to deeper green; **Ceph.** disc-shaped, eventually ± elongated, densely set·with red Br.; **Ri.** c. 11, acute; **Rsp.** to 9, to 2 cm lg., stoutly subulate, ± curving and appressed; **Csp.** (0–)1, to 2 cm lg.; **Sp.** frosted grey, sometimes tinged reddish-brownish; **Fl.** not protruding, to 5 mm ⌀, pinkish-red; **Fr.** violet-pink.—Brazil (Bahia Brejinhos, near Caëteté).

M. matanzanus León
Bo. spherical to depressed-rounded, to 8 cm h., to 9 cm ⌀; **Ceph.** c. 4 cm h., to 6 cm ⌀, Br. dense, fine, orange-reddish; **Ri.** 8–9, ± acute, prominent, sinuate; **Rsp.** 7–8, to 1.5 cm lg., spreading; **Csp.** 1, rarely longer; **Sp.** reddish at first, soon yellowish-white; **Fl.** little projecting, c. 1.7 cm lg., pink; **Fr.** pale pink (to white). Rather variable spec.—Cuba (Matanzas).

M. maxonii (Rose) Gürke
Bo. shortly conical, 10–15 cm h., dark green; **Ceph.** not large, broader than tall, Br. brown; **Ri.** 11–15, ± rounded; **Rsp.** mostly 9, sometimes several other smaller ones, spreading or bent, light or pinkish-red with a white sheen, becoming amber-coloured; **Csp.** 1(–2), short, projecting ± horizontally; **Fl.** small, pinkish-red; **Fr.** red.—Guatemala (near El Rancho and Salama).

M. melocactoides (Hoffm.) DC.
Bo. flattened-rounded, c. 8 cm h., 15 cm ⌀, light green; **Ceph.** small; **Ri.** c. 10, broad, rounded; **Rsp.** 5–8, ± curving, angular, pale brown, becoming grey; **Fl.** pink; **Fr.** to 2.5 cm lg., white (to very pale pink).—Brazil (Cabo Frio).

M. neryi K. Sch.
Bo. low-spherical, to 11 cm h., 14 cm ⌀, dark green; **Ceph.** c. 5 cm h., 7 cm ⌀, set with red Br. 2 cm lg.; **Ri.** 10, acute; **Sp.** 7–9, straight or slightly curving, grey, lowest one to c. 2.7 cm lg. and slightly furrowed, one Sp. sometimes ± central; **Fl.** c. 2.2 cm lg., carmine; **Fr.** light carmine.—Brazil (Amazonas, on the Aracá River).

M. oaxacensis (Br. & R.) Backbg.
Bo. spherical to oblong, to c. 15 cm ⌀; **Ceph.** flat, only c. 2–3 cm h.; **Ri.** 11–15, ± rounded; **Rsp.** 8–12, to 2 cm lg., ± curving; **Csp.** 1(–2), erect or porrect; **Sp.** reddish-brown at first, later grey; **Fl.** slender, deep pink; **Fr.** glossy, scarlet.—Mexico (Oaxaca).

M. obtusipetalus Lem.
Bo. spherical, then pyramidal, c. 22 cm h., 16 cm ⌀

below, greyish-green; **Ceph.** flattened-rounded, with a few purplish-red Br. overtopping the long white wool; **Ri.** 10, acute, notched; **Rsp.** 8–11, to 2.2 cm lg., stiff, ± curving, radiating, subulate, banded, whitish-brownish; **Csp.** mostly 2, upper one porrect, lower one directed downwards; **Fl.** to 2.5 cm ⌀, pink.—Colombia (Sta. Fé de Bogota, 2800 m[?]).

M. ocujalius Řiha nom. prov.
Bo. very large, to 35 cm ⌀; **Ceph.** very long. Resembles M. communis.—Cuba (Sierra Maestra).

M. onychacanthus Ritt. (FR ?), "with white claws"—not yet described.

M. oreas Miqu.
Bo. ± spherical, to c. 12 cm h., dull light to deep green; **Ceph.** flat, 4.5 cm ⌀, **Br.** ruby-red, not noticeably projecting; **Ri.** to 14 (and more); **Rsp.** to 12, upper ones 1 cm lg., bottom one to 7.5 cm lg.; **Csp.** mostly 4, to 5 cm lg.; **Sp.** stout, acicular, flexible, often curving away from the Bo., transparent horny-brown to reddish, lighter below, later frosted, yellowish with a ±darker tip; **Fl.** and **Fr.** ?—Brazil (Bahia).

M. permutabilis (FR 1331): no description available.

M. peruvianus Vpl.
Bo. spherical to slightly pyramidal and broadly rounded, greyish-green; **Ceph.** 2–8 cm h., c. 6.5 cm ⌀, with numerous pungent reddish-brown Br. projecting c. 5 cm; **Ri.** 12–14, acute, flanks slightly wavy; **Rsp.** (7–)10, mostly with 4 radiating to each side; 1 upwardly directed shortest Sp. to 1.5 cm lg., 1 downwardly directed, lowest ones to 3 cm lg.; **Csp.** 0–1, 2–4 cm lg., pointing obliquely upwards; **Sp.** very stout, stiff, very pungent, reddish-brown when wet; **Fl.** dark pink, rotate; **Fr.** red.—Central Peru (near Chosica).
Very variable in body shape and size, and spination; the following varieties are more clearly divergent:
v. **cañetensis** Rauh & Backbg.: **Bo.** low, rounded, to c. 15 cm h.; **Ceph.** c. 10 cm h. and ⌀, set with stout carmine Br., later brownish-red, and bordered by the top interlacing Sp.; **Fl.** carmine.—Central Peru (Cañete valley);
v. **lurinensis** Rauh & Backbg.: **Bo.** broadly spherical, to c. 10 cm h. and ⌀; all **Sp.** confused, interlacing and bent, very claw-like to ± loop-like, some ± compressed, brown at first; **Fl.** and **Fr.** carmine.—Central Peru (Lurin to Eulalia valleys).

M. pruinosus Werd.
Bo. spherical-ovoid, 10–12 cm h., 11–14 cm ∅, frosted green; **Ceph.** disc-shaped, to 7 cm ∅; **Ri.** 9–10; **Rsp.** 5–6 (sometimes with 2–3 smaller Ssp.), to 3 cm lg., upper ones shorter, subulate, radiating, reddish-brown; **Csp.** 1, 2 cm lg., erect; **Fl.** and **Fr.** ?—Brazil (Bahia, Sierra do Espinhaço).

M. rectispinus (FR 951): data unavailable.

M. rubrispinus (FR 1330): data unavailable.

M. ruestii K. Sch.
Bo. shortly conical to ± spherical, bluish-green, to 15 cm ∅; **Ceph.** small, high, with stiff brown Br.; **Ri.** 11–19; **Rsp.** 5–8, 2.5–3 cm lg., subulate, spreading or recurved; **Csp.** 1, to 3 cm lg., subulate; **Sp.** dark brown at first; **Fl.** small, red (description from Br. & R.)—Honduras (near Comayagua). Ceph. white-woolly, Br.-Sp. long!

M. salvadorensis Werd.
Bo. hemispherical, to 12 cm ∅, light green; **Ceph.** flattened-rounded, c. 1–2 cm h., 5–6 cm ∅, with red acicular Sp.; **Ri.** 10–12, ± acute; **Rsp.** 8–9, subulate, spreading horizontally, reddish; **Csp.** 0–1, to 2.5 cm lg.; **Fl.** and **Fr.** ?—Brazil (Bahia, San Salvador).

M. trujilloensis (trujillensis) Rauh & Backbg.
Bo. ± pyramidal-spherical, to 11 cm h., 8–11 cm ∅, light green; **Ceph.** broadly rounded, to 3 cm h. (and more?), to 6 cm ∅, with vivid carmine Br., dense and clearly projecting, fewer in the centre; **Ri.** 10; **Rsp.** 10–12, 2 cm lg., lower ones to 3 cm lg.; **Csp.** 1–4, stoutly subulate, thickened below, sometimes 1–2 upper Ssp., much shorter and thinner; **Sp.** bluish-grey to reddish, ± glassy, tipped dark brown; **Fl.** rotate, light carmine; **Fr.** thick-clavate, light carmine.—Peru (Trujillo region).
   v. **schoenii** Rauh & Backbg.: **Bo.** more elongated, to 12 cm lg., 10 cm ∅ below; **Ceph.** tall, rounded, c. 5 cm h. and ∅, with dense red Br.; **Sp.** brown to ± blackish, thickened below.

M. unguispinus Backbg.
Bo. elongated, to c. 20 cm h., mostly ± tapering above (and below); **Ceph.** flattened-hemispherical, later taller, to 5 cm h., 6 cm ∅, ± strongly set with occasionally ± interlacing Br.; **Ri.** c. 14, rather obtuse; **Rsp.** 8–9(–12), radiating, ± bent, the upper ones shortest, 1 longest Sp. directed downwards; **Csp.** 1(–3), porrect, pointing slightly upwards, thickened below; **Fl.** small, light red; **Fr.** dark red.—N. Peru (dry scrub of the E. Sechura).

M. violaceus Pfeiff.
Bo. shortly conical or spherical, to 12 cm h., to 10 cm ∅, dark green; **Ceph.** hemispherical to elongated, to 5 cm h., to 7 cm ∅, Br. stouter, red or violet; **Ri.** 10–12, acute; **Rsp.** 5–7, 0.5–2 cm lg., ± bent, sometimes straight, subulate, reddish to violet, becoming grey; **Csp.** 0–1, to 2 cm lg.; **Fl.** little projecting, deep flesh-colour; **Fr.** slender-clavate, red.—Brazil (near Rio de Janeiro).

M. zehntneri (Br. & R.) Backbg.
Bo. later cylindric, to 30 cm h., truncate above; **Ceph.** stoutly cylindric, ± as wide as the apex; **Rsp.** to 2.5 cm lg., ± curving, terete, stout, dark brown; **Csp.** 1, spreading or erect; **Fl.** pink; **Fr.** red.—Brazil (plains near Joazeiro).

Mesechinopsis Y. Ito (1957): **Pseudolobivia** Backbg. (1946).

Micranthocereus Backbg. (176)

A hitherto monotypic genus of low-growing, slender-stemmed Cerei, branching from the base, with the bluish-frosted body almost concealed, in the flowering zone, by white wool and white spines. A type of pseudo-cephalium is developed, always on the side towards the north-west, consisting of rather thick areolar wool interspersed with modified bristle-like spines. Here up to 30–40 flowers may appear simultaneously; these are small and pink, the interior of the tube with a ring of minute scales in the lower part. The fruits are glabrous, small and lidded, and the seeds glossy blackish-brown. Juvenile plants have quite long hair, and the base is ringed with golden-yellow bristles to 10 cm long, similar to Thrixanthocereus.—Distribution: Brazil (Bahia, near Caëteté). [Probably not found in cultivation.]

M. flaviflorus Buin. & Bred. 1974
Bo. columnar, offsetting from the base; **St.** to 75 cm lg., to 4 cm ∅, epidermis green, frosted blue; **Ri.** c. 16, to 6 mm br., 6 mm apart; **Ar.** oval, 3–4 mm apart, woolly at first, with white silky H. c. 10 mm lg., later glabrous; **Sp.** straight, stiff, yellowish-brown, later dirty white; **Rsp.** numerous, radiating, c. 5 mm lg., glassy; **Csp.** c. 9, middle one c. 20 mm lg., others 6–13 mm lg.; **Fl.** numerous, from the apical Ceph., tubular, yellow with a red pericarpel; **style** white; **Sti.** 4, yellow; **Fr.** berry-like, light red, slightly glossy; **S.** cap-shaped, glossy black.—Brazil (Bahia, Serra do Curral Feio, on and between rocks at c. 850 m). Discovered in 1972 by Horst and Buining.

M. monteazulensis (FR 1214): no description available.

M. multangularis (FR 1328): no description available.

M. polyanthus (Werd.) Backbg. (T.)
Bo. to 1.25 m h.; **St.** slender, to c. 5 cm $\emptyset$; **Ri.** c. 15–20, straight; **Rsp.** c. 20–30, 0.5–1.2 cm lg., ± obliquely projecting, acicular, whitish to golden-yellow; **Csp.** scarcely differentiated, usually 3–7, 1–3 of these considerably stouter, some to 3 cm lg., golden-yellow or light brownish, often also reddish; **Fl.** to 1.8 cm lg., glabrous; **Fr.** 5–7 mm lg., pinkish-red, paler below.—Distribution: see above. (Fig. 231.)

M. purpureus (FR 1329): no description available.

M. violaciflorus Buin.
Bo. to 1 m h., 4 cm thick; **Ri.** 14, 5 mm apart, acute, green, hidden by fine Sp.; **Ar.** oval, 5 mm apart, 2 mm lg., 1.5 mm br., with white to brownish H.; **Rsp.** numerous, to 25 or more, in part appressed against the Ri., partly projecting and spreading, hyaline to light brown; **Csp.** 1, to 2.5 cm lg., red; **Pseudo-Ceph.** developing on flowering-size plants, consisting of dense white to brownish wool and numerous red bristly Csp.; **Fl.** c. 23 mm lg., 7 mm $\emptyset$, cylindric, open in the daytime; **Rec.** 18 mm lg., greenish-red below, passing over into brick-red, with few small red Sc.; **Pet.** c. 2 mm lg., acute, violet outside; **Fil.** white, with yellow **An.**; **style** white; **Fr.** urn-shaped, greenish; **S.** obliquely ovoid, black.—Brazil (Minas Geraes, Chapada do Diamantina, at c. 950 m). Found in 1968 by Buining and Horst.

Micropuntia Daston (14)

Dwarf plants, simple or cushion-forming, with long-branching taproots. The cylindric or clavate stem-segments arise in part from the neck of the root, or from a short trunklet. The small leaves are (always?) reddish, the spines slender and flexible. The flowers, which appear at the stem-tips, have a thin and ± densely spiny ovary; sunken flowers have occasionally been reported (Schattat), such as have also been noted in Erdisia, Op. johnsonii, Wilcoxia albiflora etc.
The validity of this genus is in dispute. Daston gave the absence of glochids as the most vital diagnostic character. Wiegand claimed to have observed these, but they were in fact only minute spines. Investigations undertaken by Schattat, in the Botanical Garden of "Les Cèdres", showed that glochids were missing in all the four species cultivated there. L. Benson (USA) leaves the question open, in view of the absence of type-material, but suggests that the Micropuntia species might belong to the complex of forms around Corynopuntia pulchella. This is an error since the latter has unusually long glochids. Ultimately, clarification rests once again upon observations of living plants; in the case of preserved type-material it would be impossible to tell whether glochids were normally absent or if—as must certainly have happened in some instances where they were originally present—they had become detached, and been lost. "Photographic type-material with close-up photographs" would probably be helpful here, especially in colour. The flowers remain open for only one day, or half a day; they are fairly large in relation to the stem-segment, and apparently all (as far as known) are light purplish-red. But since the bodies are rather polymorphic, sometimes being so slender-cylindric that the shape alone would make it impossible to refer them to other genera, and also on account of the mostly reduced glochids (i.e. in plants on own roots), Micropuntia can be considered a valid genus. It is only in some vigorously-growing grafted plants that the otherwise reduced glochids appear, here and there, and have been observed in one species.—Distribution: USA (Utah, Nevada, California, NW. Arizona). [Plants only grow well when grafted, and do best on Opuntia tomentosa.]

M. barkleyana Daston
Bo. later clavate, with rounded Tub.; **taproot** elongated, to 10 cm lg.; **Rsp.** 4–6, c. 1 cm lg.; **Csp.** 2–3 (–4), c. 1.5 cm lg. and more, thickened below; **Sp.** compressed, dirty silvery-grey.—Utah (W. of Milford).

M. brachyrhopalica Daston (T.)
Bo. dwarf-clavate, thin below; **taproot** c. 5 cm lg., thickened-terete, **R.** branching, to 30 cm lg.; **St.** with rounded Tub., sometimes suffused reddish; **Ar.** with whitish hairlets above; **Rsp.** 5–6(?), c. 3 mm lg.; **Csp.** 1, ± curving, 0.5 cm lg. (and longer?), thickened below; **Sp.** not flattened, flexible, white.—USA (SW. Utah, near Desert Experimental Ranch, W. of Milford).

M. gracilicylindrica Wiegand & Backbg.
Bo. often with a trunklet; **Seg.** slender, long, cylindric, not becoming clavate, to 20 cm lg., 6–9 mm $\emptyset$, slightly raised around the Ar.; **Ar.** minute, scarcely visibly felty; **Rsp.** to c. 16–20, to 3(–6) mm lg.; **Csp.** 1, thickened in the lower part; all **Sp.** appressed, mostly pointing downwards; **Fl.** pinkish-red, open only for one morning; **Ov.** with fine white Sp.—USA (Nevada). (Fig. 232.)

M. pygmaea Wiegand & Backbg.
Bo. arising from the upper part of the root-neck, or from a very thin trunklet; **Seg.** elongated-spherical, to only 2.5 cm lg., c. 6 mm $\emptyset$, slightly raised around

the Ar.; **Rsp.** to c. 12–14, to 2 mm lg., very thin, acicular, weakly projecting; **Csp.** 0(–1), longer, to 1.4 cm lg., variable; **Sp.** white; **Fl.** purplish-pink, open only for 1 day.—USA (Nevada). It has not yet been possible to establish with any certainty whether this spec. is identical with any of Daston's plants. (Fig. 233.)

M. spectatissima Daston: regarded by Wiegand as a juvenile form: **Taproot** c. 10 cm lg., 2.5 cm ⌀; **Sp.** absent or, if present, 2–4, slender; **Fr.** densely white-spined.

M. tuberculosirhopalica Wiegand & Backbg.
Bo. clavate, slender; **Seg.** ± tuberculate, to c. 4 cm lg., c. 2.5 cm ⌀ above; lower **Ar.** spineless, upper ones with light flock; **Rsp.** said mostly to be missing; **Csp.** c. 3–4, to 1.3 cm lg., spreading, projecting, thin but firm, brown to black; **Fl.** pinkish-red; also reported as being sunken (perhaps anomalous?).—USA (Utah, Arizona). (Fig. 234.)

M. wiegandii Backbg.
Bo. forming cushions averaging 20 cm ⌀, but considerably larger ones have been reported; **Seg.** slender-clavate, 10–15 cm lg., c. 1.25 cm ⌀, with oblong Tub.; **Sp.** scarcely differentiated, c. 12, 1–3 as centrals, 1 broader and more flattened, to 3 cm lg., all very flexible, ± strongly contorted, interlacing, almost all of them ± flattened, mostly light (to darker.—USA (Nevada, California). (Fig. 235.) It is apparent from more recent collections that the plants are more variable than the first descriptions suggested.

Mila Br. & R. (52)

Dwarf-cereoid plants forming colonies or groups. The stems are soft-fleshed and either straight or curving, the spination being variable: stout, ± subulate to acicular, stiff to weak or bristle-like; some species also have hair-like bristles. The flowers, borne ± apically, are small-funnelform, yellow or sometimes creamy-white, the tube is short, it or the ovary having felt and some fine hairlets. The ± naked fruit is a juicy small berry. Seeds are black.—Distribution: Central Peru (Valleys of Eulalia, Rimac, Cañete, Santa and Rio Fortaleza). [(R).]

M. albisaetacens (albisetacea) Rauh & Backbg.
Bo. greyish-green; **St.** to 15 cm lg., to c. 3 cm ⌀; **Ri.** 9–10; **Ar.** small, pale brownish; **Rsp.** numerous, ± hair-like, sometimes mingled with H., interlacing; **Csp.** 3–5, whitish, some later 1.2–3.5 cm lg. and rather firmer, ± directed downwards; apical **Sp.**

sometimes ± pale brownish, soon becoming whitish, all are sometimes hair-like.—Peru (Santa valley).

M. albo-areolata Akers
Bo. dark green; **St.** to c. 8 cm lg., to 2.5 cm ⌀; **Ri.** 10–12; **Ar.** very white-woolly above; **Rsp.** c. 30–35, 4–7 mm lg., appressed in all directions, whitish; **Csp.** 3–5, to 2 cm lg., yellow, tipped black; **Fl.** ± rotate, golden-yellow; **Fr.** yellowish to reddish olive-green, with light veins.—Peru (near Imperial, S. of Lima).

M. breviseta Rauh & Backbg.
Bo. matt greyish-green; **St.** short, ± bent, to c. 2.5 cm ⌀; **Ri.** c. 13; **Ar.** with delicate yellowish-brown felt; **Sp.** to c. 50, very short, bristly, some hair-like Br. later projecting, longer, **centrals** brownish-coloured or tipped so, especially at the apex, later white.—Peru (Eulalia valley).

M. caespitosa Br. & R. (T.)
Bo. at most to 15 cm h.; **St.** to 3 cm ⌀; **Ri.** c. 10; **Ar.** with dense brown felt, later white-woolly; **Rsp.** 20 (and more), to 1 cm lg.; **Csp.** several, longest ones to 3 cm lg., stouter; **Sp.** yellowish at first, tipped brown, soon concolorous brown; **Fl.** to c. 1.5 cm lg., yellow, fading to reddish.—Peru (lower Rimac valley). (Fig. 236.)

M. cereoides Rauh & Backbg.
Bo. forming lax colonies; **St.** to 30 cm lg., 5 cm ⌀, ± cereoid, ascending, slightly bent at the base; **Ri.** c. 13; **Ar.** with yellowish-brown felt; **Rsp.** c. 18, later more, to c. 1 cm lg. eventually, bristly, ± curly and interlacing; **Csp.** to c. 11, 4 ± cruciform and stouter, slightly thickened below, to c. 2 cm lg., golden-brown, sometimes blackish-brown at first.—Peru (Rio Fortaleza valley).

M. densiseta Rauh & Backbg.
Bo. fresh green; **St.** to 25 cm lg., c. 4 cm ⌀, prostrate, with shoots from the upperside; **Ri.** 12–15; **Sp.** numerous, ± interlacing and ± completely concealing the Bo., 0.6–2 cm lg., bristly, rather stiff, slightly yellowish to light brownish in the apex, becoming white, later with slightly curly, erect, hair-like Br. below, to c. 1.3 cm lg.; **Csp.** not distinguishable.—Peru (Pisco valley).

M. fortalezensis Rauh & Backbg.
Bo. matt greyish-green, to 10 cm h.; **R.** napiform; **St.** ± spherical, to 8 cm lg.; **Ri.** 11–13; **Rsp.** numerous, fine, interlacing; **Csp.** 6–8, 1 darker Sp. at first pointing upwards, later sometimes 1 longer Sp. pointing downwards; **Sp.** brownish to darker at first, later more dirty-white; **Fr.** very small, greenish.—Peru (Rio Fortaleza valley).

M. kubeana Werd. & Backbg.
Bo. forming large colonies, fresh green, to c. 15 cm h.; **St.** later ± prostrate; **Ar.** yellow-felted at first, soon glabrous; **Rsp.** 9–16, bristly, flexible, to c. 1 cm lg., white; **Csp.** to 4, scarcely differentiated as to length and thickness, light brown, ± darker-tipped, mostly thickened below, sometimes 1 lowest Sp. longer, pointing obliquely downwards; **Fl.** satiny, light yellow; **Fr.** glossy, olive-green, wine-red when ripe.—Peru (Rimac valley, near Matucana).

M. lurinensis Rauh & Backbg.
Bo. fresh greyish-green; **St.** small-cereoid, to 10 cm lg., 3 cm ∅; **Ri.** 10–14; **Ar.** with yellowish-white felt; **Rsp.** to 40, very fine, only 5 mm lg., whitish, often interspersed with stouter Sp., brownish-black above on new growth; **Csp.** 2–3 (and more), to 2.5 cm lg., white, dark-tipped or whitish below and deep blackish-brown above.—Peru (Lurin valley).

M. nealeana Backbg.
Bo. greyish-green; **St.** often to 30 cm lg., c. 3 cm ∅; **Ri.** 11–14, ± tuberculate; **Ar.** with white to brownish felt; **Rsp.** to 30, c. 5 mm lg., very thin, white, tipped brownish; **Csp.** 4–7, stouter, 1(–2) of these longer, to 2 cm lg., projecting and later pointing strongly downwards, light brownish at first, tipped darker, later white, ± dark-tipped; **Fl.** brilliant yellow; **Fr.** green.—Peru (Eulalia, Rimac and Cañete valleys).

v. **tenuior** Rauh & Backbg.: **Bo.** rather darker green, more slender than the type; **St.** shorter; **Rsp.** yellowish at first, brown-tipped; **Csp.** 1–2, to 2.5 cm lg.—Rimac valley.
Ritter's Mila sp. No. 1, which is similar, has creamy-white Fl., and could be referred here as v. albiflora.

M. pugionifera Rauh & Backbg.
Bo. intense dark to bluish-green; **St.** ± cylindric, to 20 cm lg., to 4 cm ∅; **Ri.** mostly 11, thickened around the Ar.; **Rsp.** 7(–20), c. 5 mm lg., pungent, mostly with 3 pairs on either side and 1 central in the upper part of the Ar.; **Csp.** mostly 4, cruciform, 1 porrect, 3 directed downwards, thickened below, stout, the most robust in the G., honey-coloured on new growth, or reddish to blackish, later grey; **Fl.** c. 3 cm lg., pale yellow.—Peru (Santa valley).

M. sublanata Rauh & Backbg.
Bo. forming lax colonies; **St.** to 15 cm lg., only c. 1.5–2 cm ∅; **Ri.** c. 12; **Ar.** with yellowish-white felt; **Rsp.** 30–40, densely interlacing, bristly; **Csp.** mostly 1, thin, elongated, to 2 cm lg., light brownish, ± black in the apex, later hyaline-grey, lower St. ± concealed by interlacing Br.-Sp.—Peru (Rio Fortaleza valley).

v. **pallidior** Rauh & Backbg.: **St.** slender-cylindric; **Ar.** with light brown felt; **Sp.** not differentiated, all soon white, not greying, some tipped ± brownish and arranged more centrally.

Mirabella Ritt.
M. albicaulis Ritt. (FR 1237): no description available.

Mitrocereus (Backbg.) Backbg. (163)

(Pseudomitrocereus H. Bravo & F. Buxb.)

Very large, trunk-forming Cerei with erect stout branches; when flowering age is reached, there develops at the apex a woolly mass which is not very prominent and which is interspersed with bristles or consists of modified spines. The nocturnal flowers are stoutly bellshaped, they and the bellshaped fruits set with felt and bristles; the fruits are alike in both species of the genus, which were earlier referred to Pachycereus or in part to Neobuxbaumia.
Backebergia H. Bravo is distinguished by a completely different type of cephalium-development, while the flowers and fruit are also different, both in shape and indumentum. To include this latter genus in Mitrocereus (sensu H. Bravo) cannot be admitted; in the first place the generic diagnosis is not applicable to Backebergia, and secondly this was presumably due to Buxbaum's attempt to replace Mitrocereus by Pseudomitrocereus, which misrepresents the facts and is superfluous, since the name of Britton & Rose's type-species: "Pilocereus chrysomallus Lem." (based on an error) could easily be rectified by adding "sensu Br. & R. non Lem.". This was Buxbaum's procedure with Jasminocereus Br. & R.; his treatment of Mitrocereus is thus illogical for logic would require him to rename Jasminocereus as Brachycereus, and then to erect "Pseudobrachycereus" for the latter: an example of the consequences of ill-considered new combinations.—Distribution: Mexico (Puebla and Oaxaca). [(R).]

M. chrysomallus (sensu Br. & R.) Backbg.: **Mitrocereus fulviceps** (Web.) Backbg.

M. columna-trajani sensu Dawson: **Mitrocereus fulviceps** (Web.) Backbg.

M. fulviceps (Web.) Backbg. (T.)
Bo. to 18 m h., greyish-green; **trunk** to 1 m ∅; **branches** from fairly close to the base, parallel, ascending, to 30 cm ∅; **Ri.** 11–14 (and more); **Rsp.** c. 12, thin, radiating; **Csp.** 3 (and more), 1 longer,

to 13 cm lg., all stiff, straight, stout, those towards the apex thinner, longer, ± curving, yellowish; apex more strongly felty; **Fl.** c. 8 cm lg., creamy-white, covered with dense H. and Br.; **Fr.** with large Sc., curly H. and Br.—Mexico (Puebla and Oaxaca). (Fig. 237, 238.)

M. ruficeps (Web.) Backbg.
Bo. to 15 m h.; **trunk** to 40 cm $\varnothing$; **branches** arising from c. 2 m above the soil, straight, erect; **Ri.** c. 26; **Rsp.** 8–10, to c. 1 cm lg., stiff, straight, grey; **Csp.** 1–2, 1 longer, to 5 cm lg., stout, porrect or downcurving; all **Sp.** red at first; when flowering is reached the Sp. near the apex are more strongly modified, sometimes up to 80 being produced, these hair-like, thin, reddish and to 8 cm lg.; **Fl.** c. 5 cm lg., pinkish-white; **Br.** on the Fl. ± hidden by the Sc.; **Fr.** with felty flock and recognizable Br.—Mexico (Puebla, near Tehuacan). This spec., with its apical Fl. and inconspicuous tufted cephalium, was referred by Buxbaum to Neobuxbaumia as N. macrocephala (Web.) F. Buxb. There are no grounds for this in view of my Fig. in "Die Cact.", IV: 2240–43 and the drawings of the fruit by H. Bravo who, as early as 1954, regarded this latter name as synonymous with Mitrocereus ruficeps; she also established that the characters of the fruit were virtually identical in the two species, and differed to a considerable extent from Neobuxbaumia.

Monvillea Br. & R. (171)

Slender columnar plants, ± prostrate to erect, low-growing to quite tall. The nocturnal, ± funnelform flowers are of medium size, white, sometimes slightly greenish, scaly but otherwise glabrous, with the dried floral remains sometimes persisting. The genus is divided into 3 subgenera, based on differences of flower, ovary and fruit:

SG.1: **Monvillea**: Tube slender; ovary spherical, fruit ± spherical;
SG.2: **Ebneria** Backbg.: Tube slender; ovary cylindric; fruit ellipsoid;
SG.3: **Hummelia** Backbg.: Tube stout, ± curving; ovary oblong; fruit slender-ovoid, shortly pear-shaped or ovoid.

The figure in brackets after each specific name indicates the appropriate subgenus. (Fig. 239.)—Distribution: E. Brazil, Venezuela (coast), Ecuador (S. coast), Peru (in the N. and NE.), Bolivia, N. Argentina, Paraguay. [(R).]

M. alticostata Ritt. (FR 1015): no description available.

M. amazonica (K. Sch.) Br. & R. (3)

Bo. erect at first, to 5 m lg.; **Ri.** 7; **Sp.** c. 15, c. 8 mm lg., weak; **Fl.** c. 8 cm lg., c. 2.5 cm $\varnothing$, whitish; **Fr.** c. 5 cm lg., slender-ovoid, 2 cm $\varnothing$, furrowed, clearly scaly, with Fl.-remains.—NE. Peru (Loreto, near Tarapato).

M. anisitsii (K. Sch.) Berg.: **Monvillea spegazzinii** (Web.) Br. & R. In Berger, the description given in error under this name in fact applies to Monvillea lindenzweigiana (Gürke) Backbg.

M. apoloensis Card. (3?)—C. & S.J. (US), XXXIII: 3, 74. 1961.
Bo. erect or prostrate, 2–3 m h., matt green; **St.** 3–4 cm $\varnothing$; **Ri.** c. 8; **Rsp.** 10–13, 5–10 mm lg., spreading, thin, acicular, tipped blackish-grey; **Csp.** 1, 2–3 cm lg., directed downwards, grey to blackish; **Fl.** 7–7.5 cm lg.; **Sep.** green, reddish below; **Pet.** greenish-yellow; **Fr.** ?—Bolivia (Prov. Caupolican, between Apolo and Santa Cruz del Valle Ameno).

M. ballivianii Card. (3)
Bo. to 50 cm h. (and more?), light green; **St.** 1.5–2 cm $\varnothing$; **Ri.** 6; **Rsp.** 7–8, 4–7 mm lg., or to 1 cm lg., acicular, thin; **Csp.** 1, 2–3 cm lg., porrect; **Sp.** light grey, Csp. tipped blackish; **Fl.** c. 10 cm lg., 4.5 cm $\varnothing$; **Sep.** light green, brownish in the middle; **Pet.** greenish-white; **Fr.** 3 cm $\varnothing$, salmon-red.—Bolivia (Prov. Ballivian, Dept. Beni, near Salitral de Reyes).

M. brittoniana (Werd.) Borg: **Monvillea maritima** Br. & R.

M. calliantha Fuaux & Backbg. (3?)
Bo. forming a large shrub(?), erect (later prostrate?), robust; **St.** 4–5 cm $\varnothing$; **Ri.** 8–9; **Rsp.** 6–9, stiffly acicular, 3–4 lower ones bristly; **Csp.** mostly 3, upper ones to 4 cm lg., porrect or inclined downwards, bottom one 1.5 cm lg., decurved, all Csp. thickened below; **Sp.** light grey, darker-tipped; **Fl.** c. 7 cm lg., light yellow to cream-coloured; **Fr.** ?—Origin ?

M. campinensis (Backbg. & Voll) Backbg. (SG. ?; perhaps in a new SG.)
Bo. a dense tall shrub, erect, to 5 m h., rarely arching over; **branches** to 6 cm $\varnothing$; **Ri.** 7–9; **Sp.** 7–11, c. 5–15 mm lg., grey, black-tipped, 2–3 of these bristly, others acicular; **Fl.** to 10 cm lg., more bellshaped-funnelform, c. 6 cm $\varnothing$, greenish-white; **Tu.** ± grooved, Sc. broadly rounded, dark-tipped, long-decurrent at the base; **Fr.** ?—Brazil (São Paulo, between Campinas and Mogy Mirim). Plants can be seen in cultivation at the Jardin Exotique, Monaco.

M. cavendishii (Monv.) Br. & R. (1) (T.)

318

Bo. semi-erect to clambering, sometimes curving; **St.** mostly to 2 cm $\emptyset$; **Ri.** to c. 9; **Rsp.** 8–10, radiating in all directions, bristly-thin, whitish; **Csp.** 1 (and more), sometimes much longer, light to darker, all Sp. later whitish-grey; **Fl.** c. 10 cm lg., white; **Fr.** 4–5 cm $\emptyset$, without Sc.—S. Brazil, N. Argentina, Paraguay (?).

M. diffusa Br. & R. (3)
Bo. erect at first, then arching over, forming thickets; **branches** 4–5 cm $\emptyset$; **Ri.** c. 8; **Ar.** greyish-white, felty, sometimes more strongly white-felty; **Rsp.** 6–10, 6–12 mm lg., spreading, differing in length and thickness; **Csp.** sometimes scarcely differentiated, 1–3(–4), 1(–2) usually much longer, 2–3 cm lg., directed upwards and downwards, stoutly subulate, whitish-grey, black-tipped; **Fl.** 7.5 cm lg.; **Tub.** strongly ribbed and curving; **Fr.** shortly pear-shaped, without floral remains.—S. Ecuador (Catamayo valley), N. Peru (Saña and Olmos valleys).

M. euchlora (Web.) Backbg. (1)
Bo. erect, branching from the base, dark green; **branches** to 2.5 cm $\emptyset$, apex pointed, with a projecting tuft of Sp., new growth with wavy longitudinal furrows; **Ri.** to 8; **Ar.** little felty; **Rsp.** 10–14, to 1 cm lg., radiating, bristly, white, brownish-tipped; **Csp.** 1(–2), porrect or spreading upwards and downwards, brownish below; **Fl.** c. 10 cm lg., white; **Tu.** with indistinct lengthwise furrows; **Fr.** c. 4 cm $\emptyset$; **S.** black, smooth.—Brazil (São Paulo), Paraguay.

M. haageana Backbg. (2)
Bo. to over 3 m h., strongly branching, inclined and ascending, bluish-green, not marbled; **branches** 2–3 cm $\emptyset$, tapering at the tip; **Ri.** c. 5; **Ar.** small, white-felty; **Sp.** 5–8, to 2 mm lg., the lowest (or more central) one to 4 mm lg., thickened below; **Sp.** thin, blackish-brown; **Fl.** to 12 cm lg., white to greenish-white; **Ov.** weakly scaly.—Paraguay. (Fig. 240.)

M. insularis Br. & R.: **Cereus insularis** Hemsl.

M. jaenensis Rauh & Backbg. (3)
Bo. to 6 m h., little branching, deep green; **branches** erect, 5–10 cm $\emptyset$; **Ri.** 11–14; **Rsp.** c. 20, to 1 cm lg., thin, sometimes $\pm$ bristly, light yellowish-brownish, darker-tipped, apical Sp. sometimes pinkish-brown, all later whitish-grey; **Csp.** 1–3(–4), 1 longer, to 5 cm lg., stouter, $\pm$ subulate, thickened below, brownish-tipped; **Fl.** c. 6 cm lg., white; **Fr.** c. 4 cm lg., c. 1.5 cm $\emptyset$, weakly frosted.—N. Peru (Jaén).

v. **paucispina** Rauh & Backbg.: **Bo.** to only 3 m h., forming larger bushes; **branches** only to 5 cm $\emptyset$; **Ri.** 9; **Rsp.** to 12, bristly or stouter, blackish-brown; **Csp.** 0–1–3, 2–4 cm lg., blackish-brown at first; **Fr.** to 3 cm lg.; **S.** 1–2 mm lg., semi-kidneyshaped, black, reticulate-pitted.—N. Peru (Huancabamba valley).

M. lauterbachii (K. Sch.) Borg (1)
Bo. erect; **St.** to 2.5 cm $\emptyset$, tapering above, with erect Sp.; **Ri.** c. 6; **Rsp.** to 9, few at first, fine, one or two directed upwards, several downwards; **Csp.** c. 4, 1 longer, pointing obliquely downwards, dark above midway, becoming grey; **Fl.** c. 11 cm lg., 9 cm $\emptyset$, white.—Origin ?

M. lindenzweigiana (Gürke) Backbg. (2)
Bo. as for M. spegazzinii (Web.) Br. & R.; **branches** more terete, with faint marbling; **Fl.** to 19 cm lg.; **style** red.—Paraguay.

M. maritima Br. & R. (3)
Bo. $\pm$ simple or little branching, $\pm$ erect to arching over, often clambering high; **branches** 4–5 m h., 5–8 cm $\emptyset$, few; **Ri.** 4–6; **Rsp.** 6–8, irregularly placed, unequal; **Csp.** 1–2, stouter, much longer, to 6 cm lg.; all Sp. grey, black-tipped, subulate; **Fl.** c. 6 cm lg.; **Ov.** faintly angular; **Fr.** oblong, not clearly scaly, without floral remains.—S. Ecuador (near Santa Rosa) and N. Peru (Sechura Desert).

v. **spinosior** Backbg.: Differs in the more numerous Sp., 12–13, the centrals shorter than in the type.—S. Ecuador (near Guayaquil).

M. marmorata (Zeiss.) Frič & Krzgr.: **Monvillea spegazzinii** (Web.) Br. & R.

M. parapetiensis Ritt. (FR 1114): no description available.

M. paxtoniana (Monv.) Borg (1)
Bo. erect; **St.** to 1 m h., to 3.5 cm $\emptyset$, little branching, dark glossy green; **Ri.** c. 9; **Rsp.** 7–9, 5–10 mm lg., radiating regularly, bristly, thin, pale yellow, becoming milky-white; **Csp.** 1–4 (and more), to c. 1.5 cm lg., yellowish-brown at first, changing to pale yellow to white; **Fl.** white, to c. 12 cm lg.—Brazil?

M. phatnosperma (K. Sch.) Br. & R. (2)
Bo. creeping, light green; **St.** to 2 m lg., to 2.5 cm $\emptyset$, tapering above; **Ri.** 4–5; **Rsp.** 5–6, to 1.5 cm lg., radiating; **Csp.** 0–1, to 2.5 cm lg., straight or $\pm$ bent; **Sp.** subulate, brown, later horn-coloured; **Fl.** 12 cm lg., white; **Ov.** with traces of felt! (always?); **Fr.** 7 cm lg., 2 cm $\emptyset$, $\pm$ naked, or without Sc.; **S.** 1.5 mm lg., glossy, black.—Paraguay (near Porongo).

M. rhodoleucantha (K. Sch.) Berg (2)
Bo. erect, later arching over or creeping, or

inclined, dark green; **St.** to 2 m lg., 2–4 cm $\emptyset$, tapering above; **Ri.** 7–9; **Rsp.** 6–7(–12), to 7 mm or later 1 cm lg., subulate, yellowish-brown at first, then white, black-tipped; **Csp.** 1–3, scarcely longer, sometimes to 2 cm lg. and then thicker; **Fl.** 11–13 cm lg.; **Sep.** pinkish-red; **Pet.** white; **Fr.** to 7 cm lg., red; **S.** c. 2 mm lg., glossy, black.—N. Paraguay.

M. saxicola (Mor.) Berg. (2)
Bo. inclined, glossy, bluish-green, not frosted; **St.** 1.5–3 cm $\emptyset$; **Ri.** 6–9; **Rsp.** 7(–11), 2–6 mm lg., acicular, white, black-tipped; **Csp.** 1, later also 2–3, to 1.5 cm lg., acicular; **Fl.** 12 cm lg., greenish-white; **Fr.** c. 5 cm lg., 3 cm $\emptyset$.—Paraguay (near Trinidad).

M. smithiana (Br. & R.) Backbg. (3)
Bo. shrubby, erect to clambering, leaf-green; **branches** 4(–8) cm $\emptyset$, tapering; **Ri.** 8(–9–11); **Sp.** scarcely differentiated, to 13, longest centrals 3–4 cm lg., dark, later whitish-grey, dark-tipped; **Fl.** 6–8 (and more) cm lg., **Per.** ± bellshaped and widened, only c. 4 cm $\emptyset$, white; **Fr.** ovoid, red.—Venezuela (near La Guayra and Puerto Cabello).

M. spegazzinii (Web.) Br. & R. (2)
Bo. shrubby, creeping or ascending, then also arching over, bluish-green, marbled; **branches** c. 1.5 cm $\emptyset$, later to 2 cm $\emptyset$; **Sp.** on young shoots mostly 3, 2 directed upwards and 1 downwards, stiff, thickened below, blackish; **Rsp.** later to 5, **Csp.** 1, to 1.5 cm lg.; **Fl.** 1–13 cm lg., whitish; **Pet.** reddish; **style** white; **Fr.** frosted.—Paraguay.

M. vargasiana and M. pucuraensis, both hort. Johnson, are not sufficiently or validly described; M. pucarensis Ritt. similarly.

Morawetzia Backbg. (78)

Low-growing Cerei forming broad bushes, their stems laxly hairy or rarely hairless, the tips ± clavately thickened when flowering-age is reached. Morawetzia is distinguished from its close relative Oreocereus by a woolly and bristly apical cephalium; from this arise the strongly zygomorphic bluish-carmine flowers with terete and laxly hairy tubes. The yellowish-green, hollow fruits dehisce basally; seeds are black. Kimnach's inclusion in Borzicactus Br. & R. cannot be admitted because of the cephalium-development and the hollow fruit.—Distribution: Central Highlands of Peru (region of Rio Mantaro and Rio Huanta). [(R).]

M. doelziana Backbg. (T.)
Bo. branching from the base to form large groups, dark green; **St.** to c. 1 m h., to c. 8 cm $\emptyset$, the clavate thickening of the apex often twice as thick as the base; **Ri.** c. 11; **Ar.** circular, grey-felty, those towards the apex with lax **H.**; **Sp.** scarcely differentiated at first, to c. 20, to c. 3 cm lg., pungent; **Csp.** later 4, cruciform, to 4 cm lg., 1 pointing upwards and 1 downwards, stouter; **Sp.** yellowish to dark or reddish-brown, later grey; **Ceph.** to c. 5 cm lg.; **Fl.** c. 10 cm lg., c. 3 cm $\emptyset$.—Central Peru (near Mariscal Caceres, in the direction of Ayacucho). (Fig. 241.)

v. **calva** Rauh & Backbg.: distinguished by the absence of **H.**; apical tuft made up of fairly firm **Br.**—Central Peru (La Mejorada, in the Mantaro valley, dry region near Huanta);

v. **fuscatispina** Backbg. n.v.:
St. becoming longer; **Sp.** lighter brown; **Ceph.** appearing more rarely and much later than in the type. I studied this variety for years in the Marnier-Lapostolle collection, and initially regarded it as a hybrid; however, the many-stemmed groups at "Les Cèdres" proved to be a valid variety.

M. sericata Ritt. (FR 1309), "more attractive than M. doelziana": not yet described.

× Myrtgerocactus R. Moran gen. hybr.— C. & S.J. (US), XXXIV: 6, 184–188. 1962.

A new hybrid genus, found by Lindsay in Baja California in 1950, and considered to be a cross between Myrtillocactus cochal and Bergerocactus emoryi, since the only known specimen comes from a region where both these Cerei occur. This hybrid is listed here on account of its interesting habit and singular flower, which is more reminiscent of Bergerocactus; but no generic reference-number is attached to it; it has also been included in order to draw attention to the question of whether the erection of hybrid genera can be justified, and how they should be treated. They are called for in the case of the "Epiphyllum" hybrids. In the case of the rest of the Cactaceae, they have a special position in relation to other hybrid genera, since too little is known about them. Apart from the hybrid species listed below, there are other interesting plants, sometimes of horticultural value, such as the superb cross raised by Hummel which I have called Trichoechinopsis, which grows quickly and produces enormous flowers. R. Gräser is said to have raised a quite sensational cross between Aporocactus and Trichocereus, of which virtually nothing is known. Apart from other crosses by the same grower, there must be others which are not generally known. Ritter, for instance, claims to have found crosses between Haageocereus and Pseudoespostoa, resembling species of Neobinghamia, but not identical with any described species of this genus. It would be worth while recording all known crosses, subjecting them to closer investigation and then providing some standardized form of publication for them, because quite obviously they are not appropriate in a Handbook of naturally occurring species.

× **M. lindsayi** R. Moran

Bo. to 2.5 m h., little branching; **St.** to 5 cm ⌀; **Ri.** 11–13; **Ar.** 3–8 cm apart; **Sp.** at first 24–32, later to 60, yellowish-brown, terete or slightly angular, to 3 cm lg., thickened below; **Fl.** solitary, to 3.3 cm lg., 3.1 cm ⌀, yellow; **Pet.** numerous, c. 30; **Tu.** short; **Ov.** with crowded, felty and shortly spined Ar.; **Fr.** sterile, 1 cm ⌀, spiny.—Mexico (Baja California, S. of El Rosario; now in the collection of Gates Cactus Inc., Norco, Cal.).

In my opinion it is not firmly established whether this is a cross or a solitary survivor. Crosses do not always have sterile fruits; and self-sterile species which have not been pollinated may produce fruits without any seeds—a fact which can quite commonly be observed in the Neochilenia species. Thus a solitary self-sterile specimen could probably, in certain circumstances, set sterile fruits; but it cannot be assumed from that fact that it is a hybrid.

Myrtillocactus Cons. (168)

Large shrubs with upwardly bent branches, later developing a stout trunk; shoots in part fiercely spined, in some cases blue-frosted, with ribs which can be acute or rounded. Up to 9 flowers can sometimes develop simultaneously from a single areole; these open by day and probably also by night; they are small and shortly funnelform, greenish or creamy or reddish-white, with a spherical ovary having rudimentary scales. The small spherical, glabrous fruits are edible; they are sometimes offered for sale in the markets by the natives. Seeds are small and black.—Distribution: Mexico (Baja California and the Central Highlands) to Guatemala. [(R); in Japan sometimes used as grafting stock for young plants.]

M. cochal (Orc.) Br. & R.

Bo. to 5 m h., strongly branching; **trunk** to 30 cm ⌀; **branches** not strongly frosted but the tips distinctly zoned, to 9 cm ⌀; **Ri.** 6–9, rounded; **Rsp.** mostly c. 5, short; **Csp.** short, rarely to 4 cm lg.; **Sp.** can number to 9 in all, sometimes reddish at first, or grey to black (sometimes missing); **Fl.** 2.5 cm lg. and 3 cm ⌀, (reddish-) white; **An.** projecting brush-like beyond the spreading or revolute Per.;

Fr. 1.6 cm ⌀, red.—Mexico (Baja California). (Fig. 242.)

M. eichlamii Br. & R.

Bo. shrubby, erect, branching; **branches** deep green or faintly frosted; **Ri.** c. 6, rounded; **Rsp.** 5, thickened below; **Csp.** 1, rather longer; buds dark-purple; **Fl.** creamy-white; **Pet.** spreading; **Fr.** wine-red.—Guatemala.

M. geometrizans (Mart.) Cons. (T.)

Bo. tree-like, to 4 m h., with a distinct **trunk**; **branches** ± curving upwards, 6–10 cm ⌀, strongly bluish at first, frosted; **Ri.** c. 5–6, ± acute; **Rsp.** 5(–8–9), c. 2 mm lg., (rarely to 3 cm lg.), reddish at first; **Csp.** 1, to 7 cm lg., ± curving, ± angular, to ± dagger-like, blackish; **Fl.** 2.5–3.5 cm ⌀, not revolute, greenish-white; **Fr.** bluish-purple.—Mexico (San Luis Potosí to Oaxaca).

v. **grandiareolatus** (H. Bravo) Backbg.: **branches** longer, more straightly erect, **Tub.** conspicuous, even at the base of the plant; **Ar.** large, very felty; **Csp.** not noticeably longer.—Mexico (S. Puebla, Oaxaca).

M. grandiareolatus H. Bravo: **Myrtillocactus geometrizans** v. **grandiareolatus** (H. Bravo) Backbg.

M pugionifer (Lem.) Berg.: a form of **Myrtillocactus geometrizans** (Mart.) Cons. with more dagger-like Sp.

M. schenckii (J. A. Purp.) Br. & R.

Bo. eventually tree-like, to 5 m h., freely branching; **trunk** very short; **branches** ascending, very crowded, c. 10 cm ⌀, intense green, rarely quite faintly frosted; **Ri.** 7–8, acute; **Rsp.** 5–7, to 1.2 cm lg., straight to ± curving; **Csp.** to 5 cm lg., brown; **Fl.** white to cream; **Fr.** glabrous, at least at first (acc. Purpus: "later with small Sp." [always?]), carmine.—Mexico (border between Puebla and Oaxaca).

Supplementary to the data of the original diagnosis, in "Die Cact.", 2274, 1960 I considered certain differential characters and provided an illustration of a plant in Monaco which tallied with the description of Purpus: "Ri. fairly acute, Csp. larger, to 5 cm lg."; in habit it appeared to be a Myrtillocactus, but no other description of it existed. The habitat-photo of R. Moran, reproduced in Kimnach's article (C. & S. J. [US] XXXVI: 6, 181. 1964), shows another plant which is clearly the correct one, with Ri. not really acute, Ar. conspicuously close together and the branches relatively thick. Earlier illustrations failed to provide any details of the shoots; I therefore considered the Monaco plant to be a juvenile specimen, but its identity is not satisfactorily established.

Navajoa Croiz. (207)

Small and mostly solitary plants, with approximately two-thirds of the body buried in the soil, with cylindric-conical tubercles. They are differentiated from other genera by the uniquely bent, corky, flexible and sometimes transversely fissured spines, some of these at first with microscopically fine hairlets. The white or yellow flowers are ± bellshaped to broadly funnelform; the fruit is topshaped and semi-dry, with scattered scales which are papery and curly above. The seeds are moderately large, cap-shaped, black and finely tuberculate.—Distribution: USA (Arizona, near Holbrook, and on the N. side of the Grand Canyon in Colorado). [(G).]

N. fickeisenii Backbg.
Bo. mostly to c. 4 cm lg., to c. 5 cm $\emptyset$ (to over 8 cm $\emptyset$ has been reported), bluish-green; **Tub.** conical to ± longitudinally or transversely elongated; **Ar.** oblong at first, later more circular, the Sp.-bases at first hidden by yellowish-white fibrous felt; **Rsp.** c. 5–7, to 3.5 mm lg., finer, corky, later sometimes also 1–2 uppers, stouter, longer, to 2 cm lg.; **Csp.** 1, to 3.5 cm lg., much stouter, corky, transversely fissured, ± erect then curving strongly inwards, bent inwards high above the crown, whitish to horn-coloured; **Fl.** c. 3 cm $\emptyset$, yellow; **Sep.** greenish-yellow; **Tu.** missing; **Fr.** to c. 8 mm $\emptyset$, reddish-green.—USA (Arizona, N. side of the Grand Canyon). (Fig. 243, right.)

N. maia n.nud. is a plant recently offered from the USA.: Sp. c. 6–7, radials only, ± as thin as in the preceding, appressed, ± interlacing, light horn-colour, soon grey, interlacing above the crown, the upper one longest, ± centrally placed. Appears to be only a form or variety of the preceding in which the Csp. is absent.

N. peeblesiana Croiz. (T.)
Bo. mostly simple, flattened-spherical to spherical, sometimes short-cylindric, 2.5–7 cm lg., to 2.5 cm $\emptyset$, bluish-green; **Tub.** conical to ± cylindric, later also broader; **Ar.** at first with cushions of denser fibrous felt concealing the bases of the Sp.; **Rsp.** c. 3–5, 1 longest directed downwards, all bent strongly towards the Bo.; **Csp.** 1, 5–14 mm lg., bent upwards (not erect) over the crown; **Sp.** alike, horn-coloured, later grey, pink below at first, weak and flexible, corky, with slight transverse furrows and fissures; **Fl.** to only 1.7 cm lg., whitish with a faintly pink M.-stripe; **Fr.** 8–10 mm lg.—USA

(Arizona, from Holbrook to the Grand Canyon). (Fig. 243 left, 244.)
Since these two spec. have different spination and Fl.-colour, L. Benson's reduction of the first to the status of variety of the latter is an unwarrantable name-change (see also Pediocactus).

Neoabbottia Br. & R. (133)

Plants which are shrub-like as juveniles but then develop a long stout trunk, and branch to form a large crown. Characteristic of the genus are the nocturnal flowers which give off an unpleasant odour; these are cylindric, with a very narrow limb, arising from a zone of dense apical felt, or sometimes subapically. The buds at first have longer bristly spines and dense felt; the floral tubes, only in some cases, have short bristly spinelets in the scale-axils. The fruits are green, oblong and broadly channelled, their areoles only felty.—Distribution: Hispaniola (Haiti, Dominican Republic). Needs warmth, ✳.]

N. paniculata (Lam.) Br. & R. (T.)
Bo. to 10 m h.; **trunk** to 30 cm $\emptyset$; **branches** to 6 cm $\emptyset$; **Ri.** 4–6, with sinuate notches; **Sp.** 12–20, to c. 2 cm lg., acicular, brownish to grey; **Fl.** to 5 cm lg., greenish-white; **Pet.** to only c. 1 cm lg.; **Tu.** c. 2 cm $\emptyset$, channelled, the upper Ser. of ± elongated Sc. passing over into the Per., Sc. more numerous below, felty, sometimes with short Br.-Sp.; **Fr.** to 7 cm lg., to 5.5 cm $\emptyset$, green, thick-walled; **S.** black.—Hispaniola (Haiti, Dominican Republic). (Fig. 245.)
  v. **humbertii** Backbg.: differentiated by the somewhat stouter Fl.-Tu. with fewer Sc.; Pet. creamy-pink.—Dominican Republic.

Neobesseya Br. & R. (216)

Plants ± spherical, simple or offsetting to form larger groups; tubercles furrowed, later shrivelling. The subapical flowers are yellow or pink. Distinguished from Coryphantha, which it resembles, by the fruits which are not watery but ± fleshy, red, slow to ripen, with hard black seeds; differentiated from Neolloydia which has dull-coloured fruits with walls drying to become ± papery. Plants will in part withstand quite severe frosts.—Distribution: from British Columbia through the USA to N. Mexico (Coahuila). [(R).]

N. asperispina (Böd.) Böd.
Bo. simple, spherical, to 6 cm $\emptyset$, matt dark bluish-green; **Tub.** acute-conical, lax, lower ones curving ± upwards; **Ar.** ± white-woolly, soon glabrous;

Rsp. 9–10, to 1 cm lg., thin-subulate, radiating all round, later curving to the Bo., woolly-rough, grey-whitish; **Csp.** 0–(–1), shorter, rather stouter; **Fl.** c. 2.8 cm lg., 2.5 cm ⌀, pale greenish-yellow; **Fr.** spherical.—Mexico (Coahuila).

N. cubensis (Br. & R.) Hest.: **Neolloydia cubensis** (Br. & R.) Backbg.

N. missouriensis (Sweet) Br. & R. (T.)
Bo. simple to forming smaller cushions; single heads to 6 cm h., to 8 cm ⌀; **Tub.** 1–1.5 cm lg., ± spiralled; **Ar.** woolly; **Rsp.** (9–)14(–20); **Csp.** 0–1; **Sp.** pubescent, acicular, often curving, grey, brown-tipped; **Fl.** c. 2 cm lg., c. 2.5 cm ⌀, greenish-yellow; **Fr.** spherical, light red.—USA (N. Dakota, Montana to Texas [?]).

N. muehlbaueriana (Böd.) Böd.: **Escobaria muehlbaueriana** (Böd.) Knuth.

N. notesteinii (Britt.) Br. & R.
Bo. simple or offsetting, single heads ovoid, only c. 3 cm ⌀; **Tub.** ± hemispherical; **Rsp.** 12–18, 8–12 mm lg.; **Csp.** 1, often red-tipped; **Sp.** weak, thin, puberulent, white, greying; **Fl.** 1.5–2.5 cm ⌀, greyish-pink; **Fr.** obovoid.—USA (Montana, near Deer Lodge).

N. odorata (Böd.) Werd.: **Neolloydia odorata** (Böd.) Backbg.

N. rosiflora Lahm.
Bo. only moderately offsetting, single heads spherical to shortly cylindric, to 5–7 cm h., to 5.5 cm ⌀, light green; **Tub.** ± rounded, lax; **Ar.** elliptic, white-woolly; **Rsp.** 13–15, upper two hair-like; **Csp.** 1, appressed upwards; **Sp.** fine, white, brown-tipped; **Fl.** c. 4 cm ⌀, pale pink; **Pet.** very narrow, "± filiform"; **Fr.** ovoid to spherical, carmine.—USA (Oklahoma, W. of Tulsa). (Fig. 246.)

N. similis (Eng.) Br. & R.
Bo. forming groups to 15 cm h., 20–30 cm ⌀, deep green; single heads spherical, 6–10 cm ⌀; **Tub.** cylindric, to 2 cm lg.; furrow white-woolly in new growth; **Rsp.** 12–15, c. 1 cm lg., spreading, subulate, often finely hairy, dirty white, brown-tipped; **Csp.** 0–1, stouter, longer; **Fl.** 5–6 cm lg., light yellow; **Fr.** ± spherical, to 2 cm ⌀, red.—USA (E. Texas).

N. wissmannii (Hildm.) Br. & R.
Bo. simple, or forming groups to 30 cm ⌀, bluish-green, single heads to 10 cm h., hemispherical; **Tub.** cylindric-conical, lax, directed quite strongly upwards, to 2.5 cm lg.; **Ax.** white-woolly; **Ar.**

white-woolly at first; **Rsp.** 7–14, later 15–20, 1.5–2 cm lg., projecting ray-like, white to brownish (or yellowish-white, tipped reddish, acc. Berger), later grey with a thickened yellow base; **Csp.** 0–3, scarcely longer, rather stouter; **Fl.** 4–5 cm lg., glossy, dark to lighter yellow; **Pet.** apiculate; **Fr.** spherical, c. 8 mm ⌀.—USA (Central Texas).

N. zilziana (Böd.) Böd.: **Escobaria zilziana** (Böd.) Backbg.

Neobinghamia Backbg. emend. Backbg. (182)

Robuster Cerei from Peru, branching from the base and sometimes to more than 2 m tall, with step-like, broadly annular or long-decurrent cephalioid development in the flowering zones which may be fur-like or tufted. Flowers funnelform, opening towards evening and remaining open all night, borne ± apically or from lower woolly-hairy development, sometimes conspicuously in stages, one above the other; the tubes are stout, scaly and hairy. The ± spherical hairy fruits contain small, ± glossy black seeds. Hair-development at the base of the filaments has been noted only in the type-species so that—as in other Peruvian cerei—this is not a diagnostic character.—Distribution: Central Peru (Eulalia, Churin, Lurin valleys) and further N. (Rio Fortaleza to the Olmos valley). [(R).] Ritter held the erroneous view that the genus was of hybrid origin. Nevertheless, plants raised from "hybrid-seed" of Winter's Catalogue: Nos. 147–149, proved not to be referable here.

N. climaxantha (Werd.) Backbg. (T.)
Bo. to over 1 m h.; **St.** 6–8 cm ⌀, dull light green; **Ri.** 19–27; **Ceph.**, below a woolly apical tuft, arranged in stepped lax annular zones, white; **Rsp.** c. 50–70, c. 5–8 mm lg., ± interlacing sideways, acicular, honey-coloured, later dirty greyish-brown; **Csp.** c. 1–3, 2 uppers pointing obliquely upwards, lower one downwards, to 2 cm lg., subulate, pungent, transparent, honey-yellow, often banded, later also greyish-brown; **Fl.** deep pink; **Fr.** to 3 cm ⌀, brownish-red.—Peru (Eulalia valley). (Fig. 247.)
v. **armata** (Ak.?) Rauh & Backbg.: **Bo.** to 1.5 m h.; **Ri.** c. 20; **Csp.** much longer, to 5 cm (and more) lg., thinner, sometimes decurved; apical **Ceph.** yellowish-white, laxer in the Fl.-zone; **Fl.** white(?)—Peru (Churin valley);
v. **lurinensis** Rauh & Backbg.: **Csp.** to c. 4 cm lg., later pointing downwards; **apex** shortly hairy; **Fl.**-zone starting just below the apex, ± one-sided; **Fl.** carmine.—Peru (Lurin valley);
v. **subfusciflora** Rauh & Backbg.: **Fl.** brownish.—Peru (Eulalia valley).

N. mirabilis Rauh & Backbg.
Bo. to c. 2 m h.; **St.** 8–10 cm ∅; **Ri.** 22; **Ceph.** resembling a series of collars encircling the St. at intervals, to 10 cm deep, consisting of dense long tufts; **Rsp.** c. 50, to 2 cm lg., thin; **Csp.** 1–2, longer, subulate; **Sp.** dark to brownish-red, then grey, longer ones darker-tipped; **Fl.** to 6 cm lg., narrow-funnelform; **Sep.** purple; **Pet.** carmine.—Peru (near Olmos).

N. multiareolata Rauh & Backbg.
Bo. to 1.2 m h.; **St.** to c. 10 cm ∅; **Ri.** c. 22; **Ceph.** shortly tufted, one-sided, broad, lax, extending over 8–10 Ri., long-decurrent; **Rsp.** to c. 80, to 5 mm lg., very thin, yellowish; **Csp.** 1(–2), c. 2 cm lg., on new growth often to 6 cm lg., directed laterally or downwards, amber-yellow; **Fl.** white(?).—Peru (Rio Fortaleza valley).
   v. **superba** Rauh & Backbg.: taller, stouter, to 2.5 m h., to 15 cm ∅, main **Sp.** erect at the apex, sometimes ± curving, to 4 cm lg. (and more).

N. villigera Rauh & Backbg.
Bo. to 1.3 m h.; **St.** to 10 cm ∅; **Ri.** 20; **Ceph.** like a continuous furry mat (hence the name), sometimes ± in stages, covering 9–14 Ri., crown densely woolly-felty; **Rsp.** c. 80, thin; **Csp.** 1–2, longer, 1 to c. 4 cm lg. (and more), ± downcurving, yellowish; **Fl.** 6.5 cm lg., 4 cm ∅, pale greenish-white.—Central Peru (Churin valley). (Fig. 248.)

Neobuxbaumia Backbg. (155)

Large columnar cacti, simple to scarcely or freely branching, mostly with many ribs. The flowers, borne apically or sometimes quite low on the stems, are whitish or reddish, and the ovary can be constricted or not. The felt and small bristles or thin spines of the ovary and the very scaly fruit may be ± reduced. Seeds glossy black. The genus is subdivided into 2 subgenera according to flower-shape:
   SG.1: **Neobuxbaumia**: Flowers cylindric-funnelform; ovary not constricted; fruit in part shortly and finely spiny and felty; spines may be ± reduced;
   SG.2: **Crassocereus** Backbg.: Flowers cylindric-bellshaped; ovary constricted; fruit finely bristly-spiny to spineless.
For Neobuxbaumia mezcalaensis (H. Bravo) Backbg., see also under Rooksbya. Efforts to unite species—quite often as a result of insufficient knowledge of the characters—has often hindered the ascertaining and exact description of floral differences. The large Mexican Cerei clearly demonstrate the drawbacks inherent in the "lumping" process. In most cases I have been able to

throw some light, but in the case of Neobuxbaumia it was perhaps insufficient, because here there are unmistakable divergences of floral characters which may make it necessary not merely to exclude N. mezcalaensis, but even to limit the genus to the type-species, N. tetetzo, while raising the Subgenus Crassocereus to generic rank. Many factors favour such a treatment. In any event N. scoparia is still insufficiently clarified regarding its flowers and fruits, while its freely branching and tree-like habit does not occur in any other species of Neobuxbaumia. For the time being, however, the present classification must stand. On that basis, 4 species with 3 varieties have been described.—Distribution: Mexico (Guerrero, Tehuantepec, Oaxaca, Puebla, Vera Cruz). The appropriate subgenus is indicated in brackets after the specific name. [(R).]

N. euphorbioides (Haw.) F. Buxb.: **Rooksbya euphorbiodes** (Haw.) Backbg.

N. macrocephala sensu Daws.: **Mitrocereus ruficeps** (Web.) Backbg.

N. mezcalaensis (H. Bravo) Backbg. (1)
Bo. probably always simple, to 7 m h., to 30 cm ∅, yellowish to pale greyish-green; **Ri.** c. 15, narrow, c. 2 cm h.; **Ar.** yellow-felty, 2 cm apart; **Rsp.** 6–7, to 1 cm lg., straight, spreading, white to faintly yellowish, brown-tipped, soon grey; **Csp.** 1, c. 1.3 cm lg.; **Fl.** c. 5.5 cm lg., c. 3.5 cm ∅, greenish-white; **Ov.** without Sp. or Br., but acc. Dawson these are sometimes present; **Fr.** c. 5 cm ∅, spherical, carmine, finally with Br.-Sp.—Mexico (Guerrero, near Mezcala; Puebla, near Zapotitlán; Oaxaca, Rio Atoyac and southwards).
   v. **multiareolata** (Daws.) Daws.: distinguished by its lower habit and longer, thinner, more erect **Sp.**; **Ri.** lower; **Ar.** only 1 cm apart.—Mexico (Guerrero, Acahuitzotle);
   v. **robusta** (Daws.) Backbg.: taller, to 12 m h., to 40 cm ∅; **Ri.** later broader, more rounded; **Sp.** longer, stouter; **Ar.** larger, less crowded.—Mexico (Puebla, Rio Atoyac).
In the light of the number of characters shared with Rooksbya euphorbioides—simple habit, funnelform flowers, resemblance between juveniles of the 2 spec., relatively light armature and narrow ribs—it is possible that closer study will show the preceding species must be transferred to Rooksbya.

N. polylopha (DC.) Backbg. (2)
Bo. simple, to 13 m h., 30 cm ∅ (and more), rounded above, light green, becoming grey; **Ri.** to c. 50, weakly rounded; **Ar.** at first with thick white wool, 6–8 mm apart; **Rsp.** mostly 7–8, to 2 cm lg.,

spreading, more erect at the apex; **Csp.** 1; **Sp.** light honey-coloured, tipped brownish, then white and soon falling, in the flowering-zone sometimes to 7 cm lg.; **Fl.** lighter to darker red, often borne low on older parts of the St.; **Tu.** with downwardly directed, fleshy Sc.; **Ov.** glabrous; **Fr.** spiny.— Mexico (Hidalgo, Valle de Zimapan, Meztitlan, Tlacolula). (Fig. 249.)

N. scoparia (Pos.) Backbg. (1)
Bo. freely branching, to 7.5 m h., dark leaf-green, later dark greyish-green; newer **St.** with **Ri.** 12–15, rounded; **Ar.** to 2.4 cm apart, glabrous; **Rsp.** 5, to 8 mm lg., down-curving; **Csp.** 1, stouter, curving upwards, to 2.5 cm lg., blackish, later whitish; **flowering shoots** more slender, Ri. 20–25, lower; **Ar.** c. 1 cm apart, with white woolly felt; **Rsp.** 5–7, 2–3 cm lg.; **Csp.** 1, 2–3 cm lg.; **Sp.** honey-yellow at first, pungent, thin-subulate, all those in the flowering zone bristly, brown; **Fl.** reddish, small; **Ov.** with broad flat Sc.; **Fr.** red, glabrous!—Mexico (Vera Cruz: Oaxaca, near Juchitan).

N. tetetzo (Web.) Backbg. (1) (T.)
Bo. simple to little branching up to several metres above the base, 8–15 m h., to 30 cm ∅, grey; **branches** parallel, ascending; **Ri.** numerous, rounded; **Ar.** shortly grey-felty, later glabrous; **Rsp.** 8–13, 10–15 mm lg., radiating; **Csp.** 3, 1 of these longer, to 5 cm lg., porrect; **Sp.** straight, stiff, blackish; **Fl.** subapical, c. 6 cm lg., whitish; **Tu.** and **Ov.** glabrous; **Fr.** fig-like, 2–3 cm lg., green, with pads of felt and several Br.—Mexico (Puebla, near Zapotitlán, to Oaxaca, Rio Totolapan and beyond). (Fig. 250.)
   v. **nuda** (Daws.) Daws.: Bo. freely branching; Rsp. only, 1–3, decurved, set along the lower Ar.-border, the middle one longest; Fl. and Fr. unknown.—Mexico (Oaxaca, W. of Tehuantepec).

Neocardenasia Backbg. (56)

Plants very large-columnar, later forming a trunk; flowering areoles larger, prominent, sometimes producing 2 flowers simultaneously. Flowers diurnal, pink, cylindric, ± constricted above the ovary, this and the tube densely set with long, ± stouter bristles; the fruit is ovoid, bristly, with pink flesh. The seeds are dark brown. The genus is at present monotypic, although attempts have been made to unite it with Neoraimondia. A cogent argument against this is the observable fact that members of the Cactaceae which are separated by high mountains, so that the distributions are quite distinct, never exhibit the same characters. In any event, the resemblance between these two genera is

not a close one: Neocardenasia forms a trunk, Neoraimondia branches from the base; Neocardenasia does not produce short flowering shoots, but instead the areoles are thickened; further the cylindric floral tube is long and densely stiff-bristly, and this is not so in Neoraimondia. The appearance of 2 flowers simultaneously from an areole cannot be regarded as a diagnostic character, since this phenomenon is known to occur in other genera.—Distribution: Bolivia (Cochabamba and Chuquisaca). [(R).]

N. herzogiana Backbg. (T.)
Bo. to 10 m h., **trunk** stout, branching from the upper third; **Ri.** 6–7; **Ar.** 3–4 cm apart, strongly brown-felty at first; **Sp.** 11–14, the outer ones in new growth light, the inner ones deeper brown, centrals scarcely distinguishable, darker brown, **Rsp.** 2 cm lg., and the occasional **Csp.** to 18 cm lg.; **Fl.** 6–7 cm lg., pink, densely long-bristly; **Fil.** short, only on the upper part of the throat; **style** somewhat projecting; **Fr.** to 6 cm lg.—Bolivia (see above). (Fig. 251.)

Neochilenia Backbg. (121)*

Plants with bodies ± spherical to elongated, sometimes dwarf, in the latter often from a stout taproot. The ribs can be straight, or sometimes tuberculate; the tubes of the open-funnelform, whitish, yellowish or ± red flowers are ± woolly or hairy. The berry-like hollow fruit is ± hairy with woolly flock; the seeds are dropped from a basal opening.
The species were earlier referred to Neoporteria, but in the latter the flowers are always light reddish, with the inner petals curving towards one another until the flower fades. This unique character, added to a stem-like tube and extreme reduction of the indumentum, contrasts with the open funnel form of Neochilenia, which also has recognisable hair-development; although the latter is relatively slight in the most extreme cases, it is never reduced to felt, but is usually quite distinct, even at the bud-stage, and is sometimes very marked. This character also segregates the genus from Horridocactus with ± broadly funnelform flowers, in which the floral indumentum shows the same extreme reduction as Neoporteria.
In Neochilenia there is every transitional stage between the larger and the dwarf species, so that Ritter's segregation of his genus Chileorebutia (see

---

* This generic name is invalid under the Code of Botanical Nomenclature. Most taxonomists nowadays reject the segregation of this genus from Neoporteria; but if recognized as a separate genus, the name Neochilenia should be replaced by: **Nichelia** Bullock. Translator.

this also, itself a synonym of Thelocephala Y. Ito) cannot be maintained since the same degrees of indumentum occur in the ribbed as in the tuberculate species; and where species of "Chileorebutia" have been grafted, the tubercles quite often eventually become confluent to form more distinct ribs.

Ritter was therefore later obliged to refer some of his "Chileorebutia" species to Pyrrhocactus; there are no arguments to support Ritter's maintenance of Chileorebutia and his rejection of Neochilenia. The situation was further complicated by his inclusion of some Chilean species in Pyrrhocactus, because some of the species of "Pyrrhocactus sensu Ritt." from Chile resemble quite typical Neochilenias in flower form and indumentum, but most of them bear no resemblance to the E. Andean Pyrrhocactus.

Details of floral indumentum, in Ritter's species described as Pyrrhocactus in "Taxon" XII: 1, 1963, are insufficient, particularly as regards the degree of hair-development, which is of course the aspect which affects the relationship to Neochilenia. This may be intended to draw attention away from the fact that Chileorebutia is also a synonym of the latter genus, and that the Chilean species of "Pyrrhocactus", with their hairy-floccose flowers and ovaries, are also referable there. Regarding the tube and ovary of flowers of "Pyrrh. rupicolus and intermedius", Ritter says: "haud setosis", and of P. echinus "esetosis". The latter, in the absence of any details as to hair-development, could be attributed to Horridocactus, whereas Ritter compares "P. rupicolus and intermedius" with "P. pygmaeus" which has strongly hairy and bristly flowers, and is thus generically compatible with Neochilenia, while saying that the other two species are "haud setosis". Perhaps his "P. pygmaeus" should therefore be placed in Reicheocactus, unless traces of bristles can be observed. Given his comparison with Neoch. pygmaea, I must in the meantime retain his species in Neochilenia. This example proves the importance of exact data on indumentum when establishing generic relationships—a difficult enough problem with the globose Chilean cacti, and one which Ritter's treatment does little to clarify.

The only satisfactory solution (as I have long proposed) is the more or less conventional one of segregating the species of the East Andean zone from those of the Western one; this procedure has already been applied to the plant and animal kingdoms (see Hellmich: "Die Bedeutung des Andenraumes im biographischen Bilde Südamerikas", 1940). This systematic division reflects in every way the natural phenomena. If the most important diagnostic characters of the Pacific genera of Neochilenia and Horridocactus, on the one hand, are compared with those of the East Andean genus Pyrrhocactus on the other, considerable differences emerge as to flower shape and indumentum within the enlarged genus Pyrrhocactus sensu Ritter, even although there are also certain similarities. However, it must be borne in mind that the Andes of South Chile are a very ancient elevation, so that from time immemorial they have played an effective role as a limiting factor; and Rowley points out, in his contribution to "Die Cact." VI, Section I, that with "re-synthesized species" it is not always possible to tell whether they represent natural species or hybrids, even when in flower. It is therefore quite conceivable that the West Andean group of species, and its East Andean counterpart—presumably both of very great age—must have gone their separate evolutionary ways simply as a result of the Andean elevation; consequently the reasonable course is to treat them as separate genera.—Distribution: restricted to Chile. [(G): (R).]

N. aerocarpa (Ritt.) Backbg.
Bo. (of cultivated seedlings) later cylindric, brownish; **Ri.** resolved into Tub.; **Ar.** oblong, at first with short white flaky wool; **Rsp.** c. 10, 4–10 mm lg., subterete, ± pectinate, thickened below, horn-coloured to ± reddish-brown, darker-tipped, apical Sp. darker brownish, the lower part of the Ar. with several very thin Ssp.; **Csp.** 0–2, one directed upwards, blackish, one strongly downwards, ± twice as long as the Rsp.; **Fl.** 3(–5) cm lg. and ∅, carmine; **Tu.** and **Ov.** strongly woolly, with brown Br.; **Fr.** to 2 cm lg., 1.5 cm ∅, reddish.—Chile (Dept. Freirina) (FR 498).

v. **fulva** (Ritt.) Backbg.: **Ar.** more crowded, narrower; **Sp.** lighter, or whitish, ± bent; **Csp.** mostly 0, sometimes 1, shorter (FR 500).

N. ambigua (Hildm.) Y. Ito: **Weingartia ambigua** (Hildm.) Backbg.

N. andreaeana Backbg.
Bo. becoming oblong, to 15 cm h., 5 cm ∅, dark greyish-green; **Ri.** 14, scarcely tuberculate; **Rsp.** c. 8, to 1 cm lg., whitish-grey; **Csp.** 4, to c. 2.2 cm lg., stouter, brown at first, reddish below, later greyish-brownish; **Fl.** 3 cm lg., 3.7 cm ∅, satiny, light scarlet to coppery-red, bordered yellowish; **throat** greenish-white.—Chile (Fig. 252.)

N. aricensis (Ritt.) Backbg.—Descr. Cact. Nov. III: 9. 1963 (Pyrrhocactus aricensis Ritt., "Taxon", XII: 1, 32. 1963).
Bo. rather oblong, to 10 cm ∅, dark green; **R.** napiform, very long; **Ri.** 13–21, less noticeably notched than N. iquiquensis; **Ar.** grey; **Rsp.** 10–16, 8–15 mm lg.; **Csp.** 5–12, 1–3 cm lg.; **Fl.** pale yellow;

Fil. in 2 Ser., both inserted basally; **Fr.** 1.5 cm lg., $\pm$ spherical; **S.** 1.4 mm lg., very rough, dark brown.—N. Chile (sea-cliffs near Arica, rare) (FR 268).

N. aspillagai (Söhr.) Backbg.
Bo. $\pm$ spherical, to 15 cm $\varnothing$, dark green; **Ri.** 14, plumply tuberculate; **Rsp.** 4–12, to 2 cm lg., acicular, curving; **Csp.** 1–4, 2–3 cm lg., stouter, mostly straight; **Sp.** white at first, dark-tipped, later grey, Csp. darker; **Fl.** 4 cm lg., light yellow, pink outside, with much white flaky wool and several white Br.—Chile (Hacienda Tanumé).

N. atra Backbg.—Descr. Cact. Nov. III: 9. 1963.
Bo. spherical, to c. 8.5 cm $\varnothing$, black; **Ri.** numerous, completely resolved into spiralled, fairly slender Tub., with a small chin-like projection below the Ar.; **Ar.** narrow, oval, fairly long, white-woolly; **Rsp.** c. 10–11, all $\pm$ equal, a few mm lg., fine, thin, light-coloured; **Csp.** mostly missing, rarely 1 in the upper part of the Ar., rather longer and stouter, bent slightly to the crown or $\pm$ projecting; **buds** blackish-red, with flaky white H. below; **Fl.** c. 4 cm $\varnothing$, with a short Tu., pale yellow, or lighter above, greenish towards the centre; **Sep.** blackish-red in the middle, border lighter; **Tu.** short, with flaky white H. and with curly thin light Br. above; **style** red; **Sti.** pale pink. Unique on account of the black Bo. and the finely tuberculate Ri.—Import: Uebelmann; type-plant in the collection of J. Marnier-Lapostolle.—Chile. (Fig. 253.)

N. calderana (Ritt.) Backbg.—Descr. Cact. Nov. III: 9. 1963 (Pyrrhocactus calderanus Ritt., Succulenta, 2: 13–14. 1961).
Bo. simple, hemispherical, later more elongated, 5–8 cm $\varnothing$, green; **R.** napiform; **Ri.** 13–15, with chin-like Tub.; **Ar.** oblong, white-woolly; **Rsp.** 8–10, 1–3.5 cm lg., rather thin, curving $\pm$ upwards; **Csp.** 3–5, similar, $\pm$ flattened, $\pm$ upcurving, 2–4 cm lg.; **Sp.** greyish-brown to blackish; **Fl.** c. 3.5 cm lg. and $\varnothing$, yellowish-white, with white flaky wool, with several white hair-like Br. above; **Fr.** yellowish; **S.** dirty grey.—N. Chile (Caldera) (FR 496).

N. carneoflora Kilian n.sp.
Bo. simple (always?), brown-olive; **Ri.** 18, slightly spiralled, 1 cm br. below; **Tub.** rounded, obtuse, chin-like, 5 mm br. above; **Ar.** 3 mm lg., 2 mm br., obovate, elongated above, with white to creamy woolly felt, this more noticeable towards the crown and covering it, slightly overtopped by the Sp.; **Rsp.** 6–8, projecting $\pm$ laterally or bent to the Bo., horn-coloured at first, brown-tipped, then $\pm$ brownish-grey to grey, c. 5 mm lg.; **Fl.** 3.5 cm lg., 3 cm $\varnothing$, flesh-coloured; **Tu.** green, with Sc. which are green, flesh-coloured above, with white wool, with

several white Br. above; **Ov.** 6 mm lg.; **Pet.** lanceolate, with a darker M.-stripe; **Fil.** white to greenish or whitish-yellow; **style** carmine-pink; **Sti.** flesh-coloured; **throat** green; **Fr.** ?—Chile (collected by Ritter ?). (Fig. 254.)

N. chilensis (Hildm.) Backbg.
Bo. simple or branching from below, spherical at first, becoming columnar, pale green; **Ri.** 20–21, $\pm$ notched; **Rsp.** c. 20, c. 1 cm lg., acicular; **Csp.** 6–8, to 2 cm lg.; **Sp.** hyaline, glossy, white to yellowish, densely covering the Bo.; **Fl.** 5 cm $\varnothing$, pinkish-red, felty, with long white H.; **Br.**-colour ?—Chile.
v. borealis: only a name?

N. chorosensis (Ritt.) Backbg.
Bo. simple, flattened-spherical, to 6 cm $\varnothing$, greyish-green; **R.** napiform; **Ri.** 13–16, made $\pm$ tuberculate by constrictions between the Ar.; **Ar.** to 0.75 cm lg.; **Rsp.** 5–7, 2–10 mm lg., greyish-black; **Csp.** mostly 0, rarely 1, 1–2 cm lg., porrect; **Fl.** c. 4.75 cm lg., 4 cm $\varnothing$, light yellow, M.-stripe light red; with dense white flaky wool and numerous white Br.-H.; **Fr.** dark reddish-brown; **S.** blackish-brown.—Chile (Choros) (FR 489).

N. confinis (Ritt.) Backbg.—Descr. Cact. Nov. III: 9. 1963 (Pyrrhocactus confinis Ritt., Succulenta, 1:4–5. 1961).
Bo. simple, hemispherical, later elongated, 6–8 cm $\varnothing$, green; **R.** shortly napiform; **Ri.** 13–15, $\pm$ tuberculate; **Ar.** large, with white to grey felt; **Rsp.** 10–12, 1–2.5 cm lg., $\pm$ appressed, the lowest one very fine, topmost one stouter, longer; **Csp.** 4–7, to 4 cm lg., not flattened, projecting or pointing upwards; **Fl.** c. 4 cm lg., 3 cm $\varnothing$, funnelform, glossy, white with a reddish M.-stripe, reddish outside, with white flaky wool and H., with fine white Br.; **Fr.** with white H. and woolly flock; **S.** brown to black.—N. Chile (near Copiapó) (FR 494).

N. deherdtiana Backbg.—Descr. Cact. Nov. III: 9. 1963.
Bo. broadly spherical, ashy-grey to greenish; **Ri.** c. 12, with oblong tubercular swellings around the Ar.; **Ar.** oblong, with yellowish to white felt at first; **Sp.** to c. 6, erect at first, black, sometimes lighter below, rather short, to c. 1 cm lg.; **Fl.** appearing when the plant is only c. 3.5 cm $\varnothing$, funnelform, yellow, reddish-yellow outside, fairly large, on younger plants and even when half-open with the length equalling the plant's $\varnothing$; **Tu.** densely scaly, with curly H., these fairly dense on the bud.—Chile (locality ?). (Fig. 255, above.)
Plants in the collection of Saint-Pie, Asson (France) under Ritter's number FR251 as "Copiapoa fieldleriana"; there also under number FR

529. Either these numbers are the result of some confusion, or the plant closely resembling Cop. fiedleriana was identified by Ritter when not in flower. I have named it for the collector De Herdt of Mortsel, Antwerp, whom I have to thank for many careful observations.

N. dimorpha (Ritt.) Backbg.—Descr. Cact. Nov. III: 9. 1963 (Pyrrhocactus dimorphus Ritt., Succulenta, 1: 3–5. 1962).
Bo. hemispherical, 2–6 cm ∅, almost black; **R.** napiform, neck constricted; **Ri.** divided at first into Tub., later recognisably 13–16, very obtuse; **Ar.** white-felty; **Sp.** on new growth 6–10, 2–5 mm lg., all radials, thin, spreading laterally or appressed, black to ± white; on older St., Rsp. 8–12, to 2 cm lg., black to yellowish or light, upper ones sometimes longer, ± curving; **Csp.** 1–3, projecting, black to brownish, also horn-coloured and de-curved; **Fl.** to 3.5 cm lg., broadly funnelform, white-woolly below, Br. fine, yellowish; **Pet.** light to brownish-yellow, bordered whitish; **Sti.** reddish; **Fr.** 1.5 cm lg., red, hairy; **S.** dark brown. —Chile (Coquimbo). (Fig. 255, below) (FR 707.)

N. dueluta hort. Ritt.?
Bo. 45 mm ∅, 50 mm h., spherical, later oblong, simple, brownish to blackish-green; **Ri.** 13, spiral-led, divided into rounded Tub., with an obtuse projection below the Ar.; **Ar.** round, sparsely woolly; **Rsp.** c. 8–15, to 6 mm lg., radiating, ± bent, grey, darker towards the tip; **Csp.** (0–)1, bent upwards, dark reddish to blackish, 7–10 mm lg.; **Fl.** pale yellow, with white wool and Br. outside; **Fr.** with white wool and Br.; **S.** brown.—Chile.

N. duripulpa (Ritt.) Backbg.—Descr. Cact. Nov. III: 9. 1963 (Chileorebutia duripulpa Ritt., "Taxon", XII: 3, 123. 1963).
Bo. mostly simple, spherical, elongated in culti-vation, greyish-green to olive, 3–4.5 cm ∅; **R.** napiform, to 20 cm lg. and 3 cm ∅; **Ri.** resolved into Tub. 2–3 mm h., 3–5 mm br.; **Ar.** 1.5–3 mm apart; **Rsp.** 2–6(–10) mm lg., pectinate, fairly robust white or brown, appressed; **Csp.** mostly 0(–1); **Fl.** to 3.3 cm lg., 2.5 cm ∅, scented; **Ov.** white-woolly, without Br.; **Tu.** with several Br. 1 cm lg.; **Pet.** to 1.5 cm lg., sulphur-yellow, spotted brown; **Fil.** pale yellow; style purple below, pink above; **Fr.** red; **pulp** hard; **S.** 1.5 mm lg., matt brown.—N. Chile (Huasco) (FR 1056). (Fig. 256.) The Fr., acc. Ritter, is "hard-fleshed"; this could signify (cf. N. recondita) one of the many possible modifications, or else that there are only un-important differences between the more fleshy Fr. of the Reicheocactus-type, and the hollow Fr. of, say, R. neoreichei, which in turn affects the question of classification, even within any genus.

N. duripulpa bears Ritter's number FR 1056; the above description was made on the basis of living material I saw in the collection of the skilful Dutch collector, W. van Marle, who met his early death in an accident.

N. ebenacantha (hort. non Monv.) Backbg.: **Neochilenia hankeana** (Först.) Dölz.

N. eriocephala Backbg.
Bo. small-spherical, dark in colour, offsetting; **Ri.** resolved into small Tub.; **Ar.** with strong white hairy felt, forming a white tuft in the crown; **Sp.** scarcely differentiated, c. 10–12, irregularly placed, flexible, ± projecting, sometimes slightly curving, light to dirty white (also darker?); **Fl.** and **Fr.** ?— Chile.

N. eriosyzoides (Ritt.) Backbg.
Bo. hemispherical, later elongated, to 14 cm ∅, bluish to greyish-green; **R.** forming a longer woody taproot; **Ri.** 13–17, chin-like below the Ar.; **Ar.** to 1 cm lg.; **Rsp.** c. 10–15, 1.5–4 cm lg.; **Csp.** 4–7, 2–5 cm lg.; **Sp.** curving upwards, sometimes strongly bent, Rsp. also later spreading laterally, all rather variable in colour, ± yellowish-brownish, some-times darker tipped or greyish-black; **Fl.** c. 3.25 cm lg., 3 cm ∅, satiny, light brownish-yellow, with a carmine M.-stripe, with white flocky H. and pungent Br.-Sp.; **Fr.** c. 2 cm lg., ± reddish-green to red, very white-woolly.—Chile (Huanta). A parti-cularly attractive spec.; seedling plants are more laxly spined, some Sp. being stouter, bent upwards. (FR 484).

N. esmeraldana (Ritt.) Backbg.—Descr. Cact. Nov. III: 9. 1963 (Chileorebutia esmeraldana Ritt., "Taxon", XIII: 3, 123. 1963).
Bo. ± broadly spherical, offsetting, dark to reddish; **Ri.** resolved into ± chin-like Tub. 2.5 mm br.; **Ar.** to 1.5 mm ∅, oval, white at first; **Rsp.** 4–12, 2–7 mm lg., yellow, brown or (rarely) black; **Csp.** 1 (or few); **Fl.** 4.5–5 cm lg.; **Ov.** with brownish-green Sc. and lighter or darker Sp.; **Sep.** greenish; **Pet.** to 2.5 cm lg., pale greenish-yellow; **Tu.** to 15 mm lg., with pale red Sc.; **Fr.** red.—N. Chile (Esmeraldas; rare). (Fig. 257.)

N. floccosa (Ritt.) Backbg.—Descr. Cact. Nov. III: 9. 1963 (Pyrrhocactus floccosus Ritt., "Taxon", XII: 1. 32. 1963).
Bo. to 6 cm ∅, to 30 cm lg., green; **R.** scarcely napiform; **Ri.** 13, 7–10 mm h., notched, ± obtuse, Tub. small; **Ar.** 5 mm lg., a few mm apart, set with many white H. to 2 cm lg.; **Sp.** black or greyish-brown, acicular, straight; **Rsp.** 8–10, 7–20 mm lg.; **Csp.** 1–2(–4), 10–25 mm lg.; **Fl.** to 3.3 cm lg., white; **Fil.** white; **Tu.** with many white H. and some white

Br.; **style** red; **Sti.** golden-yellow; **Fr.** oblong, red above, green below; **S.** dark brown.—N. Chile (coast, Prov. Antofagasta) (FR 545).

N. fobeana (Mieckl.) Backbg.
Bo. spherical, somewhat caespitose, to 10 cm h., 8 cm ∅, blackish-green; **Ri.** 14, spiralled; **Ar.** white-felty; **Rsp.** 8–9, middle ones longer, 10–12 mm lg., radiating, intense black at first, tipped ± brownish-white; **Csp.** 1–2, often absent; there is also a lighter-spined form; **Fl.** pale yellow, with white wool, with Br.—Chile (origin ?).

N. fulva: see **Neochilenia aerocarpa** v. **fulva** (Ritt.) Backbg.

N. fusca (Mühlpf.) Backbg.
Bo. eventually elongated, dull brown; **Ri.** 13, tuberculate; **Ar.** white-woolly; **Rsp.** c. 7, to c. 1.7 cm lg., uppers and laterals terete, 3 lower ones flattened-terete, middle one pressed downwards, black, soon ± light grey; **Csp.** mostly 1, longer, bent ± upwards; **Fl.** glossy, delicate yellow, dirty reddish outside. There are forms with the Bo. more greyish-brown, and Fl. white to pink.—Chile. Horridocactus taltalensis Ritt. (FR 212), with brown Bo. and whitish Fl., is synonymous.

N. glabrescens (Ritt.): perhaps a form or variety of **Neochilenia mitis** (Phil.) Backbg. or N. napina (Phil.) Backbg.

N. glaucescens (Ritt.) Backbg.—Descr. Cact. Nov. III: 9. 1963 (Pyrrhocactus glaucescens Ritt., "Taxon", XII: 1, 33. 1963).
Differs from N. floccosa in the following: **Bo.** bluish-green; **R.** short-napiform; **Ri.** more strongly notched; **Ar.** with shorter white woolly H.; **Tub.** stouter; **Sp.** black; **Rsp.** 8–13; **Csp.** 1–4, 1.5–3 cm lg.; **Tu.** and **Ov.** less hairy; **S.** 1 mm lg.—N. Chile (coast, El Cobre) (FR 538).

N. gracilis (Ritt.) Backbg.—Descr. Cact. Nov. III: 9. 1963 (Pyrrhocactus gracilis Ritt., Succulenta, 12: 129. 131. 1961).
Bo. flat to hemispherical, 3–5 cm ∅, blackish-green; **Ri.** 13–16, notched; **Ar.** white-felty; **Rsp.** 10–16, 0.7–1.5 cm lg., hair-like, straight, appressed, ± white; **Csp.** 4–5, 1.5–2.5 cm lg., stouter, acicular, upcurving, greyish-brown to greyish-black; **Fl.** c. 2.7–3.3 cm lg., white, with white woolly H.; **Sep.** purple, bordered white, over 1 cm lg.; **Br.** white; **Fr.** small, green; **S.** dark brown.—N. Chile (near Caldera) (FR 495).

N. hankeana (Först.) Dölz
Bo. spherical at first, then oblong, leaf-green; **Ri.** 12–13, divided by transverse furrows into chin-like

Tub.; **Ar.** yellowish-white, large; **Rsp.** c. 7; **Csp.** 1–4, the only one (or the uppermost) to 3 cm lg., bent upwards; **Sp.** black at first, later becoming concolorous whitish-grey from the base up; **Fl.** 3–4 cm lg. and ∅, creamy-white, with H. and darker Br.; **Sep.** with a pink to brownish M.-stripe.—Chile.
   v. **minor** (Oehme) Backbg.: differs in having shorter **Sp.**
   v. **taltalensis** (Ritt.) Backbg.: **Sp.** fewer, lighter; **Tu.** with longer H.; **Fl.** more yellowish to yellow (FR 212).

N. huascensis (Ritt.) Backbg.—Descr. Cact. Nov. III: 9. 1963 (Pyrrhocactus huascensis Ritt., Succulenta, 6: 57–58. 1961).
Bo. hemispherical, later oblong, to 8 cm ∅, greyish-green; **R.** napiform, white; **Ri.** 12–16, with chin-like Tub.; **Ar.** large; **Rsp.** 5–8, 1.5–3 cm lg., slightly bent; **Csp.** 1–4, projecting to upcurving; **Sp.** black to brown; **Fl.** to c. 4.5 cm lg., carmine-reddish, bordered white, with white wool and numerous white Br.; **Fr.** white-woolly; **S.** brown.—N. Chile (near Huasco) (FR 260).

N. hypogaea (Ritt.) Backbg.: **Copiapoa hypogaea** Ritt.

N. imitans Backbg.
Bo. dwarf, compressed-spherical to spherical, to c. 4–5 cm ∅, olive-green; **R.** thick-napiform, constricted above; **Ri.** in spiralled Tub.; **Ar.** and **crown** with slight greyish-white felt; only **Rsp.** present, 5 main ones to 2 mm lg., straight, yellowish to whitish-hyaline at first, rather darker below, 1–3 Ssp. in the upper part of the Ar., very fine; **Fl.** c. 2.5 cm lg., 4 cm and more ∅, yellowish, densely hairy, with Br. above. Outstanding because the Fl. are sometimes larger than the Bo.—Chile. Chileorebutia odieri sensu Ritt. is probably identical.

N. intermedia (Ritt.) Backbg.—Descr. Cact. Nov. III: 9. 1963 (Pyrrhocactus intermedius Ritt., "Taxon", XII: 1, 32. 1963).
Bo. ± oblong, 4–10 cm ∅, dark green; **R.** napiform, white; **Ri.** higher than in N. rupicola, more deeply notched, Tub. more acute; **Ar.** larger; **Rsp.** 10–15, 8–30 mm lg., acicular; **Csp.** 4–7, stouter, straight or ± incurving, 2–4 cm lg.; **Fl.** borne in summer; **Ov.** and **Fr.** less hairy, scarcely bristly (?), but Tu. white-bristly above; **Pet.** 1 cm lg., 3 mm br., colour ?; **Fil.** white; **S.** dark brown.—N. Chile (mountains N. of Chañaral air-strip) (FR 213c).

N. iquiquensis (Ritt.) Backbg.—Descr. Cact. Nov. III: 9. 1963 (Pyrrhocactus iquiquensis Ritt., "Taxon", XII: 1, 32: 1963).

Bo. hemispherical, to 6 cm ∅, bluish-green; **R.** napiform, short; **Ri.** 10–16, 5–8 mm h., deeply notched, Tub. ± chin-like; **Ar.** to 6 mm lg., brownish; **Sp.** greyish-brown; **Rsp.** 8–10, 3–10 mm lg., straight; **Csp.** 2–4(–6), 6–12 mm lg., slightly incurving; **Fl.** c. 2.3 cm lg., pale yellow; **Tu.** funnelform to ± beaker-shaped, with white H. and some short Br.; **Fil.** white; **style** pale yellow, Sti. similarly; **Fr.** dark chestnut-brown, ± oblong; **S.** 1.2 mm lg., dark, rough, hilum small, white.—N. Chile (near Iquique) (FR 201).

N. jussieui (Monv.) Backbg. (T.)
Bo. ± spherical, brownish to blackish-green to dark reddish; **Ri.** 13–16, tuberculate; **Ar.** with slight yellow felt; **Rsp.** 7–14, upper ones stouter; **Csp.** 1–2, to 2.5 cm lg.; **Sp.** white, becoming brownish to horn-coloured, dark-tipped, curving ± upwards; **Fl.** to 4 cm lg. and ∅, Pet. pale pink, with a darker M.-stripe; Tu. distinctly hairy, with Br. above.—Chile.

N. krausii (Ritt.) Backbg.
Bo. small-spherical, to c. 4 cm ∅, freely offsetting, ± greyish-green to yellow; **R.** long-napiform; **Ri.** completely resolved in small Tub.; **Ar.** very white-woolly, confluent above to form a white apical tuft; **Rsp.** to 10, minute, subulate, ± projecting and spreading in all directions, not pubescent, ± hyaline below, darker-tipped; **Csp.** mostly 1, little longer, porrect; **Fl.** to 3.5 cm lg. and ∅, delicately perfumed, light to greenish-yellow, with very tufted H. and thin twisted brownish-red Br.; **Fr.** pale red, very woolly and fine-bristly; **S.** black.—Chile (Dept. Copiapo) (FR 502).

N. kunzei (Först.) Backbg.
Bo. becoming oblong, to c. 20 cm h. and 7.5 cm ∅, green; **Ri.** 16 (acc. K. Sch., to 21), tuberculately notched, Tub. confluent and acute; **Ar.** elliptic, weakly felty; **Rsp.** 10–12, to 4 cm lg.; **Csp.** 2–4, to 5 cm lg., stouter; **Sp.** ± upcurving, yellowish to dark above, especially in the crown; **Fl.** (acc. Oehme) 3.5 cm lg. and ∅, glossy, yellowish-white with much white wool and several black Br.—Chile (Prov. Coquimbo, Copiapo).

N. lembckei Backbg.
Bo. dwarf-spherical, probably always simple, greyish-green; **R.** long-napiform, constricted; **Ri.** completely resolved into minute spiralled Tub.; **Ar.** with greyish to yellowish-white felt, forming a ± dense woolly cap in the crown; **Sp.** radial only, c. 8, paired, sometimes 1 lower one, all very short and thin, rough, bent, appressed; **Fl.** not known.—Chile.

|N. longirapa Ritt. (FR 1321): no description available.

N. malleolata (Ritt.) Backbg.—Descr. Cact. Nov. III: 9. 1963 (Chileorebutia malleolata Ritt., "Taxon", XII: 3, 123. 1963)
Bo. greyish-green, caespitose; **Ri.** divided into Tub. 4–8 mm lg., 3.6 mm br., 3–4 mm h., with an obtuse chin; **Ar.** 2–4 mm lg.; **Rsp.** 4–8, 2–4 mm lg., incurving, brownish to yellowish; **Csp.** 0; **Fl.** 4 cm lg.; **Ov.** with brown Sc. and pale Br.; **Tu.** 1 cm lg., with longer and still paler Sc.; **Sep.** and Pet. ± linear, 2 cm lg., pale brownish-yellow; **Fil.** pale yellow; **S.** 1 mm lg., reddish-black.—Chile (N. of Chañaral) (FR 517).
  v. **solitaria** Ritt. (FR 517a)—l. c.: **Bo.** not caespitose; **Tub.** less crowded; **Rsp.** 4–12, 2–7 mm lg., yellow or brown, rarely black; **Csp.** sometimes 1; **Fl.** 4.5–5 cm lg.; **Ov.** with brownish-green Sc.; **Br.** pale or darker; **Tu.** to 15 mm lg.; **Br.** pale red; **Sep.** and **Pet.** pale greenish-yellow, with still paler borders; **Fr.** red; **S.** 1 mm lg.—Chile (Esmeralda; very rare).

N. mebbesii (Hildm.) Backbg.
Bo. subspherical, later ± oblong, green; **Ri.** c. 14, with many chin-like Tub.; **Rsp.** 7–10, to c. 0.5 cm lg., ± appressed, horn-coloured, ± darker-tipped; **Fl.** c. 5 cm ∅, white to pink, white-woolly.—Chile.
  v. **centrispina** Backbg.: **Csp.** 1–3, considerably darker, especially in the crown, ± black-tipped.

N. mitis (Phil.) Backbg.
Bo. simple, very small-spherical, c. 3.5 cm ∅, brownish to greyish-green; **R.** napiform; **Ri.** (only in seedlings?) forming low, sinuately divided surfaces, not tuberculate; **Ar.** weakly felty; **Sp.** 6–8, only 1–1.3 mm lg., radiating, appressed; buds green; **Fl.** 3.5–4 cm lg., 4 cm ∅, variable in colour: white (acc. Ritter: to pink, ± carmine or brownish), very white-hairy, with a few thin dark straight Br. above; **Fr.** red, very woolly; **S.** dark.— Chile (Dept. Copiapo). (Fig. 258.)

N. monte-amargensis Backbg.—Descr. Cact. Nov. III: 9. 1963.
Bo. depressed-spherical, offsetting freely from below, to c. 5 cm ∅, olive-green; **R.** napiform; **Ri.** c. 16, divided into elongated Tub., these more confluent at the base in age, to 5 mm lg. and h.; **Ar.** glabrous in the crown, 6 mm apart, rather sunken, later with dirty white felt, eventually becoming grey; **Rsp.** c. 11, radiating, not projecting, to 3 mm lg., ± rough, horn-coloured, soon dark; **Csp.** 0 at first, later 1(–2), the upper one ± curving to the crown, brownish, to 1 cm lg., the lower one projecting, to 6 mm lg.; **Fl.** ?—Chile (Monte Amargo: found by Lembcke). Noticeable on account of the broadly spherical shape and freely caespitose habit. (Fig. 259.)

N. napina (Phil.) Backbg.
Bo. small-spherical, quite elongated if grafted, greyish-green, sometimes suffused reddish; **R.** long-napiform, constricted above; **Ri.** c. 14, ± strongly tuberculate; **Tub.** prominent and chin-like; **Ar.** weakly felty to glabrous; **Rsp.** mostly 3–9, at most 3 mm lg., appressed to projecting, black; **Csp.** occasionally 1, blackish; buds brownish; **Sep.** bordered pale yellowish; **Fl.** 3–3.5 cm lg., pale yellow, with long flocky H., with dark curly Br. above; **Fr.** spherical to elongated, moderately woolly.—Chile (near Huasco). Grafted plants are more distinctly ribbed. (Fig. 260.) A variable spec., particularly in the spination. The following is more strongly differentiated:
   v. **spinosior** (Backbg.) Backbg.; **Rsp.** c. 10; **Csp.** to 4, stout, projecting, sometimes distinctly cruciform, black, at first lighter below; **Fl.** at first (or outside) ± suffused pink.
The plant illustrated on the cover of "Succulenta", 9 as Neoporteria napina v. spinosior, is in fact a completely different plant—Neoporteria microsperma Ritt.; this shows the importance of segregating Neoporteria and Neochilenia, because if this had been done, the confusion could not have arisen.
The true Neochilenia napina v. spinosior, with stouter, uniformly dark Sp., is illustrated in "Kaktusweelde", 9: 10, 11. 1963.

N. neofusca Backbg.
Bo. ± spherical, blackish-green, frosted white; **Ri.** at first strongly tuberculate; **Rsp.** 5–7; **Csp.** 1; **Sp.** stoutly subulate, those in the upper part of the Bo. bent more strongly upwards, thickened below, glossy, black; **Fl.** dull yellow, with woolly H.—Chile. Since Ritter (to whom I left the task) has not yet provided a detailed description, the above is taken from the short Latin diagnosis in "Die Cact.", III: 1811. 1959.

N. neoreichei Backbg.: **Reicheocactus neoreichei** (Backbg.) Backbg.

N. nigricans (Dietr.) Y. Ito: **Horridocactus nigricans** (Dietr.) Backbg. & Dölz.

N. nigriscoparia Backbg.
Bo. simple, to 4 cm h., 6 cm ∅, deep green to greyish-green; **R.** ± napiform; **Ri.** 15–19, later divided into chin-like Tub.; **Ar.** weakly felty; **Sp.** to 3.8 cm lg., stiff-bristly and stouter, erect, ± interlacing, black to brownish-black, sometimes densely covering the Bo., sometimes lighter below; **Fl.** bellshaped-funnelform, to 3 cm lg., 2.5 cm ∅, light pink, with fine H. and some twisted white Br.; **Fr.** hairy; **S.**. black.—Chile.

N. occulta (Phil.) Backbg.
Bo. dwarf, 1.3–2.5 cm ∅, sometimes caespitose, yellowish-brownish to blackish; **Ri.** 8–10, very warty; **Ar.** weakly felty; **Rsp.** 6–10, some fine, only 4 mm lg., the lowest one twice as long; **Csp.** 0–1, to 1.7 cm lg. (and more); **Sp.** spreading to ± bent, black, becoming grey; **Fl.** c. 2.5 cm lg., pale golden-yellow, with long white wool, with pale yellow Br.—Chile (Copiapo to Cobre).

N. odieri (Lem.) Backbg.
Bo. subspherical, later ± oblong, to 6 cm ∅, greyish to reddish-brown; **Ri.** c. 13, very tuberculate above, **Tub.** blistery, ± spiralled, Ri. ± continuous lower down; **Ar.** weakly felty; **Rsp.** 6–10, to 0.5 cm lg., thin, ± reddish-brown, blackish at first, ± appressed; **Csp.** 0; **Fl.** c. 5 cm ∅, white (to pink), white-woolly.—Chile (Copiapo, Huasco).

N. odieri v. mebbesii (Hildm.) Y. Ito: **Neochilenia mebbesii** (Hildm.) Backbg.

N. odoriflora (Ritt.) Backbg.
Bo. simple, flattened-spherical to hemispherical, dark greyish-green; **Ri.** 10–16, scarcely tuberculate, thick, obtuse; **Ar.** c. 1 cm lg., grey-felty; **Rsp.** 7–10, mostly over 2 cm lg., greyish-brown, greying; **Csp.** 4–7, 2–3 cm lg., ± flattened, strongly spreading, curving; **Fl.** 4–5 cm lg., 5–6 cm ∅, white with a pink M.-stripe, very white-woolly, with numerous white, long, fine Br.; **Fr.** red, white-woolly.—Central Chile (above Pichidangui) (FR 470).

N. paucicostata (Ritt.) Backbg.
Bo. simple, hemispherical, later ± elongated, with a thicker taproot, bluish or greyish-green, suffused whitish; **Ri.** 8–12, ± tuberculate, **Tub.** in the lower part ± prominent and chin-like; **Ar.** greyish to white-felty, medium-sized; **Rsp.** 5–8, 1–2 upper ones shorter and thinner, slightly angular, ± recurved; **Csp.** 1 at first, later to 4, to 4 cm lg., ± upcurving; **Sp.** greyish-black, lighter later; **Fl.** c. 3–5 cm lg., to 5 cm ∅, reddish-white, or white, and only reddish outside, hairy, with several brown to black Br.; **Fr.** reddish, white-hairy.—N. Chile (near Paposo) (FR 521).
Ritter's original photograph shows how necessary it is to show the plants in habitat and also in cultivation; in the former, the dense and rigidly projecting spines interlace to conceal the body; the spination of cultivated plants is much laxer.
   v. **viridis** (Ritt.) Backbg.: **Bo.** darker pure green; **Ri.** 13; **Rsp.** almost always 8; the **Fl.** I have seen were pinkish-white; transitional to N. hankeana (FR 521a).

N. pilispina (Ritt.) Backbg.—Descr. Cact. Nov. III:
9. 1963 (Pyrrhocactus pilispinus Ritt., Succulenta,
4: 42–44. 1962).
Bo. simple, hemispherical, 4–5 cm ∅, blackish-
green, with a long taproot; **Ri.** 13–16, spiralled,
with chin-like protuberances; **Ar.** sunken; **Rsp.** c.
6, 0.5–2 cm lg., **Csp.** 2–3, 1–3 cm lg.; **Sp.** very thin,
curving upwards and twisted, brown to black; **Fl.**
2.5–3 cm lg., borne close to the apex, ± scented,
white, with acuminate Sc., lax H. and yellowish
Br.; **Fr.** reddish to olive-brown above, with white
flock; **S.** brownish-black.—N. Chile (Atacama).
(Fig. 261.) Very close to Neoch. pygmaea (Ritt.).

N. pseudoreichei Lembcke & Backbg.
Bo. simple, to c. 4.5 cm ∅, very flat, olive-green,
later greying; **R.** stout-napiform, not constricted;
crown sunken, weakly felty; **Ri.** divided into
oblong-conical Tub. which are ± prominent below
the Ar.; **Rsp.** 10, to 2 mm lg., pectinate; **Csp.** later 1
to 3.5 mm lg., projecting ± towards the apex; **Sp.**
rather rough, pale yellowish at first, later grey-
hyaline; **Fl.** not known.—Chile.

N. pulchella (Ritt.) Backbg. (Ritter: Pyrrhocactus): not described (perhaps a form of
Neochilenia pygmaea?)
This spec. is no longer featured in the newer Winter
catalogues: **Bo.** strong, dark, brownish-green, ±
broadly spherical; **Sp.** mostly curving towards the
apex but not completely covering this, c. 12, some
of them more central, all at first partly dark brown,
partly lighter horn-coloured; **Fl.** and **Fr.** more
strongly white-hairy.—Chile.

N. pygmaea (Ritt.) Backbg.—Descr. Cact. Nov.
III: 9. 1963 (Pyrrhocactus pygmaeus Ritt.,
"Taxon", XII. 1, 32. 1963).
Bo. flat, bluish-grey or green, 3–5 cm ∅; **R.**
napiform, short, conical; **Ri.** (10–)11–13(–16), with
rather obtuse chin-like Tub.; **Ar.** 2–4 mm lg.,
white; **Sp.** dark brown or black; **Rsp.** 7–12, thin,
5–20 mm lg.; **Csp.** 1–4, stouter, 10–14 mm lg.; **Fl.** in
spring, 3 cm lg., white to greenish, with white hair,
bristly; **Fil.** bluish-green; **Fr.** with similar indumentum, red; **S.** 0.9 mm lg., hilum white.—N. Chile
(20 km N. of Chañaral, on the coast) (FR 519).

N. recondita (Ritt.) Backbg.—Descr. Cact. Nov.
III: 10. 1963 (Pyrrhocactus reconditus Ritt.,
Succulenta, 3: 27–29. 1962; earlier referred to
Chileorebutia).
Bo. dwarf, rarely offsetting, flat to hemispherical,
2.5–4.5 cm ∅, bluish or greyish-green; **R.** nap-
iform, constricted; **Ri.** 10–12, divided into chin-like
Tub.; **Ar.** white-felty, sunken; **Rsp.** 6–10, 0.5–1 cm
lg., fine, acicular, appressed to ± projecting; **Csp.**
1–2, 1–1.5 cm lg., stouter, ± upcurving; **Sp.** black

at first, greying; **Fl.** very close to the apex, 3.5–4.5
cm lg., c. 2.5–3.5 cm ∅, white to slightly yellowish;
Sep. reddish, bordered white, with white wool and
dense fine Br. which are curving to ± projecting,
brown to black, over 1 cm lg.; **Fr.** ± carmine, to 4
cm lg., hollow, as is common in the genus, but the **S.**
remaining attached and released only when the Fr.
has dried (FR 204). The fact that the fully ripe S.
still remain in the Fr., reveals Ritter's term
"Windfrucht" to be a fiction; here, yet again,
Nature has created one more variant, and I have
therefore preferred the more appropriate term:
"hollow Fr.".

N. reichei (K. Sch.) Backbg. (Chileorebutia reichei
[K. Sch.] Ritt., "Taxon", XII: 3, 124. 1963).
Bo. dwarf, simple, depressed-spherical, ± greyish-
green; **crown** sunken, concealed by much woolly
flock and interlacing small Sp.; **Ri.** completely
divided into Tub.; **Ar.** white-felty, soon glabrous;
Sp. 7–9, to 3 mm lg., radiating, appressed, not
pungent, straight or slightly bent, hyaline or white,
greying; **Fl.** to 3.3 cm lg., 3–4 cm ∅, glossy, yellow,
with white wool and several fine Br.—Chile.

Ritter (l. c.) states: **Sp.** 10–14; **Fl.** with grey or black
H.; **Pet.** greenish or reddish; **Sti.** red; **Fr.** more
strongly woolly. Since the FR number is missing
here, and the earlier number FR 501 of the same
name was a bristle-less spec. of Reicheocactus in
which the data regarding Sp. and Fl. differed from
Schumann's description, Ritter's new combination
as above remains from several points of view a
nomen dubium.

N. residua (Ritt.) Backbg.—Descr. Cact. Nov. III:
10. 1963 (Pyrrhocactus residuus Ritt., "Taxon",
XII: 1, 33. 1963).
Differentiated as follows from N. recondita: **Bo.**
4–8 cm ∅; **Ri.** 12–14; **Tub.** rather obtuse; **Ar.** grey;
Sp. pale or dark brown; **Rsp.** 10–12; **Csp.** 2–5(–8),
1–3 cm lg.; **Tu.** with white H. and white Br.; **Ov.**
white-hairy, without Br.; **Fr.** similarly.—N. Chile
(coastal ranges near Antofagasta) (FR 203). (Fig.
263.)

N. robusta (Ritt.) Backbg. and v. vegasana (Ritt.)
Backbg.: **Horridocactus robustus** Ritt. and v.
vegasanus Ritt.

N. rostrata (Jac.) Backbg.: **Neoporteria subgibbosa**
(Haw.) Br. & R.

N. rupicola (Ritt.) Backbg.—Descr. Cact. Nov. III:
10. 1963 (Pyrrhocactus rupicolus Ritt., "Taxon",
XII: 1, 32. 1963).
Bo. to 8 cm ∅; **R.** not napiform; **Ri.** with larger
chin-like Tub.; **Ar.** to 10 mm lg., grey; **Sp.** dark;
Rsp. 10–20, moderately thin, quite strongly ap-

pressed, 8–20 mm lg.; **Csp.** 6–12, 3–5 cm lg.; **Fl.** in winter, quite moderately woolly, scarcely bristly(?), purple, bordered white or pink; **Fil.** white or purplish-pink; **An.** white or pale yellow; **S.** minutely tuberculate.—N. Chile, between Alorro (N. of Caldera) and Paposo, on cliffs and mountains (FR 213).

N. saxifraga (Ritt.) (Chileorebutia Ritt.): not described.

N. scoparia (Ritt.) Backbg. n. comb. (Pyrrhocactus scoparius Ritt., Succulenta, 5: 51–53, 1962).
Bo. simple, greyish to blackish-green, 3–6 cm ⌀, hemispherical; **R.** napiform, short, not constricted; **Ri.** 10–13, strongly divided into chin-like Tub.; **Ar.** deeply sunken, white-felty; **Rsp.** c. 5–10, 5–10 mm lg., very fine, or stouter and acicular, spreading sideways, to ± curving, light brown to almost white; **Csp.** 1–4, 1–1.5 cm lg., rather stouter, mostly straight, projecting; **Fl.** very close to the crown, c. 2.5 cm lg., light purple, bordered white, with white wool and several light Br.; **Fr.** c. 1 cm lg., light purple below, greenish-brown above.—Chile (Atacama).

N. setosiflora (Ritt.) Backbg.—Descr. Cact. Nov. III: 10. 1963 (Pyrrhocactus setosiflorus Ritt., Succulenta, 6:70–72, 1962).
Bo. flat to hemispherical, c. 4–6 cm ⌀, dark greyish-green; **R.** napiform, large, constricted above; **Ri.** 13–17, with obtuse chin-like Tub.; **Ar.** white-felty; **Rsp.** 12–14, 0.8–2 cm lg., straight, acicular, slightly yellowish, occasionally thinner and even black; **Csp.** 1–4(–10), stouter, 1.5–4 cm lg., light yellowish; **Fl.** 4–6.5 cm lg., faintly yellow, greenish-yellow to more purple, with white wool and Br.; **Fr.** reddish.—Central Chile (coast) (FR 708).
    v. **intermedia** (Ritt.) Backbg.—Descr. Cact. Nov. III: 10. 1963 (Ritter: Pyrrhocactus,—var., Succulenta, 6: 70. 1962): **Bo.** smaller; **Ar.** smaller; **Sp.** shorter; **Fl.** smaller; **Pet.** more obtuse; **Br.** few (FR 708a).

N. simulans (Ritt.) Backbg.—Descr. Cact. Nov. III: 10. 1963 (Pyrrhocactus simulans Ritt., Succulenta, 4: 35–36. 1961).
Bo. simple, hemispherical, later elongated, greyish-green; **crown** flat, with greyish-white wool; **R.** napiform; **Ri.** 11–13, little tuberculate; **Ar.** large, with orange-brownish felt; **Rsp.** 8–12, 1–3 cm lg., ± straight, fairly robust, occasionally finer; **Csp.** (1–)4–8, 2–4 cm lg., straight to ± curving; **Sp.** black, greying; **Fl.** 4–4.5 cm lg., carmine, bordered light yellowish, satiny, with much white wool, with white Br.; **Fr.** c. 1.5 cm lg., red.—N. Chile (FR 488).

N. taltalensis (Hutch.) Backbg.
Bo. simple, spherical, to 8 cm ⌀, matt dark green; **Ri.** 13, with chin-like Tub.; **Ar.** at first with light yellowish-brown felt; **Sp.** with radials merging into centrals; **Rsp.** c. 6–12, 0.3–2 cm lg., thin, ± flexible, straight, curving to twisted, brownish, later white; **Csp.** 6–12, to 3 cm lg., the innermost 1–4 to 3(–4) cm lg., thicker, stiffer, ± erect, slightly bent, at first dark greyish-brown to blackish; **Fl.** 3 cm lg., 2.5 cm ⌀ and more, fuchsia-purple, with white hairy wool, with twisted Br. above; **Fr.** ± purplish-blackish.—Chile (Taltal, Sierra Esmeralda). This must be Ritter's No. FR 212: "Pyrrhocactus taltalensis n.sp., red-flowered" (not to be confused with the more strongly yellowish-flowered Neochilenia hankeana v. taltalensis [Ritt.] Backbg.)
Ritter adds: "v. flaviflorus: yellow Fl."; the name should therefore read: **Neochilenia taltalensis v. flaviflora** (Ritt.) Backbg.: **Bo.** deep dark green; **Ri.** c. 14, with acute chin-like Tub.; **Rsp.** c. 18–20, uppers to 6, very thin, all ± curving; **Csp.** 4(–6), scarcely differentiated, all ± bent up or down, light-coloured; **Fl.** rather large, light yellow, reddish-yellow outside.—Chile (neighbourhood of Taltal). Description taken from seedling-plants. (Fig. 262, right.)

N. tenebrica Ritt. (FR 1092)
No detailed description available. **Bo.** dark; **Ri.** tuberculate; **Ar.** crowded, shortly white-woolly; **Rsp.** small; **Csp.** absent; **Fl.** whitish-yellowish, to 4 cm ⌀. Closely resembles N. nuda (FR 1425).

N. totoralensis (Ritt.) Backbg.—Descr. Cact. Nov. III: 10. 1963 (Pyrrhocactus totoralensis Ritt., Succulenta, 12: 131–132. 1961).
Bo. flat to hemispherical, 2–4 cm ⌀, dark bluish to greyish-green; with a constricted **taproot**; **Ri.** 12–14, Tub. strongly chin-like; **Ar.** white-felty; **Rsp.** 6–8, 1.5–3 cm lg., thin, spreading laterally, ± curving to the Bo., young plants sometimes with several very fine shorter **Ssp.**; **Csp.** 0–1(–2–3), 2–3 cm lg., rather stouter, curving strongly ± upwards; **Sp.** ± black at first, greying; **Fl.** c. 4 cm lg., white to light yellow, M.-stripe purple, with dense white wool and long white Br.; **Fr.** red.—Chile (Atacama, Totoral Bajo) (FR 495).

N. transitensis (Ritt.) Backbg.—Descr. Cact. Nov. III: 10. 1963 (Pyrrhocactus transitensis Ritt., "Taxon", XII: 1, 33. 1963).
Distinguished as follows from N. eriosyzoides: **Bo.** to 11 cm ⌀, greyish-green; **R.** very long-napiform, not constricted above; **Ri.** less prominent, without chin-Tub.; **Ar.** pale brownish, 8–13 mm lg.; **Sp.** stoutly acicular, curving inwards, to 3 cm lg., dark brown, later whitish-brown below, greyish-black above, becoming ash-grey; **Rsp.** 8–14; **Csp.** 4–7; **Fl.**

pale sulphur-yellow, sometimes with a red stripe; **Tu.** with soft Br.; **style** purple; **Sti.** golden-yellow; **Fr.** ± white-woolly; **S.** brown.—N. Chile (near Transito) (FR 485).

N. trapichensis Ritt. (Horridocactus, ace. Ritter): not described. [Haage adds: (FR 252 C): perhaps referable to Pyrrhocactus?]

N. wagenknechtii (Ritt.) Backbg.
Bo. simple, ± greyish-green, hemispherical; **R.** napiform, thick, yellowish; **Ri.** 18–22, fairly tuberculate; **Ar.** large, white-woolly; **Rsp.** 6–8, 1–2 cm lg.; **Csp.** 1–4, 2–3 cm lg., stouter, ± terete; **Sp.** probably variable, light to darker and ± blackish; **Fl.** 3–4 cm lg., to c. 3.5 cm ∅, from greenish to brownish-yellow, to yellow and red, to brownish-red or ± reddish-white; **Sep.** ± carmine.—Chile (near La Serena) (FR 487).

Neodawsonia Backbg. (164)

Cerei which, with one exception, are not branching but offset from below; dense white woolly hairs are developed in the apical flowering zone, with new growth continuing through this, so that the wool persists as a ring for some time. The ± funnelform-tubular flowers are pink and only moderately long, with scales and hairs on ovary and tube; the latter sometimes has short bristles. The fruit, as far as known, is small, pink, hairy, and shortly spiny, and dehisces above. The seeds are dark brown and finely pitted.—Distribution: Mexico (SW. Oaxaca).

N. apicicephalium (Daws.) Backbg. (T.)
Bo. simple at first, then branching from ± close to the base, 1–3 m h., dark bluish-green; **branches** to 10, 6.5–10 cm ∅, somewhat thickened at the apex of each annual growth; **Ri.** 22–27; **Ceph.** stoutly white-woolly, forming a woolly cap up to 4 cm. deep from the apex; **Ar.** elliptic; **Rsp.** 9–12, 1 cm lg. in the lower part of the Ar., or 2–3 cm lg., thin, bristly, ± curving to twisted; **Csp.** 2–4–6, 2–4 cm lg., decurved, 1 of these projecting and ± straight, stiffer, longest; **Sp.** straw-coloured at first, then dark brown; **Fl.** 5–6 cm lg., to 3 cm ∅, pink, tinged yellowish; **Ov.** with several thin flexible H.; **Fr.** and **S.** ?—Mexico (Oaxaca).

N. guiengolensis H. Bravo: **Neodawsonia apicicephalium** (Daws.) Backbg.

N. nana H. Bravo: **Neodawsonia apicicephalium** (Daws.) Backbg.

N. nizandensis H. Bravo & Th. MacDoug.

Bo. simple at first, to 3 m h., later branching above, light green; **branches** slightly curving, 12–15 cm ∅, thickened around the previous Fl.-zones; **Ri.** 25–28; **Ar.** circular to oval, white-woolly at first; **Ceph.** of dense, light yellowish-brown, silky H. and Br.; **Rsp.** c. 16, 1.5–3 cm lg., very thin, flexible, acicular, thickened below; **Csp.** c. 6, 1 stouter, 1 cm lg., projecting upwards, yellow; **Fl.** 4 cm lg., pink; **Ov.** with flexible H.; **Tu.-Sc.** with several H. and sometimes 1 Br.; **Fr.** and **S.** ?—Mexico (Oaxaca, between Nizanda and Chivela).

N. totolapensis H. Bravo & Th. MacDoug.
Bo. simple, to 8 m h., 12–15 cm ∅, greyish-green, thickened around previous Fl.-zones; **Ri.** c. 28; **Ar.** circular, with greyish-white felt; **Ceph.** yellowish, tinged ± brownish; **Rsp.** 10–13, 0.5–1.3 cm lg., lower ones longest, white, red-tipped; **Csp.** 3–6, similar to the Rsp. but slightly stouter; **Fl.** to 3.5 cm lg., pink; **Ov.** with long flexible white H.; **Tu.-Sc.** with few H. and stiff Br.; **Fr.** 2.5–3 cm ∅, pink, small-scaly, hairy, with short white Br.-Sp.; **S.** c. 2 mm lg., dark brown.—Mexico (Oaxaca, near Totolapan). (Fig. 264.)

Neoevansia Marsh., or N. diguetii (Web.) Marsh.: **Peniocereus** (Berg.) Br. & R., or **P. diguetii** (Web.) Backbg.

Neogomesia Castañ. (194)

Solitary smaller plants, with a thick, ± spherical taproot, with strongly elongated, leaf-like tubercles which are wrinkled and transversely fissured and rounded below. Spines are usually completely absent; if present, they are very short. The unique character is the position of the large, very woolly areoles, on the upper surface of the tubercles, at some distance from the tip. The pink, bellshaped to funnelform flowers, with a naked tube, arise from the newest areoles through the stout felt of the apex. The fruit is red, subspherical to clavate, with a kind of lid.—Genus monotypic at present.—Distribution: Mexico (Tamaulipas). [(G).] See introductory remarks on Ariocarpus regarding Anderson's attempts to unite Neogomesia with Ariocarpus.

N. agavioides Castañ. (T.)
Bo. above ground to c. 8 cm ∅, dark green, later greyish-green; **Tub.** to c. 4 cm lg., to c. 6 mm br., gradually tapering towards the ± recurved tip; **Ar.** to c. 1 cm ∅; **Sp.** only occasionally present, 1–3, at most 3–5 mm lg., white to horn-coloured, subulate, appressed; **Fl.** lasting only one day, to 5 cm lg.; **Sep.** few, scale-like; outer **Pet.** white with a pink centre, inner ones ± intense pink, white at the base; **Tu.** 2

cm lg. (and more), naked; **Fr.** to 2.5 cm lg., pink to purple, hilum sunken; **S.** black, pear-shaped, finely tuberculate, to 1.5 mm lg.—Mexico (near Tula, on limestone hills at 1200 m altitude). (Fig. 265.) Cutak sent me photos of a long-taprooted plant with longer slender Tub. and white-woolly Ar.; no precise data regarding Fl.; this may be referable to the preceding spec., which has never been re-collected.

Neolloydia Br. & R. (215)

A genus related to Coryphantha; plants in part mat-forming, with bodies ± cylindric, the tubercles furrowed. The flowers are medium-large, greenish-yellow, yellowish-pink, yellow or purplish-violet. The fruit, which is not watery, is rather dull in colour, and becomes papery as it dries. The species are divided into 2 subgenera:

SG.1: Neolloydia: Plants not mat-forming, the furrow running the entire length of the tubercle, seeds matt black;

SG.1: Cumarinia (Knuth) Backbg.: Plants mat-forming, furrow not as long as the tubercle, seeds shiny to semi-matt, black.

The appropriate subgenus is indicated in brackets after the specific name.—Distribution: USA to Mexico, Cuba. [(R) but grafting recommended.]

Neolloydia beguinii (Web.) Br. & R.: **Gymnocactus beguinii** (Web.) Backbg.

N. ceratites (Quehl) Br. & R. (1)
Bo. ovoid, simple or in small groups, to 10 cm h., to 5 cm ∅; **Tub.** in 10 spiralled R., ± rhomboid; **Ar.** round, weakly woolly at first; **Rsp.** c. 15, to 1.5 cm lg., bulbously thickened below, spreading, whitish-grey (appearing frosted), translucent, sometimes tipped dark brown; **Csp.** 5(–6), in a circle, 1 middle Sp. projecting, straight to ± curving, thickened below, whitish-grey or horn-coloured or light to dark brown, mostly black-tipped; **Ax.** white-woolly; **Fl.** 3–3.5 cm lg., purple.—Mexico. (Fig. 266, right.)

N. clavata (Schweidr.) Br. & R.: **Coryphantha clavata** (Scheidw.) Backbg.

N. conoidea (DC.) Br. & R. (1) (T.)
Bo. simple to offsetting, either from the base or laterally, ± ovoid-conical, 7–10 cm h., 5–7 cm ∅, light to greyish-green; **Ax.** strongly woolly; **Tub.** rather lax, ovoid, obtuse; **Rsp.** c. 16, 0.8–1 cm lg., thin, stiff, radiating white, greying; **Csp.** 4–5, 1–3 cm lg., spreading, black; **Fl.** to 6 cm ∅, purplish-violet.—USA (Texas), Mexico (Zacatecas,

Hidalgo).

N. cubensis (Br. & R.) Backbg. (2)
Bo. later mat-forming, individual heads depressed-spherical, 2–3 cm ∅, dull green; **Tub.** numerous, compressed, 6–7 mm lg.; **Rsp.** to c. 10, 3–4 mm lg., acicular, weak, spreading sideways; **Csp.** 0–1, short; **Sp.** whitish; **Fl.** c. 1.6 cm lg., pale yellowish-green; **S.** semi-matt.—Cuba (Prov. Oriente).

N. emskoetteriana (Quehl) Craig: **Escobaria emskoetteriana** (Quehl) Backbg.

N. gielsdorfiana (Werd.) Knuth: **Gymnocactus gielsdorfianus** (Werd.) Backbg.

N. grandiflora (O.) Berg. (1)
Bo. cylindric, to 10 cm h.; **Tub.** only moderately lax, rather short; **Ax.** and young **Ar.** freely white woolly; **Rsp.** to c. 25, radiating horizontally, ± curving, flattened laterally, ± white below; **Csp.** 0–1–2, porrect, stout, black; **Fl.** large, widely opening, purple.—USA (Texas) to Mexico (Tamaulipas, near Jaumave). (Fig. 266, left.)

N. horripila (Lem.) Br. & R.: **Gymnocactus horripilus** (Lem.) Backbg.

N. knuthiana (Böd.) Knuth: **Gymnocactus knuthianus** (Böd.) Backbg.

N. matehualensis Backbg. (1)
Bo. cylindric, offsetting from the base, to 15 cm h., 5 cm ∅, pale greyish-green; **Tub.** inclined upwards and appressed, flattened, c. 2 cm across the base; **Ax.** weakly white-felty; **Ar.** white-felty, soon glabrous; **Rsp.** c. 10(–12), to 1 cm lg., hyaline, greyish-white; **Csp.** 2 at first, to 2.2 cm lg., 1 directed upwards, 1 downwards, later to 3 Sp., thickened below; **Fl.** ? (purple?).—Mexico (San Luis Potosí, near Matehuala).

N. odorata (Böd.) Backbg. (2)
Bo. offsetting from the base to form mats, single heads ± spherical, to 3 cm ∅, glossy, dark leaf-green; **Tub.** cylindric, c. 1 cm lg., strongly rounded-truncate above; **Ar.** not white-felty or only at first; **Rsp.** 7–9, to 1 cm lg., spreading horizontally, straight, stiff, thin-acicular, slightly rough and appearing frosted, white, sometimes tipped dark brown or honey-colour; **Csp.** 3–4, 2–2.5 cm lg., strongly and irregularly radiating, stouter-acicular, straight, stiff, rough, thickened below, all hooked, reddish to blackish-brown; **Fl.** c. 1.5 cm lg., to 1 cm ∅, yellowish-pink; **S.** shiny, black.—Mexico (Tamaulipas, San Luis Potosí).

N. orcuttii Rose: **Escobaria orcuttii** Böd.

N. pilispina Br. & R. non J. A. Purp. (?)
Bo. forming groups; **Tub.** ± angular, no data regarding furrows; **Ar.** with much white wool on new growth, this covering the apex; **Rsp.** 6–7, 5–6 mm lg., weak, spreading, upper ones c. 2 cm lg., bending together over the crown, white, tipped blackish; **Csp.** 0–1; **Fl.** 1.5–2 cm lg., purple; **Fr.** and **S.** ?—Mexico (San Luis Potosí, Minas de San Rafael).

N. pulleineana Backbg. (1)
Bo. clavate-cylindric, thin at first, ± twisted, to c. 20 cm lg., 1.5 cm ∅, later also branching, dark green; **R.** long-napiform; **Tub.** rounded-conical, ± compressed; **Rsp.** to 18, to 1.2 cm lg., stiff, subulate, interlacing, dirty grey; **Csp.** 3(–4), 3 stouter, 1 averagely so, erect, thickened below, longest one to 2 cm lg., directed obliquely upwards, later ± downwards, very stiffly subulate, all dirty greyish-brown, the longest one ± banded; **Fl.** yellow. —Mexico (San Luis Potosí, near Matehuala).

N. roseana (Böd.) Knuth: **Escobaria roseana** (Böd.) Backbg.

N. saueri (Böd.) Knuth: **Gymnocactus saueri** (Böd.) Backbg.

N. texensis Br. & R.: acc. Bödeker, this is the Texan form of **Neolloydia conoidea** (DC.) Br. & R.

N. viereckii (Werd.) Knuth: **Gymnocactus viereckii** (Werd.) Backbg.

N. warnockii Benson (=**Echinomastus** Glass & Foster)
Bo. simple, bluish-green, ovoid, 7–11 cm lg., 5–7.5 cm ∅; **Ri.** 13–21; **Tub.** 9 mm lg.; **Ar.** elliptic, 3 mm lg., 9 mm apart; **Sp.** dense, covering the Bo., matt light brown; **Csp.** 4, tipped chalky-blue, or brown in part, longer ones directed upwards, 1.2–2.5 cm lg.; **Rsp.** 12–14, spreading, weakly curving; **Fl.** c. 2.5 cm lg. and ∅; **Sep.** white to pink, with a green M.-stripe, longest ones lanceolate, 9–12 mm lg.; **Pet.** pink, to 12 mm lg.; **Fr.** green, brownish at maturity, with few Sc.; **S.** black.—Mexico (Chihuahua), USA (Texas, New Mexico); at altitudes of 560–1200 m. Named for Dr. B. H. Warnock who has collected the spec. on several occasions since 1947.

Neolobivia Y. Ito non Backbg.: an invalid generic name for **Pseudolobivia** Backbg. **pro parte.**

Neomammillaria Br. & R.: **Mammillaria** Haw. non Stackhouse.

Neoporteria Br. & R. emend. Backbg. (125)

Chilean species of spherical, subspherical to mostly ± cylindric cacti, in part almost cereoid, in one case very low-growing, with variable spination. In all species the flowers are ± carmine-pink, with narrow-lanceolate, tapering petals, the inner ones remaining connivent until the flower starts to fade. The stem-like tube and ovary show only traces of felt, with bristles above. The oblong fruit has only traces of felt, and is hollow at maturity; the seeds are released by means of a basal pore. 22 species described. Although all of these have the same floral characters, including the distinctive perianth-colour, thus making Neoporteria one of the most uniform genera in the Cactaceae, my views regarding the segregation of Neochilenia seem not to be shared in the USA (see also Neochilenia; Britton & Rose included the species of both genera in Neoporteria only because at that time they were not in possession of sufficient data regarding the Chilean species). Thus Hutchison, for instance, refers some species of Neochilenia to Neoporteria, and presumably Horridocactus similarly: i.e. funnelform flowers with ± distinct hair-development, and differently coloured perianths. Instead of undertaking new "revisions", such as that of Pediocactus sensu Benson, or Ariocarpus sensu Anderson, it would have been preferable here to follow my much-needed revision of Neoporteria Br. & R. After all, what are the consequences if the Neochilenia species are referred to the present genus? The Horridocactus species could no longer be excluded, still less the species of Pyrrhocactus sensu Ritt.—in other words the Chilean and the E. Andean species of the genus. The result is a classical example of failure to follow my arguments: a synthetic over-sized genus which cannot be clearly envisaged, and which ignores geographical realities.—Distribution: Central to N. Chile. [(R); grafting speeds growth and encourages flowering.]

N. acutissima (O. & Dietr.) Berg.: **Neoporteria subgibbosa** (Haw.) Br. & R.

N. ambigua (Hildm.) Backbg.: **Weingartia ambigua** (Hildm.) Backbg.

N. aricensis (Ritt.) Don. & Rowl. = **Neochilenia aricensis** (Ritt.) Backbg. 1963.

N. aspillagai (Söhr.) Backbg.: **Neochilenia aspillagai** (Söhr.) Backbg.

N. atrispinosa (Backbg.) Backbg.
Bo. small-spherical, later oblong to cylindric, dark

leaf-green; **R.** napiform, with a neck-like constriction; **Ri.** c. 15, at first divided into spiralled Tub., these later becoming confluent; **Ar.** yellow-felty at first; **Sp.** variable, those on juveniles numerous, soft-bristly to hair-like, later 3–7, to 3.5 cm lg., erect at first, harder but still flexible, some fine and bristly, later up to 30, ± dense, 9 of these stouter, more centrally placed, stiff, pungent; those on adult plants fairly stiff-acicular; **Sp.** dark brown to black; **Fl.** pinkish-red; **Fr.** greenish-pink; **S.** matt black.—N. Chile.

N. castanea Ritt.—"Taxon", XII: 1, 34. 1963.
Bo. oblong, to 15 cm ∅; **Ri.** 15–24, notched into chin-like Tub.; **Ar.** to 14 mm lg., 1–1.5 cm apart; **Sp.** straight, chestnut-brown; **Rsp.** 10–14, rough, to 15 mm lg.; **Csp.** 4–8, 15–30 mm lg., subulate; **Fl.** purple; **Tu.** or **Ov.** and **Fr.** virtually without flock, only sometimes with a few Br.; **Fr.** red; **S.** dark brown, finely tuberculate.—Chile (Prov. Talca, near Villa Prat) (FR 236).
   v. **tunensis** Ritt.—"Taxon", XII: 1, 34. 1963: **Sp.** rather longer, weaker, more tufted; **S.** less finely tuberculate.—Chile (Tuna, near San Fernando) (FR 236a).

N. castaneoides (Cels) Werd.
Bo. spherical, later oblong, greyish-green; **Ri.** 15–20, acutely furrowed; **Ar.** thickly white-felty at first; **Rsp.** to 20, to c. 1.8 cm lg., crowded; **Csp.** to 6, rather longer, erect; **Sp.** concolorous light golden-yellow to golden-brown; **Fl.** carmine-pink, white below; **Fr.** reddish-green to faintly pink.—Chile (neighbourhood of Copiapo).

N. cephalophora (Backbg.) Backbg.
Bo. dwarf, subspherical, fresh green; **R.** napiform, not strongly constricted; **Ri.** at first in spiralled Tub.; **Ar.** small; **Sp.** short, hair-like, to 1.2 cm lg., ± tuft-like above, ± light yellow to whitish; **Fl.** (acc. Simo) smaller than that of any other Neoporteria.—N. Chile (coast).

N. chilensis (Hildm.) Br. & R.: **Neochilenia chilensis** (Hildm.) Backbg.

N. clavata (Söhr.) Werd.
Bo. spherical, becoming columnar, to 1.5 m h., light green, soon grey; **Ri.** to 10, straight, ± obliquely notched; **Ar.** elliptic, with much whitish-grey felt; **Rsp.** 5–7, to 3 cm lg., very stout, subulate, straight to ± curving, spreading horizontally; **Csp.** 1, straight, porrect or pressed downwards, rather longer; **Fl.** red.—Chile (Fig. 267.)
   v. **procera** Ritt.—"Taxon", XII: 1, 34. 1963: **Bo.** tall; **R.** not napiform; **Ar.** smaller, more distant; **Sp.** thinner, shorter; **Fl.** smaller; **Tu.** with less

flock or fewer Br.; **S.** smaller.—N. Chile (E. of La Serena) (FR 716).
Ritter re-collected this insufficiently clarified spec. (FR 482); acc. to Winter's catalogue, he also listed the following varieties: v. grandiflora (FR 482a), "very large Fl., cereoid habit"; and v. parviflora (FR 482b).

N. coimasensis Ritt.—"Taxon", XII: 1, 34. 1963.
Bo. to 12 cm ∅; **R.** napiform, small; **Ri.** 15–21, notched, with long chin-like Tub.; **Ar.** to 1 cm lg., 5–12 mm apart; **Sp.** variable, greyish-yellow to dark grey; **Rsp.** 15–30, 1–4 cm lg., straight or curving; **Csp.** 8–20, mostly curving, 2–4(–7) cm lg.; **Fl.** purplish-pink, with some Br. above; **Fr.** red or yellowish; **S.** dark brown, very wrinkled.—Chile (Prov. Aconcagua, Las Coimas) (FR 473).

N. coquimbana Ritt. (FR 218): see **Neoporteria nigrihorrida** v. **coquimbana** Ritt.

N. crassispina Ritt. (FR 481): see **Neoporteria nigrihorrida** v. crassispina Ritt. (or v. **major** [Backbg.] Backbg.).

N. curvispina v. variicolor Hutch. (undescribed?): probably identical with Horridocactus curvispinus (Bert.) Backbg.

N. densispina (Backbg.) Y. Ito: with very dense light Br., resembling Neoporteria nidus (Söhr.) Br. & R., or possibly referable there.

N. exsculpta (O.) Borg: **Neoporteria subgibbosa** (Haw.) Br. & R.

N. fobeana (Mieckl.) Backbg.: **Neochilenia fobeana** (Mieckl.) Backbg.

N. fusca (Mühlpf.) Br. & R.: **Neochilenia fusca** (Mühlpf.) Backbg.

N. gerocephala Y. Ito
Bo. remaining ± spherical, sometimes later elongated but not strongly cylindric; **Ri.** tuberculate, Tub. prominent; **Sp.** numerous, thick and bristly, soft, tangled and densely interlacing, white to blackish, all soon white; **Fl.** c. 5 cm lg.; **Tu.** long.—Chile (neighbourhood of Ovalle). (Fig. 268.)
Distinguished from N. nidus by the larger Fl.
N. multicolor Ritt., described by Ritter ("Taxon", XII: 1, 33. 1963) as a distinct species, but with no mention of Fl.-size, must be referred here. The Fl. is as large as in the preceding spec., with white flock and Br. The Fl. of N. nidus is only half as long, but the variability of spination and spine-colour matches Ritter's description of N. multicolor, i.e.

the colour ranges from white to yellowish, brownish, reddish-brown to black, just as in N. nidus. The locality ("neighbourhood of Ovalle") was imprecise. Ritter states "vicinity of Coquimbo (FR 243)".

N. heteracantha (Backbg.) Backbg.
Bo. flattened-spherical, to 11 cm ⌀, dark green; **Ri.** c. 19, weakly tuberculate; **Rsp.** c. 20, to c. 2.2 cm lg.; **Csp.** c. 6, to 4.5 cm lg.; **Sp.** crowded, brushlike, slightly curving, stiff-bristly, dirty white to brownish-grey; **Fl.** carmine-pink, white below; **Fr.** small, red.—N. Chile.

N. jussieui (Monv.) Br. & R.: **Neochilenia jussieui** (Monv.) Backbg.

N. kesselringiana (Dölz) Hutch.: **Horridocactus kesselringianus** Dölz.

N. kunzei (Först.) Backbg.: **Neochilenia kunzei** (Först.) Backbg.

N. laniceps Ritt. 1963
Bo. green or brown, 3–4 cm ⌀, later to 20 cm lg., firm, crown sunken; **R.** large, napiform; **Ri.** at first strongly tuberculate, later 13–17, spiralled, deeply notched, Tub. c. 2 mm br.; **Ar.** sunken, white-felty, 2–4 mm lg., c. 2 mm br., 3–5 mm apart; **Sp.** hairlike, sometimes stouter, ± curving and bent; **Csp.** brown to black, coarser than the Rsp., 2–4 cm lg.; **Rsp.** little shorter, lighter to grey, projecting, 20–50; **Fl.** apical, 28 mm lg., slender-funnelform, Cor. 2 cm ⌀, remaining open day and night for several days, unperfumed, reddish outside, with several small acute red Sc., these with axillary white flocky wool and hair-like yellowish twisted Br.; **style** white, 21 mm lg., with 7 **Sti.**; **Fr.** intense carmine, 12 mm lg., 7 mm thick; **S.** round, matt black.—N. Chile (Totora Bajo).
Related to N. villosa. Because of a printer's error, the name was incorrectly given as N. planiceps.

N. litoralis Ritt.
Bo. hemispherical, later columnar, 3–8 cm ⌀, grass-green; **Ri.** 14–21, strongly divided into Tub.; **Ar.** oval, with whitish to yellowish felt; **Rsp.** c. 30, 0.75–2 cm lg., hair-like, radiating; **Csp.** 8–12, 1.5–3 cm lg., spreading, straight or slightly curving; **Sp.** variable in colour, yellowish-white to yellowish-brown, brown, to blackish; **Fl.** to 2.75 cm lg., carmine-pink; **Fr.** 2 cm lg., carmine.—Chile (Coquimbo, along the shore). (FR 219.)

N. mamillarioides (Hook.) Backbg.
Bo. eventually long-cylindric, to c. 10 cm ⌀, light to greyish-green; **Ri.** to over 15, divided into stout oblong Tub.; **Ar.** oval, large, thickly felty; **Sp.**

scarcely differentiated, 4 lower ones cruciform, stoutly subulate, several thinner and thicker ones on the Ar.-margin, variable in thickness and length, sometimes rather curving, thickened below, whitish to reddish-brown; all **Sp.** robust, fierce; **Fl.** to 6 cm lg., probably the largest in the genus; **Tu.** stout, somewhat channelled.—Chile (Estancia Frai Jorge).

N. microsperma Ritt.—Succulenta, 42: 1, 6. 1963.
Bo. becoming oblong; **Ri.** less strongly notched, forming a small chin-like projection; **Ar.** 3–5 mm apart; **Sp.** dense, ± curving, black at first, **Csp.** only developing later above; **Tu.** longer, rather bristly; **S.** smaller.—N. Chile (15 km E. of La Serena) (FR 535). Acc. Ritter, the data record the differences from N. wagenknechtii.
v. **serenana** Ritt.—l. c.: **Bo.** larger; **Ri.** broader, higher; **Ar.** larger; **Sp.** stouter.—Same locality (FR 716a).

N. multicolor Ritt. (FR 243), not described: "**Sp.** dense, curly, concealing the Bo., yellow to whitish or chestnut-brown." Cannot be segregated from Neoporteria gerocephala Y. Ito; **Fl.** of the same size.

N. napina (Phil.) Backbg. and v. spinosior Backbg.: **Neochilenia napina** (Phil.) Backbg. and v. **spinosior** (Backbg.) Backbg.

N. napina v. **lanigera** Hutch.: Neochilenia spec. (close to N. eriocephala?).

N. nidus (Söhr.) Br. & R.
Bo. spherical, later clavate-cylindric; **Ri.** to 18; **Sp.** scarcely differentiated, to 3 cm lg. (and more), ± bristly to stiffer, often straight and lax, mostly densely interlacing, variable also in colour from whitish to yellowish or darker to blackish, especially the centrals; **Fl.** only c. 3 cm lg.—Chile (neighbourhood of Ovalle). Distinguished from N. gerocephala by the considerably smaller Fl.

N. nigrihorrida (Backbg.) Backbg.
Bo. spherical, later moderately elongated, matt dark greyish-green; **Ri.** to 18, divided into acute chin-like Tub.; **Rsp.** c. 16, to 1.5 cm lg., radiating sideways, interlacing, stiff; **Csp.** 6–7, to 3 cm lg., very stout, pungent, subulate; **Sp.** pitch-black at first, then dirty silvery-grey; **Fl.** 4 cm lg., light carmine, white below; **Fr.** reddish-green.—Chile (S. of Coquimbo).
v. **coquimbana** Ritt., not described, earlier called N. coquimbana; probably only a form of N. nigrihorrida;
v. **crassispina** Ritt., not described; probably **N. nigrihorrida** v. **major** (Backbg.) Backbg.;

338

v. **major** (Backbg.) Backbg.; **Ri.** c. 13, more strongly thickened around the Ar.; **Ar.** larger; **Rsp.** c. 18, to 2 cm lg., projecting and then curving to the Bo.; **Csp.** c. 10, very coarse, bent upwards at the tip; **Sp.** dark grey, quite black when moist;

v. **minor** (Backbg.) Backbg.: **Bo.** smaller, more flattened-spherical at first; **Rsp.** c. 16, to 1 cm lg., thinner; **Csp.** 8, to 1.8 cm lg.

N. occulta (Phil.) Br. & R.: **Neochilenia occulta** (Phil.) Backbg.

N. odieri (Lem.) Berg. and v. **mebbesii** (Hildm.) Backbg.: **Neochilenia odieri** (Lem.) Backbg. or **Neochilenia mebbesii** (Hildm.) Backbg.

N. planiceps Ritt.—"Taxon", XII. 1, 34. 1963.
Bo. to 20 cm lg., to 40 cm ∅; **R.** napiform, large, yellow, constricted above; **Ri.** at first tuberculate, later notched, 13–17, Tub. flattened above and chin-shaped; **Ar.** to 4 mm lg., to 5 mm apart, white; **Sp.** 25–50, hair-like, curving or curly; **Csp.** 2–4 cm lg., brown or dark, radials lighter; **Fl.** 2.8 cm lg., carmine; **Tu.** with white flock and several soft hair-like yellowish Br.; **style** white; **Sti.** pale yellow; **Fr.** beaker-shaped, indumentum as the Tu.; **S.** blackish, very wrinkled.—N. Chile (Tororal Bajo, rare) (FR 483). [Haage adds: Ritter says this name is a misprint and should correctly be "laniceps".]

N. polyrhaphis (Pfeiff.) Backbg.
Bo. eventually elongated, dark greyish-green; **Ri.** c. 16; **Sp.** numerous, scarcely differentiated, bristly-thin in the apex, eventually firmer, stouter, pungent, erect, but also interspersed with others which are bristly, centrals brown; **Fl.**-data insufficiently clarified, and since the plant is scarcely represented nowadays in collections, its relationship to Neoporteria must remain open.—Chile.

N. procera Ritt.: **Neoporteria clavata** v. **procera** Ritt. (FR 716).

N. rapifera Ritt. (FR 714), not described: **Bo.** ± spherical, green, with numerous fine Sp.; or dark green, with fewer stouter Sp.; according to the name, the **R.** must be napiform; **Sp.** mostly curving, yellow at first below, then ± orange, tipped dark brown to black, or sometimes light brown in the case of the lighter green plants; **Rsp.** to 10–20, also several **Csp.**; **Fl.** pinkish-red.—Chile.

N. robusta Ritt.—"Taxon", XII. 1, 34. 1963.
Bo. 8–15 cm ∅, oblong; **R.** not napiform; **Ri.** 13–18, with short Tub.; **Ar.** to 15 mm lg., to 1 cm apart; **Rsp.** 15–22, 1.5–4 cm lg., acicular, pale

brown, soon white; **Csp.** 8–16, 2–7 cm lg., subulate, brown to almost black; **Fl.** purple, with white flock and Br.; **S.** dark brown, very wrinkled.—Chile (Prov. Santiago, E. of Montenegro) (FR 473c).

N. senilis (Phil.) Backbg.: **Neoporteria gerocephala** Y. Ito.

N. sociabilis Ritt.—Succulenta, 42: 1, 3. 1963.
Bo. oblong, to 8 cm ∅, not taprooted; **Ri.** 13–21, to 1.5 cm h., narrow, tuberculate; **Ar.** to 1 cm lg., 6 mm br., 5–10 mm apart; **Sp.** acicular, straight, dark grey; **Rsp.** 16–20, to 2 cm lg.; **Csp.** 7–14, to 3 cm lg.; **Fl.** to 3.3 cm lg., purple, bordered white; **Sep.** recurved; **Fr.** pale red, oblong; **S.** 1.3 mm lg., with a minute hilum.—N. Chile (Totoral Bajo) (FR 655).

v. **napina** Ritt.—l. c.: **R.** napiform, with a neck-like constriction; **Ri.** 11–18; **nectary** not reddish below (as in the type); **Fil.** white (pale purple in the type) (FR 655a).

N. subcylindrica (Backbg.) Backbg.
Bo. soon becoming cylindric, dark green; **Ri.** 16, narrow; **Rsp.** thin, interlacing sideways; **Csp.** 6, irregularly arranged, confused and interlacing, dark brown, becoming straw and later grey.—Chile.

N. subgibbosa (Haw.) Br. & R. (T.)
Bo. spherical, later to 1 m lg. and more, to 10 cm ∅, light then greyish-green; **Ri.** to 20, ± compressed, fairly tuberculate; **Ar.** large, white-woolly at first; **Rsp.** c. 24, stout, directed sideways; **Csp.** 4, stiffly subulate; **Sp.** light amber, later darker, with a lighter base, sometimes ± reddish-brown; **Fl.** c. 4 cm lg., carmine-pink.—Chile (near Valparaiso).

v. **intermedia** Ritt., not described: later regarded by Ritter as a variety of N. litoralis (just as with N. procera v. serenana, which he later described as a variety of N. microsperma). I give the name here because I am in doubt as to where it should correctly be placed, or whether it is indeed a good variety, because Ritter's fairly frequent name-changes make it difficult to reach a final judgment.

N. taltalensis Hutch.: **Neochilenia taltalensis** (Hutch.) Backbg.

N. thiebautiana (Backbg.) Y. Ito, with firm black Sp. curving upwards, is probably only a form of **Neoporteria nidus** (Söhr.) Br. & R.

N. villosa (Monv.) Berg.
Bo. eventually oblong to cylindric, to c. 15 cm h., 8 cm ∅, greyish-green, later suffused violet to blackish; **Ri.** 13–15, divided into oblong-rounded

and chin-like Tub.; **Ar.** ± strongly white-felty to woolly; **Sp.** scarcely differentiated, numerous, hair-like to fine-bristly, lighter or darker or blackish, especially the 4 rather stouter, more central Sp. to 3 cm lg., sometimes mingled with sulphur-yellow ± bent hair-like Sp.; **Fl.** c. 2 cm lg., white inside below.—Chile (vicinity of Huasco).

N. villosa v. polyrhaphis (Pfeiff.) Borg: **Neoporteria polyrhaphis** (Pfeiff.) Backbg.

N. wagenknechtii Ritt.—Succulenta, 42: 1, 5. 1963. **Bo.** to 30 cm h., to 11 cm ∅, greyish-green; **R.** not napiform; **Ri.** 11–17, very obtuse, with chin-like projections; **Ar.** 6–13 mm lg., to 7 mm br., 5–10 mm apart, grey or brownish; **Sp.** acicular; **Rsp.** 10–14, to 2.5 cm lg., straight, dark grey; **Csp.** 3–6, 2–3 cm lg., greyish-brown; **Fl.** 2.2 cm lg., purple, with slighter white felt, Br. missing (always?); **Fil.** white; **style** white below, red or brownish above; **Fr.** barrel-shaped, green or reddish; **S.** brown.—N. Chile (N. of La Serena, Juan Soldado). If Br. are missing(?), and given the complete uniformity of the other floral characters of colour and construction, then this factor is of as little significance in Neoporteria as in Parodia, but the typically very bristly flowers of Neochilenia must be segregated from those of Reicheocactus, in which bristles are lacking, in order to avoid confusion such as had earlier arisen between Neochilenia reichei and Reicheocactus pseudoreicheanus. Generic segregation cannot always be completely uniform, but must be adapted to the facts of any particular situation. (FR 715).

v. **napina** Ritt.—l. c.: **R.** large, napiform, with a constricted neck; **Sp.** longer, curving; **Fl.** larger; **Tu.** with some white Br.(!).—N. Chile, mountains of Choros Bajos, N. of La Serena) (FR 714).

Comparison of the Br.-development shows clearly that reduction has occurred in the type of the species, and regard for this fact is an essential aid to classification.

Neoraimondia Br. & R. (55)

Robust cerei, medium-tall to very tall, branching from the base, branches mostly erect and candelabra-shaped, stout and few-ribbed, of ± divergent habit in only one species. When flowering is reached, remarkable short shoots are developed, these being densely felty, rounded or cylindric, rarely spiny and then only on older shoots; from these shoots 2 diurnal flowers may arise simultaneously; these are rather shortly funnelform, the tube is shortly hairy, the hairs intermingled in the lower part with at most some inconspicuous spines.

The spherical to oblong fruit has round brown cushions of felt, and short spines. This genus, together with Corryocactus brevistylus, has the longest spines known in the Cactaceae. The seeds are matt black and finely pitted.—Distribution: from N. Peru to N. Chile. (Fig. 271.)
Neocardenasia Backbg. is sometimes referred here, despite the considerable differences; see under that generic name.

N. arequipensis (Meyen) Backbg. (T) **Bo.** greyish-green, to 10 m h., trunk to 40 cm ∅; **branches** somewhat bent below, then ascending and parallel, 20 cm ∅ and more; **Ri.** 8; **Ar.** at first to 2 cm ∅, later elongating to form a ± spherical or cylindric short shoot; **Sp.** irregularly 1–2–4–7, terete, subulate, very flexible, scarcely pungent, to 25 cm lg.; **Fl.** greenish-white; **Fr.** c. 7 cm lg., purple outside and in, the felt-cushions and Sp. dropped at maturity.—Peru (S. of Mollendo to the Nazca and Puquio valleys).
v. **rhodantha** Rauh & Backbg.: **Bo.** to c. 5 m h., fresh green; **Ri.** mostly 7; **branches** 30–40 cm ∅; **Ar.** with brownish wool, especially in the apex; **Fl.** pinkish-red, 4.5–5 cm lg.—S. Peru (around Arequipa); v. **riomajensis** Rauh & Backbg.: differentiated from v. rhodantha by the lower **Ri.**-count, 4–6; **Fl.** light carmine.—S. Peru (Rio Majes).

N. aticensis Raugh & Backbg. **Bo.** to 4 m h. and more; **branches** not parallel but ascending and somewhat diverging, sometimes tapering above; **Ri.** (6–)7(–8); **Fl.** ?—S. Peru (near Atico). (Fig. 269.) Distinguished from the other spec. by the more spreading habit and the tapering branches.

N. gigantea (Werd. & Backbg.) Backbg. **Bo.** to 8 m h.; **branches** erect and closely spaced; **Ri.** mostly 4(–5); **Ar.** very crowded, flowering ones ± conically elongated; **Fl.** and **Fr.** purplish-red.—N. Peru (W. of Morropon; near Yequetepeque). (Fig. 270.)
v. **saniensis** Rauh & Backbg.: **Bo.** only c. 4 m h.; **branches** broader, laxer, but parallel and ascending; **Ri.** 4–5; **Fl.** light wine-red.—N. Peru (Rio Saña valley).

N. macrostibas (K. Sch.) Br. & R.: **Neoraimondia arequipensis** (Meyen) Backbg.

N. macrostibas v. gigantea (Werd. & Backbg.) Backbg.: **Neoraimondia gigantea** (Werd. & Backbg.) Backbg.

N. macrostibas v. rosiflora (Werd. & Backbg.)

Backbg.: **Neoraimondia roseiflora** (Werd. & Backbg.) Backbg.

N. roseiflora (Werd. & Backbg.) Backbg.
Bo. to only c. 2 m h.; **branches** thick, ± curving below, ascending and parallel; **Ri.** mostly 5; **Ar.** spherical or oblong when flowering age is reached; **Fl.** light pinkish-red, M.-stripe dark.—Central Peru (near Chosica and in the Pisco valley).
    v. sayanensis Ritt., undescribed: a very short-spined form or variety.

Neotanahashia Y. Ito, or Neotanahashia reichei Y. Ito non K. Sch.: **Reicheocactus** Backbg., or **Reicheocactus pseudoreicheanus** Backbg.

Neowerdermannia Frič (119):
Weingartia Werd.

Small globose cacti with an edible thick fleshy taproot, without any neck-like constriction. Ribs ± strongly divided into tubercles which are sometimes chin-like, the areoles then being sunken. The main spines are ± curving or sometimes even hooked, especially in juvenile plants of the one Chilean species (which appears to have a distribution extending as far as S. Peru). Flowers relatively small, white or lilac-pink, with a short tube and glabrous. The small fruits are also glabrous and contain very few seeds. Several flowers have been observed to arise simultaneously from one areole. On the basis of these characters, Neowerdermannia cannot be separated from the Genus Weingartia, and the two specific names must be recombined, to be known as Weingartia chilensis (Backbg.) and Weingartia vorwerkii (Frič), the latter including v. erectispina (Hoffm. & Backbg.) and v. gielsdorfiana (Backbg.). In any event this name-change is better founded than Hutchison's inclusion of Weingartia in Gymnocalycium. I have listed the genus separately here because the name is still in common use, even although it cannot be justified. In my handbook "Die Cact.", III: 1795, 1959, I drew attention to the fact that the species of this genus are more appropriately referred to Weingartia; Dr. Simo confirmed this in 1963 in the monthly journal of the Ges. Oesterr. Kakteenfreunde, VII:1. Because of this, the following Neowerdermannia-names will be followed by the names under the new combination which should in future be regarded as valid.—Distribution (in general as for Weingartia): N. Argentina, Bolivian highlands to those of N. Chile and neighbouring S. Peru. [(R); grafting is recommended. Prone to attack by woodlice.]

N. chilensis Backbg.—**Weingartia chilensis**

(Backbg.) Backbg.—Descr. Cact. Nov. III: 15. 1963.
Bo. dark bluish-green, often suffused slightly brownish or reddish; **R.** napiform, tapering; **Ri.** c. 15, narrow, Tub. narrow, long; **Rsp.** c. 20, 0.8–2.2 cm lg., radiating, flexible, mostly straight, rarely ± curving or bent, at most one lower longer Sp., blackish or violet-brown, the remainder pinkish-grey to darker; **Csp.** 1, straight, stiff, erect, never hooked, blackish to violet-brown; **Sp.** sometimes all lighter, shorter at first, Rsp. later sometimes interlacing; **Fl.** white.—N. Chile (Ticnamar).

N. peruviana Ritt. & Krainz, not described: **Weingartia chilensis** (Backbg.) Backbg.

N. vorwerkii Frič—**Weingartia vorwerkii** (Frič) Backbg.—Descr. Cact. Nov. III: 15. 1963, similarly the varieties:
Bo. broadly to flattened-spherical, passing over into the tapering **R.**, scarcely rising above the soil; **Ri.** 16 and more, divided into acute, chin-like, spiralled Tub.; **Ar.** in the depressions between the Tub.; **Sp.** to c. 10, to 1.5 cm lg., bent sideways and ± projecting or ± appressed, 1 directed upwards, 1 downwards, to c. 4 cm lg., ± strongly bent above; **Fl.** white, with a light lilac-pink stripe.—N. Argentina to N. Bolivia.
    v. **erectispina** Hoffm. & Backbg.: **Tub.** more slender; **Sp.** long, erect, crowded and projecting, often ± wavy or twisted, thinner than in the type, the lowest one longest, sometimes more strongly bent above, all fairly weak.—Bolivia (near Viacha).
    v. **gielsdorfiana** Backbg.: **Bo.** mostly smaller than in the type; **Tub.** more rounded; **Sp.** shorter; **Fl.** light violet to white.—N. Bolivia.
In view of the new combination with **Weingartia**, the citations for the above two varieties are correctly: v. **erectispina** (Hoffm. & Backbg.) Backbg., and v. **gielsdorfiana** (Backbg.) Backbg., in accordance with the amendments published in Descr. Cact. Nov. III: 16. 1963.

Nichelia Bull.: **Neochilenia** Backbg.

Nopalea SD. (18)

Bushy to almost tree-like plants, resembling Opuntia, with glochids, the leaves small and soon dropping. The shoots are flattened, fleshy and often narrow; spines without sheaths are produced singly or in clusters. The flowers are ± red and borne on the margins, the petals are erect and connivent, with the filaments projecting and the style mostly quite strongly thickened below. The tuberculate ovary is predominantly spineless, the fruit mostly similarly; the latter is a juicy red berry.— Distribution: from Mexico to Panama. [(R).]

N. angustifrons Lindbg.: **Nopalea dejecta** (SD.) SD.

N. auberi (Pfeiff.) SD.
Bo. to 10 m h., with a cylindric **trunk**; **branches** often placed at right angles, sparsely spiny, bluish-green, ± frosted; **Ar.** round, with short wool and later brown Glo.; **Sp.** 0, or 1–2, subulate, the longer upper one to 3 cm lg., the lower one only half as long, whitish, tipped brownish; **Fl.** c. 9 cm lg., pinkish-red; **Ov.** with noticeable but low Tub., with numerous Glo. in the Ar., to 1 cm lg.—Central and S. Mexico.

N. cochenillifera (L.) SD. (T.)
Bo. often 3–4 m h., **trunk** to 20 cm ∅; **branches** oblong, ascending or spreading, to 50 cm lg., ± light green at first, spineless or with only minute Sp. on old shoots; **Glo.** numerous, soon dropping; **Fl.** c. 5.5 cm lg., scarlet; **Ov.** with long, lozenge-shaped Tub. and many Glo.— Tropical Central America and Jamaica (its true homeland?).

N. dejecta (SD.) SD.
Bo. to 2 m h., bushy at first, later forming a **trunk**; **branches** linear-oblong, often arching over, to 15 cm lg., only moderately thick, light green even when old, very spiny; **Sp.** 6–8 from old Ar., mostly only 2, to 4 cm lg., spreading, pale yellow or reddish, later grey; **Fl.** c. 5 cm lg., dark red.— Panama?

N. escuintlensis Matuda
Bo. to 1.3 m h., bushy; **branches** squarrose, erect, obovoid or ± circular, tapering below, 15–20 cm lg., to 10 cm br., dark green; **Ar.** yellowish-felty; **Glo.** later numerous; **Sp.** 1–3, to 2.5 cm lg., yellowish-white; **Fl.** 8–11 cm lg., yellowish to scarlet; **Ov.** tuberculate, spineless, very slender-clavate; **Fr.** 5–7 cm lg.—Mexico (Chiapas, Rio Cintalapa, near Escuintla).

N. gaumeri Br. & R.
Bo. to 3 m h., freely branching; **branches** linear-oblong to ± lanceolate, only 6–12 cm lg., to 3 cm br.; **Sp.** 4–12, very dissimilar, 0.5–2 cm lg., fairly stout, often ± backwardly curving; **Fl.** only 4 cm lg.; **Fr.** with numerous Ar., spiny, with yellow Glo.—Mexico (Yucatan, near Sisal).

N. guatemalensis Rose
Bo. 5–7 m h., tree-like, often branching from close to the base; **branches** ovoid to oblong, to 20 cm lg., bluish-green; **Ar.** numerous, shortly white-woolly; **Sp.** 5–8, longest ones to 3 cm lg., unequal, thin, acicular at least on new growth, white or pink; **Fl.** only 5–6 cm lg., red; **Fr.** to 5 cm lg., without longer Glo.—Guatemala (near El Rancho).

N. inaperta Schott
Bo. to 7 m h., often bush-like; **trunk** very spiny; **branches** ± ovoid, 6–17 cm lg., very tuberculate, glossy, green; **Sp.** 4–12, usually 3–6 at first, to 2 cm lg., yellowish-brown; **Fl.** only 4 cm lg.; **Fr.** c. 1.5 cm lg.— Mexico (Yucatan).

N. karwinskiana (SD.) K. Sch.
Bo. to 2 m h., sometimes more, with a branching, spiny **trunk**; **branches** oblong, 15–30 cm lg., light matt green, faintly frosted; **Sp.** 3–7, 1–2 cm lg., spreading, pale yellow to ± white; **Glo.** numerous, yellow; **Fl.** to 12 cm lg., red.— Mexico.

N. lutea Rose
Bo. to 5 m h., with a short trunk; **branches** spreading, ± ovoid, elliptic or oblong, pale green, slightly frosted, 6–12 cm lg., to 3 cm br.; **Ar.** large, shortly brown-woolly; **Sp.** to 4 cm lg., weak, acicular or bristly, yellow, becoming brown; **Fl.** 5 cm lg.; **Ov.** with many Ar. with yellow Glo.; **Fr.** c. 4 cm lg.—Guatemala (near El Rancho), Honduras and Nicaragua. Sometimes more bush-like in habit.

N. moniliformis K. Sch.: **Consolea moniliformis** (L.) Britt.

N. nuda Backbg.
Bo. to only c. 80 cm h., shrubby, **primary shoots** later subterete, becoming corky; **branches** c. 12 cm lg., 5 cm br., rounded above, tapering below, weakly tuberculate, deep leaf-green; **Ar.** with white to light brownish felt; **Sp.** absent; **Fl.** c. 3.5 cm lg., light carmine; **Ov.** spherical; **Fr.** broadly spherical, 2 cm ∅, dark violet.—Mexico(?). (Fig. 272.)

Nopalxochia Br. & R. (38)

Epiphytic plants with flat shoots, or with small terete stem-like sections, the leaf-like segments with ladder-like notches. The fairly large diurnal flowers are pink or mid-red and open funnelform; the species with pink flowers has a second inner series of petals which are ± connivent. The glabrous and spineless tube and ovary are set with narrow scales which, in the bud-stage, are at first noticeably recurved. N. phyllanthoides, because of the slow development from attractive bud to fully open flower, is particularly attractive; it sometimes has a second flowering season in the year, with numerous blossoms in the main season; both it and the second species have contributed to the development of many Epicactus cultivars. (Fig. 274).— Distribution: Mexico (Chiapas; Oaxaca; Jalapa(?) and near Tlacolula[?]). [(R); only the second species should be kept outdoors in summer; in cool weather both species tend to mark.]

N. ackermannii (Haw.) Knuth

Bo. arching over, without long stem-like sections; **branches** lanceolate, with sinuate notches, ± weak, more leaf-green; **Fl.** large, rather lax, mid-red; **Tu.** slender, angular, furrowed, with reddish projecting Sc.—Mexico (Chiapas, Oaxaca).

One form has more fleshy branches, while those of another form are thinner, and Fl.-colour varies from deeper mid-red to bluish-red to more orange-red; Fil. red above, ·whitish to greenish below, throat similarly (acc. colour photos by Buchenau).

N. conzattianum T. M. MacDoug.: **Pseudonopalxochia conzattianum** (T. M. MacDoug.) Backbg.

N. phyllanthoides (DC.) Br. & R. (T.)

Bo. arching over, with long "stems"; **branches** lanceolate, tapering, with flat step-like notches, with distinct median and secondary veins, darker greyish-green; **Fl.** c. 10 cm lg., pink, light pinkish-red inside; **Tu.** short, with red Sc.—Mexico (Jalapa?; Tlacolula; Puebla, Rio Acapulco). (Fig. 273.) There is a well-known cultivar, "Deutsche Kaiserin". Acc. Bornemann, this was a cross between Epiphyllum ackermannii hybridus (seed-parent), and Nopalxochia phyllanthoides; Fl. with out Br.; first introduced to the trade by the Berlin nurseryman Kohlmannslehner under the above cultivar-name. Other crosses have ± spiny Tu. or Ov. and Fr., in other words, characters of Pseudonopalxochia (see the latter).

Notocactus (K. Sch.) Berg. emend. Backbg. (111)

Globose to shortly columnar, ± caespitose plants, the flowers predominantly yellow, rarely reddish; stigmas, with very few exceptions, light reddish to dark purple. Spination sometimes weak, less robust, mostly attractively coloured, ± variable. Flowers usually large and conspicuous. I divide them into the following subgenera on the basis of differences in the fruits:

  SG.1: Notocactus: fruits fleshy, dehiscing by a
     longitudinal tear;
  SG.2: Neonotocactus Backbg.:fruits elongating,
     thin-walled, flaccid, sometimes hollow
     and disintegrating basally.
The figure after each specific name indicates the appropriate subgenus. The seeds are matt, black.

The flowers are differentiated from Eriocactus by the longer tube; in the latter, moreover, there is a development of apical wool such as never occurs in Notocactus, and the fruits are dissimilar. For reasons which are far from apparent, Brasilicactus is also sometimes included in Notocactus, although the small flowers and fruits of the former are more strongly spiny and thus clearly differentiated from those of Notocactus—in fact unique among the spherical cacti of S. America.—Distribution: from N. to southern central and E. Argentina, through Uruguay, to S. Brazil. [(R): grafting speeds growth and produces more Fl.]

N. acutus v. depressus (FR 1377): rather dwarf plant; no description available.

N. allosiphon Marchesi

Bo. spherical, dull green, 11–13 cm ∅, 8–12 cm h., crown slightly sunken; **Ri.** 15–16, straight, 1.8–2.3 cm br., flanks flat to concave; **Tub.** rounded, sometimes ± compressed laterally, 2–3 mm h.; **Ar.** 7–9 mm apart, in depressions between the Tub.; **Rsp.** shorter and thinner than the centrals but otherwise very similar; **Csp.** 4, upper one erect, bottom one appressed against the Tub., 2 laterals thin, acute, dark red, later greying, tipped blackish, 9–19 mm lg.; **Fl.** pale yellow, numerous, subapical, 5.5 cm lg. and 5 cm ∅, densely covered with appressed wool, greyish to chestnut-brown and white below, with pale flesh-coloured Sc. 2–2.5 mm lg., also blackish-brown Br. 10 mm lg., 13 mm lg. above; **Sep.** with a pink M.-line on the underside; **Pet.** oblong to elliptic-lanceolate, rounded above, 8–11 mm br.; **Tu.** funnelform, only 12–14 mm lg.; **Fil.** light cream; **Sti.** purple, 11–13; **style** white; **S.** flattened-spherical, black, densely tuberculate.— Uruguay (Rivera, Valle Ar. Platon).

N. apricus (Ar.) Berg. (2)

Bo. caespitose, broadly spherical, light green; **Ri.** to 20, slightly tuberculate, low; **Ar.** 3–4 mm apart; **Rsp.** 18–20, bristly, bent, ± interlacing sideways, yellowish-grey; **Csp.** 4, to 1.5 cm lg., 1 often bent downwards, yellowish-grey to yellowish, reddish below, ± darker-tipped; **Fl.** large, c. 8 cm lg., yellow; outer **Pet.** and **Sep.** sometimes reddish in the middle; **Tu.** stout; **style** sometimes red below, white above; **Fil.** yellow (uppers) and red (lower ones).—Uruguay. (Fig. 275.)

Very variable spec.; Fl. 6–8 cm lg.; Pet. more crowded or laxer, pointed or rather obtuse; Sp. yellowish to ± reddish; the Tu. can also be more slender.

N. arachnites Ritt.

Bo. simple, spherical, green, 4–9 cm ∅, crown spiny; **Ri.** 14–16, 3–6 mm h., slightly notched; ·**Ar.**

round, white, 3–7 mm apart; **Sp.** thin, whitish-brown, red when young; **Rsp.** 10–14; **Fl.** c. 37 mm lg., sulphur-yellow; **Pet.** lanceolate; **Fil.** lemon-yellow, 10 mm lg.; **Fr.** green; **S.** black, hemispherical.—Brazil (Rio Grande do Sul, Serra do Herval).

v. **minor** Ritt.: **Bo.** smaller, 3–5 cm ⌀; **Ar.** 2–3 mm ⌀, 2–4 mm apart; **Sp.** thin, short; **Fl.** same size as the type; **Sti.** blackish-purple; **Pet.** broader, less acute; **S.** rather larger.—Brazil (Rio Grande do Sul, W. of St. Ana de Boa Vista). (FR 1395a.)

N. araneolarius (Reichb.) Hert.: "Csp. 5–7, very short, purple, Rsp. 15–17, yellow, Fl. not known": a plant of unclarified status, from the Montevideo area.

N. buenekeri (from Brazil): see **Parodia buenekeri** Buin. 1962.

N. buiningii (SG. Malacocarpus) Buxb.
Bo. flattened-spherical, simple, to 8 cm h., 12 cm ⌀, light grass-green*; crown lacking wool; **Ri.** c. 16, c. 2 cm h., divided into thin acute Tub. projecting chin-like over the Ar. beneath; **Ar.** oblong at first, 3–7 mm lg., white-woolly, soon glabrous; **Sp.** 4, cruciform, with Ssp., yellowish and glassy at the tip, thickened and dark brown below; **Fl.** yellow, 7 cm lg., 8 cm ⌀; **Tu.** with brown wool; **Fil.** yellow; **style** 25 mm lg., with 9 red **Sti.**; **S.** bellshaped, with a large hilum and matt black, finely tuberculate testa.—Uruguay (along the Brazilian frontier, near Livramento/Riviera, rare). Named for the late A. F. Buining, who discovered it during his 1966 expedition. (Fig. 493.)

N. caespitosus (Speg.) Backbg.: characters largely identical with those of Notocactus minimus Frič & Krzgr., which has also been reported from Uruguay. The latter may indeed be identical with this plant.

N. carambeiensis Buin. & Bred.
Bo. spherical, later shortly cylindric, to 10 cm h., 8 cm ⌀, dark matt green, offsetting from below, crown woolly; **Ri.** 12–14, vertical, to 10 mm h., 12–16 mm br. below; **Ar.** round to oval, woolly at first, later glabrous, to 10 mm apart; **Sp.** black to blackish-brown, later greyish-brown, dark-tipped; **Rsp.** 6–8, ± appressed, to 20 mm lg., sometimes with one small Ssp.; **Csp.** 4, cruciform, lowest one to 3 cm lg., laterals to 2.5 cm, upper one to 2 cm lg.; **Fl.** 25 mm lg. and ⌀, deep yellow, ± bellshaped,

pericarpel with a few Sc. 2 mm lg., short white H. and sometimes a blackish-brown Br. 4 mm lg.; **Sep.** and **Pet.** acute, spatulate, deep yellow; **Fil.** yellow; **An.** creamy-white; **Sti.** 8, purplish-red; **Fr.** to 12 mm lg., dehiscing laterally; **S.** cap-shaped, matt black.—Brazil (Paraná, N. of Ponto Grossa near Carambei at c. 1000 m, mostly on black rocks or grassy slopes with a humus-rich soil, pH 4–5). Found by Horst and Buining, 1966. (Fig. 494.)

N. concinnus (Monv.) Berg. (2)
Bo. usually simple, flattened-spherical, to 10 cm ⌀, 6 cm h., glossy, green, crown spineless; **Ri.** c. 18, with low Tub.; **Ar.** 5–7 mm apart; **Rsp.** 10–12, to 7 mm lg., bristly, thin, light yellow; **Csp.** 4, cruciform, to 1.7 cm lg., ± down-curving, lowest one stoutest, yellowish or brownish; **Fl.** c. 7 cm lg., canary-yellow; **Sti.** red.—S. Brazil, Uruguay.

N. concinnus v. **joadii** (Ar.) v. Osten & Y. Ito: Notocactus joadii (Hook.) Hert. (see the latter).

N. crassigibbus Ritt. (FR 1394)
Bo. spherical, simple, green*, crown glabrous; **Ri.** 10–15, obtuse, strongly tuberculate, 5–20 mm h.; **Ar.** set between the Tub., round, white, 2–8 mm ⌀, 8–15 mm apart; **Sp.** pale yellow, flexible, mostly bent; **Rsp.** 7–10, appressed, 10–25 mm lg.; **Csp.** mostly 1, directed downwards, 15–30 mm lg.; **Fl.** 50–60 mm lg.; **Ov.** strongly white-woolly, with a few thin Br.; **Fil.** pale golden-yellow, 10 mm lg.; **An.** buttercup-yellow; **style** pale yellow, 25 mm lg., with 11 purple Sti.; **Pet.** sulphur-yellow, lanceolate; **Fr.** green, with white wool and yellow Br.; **S.** black, hemispherical.—Brazil (Rio Grande do Sul, Lavras).

N. eremiticus (FR 1390): no description available.

N. floricomus (Ar.) Berg. (2)
Bo. eventually ± columnar, to c. 30 cm h., c. 13 cm ⌀, **crown** depressed; **Ri.** c. 20, Tub. conical, ± crowded; **Ar.** weakly white-felty, close together; **Rsp.** c. 20, ± firm, ± projecting, whitish or grey, reddish below; **Csp.** 4–5, 2–2.5 cm lg., stouter, subulate, spreading, the middle one porrect, grey to lighter; **Fl.** to 5 cm lg. and more, yellow; **Sti.** blackish-red.—Uruguay.

v. **flavispinus** Backbg.: **Csp.** pale yellow;

v. **rubrispinus** Backbg.: **Csp.** brilliant red;

v. **spinosissimus** Frič ex Buin.: **Sp.** scarcely differentiated, dense, brown;

---

*Translator's note: the photograph (493) much more accurately represents the Bo.-colour of cultivated plants; all the plants I have seen have been a most unusual light near-grey. Apparently not self-fertile.

*One of the distinctly "gymnocalycioid" Notocacti; Bo. conspicuously glossy, deep green; Fl. often larger than stated (in one of my plants to 100 mm) and more lemon-yellow than sulphur-yellow; a magnificent glossy Fl., probably the largest of any Notocactus spec., remaining open for 3–4 days. Not self-fertile. (Translator.)

v. **velenovskyi** (Frič ex Backbg.) Krainz: **Sp.** finer; **Rsp.** more numerous, glossy, whitish; **Ar.** at first noticeably woolly.

N. fuscus (FR 1379): name means "reddish-brown". Habit reminiscent of a Neoporteria. (HU 29.)

N. glaucinus (FR 1376a): v. gracilis (FR 1378 and 1426); and v. miniatispinus (FR 1376).

N. globularis (FR 1388).

N. herteri Werd. (2)
Bo. spherical to $\pm$ elongated, to c. 15 cm $\varnothing$, pale green; **Ri.** c. 22, strongly tuberculate; **Tub.** $\pm$ conical; **Ar.** to 1.5 cm apart; **Rsp.** 8–11, acicular, flexible, erect at first, later radiating; **Csp.** 4(–6), mostly cruciform, to 2 cm lg., stouter, subulate, brownish-red, sometimes banded; **Fl.** c. 4 cm lg., purplish-red; **Sti.** brownish-red.—Uruguay (Dept. Rivera, Cerro Galgo).

N. hypocrateriformis (O. & Dietr.) Hert.: probably identical with **Notocactus mammulosus** (Lem.) Berg.

N. intricatus (Lk. & O.) Hert.: judging by all the characters, this is probably a Wigginsia (Fl. and Fr. not known); possibly the earliest name of (Malacocarpus) **Wigginsia arechavaletai** (K. Sch. ex Speg.) D. M. Port.

N. joadii (Hook.) Hert.: an unclarified spec.

N. linkii (Lehm.) Hert.: **Notocactus ottonis** v. **linkii** (Lehm.) Berg.

N. maldonadensis (Hert.) Hert.: **Wigginsia arechavaletai** (K. Sch. ex Speg.) D. M. Port. (see under Malacocarpus).

N. mammulosus (Lem.) Berg. (2)
Bo. later $\pm$ elongated, to 10 cm h., 6 cm $\varnothing$, greyish to mid-green to darker; **Ri.** 18–20, with very prominent chin-like Tub.; **Ar.** broad, to 6 mm apart; **Rsp.** 10–13(–15), scarcely 5 mm lg., thin, yellowish-whitish, mostly brown at the tip and base; **Csp.** 3(–4), $\pm$ subulate, longer, 1–1.4 cm lg., stouter, yellow, brown-tipped; **Fl.** to c. 4 cm lg., strongly white-woolly, with brown or black Br., canary-yellow; **Sti.** purplish-red.—Argentina, Uruguay.
    v. pampeanus (Speg.) Cast. & Lelong: **Notocactus submammulosus** v. **pampeanus** (Speg.) Backbg.;
    v. submammulosus (Lem.) Y. Ito: **Notocactus submammulosus** (Lem.) Backbg.

Further varieties are listed by Y. Ito, but some of these are synonyms while others are based on undescribed names.

N. megapotamicus Ost. ex Hert. (2)
Bo. offsetting, eventually oblong, sap-green; **Ri.** 13–15, indistinctly tuberculate; **Ar.** woolly at first, to over 1 cm apart; **Rsp.** to c. 13, c. 1.5(–1.7) cm lg., appressed, interlacing laterally, yellowish to reddish or darker at first; **Csp.** 3–4, to over 1.3 cm lg., blackish-brown at first; **Sp.** slightly rough, stoutly bristly, $\pm$ twisted and curving, later greying; **Fl.** c. 3 cm lg., 4 cm $\varnothing$, satiny, sulphur-yellow; **Sti.** pink.—S. Brazil (Rio Grande do Sul). Acc. Buining, a variety of N. ottonis(?).

N. minimus Frič & Krzgr. (2)
Bo. very small-cylindric; **R.** $\pm$ napiform; **Ri.** 12–15, narrow; **Rsp.** 15–17, 4 of these directed upwards, 6 towards each side, 1 downwards, stiff-bristly, hyaline; **Csp.** 3(–4), 2 side ones bent upwards, 1(–2) projecting sideways, 5–6 mm lg., sometimes bent upwards to $\pm$ hooked, brown; **Sp.** densely covering the Bo.; **Fl.** to 2.7 cm lg., 4 cm $\varnothing$, yellow, with white wool and reddish-brown Br.; **Sti.** red.—Uruguay.
Quite distinct from all other spec. because of the occasionally hooked Sp. and the small, later cylindric, habit (grafted plants have been noted to 8 cm h.!). Ar. rather crowded.

N. mueller-melchersii Frič ex Backbg. (2)
Bo. $\pm$ elongated-spherical, c. 8 cm h., 6 cm $\varnothing$, matt green; **Ri.** c. 22; **Ar.** c. 5 mm apart, white-felty at first; **Rsp.** 15–18, to 8 mm lg., finely acicular, radiating sideways, yellowish-white; **Csp.** 1, to 2 cm lg., subulate, pungent, directed $\pm$ downwards, light horn-coloured to yellowish, dark-tipped, reddish-brown below; **Fl.** c. 3 cm lg., 5 cm $\varnothing$, pale golden-yellow; **Sti.** pale carmine.—Uruguay (Sierra de los Animos).
    v. **gracilispinus** Krainz: **Csp.** 2–3, shorter, sometimes 4, to 7 mm lg., often scarcely differentiated; **Fl.** rather smaller.

N. mueller-moelleri Frič (not validly described) (2)
Bo. hemispherical, later oblong, dark green; **Ri.** 22, low, divided into rounded Tub.; **Ar.** white-felty, later almost 1 cm apart; **Rsp.** c. 20, to 6 mm lg., fine, appressed, radiating in all directions; **Csp.** to 4 and then cruciform, to c. 5 mm lg., lowest one stouter, subulate, reddish, pointing $\pm$ downwards; the stouter **Sp.** unusual in that they stand up erectly around the crown at first; **Fl.** and **Fr.** ?—Uruguay. A distinctive plant, probably close to N. mueller-melchersii.

N. muricatus (O.) Berg. (2)
Bo. sometimes offsetting, ovoid to ± columnar, to 20 cm and more has been reported, green; **Ri.** 16(–20); **Tub.** broad, flat; **Ar.** crowded; **Rsp.** 10–14(–20), to 8 mm lg., bristle-like, spreading to ± appressed, whitish; **Csp.** 1–4, to 1.3 cm lg., ± projecting, amber to whitish, 1 chestnut-brown to ruby-red; **Fl.** to c. 3 cm lg., sulphur-yellow; **Sti.** purplish-red. Descriptions by Pfeiffer, Rümpler and K. Schumann differ as to length and colour of the Sp., size of the Fl. and size and colour of the Bo.—S. Brazil.

N. ottonis (Lehm.) Berg. (1) (T.) v. **ottonis**
Bo. ± flattened-spherical, 5–11 cm ∅, deep green; **Ri.** 8–12, rounded, weakly tuberculate; **Ar.** c. 1 cm apart; **Rsp.** 10–18, acicular, yellow; **Csp.** (0–)3–4, to c. 2.5 cm lg., somewhat stouter, ± reddish-brown, lighter-tipped; **Fl.** 4–6 cm lg., rather broader, deep glossy yellow; **Sti.** dark red.—S. Brazil, Uruguay, Argentina. A very variable spec. The following varieties have been described:
v. **albispinus** Backbg.: **Ri.** c. 13; **Rsp.** mostly 7(–9); **Csp.** mostly only 1, ± brownish, soon whitish like the other Sp.; **Fl.** c. 3 cm lg.; **Sti.** light red; **buds** with longer Br. than the type;
v. **arechavaletai** (Speg.) Buin.: **Ri.** fewer than 10; **Fl.** to 8 cm ∅; **Sti.** dark purple;
v. **brasiliensis** (Hge. Jr.) Berg.: **Rsp.** more erect, yellowish-brown; **Csp.** shorter, straighter, brownish; **Pet.** ± cordately notched; **Sti.** 11, yellow;
v. **buenekeri**: no further details available; at present only a name of Ritter's;
v. **elegans** Backbg. & Voll: **Tub.** longer; **Ar.** somewhat more widely spaced; **Fl.** with laxer, very narrow, tapering Pet.;
v. **linkii** (Lehm.) Berg.: **Ri.** more numerous, narrower, more acute; **Rsp.** 9–10, white at first, later brown-tipped; **Csp.** smaller, blackish at first, later brown; **Fl.** c. 5 cm ∅; **Sti.** purple;
v. megapotamicus (Ost. ex Hert.) Buin.: **Notocactus megapotamicus** Ost. ex Hert.;
v. **multiflorus** Frič ex Buin.: **Ri.** acute; **Sp.** under 2 cm lg.; **Fl.** under 2 cm ∅; **style** and **Sti.** orange;
v. **paraguayensis** (Heese) Berg.: **Ri.** (or Tub.) more acute; **Sp.** project, thin-acicular, redder;
v. **schuldtii** Krzgr.: **Ri.** fewer than 10; **Fl.** to 10 cm ∅; **Sti.** orange-yellow;
v. **stenogonus** Backbg.: **Bo.** to 8 cm h.; **Ri.** c. 10, narrower; **Rsp.** mostly 8, to c. 1 cm lg., brownish at first, later pale horn-coloured; **Csp.** mostly 3, to 1.2 cm lg.; **Fl.** c. 2 cm lg., 2.5 cm ∅; **Sti.** light red; **buds** noticeably weakly woolly, at first appearing ± glabrous;
v. **tenuispinus** (Lk. & O.) Berg.: **Sp.** finer, bristly, lighter; **Csp.** unequal, ± twisted; **Fl.** smaller, paler; **Fl.**-indumentum slighter;
v. **tortuosus** (Lk. & O.) Berg.: **Bo.** ± dark green;

Sp. shorter, stouter, ± radiating; **Csp.** 4–6, stouter, erectly radiating, 1 often pointing ± downwards;
v. **uruguayus** (Ar.) Berg.: **Ri.** 11, more broadly tuberculate; **Ar.** more distant; **Sp.** spreading, spidery; **Csp.** 0, or scarcely differentiated;
v. **villa-velhensis** Backbg. & Voll: **Bo.** yellowish-green, more caespitose; **Ri.** sometimes ± spiralled; **Tub.** ± warty, prominent; **Sp.** yellow; **Csp.** 0 to several, darker; **Fl.** c. 3 cm lg.

N. oxycostatus Buin. & Bred.
Bo. simple or offsetting from the base, ± depressed-spherical at first, later spherical, to 9 cm h. and ∅, ± greyish-green; **Ri.** 6–7, acute, 3.5–4 cm br. below, 2–2.2 cm h., often with an acute, chin-like or hatchet-shaped prominence between the Ar.; **Ar.** ± round, c. 7 mm ∅, very white-woolly at first, later with greyish-white felt and finally glabrous, c. 1 cm apart; **Sp.** reddish-brown, slightly glossy, flat, laxly twisted or curving, never straight; **Rsp.** 2 on either side and one directed downwards, 16–25 mm lg.; **Csp.** pointing straight down or variously directed, to 20 mm lg., also up to 8 small Ssp.; **Fl.** 5 cm lg., 4.5 cm ∅, bellshaped to funnelform, yellow; **Ov.** 15 mm lg., with Sc. up to 3 mm lg., with Br. to 10 mm lg.; **Sep.** glossy yellow, 24 mm lg., spatulate, minutely notched at the tip; **Pet.** glossy yellow, similarly shaped; **Fil.** yellowish-white; **An.** 1.5 mm lg., yellow; **style** yellowish-white, with 12 red, acutely tapering, papillose **Sti.**; **Fr.** with yellowish-grey H. and reddish-brown Br.; **S.** cap-shaped, testa glossy, black, hilum ochreous. Very floriferous.—S. Brazil (Rio Grande do Sul, E. of Sao Gabriel, in hilly terrain, among rocks and pampas grass under shrubs and brushwood, at c. 300 m). This outstanding spec. of the N. ottonis complex was found by Horst and Buining in 1968, at an isolated locality.

N. pampeanus (Speg.) Backbg.: **Notocactus submammulosus** v. **pampeanus** (Speg.) Backbg.

N. pseudoherteri Buin.
Bo. flattened-spherical, green, c. 20 cm ∅, 12 cm h.; crown glabrous; **R.** fibrous; **Ri.** c. 26, tuberculate, 2–2.5 cm apart; **Ar.** 6–8 mm lg., 5–6 mm apart, white-woolly at first, soon glabrous, sunken in the Tub.; **Sp.** c. 14, dark brown at first, later greying, arranged in 5 lateral pairs to 2.3 cm lg., ± appressed against the Bo. or ± erect, with one shorter and weaker Sp. above and below on the Ar.; **Csp.** 4, cruciform, rather stouter, bulbously thickened below, to 3 cm lg.; **Fl.** to 5 cm lg. and 5–5.6 cm br. when fully open, self-fertile; **pericarpel** 6 mm lg., 5 mm br. inside; **Sc.** with brown wool and one solitary black Br.; **nectary** 1–1.5 mm lg.; **Fil.** colourless, in 2 R., 10 mm lg.; **An.** intense yellow;

style with 12 purplish-red **Sti.**; **Tu.** with brown wool and black **Br.**; **Pet.** pale yellow, lanceolate or broadly tapering; **Fr.** at first a soft red berry, shrinking at maturity, with floral remains persisting; **S.** roundish, rather larger than in N. herteri.— Uruguay (on the E. slopes of the Cochilla Negra, at 150–200 m, among grasses, on open rocky surfaces). Discovered by Horst and Buining. (Name = "false N. herteri".)

N. pulvinatus (SG. Malacocarpus) van Vliet
Bo. caespitose, forming groups to 50 cm across, single St. spherical, to 15 cm ∅, crown covered with white wool and Sp.; **Ri.** 14–24, acute, scarcely notched, to 15 mm h., 20 mm br.; **Ar.** round, 4 mm ∅, to 18 mm apart, grey-felty; **Sp.** sharp, golden to pale brown; **Rsp.** 7–15, to 2 cm lg., lower ones stoutest; **Csp.** 1 to 2.5 cm lg., directed upwards at first and later down; **Fl.** funnelform, to 4 cm lg., 4.5 cm ∅, apical, self-fertile; **Tu.** and **Ov.** densely woolly; **Sep.** and **Pet.** lanceolate, lemon-yellow, style light yellow, with 9 red **Sti.**; **Fr.** oblong, pale pink to pale green, woolly; **S.** bellshaped, tuberculate, hilum white.—Uruguay (Cerro Largo, among grasses, on lichen-covered stones). Sp.-colour exceedingly variable. Specific name = "cushion-forming".

N. purpureus Ritt.
Bo. spherical, later elongated to clavate, to 14 cm thick, often offsetting from the base; **crown** ± depressed, woolly; **Ri.** 14–19, straight, 7–15 mm h., notched, obtuse, Tub. 2–3 mm h.; **Ar.** round, white, set between the Tub., 3–5 mm ∅, 5–8 mm apart; **Sp.** sharp; **Rsp.** c. 15, white, straight, 6–14 mm lg.; **Csp.** 4–6, reddish-yellow, straight to curving, 8–20 mm lg.; **Fl.** apical, 4 cm lg.; **Ov.** with white wool but no Br., nectary 1.5 mm lg., half-closed; **Tu.** beaker-shaped, 12 mm lg., with brown Br. above; **Fil.** pale yellow; **An.** dark golden-yellow; **style** pale yellow; **Sti.** c. 10, 7–8 mm lg., whitish; **Pet.** purplish-pink, 18 mm lg., 4–5 mm br.; **Fr.** greenish-red; **S.** 1 mm lg., black, hilum protruding.—Brazil (Rio Grande do Sul, S. of Serra Geral).*

N. rauschii van Vliet: named for the collector, Walter Rausch, of Vienna.

N. rechensis Buin.
Bo. fresh green, spherical to shortly cylindric, to 7 cm lg., 3–5 cm ∅, offsetting freely from the base; **Ri.** c. 18, 4 mm h., to 7 mm apart; **Ar.** round, c. 2 mm ∅, white-woolly in the crown, later glabrous, to 4 mm apart; **Sp.** varying from white to yellow, forming upright clusters in the crown and conceal-

ing this; **Rsp.** 4–6, radiating, whitish-yellowish, 6–7 mm lg., 2–4 directed downwards and sideways; **Csp.** 3–4, darker yellow, one pointed downwards, all rather stouter and longer, especially the lowest one; **Fl.** c. 3 cm lg., 3–3.5 cm ∅, yellow; **Tu.** with lanceolate Sc., wool and white Br.; **Sep.** lanceolate, M.-stripe ± reddish; **Pet.** lemon-yellow, 15 mm lg., 2 mm br.; style c. 2 cm lg., with c. 10 white **Sti.** 2 mm lg.; **Fr.** red, with floral remains; **S.** cap-shaped, 1 mm lg.—Brazil (Rio Grande do Sul, on rocks near Ana Rech). Found by H. Büneker of Corvo.

N. roseoluteus van Vliet
Bo. spherical, to 18 cm ∅ and h., coppery-green, crown covered with white wool which is pierced by the new Sp.; **Ri.** 15–18, triangular in section, with noticeably round Tub. between the Ar.; **Ar.** depressed, 5 mm ∅, 10 mm apart, round, with white wool, this soon disappearing; **Rsp.** to c. 8, to 15 mm lg., mostly shorter, light brown, brown below and at the tip; **Csp.** 4, cruciform, sometimes flattened, the stoutest one directed downwards, to 3 cm lg., coloured as the Rsp.; **Fl.** bellshaped, to 8 cm ∅, borne on new Ar. in the crown, glossy, light salmon-coloured, with a darker M.-stripe, light yellow below, with lilac to lilac-brown Sc. on the outside; **style** light yellow, with 9 salmon **Sti.**; **Fr.** berry-like, light green to light pink; **S.** cap-shaped.—Uruguay (near Tranqueras). Van Vliet describes this spec. as a transitional form between N. mammulosus and N. herteri; in habitat it grows in full sun on stony ground and in the crevices of rocks. S. of this spec. were earlier distributed under the name N. cupreatus. (Fig. 495.)

N. rubriflorus Kol.
Bo. spherical, becoming columnar, light green, becoming slightly corky below; **Ri.** 21–27, tuberculate; **Ar.** white-woolly; **Rsp.** c. 12, glassy, yellow, lighter, thinner and shorter than in N. herteri; **Csp.** 4, cruciform, yellow, reddish below; **Fl.** red with a light throat, c. 4 cm lg. Very close to N. herteri, but imported much earlier; in the Haage collection at Erfurt there are specimens 50 years old.—Uruguay.

N. rutilans Dän. & Krainz (2)
Bo. spherical to elongated, c. 5 cm h., dull bluish-green; **Ri.** (18–)24, spiralled, Tub. small, chin-like; **Ar.** to 7 mm apart, at first strongly white-woolly; **Rsp.** 14–16, to 5 mm lg., stiff, pungent, white below, brownish-red above, later yellowish to grey; **Csp.** 2, upper one thinner, shorter, lower one stouter, straight or pointing downwards, longer, to 7 mm lg., brilliant brownish-red; **Fl.** 3–4 cm lg., to 6 cm ∅, variable in size, pinkish-carmine, lighter to yellowish-white towards the throat, with white wool and reddish-brown Br. to 5 mm lg.; **Sti.**

* Translators note: Resembles N. horstii, to which some authors refer it as a variety. Probably not self-fertile.

purple, sometimes also yellow.—Uruguay (Cerro Largo).

N. schlosseri van Vliet 1974
Bo. simple, vivid green, reversed pear-shape, later shortly cylindric, to 18 cm lg., to 11 cm ∅; **crown** depressed, surrounded by reddish-brown Sp. and covered with sparse white wool; **Ri.** c. 22, 8 mm h., with chin-like Tub. between the Ar.; **Ar.** little sunken, 7 mm apart, 2 mm ∅, round, with white woolly felt, soon becoming glabrous; **Csp.** 4, cruciform, straight, flattened, stiff, sharp, one of these directed upwards, to 24 mm lg., another pointing downwards, 17 mm lg., all scarcely distinguishable from the Rsp., reddish-brown, blackish-brown below, later greying, often curving; **Rsp.** c. 34, straight, sharp, hyaline, with light brown tip and base, c. 11 mm lg.; **Fl.** borne around the crown, 4.5 cm lg., 5 cm br., not self-fertile; **Tu.** bellshaped, glossy, light lemon-yellow, with pink and greenish Sc. outside, also brown wool and dark brown bristly H.; **Pet.** spatulate, ± fringed above, glossy lemon-yellow, with a light green M.-stripe; **Fil.** light yellow; **style** almost 14 mm lg., with 10 dark purple **Sti.**; **Fr.** dehiscing vertically, with c. 400 **S.**, these with a black glossy tuberculate testa and a hilum with a light, wavy margin.—Uruguay (E. parts of Dept. Maldonado, near Garzon).

N. scopa (Spreng.) Berg. (1)
Bo. spherical, becoming cylindric, to 25 cm h. (and more), to 10 cm ∅, fresh green; **Ri.** 30–35, weakly tuberculate; **Ar.** 5–8 mm apart; **Rsp.** to 40, to 7 mm lg., thin, white, completely concealing the Bo.; **Csp.** 3–4, rather stouter, ± brownish-red, or often to white; **Fl.** c. 4 cm lg. and ∅, canary-yellow, with brown wool and black Br.; **Sti.** red.—S. Brazil, Uruguay.
　　v. **daenikerianus** Krainz: **Rsp.** and **Csp.** yellow or honey-coloured, to 1 cm lg.; **Fl.** c. 3 cm lg., scarcely broader.—Uruguay(?), S. Brazil (?);
　　v. **glauserianus** Krainz: **Rsp.** light yellow; **Csp.** orange to brownish-yellow (lighter above), or chestnut-brown.—Uruguay;
　　v. **ramosus** (v. Osten) Backbg.: **Bo.** more freely offsetting to cushion-forming.

N. securituberculatus (FR 1375): no description available.

N. submammulosus (Lem.) Backbg. (2)
Bo. hemispherical, later sometimes ± oblong, stout or large, mid-green; **Ri.** c. 13, with prominent and chin-like Tub.; **Rsp.** c. 6, upper ones to 7 mm lg., ± subulate, radiating horizontally or directed ± upwards; **Csp.** 2, to 2 cm lg., 1 directed upwards, 1 downwards, flattened, the lower one stouter; **Sp.** light yellowish, tipped brown, stouter ones ruby-

red below, later greying; **Fl.** c. 4 cm lg., yellow; **Sti.** purple.—Uruguay, Argentina.
　　v. **pampeanus** (Speg.) Backbg.: **Bo.** glossy, darker green; **Rsp.** 5–10, whitish; **Csp.** 2(–3), strongly flattened, in part twisted, pale horn-coloured.

N. sucineus Ritt. (FR 1399)
Bo. spherical, later oblong, glossy green, soft, 3–7 cm ∅, simple, crown sunken, spiny; **Ri.** 18–24, 2–3 mm h., notched; **Ar.** round, white, 1–2 mm ∅, 2–4 mm apart, set in the hollows between the Tub.; **Sp.** sharp, straight; **Rsp.** amber-coloured, c. 15–30, 3–6 mm lg.; **Csp.** golden-yellow, 8–12, 7–20 mm lg.; **Fl.** apical, 35 mm lg.; **Ov.** with white wool, with yellow Br. above; **nectary** 1 mm lg.; **Tu.** beaker-shaped, 10 mm lg.; **Fil.** lemon-yellow; **An.** pale yellow; **style** purple, 20 mm lg.; **Sti.** blackish-purple; **Pet.** sulphur-yellow, 18 mm lg., 3–4 mm br., inner ones acute, outer ones rounded; **Fr.** covered with white wool, pulp pink; **S.** less than 1 mm lg., black, slightly tuberculate; hilum basal.—Brazil (Rio Grande do Sul, Sao Gabriel).

N. tabularis (Cels ex K. Sch.) Berg. (2)
Bo. flattened-spherical, to c. 8 cm ∅, bluish-green; **Ri.** 16–23, low, obtuse; **Ar.** 4–5 mm apart; **Rsp.** 16–18, to 1 cm lg., thin-acicular, spreading, hyaline; **Csp.** 4, cruciform, upper one to c. 1.2 cm lg., slightly curving, others shorter, white, brown-tipped; **Fl.** only 6 cm lg.; **Pet.** linear, glossy, yellow; **Sti.** carmine.—Uruguay.

N. tenuicylindricus Ritt. (FR 1361)
Bo. simple, columnar, 2–3 cm thick, 4–8 cm h., green to bluish-greyish; **Ri.** 13–21, 3–4 mm h., notched, tuberculate; **Ar.** in the hollows between the Tub., 1–1.5 mm ∅, white-woolly, 1.5–3 mm apart; **Sp.** straight, stout, sharp; **Rsp.** 10–15, pale yellow, 3–4 mm lg.; **Csp.** 2–4, brownish-red, 3–6 mm lg.; **Fl.** 42 mm lg.; **Ov.** spherical, mostly covered with white wool overtopped by yellow Br.; **nectary** pale yellow; **Tu.** beaker-shaped, 15 mm lg., lemon-yellow; **An.** pale yellow; **Sti.** carmine; **Pet.** 28 mm lg., 5 mm br., brilliant lemon-yellow; **S.** oblong, black, slightly tuberculate, hilum basal, large.—Brazil (Rio Grande do Sul, S. of Alegrete).

N. tenuispinus (Lk. & O.) Hert.: **Notocactus ottonis** v. **tenuispinus** (Lk. & O.) Berg.

N. uebelmannianus Buin.
Bo. flattened-spherical, not offsetting or only rarely, glossy dark green, to 17 cm ∅, to 12 cm h.; **Ri.** 12–16, to 3.5 cm br., rounded, tuberculate, Tub. chin-like, prominent; **Ar.** to 10 mm br., to 8 mm lg., with white wool at first, later glabrous, to 2.5 cm apart, with a small transverse groove beneath the Ar.; **Sp.** mostly appressed; **Rsp.** c. 6, 1–3 cm lg.,

some directed downwards, other shorter ones upwards, white to whitish-grey, unequal, sometimes interlacing; **Fl.** glossy wine-red, to 5 cm br., 4.5 cm lg. when closed; **Tu.** covered with brown wool; **Fil.** creamy-yellow; **style** whitish, sometimes reddish above; **Sti.** red; **Pet.** acute, 2 cm lg., to 4 mm br.; **Fr.** glossy red at maturity; **S.** small, capshaped.—Brazil (Rio Grande do Sul, near Cacapava; found by L. Horst in 1965 only on a single mountain-peak). (Fig. 496.) Named for W. Uebelmann who first imported this fine spec.

v. **flaviflorus** Buin.: **Fl.** yellow; **Fr.** not flat but spherical, otherwise as the type. Grows in mixed companies with the red-flowered type, with c. 20 % of the populations yellow-flowered.

N. **uruguayus** (Ar.) Hert.: **Notocactus ottonis** v. **uruguayus** (Ar.) Berg.

N. vanvlietii Rausch
Bo. simple, reversed pear-shape, to 10 cm h., 6 cm ∅, dark green, crown sunken, with white felt; **Ri.** to 30, vertical, with chin-like **Tub.**; **Ar.** round, c. 2 mm ∅, set in the hollows between the **Tub.**, whitefelty, later glabrous; **Rsp.** 13–15, to 8 mm lg., appressed, interlacing around the **Bo.**; **Csp.** 1–4, bottom one curving downwards, to 15 mm lg., all **Sp.** bristly, weak, reddish to blackish-brown, dark below; **Fl.** self-sterile, in a ring around the crown, 50 mm lg., 57 mm ∅; **Ov.** and **Tu.** yellowish, with pink **Sc.** and brown **Br.**; **Pet.** lanceolate or spatulate, somewhat notched, glossy, light lemon-yellow with a pink M.-stripe, passing over to greenish below, **Sc.** dark green with brown dots, with brown wool and **Br.**; **Tu.** broadly funnelform, yellow, orange-yellow below; **Fil.** white; **style** yellow; **Sti.** 11, violet to purplish-red; **Fr.** spherical, light green; **S.** irregularly bellshaped; Fr. and S. as in N. werdermannianus but smaller in all the parts, while the Sp. are also divergent.—Uruguay (Chuchilla de los once Cerros).

v. **gracilior** Rausch: **Bo.** only 4 cm h., 5 cm ∅; **Ri.** to 25, vertical; **Sp.** yellowish-white to pink, curly; **Rsp.** 13–15; **Csp.** 3–4; **Fl.** yellow to orange-yellow.—Uruguay (between Minas de Corales and Ansina).

N. **velenovskyi** Frič: **Notocactus floricomus** v. **velenovskyi** (Frič ex Backbg.) Krainz.

N. werdermannianus Hert. (2)
Bo. ± spherical, later somewhat broader above, to c. 13 cm h., 10 cm ∅, yellowish-green; **Ri.** c. 40, with numerous smaller chin-like **Tub.**; **Ar.** 5 mm apart; **Rsp.** c. 16, c. 5 mm lg., projecting, yellowish-white; **Csp.** 4, the lowest one longest, c. 1.5 cm lg., directed downwards, stoutly acicular, scarcely pungent, yellowish at first; **Fl.** c. 6 cm lg., over 7 cm

∅, sulphur-yellow, glossy; **Sti.** light purple.—Uruguay (Tacarembó).

Ritter mentions a "novelty, with orange-red Fl." (FR 1269).

Nyctocereus (Berg.) Br. & R. (139)

Thin-stemmed plants, erect, inclined or prostrate, mostly with narrow low ribs, these in one species winged and more prominent. Spination predominantly thin-acicular. Flowers nocturnal, fairly large, white, their tubes and ovaries set with bristly-fine but sharp spines; flowers sometimes arising from the thickened apical zone of the previous year's growth, and thus borne simultaneously both at the tip and lower down. The tube expands into the broad perianth which is not down-curving. Fruit fleshy, spiny or bristly. Seeds large, mostly black.—Distribution: Mexico, Guatemala, Nicaragua. [(R).]

N. chontalensis Alex.
Bo. prostrate, or hanging down over rocks, to 1 m lg. (and more), yellowish-green; **St.** to 40 cm lg., to 5 cm ∅; **Ri.** (4–)5–6, winged, the angles acute, often reddish; **Rsp.** 5–7; **Csp.** 1–4; **Sp.** 0.5–1 cm lg., thin-acicular, centrals rather stouter, ± light brown, later blackish-brown, on stouter growths also 3–4 finer **Br.** in the lower part of the **Ar.**; **Fl.** 6–8 cm lg., strongly perfumed; **Ov.** and **Tu.** only hairy; **Fr.** spherical, c. 2 cm ∅, **Br.** yellow to golden-brown.—Mexico (Oaxaca, between Nejapa and Tehuantepec).
Because of the main floral characters, this plant appears to be referable to Nyctocereus despite the conspicuously low rib-count and stronger reduction of floral Br.; this has its counterpart, e.g. in Parodia and Samaipaticereus inquisivensis.

N. guatemalensis Br. & R.
Bo. ascending, arching over or creeping, 1 m lg. (and more); **St.** 3–6 cm ∅; **Ri.** 8–12, very low, ± rounded; **Rsp.** c. 10; **Csp.** 3–6, mostly much longer than the Rsp., to 4 cm lg. but thinner; **Fl.** 4–7 cm lg., strongly scented; **Ov.** ± tuberculate, with pink or brownish **Sp.**; **Tu.** spiny, crimson outside, carmine inside; **S.** glossy, black.— Guatemala (El Rancho).

N. hirschtianus (K. Sch.) Br. & R.
Bo. columnar, erect, later inclined; **St.** 1–1.5 cm ∅, freely branching; **Ri.** 10, ± acute, scarcely notched; **Rsp.** 7–9, to 9 mm lg., radiating, the lowest one shorter; **Csp.** 3–5, the top one to 2 cm lg., spreading; **Sp.** acicular, stiff, pungent, the larger ones with a bulbous thickening below, reddish to horn-coloured; **Fl.** 4–7 cm lg.; **Tu.** and **Ov.** very spiny.—Nicaragua.

N. neumannii (K. Sch.) Br. & R.
Bo. ascending or bending downwards, to 1 m lg.; **St.** to 3 cm ∅; **Ri.** 13, slightly notched; **Sp.** scarcely differentiated, 10–14, to 4 cm lg., brownish, later greyish; **Fl.** c. 10 cm lg.; **Ov.** tuberculate, with brown or reddish **Sp.**— Nicaragua (near Chiquitillo, Metagalpa).

N. oaxacensis Br. & R.
Bo. ± prostrate; **R.** thick-napiform; **St.** thin, to 3 cm ∅; **Ri.** 7–10, very low; **Rsp.** 8–12, 0.4–1.5 cm lg., thin; **Csp.** 3–5, rather stouter; **Sp.** brownish to brown; **Fl.** reddish or dirty purple outside, only the innermost **Pet.** white; **Ov.** densely set with brownish **Br.**—Mexico. (Fig. 276.)

N. serpentinus (Lag. & Rodr.) Br. & R. (T.)
Bo. erect at first, then arching over, to hanging or creeping, to 3 m lg., branching; **St.** 2–5 cm ∅; **Ri.** 10–13, low, rounded; **Sp.** c. 12, 1–3 cm lg., acicular, pink at first, then whitish to brownish, ± darker-tipped; **Fl.** 15–20 cm lg., **Pet.** reddish-green outside, middle ones carmine-pink, innermost ones white; **Fr.** red, spiny; **S.** 5 mm lg. and more, glossy, black.—Mexico (never re-collected in the wild).
v. **ambiguus** (DC). Berg.: **Bo.** robust, erect with yellow Sp. above; **Fl.** large, deeper carmine-red (presumably the Sep.);
v. **pietatis** H. Bravo 1972: **Bo.** to 1.3 m h., little branching; **St.** to 2 m lg., 6 cm ∅; **Ri.** 16; **Ar.** 1 cm apart, round, with white wool; **Sp.** tangled; **Rsp.** 14, 15 mm lg.; **Csp.** 4–5, 2.5–3 cm lg., intense yellow at first, later whitish; **Fl.** white, nocturnal, 15 cm lg.; **Fr.** 6 cm lg. and 4.5 cm ∅, with numerous Ar. with dark beige felt and Sp. 2.5 cm lg.*—Mexico (Michoacan, La Piedad).
v. **splendens** (DC.) Berg.: **St.** deep glossy green; **Sp.** short, weak, white;
v. **strictior** (Först.) Berg.: **Sp.** flecked blackish-red in the upper part; outer **Pet.** light tawny.

Obregonia Frič (205)

A monotypic genus, conspicuous for the tubercles which are modified into thick, angular scales with the upper part bent outwards. Flowers produced centrally, moderately large, opening widely; apart from the floral remains which persist at the tip of the tube, this is glabrous, similarly the clavate, berry-like, fleshy fruit which dehisces basally; seeds black. The flower-form shows some resemblance to Strombocactus which also possesses unusual angular tubercles, only here the tips appear truncate. In both genera the weak spines soon

* I queried this figure with Mr. Haage but received no reply, so I think it must be treated as suspect. Translator.

drop. In Strombocactus, however, the upper part of the floral tube has dry-bordered scales, the fruit dries up, and the seeds are dust-fine. Despite this, Berger united Obregonia with Strombocactus, while Marshall included it in Ariocarpus. This same procedure has recently been adopted in the USA with the genus Toumeya. These transfers were the result of attempts at systematic simplification; nevertheless they represent synthetic groupings, admittedly of related groups of species, but they do not represent the uniform "generic" characters created by Nature, which are the only ones giving an immediately recognizable natural grouping. Precise segregation into small genera is thus an arrangement which is independent of any theorising, and one which makes the distinguishing features clearly apparent. Moreover, no method can be acceptable if it rests on the piecemeal treatment of small groups of species.— Distribution: Mexico (in the NE.) [✷; cannot be grafted.]

O. denegrii Frič (T.)
Bo. broadly rounded, greyish to dark green, to 12 cm ∅; **Tub.** thick, triangular, to 2.5 cm across the base, to 1.5 cm lg., flat on the upper surface, keeled on the underside; **Ar.** at the tip of the Tub., woolly at first, with 2–4 scarcely pungent and rather weak Sp. to 1.5 cm lg., wool and Sp. soon dropping; **Fl.** white or pale pink, c. 2.5 cm ∅; **Fr.** a white berry.— Mexico (Tamaulipas, San Vicente near Ciudad Victoria). (Fig. 277.)

Opuntia (Tournef.) Mill. (17)

This is the second largest genus in the Cactaceae, with the most extensive north–south distribution in the family; two major areas of distribution are clearly distinguishable, as in the quite closely related cylindric and globose genera: Cylindropuntia-Austrocylindropuntia; and Corynopuntia-Tephrocactus; however the southern "platyopuntioid" group (only c. 45 species) consists of an appreciably smaller number of species than the northern one with c. 200 species. The former genus Opuntia, which previously included not only the genera mentioned but at one time also Consolea, Brasiliopuntia, Nopalea and Grusonia, was a synthetic and unmanageable omnibus genus: unmanageable, since the defining of group-characters was impossible; and synthetic, in that it combined species with flattened or cylindric stems with those having short-clavate to spherical shoots, with a clear geographical division within the two major zones of distribution, the plants in some instances being the sole members of their subfamily. Britton and Rose saw the need for a considerable fragmentation of the old collective genera, principally among the Cereoideae, so that inevitably the same became necessary with the Opuntioideae. Lemaire made a start with Tephrocactus; in 1935 F. M. Knuth segregated Corynopuntia and Cylindropuntia; and the first step was taken towards a more intelligible classification. Austrocylindropuntia had to come next, since the southern cylindric species could not be excluded from this separation into two major distributions. Opuntia nowadays thus contains only species with ± flat and circular stem-segments, with the "dwarf, in part ± rounded" species forming natural stages of reduction. The flowers are ± rotate and very uniform (i.e. Section I: Macranthae [A–1]); in the mostly smaller-flowered species (Section II: Micranthae [A–2]) the petals are ± erect, sometimes abbreviated and narrower, forming a transition to the northern Series "Stenopetaleae" where they are very narrow, and the flowers are sometimes dioecious, although this has no significance as this feature also occurs in some members of Mammillaria and Gymnocalycium. There is great variability in the colour of stems, spines and fruits, as well as the degree of development of glochids or spines, including that of the flowers. Even within a species there can be a considerable range of variability as to a plant's height and flower-colour; in O. lindheimeri for instance the flowers range from yellow to red, and the fruits are polymorphic,—from broadly spherical to oblong; the latter, like the flowers, usually appear in quite large numbers, with the fruit-colour running from various shades of green, through yellow and orange, to red to almost blackish-purple. The fruits in fact can be a longer-lasting adornment to the plant than the flowers, since their colour sometimes alters as the fruit ripens, and this can take up to 2 years in certain instances. Sterile fruits have been reported, as well as others containing very few seeds. The latter are subspherical to flat and round, with a hard testa, and sometimes ± hairy. The scale-leaves of the ovaries and fruits may be quite long and bent outwards, or they can be more strongly or even extremely reduced; glochids (readily detached short spines) are ± always present. Most Opuntias bear their flowers along the margins of the stem-segments although there are species in which they are borne on the flat surface of the pad. The epidermis is smooth, matt, glossy or—a diagnostic character in some species—velvety. Many Opuntias are characterised by abundant flowers; for this reason and because of their variety of colour and their bizarre forms, they are often used for ornamental plantings in tropical to subtropical countries, and in S. Europe. Some species have thus become naturalised; and given their capacity for rapid propagation, they have become a serious nuisance in Australia, India and S. Africa. But in their homelands and in several parts of the warmer countries of the world they represent an important source of animal-fodder, particularly for donkeys; in Mexico they were formerly eaten as a vegetable; they are still the raw material for a beverage, and are made into sweetmeats, while the edible fruits of a number of species are quite often offered for sale in the markets; they are therefore often planted as a commercial crop.

The Opuntias of the Galapagos Islands offer an interesting problem since it is not known how their distribution originated, or that of the genera of Cerei which are now endemic there; however that may be, related genera and species of Opuntioideae and Cereoideae are found on the nearer parts of the S. American continent. The Opuntias of the Galapagos must belong to the northern area of major distribution, as is shown by the fact that certain characters are common to both. A moderately branched specimen of O. galapageia bears a confusing resemblance to many plants of O. chlorotica, and it also flowers quite freely from the pad-surface. (O. bonplandii from Ecuador, which grows to 2–4 m high and has pale yellow acicular spines, may represent a surviving connecting link from former times when the distribution covered a wider area.) At one time botanists knew only one species, with one variety. Then K. Schumann, Weber, Stewart and J. T. Howell erected further species, some of them especially large and trunk-forming plants, and others without any trunk, while further species had larger fruits and seeds. For reasons of logic I feel obliged to gather them all together again. There is, without any question, every sort of gradation regarding plant-height and spination. Differences of height are not a diagnostic character since in O. lindheimeri, for instance, there are forms which are low-growing and broadly branching, while others are tree-like and may reach 4 m in height; the same differences arise in O. dobbieana from Ecuador, and in O. dillenii, while Tephroc. lagopus, for example, may bear either oblong or broadly spherical fruits. Even larger fruits and seeds do not of necessity constitute a differential character at specific level; cytological studies have still to be made. In this case, therefore, it has been necessary to follow the "lumping" treatment which is common in the USA. However, Y. Dawson recently visited the Galapagos Islands and he has restored the old specific demarcations while adding new varieties of O. echios based on differences of the fruits or their size; but as he himself remarks: "Opuntia has developed some remarkable forms here, probably from more than one ancestor". While the Cerei of the Galapagos are much more strongly distinct generically, the Opuntias from these islands in general show much more uniformity of characters, or intermediate stages, so that in view of a certain parallelism with continental species, differences of height or fruit-form cannot reasonably be given exceptional status and elevated to specific characters; I have therefore made no changes to my classification of these Opuntias.—Distribution: from Canada to S. Argentina, in the W. Indies and on the Galapagos Islands. The two major zones of distribution lie on either side of a line from southern N. Peru across to N. Brazil where (as in more southern Pacific Peru and in Chile) no single flat-stemmed species occurs, although they are found again from the S. Peruvian highlands to the SE. or to the S. [○, (R).] To simplify the finding of any particular species, each specific name is followed by a reference based on the following analysis:

A: Northern Group:
  1: Flowers larger
    a: Low and often ± creeping plants, with subterete or narrow stems
    b: Larger-stemmed plants but not large-shrubby to treelike, with circular to broadly oblong segments
    c: Species which form taller shrubs or are treelike
  2: Flowers mostly smaller, petals ± erect
    a: Petals broader
    b: Petals narrower ("Stenopetalae")
B: Southern Group:
  1: Low-growing species with small stems, forming denser groups ("Airampoae")
  2: Larger species but ± creeping to mostly prostrate
  3: Erect, shrubby to ± treelike species.

If a specific name cannot be found here, look under Cylindropuntia, Austrocylindropuntia, Corynopuntia or Tephrocactus; it might also be found under Brasiliopuntia or Consolea or, in one case, under Marenopuntia.

O. abjecta Small (A1–a)
Bo. prostrate, irregularly branching, light green; **Seg.** circular to ± oval, thick; **Glo.** yellowish; **Sp.** thin and bristle-like, solitary, brown to reddish, to 6 cm lg.; **Fl.** mostly solitary; **Fr.** red to purple, 1.5 cm lg.—USA (Florida, Big Pine Key).

O. acaulis Ekm. & Werd. (A1–b)
Bo. to 2 m h., without a trunk; **Seg.** dirty yellowish-green, ovate to oblong, to 20 cm lg., to 13 cm br.; **Sp.** (3–)5–6(–7), 1–2 of these to 4 cm lg., the others to 2 cm lg., greyish-yellowish, stoutly acicular, ± flattened; **Glo.** brownish; **Fl.** yellow, to 7 cm lg., 1.5 cm br.; **Ov.** with Ar. with 1–2 Sp., to 1 cm lg.; **Fr.** ?—Haiti (in the NW.)

O. aciculata Griff. (A1–b)

Bo. to 1 m h., forming clumps to 3 m br.; **Seg.** erect, ± ovate, to 20 cm lg., rounded, dull dark green, ± frosted; **Ar.** large, fairly crowded; **L.** subulate, 7 mm lg.; **Sp.** several, mostly 2, thin-acicular, to 5.5 cm lg., brown below, yellow above, often recurved; **Glo.** numerous, long-persisting; **Fl.** to 10 cm ∅, golden-yellow, green in the centre; **Pet.** broad; **Fr.** pear-shaped, purple.—USA (Texas, Laredo).
  v. **orbiculata** Backbg.: **Seg.** glossy, more circular; **Glo.** in similar thick tufts in the large Ar.; **Fl.** brilliant deep red.

O. adpressa Ritt. (FR 892): no description available.

O. aequatorialis Br. & R. (A1–b)
Bo. to 1.5 m h., bushy, strongly branching; **Seg.** oval to narrowly oblong, to 20 cm lg., 3–8 cm br., fairly easily detached; **Sp.** stiff, subulate, pale yellow, 2–4 at first, later more, 2.5–6 cm lg.; **Fl.** orange-red.—Ecuador (Sibambe).

O. affinis Griff. (A1–b)
Bo. to 1.25 m h., sometimes to 2 m, forming a low tree; **Seg.** ± oval, 13–35 cm lg., broadly rounded above, tapering below, velvety; **Ar.** grey or white, to 3 cm apart; **Sp.** angular to twisted, absent at the base of the shoot, 1–5 above, straw-coloured, becoming white in the 2nd year, one of these to 3 cm lg., others much shorter; **Glo.** light straw; **Fl.** orange outside, centre red; **Fr.** red, rather small-spherical.—Mexico (Oaxaca).

O. albata hort.
Possibly a variety of O. microdasys, with the great advantages that it lacks sharp **Glo.** while also readily producing large numbers of yellow **Fl.**; **Sti.** green.—Mexico.

O. albisaetacens Backbg. (B1)
Bo. with small Seg., freely branching, forming low colonies; **Seg.** oblong, tapering above, to c. 4 cm lg., 2.5 cm br.; **Sp.** later to 10, snow-white, flexible, to 6 cm lg., often tangled and interlacing; **Fl.** red(?).—S. Bolivia (near Tupiza).
  v. **robustior** Backbg.: **Seg.** stouter, to 7.5 cm lg., 3.5 cm br., thicker, 1.5 cm thick; **Ar.** brownish on older Seg., white on new growth, c. 1.6 cm apart; **Sp.** mostly directed downwards, sometimes curving to sharply bent, subterete to compressed and twisted, fairly robust, to 6 cm lg., dirty whitish; **Glo.** whitish; **Fl.** ?

O. alko-tuna Card. (B3)
Bo. erect, with a trunk, branching strongly, to 1.3 m h., trunk to 10 cm ∅; **Seg.** green, thick, ovate to flattened-rounded, tuberculate, to 18 cm lg., 11 cm br.; **Ar.** grey; **Sp.** 2–6, subulate, 1–5 cm lg., grey;

Glo. brownish; **Fl.** rotate, 6–7 cm lg.; **Ov.** with yellow Glo. and small brown Sp.; **Fr.** pear-shaped, firm, 4 cm $\varnothing$, hard inside, green; **S.** yellowish-brown.—Bolivia (Sierra de Tunari, Santa Rosa).

O. allairei Griff. (A1–a)
Bo. prostrate; **R.** napiform; **Seg.** bluish-green, to 15 cm lg.; **Sp.** 0–3, to 2.5 cm lg., yellowish-brown; **Fl.** to 7 cm $\varnothing$, yellow with a red centre; **Fr.** dark red, to 5 cm lg.—USA (Texas, mouth of Trinity River). Probably only a form of O. macrorhiza.

O. ammophila Small (A1–c)
Bo. erect, $\pm$ branching, to 2 m h., finally with a trunk 25 cm $\varnothing$; **R.** napiform; **shoots** from the upper part of the trunk, primary shoots elongated to $\pm$ cylindric, terminal shoots elliptic or oval, to 17 cm lg.; **L.** 1 cm lg., green; **Sp.** slender, 1–2, later mostly along the margin, 2–6 cm lg., $\pm$ terete, more rarely twisted, reddish or red; **Glo.** noticeably heap-like; **Fl.** to 8 cm $\varnothing$, yellow; **Fr.** ovoid, 3 cm lg., $\pm$ purple.—USA (Florida, Fort Pierce).

O. amyclaea Tenore (A1–c)
Bo. erect; **Seg.** matt green, thick, $\pm$ pruinose, oblong to elliptic, to 40 cm lg., half as wide; **Ar.** with 1–2 appressed hairlike Br.; **Sp.** 1–4, white or horn-coloured, stiff, usually under 3 cm lg., the stoutest ones angular; **Glo.** brown; **Fl.** yellow; **Fr.** yellowish-red, not very juicy.—Mexico (Hidalgo, often planted as a crop). Plants of this name in Europe appear to be crosses of O. ficus-indica with O. streptacantha.

O. anacantha Speg. (B2)
Bo. prostrate or inclined to ascending; **branches** to 2.5 m lg.; **Seg.** dark green, oblong, acuminate, 15–40 cm lg., 3.5–7 cm br.; **Ar.** with a red mark; **Sp.** 0 (or 1, rudimentary); **Fl.** 5 cm $\varnothing$, yellow; **Fr.** red, 3 cm lg., yellowish or white inside; **S.** disc-shaped.—Argentina (S. Chaco; Santiago del Estero).

O. anahuacensis Griff. (A1–a)
Bo. low to prostrate, to 1.5 m br., at most 50 cm h.; **Seg.** glossy yellowish-green, oblong, to 27 cm lg., to 13 cm br.; **Sp.** 1–2, porrect, 2–3 cm lg., flattened or twisted; **Fl.** yellow; **Fr.** dark purple, pear-shaped, 7 cm lg.—USA (Texas, Anahuac, mouth of Trinity River).

O. angustata Eng. (A1–b)
Bo. erect; **Seg.** to 25 cm lg., tapering below, half as wide as long, but rather thick; **Ar.** c. 2.5 cm apart; **Sp.** over all the Seg.-surface, sharply angular, 2.5–3.5 cm lg., straw to whitish, darker below; **Glo.** brown; **Fl.** yellow; **Fr.** $\pm$ ovoid, to 3 cm lg.—USA (Arizona, Bottoms).

O. antillana Br. & R. (A1–a)
Bo. $\pm$ prostrate, in colonies 1 m br.; **Seg.** $\pm$ ovate, to 20 cm lg., narrow, $\pm$ terete below, quite readily detached; **Sp.** terete, stiff, 3–6, unequal, 1–6 cm lg., yellow, white eventually; **Glo.** numerous, yellow; **Fl.** 5–7 cm lg., yellow, becoming reddish when fading; **Fr.** purple, 4 cm lg.—Hispaniola and central Antilles.

O. arechavaletai Speg. (B3)
Bo. erect, $\pm$ treelike, to 2 m h., freely branching; **Seg.** dark green, oblong-oval, 25–30 cm lg., 8–12 cm br.; **Ar.** white, without a mark; **Sp.** 1(–3), white, brownish-tipped; **Fl.** 6–7 cm $\varnothing$, lemon-yellow; **Pet.** few; **Fr.** $\pm$ clavate-cylindric, 7 cm lg., purple inside and out.—Uruguay (Montevideo).

O. arenaria Eng. (A1–a)
Bo. prostrate, to 30 cm lg., branching; **R.** spindle-shaped; **Seg.** strongly swollen during the growing period, flattened-terete, flatter during the dry season, to 8 cm lg., half as wide; **Ar.** brown, large, numerous; **Sp.** 5–8, 2–3 of these much longer, to 4 cm lg.; **Glo.** brown; **Fl.** red, 7 cm $\varnothing$; **Fr.** dry, spiny, 3 cm lg.; **S.** large.—USA (Texas; S. New Mexico).

O. armata Backbg. (B1)
Bo. low-growing, forming dense colonies; **Seg.** erect to spreading, terete at first, flattened when older, to 3.5 cm lg., 2 cm thick; **L.** reddish; **Sp.** erect at first, tinged reddish, soon white or milky, to 9, to c. 2.3 cm lg., irregularly spreading; **Glo.** resembling thinner Sp.; **Fl.** ?—N. Argentina (?).
    v. panellana Backbg.: see **Opuntia panellana** (Backbg.) Backbg.

O. arrastradillo Backbg. (A2–b)
Bo. low-shrubby; **Seg.** green, very oblong; **L.** olive-green; **Ar.** numerous, crowded; **Sp.** 1–2, thin, flexible, to 7 mm lg., mostly soon dropping; **Fl.** light orange; **Fr.** ?—Mexico (Zacatecas ?).

O. assumptionis K. Sch. (B3)
Bo. erect, $\pm$ treelike, to 1 m h.; **Seg.** leaf-green, obovate, c. 10 cm lg., 5.5 cm br. eventually; **Ar.** without a spot; **Sp.** 1(–2), brown; **Glo.** scarcely projecting; **Fl.** only 2.5 cm br., lemon-yellow; **Fr.** $\pm$ shortly pear-shaped, 3.5 cm lg., 2.5 cm $\varnothing$; **S.** grey, pubescent.—Paraguay (near Asunción).

O. atrispina Griff. (A1–b)
Bo. low-growing, or an erect shrub, to 60 cm h., forming groups to 2 m br.; **Seg.** light green, to 15 cm br., spineless below; **Sp.** 2–4, spreading, stiff, stout, dark brown, blackish below, longest ones flattened; **Glo.** yellowish at first, then brown; **Fl.** yellow; **Fr.** purplish-red.—USA (Texas, Devil's River).

O. atrocapensis Small (A1–a)
Bo. low-growing, ascending, freely branched but prostrate; **Seg.** ± ovoid, ± glossy deep green, to 10 cm lg., not frosted; **L.** thick-subulate, to 4 mm lg.; **Ar.** small; **Sp.** usually 1, light yellow, later white, straw-coloured when wet, sometimes flecked brown, to 2–3.5 cm lg.; **Fl.** pale yellow, to 5 cm ∅; **Pet.** few; **Fr.** slender-ovoid, to 3.5 cm lg., reddish-purple; **S. c.** 3–3.5 mm lg., flat.—USA (Florida, dunes near Cape Sable).

O. atrofusca hort.: offered commercially, but not described.

O. atropes Rose (A1–c)
Bo. freely branching, to 3 m h.; **Seg.** oblong to ± ovate, deep green, to 30 cm lg., faintly velvety; **L.** to 5 mm lg., velvety; **Ar.** light brown; **Sp.** 3–6 cm lg., whitish or yellowish at first, the base later dark yellow to brown, lighter to white above; **Glo.** yellow, long, numerous; **Fl.** red; **Ov.** ± spineless.—Mexico (Morelos, Yautepec).

O. atro-virens Speg.: probably only a variety of O. mieckleyi K. Sch.: **Seg.** ± spineless, dark green, ± cylindric below; **Sp.** to 15, minute, whitish, dropping; **Fl.** crimson.—Argentina (Corrientes).

O. aulacothele Web. (B1)
Bo. strongly branching, small; **Seg.** greyish to brownish-green, 4–6 cm lg., 2–3 cm br.; **Ar.** without Glo.; **Sp.** 8–10, white, terete, little pungent, upper 4 stouter, to 2–3 cm lg., lower ones very white, only c. 6 mm lg.; **Fl.** ?—Origin ? An insufficiently clarified spec.

O. aurantiaca Lindl. non Gill. (B2)
Bo. not tall, densely bushy, erect to ± prostrate, 15–30 cm h.; **Seg.** linear at first to ± clavate, to 15 cm lg., 10–15 mm br., 8–10 mm thick, dark green; **Ar.** whitish-grey; **Sp.** to 6, 3 uppers stouter, one to 1.5 cm lg., lower ones decurred, bristly, thin, to 2 cm lg., all dirty brownish; **Fl.** orange (yellow also reported); **Fr.** to 3 cm lg., purplish-red inside and out, strongly spiny.—Uruguay (near Montevideo).

O. austrina Small (A1–b)
Bo. erect to ascending; **R.** fibrous or tuberous, tuber to 15 cm lg., 6 cm thick; **Seg.** narrowly ovate or elongated, thick, tuberculate, sinuate, light green, to 12 cm lg.; **L.** to 1 cm lg.; **Sp.** in the upper half of the shoot, or on its margins, (1–)2(–6), sometimes absent, twisted, whitish to pink, darker above and below; **Fl.** to 7 cm ∅, light yellow; **Fr.** to 3 cm lg.—USA (Florida, S. part of the peninsula).

O. azurea Rose (A1–b)
Bo. with spreading branches above a short trunk;

Seg. faded bluish-green, mostly circular to rounded-oblong, to 15 cm ∅, frosted; **Sp.** mostly only in the upper half of the Seg., 2–3 cm lg., ± decurved, ± black when old; **Glo.** brown, numerous; **Fl.** deep yellow, with a red centre; **Fr.** carmine, spherical to ± ovoid, spineless.—Mexico (Zacatecas; Durango ?).

O. bahamana Br. & R. (A1–b): not sufficiently described. Since it has no trunk, it cannot belong in Consolea to which Britton and Rose attributed it. **Seg.** oblong, rather large, but the plant is only to 1.5 m h.; **Sp.** 0 or 1–4, yellow, to 2 cm lg.; **Fl.** 6 cm ∅, ± funnelform, ± pinkish-yellow, more pink inside.—Bahamas (Rocky Slopes, The Bright, Cat Island). Perhaps a cross between Consolea and Opuntia.

O. ballii Rose (A1–a)
Bo. low-growing, spreading; **Seg.** rather thick, pale green, frosted, ± ovate, 6–10 cm lg.; **Sp.** 2–4, brownish, ± flattened, mostly erect, longest ones 4–7 cm lg.; **Glo.** conspicuous; **Fl.** ?; **Fr.** small, spherical, frosted, c. 2 cm lg., spineless; **S.** fairly thick.—USA (W. Texas, Pecos).

O. basilaris Eng. & Big. (A1–a) (A1–b)
Bo. mostly low-growing, with ± erect branches from the base; **Seg.** greyish to bluish-green, often reddened around the Ar., finely velvety, ± ovate, 12–20 cm lg., sometimes more circular; **L.** minute; **Ar.** yellowish; **Sp.** absent; **Glo.** fine, numerous, reddish-brown, soon dropping; **Fl.** purplish-reddish, 5 cm ∅; **Fr.** shortly ovoid, dry, velvety; **S.** large, thick.—USA (SW.) to N. Mexico (Sonora);
v. **cordata** Fobe: **Seg.** cordate above;
v. **humistrata** (Griff.) Marsh.: **Seg.** sometimes elongated, ± ovate to elliptic, rounded above, to 18 cm lg.;
v. **longiareolata** (Clov. & Jott.) L. Benson: **Ar.** more oblong on older **Seg.** which are more spatulate, to 12.5 cm lg., c. 5 cm br.; **Glo.** dropping even on new growth, surrounded by white Ar.-wool.—USA (N. Arizona, Grand Canyon, Granite Rapids);
v. **ramosa** Parish: **Seg.** smooth, oblong, flatter, re-branching also above to form bushy plants.—USA (California, Bear Valley, San Jacinto Plains).
O. basilaris sanguinea hort. is an attractive cultivar: **Seg.** faded bluish-green, oblong to circular, strongly reddened around the Ar.

O. beckeriana K. Sch. (A1–b) may be a cultivar: **Bo.** a low-growing, freely branching shrub; **Seg.** grass-green, to 10 cm lg.; **Sp.** 2–6, straight, yellowish, banded darker to white, to 1 cm lg.; **Fl.** 7–8 cm br., dark yellow.

O. bella Br. & R. (A1–b)
Bo. shrubby, to 1.2 m h., forming dense thickets; **Seg.** matt dark green, to 16 cm lg.; **Sp.** white, 2–6, unequal, acicular, to 2 cm lg.; **Glo.** brown; **Fl.** 5 cm lg., sulphur-yellow, orange when fading; **Fr.** small, greenish-yellow.—Colombia (Dagua).

O. bensonii Sanchez-Mejorada 1972
Bo. treelike, 2–4 m h., with a trunk; **branches** 30 cm lg., 20 cm ∅, reddish-green; **Ar.** 3–4 cm apart, white-felty; **Glo.** golden-yellow; **Sp.** 5–8, to 35 mm lg., whitish, tipped darker; **Fl.** intense yellow; **Fr.** obconical, 6–7 cm lg., dark purple, Ar. with numerous yellow Glo.; **S.** disc-shaped, 4 mm ∅.—Mexico (Michoacan, Palo Pintado, 350 m).

O. bergeriana Web. (A1–c)
Bo. to 3.5 m h., with a **trunk** to 40 cm ∅, strongly branching; **Seg.** narrowly oblong, to c. 25 cm lg.; **Sp.** 2–3–5, subulate, brown or yellowish below, to 4 cm lg., ± flattened; **Glo.** yellow to brownish; **Fl.** intense red; **Fr.** to 4 cm lg., red; **S.** flattened.—Origin? (Known only in cultivation.)

O. bernichiana hort. (A1–b): probably a cross between O. compressa and O. stricta; often seen in S. European collections and particularly recommended for planting in the open, in beds or for ornament, since it produces a prodigious wealth of blossoms. **Bo.** spineless, densely branching; **Seg.** obovate; **Fl.** fairly large, yellow; **Fr.** red, oblong, spineless.—Origin can no longer be established (mentioned in the catalogue of the Marnier-Lapostolle collection). (Fig. 278.)

O. bisetosa Pitt. (A1–b)
Bo. shrubby; **Seg.** oval to oblong, pale green; **Rsp.** several; **Csp.** 1, porrect; **Sp.** all white, the central one longest, twisted.—Venezuela.

O. bispinosa Backbg. (B2)
Bo. prostrate, light to greyish-green; **Seg.** ovate-linear, to 20 cm lg., to 8 cm br., narrower at first; **Ar.** with a violet spot; **L.** short, light green; **Sp.** mostly 2, the longer to 5.5 cm lg., mostly porrect, the second one pointing ± downwards, to 1.3 cm lg., all at first brown to brownish-white, then whitish-grey; **Fl.** intense orange, c. 6 cm lg., 4 cm ∅; **Fr.** ± oblong-spherical, red, to 5.5 cm lg.; **S.** pubescent.—NE. Argentina. (Fig. 279.)

O. boldinghii Br. & R. (A1–b)
Bo. erectly bushy, to 2 m h.; **Seg.** matt, green, ± frosted, ± ovate, to c. 20 cm lg.; **Ar.** large, brown; **Sp.** mostly absent or quite short, brown; **Fl.** 5 cm lg., pinkish-red, rotate; **Fil.** pink; **Fr.** c. 4 cm lg., spineless, ± ovoid.—Venezuela (NW. coast), Curaçao, Trinidad.

O. boliviensis Backbg. (B1)
Bo. in low-growing colonies; **Seg.** light bluish-green, not clearly tapering below, to 6 cm lg., 3.5 cm br., 2 cm thick below, tapering above and more flattened; **Ar.** light brown; **Sp.** to the base of the shoot, **Rsp.** to 5, small, light brownish to whitish; **Csp.** 1–2 or more, whitish, darker-tipped, one Sp. mostly spreading downwards; **Fl.** yellow; **Fr.** with red juice.—Bolivia (E. of Oruro).

O. bonplandii (HBK.) Web. (A1–c)
Bo. a tall shrub, to 4 m h., with a lax crown; **Seg.** ovate or ± so, to 30 cm lg., dull green; **Sp.** 2–7 at first, to 1.6 cm lg., acicular, pale yellow, soon dropping; **Fl.** orange, c. 6 cm lg. and ∅.—Ecuador (Cuenca).

O. borinquensis Br. & R. (A1–a)
Bo. little branching, forming groups to 2 m br., 0.5 m h.; **Seg.** oblong-ovoid, matt, green, compressed-rounded, to 8 cm lg., 4 cm br., 1.5 cm thick; **Ar.** small; **Sp.** at first only 2–3, to 6 cm lg., brown at first, becoming white; **Fl.** ?; **Fr.** ± ovoid, 1.5 cm lg.—Puerto Rico.

O. brachyclada Griff. (A1–a)
Bo. dwarf, much branching; **Seg.** broadly rounded to ± cylindric, small, grey, suffused red; **Ar.** ± prominent; **Sp.** 0; **Glo.** light brown; **Fl.** and **Fr.** ?—USA (California, San Bernardino Mountains, San Gabriel).

O. bravoana Baxt. (A1–b)
Bo. shrubby, to 2 m h., branching from the base; **Seg.** oblong to ± ovate, to 36 cm lg., 14 cm br., smooth or somewhat velvety-papillose, ± tuberculate at first; **Sp.** 0 to several, mostly 2–3, later 5, flattened, weakly twisted, 2–6 cm lg., sometimes decurved, yellowish, later grey, darker below; **Glo.** yellow; **Fl.** 8 cm ∅, yellow with a reddish tint.—Mexico (Baja California, S. of La Paz.)

O. brunnescens Br. & R. (B2)
Bo. forming a low spreading bush, to 1 m h., without a trunk; **Seg.** fairly glossy, oblong to elongated or more circular, dull green, 15–30 cm lg.; **Ar.** with a violet spot; **Sp.** 2–5, brownish, mostly 3, directed sideways and downwards, stout, often twisted, later to 4.5 cm lg.; **Fl.** yellow; **Fr.** red, with Glo. but scarcely spiny, floral scar sunken, red.—N. Argentina (Córdoba).

O. calcicola Wherry (A1–a)
Bo. creeping, ascending; **R.** fibrous; **Seg.** elongated to ± ovate, to 21 cm lg., 4–8 cm br., to 9 mm thick, matt greyish to yellowish-green, weakly frosted at first; **L.** to 8 mm lg., soon dropping; **Sp.** 0, present only on seedlings and then minute, white; **Glo.**

numerous, light greyish-yellow or orange-yellow; **Fl.** numerous, 7–10 cm ⌀, mid to lemon-yellow; **Fr.** slender-ovoid, to 4.5 cm lg., greyish-red; **S.** greyish to orange-yellow.—USA (W. Virginia, N. of Bolivar).

O. camanchica Eng.: **Opuntia phaeacantha** v. **camanchica** (Eng.) Borg.

O. candelabriformis Mart. (A1–b)
Bo. to c. 1 m h., shrubby; **Seg.** to 20 cm lg., 9 cm br., ± obovate; **Ar.** 3 mm ⌀, brownish at first, then white; **Glo.** white; **Sp.** 4–5, 3 of these stout, white, one to 3 cm lg., downcurving, compressed; **Fl.** 8 cm lg., to 7 cm ⌀, carmine; **Fil., style** and **Sti.** carmine.—Mexico (acc. K. Schumann).

O. canina Speg. (B1)
Bo. prostrate or creeping, ± erect at first, **branches** to 3 m lg.; **Seg.** ± linear, light green, 23–35 cm lg., 4.5 cm br.; **Sp.** 0(–2), whitish; **Ar.** without a spot; **Fl.** to 5 cm br., orange; **Fr.** oblong-ovoid, red outside, greenish-white inside; **S.** white.—Argentina (Jujuy, Pampablanca).

O cantabrigiensis Lynch (A1–b)
Bo. erectly shrubby, to 2 m h.; **Seg.** circular to ± ovate, 12–20 cm lg., rather pale bluish-green; **Ar.** brown; **Sp.** acicular, mostly 3–6 or more, rather spreading, brown or reddish below, yellow above, to 4 cm lg.; **Glo.** numerous, 1 cm lg. or more, yellowish; **Fl.** to 6 cm lg., yellowish with a reddish centre; **Ov.** with longer Br.-Sp. above; **Fr.** spherical, 4 cm ⌀, purple; **S.** small.—Mexico (San Luis Potosí; Hidalgo; Querétaro).

O. canteri Arech. (B1)
Bo. erectly bushy, to 1 m h.; **Seg.** glossy green, slender-oblong, to 20 cm lg., 4–6 cm br., tapering to the base; **Sp.** 0(–1–2), 2 cm lg., whitish, brownish-tipped; **Ar.** with a violet spot; **Fl.** c. 4.5 cm ⌀, orange; **Fr.** ± pear-shaped, 5 cm lg.; **S.** flattened.—Uruguay (coast).

O. caracasana SD. (A1–b)
Bo. bushy, to 1.2 m h.; **Seg.** ± oblique-oblong, tapering above and below, to 12.5 cm lg., thick, pale green; **Sp.** 2–4, unequal, 2.5–4 cm lg., pale yellow; **Fl.** and **Fr.** ?—Venezuela (Caracas, in the mountains).

O. cardiosperma K. Sch.(B2)
Bo. erectly shrubby; **Seg.** leaf-green to lighter, oblong to narrowly obovate, tapering below, to 15 cm lg.; **Sp.** 0(–1–2), 1 cm lg., brownish, becoming white; **Ar.** with a dark green spot; **Fl.** ?; **Fr.** slender pear-shaped, 7.5 cm lg., only Glo. present; **S.** heart-shaped, flattened, border hairy.—Paraguay (Recoleta near Asunción).

O. cardona Web.: an undescribed plant which Weber himself regarded as synonymous with O. streptacantha Lem., although the latter flowers yellow to orange, while O. cardona has red Fl.; both have a ± tree-like habit. Possibly it is a cross of O. streptacantha with a red-flowered species of the "Streptacanthae".

O. catingicola Werd.
Bo. shrubby, to 1.5 m h.; **Seg.** oblong, to 15 cm lg.; **Sp.** to 5, acicular, yellowish; **Fl.** light mid-red, relatively small.—Brazil (Bahia, between Mondo Nuevo and Ventura, 600 m).
v. **fulviceps** Backbg.: **Seg.** rounded, to 8 cm br. also broadly rounded, intense to darker green; **Ri.** c. 20, strongly spiralled; **Tub.** discrete or ± connected at the base to ± rounded; **Ar.** c. 3–4 mm lg., light brownish; **Sp.** scarcely differentiated, 5 or more ± centrally arranged, light to dark or reddish-brown at first, longest ones curving ± towards the apex or erect and bent ± outwards, c. 1.5–5 cm lg., or more flexible if longer.

O. cedergreniana Backbg. (B1)
Bo. forming low, lax colonies; **Seg.** chain-like, creeping, suffused reddish, only moderately tapering below, to 10 cm lg., 6 cm br.; **Ar.** set on flat Tub.; **Sp.** to 6, longest ones to 7 cm lg., light reddish-brown or flecked with that colour, others to 3.8 cm lg., some sometimes very short and thin, reddish at first; **Fl.** yellow; **S.** yellowish, wrinkled.—N. Argentina (Los Andes).

O. chaffeyi Br. & R. (A1–a)
Bo. dwarf, in habitat with the growth above-ground probably only annual; **R.** large, fleshy, deep in the ground, to 35 cm lg., 4 cm thick; **St.** to 15 cm lg., to 25 cm lg. in cultivation, often flaccid, prostrate, freely branching; **Seg.** to 5 cm lg., 7 mm thick, slightly flattened, pale bluish-green or reddish, smooth; **L.** minute; **Ar.** with wool brown first, later white; **Sp.** 1(–2–3), acicular, to 3 cm lg., white or pale yellow; **Glo.** numerous, yellow; **Fl.** lemon-yellow; **Fr.** ?—Mexico (Zacatecas, Mazapil).

O. chakensis Speg. (B3)
Bo. ± tree-like, with a ± spineless trunk, to 3 m h.; **Seg.** dark green, slender-lanceolate, tapering to both ends, to 30 cm lg., 9–12 cm br.; **Sp.** 0(–1–2), whitish; **Ar.** without a spot; **Fl.** 6 cm ⌀, dark yellow to orange-yellow; **Fr.** pear-shaped, purple, green inside; **S.** lens-shaped.—N. Argentina (N. and S. Chaco).

O. charlestonensis Clokey: **Opuntia phaeacantha** v. **charlestonensis** (Clokey) Backbg.

O. chlorotica Eng. & Big. (A1–b)
Bo. erectly shrubby, with a trunk, to 2 m h., branches erect; **Seg.** ovate to circular, sometimes even broader than long, to 20 cm lg., bluish-green, ± frosted; **L.** subulate, small, red-tipped; **Sp.** several, mostly decurved to appressed, ± bristly-fine to stiffer, 3–4 cm lg., mid-yellow; **Glo.** fairly numerous, yellow, long; **Fl.** yellow, to 7.5 cm ∅, throat green, turning red as Fl. fades; **Fr.** purple, white inside, 4 cm lg., shortly spined; **S.** small.— USA (New Mexico to Nevada and California).

O. cochabambensis Card. (B3)
Bo. forming small trees, to 1.2 m h., **trunk** 3–4 cm ∅, with Sp. up to 40 or more in number, very thin, appressed, to 2 cm lg.; **Seg.** to 30 cm lg., to 4–5 cm br., flat; **Ar.** white; **Sp.** 3–5, acicular, 2–3 cm lg., whitish, more appressed or more spreading; **Fl.** rotate, 5 cm lg., lemon-yellow; **Ov.** with yellow Glo. and Sp.; **Fr.** 3 cm ∅, purple, Ar. with white felt and crowded Glo.—Bolivia (Cochabamba).

O. comonduensis (Coult.) Br. & R. (A1–a)
Bo. low-growing, forming groups to 20 cm h.; **Seg.** ovate to circular, to 15 cm br., delicately velvety; **Ar.** brown; **Sp.** in the upper part of the Ar., 1–2(–3) at first, later to 10, to over 3–5 cm lg., yellow; **Glo.** yellow; **Fl.** yellow to whitish, 6 cm lg.; **Fr.** purple, 4 cm lg., spineless; **S.** thick.—Mexico (Baja California, Comondu).

O. compressa (Sal.) Macbr. (A1–a) (T.)
Bo. spreading-prostrate; **R.** fibrous; **Seg.** ovate or ± circular, light or pale green, 5–10 cm lg., 5–6 cm br.; **L.** mostly appressed; **Sp.** mostly 0, rarely 1, stouter, brownish to light-coloured, to 2.5 cm lg.; **Glo.** greenish; **Fl.** 5 cm ∅, pale yellow.—USA (on the plains E. and SE. of the Alleghanies). See O. humifusa Raf.!

O. (Platyopuntia) conjungens (FR 895): no description yet available.—Bolivia.

O. cordobensis Speg. (B3)
Bo. erectly shrubby, almost tree-like, to 2 m h., with a robust spiny **trunk**, to 20 cm ∅; **Seg.** elliptic to rhombic, greyish-green, to c. 30 cm lg., not very thick; **Ar.** fairly numerous; **Sp.** 1–6, white, subulate, sometimes ± compressed and twisted; **Fl.** mostly borne on the margins, yellow, c. 8 cm ∅; **style** orange; **Fr.** pale yellow inside and out, c. 8 cm lg., top-shaped, sometimes tinged slightly pink, often empty of S.; **S.** 3 mm lg.—N. Argentina (Córdoba).

O. covillei Br. & R. (A1–b)
Bo. erectly shrubby, forming thickets; **Seg.** circular to ± ovate, pale green, 10–20 cm lg. or more, ± frosted, also reddish; **Ar.** 4 cm apart; **Sp.** 3–4(–5), white at first, later brown, thin, unequal, to 6 cm lg.; **Fl.** large, yellow.—USA (S. California). O. occidentalis, with which this spec. is often confused, grows larger and is found nearer the coast; Sp. directed more downwards, ± bent.

O. crassa Haw. (A1–b)
Bo. erectly shrubby, somewhat branching; **Seg.** frosted, bluish-green, ovate to oblong, thick, to 12.5 cm lg.; **Ar.** brown; **Sp.** mostly 0, never more than 2, to 2.5 cm lg.; **Fl.** yellow; **Fr.** spherical, wine-red.—Origin ? (Often cultivated in tropical America).

O. cretochaeta Griff. (A1–c)
Bo. tree-shaped, to 4 m h., with a lax crown, with a **trunk** to over 1 m lg.; **Seg.** ± ovate, to 32 cm lg., 17 cm br., broadest above midway, dark green, then yellowish-green, smooth; **L.** conical; **Ar.** grey; **Sp.** 1 at first, then 2–5, to 5 cm lg., ± curving, white, or sometimes flattened, twisted; **Glo.** light yellow; **Fl.** deep orange, 5.5 cm ∅; **Fr.** light purple, to 5.5 cm lg., Ar. with 1 white Sp.—Mexico (Dublan).

O. crystalenia Griff. (A1–b–c)
Bo. erect, to 2.5 m h.; **Seg.** bluish-green, frosted, ± broadly ovate, to 25 cm lg.; **L.** subulate; **Sp.** only in the upper part of the shoot, (1–)2(–4), the longest ones to 1.5 cm lg., white; **Glo.** yellow; **Fl.** yellow; **Fr.** ± spherical, c. 4.5 cm ∅, mauve, with thin Sp.—Mexico (Cardenas).

O. cumulicola Small (A1–b)
Bo. erect, to over 1 m h.; **Seg.** light green, elliptic to ± circular or ovate, to 30 cm lg., thick; **L.** subulate; **Sp.** over all the surface, or the margins only, mostly 1, or with a second, very small, not over 3 cm lg., light yellow at first, then light grey or whitish; **Fl.** to 11 cm ∅, deep yellow; **Fr.** ± ovoid, to 5 cm lg., purple; **S.** numerous.—USA (Florida, sand-dunes in the S.)

O. curassavica (L.) Mill. (A1–a)
Bo. half-creeping, low-growing, little branching, also pendant; **Seg.** not tuberculate, always smooth, oval to oblong, distinctly flattened, light green; **Sp.** 4 at first, later numerous and white, to 2.5 cm lg., with white H.; **Glo.** developing later; **Fl.** to 5 cm ∅, yellow, with a slight brownish tinge; **Fr.** ?— Curaçao archipelago.

v. **colombiana** Backbg.: differs from the type as follows: **Seg.** rather shorter; **Sp.** brown (not yellowish).—Colombia (Straits of the Rio Magdalena).

O. curvospina Griff. (A1–c)
Bo. ± tree-like, to 2.4 m h., with a distinct **trunk** and a rounded crown; **Seg.** ± circular, to 22 cm ∅, smooth, frosted, greyish-green, later yellowish-green; **Ar.** light brown at first; **Sp.** numerous, porrect, mostly 6, 4 of these yellow and 2 white, to 5 cm lg., flattened, twisted, pointing in all directions; **Glo.** yellow; **Fl.** to 7 cm ∅, yellow, ± reddish in the centre; **Fr.** dark red, colourless inside, to 10 cm lg., Sp. dropping.—USA (California, Nipton; Nevada, Searchlight).—Possibly only a form of O. chlorotica.

O. cymochila Eng.: **Opuntia tortispina** v. **cymochila** Eng.) Backbg.

O. darrahiana Web. (A1–a)
Bo. in low colonies, to 25 cm h., 40 cm br., freely branching; **Seg.** green to sea-green, rather flat, oval, 8 cm lg., 5 cm br.; **Sp.** c. 6, to 4.5 cm lg., white to greyish-white, brownish-tipped, ± erect; **Glo.** absent ?; **Fl.** and **Fr.** ?—Bahamas (Turks Islands).

O. deamii Rose (A1–b)
Bo. erect, to c. 1 m h., with a trunk; **Seg.** few, ascending, spreading, very large, to 30 cm lg., ± ovate to lanceolate, smooth, light leaf-green, later dark green; **Ar.** small; **Sp.** 2–6, mostly 4, white or matt yellow, 3–5.5 cm lg., stiff, somewhat flattened, spreading, subulate; **Fl.** 7 cm lg., reddish; **Fr.** 6 cm lg., oblong, wine-red, with a few Sp. above, red inside; **S.** small.—Guatemala (Fiscal, Sanarata).

O. decumbens SD. (A1–a)
Bo. low to creeping or to c. 40 cm h.; **Seg.** to c. 20 cm lg. or less, oval to oblong, finely velvety; **Ar.** yellow with a red spot; **Sp.** 0–1 or more, thin, stiff, to 4 cm lg., yellow; **Fl.** numerous, to 4 cm lg., dark yellow; **Fr.** intense purple, juicy.—Mexico and Guatemala.

O. delaetiana (Web.) Web. (B3)
Bo. shrubby to tree-like, height unknown; **Seg.** thin and spineless, becoming stouter, vivid green, narrowly oblong, somewhat sinuate, to 25 cm lg., 8 cm br.; **Sp.** (0–)3–4, horn-coloured; **Fl.** 8 cm ∅, orange-yellow; **Fr.** oblong to pear-shaped, to 7 cm lg.—Paraguay, NE. Argentina.

O. delicata Rose (A1–a)
Bo. prostrate; **Seg.** ovate to subcircular, thin, bluish-green, ± frosted, 4–9 cm br.; **Sp.** in the upper Ar. of the Seg., 1–3, thin, brown, 3–4 cm lg.; **Glo.** brown; **Fl.** 5 cm lg., 6 cm ∅, yellow; **Fr.** oblong, to 3 cm lg.; **S.** small.—USA (SE. Arizona).

O. depauperata Br. & R. (A1–a)
Bo. to only 20 cm h.; **Seg.** slightly flattened, not tuberculate, velvety, dark green, to 12 cm lg.; **Sp.** 2–3, reddish to pale brown, to 2.5 cm lg.; **Glo.** developed later, yellow; **Fl.** ?—N. Venezuela (Zig Zag).

O. depressa Rose (A1–a–b)
Bo. low-growing, spreading and creeping, sometimes to 60 cm h., forming colonies to 4 m br.; **Seg.** velvety at first, dark green, ± oval, 20 cm lg.; **Sp.** mostly 1, or 1–3 shorter Ssp., yellowish; older shoots to 30 cm lg., with 4–5 Sp.; **Fl.** red; **Fr.** small, spherical, with large clusters of brown Glo.—S. Mexico (Tehuacán).

O. dillenii (Ker-Gawl.) Haw. (A1–b–c)
Bo. low-growing, spreading to form thickets, or erect, large and much-branching, to 3 m h. and then forming a trunk; **Seg.** subovate to oblong, to 40 cm lg., sometimes wavy, bluish-green, somewhat frosted, glossy green at first; **Ar.** large, brown or white, distant; **L.** ± bent; **Sp.** very variable, sometimes absent, to 10 on new shoots, ± flattened, curving or straight, sometimes terete, yellow, or banded and/or spotted brown, to 7 cm lg., mostly shorter, later brownish; **Fl.** to 8 cm lg., sometimes reddish at first, normally lemon-yellow; **Fr.** spherical to pear-shaped, 5–7.5 cm lg., purple, spineless, juicy.—USA (SE. coast), Bermudas, W. Indies, N. Venezuela. Naturalised in S. India and Australia.

v. **tehuantepecana** H. Bravo—Cact. y. Suc. Mex., IX: 3, 55–56. 1964. **Bo.** tall, shrubby to ± tree-like, in part like the type, but differing as follows: **Seg.** more yellowish-green, 30 cm lg., 20 cm br.; **Sp.** only 1–3, 2–3 cm lg., white or tipped whitish-brown, banding absent; **Fl.** larger, greenish-yellow; **Fil.** greenish-yellow, shorter; **style** rather elongated, little projecting, green; **Fr.** long pear-shaped, tapering below, to 10 cm lg., yellowish-green, with Ar. 2 mm lg., with 1 coffee-coloured Sp. above, 5 mm lg.; **S.** 4 mm lg., horn-coloured, surface hairy.—Mexico (Oaxaca and Chiapas, Isthmus of Tehuantepec). Fl. can also be almost white.

O. discolor Br. & R. (B1)
Bo. creeping, with tangled branches; **Seg.** of irregular length, dark green, thickish, narrow-elongated, 3–12 cm lg., 1.5–2.5 cm br.; **Sp.** 1–6, brownish, to 3 cm lg.; **Glo.** developing later, numerous; **Fl.** 3 cm ∅, light to orange-yellow; **Fr.** small, red.—Argentina (Tucumán, Santiago del Estero).

O. distans Br. & R. (B3)
Bo. erect, tree-like, to 4 m h., with a short **trunk** to 15 cm ∅; **Seg.** flat, bluish-green, later greyish-green, long-oval, to 25 cm lg., 15 cm br.; **Sp.** 0; **Fl.** 4

cm lg. and ∅, orange-red.—Argentina (Cata-marca).

O. dobbieana Br. & R. (A1–b–c)
Bo. forming a low bush, or large and up to 4 m h.; **Seg.** circular to shortly oblong or ± ovate, 10–25 cm lg., pale green, very spiny; **L.** minute; **Ar.** small; **Sp.** 5–12, ± acicular at first, white, later subulate, 1–3 cm lg., with 2–4 recurved H. in the lower part of the Ar.; **Fl.** to 6 cm lg., chocolate-brown (?); **Fr.** red, juicy, to 5 cm lg., spiny at first.—Ecuador (between Huigra and Sibambe).

O. drummondii Graham (A1–a)
Bo. prostrate, spreading, to 20 cm h.; **R.** with bead-like thickenings; **Seg.** thick, variable, linear to broadly oblong or obovate, c.12 × 6 cm, sometimes darker around the Ar.; **Sp.** 0–4, to 4 cm lg., brownish-red to grey; **Fl.** 6 cm ∅, yellow; **Fr.** red, clavate to ovoid, 3.5 cm lg., spineless.—USA (N. Carolina to Florida).

O. durangensis Br. & R. (A1–b)
Bo. rarely more than 1 m h., occasionally larger, relatively little branching; **Seg.** circular to oval, to 20 cm br., weakly velvety, frosted; **Ar.** numerous; **Sp.** 3–5, to 1.5 cm lg., yellow, at least below, later darker, pungent; **Glo.** yellow or brown; **Fl.** amber-yellow, 5 cm lg.; **Ov.** finely velvety; **Fr.** white or red, shortly spiny.—Mexico (city of Durango and surrounding mountains).

O. eburnispina Small (A1–a)
Bo. prostrate, forming low colonies; **R.** napiform; **Seg.** oval or subcircular, pale green, to 13 cm lg., slightly glossy; **L.** pale green, subulate, somewhat curving; **Sp.** 1–2–4, stout, ivory-white, yellow-tipped at first, then dark grey, greenish when wet; **Fl.** 4–5 cm ∅, yellow; **Fr.** subovoid, to 2 cm lg.—USA (Florida: on sand, near Cape Romano).

O. echios How.: **Opuntia galapageia** v. **echios** (How.) Backbg.

O. eichlamii Rose (A1–c)
Bo. eventually tree-like, with the principal branches ± erect; **Seg.** glossy, green, circular to ± ovate, to 20 cm lg., ± frosted; **L.** minute; **Ar.** small; **Sp.** 4–6, unequal, to 2 cm lg., pink at first, soon becoming white, spreading, larger ones flattened; **Glo.** brown; **Fl.** 3.5 cm lg., carmine; **Fr.** 4 cm lg., tuberculate, not edible.—Guatemala (near the capital).

O. ekmanii Werd. (A1–a)
Bo. low, to 30 cm h., segmented; **Seg.** not tuberculate, 10 cm lg., 3.5 cm br.; **Ar.** distant, with grey to yellowish flocky felt; **Sp.** 2–4(–5), acicular,

to 5 cm lg., rarely with several small Ssp.; **Glo.** light to reddish yellow; **Fl.** 4–7 cm lg., c. 4 cm ∅, yellow; **Fr.** pear-shaped, 4 cm lg.—Haiti (in the NW.)

O. elata Lk. & O. (B3)
Bo. erectly shrubby, to 1–2 m h.; **Seg.** deep green, oblong to obovate, to 25 cm lg., to 15 cm br., rather thick; **Ar.** with a dark spot; **Sp.** 0–1, white; **Fl.** c. 8 cm ∅, orange; **Fr.** clavate, wine-red.—Paraguay.

O. elatior Mill. (A1–c)
Bo. tall-shrubby, to 5 m h.; **Seg.** olive-green, oval to ± round, 10–40 cm lg.; **L.** green, red-tipped; **Sp.** 2–8, acicular, mostly terete, 2–7 cm lg., dark brown; **Fl.** 5 cm ∅, dark yellow, striped red or (when fading?) pink; **Fr.** subovoid, reddish, dark red inside.—Panama, Colombia, Curaçao, Venezuela.

O. ellisiana Griff.: generally regarded as an ecotype of Opuntia lindheimeri Eng.; **Seg.** spineless, at least at first; **Ar.** white-felty; **L.** bent strongly outwards; **Fl.** light orange-yellow; **Fr.** obovoid, glabrous, mauve, floral scar flat, Ar. whitish.—USA (Texas).

O. engelmannii SD. (A1–b)
Bo. erect-shrubby, without a trunk, to 2 m h., mostly lower; **Seg.** circular to oblong, pale green, to 30 cm lg.; **Ar.** becoming large; **Sp.** often missing in the lower part of the shoot, otherwise 1–4, later to 10, ± spreading, whitish, darker below, to 5 cm lg.; **Glo.** brown, yellow-tipped; **Fl.** large, yellow; **Fr.** 4 cm lg., red, spineless.—USA (S. States) to N. Mexico (Durango to Sonora).

v. **discata** (Griff.) C. Z. Nels.; **Seg.** bluish-green, to 25 cm br.; **Ar.** brown; **Sp.** 2–7, 2–5 cm lg., grey with a dark base, or dark to blackish brown.—USA (S. Arizona), Mexico (N. Sonora).

O. erectoclada Backbg. (B1)
Bo. low, ± creeping, forming colonies; **Seg.** dark green, to c. 5 cm lg., 4 cm br., larger in grafted plants; **L.** red; **Sp.** at first very small, very thin, 2 at first, later more, 2–3, pungent, spreading, light-coloured; **Fl.** c. 4 cm ∅, glossy, deep carmine; **Fr.** 3 cm lg., with several brownish Sp., carmine inside and out; **S.** ± wrinkled, kidney-shaped.—N. Argentina (Salta, Cachipampa). (Fig. 280.)

O. erinacea Engl.: an unclarified spec. The plant to which this name is usually attributed is **Opuntia hystricina** v. **bensonii** Backbg.

O. excelsa Sanchez-Mejorada 1972
Bo. tree-like, 8–12 m h., with a woody trunk 5–6 m h., 40 cm ∅; **branches** oblong to truncate, 30 cm lg., 22 cm br., dark green, sometimes quite spineless; **Ar.** 23–28 mm apart, elliptic; **Glo.** short, ochreous;

Sp. 1–3, rarely 3–5, 4–18 mm lg., greyish-white, darker-tipped; **Fl.** orange-pink to yellowish-salmon, with a magenta-red M.-line; **Fr.** pear-shaped, 7–8 cm lg., 4 cm $\emptyset$, purplish-red suffused greenish; **S.** numerous, 4 mm lg., 2 mm thick. Individuals have been known to reach 14 m h.—Mexico (Jalisco, Playa Blanca, La Huerta).

O. feroacantha Rose (A1–c)
Bo. tall-shrubby, to 3 m h., trunk with large Sp.; **Seg.** oblong or subovate, to 20 cm lg., smooth; **Ar.** few, brown; **Sp.** 1–2(–3–4), matt white, one usually very short, later brown below; **Fl.** 4 cm $\emptyset$, colour ?—Mexico (Sinaloa, Nayarit).

O. ficus-indica (L.) Mill. (A1–c)
Bo. tall-shrubby, to $\pm$ tree-like and then with a trunk, to 5 m h., and usually with a larger crown; **Seg.** oblong to $\pm$ spatulate, fairly broad, to c. 50 cm lg.; **Ar.** small; **Sp.** 0; **Glo.** numerous, yellow, soon dropping; **Fl.** to 10 cm $\emptyset$, yellow or orange-red (and the Fr. then red); **Fr.** usually reddish with a yellow tint.—Origin? Extensively planted in the tropics, subtropics and S. Europe, also for its edible fruits. The following are distinguished by the divergent colour or form of the Fr.:

v. alba: Fr. whitish; a form with rudimentary S. is v. asperma, and a still smaller one is subv. minor; v. lutea has yellow Fr.; in v. pyriformis the Fr. are pear-shaped with a "stem", nankeen-yellow inside, yellow outside, with reddish or violet veins, to over 12 cm lg., with few S.; v. rubra has a carmine Fr.; in v. serotina the Fr. is oval, nankeen-yellow or yellow with a reddish tint (names in Borg's "Cacti", all of them merely garden-names).
v. **splendida** Web. is reputedly a form which never flowers and is thus sterile; at one time much used in the production of cochineal;
O. ficus-indica f. **reticulata** Backbg. is an interesting form, with a net-like pattern outlined in brownish felt.

O. flavescens Peebles (A1–b)
Bo. shrubby; **Seg.** yellowish-green, circular to obovate, to 22 cm lg., 17 cm br.; **Sp.** 1–4, only in the upper part of the Seg., to 2.5 cm lg., stout and stiff, yellowish-tipped, brownish below, or white to faded grey with a red or reddish-brown base; **Glo.** brown; **Fl.** yellow; **Fr.** red to purple, yellowish-green inside; **S.** straw-coloured, compressed.—USA (Arizona, Sells).

O. fosbergii C. B. Wolf: a hybrid between Cylindropuntia bigelowii and C. echinocarpa.

O. fragilis (Nutt.) (A1–a)
Bo. low, branching, forming colonies to 20 cm h.,

40 cm br.; **Seg.** $\pm$ without Tub., subterete or often $\pm$ flattened, mostly dark green, to 4 cm lg,; **Ar.** small, white; **Sp.** mostly 1–4, upper one angular, stout, to 3 cm lg., yellowish-brown, often lighter above; **Glo.** yellowish-whitish; **Fl.** 5 cm $\emptyset$, pale yellow to pale reddish-yellow; **Fr.** dry, tuberculate, very spiny; **S.** yellow, flat.—British Columbia; USA (Washington; Oregon to Arizona and NW. Texas). (Fig. 281.)
v. **brachyarthra** (Eng.) Coult.: Seg. with swollen Tub.; Sp. 3–5, stouter, terete; Fl. 2.5 cm $\emptyset$;
v. **denudata** Wiegand & Backbg.: Seg. rather thick, more strongly flattened, to c. 3.75 cm br., usually spineless but sometimes with an occasional, quite short Sp.; Fl. yellow to pink.—USA (Utah);
v. **parviconspicua** Backbg.: Seg. ovate to round, small, weakly tuberculate, scarcely flattened, bluish-green, $\pm$ reddish at first, to 5 cm lg., 2.7 cm br., 1.7 cm thick, Sp. mostly missing, or fine and short, to 1 cm lg., white, brown-tipped; Glo. tufted in older Ar., younger Ar. white-felty; Fl. yellow, c. 5 cm $\emptyset$.—USA (locality ?)

O. fuliginosa Griff. (A1–c)
Bo. tree-shaped, strongly branching, to 4 m h.; **Seg.** circular to oblong, to 30 cm lg., glossy; **Ar.** distant; **Sp.** few, rarely to 6, thin, acicular, dark brown, to 4 cm lg., also horn-coloured; **Glo.** yellow to brown; **Fl.** yellow at first, becoming red, to 6 cm lg.; **Fr.** pear-shaped, red, to 4 cm lg.—Central Mexico.

O. fuscoatra Eng. (A1–a)
Bo. low, with spreading branches; **Seg.** circular to subovate, tuberculate, to 8 cm lg.; **Sp.** 1–2–3, to 3 cm lg., one Sp. rather stout, rarely yellowish, mostly darker brown to $\pm$ black, sometimes $\pm$ flattened; **Fl.** 7.5 cm $\emptyset$, yellow; **Fr.** to 5 cm lg., red.—USA (E. Texas).

O. fusicaulis Griff. (A1–c)
Bo. to 5 m h.; **Seg.** bluish-green, frosted, to 40 cm lg., longer than broad, tapering at the ends, spineless; **Glo.** often missing; **Ar.** small, brownish; **Fl.** ?; **Fr.** greenish-white.—Origin ?

O. galapageia Hensl. (A1–b, 1–c)
In the text introducing this genus I stated my views on the question of whether the Galapagos Opuntias consist of only one species with several varieties, or of several distinct species; however the following remarks deserve mention here: In the Botanical Garden of "Les Cèdres" (Marnier collection) I was able to study the fairly extensive living material; this came from a number of the islands, including many juvenile plants, and was forwarded by Mr. Brosset of UNESCO's "Charles

Darwin" station in Quito. This material, in particular the habitat spination, clearly showed that here was one species only, with numerous intermediates. The former specific names erected by Weber, Schumann, Stewart and Howell can therefore no longer be maintained as such, and are listed below as varieties. Dr. Baur recognised (1891–92) that O. galapageia had a tall trunk in the south, this trunk-development reducing as one goes northwards until, in the northernmost islands, it is entirely absent. My observation of individuals, taken in conjunction with the more recent reports of Y. Dawson on the size and indumentum of flowers and fruits, show that in each of the islands—which had been separated long ago—a characteristic modification had arisen. For ready identification, either of older specimens or juvenile plants, it is therefore essential to know from which island they come and, in the case of the tree-like species, their flower-size. Otherwise the task is impossible, particularly in the case of younger plants. For this reason I am unable to follow Dawson in his recent attempt to segregate the species once more. This was also the view of Dr. Baur after his visit to many of the islands; but until the present time sufficient material has never been available to prove the point.

Accordingly I have segregated these Opuntias as follows:

v. **galapageia**: **Bo.** tree-like, **trunk** thick, to 45 cm ∅, to 2 m h., **crown** broad and laxly spreading; **Seg.** at first intense dark green (new growth), then ± bluish-green, subcircular to oblong or ± oval, to 40 cm lg., 30 cm br.; **Ar.** to 4.5 cm apart; **Sp.** to 20 or more, curly at first, weak, not sharp or only later, finely acicular; **Glo.** present or absent; **Fl.** only c. 2.5 cm ∅, yellow; **Fr.** 2.5 cm lg., broadly spherical, dropping and ripening on the ground.—Islands: Abingdon, James, Bartholomew, Jervis (Duncan?).

v. **brossetii** Backbg. n.v.

Bo. (since it originates on Charles) probably tree-like; **Seg.** oblong, epidermis blackish; **Sp.** firm, pungent, whitish-yellowish to straw-coloured; **Fl.** and **Fr.** unknown.—Charles Island. (Fig. 282.);

v. **echios** (How.) Backbg.: **Bo.** still taller than the type, in part to 8 m h., **trunk** to 4 m lg., **crown** ± erect, lax, sometimes ± pendant; **Seg.** light green, ± oval to elliptic; **Ar.** fairly crowded, brownish; **Sp.** stiffly acicular, pungent, 11–13 cm lg., straw-yellow to brownish, to 13; **Glo.** brown; **Fl.** c. 7 cm lg., tapering conically below; **Ov.** 3.5 cm lg.; **Pet.** yellow; **Fr.** to 6 cm lg., dropping, weakly spiny.—Indefatigable Island (Conway Bay) and the nearby island of Plaza. (Fig. 283.);

subv. **barringtonensis** (Daws.) Backbg. n.comb. (O. echios v. barringtonensis Daws.,

C. & S. J. [US], XXXIV: 4, 104. 1962). **Seg.** more pendant, trunk rather stouter; **Fr.** spineless, 5.5–8 cm lg., tapering below.—Barrington Island;

subv. **inermis** (Daws.) Backbg., n. comb. (O. echios v. inermis Daws., l. c. 103, 1962). **Fl.** 7.2 cm lg.; **Ov.** 4.8 cm lg.; **Fr.** spineless, spherical, 2–4 cm lg.—Albemarle Island;

subv. **prolifera** (Daws.) Backbg. n.comb. (O. echios v. prolifera Daws., l. c. 104. 1962). **Bo.** with a more erect crown; **Seg.** in part pendant; **Fl.** only 2.2 cm br.; **Ov.** 4 cm lg.; **Fr.** to 6.5 cm lg., remaining attached and then with mostly only unripe **S.**, or dropping and rooting to form young plants.—Indefatigable Island;

v. **gigantea** (How.) Backbg.: **Bo.** tree-like, with a long **trunk**, **crown** stout, sometimes hanging down to the ground, overall height to 4–8–10 m.; **Seg.** to 30 cm lg., 20 cm br., intense green; **Ar.** not very crowded; **Sp.** 2.5–3 cm lg., or absent; **Fr.** ± spherical, spiny.—Indefatigable Island (Academy Bay). **S.** at maturity only in the upper part of the **Fr.** (acc. Howell), or else filling the entire cavity (acc. Dawson's illustration);

v. **helleri** (K. Sch.) Backbg.: **Bo.** shrubby, without a trunk, ± prostrate, freely branching; **Seg.** elliptic to oblong or broadly lanceolate, pale yellowish-green to frosted bluish-green, deep green at first, to 35 cm lg., 18 cm br.; **Ar.** 2 mm lg., yellow, with a few **H.**; **Sp.** c. 20, yellowish-brown, to 5 cm lg. below on juveniles, later to only 1.5 cm lg., not pungent; **Glo.** few, fairly inoffensive; **Fl.** to 5.5 cm lg., 3.5 cm ∅, yellow; **Ov.** c. 3 cm lg., with bristly-fine brownish-yellow **Sp.** 2 cm lg.; **Fr.** 3–5 cm lg., with Br.-Sp.—Islands: Tower, Bindloe, Wenman (type-locality), Culpepper;

v. **insularis** (Stew.) Backbg.: **Bo.** mostly to 2 m h., rarely to 4 m, little branching, always with a recognisable **trunk** which is spiny (often smooth in other forms), **crown** to 1 m h.; **Seg.** broadly ovate, tapering and rounded above, greyish-green, to 30 cm lg., 20 cm br.; **Ar.** fairly crowded; **Sp.** rather stiff, thin, shorter; **Glo.** missing, at least later; **Fl.** only 3.5 cm ∅; **Fr.** 2–4 cm lg.—Albemarle Island. This variety must be regarded as an intermediate form between the southern to central variety with quite a tall trunk—O. echios v. inermis, which also occurs on Albermarle—and those with a short trunk (v. saxicola, also found on Albermarle) to those lacking any trunk (v. helleri and v. zacana); the latter occur on the islets close to the main northern islands;

v. **myriacantha** (Web.) Backbg.: Synonym: Opuntia megasperma How.: **Bo.** tree-like, to c. 4 m h., **trunk** to c. 2 m lg., **crown** broad, rounded, dense; **Seg.** yellowish-green, to

35 cm lg., 20 cm br.; **Ar.** 1–2 cm apart; **Sp.** later to 10 cm lg., yellow, ± downwardly directed; **Glo.** to 5 mm lg. or missing (Dawson); **Fl.** c. 8 cm lg. (Schumann; 7 cm lg. acc. Dawson), yellow; **Fr.** not dropping, pear-shaped, ± unarmed, c. 8.2–17 cm lg.; **S.** few, large, compressed.— Islands: Chatham, Hood with Gardner, Charles, Champion;

> subv. **orientalis** (How.) Backbg.: **Fl.** somewhat smaller, to 5.5 cm ∅; **Fr.** 6–8 cm lg.; **S.** to 8 mm lg., 4 mm thick.—Gardner Island (Howell), Chatham (Dawson). **Fl.** (acc. Dawson) 5.5 cm lg., c. 4 cm ∅, not opening widely. (Fig. 284.)

The fruits of the above variety and subvariety do not ripen until the second year; all others in the first year. These representatives from the SE. islands must undoubtedly be attached to Weber's O. myriacantha, although Howell, in his work on the Galapagos Opuntias, dropped the name as being "dubious", or referred it to O. echios typica as a synonym. In this, he overlooked Weber's further description in Schumann's "Gesamtbschrbg.", Appendix, 161. 1903, which mentions "tree-like habit" and "flowers 8 cm lg.", with the ovary 5 cm lg. The locality first given for it is Charles Island. O. megasperma also originated there, or in the southern islands. Confusion with the tree-like O. echios found on Indefatigable is therefore excluded. Given Weber's adequate descriptions, it was possible to establish which Opuntia was intended, and that left only the similar plant Howell had described as O. megasperma.

Dawson also made a classification based on the fruits. All comparative observations have demonstrated the unreliability of this approach, moreover Howell gives "O. megasperma" as having fruits 13–17.5 cm lg., while others were only 9.5 cm lg. The thickness of the fruit-wall is equally variable, acc. Howell from 9–13 mm. Furthermore, both colour and size of the shoots tallies in the two plants. Weber's name must therefore be retained, because his description is just as precise as that of Howell;

v. **saxicola** (How.) Backbg.: **Bo.** with a short trunk to semi-shrubby, with a fairly dense crown, rarely taller; **Seg.** not pendant, nearly circular, green to greyish-green, elliptic to ± ovate, to c. 30 cm lg., 20 cm br.; **Ar.** brown, not very crowded; **Sp.** mostly more than 20, to 9 cm lg., fairly stiff, pungent; **Fl.** 5.5 cm br.; **Fr.** to 4 cm lg., 3 cm ∅; **S.** 3.5 mm lg.—Albemarle Island; v. **zacana** (How.) Backbg.: **Bo.** erect and shrubby, without a trunk, to 1.5 m (rarely to 2.5 m) h.; **Seg.** ±ovate, ± tapering below, to 35 cm lg., 25 cm br., light green; **Ar.** not very crowded; **Sp.** to c. 10, to 1 cm lg., short and stiff; **Glo.** ?; **Fl.**

not described; **Fr.** to 8.5 cm lg., 4.5 cm ∅, rarely with short Sp.—North Seymour Island.

The progressive reduction in trunk-length from south to north, the uniformity of colour in flowers and spines, as well as a comparison of shoot-size, testify to the Galapagos Opuntias being a single, ± variable species. Howell himself said that O. saxicola and O. insularis, for instance, were closely related to O. galapageia.

O. glaucescens SD. (A2–b)
Bo. forming a low erect bush; **Seg.** oblong to subovate, to 15 cm lg., to over 5 cm br., ± frosted, greyish-green, usually reddish at first around the Ar.; **Ar.** grey; **Sp.** 1–4, mostly elongated, to 2.5 cm lg., not very stout, light to ash-grey, eventually also blackish; **Glo.** brown to pink; **Fl.** small, flame to orange, even on the same plant; **Pet.** very erect; **Ov.** green with red Br.—Mexico. Variable: new growth sometimes bluish-green and Sp. light horn-coloured, to 4.5 cm lg., also with very short Ssp.; **Seg.** broadly spatulate, probably transitional to the type.

O. gomei Griff.: a form of **Opuntia lindheimeri** Eng.

O. gorda Griff.: **Opuntia robusta** Wendl.

O. gosseliniana Web. (A1–b)
Bo. erect-shrubby, to c. 1 m h., branching from low down; **Seg.** often broader than long, to 20 cm br., rather thin, mostly ± reddish; **Sp.** mostly very flexible, not stout, projecting, 4–10 cm lg., mostly 1–2, less often 3 but occasionally more, light-coloured to ± reddish-brown, sometimes absent in the lower part of the Seg.; **Fl.** yellow; **Fr.** 4 cm lg., spineless, with numerous Glo.—Mexico (Baja California; Sonora).

> v. **santa-rita** (Griff. & Hare) L. Bens.: **Seg.** circular, bluish-green, reddish only along the margins or around the Ar.; **Sp.** 0–1, dark; **Fl.** mid-yellow, 7 cm ∅.—USA (SE. Arizona).

O. grandiflora Eng. (A1–a)
Bo. prostrate, somewhat ascending, darker green; **Seg.** 12.5–15 cm lg.; **Sp.** 0; **Glo.** thin; **Fl.** yellow, to 12.5 cm ∅, centre red; **Fr.** oblong, 6 cm lg.—USA (Texas, Brazos).

O. grandis Pfeiff. (A2–b)
Bo. low-growing to erect-shrubby, to over 60 cm h.; **Seg.** more circular than oblong, to 18 cm br., reddish at first; **L.** pink; **Sp.** mostly 4, not very stout, usually pointing ± downwards, whitish; **Fl.** 2 cm br., orange-reddish; **Fr.** spherical, c. 3.5 cm ∅, ± spiny, purple inside.—N. Mexico. Variable, with insignificant differences (forms).

O. greenii: see **Opuntia humifusa** Raf.

O. griffithiana Macks.: a form of **Opuntia lindheimeri** Eng.

O. guatemalensis Br. & R. (A1–a)
Bo. low, spreading, resembling O. decumbens but **Seg.** glossy not velvety, deep green; **Ar.** brown, with dark spots; **Sp.** 1–3, terete, acicular, glossy white, dark-tipped soon greying, usually ± spreading and downcurving; only 2.5 cm lg., lemon-yellow.—Guatemala.

O. guerrana Griff. (A1–b)
Bo. erect-shrubby, to 1.2 m h.; **Seg.** ± circular to ± oblong, 15–25 cm lg., thick, frosted; **Ar.** brownish; **Sp.** 1–6, flattened and twisted, white to yellowish; **Fl.** yellow; **Fr.** spherical, "greenish-white" (perhaps refers to unripe Fr., since it has also been reported as being mauve, spiny.)—Mexico (Hidalgo, Dublán). Perhaps only an ecotype of O. robusta Wendl.?

O. guilanchi Griff. (A1–b)
Bo. erectly shrubby, sometimes forming a sort of **trunk**; **Seg.** broadly ovate, to 24 cm lg., to 16 cm br., distinctly velvety; **Fl.** ?; **Fr.** ± spherical, 4 cm ∅, variously coloured.—Mexico (Zacatecas).

O. hanburyana Web. (A1–b)
Bo. bushy, to 2 m h.; **Seg.** narrowly oblong, to 30 cm lg., light green, glossy; **Ar.** brown or blackish; **Sp.** several, acicular, spreading, ± flattened and twisted, to 3 cm lg., yellowish-brown to lighter; **Fl.** small, yellow; **Fr.** small.—Origin ?

O. heliae Matuda (A1–a)
Bo. low, branches ± pendant, to 50 cm lg.; **Seg.** oblong to ovate or ± circular, to 10 cm lg., 8 cm br., pale green, finely hairy; **Sp.** often absent, more rarely 1–2, to 1.5 cm lg.; **Glo.** reddish-yellow; **Fl.** yellow, 3.2 cm ∅.—Mexico (Chiapas, Monte Ovando, on cliffs).

O. helleri K. Sch.: **Opuntia galapageia** v. **helleri** (K. Sch.) Backbg.

O. hernandezii DC. (A1–b)
Bo. shrubby; **Seg.** dark green, to 25 cm lg., somewhat tuberculate, rounded above; **Sp.** c. 2–4 and more, acicular, thin, 2 equally long, 2 shorter; **Fl.** pink; **Fr.** small, green, not very juicy.—Origin ? Perhaps a hybrid.

O. herrfeldtii Kupp.: **Opuntia rufida** Eng.

O. hitchcockii G. Ortega (A1–b)
Bo. low-shrubby, to 50 cm h.; **Seg.** light green,

mostly circular; **Sp.** numerous, 2–3 cm lg. or more, white; **Fl.** yellow; **Fr.** red.—Mexico (Mazatlán, on the coast).

O. hoffmannii H. Bravo (A1–a)
Bo. very low, stongly branching; **Seg.** 2 cm br. or thick, 6–10 cm lg., ± tuberculate, velvety; **Sp.** 3–5 at first, 1–3.5 cm lg., banded light brown and yellow, later white, very pungent; **Fl.** yellow with a faint orange-reddish tint; **Ov.** velvety, with yellow wool and Sp.; **Fr.** reddish 4.3 cm lg.; **S.** yellow, circular—Mexico (Puebla: Tehuacán, Zapotit-lán).

O. hondurensis P. C. Standl. (A1–c)
Bo. tree-like, **trunk** to 30 cm ∅, to 9 m h.; **Seg.** ± ovate to elongated-obovate, 13–22 cm lg., to 7 cm br., pale green; **Sp.** to c. 12, unequal, thin, subterete, reddish-brown to rust-coloured, spreading, longest ones 2–2.5 cm lg.; **Fl.** and **Fr.** ?—Honduras (Aguan valley).

O. horstii W. Heinr.—Descr. Cact. Nov. III: 10. 1963 (A1–b)
Bo. erectly shrubby, low-growing; **Seg.** circular, each set at an angle to the preceding one, to c. 6.5 cm ∅, 6 mm thick, finely pitted, light matt bluish to greyish-green, suffused violet towards the margins and around the Ar., older shoots more strongly coloured; **Ar.** later c. 1.5 cm apart, to 3 mm lg., weakly grey-felty; **L.** to 5 mm lg., reddish to greyish-green; **Glo.** very small, c. 2 mm lg., or sometimes more densely clustering, to 4 mm lg., brilliant reddish-brown; **Sp.** occasionally present on marginal Ar.; **Rsp.** to 3 mm lg., brownish-red, somewhat acicular, **Csp.** stouter, 0–1, to 5 cm lg., upper third light to greyish-white, tip 2 mm lg., blackish-red to brown, bottom of the Sp. similarly coloured; **Fl.** and **Fr.** ?—Origin ? (Fig. 285.)
Holotype in the Botanical Garden of Leipzig University, origin not known; named for the curator, Horst, who rebuilt the war-damaged Leipzig Collection of cacti.
While the plant appears close to O. macrocentra, the latter has larger shoots and lacks Rsp., and the shoots are not so regularly set at an angle to one another.

O. howeyi Purp. (A1–a)
Bo. semi-prostrate, bushy, low, spreading; **Seg.** ± circular, medium-sized; **Sp.** stiff, greyish-white, brown below, to 2.5 cm lg.; **Fl.** pale yellow, greenish inside, limb reddish; **Fr.** spherical, red, spiny.—Mexico (Salinas).

O. huajuapensis H. Bravo (A1–c)
Bo. tree-like; **Seg.** fairly large, to 35 cm lg., 28 cm br., subovate to circular, dark bluish-green, faintly

velvety; **Ar.** grey; **Sp.** several, 4–5 in the upper part of the Ar., 1 cm lg., 3 in the lower part, 3–4 cm lg., yellowish-white, somewhat flattened, spreading downwards or curving; **Glo.** large, yellow, only in the marginal Ar., also 4–6 Br. 5 mm lg., white, twisted; **Fl.** 5–6 cm lg., yellow.—Mexico (Oaxaca, Huajuapán de León; Puebla, Tecamachalco).

O. humifusa Raf. (A1–a)
Bo. creeping, spreading; **R.** fibrous; **L.** spreading; **Seg.** dark green(!), circular to subovate, 7.5–12.5 cm lg.; **Sp.** mostly missing, sometimes 1, stiff, terete, to 2.5 cm lg., also 1–2 small Ssp., whitish, often reddish above and below; **Glo.** reddish-brown; **Fl.** sulphur-yellow, to 8.5 cm br., often with a reddish centre; **Fr.** clavate, glabrous, to 5 cm lg.; **S.** compressed.—USA (from the SE. to far north). See O. compressa (Sal.) Macbr. Synonyms: O. mesacantha Raf., O. rafinesquei Eng.; O. greenei Eng. (often regarded as a variety of the latter), O. oplocarpa Eng. and O. rafinesquei v. microsperma Eng., are at most forms with only slight differences. Eng. (often regarded as a variety of the latter), O.

O. hyptiacantha Web. (A1–b)
Bo. erectly shrubby, to over 1 m h., much branching; **Seg.** pale green, fresh green at first, oblong to suboval, to 30 cm lg.; **Sp.** solitary at first, with 2–3 white Br.-H., slightly pungent, later 4–6(–10) Sp. 1–2 cm lg., spreading or appressed; **Glo.** brownish; **Fl.** red; **Fr.** spherical, yellowish, with long weak Glo.—Mexico (Oaxaca).

O. hystricina Eng. & Big. (A1–a)
Bo. prostrate, spreading; **Seg.** erect, 6–10 cm lg., to 6 cm br., or circular; **Ar.** 1 cm apart; **Sp.** numerous, pale brown to white, 3–10 cm lg., flattened, often down-curving if longer, stiffer, not hair-like or bristly, Ar. with Sp. throughout; **Glo.** yellow; **Fl.** 6 cm lg., 7 cm $\varnothing$, orange or pink; **Fr.** 3 cm lg., dry, ovoid to oblong, spiny above.—USA (New Mexico, Arizona, SW. Colorado, Nevada).
v. **bensonii** Backbg.: forming groups to 30 cm br., 20 cm h.; **Seg.** to 20 cm lg., to 7.5 cm br., more elongated than in the type; **Sp.** 4–9, to 5 cm lg., somewhat flattened, moderately stiff, white or pale grey; **Glo.** to 3 mm lg.; **Fl.** yellow, white, intense pink or red, to 6.5 cm $\varnothing$; **Fr.** 3 cm lg., cylindric, spiny.—USA (Arizona to Utah and California: Mojave Desert);
v. **nicholii** (L. Bens.) Backbg.: groups to 1.8 m br., to 20 cm h., prostrate; **Seg.** subcircular or narrower, 12.5–20 cm lg., 5–12 cm br.; **Ar.** 2 cm apart; **Sp.** in every Ar., 4–7, longer ones in the upper part of the Seg., much flattened, $\pm$ flexible, often reddish at first, then white or grey; **Fl.** ?—USA (Arizona, Colorado Canyon);
v. **ursina** (Web.) Backbg.: in lax low groups; **Seg.**

oblong to $\pm$ ovate, to 15 cm lg., 7.5 cm br.; **Sp.** in every Ar., usually 6–14, 7.5–20 cm lg., very flexible, only slightly compressed, very thin, of even length throughout the shoot, $\pm$ thread-like, white or pale grey, sometimes to 20 bristle-like Sp., reddish-white to brownish; **Fl.** mostly yellow.—USA (SE. California to Arizona). Popularly known as the "Grizzly Bear" cactus.

O. impedata Small (A1–a)
Bo. prostrate, densely branching; **Seg.** fairly thick, oblong to elliptic, to 15 cm lg.; **Sp.** 1–2 or more, light grey, brown-tipped when moist, sometimes salmon-coloured and slightly striped; **Fl.** to 5.5 cm br., light yellow; **Fr.** clavate, 3 cm lg.—USA (Florida: dunes, Atlantic Beach).

O. inaequilateralis Berg.: a cultivar from La Mortola, c. 1.2 m h., which is probably now lost; **Seg.** fresh green, obliquely oblong, to c. 30 cm lg., not frosted, lighter at first; **Sp.** 3–7, acicular to stiffer, later to 15, to 4 cm lg., yellow at first, then white; **Glo.** brown, in dense tufts; **Fl.** large, yellow; **Fr.** oblong, reddish, juicy and sweet.—Origin ?

O. inamoena K. Sch. (A2–a)
Bo. forming low groups to 1 m br., sometimes to 60 cm h.; **R.** fibrous; **Seg.** bluish to deep green, sometimes lighter at first, circular to oblong, to 3 cm $\varnothing$, often thicker below; **Sp.** normally absent; **Glo.** numerous at first, yellowish-brown, new Ar. white, also with downwardly directed hairlets, Glo. and H. soon falling; **Fl.** to 3.5 cm lg., 4 cm $\varnothing$, orange-yellow or orange-reddish; **Fr.** orange, to 3 cm $\varnothing$.—Brazil (Pernambuco).
v. **flaviflora** Backbg.: **Fl.** light yellow, changing to orange-reddish only when fading; **Fr.** numerous, dark violet.

O. insularis Stew.: **Opuntia galapageia** v. **insularis** (Stew.) Backbg.

O. jaliscana H. Bravo 1972
Bo. tree-like, 4 m h., with a trunk, freely branching; **branches** oblong, 20 cm lg. and 8–9 cm $\varnothing$, light green; **Ar.** 2.5 cm apart, round, scarcely felty; **Glo.** short, yellow; **Sp.** 1–3, yellow, 5–15 mm lg.; **Fl.** reddish-orange.—Mexico (Jalisco, Zapotlanejo).

O. jamaicensis Britt. & Harr. (A1–b)
Bo. erectly shrubby, sometimes with a short trunk, moderately branching; **Seg.** matt green, $\pm$ ovate, tapering below, flat, thin, readily detached, to 13 cm lg., 5–7.5 cm br.; **Sp.** 1–5, mostly 2, acicular, white, to 2.5 cm lg.; **Fl.** 4 cm $\varnothing$, light sulphur-yellow with a $\pm$ reddish M.-stripe.—Jamaica (S. of Spanish Town).

O. johnsonii hort.: undoubtedly referable to **Opuntia macbridei** Br. & R. or its v. **orbicularis** Rauh & Backbg.; at most a form, scarcely differentiated; both plants are prostrate to ± creeping, with the first Fl. of the season sunken on any shoot. The type, however, can grow to 60 cm h.

O. juniperina Br. & R. (A1–a)
Bo. low, spreading, not completely prostrate; **Seg.** subovate, fairly flat, to 12 cm lg., broadly rounded above; **Sp.** only in the upper Ar. of a shoot, 1 main Sp. stouter, brown, to 4 cm lg., also several short Ssp.; **Fl.** light yellow; **Fr.** 3 cm lg., dry, spineless, red; **S.** large, irregular.—USA (New Mexico, near Cedar Hill).

O. keyensis Britt. (A1–b)
Bo. erectly shrubby, in groups to 3 m br.; **R.** fibrous; **Seg.** elliptic, ovate to ± spatulate, to 30 cm lg., light green, thick; **Ar.** often quite large and prominent; **Sp.** 4–13, very short, mostly concealed by the Ar.-wool and Glo., pink at first, then salmon-coloured, somewhat flattened; **Fl.** beaker to bellshaped, salmon-red, to 3.5 cm br.; **Fr.** ovoid, to 6 cm lg., purple; **S.** numerous.—USA (Florida, Hammocks, Keys).

O. kiska-loro Speg. (B1)
Bo. prostrate, in broad colonies, branches rooting, to 3 m lg.; **Seg.** light green, ± linear, to 35 cm lg., 4.5 cm br.; **Sp.** 0(–1–2), whitish; **Fl.** 4–5 cm br., orange; **Fr.** 5 cm lg., purple-violet, white inside.—Argentina (more northern areas) to E. Bolivia.

O. laetevirens Backbg. (B1)
Bo. prostrate; **Seg.** glossy, mid-green, to c. 6 cm lg., 4 cm br., irregularly pitted; **Ar.** brownish; **Sp.** unequal, pale yellow at first, then stouter and yellowish, to c. 4, to c. 1.7 cm lg.; **Glo.** light, longer; **Fl.** ?—Origin ? (S. Bolivia or N. Argentina ?).

O. laevis Coult. (A1–b)
Bo. laxly shrubby, to 2 m h., mostly lower in cultivation; **Seg.** oblong to ± ovate, 15–30 cm lg., light green; **Sp.** often 0, mostly 1–3, short, to 1 cm lg., only in the upper part of the Seg., whitish-grey; **Fl.** to 7 cm ∅, lemon-yellow, suffused pink; **Fr.** ovoid, to 7 cm lg.—USA (Arizona), probably also N. Mexico (N. Sonora).
    v. **cañada** (Griff.) Peebl.: **Bo.** to only 1 m h., with a broad crown; **Seg.** to only 22 cm lg., glossy; **Sp.** dissimilar, white to yellow, flattened, sometimes twisted; **Glo.** often numerous at first; **Fl.** yellow, centre red or orange; **Fr.** red.—USA (SE. Arizona).

O. lagunae Baxt. (A1–b)
Bo. shrubby, to over 1 m h.; **Seg.** light mid-green, not bluish-green, young growth never reddish; **Sp.** thinner than in O. robusta and other similar spec.; **Fr.** smaller, spherical, mauve, weakly spiny.—Mexico (Baja California, Sierra de la Laguna).

O. lanceolata Haw. (A1–c)
Bo. eventually ± tree-like; **Seg.** oblong-lanceolate, more or less, matt green, not frosted, to c. 35 cm lg., somewhat tuberculate; **Ar.** small, distant; **Sp.** 0 or few, to only 1 cm lg.; **Glo.** yellow; **Fl.** large, yellow.—Origin ? Possibly only a form or variety of O. ficus-indica, and clearly sharing its characters in part.

O. lasiacantha Pfeiff. (A1–b–c)
Bo. large, shrubby, ± forming a trunk; **Seg.** matt green, oblong to ± subovate, 20–30 cm lg.; **Ar.** small; **Sp.** mostly 1–3, acicular, 2–4 cm lg., white, rather spreading; **Glo.** numerous, dirty yellow to brown; **Fl.** to 8 cm ∅, yellow to intense orange; **Fr.** purple, inside also.—Central Mexico.

O. lata Small (A1–a)
Bo. prostrate, forming colonies to 1 m br., somewhat ascending; **R.** stout; **Seg.** elliptic to narrowly oval, thick, 4–15 cm lg., intense green, rather frosted, especially initially; **Sp.** mostly on the margins of the shoots, thin, mostly 2, pink or banded red, terete, sometimes ± twisted; **Glo.** numerous; **Fl.** yellow, 7–9 cm ∅; **Fr.** clavate, to 6.5 cm lg., red to purplish-reddish; **S.** numerous.—USA (Florida, N. part of the peninsula).

O. lemaireana Cons.: **Opuntia vulgaris** v. **lemaireana** (Cons.) Backbg.

O. leucotricha DC. (A1–c)
Bo. in habitat to 5 m h., with a **trunk**, the latter and branches covered with long Br.-Sp.; **Seg.** circular to oblong, 10–20 cm lg., velvety; **Ar.** moderately crowded; **Sp.** more in the lower part of the Ar., 1–3, white, to 8 cm lg., flexible, weak but somewhat pungent, stiffer at first; **Glo.** yellow; **Fl.** yellow, 6–8 cm ∅; **Fr.** spherical, 4–6 cm lg., variable in colour, white to red or ± violet.—Mexico (Durango, central plateau).

O. lindheimeri Eng. (A1–b–c)
Bo. variable in habit, shrubby to ± tree-like, to 2–4 m h. and then with a recognisable trunk, but also much less; **Seg.** green to leaf-green, sometimes ± frosted, circular to subovate, to 25 cm lg.; **L.** subulate, ± flattened; **Ar.** distant; **Sp.** mostly 1–6, often only 2, to 4 cm lg. and more, projecting, or shorter and only somewhat spreading, pale yellow to whitish, also brownish and dark below, or Sp. sometimes absent; **Glo.** yellow to brownish; **Fl.**

yellow to dark red; **Fr.** ± pear-shaped, purple, sometimes oblong, 3.5–5.5 cm lg.—USA (SW. Louisiana, SE. Texas), NE. Mexico (Tamaulipas). An exceedingly variable spec. The tree-form was named O. alta Griff., and an ecotype without Sp. was called O. ellisiana Griff. (see this also).

v. **chisosensis** M. Anth.: more probably related to O. phaeacantha because of its low, compact habit to 1 m h. and the following characters: **Seg.** to c. 29 cm lg., 22 cm br.; **Sp.** 1–5, yellow at first, sometimes reddish-orange; **Fl.** ?; **Fr.** frosted, small, spherical, c. 4 cm lg., red inside.—USA (Texas, Big Bend, Chisos Mountains).

O. linguiformis Griff. (A1–b)
Bo. bushy, to 1 m h.; **Seg.** conspicuously elongated, oblong or lanceolate, to over 40 cm lg., several times longer than broad, expanding above or else more strongly tapering; **Sp.** few, often only 1–2, to c. 16 mm lg., yellow, thin to firmer, occasionally longer; **Fl.** 7–8 cm ∅, yellow, reddening as it fades; **Fr.** purplish-reddish.—USA (S. Texas, near San Antonio).

O. littoralis (Eng.) Cock. (A1–b)
Bo. shrubby, fairly low or to 1.2 m (–2 m) h.; **Seg.** circular to oblong, thick, 15 cm lg. or more, dull green; **Ar.** large; **Sp.** numerous, yellow, 1–2 cm at first, later much longer, also flattened, acicular, sometimes to 7 cm lg., ± downwardly directed or bent; **Fl.** yellow, 8–12 cm br.; **Fr.** red, juicy, spiny.—USA (coast and islands of south California).

O. longispina Haw. (A1–a)
Bo. very low-growing, forming dense colonies; **Seg.** disc-shaped to thicker below, also obliquely oblong to subcircular, 2–3.5 cm lg.; **Sp.** all ± purple, scarcely differentiated, the outer ones (Rsp.) more numerous and shorter, thin, ± appressed, the inner ones (Csp.) unequal, stouter, obliquely projecting, to c. 1 cm lg. or more, to c. 4; **Fl.** golden-yellow; **Fr.** ?—NW. Argentina (Mendoza to Salta).

v. **agglomerata** Backbg.: **Seg.** crowded, more circular, weakly compressed, tuberculate; **Sp.** greyish-white, (1–)2–3, rather short, one considerably longer;
v. **brevispina** Backbg.: **Ar.** without more numerous outer Rsp. at first; **Glo.** later in large clusters, thin, with fine bristly Ssp., sometimes 1–2 which are longer, light horn-coloured, older ones to 1 cm lg.;
v. **corrugata** (Pfeiff.) Backbg.: **Seg.** oblong to subcircular; **Sp.** almost all white; **Fl.** 2.5 cm lg., peach-coloured (resembles O. multiareolata which has oblique shoots and white Sp., but the latter is chain-like in habit, like O. picardoi and O. obliqua which are close to it);

v. **flavidispina** Backbg.: **Sp.** mostly all yellow; **Fl.** yellow;
v. **intermedia** Backbg.: **Rsp.** yellowish; **Csp.** whitish; **Fl.** light yellowish or peach-coloured.

O. lubrica Griff. (A1–b)
Bo. forming low bushes to 45 cm h.; **Seg.** subcircular to ± subovate, to c. 20 cm br., leaf-green, glossy, papillose; **Ar.** prominent; **Sp.** variable, 0–1–3, sometimes to 16, to 1.2–2.5 cm lg., yellowish, translucent, sometimes darker below; **Glo.** to c. 5 mm lg.; **Fl.** 5–6 cm ∅, yellow, turning reddish as it fades, especially in the throat; **Fr.** light red, red inside, acid; **S.** small.—Mexico (Alonzo).

v. **aurea** (Baxt.) Backbg.: **Seg.** c. 12 cm br. and lg., 2.75 cm thick, light green, finely papillose; **Sp.** 0–1 or more, colourless; **Glo.** golden-brown, prominent; **Fl.** yellow or (when fading?) pink, c. 4 cm ∅; **Fr.** slender-ovoid, fleshy, rarely with one Sp.—USA (SW. Utah, NW. Arizona, California).

O. macateei Br. & R. (A1–a)
Bo. prostrate; **Seg.** 2.5–6 cm lg., circular to subovate, dull green, smooth, later ± tuberculate; **Sp.** 1–3, to 2.5 cm lg., brownish; **Fl.** to 10 cm lg., 8 cm ∅, yellow with a red centre; **Ov.** ± cylindric, to 6 cm lg., with Br. to 12 mm lg.—USA (Texas, Rockport).

O. macbridei Br. & R. (A1–b)
Bo. low-bushy, sometimes forming impenetrable thickets; **Seg.** obovate, 6–8 cm br., to 15 cm lg., smooth, light green, becoming darker green; **Ar.** brown at first; **Sp.** 2–4, grey to whitish or horn-coloured, tipped yellowish, unequal, to 5 cm lg., stiffly subulate; **Fl.** small, orange-reddish; **Pet.** obliquely erect; **Fr.** red to purple.—Peru (Huanuco). (Fig. 286.)

v. **orbicularis** Rauh & Backbg.: **Bo.** prostrate to creeping; **Seg.** succeeding one another like beads, circular, faded greyish-green; **Fl.** scarlet.—N. Peru (Olmos-Jaén valley).
Opuntia johnsonii hort. is at best a more weakly spined form; in all of them the first flowers of the annual growth can be sunken.

O. macdougaliana Rose (A1–c)
Bo. tall-shrubby to tree-like, to 4 m h., branching from near the base; **Seg.** oblong, to 30 cm lg., 8–10 cm br., finely velvety; **Ar.** more distant; **Sp.** mostly 4, 2.5–4 cm lg., one of these longer, somewhat flattened, yellowish, later whitish; **Glo.** short, numerous, yellow; **Fl.** dark orange, almost reddish; **Fr.** spherical, 5 cm lg., red.—Mexico (Oaxaca; S. Puebla).

O. mackensenii Rose (A1–a)

Bo. low-growing; **R.** napiform; **Seg.** 10–20 cm lg., rarely broader than long, frosted pale green at first, later deep green; **Ar.** small; **Sp.** 1–4, white or brown, or white with a brown base, to 5 cm lg., somewhat flattened and twisted; **Glo.** brown; **Fl.** to 8 cm ∅, yellow, brownish-red at the centre; **Fr.** spineless, to 6 cm lg., purplish-pink.—USA (Texas, near Kerville).

O. macrarthra Gibb. (A1–a)
Bo. prostrate to ascending; **Seg.** oblong or oblong-ovate, pale green, thick, weakly glossy, 12–35 cm lg.; **L.** subterete; **Ar.** brown; **Sp.** 0–1, to 2.5 cm lg.; **Glo.**, when present, yellow; **Fl.** ?; **Fr.** to 6 cm lg. Seg. are longer than broad.—USA (S. Carolina, coast).

O. macrocalyx Griff. (A1–b)
Bo. erectly bushy, to 1 m h. and br.; **Seg.** oblong-ovate, greyish-green, velvety, 9–22 cm lg.; **Ar.** 1 cm apart; **Fl.** yellow, greenish outside; **Fr.** red, greenish inside, 7 cm lg.—Mexico (Coahuila, Saltillo).

O. macrocentra Eng. (A1–b)
Bo. shrubby, to 90 cm h.; **Seg.** circular or somewhat oblong, to 20 cm lg., often washed bluish or purple; **Sp.** 0, or if present, only in the upper part of the shoot, 1–2(–3), thin, erect, to 7 cm lg., variable in colour: brown or blackish or whitish above; **Fl.** yellow, turning reddish when fading, 7.5 cm ∅; **Fr.** 6 cm lg., purple.—USA (W. Texas; E. Arizona) to N. Mexico (Chihuahua).
v. **martiniana** L. Bens.: **Seg.** with Sp. at every Ar.; **Sp.** yellow, light brown or reddish-brown below, somewhat flattened.—USA (NW. Arizona);
v. **minor** M. Anth.: **Bo.** without a trunk, ascending and spreading; **Seg.** shortly obovate, 6–10 cm lg., 5–7 cm br.; **Sp.** 2–7, mostly 3–4, acicular, angular, twisted, present only in the upper Ar., brownish-red at first below, then white and tipped orange, older Sp. brownish-red, tipped orange, 2.5–6 cm lg.; **Glo.** numerous, orange, then yellow and brownish-red with a yellow base; **Fl.** ?—USA (Texas, Big Bend Region).

O. macrorhiza Eng. (A1–a)
Bo. prostrate, in colonies to 1 m br.; **R.** napiform; **Seg.** bluish-green, to 16 cm lg., 1 cm thick, matt, ± circular; **Ar.** fairly large; **Glo.** numerous, yellow or brown; **Sp.** sometimes missing, otherwise to 4, unequal, to 2.5 cm lg.; **Fl.** to 8 cm ∅, yellow with a red centre; **Fr.** to 5 cm lg., purple or red; **S.** 5 mm lg.—USA (Missouri and Kansas, to Texas).

O. magnifica Small (A1–b)

Bo. shrubby, to 2 m h., broadly branching; **R.** fibrous, quite thick; **Seg.** elliptic, oval or obovate, to 50 cm lg. and more, light green, frosted; **Ar.** inconspicuous; **Sp.** 1(–2–3), thin to weak, pale yellow, faintly striped, to 1.5 cm lg.; **Fl.** intense yellow, 9–12 cm ∅; **Fr.** conical, 9.5 cm lg., purple; **S.** very numerous.—USA (Florida, Amelia Island).

O. maldonadensis Arech.: regarded as an uncertain spec.; **Bo.** erect, densely bushy; **Seg.** dark green to olive, cylindric at first, to 10 cm lg. and br., terminal Seg. subovate; **Ar.** with a violet mark; **Sp.** 5 or more, to 2.5 cm lg., spreading, reddish to brown.—Uruguay (Maldonado, Punta Ballena). Perhaps a hybrid of O. aurantiaca?

O. marnierana Backbg. (A2–b)
Bo. low-bushy; **Seg.** flattened ovate to oblong, to 18 cm lg. and 14 cm br., bluish-green, not frosted; **Sp.** mostly 2, curving ± strongly downwards or revolute, ± flattened, reddish-brown, brown-tipped, 1–3 cm lg., often 1–2 shorter Ssp.; **Glo.** dark brown; **Fl.** unisexual, orange-reddish; **Pet.** very narrow, quite strongly erect.—Mexico.

O. maxima Mill. non SD. (A1–c)
Bo. large-shrubby, strongly branching; **Seg.** pale green, elongated, ± broadly oval, rounded above, not tuberculate, to 35 cm lg., to over 18 cm br.; **Ar.** small, distant; **Sp.** 0–1–2, short, white, to 12 mm lg.; **Glo.** yellow to brown; **Fl.** orange, to 8 cm ∅; **Fr.** ± oblong, reddish.—Origin ? (Known only in cultivation). O. maxima SD. was no more than a name.

O. maxonii G. Ortega (A1–a–b)
Bo. low, to 50 cm h.; **Seg.** fairly large, reddish to reddish-green; **Ar.** crowded; **Sp.** 1–2, 2–3 cm lg.; **Glo.** numerous, yellow; **Fl.** intense yellow; **Fr.** 2 cm lg., pulp strongly coloured.—Mexico (Sinaloa).

O. megacantha SD. (A1–c)
Bo. tree-like, to 5 m h. or more, developing a trunk; **Seg.** pale green, matt, subovate to oblong, also asymmetrical, younger ones to c. 17 cm lg., old ones to 40(–60) cm lg., to over 7.5 cm br., considerably smaller in cultivation, slightly frosted; **L.** small, 3 mm lg.; **Ar.** small, distant, brown at first; **Sp.** white, mostly 1–5, c. 2–3 cm lg., sometimes only in the upper Ar.; **Glo.** few, yellow, dropping; **Fl.** yellow to orange, c. 8 cm ∅; **Fr.** to 8 cm lg., whitish-yellow.—Mexico (Central Highlands; cultivated in Jamaica and California; naturalised in Hawaii).

O. megalantha Griff. (A1–b–c)
Bo. erect, shrubby, to over 2 m h.; **Seg.** ± ovate, frosted, greyish-green, to over 20 cm lg., 14 cm br.; **Sp.** 1–3, longest ones to 4–5 cm lg., yellow; **Fl.**

367

yellow, 10–11 cm $\emptyset$; **style** white; **Sti.** white or greenish; **Fr.** dark red.—Origin ? (Hybrid; **Sp.** said to be flattened in some cases.)

O. megapotamica Arech. (B3)
Bo. erect, forming a small shrub to c. 1 m h.; **Seg.** faded green, circular to $\pm$ oblong, to c. 10–12 cm lg. and almost as broad; **Ar.** with a dark spot; **Sp.** 0 (rarely 1, short); **Fl.** orange; **Fr.** red, oblong.—Uruguay.

O. megarhiza Rose (A1–a)
Bo. low, to 30 cm h., strongly branching; **R.** to 6 cm thick, to 60 cm lg.; **Seg.** thin, to 30 cm lg., 3 cm br.; **Sp.** to 2.5 cm lg., brown; **Fl.** lemon-yellow, often washed pink, 5 cm $\emptyset$; **Fr.** and **S.** ?—Mexico (San Luis Potosí, near Alvarez).

O. megasperma How. and v. orientalis How.: **Opuntia galapageia** v. **myriacantha** (Web.) Backbg. and subv. **orientalis** (How.) Backbg.

O. melanosperma Svenson (A1–b)
Bo. bushy, to 1.2 m h.; **Seg.** semi-erect to prostrate, flat, light green, obovate, to 15 cm lg., to 9 cm br.; **Ar.** delicate brown; **Sp.** 1–3, yellow, straight, acicular, to 2 cm lg.; **Glo.** yellowish; **Fl.** orange-yellow, reddish when fading, 6 cm $\emptyset$; **Fr.** 4 cm lg., reddish; **S.** dark.—Ecuador (Punta Ayangue).

O. mesacantha Raf. and var.: **Opuntia humifusa** Raf.

O. microdasys (Lehm.) Pfeiff. (A1–b)
Bo. moderately high bushes, densely and more broadly branching, sometimes prostrate, at times to 60 cm h.; **Seg.** subcircular to $\pm$ oblong, to 15 cm lg., mostly pale green, softly velvety, spineless; **Ar.** (**Glo.**) light yellow on new growth, later deeper yellow, numerous, dense; **buds** greenish; **Fl.** numerous, 4–5 cm lg., pure yellow, reddish-yellow when fading; **Fr.** oblong, to 4.5 cm lg., light violet-red.—Mexico (in the N. and to Zacatecas, N. Hidalgo). There is a form with smaller shoots and Fl. (Rivière No. 8210).
   v. **albispina** Fobe: **Seg.** mid-green; **Glo.** white, $\pm$ falling; **buds** reddish; **Fl.** whitish-yellow; **Fr.** darker violet-red, outside and inside; f. alba hort. is a form with light greenish buds; form "Angel's Wings" (nom. prop.: f. laxiglochidiata) has finely flocky Ar.; **Fl.** greenish-yellow; f. albata hort. ("Polka Dot") is said to have harmless Glo., but these are dropped in full sunshine at higher temperatures. There is also f. **minima**, with **Seg.** lighter green and very small;
   v. aurantiaca hort., with larger Seg. and brownish-yellow, rather more distant and larger

Ar., may be a cross with O. rufida or O. macrocalyx;
   v. gracilior hort.: v. **laevior** SD.;
   v. hildmannii hort.: only a name of Schelle's;
   v. **laevior** SD.: **Seg.** darker green, lighter at first, smaller, freely branching; **Ar.** golden-yellow to golden-brown (**Glo.**); **buds** reddish; **Fl.** light yellow; **Fr.** oblong, light red inside and out, smaller than in the type;
   v. lutea hort.: an American name, perhaps for v. aurantiaca hort.?
   v. minima hort.: probably identical with v. **rufida** f. **minima** hort.;
   v. minor SD.: at most an ecotype of the type;
   v. **pallida** hort.: **Seg.** greyish-green; **Glo.** pale yellow, later brownish; **buds** greenish to reddish; **Fl.** light yellow; **Fr.** more strongly oblong to $\pm$ clavate, lighter red; pulp glassy-white(!);
   v. **rufida** K. Sch. (non Op. rufida Eng.): **Seg.** more distinctly oblong-oval, deeper green; **Ar.** crowded, brownish (**Glo.**); **buds** reddish; **Fl.** yellowish;
      sv. **albiflora** Backbg.: **Ar.(Glo.)** somewhat larger; **buds** greenish-yellow; **Fl.** pure white; **Fr.** yellowish;
   v. **rufida** f. **minima** hort.: dwarf form; **Seg.** relatively minute; **Fl.** faintly yellowish, throat more intensely yellowish, white outside; **Fr.** reddish, glassy-green inside.
   v. (f.) undulata hort.: a form with wavy Seg.
Very variable spec., with further divergent forms; v. pallida, for instance, is one with light green buds, and Fr. light red and more spherical than in v. microdasys; also a form of v. microdasys with yellow buds and smaller Fr.

O. microdisca Web.: **Opuntia longispina** Haw.

O. mieckleyi K. Sch. (A1–b)
Bo. low-shrubby, erect; **Seg.** darker green, narrowly oblong, 15–25 cm lg., 4–6 cm br. (terminal shoots); **Ar.** with a dark spot; **Sp.** 0(–1–2, dark); **Fl.** 6 cm $\emptyset$, orange to brick-red.—Paraguay (San Salvador, Estancia Loma).

O. militaris Br. & R. (A1–a)
Bo. low-growing, to 30 cm h., slightly spreading; **Seg.** narrowly oblong to subovate, rather thick, $\pm$ glossy at first; **Sp.** 1–2 at first, sometimes more; **Fl.** only 3 cm lg., greenish to cream; **Ov.** spineless.—Cuba (Guantánamo Bay).

O. missouriensis DC.: **Opuntia polyacantha** Haw.

O. mojavensis Eng.: **Opuntia phaeacantha** v. **mojavensis** (Eng.) Fosb.

O. monacantha Haw.: **Opuntia vulgaris** Mill.

O. montevidensis Speg. (B2–3)
Bo. bushy, semi-erect to prostrate, to 50 cm h., to 75 cm br.; **Seg.** ± ovate-elliptic, rather flat, to 10 cm lg., to 3.5 cm br., to 8 mm thick; **Ar.** with a dark spot; **Sp.** typically 5, 1–3 of these Csp. to 3 cm lg., stout, radials bristly, thin, whitish, ± appressed, all at first honey-coloured; **Fl.** 3.5 cm lg., orange; **Fr.** 4 cm lg., ± clavate, purple outside and in. — Uruguay (Cerro near Montevideo).

O. multiareolata Backbg. (B1)
Bo. creeping; **Seg.** small, branching to form chains, set obliquely, c. 2.5 cm lg., 2.3 cm br., tapering below, green; **Ar.** rather prominent, crowded, with greyish-white felt; **Sp.** (2–)6–7, thin, whitish, to 3 mm lg., little projecting; **Fl.** ? — NW. Argentina.

O. × munzii C. B. Wolf: **Cylindropuntia × munzii** (C. B. Wolf) Backbg.

O. myriacantha Web.: **Opuntia galapageia** v. **myriacantha** (Web.) Backbg.

O. nejapensis H. Bravo 1972
Bo. tree-like, forming a trunk; **Seg.** 30–35 cm lg. and 20–25 cm ∅, yellowish-green, thick, ± wavy; **Ar.** few, 5–7 cm apart; **Sp.** 3, upper one 5–8 cm lg., lower ones 2–3 cm lg., white, tipped yellowish; **Fl.** not known; **Fr.** large, fig-like, 7–8 cm lg., 5 cm ∅; **S.** light beige, 5 mm ∅. — Mexico (Oaxaca, between Camarones and Nejapa).

O. nemoralis Griff. (A1–a)
Bo. prostrate, in colonies to 1 m br., to 30 cm h.; **R.** fibrous; **Seg.** ± ovate, to 9 cm lg., not tuberculate, smooth; **Ar.** sometimes with a red spot; **Sp.** ± subulate, whitish, to 2.5 cm lg.; **Glo.** yellow; **Fl.** yellow; **Fr.** ovoid to pear-shaped, 3 cm lg., light red. — USA (Texas, Longview).

O. nicholii L. Bens.: **Opuntia hystricina** v. **nicholii** (L. Bens.) Backbg.

O. nitens Small (A1–b)
Bo. bushy, to 1 m h.; **R.** fibrous; **Seg.** obovate, 6–15 cm lg., glossy, green, not frosted, rather thick; **Ar.** ± prominent; **Sp.** 1(–4), brown, lighter-tipped, later dark grey; **Fl.** light yellow, to 6.5 cm ∅; **Fr.** ovoid to clavate, 4 cm lg., purple. — USA (Florida, W. bank of the Halifax River).

O. obliqua Backbg. (B1)
Bo. very low-growing, creeping, spreading, similar to O. picardoi but with the epidermis faintly spotted; **Seg.** obliquely set, to 4 cm lg.; **Ar.** brownish at first; **Sp.** mostly 5–7, at first white flecked brown, later grey, fairly long; **Glo.** longer,

brownish, in projecting tufts; **Fl.** red. — N. Argentina.

O. occidentalis Eng. & Big. (A1–b)
Bo. erect, shrubby, forming large thickets, over 1 m h.; **Seg.** oblong-ovate, 20–30 cm lg.; **Sp.** 2–7, longest ones to 5 cm lg., ± flattened, brown to lighter and sometimes whitish, or the shorter ones whitish; **Glo.** brown; **Fl.** yellow, large, to c. 10 cm lg.; **Fr.** large, purple. — USA (S. California, W. slopes of the mountains), Mexico (Baja California).

O. occidentalis v. piercei (Fosb.) Munz: **Opuntia phaeacantha** v. **piercii** Fosb.

O. ochrocentra Small (A1–b)
Bo. shrubby, freely branching, to 1 m h.; **R.** fibrous; **Seg.** elliptic to oval, light green, rather thick, to 30 cm lg.; **Ar.** prominent; **Sp.** 5–6, yellow, stiff, subulate, to c. 5 cm lg., recurved; **Fl.** light lemon-yellow, to 8.5 cm ∅; **Fr.** ± ovoid, c. 2 cm lg., red. — USA (Florida, S.E. of Big Pine Key).

O. orbiculata SD. (A1–b)
Bo. shrubby, c. 1 m h., without a trunk; **Seg.** green to bluish-green, circular to ± ovate, sometimes spatulate, to 15 cm lg.; **Ar.** with fairly long H. persisting for some time; **Sp.** to 6, acicular or sometimes twisted, 4 cm lg., yellowish at first, then white to grey; **Fl.** to 10 cm ∅, yellow, washed ± reddish. — N. Mexico. A robust and very frost-resistant stock, useful in horticulture for speedy growth.

O. oricola Philbr. — C. & S. J. (US) XXXVI: 6, 163–165. 1964 (A1–c)
Bo. ascending, branching, to 3 m h., branches in part bent downwards at the tips; **Seg.** 15–25 cm lg., 12–19 cm br., circular to elliptic, colour of epidermis not known; **Sp.** yellow at first, translucent, number not known; **Fl.** c. 7 cm lg. and ∅, yellow; **Sep.** irregularly dentate; **Pet.** moderately broad, often apiculate; **Fr.** spherical, c. 5 cm lg., 4.5 cm ∅, with fine, longer, projecting Sp. (Glo.?); **S.** ? — USA (type-locality San Ysidro Canyon (California), to Mexico (Baja California, S. of Enseñada); also the Californian Channel Islands and the Mexican Los Coronados Islands). The brief description made no mention of spine-count, or the colour of Fr. and Seg. Restricted to areas close to the sea.

O. orurensis Card. (B1)
Bo. very low, to 10 cm h., in groups to 50 cm br.; **Seg.** elliptic, ± curving, ± cylindric below, flattened above, rounded at the tip, tuberculate, readily detached; **Sp.** scarcely differentiated, lower Ar. with 6–8, some reddish-brown, others white

and red-tipped, upper **Ar.** with 4–8 purplish-brown **Sp.**, all acicular, pungent, erect, 5–22 mm lg.; **Glo.** numerous, yellow and brown; **Fl.** sulphur-yellow, 4 cm lg.; **Fr.** to 2 cm lg., ± conical, purple, mostly sterile.—Bolivia (Dept. Oruro).

O. pachona Griff.: said to be an ecotype of **Opuntia streptacantha** Lem.

O. pailana Wgt. (A1–b)
Bo. erect, shrubby; **Seg.** circular to ± ovate, to 10 cm lg., 9 cm br., bluish-green, smooth, slightly glossy, later more yellowish-green; **Ar.** brown; **Sp.** 3 at first, later 6–8, to 3 cm lg., one of these white at first, then with dark flecks and finally brown, the others white, brown-tipped, with H. which are later fairly long; **Glo.** greyish-yellow; **Fl.** ?—Mexico (Coahuila, Sierra de la Paila). Not re-collected for a long time. Perhaps identical with O. crinifera SD.?

O. palmadora Br. & R. (A2–a)
Bo. tall, shrubby, to 3.5 m h., but often low-growing, sometimes with a trunk to 9 cm ∅, often very spiny; **Seg.** numerous, very thin, narrow, to 15 cm lg., mostly erect; **Ar.** white; **Sp.** mostly 1–4(–6), yellow at first, later white, to 3 cm lg.; **Fl.** moderately large; **Pet.** erect, brick-red; **Ov.** with longitudinal Tub.; **Fr.** small; **epidermis** papillose, particularly when dry.—Brazil (Bahia, occurring frequently in the Caatinga).

O. palmeri Eng. (A1–b)
Bo. shrubby; **Seg.** pale bluish-green, oval, smooth, to 25 cm lg., to 20 cm br.; **Ar.** pale brown at first; **Sp.** 5–7, only 1–3 in lower Ar., straw-coloured, thin, flattened to compressed, decurved to spreading; **Fl.** and **Fr.** ?—USA (Utah, St. George).

O. panellana (Backbg.) Backbg. (B1)
Bo. low-growing, forming squarrose groups; **Seg.** ± circular to moderately flattened, to 3 cm lg., to 1.5 cm br., ± tapering to both ends; **Ar.** often set in a reddish zone; **Sp.** to c. (5–7–)9, 0.6–2 cm lg., thin, stiff, unequal, reddish-white at first, later dirty white and reddish above and below, sometimes weakly compressed and ± twisted, sometimes also straw-coloured; **Glo.** light brown to whitish, erect.—Origin?

O. paraguayensis K. Sch. (B3)
Bo. erectly shrubby, freely branching, 1–2 m h.; **Seg.** light green, obovate, to 21 cm lg., 5–8.5 cm br.; **Sp.** 0, rarely one, light-coloured; **Glo.** yellowish; **Fl.** 8 cm ∅, orange; **Fr.** conical, to 7 cm lg., dark purple; **S.** round.—Paraguay (near Escoban).

O. pascoensis Br. & R. (A1–a)

Bo. low-shrubby, to 30 cm h.; **Seg.** to 4 cm br., to 12 cm lg., not tuberculate, circular, little flattened; **Ar.** brown with a dark spot and white H.; **Sp.** 4–5 at first, to 2 cm lg., yellow; **Glo.** numerous, short, yellow, only developing later; **Fl.** ?; **Fr.** spherical, 1.5 cm ∅, spiny above.—Peru (Matucana, Pasco). Resembles O. pestifer which has tuberculate shoots, is not velvety and lacks H.

O. peckii Purp. (A1–b[a])
Bo. a low-growing spreading shrub; **Seg.** small, circular, densely spiny; **Sp.** brown below, white above; **Fl.** large, pale yellow, darker yellow inside.—USA and/or Mexico ? Description inadequate. Perhaps only a form or variety of O. howeyi Purp.?

O. penicilligera Speg. (B2)
Bo. forming ± prostrate groups; **Seg.** flattened, circular to broadly ovate, to 12 cm lg., to 10 cm br., dark green; **Sp.** thin, twisted, (1–)3, one Csp. 1–5 cm lg., radials 0–3–4, shorter, all of them white; **Glo.** rusty-red, developing later, to 6 mm lg., tufted; **Fl.** lemon-yellow; **Ov.** with many Ar. and Glo.; **Fr.** clavate, reddish, to 4.5 cm lg.; **S.** small, kidney-shaped, with felty H.—Argentina (Rio Negro, Rio Colorado, Pampa Sanquil-co, to Bahia Blanca).

O. pennellii Br. & R. (A1–a)
Bo. prostrate; **Seg.** ± ovate, smooth, thick, to 15 cm lg.; **Sp.** 1–7, subulate, to 3.5 cm lg., white dark-tipped; **Glo.** inconspicuous, yellowish; **Fl.** yellow?—Colombia (Magangue, on the plains).

O. pes-corvi Le Conte (A1–a)
Close to O. drummondii Grah.; **Sp.** only 1–3; **Fl.** only 4 cm ∅; **Fr.** to only 14 mm lg., purplish-pink.—USA (Florida).

O. pestifer Br. & R. (A1–a)
Bo. ± prostrate, forming a squarrose shrub, to 20 cm h. and more; **Seg.** flatter, less so later, not velvety, tuberculate, to 3 cm br., to 5 cm lg. and more; **Sp.** 2–5 at first, brownish, to 3 cm lg.; **Glo.** yellow; **Fl.** light yellow, c. 4 cm lg. and ∅.—Central Ecuador to Central Peru.

O. phaeacantha Eng. (A1–a to 1–b)
Bo. shrubby, low to taller, the type to c. 1 m h., quite broadly spreading; **Seg.** longer than broad, 10–15 cm lg., mostly spineless below; **Ar.** more distant; **Sp.** 1–4, ± compressed, to 6 cm lg., mostly fairly stout, brown below, lighter to whitish above, sometimes yellowish, sometimes decurved; **Glo.** numerous, brown to yellow; **Fl.** 5 cm ∅, yellow; **Fr.** pear-shaped, tapering below, to 3.5 cm lg., reddish.—USA (Texas to Arizona), N. Mexico (Chihuahua).

v. albispina hort.: **Sp.** whitish above; **Fr.** carmine to reddish;

v. **camanchica** (Eng.) Borg: dwarf, sometimes prostrate; **Seg.** circular to ovate, to 17.5 cm lg. and br.; **Ar.** mostly with **Sp.**; **Sp.** 1–3(–6), compressed, reddish to blackish-brown, lighter-tipped, 3.5–7.5 cm lg.; **Glo.** green or yellowish-brown; **Fl.** 6–7 cm $\emptyset$, yellow, orange or (when fading?) pink; **Fr.** ovoid, purple, juicy, edible.—USA (from S. Colorado to the S. border);

v. **charlestonensis** (Clokey) Backbg.: **Seg.** to 18 cm lg., 12 cm br., yellowish-green to purple; **Sp.** 4–6, white, brown below, acicular, not compressed; **Fl.** light yellow, later salmon-coloured, 4 cm $\emptyset$; **Fr.** ovoid.—USA (Nevada);

v. gigantea hort.: **Seg.** to 15 cm br.; v. longispina hort.: **Sp.** to 7 cm lg.; v. minor hort.: **Seg.** small, very spiny;

v. **mojavensis** (Eng.) Fosb.: $\pm$ prostrate; **Seg.** circular; **Sp.** 2–6, robust, sharply angular and compressed, $\pm$ curving, reddish-brown, paler above, 3.5–6 cm lg., also 1–3 smaller Ssp.; **Fr.** 4.5 cm lg., oblong, dark mauve.—USA (Mojave Desert).

v. pallida hort.: **Fl.** creamy-white, greenish inside;

v. **piercei** Fosb.: **Seg.** to 20 cm lg., light green to reddish; **Sp.** mostly 1, dark reddish-brown to whitish; **Fl.** pale yellow, 6 cm $\emptyset$; **Fr.** slender, red, 5 cm lg.—USA (California, Gold Mountain).

v. rubra hort.: **Fl.** reddish-brown; **Fr.** reddish;

v. salmonea hort.: **Fl.** brownish to salmon-coloured.

O. picardoi Marn.-Lap. (B1)
Bo. prostrate, branching to form chains; **Seg.** obliquely oval, flat, to 7 cm lg., 3.5 cm br., somewhat glossy, green, sharply pitted; **Ar.** yellowish-brown; **Sp.** to 10, white, yellow-tipped, to 3.5 mm lg.; **Glo.** yellow; **Fl.** 4 cm $\emptyset$, red; **Fr.** yellowish to red, to 1.2 cm lg.—N. Argentina (Salta; Catamarca, acc. Fechser).

O. pilifera Web. (A1–c)
Bo. eventually tree-like, to 5 m h., with a trunk and a broad crown; **Seg.** pale green, broadly oval to circular, 10–30 cm lg.; **Ar.** 2–3 cm apart; **Sp.** stoutly acicular, weakly spreading, 2–9, 5–15 mm lg., white, yellowish-tipped, also with numerous whitish H. to 2–3 cm lg., set along the edge of the Ar. and $\pm$ soon dropping; **Fl.** dark red, 6 cm $\emptyset$; **Fr.** red, 4–5 cm lg., juicy.—Mexico.

v. **aurantisaeta** Backbg.: **Sp.** bristle-like at first, light golden-brown, later white; **Fl.** lighter carmine; **Fr.** very spiny, as in the type.

O. pisciformis Small (A1–a)
Bo. prostrate, densely branching, forming colonies

to 4 m br.; **R.** fibrous; **Seg.** narrowly elliptic, linear or spatulate, 10–30 cm lg., very thick, deep green; **Sp.** 2–3, creamy, then grey and dark-tipped, to 6 cm lg., salmon-coloured when moist; **Fl.** numerous, light yellow, to 7.5 cm $\emptyset$; **Fr.** broadly top-shaped, purple, to 4 cm lg.—USA (Florida, Atlantic Beach, growing on dunes).

O. pittieri Br. & R. (A1–c)
Bo. eventually tree-like, to 5 m h., with a spiny trunk; **Seg.** twice to 4 times as long as broad, 25–50 cm lg., green; **Ar.** dark brown to purple, to 3 cm apart; **Sp.** 3–6, acicular, weakly spreading, 2–5 cm lg., white; **Glo.** missing, or developing slowly; **Fl.** intense orange to scarlet (when fading).—Colombia (W. Cordillera, Venticas del Dagua).

O. pituosa Ritt. (FR 1036): no description available.

O. plumbea Rose (A1–a)
Bo. low, creeping to 10 cm h., in groups to 30 cm br., little branching; **Seg.** $\pm$ circular, to 5 cm $\emptyset$, matt, leaden-greenish; **Ar.** fairly large; **Sp.** mostly 2(–4), to 3 cm lg., pale brown, sometimes missing; **Fl.** very small, red; **Fr.** to 2 cm lg., spineless.—USA (Arizona, San Carlos Reservation).

O. poecilacantha Backbg. (B1)
Bo. low, branching and re-branching; **Seg.** broad at the base, slightly tapering above, greyish-green, strongly tuberculate, to c. 5 cm lg.; **Ar.** white; **Sp.** unequal, c. 10–12, some much longer than the others, 1.5–4 cm lg., brownish, flecked or banded $\pm$ golden-brown, longer Sp. sometimes pointing downwards or curving, subulate; **Glo.** stiff, to 6 mm lg., spine-like, brown, also similarly coloured normal Glo.; **Fl.** ?—Bolivia.

O. pollardii Br. & R. (A1–a)
Bo. prostrate; **R.** thick; **Seg.** bluish-green, swollen, broadly oval, frosted, 5–16 cm lg., 1–2 cm thick; **Sp.** 1, mostly in upper part of the Ar., stiff, pungent, 2.5–4 cm lg.; **Glo.** numerous, yellow; **Fl.** yellow, 6–8 cm $\emptyset$; **Fr.** 2.5–4 cm lg.—USA (N. Carolina to Florida, Alabama, Mississippi). Distinguished from O. compressa as follows: **Seg.** frosted, dissimilar in colour, larger; longest **Sp.** longer; **S.** thicker.

O. polyacantha Haw. (A1–a)
Bo. prostrate, bushy, branching; **Seg.** obovate, not very thick, with Sp. in each Ar., to c. 10 cm lg., 7.5 cm br.; **Ar.** c. 1 cm apart; **Sp.** curving to the Bo., c. 6–12, not flattened, to 2.5 cm lg., the lower part of the Seg. without any bristly elongated Sp., those on the upper margin probably erect, white, brown or in both colours; **Fl.** 7 cm lg. and $\emptyset$, yellow, orange

to pink (when fading?); **Fr.** ± spherical, 1 cm ∅, dry, with Glo. and Sp.; **S.** flat, yellow.—USA (throughout central zones, from Washington to Texas and Arizona).

v. **schweriniana** (K. Sch.) Backbg.: **Seg.** smaller, to 5 cm lg., mostly to 2.5 cm lg., 1.5–3 cm br.; one **Sp.** to 2 cm lg., remainder shorter and directed downwards; **Fl.** greenish-yellow to pink; **Fr.** spineless.—USA (Colorado, in the NW.)

v. **trichophora** (Eng. & Big.) Coult.: in colonies to 1 m br.; **Seg.** circular to ± ovate, 6–10 cm ∅; **Ar.** crowded; **Sp.** unequal, very numerous, longest one to 4 cm lg., acicular, pale, often white, the base of older Seg. often with long Sp. like bristly H.; **Fl.** 7 cm ∅, yellow or pink; **Fr.** 2 cm lg., 1 cm br., with pale Br.-Sp.—USA (Texas; New Mexico; Oklahoma; W. Colorado, Wet Mountain Valley).

O. polycarpa Small (A1–b)
Bo. erectly shrubby, to 1 m h., densely branching; **Seg.** elliptic to narrowly rhombic or broader, to 40 cm lg., light green; **Sp.**, if present, 1–3, fairly thin, pale yellow, sometimes with darker markings or salmon-coloured below, later grey, brown-tipped, 2–3 cm lg.; **Ar.** with or without recognisable Glo.; **Fl.** light yellow, to 7.5 cm lg.; **Fr.** ± ovoid, to 5 cm lg., ± purplish-red'—USA (Florida).

O. pottsii SD. (A1–a)
Bo. low, spreading, to 30 cm h,; **R.** often like beads, thickened to 3 cm ∅; **Seg.** broadly ovate, to 12 cm lg., pale green to bluish-green; **Sp.** 1–2, 2–4 cm lg., mostly white or purplish-red; **Fl.** 6–7 cm ∅, deep purple; **Fr.** spineless.—USA (Texas; New Mexico) to Mexico (Central Chihuahua).

O. prasina Speg. (B3)
Bo. erectly shrubby, to c. 2 m h.; **Seg.** yellowish-green, later tinged reddish, also greyish-green, elliptic-lanceolate, to 25 cm lg., to 14 cm br.; **Sp.** 0(–1–3, whitish); **Fl.** 10 cm ∅, orange; **Fr.** top to pear-shaped, wine-red outside, purple inside.—Argentina (Entre Rios, Rio Parana).

O. procumbens Eng. (A1–a)
Bo. low, not ascending, in large colonies; **Seg.** circular, 20–50 cm br., yellowish-green, ± frosted; **Ar.** large, not closely spaced; **Sp.** 1–5, spreading, 2.5–5 cm lg., yellow, lighter above, flattened; **Glo.** yellow, long; **Fl.** yellow; **Fr.** clavate, c. 7 cm lg., red, juicy.—USA (N. Arizona).

O. pubescens Wendl. (A1–a[b])
Bo. low, shrubby, strongly branching, sometimes to 40 cm h.; **Seg.** ± tuberculate, velvety or smooth, ± cylindric at first, later flatter, to 7 cm lg.; **Sp.** 3–7 at first, or more, rather short, brownish; **Fl.** lemon-yellow; **Fr.** to 2.5 cm lg., red, somewhat spiny.—Mexico (from the N., southwards) to Guatemala.

O. pumila Rose (A1–a)
Bo. forming low, much-branched bushes; **Seg.** always velvety, flatter at first, becoming less so, tuberculate, to 20 cm lg.; **Sp.** 1–3 at first, later more, yellowish, to 3 cm lg.; **Fl.** yellow, suffused red; **Fr.** spherical, red, 1.5 cm lg.—Central and S. Mexico.

O. pusilla Haw. non SD. (A1–a)
Bo. low to prostrate; **Seg.** oval, little flattened, weakly tuberculate, light green, variable in length; **Ar.** distant; **Sp.** 1–2 at first, brownish, later straw-coloured; **Fl.** pale yellow, rather large, with few Pet.; **Fr.** ?—Origin ? (W. Indies?)

O. pusilla SD.: probably **Tephrocactus weberi** v. **setiger** (Backbg.) Backbg.

O. pycnantha Eng. (A1–b)
Bo. erectly bushy, to only medium-high; **Seg.** circular to more oval, 12.5–15 cm lg., to 12.5 cm br., velvety or papillose; **Ar.** more numerous; **Sp.** 3–7 at first, pale straw-coloured, to 2.5 cm lg., later more, to 20, longer and stiffer, finally grey or brownish; **Glo.** numerous, weak; **Fl.** greenish-yellow; **Fr.** 4 cm lg., very prickly.—Mexico (Baja California, Magdalena Bay).

v. **margaritana** Coult.: **Ar.** brownish-felty, later grey; **Sp.** pointing down, light reddish-brownish at first, then pale, to c. 10, mostly subulate, some thinner, rather unequal, to c. 1 cm lg.; **Glo.** in the Ar.-felt, reddish-brown; **Fl.** sulphur-yellow to lighter.—Mexico (Baja California, Santa Margarita Island).

O. pyriformis Rose (A1–c)
Bo. tall, to 5 m h., with widely spreading branches, lower ones to 5 m lg., spreading over the soil; **Seg.** ± ovate, thick, to c. 18 cm lg., or more; **Ar.** small, relatively close; **Sp.** 1–2, later usually more, normally projecting strongly downwards, thin, weak, yellow, fairly short, 1–2.2 cm lg.; **Fl.** yellow; **Fr.** 4 cm lg., spineless.—Mexico (Zacatecas, Hacienda de Cedros).

O. quimilo K. Sch. (B3)
Bo. ± tree-like, to 4 m h., strongly branching, **trunk** with up to 8 Sp.; **Seg.** greyish-green, to 3 cm thick, elliptic to obovate, to 50 cm lg., to 25 cm br.; **Sp.** 1(–2–3), white, ± twisted and compressed; **Fl.** c. 4.5 cm br., ± brick-red; **Fr.** pear-shaped to spherical, to 7 cm lg., greenish-yellow; **S.** 8 mm lg.—N. Argentina (Santiago del Estero, La Banda).

O. quipa Web. (A2–a)

Bo. a small, laxly branching shrub; **Seg.** obovate to oblong, to c. 6 cm lg., to 4 cm br., light or yellowish-green, little spiny, new growth with thin prickles, soon dropping, and **H.** hanging down from the woolly **Ar.**, **Seg.** swollen around the **Ar.**; **Sp.** later 0–2–3, weak, short, appressed; **Fl.** orange-red, small; **Pet.** erect; **Fil.** erect, closed around the style; **Fr.** pale orange, edible, 2 cm ∅, 2.5 cm lg., spineless, floral scar sunken, **Glo.** short, yellowish-brown.—Brazil (Pernambuco). (Fig. 287.)

O. quitensis Web. (A2–a)
Bo. bushy, to 2 m h., in thickets, low-growing in exposed positions; **Seg.** therefore variable, 10–40 cm lg.; **Ar.** small, white; **Sp.** 0 or 1–3(–4), yellowish-brown or whitish at first, acicular, flexible, 2–3 cm lg.; **Fl.** red, 1.2–1.5 cm br.; **Pet.** erect; **Fr.** obovoid, red, ± spineless, c. 2 cm lg.; **S.** 3 mm lg.—Ecuador (Quito to the Chanchan valley, above Huigra). Closely related to O. macbridei, but the latter has subulate **Sp.**; both spec. are variable in habit.

O. rafinesquei Eng.: **Opuntia humifusa** Raf.

O. rastrera Web. (A1–a)
Bo. creeping; **Seg.** circular to ± ovate, to 20 cm ∅; **Sp.** 0–1 to several, white, to 4 cm lg.; **Glo.** yellow; **Fl.** yellow; **Fr.** purple, ovoid, acid.—Mexico (San Luis Potosí; Oaxaca, Puerto Angel).

O. repens Bello non Karw. (A1–a)
Bo. a smaller, more erect shrub, to 50 cm h., forming thickets to 4 m br., freely branching, sometimes prostrate and ascending; **Seg.** green, velvety or smooth, not tuberculate, to 16 cm lg., to 3.5 cm br., mostly quite strongly flattened; **Ar.** brown, with several **H.**; **Sp.** more numerous, reddish at first, then brown, to 3.5 cm lg.; **Glo.** numerous, yellow, developing late; **Fl.** 4 cm ∅, light yellow to salmon-red; **Fr.** red, to 3 cm lg., with or without **Sp.**—W. Indies (smaller central islands).

O. retrorsa Speg. (B2)
Bo. creeping, forming confused groups, branches irregular in length; **Seg.** light green, 10–25 cm lg., 2–3.5 cm br., flat; **Ar.** with a violet spot; **Sp.** 1–3, white, reddish above; **Fl.** yellow, 4–5 cm ∅; **Fr.** 2 cm lg., purple outside, light pink inside; **S.** ± hairy.—Argentina (S. Chaco, dry grasslands).

O. retrospina Lem. (B1)
Bo. prostrate, branching, in groups; **Seg.** light yellowish-green, ± glossy, oblong, ± curving, tapering to both ends, to 5 cm lg., ± wrinkled, often washed reddish below the Ar., grafted plants larger; **Ar.** light brownish; **Sp.** 3–5 at first, to 6 mm lg., ± yellowish horn-coloured, later also 2–3 Sp. curving downwards, to 9 mm lg., and 1–3 more

central, to 4 cm lg., irregularly spreading, also twisted and contorted; **Fl.** flame-coloured; **Fr.** ?—N. Argentina?

O. rhodantha K. Sch. (A1–a)
Bo. prostrate, strongly branching, to 30 cm h.; **Seg.** ascending, ± ovate, to 16 cm lg., to 7 cm br. or rather more, intense green, ± tuberculate; **Sp.** mostly only in the upper part of the Seg., 1–4, 3–6 cm lg., projecting to radiating, subulate, white, yellow or brown; **Fl.** 8 cm lg. and br., purplish-pink, orange or yellow; **Fr.** oblong, dry, ± spiny.—USA (from W. Colorado to California). A hardy spec. with attractive Fl.
    v. pallida: Fl. yellow;
    v. **pisciformis** Späth: Seg. narrower, deep green; Sp. yellow; **Fl.** smaller, light carmine.
The following garden-names have been based on the considerable variability of Fl.-colour:
    v. rosea, with pink Fl.; v. rubra, with brilliant red Fl.; v. salmonea, with salmon-pink Fl.; v. schumanniana Späth, with deep carmine Fl.;
    v. spinosior Boiss. & Davids.; **Sp.** at least 4, long, robust.—USA (desert of SW. Colorado).

O. ritteri Berg. (A1–b)
Bo. bushy; **Seg.** subcircular to ± ovate, light green, finely velvety; **Sp.** numerous, acicular, light yellow, ± projecting, to 1.5 cm lg.; **Fl.** large, light red.—Mexico (Zacatecas). The plant commonly met in collections under this name is freely branching and up to c. 60 cm h., with similarly coloured Sp., but the shoots not velvety; **Fl.** light yellow. Perhaps a hybrid?

O. riviereana Backbg. (A2–b)
Bo. prostrate to ascending, low-growing, in colonies; **Seg.** circular to obovate, to 22 cm lg., 14 cm br., 3 cm thick, new growth and Ov. (only in this spec. of the "Stenopetalae") tinged strongly purple; **Ar.** whitish at first, later black; **Sp.** mostly (1–)2(3–4), to 3 cm lg., straight or directed slightly downwards, Ssp. when present thin, to 7 mm lg., ± compressed below; **Glo.** brown; **Fl.** c. 4 cm lg., 2 cm ∅, orange-red, unisexual; **Ov.** purple.—Mexico.

O. robinsonii G. Ortega (A1–b)
Bo. shrubby, to 1 m h., with a small stouter **trunk**, with up to 10 Sp.; **Seg.** light green, 15–20 cm br.; **Sp.** 0–1, downcurving, 1–2 cm lg., dark below, white at midway, yellow-tipped; **Fl.** 8–9 cm lg., lemon-yellow; **Fr.** pear-shaped, purple, to 6 cm lg., sweet; **S.** dirty white, to 4 mm lg.—Mexico (Sinaloa, near Arroyo Chiquerite).

O. roborensis Card. 1966
Bo. shrubby, branching, 0.5–1 m h.; **Seg.** oval to elliptic, 7–10 cm lg., 2.5–3.5 cm br.; **Ar.** 2–2.5 cm apart, grey-felty, with light brown Glo.; **Sp.** 1–3,

appressed, whitish-grey, tipped brown, 1–3 cm lg.; **Fl.** numerous, apical, 4 cm lg.; **Ov.** 2 cm lg., dark green; **Pet.** broadly spatulate, golden-yellow; **style** white; **Fr.** purple; **S.** whitish, 3 mm ∅.—Bolivia (Chiquitos, Santa Cruz, near Roboré, 600 m). Somewhat resembles both O. retrorsa and O. canina.

O. robusta Wendl. (A1–c)
Bo. forming a lax tall shrub, occasionally to 5 m h.; **Seg.** large, circular to rather oblong-circular, to 25 cm br. and more, sometimes less, thick, frosted, light bluish-green; **L.** reddish; **Sp.** 8–12, stout, unequal, to 5 cm lg., sometimes absent, white, brown or yellowish below, terete; **Fl.** 5 cm lg. and ∅, yellow; **Fr.** spherical to ellipsoid, to 9 cm lg., deep red.—Central Mexico.
  v. **longiglochidiata** Backbg.: **Glo.** on new growth in projecting tufts, brownish-yellow, often as long as the Sp.;
  v. **maxima** hort.: with whiter **Sp.**; **Fl.** yellow; **Seg.** to 40 cm br. have been reported, certainly larger than in the type which itself is variable; **Fr.** mauve, spherical, 6 cm ∅. Schelle says: **Fl.** 7 cm lg. and ∅, **Fr.** brownish-red, sometimes the size of an apple;
  v. **viridior** SD.: not validly described; **Bo.** greenish, rather more oblong; **Sp.** shorter, mostly 3–5; **Fl.** yellowish, turning ± salmon-pink when fading; **Fr.** red inside and out (possibly a hybrid?).

O. rubiflora Griff. non Davids. (A1–b)
Bo. to 45 cm h., groups to 1 m br.; **Seg.** ± ovate, to 18 cm lg.; **Sp.** few, to 5 cm lg., white, brown or straw below; **Fl.** pink.—Origin? (Hybrid?; classifiable with the "Phaeacanthae".) If it is a good spec., then the name needs to be changed because it had already been used a little earlier by Davidson for another plant.

O. rubrifolia Eng.: indistinguishable in its characters from O. tortispina; Fl. and Fr. unknown.—USA (Utah, St. George).

O. rufida Eng. (A1–b)
Bo. shrubby, erect, to 1.5 m h., forming a small trunk; **Seg.** ± circular, 6–25 cm br., fairly thick, dull greyish-green, velvety; **L.** tipped reddish; **Sp.** 0; **Glo.** numerous, darker to reddish-brown; **Fl.** yellow to orange (? when fading), to 5 cm lg.; **Fr.** light red.—USA (Texas), N. Mexico (Durango). Often known better by its synonym, Opuntia herrfeldtii Kupp.; the following are very attractive crosses: O. rufida × rubra hort., with the new growth concolorous red; and O. rufida × rubrifolia hort., with the Seg. light green, becoming bluish-green; L. entirely red; minute Sp. sometimes present.

O. rutila Nutt. non Clov. & Funst. (A1–a)
Bo. low-growing, spreading; **Seg.** flat to three-sided, cylindric or ovate, later more flattened, young Seg. readily detached and almost spineless, 4–10 cm lg., 2–5 cm br.; **Ar.** to 1.5 cm apart; **Sp.** 1–6, 1–3 cm lg., spreading sideways or upwards, often only in the upper Ar., white, brown or both colours together; **Fl.** 6 cm ∅, pinkish-red, yellow or intermediate shades; **Fr.** 3.5 cm lg., clavate, yellow, sometimes spiny.—USA (W. Colorado; Wyoming).

O. salagria Cast. (B2)
Bo. shrubby, mostly to 2 m h.; **Seg.** subcircular to ± spatulate, to 30 cm lg., 17 cm br., 1.8 cm thick, leak-green; **Sp.** mostly 1(–2), slender, stiff, 3.5–4 cm lg.; **Glo.** brown, short; **Fl.** borne mostly along the upper margin of the shoot, to 10 cm lg. and br., orange-red; **Fr.** clavate, 7 cm lg., dark violet-red, green inside.—Argentina (Sierra Chica de Córdoba; Prov. San Luis).

O. salvadorensis Br. & R.(A1–a)
Bo. low, branching freely and spreading, to 10 cm h.; **Seg.** circular to ± oblong, flat, 10–15 cm lg., smooth; **Ar.** small; **Sp.** mostly 3, thin-acicular, unequal, to 6 cm lg.; **Fl.** yellow, c. 2 cm lg.—Salvador (Dept. Usulután, Hacienda La Concordia).

O. santa-rita Rose: **Opuntia gosseliniana** v. **santa-rita** (Griff. & Hare) L. Bens.

O. saxatilis Ritt. (FR 1035): no description available.

O. saxicola How.: **Opuntia galapageia** v. **saxicola** (How.) Backbg.

O. scheeri Web. (A1–b)
Bo. erectly shrubby, densely branching, to c. 90 cm h.; **Seg.** bluish-green, subcircular to oblong, 15–30 cm lg.; **Sp.** 10–12, thin-acicular, yellow, 1 cm lg., mixed with white or yellowish Br.-H.; **Glo.** brownish-yellow; **Fl.** c. 10 cm ∅, pale yellow, salmon-coloured when fading; **Fr.** spherical, red; **S.** small.—Mexico (Querétaro, El Pueblito).

O. schickendantzii Web. (B3)
Bo. bushy, to 1–2 m h., bluish-green; **Seg.** terete at first or only below, later flattened, narrow, long, mostly slightly curving, fairly flat, to c. 20 cm lg., slightly tuberculate; **L.** reddish; **Sp.** 1–2, thin-subulate, white, to 2 cm lg., later more numerous; **Fl.** 4 cm ∅, satiny, yellow; **Fr.** spherical, spineless, green, sterile.—Argentina (frontier region, Tucuman-Salta; Catamarca, acc. Fechser). (Fig. 288.)

O. schickendantzii similis n.n.: a more yellowish-green plant with rather longer and broader **Seg.**; **Sp.** pale brownish; **Fr.** reddish at maturity, shortly spiny, its few **S.** 3 mm lg., flat, circular. This plant has long been known in collections under the name of the true spec. which was only recently re-collected by Fechser. Either the fertile spec. is a hybrid, or there are in fact two spec. since the former has also been reported from Catamarca and Córdoba, and the differences may have been overlooked.

O. schumannii Web. (A1–b)
Bo. bushy, to c. 2 m h.; **Seg.** matt, dark green, subovate to oblong, 15–25 cm lg.; **Ar.** distant; **Sp.** 2–10, unequal, to 4.5 cm lg., ± twisted, flattened, somewhat spreading, dark brown; **Glo.** few, soon dropping; **Fl.** 6 cm lg., yellowish to orange, red when fading; **Fr.** dark purple, juicy.—N. zones of S. America.

O. schweriniana K. Sch.: **Opuntia polyacantha** v. **schweriniana** (K. Sch.) Backbg.

O. securigera Borg (B2)
Bo. prostrate, to 20 cm h.; **Seg.** dark green, to 8 cm lg., to 6 cm br.; **Rsp.** bristle-like, 15 and more, length ?; **Csp.** 1–3, to 5 cm lg., thin, white; **Glo.** brownish; **Fl.**, **Fr.** ?—Argentina (Patagonia). Possibly identical with O. penicilligera Speg., or a form or variety of the latter.

O. senilis Parm.: regarded as a synonym of **O. orbiculata** SD., which Pfeiffer held to be identical with O. crinifera SD.; this was described separately and was itself perhaps O. pailana Wgt. (?).

O. setispina Eng. (A1–b)
Bo. an erect shrub to c. 60 cm h., to 1.2 m br.; **Seg.** deep bluish-green, somewhat frosted, also tinged purple, at least around the Ar., circular to ± oval, 5–15 cm lg. and br.; **Ar.** large; **Sp.** 1–6, 2–3 cm lg., white; **Glo.** yellow, later conspicuous; **Fl.** yellow; **Fr.** 4 cm lg., purple.—Mexico (W. Chihuahua).

O. soederstromiana Br. & R. (A1–b)
Bo. bushy, erect, small tree-like, 60 cm to 1 m h., very spiny; **Seg.** subovate, slightly frosted, or glossy, green, 20–40 cm lg., later greyish-green; **L.** small-subulate, reddish above; **Sp.** 2–5 at first, later to 10, to 4 cm lg., at first pink or reddish below, paler above, soon uniformly grey; **Fl.** yellow at first, soon orange to brick-red, 5–6 cm lg.; **Fr.** oblong-ovoid, to 5 cm lg., mostly spiny, red, juicy.—Ecuador (Quito, San Antonio).

O. soehrensii Br. & R. (B1)
Bo. forming low colonies, sometimes to 1 m br.,

rather variable as to size and colour of Bo. and Sp.; **Seg.** creeping and rooting, ± tuberculate, flattened-rounded or rather flatter, tapering below or ± curving, lighter to greyish or bluish-green; **Sp.** variable, yellowish to brownish or greyish-whitish, mostly in the upper part of the shoot, or longer there (especially in cultivated plants), unequal, variable in number, longer ones often later directed ± downwards; **Fl.** light yellow, 3 cm lg.; **Fr.** glabrous or spineless (perhaps also spiny and red inside?).—S. Peru to Bolivia.

O. sphaerocarpa Eng. & Big. (A1–a)
Bo. low, spreading; **Seg.** light green, sometimes reddish, circular, to 7 cm br., rather thick, very tuberculate; **Ar.** to 1 cm apart; **Sp.**, when present, mostly only in the upper Ar., or few and short, to 2 cm lg., acicular, thin; **Fl.** ?; **Fr.** 1.8 cm ∅, spineless, dry.—USA (New Mexico, near Albuquerque).

O. spinalba Raf., from Florida: an unclarified spec.

O. spinosibacca M. Anth. (A1–b)
Bo. shrubby, to 1.5 m h., sometimes developing a trunk to 60 cm h., to 18 cm ∅; **Seg.** somewhat ascending to spreading, very frosted, green, ovate to oblong, 10–24 cm lg., 7.5–11 cm br.; **Sp.** 2–5, missing in the lowest Ar., slightly twisted, at first white, red below, then reddish-brown to orange, paler-tipped, finally grey, 1–4 of the Sp. 3.5–7 cm lg., 1, to 2 cm lg., mostly 2 bristly-fine, to 1.2 cm lg.; **Fl.** 5.5 cm lg., 5 cm ∅, yellow, red inside; **Fr.** drying, proliferating, 3.5 cm lg., pale purple, with 1–4 brownish-red or white subulate Sp.—USA (Texas, Big Bend).

O. spinulifera SD. (A1–c)
Bo. eventually tree-like, large, strongly branching; **Seg.** broadly oval to circular, smooth, ± frosted, 20–30 cm lg. or br.; **L.** red; **Sp.** 0, or 1–3 (on older shoots), thin, white, some of them ± bristly, fine, sometimes yellowish-white; **Fl.** yellow; **Fr.** turning light red, shortly spiny.—Mexico. Spec. has proved to be fairly hardy during cold winters on the Riviera and Costa Brava, surviving temperatures down to − 10°C.

O. spranguei G. Ortega: **Opuntia tomentosa** v. **spranguei** (G. Ortega) Backbg.

O. stenarthra K. Sch. (B2)
Bo. prostrate, ascending, to 80 cm h., branches to 2 m lg.; **Seg.** yellowish-green, thin, narrowly oblong, 8- 25 cm lg., 2.5–5(–7) cm br.; **Sp.** 0(–1–3–5, 0.6–3.5 cm lg., horn-coloured at first, then white); **Fl.** 3 cm ∅, lemon-yellow, to 3 cm lg.; **Fr.** pear-shaped, to 2.5 cm lg., with brown Glo.; **S.** round, grey, very hairy.—Paraguay (Estancia Tagatiya).

O. stenochila Eng. (A1–a)
Bo. prostrate; **Seg.** subovate, 10 cm lg., 7.5 cm br.;
Sp. mostly 1, longer, to 3 cm lg., also 1–2 short
recurved Ssp., all light, almost white; **Glo.** light to
greenish-yellow; **Fl.** yellow, to 5 cm lg.; **Ov.** ±
conical; **Fr.** to 5 cm lg., clavate, very juicy.—USA
(W. New Mexico, Zuñi Canyon; Arizona).

O. stenopetala Eng. (A2–b)
Bo. low, bushy; **Seg.** oblong-ovate, greyish-green,
not normally frosted; **Sp.** 1–2 or more, blackish,
then grey, to 5 cm lg.; **Fl.** orange-reddish,
unisexual, c. 2 cm br.; **Fr.** scarlet, ovoid, with or
without Sp., peach-colour inside; **S.** light brown,
small, flat.—Mexico (Fig. 289.)

O. streptacantha Lem. (A1–c)
Bo. eventually tree-like, to 5 m h., freely branching,
trunk to 45 cm ∅; **Seg.** circular to ovate, 25–30 cm
lg., dark green; **Ar.** fairly crowded; **Sp.** quite
numerous, spreading, some appressed, also 1–2
Br.-H., pressed downwards; **Fl.** to 9 cm ∅, yellow
to orange; **Fr.** spherical, 5 cm ∅, dark red,
sometimes yellowish, inside and out.—Mexico
(Central Highlands).

O. stricta Haw. (A1–b)
Bo. a low shrub to 80 cm h., often in larger colonies;
Seg. oblong to ovate, mostly 8–15 cm lg., but also
considerably elongated, to 30 cm lg., green or
bluish-green, smooth; **Sp.** 0, or 1–2, terete, to 4 cm
lg., yellow; **Ar.** and **Glo.** brownish; **Fl.** to 7 cm lg.,
yellow; **Fr.** purple, tapering below, 6 cm lg.—USA
(S. Texas, Florida) to Cuba.

O. strigil Eng. (A1–b)
Bo. a smaller shrub, to 60 cm h.; **Seg.** subcircular,
10–12.5 cm lg.; **Ar.** crowded; **Sp.** 5–8, spreading,
several appressed and directed downwards,
reddish-brown to brown, light-tipped, to 2.5 cm
lg.; **Glo.** numerous; **Fl.** yellow to creamy-yellow, 7
cm ∅; **Fr.** small, spherical, 1.2 cm ∅, red.—USA
(Texas).

O. subsphaerocarpa Speg. (B3)
Bo. erect, shrubby; **Seg.** dark green, fairly glossy,
long-oval, rounded above, to 20 cm lg., to 5.5 cm
br.; **Sp.** 0(–1, white, 1.5–2.5 cm lg.); **Fl.** 5 cm ∅,
yellow; **Fr.** ± spherical, wine-red, whitish-green
inside; **S.** with long dense H.—Argentina (Misiones).

O. sulphurea G. Don (B2)
Bo. prostrate to erect, shrubby, to 30 cm h., in
colonies to 2 m br.; **Seg.** flattened, thick, very
tuberculate, oblong to ovate, to 25 cm lg., green to
greyish-green, sometimes tinged red; **Sp.** 2–8,
sometimes curving, twisted, spreading, to 10 cm lg.,

brownish to red, often paler at first; **Fl.** 4 cm lg.,
yellow; **Fr.** yellow, small, ± scented.—W. Argentina (from San Luis to the Chubut River).
Shows the following variations: some plants have
Fr. which only change colour to red in the 2nd
year; some have greyish-green shoots to 20 cm lg.,
10 cm br., grey Sp. to 6.5 cm lg., and Fl. yellowish
with a somewhat pink centre, and the Fr.-pulp then
greyish-white; in other plants, where the shoots are
more mid-green, to 15 cm lg. and 10 cm br., the Fl.
are smaller, ± whitish-yellow, and the Fr.-pulp is
red.
    v. **hildmannii** (Frič) Backbg.: **Seg.** greatly
thickened below, sub-circular; **Sp.** rather shorter, fewer, sometimes irregularly curving, brilliant red; **Fl.** yellow; **Fr.** yellow.—NW. Argentina;
    v. **pampana** (Speg.) Backbg.: colonies to 50 cm
h.; **Seg.** to 8 cm lg., light green, to 6 cm br., later
± circular, to 2 cm thick, tuberculate; **Ar.**
whitish; **Sp.** only 1 at first, later downcurving,
later to 4, the lowest one to 3 cm lg., rather
twisted, stiff, pungent, white, the tip red at first,
later black; **Fl.** small, yellow, spineless; **Fr.**
ovoid, 3.5 cm lg., unscented, yellow with a pink
sheen, acid, little juicy.—Argentina (Sierra
Ventana, Sierra Tandil etc.).

O. **tajapayensis** Ritt. (FR 897): no description
available.

O. tapona Eng. (A1–b)
Bo. shrubby, to 60 cm h.; **Seg.** smooth, circular to
ovate, to 25 cm br.; rather thick, pale green; **Sp.**
(1–)2–4, yellow, longest one to 7 cm lg., thin,
porrect, sometimes pointing downwards; **Glo.**
brownish; **Fl.** light orange-yellow; **Fr.** dark purple,
4–6 cm lg., red inside.—Mexico (Baja California:
Loreto Island).

O. tardospina Griff. (A1–a)
Bo. low, spreading, mostly prostrate; **Seg.** matt,
darker green, circular to ovate; **Ar.** large, 4 cm
apart; **Sp.** 1(–2), to 5 cm lg., darker brown, lighter-
tipped; **Glo.** brown, numerous; **Fl.** ?; **Fr.** 6 cm lg.,
red.—USA (E. Texas).

O. tayapayensis Card. (A1–a)
Bo. low, to 30 cm h., with a small subterete trunk;
Seg. velvety, ± circular to ± flattened, 2–3 cm lg.,
later to 8 cm lg., pale green; **Sp.** mostly 1–3, to 2 cm
lg., also a few whitish wavy H.; **Glo.** few; **Fl.** rotate,
4 cm lg., light yellow; **Fr.** spherical, yellow, rather
velvety.—E. Central Bolivia (Tayapaya).

O. taylori Br. & R. (A1–a)
Bo. prostrate, broadly branching; **Seg.** light green,
smooth or velvety, not tuberculate, to 2 cm br., to

12 cm lg.; **Sp.** 3–6 at first, yellowish-brown, later white, to 4 cm lg.; **Fl.** small, yellow; **Fr.** pear-shaped, to 1.5 cm lg., spineless, with a few Br.—Haiti; Santo Domingo. The plants in Santo Domingo are reputedly always velvety; perhaps a variety?

O. tenuiflora Small (A1–b)
Bo. shrubby, prostrate to erect, freely branching; **R.** fibrous; **Seg.** spatulate to ± elliptic or narrower, mostly 15–40 cm lg., rather thick, deep green, often ± frosted; **Sp.** mostly 3–6, pale yellow, later dirty yellow, curving, 2–5 cm lg.; **Fl.** deep salmon-colour, bellshaped, c. 3 cm ⌀; **Fr.** thick-clavate, to 7 cm lg., purple, stem-like below; **S.** numerous.—USA (Florida, Hammocks, upper Keys of Florida).

O. tenuisipina Eng. (A1–a)
Bo. low, spreading, to 30 cm h.; **Seg.** ± ovate, tapering below, 7–15 cm lg., light green; **Sp.** 1–3, thin, to 5 cm lg., white or brown; **Glo.** brown; **Fl.** to 7.5 cm ⌀; **Fr.** oblong, 2.5–4 cm lg.; **S.** irregular in shape.—USA (SW. Texas; New Mexico; Arizona).

O. tilcarensis Backbg. (B1)
Bo. low, branching like a string of beads, forming colonies; **Seg.** readily detached, more flattened above, rounded, base subterete and often elongated, light green, to 5 cm lg., and more, 4–5 cm br., 1.5 cm thick (stouter when grafted), tuberculate; **Ar.** small; **Sp.** few to several, 1–4 longer, sometimes to 7 cm lg., pungent, often other small, thinner, light yellow Sp., variously spreading, mostly porrect; **Fl.** c. 5 cm ⌀, yellow to reddish-orange, glossy.—N. Argentina (Tilcara). [Probably the plant Haage gives as FR 63, without description.]
v. **rubellispina** Backbg.: **Seg.** more bluish-green; **Sp.** pale pinkish-white at first, sometimes with red marks below, reddish-brown at the base, mostly to 4 longer Sp., usually to c. 4.5 cm lg., individuals also longer, ± porrect, very flexible, sometimes also several shorter or bristle-like Sp., less spreading, whitish; **Ar.** brownish; **Glo.** chestnut-brown; **Fl.** ?

O. tomentella Berg. (A1–c)
Bo. a taller shrub, without a trunk; **Seg.** oblong to obovate, 20–30 cm lg., lighter green, 9–15 cm br., ± glossy at first but with recognisably velvety H., these shorter than in O. tomentosa; **Sp.** 1–2, acicular, projecting, 7–10 mm lg., whitish, sometimes missing; **Fl.** carrot-coloured; **style** pink; **Fr.** and **S.** smaller than in O. tomentosa.—Guatemala (Antigua, Moran, Amatitlán).

O. tomentosa SD. (A1–c)
Bo. eventually tree-like, to 6 m h., with a spineless trunk to 30 cm ⌀; **Seg.** greyish-green, oblong to narrowly ovate, 10–20 cm lg., very velvety; **Sp.** 0–1(–3), rather short; **Glo.** yellow; **Fl.** to 5 cm lg., orange; **style** purple; **Fr.** ovoid, red, spineless, sweet; **S.** 4 mm ⌀.—Mexico (Central Highlands).
v. **rileyi** (G. Ortega) Backbg.: **Bo.** to 3 m h.; **trunk** short, very spiny; **Sp.** white or grey; **Seg.** narrowly ovate, 10–14 cm lg. or more, velvety; **Ar.** white; **Sp.** mostly 1, curving downwards; **Glo.** yellow; **Fl.** 7 cm ⌀, yellow; **style** white; **Fr.** ?—Mexico (Sinaloa, coast between Rio San Lorenzo and Rio Elota);
v. **spranguei** (G. Ortega) Backgg.: **Bo.** to 3 m h., **trunk** short; **Seg.** dark green, shortly white-velvety; **Ar.** white; **Glo.** yellowish-green; **Fl.** 6 cm ⌀, yellow, spotted red in the centre.—Mexico (Sinaloa, coast between Rio San Lorenzo and Rio Elota).

O. tortispina Eng. (A1–a)
Bo. prostrate and ascending; **Seg.** circular or ovate, 14–20 cm lg., darker green; **Sp.** 3–5, white, often twisted, angular and grooved, 3.5–6 cm lg., with 2–4 thinner lower Ssp. 1–2.5 cm lg.; **Glo.** yellowish; **Fl.** sulphur-yellow, 6–7.5 cm ⌀; **Fr.** ovoid, to 5 cm lg.—USA (Nebraska to N. Texas).
v. **cymochila** (Eng.) Backbg.: **Seg.** circular, to 8.5 cm br.; **Sp.** 1–3, stout, white, often reddish-brown below, 2.5–5 cm lg., spreading or down-curving, somewhat compressed or twisted; **Fr.** to 3 cm lg.—USA (Kansas; Texas; New Mexico; Arizona).

O. tracyi Britt. (A1–a)
Bo. low, prostrate, freely branching, to 20 cm h.; **Seg.** pale green, ± terete at first, later linear-oblong, c. 1 cm thick, to 8 cm lg., 3.5 cm br.; **Sp.** 1–4, to 3.5 cm lg., ± white, dark-tipped; **Glo.** numerous, brown; **Fl.** mid-yellow, 4 cm ⌀.—USA (S. Mississippi; SE. Georgia; N. Florida).

O. treleasii Coult. (A1–a)
Bo. low, branching from the base, to 30 cm h.; **Seg.** pale bluish-green, ovate, to 15 cm lg. or more, fleshy, smooth; **Sp.** absent (type) or numerous (v. **kernii** Griff.); **Glo.** dirty yellow; **Fl.** pink, sometimes spiny; **S.** large.—USA (S. California, above Caliente [unarmed] or below it [spiny]).

O. triacantha (Willd.) Sweet (A1–a)
Bo. low-growing; **Seg.** smooth, matt, green, fairly thick, 4–8 cm lg., fairly easily detached; **Sp.** mostly 3, to 4 cm lg., white at first, later sometimes yellowish, thin; **Fl.** 5 cm lg., brownish-yellow to cream, washed pink; **Fr.** 2.5 cm lg., red, spineless.—Lesser Antilles (St. Thomas to Guadeloupe; Puerto Rico; Cuba, near Guantánamo).

O. tuna (L.) Mill. (A1–b)
Bo. shrubby, to 90 cm h.; **Seg.** light green, oblong to oval, smaller or to 16 cm lg., dark above the large Ar.; **Sp.** 2(–3–5–)6, somewhat spreading, light yellow; **Glo.** yellow; **Fl.** c. 5 cm ⌀, light yellow, centre ± reddish; **Ov.** slender-clavate; **Fr.** ovoid, 3 cm lg., red.—Jamaica (in the S.) Very free-flowering.

O. tuna-blanca Speg. (B3)
Bo. erectly shrubby, to 1.5 m h.; **Seg.** pale yellowish-green, broadly lanceolate, 12–24 cm lg., 5–9 cm br.; **Sp.** 0 (rarely 1); **Fl.** 8–9 cm ⌀, orange; **Fr.** ?—Argentina (Jujuy, Humahuaca).

O. turbinata Small (A1–b)
Bo. shrubby, erect, under 1 m h., freely branching; **R.** fibrous, stout; **Seg.** oval, circular or obovate, to 15 cm lg., light green, thick, frosted; **Ar.** prominent; **Sp.** 1(–2–5), to 2–3 cm lg., pale to light yellow at first, later brownish; **Fl.** light yellow, to 5.5 cm ⌀; **Fr.** spherical to top-shaped, to 4 cm lg., purple.—USA (Florida, coastal dunes in the NE.).

O. turgida Small (A1–b)
Bo. small, shrubby, erect, to 0.5 m h.; **R.** fibrous; **Seg.** elliptic to ovate, to 12 cm lg., deep green, rather thick, sometimes frosted at first; **Sp.** 0; **Glo.** dense; **Fl.** to 6.5 cm ⌀, light yellow; **Fr.** ± ovoid, to 2.5 cm lg., greenish-purple; **S.** numerous.—USA (Florida, on the Halifax River, S. of Daytona; Hammocks).

O. undulata Griff. non Lk. & O. (A1–c)
Bo. eventually tree-like, large, robust, with a trunk to 30 cm ⌀; **Seg.** broadly circular, to over 50 cm br., firm, glossy and ± wavy, light green, becoming darker green; **Ar.** to 6 cm apart; **Sp.** 0 or mostly 1, rarely to 4, short, flattened, sometimes twisted, to 15 mm lg.; **Fl.** creamy-white; **Ov.** ± cylindric, spineless; **Fr.** large, to 10 cm lg., dark red to pale orange, reddish to orange inside.—Mexico (Aguascalientes and sporadically on the Central Plateau).

O. urbaniana Werd. (A1–b)
Bo. bushy; **Seg.** oblong-linear, to 20 cm lg., 5.5 cm br.; **Sp.** 1(–2), 1 of these to 5 cm lg., others smaller if present, all light horn-coloured at first, then yellowish, acicular, rarely flattened and twisted; **Glo.** honey-coloured; **Fl.** to 7 cm lg., 3 cm ⌀, yellow; **Fr.** ?—Santo Domingo (valley of Cibao). The spec. has been regarded as a Consolea, but it lacks a trunk; possibly it is a hybrid, or a spec. of Opuntia from the complex: O. bahamana and O. acaulis.

O. utkilio Speg. (B1)
Bo. prostrate, **branches** to 2.50 m lg.; **Seg.** elliptic-

linear, 15–30 cm lg., 5–6 cm br., fresh green at first, later darker; **Ar.** with a violet spot; **Sp.** 2(–3), white, later sometimes more; **Fl.** to 4 cm ⌀, yellow; **Fr.** 3 cm lg., violet-red outside and inside.—Argentina (Tucuman; Santiago del Estero).

O. vaseyi (Coult.) Br. & R. (A1–a–b)
Bo. bushy, low to erect; **Seg.** to c. 12 cm lg. (or more), ± ovate, pale green, ± frosted at first; **Ar.** fairly large; **Sp.** 1–3, spreading, at most 2 cm lg., greyish or light brown, yellowish to whitish at the tip, rather flat, new growth sometimes with only 1 Sp., brown; **L.** reddish, short; **Fl.** deep salmon-colour, attractive, large; **Fr.** spherical, to 5 cm lg., purple.—USA (S. California, San Bernardino and Orange Counties). Often found in masses; one of the few red-flowered spec.

O. velutina Web. (A1–c)
Bo. tree-like, to 4 m h., sometimes with a stout trunk; **Seg.** oblong to ovate, 15–20 cm br., pale green, velvety; **Ar.** white; **Sp.** 2–6, yellow, later white, subulate, to 4 cm lg.; **Glo.** yellow, later brown; **Fl.** small, yellow; **Fr.** red.—Mexico (Guerrero, e.g. Canyon del Zopilote).

O. vulgaris Mill. (A1–c)
Bo. tree-like to shrubby, to 6 m h., **trunk** to 15 cm ⌀, spiny or not; **Seg.** thin, glossy, fresh green, broader oval to oblong, constricted below, 10–30 cm lg., 8–15 cm br.; **Sp.** 1–2 (if present on the trunk, then to 10), yellowish-brown to dark reddish-brown; **Fl.** to 9 cm ⌀, sulphur-yellow, in Argentina and Uruguay more orange-yellow; **Fr.** clavate, to spherical with a "stalk", to c. 7.5 cm lg., sometimes proliferating, reddish-purple.—Brazil to Argentina.
This name was for a long time erroneously applied to O. compressa, with O. monacantha Haw. as a synonym. The attractive variegated form which has been known as Opuntia monacantha f. variegata is thus more correctly **Opuntia vulgaris** f. **variegata**; this has shoots marbled yellowish and green, the Ov. is similarly coloured; the Fl. has reddish Sep.; the immature Fr. is also variegated, but yellow when ripe. There is also a (polyploid?) form with larger and thicker Seg., Sp. to 4, Fr. much larger, oblong, proliferating.
    v. **lemaireana** (Cons.) Backbg.: **Seg.** and **Fl.** smaller.

O. vulpina Web. (B2)
Bo. low-bushy; **Seg.** thinner than in O. sulphurea, more elongated, to c. 15 cm lg., 6 cm br.; **Fl.** deeper yellow; **style** slender-clavate (in O. sulphurea, thick-clavate below); **Fr.** oblong, 3 cm lg., pulp carmine.—Argentina.

O. wentiana Br. & R. (A1–b)
Bo. shrubby, to 2 m h., freely branching; **Seg.** ±
oval to elliptic, rather thin, to 25 cm lg., pale green,
faintly frosted; **Sp.** mostly 3 at first, later 4–5, pale
yellow, soon white; **Fl.** 6–7 cm lg., c. 6 cm ∅, pale
yellow; **Fr.** small, red.—Venezuela and Curaçao
Islands.

O. whetmorei Br. & R.: **Tephrocactus glomeratus** v.
andicola (Pfeiff.) Backbg.

O. whitneyana Baxt. (A1–a)
Bo. low, branching, to 40 cm h.; **Seg.** to 15 cm lg., to
10 cm br., 2.5 cm thick, sometimes quite circular to
obovate, not velvety, reddish; **Ar.** more sunken;
Sp. 0; **Fl.** 7.5 cm ∅, red; **Fr.** dry.—USA (California, Sierra Nevada Mountains).
    v. **albiflora** Baxt.: **Seg.** green, never reddish; **Fl.**
white, fairly large. Both spec. and variety are
readily distinguished from O. basilaris by the
thickened, circular and non-velvety shoots.

O. wilcoxii Br. & R. (A1–b)
Bo. erectly shrubby, to 2 m h., freely branching;
Seg. oblong, rather thin, dark green, to 20 cm lg.,
finely velvety, reddish around the Ar.; **Sp.** 1–3,
longest one to 6 cm lg., white or yellowish; **Glo.**
yellow; **Fl.** 6 cm lg., yellow; **Fr.** 4 cm lg., velvety.—
Mexico (from S. Sonora to Sinaloa).

O. woodsii Backbg. (A1–b)
Bo. shrubby; **Seg.** rhombic; **Fl.** red.—USA
(Nevada, Zion National Park). Habit similar to O.
engelmannii, from which it is distinguished by the
rhombic shoots and red Fl.

O. zacana How.: **Opuntia galapageia** v. **zacana**
(How.) Backbg.

O. zacuapanensis Berg.: a little known spec.,
differing little from O. lasiacantha apart from
having only 2 white Sp. which are yellowish at base
and tip. Origin not known.

O. zebrina Small (A1–b)
Bo. shrubby, to 1 m h.; **R.** fibrous; **Seg.** deep green,
sometimes ± frosted, ± ovate, often spineless
below; **Sp.** 1–4, subulate, ± twisted, reddish-brown,
finely zoned; **Fl.** to 7 cm ∅, yellow; **Fr.** reddish-
purple, shortly ovoid, to 4.5 cm lg.—USA (Florida,
Cape Sable and Keys).

Oreocereus (Berg.) Ricc. (77)

A genus of predominantly more strongly hairy
Cerei, forming low groups, ± dense colonies of
medium height, stouter columns, or shrubs with
slender branches. Flowers mostly subapical, except

in O. trollii where they arise lower down the flanks.
Diagnostic characters are the longer, ± cylindric
tube and longer-projecting style of the zygomorphic flower, and above all the yellowish-green
spherical hollow fruit which dehisces basally to
show the fairly large and laxly arranged matt black
seeds. Elsewhere among the Cerei a fruit of this
type occurs only in Morawetzia, which develops a
cephalium but is closely related to Oreocereus. In
both genera the hair-development is sometimes
greatly reduced. To include this genus in Borzicactus, as done by Kimnach (USA), is an untenable
thesis in the light of the completely divergent fruits,
and the cephalium in Morawetzia. Riccobono's
type-species was O. celsianus, but the plant of
Lemaire's name in Cels's catalogue suffered
confusion with O. trollii at the hands of Salm-
Dyck, so that after the description of O. trollii the
taller columnar species had to be re-named, since it
could not be established which plant should be
regarded as the type-species.—Distribution: from
N. Argentina through Bolivia to N. Chile and S.
Peru. [(R).]

O. celsianus (Berg.) Ricc. pro parte: **Oreocereus
neocelsianus** Backbg.

O. crassiniveus Backbg.: **Oreocereus trollii** v.
crassiniveus Backbg.

O. doelzianus (Backbg.) Borg: **Morawetzia doelziana** Backbg.

O. fossulatus (Lab.) Backbg.
Bo. shrubby, to 2 m h., laxly branching; **shoots** to c.
8 cm ∅; **Ri.** 11–14, thickened around the Ar. which
are surmounted by a V-notch; **H.** somewhat wispy;
Ar. thickly felty at first; **Rsp.** to c. 16; **Csp.** 1–4,
subulate, to c. 4 cm lg., yellowish to brownish,
or dark below; **Fl.** violet-reddish.—Bolivia
(Chuquisaca). Sometimes branching from the flanks.
    v. **gracilior** (K. Sch.): **Sp.** c. 14, Csp. mostly
solitary, to 5 cm lg., all Sp. amber-coloured; **Fl.**
greenish to violet-pink.—Bolivia (above La
Paz).

O. hendriksenianus Backbg.
Bo. forming large, moderately tall groups or
colonies, branching from below, to c. 1 m h.; **St.**
robust, to almost 10 cm ∅; **H.** ± wispy, densely
tangled, often coffee-coloured at the apex; **Ri.** c. 10,
to 2.5 cm br., with shallow transverse furrows
between the Ar.; **Ar.** with yellow felt at first, later
blackish-grey; **Rsp.** c. 8–9, to 15 mm lg.; **Csp.** (1–)4,
horn-coloured, at first sometimes darker or flecked,
to 7 cm lg.; **Fl.** carmine, 7 cm lg.—S. Peru to N.
Chile.
    v. **densilanatus** Rauh & Backbg.: **H.** pure white,

dense, in long tufts; **Sp.** finer, shorter, less conspicuous, yellow.—S. Peru (Puquio valley);
v. **spinosissimus** Rauh & Backbg.: **H.** white to yellowish; **Csp.** 10–15 cm lg., porrect, brilliant yellow.—S. Peru (Puquio valley).

O. maximus Backbg.
Bo. branching from the base and sides, to over 3 m h.; **branches** not numerous, to 20 cm thick; **H.** laxly wispy, little projecting, often curly; **Ar.** large, oblong, with thick brown felt; **Sp.** scarcely differentiated, stout, terete, straight or $\pm$ curving, 2 lower ones rather thinner, 1 or several more central Sp. longer, very stout, in various colours from light yellow to orange-brown; **Fl.** to c. 9 cm lg., dull pink.—Bolivia (Tupiza).

O. neocelsianus Backbg. (T.)
Bo. lower than the preceding, but over 1 m h., light to darker to greyish-green; **St.** 8–12 cm thick; **Ri.** 10–17, obtuse, swollen around the Ar.; **H.** wispy, tangled, $\pm$ dense to fairly so, rarely brownish above, to 5 cm lg.; **Ar.** large; **Rsp.** c. 9, stiffly subulate, to 2 cm lg.; **Csp.** 1–4, stouter, to 8 cm lg., variously coloured; **Fl.** to 9 cm lg., dull pink.—S. Bolivia to N. Argentina (to Humahuaca). Branching mostly from the base.

O. ritteri Cullm.: **Oreocereus hendriksenianus** v. **densilanatus** Rauh & Backbg.

O. tacnaensis Ritt.: **Oreocereus variicolor** v. **tacnaensis** Backbg.

O. trollii (Kupp.) Backbg.
Bo. in low groups, laxly branching from the base, rarely over 60 cm h., mostly less; **St.** thick; **Ri.** 15–25, low; **H.** dense, fine, white, to 7 cm lg.; **Sp.** scarcely differentiated, radials 10–15, $\pm$ bristly-fine, to subulate, Csp. 1 to several, stoutly subulate, brilliant brownish-red at first, later yellow to reddish-brown; **Fl.** to over 4 cm lg., pinkish-red to carmine, bluish-carmine inside.—N. Argentina (frontier zone: Humahuaca and northwards). (Fig. 290.)
v. **crassiniveus** (Backbg.) Backbg.: **St.** later prostrate, quite long; **H.** pure white; **Sp.** not very stout, light.—S. Bolivia (N. of Tupiza);
v. **tenuior** Backbg.: **Bo.** densely branching, more slender, to 60 cm h., 9 cm $\emptyset$; **Sp.** stiff but thin, acicular to subulate.—Bolivia (Huari-Huari).

O. variicolor Backbg.
Bo. erectly columnar, moderately branching; **St.** arising from the base; **Ri.** c. 12, rounded; **Ar.** large, brownish-white; **H.** rarely present, or few and then short; **Rsp.** c. 15, variously stout; **Csp.** 4, much longer, stoutly subulate, from near-white to dark

blood-red; **Fl.** c. 6 cm lg., red.—N. Chile (at high altitudes, near Ticnamar).
v. **tacnaensis** (Ritt.) Backbg.: **Bo.** dull bluish-green; **Ri.** 10 at first, without any notch or transverse division; **Sp.** more numerous, c. 3–4 mm lg., **Rsp.** (seedlings) c. 15, lighter or hyaline, **Csp.** scarcely recognisable, c. 10, longer, stouter, 12 mm lg. and more; **H.** virtually missing; **Ar.** long-oval. **Sp.** increasing later in both thickness and number.—S. Peru (Tacna frontier region). Probably forms colonies.

Oroya Br. & R. (115)

Spherical species, the largest to 25 cm $\emptyset$, mostly offsetting, the spine-colour rather variable in some species. Bodies often set low in the soil, sometimes with stout main roots. Occurrence restricted to altitudes over 3500 m. Flowers relatively small, with the inner petals curving $\pm$ inwards; ovary and fruit with only traces of felt; the fruit is a small hollow berry, with the seeds laxly arranged inside it. (Similar characters of flower and fruit also found in the Chilean genus, Neoporteria. When Kimnach (USA) seeks to include in Borzicactus the genera Oreocereus and Morawetzia, with their hollow fruits, and at the same time also the genus Matucana which, in habit, resembles Neoporteria from Chile, then logically he should also include Oroya since Borzicactus sensu Kimn. likewise possesses rather narrow flower-openings; this demonstrates the effects of synthetic groupings as opposed to natural ones. These confusions cannot arise where groups of species with naturally uniform characters are segregated.—Distribution: Peru, High Andes, from the Cordillera Negra to the Mantaro region. [G.]

O. borchersii (Böd.) Backbg.
Bo. broadly spherical, fairly deep in the ground, to over 20 cm $\emptyset$, 20–30 cm h., fresh green; **Ri.** to c. 30; **Ar.** light brown; **Rsp.** $\pm$ pectinate, thin-acicular to bristly, 15–25; **Csp.** 1–3(–5) or more, scarcely differentiated; **Sp.** to c. 2–2.5 cm lg., (greenish to) amber-coloured; **Fl.** numerous, 2 cm lg., 1 cm $\emptyset$, lemon-yellow; **Fr.** $\pm$ clavate, yellowish-green, to 2.5 cm lg.—N. Peru (Cordillera Blanca and Cordillera Negra).
v. **fuscata** Rauh & Backbg.: Sp. reddish-brown.

O. gibbosa Ritt., with noticeable swellings around the Ar. and $\pm$ chin-like tuberculate protuberances, has been shown by recent observations to be **Oroya peruviana** (K. Sch.) Br. & R. which shows similar variability of habit. Imported plants of Ritter's were indistinguishable from O. peruviana in Werdermann's colour photo in "Blüh. Kakt.

u.a.sukk. Pflz.", plate 166, 1939; moreover it is just as floriferous in cultivation, but this cannot be said for any other species.

O. laxiareolata Rauh & Backbg.

Bo. mostly simple, elongated in age, to c. 15 cm h., 10 cm ∅ or more, greyish-olive to leaf-green; **Ri.** 24–30, variable in width, with transverse indentations above the Ar.; **Ar.** narrow, elongated, yellowish to white; **Sp.** pectinate, directed stiffly sideways, pale yellowish, reddish or dark below; **Rsp.** c. 16–24; **Csp.** mostly 0, sometimes 1, porrect, more elongated; **Fl.** pale carmine, mid-yellow towards the centre.—Central Peru (Mantaro terraces, S. of Oroya).

v. **pluricentralis** Backbg.—Descr. Cact. Nov. III: 10. 1963: **Csp.** to c. 7, in a vertical R., the longest one noticeably porrect, others pointing ± upwards, dark below, otherwise deeper yellow; **Rsp.** in part (uppers) yellower than in the type; **Sp.** usually enveloping the Bo. fairly closely; **Ar.**, as in the type, fairly distant. (Fig. 291.)

O. neoperuviana Backbg.

Bo. eventually larger-spherical, to c. 40 cm h., 20 cm ∅, green to dark green; **Ri.** 24–35; **Rsp.** c. 20–30, acicular, interlacing, to c. 1.5 cm lg.; **Csp.** to 5, 1–2 often more noticeable, otherwise scarcely differentiated; **Sp.** honey-yellow, brown below, sometimes rather variable in colour, to lighter yellow; **Fl.** to 2 cm lg., numerous, carmine to paler above, yellowish inside.—Central Peru (Oroya). Like most other spec. or varieties, this plant is harder to flower in cultivation than the type-species.

v. **depressa** Rauh & Backbg.: **Bo.** depressed-spherical, to c. 10 cm h., 20 cm ∅, projecting little above the soil; **Ri.** 15–20; **Rsp.** c. 20; **Csp.** mostly 1, to 2 cm lg.; all **Sp.** reddish-brown.— Central Peru (Andahuaylas);

v. **ferruginea** Rauh & Backbg.: **Fl.** smaller, more intensely red. Apparently rather variable. I have seen one plant with a dark green epidermis; **Sp.** c. 13, somewhat bent, ± chocolate-brown, tips ± black; Csp. 0;

v. **tenuispina** Rauh: **Bo.** light green; **Ri.** narrow; **Rsp.** numerous, thin, to 2.5 cm lg., pectinate; **Csp.** often present but scarcely distinguishable as such; **Sp.** pale yellowish to whitish or brownish-reddish, darker below.

O. peruviana (K. Sch.) Br. & R. (T.)

Bo. depressed-spherical to subspherical, to c. 14 cm ∅, bluish-green; **Ri.** to c. 21, at first ± tuberculate, later with transverse indentations between the Ar., often (or in age) with a ± chin-like protuberance below the Ar.; **Ar.** to over 1 cm lg., white; **Rsp.** c. 15–16, pectinate and ± spreading; **Csp.** c. 4–5, subulate, to c. 2 cm lg.; **Sp.** reddish-brownish,

mostly black below; **Fl.** numerous, to 2.5 cm lg., 2.2 cm ∅, carmine-reddish, yellow inside or below; **Fr.** virtually glabrous.—Central Peru. Mature plants cannot be distinguished from O. gibbosa Ritt., so that Ritter must know the type-locality for the type-species, which has not yet been satisfactorily established. Floriferous spec.

O. subocculta Rauh & Backbg.

Bo. broadly spherical, sunken mostly in the soil, rarely offsetting, to 15 cm h., 20 cm ∅, passing over into the taproot; **Ri.** 20–30; **Ar.** to 1.5 cm lg.; **Rsp.** c. 10, pectinate; **Csp.** 0–1–2, stouter, porrect, to 2 cm lg.; **Sp.** yellowish, reddish below; **Fl.** 2.5 cm lg., 1.5 cm ∅, light carmine to crimson, yellowish below.—Central Peru (S. of Oroya).

v. **albispina** Rauh & Backbg.: **Sp.** white, strongly appressed, centrals missing or to 3, to 3.3 cm lg.; **Fl.** 3 cm lg., 2.5 cm ∅;

v. **fusca** Rauh & Backbg.: **Ri.** to 32; **Sp.** intense reddish-brown at first, glassy above, less interlacing, centrals mostly absent; **Fl.** 1.5 cm lg., deep red.

Ortegocactus Alex. (223)

Small spherical plants, mostly caespitose, resembling Coryphantha except that the stout tubercles have no furrow. As in Mammillaria, the flowers arise from the newer axils and are hairy. The longer-persisting fruit is dry, the seeds black and finely pitted. This genus shows particularly clearly that the reduction of floral indumentum by innumerable stages conforms to evolutionary laws, and that it is of decisive importance for a systematic classification. Ortegocactus, with its hirsute axillary flowers, stands before Mammillaria in the line of reduction, but between the Groups Boreoechinocacti and Mammillariae.—Distribution: Mexico (Oaxaca). (?)

O. macdougallii Alex. (T.)

Bo. broadly spherical, light greyish-green, to only c. 4 cm ∅; **Tub.** rhomboid to depressed-rounded, to 12 mm br., finely pitted, spiralled; **Ar.** shortly woolly; **Rsp.** 7–8, 5–10 mm lg.; **Csp.** 1, 4–5 mm lg.; all **Sp.** black to whitish, black-tipped; **Fl.** to 3 cm lg., to 2.5 cm ∅, mid-yellow; **Tu.** short; **Ov.** not scaly, with weak H.; **style** greenish-yellow; **Sti.** 4, deep green; **Fr.** spherical-ellipsoid, dry, dark red, thinly hairy; **S.** 0.9 mm lg.—Mexico (Oaxaca, near the village of San José Lacheguiri). (Fig. 292.)

× **Pachgerocereus orcuttii** (K. Brand.) R. Moran— Cact. y Suc. Mex., VIII: 3, 59. 1963.
A natural hybrid between Pachycereus pringlei and Bergerocactus emoryi, or identical with Pachy-

cereus orcuttii (K. Brand.) Br. & R. (see latter for description). The hybrid genus (l. c.) is given as: × Pachgerocereus R. Mor.

Pachycerei Berg. emend. Backbg.: for comments on the Group, see under Polaskia Backbg.

Pachycereus (Berg.) Br. & R. (149)

Large to very stout columnar Cerei, sometimes with a trunk, always fairly freely branching, those without a trunk branching from near the base. Flowers nocturnal, ± bellshaped-funnelform to funnelform; the relatively stout tube is fairly densely scaly; the ovary has stronger wool-development, with bristles present to completely reduced; the fruit shows a comparable line of reduction, similar to that seen in some closely related species: from a dense covering of longer spines, to fine and short spines; it opens above or splits open; while there is no actual fruit-pulp, the funicles are often fleshy and contain a pectinose substance. The fruit dries very quickly. In some species the new areoles are connected by bands of felt, these disappearing later. Seeds are large, mostly matt black, but shiny in some cases.—Distribution: Mexico (from Baja California and Sonora, near the coasts, southwards to Tehuantepec, and the Highlands in Guerrero, Morelos, Puebla and Oaxaca). [(R).]

P. calvus (Eng.) Br. & R.
Bo. strongly columnar, with a **trunk**; **branches** very stout, ± curving and frosted; **Ri.** to c. 20 and more; **Sp.** fairly stout at first, those of the flowering zone greatly reduced, short or missing; **Ar.** discrete towards the apex; **Fl.** clearly funnelform, white; **Fr.** very spiny, oblong, Sp. red, pale-tipped, funicles red, pectinose.—Mexico (Baja California, from Cape San Lucas northwards). (Fig. 294, right, 295.)

P. chrysomallus sensu Br. & R.: **Mitrocereus fulviceps** (Web.) Backbg.

P. columna-trajani sensu Br. & R.: **Haseltonia columna-trajani** (Karw.) Backbg.

P. columna-trajani sensu Daws.: **Mitrocereus fulviceps** (Web.) Backbg.

P. gaumeri Br. & R.: **Anisocereus gaumeri** (Br. & R.) Backbg.

P. gigas (Backbg.) Backbg.
Bo. giant-cereoid, forming a long trunk, broadly branching above that, with no noticeable constriction; **trunk** to 1 m ∅; **branches** matt greyish-green, growing out sideways from the trunk and then ascending, parallel and vertical, to c. 15 cm ∅; **Ri.** c. 10, very broad, not prominent; **Sp.** not modified in the flowering-zone, stoutly subulate; **Rsp.** moderately lg., 1 central dark, flattened; **Fl.** ? **Fr.** dry, with dense and longer Sp.—Mexico (Guerrero, Zopilote Canyon).

P. grandis Rose
Bo. enormous, to over 10 m h.; **branches** dense, ascending steeply or obliquely, sometimes somewhat constricted; **trunk** to 1 m ∅, **branches** stout, pale green, at first with frosted stripes; **Ri.** 9–11, prominent, fairly acute; **Rsp.** 9–10; **Csp.** 3, the lowest one longest, to 6 cm lg., somewhat flattened; all **Sp.** subulate, grey to white, black-tipped, modified in the flowering-zone, acicular to bristly; **Fl.** only 4 cm lg.; **Ov.** with Br. and weak H.; **Fr.** large, with yellow Br. and yellow felt.—Mexico (Morelos near Cuernavaca).

P. lepidanthus (Eichl.) Br. & R.: **Anisocereus lepidanthus** (Eichl.) Backbg.

P. marginatus (DC.) Br. & R.: **Marginatocereus marginatus** (DC.) Backbg.

P. orcuttii (K. Brand.) Br. & R.
Bo. branching from below, to 3 m h.; **branches** to 15 cm ∅; **Ri.** 14–18, 1 cm h.; **Ar.** 6 mm ∅, light grey; **Rsp.** c. 12–20, c. 12 mm lg.; **intermediate Sp.** c. 10, 16–24 mm lg., one upper often to 7 cm lg.; **Csp.** 5, porrect, rather longer; **Fl.** greenish-brown, c. 4 cm lg.; **Ov.** densely felty, with brown Br. to 6 cm lg.; **Fr.** 5 cm lg. and ∅, dry, with dense long thin yellow Sp. to 2.5 cm lg.—Mexico (Baja California, around El Rosario).
Acc. Reid Moran's more recent investigations, this is a natural hybrid between Pachycereus pringlei and Bergerocactus emoryi, which he named × **Pachgerocereus orcuttii** (K. Brand.) R. Mor.; another hybrid of the latter is × Myrtgerocactus lindsayi R. Mor.; see also under this.

P. pecten-aboriginum (Eng.) Br. & R.
Bo. tree-like, to 10 m h., with a **trunk** to 2 m lg., 30 cm ∅; **branches** steeply or obliquely ascending, stout; **Ri.** 10–11; **Ar.** shield-shaped, connected at least for a time by a band of felt; **Sp.** at first 8 radials to 1 cm lg., subulate, 1 laterally compressed Csp. to 3 cm lg., mostly shorter; all apical Sp. dark, soon whitish-grey and black-tipped, those in the flowering zone modified to golden-brown Br., tufted, to 2.5 cm lg.; **Fl.** to 8.5 cm lg.; **Tu.** and **Ov.** with longer-projecting Sc., drying to black; **Ov.** more strongly yellow-woolly, sometimes with small Br.; **Pet.** pure white; **Fr.** to 7.5 cm ∅, densely set with yellow felt and stiff yellow Br. to 6 cm lg.; **S.**

glossy, 6 mm lg.—Mexico (Sonora, to the Gulf of Tehuantepec). The fruit was formerly used by the Mexican Indians as a comb, hence the specific name meaning "natives' comb".

P. pringlei (S. Wats.) Br. & R. (T.)
Bo. mostly tree-like, to 11 m h., with a **trunk** to 2 m lg. and 60 cm thick which eventually becomes woody and glabrous; **branches** obliquely ascending, very stout, curving and frosted at first; **Ri.** c. 13; **Ar.** (in particular the flowering ones) large, those in the flowering zone confluent, connected at first by a band of felt; **Sp.** white, black-tipped, scarcely differentiated, c. 20, mostly to c. 2 cm lg., stout, later sometimes to 12 cm lg., concolorous black, those in the flowering zone dropping or ± absent; **Fl.** bellshaped-funnelform, to 8 cm lg., white; **Tu.** and **Ov.** more strongly felty, without any recognisable Sp.; **Fr.** oblong-spherical, with shortly spined Ar. and some felt; **S,** with fleshy funicles.—Mexico (Sonora to Nayarit, near the coast, Baja California and neighbouring islands). (Fig. 293, 294 left.) On the islands of Tortuga, La Catalana etc. there are shorter ± trunkless forms, but little is known of these.

P. queretaroensis (Web.) Br. & R.: **Ritterocereus queretaroensis** (Web.) Backbg.

P. ruficeps (Web.) Br. & R.: **Mitrocereus ruficeps** (Web.) Backbg.

P. tehuantepecanus MacDoug. & H. Bravo: **Pachycereus pecten-aboriginum** (Eng.) Backbg.

P. tetetzo (Web.) Br. & R.: **Neobuxbaumia tetetzo** (Web.) Backbg.

P. weberi (Coult.) Backbg.
Bo. tree-like, to over 10 m h., **trunk** to 1 m lg.; **branches** numerous, ascending and parallel, ± frosted, dark bluish-green, regularly constricted; **Rsp.** 6–12, to 2 cm lg., acicular; **Csp.** 1, to c. 10 cm lg., flattened, dark reddish-brown to blackish; **Fl.** to 10 cm lg., yellowish-white; **Ov.** with much woolly felt; **Tu.** with narrow thin Sc. and long brown H.; **Fr.** oblong, to 7 cm lg. and more, virtually dry, with small deciduous Sp.—Mexico (Puebla; Oaxaca). Diverges from P. grandis by its broad crown; and from P. gigas by the longer solitary Csp., shortly spiny Fr., different epidermis-colour and more conspicuous constriction of the shoots.

Parodia Speg. (108)

A genus of some of the most attractive globose cacti of S. America; in 1923 only a single species was known, whereas there have been numerous discoveries in more recent times. Bodies from spherical to elongated, with spines variable as to thickness, shape and colour; central spines range from ± hooked, to very curving or straight. The flowers have a short tube, with slender scales, which is ± very woolly and with or without bristles above, these sometimes also lower down or only in a ring above; the woolly indumentum of the ovary is in part ± reduced. Since the bristles can be much reduced to absent, there is a clear line of reduction in indumentum which is not parallelled in the Chilean species; this shows that the question must be studied separately for each genus. The seeds show similarly conspicuous differences: they can be light-coloured and very fine, or larger and black, which shows—in the face of the very uniform nature of the genus—that seeds are not a good basis for systematic classification. The fruits dry to become thin-membranous, and then open basally or disintegrate. The rib-form is also variable; ribs may be continuous, or completely divided into tubercles, with intermediate stages. Some 14 undescribed species must be given at least a brief mention here since seeds are available, and therefore plants are also found in collections.— Distribution: Bolivia to N. Argentina, Paraguay, Central to S. Brazil. [(G) or (R); some spec. prosper on their own roots, and some—e.g. P. comosa— cannot be successfully grafted; other spec., however are more difficult when on their own roots, so that most grafted plants grow faster and flower more freely, although the genus as a whole is free-flowering.] The species are divided as follows on the basis of their central spines:

1. Species with hooked centrals;
2. Species with the centrals ± curving above;
3. Species with straight centrals.

For readier identification the appropriate group is shown in each case by the figure after the specific name. There are however plants where the spination is not always uniform.

P. agregia Wesk. (nom. prov.)
Bo. oblong, dark green, 10 cm h., 6 cm ∅; **Ri.** 13, spiralled, Tub. round; crown covered with white wool; **Ar.** 6 mm apart, long remaining woolly; **Rsp.** white, 10, appressed; **Csp.** 7, brownish-yellow, 2 laterals and the bottom one strongly hooked; **Fl.** red, 5 cm ∅; **Fr.** broad, golden-yellow; **S.** round to oval, dark, glossy as if varnished.—Argentina. Found by Fechser. A form of Parodia dichroacantha.

P. alacriportana Backbg. & Voll (1)
Bo. simple, spherical to elongated, to 8 cm ∅, dark green; **Ri.** c. 23; **Rsp.** to c. 20, to 8 mm lg., thin; **Csp.**

4–7, to 7 mm lg., one to c. 1 cm lg., hooked; **Sp.** white at first, laterals bristly fine, centrals yellow; **Fl.** medium-sized, yellow.—S. Brazil (Rio Grande do Sul, in the mountains near Porto Alegre).

P. amambayensis (Werd.) Borg: **Parodia paraguayensis** Speg.

P. andreae Brandt (syn. P. subtilihamata Ritt.)
Bo. broadly spherical, dark grass-green, to c. 15 cm h., 14 cm ∅; **Ar.** slightly tuberculate, covered with short wool, c. 7–10 mm lg., in old plants the Ar. are contiguous, forming an unbroken band of white wool; **Ri.** 13; **Rsp.** c. 20, whitish, often golden-brown later, very fine, 10–15 mm lg.; **Csp.** 7, straight, the middle one projecting stiffly away from the Bo., all Csp. light brown to honey-coloured, c. 20–25 mm lg.; **Fl.** golden-orange, c. 4–5 cm ∅, throat orange-pink; **Tu.** short; **style** and **Sti.** yellow; **Fr.** brownish, c. 4 mm ∅; **S.** dark reddish-brown, almost black, glossy.—Bolivia (Prov. Mendez, near Cieneguilla and probably also in the mountains near Tarija). Seedlings of this spec. also appear in sowings reputedly of P. subtilihamata and P. tredecimcostata. (Fig. 497.)

P. atroviridis Backbg.—Descr. Cact. Nov. III: 10. 1963 (1–2–3)
Bo. simple, dark green, to 7 cm h., 6.5 cm ∅; **crown** felty; **Ri.** spiralled, c. 13, tuberculate; **Ar.** c. 9 cm apart; **Rsp.** c. 10, 5 mm lg., white; **Csp.** 4, brown, upper ones thinner, lower one 1.3 cm lg., straight to ± hooked; **Fl.** c. 2.3 cm lg., 3 cm ∅; **Pet.** yellow, numerous, c. 2.5 mm br.; **style** light green.—N. Argentina (no more precise locality given; found by Fechser). (Fig. 296.)

P. aureicentra Backbg. (2[1])
Bo. spherical to elongated, to 15 cm ∅, mostly grouping, single plants sometimes also ± flattened-spherical; **Ri.** c. 13–15, ± tuberculate; **Ar.** at first strongly white-woolly; **Rsp.** bristle-like, to c. 40, interlacing laterally; **Csp.** stouter, 6–10, to 2–2.5 cm lg., one or several of the 4 strongest straight to ± curving at the tip or even hooked; lateral **Sp.** white, centrals lighter to darker golden-brown; **Fl.** c. 4 cm ∅, light blood-red.—N. Argentina (Salta, Cachipampa).
Spec. with very variable spination. Ritter described v. albifusca Ritt., which scarcely diverges from the above description, also a v. omniaurea Ritt. with strongly hooked Csp., spination finer, overall yellowish-brownish, with only 22–26 Rsp.; but there are also very fine-spined intermediates with white Rsp., all Sp. finer, and a form with c. 18 Rsp., golden-brown like the 5 strongly hooked Csp. which are 2.5 cm lg. The number of centrals is just as variable as the stoutness and colour of the Rsp.

or the Csp., while the smaller flower-size of v. albifusca (to 4 cm lg.) is of little importance since Ritter himself gives variations of 4–4.5–5 cm for both the type and v. omniaurea. Because of the numerous intermediates, these two varieties cannot be segregated, but the following seems admissible on account of the divergence of Fl.-colour:
  v. **lateritia** Backbg.: Fl. brick-red.

P. aureispina Backbg. (1)
Bo. spherical, fresh green, to 6.5 cm ∅; **Ri.** to c. 16 or more, spiralled, tuberculate; **Rsp.** c. 40, bristly-fine, white; **Csp.** c. 6, to c. 15 mm lg., ± golden-yellow, 4 of these cruciform, all stouter, the lowest one or several hooked; **Fl.** to 3 cm ∅, golden-yellow; **S.** minute, brown.—N. Argentina (Salta).
  v. **australis** Brandt: closely resembles P. rubriflora, differing as follows: areolar wool pure white; **Csp.** mostly 8, darker carmine, especially the 6 lower stoutest ones, not fading with age as in v. rubriflora, outer upper ones sometimes tipped darker, and lighter below; **Fl.** not flame-coloured with a golden sheen, but dark blood-red with a bluish-violet sheen. In v. australis the Fl. are 6 cm ∅. This is the most southerly of the aureispina varieties, as indicated by the name (Fig. 498);
  v. **elegans** Backbg.: **crown** more strongly white-woolly; all **Sp.** fine, with additional finer hair-like Br. to 2.2 cm lg., but one lower Csp. clearly hooked. Backeberg's v. elegans is a hybrid, acc. F. Brandt and others, since it does not come true from seed;
  v. **vulgaris** Brandt: **Bo.** hemispherical, later elongated, compact, intense bluish-green; **crown** slightly sunken, with tufted Sp.; **Ri.** (19–)21(–29), spiralled, divided into small Tub.; **Ar.** weakly woolly, pure white, very slowly becoming glabrous, c. 8 mm apart; **Rsp.** c. 20–40, radiating, white, c. 10 mm lg.; **Csp.** 6–10, the lowest one stoutest, hooked, c. 15 mm lg., whitish-yellow, the 4 or more stoutest tipped dark to brownish-red; **Fl.** several together in the crown, c. 4–5 cm ∅, pericarpel smooth in the lower part, glabrous, green, areolate above, set with Sc. with whitish wool; **Sep.** mid-green, paler in the centre; **Pet.** golden-yellow; **Fil.** and **An.** yellow; **style** cream; **Fr.** small, thin-membranous; **S.** small, glossy, light brown.
There are also Fl. with a dark throat. F. Brandt has also described v. scopapoides and v. rubriflora.—N. Argentina (Salta). (Fig. 499.)

P. aurihamata hort.: a more golden-yellow form of **Parodia mutabilis** Backbg.

P. aurinana Ritt. (FR 922): an unclarified spec.,

cited in 1966 by Weskamp.—Argentina (Salta, at low altitudes).

P. ayopayana Card. (3)
Bo. spherical, to 8 cm h., 9 cm ⌀, fresh green; **Ri.** c. 11, 2 cm h. and br., weakly tuberculate and somewhat angular; **Ar.** white; **Rsp.** 10–11, to 2 cm lg., white, acicular; **Csp.** 4, subulate, light brown, thickened below, straight, mostly 3 cm lg., one to 3.5 cm lg.; **Fl.** 3 cm lg., golden-yellow; **Fr.** 1–4 cm lg., white-woolly; **S.** fine, brownish to black.—Bolivia (Puente Pilatos).
    v. elata Ritt. (FR 746a): only a name.

P. backebergiana Brandt
Bo. flattened-spherical, bluish-green, 5 cm h., 8 cm ⌀; **Ri.** 13, spiralled, acute, c. 1 cm h., to 2 cm apart, tuberculate; **Ar.** with much white wool; **crown** depressed, covered with white stranded wool to 1 cm lg.; **Rsp.** c. 8, subulate, brown, stout, c. 3–5 mm lg., erect, ± curving; **Csp.** 1, c. 1 cm lg., stouter, more bent at the tip; **Fl.** c. 3 cm ⌀, deeply embedded in the white apical wool, brilliant blood-red, opening widely; throat greenish-yellow; **pericarpel** orange-yellowish, c. 3 cm ⌀, with scattered woolly hairlets; **Rec.** only a few mm lg.; **style** with 8 yellowish **Sti.** (Fig. 500).—Bolivia (Oropeza, on the road from Sucre to Tarabuco, in company with P. otuyensis Ritt.).

P. bilbaoensis Card. 1966
Bo. shortly cylindric, 4–5 cm h., 5–6 cm ⌀, light green; **Ri.** c. 13, slightly spiralled, 8 mm h., to 13 mm br.; **Ar.** 5 mm apart, round, 2 mm ⌀, grey-felty; **Rsp.** 18–20, appressed or ± spreading, very thin, acicular, 6–8 mm lg., white; **Csp.** 4, spreading, 12–20 mm lg., white to brownish, straight; **Fl.** 2.5 cm lg., golden-yellow; **style** light yellow; **Sti.** 5, yellow.—Bolivia (Bilbao, Dept. Potosí, near Mollenvillque, at 2200 m, in rock-crevices under bushes). Differentiated from P. taratensis, which occurs in the same area, by the more numerous and shorter Rsp. and almost straight Csp.

P. borealis Ritt.—"Taxon", XIII: 3, 116. 1964 (3)
Bo. hemispherical, later elongated, greyish-green, to 3.7 cm ⌀; **Ri.** c. 13, later also to 15, c. 7 mm h.; **Rsp.** (as in P. comosa) 7–20 mm lg., hair-like, white or yellow-brown, lowest ones shortest; **Csp.** 4, acicular, to 2.5 cm lg., stiff, mostly dark brown, blackish or yellowish-brown to grey; **Fl.** to 2 cm lg., golden-yellow; **Sep.** reddish; **Tu.** with reddish-brown or black Br. above; **Fr.** carmine; **S.** 0.5 mm lg., purse-shaped.—Bolivia (Prov. Larecaja-Muñecas, frontier, in the Rio Consata gorge, Dept. La Paz) (FR 120).

P. brasiliensis Speg. (Notocactus, acc. Haage)

Presumably now lost. Described as follows: **Ri.** c. 15, tuberculate; **Rsp.** 8–10, thin, whitish-yellowish, 4–5 mm lg.; **Csp.** only 1, to 1 cm lg., stout, brown, bent downwards at the tip; **Fl.** 2.5 cm lg., whitish or pale pink.—Brazil (Santos).

P. brevihamata W. Hge. (1)
Bo. slender-spherical, 3–4 cm ⌀, later elongated, olive-green, tinged ± purplish in the sun; **Tub.** in 22 R., very slender; **Ar.** white or yellowish; **Rsp.** c. 16, to 3 mm lg., yellowish-white; **Csp.** 4–6, to 4 mm lg., thickened below, yellow, brownish-red above, one Sp. concolorous dark red at first, decurved, hooked; **Fl.** golden-yellow.—S. Brazil (Rio Grande do Sul).
Matthes has reported 2 forms to me: type-species with a darker Bo., Ar. more strongly woolly, Fl. shorter, Pet. broader and sometimes more rounded; the other form has a greener Bo., longer Rsp., larger Fl., Pet. laxer and more lanceolate; both have pungent Br. My own cultivated plant is dark, readily becomes violet-green, the Fl. are lax, fairly large, the Pet. broad, tapering.
The spec. is thus variable as shown above; the amount of areolar felt is also variable.

P. buenekeri Buin.—Succulenta, 41: 8, 99–101. 1962 (1–2)
Bo. spherical, to c. 5 cm h., 6 cm ⌀, intense green; **Ri.** c. 20, divided above into short Tub.; **Ar.** ± greyish-whitish; **Rsp.** to c. 13, 6–23 mm lg., whitish, not quite straight, thin, ± interlacing sideways; **Csp.** 5–6, ± colourless at first, then brownish, to 3 cm lg., thickened below, later occasionally recognisably hooked; **Fl.** to 4 cm lg. and ⌀, glossy, golden-yellow, set with many dark Br.; **Fr.** 8 mm lg., with wool and white Br.; **S.** 1 mm lg., brownish-black.—S. Brazil (border between Rio Grande do Sul and Santa Catarina). (Fig. 297.)
The original description gave the Csp. as at most having the tips bent, but I have also seen plants where they were distinctly hooked.

P. buiningiana: mentioned by Ritter (FR 1096), belonging to the microsperma group.

P. cafayatensis n.nud.: **Parodia microsperma** v. **cafayatensis** Backbg.

P. camargensis Buin. & Ritt.—Succulenta, 41: 2, 18–21. 1962 (2–3)
Bo. simple or caespitose, to 13 cm ⌀, 25 cm h.; **Ri.** 10–15, rather obtuse; **Rsp.** 8–11, 2–4 cm lg., lower ones longer, stouter; **Csp.** 3–4, 2.5–5 cm lg.; **Sp.** straight or ± curving, all stiff and yellowish-brown; **Fl.** to 3.5 cm lg., carmine, bordered brownish-yellow, with whitish to brownish H.; **S.**

black, 1.5 mm lg.—Bolivia (S. Cinti, Camargo) (FR 86).

v. **camblayana** Ritt. (1–2): **Bo.** with more white woolly H. in the crown; **Ar.** smaller; **Csp.** 7–9, thinner, 1–4 lowest ones stouter, reddish-brown, sometimes hooked; **Fl.** larger, yellow-ochre, with or without a reddish M.-line (FR 724);

v. **castanea** Ritt.: **Ri.** 10–18; **Sp.** thinner, chestnut to blackish-brown or black; **Rsp.** 7–9; **Csp.** 1–4; **Fl.** and **S.** rather smaller (FR 723);

v. **prolifera** Ritt.: **Sp.** reddish-brown; **Rsp.** 6–8; **Csp.** 1–4; **Fl.** to 3 cm lg.; **S.** rather smaller (FR 726). (Fig. 312, above.)

P. camblayana Ritt.: **Parodia camargensis** v. **camblayana** Ritt.

P. **cardenasii** Ritt.—Succulenta, 43: 4, 58. 1964 (3) **Rsp.** 8–14, whitish; **Csp.** 3–5, white, tipped chestnut-brown; **Fl.** 3 cm lg., sulphur-yellow; **Tu.** to 12 mm lg.; **Ov.** without Br.; **Sep.** with a red M.-line and tip; **Pet.** 1.5 cm lg., to 6 mm br.; **Fil.** coppery-yellow above, almost white below.—Bolivia (Prov. O'Connor, Angosto de Villamontes) (FR 914).
Ritter's description gives the data distinguishing this plant from P. formosa.

P. **carminata** Backbg. (1)
Bo. oblong-spherical, dull bluish-green; **Tub.** spiralled; **Rsp.** c. 18, bristly, fine, white, to 8 mm lg.; **Csp.** several, 4 cruciform, more clearly recognizable, dark to blackish-brown, lowest one hooked; **Fl.** 2.5 cm ∅, glossy, carmine.—N. Argentina (Salta).

P. **carrerana** Card.—"Cactus", 18: 93–94. 1963 (3) **Bo.** to 7 cm h., 10 cm ∅, greyish-green; **Ri.** c. 14, ± spiralled, 1 cm h., 1.5 cm br.; **Ar.** 1 cm apart, 6 mm ∅, round, grey; **Rsp.** c. 17, interlacing, appressed, 1.5–3 cm lg.; **Csp.** 3–4, projecting, 2.5–3 cm lg.; all **Sp.** white, red at first above; **Fl.** rising from a tuft of white wool, to 4 cm lg., 2.5 cm ∅, salmon-red; **Tu.** 2 cm lg., reddish, with white wool, with brown Br. above; **Pet.** narrowly spatulate; **Fil.** light yellow, very fine; **style** yellow; **Sti.** yellow.—Bolivia (Chuquisaca, Las Carreras-Chaupi Unu, 2300 m). Distinguished from P. tarabucina Card. by the white Sp.

P. castanea Ritt.: **Parodia camargensis** v. **castanea** Ritt.

P. **catamarcensis** Backbg. (1)
Bo. spherical to oblong; **Ri.** divided into Tub.; **Ar.** more strongly white-woolly at first; **Rsp.** c. 9, bristly, thin, white; **Csp.** 4, often fairly stout, dark

red, lowest one hooked towards the Bo. and claw-like; **Fl.** light yellow, medium-sized.—N. Argentina (Catamarca?). (Fig. 298.)

v. **rubriflorens** Backbg.—Descr. Cact. Nov. III: 10. 1963: **Bo.** soon becoming oblong, c. 3.5 cm ∅; **Ri.** 21, in spiralled R. of Tub.; **Rsp.** c. 10, white, ± acicular-subulate when seen under a lens; **Csp.** 1, to c. 6 mm lg., hooked downwards and strongly towards the Bo., claw-like, light flesh-colour at first, rarely also 2 further Sp., straight, directed upwards; all **Sp.** very finely rough; **Fl.** red ("erythrantha", acc. Fechser).—N. Argentina.

P. **chaetocarpa** Ritt.—Succulenta, 43: 4, 58. 1964 (3)
Bo. light green, to c. 8 cm ∅; **Ar.** 2–4 mm apart; **Rsp.** 10–15, white; **Csp.** 4–7, 8–20 mm lg., pale or dark brown; **Fl.** to 2.5 cm lg., coppery-yellow; **Tu.** to 8 mm lg.; **Ov.** densely bristly; **Sti.** c. 12; **S.** rather larger, not so smooth.—Bolivia (Prov. Cordillera, Salinos) (FR 1135).
Ritter's description shows the differences from P. formosa.

P. **challamarcana** Brandt
Bo. spherical, light to dark green, c. 10 cm h., 8 cm ∅; **Ri.** 13, spiralled, 1 cm h., acute, glossy; **Ar.** white-woolly, c. 5 mm ∅, set on flat Tub.; **Rsp.** 9–10, radiating, projecting, lower ones shorter, tipped ± brownish; **Csp.** 4, thin, light below, otherwise brown, longest one directed upwards, to 3.5 cm lg.; **Fl.** c. 4 cm ∅, light to golden-yellow, with a lighter throat; **Sc.** to 3 mm lg., brownish to yellow, Sc.-Br. rusty brown, c. 1 cm lg.; **Fil.** glossy silvery-white; **An.** creamy-white; **style** 2.4 cm lg., creamy-white; **Fr.** 5 mm ∅, hard-skinned, covered with woolly H.; **S.** 5 mm ∅, ± oval.—Bolivia (S. Cinti, Challamarca). (Fig. 501.)
Acc. Lau, this spec. occurs at the confluence of the Rio Challamarca with the Rio Camblayo, and only on schistose rocks. Ritter, approaching the area from the other side, found P. procera in the same locality.

P. **chrysacanthion** (K. Sch.) Backbg. (3)
Bo. broadly spherical at first, in age sometimes more strongly elongated, light green; **Ri.** c. 24, tuberculate, spiralled; crown later very woolly; **Ar.** white; **Rsp.** bristle-fine, numerous, pungent, brittle; **Csp.** rather stouter, 8–10 mm lg., the innermost one to 2 cm lg.; all **Sp.** golden-yellow; **Fl.** rather small, bellshaped-funnelform, yellow; **S.** dark to blackish, small but not dust-fine.—N. Argentina (Jujuy).
There are also forms with very light Sp.: v. leucocephala hort.

P. cintiensis Ritt.—Succulenta, 41: 9, 122. 1962 ([2–]3)
Bo. oblong, to 35 cm h., 10 cm ⌀, woolly above; **Ri.** 18–23, more tuberculate at first; **Ar.** white to brownish; **Rsp.** 12–20, thin-acicular, white to light brown, 1.5–3 cm lg.; **Csp.** scarcely distinguishable as such, lowest one stoutest, ± bent above on new growth, all later straight, light brown, 2–4 cm lg.; with c. 3 fine, ± projecting Ssp. above; **Fl.** to 3.25 cm lg., blood-red with reddish-brown wool, white-woolly below; **Fr.** blood-red, with dense white wool; **S.** black, 1 mm lg.—Bolivia (S. Cinti, Impora) (FR 85a).
Fl. more campanulate, as also in P. camargensis (likewise from S. Cinti) to which the above spec. is related.

P. columnaris Card. (3)
Bo. short-columnar to ± clavate, to 30 cm h., 7 cm ⌀, matt green; **Ri.** 12–13, with slight transverse depressions; **Ar.** white at first; **Rsp.** 7–8, appressed, pungent, acicular, grey, to 1.8 cm lg.; **Csp.** 1, grey, to 2 cm lg., bent somewhat downwards; all **Sp.** stiff, bristly; **Fl.** to 2 cm lg., 3 cm ⌀, bellshaped, light yellow, white-woolly below, with brown wool and brown Br. above; **Fr.** dry, 4 mm lg., white-hairy; **S.** glossy, black, small.—Bolivia (Cochabamba, Angosto de Perez).

P. comarapana Card. (3)
Bo. spherical, quite low in the soil, to 5 cm h., 8 cm ⌀; **Ri.** 18–20, tuberculate; **Ar.** whitish; **Rsp.** 18–23; **Csp.** scarcely differentiated but 3–4 more distinctly so, individuals longer; **Sp.** 0.3–2 cm lg., all thin, yellow, brownish-tipped; **Fl.** 2.5 cm lg., 0.5 cm ⌀, orange-yellow, with white H., with brown Br. below; **Fr.** spherical, 8 mm ⌀, dry, greenish-white, pink below; **S.** blackish-brown, 1 mm lg.—Bolivia (N. Comarapa).
  v. **paucicostata** Ritt.—"Taxon", XIII: 3, 117. 1964.
  Bo. rather more slender, 3–6 cm ⌀, freely offsetting; **Ri.** fewer, 12–16; **Fl.** orange to ochreous-yellow, more obtuse above; **Tu.** yellowish inside, pale carmine outside; **Fil.** greenish-yellow; **Ov.** with red Sc.—Bolivia (Mataral) (FR 743a).

P. comata Ritt., not described: "Sp. tufted, weak; Fl. blood-red to carmine" (FR 932).

P. commutans Ritt.—Succulenta, 43: 2, 22. 1964 ([1–]2–3)
Bo. spherical, later elongated, to 16 cm ⌀, 30 cm lg., **crown** with white wool; **Ri.** 13(–14), straight, scarcely notched; **Ar.** white, to 1.2 cm apart; **Rsp.** c. 12 at first, thin, appressed, white, 5–10 mm lg., later brownish or golden-yellow (Csp. similarly), 14–16,

straight, 1–3 cm lg.; **Csp.** 2–4 at first, yellowish-brown, flexible, lower ones 2–5 cm lg., strongly curving, hooked above, in age 4(–6), ± straight, subulate, lower ones 4–6 cm lg.; **Fl.** to 3.5 cm lg., yellow to coppery-yellow; **Tu.** to 1.1 cm lg., white-woolly, sometimes with yellow or brown Br.; **Ov.** with white wool and small yellowish or reddish Sc.; **Pet.** to 16 mm lg., 5 mm br.; **Fr.** cylindric, to 5 cm lg., pale green or yellow or carmine; **S.** black, 0.75 mm lg., hilum white.—Bolivia (borders, S. Cinti and S. Chicas, near Impora) (FR 729).

P. comosa Ritt.—"Cactus" (Paris), 75: 21. 1962(3)
Bo. elongated, to c. 30 cm h., to 7 cm ⌀, with a woolly crown; **Ri.** 8–12, rounded; **Rsp.** 14–18, very thin, 8–15 mm lg., white; **Csp.** 6–9, brown, thin, straight, to 2 cm lg.; **Fl.** to 2.5 cm lg., golden-yellow below, ochreous-yellow in the upper part, 5–6 mm* ⌀; **Tu.** brown-woolly; **Fr.** to 3 cm lg., red, white-woolly; **S.** black, 0.6 mm lg.—Bolivia (borders, S. Yungas and Loayza, gorge of the Rio de la Paz). (FR 111.)

P. compressa Ritt.—"Cactus" (Paris), 73–74: 9. 1962 (2–3)
Bo. elongated, to 15 cm h., to 6 cm ⌀, offsetting freely, dark green; **Ri.** 14–22, at first ± tuberculate and then rather obtuse and narrow, with horizontal depressions; **Ar.** white; **Rsp.** 6–9, 4–12 mm lg., stiff, stout; **Csp.** 1–4, to 8 mm lg., fairly robust; all **Sp.** greyish or violet-red, straight or slightly curving; **Fl.** to 3 cm lg., 2 cm ⌀, pale crimson to white; **Tu.** white-woolly, with pale yellow Br.; **Ov.** white-woolly; **Fr.** crimson, woolly; **S.** glossy, black, 0.5 mm lg.—Bolivia (Prov. Oropeza, Rio Chico) (FR 385).
The above floral data are those of the first description in French. In Kakt. u. a. Sukk., 6: 111. 1964, Ritter states: "outer Pet. carmine outside, ± paler inside; inner Pet. concolorous pure light carmine" (FR 385); "P. ocampoi, which is related to it, is separated from it principally by the Fl.-colour, pale to ochreous-yellow (never red) (FR 738)". No explanation was given as to why the first description gave the Fl.-colour as "pale crimson to white". The Fr., first given as "crimson", then became "carmine". These changes should be explained so that it is clear which spec. Ritter had in mind when giving the above floral data or whether the original description was erroneous. The other data are generally in harmony.

P. cruci-albicentra (Frič) hort.: **Parodia nivosa** Frič ex Backbg.

---

* One dimension for the Fl. must be considered suspect (Translator).

P. cruci-nigricentra (Frič) Sub. and v. sibalii Sub. are forms of **Parodia faustiana** Backbg., with dark or black Sp., the Csp. fairly long and stout, black. Parodia culpinensis Ritt., not described, (1): belongs. together with P. camargensis v. camblayana Ritt. and P. fulvispina Ritt., to the complex of P. maassii in which both straight and strongly hooked Sp. occur, just as P. camargensis v. camblayana can have strongly hooked Csp. and probably also variations of colour, even if Ritter's description makes no mention of hooked Sp. In view of the wide range of variability in P. maassii and its vast distribution, all these plants could quite well be reduced to synonymy, as varieties of the last-named spec. (Colour photo in "Die Cact.", Vol. VI: Fig. 3407).

P. culpinensis has only warty protuberances, Rsp. c. 10, Csp. 3, 2 of these erect, 1 porrect, fairly long, hooked, all dark reddish-brown (FR 730). (Fig. 502.)

P. dextrohamata Backbg.—Descr. Cact. Nov. III: 10. 1963 (1)
Bo. simple, to c. 5 cm lg., 3.5 cm ∅, dark greyish-green, **crown** weakly felty; **Ri.** spiralled, small-tuberculate; **Ar.** 5 mm apart, soon becoming glabrous; **Rsp.** c. 10, rather rough, c. 3–4 mm lg., mostly radiating sideways, also 1 directed upwards and 1 downwards, white; **Csp.** mostly 1, directed downwards, pale red, hooked towards the right, to 6 mm lg.; **Fl.** c. 2.5 cm lg., 2 cm ∅; **Sep.** yellow, with a dorsal red line; **Pet.** yellow, spatulate, c. 3.5 mm br.; **Fil., style** and **Sti.** whitish; **Tu.** white-woolly, with a few pale Br.—N. Argentina (no precise locality given; found by Fechser). (Fig. 299.)

v. **stenopetala** Backbg.—l. c.: **Rsp.** 7–10, 2 upper ones almost central, to 4.5 mm lg.; **Csp.** 1, reddish-brown, to 6 mm lg.; **Fl.** 1.5 cm lg., 3.5 cm ∅; **Pet.** and **Sep.** golden-yellow, narrow, pointed, c. 2.5 mm br.; **Tu.** 9 mm lg., with white H. and several blackish Br. (Fig. 300). Csp. here likewise hooked to the right, but the Pet. are considerably narrower than in the type.

P. dichroacantha Brandt & Wesk. (Syn. P. kilianana Backbg.)
Bo. hemispherical, later elongated, dark green; crown slightly depressed, with white wool; **Ri.** 13, spiralled, tuberculate; **Ar.** white-felty, tinged slightly reddish, soon becoming glabrous, c. 8 mm apart; **Rsp.** (9–)10, radiating, projecting, 7–10 mm lg., 4–5 upper ones brownish-red, rather stouter than the lower white Sp.; **Csp.** 1, porrect, hooked, c. 13 mm lg., brownish-red; **Fl.** apical, c. 60 mm ∅; **Pet.** c. 30 mm lg., 4–5 mm br., spatulate, tapering above, brilliant red with a faint violet M.-stripe outside; **Tu.** with whitish-grey wool and a few blackish Br.; **Fil.** golden-yellow below, carmine above; **An.** pale yellow; **style** creamy-white to reddish; **Sti.** 10, 7 mm lg., creamy-white; **Fr.** c. mm ∅, golden-yellow; **S.** very fine, round, brown.—N. Argentina (N. of Tucuman and Salta, sometimes in rock-crevices in red earth, at c. 1000 m). Found by Fechser. Resembles P. atroviridis.

P. echinus Ritt.—"Taxon", XIII: 3, 117. 1964 (2–3)
Bo. diverges from P. comosa by the initially hemispherical habit and lesser height, eventually to 25 cm, greyish-green; **Ri.** only 11–16; **Ar.** 1–3 mm apart; **Sp.** 12–15, 7–20 mm lg., pale yellow or pale brownish-yellow, never white, lowest ones shortest; **Csp.** 4, cruciform, yellowish or chestnut-brown, straight or slightly curving, stiffly acicular, interspersed with 1–4 rather thinner Sp.; **Fl.** to 2.5 cm lg., yellowish in the bud-stage, later ochreous-orange; **Tu.** with brown or black Sp. above; **Ov.** pale yellow or greenish; **Fr.** to 6 mm lg., pink; **S.** 0.8 mm lg., purse-shaped.—Bolivia (borders, Prov. Murillo and Loayza, Dept. La Paz, La Paz gorge) (FR 747). (Fig. 301.)

P. elegans Fechs. n.nud.
Bo. spherical, caespitose; **Ri.** tuberculate; **Sp.** white, reddish-brown at first above midway, sometimes a single longer **Csp.**, straight to clawlike and hooked above; **Fl.** yellow, larger than in P. erythrantha (Speg.) Backbg.—N. Argentina (no locality stated). Collected by Fechser. (Fig. 302.)

P. erythrantha (Speg.) Backbg. (1)
Bo. fairly small-spherical; **Ri.** tuberculate, spiralled; **Ar.** white-woolly at first; **Rsp.** c. 20, bristly fine, white, shorter, interlacing; **Csp.** 4, white below, reddish above, thin, one of these hooked; **Fl.** ± brick-red, to 3 cm ∅; **Fil.** red.—N. Argentina (Salta).

v. **thionantha** (Speg.) Backbg. n. comb. (Echinocactus microspermus v. thionanthus Speg., Cact. Plat. Tent. 498, 1905): **Bo.** eventually somewhat elongated, to c. 4 cm ∅; **Rsp.** c. 15, white, bristle-fine, interlacing; **Csp.** (2–)4, rather thin, to 1 cm lg., thickened below, whitish below, or pale red to higher up, or uniformly reddish, one Sp. strongly hooked; **Fl.** 3 cm lg. and ∅, mid-yellow; **Tu.** white-woolly, with dark Br.; **Fil.** yellow. (Fig. 303.)

P. escayachensis (Vpl.) Backbg. n. comb. (Echinocactus escayachensis Vpl., MfK. 26: 125. 1916 (3)
Bo. spherical, to 12 cm ∅, with the crown brownish-yellow; **Ri.** c. 15, flatly tuberculate; **Ar.** short-felty; **Sp.** c. 20, subulate, terete or ± flattened, thickened below, unequal, to 2 cm lg., centrals scarcely distinguishable as such, yellowish-brown to grey, in part ± curving, the longest one to 4 cm lg.; **Fl.** 2.5 cm lg., light flesh to dark salmon-

colour.—S. Bolivia (Tarija, Iscayachi). [Haage adds: The name, so as to correspond with the type-locality, should correctly be "iscayachensis".] Ritter regards this spec. (Succulenta, 12: 180. 1963) as a synonym of P. maassii v. maassii, and names v. shaferi as the plant which Britton and Rose took for their description. In my opinion, this is not justified. Vaupel was familiar with both species, and illustrated (MfK, 25: 45. 1915) the plant available to Heese for the original description; of this plant, Heese himself (l. c. 19; 128. 1909) stated: "The Fl. has a certain resemblance to that of Echus. microspermus" (and it is well-known that this can be ± orange-yellow). The first description, like the illustration, was inadequate. The best one can do, in the circumstances, is to rely on Vaupel's illustration of the living material in Berlin. Since no type-plant is available for P. maassii it is out of the question to take as its v. typica P. escayachensis with fairly straight Sp., which Vaupel described as having "light flesh to dark salmon-coloured Fl." (in the quotation above, when referring to the differently coloured Fl. of Heese's plant). Ritter described other closely related plants of this complex, according them specific rank. The above plant is the only one with flesh-coloured Fl., so that I continue to list it; Ritter makes no mention anywhere else of a Fl. with this colour, so it appears doubtful whether he in fact saw the above spec.

P. faustiana Backbg. (3)
Bo. simple, subspherical, to 6 cm ∅, pale grass-green; **Ri.** spiralled, divided into moderately large Tub.; **Rsp.** bristly fine, c. 20, hyaline, to 1 cm lg., interlacing; **Csp.** (3–)4, much stouter, to over 2.5 cm lg., straight, brown to darker, stiff; **Fl.** scarlet outside, golden-yellow inside.—N. Argentina (Salta).
v. **tenuispina** Backbg.: **Csp.** fine; **Fl.** red to blood-red.
Plants with dark to blackish Csp. were named P. cruci-nigricentra (Frič) Sub., and v. sibalii Sub.; but in view of the colour-range they are probably not even valid varieties, and are only forms.

P. fulvispina Ritt.: not described (2); shows few differences from P. camargensis v. camblayana; with Csp. reddish-brown, ± straight to curving above, sometimes ± hooked; Fl. ?

P. fechseri Backbg.—Descr. Cact. Nov. III: 11. 1963 (3)
Bo. simple, oblong, to c. 8 cm lg., 4 cm ∅, vivid green; **crown** white-woolly; **Ri.** c. 15, spiralled, tuberculate; **Rsp.** c. 9–10, white, interlacing, to 8 mm lg., one directed upwards, all bristly, fine; **Csp.** 3–4, flexible, brown to pink, to 2 cm lg., porrect, straight or curving upwards, thinner or stouter; **Fl.**

yellow, c. 3–3.5 cm lg., 4 cm ∅.—N. Argentina (no more precise locality known; found by Fechser). (Fig. 304.)

P. formosa Ritt.—Succulenta, 43: 4, 57. 1964 (3)
Bo. spherical, to 8 cm ∅, light green, **crown** glabrous; **Ri.** 13–26, ± completely divided into Tub. 3–6 mm h.; **Ar.** 2–8 mm apart, to 1.5 mm ∅, white; **Sp.** acicular, straight; **Rsp.** 20–30, 3–8 mm lg.; **Csp.** 6–12, 3–12 mm lg., reddish-brown; **Fl.** to 4 cm lg., sulphur-yellow; **Tu.** to 1.6 cm lg., with white wool, with several thin Br. above; **Ov.** similarly; **Pet.** to 1.8 cm lg., 3–6 mm br.; **style** sulphur-yellow; **Sti.** pale yellow; **Fr.** ± spherical; **S.** 0.5 mm lg., light chestnut-brown.—Bolivia (Prov. O'Connor, Margarita) (FR 735).

P. fričiana Brandt
Bo. simple, erect, matt light green, c. 15 cm h., 9 cm ∅; **Ri.** 15, slightly spiralled; **Ar.** on small Tub., densely woolly; **Rsp.** c. 16–20, stout, light brown, horn-coloured below, c. 15 mm lg., erect; **Csp.** 8, scarcely differentiated, light brown, stout; **Fl.** c. 5 cm ∅, carmine-pink; **pericarpel** ochreous pink, c. 4 mm ∅, with dense white wool and carmine-pink Sc. without Br.; **Sep.** red, suffused carmine; **Pet.** carmine-pink, c. 2 cm lg., 4 mm br., throat lighter; **Fil.** light pink; **An.** yellow; **style** yellowish with short yellowish **Sti.**; **Fr.** ochre-coloured, with white wool; **S.** tuberculate, testa black, glossy.—Argentina (Jujuy, S. of Tilcara, near Maimara). Discovered by Frau Muhr. (Fig. 503.)

P. fulvispina Ritt.—"Cactus", 17: 76, 54–55. 1962 (1–2)
Bo. to 30 cm lg., to 12 cm ∅, greyish-green, **crown** white-woolly; **Ri.** 18–21, rather obtuse, slightly tuberculate; **Ar.** 2–5 mm ∅, 0.5–1.2 cm apart; **Sp.** golden-yellow to brownish-red, mostly brownish-yellow, not greying; **Rsp.** 9–12, 2–4 mm lg.; **Csp.** 4, 2.5–4 cm lg., lower one longest, to 5 cm lg.; **Fl.** c. 3–3.7 cm lg.; **Pet.** carmine, bordered brownish-yellow; **Tu.** with white H. and brown Br.; **style** yellow; **Fr.** pink to blood-red, to 1 cm ∅; **S.** 0.6 mm lg., black, slightly glossy.—Bolivia (Prov. Mendez, Carrizal) (FR 727).
Belongs to the P. maassii complex, since the Csp. are ± straight to ± hooked; could be regarded as a variety of the latter.
v. **brevihamata** Ritt.—l. c.: **Ri.** 15–21, less prominent, more clearly tuberculate; **Sp.** shorter, weaker; **Csp.** equal, to 2.5 cm lg.; **Fl.** pale ochre, with a reddish M.-line; **S.** more glossy.—Bolivia (Dept. Tarija, near Tojo) (FR 727a).

P. fuscato-viridis Backbg.—Descr. Cact. Nov. III: 11. 1963 ([1–]2–3)
Bo. simple, spherical, c. 4–5 cm ∅, brownish-

green; **crown** weakly felty; **Ri.** spiralled, c. 17, divided into small, ± rhombic, white-spotted Tub.; **Ar.** weakly woolly at first, soon glabrous; **Rsp.** 9–10(–11), c. 3.8 mm lg., white, or sometimes also pink or brownish at first, or tipped brownish and yellowish below; **Csp.** mostly 1, directed downwards, reddish or brownish, mostly bent or hooked above; **Fl.** 3 cm lg., 3.5–6 cm br., rotate, with red Sc., white H. and flexible black Br. c. 1 cm lg.; **Pet.** 7 mm br., yellow; **Tu.** c. 1.8 cm lg.; **Fil.** yellow.; **style** white; **Sti.** 10, white, papillose, 5 mm lg.; **S.** dark brown, minute, glossy, hilum large.—N. Argentina (grows in company with P. saint-pieana; found by Fechser). (Fig. 305.)

P. gibbulosa Ritt., not described (2); this spec. also is closely related to the P. maassii complex. The plants I have seen were bluish-green; **Ri.** only tuberculately swollen around the Ar., c. 14; **Rsp.** c. 9, radiating, pale horn-coloured; **Csp.** (1–)4, dark at first, 3 directed upwards, 1 appreciably longer, ± bent or only curving above and sometimes straight, later horn-coloured; crown white-woolly; **Fl.** rather large, yellow. (FR 736) (Fig. 306.) [Haage adds: Described by Backeberg as resembling P. maassii; however Fig. 306 shows the later P. gibbulosoides. Ritter himself pointed out that P. gibbulosa—on the basis of the S.—was not even a Parodia, since it lacked a strophiole.]

P. gibbulosoides Brandt
Bo. broadly spherical, 10 cm ∅; **Ri.** to 26, tuberculate; **Bo.** and crown enveloped in dense white wool; **Rsp.** 9; **Csp.** 1, straight, 5 mm lg.; **Fl.** small, 1 cm ∅, many appearing together; **S.** 0.2 mm ∅, with a distinct bi-partite strophiole.—Bolivia, Dept. of Cochabamba, Prov. Campero, in the mountains N. of the Rio Grande. (Figs. 306 and 504.)

P. gigantea Krainz: a name or a description for a plant scarcely distinguishable from P. tilcarensis; the latter was also the first known spec. which eventually becomes quite large. Spination originally said to be honey-coloured, and the Fl. coral-pink; these two characters offer no significant diagnostic difference (see P. tilcarensis).

P. glischrocarpa Ritt., undescribed: "Ri. prominent, Fr.-pulp sticky" (FR 923) (Fig. 307).

P. gokrauseana W. Heinr.
Described in 1967 from old cultivated plants in the collection of the late Hans Neumann of Brieselang; named for Gottfried Krause. Shortly afterwards, several Parodia-experts established that this plant was in fact the long-familiar P. tilcarensis (Werd. & Backbg.) Backbg. v. gigantea (Frič ex Krainz)

Backbg. (Kakteen/Sukkulenten, 1968, p. 51.)

P. gracilis Ritt.—Succulenta, 43: 2, 23. 1964 (1–2) Differentiated from P. procera Ritt. as follows: **Bo.** spherical, later slightly elongated, 5–10 cm ∅; **Ri.** 13–19, 5–8 mm h., later ± tuberculate; **Sp.** brown; **Rsp.** 14–22; **Csp.** 4–10, sometimes hooked in juveniles.—Bolivia (Prov. Mendez, Alta España) (FR 740).

P. gummifera Backbg. & Voll (3)
Bo. simple, spherical to slightly taller, to 10 cm h., 6 cm ∅, greyish-green; **Ri.** c. 32, tuberculate at first, later narrow, unbroken, tuberculate above; **Ar.** small, with thick yellowish-grey wool at first; **Rsp.** 2 shorter laterals, 1 longer Sp. directed downwards, to 5 mm lg., sometimes also 2 minute Ssp. above; **Csp.** 1, ± subulate, straight, light grey, later darker grey, tipped brownish; **Fl.** 2 cm lg., 1.5 cm ∅, sulphur-yellow; **S.** small, matt, black.—Brazil (Minas Geraes, Serra da Ambrosia).

P. gutekunstiana Backbg. (2)
Bo. becoming oblong, to c. 15 cm lg., 5 cm ∅; **Ri.** 22, tuberculate; **Rsp.** 18–20, to 7 mm lg., very thin, appressed, reddish, later whitish; **Csp.** 4, reddish, to 15 mm lg., the lowest one only bent to semi-hooked; **Fl.** 3.5 cm lg., c. 3 cm ∅, yellow inside, more orange-reddish above, sometimes with a reddish M.-stripe; **Pet.** laxly spreading; **Tu.** and **Ov.** with white wool below, reddish-brown wool above, Br. scarcely discernible.—Argentina(?).

P. haematantha Y. Ito: **Parodia sanguiniflora** Frič ex Backbg.

P. hausteiniana Rausch
Bo. simple, spherical to shortly cylindric, c. 50 mm ∅; **Ri.** c. 13, slightly spiralled; **Ar.** round, 3 mm ∅, 6 mm apart, white-felty; **Rsp.** 26–30, 8 mm lg., radiating, appressed, thin, yellow, later white; **Csp.** 4, cruciform, stouter, yellow, the brown tip rolled inwards and downwards, thickened below, the lowest of the Csp. longest, to 13 mm lg.; **Fl.** c. 10 mm lg. and ∅; **Ov.** and **Tu.** green, with dark green Sc. and brown Br. 4 mm lg.; **Pet.** yellow, bordered dark yellow; **throat** and **Fil.** golden-yellow; **style** and **Sti.** long-projecting, golden-yellow; **Fr.** oval, 3–4 mm lg., olive-green; **S.** oblong-oval, dark brown, testa finely tuberculate.—Bolivia (near Mizque, at 2200 m). Named for Dr. E. Haustein of Erlangen.

P. heteracantha Ritt., not described: "In the P. microsperma group; Rsp. small, fine, white; Csp. long, reddish-brown, mostly straight" (FR 926).

P. ignorata Brandt (syn. P. sotomayorensis Ritt.)

Bo. simple, light green, c. 10 cm h., 7 cm $\emptyset$; **Ri.** spiralled, c. 1 cm h., 2 cm br.; **Ar.** 5 mm lg., oval, 1 cm apart, very woolly; **crown** woolly; **Rsp.** 10–12, light brown, 1.3–2 cm lg.; **Csp.** 4, upper 3 directed upwards, to 2 cm lg., the other stoutest, projecting, hooked, all light brown, as the Rsp.; **Fl.** appearing from the dense apical wool, pale yellow, c. 3 cm $\emptyset$; **pericarpel** c. 6 mm $\emptyset$, whitish-yellow, with white H.; **Rec.** sparsely white-woolly, the brownish Sc. without Br.; **Tu.** c. 1.5 cm lg.; **Sep.** 2 cm lg., pale yellow; **Pet.** similarly, 3 mm br.; **Fil.** and **An.** cream; **style** light greenish to cream, c. 2.2 cm lg.; **Sti.** 3 mm lg.; **Fr.** light green, white-woolly, c. 6 mm $\emptyset$; **S.** with black, $\pm$ glossy testa.—Bolivia (riparian region of the Rio Pilcomayo, in the mountains around Sotomayor). (Fig. 505.) Fl. resembles that of P. ocampoi, from which this spec. is distinguished by the claw-like lowest Csp.

P. jujuyana Frič ex Subik (1)
Bo. oblong, to 12 cm h., 5 cm $\emptyset$; **Ri.** 18, oblique, tuberculate; **Rsp.** 16, grey, pale brown at the tip; **Csp.** 4, brown at first, then grey, all hooked; **Fl.** 2 cm $\emptyset$, red; **Fil.** purple; **Sti.** yellow.—N. Argentina.

P. kilianana Backbg.—Descr. Cact. Nov. III: 11. 1963 (1–3)
Bo. simple, spherical, green, to 9 cm h., 7 cm $\emptyset$; **crown** white-felty; **Ri.** c. 21, spiralled, divided into quite small Tub.; **Ar.** c. 5 mm apart, woolly, soon glabrous; **Sp.** very variable, longer or shorter, thinner or stouter, $\pm$ straight or $\pm$ hooked; **Rsp.** mostly 7, rather rough, arranged in the lower semi-circle of the Ar., slightly curving or straight, c. 2–6 mm lg., white, yellowish below, reddish-tipped; **Csp.** 4, 3 curving upwards, to c. 1.2 cm lg., lower one later porrect or directed downwards, to c. 1.8 cm lg., straight, curving or hooked above, reddish to brown, lighter below; **Fl.** c. 2.5 cm lg. and $\emptyset$, orange-red to brick-red; **Fil.** red.—N. Argentina (Quebrada del Toro; found by Rausch) (Fig. 308, 506.) [Haage adds: Syn. P. dichroacantha Brandt & Weskamp.]

P. koehresiana Brandt (1972)
Bo. simple, erect, dark green, c. 12 cm h., 8 cm $\emptyset$; **Ri.** 13, straight, acute, c. 1 cm h., 1.5 cm br.; **Ar.** on small Tub., 8 mm $\emptyset$, densely white-woolly, not becoming glabrous; **crown** densely woolly; **Rsp.** c. 8, brilliant brown, 2.5–3 cm lg., straight, stout, set around the Ar.; **Csp.** 1, c. 3 cm lg., brilliant brown, straight; **Fl.** c. 3 cm $\emptyset$, yellowish or reddish-orange; **pericarpel** c. 5 mm $\emptyset$, greenish-pink with whitish and brownish wool; **Tu.** and **Sc.** yellowish-pink; **Sep.** and **Pet.** ochre, with an orange-red M.-stripe; **style** and **Sti.** yellowish, 3 mm lg.; **Fr.** brownish, 4 mm $\emptyset$, hard-skinned; **S.** brown, testa glossy.—Bolivia (San Juán, in the mountains W. of

Rio San Juán). Named for the cactus-nurseryman, Gerhard Köhres. (Fig. 507.)

P. krasuckana Brandt
Bo. simple, flattened-spherical, occasionally caespitose, c. 8 cm h., 10 cm $\emptyset$, fresh green; **Ri.** c. 15, spiralled, c. 1 cm h., 1.5 cm br.; **Ar.** oval, 5 mm lg., 1 cm apart, set on protuberances in the Ri., covered with white thread-like wool; **Rsp.** 8–12, white with a brownish tip at first, later light brown, upper ones stout, 1–2 cm lg.; **Csp.** 4, all light brown, 1–2 cm lg., stout, bottom one 2 cm lg., with a claw-like tip; **Fl.** apical, an intense brilliant blood-red, opening only to funnelform, c. 3 cm $\emptyset$, 4 cm lg.; pericarpel 4 mm $\emptyset$, green, with scattered white H. below, with small Sc. 4 mm br.; **Rec.** 1 cm lg., light blood-red, with few red Sc. and H. only 2 mm lg., Br. lacking; **Sep.** narrow, 2 mm br., 1.5 cm lg., brilliant blood-red; **Pet.** similarly brilliant blood-red, 2 cm lg., 3 mm br.; **Fil.** red, lower ones sometimes yellowish; **Fr.** olive, hard-walled, 4 mm $\emptyset$, white-woolly.—Bolivia (Dept. Chuquisaca, between Tarabuco and Zudañez, collected by W. Rausch). (Fig. 508.) Named for the grower, W. Krasucka, these plants formed part of a consignment of imported plants said to be Parodia suprema Ritt.!

P. laui Brandt 1973
Bo. simple, flat, green, 7 cm h., 9 cm $\emptyset$; **Ri.** 13, spiralled, acute and prominent, robust, 1.5 cm h., 2 cm apart; **Ar.** set on Tub., 6 mm $\emptyset$, with dense white wool c. 3 mm lg.; **crown** sunken; **Rsp.** c. 20, white, tipped reddish-brown, to 1.5 cm lg., thin; **Csp.** 6, 4 lower ones cruciform, 3 of them hooked, the upper one straight, the 2 other Sp. straight, thinner, set in the upper part of the Ar., all 6 Csp. reddish-brown, c. 2–2.5 cm lg.; **Fl.** 3.5–4 cm $\emptyset$, salmon to red, glossy, with white wool and black Br. outside; **Sep.** salmon-red, with a carmine M.-stripe; **Pet.** salmon-reddish tipped carmine, passing over below into yellowish-reddish, glossy, c. 2 cm lg., 3 mm br.; **Fil.** salmon-red; **An.** cream; **style** yellowish; **Sti.** yellow; **Fr.** brownish, with a hard shell; **S.** oblong, 1 mm lg., testa matt black.—Bolivia (Campero, among the mountains on the road Mizque—Mine Asientos, high above the Rio Caine at 2700 m). (Fig. 509.)

P. maassii (Heese) Berg. (1–3)
Bo. spherical to elongated, to 15 cm $\emptyset$, fresh green, **crown** white-woolly; **Ri.** 13–21, spiralled, $\pm$ tuberculate above; **Ar.** white-woolly at first; **Rsp.** 8–10(–15), 5–10 mm lg., even to 3 cm lg. in the extreme forms, $\pm$ honey-coloured at first, later lighter; **Csp.** 4, much stouter, lowest one to over 3(–7) cm lg., projecting, twisted, $\pm$ bent to hooked, light brown to paler, more thickened below than the Rsp.; **Fl.** coppery yellowish-red, moderately

large; **Fr.** dry; **S.** matt, black.—S. Bolivia to N. Argentina.

v. **albescens** Ritt.—Succulenta, 12: 179. 1963: **Sp.** pale brown, soon grey; **Rsp.** 10–14, 2–3 cm lg.; **Csp.** 4, lowest one 4–6 cm lg., hooked at first, later curving.—Bolivia (S. Cinti, between Puente San Pedro and Culpina) (FR 46d);

v. atroviridis Backbg.: name given to a very dark green form with long and very curving Sp. The type varies, and sometimes has very long Csp.;

v. auricolor Ritt., not described: Tub. longer-persisting, less confluent below into Ri., spiralled; all Sp. golden-brown at first, denser, finer, Csp. to 2 cm lg., sometimes hooked (in seedling-plants). Juvenile plants soon becoming oblong; an attractive variety;

v. **carminatiflora** Ritt.—Succulenta, 42: 12, 179. 1963: **Sp.** yellowish to reddish-brown; **Rsp.** 15–18, 3–4 cm lg.; one lower **Csp.** 4–6 cm lg., hooked at first, curving later; **Fl.** dark carmine.—N. Argentina (Salta, S. of Tres Moros) (FR 46c);

v. **intermedia** Ritt.—l. c.: **Sp.** brown, reddish-brown or greyish-black; **Rsp.** 11–16, 2–4 cm lg.; lowest **Csp.** little bent; **Fl.** blood-red.—Bolivia (Mendez, Cieneguillas) (FR 46e);

v. **rectispina** Backbg.—C. & S. J. (US) XXIII: 3, 84. 1951: all **Sp.** straight; **Fl.** more red.—Bolivia (collected by Ritter near Betanzos, Prov. Saavedra, and by myself E. of Tupiza) (FR 46 g);

v. **shaferi** Ritt.—Succulenta, 42: 12, 179. 1963: **Ri.** 10–15; **Rsp.** 8–12, 2–3 cm lg.; lowest **Csp.** 4–7 cm lg.—N. Argentina (Jujuy, La Quiaca) (FR 46). More likely to be P. maassii v. maassii.

See also under Parodia escayachensis.

P. mairanana Card. (1)
Bo. broadly spherical, to over 5 cm ∅, olive to greyish-green; soon offsetting, sometimes from high on the flanks; **Ri.** 13–14, scarcely tuberculate, **Ar.** light brownish-white; **Rsp.** 9–14, ± appressed, 3–12 mm lg.; **Csp.** 1 (later sometimes to 3), ± curving either above or throughout, to ± hooked, to 2 cm lg.; all **Sp.** light brownish at first, Rsp. soon whitish, Csp. horn-coloured, rather stouter; **Fl.** to 3.5 cm ∅, 1–2 cm lg., orange to golden-yellow, white-hairy; **Pet.** sometimes with a finer reddish M.-line, ± red-tipped; **Ov.** with salmon-coloured H.; **Tu.** sometimes reddish; **Fr.** brownish-red, with white H.; **S.** 1 mm lg., dark brown. Plant tends to offset quite freely. Very floriferous and rather variable spec., i.e. there are transitional forms to the darker green, dark-spined variety (often with darker Fl.-colour); this has to be segregated in order to define the variability of the type. Cardenas, in his diagnosis of the type, gives no data regarding floral Br., but individual dark Br. are in

fact present on the upper part of the Tu. The buds have light brown H.

v. **atra** Backbg.—Descr. Cact. Nov. III: 11. 1963: **Bo.** glossy, intense dark green; **Ri.** c. 13; **Ar.** light dirty white, felt longer-persisting; **Rsp.** c. 8–9, thin, to c. 5–6 mm lg.; **Csp.** 1, to c. 8 mm lg., ± strongly curving and ± bent above or arcuate; **Sp.** at first (greyish-)black, soon lighter, Csp. also somewhat reddish or greyish-black, or bleached horn-colour; **Fl.** c. 2.2 cm lg., 2–3 cm ∅, orange-yellow, ± bellshaped or funnelform, encircled above with a ring of dark erect Br.; **Pet.** without a M.-line, tipped deep red; **Sti.** c. 12; **buds** at first with dense reddish-brown H.—E. Bolivia. (Both type and variety originated with Cardenas; type-locality: Prov. Florida, Dept. Santa Cruz, Mairana, 1500 m). (Fig. 309, above.)

P. malyana Rausch
Bo. to 6 cm h., 5 cm ∅, leaf-green; **Ri.** 20–26; **Ar.** round, 2 mm ∅, 3 mm apart, with white to yellowish-brown felt; **Rsp.** 20–24, 5–6 mm lg., straight, appressed and interlacing laterally, hyaline; **Csp.** 6–8, 8–9 mm lg., straight, projecting, white, yellow below and tipped brownish-red, brittle; **Fl.** 35–40 mm lg. and ∅; **Ov.** and **Tu.** yellowish, greenish or pink; **Sc.** tipped reddish, with white H. and brown Br.; **Sep.** lanceolate, yellowish, red inside; **throat** and **Fil.** orange to red; **style** and **Sti.** yellowish-white; **Fr.** 3 mm lg., ovoid; **S.** brown, smooth, glossy.—Argentina (Catamarca, near Ancasti, at 1000 m). Named for the Austrian nurseryman, G. L. Maly.

f. **citriflora**: Fl. lemon-yellow.

P. matthesiana Heinr.
Bo. deep blackish-bronze with the Csp. and buds overtopping the crown in a tuft, 39 mm h., 43 mm ∅, ± spherical; **Ri.** 21, spiralled, c. 5 mm h., divided into rounded Tub.; **Isp.** 13:21; **Ar.** to 3 mm ∅, hemispherical, white-woolly, 8 mm apart; **Rsp.** stiff, bristly, c. 8 mm lg., whitish; **Csp.** 1 hooked, directed downwards, to 24 mm lg., also 3–4 shorter ones, thin-acicular, dark reddish-brown; **Fl.** around the crown, c. 53 mm lg., 45 mm ∅, brilliant yellow, reddish when fading, appearing semi-double; **Tu.** with narrow, acute, brown Sc.; **Fil.** light yellow; **style** yellow; **Sti.** 9, 6–7 mm lg., orange-yellow at midway; **Fr.** a reddish berry with wool and Br.—Origin not known. Named for the cactophile, Richard Matthes.

P. maxima Ritt.—Succulenta, 43: 2, 23. 1964 (2)
Distinguished from P. commutans as follows: **Bo.** to 23 cm ∅; **Ri.** 13–20, straight or ± spiralled; **Ar.** 1–7 mm apart; **Csp.** strongly bent in young plants, but not so hooked; **Sp.** on older plants pale brown to whitish, Rsp. 18–28, 1.5–5 cm lg., Csp. rather

curving, lower ones 5–11(–14) cm lg.; **Fl.** 3.2–4 cm lg.; **Ov.** with white Sc.; **Tu.** without Br., to 1.5 cm lg.; **Fr.** carmine.—Bolivia (Prov. Mendez, Dept. Tarija, Cieneguillas) (FR 87). Pet.-size not given here since they fall within those of P. commutans.

P. microsperma (Web.) Speg. (1) (T.)
Bo. spherical, little offsetting, later to 20 cm h., to 10 cm ∅; **Ri.** tuberculate, c. 15–20; **Rsp.** 11–25, thin, white, to 6 mm lg.; **Csp.** 3–4, red to brown, stouter to almost subulate, to c. 1 cm lg.; **Fl.** yellow, to 4 cm ∅; **S.** 0.5 mm lg.—N. Argentina (Tucuman).
  v. brunispina hort.: at most a form;
  v. **cafayatensis** Backbg. n.v.: **Ri.** with the Tub. more coherent; **Sp.** darker at first, the 3 upper Csp. fine, sometimes rudimentary, Rsp. slightly reddish-brownish above, c. 8–12; **Sep.** yellow, at most with a reddish M.-stripe; **Pet.** mid-yellow; **Fl.** 4 cm lg., 3 cm ∅; **throat** and **Fil.** mid-yellow.—N. Argentina (near Cafayate). (Fig. 310.) Distinguished above all by the more distinct Ri. and the mid-yellow colour of the Fl. The P. microsperma complex is a fairly large one, and the overall area quite extensive. Ritter named different forms, but these have not been described;
  v. **macrancistra** (K. Sch.) Borg: **Csp.** hooked, much longer, to 5 cm lg.

P. microthele Backbg. (3)
Bo. spherical to elongated, green, to 6 cm h., 4.5 cm ∅; very slender **Tub.** replace the Ri.; all **Sp.** bristly-fine, short, only to 5 mm lg., yellowish to brownish-white at first, interspersed with white Br.-Sp., all later whitish; **Fl.** glossy, reddish-orange.—Argentina. Often seen in collections as P. microsperma.

P. miguillensis Card.—C. & S. J. (US), XXXIII: 4, 109. 1961 (3)
Bo. simple, ± clavate, pale green, 6 cm lg., 4 cm ∅; **Ri.** 13, moderately acute; **Ar.** pale brown; **Sp.** 16–20, 2–10 mm lg., acicular, yellowish-white to pale brown, **Csp.** not distinguishable as such, but some Sp. rather stouter and longer, projecting, spreading; **Fl.** 18 mm lg., 7 mm ∅, bellshaped, pale yellow, white in the centre; **Tu.** with brown H. and brown Br.; **Ov.** white-hairy; **Fr.** ?—Bolivia (S. Yungas, Miguilla—La Plazuela).

P. minima: not described, only mentioned by Ritter. Plants with this name are referrable to the P. formosa group.

P. minuta Ritt.: not described ("small spec.") (FR 737).

P. multicostata Ritt., not described ("c. 20 crowded Ri.") (FR 733).

P. mutabilis Backbg. (1)
Bo. spherical, to 8 cm h. and ∅, or more; **Ri.** divided into spiralled Tub.; **Rsp.** bristly, fine, c. 50, white; **Csp.** 4, stout, to 1.2 cm lg., one of these hooked, reddish to orange-brown; **Fl.** light to golden-yellow, large, to over 3 cm ∅, **throat** white or reddish; **S.** very fine, brown.—N. Argentina (Salta).
  v. **carneospina** Backbg.: **Tub.** larger; **crown** with much white wool; **Rsp.** bristly, to over 50; **Csp.** light brown to flesh-coloured, tips darker;
  v. **elegans** Backbg.: **Tub.** more slender; **Csp.** finer;
  v. **ferruginea** Backg.: **Csp.** rust-brown.

P. neglecta Brandt 1973
(Syn.: P. formosa v. prolifera)
Bo. bluish-green, c. 7 cm h. and ∅, very freely offsetting; **Ri.** c. 16, spiralled, c. 8 mm h., furrowed and tuberculate at the Ar.; **Ar.** 2 mm br., 4 mm lg., oval, covered with white wool 2 mm lg.; **Rsp.** set around the Ar., c. 20–35, directed more upwards, fine, white, to 6 mm lg.; **Csp.** c. 8, to 10 mm lg., whitish below, reddish-brownish above, acute, straight, sharp; **Fl.** golden-yellow, c. 2 cm ∅; **Ov.** greenish-brown, covered with white wool; **Rec.** c. 1 cm lg., with carmine Sc.; **Br.** blackish-brown, 7 mm lg.; **Sep.** golden-yellow with a carmine M.-stripe and tip; **Pet.** golden-yellow, throat pink; **Fil.** golden-yellow; **An.** yellow, 10 mm lg.; **style** and **Sti.** golden-yellow; **Fr.** hard-walled, ochre-coloured, with dense white wool; **S.** brownish-black, hilum light.—Bolivia, vicinity of the Rio Chulon, N. of the Rio Mizque, at 1000 m). (Fig. 510.)

P. neglectoides Brandt 1973
(Syn: P. comarapana v. paucicostata Ritt.)
Bo. spherical, erect, green, c. 8 cm h., 7 cm ∅, freely offsetting; **Ri.** 16, mostly straight and vertical, sometimes spiralled, with considerable tuberculate thickening of the Ar., to 1 cm h.; **Ar.** subglabrous, c. 1 mm lg.; **Rsp.** c. 20, to 1 cm lg., upper ones shorter, lower and lateral ones stouter and longer, whitish horn-coloured, sometimes brown-tipped; **Csp.** 6, to 1.8 cm lg., straight, acute; **Fl.** bellshaped, buttercup-yellow, to 3 cm ∅; **Rec.** pink, Sc. carmine, Br. black, sinuate; **style** and **Sti.** golden-yellow; **Sep.** dark buttercup-yellow, sometimes pink-tipped; **Pet.** darker golden-yellow, very acute; **Fr.** light brown, hard-walled, densely white-woolly; **S.** with a brownish-black, tuberculate, glossy testa.—Bolivia (upper course of the Rio Vallegrande, in the mountains around Mataral, at 1000–1300 m). (Fig. 511.)

393

P. nivosa Frič ex Backbg. (3)
Bo. spherical to oblong, to 15 cm h., 8 cm ∅; **Ri.** divided into conical Tub., light green; **Ar.** densely white-woolly at first; **Rsp.** bristly, fine, numerous, snow-white; **Csp.** 4, stouter, straight, snow-white, one of these usually darker below; **Fl.** to 5 cm ∅, flame-coloured.—N. Argentina (Salta). There is said to be a yellow-flowered form.*

v. **cruci-albicentra** (Frič) Buin.: a more greyish-white form.

P. obtusa Ritt.—Succulenta, 43: 3, 44. 1964 (1)
Bo. to 80 cm h., 8–17 cm ∅, crown white; **Ri.** 13–21, 1–2 cm h., Tub. obtuse; **Ar.** to 1 cm lg., white, 1–1.5 cm apart; **Sp.** pale yellow or pale brown, subulate; **Rsp.** 6–9, 2–6 cm lg.; **Csp.** 1–3, 4–7 cm lg., only 1 at first, claw-like; **Fl.** to 3.7 cm lg., sulphur to golden-yellow, Pet. to 5 mm br.; **Tu.** without Br., with white wool; **S.** 0.7 mm lg., greenish.—Bolivia (N. Chichas, Cotagaita) (FR 1125).

P. ocampoi Card. (3)
Bo. shortly cylindric, to 7 cm h., 6 cm ∅, dark green, caespitose, forming cushions to 40 cm br.; **Ri.** c. 17, acute; **Ar.** grey; **Rsp.** 8–9, 1 cm lg.; **Csp.** 1, to only 5 mm lg.; all **Sp.** at first reddish to light brown, later horn-grey; **Fl.** c. 3 cm lg., golden-yellow; **Tu.** with white and brown H.—Bolivia (Cochabamba, Puente Arce) (FR 738).

v. **compressa** Ritt.: only a catalogue-name; see P. compressa Ritt.

P. occulta Ritt.
No detailed description available, the specific name means "hidden", and this plant is the smallest of the P. maassii complex, possibly = P. challamarcana Brandt.—Bolivia.

P. omniaurea Ritt. 1962: "all golden-yellow Parodia". Held to be a form of P. aureicentra Backbg., and may be identical with P. rauschii. Since P. omniaurea Ritt. is only described as a variety while P. rauschii has been given specific rank, the latter name has priority.

P. otaviana Card.—"Cactus", 18:95. 1963 (3)
Bo. to 12 cm ∅; **Ri.** 13; **Ar.** elliptic, grey, 8 mm lg., creamy above; **Sp.** 9–15, to 1.5–3.5 cm lg., white, thickened below; **Csp.** not always present, sometimes 1–3; **Fl.** arising from tufts of white wool, few, orange-yellow, 3 cm lg., 2 cm ∅; **Tu.** yellowish-red, with white and brown H.; **Fil.** and **style** light yellow; **Sti.** 8, whitish-yellow.—Bolivia (Potosí, Pampa de Otavi, 3400 m).

P. otuyensis Ritt.—"Cactus", 17: 76, 52–53. 1962 (1)
Bo. simple, rarely offsetting, flattened-hemispherical, to 11 cm ∅, greyish-green; **R.** short, fleshy; **crown** not very woolly; **Ri.** in young plants divided into rounded Tub. c. 7 mm h., later less so, ± spiralled, 13–20, 7–10 mm h.; **Ar.** round, white; **Sp.** brown to blackish, greying; **Rsp.** 7–9, equal at first, to 1 cm lg., sometimes ± curving, upper one later to 2.5 cm lg.; **Csp.** 1, stouter, 1.5–2.5 cm lg., hooked; **Fl.** to 2.7 cm lg., to 3 cm ∅, carmine, Pet. bordered violet or brownish-yellow; **Tu.** red inside and out, with brown wool, with a few blackish Br.; **style** yellowish; **Fil.** white, reddish above; **Fr.** spherical, to 6 mm ∅, red below, green above; **S.** 1.25 mm lg., matt, black.—Bolivia (Prov. Saavedra, Dept. Potosí, near Otuyo) (FR 913). (Fig. 309, below.) P. sotomayorensis Ritt. is said to be very close to the preceding, but has not yet been published.

P. paraguayensis Speg. (1)
Bo. spherical, simple or offsetting, to 4.5 cm ∅, low in the soil, greyish-brown or earth-coloured; **Ri.** 8–12, tuberculate; **Ar.** at first only slightly woolly; **Rsp.** 5, 5–10 mm lg., sometimes curving downwards; **Csp.** 1, much stouter, to 2 cm lg., hooked; **Sp.** ash-grey at first, scaly, later more honey-coloured; **Fl.** to 2.5 cm lg., golden-yellow, with rust-coloured wool and Br.—Paraguay (Sierra de Amambay).

P. penicillata Fechs. & v. d. Steeg (3)
Bo. to 12 cm ∅, later to 70 cm lg., fresh-green; **Ri.** 17, spiralled, tuberculate; **Ar.** distinctly woolly; **Rsp.** c. 40, thin, appressed; **intermediate Sp.** c. 8; **Csp.** scarcely differentiated, but c. 15–20 more central Sp., very thin, some rather longer, 4–5 cm lg.; **Sp.** yellow to yellowish-white or even hyaline; **Fl.** rather small, ± bellshaped, red.—Argentina (Salta, Cafayate). (Fig. 311.) Often grows in a hanging position.*

v. **fulviceps** Backbg.: **Bo.** subspherical, to 8 cm ∅, dark green; **Ri.** c. 20, strongly spiralled; **Tub.** rather coarser, ± round; **Ar.** 3–4 mm lg., light brownish; **Sp.** in number as the type, but 5 of them more central, light to reddish-brown; **Fl.** as in the type, 5 cm lg., 4 cm ∅, orange-red to flame-coloured.

v. **nivosa** Fechser: **Bo.** over 20 cm lg., 8 cm ∅, mostly oblong, tapering carrot-like at the base, often growing pendant, bluish-green; **Ri.** spiralled, with Tub. ± in Isp. 15:25; **Tub.** to 9 mm br.,

---

* Buds on my plant are bright yellow—but the flowers open to bright red. Translator.

* The very distinctive feature of the plants I have seen is that the Sp. in the crown (radials and intermediates) are already almost their full length and project in a tight cluster, like a tufted brush. Translator.

to 6 mm lg.; **Ar.** rounded, c. 3–4 mm lg., pale yellowish-brownish; **Sp.** stiff-bristly, to over 40, c. 10 centrals rather stouter, outer ones finer, all concolorous white except that the Csp. have a thickened, pale yellowish-brown base, to over 4 cm lg., outer ones shorter, mostly at least 2 cm lh., all thickened and fur-like and often brown below; **Fl.** orange-red to flame, 3–4 cm lg., to 4 cm $\emptyset$; **S.** 0.50–0.75 mm lg., dark brown, glossy, one end of the light hilum being beak-like.—N. Argentina (Salta; no more precise locality stated; collected by Fechser).
The varieties of P. penicillata are not always true from seed; the validity of this variety is dubious.

P. peruviana
Author not known; plants found in collections in the ČSSR.
Bo. simple, spherical, c. 5 cm $\emptyset$, dark green, lighter at the apex which later becomes weakly white-woolly; **Ri.** spiralled, c. 20–22, with rounded Tub.; **Ar.** weakly white-woolly, later glabrous; **Rsp.** 9–10, white; **Csp.** 3, 2 of these straight, directed upwards, 1 hooked and pointing downwards, brown; **Fl.** 3 cm lg., 2.5 cm $\emptyset$, intense orange-yellow; **Sep.** with a M.-stripe widening above the tip bordered red; **Pet.** concolorous; **Tu.** white-woolly, with 2–3 brown Sp. above, these 4 mm lg.; **Sti., style** and **Fil.** yellow.—Origin not known but Peru seems improbable.

P. pluricentralis Backbg. & Brandt (1)
Bo. bluish-green, suffused brownish, c. 12 cm h., 4–5 cm $\emptyset$; **Ri.** 13(–18), consisting of R. of stout Tub.; **Ar.** c. 7 mm apart, very woolly, later glabrous; **Rsp.** 9–11, directed sideways and downwards, white, dark-tipped, c. 8 mm lg.; **Csp.** 4–6, stout, brownish-red, 3 directed upwards, c. 1 cm lg., 1 stouter, downwardly directed, 1.5 cm lg., hooked; **Fl.** golden or light yellow, reddish-brown outside, c. 5 cm $\emptyset$; **Sc.** reddish-brown; **Br.** black; **style** and **Sti.** white; **Fr.** thin-skinned, brownish, c. 3 mm $\emptyset$; **S.** very small.—Argentina (Salta, near Amblayo, N. of Cafayate). (Fig. 512.)

P. procera Ritt.—"Taxon", XIII: 3, 117. 1964 (1–2)
Bo. diverging from P. camargensis by the lesser diameter, 3–5 cm $\emptyset$, and the greater length of old plants, 30(–50) cm; **crown** white-woolly; **Ri.** (10–)13, 7–12 mm h.; **Ar.** 2.5–5 mm apart; **Rsp.** c. 7–9, 7–15 mm lg., hair-like, white, sometimes brown-tipped; **Csp.** 4, cruciform, 1.5–2 cm lg., chestnut-brown or lighter, the lowest one sometimes hooked; **Fl.** to 3 cm lg., lemon-yellow; **Pet.** ochreous-yellow at the tip; **Tu.** pale green, with white H. below, with brown H. and brown Br. above; **Fr.** to 8 mm $\emptyset$, with long white wool; **S.** 0.5

mm lg., 1.3 mm br. (13 mm, as in "Taxon", is a printer's error), semi-matt, hilum white.—Bolivia (Dept. Chuquisaca, Prov. S. Cinti, mouth of the Rio Challamarca) (FR 742).

P. prolifera Ritt., not described ("stout, caespitose plants, forming cushions; **Sp.** robust, light") (FR 723). (Fig. 312 above.)

P. pseudoayopayana Card. 1969
Bo. flattened-spherical, greyish-green or dark green, 2–3 cm h., 4–5 cm $\emptyset$; **Ri.** 13, acute to slightly rounded, 5–8 mm h., 8–10 mm br., straight; **Ar.** 5–8 mm apart, round, 2–2.5 mm $\emptyset$, newer ones prominent; **Rsp.** 8–9, radiating or appressed, 4–5 mm lg., greyish-white; **Csp.** 1, straight, 5–6 mm lg., brownish, directed upwards; all **Sp.** sharp, thin; **Fl.** apical, few together or solitary, 2.5 cm lg., 1.5 cm $\emptyset$, light orange-yellow; **Ov.** and **Tu.** densely white-woolly, Ov. 5 mm lg., light green below, purple above; **Sep.** broad-spatulate, 8×2 mm; **Pet.** spatulate, 12×3 mm; **style** 14 mm lg., brilliant orange, with 9 yellow **Sti.**; **Fr.** cylindric, 1.2–2 cm lg., pink with tufts of white H. Like P. ayopayana it grows along the river-bank, but it is smaller, has notched Ri., spination in part shorter, thinner, and only 1 instead of 4 Csp. Fr. similar. Intermediates have been found.—Bolivia (Prov. Ayopaya, Dept. Cochabamba, near Cotacajes, at 1500 m).

P. pseudoprocera Brandt
Bo. deep green, clavate, scarcely over 10 cm h., 7 cm $\emptyset$; **Ri.** 13, to 1 cm h., 1.5 cm apart; **Ar.** white-woolly, oval, c. 5 mm $\emptyset$, set on small Tub.; **Rsp.** c. 9–10, slightly sinuate, stout, white, to 1 cm lg.; **Csp.** 4, light brown to brown, the bottom one with a slightly incurving tip, the 3 others directed laterally and upwards, all 4 later more upwards and straight, 1.5 cm lg.; **Fl.** bellshaped, 2.5 cm $\emptyset$, often several together, central, enveloped in white and brown wool; **Pet.** tipped golden-yellow, yellowish at midway, white below; **Sc.** brownish; **Br.** dark brown, 6 mm lg.; **Fil., style** and **Sti.** cream; **Fr.** brownish; **S.** round, black, matt. 0.5 mm $\emptyset$.—Bolivia (Dept. Chuquisaca). Extremely free-flowering, even when plants are only 4 cm $\emptyset$. (Fig. 513.)

P. pseudostuemeri Backbg.—Descr. Cact. Nov. III: 11. 1963 (2–3)
Bo. simple, bluish-green, hemispherical at first, later to 25 cm h., c. 12 cm $\emptyset$; **crown** with dirty white felt; **Ri.** c. 21, continuous, constricted between the Ar.; **Ar.** c. 1 cm apart, felty at first, soon glabrous; **Rsp.** 25–35, somewhat interlacing, greyish-white, to 8 mm lg., bristly-fine, flexible, straight or curving, sometimes $\pm$ projecting; **Csp.** 4, cruciform, quite characteristic because of the initially

violet-grey colour, later darker, with a dark thickened base, c. 11 mm lg., acicular, also 3(–4) Ssp. in the upper part of the Ar., erect, greyish-white, dark-tipped, blackish below; **Fl.** 2.5 cm lg., 2.5 cm ∅, red.—N. Argentina (Molle Punco; found by Frau Muhr.) (Fig. 312, below.)

P. punae Card. 1967
Bo. spherical, 7–8 cm h., 6–7 cm ∅, greyish-green; **Ri.** c. 15, acute, slightly spiralled, 8 mm h., 10 mm br. below; **Ar.** 5–8 mm apart, round or elliptic, 2 mm ∅, white-felty; **Rsp.** 8–10, spreading to appressed, 5–7 mm lg.; **Csp.** 1, 8–11 mm lg., whitish, tipped pink, hooked; all **Sp.** thickened below; **Fl.** from the apical wool, numerous, c. 2 cm lg., 2 cm ∅; **Ov.** elliptic, 6–7 mm lg., 4 mm br., woolly, scaly; **Tu.** short; **buds** white-hairy, reddish-brown above; **Pet.** lanceolate, 9 × 2 mm, dark orange; **style** light yellow; **Sti.** 8, light orange; **Fr.** spherical, 3–3.5 mm ∅; **S..** round, matt black, minutely pitted.—Bolivia (Prov. Mizque, Dept. Cochabamba, mines of Asientos, at 2400 m) (Fig. 514.) Named for its discoverer, Dr. Oskar Puna.

P. purpureo-aurea Ritt.—Succulenta, 43: 4, 57. 1964. (3)
Bo. ± greyish-green; **R.** ± napiform; **Ar.** 2–3 mm lg., with white or brown wool; **Rsp.** 10–18, white; **Csp.** 4–7, 4–25 mm lg.; **Fl.** to 2.8 cm lg., golden-yellow; **Tu.** to 1 cm lg.; **Pet.** to 1.5 cm lg., to 4 mm br.; **Sep.** red-tipped; **Fil.** brownish-crimson.— Bolivia (E. part of Prov. O'Connor) (FR 1134). Ritter's description shows the characters distinguishing the spec. from P. formosa.

P. rauschii Backbg.—Descr. Cact. Nov. III: 11. 1963 (1)
Bo. simple, green, to 25 cm lg., 15 cm ∅; **crown** covered with white wool and Sp.; **Ri.** c. 13, continuous but constricted between the Ar., ± spiralled; **Rsp.** thin, c. 25, whitish or yellowish, 1–1.2 cm lg.; **Csp.** specially characterised by being 6, stouter, 3 of these erect, straight, 2 laterals projecting, to c. 2.2 cm lg., slightly curving, yellow to golden-yellow, longest one directed downwards, hooked, to (3–)10 cm lg., ± yellow; **Fl.** orange-red to red.—N. Argentina (Salta, Quebrada del Toro; found by Rausch). (Fig. 313.) Distinguished from P. aureicentra by the larger or longer Bo., fewer Rsp. and the bottom Csp. which is hooked and much longer.

P. rigida Backbg.—Descr. Cact. Nov. III: 11. 1963 (2)
Bo. spherical to oblong, intense green, to c. 4.5 cm h., 4.5 cm ∅; **crown** moderately woolly; **Ri.** c.

16–20, very tuberculate, coherent below; **Rsp.** 7–9, directed sideways and downwards, thin-subulate, to c. 5 mm lg.; **Csp.** 3–4, pale pink to reddish-brownish at first, stoutly subulate, rather rough, 2–3 erect, straight, 1 directed strongly downwards, to 8 mm lg., not completely hooked; **Fl.** c. 2 cm lg. and ∅, mid-yellow, with white H., with blackish Br.—N. Argentina (Tolombon). (No. Ue 1000 in Uebelmann's collection). (Fig. 314, left.)

P. rigidispina Krainz (3)
Bo. eventually ± oblong-spherical, c. 5 cm ∅, matt, greyish-green; **crown** with white wool; **Ri.** 20–21, tuberculate; **Rsp.** 10–11, 5 mm lg., thin, hyaline, firm, bristly; **Csp.** 4, cruciform, flesh-coloured, dark-tipped, with a grey sheen, 4–7 mm lg., lowest one often only 4 mm lg., stiff, thin-acicular; **Fl.** 3.7 cm lg., glossy, light yellow, smelling of iodine; **Fr.** small, spherical; **S.** minute, glossy, brown.—N. Argentina.
v. major Krainz, not described: **Sp.** stouter, brownish-red.

P. rigidissima (Frič) Y. Ito: **Parodia rigidispina** Krainz; v. rubriflora (Frič) Y. Ito is based on an undescribed name of Frič and cannot be identified.

P. riojensis Ritt., not described (P. microsperma group: "Sp. weak, pinkish-white") (FR 917).

P. ritteri Buin. (3)
Bo. eventually columnar, to 50 cm h., 10 cm ∅, simple, grass-green; **Ri.** 15–21, tuberculate at first, later less so, Tub. rather obtuse; **Ar.** white to brownish; **Rsp.** 10–14, 1.5–4 cm lg., semi-erect; **Csp.** 1 at first, later to 4, equal to the Rsp. and little differentiated, later ± slightly curving above; **Sp.** pink at first, white below, then white with red dots; **Fl.** to 3.25 cm lg., blood to brownish-red, bordered yellowish; **Ov.** red, white-hairy; **Fr.** carmine, white-woolly; **S.** black.—Bolivia (Tarija, El Puente).
v. cintiensis Ritt., n.nud.: later described as P. cintiensis;
v. hamata Ritt. (FR 85b): not yet described.

I P. robustihamata Ritt.: **Parodia rauschii** Backbg.

P. roseoalba Ritt.—Succulenta, 43: 2, 23. 1964 (3)
Differentiated from P. ritteri Buin. as follows: **Bo.** shorter, 10–15 cm ∅; **Ri.** 13–19, 10–15 mm h.; **Ar.** 5–10 mm apart; **Sp.** 3–7 cm lg., pink, brownish or pale yellow; **Rsp.** 9–11; **Fl.** yellow; **Tu.** 11–15 mm lg., white below, densely white-woolly above, Br. brownish-red to brown, or some dark brown; **S.** 1.5 mm lg., or 1 mm br.—Bolivia (Prov. N. Chichas, Dept. Potosí, road from Cotagaita to Tupiza) (FR 728).

P. rostrum-sperma Brandt 1973

Bo. simple, compressed, greyish-green, matt, 12 cm h., 8 cm ∅; **Ri.** 16, c. 10 mm h., 12 mm br., straight; **Ar.** c. 6 mm lg., 4 mm br., 10 mm apart, set on small Tub., densely white-woolly; **Rsp.** c. 11–13, whitish, upper ones longest, to 20 mm, brownish when older; **Csp.** 4, brownish, 3 directed upwards, 20–30 mm lg., the fourth claw-like or ± straight, 25–30 mm lg.; **Fl.** 30 mm ∅, orange, inner **Pet.** glossy orange with a reddish M.-stripe, c. 20 mm lg., 3 mm br.; **Fil., An.,** style and **Sti.** creamy-white; **Fr.** ochreous, 4 mm ∅, white-woolly, hard-shelled walls; **S.** 1.2 mm lg., testa black, tuberculate, strophiole with a long, ± sword-like tip, a form unique among Parodias.—Bolivia (Dept. Tarija, Prov. Avilez, in the mountains near Tojo, at 2500 m; collected by Rausch). (Fig. 515.)

P. rubellihamata Backbg.—Descr. Cact. Nov. III: 11. 1963 (1)

Bo. similar to P. sanagasta, but not woolly in the crown; **Ri.** tuberculate only towards the apex, later more coherent; **Ar.** c. 3 mm lg., white-woolly; **Rsp.** c. 10, spreading, white at first, tipped ± reddish, to c. 1 cm lg.; **Csp.** reddish, to 1.3 cm lg., 4 in all, 3 of these spreading upwards, 1 porrect, hooked, reddish; **Fl.** intense red.—N. Argentina (Sanagasta?; found by Fechser). (Fig. 314, right.) Probably identical with the following: P.rubellihamata Ritt. (FR 919), undescribed; v. chlorocarpa Ritt. (FR 921) and v. paucicostata Ritt. (FR 920).

v. **aureiflora** Backbg. n.v.: **Bo.** as in the type; **Ri.** c. 17, unbroken, weakly tuberculate; **Rsp.** 12–14, to 1 cm lg., white, projecting; **Csp.** (2–3–)4, 1.2–1.6 cm lg., rather stouter but relatively thin, one of these hooked; **Sp.** all minutely rough; **Fl.** c.2.7 cm lg., 3–3.5 cm ∅, golden-yellow; **Tub.** reddish, with grey **H.**, with black **Br.** above, Sc. reddish; **Fil.** carmine; **style** and 10 **Sti.** cream-coloured.—From a consignment of imports of the type-species U.2010 (Uhlig); found by Fechser.

P. rubida Ritt.—Succulenta, 43: 3, 43. 1964 (2)

Bo. rather oblong-spherical, deep green, to 10–16 cm ∅, **crown** white; **Ri.** mostly 13, to 2 cm h., with more slender Tub.; **Ar.** white; **Rsp.** c. 12–16, 2–5 cm lg., thin, whitish; **Csp.** 3–6, bottom one to 3–7 cm lg., at first strongly bent above, later more curving, brownish-black, then pale brownish-reddish, finally whitish; **Fl.** with carmine Pet., bordered brownish-yellow, 2–4 mm br.; **Tu.** to 1.5 cm lg., with light wool, often without Br.; **Ov.** and **Fr.** white-woolly.—Bolivia (S. Cinti, La Torre) (FR 725).

P. rubistaminea Ritt. (1): undescribed; of the P.

microsperma group, "Ri. tuberculate, with 1 to several fine hooked Sp.; Fl. yellow with red Fil." (FR 924). [Haage adds: = **Parodia sanagasta** Wgt.]

P. rubricentra Backbg. (3)

Bo. at first broadly spherical, later oblong; **Ri.** c. 16, spiralled, tuberculate for half the height; **Rsp.** bristly, numerous, white, longer; **Csp.** several, stiffer but flexible, often slightly bent, pink-tipped, crowded in the crown, the centre thus appearing red; **Fl.** pale coppery-orange.—N. Argentina (Salta).

P. rubriflora Backbg.—Descr. Cact. Nov. III: 12. 1963 (1)

Bo. broadly spherical, to c. 6.6 cm ∅, c. 3 cm h., leaf-green; **Ri.** c. 19, spiralled, with Tub. c. 5 mm br.; **Ar.** at first greyish-white, felty, later also brownish in the centre or below; **Rsp.** to c. 20, bristly, white, to 6 mm lg.; **Csp.** 4, cruciform, 1 of these hooked, stoutly acicular, to 12 mm lg., dark reddish-brown at first, then lighter, reddish above, sometimes ± yellowish-reddish or lighter below, also up to 3 further Sp. situated over the 4 true Csp., the lowest of these hooked, the upper Csp. directed towards the crown, rather stouter than the Rsp., white, tipped pale brownish; **Fl.** flame-coloured with a slight golden shimmer, c. 1.5 cm lg., 3.3 cm ∅; **Fil.** carmine; **style** whitish; **Sti.** c. 12, sometimes ± cleft above, 3.5 mm lg., whitish.—N. Argentina. (Fig. 315.) The Fl. are shorter and narrower than in P. sanguiniflora which also lacks the extra Csp.

P. rubriflora Frič: Neue u. selt. Sukk., 8. 1947: only a name.

P. rubrifuscata Ritt.? (2), not described. I saw plants as follows:
Bo. spherical, dark green; crown white-woolly; **Ri.** divided into large conical Tub.; **Ar.** soon glabrous; **Rsp.** 9–10, radiating, one rarely directed upwards, white, sometimes slightly curving; **Csp.** 4, much longer, dark brown at first, soon light brown then horn-coloured, sometimes rather darker-tipped, all projecting, thickened below, the middle one bent more upwards and the lower one more downwards and sometimes bending up again, or doubly curving, the tip not bent, at most shortly curving; **Fl.** ? (Fig. 316.)

P. rubrihamata Y. Ito: apparently only a name.

P. rubrispina, and v. intermedia hort.: only names.

P. saint-pieana Backbg. (3)

Bo. depressed-spherical, grafted plants more

oblong and freely offsetting, to 6 cm $\emptyset$; **Ri.** divided into slender Tub., leaf-green; **Sp.** c. 17, centrals scarcely distinguishable as such, at first erectly clustering, then more radiating, one robuster and mostly porrect, all brownish, at first yellow below; **Fl.** 2.5 cm lg., yellow; **Fr.** subspherical.—N. Argentina (Jujuy).

P. salmonea Brandt 1973
Bo. erect, compressed, green, to 14 cm h., 11 cm $\emptyset$; **Ri.** 20, c. 10 mm h., 15 mm apart, narrow, acute, $\pm$ spiralled; **Ar.** on Tub. along the Ri., creamy-white, with long wool; **crown** flat, densely woolly; **Rsp.** c. 7, light brown, 5–7 mm lg.; **Csp.** 4, c. 10 mm lg., 3 upwardly spreading and resembling the Rsp., the fourth stoutest, claw-like, 15 mm lg.; all **Sp.** brownish; **Fl.** c. 4 cm $\emptyset$, salmon-pink to light pink; **pericarpel** c. 4 mm $\emptyset$, yellowish-green with white wool; **Pet.** 10 mm lg., reddish above; **Sc.** salmon-reddish, with white and brownish wool, lacking Br.; **Sep.** salmon-red, yellowish-red below, 1.5 cm lg., 2 mm br.; **Fil.** and **An.** yellowish; **style** and **Sti.** cream; **Fr.** brownish; **S.** with a glossy black testa.—Bolivia (Chuquisaca, in the mountains between Tarabuco and Zudañez, at 2500 m; collected by W. Rausch). (Fig. 516.)

　v. **carminata** Brandt: **Bo.** more bluish-green, **Sp.** darker brown; **Fl.** c. 3 cm $\emptyset$, blood-red to carmine, with a carmine sheen.—Mountains near Tarabuco at 3000 m.

P. salmonea has dense cranial wool but the floral Ar. are only weakly woolly; it resembles P. multicostata nom. nud.

P. sanagasta (Frič) Wgt. (1–2)
Bo. spherical, to c. 5 cm $\emptyset$; **Ri.** 15, spiralled, tuberculate; **Ar.** very woolly at first, glabrous after 2 years, to 4 mm $\emptyset$; **crown** white-woolly; **Rsp.** 7–9 (rarely 10–11), white or faintly pink, 4–8 mm lg.; **Csp.** 4, 1 of these hooked, reddish (blood to ruby-red), to 1.5 cm lg., later, or only below, appearing whitish or pale reddish, all Csp. fairly firm; **Fl.** yellow, resembling P. microsperma; **style** and **Sti.** light yellow; **Fr.** small; **S.** minute.—N. Argentina (Salta ?). The type easily becomes slightly more reddish; the hooked Sp. are sometimes incompletely bent. The plants are clearly variable; some remain green, even in the sun (corresponding to the above description as to characters, but Rsp. somewhat fewer), as mentioned in Succulenta, 69. 1954:

　v. **viridior** Backbg.—Descr. Cact. Nov. III: 12. 1963: **Bo.** spherical to oblong, remaining green; **crown** very woolly; **Ar.** large, white, felt longer persisting; **Rsp.** 7–9; **Csp.** to 11 mm lg., as in the type, finer or rather stouter, paler or intense reddish-brownish; **Fl.** rotate, light yellow, 4–5.5

cm $\emptyset$; **Fil.** yellow; **style** and c. 12 **Sti.** cream. (Fig. 317.)

Plants distributed by Fechser, Buenos Aires, as P. sanagasta, without cranial wool, and with deep red Fl.: see under P. rubellihamata Backbg. n.sp. P. rubellihamata Ritt. may be identical with the latter. The following are at present only names: P. sanagasta v. grandiflora Ritt.: "Spination variable; Fl. much larger than in the type" (but, as with P. microsperma, possibly not really distinct); P. sanagasta v. minimiseminea Ritt.: "Neat little plant with slender little Tub. (!)": crown $\pm$ woolly, whereas in P. rubellihamata (Ritt.?) Backbg. it is depressed and not woolly. [Haage adds: v. tenuispina Ritt. (FR 929): no description available.]

P. sanguiniflora Frič ex Backbg. (1)
Bo. simple, depressed-spherical at first, later more spherical, to over 5 cm $\emptyset$; **Ri.** in spiralled Tub.; **Ar.** with whitish woolly felt at first; **Rsp.** c. 15, bristly, fine, white, c. 6–8 mm lg.; **Csp.** 4, cruciform, brownish, lowest one longest, hooked, to 2 cm lg.; **Fl.** blood-red, to 4 cm $\emptyset$, glossy; **S.** minute, brown.—N. Argentina (Salta). In Saint-Pie's collection I saw plants (said to be from Tarija, Bolivia) which accorded with the above as to number of Sp., and Fl., but with more golden-brown Csp.; perhaps a variety. (Fig. 319.)

　v. **violacea** (Frič) Borg: **Fl.** violet-red, more bluish-red than in the type. Perhaps only a form with intermediates?

P. schuetziana Jajó (1)
Bo. $\pm$ broadly spherical, to 11 cm $\emptyset$; **Ri.** spiralled, tuberculate; **Ar.** fairly strongly white-woolly towards the crown; **Rsp.** c. 15, radiating, interlacing; **Csp.** rather stouter, slightly or much longer, $\pm$ bent or curving upwards, soon white or brown at first above, variable and also whitish-yellow or brown; **Fl.** c. 2 cm lg., red.—N. Argentina (Jujuy).

P. schwebsiana (Werd.) Backbg. (1)
Bo. spherical, later $\pm$ oblong, to c. 11 cm h., 7 cm $\emptyset$, slightly glossy, green; **crown** with much white wool; **Ri.** 13–20, weakly tuberculate, spiralled; **Ar.** white-woolly at first; **Rsp.** c. 10, light horn-coloured, then grey; **Csp.** 1, bent downwards, hooked at the tip, to 2 cm lg., pale brownish at first; **Fl.** 2 cm $\emptyset$, wine to rust-red.—Bolivia (near Cochabamba).

　v. **applanata** Hoffm. & Backbg.: **Bo.** to c. 7 cm $\emptyset$, 2.3 cm h.; **crown** woolly; **Ri.** c. 17; **Rsp.** 6–8, sometimes only 5, 5–7 mm lg.; **Csp.** 1, curving down towards the Bo., $\pm$ hooked at the tip, to c. 13 mm lg.; **Sp.**: the 3 upper ones later rather stouter, can be regarded as Csp., the middle one

± equal in thickness to the hooked Sp., both thickened below, all Sp. reddish-brown at first, soon paling to horn-coloured; **Fl.** c. 2.5 cm ∅, intense bluish-carmine; **Tu.** reddish-brown, with brown Br.; **Ov.** white-hairy.—Bolivia (road from Cochabamba to Comarapa). (Fig. 318, above.)

v. **salmonea** Backbg.: **Fl.** pale salmon-red.

P. scopaoides Backbg. (1)
Bo. subspherical at first, later elongated, to c. 6 cm ∅, to over 10 cm h., deep green; **Ri.** in numerous spirals, divided into slender Tub.; **Ar.** and **crown** white-woolly, Ar. soon less woolly; **Rsp.** numerous, bristly, fine, hyaline; **Csp.** several, 4 rather stouter, mid-red, lowest one hooked, to c. 15 mm lg.; **Fl.** c. 3 cm ∅, orange-yellow, throat red.— N. Argentina (Salta).

| Parodia scoparia (FR 915): only a name.

P. setifera Backbg. (1)
Bo. broadly spherical to spherical, to c. 5 cm ∅; **Ri.** c. 17, indistinctly tuberculate above; **Ar.** strongly white-woolly at first; **Rsp.** bristly-fine, c. 20, to 8 mm lg., pure white; **Csp.** 3–4, flesh-coloured to black, one longer, pointing obliquely sideways or downwards, all Sp. at first forming an erect tuft, flesh-coloured to black, very flexible; **Fl.** to 4 cm ∅, yellow to light yellow.—N. Argentina (Salta).

v. **longihamata** Werd.: **Bo.** to c. 7 cm h., 8 cm ∅, light green; **Ri.** 18–20; **Rsp.** to 10, white, tipped brown; **Csp.** 1, to 5 cm lg., light horn-coloured, dark-tipped, hooked downwards; **Fl.** yellow, 3.5 cm lg.; **Tu.** with grey wool and brown Br.
The following have not been completely validly described: v. nigricentra Backbg., with ± dark hooked Sp.; v. orthorhachis Backbg.: Bo. with narrow, straight Ri.

P. setispina Ritt.—Succulenta, 43: 4. 57–58. 1964 (3)
Bo. to 30 cm h.; **Ar.** 1–3 mm ∅, 6–10 mm apart; **Sp.** ± hair-like; **Rsp.** 9–15, white, tipped brown, 7–12 mm lg.; **Csp.** 1–6, 1–3 cm lg., brown or black, whitish below; **Fl.** sulphur-yellow; **Tu.** 1.3 cm lg.; **Pet.** to 2.2 cm lg., to 7 mm br.; **Fil.** golden-yellow.—Bolivia (eastern Prov. O'Connor) (FR 1153). Acc. Ritter, the above description shows the differences from P. formosa.

P. setosa Backbg.—Descr. Cact. Nov. III: 12. 1963 (3)
Bo. simple, bluish-green, to 25 cm h., 12 cm ∅; **crown** white-woolly; **Ri.** to c. 35, much constricted between the Ar., ± straight; **Rsp.** bristly, interlacing, straight or curving, to 40 or more, sometimes ± projecting, to 2 cm lg., greyish-white, dark

below; **Csp.** characteristically 4, sometimes with several Ssp., all erect, brownish, bristly at first, later rather stouter, to 11 mm lg.; **Fl.** not known.—N. Argentina (Tumbaya; found by Frau Muhr). (Fig. 318, below.) Spec. conspicuous for its light, bristle-like spination and strongly woolly crown.

P. sotomayorensis Ritt.: not yet described (see P. otuyensis).

P. spegazziniana Brandt
Bo. simple, greyish-green, c. 9 cm h., 7 cm ∅; **Ri.** 21, consisting of R. of Tub., spiralled; **Ar.** and **crown** with dense white wool, not becoming glabrous; **Rsp.** c. 10, to 1.5 cm lg., those at the apex falcate-erect, later appressed, white; **Csp.** 4, 3 uppermost ones curved up, sickle-shaped, c. 2.2 cm lg., the fourth stouter, projecting, 2.5 cm lg., with a very claw-like tip, all Csp. light pinkish-brownish below, violet-grey to blackish above midway, often confused and spreading; **Fl.** c. 5 cm ∅, dark golden-bronze with a red M.-stripe, bordered and tipped carmine; **Fil.** golden-yellow; **An.**, style and **Sti.** cream; **Fr.** thinly membranous, brownish, c. 3 mm ∅; **S.** very small, glossy, light brown.— Argentina (Prov. Jujuy). Named for Prof. Carlos Spegazzini. Initially distributed under the name P. gigantea v. jujuyana (Fig. 517).

P. splendens Card.—C. & S. J. (US) XXXIII: 4. 109. 1961 (2–3)
Bo. simple, c. 10 cm h., 11 cm ∅, ± pale bluish-green; **Ri.** c. 13, unbroken, spiralled; **Ar.** grey or brown; **Rsp.** 12–14, thin-acicular, compressed, 2–4 mm lg.; **Csp.** 1–3, subulate, 4–10 cm lg.; all **Sp.** white, brownish below, longest ones sinuate; **Fl.** 4 cm lg., yellow, with white H.; **Fr.** ?—Bolivia (S. Cinti, Chuquisaca, road from Las Carreras to Chaupi).

P. steinmannii hort.: not described; Bo. broadly spherical; Ri. divided into stouter Tub.; crown white-woolly; Rsp. c. 12–14; Csp. presumably several but only 1 stouter, hooked; Fl. ?—Origin ?

P. stuemeri (Werd.) Backbg. (2)
Bo. spherical, later oblong, rarely caespitose, matt, light green, to c. 20 cm h., c. 15 cm ∅; **crown** with whitish to brownish felt; **Ri.** 20 or more, flat, ± divided into rather conical Tub.; **Rsp.** to c. 25, thin-acicular, to 2 cm lg., noticeably interlacing laterally, white; **Csp.** mostly 4, stiffly acicular, rather stouter than the Rsp., to 2.5 cm lg., brownish to violet-grey or black, tufted in the crown, soon much lighter or ± white below and reddish-brownish above; **Sp.** later often concealing the Bo.; **Fl.** 4 cm lg., pale golden-yellow to coppery-orange, also brownish to light orange above; **Tu.** with

reddish-brown wool, with Br.; **Ov.** white-woolly.—N. Argentina (Salta). (Fig. 320.) Spec. variable as to strength and colour of the Sp.

v. **robustior** Backbg.—Descr. Cact. Nov. III: 12. 1963: differentiated from the type by c. 12–13 rather stouter **Rsp.**, sometimes brownish below; **Csp.** 4, stouter, to 1.5 cm lg., horn-coloured, light brown above; **Fl.** red, 2 cm lg., 2–5 cm ∅, brown-woolly.—N. Argentina (Maimara, found by Frau Muhr). (Fig. 321, left.)

P. subterranea Ritt.—Succulenta, 43: 3. 43. 1964 (1–2)
Bo. flat-spherical, to 6 cm ∅, dark to olive-green, **crown** with white wool; **Ri.** 11–13, 4–7 mm h., divided into very conical Tub., united below; **Ar.** white, soon glabrous; **Rsp.** c. 10, 5–8 mm lg., radiating and appressed, whitish to horn-coloured or the upper ones blackish-grey, grey to blackish at first; **Csp.** 1(–4), stout, 7–14 mm lg., suberect or projecting, black, one at first hooked, later straighter; **Fl.** to 3 cm lg., purple; **Tu.** with white to brown H., with black Br. above; **Fr.** red or green, white-hairy.—Bolivia (S. Cinti, La Cueva) (FR 731). (Fig. 322.)

P. subtilihamata Ritt. (FR 741): only a name of Ritter's, no description available. Brandt's published description, based on seedling plants, appears applicable to adult plants of P. andreae Brandt.

P. sulphurea hort.: only a name; probably referable to P. aureispina Backbg.

P. superba Brandt
Bo. cylindric, green, over 10 cm h., c. 7 cm ∅; **Ri.** 13, spiralled, tuberculate; **Tub.** to 6 mm h., stout, flattening in age; **Ar.** 7 mm ∅, c. 1 cm apart, covered with much downy wool which is white, silky, dense and glossy; **Rsp.** c. 7, tipped pink, laterals directed upwards, curving and sickle-shaped, c. 1.5 cm lg.; **Csp.** 4, the 3 upper ones directed upwards, sickle-shaped, c. 1.5 cm lg., the bottom one stoutest, longest, thickened below, to 2 cm lg. and more, strongly hooked, all Csp. brownish-pink; pericarpel olive-green, densely woolly, c. 5 mm lg. and br.; **Rec.** c. 1.5 cm lg., 8 mm ∅, light green; **Sc.** olive-brownish, with dense whitish wool and brown Br., the longest to 8 mm; **Sep.** golden-yellow, striped and tipped carmine, greenish-yellow below; **Pet.** golden-yellow, crowded, 2.5 cm lg., 6 mm br.; **Fl.** c. 5–6 cm ∅; **Fil.** golden-yellow; **An.** cream; **style** with 7 Sti., yellowish; **Fr.** brownish, 3 mm ∅; **S.** round, dark brown very small.—N. Argentina. First distributed incorrectly as P. dextrohamata. (Fig. 518.)

P. suprema Ritt.—"Cactus", 17: 76. 51–52. 1962 (1–3)
Description completed from plants raised in Holland from Ritter-collected seed: **Bo.** spherical, light bluish-green; **crown** broad, white-woolly, overtopped by the Sp. around the margin; **Ri.** 13–20, with slender Tub. at first, then only slightly tuberculate; **Rsp.** (9–) 11–16, radiating, thin, light horn-coloured, soon white, or horn-coloured above, to 2 cm lg.; **Csp.** 4, brown to black, not longer at first, then 2–4.5 cm lg., lowest one longest, hooked at first, later ± straight; **Fl.** 3.5 cm ∅, scarlet, Pet. bordered ± violet; **style** yellow to brownish; **Fr.** to 8 mm lg., carmine to brownish-red, probably (although not so stated) it and the Tu. with brownish wool and black Br.; **S.** 1 mm lg., glossy, black.—Bolivia (Dept. Tarija, San Antonio, 3500 m) (FR 912). Better regarded as a variety of P. maassii, particularly in view of Ritter's information that an intermediate is to be found in the vinicinity.

P. tabularis hort.: only a name current in the USA.

P. tafiensis Backbg.—Descr. Cact. Nov. III: 12. 1963 (1–3)
Bo. simple, spherical, green; **crown** white-woolly; **Ri.** tuberculate; **Ar.** white, c. 8 mm apart; **Rsp.** thin, 10, to 7 mm lg., white; **Csp.** 4, cruciform, to 1 cm lg., brown; **Fl.** c. 3 cm lg., 4 cm ∅, fiery carmine; **Fil.** and **style** carmine; **Sti.** erect, c. 4, pink.—N. Argentina (Tafi, Km 90; found by Lembcke). (Fig. 321, right.) Distinguished from P. sanguiniflora by fewer Rsp., rather smaller Fl. and pink Sti. (these creamy-white in P, sanguiniflora).

P. tarabucina Card.—C. & S. J. (US), XXXIII: 4, 108–109. 1961 (2)
Bo. spherical, to 20 cm h., 25 cm ∅; **Ri.** unbroken, spiralled, c. 13; **Ar.** elliptic, grey-felty; **Rsp.** 12–13, thin-acicular, compressed, 1–3 cm lg.; **Csp.** 1, ± bent above, subulate, 5–7 cm lg.; upper Sp. brownish, then whitish; **Fl.** 5 cm lg., 4 cm ∅, salmon to purple; **Tu.** with purplish, reddish or yellowish H.; **Ov.** white-woolly; **Fr.** ?—Bolivia (Oropeza, road from Sucre to Tarabuco).

P. taratensis Card.—C. & S. J. (US), XXXVI: 1, 24–25. 1964 (1)
Bo. spherical, 3 cm h., 4–5 cm ∅, light green; **Ri.** c. 13, spiralled; **Ar.** to 8 mm apart, grey; **Rsp.** c. 17, very thin-acicular, spreading, white, 3–15 mm lg.; **Csp.** 4, cruciform, 1.5–2.5 cm lg., hooked, acicular, whitish below, brownish above; **Fl.** rising from the loose apical wool, 3 cm lg., 1.5 cm ∅; **Ov.** with white Sc., with brown Br.; **Tu.** with pink Sc., white wool and brown Br.; **Pet.** golden-yellow, 1.5 cm lg.; **Fil.** yellow, **style** and the 8 Sti. similarly.—

Bolivia (Prov. Tarata, Dept. Cochabamba, road from Tarata to Rio Caine, 2200 m).

P. thionantha Brandt
Bo. bluish-green, cylindric, c. 16 cm h., to 10 cm $\emptyset$; **Ri.** 21, spiralled, tuberculate; **Ar.** densely woolly, especially in the crown; **Rsp.** c. 10, white, radiating, to 6 mm lg.; **Csp.** always 4, the 3 upper ones to 10 mm lg., the fourth stoutest, to 1.5 cm lg., hooked, all dark carmine; **Fl.** light golden-yellow, c. 4–6 cm $\emptyset$; **Fil.** yellow, sometimes red; **Sti.** and **style** whitish to cream; **Tu.** white with blackish Br.—N. Argentina (Salta, on the borders of Tucuman). Backeberg listed this plant as P. erythrantha var. thionantha, whereas Brandt sees it as an independent species. (Fig. 519.)

P. tilcarensis (Werd. & Backbg.) Backbg. (3)
Bo. eventually elongated, to over 15 cm h., sometimes of similar diameter, matt, leaf-green; **Ri.** scarcely tuberculate above, $\pm$ spiralled; **Ar.** white-woolly at first, those in the crown crowded; **crown** white; **Rsp.** 9–15, fine, slightly thickened and dark below; **Csp.** 4, brownish to dark brown, $\pm$ bulbously thickened below, to c. 2.5 cm lg., later sometimes darker-tipped, straight to slightly curving; **Fl.** c. 3 cm lg. and $\emptyset$, $\pm$ bellshaped-funnelform, bronzey-red to $\pm$ blood-red; **S.** rather larger, black.—N. Argentina (near Tilcara).
    v. gigantea (Krainz) Backbg.: Fl. coral-pink. Bo. later stout (like the type): Sp. honey-brown: probably scarcely differentiated. The following has not been validly described: v. jujuyana Frič, (also written as v. jujuyensis Frič): crown with blackish Sp. Spec. appears to be just as variable in Sp.-colour as, for instance, P. stuemeri. (See also P. gigantea Krainz).

P. tredecimcostata Ritt. (FR 739): undescribed species, constantly 13-ribbed; v. minor and v. aurea are only ecotypes.

P. tuberculata Card. (1)
Bo. simple, broadly spherical, to 7 cm br., 5 cm h., greyish-green; **Ri.** c. 13, spiralled, divided into plump Tub. to 1 cm br.; **Ar.** grey; **Rsp.** 10–11, acicular, to 1 cm lg., $\pm$ appressed; **Csp.** 4, to 18 mm lg., one hooked downwards; **Sp.** all grey, frosted white, thickened below; **Fl.** shortly bellshaped, 1.8 cm lg., yellowish-red; **Ov.** white-woolly; **Fr.** spherical, to 7 mm $\emptyset$, with white H.; **S.** 0.8 mm lg., black.—Bolivia (Oropeza, near Quebrada de Villa Maria, Hacienda Ressini).

P. tuberculosi-costata Backbg. n.sp. (1)
Bo. broadly spherical, deep green; **Ri.** c. 16, $\pm$ tuberculate; **Rsp.** c. 12, light brownish at first, soon lighter, $\pm$ brownish-tipped, c. 5–7 mm lg.; **Csp.** 4,

bottom one hooked, stouter, deeper brown, to 2.3 cm lg.; **Fl.** golden-yellow, 2.5 cm lg., c. 3 cm $\emptyset$; **Sep.** with a red M.-line; **Pet.** slightly red-tipped; **Tu.** orange-yellow, 2 cm lg., with red Sc., with a reddish line below the Ar., wool light fawn, with a few black Br. above; **Fil.** yellow; **style** and 10 long **Sti.** cream; **Fr.** ?—N. Argentina (found by Fechser, with no precise locality given. Uhlig No. U 2200).

P. uebelmanniana: perhaps = Notocactus Buxb. No description available.

P. uhligiana Backbg.—Descr. Cact. Nov. III: 12. 1963 (2–3)
Bo. simple, spherical, to 10 cm $\emptyset$, greyish-green; **crown** $\pm$ white-woolly, overtopped by the Sp.; **Ri.** $\pm$ spiralled, to c. 20, tuberculate; **Ar.** 1 cm apart, soon glabrous; **Rsp.** c. 35, thin, $\pm$ straight, whitish, to 1 cm lg.; **Csp.** 4–8, thickened below, 4 of these stouter, straight or $\pm$ curving, mostly 1 much longer, to 5 cm lg., more thickened below, light to dark brown; **Fl.** coppery-red; **S.** small, glossy, black, hilum small, corky.—N. Argentina (Salta, Quebrada El Toro; found by Rausch). (Fig. 323.) A very fine-spined form has been called v. stuemerioides: Csp. sometimes more bent above.

P. vacae Rausch, nom. prov.: description not available.

P. variicolor Ritt.—"Taxon", XIII: 3, 117. 1964 (1–2)
Bo. differing from P. aureicentra by its greater length, to 28–42 cm lg.; **Rsp.** fewer, **Sp.** stouter, coloured similarly to the **Csp.** or as in P. aureicentra; **Pet.** blood-red, bordered brownish-red; **S.** thinner, longer, glossy.—N. Argentina (N. of Cachi, road to Poma, Prov. Salta) (FR 916a).
    v. **robustispina** Ritt.—l. c.: **Sp.** slightly glossy, honey to blackish; **Csp.** much longer and stouter, to 4–7 cm lg., often curving or more hooked.—N. Argentina (mountains E. of Cachi, 3000 m and higher, Prov. Salta) (FR 916b).
It is not yet clear how close this spec. is to P. rauschii, and whether together they form a complex.

P. weberiana Brandt 1969
Bo. simple, broadly spherical, grass-green, c. 7 cm h., 10 cm $\emptyset$, crown depressed, not woolly; **Ri.** 21, spiralled, tuberculate; **Ar.** small, oval, c. 3 mm lg., $\pm$ without wool; **Rsp.** 15, set around the Ar., radiating, very unequal, to 1 cm lg., thin, yellowish-white; **Csp.** 4, 3 of these directed upwards, to 1.2 cm lg., thin, straight, pale brownish, lighter below, darker-tipped, the fourth Sp. pointing downwards, stoutest, c. 1.5 cm lg., hooked, darker; **buds** grass-green, without wool; **Fl.** golden-yellow, pericarpel

brownish-pink; **An.**, **style** and **Sti.** white; **Sc.** green, c. 7 mm lg.; **Fr.** brownish, oval, 5 mm lg.; **S.** round, very small, testa smooth, brownish, glossy.

Named for Dr. A. Weber who described in 1896 the first species later to be referred to the newly erected genus Parodia. Spination variable in colour, while the Fl. can also be golden-orange and reddish-orange; in the latter case the buds also are more reddish.—N. Argentina (Fig. 520.)

P. yamparaezi Card.—"Cactus" (Paris), 19: 82, 43–44. 1964 (2–3)

Bo. simple, broadly spherical, to 10 cm h., 14 cm ∅; **Ri.** 14–20, spiralled; **Ar.** 1 cm apart, grey; **Rsp.** 7–9, radiating to appressed, 4–12 mm lg., thin-acicular; **Csp.** 1, to 2.5 cm lg., subulate, curving at the tip; **Sp.** light grey to white; **Fl.** 2.5 cm lg., glossy, blood-red, with white and brown H.; **style** and **Sti.** white; **Fil.** ± creamy-white.—Bolivia (Chuquisaca, near Yamparaez).

P. zaletaewana Brandt 1973

Bo. compressed, spherical, to over 15 cm h. and c. 12 cm ∅, blackish or dark green; **Ar.** oval, c. 7 mm lg., set on small Tub., with much silky white wool which covers the Ar. so that they appear to form a stripe; **Ri.** 13, 15 mm h., 25 mm apart, slightly spiralled; **Rsp.** c. 15, to 20 mm lg., rigid, straight, the upper ones longest, darkest, often tipped blackish, directed sideways and up, only one of them pointing downwards; **Csp.** 4, sometimes ± cruciform, 3 of them directed upwards, those in the crown dark brown to blackish, becoming lighter, and then more brownish-grey, c. 2 mm lg., the downward-pointing Csp. is to 3.5 cm lg., thick, stout, slightly curved at the tip but not hooked; **Fl.** purple to carmine, c. 50–60mm ∅, opening to cup-shaped; **Ov.** and **Tu.** carmine with carmine Sc., densely set with pink wool, with short blackish-brown Br. above; **Sep.** carmine, narrow-lanceolate; **Pet.** bordered light reddish, with a dark purplish-red M.-stripe; **Fil.** golden-yellow; **An.** yellow; **style** and **Sti.** yellowish; **Fr.** carmine-pink, 6 mm ∅, with light pink wool; **S.** blackish, strophiole light.—Bolivia (Dept. Chuquisaca, near Salitre and Culpina). This plant, which came from Ritter, was at first distributed under the names: Parodia culpinensis and Parodia gibbulosa. (Fig. 521.)

Parviopuntia Marn.-Soul.: **Tephrocactus** Lem.

Pediocactus Br. & R. (202)

A genus of plants which, in habitat, are frost-resistant; the bodies have tubercles replacing ribs, the flowers are only medium-sized; the scales of the tube are not ciliate, ovaries and fruits are naked,

fruits dry and laterally dehiscent. The flowers, so far as is known, are borne not in, but around, the meristem; they open during the day and close somewhat at night, and are broadly funnelform. Acc. Schumann the fruits open in part by means of a circular slit near the base, or they drop, or they split irregularly. Variable types of dehiscence are known to occur also in other genera. Flower-colour is sometimes variable, from yellowish through pink to white. Seeds are dark brown to black, finely tuberculate, with a large sub-basal hilum.

L. Benson recently united Utahia sileri (Eng.) Br. & R., Toumeya Br. & R. and Pilocanthus paradinei (B. W. Bens.) B. W. Benson & Backbg. with this genus. In accordance with the systematic considerations applied in this work, the separation of these genera is maintained here, both because of the differential characters set out in the Systematic Survey, and the following facts: Pediocactus has no ciliate scales on the tube, ovary and fruit are naked, the flowers do not arise centrally; Utahia has centrally borne flowers, tube and ovary densely set with dry ciliate scales, and the fruit has small scales; Pilocanthus has differently shaped flowers borne ± centrally (as shown in my Fig. 2707, "Die Cact.", p. 2879, 1961), and the spination is as distinctive among the spherical cacti of the northern distribution as that of Navajoa. Croizat saw this as an important argument for segregating the latter, and the same consideration applies even more strongly to Pilocanthus; but if all these genera are united—or even simply Utahia and Pediocactus—then logically the process cannot stop there, and Toumeya for instance must also be included. H. Bravo and Marshall, while maintaining Toumeya as an independent genus, have again included Navajoa and even Turbinicarpus. This shows firstly the dangers of "lumping", which leads to differing views on delimitation as the above example clearly shows, and which—carried to its logical conclusion—threatens to produce massive and chaotic combinations; secondly it demonstrates that the small genus is a safeguard against quite open-ended developments such as the above. To the type-species of Pediocactus, L. Benson also adds P. simpsonii v. caespiticus as "n.nud.". In view of the details in my illustrations he should have been able to satisfy himself that this variety is sufficiently divergent from the type and even has claims to specific status. The name is, moreover, not a "n.nud.", since "Die Cact.", Vol. V, 2846. 1961 contains a Latin diagnosis for the principal diagnostic difference. Clearly L. Benson does not know this plant, and the inclusion of the name cannot be justified, even on the basis of failure to name a type-species. Such detailed photos are perfectly admissible under the Code of Nomenclature 1954 (German edition), particularly in view of the much-enlarged views of the spines. I regard the deposition of type-material as only being justified when the original description does not include adequate illustrations. As against this, a Latin diagnosis has not been provided for Pediocactus knowltonii L. Bens. which was first mentioned in the American journal, 193. 1961, with a short description in English, and again in C. & S. J. (US) 52. 1961, also without a Latin diagnosis. I have provided this now for v. knowltonii since it belongs to P. bradyi L. Bens.; both plants are very small, with similar spination and no central spines. If a v. minor is to be added to P. simpsonii, then the same must be done with P. bradyi, for the latter and its v. knowltonii occur much closer to one another than P. simpsonii and its variety. Two valid species are thus known.—Distribution: from NW. USA (Washington-Montana (E. Wyoming?), through the central States to N. Arizona and New Mexico. [Cultivation in Europe is seldom successful, probably because P. simpsonii is subjected in the wild to winter-cold; even grafted plants rarely do well.]

P. bradyi L. Benson—C. & S. J. (US), XXXIV: 1, 19. 1962.
Bo. mostly simple, rarely two-headed, ± spherical to ovoid, to c. 6 cm lg., to 5 cm ∅, often smaller; **crown** moderately woolly; **Rsp.** to c. 15, 3–6 mm lg., ± appressed, smooth, somewhat cartilaginous, white to yellowish-brownish; **Csp.** 0; **Fl.** ?; **Fr.** broadly top-shaped, to 6 mm lg., dehiscence as in the type-species; **S.** black, with minute papillae on irregular prominences, c. 2.3 mm lg.—USA (Colorado Plateau, at 1200 m; N. Arizona, near Marble Canyon on the Colorado River).
v. **knowltonii** (L. Bens.) Backbg.—Descr. Cact. Nov. III: 12. 1963 (see introduction; given by L. Benson as P. knowltonii, l. c., 19. 1962, but without Latin diagnosis): **Bo.** small-spherical, to 3.8 cm h., to almost 2 cm ∅ (L. Benson). My own plant is 2.5 cm ∅; little offsetting, mostly simple; **Tub.** very tiny; **Rsp.** 18–23, white, fine and hairlike, to 1.4 mm lg., white to reddish-brownish, or tipped thus; **Csp.** 0; **crown** with slight wool; **Fl.** c. 1 cm lg., pink; **Fr.** to 4 mm lg.; **S.** black, 1.5 mm lg.—USA (Colorado, juniper-pinyon woodland: New Mexico, near Los Piños River). (Fig. 324.) Pubescence of the Sp. is not a sufficient character for specific segregation since this feature can be very variable, i.e. in some Mammillarias. Colour photo in Kakt. u.a. Sukk., 13: 11, 182. 1962.

P. simpsonii (Eng.) Br. & R. (T.)
Bo. spherical to ± elongated, mostly simple,

normally to 15 cm ∅ (and then to 22 cm h.); **Ri.** tuberculate; **Ar.** quite strongly woolly at first; **Rsp.** 15–25(–30), to 0.8–1 cm lg., white to cream; **Csp.** 5–8(-11), 0.4–1.8(–2.65) cm lg., straight or slightly curving, ± reddish-brown, lighter or darker, sometimes also cream to yellowish below; **Fl.** to 2 cm lg., to c. 3 cm ∅ (1.9–2.5 cm ∅), yellowish, yellowish or greenish-pink, pink or white; **Fr.** ± spherical, to c. 7 mm lg., virtually naked, dry, green, splitting irregularly or with a circular slit below and dropping.—Despite numerous supporting statements, L. Benson's treatment is inaccurate in several details. He attaches v. minor and v. robustior to P. simpsonii v. simpsonii. He has the following to say regarding the distribution of the type or v. simpsonii: S. Idaho, Montana to Central Nevada, N. Arizona, W. Kansas and New Mexico (Fig. 325); but he does not mention its occurrence in Colorado, or that Boissevain found the type widespread in NW. Colorado and numerous on the Monarch Pass. The illustration from this locality shows both broadly spherical and very oblong forms, whereas Benson says only "spherical to broadly ovoid", with v. simpsonii to 15 cm lg., and v. robustior to only 12.5 cm lg. Polaski actually reported plants to 22 cm lg. Since Coulter gave v. robustior Coult. as "larger in all parts, especially the Tub., Rsp. to 2.3 cm lg., Csp. to 2.3 cm lg.", while Benson gives v. simpsonii as having "Csp. 1.2–1.9 cm lg.", and Boissevain describes those of the type as "to 1.8 cm lg.", I see no prospect of segregating v. typica and v. robustior unless on Fl.-∅ acc. Benson: in v. typica to 2.5 cm ∅, and in v. robustior to c. 3.1 cm ∅; on the other hand, Boissevain observed to 3 cm ∅ in the type!
It was perhaps because of this difficulty of demarcation that L. Benson does not quote Boissevain's data and fig. The following localities should therefore be added: (for v. robustior) E. Washington, E. Oregon, W. Idaho, NE. Nevada; the type-species came from Butte Valley in Utah and the eastern Kobe Valley. The lectotype came from here, and from Butte Valley a plant which "more or less approximated to v. robustior". In other words here again a transitional form. L. Benson makes no mention in his treatment of Utah, either for v. typica, or even for v. robustior from Utah.
v. **caespiticus** Backbg. Not admitted in L. Benson's articles in C. & S. J. (US), 49–54. 1961, and 17–19. 1962, where it is incorrectly cited as nom. nud. (see above) and reduced to synonymy with v. simpsonii and even with v. hermannii, a curious and inaccurate combination since the characters of v. caespiticus are as follows: **Bo.** only the size of a goose egg, sometimes flattened, freely caespitose, in groups to 30 cm ∅ and 50 cm h.; **Rsp.** to 24; **Csp.** to 8; **Sp.** on new growth,

especially the Csp., ± white.—USA (Colorado, Salida, 2700 m);

v. **hermannii** (Marsh.) Wieg. & Backbg.: **Bo.** hemispherical; **Rsp.** 14–16; **Csp.** 3–5 (variety with the fewest Csp.); **Fl.** more bellshaped, white to cream to pink; **Sp.**: radials ± hair-like and thin, centrals to only 1 cm lg. and red.—USA (Utah: Garfield County, on flat surfaces whereas Pediocactus is normally a plant of the mountains, found at 2400–3000 m; this variety grows at only c. 1800 m; **Csp.** much finer);

v. **minor** (Eng.) Cockerell—Torreya 18: 180. 1916: **Bo.** smaller; **Rsp.** 20–28, to 6 mm lg., white to cream; **Csp.** 5–8, to c. 1.3 cm lg.; **Fl.** 1.2–1.9 cm ∅.—USA (Central Colorado, highlands);

v. nigrispinus Marsh. (Cactaceae, 140, 1941, without Latin diagnosis):

Bo. depressed-spherical, mostly caespitose; Rsp. projecting, these and the Csp. blackish.—USA (Washington, Priest's Rapids). Mentioned already by Britton & Rose, "The Cactaceae", III: 91. 1937, as a form; it could be considered a new spec. In view of the variability of Sp.-colour common in Pediocactus, as well as the depressed-spherical and freely offsetting habit, and the distances separating the respective distributions (see Benson's data regarding v. robustior), it is possible that this variety is identical with v. caespiticus. However a valid description and closer investigations have still to be undertaken. Since L. Benson nowhere mentions black Rsp., the smaller v. nigrispinus Marsh., as described by Marshall, is particularly unsuitable for referral to v. robustior, as done by Benson.

In C. & S. J. (US), XXXIV: 2, 57–61. 1962, L. Benson completes the inclusion of Navajoa Croiz. and Toumeya Br. & R., as discussed here in the introduction to this genus; this was inevitable with such a broad generic concept. In so doing, he erected the following Sections: 1: Pediocactus, 2: Navajoa, 3: Toumeya.

A vital point here is that in his Key to the Sections, l. c. p. 57, Benson bases his classification solely on the nature of the Sp. but then, surprisingly, ignores the uniquely hair-like spination of Pilocanthus. His sectional classification: "Spines not strongly flattened", is thus insufficient; for when acicular-subulate spines are separated from those which are bast-like and others which are cartilaginous, it becomes more important than ever to distinguish the long hair-like spines of Pilocanthus which are quite unique in the entire northern distribution of the spherical cacti. This appears not to suit L. Benson's concept so he treats it in the same way as he does the inclusion of Turbinicarpus F. Buxb. & Backbg. in Toumeya, by Helia Bravo and Marshall; in other words he overlooks that also, despite the fact that in the same journal, 3: 1961 in the

cover-picture, and l. c. 98. 1961, a "Toumeya krainziana Frank" (i.e. a spec. of Turbinicarpus) is illustrated or discussed. Detailed consideration of the question: "What is to be done with Turbinicarpus?" should thus not have been omitted, since the Sections were keyed out strictly on spine-characters; and in that case those of Pilocanthus and Turbinicarpus should also have been considered. L. Benson seems to have discovered here the consequences liable to ensue from his classification which ignores the facts, for then inevitably Aztekium and Lophophora would have had to be included, and a number of other genera could no longer have remained distinct.

It is easy to understand why L. Benson, whose classification in "Arizona Cacti" is still based only on Echinocactus and Mammillaria (including Coryphantha!), was slow to alter his views. But the inadequacy of the treatment is no reason for allowing it to pass unchallenged. Let it be said in conclusion that Toumeya and Utahia (combined by L. Benson in Pediocactus, l. c. XXXII: 2. 50. 1961) were erected by Britton and Rose, both of them experienced authors, for sound reasons based on their overall concepts, just as I did with Pilocanthus; in the same way as the latter is segregated by its unique hair-development, so Utahia is separable from Pediocactus by its quite distinctive floral characters. The views of other authors cannot simply be ignored when revisions are made within a restricted field. Logic demands that what is done in one instance should be applied universally; moreover, we have worked well with the known genera for decades, so that there is no need for any sudden unification within a dubious comprehensive genus. "Revisions" such as this must be looked at critically since they touch the basic problems of present-day cactology, and a solution of this kind is an over-simplification of the facts.

The small number of N. American authors—whose work has never recognised the existence of varieties, and thus fails to satisfy the geo-botanist—all proceed along similar lines. No uniform guide-lines are accepted, so that synthetic "revisions" appear one after the other, e.g. Kimnach's particularly questionable treatment of Rauh's discoveries in Peru; and Anderson in his no less brutal "revision" of Ariocarpus, Roseocactus and Neogomesia. One is left with the impression that the important thing is to do something different at all costs; this approach has no clear goal; it produces utter confusion in the nomenclature which is not dispelled by the impressive assembly of supporting citations. These authors appear to lack any understanding of the consequences, or sufficient knowledge either of the total corpus of knowledge, or of the problems it poses. There even seems to be a deliberate ignoring of the basis for classification provided by Nature herself, in the line of shoot-reduction seen in flower and fruit. Artificial concepts within restricted fields are taken as the working basis instead of the many-faceted workings of Nature, using the means she provides.

Because of the importance of these general problems, the Genus Pediocactus Br. & R., and sensu L. Benson, has had to be studied at greater length since it shows why I have left Pediocactus, Utahia, Toumeya, Navajoa and Pilocanthus as independent genera. It also obviates the need for detailed examination of Turbinicarpus or of other questions inevitably resulting from piecemeal combinations.

Peireskia (Plum.) Mill. (1)

This genus was long regarded as the ancestral form of the Cacti; but since its members have continued to bear unmodified leaves, even in very dry zones, i.e. without any environmental adaptation towards more succulent forms, the genus has to be seen as a conservative stage in the broad lines of evolution of the Cactaceae, with a strong similarity to other leaf-bearing plants. The development of the ovary at the base of the style is seen as primitive, but in the face of its conservative retention over unconscionably long periods of time, one could equally well say that it is the simplest possible stage in the infinite variety of forms which Nature has developed. However, seed-development at the base of the style and true (i.e. inferior) seed-cavities constitute such significant differences that Berger segregated a subgenus on that basis; and Knuth, quite logically within the framework of modern classification, raised it to the status of genus with the name Rhodocactus. Conspicuous differences between the species with superior ovaries make it necessary to distinguish also the following subgenera:

SG.1: Peireskia: Flowers larger, not sessile;
SG.2: Neopeireskia Backbg.: Flowers very small, very shortly pedunculate or sessile, corolla cup-shaped.

The genus could not be subdivided on the basis of similar arrangement of the ovaries. The figure after each specific name indicates the appropriate subgenus. Fruits, depending on flower-size, are small or much larger; the latter are particularly fleshy, and are sometimes eaten as dessert-fruit. The seeds have a thin testa and are glossy black. The genus was named for the Provençal scholar Peiresc, and because of the French pronunciation of the name it was first written as Pereskia; but for the last 100 years, i.e. since Salm-Dyck, it has been pointed out that where a name commemorates a person, the name should be written correctly; if an intrinsically invalid generic name can be validated as a nomen conservandum, then logically one should do the same and substitute the correct spelling for any generic name based on a personal name. It is a dubious honour if the name is incorrect or corrupt. The above spelling has been retained since it is the form of the name most commonly used by authors, although the Code requires it should be "Pereskia". Of the 8 species hitherto described, 4(–5?) belong to SG.2. Acc. N. H. Boke, C. & S. J. (US), XXXV: 1, 3 pp., 1963, P. tampicana is only a variant of P. grandifolia; P. lychnidiflora and P. zinniaeflora have never been re-collected; and P. conzattii must be regarded as a synonym of P. pititache, which Britton & Rose erroneously attributed to Peireskiopsis. The descriptions of the former species have been left in Rhodocactus pending clarification (see Rhodocactus). Distribution: From the USA (Florida) through Tropical America inclusive of the W. Indies, to Peru, Paraguay and N. Argentina. [Vigorous; sometimes used as grafting stock.]

P. aculeata (Plum.) Mill. (1) (T.)
Bo. a scrambling shrub, to 10 m lg.; **branches** thin; **L.** shortly petiolate, lanceolate to oblong or ovate, to 7 cm lg., green on both surfaces; **Sp.** 1–3 below, paired in the L.-axils, recurved; **Fl.** clustered, to 4.5 cm ∅, white, pale yellow or pinkish; **Ov.** leafy, often spiny; **Fr.** light yellow, to 2 cm ∅; **S.** black, rather flat, to 5 mm lg.—Distribution as above, probably also naturalised in Mexico; H. Bravo suggests the original homeland is Venezuela. (Fig. 326.)

v. **godseffiana** (Sand.) Knuth: a plant with ± peach-coloured L. which is perhaps referable to v. rubescens as a form, although it is sometimes green; L. mostly red on the underside;

v. **rubescens** (Pfeiff.), with no valid combination: "Ar. very woolly, the ovate L. violet-red below"; however the type also becomes more hairy when in a very dry situation, while a slight reddening of the L.-underside also occurs.

P. amapola Web.: **Rhodocactus sacharosa** (Griseb.) Backbg.

P. argentina Web.: **Rhodocactus sacharosa** (Griseb.) Backbg.

P. autumnalis (Eichl.) Rose: **Rhodocactus autumnalis** (Eichl.) Knuth.

P. bahiensis Gürke (1)
Bo. shrubby at first, later a tall tree, to 8 m h., with a **trunk**; **branches** without Sp. at first; **L.** lanceolate, to 9 cm lg.; **Sp.** later to 40, to 9 cm lg.; **Fl.** in small

clusters, pink; **Ov.** with large L.; **Fr.** often proliferating, to 4 cm lg., irregularly angular, leafy; **S.** oblong, black, to 5 mm lg.—Brazil (E. Caatinga).

P. bleo (HBK.) DC.: **Rhodocactus bleo** (HBK.) Knuth.

P. colombiana Br. & R.: **Rhodocactus colombianus** (Br. & R.) Knuth.

P. conzattii Br. & R.: **Peireskia pititache** Karw.

P. corrugata Cutak: **Rhodocactus corrugatus** (Cutak) Backbg.

P. cubensis Br. & R.: **Rhodocactus cubensis** (Br. & R.) Knuth.

P. diaz-romeroana Card. (2)
Bo. shrubby, to 1.2 m h., freely branching; **R.** tuberous, woody; **branches** spreading ± horizontally; **Ar.** grey and white; **Sp.** 5 at first, later to 12, 0.5–2 cm lg., rather flattened, whitish or yellowish; **L.** sessile, dark green, ovate-elliptic, to 2.5 cm lg., 1 cm br.; **Fl.** to 1 cm lg., wine-red; **Ov.** glabrous, 5-lobed; **Fr.** to 5 mm $\varnothing$, blackish to wine-red.—E. Bolivia (near Cochabamba, Ttacko Laguna).

P. foetens Speg. and P. fragrans Lem.: forms of **Peireskia aculeata** (Plum.) Mill.

P. grandifolia Haw.: **Rhodocactus grandifolius** (Haw.) Knuth.

P. guamacho Web.: **Rhodocactus guamacho** (Web.) Knuth.

P. higuerana Card.: **Rhodocactus higueranus** (Card.) Backbg.

P. horrida (HBK.) DC. non Parodi: **Peireskia humboldtii** Br. & R.

P. humboldtii Br. & R. (2)
Bo. tree-like, to 6 m h.; **branches** subterete, slender; **L.** solitary, narrowly oblong, sessile, 3 cm lg.; **Sp.** often solitary, to 2–3, to 3 cm lg., dark; **Fl.** c. 1 cm lg., red to orange, 5-lobed, shortly pedunculate; **Fr.** small, with many **S.**—N. Peru (Jaën, on the Marañon River).

P. lychnidiflora DC.: **Rhodocactus lychnidiflorus** (DC.) Knuth.

P. moorei Br. & R. (1)
Bo. shrubby, 1 m h.; **L.** subcircular, to 8 cm lg.; **Ar.** grey; **Sp.** 2–4, unequal, to 7.5 cm lg., ash-grey,

blackish above; **Fl.** c. 4.5 cm $\varnothing$, pinkish-red, with **Br.**; **Ov.** with black **Sp.** and **L.** to 3 cm lg.—Brazil (Corumba).

P. nicoyana Web.: **Rhodocactus nicoyanus** (Web.) Knuth.

P. opuntiaeflora DC.: **Peireskiopsis opuntiaeflora** (DC.) Br. & R.

P. panamensis Web.: **Rhodocactus bleo** (HBK.) Knuth.

P. pflanzii Vpl.: **Quiabentia pflanzii** (Vpl.) Vpl.

P. pititache Karw.—In Pfeiffer, En. Diagn. Cact., 176. 1837 (1)
Bo. tree-like, to over 20 m h. (P. conzattii, acc. MacDougall); **trunk** to 35 cm; **L.** oval to subovate, pointed, firm, with entire margins and a short petiole; **Sp.** 1–8 or more later, variously long; **Fl.** only on older plants, opening only in sunshine during June–July, orange-red, with peduncles c. 3 cm lg.; **S.** black, smooth.—Mexico (Tehuantepec), Guatemala ? Description acc. N. H. Boke, who established the correct genus. Acc. H. Bravo the ovary is superior. P. conzattii Br. & R. is a synonym.

P. portulacifolia (L.) Haw.: **Rhodocactus portulacifolius** (L.) Knuth.

P. rotundifolia DC.: **Peireskiopsis rotundifolia** (DC.) Br. & R.

P. saipinensis Card.: **Rhodocactus saipinensis** (Card.) Backbg.

P. sparsiflora Ritt. (2)
Valid diagnosis, with Latin text, still awaited; only the following data are available: Bo. shrubby; R. tuberous, woody; branches and L. of similar colour; L. polymorphic, in favourable conditions twice as large as when unfavourable, oval, tapering towards both ends or sometimes rounded above; Sp. to 8, more radial Sp. c. 6, light yellowish, thinner, 3 of these c. 1 cm lg.; 1–2 stouter, more central Sp. to 13 mm lg., horn-yellow, light brownish and thicker below; Ar. with sparse H.; Fl. said to be solitary, no colour given.—NE. Peru (FR 640).
It has not been established whether or not this is Rhodocactus antonianus Backbg.

P. spathulata Otto: **Peireskiopsis spathulata** (O.) Br. & R.

P. tampicana Web.: **Rhodocactus tampicanus** (Web.) Backbg.

P. vargasii H. Johns. (2)
Bo. eventually tree-like, to 4 m h., also prostrate; **L.** more rounded below, tapering above, ± sessile, to 2.5 cm lg.; **Ar.** white-felty, with H. to 1 cm lg.; **Sp.** 1–3, pungent, to 2.5 cm lg., pale straw-coloured at first, later grey, black-tipped; **Fl.** several together, sessile, small, to 1.5 cm ∅, calyx lobed, white; **Fr.** under 6 mm lg., wine-red to blackish; **S.** glossy, black, 1.5 mm lg.—NE. Peru (Jaën, Bellavista).
   v. **longispina** Rauh & Backbg.: **Bo.** shrubby, to c. 2 m h.; **L.** similar to those of the type, light green; **Sp.** to 3, to 5 cm lg., pale yellow; **Fl.** 1–3 together, 0.7 cm ∅, white, with a green M.-stripe; **Fr.** 4 mm ∅, green;
   v. **rauhii** Backbg.: **Bo.** only 1.5 m h.; **Sp.** to 10; **Fl.** small, white.

P. verticillata Vpl.: **Quiabentia verticillata** (Vpl.) Vpl.

P. weberiana K. Sch. (2)
Bo. 1–3 m h., shrubby; **L.** to 3 cm lg., 2 cm br., sessile, broadly elliptic or ± ovate, acuminate; **Ar.** white; **Sp.** 1 at first, later to 5, longest one c. 1.5 cm lg., yellowish-brown to horny-yellow; **Fl.** several together, 1 cm lg., white, 2 cm ∅.—Bolivia (Tunari Mountains). The distribution of SG. Neopeireskia in N. Peru and E. Bolivia leads one to suppose that it must also occur intermediately.

P. zehntneri Br. & R.: **Quiabentia zehntneri** (Br. & R.) Br. & R.

P. zinniaeflora DC.: **Rhodocactus zinniaeflorus** (DC.) Knuth.

Peireskiopsis Br. & R. (5)

At first regarded as Peireskia because of the similarly leafy habit, but the flower-shape and even more especially the presence of glochids and the larger, hard, pubescent seeds showed the relationship to the Opuntioideae. In some cases at least, the ovary may be stalked; but in general relatively little is known of either flowers or fruits. An interesting point to note is Diguet's information tending to show that P. aquosa is more nocturnal than diurnal since the flowers, wide open at daybreak, close rapidly as the sun rises. However, this does not appear to be the case with all the species. P. spathulata and P. velutina have proved to be excellent grafting stocks for seedlings; even the smallest plantlets grow extraordinarily quickly on them, but they do need to be re-grafted; the stumps then produce further shoots, and this procedure is vital when raising rarities (see Fig. in the introductory section).—Distribution: Mexico and Guatemala. [(R).]

According to the Code of Nomenclature, the correct spelling is "Pereskiopsis", but this has of necessity been amended by Berger and other authors to correspond to "Peireskia" (see under the latter).

P. aquosa (Web.) Br. & R.
Bo. shrubby; **branches** bluish-green; **L.** brilliant green, ± elliptic, ± twice as lg. as br.; **Ar.** at first with long white H.; **Sp.** mostly only 1, white; **Glo.** few, yellow; **Fl.** yellow, flecked red outside; **Fr.** pear-shaped, to 5 cm lg., to 2.5 cm ∅, yellowish-green.—Mexico (Guadalajara).

P. autumnalis Eichlam: **Rhodocactus autumnalis** (Eichl.) Knuth.

P. blakeana G. Ortega
Bo. to 3 m h., sometimes with a trunk; **branches** to 5 cm thick, green at first, then brown; **Ar.** with whitish-yellow felt; **Sp.** 2, grey above, black below; **Glo.** yellow; **Fl.** ?; **Fr.** ?; **S.** 2 mm lg., pink, lens-shaped.—Mexico (Sinaloa, Abuya near Culiacan).

P. brandegeei Br. & R.: **Peireskiopsis porteri** (Brand.) Br. & R.

P. chapistle (Web.) Br. & R.
Bo. shrubby, to 4 m h.; **branches** smooth; **L.** round to elliptic, to 4 cm lg.; **Ar.** white; **Sp.** mostly 1, white, to 6 cm lg.; **Fl.** yellow to pink; **Fr.** red.—Mexico (Oaxaca: Morelos ?).

P. diguetii (Web.) Br. & R.
Bo. a large shrub; **branches** downy, green at first, reddish when older; **L.** elliptic-ovate, to 5 cm lg.; **Ar.** at first with dense white felty H., later with short black wool; **Sp.** mostly 1, rarely to 4, to 7 cm lg., blackish at first; **Glo.** few, brownish; **Fl.** yellow; **Fr.** 3 cm lg., red, sometimes spiny; **S.** white, 5 mm lg.—Central Mexico (Jalisco; Guadalajara; Oaxaca).

P. gatesii Baxt.
Bo. a clambering shrub; **shoots** pale green, **branchlets** to 7 cm lg.; **L.** scarcely longer than br.; **Ar.** dark; **Sp.** 1 to several, to 5 cm lg., grey to nut-brown below, tip dark brown to black, with thin, similarly coloured Sh.; **Glo.** brown; **Fl.** ?; **Fr.** deep pink, 2 cm lg., 1 cm ∅, leafy, mostly sterile, with few brown Sp.—Mexico (Baja California).

P. kellermannii Rose
Bo. a clambering shrub; **shoots** to 5 m lg., c. 2 cm ∅, green at first; **L.** glossy, green, elliptic to ± oblong or subcircular, also tapered at both ends,

twice to 3 times as lg. as br., to c. 5 cm lg.; **Ar.** with white felt and **H.**; **Sp.** 0–1, stout, blackish, to 3 cm lg., old shoots with 1 to several, sharp, brown; **Glo.** brown; **Fl.** ?; **Fr.** red, smooth, leafy, with brown Glo.; **S.** pubescent.—Guatemala (Trapichite).

P. opuntiaeflora (DC.) Br. & R.
Bo. tree-like; **branches** with a brown rind in age; **L.** solitary or paired, fleshy, greyish-green, ovate, truncate, emarginate or shortly tapering, sometimes with a very short petiole, to 3.5 cm lg., 3 cm br.; **Ar.** grey; **Sp.** missing or sometimes only 1, stout, terete, sharp, to 6 cm lg.; **Fl.** solitary, with a peduncle to 5 mm lg., overall length 3 cm, yellow with a mixed reddish-yellow stripe; **Ov.** pear-shaped, with minute Sc.—Mexico.

P. pititache (Karw.) Br. & R.: **Peireskia pititache** Karw.

P. porteri (Brand.) Br. & R. (T.)
Bo. shrubby, to 1.2 m h.; **branches** to 3 cm ∅; **L.** sessile, to 3 cm lg., apiculate, ovate, narrower in cultivation; **Sp.** 0 at first, then 1–2, brown, 3–8 on older shoots, 3–5 cm lg., to 20 on oldest growth; **shoots** brownish by the 2nd year; **Glo.** brown; **Fl.** c. 4 cm ∅, yellow; **Fr.** oblong, to 5 cm lg., orange, with large Ar. and brown Glo.; **S.** few, with deciduous white H.—Mexico (Sinaloa; Baja California). (Fig. 327.)

P. rotundifolia (DC.) Br. & R.
Bo. with woody St.; **branches** slender, smooth; **L.** ± circular, shortly apiculate; **Sp.** 1, longer; **Ar.** white; **Glo.** few or absent; **Fl.** 3 cm ∅, reddish-yellow; **Fr.** ± ovoid, red, leafy.—Mexico.

P. scandens Br. & R.
Bo. a clambering shrub, to 10 m lg.; **branches** grey, terete, smooth; **L.** ovate, to 2 cm lg., smooth, tapering; **Ar.** white-woolly; **Sp.** 1, short, 5 mm lg.; **Glo.** brown; **Fl.** yellow; **Fr.** slow to mature, slender, to 7 cm lg., ± tuberculate; **S.** few.—Mexico (Yucatan, Izamal and Merida).

P. spathulata (O.) Br. & R.
Bo. shrubby, to 2 m h.; **branches** bluish-green, downy; **L.** spatulate, thick, green, to 3 cm lg.; **Ar.** hairy at first; **Sp.** 1–2, stiff, white below, to 2.5 cm lg.; **Glo.** brown; **Fl.** red; **S.** white.—S. (?) Mexico.

P. velutina Rose
Bo. forming dense bushes, to over 1.2 m h.; branches green; **L.** elliptic to ± ovate, 2–6 cm lg., to 2.5 cm br., dark green, downy on both surfaces; **Sp.** few, short; **Glo.** present; **Ar.** with longer white H.; **Fl.** sessile, brilliant yellow; **Fr.** ?—Mexico

(Querétaro; Central Mexico).

Pelecyphora Ehrenbg. (222)

It is apparent in this genus, as for instance in the three basic growth-forms in Opuntia, that the floral characters are insufficient in themselves for the precise delimitation of naturally-occurring groups of species; in the present genus this demarcation only recently became possible. At this time only 2 described species can be included with certainty; in both of these the tubercles are compressed laterally—hence the name "hatchet-bearer"—and the areoles are correspondingly elongated, with the spines clearly pectinate and appressed; in both species the tubercles later harden; both also have an almost napiform basal part, and sit rather low in the ground. In both species there is also a minute but ± distinct areolar furrow, to which Schumann drew attention in part. The fruits disintegrate in the upper part; they are small and soft, and the seeds are black. The flower resembles that of En-cephalocarpus; it and the fruit are naked. Solisia pectinata bears a conspicuous resemblance to the second species, so that the former was first described as Pelecyphora although the flowering position and fruit are quite dissimilar; the tubercle-shape and spine-arrangement are alike. This shows the importance of a clear-cut delimitation of characters, with the small genus more accurately representing the facts of Nature. This delimitation does not allow the inclusion of "Echinocactus valdezianus" since the resemblance is in fact only a rather distant one; it must instead be referred to Gymnocactus. The type-species grows well and is quite frequently seen in collections, while the second species is less common.—Distribution: Mexico (N. Mexico and San Luis Potosí). [(R).]
The type-species was used as a remedy by the Mexican Indians who called both it and Loph-ophora "Peyote" or "Peyotillo".

P. aselliformis Ehrenbg. (T.)
Bo. spherical-clavate, to c. 10 cm h., 5.5 cm ∅, later offsetting to form groups, greyish-green; **Tub.** spiralled, to 5 mm h.; **Ar.** long; **Sp.** not pungent, ± strongly united apart from the tips which are free, very small, longest in the centre of the Ar.; **Fl.** 3 cm ∅ and more, bellshaped-funnelform, carmine-violet; **S.** kidney-shaped.—Mexico (San Luis Potosí).

P. pseudopectinata Backbg.
Bo. simple, spherical to ± oblong, to c. 6 cm h., 4.4 cm ∅; **Tub.** ± 4-sided below, strongly flattened above; **Ar.** elongated; **Sp.** very fine, short, free, pectinate, hyaline, ± greyish-yellowish below, c.

1.25 mm lg.; **Fl.** c. 2 cm lg., 1.5 cm ⌀, pale whitish-pink with a deep reddish-brown M.-stripe; **Fil.** and **style** pink; **Fr.** small, dark green.—Mexico (Palmillas, N. Mexico). (Fig. 328.)

P. valdeziana and v. albiflora Paž.: **Gymnocactus valdezianus** (Möll.) Backbg. and v. **albiflorus** (Paž.) Backbg.

Peniocereus (Berg.) Br. & R. (131)

Rather slender-stemmed Cerei with thick, tuberous to napiform roots which in the type-species can weigh up to 125 lbs. (c. 60 kg). Some species show dimorphic habit: the shoots normally have several angles at first, later becoming in part terete; however there also angular stem-sections on terete shoots, possibly marking the new season's growth. Precise data are still missing on this point. The flowers are nocturnal and mostly white, but sometimes varying towards yellowish or light pink. Tube and ovary are set with ± stiff, ± bristly fine spines, the red oblong fruit similarly. The status of the genus in Britton and Rose's Key is not satisfactory, since it would preclude the segregation of Acanthocereus and Peniocereus; the same applies to the floral sketch, Fig. 167, Vol. II, "The Cactaceae", with the note: "funnel-like". There is the additional point that Wilcoxia, judged by the same criteria, is equally difficult to delimit since this genus appears to have flowers which are also open at night; this has resulted in some species being little clarified (P. marianus), in fact even in the erection of a new genus (Neoevansia), but still without any clear demarcation between Acanthocereus and Peniocereus. This reinforces the argument that the small genus demands precise observations; in the meantime it has been found that in Peniocereus alone the perianth is directed strongly downwards at anthesis while the anthers, closely grouped around the style, are still erect! This feature is unknown in Acanthocereus, or in Wilcoxia with its funnelform flowers, which must be regarded as day-flowering even although the blooms are, in one instance, open at night; however this occurs in other day-flowering genera. Until such time as the typical perianth-positions in Acanthocereus and Peniocereus have been clarified, it remains problematical to which genus Acanthocereus maculatus should be referred; Cutak had referred it to Peniocereus; but recently it was found that the inner petals stand ± erect at anthesis, giving a funnel-like form, instead of being bent downwards. This proved that Weingart and H. Bravo had correctly included the species in Acanthocereus.—Distribution: USA (S. States but not California), W. Mexico to the Rio Tehuan-

tepec. [Grafting advisable because of the stout roots; the plants then grow much better; P. haackeanus and P. marnieranus are perhaps exceptions.]

P. diguetii (Web.) Backbg.
Bo. forming a bush; **R.** napiform, thick, to 40 cm lg.; **branches** thin, scarcely exceeding 1 m(?) in length, c. 8 mm ⌀, to over 3 m lg. has been observed on grafted plants, tips (seen under a lens) with dense H. and bristly Sp., **epidermis** not downy; **Ri.** 6–9, very narrow and low, rounded; **Ar.** white; **Rsp.** c. 10, bristly, white, to 4 mm lg., appressed, dark-tipped; **Csp.** 2, shorter; all **Sp.** later falling; **Fl.** to 9.5 cm lg., 6 cm ⌀, perfumed, white to delicate pink; **Fr.** pear-shaped, scarlet, to 5 cm lg., 2.5 cm ⌀; **S.** small, glossy, black.—USA (S. Arizona), Mexico (Sonora; Sinaloa, in the NW., with P. marianus).

P. fosterianus Cut.
Bo. to 2 m h., shrubby; **R.** consisting of a main R. with several carrot-like R.; **branches** to 1 m lg., arising from a very small trunk, 3–5-angled at first, later cylindric, pencil-thick; **Ar.** ± glabrous; **Sp.** minute, mostly 6, in part subulate and thickened below, 1 more central, all dark brown to black, at first also 6–8 Br.-Sp., white to yellowish-brown, to 3 mm lg.; **Fl.** to 10 cm lg., white; **Fr.** ?—Mexico (Guerrero, S. of Tierra Colorada).

P. greggii (Eng.) Br. & R. (T.)
Bo. a lax shrub, to 3 m h.; **R.** to 60 cm ⌀; **branches** from a short little trunk, to 2.5 cm ⌀, downy at first, 3–6-angled, angles acute; **Sp.** short, firm, at most 2 mm lg., Rsp. 6–9, quite often also 1–2 Csp., thickened below, mostly dropping, blackish; **Fl.** 15–20 cm lg., white or yellowish-white; **Fr.** scarlet, beaked-ovoid, slender, to 6.5 cm lg., with deciduous Sp.; **S.** black.—USA (S. States except California), Mexico (Sonora; Chihuahua; Zacatecas).
Engelmann distinguished a v. **transmontanus** (Eng.) with the Tu. much more slender than in the type, and narrower Pet.
In habitat simultaneous flowering has been noted, i.e. most plants of the spec. flower at the same time.

P. haackeanus Backbg.—Descr. Cact. Nov. III: 12. 1963.
Bo. an ascending shrub; **R.** probably napiform; **branches** to over 40 cm lg., c. 2–2.5 cm ⌀, green; **Ri.** narrow, rounded, 7–9 at first, later also to 10, 5 mm h.; **Ar.** 1.3–1.5 cm apart, whitish; **Sp.** c. 12–18, 3–3.5 mm lg., longer ones pointing downwards, stiff-bristly, whitish, without any distinguishable Csp.; **Fl.** to 11 cm lg., 7.5 cm ⌀; **Pet.** pale pink; **Sep.** ± brownish-red; **nectary** narrow, long; **Tu.**

brownish to dark green, Ar. fairly distant; **Ov.** densely tuberculate, with c. 7–11 thin Br.-Sp., Ar. white; **Fl.** with a rather acid but agreeable perfume; **Fr.** ± ovoid, to c. 7 cm lg., to 5 cm $\emptyset$, purple inside and out; **S.** c. 4 mm lg., 2.8 mm thick, smooth, glossy, black.—Mexico (?). (Fig. 329, 330.) Has the finest Fl. of the genus; named for the nurseryman, W. Haacke, of Antibes, France. The type-plant is in the collection of J. Marnier-Lapostolle, St.-Jean, Cap-Ferrat.

P. johnstonii Br. & R.
Bo. a clambering shrub, to 3 m lg.; **R.** a massive taproot, weighing to 14 lbs. (c. 7 kg).; **branches** (and St.) 3–5-angled, not downy at first; **Ri.** 3–5, angles sinuate; **Ar.** rather prominent at first; **Rsp.** 9–12, brown to black, or the upper ones black, thickened below, 2 lower Sp. light brown, elongated, bristly-fine, recurved; **Csp.** 1–3, subulate, to 8 mm lg.; **Fl.** c. 15 cm lg., colour not known; **Tu.** with brownish felt and Br.-Sp.; **Fr.** oblong-ovoid, 6 cm lg., with black Sp.; **S.** glossy, black.—Baja California (in the S. and on San José island).

P. macdougallii Cut.
Bo. shrubby, to 3 m lg.; **R.** large, napiform; **branches** 3-angled, arising from a small thick trunk to 6.5 cm thick, to 1.35 m lg., angles scarcely sinuate, young shoots sometimes with up to 6 angles; **Ar.** to 4 cm apart, white at first; **Sp.** mostly 3–4, sometimes inconspicuous, often quite elongated and fairly stoutly acicular; **Fl.** to 9 cm lg., scarcely perfumed, greenish-white; **Tu.** reddish-green, brown-felty, with fine whitish-reddish Sp.; **Ov.** dark green.—Mexico (Oaxaca, Cerro Arenal, Rio Tequisitlan, Rio Tehuantepec).

v. **centrispinus** Backbg.: **Ri.** narrow, rounded above, relatively prominent, 4, dark green; **Rsp.** in number ± as in the type, to 1.5 cm lg., white; **Csp.** 1, to 2.5 cm lg.; **Fl.** 8 cm lg., 4–4.5 cm $\emptyset$, white; **Sep.** and **Tu.** brownish-red, Sp. reddish.—Mexico (in the S.?).
The plant illustrated in "Die Cact.", Vol. VI, p. 3843, Fig. 3480 left, with 3 Ri. and very crowded Ar., is **not** a sterile shoot of the variety, but probably a new and undescribed spec.

P. maculatus (Wgt.) Cut.: **Acanthocereus maculatus** Wgt.

P. marianus (Gentry) H. Sanchez-Mej.—Cact. y Suc. Mexicanas 7: 4, 85–91. 1962 (Wilcoxia mariana Gentry, Publ. Carn. Inst. Wash. No. 527 (Rio Mayo Pl.), 191. 1942).
Bo. little branching, squarrose-shrubby, ± erect (acc. photo, Sanchez-Mej.); **Ri.** slightly tuberculate, with projecting Sp.; **Fl.** white; **Tu.** strongly tuberculate, Tub. crowded throughout the entire

length.—Mexico (Sonora, Cerros de Topolobampo, Navachiste and Rio San Miguel, on the right bank down to the sea.) Fl. open at sundown, close towards 10 o'clock the following day.

P. marksianus Schwarz, a catalogue-name 1955; not described.

P. marnieranus Backbg. n.sp.
Bo. shrubby, climbing, dimorphic; **branches** short at first, to c. 12 cm lg., brownish, 3–4-angled, clustered, readily detached and thus propagating rapidly; **Ar.** very crowded, almost forming a stripe; **Sp.** whitish, appressed; later, from the young growths which are constricted above, there arise the actual 4-angled **shoots** to c. 3.5 cm $\emptyset$, rarely with 5 Ri.; **Ri.** ± pressed sideways above; **Sp.** carmine at first, c. 5, projecting, sometimes with 2–3 Br. c. 2 mm lg., all soon whitish; **Rsp.** 5, thin-subulate, 5–18 mm lg., scarcely thickened below; **Csp.** 1, porrect, to c. 2 cm lg., ± thickened below; **Fl.** 5.2 cm lg., 4 cm $\emptyset$, with the Per. bent downwards; **Sep.** brownish; **Pet.** faintly brownish-white; **Tu.** 4.5 cm lg., 1 cm $\emptyset$, dirty reddish-green, with thin pale Sp.; **Ov.** ± oblong, spineless, Ar. very crowded, with brownish felt-cushions; **Fr.** ?—Mexico (found by MacDougall, no locality stated). (Fig. 331 and 5, right.)
The type-plant, which I saw in the Botanical Garden "Les Cèdres", is remarkable for its wealth of Fl. which are often closely ranged, one above the other, resembling a chain. I named the spec. for Mr. J. Marnier-Lapostolle who allowed me, over a long period of time, to check the text of this Lexicon, or to supplement it, from his ample living material.

P. occidentalis H. Bravo—Cact. y. Suc. Mex., VIII: 4, 79–82. 1963.
Bo. an erect shrub; **Ri.** winged, 4–5 at first, later 6–7, dark green, smooth; **Ar.** small, with yellowish wool; **Rsp.** 5 at first, later to 10, 2–4 mm lg.; **Csp.** 1 at first, later to 3, 3–4 mm lg., all dark brown; **Fl.** funnelform, to 8 cm lg.; **Tu.** dark brownish-green; **Ov.** dark green, with Sp. 1–2 mm lg., those on the Tu. 1–2, to 5 mm lg., they and the Ar. pale brownish; **Pet.** cream with a pink sheen, cream above; **style** cream; **Sti.** 8, cream; **Fr.** ovoid, 3.5 cm lg., red with a purple tinge, with 8 greyish-brown Sp. to 1 cm lg.; **S.** 3.5 mm lg., glossy, black.—Mexico (Oaxaca, 20 km from Pochutla on the coastal road to Rio Copalito, in dry scrub, also in the vicinity of Puerto Escondido). Shoots in this spec. are never terete; Sp. fairly short.

P. rosei G. Ortega
Bo. erect, to 2 m lg., shoots recurved; **R.** conical-napiform, to 10 cm $\emptyset$; **branches** 30–80 cm lg., to 1.5 cm $\emptyset$, with slight, distant marbling, or light green

with dark marks beneath the Ar.; **Ri.** 4–5, but the branches soon becoming cylindric; **Sp.** 1–2 at first, later 8–9, also longer ones directed downwards, yellow, thin, all sometimes completely absent; **Fl.** 10 cm ⌀, white; **Pet.** described as "± erect, with recurving Sep.", so probably not seen at anthesis, but long and narrow, typical of the genus; **Fr.** 3 cm lg., red, spiny; pulp red; **S.** coffee-brown.—Mexico (Sinaloa, close to the sea).

Pereskia and Pereskiopsis: see under **Peireskia** and **Peireskiopsis**.

Peruvocereus Akers: **Haageocereus** Backbg.

Pfeiffera SD. (51)

Small erect cereoid shrubs, growing on rocks or epiphytic, but without aerial roots. Ribs few in number. The small diurnal flowers have only a very short tube, the ovary and the small fruit are spiny. Distribution: Bolivia (Chaco or SE. region) to N. Argentina (NE. to Catamarca and La Rioja). [(R).]

P. erecta Ritt.—"Taxon", XIII: 3, 116. 1964.
Bo. erect, to 30 cm h., little branching; **shoots** 6–12 mm ⌀; **Ri.** 5–7, to 2.5 mm h.; **Ar.** white, round, 3–5 mm apart; **Sp.** 12–16, thin, whitish, 4–10 mm lg.; **Fl.** 1.5 cm lg., white; **Pet.** obtuse above, emarginate; **Tu.** without a nectary; **Ov.** with minute red Sc. and fine white Br.; **Fil., style** and **Sti.** white; **Fr.** 1 cm lg., dark green, with thin white Br.; **S.** 1.5 mm lg., glossy, black, smooth.—Bolivia (Dept. Santa Cruz, Prov. Valle Grande, W. of Valle Grande, on the slopes down to the Rio Mizque) (FR 883).

P. ianthothele (Monv.) Web. (T.)
Bo. erect to hanging, moderately branching; **branches** pale green, to c. 50 cm lg., to 2 cm thick, often suffused violet near the Ar.; **Ri.** (3–)4, acute, sinuate; **Ar.** round, white-felty, with deciduous little Sc.; **Sp.** bristly, 6–7, under 5 mm lg., yellowish; **Fl.** to 2.2 cm lg., to 1.5 cm br.; **Sep.** purplish-red to pink; **Pet.** creamy-white; **Ov.** obtusely 5-angled, brownish-green, with white prickles; **Fr.** 1 cm ⌀, spherical, translucent, pinkish-red; **S.** numerous, small, black.—Bolivia, Argentina. (Fig. 332.)

P. mataralensis Ritt.—"Taxon", XIII: 3, 115. 1964.
Bo. hanging from trees, to 20 cm lg., branching; **shoots** 7.5–12.5 mm br.; **Ri.** (3–)4–7(–8), 3–5 mm h., sometimes as prominent as in the type-species; **Ar.** white, 5–10 mm apart; **Sp.** 9–15, 4–8 mm lg., thin-acicular, yellow or brown, finest ones white; **Fl.** to

1.7 cm lg., apical, white; **Pet.** rounded; **Tu.** 1 mm lg., nectary scarcely recognizable; **Ov.** 6 mm lg. and to 6 mm br.; **Fil., style** and **Sti.** white; **Ov.** green; **Fr.** 1.5 cm lg., spherical, yellowish-green, white-bristly; **S.** 1.2 mm lg., semi-matt, black, curving.—Bolivia (Dept. Santa Cruz, Prov. Florida, Mataral) (FR 363).

v. **floccosa** Ritt.—l.c.: **Ar.** larger, more woolly, to 2 mm ⌀ (in v. mataralensis only 1.5 mm ⌀); **Sp.** rather stouter.—Bolivia (Dept. Cochabamba, Prov. Campero, Quiroga) (FR 881).

P. multigona Card.—"Cactus" (Paris), 19–82, 51–52. 1964.
Bo. hanging; **shoots** thin, rounded, to 25 cm lg., pale green, to 1 cm ⌀; **Ri.** c. 7, tuberculate; **Ar.** to 7 mm apart, round, prominent, pale brown; **Sp.** acicular, very thin, 6–7, 3–10 mm lg., pale brown; **Csp.** occasionally 1; **Fl.** apical, 1.5 cm lg., white; **Pet.** c. 9; **Fr.** spherical, pale yellow, c. 1 cm ⌀, watery; **S.** 1.2 mm lg., glossy, black.—Bolivia (Prov. Azero, Dept. Chuquisaca, road from Monteagudo to Camiri, 1100 m). An interesting spec., clearly differentiated by its subterete and finely tuberculate shoots.

Ritter also mentions the following newly named spec.: P. gibberosperma Ritt.; P. gracilis Ritt., "very slender, with many Ri. and thin Sp."; P. tarijensis Ritt., "weakly spined", Ri. fairly low (FR 880).

Phellosperma Br. & R. (229)

Mammillaria-like plants, becoming oblong eventually, spination in habitat dense and white, with long-projecting dark hooked spines. The funnelform flowers appearing from older axils have a fairly long tube; the seeds have a large corky aril almost as large as the seed itself; only Blossfeldia seeds show a comparable structure. Britton and Rose named the genus from this corky appendage, since it signifies "cork-seed"; it has been used for quite 40 years and is retained here on account of this unique principal feature, and because any attempt to re-classify it would demand corresponding treatment for many other groups of species within the entire family; and this is neither possible nor necessary. These attractive plants seldom last long in cultivation on their own roots, yet they become bloated if grafted.—Distribution: USA (S. Utah, SE. California, Arizona, reputedly also in Nevada), Mexico (N. Baja California). [(G).]

P. tetrancistra (Eng.) Br. & R. (T.)
Bo. simple or caespitose, to 30 cm lg., to 7 cm ⌀; **Tub.** rounded; **Isp.** 8: 13; **Ax.** naked; **Rsp.** 30–60,

white, sometimes brown-tipped, 5–10 mm lg., densely interlacing; **Csp.** (1–)4, stouter, tipped brown to black, lighter below, upper ones to 7 mm lg., lower one hooked, to 9 mm lg.; **Fl.** to 4.5 cm lg., 3.5 cm ∅, purple with a lighter border; **Fr.** red, oblong, to 3.5 cm lg.; **S. c.** 2 mm lg.—Distribution: as above. (Fig. 333.)

Philippicereus Backbg. (84)

This genus is closely related to Eulychnia, as evidenced by the top- to bell-shaped flower. A tube in the true sense is virtually missing; half the overall length of the flower is taken up by the rather large seed-cavity. An unusual character, and one which is of vital diagnostic importance to the genus, is the long and rather stoutly bristly, almost spiny indumentum of the nocturnal flower; this is absent in all the Eulychnia species, so that Philippicereus must be placed before the former genus in the line of reduction of shoot-characters. At one time the relatively low habit and the formation of large colonies were considered to be diagnostic features, but this has more recently been noted as occurring also in Eulychnia procumbens. Earlier descriptions gave bristles as occurring only in the upper part of the fruit; however the herbarium material I examined showed that the bristly indumentum is at least variable, i.e. it may be present lower down also.—Distribution: Chile (von Los Molles to Los Vilos). [(R).]

P. castaneus (Phil.) Backbg. (T.)
Bo. to 1 m h., in colonies up to 20 m br.; **St.** to 8 cm ∅, branching from the base, sometimes decumbent; **Ri.** 9–11, low, rounded; **Ar.** large, round; **Rsp.** 8–10, 5–20 mm lg.; **Csp.** 1, 6–10 cm lg., stout, porrect; all **Sp.** yellow at first, brown-tipped, later greyish-white; **Fl.** 3–5 cm lg., very woolly, white or pink, with stout brown Br. c. 1.5 cm lg.; **Fr.** 5 cm lg., bristly and woolly; **S.** 1.5 mm lg., matt, black.—Chile (as above, and in Coquimbo, near Taliney). (Fig. 334.)

Phyllocactus Lk.: **Epiphyllum** (Herm.) Haw.

Pilocanthus B. W. Bens. & Backbg. (208)

Plants mostly solitary, the spines short at first but succeeded by others which are very long and hair-like, and unique among the spherical cacti. The fact that L. Benson, in his classification into sections according to spine-character, united this particular genus with Pediocactus, says little to justify his

"revision" (see Pediocactus). The rotate flowers arise just below the meristem; they are densely scaly and glabrous, as are also the naked, dry fruits which dehisce by a gaping lateral split.—Distribution: W. Arizona.

P. paradinei (B. W. Bens.) B. W. Bens. & Backbg. (T.)
Bo. spherical, with a longer basal section, to 4 cm h., to 8 cm ∅, greyish or bluish-green; **R.** napiform, to 15 cm lg.; **Tub.** 5 mm h.; **Rsp.** at first (in juveniles) c. 16, at most 16 mm lg., later to c. 20; **Csp.** eventually to 6, scarcely differentiated, some to 7 cm lg., all hyaline, sometimes indistinctly flecked above; **Fl.** rotate, 1.2 cm lg., 2.2 cm ∅, creamy-white, sometimes with a pink M.-stripe; **Fr.** small-ovoid; **S.** matt, black, to 3 mm lg.—USA (Arizona, House Rock Valley, NE. Mohave County, N. Kaibab Plateau). [G.] (Fig. 335.)

Pilocereus K. Sch. non Lem.: **Pilosocereus** Byl. & Rowl.

Pilocereus Lem.: **Cephalocereus** Pfeiff.

Pilocereus houlletii Lem.: see Pilosocereus sartorianus (Rose) Byl. & Rowl.

Pilocopiapoa Ritt. (128)

Plants forming large mounds, resembling the species of Copiapoa in flower-form and dehiscence of the fruits, but the ovaries, tubes and fruits are hairy. This genus is particularly interesting since in this case Ritter has followed my principle for segregation, i.e. on the successive reduction of the indumentum. Seeds glossy, black.—Distribution: Chile (lat. 24°, inland). [Cultivation: ?; seedlings appear to grow well.]

P. solaris Ritt. (T.)
Bo. with many heads, forming tall mounds, to over 1 m h. and 2 m ∅, single heads to 12 cm ∅, greyish-green, not frosted; **crown** woolly, flat; **Ri.** (8–)9(–11), not tuberculate; **Ar.** yellowish-brown at first; **Rsp.** 7–10, 1.5–5 cm lg.; **Csp.** 2–5, 2–6 cm lg.; **Sp.** light yellowish-brownish at first, stout, rigid, minutely rough, ± curving; **Fl.** to 3 cm lg. and ∅, perfumed, pinkish-yellow to carmine; **Fr.** green to red, to 1.5 cm lg., with acute dry Sc. and white wool.—N. Chile (E. of Cobre). (Fig. 336.)
Rümpler describes Echus. bridgesii as having a hairy Fl., so it may be identical with the above, or possibly it is a further spec. (see also under Copiapoa bridgesii).

Pilosocereus Byl. & Rowl. (175)

A genus with a very wide distribution; flowers ±
bellshaped-funnelform and glabrous apart from
the rudimentary indumentum in SG.1—
characteristic of the reduction-process in the
hairiness of the flowering zone which is very
variable in the genus: the apical areoles have longer
hairs, the lateral areoles show ± longer hair-
development in the flowering region, but this is
similarly variable, i.e. the species may at times
flower lower down on the sides, or only in the upper
part of the stem. The hairs of the flowering
zone can also vary in length and density, with or
without spine-modification. In some species, and
quite independently of the hairs in the flowering
sections, a veritable cap of hairs develops at the
apex. There are thus all degrees of hair-
development, with their reduction to the point of
absence, so that there is no constant cephalium-
formation such as exists in the genera bearing true
cephalia; while these may vary very widely in form,
they are constant throughout the species of any
genus; for this reason the term "pseudo-
cephalium", often used in rather different senses, is
strictly applicable only to Pilosocereus. A similar
line of reduction is apparent in the height of the
plants: from large, much-branching trees down to
plants attaining only ½-metre in height. The
glabrous fruit, however, shows great uniformity
within the genus; it is always depressed-spherical
and, so far as known, it is ± furrowed or wrinkled
above, with persistent floral remains; the pulp is
often red, the seeds uniformly of average size and
± glossy black or dark brownish. Unification
within Cephalocereus Pfeiff., or some collective
genus of this name, is unacceptable in view of the
foregoing. Of the described species, 4 have not been
satisfactorily clarified. I have subdivided the genus
as follows, on the basis of the incomplete or
complete reduction of areolar hair or felt:

SG.1: Mediopilocereus Backbg.: flowers with
traces of felt; hair absent on the stems.
SG.2: Pilosocereus: flowers completely glabrous:
A: Areolar hair completely missing
B: Areolar hair present:
a: flowering zone with modified bristly
spines
b: flowering zone without modified bristly
spines

The figures and letters in brackets after the specific
names refer to the above divisions.—Distribution:
from Mexico, through Central America and the W.
Indies, to N. Peru and Central Brazil. This range
almost completely overlaps that of Melocactus,
with the same extension south of the Equator, and
challenges us to attempt some reconstruction of

earlier distributions, or the processes contributing
to their present occurrence.
The species of this genus are mostly very vigorous
and not nearly as difficult as was once assumed on
the basis of their origin in warmer latitudes. For
this reason they need only be grafted if growth has
to be speeded up; where they are planted out,
grafting is not necessary. Species from warmer
regions should not be kept too cool in winter.

P. alensis (Web.) Byl. & Rowl. (2B-b)
Bo. to 6 m h., branching from the base; **St.** bluish-
green, fairly slender; **Ri.** 12–14; **Sp.** 10–14, acicular,
c. 1–1.5 cm lg., brownish; **Pseudo-Ceph.** yellowish
to whitish, to 5 cm lg., inconspicuous at the apex,
stronger in the long, ± one-sided flowering zone;
Fl. light purple to purplish-green.—W. Mexico
(Jalisco, Sierra de Alo).

P. arenicola (Werd.) Byl. & Rowl. (2B-b)
Bo. to 5 m h., tree-like; **branches** greyish-green, to 7
cm ∅; **Ri.** 6(–7); **Ar.** thick, grey; **Rsp.** 8–9; **Csp.** c.
6; all **Sp.** to c. 1.5 cm lg., yellow to brownish;
Pseudo-Ceph. whitish to yellowish in the apex,
longer, more flocky and dense on the flanks; **Fl.** ±
subapical, colour ?—Brazil (N. Bahia, between
Saure and Aracy).

P. arrabidae (Lem.) Byl. & Rowl. (2B-b)
Bo. shrubby, sometimes to 3 m h., branching from
below; **branches** pale green, to 10 cm ∅, frosted,
bluish; **Ri.** c. 6–8, ± tuberculate; **Ar.** soon
glabrous; **Sp.** 5–10, unequal, 8–9 radials, 1–2 Csp.
to 4 cm lg., subulate, other Sp. acicular; **Pseudo-
Ceph.** longer at the apex, lax, soon falling, missing
in the flowering zone; **Fl.** high on the flanks, to 7 cm
lg., white; **Fr.** 5 cm ∅.—Brazil (around Rio de
Janeiro).

P. aurilanatus Ritt. (FR 1325): not yet described;
"Fl.-shoots with golden wool".

P. aurisetus (Werd.) Byl. & Rowl. (2B-a)
Bo. to 1 m h., branching from below; **branches** to 6
cm ∅, frosted, blue, to 6 cm ∅; **Ri.** c. 15, flat; **Ar.**
whitish-grey, with H. 1 cm lg.; all **Sp.** finely
acicular, numerous, to 2.5 cm lg., to 5 cm lg. and
bristly in the flowering zone, translucent, golden-
yellow; **Pseudo-Ceph.** longer in the flowering zone;
Fl. to 5 cm lg., whitish; **Fr.** and **S.** ?—Brazil (Minas
Geraes, Serro do Cipó).

P. backebergii (Wgt.) Byl. & Rowl. (2B-b)
Bo. tree-like, to 5 m h.; **branches** green, blue-
frosted, 7–12 cm ∅; **Ri.** 9; **Rsp.** 6–9, pungent, thin,
to 1.5 cm lg.; **Csp.** 1, to 3 cm lg.; Sp. white, horn-
coloured below; **Pseudo-Ceph.** lax to dense and
longer above, the Ar. of the flowering zone with

discrete tufts of white H.; **Fl.** higher or lower on the shoot, yellowish-green, whitish inside; **Fr.** violet-red.—Venezuela (Puerto Cabello).

P. bahamensis (Britt.) Byl. & Rowl. (2B-b)
Bo. tree-like, to 4 m h.; **branches** to 9 cm ∅, matt, green; **Ri.** 10–11; **Sp.** acicular, spreading, ascending, to 3 cm lg., yellow at first, dark below, then yellowish-brown to brown; **hair-development** short to missing in the crown, sparse or missing in the flowering zone; **Fl.** high on the flanks, to 6 cm lg., white washed pink; **Tu.** bluish.—Bahamas (Berry Islands).

P. barbadensis (Br. & R.) Byl. & Rowl. (2B-b)
Bo. shrubby, ascending, to 6 m h.; **branches** glossy, green; **Ri.** 8–9, fairly prominent; **Sp.** numerous, acicular, light brown, to 4 cm lg.; **Pseudo-ceph.** inconspicuous at the apex, laterally in ± contiguous tufts of sometimes longer H.; **Fl.** to 6 cm lg., light pink; **Tu.** greenish below, red above.—Barbados.

P. bradei (Backbg. & Voll) Byl. & Rowl. (2A)
Bo. shrubby, 2 m h.; **branches** frosted, sky-blue, to 8 cm ∅; **Ri.** c. 10, acutely cross-furrowed; **Ar.** grey; **Sp.**: on sterile shoots c. 6 Rsp. and 1–2 Csp., to 2 cm lg., all chocolate-brown, fertile shoots often spineless; **Pseudo-Ceph.** absent; **Fl.** c. 7 cm lg., 3 cm ∅, greenish-white.—Brazil (Diamantina).

P. brasiliensis (Br. & R.) Backbg. (2B-b)
Bo. shrubby, branching from below, to 3 m h.; **branches** greyish-green, at most slightly frosted at first; **Ri.** 4–5, fairly prominent, becoming flatter below; **Ar.** crowded, surmounted by ascending furrows; **Rsp.** few, very short, brown, acicular; **Csp.** 1(–2) to 2 cm lg., brown; **Pseudo-Ceph.** denser in the crown, to 2 cm lg., weak and inconspicuous in the flowering zone; **Fl.** 5 cm lg., white.—Brazil (near Rio de Janeiro).

P. brooksianus (Br. & R.) Byl. & Rowl. (2B-b)
Bo. branching from below, to 6 m h.; **branches** robust, frosted, bluish-green; **Ri.** 8–9; **Ar.** closely spaced, ± confluent in the flowering zone; **Sp.** to 16, yellow, thin, to 3 cm lg., ± equal; **Pseudo-Ceph.** silky and dense in the crown, in thick, longer, rounded tufts in the flowering zone; **Fl.** to 6 cm lg., high on the flanks, unscented, purple.—Cuba (Oriente and Santa Clara).

| P. carolinensis (FR 1217): no description available.

P. catalani (Ricc.) Byl. & Rowl. (2A)
A scarcely known spec. Overall height and colour of shoots not known; **Ri.** 6, obtuse, thick; **Rsp.** 6–8; **Csp.** 1–2; **Sp.** greyish-black, c. 5 mm lg., Csp. rather

longer and stouter; **Fl.** to 10 cm lg., bellshaped, dirty greenish-white, arising from a hairless flowering zone.—Origin? Perhaps a hybrid or, because of the relatively long Fl., not referable here?

P. catingicola (Gürke) Byl. & Rowl. (2B–b)
Bo. tree-like, to 8 m h., with a thick **trunk**; **branches** greyish-green, not frosted, 8–12 cm ∅; **Ri.** c. 4–5, to 4 cm h.; **Ar.** greyish-white; **Rsp.** 8–12, to 1 cm lg., ± appressed; **Csp.** 5–8, to 10 cm lg. on the trunk, elsewhere to 3 cm lg.; all **Sp.** subulate, yellowish to horn-coloured; **Pseudo-Ceph.** denser and to 2 cm lg. at the apex, weak in the flowering zone; **Fl.** 8 cm lg., white.—Brazil (Bahia, in the Catinga).

P. chrysacanthus (Web.) Byl. & Rowl. (2B–b)
Bo. branching from the base, to 5 m h.; **branches** green, frosted blue towards the tip; **Ri.** 9–12; **Sp.** 12–15, to 4 cm lg., yellow; **Pseudo-Ceph.** strong and white at the tip, stout and flocky in the flowering zone; **Fl.** subapical, whitish to ± pinkish-red.—Mexico (Puebla, Tehuacan; Oaxaca).

P. chrysostele (Vpl.) Byl. & Rowl. (2B–b)
Bo. freely branching, to 5 m h., sometimes with a small trunk; **branches** fresh green, to 9 cm ∅; **Ri.** 20–30; **Ar.** with a few H. to 2 cm lg.; **Sp.** c. 30, not differentiated, those in the flowering zone modified, bristly and to several cm lg., otherwise brownish, finely acicular, to 2 cm lg.; Br.-Sp. of the flowering zone borne only on the west side; **Pseudo-Ceph.** consisting of longer H. in the flowering zone; **Fl.** 5 cm lg., olive-green to whitish.—Brazil (Pernambuco, in the interior).

P. claroviridis (Backbg.) Byl. & Rowl. (2B–b)
Bo. tree-like, several m h.; **branches** light green, weakly frosted, 6–8 cm ∅; **Ri.** c. 7; **Ar.** white; **Rsp.** 10–12, thin, yellowish, irregularly long, sometimes appressed; **Csp.** 1–3, similarly; **Pseudo-Ceph.**: short decurrent discrete tufts of white H., apex moderately hairy; **Fl.** also appearing lower on the flanks, probably as in P. moritzianus.—Venezuela (below Caracas).

| P. coerulescens (FR 1326): no description available.

P. collinsii (Br. & R.) Byl. & Rowl. (2B–b)
Bo. shrubby, to 3 m h.; **branches** bluish-green, frosted above, to 4 cm ∅; **Ri.** c. 7, moderately prominent; **Ar.** fairly close; **Sp.** numerous, acicular, c. 10 Rsp., 1 stouter Csp., mostly to c. 2.2 cm lg., longest ones sometimes 3–4 cm lg., all dark brown, soon black; **Pseudo-Ceph.**: strong H.-development at the apex, white, that of the flowering zone moderately strong, flocky; **Fl.**

subapical, 5 cm lg., whitish.—Mexico (Oaxaca, Tehuantepec).

P. colombianus (Rose) Byl. & Rowl. (2B–b)
Bo. to 6 m h., branching from midway; **branches** erect; **Ri.** 7, rather obtuse; **Sp.** 25 and more, long, thin; **Pseudo-Ceph.** rather long, white, lax, extending down for 1 m below the apex; **Fl.** 7 cm lg., pale pink.—Colombia (Venticas del Dagua).
Rose provided insufficient data. A spec. from the N. coast, as follows, is more probably not referable here: **Bo.** tree-like; **branches** light to leaf-green, variable; **Ri.** 8; **Ar.** with pendant H.; **Sp.** to 10 Rsp., Csp. scarcely differentiated, 1–4, brown, to 5 cm lg.; **Fl.** 7 cm lg., whitish, arising from only moderately hairier Ar.; **Fr.** flattened-spherical, red inside and out.—Colombia (Pto. Colombia).
I proposed this spec. should be named P. klusacekii; Sp. on newer growth are reddish-brown.

P. cometes (Scheidw.) Byl. & Rowl. (2B–b)
Bo. shrubby, laxly ascending, several m h.; **branches** to c. 10 cm ∅, greyish-green; **Ri.** c. 12–15; **Sp.** 12–15, yellowish, to 2 cm lg., later also longer and ± pointing downwards; **Pseudo-Ceph.** lax and longer at the apex, the flowering zone with tufts of whitish wool at intervals; **Fl.** high on the flank, white; **Fr.** green.—Mexico.

P. cuyabensis (Backbg.) Byl. & Rowl. (2B–b)
Bo. shrubby, height ?; **branches** greyish-green, to 6 cm ∅, faintly frosted; **Ri.** 10(–11), to 8 mm h.; **Ar.** 3 mm apart; **Sp.** c. 15, **Csp.** not differentiated, all acicular, yellowish-brown, longest ones to 1.8 cm lg.; **Pseudo-Ceph.** denser but still lax on the more frosted shoot-tip; **Fl.** white.—Brazil (near Cuyabá).

P. deeringii (Small) Byl. & Rowl. (2B–b)
Bo. shrubby, to 10 m h.; **branches** erect, rather slender, few, deep green to lighter; **Ri.** (9–)10; **Sp.** 25–30, to 1 cm lg., acicular; **Pseudo-Ceph.**: H. moderately long and lax at the apex, flowering zone with woolly tufts, either more crowded or more distant; **Fl.** 6 cm lg., probably white; **Fr.** dark red.—USA (Florida, Rocky Hammocks).

P. densiareolatus Ritt., not described: "blue" (FR 957).

P. densilanus Ritt. (FR 960), not described: "with white H.".

P. diamantina Ritt., not described (perhaps Pilosocereus sp. 3 in "Die Cact.", Vol. 4. 2467. 1960 ?)

P. floccosus Byl. & Rowl. (2B–b)

Bo. shrubby, branching from the base, to 2 m h.; **branches** first greyish then yellowish-green, to 10 cm ∅; **Ri.** 5; **Ar.** grey; **Rsp.** 6–8; **Csp.** 0–6; all **Sp.** irregular, first light brown, darker below, in the flowering zone to 11, equal, 1 cm lg., enveloped in wool; **Pseudo-Ceph.**: apex and upper Ar. with greyish-brownish to brownish wool 4–5 mm lg., flowering zone with laxly decurrent, flocky-hairy tufts; **Fl.** 5 cm lg., greenish-white.—Brazil (Diamantina). Originally described as Pilocereus floccosus Backbg. & Voll non Lem.

P. gaumeri (Br. & R.) Backbg. (2B–b)
Bo. shrubby, to 6 m h.; **branches** light green, to c. 3 cm ∅, rarely to 6 cm ∅; **Ri.** 8–9; **Sp.** numerous, acicular, 15–25, 1–5 cm lg., yellowish-brown at first; **Pseudo-Ceph.** laxly web-like at the apex, flowering zone with scattered tufts of H.; **Fl.** 5–7 cm lg., light green.—Mexico (Yucatan).

P. gironensis Rauh & Backbg. (2B–b)
Bo. shrubby, squarrosely branching, from the base and higher; **branches** curving and ascending, often unsightly, ± frosted, bluish-green; **Ri.** to 8, with shallow cross-furrows; **Rsp.** later c. 9; **Csp.** 1–2; **Sp.** acicular-subulate, later also to 14, some stouter; **Pseudo-Ceph.** lax or dense and rather longer at the apex, flowering zone with mop-like pendant skeins.—Ecuador (Giron Pasaje).

P. glaucescens (Lab.) Byl. & Rowl. (2B–b)
Bo. tree-like, to 6 m h., with a trunk; **branches** frosted, light blue, to 10 cm ∅; **Ri.** 8–10; **Ar.** silvery-grey, with some pendant H. to 2 cm lg.; **Rsp.** 13–18; **Csp.** 5–7; all **Sp.** equal, to 1.5 cm lg., outer ones yellowish-white, inner ones brownish, ± thickened below; **Pseudo-Ceph.** sparse and short at the apex, flowering zone strongly white-woolly; **Fl.** to c. 7 cm lg., white.—Brazil (Central Bahia to Central Minas Geraes, Diamantina).

P. glaucochrous (Werd.) Byl. & Rowl. (2B–b)
Bo. erectly shrubby, moderately branching, to 4 m h., frosted, light blue; **branches** slender, to 7 cm ∅ at most; **Ri.** acutely cross-furrowed, to c. 9; **Ar.** in the crown with white wool to 4 cm lg., with whitish-grey felt, flowering zone with H. to c. 3 cm lg.; **Rsp.** 9–12, to 1.5(–2) cm lg.; **Csp.** c. 3–4, sometimes to 5 cm lg., stouter; all **Sp.** translucently straw-coloured; **Pseudo-Ceph.**: to 3 cm lg. at the apex, otherwise tufted; **Fl.** to 5.5 cm lg.; **Pet.** pink to whitish; **Fr.** to 5 cm ∅, frosted greenish or faintly reddish; **S.** over 1 mm lg., black, glossy.—Brazil (Bahia, Serra d'Espinhaço, near Morro Chapéo).

P. gounellei (Web.) Byl. & Rowl. (2B–b)
Bo. to 2–3 m lg., with a short **trunk** over 8 cm ∅; **branches** often spreading horizontally, then curv-

ing upwards or sometimes prostrate, to 8 cm $\emptyset$; **Ri.** 10–11, ± tuberculate; **Ar.** large, upper ones 1.5 cm across; **Rsp.** c. 15–24, brown; **Csp.** 4–6, brown, rigid, pungent, to 10 cm lg., subulate; **Pseudo-Ceph.**: a meagre white tuft in the apex, flowering zone with flocky white to brown tufts of H.; **Fl.** to 9 cm lg., whitish; **Fr.** green at first, then red.—Brazil (Pernambuco, Bahia).

 v. **zehntneri** (Br. & R.) Byl. & Rowl.: **branches** more slender, to 4 cm $\emptyset$; **Ar.** rather more distant; **Sp.** to 30, light yellow, **Csp.** scarcely differentiated, mostly not longer but occasionally to c. 3–4 cm lg.—Brazil (Bahia, Serra de Tiririca).

P. guerreronis (Backbg.) Byl. & Rowl. (2B–b)
Bo. shrubby, to 4 m h.; **branches** ascending, light green, not frosted; **Ri.** 9–10, to 1.4 cm h.; **Sp.** 10–15, scarcely differentiated, unequal, 0.2–5 cm lg., pungent, chestnut-brown; **Pseudo-Ceph.** moderately long or dense in the apex, flowering zone near the apex with quite strongly woolly tufts of H. which do not hang down far and are longer-persistent; **Fl.** also from lower on the flank, whitish.—Mexico (Guerrero).

P. gutarianensis (FR 1218): no description available.

P. hapalacanthus (Werd.) Byl. & Rowl. (2B–b)
Bo. shrubby, to 5 m h.; **branches** ascending, vivid green, not frosted; **Ri.** c. 12; **Ar.** with sparse grey felt, those near the apex with H. 2 cm lg.; **Sp.** scarcely differentiated, 15–20, rarely one over 1 cm lg., yellowish to golden-brown; **Pseudo-Ceph.**: fairly short and tufted at the tip, flowering zone weakly hairy, H. to 2 cm lg.; **Fl.** c. 6 cm lg., translucent, cream-coloured; **Fr.** dark green.—Brazil (coast, N. of Recife).

P. hermentianus (Monv.) Byl. & Rowl. (2B–b)
Bo. erect, over 3 m h.; **branches** light green, 5–7 cm $\emptyset$; **Ri.** c. 19, weakly tuberculate, with horizontal folds; **Sp.** c. 20, small, thin, yellowish, of these c. 14–16 are Rsp., Csp. 4–6, all 3–6 mm lg.; **Pseudo-Ceph.** of silky, pendant, persistent H., sometimes flocky, from brownish Ar.; **Fl.** to 6 cm lg., 3 cm $\emptyset$.—Mexico or Haiti. Insufficiently known spec.; Haiti as its origin is dubious.

P. (Pilocereus) **houlletii** (Lem.): see comments under Pilosocereus sartorianus (Rose) Byl. & Rowl.

P. keyensis (Br. & R.) Byl. & Rowl. (2B–b)
Bo. shrubby, to 6 m h., with a trunk-like section to 12 cm $\emptyset$, moderately branching; **branches** erect, bluish-green, strongly frosted, 5–6 cm $\emptyset$; **Ri.** 9–10;

Sp. c. 15, to 1.5 cm lg., acicular, yellow; **Pseudo-Ceph.**: apical H. very short to missing, those in the flowering zone only short, white, becoming grey; **Fl.** high on the flanks, brownish-purple, 6 cm lg.; **Fr.** reddish.—USA (Florida, on the Keys). Probably no longer growing wild.

P. klusacekii Backbg.: see Pilosocereus colombianus (Rose) Byl. & Rowl.

P. lanuginosus (L.) Byl. & Rowl. (2B–b)
Bo. a tall shrub to 8 m h., with a **trunk** to 25 cm $\emptyset$, ± freely branching; **branches** to 8 cm $\emptyset$, bluish-green, strongly blue at first; **Ri.** (7–)8(–13); **Ar.** with H. to 2 cm lg.; **Sp.** 10–20, 9–15 of these Rsp., Csp. c. 1–5, all acicular, 1.5–5 cm lg., yellow to yellowish-green, becoming brownish to black, sometimes contorted or fibrous; **Pseudo-Ceph.** with lax H. to 2 cm lg. at the apex, flowering zone with more generous, decurrent hair-development; **Fl.** 6 cm lg., creamy-white; **Fr.** green to reddish, red inside.—Curaçao and neighbouring islands, NE. Colombia, NW. Venezuela.

P. leucocephalus (Pos.) Byl. & Rowl. (2B–b)
Bo. tree-like, densely branching, with a shorter **trunk**; **Ri.** c. 7–8; no data available on **Sp.**, **Fl.** and **Fr.** of the true spec. which Lindsay re-discovered, and which I illustrated in "Die Cact.", IV: Fig. 2333 (p. 2446) 1960.—Mexico (Sonora, Navajoa). This plant has a conspicuous, longer-decurrent cap of white H., and it is clearly distinguishable in habit from P. palmeri, sartorianus or houllettii, with which it has continually been confused since Rümpler's time—or even with P. alensis. The specific name is far more apt for this plant, whose Fl. appear at the apex through a dense mass of woolly H., than it is for any of the other spec. mentioned. This plant merits re-collection and should be accurately described.

P. luetzelburgii (Vpl.) Byl. & Rowl. (2B–b)
Bo. to 1 m h., at first ± clavate, then with the upper part narrowed like the neck of a bottle, and bent towards the west, on which side the Pseudocephalium is also probably present; **branches** sparse; **Ri.** 13–16; **Ar.** white; **Rsp.** 15–18, appressed, acicular, to 1.5 cm lg.; **Csp.** c. 4 or somewhat more, indistinctly differentiated, rather stouter, to 3 cm lg.; all **Sp.** horn-yellow at first, then grey; **Pseudo-Ceph.** tufted, to 2 cm lg. at the apex, similarly in the flowering zone; **Fl.** to 5 cm lg., whitish; **Fr.** 3.5 cm $\emptyset$.—Brazil (Central Bahia, on several mountain-ridges).

P. machrisii (Daws.) Backbg. (2B–b)
Bo. shrubby, branching from the base, to 3.5 m h.; **branches** erect, to 8 cm $\emptyset$, frosted blue above; **Ri.**

11–13; **Ar.** with yellowish-brown wool, and H. to 4 mm lg.; **Rsp.** c. 12–13, to 8 mm lg.; **Csp.** c. 2–4, scarcely differentiated, to 1.5 cm lg.; all **Sp.** yellow to brown; **Pseudo-Ceph.** of dense brownish wool 4 mm lg. at the apex, the flowering zone with woolly H. in distinct projecting tufts, these white in cultivation; **Fl.** c. 4.5 cm lg., 3.5 cm ∅.—Brazil (Goayaz, S. of Uruacú).

P. magnificus Buin.
Bo. noticeably candelabra-shaped, branching almost from the base, 1.5–2 m h.; **branches** 7 cm ∅, frosted azure-blue; **Ri.** 6–7, to 2 cm h., 2.2–2.5 cm br.; **Ar.** round, 4 mm ∅, 4–5 mm apart, with white H. at first, later naked, only flowering Ar. with H. to almost 1 cm lg.; **Sp.** c. 25, 5–10 mm lg., thin, yellowish at first, then reddish-brown and greyish-brown; **Fl.** 44 mm lg., 27 mm ∅, frosted bluish outside; **Sep.** 3–7.5 mm br., 3–11 mm lg., greenish, with a dark green M.-stripe; **Pet.** 5–6 mm br., 9–11 mm lg., thin, greenish-white, borders denticulate; **Fil.** creamy-white; **Fr.** 26 mm ∅; **S.** black.—Brazil (Minas Geraes, on flat rock-slabs on the Rio Jaquitihonda, 370 m). (Fig. 523).
Requires above-average temperatures in cultivation.

P. maxonii (Rose) Byl. & Rowl. (2B–b)
Bo. tree-like, to 3 m h., with a short **trunk**; **branches** obliquely ascending, frosted blue; **Ri.** 6–8; **Sp.** c. 10, thin, yellow, one Csp. 4 cm lg.; **Pseudo-Ceph.**: a stronger white cap in the apex, stronger also in the flowering zone which extends downwards for up to 30 cm, here ± concealing the Sp.; **Fl.** 4 cm lg., purple; **S.** brownish(!).—Guatemala (El Rancho, Salama).

P. millspaughii (Britt.) Byl. & Rowl. (2B–b)
Bo. to 6 m h., to 20 cm ∅ at the base; **branches** obliquely erect, to 12 cm ∅, pale greyish-green, frosted; **Ri.** 8–13; **Sp.** c. 20, acicular, yellow to yellowish-brown, dark below, becoming greyish-brown, to 2 cm lg., or up to 3–7 cm lg. in the flowering zone; **Pseudo-Ceph.** ± unilateral, decurrent from the apex, of thicker tufts of H., often as long as the Sp., 5 cm lg.; **Fl.** to 7 cm lg., waxy-stiff, white.—Cuba and Bahamas.

P. minensis (Werd.) Byl. & Rowl. (1)
Bo. shrubby, to 2 m h.; **branches** vivid green, to 4 cm ∅; **Ri.** c. 13; **Ar.** more felty at first; **Sp.** to 20, to 2 cm lg., one to 3 cm lg., all yellowish at first, then brownish and finally black; **Pseudo-Ceph.** absent; **Fl.** 5 cm lg., 3 cm ∅, greenish-white, with traces of felt; **Fr.** blue; **S.** dark brown.—Brazil (Minas Geraes).

P. monoclonos (DC.) Byl. & Rowl. (2B–b)

Bo. simple, erect; **Ri.** mostly 8; **Sp.** to 16, short, spreading, equal; **Pseudo-Ceph.** only short, both at the apex and in the flowering zone; **Fl.** long-bellshaped, white; **Fr.** purple.—W. Indies (said to occur in Hispaniola, but never re-collected there; perhaps from elsewhere?)

P. moritzianus (O.) Byl. & Rowl. (2B–a)
Bo. tree-like with a trunk: **branches** ascending obliquely, green, somewhat frosted; **Ri.** 7–8(–10), obtuse, ± tuberculate at the tip; **Rsp.** 6–8(–10), short; **Csp.** 1–3, to 1.5 cm lg.; **Sp.** light at first, then dirty yellow, above and in the flowering zone short, bristly, clustered, white; **Pseudo-Ceph.** short in the crown, longer in juvenile plants, flowering zone with decurrent discrete tufts of moderately long white H. rising from brown areolar felt; **Fl.** 5 cm lg., white; **Fr.** violet, white inside.—Venezuela.

P. mortensenii (Croiz.) Backbg. (2B–a)
Bo. tree-like; **branches** bluish at first, then blue; **Ri.** c. 9; **Ar.** with woolly felt, hairy in the crown; **Rsp.** 5–7, 1–1.5 cm lg., thin, pungent, brown or grey; **Csp.** mostly 1, sometimes 2, stout, dirty yellow to grey, 3–4 cm lg.; **Pseudo-Ceph.** consisting of only inconspicuous lax H. at the tip, flowering zone with more plentiful H.; **Fl.** to 6 cm lg., 3.5 cm ∅.—Venezuela (State Lara).
If a plant discovered by Humbert is referable here, then the Sp. at the apex can be longer, bristly-fine, dense and erect.

P. multicostatus Ritt., undescribed: "bluish-green" (FR 1346).

P. nobilis (Haw.) Byl. & Rowl. (2B–b)
Bo. a dense and freely branching shrub; **branches** glossy to light green, also darker, to violet-green or almost black, 3–7 cm ∅, not frosted; **Ri.** 5–7(–10); **Ar.** brownish-yellow; **Rsp.** c. 9, spreading, to 1 cm lg.; **Csp.** 2–4, stouter or only acicular, to 3.5 cm lg.; **Sp.** yellow, brown-tipped, then brown; **Pseudo-Ceph.** inconspicuous and lax at the apex, in the flowering zone hairy white, tufted, to 2 cm lg.; **Fl.** 4–6 cm lg., purplish-pink; **Fr.** red.—W. Indies (from St. Christopher to Grenada).

P. oligolepis (Vpl.) Byl. & Rowl. (2B–b)
Bo. little branching, to 1 m h.; **branches** greyish-green, not frosted; **Ri.** 5; **Rsp.** 8–10, scarcely 5 mm lg., thin, spreading; **Csp.** 1, rather stouter, to 2 cm lg.; **Pseudo-Ceph.** of areolar H. 1 cm lg., laxly enveloping the apex, flowering zone moderately hairy; **Fl.** 6 cm lg., whitish.—Brazil (Amazonas) and a small zone on the Venezuela-Guayana frontier.

I P. oreas (FR 1226): no description available.

P. pachycladus Ritt. (FR 1223, 1290): no description available.

P. palmeri (Rose) Byl. & Rowl. (2B–b)
Bo. ascending, to 6 m h., with up to 20 **branches** to 8 cm ⌀, dark green, bluish and frosted above; **Ri.** 7–9, rounded; **Sp.** brown to grey; **Rsp.** 8–12, thin, 2–3 cm lg.; **Csp.** 1, 3 cm lg.; **Pseudo-Ceph.** of thick areolar wool, sometimes joining to form decurrent skeins, making a dense cap over the apex, long in the flowering zone and arranged in tight balls; **Fl.** purple (colour photo in "Die Cact.", IV, Fig. 2328).—E. Mexico (Tamaulipas, between Matamoros and Tampico). Only yellow-spined in the seedling-stage; P. sartorianus has straw-coloured Sp.
> v. **victoriensis** (Vpl.) Backbg. n. comb. (Cereus victoriensis Vpl. MfK. 24. 1913): **Fl.** white, washed faintly pink or pale violet (colour photo by Werdermann in "Blüh. Kakt. u.a. sukk. Pflanzen", Plate 37 (1932): Sp. also brown(!)

P. pentaedrophorus (Lab.) Byl. & Rowl. (2A)
Bo. a lax shrub, to 10 m h.; **branches** erect, to 3 cm ⌀ or rather more, frosted, vivid blue; **Ri.** 4–6, rarely more; **Ar.** with sparse felt and no H.; **Sp.** to 12, yellowish to greyish-brown, **Csp.** sometimes to 4 cm lg., otherwise unequal; **Pseudo-Ceph.** absent; **Fl.** to 5 cm lg., white; **Fr.** greenish or reddish, purplish-violet inside.—Brazil (Pernambuco, Bahia).

P. perlucens (K. Sch.) Byl. & Rowl.: **Cereus perlucens** K. Sch.

P. piauhyensis (Gürke) Byl. & Rowl. (2B–b)
Bo. tree-like, to 10 m h., **trunk** to 50 cm ⌀; **branches** numerous, to 100, bluish-green to vivid blue; **Ri.** (12–)16; **Rsp.** 25–30 or more; **Csp.** 1, to 3 cm lg.; all **Sp.** yellowish-brown, acicular, rigid, pungent, Csp. rather stouter; **Pseudo-Ceph.** of rather longer, tufted, whitish-grey H., only in the flowering zone; **Fl.** to only 4 cm lg., white; **Fr.** reddened, frosted.—Brazil (Pernambuco, Piauhy).

P. polygonus (Lam.) Byl. & Rowl. (2B–b)
Bo. simple at first, eventually tree-like, to over 3 m h., **trunk** to 1.5 m lg.; **branches** ascending, at first often quite strongly blue; **Ri.** 5–13, rather narrow, ± furrowed on the flanks; **Sp.** on young growth acicular or bristly, to 1.5 cm lg., yellow, later darker, with additional subulate Sp., yellowish-brown, 2–7 cm lg.; **Pseudo-Ceph.** of longer brownish H. at the apex, later falling, flowering zone with isolated tufts to 2 cm lg., these absent in places; **Fl.** to 6 cm lg., white.—E. Cuba; Santo Domingo and Haiti.
Ekman observed in Santo Domingo an un-diagnosed plant of candelabra-like habit, to 4 m h., with pale yellowish-red Fl.; possibly P. swartzii.

P. princeps (FR 1343): no description available.

P. purpusii (Br. & R.) Byl. & Rowl. (2B–b)
Bo. shrubby or simple, to 3 m h.; **St.** light green, 3–4 cm ⌀; **Ri.** 12; **Sp.** numerous, fairly dense, tawny, thickened below, acicular, to 3 cm lg.; **Pseudo-Ceph.** weak at the apex but the flowering zone, which is little lower down, has piled and prominent H.-clusters; **Fl.** 7 cm lg., pale pink, **Pet.** bordered white; **Fr.** greenish.—Mexico (coast of Sinaloa; Jalisco; N. Nayarit; S. Sonora; Islas Marías).

P. quadricentralis (Daws.) Backbg. (2B–b)
Bo. tree-like, to over 5 m h., **trunk** to 25 cm ⌀; **branches** to 10, in the bottom 1.5 m, to 8 cm ⌀; **Ri.** mostly 9; **Rsp.** 11–13, 1–2 cm lg.; **Csp.** mostly 4, spreading, 2–3.5 cm lg.; **Sp.** matt reddish-brown, soon flecked matt grey; **Pseudo-Ceph.**: a mass of longer woolly H. at the apex, these denser in the flowering zone, white at first, then grey and dirty, H. then dropping on one side of the branch; **Fl.** and **Fr.** ?—Mexico (E. Oaxaca; W. Chiapas).

P. robinii (Lem.) Byl. & Rowl. (2B–b)
Bo. tree-like, to 8 m h., with a thick **trunk**; **branches** ascending, to 10 cm ⌀, matt green, light bluish-green at first; **Ri.** 10–13; **Ar.** shortly woolly; **Sp.** 15–20, acicular, yellow, to 2.5 cm lg., **Csp.** scarcely differentiated; flowering Ar. crowded; **Pseudo-Ceph.** short to missing in the apex, flowering zone ± similarly; **Fl.** 5 cm lg., 3 cm ⌀, white; **Fr.** wine-red.—Cuba (coast of Habana and Matanzas).

P. robustus Ritt., not described: "bluish-green, with white H." (FR 1344).

P. royenii (L.) Byl. & Rowl. (2B–b)
Bo. tree-like, to 8 m h., sometimes with a short trunk to 30 cm ⌀; **branches** ascending, green or, especially at first, frosted-blue; **Ri.** 7–11; **Ar.** crowded; **Sp.** acicular, variable, sometimes only 1 cm lg., or to 6 cm lg., yellow; **Pseudo-Ceph.** of weak H. in the new Ar., flowering zone with clusters of longer white H.; **Fl.** 5 cm lg., white; **Fr.** green to reddish.—W. Indies (several islands in the Lesser Antilles).

P. rupicola (Werd.) Byl. & Rowl. (2B–b)
Bo. to 50 cm h., somewhat branching at the base; **branches** greyish-green, c. 4 cm ⌀; **Ri.** c. 9; **Ar.** at first with a cushion of dense grey wool, later glabrous; **Sp.** to 20, Csp. scarcely separable, to 1.5 cm lg., yellow, then brown to blackish-grey, thickened below, acicular, longest ones to 2 cm lg.; **Pseudo-Ceph.** tufted and short at the tip, flowering

zone subapical, with strong wool or H.-development; **Fl.** and **Fr.** ?—Brazil (Sergipe, Serra da Itabahana).

P. salvadorensis (Werd.) Byl. & Rowl. (2B–b)
Bo. tree-like, to 4 m h., with a short **trunk**; **branches** numerous, greenish or grey, with soft flesh, to 10 cm $\emptyset$; **Ri.** 7–9; **Ar.** whitish-grey; **Rsp.** 10–11, to 1 cm lg., some lower ones often bristly, others stiffly acicular; **Csp.** 4, cruciform, upper one to 2.5 cm lg., remainder 1–2 cm lg.; all **Sp.** yellow, then brownish to darker or tipped thus; **Pseudo-Ceph.** of only a few apical H. to 1.5 cm lg., flowering zone $\pm$ similarly; **Fl.** ?; **Fr.** to 5 cm $\emptyset$.—Brazil (coast of Bahia, on sand-dunes).

P. sartorianus (Rose) Byl. & Rowl. (2B–b)
Bo. to 5 m h.; **branches** strongly ascending, light or yellowish-green (to bluish-green?); **Ri.** to 7, acutely cross-furrowed on the flanks; **Rsp.** 7–8 at first, later more; **Csp.** mostly only 1; all **Sp.** straw-coloured, to only 1 cm lg.; **Pseudo-Ceph.**: all Ar. have a few to many cobwebby H., these much more plentiful in the flowering zone, to 6 cm lg., white; **Fl.** 6–8 cm lg., dirty pinkish-red; **Fr.** red.—Mexico (Vera Cruz). Often confused with P. palmeri, but the latter has brown Sp., and the Fl. are purple or, in the variety, white with a pink sheen.

Pilocereus houlletii Lem. (**Pilosocereus**) (2B–b)
(T.): mostly regarded as a synonym of P. leuco-cephalus (Br. & R.), or certainly as close to the preceding spec., since the Sp. are also described as straw-coloured; Fl., however, "violet with some pink and yellow"; flowering zone apical, consisting of dense white wool from which the Fl. arise, acc. Rümpler's drawing. A plant flowering thus was illustrated in "Die Cact.", Vol. IV, Fig. 2330 and 2331. Since in this case the wool in the lower part gradually drops, but is constantly replaced by dense new growth in the crown, and I saw the plant flowering several times, always in this fashion, this spec. cannot at present be referred elsewhere. Seeds are brownish!

P. sergipensis (Werd.) Byl. & Rowl. (2B–b)
Bo. to 3 m h., little branching; **shoots** attractively blue-frosted, to 4.5 cm $\emptyset$; **Ri.** 6; **Ar.** with white to greyish-brown felt; **Rsp.** 8–11, thin-acicular, to 1 cm lg.; **Csp.** 2–4, 2 rather stouter, to over 1 cm lg.; all **Sp.** horn-coloured, becoming blackish-brown, rather knotted below; **Pseudo-Ceph.** in the apex with many H. to 1.5 cm lg., flowering zone with lax flocky clusters of H.; **Fl.** ?; **Fr.** to 6 cm $\emptyset$.—Brazil (Sergipe, near Jaboatão). (Fig. 337.)

| P. splendidus (FR 1224): no description available.

P. sublanatus (SD.) Byl. & Rowl. (2B–b)
A little-clarified specific name. It is possibly the first name for P. arrabidae or P. catingicola, both of which have only 4–5 Ri., which is low for the Brazilian spec. Further details in "Die Cact." IV: 2413. 1960.

P. superbus Ritt., not described: "mid-blue" (FR 1347).

P. supremus Ritt., not described: "magnificent blue" (FR 1345). [Haage adds: Tallest of the genus.]

P. swartzii (Griseb.) Byl. & Rowl. (2B–a)
Bo. tree-like, to 7 m h., often with a longer trunk; **branches** matt green, not frosted, stout, fairly steeply ascending; **Ri.** 10, depressed between the Ar.; **Sp.** in young plants 20 or more, later only 8–10, to 2.5 cm lg., modified in the flowering zone into longer bristly Sp.; **Pseudo-Ceph.** of irregularly decurrent rows of skeined H. from Ar. in the flowering zone; **Fl.** 6 cm lg., pink to greenish-yellow.—Jamaica (e.g. near Port Henderson). If the plant mentioned under P. polygonus (of candelabra-like habit, with the unusual yellowish-red Fl.-colour and not identified by Ekman and Werdermann) proves to be identical with P. swartzii, then this extends its range to Santo Domingo.

P. tehuacanus (Wgt.) Byl. & Rowl. (2B–b)
Bo. tree-like, with a **trunk**; **branches** arising from the lower part of the trunk, obliquely ascending, light green but with a strong blue tinge, c. 6 cm $\emptyset$; **Ri.** 15; **Sp.** numerous, c. 25, thin, acicular, pungent, brittle, walnut-brown, **Csp.** scarcely distinguishable as such, c. 3–4, $\pm$ thickened below, to 2 cm lg.; **Pseudo-Ceph.** in the crown and reaching quite a long way down, consisting of a web of soft H., said to be bluish-grey, flowering zone with intermittent dense H.-development; **Fl.** high on the flanks, colour ?—Mexico (neighbourhood of Tehuacan (Weingart); Dawson reported plants of this type from Oaxaca, near Totolapan).

P. tuberculatus (Werd.) Byl. & Rowl. (2A)
Bo. to 4 m h., mostly branching from the base; **branches** dark green, to 4 cm $\emptyset$, horizontally spreading and then upcurving; **Ri.** c. 7, strongly tuberculate; **Ar.** large, brownish to grey, especially at the apex, H. lacking; **Rsp.** c. 9–13, acicular, to 1.5 cm lg.; **Csp.** c. 4–7, stouter, 1–2 of these to 4 cm lg., all flexible, dark-tipped, horn-coloured becoming blackish-brown; **Fl.** c. 6 cm lg., white; **Fr.** small, c. 2.5 cm $\emptyset$.—Brazil (Pernambuco, Serra Negra; N. Bahia, Aracy). Resembles P. minensis, but without

any H.-development.

P. tuberculosus Rauh & Backbg. (2B–b)
Bo. erect, shrubby; **branches** dark green, 5–10 cm
∅; **Ri.** 11–12, 1 cm br., initially divided by strong
cross-furrows, these later flattening so that the Ri.
are strongly tuberculate down to midway; **Ar.**
whitish-brownish; **Rsp.** c. 15, 3–8 cm lg.; **Csp.** to 4,
1.5–4 cm lg.; all **Sp.** brownish, often ± flecked, c. 4
mm lg. in the crown; **Pseudo-Ceph.** of curly apical
H. to 8 mm lg.; flowering zone ?; **Fl.** ?—N. Peru
(Rio Saña valley).

P. tweedyanus (Br. & R.) Byl. & Rowl. (2B–b)
Bo. a tall shrub; **branches** steeply ascending, at first
and for a longer time intensely blue, as if frosted;
Ri. 7–9; **Ar.** grey; **Sp.** very variable, either equal
and short, to 12, thin, to c. 2 cm lg., or recognizable
as 12 Rsp. and 4 cruciform Csp., the latter to 4 cm
lg., usually directed ± downwards (in P. gironensis: laterally and upwards!), the bottom one
often to 6 cm lg.; **Sp.** either light with a dark tip, or
mostly concolorous black at first, especially the
longer ones, or flecked, or light below, the stoutest
ones rather thickened below; **Pseudo-Ceph.** consisting of stronger H. at the apex, those in the
lateral flowering zone much longer and denser,
pure white, sometimes developing intermittently;
Fl. to 7 cm lg., white; **Fr.** red.—S. Ecuador (Santa
Rosa), N. Peru (E. Sechura).

P. ulei (K. Sch. non Gürke) Byl. & Rowl. (2B–b)
(Cephalocereus robustus Br. & R.)
Bo. treelike, to 7 m h., trunk 1–2 m ∅ (acc. K.
Sch.); **branches** pale blue above, directed horizontally, later upwards, to 10 cm ∅; **Ri.** c. 8; **Ar.**
crowded; **Sp.** more clearly differentiated on new
growth, later more intermingled, c. 10–12, subulate, dark, to c. 2 cm lg., appreciably longer in
young plants; **Pseudo-Ceph.** scarcely developed on
young plants, later in dense long tufts in the
flowering zone, brown (K. Sch.) or silvery (Werd.),
H. to 6 cm lg.; **Fl.** to 5 cm lg., white; **Fr.** reddish,
carmine inside; **S.** slightly glossy.—Brazil (Cabo
Frio). (P. robustus Ritt.?)

P. urbanianus (K. Sch.) Byl. & Rowl. (2B–b)–(2B–a)
Bo. simple or branching from below, to 4 m h.;
branches light to dark green, not frosted, 4–5 cm ∅,
to 30 cm ∅ near the base of old plants; **Ri.** 8–12;
Sp. 10–13, stoutly bristly, flexible, brownish-red at
first, then ash-grey tipped reddish, **Csp.** 3–4, to 1.5
cm lg.; **Pseudo-Ceph.**: ± white and flocky above,
flowering zone with white flocky clusters to c. 2 cm
lg., arranged on one side only, the Sp. here
increased to 25, resembling horse-hair, to 8 cm lg.;
Fl. 6 cm lg. or less, 4 cm ∅, pale or reddish-

yellow.—W. Indies (Guadeloupe, possibly also
Grenada).

Piptanthocereus Ricc.: a name taken again into use
by Ritter in part, quite unnecessarily, for the Genus
Cereus (Herm.) Mill.

Polaskia Backbg. (147)

Tree-like Cerei with stout branches and relatively
small flowers of very unusual character: the
extremely short tube and the imbricately scaly
ovary are topped by the perianth which is recurved
obliquely downwards; the anthers, which crowd
round the style, are fairly long and in erect clusters.
The small spherical fruit bears distant bundles of
short spines; the seeds are black. The genus is
monotypic.—Distribution: Mexico [(R).]
This genus starts my Group "Pachycerei Berg.
emend. Backbg.", which will be discussed briefly
here. It is remarkable that the northern distribution
includes further monotypic genera, as well as
Polaskia, in which the flowers are unusual:
Heliabravoa, Carnegiea, Lemaireocereus, Marginatocereus, Isolatocereus, Escontria and Hertrichocereus, as well as the following with cephalioid
development: Cephalocereus, Backebergia and
Haseltonia. All these are clearly differentiated by
floral characters. In other Groups I have always
included plants where the relationship is clearly
recognisable; in the "Polyanthocerei", for instance, I referred to Myrtillocactus and Lophocereus those species where both the relatively small
flowers, often with several appearing simultaneously from a single areole, and the fruits testify
to a closer relationship.
The often conspicuous differences between a
number of genera have been exposed as a result of
my published work over many years. If other
conclusions are later drawn from this work—as for
example by Buxbaum—then it can be said they rest
predominantly on unproven assumptions. But
until such time as we are able to show how the
phenomenon arose whereby individual species are
sometimes so strongly demarcated from one
another by the structure and other floral characters, the only practical possibility is to classify by
progressive reduction as explained in the Systematic Survey; and to gather into a single Group
these usually strongly stemmed species and groups
of species, even including those with evolutionary
stages of cephalium-development; that being done,
they can be classified as far as possible according to
the line of reduction of the shoot-character in the
flower. There is as yet no satisfactory explanation
as to how such strongly differentiated species as
those of Polaskia, Escontria and Heliabravoa, for

instance, came into existence within an often relatively restricted area. For the time being even the phylogeneticist can prove nothing, and we can only establish the fact that widely different forms have arisen. The reason is still not known to us, only that they have arisen in quite a narrow area within a similar environment; and this factor, as well as an assessment of the characters, argues the strong probability of a closer relationship, and allows us to draw all these Cerei into a single Group, without making any far-reaching unification. The important point has been to work out clearly the differing floral characters; even authors like Britton and Rose did not always succeed in doing this—rather surprisingly, in the face of so characteristic a flora as that of the great Mexican Cerei. This classification required individual and sometimes monotypic genera because of the principles stated in my Systematic Survey: that basically only the facts of Nature determine a classification. Any more extensive grouping, and the reasoning behind it, had been based on a purely theoretical and fictitious treatment, despite the obvious floral differences shown by these remarkable large Mexican Cerei. Obviously it would be interesting to find an explanation, based for instance on phylogenetic considerations, but the most pressing task of our times is a clear and comprehensive arrangement of the different forms developed in Nature; and such explanations, at least as they stand at present, produce more confusion than enlightenment.

P. chichipe (Goss.) Backbg. (T.)
Bo. tree-like, to 5 m h., with a short **trunk** 0.8–1 m ∅, the **crown** strongly branching; **branches** to c. 10 cm ∅, with yellowish flesh; **Ri.** mostly to 9, acute, thickened around the Ar.; **Rsp.** 6–7–9, 1 cm lg.; **Csp.** 1, somewhat longer than the radials, often thickened below; **Fl.** rather small, ± creamy-white, without Sp.; **Fr.** small, 2–2.5 cm ∅, red inside and out, **Ar.** small and short-felty, distant, with small clusters of Sp.; **S.** small, black.—Mexico (Puebla, near Tehuacan; Oaxaca, NW. of Tamazulapan). Juvenile plants are pruinose. (Fig. 338.)

Porfiria Böd. (227)

Bödeker erected the genus on the basis of the differential factors of the Systematic Survey: the carrot-like base, the sizeable flowers and the reputedly quickly maturing fruit. I consider the species attributed to this genus as being still insufficiently clarified, but I list it here since the name is still in common use; in my view it is not sufficiently distinct from Mammillaria. The name P. coahuilensis Böd. (1925–26) was changed to P.

schwartzii (Frič) Böd. (1929) because Haagea schwartzii Frič (1926) had to regarded as a valid basionym. The name P. coahuilensis v. albiflora Böd. was only a proposal; the plant in question was later described by Bödeker as Mammillaria albiarmata Böd., as a comparison of the characteristics will show.—Distribution: N. Mexico. [(R).]

Porfiria schwartzii (Frič) Böd. (T.): **Mammillaria schwartzii** (Böd.) Backbg.
Bo. simple, with a stout napiform root, c. 4 cm ∅, flattened above; **sap** milky; **Tub.** erect, c. 12 mm lg., ± 3-sided; **Ar.** woolly at first; **Ax.** ± woolly; **Rsp.** 16, thin, whitish-grey, to 6 mm lg.; **Csp.** 0–1, brownish, 6 mm lg.; all **Sp.** minutely rough; **Fl.** bellshaped-funnelform, to 3 cm ∅, whitish, with the centre a faint pink; **Fr.** clavate, crimson, large; **S.** brilliant light brown.—Mexico (Coahuila, San Pedro). [(R).]

Pseudoespostoa Backbg. (179)

Moderately large Cerei, branching from the base, with hair-development resembling white cotton-wool, and a lateral superficial cephalium of brownish-white wool, without bristles; the fruits are sizeable white berries, less hairy than in Espostoa, and the seeds are glossy black (not matt black as in Espostoa). A further important difference is the following: Espostoa forms a tall shrub or a tree, and has a grooved cephalium. These differences and the fact that unification with Espostoa often leads to E. lanata being confused with Pseudoespostoa melanostele, would appear to make segregation of the genera advisable, but Pseudoespostoa is still, quite incomprehensibly, resisted by some authors. The two genera are undoubtedly closely related, but they cannot be combined if the two types of cephalium are to be kept distinct, and obviously this should be done since these developments are constant and always similar so that they represent a good diagnostic character since they are typical of the flowering region in each genus. Where this fact has not been recognised, superfluous new combinations have resulted, and the synonymy is overloaded.— Distribution: Pacific side of Peru (from the Pisco Valley in the S., to the Rio Saña Valley in the N., with a considerable variation in altitude: from 800–2400 m above sea-level.) [(R).] See also under Espostoa (introduction) regarding the segregating of this genus from Pseudoespostoa.

P. melanostele (Vpl.) Backbg. (T.)
Bo. branching from the base, to 2 m h.; **branches** greyish-green, to 10 cm ∅; **Ri.** c. 25, divided into low Tub.; **Ar.** fairly close; **H.** at first forming a

dense cap, later becoming laxer; **Sp.** numerous, mostly thin, almost bristly, scarcely 5 mm lg., interspersed with others, usually solitary, which are much stouter and longer, to 4 cm lg., yellow; **Ceph.** yellowish-brown, extending over c. 8 Ri., not rising from a groove or seam (as in Espostoa); **Fl.** c. 5.4 cm lg., white; **Tu.** slightly hairy above; **Ov.** with a few hairlets; **Fr.** white to yellowish-white, very weakly hairy.—Peru (Rio Pisco to Rio Saña). Double-sided cephalia are known to occur. Wool and Sp. later become ± blackish, hence the specific name: "dark column". Sp. rather variable in length and character. (Fig. 339.)

    v. **inermis** Backbg.: **Bo.** mostly more strongly hairy; **Csp.** less noticeable, not clearly longer and yellow; **H.** remaining white longer.—Central Peru (Matucana);

    v. **rubrispina** Ritt., not yet described: some **Sp.** short, reddish.

Pilocereus haagei and dautwitzii, held by some authors to be identical with Vaupel's spec., can no longer be satisfactorily clarified, as Werdermann has shown.

Ritter mentions the former name, as Espostoa, in "Taxon" XIII: 4.143. 1964, giving the following divergences:

P. nana (Ritt.) Backbg. n. comb. (Espostoa nana Ritt., l.c.)

Bo. to 1.5 m h.; **branches** to 8 cm ∅; **Ar.** white or pale yellow; **Sp.** pale yellow; **Rsp.** c. 30, c. 7.5 mm lg.; **Csp.** 1; **Ceph.** white or palé yellow; **Fl.** obviously little different from that of the preceding spec.; **S.** glossy.—Peru (Dept. Ancash, below Caras, or Huallanca, in the Cañon del Pato). Possibly not a valid spec.?

The modest height and glossy seeds clearly make this plant referable to Pseudoespostoa, since these are characters common to all; equally, inclusion in Espostoa is unacceptable, since the characters mentioned are uniformly divergent.

Pseudolobivia (Backbg.) Backbg. (97)

The reasons for segregating this genus, with a summary of the principal diagnostic characters, have already been given under Echinopsis. For details, the reader is referred there. There is a stronger resemblance to Lobivia in the "hatchet-shaped" rib-tubercles, except for P. aurea and P. luteiflora in which the slender yellow diurnal flowers in themselves demand a special position. In the other species also the flowers are either open during the day only, or remain so even when they started to open towards evening on the previous day; but here differences in times of opening have little significance since these differences are also

present in Lobivia. In 2 species of Pseudolobivia the flowers are as short as in Lobivia, while in others they are as long as in Echinopsis, but more slender; this feature, together with the often vivid colours of red and yellow in addition to white, equally clearly show the intermediate status of the genus. Some species—e.g. P. ferox and P. wilkeae—cannot be satisfactorily placed except in a special genus such as this, where hooked spines occur in part, either at first or throughout, whereas in Echinopsis they are unknown.—Distribution: from the Bolivian Highlands to N. Argentina. [(R).]

P. acanthoplegma Backbg.: **Lobivia acanthoplegma** (Backbg.) Backbg.

P. ancistrophora (Speg.) Backbg. (T.)
Bo. flattened-spherical, to c. 8 cm ∅; **Ri.** 15–16; **Rsp.** 3–7, recurved and spreading, to 15 mm lg.; **Csp.** 1, sometimes to 4, stouter, sometimes rather darker at first; **Fl.** c. 12–16 cm lg., unscented, white, **Tu.** slender; **Fr.** 1.6 cm lg., green.—Argentina (Tucuman-Salta). Fl. remain open for 2 days.

P. aurea (Br. & R.) Backbg.
Bo. spherical to elongated, to 10 cm h.; **Ri.** 14–15, acute; **Ar.** brown at first; **Rsp.** c. 10, to c. 1 cm lg.; **Csp.** 1, sometimes to 4, stouter, sometimes rather flat, to 3 cm lg.; **Sp.**: radials whitish, **Csp.** dark to blackish at first; **Fl.** 9 cm lg., 8 cm ∅, lemon-yellow, deeper yellow inside.—Argentina (Córdoba, Cassafousth).

    v. **elegans** (Backbg.) Backbg.: **Pet.** narrow, ray-like, glossy;

    v. **fallax** (Oehme) Backbg.: **Ri.** 12; **Rsp.** 7–9; **Csp.** 1, to 4.5 cm lg.; all **Sp.** blackish at first, **Csp.** sometimes greyish-reddish; **Fl.** to 7 cm lg., to 6 cm ∅, lemon-yellow, pink when fading.—Argentina (Córdoba ?). Bo. matt, greyish-green;

    v. **grandiflora** (Backbg.) Backbg.: **Fl.** rotate, large; **Pet.** 1 cm br., crowded.—Same locality as the type.

P. boyuibensis (Ritt.) Backbg. n. comb. (Echinopsis boyuibensis Ritt., Succulenta 44: 2, 25. 1965).
Bo. resembling P. obrepanda; **Ri.** 10–12, less notched; **Rsp.** 2–6, 7–20 mm lg., longest ones mostly hooked; **Csp.** 0–1, 2–4 mm lg., mostly hooked; **Fl.** 9 cm lg., 6 cm ∅, probably white.—Bolivia (Dept. Sta. Cruz, W. of Boyuibe) (FR 777a). [Haage adds: **S.** purse-shaped, matt.]

P. callichroma (Card.) Backbg. n. comb. (Echinopsis callichroma Card., Kakt. u.a. Sukk., 16 : 3, 49–50. 1965).
Bo. rather flattened-spherical, to 3 cm h., to 15 cm ∅, greyish-green; **Ri.** 17–19, acute, with hatchet-

shaped Tub. c. 1 cm h., 1.2 cm br.; **Ar.** 1–2.5 cm apart, elliptic, grey; **Sp.** 12–14, centrals not distinguishable, 2–6 cm lg., flexible, thin, pungent, strongly bent, grey; **Fl.** light magenta, no size stated; **Sep.** c. 3.5 × 0.6 cm; **Pet.** broadly lanceolate, c. 3 × 0.8 cm, very light magenta or reddish-pink with a darker M.-stripe; **Tu.** to 9 cm lg., green, with brown and black wool; **Ov.** to 1.5 cm lg., green, wool as for the Tu.; **Fil.** in 2 Ser., white; **style** green below, pale yellow above.— Bolivia (Dept. Cochabamba, Prov. Tapacari, road to Cami, 2700 m).

One of those species in which the overall characters, and above all the Fl.-colour, demonstrate that unless Pseudolobivia is segregated, then it is impossible to separate Echinopsis and Lobovia.

P. calorubra (Card.) Backbg. n. comb. (Echinopsis calorubra, Card., Nat. C. & S. J., 12 : 3, 62. 1957). **Bo.** depressed-spherical, to 14 cm ∅, 6–7 cm h., light green; **Ri.** 16, divided into hatchet-shaped Tub.; **Ar.** 2.5 cm apart, in the depressions of the notches; **Rsp.** 9–13, somewhat curving, one of them yellowish; **Csp.** 1, straight, to 2.5 cm lg.; **Sp.** subulate, later grey, brown-tipped; **Fl.** to 15 cm lg.; **Sep.** lanceolate, green outside, reddish inside; **Pet.** spatulate, orange-red above, bluish-pink towards the base; **Fil.** of the lower Ser. green below, lilac-pink at midway, red above, those of the upper Ser. white below, lilac-pink at midway and red above; **style** green with yellow **Sti.**—Bolivia (Prov. Valle Grande, on the road Comarapa-San Isidro, 1900 m).

P. carmineoflora Hoffm. & Backbg. **Bo.** depressed-spherical, c. 7 cm ∅, 4 cm h., matt, dull green; **Ri.** c. 14, acute; **Ar.** ± brownish; **Rsp.** 10–12, to 2.6 cm lg.; **Csp.** (2–) 3–4, in part ± angular below, thickened below, mostly curving upwards or more strongly bent over the crown; **Sp.** horn-coloured, later grey, at first rather darker; **Fl.** c. 7.5 cm lg., carmine.—Bolivia (vicinity of Cochabamba). Fl. opens only for one morning, in sunshine. (Fig. 340) A very similar plant, with 14 similarly notched and acute **Ri.**, had only 9 **Rsp.** c. 2 cm lg.; **Csp.** 2, one above the other, to 3 cm lg.; **Sp.** pale horn-coloured, rough; **Fl.** c. 10 cm lg., almost 6 cm ∅, **Pet.** more carmine towards the throat, more salmon-coloured towards the margin, not as intensely carmine as the **Fil.** and the **style**; **Tu.** green, forming a weak S-shape, with grey and brown H.; **hymen** green. Either the spec. is rather variable, or this is a uniformly divergent plant which must be considered a valid variety. No judgment is possible on the basis of only two plants. However the type, with its Fl. opening first about 9 a.m., is very typical of the genus. Cf. also P. toralapana (Card.) Backbg.

P. ducis-pauli (Frič) Krainz, and v. rubriflora Schütz (Fričiana Rada I, 7, 1962): **Pseudolobivia longispina** (Br. & R.) Backbg., and variety.

P. ferox (Br. & R.) Backbg. **Bo.** eventually fairly large, spherical, to 20 cm lg. and ∅; **Ri.** to 30, acute, ± sharply divided into oblique Tub. to 3 cm lg.; **Rsp.** 10–12, flexible, to 6 cm lg.; **Csp.** 3–4, to 15 cm lg., upcurving, flexible; **Sp.** sometimes darker at first; **Fl.** white, moderately long; **Tu.** fairly slender below; **Per.** widely opening.—Bolivia (E. of Oruro).

P. fiebrigii (Gürke) Backbg.: **Pseudolobivia obrepanda** v. **fiebrigii** (Gürke) Backbg.

P. frankii Bosz. **Bo.** broadly spherical; **Ri.** c. 14, divided by rather deeply sunken Ar. into narrow, acute, scarcely offset Tub.; **Ar.** white, fairly large; **Rsp.** very unequal, to c. 1 cm lg., sometimes very short, whitish-grey, sometimes dark-tipped; **Fl.** ± light violet-reddish.—Origin ?

P. hamatacantha (Backbg.) Backbg. **Bo.** flattened-spherical, to 15 cm ∅, 7 cm h., leaf-green; **Ri.** to 27, acutely tuberculate; **Sp.** 8–15, 4–12 mm lg., yellowish-white to horn-coloured, several distinguishable as Csp., 1 curving to the crown and bent or even hooked; **Fl.** to 20 cm lg., white, scented; **Fr.** green, 4 cm lg.—Argentina (Salta).

P. kermesina Krainz **Bo.** hemispherical, eventually quite large, to over 15 cm ∅, deep green; **Ri.** 15–23, ± tuberculately thickened around the Ar.; **Rsp.** 11–16, to 12 mm lg., thin-subulate, rusty-yellow at first, tipped dark brown, later grey, stiff, pungent, rough; **Csp.** 4–6, projecting, straight or curving to the Bo., to 2.5 cm lg., rather stouter, coloured as the Rsp., rather darker at first; **Fl.** to c. 18 cm lg., 9 cm ∅, unperfumed, carmine to lighter.—Argentina (?)*

P. kratochviliana (Backbg.) Backbg. **Bo.** flattened-spherical, dark green, to c. 6 cm ∅, 3–4 cm h.; **Ri.** to 18, acute, divided into rather low Tub.; **Sp.** to 15–18, **Csp.** 1–2(–4), to 5 cm lg., darker at first, all later greyish-white; **Fl.** at most 5 cm lg., white, with rather plentiful blackish H.— Argentina (Salta). (Fig. 341.)

*Re-collected recently in the vicinity of Santa Victoria in Argentina, near the Rio Bermejo where it forms the frontier with Bolivia. Fl. can also be white. ("Echinopsis mamillosa var. kermesina" [Krainz] Friedrich.) Data and colour-illustration, K.u.a.S. calendar (Germany), 1977. (Translator's note.)

P. lecoriensis (Card.) Backbg. n. comb. (Echinopsis lecoriensis Card., C. & S.J. [US], XXXV: 5, 158–159. 1963).
Bo. to 60 cm h., spherical to cylindric, to 25 cm ⌀, greyish-green; **Ri.** c. 24, acute, notched; **Ar.** 2.5 cm apart, grey; **Rsp.** 12–14, pectinate, 3–7 cm lg., curving upwards; **Csp.** 2–4, to 9 cm lg., bent upwards; all **Sp.** subulate, robust, stiff, whitish-grey, tipped purplish-brown; **Fl.** apical, funnelform, 10 cm lg., 8 cm ⌀, whitish, inner Pet. tipped lilac; **style** light green; **Sti.** 11, greenish-yellow.—Bolivia (Prov. Linares, Dept. Potosí, Pampa de Lecori, 3400 m).
A typical Pseudolobivia, habit and flower-length showing they constitute a separate group of spec., as Cardenas himself pointed out. Fl., as also in many Lobivias, remain open at night.

P. leucorhodantha (Backbg.) Backbg.
Bo. flattened-spherical, brownish to greyish-green, to 7 cm ⌀, 4 cm h.; **Ri.** 18–20, acute; **Sp.** to 14, 8–10 mm lg., a few Csp. recognisable, 1 more distinct, projecting, bent at the tip; **Fl.** c. 10 cm lg., light pink outside, delicate white inside; **Fr.** oblong, 2 cm lg.—Argentina (Salta).

P. lobivioides (Backbg.) Backbg.: **Pseudolobivia pelecyrhachis** v. **lobivioides** (Backbg.) Backbg. [Haage adds: Dr. H. Friedrich has shown this should be called Echinopsis pelecyrhachis Backbg. v. lobivioides (Backbg.) H. Friedr.]

P. longispina (Br. & R.) Backbg.
Bo. large-spherical to elongated, to 25 cm ⌀; **Ri.** 25–50, acute, with Tub. 2 cm lg.; **Sp.** to 15, stoutly subulate, hooked on new growth, flexible, over 8 cm lg., yellowish to brown; **Fl.** to 10 cm lg., white; **Fr.** ± spherical.—N. Argentina (Jujuy, La Quiaca to Tilcara).
v. **nigra** (Backbg.) Backbg.: **Bo.** eventually thick-columnar, to 30 cm h., bluish-green; **Ri.** over 20, acute, Tub. to 4 cm lg.; **Sp.** 12–14, hooked at first, later to 12 cm lg., dark brown to blackish or soon thus, finally grey; **Fl.** 10 cm lg., with a stout Tu., white.—Argentina (Jujuy).
Recent Uhlig imports, with typical spination, have been very variable in colour; **Pet.** also reddish. Consequently a certain variability has to be assumed, i.e. no delimitation is practicable. Younger plants have fewer Ri. and Sp.
Pseudolobivia ducis-pauli (Frič) v. rubriflora Schütz is therefore referable here. Echinopsis ducis-pauli Först. was described without data on Fl.: "Ri. 18; Rsp. 6–8, c. 2 cm lg.; Csp. 1, of equal length; Sp. all purplish-brown at first". Frič believed he had re-collected the plant described by Förster, but the description is too brief for any identification to be made.

P. luteiflora Backbg. n. sp.
Bo. spherical, dull dark green, capable of flowering at 4.5 cm ⌀; **Ri.** 13–14, acute, 10–12 mm br., 7–10 mm h.; **Ar.** brownish-white at first, soon glabrous, c. 1 cm apart; **Rsp.** 7–9, acicular, thin to rather stouter, yellowish-white, more brownish at first, to 5–6 mm lg., ± thickened below; **Csp.** mostly 3, subulate, 2 upper ones blackish-brown or dark reddish-brown at first, to c. 6 mm lg., lower one projecting, light, with a red, much-thickened base, to 2–2.3 cm lg., stouter than the 2 others; **Fl.** c. 7 cm lg., 4–5 cm ⌀, without a ring of wool; **buds** white-hairy; **Tu.** c. 4.5 cm lg., c. 0.5 cm ⌀, with greyish-black H., with thin spiny Sc., to 4 mm lg., brownish; **Ov.** oblong, green, to 12 mm lg., 6 mm ⌀; **Pet.** 2.5 cm lg., c. 6 mm br., narrowly spatulate, acuminate; **Sep.** pale yellow outside, olive-brown inside; **Fil.** yellow, in 2 Ser.; **style** pale green, 2.5 cm lg.; **Sti.** 4 mm lg., pale green; **Fr.** ?—N. Argentina. (Fig. 97.) Found by Frau Muhr (Uhlig No. U 2185.) The only spec. of the genus with Sc. modified into Sp., but with the slender Fl. lacking a ring of wool, and thus presenting a sort of "missing link" to Acanthocalycium.

P. nigra (Backbg.) Backbg.: **Pseudolobivia longispina** v. **nigra** (Backbg.) Backbg.

P. obrepanda (SD.) Backbg.
Bo. ± depressed-spherical, glossy, dark to greyish-green, rarely offsetting; **Ri.** divided into hatchet-shaped Tub. c. 2 cm lg.; **Rsp.** 9–11, to 1 cm lg.; **Csp.** 1–3, to 5 cm lg.; **Sp.** stiff, whitish to dark brown, **Rsp.** mostly pectinate; **Fl.** to 20 cm lg., white, parsley-scented; **Tu.** ± bent.—Bolivia (Cochabamba area).
v. **fiebrigii** (Gürke) Backbg.: **Fl.** with a straight Tu.; **Pet.** more erect; perfume pleasant (not of parsley, as in the type).

P. orozasana (Ritt.) Backbg.-"Cactus", 20 : 83, 61. 1965 (Echinopsis mamillosa v. orozasana Ritt., Succulenta 44 : 1, 25. 1965).
Bo. broadly spherical, to 20 cm ⌀, capable of flowering at 7.5 cm ⌀; **Ri.** with hatchet-shaped Tub.; **Rsp.** 12–18, 1–2.5 cm lg.; **Csp.** 6–12, 0.8–3.5 cm lg., straight; **Fl.** to 20 cm lg., opening in full sunshine, c. 8 cm ⌀, pure white; **Tu.** c. 17 cm lg., slender, green, with brown H.; **Sep.** recurved, greenish, rather narrow; **Pet.** broadly spatulate; **Fil.** white; **An.** cream; **style** greenish; **Sti.** greenish-white.—Bolivia (Prov. Arce, Orozas) (FR 779). (Fig. 342.)
The characters of Ri. and Fl. suggest this is better regarded as an independent spec. Fl.-data added by me, on the basis of my observations in the Marnier Collection.

P. pelecyrhachis (Backbg.) Backbg.
Bo. flattened-spherical, green; **Ri.** c. 20, not broad, rounded above; **Tub.** oblong, sometimes ± chin-like, narrower above; **Rsp.** 9, 5–8 mm lg., white, tipped yellow; **Csp.** 0 or 1, short, ± bent; **Fl.** c. 10 cm lg., white, with whitish-grey H.—Argentina (Salta).
    v. **lobivioides** (Backbg.) Backbg.: **Bo.** sometimes elongated eventually, dark green; **Ri.** 19, acute, Tub. only slightly chin-like; **Rsp.** 14, yellow; **Csp.** missing or to 4, straight, to 1 cm lg.; **Fl.** white; **Pet.** ± erect.—Argentina (Salta).

P. polyancistra (Backbg.) Backbg.
Bo. flattened-spherical, to only c. 6 cm ∅, mostly smaller; **Ri.** 17–30, narrow, slightly rounded and tuberculate, light green; **Sp.** numerous, fine, bristly, **Csp.** scarcely distinguishable as such, often bent to hooked, sometimes only short, all irregularly arranged, to 1.2 cm lg.; **Fl.** to 10 cm lg., white, scented; **Tu.** very slender.—Argentina (Salta). (Fig. 343.)

P. potosina (Werd.) Backbg.
Bo. spherical to elongated, to c. 8 cm ∅ or more, vivid green, slightly glossy; **Ri.** c. 13, acute, divided into obliquely arranged Tub., or the Ri. discontinuous; **Ar.** to 5 cm apart, large, dirty light brown at first; **Sp.** 9–13, scarcely differentiated, whitish to rust-red, black-tipped, later brownish-grey, to 4 cm lg., very stout, often to 5 mm br., thickened below, at first hooked or curled inwards above; **Fl.** white, fairly stoutly and shortly funnelform, **Pet.** spreading.—Bolivia (near Potosí). [Haage adds: Dr. H. Friedrich's studies have shown this should be referred to as Lobivia potosina (Werd.) H. Friedr.]

P. rojasii (Card.) Backbg.
Bo. simple, spherical, to 11 cm ∅, 6 cm h., greyish-green; **Ri.** c. 16, notched, ridges sometimes reddish, tuberculate; **Ar.** grey; **Rsp.** 8–9, 5–14 mm lg.; **Csp.** 1, 15–17 mm lg., curving upwards; all **Sp.** subulate, whitish-grey, brownish-tipped; **Fl.** to 12 cm lg., pale pink, with whitish and brownish H.—Bolivia (Santa Cruz, "El Fuerte", Samaipata).
    v. **albiflora** (Card.) Backbg.: **Ri.** 14, acute; **Rsp.** 6–11, to 2 cm lg., recurved; **Csp.** 1–3, curving upwards; **Fl.** 17 cm lg., white.—Same locality.

P. toralapana (Card.) Backbg. n. comb. (Echinopsis toralapana Card., "Cactus", 19: 82, 41–42. 1964).
Bo. to 4 cm h., 16 cm ∅; **Ri.** c. 13, pale green, Tub. hatchet-shaped; **Ar.** to 3 cm apart; **Sp.** pectinate, 6–10, curving, to 5 cm lg., subulate, greyish-white; **Fl.** to 14 cm lg., bluish-red; **Fil.** pale green below, pale purple above; **style** green.—Bolivia (Prov.

Arani, near Toralapa, 3200 m). Without doubt referable to the complex of P. carmineoflora: see this latter. Possibly only a variety.

P. torrecillasensis (Card.) Backbg. (described as Echinopsis Card.)
Bo. flat, only 1–2 cm h., green, on a thick taproot to 8 cm lg.; **Ri.** 16, notched, acute; **Ar.** 8 mm apart; **Rsp.** 6–7, to 10 mm lg.; **Csp.** 1, to 1 cm lg.; all **Sp.** curving, compressed, acicular, grey; **Fl.** 8 cm lg., red to salmon-red; **Fil.** purple; **Sti.** emerald-green.—Bolivia (Santa Cruz, near Torrecillas). Sits deep in the ground.
Echinopsis torrecillasensis, raised from Cárdenas's seed—Lobivia torrecillasensis hort. europ.—does not conform to Cárdenas's drawing, and is a red-flowered variety of Lob. arachnacantha (see latter).

P. wilkeae Backbg.
Bo. hemispherical to spherical, to over 10 cm ∅, mid-green; **Ri.** 18 and more, acute, at first completely resolved into narrow hatchet-shaped Tub., straight and unbroken below; **Ar.** white; **Rsp.** 6–7, subulate, the top one more central, ± compressed, 2.3–4.5 cm lg.; **Csp.** 1–2, to 9.3 cm lg., horn-coloured, reddish below, sometimes fairly dark, one stoutest Sp. bent to hooked on new growth; **Fl.** c. 8 cm lg., 6.5 cm ∅, whitish-pink.—Bolivia (Uyuni). [Haage adds: Dr. H. Friedrich's studies have shown this should be called Lobivia wilkeae (Backbg.) H. Friedr.]
    v. **carminata** Backbg.: **Ri.** to 26; **Rsp.** 9–11, to 2 cm lg., horn-coloured, stoutly subulate; **Sp.** dark to blackish at first; **Fl.** smaller, 5 cm lg, carmine.— Same locality.

Probably the following should also be referred to this genus:
"Echinopsis (Pseudolobivia) calochrysea Ritt.", FR 985, with a large yellow Fl.

Pseudomammillaria F. Buxb.: **Dolicothele** (K. Sch.) Br. & R., emend. Backbg. Series 2: Microfloridae Tieg.; see under Dolichothele for spec.

Pseudomitrocereus H. Bravo & F. Buxb.: **Mitrocereus** Backbg.

Pseudonopalxochia Backbg. (37)

Among the Epiphyllum-like plants there is an unbroken line of reduction in the shoot-character of the flower, and the individual stages have been segregated as genera. Until recently the stage of indumentum **before** Nopalxochia was missing from the day-flowering plants; then the successful plant-collector T. M. MacDougall found and described this in 1947. The "epiphylloid" group of genera, where all the missing stages have been discovered by degrees, demonstrates the advantages of a classification based on this type of natural differentiation. The flowers of Pseudonopalxochia resemble those of Nopalxochia, but they have 1–4 whitish bristles; the fruits are also bristly.—Distribution: Mexico (Oaxaca). [Vigorous-growing.]

P. conzattianum (T. M. MacDougall) Backbg. (T.)
Bo. shrubby, epiphytic; **shoots** flat, as in Nopalxochia, only moderately broad, sometimes reddish at first; **Fl.** c. 8 cm lg., (beaker-shaped to) funnelform, brilliant red with an orange tinge; **Tu.** only to 2.8 cm lg.; **Fil.** green below, then red, whitish above; **style** red; **Ov.** and **Fr.** with white Br.; **Fr.** green, 4 cm lg., 3 cm $\emptyset$, **Br.** to 10; **S.** dark brown.—Mexico (Oaxaca, near Santiago Lachiguiri).

Pseudopilocereus Buxb.

P. fulvilanatus Buin. & Bred. 1973
Bo. columnar, branching and tree-like, to 3 m h. but often smaller; **branches** 10–11 cm $\emptyset$, green, blue-frosted above; **Ri.** 5(–6), 4 cm br. below, 3 cm h., to 9 cm apart; **Ar.** oval, c. 7 mm lg., 5 mm br.; **flowering Ar.** with thick cushions of golden-brown wool, merging to form a band, other Ar. with short grey felty H.; **Sp.** brown at first, later grey, stout, acicular, mostly pointing obliquely upwards; **Rsp.** c. 11, 10–25 mm lg., radiating; **Csp.** 1, upwardly directed, to 45 mm lg.; **Fl.** nocturnal, bellshaped, 52 mm lg., 33 mm br.; **Tu.** white, glabrous; **pericarpel** 8 mm lg., 14 mm br., thick-walled, light green; **Rec.** 38 mm lg., to 15 mm br., thick-walled, pale green with a blue tint, with Sc. 12 mm lg. above; **Sep.** to 15 mm lg., 7 mm br., light green with light brown, irregularly wavy borders, oval; **Pet.** 11–12 mm br., c. 55 mm lg., white, oval; **Fil.** light brown, lower ones pressed against the wall; **An.** light brown, 1.5 mm lg.; **style** white, c. 45 mm lg., with 8 light brown **Sti.**; **Fr.** dark brown to violet, 4.5 cm $\emptyset$; **S.** ovoid to cap-shaped, 1.5 mm lg., black, glossy.—Brazil (Minas Geraes, northern Serra do Espinhaco, 800–1000 m. Discovered 1968 by A. F. H. Buining and L. Horst). (Fig. 522.)

Pseudorhipsalis Br. & R. (23)

Plants resembling the flat-stemmed Rhipsalis. Flowers solitary, petals spreading, with a short but distinct tube. Kimnach referred these plants to Disocactus, for reasons better suited to a "genetic system", but this is not possible under the systematic arrangement used here. In any event the Disocactus species have uniformly red flowers, whereas all those of Pseudorhipsalis are white, light lemon-yellow or yellowish-white inside; no investigations have yet been made regarding this uniformity of colouring, or the extent to which it characterises the various natural groupings. Nevertheless segregation makes diagnosis simpler, and obviates name-changes which are not urgently necessary.—Distribution: Jamaica, Costa Rica and S. Mexico. [Vigorous-growing.]

P. alata (Swartz) Br. & R. (T.)
Bo. shrubby, to 5 m lg.; **shoots** broadly linear, oblong or lanceolate, also constricted, narrowing and terete below, light green, to 40 cm lg., 4–6 cm br., with a stout M.-Ri.; **Fl.** c. 1.5 cm lg., yellowish-white; **Fr.** a berry 1 cm lg.—Jamaica (W. of the island).
P. harrisii (Gürke) Y. Ito: perhaps a variety here, shoots without any stem-like constriction; Fr. only 5 mm $\emptyset$. Britton and Rose referred "Rhipsalis harrissii Gürke" to the above spec. as a synonym. As far as I know, there have been no satisfactory investigations as to whether the latter should be segregated, either as a spec. or a variety.

P. himantoclada (Rol.-Goss.) Br. & R.
Bo. shrubby, eventually forming large hanging bushes, 1 m lg. or more; **shoots** thin, flat, 4–5 cm br., with serrate margins, vivid green, glossy, tipped reddish at first, terete below, dimensions reduced as branching proceeds; **Fl.** 2.6 cm lg., white inside, pink outside.—Costa Rica (Pozo Azul).

P. macrantha Alex.
Bo. bushy, light green, with terete stemlets, hanging; **shoots** to 90 cm lg., 4.5 cm br., tapering above, notched; **Ar.** grey; **Fl.** solitary or paired, 3 cm $\emptyset$, light lemon-yellow; **Sep.** brownish-orange, reddish below; **Fr.** a spherical red berry 7–8 mm $\emptyset$.—Mexico (Oaxaca, N. of Niltepec and near La Gloria).

Pseudotephrocactus Frič & Krzgr.: an undescribed name for several spec. of Tephrocactus.

Pseudozygocactus Backbg. (28)

The genus is an interesting example of the very great variety of forms which can arise: the plant itself has a confusing resemblance to Zygocactus, but the flowers are small, as in Rhipsalis, and lack a recognisable tube. On the basis of plant-structure it has to be referred to the "Epiphylli", but the small flower is seen as showing a greater degree of reduction, as justified by atavism in Rhipsalis and

Lepismium. Furthermore the ovary is sharply 4-angled and winged as in Schlumbergera, for instance; this is never seen in Rhipsalis, and the flowers are apical.—Distribution: Brazil (Itatiaya Mountains and southwards). [Little is known regarding the cultural requirements of this spec., which is still rare in collections; it can be presumed that, like Rhipsalidopsis, it does better in a shaded position.]

P. epiphylloides (Campos-Porto & Werd.) Backbg. (T.)
Bo. an epiphytic low shrub; **branches** shortly segmented, Seg. to 2.5 cm lg., c. 1 cm br., margins strongly notched; **Ar.** naked, minute; **Fl.** solitary, apical, c. 1 cm lg.; Fl. do occur exceptionally on the margins, just as sometimes seen in Zygocactus. Inclusion in Hatiora with its spherical ovary, as suggested by Buxbaum, is not admissible because of the many points in common with the other "Epiphylli"; **Fr.** ?—Brazil (Itatiaya Mountains, at 1600 m).
v. **bradei** (Campos-Porto & Cast.) Backbg.: **Bo.** bushy, to 80 cm lg., hanging, densely branching; **Seg.** ± tongue-like and elongated, truncated above, scarcely notched on the margins, narrowing below; **Fl.** 2 cm ∅, yellow.—Brazil (Serra Bocaina). (Fig. 344.)

Pterocactus K. Sch. (7)

Small plants with thick taproots and variously shaped stems: spherical or cylindric. The flower is sunk into the apex, with the fruits similarly; as these ripen, the stems thicken above and the fruit is detached by a more or less circular slit. An unusual feature is that the seeds have a winged margin, a character unique to the genus; the width of the wing-like border varies from species to species. 7 species described.—Distribution: S. America, from near the Magellan Straits in W. Argentina to much further north. [Rather difficult on its own roots, flowers more readily if grafted.]

P. australis (Web.) Backbg.
Bo. divided into spherical to clavate Seg.; **R.** napiform, to 8 cm lg., 3 cm ∅; **Seg.** to 8 cm lg., tuberculate; **Rsp.** 10–15, to 4 mm lg., white; **Csp.** 1–2, to 2 cm lg., flattened, whitish to brownish; **Sp.** projecting; **Fl.** to 3 cm ∅, straw-coloured; **S.** wrinkled.—S. Argentina (between the Magellan Straits and Rio Sta. Cruz).
v. **arnoldianus** Backbg.: **Csp.** black, shorter, bent.

P. decipiens Gürke
Bo. with cylindric shoots to 1.2 cm ∅, with dense oblong Tub.; **Sp.** 4–7 mm lg., appressed; **Fl.** 4.5 cm ∅, Pet. with a minute recurved tip; **Sti.** purplish-red(!); **S.** with a thick non-transparent annular wing.—Argentina (near Córdoba). (Fig. 345.)
Referred in part to P. tuberosus, but latter is less tuberculate, shoots more slender, Fl. smaller, and seed-wing thin-membranous and translucent.

P. fischeri Br. & R.
Bo. oblong or cylindric; **shoots** very tuberculate, c. 1.5 cm ∅, to c. 10 cm lg.; **Rsp.** c. 12, bristly, white, c. 6 mm lg., spreading and projecting; **Csp.** c. 4, 1–1.5 cm lg., not flattened, brownish, yellowish-tipped; **Glo.** numerous, yellowish, to 4 mm lg.; **Fl.** ?; **S.** large, with a narrow wing.—S. Argentina (Rio Negro).

P. hickenii Br. & R.
Bo. spherical-clavate, more oblong; **shoots** not very tuberculate, 2–3 cm lg.; **Rsp.** c. 10–14; **Csp.** c. 3–4, scarcely differentiated; **Sp.** all c. 3 cm lg., thin, projecting, yellow above, brown below; **Fl.** to 4 cm ∅, yellowish, with a pink border and a greenish M.-stripe; **S.** 5 mm thick, with a narrow annular wing.—S. Argentina (Comodoro Rivadavia).

P. kuntzei K. Sch.: **Pterocactus tuberosus** (Pfeiff.) Br. & R.

P. marenae (Pars.) Rowl.: **Marenopuntia marenae** (S. H. Pars.) Backbg. While Marenopuntia too has sunken apical Fl., the S. here have no annular wing; moreover the habit is quite divergent from that of Pterocactus; the vast distance separating the two distributions is an argument against any closer relationship.

P. pumilus Br. & R.
Bo. low or prostrate and ascending, with ± shortly cylindric **Seg.** c. 1 cm ∅; **Tub.** virtually absent or minute; **Ar.** quite strongly woolly-felty; **Sp.** fairly short, ± appressed or only slightly projecting, weak, on the Ov. similarly; **Fl.** ?; **S.** with an annular wing 1 mm br.—S. Argentina (Chubut, Puerto Piramides).

P. skottsbergii (Br. & R.) Backbg.
Bo. with spherical Seg.; **R.** thick, napiform, to c. 10 cm lg.; **Seg.** sometimes ± elongated, mostly c. 3 cm ∅; **Ar.** with thick cushions of felt, these crowded; **Sp.** c. 10, black, tipped yellow, 1–2 cm lg., **Csp.** stouter, not flattened; **Fl.** c. 6 cm lg., in dried material reddish to reddish-green; **Ov.** with brown or blackish Sp.; **Fr.** ?—S. Argentina (Terr. Sta. Cruz, Lago Buenos Aires and northwards).

P. tuberosus (Pfeiff.) Br. & R. (T.)
Bo. slender-cylindric; **R.** thick, napiform, to 12 cm

427

lg., 8 cm ∅, sometimes several; **Seg.** brownish-reddish, ± without Tub., to 40 cm lg., 1 cm ∅, ± thickened at the tip; **Ar.** minute; **Sp.** numerous, fine, short, appressed; **Fl.** 3 cm lg., yellow; **Sti.** yellow(!); **Ov.** with numerous Br.; **Fr.** dry; **S.** to 4 mm ∅, with an annular wing to 4 mm br.—W. Argentina (Mendoza, towards the Paso Cruz).

P. valentinii Speg.: **Pterocactus australis** (Web.) Backbg.

Pterocereus MacDoug. & Mir. (156)

Large Cerei with few thinly-winged ribs and cylindric-funnelform flowers which have crowded, outwardly curving scales; the axils of the tube have plentiful brownish felt and several very short yellowish spines, this indumentum missing in the upper part, the ovary similarly. Flowers open only at night. The light carmine spherical fruit has a fleshy wall, and scales which turn red; its axils are felty, and have over 20 dark red spines to 1.4 cm lg.; the pulp is wine-red and the seeds glossy black.

The flower of Anisocereus lepidanthus (Eichl.) Backbg. has very similar scales, but from Eichlam's data the latter plant must be regarded as diurnal, or else its flowers do not close when fading but just shrivel, while the scales are straw-like and the tube, instead of short spines, bears awns 1.5 cm lg.

While Anisocereus gaumeri has few ribs and these are similarly winged, neither bristles nor spines on the flower-tube have been reported, and the flowers do not dry up in the same way, while the dry fruit is very shortly spined. The inadequacy of the description leaves the relationship of this species in doubt (see also Anisocereus).—Distribution: Mexico (Chiapas, NE. of Tuxtla Gutierrez or N. of La Chacona). [No data available regarding cultivation.]

P. foetidus MacDoug. & Mir. (T.)
Bo. to 8 m h., simple or little branching, with a cylindric trunk to 1.5 m h., to 14 cm ∅; **branches** green, suberect, with a cylindric axis; **Ri.** (3–)4, thin to 7 cm h., the ridge slightly notched; **Ar.** white or grey; **Sp.** not differentiated, 10–11(–20), subulate, grey to reddish-black, to 4.8 cm lg., spreading; **Fl.** to 9.5 cm lg., closed during the daytime, with a disagreeable smell (hence the specific name), to c. 4 cm ∅, greenish-white; **Fr.** 4.5 cm ∅; **S.** c. 5 mm lg.—Mexico (see above). (Fig. 346.)

P. gaumeri (Br. & R.) MacDoug. & Mir.: **Anisocereus gaumeri** (Br. & R.) Backbg.

Pygmaeocereus Johns. & Backbg. (91)

Very small cylindric Cerei, mostly offsetting quite freely from the base; flowers slender-funnelform, nocturnal.—Distribution: coastal regions of S. Peru. [(R).(G).]

P. akersii Johns.: only a name (illustration in "Kakt.u.a.Sukk.", 11: 162. 1961); **Sp.** more distant, **Csp.** sometimes longer; perhaps a variety of P. bylesianus, unless any transitional forms are found.

P. bylesianus Andreae & Backbg. (T.)
Bo. short, forming small groups; **St.** scarcely exceeding 10 cm lg.; **Ri.** 12–14, very low, later forming small Tub.; **Ar.** roundish; **Sp.** numerous, dark, becoming grey, radiating, not very strongly interlacing, i.e. in distinct clusters, **Csp.** not discernible; **Fl.** c. 6 cm lg., when fully open at least 6 cm ∅; **Tu.** 5 mm ∅, with flocky H. in the axils, the oblong Ov. similarly.—Peru (Fig. 348, right.)

P. densiaculeatus Backbg.—Descr. Cact. Nov. III: 12. 1963.
Bo. forming small groups by lateral branching; **St.** fairly lg., c. 1.7 cm ∅ measured over the Sp.; **Ri.** c. 18, extremely narrow and low; **Ar.** round, light brownish, only c. 2 mm apart; **Sp.** to over 30, at most 3 mm lg., interlacing, completely concealing the Bo., some of them projecting, all plumose, apical Sp. at first pale reddish, brown-tipped; **Fl.** and **Fr.** ?—Origin ? (Fig. 347.)

The manner of growth resembles that of Mammillaria viperina. The spination is so unusual and attractive that it is essential it should be named, in order that information about it remains available. It is probably referable to Pygmaeocereus, but since the Fl. has never been observed, it cannot with certainty be attributed here.

P. rowleyanus Backbg.
Bo. as in the preceding; **Ar.** round at first, then ± oblong; **Sp.** more numerous, weaker, in several Ser., all white, **Csp.** dark-tipped, clusters denser than in the type-species; **Ar.** very crowded; **Fl.** only ⅔ the ∅ of P. bylesianus and rather shorter.—Peru (Fig. 348, left.)

Pygmaeocereus nigrispinus Akers(?): only a name, probably applicable to the type-species.

Pygmaeolobivia Backbg.: formerly proposed by me as a SG. of Lobivia (1934); it included species which later, because of floral bristles, were referred to Mediolobivia as a SG. with the same name; it is sometimes invalidly used as a generic name.

Pyrrhocactus Berg. emend. Backbg. (106)

This genus occupies a key-position in the series of questions concerning the delimitation and naming of a whole group of S. American spherical Cacti. See also under Horridocactus and Neochilenia. The American authors Kimnach and Hutchison unite all the Chilean species except Copiapoa under Neoporteria, despite the fact that the flowers of the latter genus, as represented by the type-species, are completely uniform in colour, structure and extreme reduction of the indumentum, which is thus a diagnostic character for a separate genus; the views of these authors are thus ill-conceived; or they would then inevitably have to include species of "Pyrrhocactus sensu Ritt.", and the E. Andean species also could no longer be segregated. To these it would be necessary to add Austrocactus and Parodia since they all (or Parodia only in part) have bristly flowers and fruits. The result would be an outsize genus lacking cohesion, which could only cause unnecessary confusion among well-established names. The difficulty of a systematic classification of those groups of species arises from the fact that Castellanos, for instance, attributed a still undescribed species from Mendoza to Austrocactus, whereas the urn-shaped flower clearly pointed to Pyrrhocactus. If the conventional delimitation is not strictly observed, the inevitable consequence would be an unforeseeable extension of the generic concept, with incalculable results; even the characteristic of a softly fleshed body would then be no obstacle (this is only sometimes present, for example, in Lobivia). The recent American procedure would logically demand the use of the name Austrocactus—the prior claimant—for a vast genus of this kind; and for the reasons given above Neoporteria would have to be referred to it. This shows the consequences of a piecemeal treatment of the larger complex of problems which is followed by some authors.

As against this, I have already given sufficient arguments for my segregation of different genera, and no further explanations are needed here. Therefore, on the basis of the arguments advanced under Neochilenia, I include in Pyrrhocactus only the E. Andean species which, for an inconceivable length of time, have developed independently from the Pacific distribution, even despite partial convergence of floral characters. If the procedure is adopted for Rebutia-Sulcorebutia, then it must be followed here. It seems likely that the total number of species is still not known, as demonstrated by the results of recent expeditions. Three new species have been described on the basis of colour-photographs of Lembcke, since they are indisputably new, and so characteristic that the details provided will be sufficient for identification. The flowers of Pyrrhocactus are sometimes beaker-shaped, sometimes densely scaly with felt, at other times more shortly funnelform, but always more strongly woolly with a narrower limb, and clearly distinct from those of the genera Neochilenia and Horridocactus. The floral bristles may vary in number, length and density. Further comparative investigations are needed, both in the field and on living material, in order to delimit the genus more precisely. The flowers are predominantly yellow of various shades. Little information is available regarding seeds.—Distribution: W. Argentina, from Rio Colorado to Salta and Jujuy. [In general, the species do not grow very vigorously on their own R. but all, so far as known, can be grafted and they then grow better and flower more freely.]

Pyrrhocactus Berg. emend. Buxb.
Bodies mostly simple, flat-spherical or later elongated; ribs straight, stout, notched; areoles large, elliptic, felty; spines numerous, subulate, stout, often curving upwards and thickened below, ash-grey to reddish-brown to black; centrals mostly 4, cruciform. Flowers in various shades of yellow, shortly funnelform or beaker-shaped, sometimes with densely felty scales or else more strongly woolly.—Argentina (areas E. of the Andes).

Ritter's names, if not found here, should be sought under Neochilenia or Horridocactus.

P. aconcaguensis Ritt. (FR 542): **Horridocactus aconcaguensis** (Ritt.) Backbg.

P. atrospinosus Backbg.—Descr. Cact. Nov. III: 13. 1963.
Bo. spherical to elongated, bluish-green; **Ri.** to c. 20, quite strongly swollen around the Ar., especially at first; **Ar.** large, with thick brownish-white felt; **Rsp.** in 5–6 pairs, pectinate, strongly interlacing, stoutly subulate, light but also more grey at first; **Csp.** 0 at first, then usually 2 or rather more, those in the apex equal in length to the Fl. when closed, black at first, then more ash-grey, more strongly subulate, erect to porrect, fairly dense and rigidly projecting above; **Fl.** dirty coppery-yellow; **Tu.** short, it and the **Ov.** together forming a ± top-like shape, dark green, with numerous Sc., axils only shortly white-hairy, Br. only few in the upper part; **S.** 1.5 mm lg., matt, black.—W. Argentina (40 km W. of Mendoza). (Fig. 349 above.)

P. bulbocalyx (Werd.) Backbg.
Bo. simple, spherical, light greyish-green; **Ri.** c. 12, rounded, thickened around the Ar. to form round Tub., or transversely depressed; **Ar.** large, oblong, with whitish-grey or lighter felt; **Rsp.** 7–11, stout,

± curving, to 2 cm lg.; **Csp.** typically 4, over 2 cm lg., ± up-curving; **Sp.** all light to faintly reddish, tip or upper part dark; **Fl.** straw-yellow, with a red throat, urn-shaped, 4 cm lg., with several brownish Br., and whitish flock in the Sc.—N. Argentina (locality?). (Fig. 350.)

P. catamarcensis (Web.) Backbg.
Bo. simple, spherical, later columnar, to 50 cm h., to 12 cm ∅, occasionally to 1 m h., dull leaf-green; **Ri.** 13–17, thickened around the Ar.; **Ar.** whitish; **Rsp.** c. 10, light brown or whitish, stiff, subulate, curving, to 2 cm lg.; **Csp.** 4, not thickened below, stouter, more bent, yellow to glossy dark brown; **Fl.** 4.5 cm lg., lemon or golden-yellow, ± urn-shaped.—N. Argentina (San Juan and Catamarca).

P. coliquagenis Ritt. (FR 1450): no description available.

P. dubius Backbg.
Bo. becoming oblong, to c. 20 cm lg.; **Ri.** c. 13, tuberculate; **Ar.** yellowish; **Rsp.** 10–12, horn-coloured, flecked brown, or yellowish-white, dark-tipped, projecting, to 1.5 cm lg.; **Csp.** (1–)2, bent ± upwards, to 2.5 cm lg., coloured like the Rsp.; **Fl.** with a short Tu., 3 cm lg., washy greenish-yellow; **Fr.** green.—N. Argentina.
In the Famatina area Lembcke collected a plant which appears to be referable here: Sp. unequal, dissimilar; Csp. to 4, sometimes brownish at first, not always regularly central. Otherwise it resembles the preceding spec., and the divergences are not unacceptable. Seen at Uhlig: No. U 2019.

P. floccosus Ritt. (FR 545): Syn. **Neochilenia floccosa** Backbg.

P. griseus Backbg. ("Die Cact.", VI: 3906/7. 1962, Fig. 3548): on the basis of the Fl., now seen, this is **Acanthocalycium griseum** (Backbg.) Backbg.

P. melanacanthus Backbg.—Descr. Cact. Nov. III: 13. 1963.
Bo. ± spherical, leaden-grey; **Ri.** c. 12, rounded, fairly broad below, moderately swollen around the Ar., the lower Tub. sometimes with a ± chin-like projection; **Sp.** c. 10, fairly lg., those in the crown ± overtopping the half-open Fl., ± curving, ± projecting, the longest Csp. ± extending sideways, those in the crown fairly erect; **Sp.** all black at first, later ash-grey, ± interlacing; **Fl.** truncate-funnelform, lighter to intenser golden-yellow, brownish-yellow outside; **Tu.** with dense reddish Sc., enveloped in a web of curly H., but the Sc. clearly visible, with a few fine Br. above; **style** and capitately connivent **Sti.** creamy-white.—N. Ar-

gentina (San Juan). (Fig. 349 below, 351.)

P. neokrausei Ritt. (FR 1450): no description available.

P. sanjuanensis (Speg.) Backbg.
Bo. spherical to elongated, matt, dark green, later dirty grey; **Ri.** 13, ± tuberculate, more continuous below; **Ar.** fairly large; **Rsp.** 9–15; **Csp.** c. 3–7; **Sp.** ash-grey below, pink or reddish-chestnut above; **Fl.** funnelform; **Tu.** and **Ov.** densely scaly, with several Br. above, not strongly hairy; **Pet.** rather narrow.—N. Argentina (San Juan, very rare!). Fig. 1515 in "Die Cact.", III: 1572. 1959.

P. setiflorus Backbg. nom.nov.—Descr. Cact. Nov. III: 13, 1963 (P. setosiflorus Backbg., homonym of P. setosiflorus Ritt.) (T.?)
Bo. spherical to elongated, bluish-green; **Ri.** c. 15, at first strongly tuberculate, Tub. later confluent; **Ar.** large, with brownish-white felt; **Rsp.** c. 8–10, upper ones very subulate, lower ones acicular, ± curving, all blackish at first, reddish below, some Sp. lighter; **Csp.** c. 4, subulate, scarcely distinguishable from the stouter Rsp., to c. 2.5 cm lg. or more, black to brownish-black at first, reddish below; **Sp.** sometimes ± flecked; **Fl.** ± beaker-shaped, c. 3 cm lg., salmon-reddish, more orange when fading; **Tu.** and **Ov.** green, both with fairly long projecting and ± spiny Br., lower ones whitish, upper ones brownish.—W. Argentina (close to the Chilean frontier). This is perhaps "Pyrrhocactus strausianus sensu Berger", lectotype of the genus, but unquestionably not Schumann's plant, since for the genuine spec. he gave the locality as "Rio Colorado", while Berger said of the plant he described: "around Mendoza". The above-described plant is said to come from that area. Berger, it is true, gives the Fl.-length as only 1.5 cm, but these dimensions cannot always be assumed to be accurate since they may relate either to fully open or only partially open Fl.; P. setosiflorus Backbg. and P. setosiflorus Ritt. were both published in June 1962 (Ritter's plant in the Dutch journal "Succulenta"). Since my publication, although ready in MS-form a whole year earlier, was only printed on 26.6, and the June issue of "Succulenta" is dated 1.6.62 despite its only being distributed later, I gave my species a new name in order to avoid errors. Since I usually only learn of publications in journals after they have appeared, the name for my description had to be altered, even although mine was doubtless the older description.

P. setosiflorus Ritt.: **Neochilenia setosiflora** (Ritt.) Backbg.

P. strausianus (K. Sch.) Berg.

Bo. shortly columnar, to c. 16 cm h., 9 cm ∅, greyish-green, lighter at first, the crown with little felt, overtopped by the Sp.; **Ri.** 13, 2 cm h., ± tuberculate because of transverse depressions; **Ar.** yellowish at first, then grey; **Sp.** to c. 20, not clearly differentiated, the 4 innermost Sp. stoutest, to 3 cm lg., thickened below, straight or slightly bent, subulate, rigid, pungent, reddish-grey, interlacing; **Fl.** short, funnelform, moderately woolly; **Tu.** with short hyaline or yellowish, reddish-tipped Br.-Sp.—S. Argentina (N. of the middle course of the Rio Colorado). Description acc. Schumann.

The true spec. is illustrated by Weingart in "Kaktusař", title-page, No. 2. 1935. The Fl.-colour, while not stated, seems to be yellowish. The plants often have bluish to rust-coloured Sp. Britton and Rose had already described a spec. from Mendoza under the above name, Berger's description came afterwards. The length of floral Br. is very variable in both spec.

P. subaianus Backbg.

Bo. spherical to elongated; **Sp.** to c. 20, ± equal, interlacing, slightly curving, Csp. little differentiated, directed up towards the crown, thickened below, all Sp. light-coloured; **Fl.** with a conical Tu. and longer Br. above, these being erect, whitish to yellowish, to 1 cm lg.; **Pet.** yellowish; **S.** 1 mm lg., black.—Chilean Highlands.

This spec. seems to have penetrated from the E. Andes, like Weingartia chilensis. The plants, which have fairly dense and light-coloured Sp., grow near Campana at 2000 m.

Two further plants come from the same altitude: one from Horcon de Piedra, yellowish-green, to 40 cm lg.; Ri. to 30; Sp. interlacing, to 30, slightly curving; Fl. urn-shaped, metallic to greenish-yellow; the second spec. grows at the same altitude, near Chicaoma: Bo. bluish-green; Sp. rather darker at first. In my Handbook I gave them both under Horridocactus, since the Fl. seemingly have only a weak indumentum. On the basis of the urn-shaped Fl., however, both could be referable to Pyrrhocactus. Further investigation proved impossible as no further living material has been collected. Acc. to Dr. Kraus, these plants cannot be crossed with spec. of Horridocactus, which suggests they must belong to another genus.

P. taltalensis Ritt. (Horridocactus Ritt., FR 212): Plants raised in the Marnier Collection, from Ritter's seed of that number, had brown Bo. and white Fl. Acc. Winter's catalogue 1962, the Fl. are red. Have the S. been mixed up? A brown-bodied plant with a white Fl. suggests Neochilenia fusca (Muehlpfrdt.) Backbg.

I P. tenuis Ritt. (FR 1453): no description available.

P. transitensis Ritt. (FR 1432): no description available.

P. umadeave (Frič) Backbg.

Bo. spherical, to 10 cm h., to 11 cm ∅, matt, green; **Ri.** c. 18, ± spiralled; **Ar.** white; **Sp.** very numerous, Csp. later undifferentiated, to 35, all Sp. curving upwards, subulate, rigid, pungent, to 3 cm lg. and more, white to tinged brownish-pink, dark-tipped, thickened below, ± frosted, centrals stoutest; immature plants have only c. 16 Ri., shorter Sp. with 1–2(–4) Csp., ± concolorous black at first; **Fl.** to 3.5 cm lg., pale yellowish, woolly, with several yellow Br.; **Fr.** to 4 cm lg., 2 cm br., with little woolly flakes, with floral remains and stouter Br. above, dehiscing by a basal pore.—N. Argentina (Puerto Tastil; Jujuy).

v. **marayesensis** Backbg.—Descr. Cact. Nov. III: 13. 1963: **Bo.** fresh green; all **Sp.** dense, bent towards the crown, almost completely hiding the latter and the upper Bo., all stoutly subulate, concolorous black to almost bluish or greyish-black; **Fl.** white, urn-shaped, pink lower down, Br. missing or inconspicuous; **Sti.** pink; **S.** 1.25 mm lg., slightly glossy, black, finely granular.—N. Argentina (near Marayes). (Fig. 352.)

The following plants occur in the same area: Denmoza erythrocephala and Tephrocactus articulatus v. diadematus or v. papyracanthus.

P. vollianus Backbg.

Bo. cylindric, to 15 cm h., 4 cm ∅; **Ri.** 7, tuberculate; **Ar.** light brown at first; **Rsp.** 18, 3–4 of these thin, to 1 cm lg., others stouter, to 3.5 cm lg.; **Csp.** 5, cruciform with one in the centre, 3.5 cm lg., stouter than the Rsp.; **Fl.** large, yellow, ± urn-shaped, densely felty, with stout reddish-brown Br. to 1.8 cm lg.—S. Argentina.

v. **breviaristatus** Backbg.: **Ri.** 8, weakly tuberculate; **Rsp.** 12–13, some thicker, some thinner, to 2 cm lg.; **Csp.** 3 in a triangle, acicular, thickened below, light brown at first, then dull grey; **Fl.** yellow(?), smaller than in the type, with fewer Br. arranged more in the upper part.

Quiabentia Br. & R. (4)

Mostly shrubby plants, with terete branches, and fleshy leaves without a distinct middle-rib, these later deciduous; one species is tree-like. While there is a certain resemblance to Peireskiopsis, no true glochids are present in the areoles; these are replaced, as far as our present information goes, by thin subsidiary spines. The branches are usually arranged in a whorl. Cardenas has reported glochids as being present on the ovary of Q. pereziensis. Plants of this genus are rare in

European collections; to date only Q. chacoensis has flowered here, but there is no record of the flower-insertion. It is known that in 2 species the flowers are sunken into the shoot-tip and have a narrow ovary. The perianth is fairly large, and light to intense red. Seeds are large and hard, as in all members of the Opuntioideae to which this genus belongs. There is a temptation to regard the genus as primitive or ancestral, but this is contradicted by the flower-position being (as far as is known) apical. Probably Quiabentia is more accurately seen as an extreme evolutionary stage within the broad framework of the Opuntioideae, bearing a resemblance in habit to other leafy plants in the same way as is seen in the leafy Peireskioideae.—Distribution: isolated in the Brazilian catinga (one species); and from E. Bolivia to N. Argentina (Chaco to Jujuy). [(R); the plants must never be kept too cool; and during the growing period they should not be too dry.]

Q. chacoensis Backbg.
Bo. shrubby; **branches** to over 3 cm ∅, green; **Ar.** white; **L.** to 7 cm lg., spatulate, tapering, with a light border; **Sp.** to c. 9, radiating, unequal, to 5 cm lg., light, with thin, readily deciduous Ssp.; **Fl.** red, with a narrow throat; **Fil.** and **style** clustered, projecting.—N. Argentina (Chaco Austral).
v. **jujuyensis** Backbg.: differentiated by the **branches** being fewer, erect, and the **Sp.** less fierce; **L.** broader, more ovate, tapering. The terete and little-branching St. become rather corky.—N. Argentina (Jujuy, Puesto Viejo).

Q. pereziensis Backbg.
Bo. shrubby, rarely over 2 m h.; **branches** mostly projecting horizontally, readily detached; **L.** only 1.5 cm lg.; **Sp.** inconspicuous; **Fl.** 5 cm ∅, pink; **Ov.** leafy, with Glo.—Bolivia (road to Santa Cruz, in the vicinity of Perez).

Q. pflanzii (Vpl.) Vpl.
Bo. tree-like, to 15 m h., with a stout **trunk**; **Sp.** short, weak, white; **L.** oval, 4 cm lg., tapering below, thick-fleshy, 2 cm br., fairly crowded on flowering shoots; **Fl.** almost 5 cm lg., depressed at the base, pale pink; **style** stout; **Sti.** papillose.—Bolivia (Santa Isabel, 50 km down-river from Villamontes).

Q. verticillacantha (FR 902): no description available.

Q. verticillata (Vpl.) Vpl.
Bo. shrubby, rarely over 2 m h., main St. robust; **branches** verticillate, rather short, projecting ± horizontally, c. 1 cm ∅, glossy green; **Sp.** 1 or more, perpendicular to the shoot, rigid, acicular,

very sharp, to 7 cm lg., white; **L.** 5 cm lg., 1.5 cm br.; **Fl.** 1.5 cm lg., light red; **Fil.** numerous; **Sti.** papillose.—Bolivia (Laguna Santa Isabel, in company with Q. pflanzii).

Q. zehntneri (Br. & R.) Br. & R. (T.)
Bo. shrubby, to c. 3 m h., with a continuous main **St.**; **branches** ascending, long, very spiny, sometimes readily detached; **L.** to 4 cm lg., oval to circular; **Sp.** numerous, thin, ± bristly at first, white; **Ar.** shortly white-felty; **Fl.** sunken, to 4 cm lg., to 8 cm ∅, brilliant red; **Ov.** slender, to 4 cm lg.; **Fr.** to 7 cm lg., 1.5 cm ∅, with low oblong Tub., finally lacking Sp. and Br.; **S.** 5 mm ∅.—Brazil (Bahia, Bom Jesus de Lapa). (Fig. 353.)

Rapicactus F. Buxb.: spec. segregated from **Gymnocactus** Backbg. on account of their napiform R. with a neck-like constriction above (see Gymnocactus).

Rathbunia Br. & R. (146)

Shrubby, rather soft-fleshed Cerei of moderate size, with ± curving shoots. The flowers are diurnal, red, with a narrow tube and a ± oblique limb; the ovary is sometimes spiny, the fruit always so; the latter dehisces transversely and is red both inside and out; the seeds, so far as known, are fairly small, glossy, black. The floral remains persist on the fruit.—Distribution: Mexico (States along the W. coast, including Guerrero and Michoacan, then N. to Sonora where the majority of species occur). [(R).]

R. alamosensis (Coult.) Br. & R.
Bo. shrubby, to 3 m h.; **branches** erect at first, then curving upwards, c. 8 cm ∅, also bending downwards, rooting and sending out fresh shoots; **Ri.** 5–8, obtuse; **Rsp.** 11–18, spreading; **Csp.** to 4, the bottom one longest; **Sp.** all subterete or angular, the longest bottom one sometimes flattened, 2.5–3.5 cm lg.; **Fl.** scarlet, 4 cm lg., limb narrow, oblique, not longer-decurved, **An.** and **style** little-projecting; **Fr.** ?—Mexico (Sonora, Alamos).

R. kerberi (K. Sch.) Br. & R.
Bo. shrubby, to 2 m h.; **branches** subterete; **Ri.** 4, laterally compressed, later flatter; **Ar.** brownish-grey; **Rsp.** c. 12, subulate, pungent; **Csp.** 4, porrect, 4.5 cm lg.; **Fl.** c. 12 cm lg., limb elongated, recurved, zygomorphic, pinkish-red; **Fil.** red; **An.** dark purple; **style** red.—Mexico (Colima; Nayarit; Sinaloa).

R. neosonorensis Backbg.

Bo. shrubby, dark green; **branches** strongly ascending; **Ri.** c. 8; **Rsp.** 13–14, radiating sideways; **Csp.** 1–3, the lowest one longest, projecting obliquely downwards; **Fl.** 7.5 cm lg., glossy, scarlet, limb longer, more strongly revolute; **An.** and **style** close together, long-projecting; **Ov.** sometimes with some tiny **H.**; **Fr.** oblong-spherical, with short Sp.—Mexico (Sonora). (Fig. 354.)

R. pseudosonorensis (Gürke) Berg.: **Rathbunia sonorensis**/(Rge.) Br. & R.

R. sonorensis (Rge.) Br. & R. (T.)
Bo. shrubby; **branches** to 6 cm ∅, leaf to dark green; **Ri.** 8, obtuse, distinctly notched; **Ar.** white; **Rsp.** to 11, radiating horizontally, to 1.5 cm lg., snow-white, tipped dark brown; **Csp.** 1, rather longer and stouter, brown below; **Fl.** 6.5 cm lg., scarlet to carmine, limb fairly straight, not very strongly revolute; **Pet.** only short, bent somewhat outwards; **Ov.** with minute flakes of wool.—Mexico (Sonora).

Rauhocereus Backbg. (89)

Erectly shrubby, laxly branching Cerei with the ribs uniquely tessellate, forming weakly flattened tubercles. The nocturnal flowers are bellshaped-funnelform, the fairly dense scales with tufts of woolly hairs in the axils, the ovoid fruits similarly. The small seeds are glossy, black. Distribution: N. Peru (Rio Saña valley, and between Chamaya and Jaën). [(R); must not be kept too cool in winter.]

R. riosaniensis Backbg. (T.)
Bo. with a thicker trunk, to 4 m h., branching; **shoots** mostly to 8 cm ∅, bluish-green; **Ri.** to 6, transversely furrowed to form ± flattened Tub., furrows eventually less deep than at first; **Sp.** mostly 6(–8), not clearly distinguishable as Rsp. and Csp., the upper one longest, to 5 cm lg., carmine below, yellowish above, all later whitish-grey, some stout, others thinner, mostly to 2.7 cm lg., 3 shorter ones, still thinner, to 5 mm lg., sometimes 1–2 minute light brownish Ssp. above; **Fl.** to 10 cm lg., 5 cm ∅, limb rotate, white; **Fil.** and **style** white, they and the yellow **Sti.** erect and projecting; **Tu.** yellowish-green, Sc. fairly dense and large, pointed, darker green, lower part of the Tu. and the Ov. with grey H.; **nectary** brownish; **Fr.** raspberry-coloured, crimson inside.—N. Peru (Rio Saña valley). (Fig. 355–356.)
  v. **jaenensis** Rauh: **Trunk** to 20 cm ∅; **Rsp.** only 2–3, to 1.5 cm lg., very stout and pungent; **Csp.** 2, very stout, to 2 cm lg., one directed upwards, the other downwards to ± appressed.—N. Peru (between Chamaya and Jaën).

Rebulobivia Frič: only a name, predominantly for species of the Ser. "Conoideae" of the SG. Pygmaeolobivia Backbg. of the Genus **Mediolobivia** Backbg.

Rebutia K. Sch. (103)

Small plants, mostly ± depressed-spherical, with the ribs resolved into tubercles; spines finely acicular to ± bristly and fine, yellowish, white or ± brownish. The slender funnelform flowers appear fairly low on the body, usually many together; they have small scales and are otherwise glabrous. The thin-walled small fruit dries up; the seeds are matt or glossy, black. The earliest known species had red flowers, but later discoveries have blooms of violet to lilac-pink and yellow. Some species are self-fertile, others require cross-pollination. 2 subgenera have been erected, according to whether the style is completely free, or somewhat united below:
SG. 1 Rebutia: style completely free
SG. 2 Neorebutia Bew.: style shortly united at the base.
The species of SG. 2 are self-sterile; SG. 1 includes both forms. The Rebutias are ideal plants, both for nurserymen and amateurs, since they flower easily and prolifically.—Distribution: from N. Argentina to NE. Bolivia. [(R); grafted plants form larger groups and bear even more numerous Fl.]
In recent times Ritter, Donald and Buining have attempted to include Aylostera and Mediolobivia in Rebutia, while Cardenas seeks to refer even Sulcorebutia to the genus. This is just as inadmissible, for a whole variety of reasons, as Marshall's earlier attempt on the same lines. The existing delimitation has so many advantages in diagnosis and the arrangement of collections (given correct labelling, the viewer knows the characters of the indumentum, even when no flowers are present) so that this procedure has been followed universally in larger collections where it is essential to have a clear general picture. Divergent treatments seek to revive outmoded former collective genera, with the disadvantage that there has been no uniformity of procedure: for instance Ritter accepts Sulcorebutia, where all its representatives are clearly recognisable simply by the long linear areoles. The 3 accepted genera form natural groups of species; to combine them gives a synthetic category which is not based on any uniform or logical principle of classification. The new combinations under Rebutia, or the "Sections", of these authors are an unnecessary proliferation of the extensive synonymy and a purely subjective reorganisation which cannot be justified. What convincing proof has been given for

the necessity of alterations of this kind? These attempts do nothing to stabilise the nomenclature, and I am therefore unable to accept them.

My classification on the basis of the reduction of floral indumentum is shown to be a natural one, not only because the groups of species are always uniform in character, but even within Rebutia traces of reduction have been observed: a witness to a natural process which my systematic method reproduces as far as possible.

The subgeneric name Neorebutia sometimes appears as an independent genus (as with SG. Pygmaeolobivia of the Genus Mediolobivia), but this is not justified.

R. albopectinata: **Mediolobivia albopectinata** Rausch.

R. almeyeri W. Heinr. n.sp. (in MS) (1)
Diverges from comparable plants of Ser. 2 "Seniles" as follows: **Bo.** flattened-spherical, little offsetting; **Fl.** 3 cm ∅, brilliant orange-red, throat light yellow, self-fertile; **Pet.** bordered yellow; **style** yellow; **Tu.** with brownish-salmon Sc.; **Fr.** yellowish, with brown Sc.; **S.** very small.—Origin?

R. arenacea Card. (1)
Bo. simple to cushion-forming, single heads to 3.5 cm h., 5 cm ∅; **Tub.** in c. 30 spirals; **Ar.** creamy-grey; **Rsp.** white, in 6–7 pairs directed sideways, one upwardly directed Sp. 5 mm lg., its surface appearing to be covered in sand; **Fl.** yellowish-orange, 3 cm lg. and ∅; **Ov.** with traces of felt at the base.—Bolivia (Dept. Cochabamba).
Regarded by Ritter as a Sulcorebutia although the Ar. are elliptical (broader than lg.), and not linear.

R. binnewaldiana W. Heinr. n.sp. (in MS) (2?)
Differentiated from R. wessneriana and R. permutata as follows:
Bo. bluish-green, simple; **crown** ± naked; **S.** large; and from R. calliantha by the following: **style** golden-yellow; **Fil.** yellow.—Bolivia (Huari Huari).
Fl. 4.3 cm ∅, scarlet, throat orange-red, self-sterile; **Tu.** with blackish-red Sc.; **Fr.** glossy, red.

R. brachyantha (Wessn.) Buin. & Don.: **Mediolobivia brachyantha** (Wessn.) Krainz.

R. brachyantha Card.: **Sulcorebutia breviflora** Backbg. nom.nov.

R. brunescens: **Mediolobivia brunescens** Rausch.

R. brunneoradicata (FR 1109): description not available.

R. buiningiana (Aylostera) Rausch.

Bo. simple, rarely offsetting, spherical, to 5 cm ∅, greyish to light green; **Ri.** to 20, spiralled, tuberculate; **Ar.** c. 2 mm ∅, with white and brown felt; **Rsp.** 14–16, hyaline, 6–10 mm lg.; **Csp.** 2–3, set vertically, to 14 mm lg., white, brown above and below; **Fl.** lateral, 35 mm lg., 30 mm ∅, orange-pink, throat whitish-pink; **style** yellowish, with 6 yellow **Sti.**; **Fr.** brownish-red, with dark Sc. and white H.; **S.** typical of Aylostera.—Argentina (Jujuy, near Iruya, 2700 m. Found by W. Rausch and named for A. F. H. Buining). (Fig. 465.)

R. caineana (Sulcorebutia) Card.
Bo. spherical, somewhat flattened, offsetting, 1.5–2 cm h., 4–5 cm ∅, dark green; **R.** napiform; **Ri.** 13, spiralled, Tub. 5 mm h., 7 mm ∅; **Ar.** 4 mm apart, elliptic, 3 mm lg., white-felty; **Sp.** 14–16, pectinate, thin-acicular, 3–4 mm lg., appressed or spreading; **Fl.** basal, funnelform, 3.5–4 cm lg., 3 cm ∅, yellow; **Ov.** spherical, light purple, with Sc. 2 mm br.; **Tu.** expanded, yellow, tinged light purple, with purple Sc.; **Sep.** lanceolate, yellow; **An.** yellow; **style** light yellow with yellow **Sti.**—Bolivia (Tarata, Cochabamba, near the Rio Caine, 3000 m, in clefts on sandstone).
Species resembles R. brachyantha but is distinguished from it by the longer Fl., purple at the base.

R. calliantha Bewg. (2)
Bo. spherical to ± elongated; **Tub.** in up to c. 27 spirals; **Sp.** 12–21, Csp. not distinguishable as such, to c. 1 cm lg., strongly spreading, whitish; **Fl.** to 4.5 cm ∅, flame-coloured, **buds** deep dark red; **Pet.** spatulate; **Tu.** with violet Sc.; **style** pinkish-orange; **Sti.** white.—N. Argentina. (Fig. 357.)
v. **beryllioides** Buin. & Don.—Sukkde. VII-VIII (SKG), 103. 1963.
Differs in the following: **Bo.** glossy green, flat; **Sp.** yellow to golden-brown, shorter, less numerous; **Fl.** scarlet;
f. breviseta (Backbg.) Buin. & Don.: formerly **R. senilis** v. **breviseta** Backbg..; referred here by these authors (see under R. krainziana).
v. densiseta Bew. is an undescribed name for a more densely, finely spined form.

R. candiae Card.: **Sulcorebutia candiae** (Card.) Backbg.

R. caracarensis (Sulcorebutia) Card.
Bo. simple or caespitose, spherical, flattened, dark greyish-green, 1–1.5 cm h., 1.5–2.5 cm ∅, crown sunken; **R.** napiform, long; **Ri.** c. 17, spiralled, tuberculate, Tub. rounded, 4 mm ∅; **Ar.** 4 mm apart, linear, 4–5 mm lg., with ± greyish-black felt; **Sp.** 11–17, pectinate, appressed, somewhat interlacing, 3–4 mm lg., straw-yellow, thickened and blackish at the base, densely covering the crown;

Fl. lateral, funnelform, 2.5 cm lg., 2.5 cm ⌀, glossy magenta; **Ov.** with greenish-purple Sc.; **Tu.** short, with green, dark-tipped Sc.; **Sep.** spatulate, magenta, whitish below; **Pet.** lanceolate, magenta; **Fil.** magenta; **An.** yellow; **style** thin, whitish, with 4 yellowish-green **Sti.** Distinguished from R. inflexiseta by the shorter appressed **Sp.**, smaller Fl. and more numerous Pet.—Bolivia (Prov. Zudañez, Chuquisaca, Cara-Cara Mountains, 2400 m).

R. carminea Buin.: at most a form of **R. violaciflora v. knuthiana** (Backbg.) Don.

R. chrysacantha Backbg. (1)
Bo. eventually tall-spherical, to c. 6 cm h., 5 cm ⌀, fresh green; **Sp.** 25–30, Csp. little differentiated, several darker and thicker below, to 1.2 cm lg., all bristly, fine, at least the more central Sp. becoming yellow towards the end of the season; **Fl.** to 5 cm lg., yellowish-red, self-fertile; **Tu.** yellowish-orange.—N. Argentina (Salta).
    v. **elegans** (Backbg.) Backbg.: distinguished by the more whitish **Sp.**, only the tips slightly yellowish; all **Sp.** fine, dense.
    v. **iseliniana** (Krainz) Don.: see R. senilis v. iseliniana Krainz.

R. cintiensis (FR 938): no description available.

R. citricarpa Frič: **Rebutia xanthocarpa** v. **citricarpa** Frič ex Backbg.

Rebutia colorea (FR 1106): no description available.

R. corroana Card. 1971
Bo. spherical, 5 cm h., 6–7 cm ⌀, fresh green; **Ri.** c. 22, spiralled, flattened, divided into low Tub. 12 mm ⌀; **Ar.** 1 cm apart, round, 3 mm ⌀, brownfelty, projecting; **Sp.** over 25, thin, spreading, sharp, unequal, 3–15 mm lg.; crown slightly depressed, densely spiny; **Fl.** lateral, 2.5 cm lg., 1.8 cm ⌀; **Ov.** with reddish-brownish Sc.; **Tu.** short, yellow with dark red Sc.; **Sep.** golden-yellow, with brownish-red dots outside; **Pet.** sulphur-yellow; **style** yellow with 5 light yellow **Sti.**—Bolivia (Prov. Oropeza, Dept. Chuquisaca, Cuesta del Meadero, 2720 m).

R. densipectinata Ritt. (FR 758): no description available.

R. eos: **Mediolobivia eos** Rausch.

R. fiebigiana W. Heinr. n.sp. (in MS) (1)
Differentiated from others of SG. Rebutia as follows: **Bo.** larger, not caespitose, **crown** very deeply sunken; **Sp.** tipped yellowish-brown; **Fl.**

very large; **style** not united.—Bolivia (Huari Huari).
Fl. to 5 cm ⌀, brilliant red, self-sterile; **style** whitish to flesh-coloured; **Tu.** with dull dark red Sc.; **Fr.** dull red.

R. glomeriseta Card. (1)
Bo. spherical, offsetting, to c. 6 cm ⌀; **Tub.** in 20 spirals; **Ar.** light brown or white; **Sp.** numerous, bristly, 2–3 cm lg., white, strongly interlacing, covering the Bo. quite densely, some Sp. more projecting; **Fl.** 2.5 cm lg., golden-yellow; **Ov.** light yellow; **Sep.** yellow with a lilac sheen; **style** white; **Sti.** light yellow.—Bolivia (Dept. Cochabamba; Sucre, Hacienda Ressini.* (Fig. 358.)
Referred by Ritter to Sulcorebutia—unjustifiably in my view, as the Ar. are round, not linear.

R. graciliflora Backbg.—Descr. Cact. Nov. III: 13. 1963 (1).
Bo. spherical, dark green, to over 2.5 cm ⌀; **Ri.** spiralled, Tub. slender; **Rsp.** and **Csp.** not differentiated, c. 15, very short, hyaline, grey, sometimes irregularly darker to blackish (!), c. 2 mm lg., missing at first in the crown; **Fl.** only c. 1.8 cm lg., 1.7 cm ⌀, light red, slightly yellowish (colour as in Aylostera spinosissima); **Tu.** 1 cm lg., glabrous, yellowish-greenish, with pale green Sc.; **Ov.** yellowish-green, Sc. green; **Fil.** and **style** white; **Sti.** white, papillose.—N. Argentina (no locality given). (Fig. 359.) Distinguished from R. xanthocarpa v. luteirosea Backbg. by the dark green Bo., divergent colour of Csp., greenish Tu. and Ov.

R. gracilispina Ritt. (FR 1118): no description available.

R. grandiflora Backbg. (1)
Bo. larger than in R. minuscula, to c. 7.5 cm ⌀, 5 cm h.; **Tub.** in c. 26 spirals; **Rsp.** c. 25, bristly, short, whitish; **Csp.** c. 4, very short, darker, scarcely differentiated, darker below; **Fl.** larger than in R. minuscula, to 6.5 cm lg., brilliant carmine.—N. Argentina (Salta, Quebrada Escoipe).
Regarded by Krainz as a variety of R. minuscula; however its locality is isolated, and it is clearly divergent in the dimensions of Bo. and Fl., and has a longer Tu.

* [Translator's note: Acc. Donald (Ashingtonia II, 7. 138, 1976) Backeberg's habitat details are incorrect: not only is Sucre in Dept. Chuquisaca, but the true habitat is near Naranjito, above the Rio Ayopaya, Ayopaya Prov., Dept. Cochabamba; Backeberg confused Rebutia (Sulco.) glomeriseta Card. with a superficially similar plant found by Frank at Hacienda Ressini ("Rebutia spinosissima" = R. nivosa Ritt. nom.nud.), and modified the habitat of S. glomeriseta accordingly.]

R. haseltonii Card. 1966: see **Sulcorebutia haseltonii** (Card.) Donald.

R. hyalacantha (Backbg.) Backbg. (2?)
Bo. to c. 8 cm $\emptyset$, green; **Sp.** c. 25, c. 2 cm lg., **Csp.** not clearly differentiated, all crowded, glassy, yellowish-white; **Fl.** red, self-sterile.—N. Argentina (Salta).
Pollination with spec. of SG. 1 said to be unsuccessful. Since it is self-sterile, it cannot be a variety of R. senilis. Differs from R. wessneriana (with Sp. white, tipped brown) by its glassy, yellowish-white Sp. Segregation of the 2 spec. is necessary in my view, to avoid confusion.

R. inflexiseta (Sulcorebutia) Card.
Bo. spherical, simple or offsetting, 1–2.5 cm h., 2–3.5 cm $\emptyset$, crown sunken; **Ri.** 14–17, spiralled, broken into rounded Tub. 4–5 mm $\emptyset$; **Ar.** 3–4 mm apart, slightly felty; **Sp.** 14–18, pectinate, thin-acicular, flexible, or radiating and projecting, interlacing, whitish-yellow, base thickened, blackish, 5–15 mm lg.; **Fl.** basal, funnelform, 3 cm lg., 2 cm $\emptyset$, magenta; **Ov.** spherical, green, with broad Sc.; **Tu.** c. 1 cm lg., with light green Sc.; **Sep.** spatulate, magenta-lilac; **Pet.** lanceolate, magenta above, whitish below; **Fil.** dark magenta; **An.** light yellow; **style** light green, with 7 short emerald-green **Sti.**—Bolivia (Prov. Zudañez, Dept. Chuquisaca, around Prest, 2400 m). Distinguished by the long, upper Sp. which are flexible and interlacing, as well as by the Fl. of only a few Pet.

R. kariusiana Wessn.—Kakt. u.a. Sukk., 14: 8, 149. 1963 (1).
Bo. leaf-green, spherical, with a depressed and spiny crown, to c. 5 cm $\emptyset$, little offsetting; **Ri.** spiralled, tuberculate; **Ar.** c. 5 mm apart; **Rsp.** 8–10, 3–6 mm lg., light brown to white, lighter at first; **Csp.** 3–4, dark brown, thickened below, to 6 mm lg.; **bud** light green, pointed; **Fl.** c. 2.5 cm lg., 4 cm $\emptyset$, intense pinkish-red; **Pet.** lanceolate, acute, with a light brownish dorsal stripe; **Tu.** 1.2 cm lg., with pale green Sc.; **Ov.** pale to olive-green; **Fil.** yellow; **style** white above, pinkish-white below; **Sti.** yellow; **Fr.** yellowish-green when ripe, 6 mm $\emptyset$; **S.** glossy, black, hilum white.—N. Argentina (Salta?). (Fig. 360.) Said to be self-sterile.

R. krainziana Kesselr. (1)
Bo. offsetting freely, single head to 5 cm h., 4 cm $\emptyset$, light green; **Tub.** very small; **Ar.** white, relatively large, mostly rather oblong, to 2 mm lg.; **Sp.** 8–12, bristly, very thin, very short, snow-white, 1–2 mm lg.; **Fl.** intense red, yellowish below, c. 3 cm lg., 4 cm $\emptyset$; **Ov.** with brownish-violet Sc.—Bolivia.
The spec. is self-sterile, and easily recognized; R. senilis v. breviseta Backbg., which is self-fertile, is

rather similar but has thinner and $\pm$ projecting Sp. (see R. calliantha).
v. breviseta hort.: a form without Csp., with lax linear Pet.

R. kruegeri Card.: **Sulcorebutia kruegeri** (Card.) Backbg.

R. lanosiflora (FR 1116): no description available.

R. mamillosa (Aylostera) Rausch
Bo. spherical, 20 mm $\emptyset$, caespitose, dark green to brown; **Ri.** 14–16, spiralled, Tub. 3–4 mm lg.; **Ar.** 2 mm lg., brown-felty; **Rsp.** 8–10, spreading, 3–4 pairs to each side and 1 each upwards and downwards, to 4 mm lg., yellow, brown below; **Csp.** 0–1, brown, 2 mm lg.; **Fl.** lateral, c. 40 mm lg. and $\emptyset$; **Sep.** narrow, brownish-pink with a greenish M.-stripe; **Pet.** narrow, acute, red; **Fr.** spherical, 4 mm $\emptyset$; **S.** cap-shaped, 1 mm lg., testa black, glossy, Resembles Aylostera spegazziniana.—Bolivia (W. of Camargo, 3300 m).

R. margarethae Rausch 1972
Bo. simple, to 4 cm h. and 6 cm $\emptyset$, epidermis violet-brown; **R.** napiform; **Ri.** 15–17, spiralled, with c. 10 prominent round Tub.; **Ar.** oval to oblong, c. 3 mm $\emptyset$, white-felty; **Rsp.** 7–11, spreading to appressed, 15–20 mm lg., often $\pm$ curving, dark brown, yellow below, later greying; **Fl.** lateral, c. 40 mm lg. and 35 mm $\emptyset$; **Ov.** and **Tu.** yellowish-pink with green Sc.; **Sep.** pink, with a green M.-stripe; **Pet.** spatulate, red, orange inside, **throat** and **Fil.** yellow; **style** white, with 6 white Sti.; **Fr.** flat-spherical, c. 4 mm $\emptyset$; **S.** cap-shaped, 1.3 mm lg. and 1 mm $\emptyset$.—Argentina (Salta, near Santa Victoria, 3500 m). (Fig. 524.)
Named by W. Rausch for his wife, Margarethe, in recognition for her help in caring for his plants.

R. marsoneri Werd. (1)
Bo. broadly rounded, offsetting little or not at all, to 5 cm $\emptyset$, to c. 4 cm h., sometimes broader, light green; **Ar.** brownish-white; **Sp.** c. 30–35, scarcely differentiated, lower ones to 5 mm lg., more whitish, upper ones 9–15, rather stouter, c. 8–15 mm lg., reddish-brown, at least above, apparently also variable in colour, to all Sp. whitish; **Fl.** self-sterile, to 4.5 cm lg., light to intense yellow, inner Pet. also $\pm$ orange-yellow; **style** light yellow; **Sti.** white; **S.** matt, black.—N. Argentina (Jujuy).
v. brevispina Don.: nom.nud. for a short-spined form;
v. grandiflora Don.: nom.nud.; acc. to the name, must have larger Fl.;
v. **spathulata** Don.: **Pet.** spatulate; **Tu.** with violet-red Sc.; **S.** glossy, black; the so-called "false R. marsoneri";

v. **vatteri** Don.: **Fl.** self-sterile; **S.** glossy, black (Jujuy); **Pet.** broader in this and also the preceding variety; both offset more freely than the type.

R. melachlora (FR 935), from N. Argentina: no description available.

R. menesesii Card.: **Sulcorebutia menesesii** (Card.) Backbg.

R. minuscula K. Sch. (1) (T.)
Bo. depressed-rounded to spherical, simple or offsetting, to c. 5 cm $\emptyset$; **Tub.** in 16–20 spirals, light green; **Sp.** 25–30, 2–3 mm lg., whitish, Csp. not distinguishable as such; **Fl.** to 4 cm lg., bright red; **Pet.** tapering; **Ov.** pale red; **Fr.** scarlet, 3 mm $\emptyset$.— N. Argentina (Tucuman). Pink Fl. also reported.
The varietal names sometimes referred here mostly belong to varieties of small-flowered R. xanthocarpa.

R. minutissima Ritt. (FR 1124): no description available.

R. multicolor (FR 1108): no description available.

R. nitida Ritt. (FR 769): no description available.

R. patericalyx Ritt. (FR 757) and v. odontopeta Ritt. (FR 757a): no description available.

R. pauciareolata Ritt. (FR 1121): no description available.

R. permutata W. Heinr.—Descr. Cact. Nov. III: 13. 1963 (1).
Distinguished from R. wessneriana by the **Bo.** being simple or scarcely offsetting, **crown** densely white-spined (not $\pm$ spineless), Sp. not brown-tipped; the rather long, dense Sp. are off-white; **Fl.** self-sterile. The spec. comes true from seed.— Origin? (Fig. 361, right).
   f. **gokrausei** W. Heinr.—l.c., 1963: a seedling form with the **Bo.** shortly columnar, not broadly spherical as in the type. Spination finer, so that the plants resemble a juvenile Cleistocactus strausii; **Sp.** are white, long, hair-like or bristly; **Fl.** stout, the longer Tu. likewise. The form occurred in the nursery of Gottfried Krause, Dresden-Stetzsch, by cross-pollinating several parent plants of this self-sterile spec., but was not reproduced in later attempts. Since older Rebutias, like some Sulcorebutias and Aylosteras, in part show a more strongly columnar habit, this form may represent a similar reversion resulting from a possibly latent factor. (Fig. 361, left.)

R. pseudopygmaea Ritt. (FR 1122): no description available.

R. pulchera Card. = **Sulcorebutia pulchera** Card.: no description available.

R. ritteri (Wessn.) Buin. & Don., and its forms: f. peterseimii Buin. & Don. and f. hahniana Buin. & Don., all in Sukkde. VII/VIII, 103. 1963: see under **Mediolobivia ritteri** (Wessn.) Krainz or **M. nigricans** v. peterseimii (Frič); f. hahniana probably belongs to the same spec.

R. rosalbiflora Ritt. (FR 1115): no description available.

R. senilis Backbg. (1)
Listed here are all plants with larger, red or yellow Fl., with projecting, fine, $\pm$ white Sp. which, while variable in length, are never pectinate or appressed. Var. senilis is now unfortunately more or less lost, and it has the longest, densest and pure white Sp.: **Bo.** to 8 cm lg., 7 cm $\emptyset$, deep green; **Sp.** numerous, long, chalky-white, dense, c. 25, to 3 cm lg.; **Fl.** 3.5 cm $\emptyset$, self-fertile, carmine, throat white; **Pet.** pointed; **Ov.** yellowish-orange.—N. Argentina (Salta, upper Quebrada Escoipe). (Fig. 362.)
   v. **aurescens** Backbg.: **Sp.** later becoming $\pm$ yellowish, or only the Csp., all fine, thin, dense; **Fl.** large, mid-red; **Bo.** subspherical;
   v. **breviseta** Backbg.: **Sp.** very short but not pectinate, at most 4–7 mm lg.; **Fl.** mid-red;
   v. cana hort.: only a name;
   v. **iseliniana** Krainz: **Sp.** hair-like, lax, with a yellowish sheen or pure white; **Fl.** orange-red; **Bo.** rounded;
   v. **kesselringiana** Bewg.: **Sp.** laxly projecting, 30–35, 8–12 mm lg., white to pale yellowish; **Ar.** crowded; **Fl.** to 4.5 cm $\emptyset$, light yellow, inner Pet. golden-yellow; **Fr.** olive; **S.** glossy black;
   v. **lilacino-rosea** Backbg.: **Sp.** as in the type; **Fl.** light lilac-pink;
   v. **schieliana** Bewg.: **Sp.** c. 15, whitish, tipped brownish or yellowish, fairly dense; **Fl.** 4 cm lg. and $\emptyset$, outer Pet. crimson, inner ones more orange-red; **Tu.** and **Ov.** with violet Sc.;
   v. **semperflorens** Poind.: a sport which arose in cultivation; caespitose, with numerous Fl.;
   v. **sieperdaiana** (Buin.) Backbg.: **Sp.** only moderately lg., very fine; **Ar.** rather more distant than in v. kesselringiana, with the spirals of Tub. thus not so distinct; **Fl.** (self-sterile?) c. 4.5 cm lg., 3.5 cm $\emptyset$, deep yellow, pinkish-yellow outside; **Pet.** fairly broad, rounded above, or slit, or apiculate;
   v. **stuemeri** Backbg.: **Sp.** as in v. senilis, but rather laxer; **Fl.** brick-red, throat and Pet.-border often yellowish, Pet. rather laxly outspread. Further varietal names may be found

under other specific names, sometimes with specific status.

R. singularis Ritt. (FR 1423): no description available.

R. sphaerica Ritt. (FR 1140): no description available.

R. tamboensis (FR 1142): no description available.

R. tarvitensis (FR 773): no description available.

R. torquata (FR 1117): no description available.

R. totorensis Card.: **Sulcorebutia totorensis** (Card.) Ritt.

R. tropacolitica Ritt. (FR 1114): no description available.

R. tuberculato-chrysantha Card. 1971 (? Mediolobivia?)
Bo. caespitose, short-cylindric, greyish-green, 15–20 mm lg., 15–22 mm $\emptyset$; **Ri.** c. 11, tuberculate; **Ar.** 3 mm apart, elliptic, 2.5 mm lg., grey-felty; **Sp.** 8–10, pectinate, slender-bristly, white, purple below, 2 mm lg.; **Fl.** few, basal, funnelform, 30–32 mm lg., 25–30 mm $\emptyset$; **Ov.** round, 3 mm lg., light green with greenish-yellow Sc.; **Tu.** 20 mm lg., pink below, lighter above, glabrous, with yellowish Sc. 3 mm lg.; **Sep.** spatulate, 16 × 5 mm, reddish; **Pet.** lanceolate, 12 × 5 mm, golden-yellow; **Fil.** red below, yellow above; **An.** yellow; **style** 15 mm lg., white, with 7 light yellow **Sti.**—Bolivia (Prov. Chapare, Dept. Cochabamba, up to c. 3500 m).

R. turbinata hort., not described: said to resemble R. krainziana, but to have smaller Fl. and divergent spination.

R. vallegrandensis Card. (Aylostera Speg.)
Bo. spherical or short-cylindric, 4–6 cm h., 4–5 cm $\emptyset$, fresh green, crown flattened, densely spiny; **Ri.** c. 20, weakly tuberculate; **Ar.** 4–5 mm apart, rounded, prominent, white-felty; **Sp.** 30 or more, tangled, radiating and projecting, 3–10 mm lg., bristly, very thin; **Fl.** numerous, lateral or basal, funnelform, 2.5 cm lg., 2 cm $\emptyset$, red; **Ov.** spherical, 3 mm $\emptyset$, brownish-green, with Sc. and a few short white H.; **Tu.** narrow, 1 cm lg., 2 mm $\emptyset$, light red, with Sc. and short white H.; **Sep.** magenta-red, acute; **Pet.** lanceolate, blood-red; **Fil.** white; **An.** yellow; **style** white, with 5 yellow **Sti.**; **Fr.** spherical, 3.5 mm $\emptyset$; **S.** mitre-shaped, subspherical below, black, finely pitted.—Bolivia (Prov. Vallegrande, Santa Cruz, near Candellaria, at 2000 m). Collected by W. Rausch.

R. violaciflora Backbg. (1)
Bo. spherical, mostly simple, yellowish-green, small, to c. 2 cm $\emptyset$ (ungrafted); **Ar.** yellowish-white; **Sp.** c. 20, bristly, stiff, radiating, deep golden-brown, to 2.5 cm lg., **Csp.** stouter; **Fl.** c. 3.5 cm lg., 3 cm $\emptyset$, self-fertile, light violet-red.—N. Argentina (Salta, upper Quebrada Escoipe).
v. **knuthiana** (Backbg.) Don.: **Bo.** matt, pale light green, to 4.5 cm $\emptyset$; **Ar.** brown; **Sp.** hair-like, 30 and more, brown, ± interlacing sideways, mostly lighter below; **Fl.** 4.5 cm lg., dull carmine (Salta).

R. vizcarrae Card.
Bo. broadly spherical, 3–3.5 cm h., 4–5 cm br., greyish-green, crown sunken; **Ri.** c. 18, tuberculate, 4 mm h., 5 mm br.; **Ar.** 1 cm apart, elliptic, 4–6 mm lg., grey-felty; **Rsp.** c. 17, pectinate-radiating, 4–8 mm lg.; **Csp.** 2–3, radiating, 8–11 mm lg.; all **Sp.** yellowish-white or brownish, sharp; **Fl.** numerous, lateral, funnelform, dark magenta, 3.5 cm lg., 2 cm br.; **Ov.** spherical, 5 mm lg., green, with broad Sc.; **Tu.** short, only 5 mm lg., with Sc. 3–5 mm lg.; **Sep.** 20 × 2 mm, pink, tipped green; **Pet.** lanceolate, 20 × 4 mm, light magenta; **style** thin, white, with 5 yellow **Sti.**—Bolivia (Prov. Mizque, Cochabamba, near Mizque, at 2000 m). Named for Eufronio Vizcarra of Mizque. This plant is conspicuous for the straight, radiating spines.

R. wessneriana Bewg. (1)
Bo. broadly rounded, freely offsetting, crown only ± felty, virtually spineless, showing clearly through the Sp., to 7 cm h., 8 cm br., green, suffused ± violet in strong sunshine; **Ri.** not completely divided into Tub.; **Ar.** 5 mm apart; **Rsp.** and **Csp.** not differentiated, c. 25, c. 2 cm lg.; **Fl.** c. 5.5 cm $\emptyset$, blood-red; **Tu.** red, Sc. violet; **style** pinkish-orange; **Sti.** white; **Fil.** red.—N. Argentina (locality not known).
See R. hyalacantha and R. permutata for differences separating these spec.

R. xanthocarpa Backbg. (1)
Bo. subspherical, to 4.5 cm h., c. 5 cm $\emptyset$, leaf-green, offsetting from below; **Sp.** 15–20, fine, hyaline, c. 4 directed upwards, slightly yellowish and rather stouter, to c. 7 mm lg., others shorter, lowest ones only 1–2 mm lg.; **Fl.** small, to 2 cm $\emptyset$, self-fertile, carmine, rather lighter inside; **Tu.** red; **Ov.** light carmine; **Fr.** yellowish.—N. Argentina (Salta).
v. **citricarpa** Frič ex Backbg.: **Fl.** mid-carmine; **Ov.** and **Fr.** greenish-yellow;
v. **coerulescens** Backbg.: **Fl.** bluish-red; **Pet.** rather shorter, narrower (lanceolate) and laxer than in v. dasyphrissa; **Ov.** orange-yellow;
v. **dasyphrissa** (Werd.) Backbg.: **Sp.** rather

longer and whiter; **Fl.** bluish-red; **Pet.** more crowded, broader and rather longer than in the preceding variety; **Tu.** and **Ov.** olive; **Fr.** golden-yellow;

v. **luteirosea** Backbg.: **Fl.** pale yellowish-red;
v. **salmonea** Frič ex Backbg.: **Fl.** ± salmon-red; **Ov.** pale red;
v. **violaciflora** (Backbg.) Backbg.: **Fl.** like R. violaciflora in colour, i.e. deep brilliant violet, but smaller, or only as large as those of v. xanthocarpa.

A hybrid which must be mentioned here because of its significance is: Rebutia hybrida albiflora "Meisterstück"; raised by the nurseryman Stirnadel, this was a cross between a Rebutia and a spec. from the Pseudolobivia complex around P. polyancistra; the Bo. fully resembled Rebutia, but the Fl. was white, a colour not yet seen in this genus.

R. candiae Card., R. canigueralii Card., R. kruegeri (Card.) Backbg., R. menesesii Card., R. steinbachii Werd., R. taratensis Card., R. tiraquensis Card., R. totorensis Card. and R. tunariensis Card.: see **Sulcorebutia** Backbg. Rebutia-names will be found under **Aylostera** Speg. if the Fl. have H. and Br., and the style and tube are stem-like and united; otherwise see under **Mediolobivia** Backbg.
Recent names of Ritter's, published as Rebutia, belong to Aylostera and should be sought there.

Reicheocactus Backbg. (124)

A genus which is interesting from several points of view, and also a disputed one. The type-species is a plant which was long regarded as "Echinocactus reichei K. Sch.", until it was noticed that it lacked the floral bristles of Schumann's species. Yet again, the degrees of floral indumentum had proved their worth and demonstrated that "Echus. reichei hort. germ." was not the true plant; in fact it had not been described. Frau Heese, wife of the first importer, said it came from Chile. At that time, apart from Copiapoa, no Chilean species were known which did not have floral bristles, and the "false Echus. reichei" had to be given a new genus and a name: Reicheocactus pseudoreicheanus. It is characterised by a later ± barrel-shaped habit, and the ribs are divided into extremely tiny tubercles, while the spines are ± curving and appressed; the flower is short, without a discernible tube, and the filaments are not arranged in 2 series. The fruit is said to split laterally. In the meantime further bristle-less species have become known from Chile, and they must be referred provisionally to Reicheocactus.

In the genus as conceived until now, 3 species have been described.—Distribution: Chile (not completely satisfactorily established in the case of the type-species). [(R); the type-species grows very well on its own roots; other spec. do better if grafted.]

R. floribundus Backbg.
Bo. simple, bluish-green, to c. 6 cm ⌀ (acc. my only available plant); **Ri.** 13, rather spiralled, thickened around the Ar., with a deep transverse furrow between the Ar., with a strongly chin-like protuberance, sometimes washed reddish; **Sp.** scarcely differentiated, in all 10–18, 2–3 of these more central, rather stouter, to 11 mm lg., porrect, others shorter, especially the 1–3(–4) in the upper part of the Ar., all pale yellowish-brown, tipper darker; **Fl.** 2.5 cm lg., 1.8 cm ⌀, remaining half-open, mid-yellow; **Tu.** only hairy; **Fr.** violet-red; **S.** matt black, 1 mm lg.—Chile.
Self-sterile. Unpollinated Fl. produce Fr. which are always without S.

R. neoreichei (Backbg.) Backbg.
Bo. spherical, eventually oblong; **Ri.** divided into small Tub.; **Sp.** c. 18–19, hyaline at first, roughly hairy, pectinate, Csp. often absent or variously directed; **Ar.** more strongly woolly in the apex; **Fl.** densely woolly-hairy but without Br., fairly large.—Chile.
Ritter's "Chileorebutia reichei FR 501" was supposedly a re-collection of the plant described by Schumann. This cannot be correct, since "Echus. reichei K. Sch." had floral Br., and the Sp. were not rougly hairy. Ritter's data in Winter's catalogue 13. 1962: "Synonymous with Neochilenia reichei (see also the latter) and further new specific names" are thus inaccurate; moreover it would mean that Neochilenia lembckei, the above spec. and Neochilenia pseudoreichei were the same as Neochilenia or Chileorebutia reichei. My close-up photographs, Vol. III of "Die Cact.", show that the 3 spec. are clearly differentiated. Possibly Dr. Kraus re-collected the genuine Echus. reichei (Vol. III: Fig. 1755, p. 1825. 1959).

R. pseudoreicheanus Backbg. (T.)
Bo. eventually ± ovoid, to c. 7 cm h., 6 cm ⌀, rarely or little offsetting, dark greyish olive-green; **Ri.** to c. 40, completely divided into flattened-roundish little Tub., epidermis pitted; **Ar.** oblong, with sparse brown or light brownish felt, inconspicuous in the depressed crown; **Rsp.** 7–9, appressed sideways, paired, thickened below, to 3 mm lg., dark below, more yellowish above, all ± curving, the lowest one sometimes appressed downwards and thinnest; **Fl.** yellow, ± reddish-brownish outside, to 3.5 cm lg. and ⌀, shortly funnelform, without a hymen; **Tu.** extremely short,

without Br., with dense brownish-grey H.; **style** red; **Fr.** woolly, said to dehisce by splitting longitudinally.—Locality ? (Fig. 364, left; 365.) One clone is known to be a shy bloomer.

Acc. Buining, Ritter found this species again in Argentina, near the village of Famatina (FR 459). Others have since looked for it there, but have not found it.

Ritter himself has made no report on his discoveries, and did not include "Echus." famatimensis in the Winter catalogues. However he found material which was similar, although the spination was different, as shown by the close-up photographs in the illustrated section:

Reicheocactus sp.: Bo. resembling the preceding, lighter green, not barrel-shaped and slightly tapering above as in the type-spec. of Reicheocactus (unlike Lobivia famatimensis (Speg.) Br. & R.); Ri. running vertically, Tub. more crowded and the Ri. therefore more distinct; Ar. more crowded, light brownish to whitish, more densely woolly at the depressed apex; Sp. c. 9, pale yellow, reddish and thickened below; Fl. yellow, slender-funnelform, expanding sharply above the short Tu., H. more flocky and slighter than in "Echus. famatimensis Speg." (Fig. 363, 364 right.) Ritter recently said of his plants "genus?", and added a v. haematantha (FR 459c) which, from the name, must have red Fl. Since his plants can only belong to Reicheocactus, it would be appropriate (see also under Lobivia famatimensis) to name them Reicheocactus pseudofamatimensis and v. haematantha.

Rhipsalidopsis Br. & R. (26)

Small epiphytic, non-climbing and dimorphic shrubs: at first subterete 4–5-angled shoots develop, their angles with weak yellowish-white spines or bristles; later stem-segments consist predominantly or exclusively of flat-clavate sections, with broad apical areoles from which the new shoots and the small regular pink flowers appear. In the variety, the angular and bristly character of the shoot remains constant. While the genus is related to Epiphyllopsis, it has a 4-angled ovary and a 4-angled, slightly depressed fruit; the filaments are crowded only around the base of the style, and there is no nectary.—Distribution: S. Brazil (State of Paraná). [◑.(R).]
Reid Moran has also referred Epiphyllopsis to this genus; see under the latter genus for the differences.

R. gaertneri (Reg.) Lindgr. and v. tiburtii (Backbg. & Voll) Moran: **Epiphyllopsis gaertneri** (Reg.) Berg. and v. **tiburtii** Backbg. & Voll.

R. rosea (Lag.) Br. & R. (T.)
Bo. at first reddish or pale green, then darker green, matt; **Seg.** later ± reddish in the sun, to c. 3.7 cm lg., to 11 mm br. above, to 3 mm thick, margin with 2–3 notches; sometimes 3–4-angled Seg. appear between the flat ones; Seg. with slender bristly H., but not so strongly bristly as the variety; **Fl.** to 3 at once, with a very short Tu., rotate, 3.7 cm ∅, pink; **style** pinkish-red; **Sti.** 3–4, white; **Fr.** yellowish, ± depressed, faintly angular, with floral remains; **S.** brown. (Fig. 367.)

v. **remanens** Backbg.: **Bo.** with very small shoots, densely bushy; **Seg.** short, differing from the type in that later Seg. are not flat, but 4–5-angled, only very rarely 3-angled; **Br.** always plentiful, whitish, very thin, at most 2 mm lg.; extremely slow-growing in cultivation. Said to have been re-collected recently.

Rhipsalidopsis serrata Lindgr.: **Epiphyllopsis gaertneri** v. **serrata** (Lindgr.) Backbg.

Rhipsalis Gärtn. (20)*

Epiphytic plants, mostly freely branching and hanging, occasionally sprawling over rocks, sometimes climbing, forming fibrous aerial roots. Shoots very variable in shape (sometimes even within a single species): terete, angular or leaf-like, thin to broadly subcircular, sometimes with minute scales; flowering areoles not sunken, small, glabrous or with hairlets and even bristles. Flowers mostly solitary, occasionally several at the same time from a single areole, especially in the broadly leaf-like kinds; flowers always small, greenish-white, white, yellow(ish) or pink, or reddish-purple, lasting for several days. The small berry-fruits decorate the plant in various colours, from white to red to very dark, or even golden-yellow; these normally contain only few, rarely more numerous, small seeds of variable form, and from light brown to black.

4 subgenera are distinguished on the basis of shoot-shape:

SG. 1: Rhipsalis: shoots ± terete, not noticeably bristly, stouter to very thin, terminal shoots sometimes faintly angular or furrowed, especially when shrunken;

SG. 2 Ophiorhipsalis K. Sch.: shoots terete, always bristly (glabrous only in age);

SG. 3: Goniorhipsalis K. Sch.: Shoots distinctly angular or ribbed, sometimes or in part flattened;

* Haage adds here: Buxbaum states that all Lepismium spec. (except L. cruciforme, with its distinctive Fl.-structure) should now be referred back to Rhipsalis.

SG. 4: Phyllorhipsalis K. Sch.: terminal or main shoots leaf-like, only a few primary shoots 3-angled and even these often ± terete.

The figure following each specific name indicates the appropriate subgenus.—Distribution: from Florida through Mexico and the Antilles to much further south in S. America; also in the Old World: in more southern Africa, Madagascar to Ceylon (more recent studies have shown ± divergent characters so that these do not appear to be introductions). [(R).///.]

Kimnach has transferred R. angustissima, coriacea, jamaicensis, leiophloea, purpusii and ramulosa to Disocactus (see latter also), and united them all under D. ramulosus. He himself says: "all have minute flowers and fruits". His principal reason for inclusion within Disocactus was the existence of the "floral bracteoles" or—as Vaupel said of his Group "Ramulosae"—"ovaries scaly". Kimnach draws comparisons with Pseudorhipsalis, which he also transfers to Disocactus, mentions convergences, and passes on from similarities of individual characters to unification. While this work is undoubtedly interesting, it is of greater importance in the field of phylogenetics, and is fundamentally theoretical. For instance, just to quote the matter of "floral bracteoles", I have observed that in Lepismium, inter alia, flowering short shoots may possess distinct scaliness (perhaps a reversion), and shortly stem-like tubes occur in Rhipsalis. We have no certain knowledge of how the different forms arose, and we are only guessing unless we start from the basis of classification in accordance with natural phenomena.

While it is one of the tasks of a phytographic handbook to take account of the observations and opinions of other authors, it still remains most important to refrain from advancing any theory regarding the way in which our present genera, species and specific characters have arisen, because no such theory can be proved; equally, the clearest possible approach, and one most closely according with the facts of Nature, has to be chosen because of practical requirements; in the case of Rhipsalis, for instance, Schumann's division into subgenera is helpful. An overall classification on this basis does not permit the unification of species which are clearly distinct as to flower-size etc. or which have relatively widely separated distributions, merely on the grounds that they may possibly be closely related; in any case, segregation according to degrees of relationship is a matter of opinion. Since Kimnach, for example, has not provided any comprehensive classification with the necessary Keys, anyone happening to see Rhipsalis ramulosa in flower would not have known that this Rhipasalis species with its tiny flowers was now supposed to be

a Disocactus, unless he could refer to other works with the appropriate references. The phylogeneticist may have interesting observations to make, but the plant-geographer and other practical workers can make little use of them, and have to apply the customary and well-founded classifications. Kimnach's other combinations show that he is not too clear about the end-results of his treatment, or at least he makes no comment on the subject. Consider here the example of the highly questionable inclusion of Matucana in Borzicactus … whereupon Hutchison discovered a ± flattened-spherical Submatucana which, according to Kimnach, must also be referred to the cereoid Genus Borzicactus. These cases add point to my concluding words in "Die Cact." Vol. VI, in which I quoted L. Stebbins Jr. who rightly declared that phylogenetics and phytogeography are separate and distinct disciplines, each of which should pursue its own appointed tasks. Kimnach's goals are thus not in harmony with those of the present work which calls for a comprehensive classification based on naturally-occurring factors, which will assist the practical worker; because the work of Britton and Rose has been overtaken by recent discoveries, no such classification exists, and the arrangement under my Systematic Survey must therefore stand.

R. aculeata Web. (2)
Bo. branching, climbing up tree-trunks, forming numerous aerial R.; **shoots** cylindric, rigid, green; **Ri.** 8–10, indistinct; **Ar.** whitish; **Br.** 8–10, radiating, ± appressed, ± rigid, 3–4 mm lg., white; **Fl.** borne on the margins, c. 2 cm lg., 1.5 cm ∅, white; **Ov.** spherical, with small Sc.; **Fr.** dark wine-red; **S.** c. 20, spindle-shaped, brown.—Argentina, Brazil, Paraguay.

R. angustissima Web. (4)
Bo. much branching, hanging; **shoots** of two types: lower ones cylindric, woody, c. 25 cm lg., 2–3 mm ∅, later ones leaf-like, lanceolate, slightly serrate; **terminal shoots** to only 1.3 cm br., with a stout M.-nerve, brownish-red at first, then glossy dark green; **Ar.** sparsely white-felty; **Fl.** 4–5 mm lg., carmine outside, lighter inside; **Ov.** spherical, with some carmine Sc.; **Fr.** matt, white; **S.** numerous, oblong, apiculate, very glossy, black.—Costa Rica (near Caché).

R. bermejensis Ritt. (FR 364): not described; somewhat resembles R. madagascarensis.

R. boliviana (Britt.) Lauterb. (4)
Bo. with primary shoots ± 4-angled, narrowly winged below; **terminal shoots** leaf-like, to 2 cm br., irregularly notched, thin, flat; M.-rib robust; **Ar.**

very woolly-felty, **Br.** to 10, 2 mm lg.; **Fl.** solitary, rarely paired or in 3's, c. 1.5 cm lg., yellow; **Fr.** spherical, colour not known.—Bolivia.

R. burchellii Br. & R. (1)
Bo. hanging, branching in whorls or forking; **shoots** threadlike, 4–10 cm lg., primary ones to 60 cm lg., terminal ones to only 6 cm lg., 1–2 mm thick, if verticillate, then in 3's or 4's, all ± clavate, light green to reddish; **Ar.** with woolly felt at first, without **Br.**; **Fl.** close to the apex, numerous, 1.5 cm lg., bellshaped, whitish; **Ov.** without Sc.; **Fr.** pink.—Brazil (São Paulo; Serra de Mar to Cerras de Caldas).

R. campos-portoana Löfgr. (1)
Bo. shrubby, hanging or curving; **shoots** cylindric, paired, or the terminal shoots in whorls of 3–4, only 4.5 cm lg., to 2.5 mm thick; **Ar.** glabrous; **Fl.** subapical, not widely opening, whitish; **Ov.** without Sc.; **Fr.** light red.—Brazil (Rio de Janeiro: Itatiaya).

R. capilliformis Web. (1)
Bo. shrubby, hanging; **shoots** weak, very thin, branching and bushy, terminal shoots only 2–3 mm thick, sometimes faintly 4-angled, tapering at the tip; **Fl.** lateral, only (6–)8 mm ∅, white; **Ov.** subspherical, without Sc., green; **Fr.** white; **S.** dark brown.—E. Brazil (not re-collected in the wild).

R. cassutha Gärtn. (1) (T.)
Bo. weak, hanging, freely branching, sometimes growing on rocks, to 3 m lg.; **shoots** forking, rarely whorled, 10–15–50 cm lg., 2–3 mm thick, (light) green; **Ar.** spiralled, sparsely grey-felty, mostly with 1–2 minute black Br.; **Fl.** lateral, to 5.5 mm lg., rather fleshy, spreading, whitish to cream; **An.** 9–12, on a ring; **Ov.** without Sc.; **Fr.** glabrous, spherical, white or pink.—Tropical zones of both the New and the Old World (Africa to Ceylon).

R. cassuthopsis Backbg. (1)
Bo. weak, hanging, very freely branching; **shoots** forking, rarely whorled, 10–60 cm lg., oldest ones 8 mm thick, newest growths only 2–3 mm thick, greenish-yellow; **Ar.** not felty, with minute red Br. only at flowering; **Fl.** numerous, lateral, semi-bellshaped, 6–7 mm lg., to 7 mm ∅, greenish-white; **An.** 6–8; **Ov.** without Sc.; **Fr.** translucent greenish-white, elliptic.—Brazil (Pará, in forests near Belém).

R. çereoides Backbg. & Voll (3)
Bo. with greater or lesser development of aerial **R.** at the nodes and then resembling small Hylocerei; **shoots** acutely 3-angled, rarely 4-sided, 4–10 cm lg., to 1.7 cm thick, the angles often offset on successive

Seg.; **Ar.** small, Sc. minute, with traces of felt, with 2–4 short weak Br.; **Fl.** to 3–4 at one time, c. 2 cm ∅, white, spreading, Pet. convex; **Fr.** spherical, olive-green at first, then transparent light pink; **S.** glossy, dark brown, numerous.—Brazil (around Rio de Janeiro).

R. cereuscula Haw. (1)
Bo. shrubby-bushy, mostly hanging, to c. 60 cm lg.; **long shoots** 20–30 cm lg., 3–4 mm thick, dark green; **short shoots** dense, spiralled or in whorls each of a few shoots, elliptic or shortly cylindric, 4–5-angled, 1–3 cm lg., light green; **Ar.** sparsely felty, with 2–4 short white Br.; **Fl.** subapical, rarely paired, bellshaped, c. 1.5 cm lg., 2 cm ∅, white; **Ov.** without Sc.; **Fr.** obconical, white.—Brazil (São Paulo), Argentina (Entrerios), Uruguay, Paraguay.
v. **rubrodisca** (Löfgr.) Cast.: **Fl.** only c. 1 cm ∅; **disc**, **Ov.** and base of **An.** red.—Brazil (São Paulo, near Caldas).

R. chloroptera Web. (4)
Bo. shrubby; small **trunk** often 3-angled, angles acute, ± winged; **shoots** of two types: oblong, to 20 cm lg., to 2 cm br. above, tapering below, or spatulate, ovate or lanceolate, serrate-notched, 8–16 cm lg., 1.5–6 cm br., leaf-green, often bordered red; **Ar.** with little felt, with solitary or paired Br.; **Fl.** not numerous, c. 1.5 cm lg., widely opening, yellow, darker when fading; **Ov.** cylindric, without Sc.—Brazil (?).

R. clavata Web. (1)
Bo. erect at first, soon hanging, strongly branching, forking or in whorls of 2–7 shoots, c. 1 m lg.; **shoots** thin-clavate above, to c. 5 cm lg., 2 mm thick, 3 mm thick at the tip, yellowish, later green, ± suffused reddish; **Ar.** only at the shoot-tip; **Fl.** subapical, c. 1 cm ∅, ± bellshaped, white; **Ov.** spherical, without Sc.; **Fr.** spherical, greenish-white; **S.** large, beaked, dark brown.—Brazil (Rio de Janeiro).
v. **delicatula** Löfgr.: more slender in all parts than the type; **Bo.** ± light green; **bud** white (yellow in the type); **Fl.** hemispherical to ± bellshaped, Pet. not revolute; very floriferous.—Brazil (Rio de Janeiro: Tijuca).

R. coralloides Rauh (provisional description, not yet fully valid) (2)
Bo. bushily branching, **branches** 1–4, forming larger cushions, to 10 cm h.; annual growth very short, 0.5–1.5 cm lg., 0.5–0.8 cm ∅, (5–)6(–7)-angled, new growth ± reddened, eventually greyish-green, constricted at the end of season's growth, ± chain-like; **Ar.** with (6–)8(–10) Br., these thin, silvery-white, erect at the apex, dying off on old shoots; **Fl.** and **Fr.** ?—Madagascar (SE.

coast, between Fort Dauphin and Manantenina, on gneiss rock-formations). (Rauh No. 1385.) A similar plant (Rhipsalis sp. M 1298) was also found by Rauh: Fl. only 4 mm br., Pet. revolute, ± transparent, white.—Madagascar (20 km NW. of Fort Dauphin, on gneiss). (R. pilosa?, R. saxicola?).

R. coriacea Polak. (4)
Bo. strongly branching, hanging down for 4–8 m; **trunks** woody, terete below; **shoots** thin, lanceolate, pointed, weakly serrate, to 20 cm lg., to 3.5 cm br.; **terminal shoots** with a long "stem"; **Ar.** on the trunk, and sometimes on the shoots, with 2–7 long Br.; **Fl.** lateral, to c. 1.2 cm lg., rather narrow, greenish-white to pink; **Ov.** with Sc.; **Fr.** white; **S.** black. New growth red at first.—Costa Rica (near Cartago).

R. cribrata Lem. (1)
Bo. densely shrubby, erect at first, then hanging, but more spreading; **shoots** threadlike, to 20 cm lg.; **short shoots** in whorls or spirals, smallest ones only 1 cm lg., 2 mm thick, yellowish-green; **Ar.** scarcely woolly, sometimes with 1 minute Br.; **Fl.** at the tip of the short shoots, to 1.5 cm lg., bellshaped, white, slightly reddened above; **Ov.** ± spherical, without Sc.; **Fil.** arising from a red ring; **Fr.** purple; **S.** black.—Brazil.

R. crispata (Haw.) Pfeiff. (4)
Bo. shrubby, freely branching, to 40 cm lg.; **shoots** mostly from the tip of older shoots, oblong or elliptic, tapering below, margins wavy, deeply notched, to 12 cm lg., 7 cm br., dark (or yellowish-) green; **Ar.** weakly grey-felty, with a few black Br. on newer shoots; **Fl.** 1–4 at the same time, lateral, c. 1.4 cm lg., rotate, creamy-yellow; **Ov.** light green; **Fr.** white, containing few **S.**—Brazil (Rio de Janeiro to São Paulo).

R. crispimarginata Löfgr. (4)
Bo. hanging; **trunk** subterete, woody; **shoots** from the tip of older growths, sometimes clustered, leaf-like, very wavy, the stout M.-nerve sometimes similarly, oblong-oval, narrowed to ± stem-like at the base, margin irregularly notched, wavy; young shoots with pinkish-red, translucent borders; **Ar.** small; **Fl.** solitary or in 2's and 3's, rotate, white; **Ov.** with sparse felt and sometimes 1 Br.; **Fr.** pink, translucent.—Brazil (Rio de Janeiro; Ilha Grande).

R. cuneata Br. & R. (4)
Bo. probably hanging; **shoots** continuing from the tip of the preceding ones, oblong to spatulate, strongly notched, 8–12 cm lg., thin, green; **Ar.** sometimes with 1–2 Br.; **Fl.** solitary, as far as

known; **Fr.** spherical, 4 mm ⌀.—Bolivia (at c. 1700 m, above San Juan). Spec. inadequately described, or only from herbarium material.

R. densiareolata Löfgr. (1)
Bo. shrubby, trunk ± erect at first, then hanging, to 60 cm lg., 1–1.2 cm thick; **shoots** 6–7 together, never whorled, 20–60 cm lg., 5–7 mm thick, ± tapering at the tip, light yellowish-green, later grey; **Ar.** crowded, spiralled, on younger shoots with Br. 1–1.5 mm lg.; **Fl.** very numerous, c. 9 mm ⌀, white; **Ov.** without Sc.; **Fr.** pinkish-red, ovoid.—Brazil (Rio de Janeiro, near Tijuca).

R. elliptica Lindbg. (4)
Bo. shrubby, branching, hanging, over 1.5 m lg.; **shoots** in 3's or 4's, in a row, separated by constrictions, leaf-like, oblong-elliptic, 6–15 cm lg., 2.5–6 cm br., dark green, border slightly wavy and notched, occasionally entire; **Ar.** sparsely felty, sometimes with 1 Br.; **Fl.** lateral, 8–9 mm lg., white; **Ov.** ± angular, without Sc.; **Fr.** pink, spherical.—Brazil (coast, Rio de Janeiro to Santa Catharina and sometimes inland).
  v. **helicoidea** Löfgr.: **shoots** smaller, more terete, always contorted around the axis, green at first, later coppery-red (Rio de Janeiro: Ilha Grande).

R. erythrocarpa K. Sch.: see Rhipsalis lindbergiana K. Sch.

R. fasciculata (Willd.) Haw. (2)
Bo. branching freely, in whorls, from the tip of the previous year's growth; **shoots** short, fleshy, 4–5 mm thick, with 6–10 little prominent Ri., to terete, at first ± completely cylindric; **Ar.** with a cluster of brittle, whitish, later darker Br.; **Fl.** numerous, little opening, 6–8 mm lg., 5 mm ⌀, greenish-white; **Ov.** spherical, some Ar. with 2–3 Br.; **Fr.** with felty and bristly Ar., white to pale greenish, translucent; **S.** ?—Brazil (Bahia).
Vaupel's statement that the S. are "brown", and Pfeiffer's that they are "black", were clearly based on Madagascan plants. No data available from Zehntner, who re-discovered this spec. Description acc. Vaupel, who includes the Madagascan spec., as is obvious from his synonymy. The original description was incomplete, giving no details of Fl., Fr.-colour or S.; Rauh's discoveries in Madagascar (see notes at the end of this genus) show that inclusion in R. fasciculata cannot be admitted, at least while the latter remains unclarified and inadequately described. See also R. madagascarensis.

R. goebeliana (hort. ?) Backbg. (4)
Bo. bushy, hanging; **primary shoots** narrow, flat,

with a robust nerve, 8 mm br. above, terete below, vivid green; **terminal shoots** narrowly oblong, ± tapering above, c. 8–13 cm lg., 2.5–3 cm br., sometimes slightly wavy; **Fl.** pinkish-white; **Ov.** oblong, with Sc.; **Fr.** greenish-white.—Origin ?

R. gonocarpa Web. (4)
Bo. strongly branching, weakly erect or hanging; **trunk** flat, winged, sometimes 3-angled, notched; **shoots** lateral, c. 30 cm lg. (and more), to 3 cm br., sometimes narrowing and stem-like and then to 60 cm lg., notches rounded, shoots mostly bordered dark red; **Ar.** weakly white-felty; **Fl.** along the entire length of the shoot, to 1.5 cm lg., little opening, white; **Ov.** 3–4–5-angled; **Fr.** spherical, weakly angular, blackish-purple.—Brazil (São Paulo).

R. hadrosoma Lindbg. (1)
Bo. shrubby, freely branching, creeping, on trees and rocks; **trunk** 10–15 cm lg.; terminal **shoots**, solitary, or in 2's or 3's, cylindric, to 10 cm lg., 1.5–2 cm thick, rounded, truncate above, matt, light green, bristly at first; **Ar.** little felty, surrounded by a red ring; **Fl.** lateral, numerous, to 2 cm ∅, opening widely, Pet. strongly revolute, white; **Fr.** to 1 cm ∅, dark purple.—Brazil (São Paulo).

R. heptagona Rauh & Backbg. (3)
Bo. hanging, long; **shoots** slender, 7-ribbed, to 5 mm ∅, very finely grooved, greyish-green, light-pitted, single ones to 25 cm lg., then in whorls or one above the other, sometimes branching very freely; **Ar.** with yellowish felt; **Fl.** solitary, small, yellowish-white; **Fr.** red, spherical, 5 mm ∅, with floral remains.—N. Peru (Jaën).

R. heteroclada Br. & R. (1)
Bo. shrubby, rigid and often erect; **shoots** in whorled clusters, cylindric; **terminal shoots** 1.5–2 mm ∅, dark green, ± reddish at the tip; **Ar.** red, sometimes with 1 Br.; **Fl.** lateral, subapical, small, white to greenish; **Ov.** without Sc.; **Fr.** spherical, white.—Brazil (Ilha Grande).

R. horrida Bak. (2)
Bo. branching freely from the base, later also from towards the apex; **shoots** 10–50 cm lg., 5 mm ∅, with c. 8 Ri., pale green; **Ar.** with dense, ± glassy, brittle, reddish-brown Br.-Sp. c. 5 mm lg., those in the apex forming a dense tuft; **Fl.** ?, probably up to 3 together from an Ar.; **Fr.** 1–3 together, spherical, sometimes with Ar. and Br.—Madagascar.

R. houlletiana Lem. (4)
Bo. shrubby, to 2 m lg. and more, hanging; **shoots** at first cylindric or terete and stem-like below, leaf-

like above, often with these 2 shapes alternating; **primary shoots** to 2 mm thick; **terminal shoots** ± terete below, to 40 cm lg., 3–5 cm br., vivid green, deeply serrate with teeth to 3 cm lg. and 1 cm br., border not wavy, ± suffused red; **Ar.** scarcely felty, without Br.; **Fl.** nodding, c. 2 cm lg., white; **Ov.** shortly cylindric, 4–5-angled, light green; **Fr.** spherical, carmine.—Brazil (Rio de Janeiro; São Paulo, Minas Geraes). (Fig. 368.)
Spec. variable as to dentation and red colouring; Br. & R. describe the Fl. as cream-coloured, later yellowish, and the Fr. as appreciably smaller.

R. incachacana Card. (4)
Bo. freely branching, to 1.5 m lg., hanging; **shoots** 20–30 cm lg., 4–6 cm br., ± wavy, green; **Ar.** in the indentations (sunken?), with light brown felt and tufts of Br.-H. to c. 1.8 cm lg., light brown to whitish; **Fl.** 1–2 from amid the Br., c. 1 cm lg., dark purplish-violet above, lighter below; **Ov.** with stiff white H. below, with large purple Sc. with a few axillary H.; **Fr.** 5-angled, angles reddish.—Bolivia (Prov. Chapare, Dept. Cochabamba, Incachaca).
If the Ar. are sunken, then the spec. is referable to Lepismium, which would tally with the Pet. being united and tube-like below.

R. jamaicensis Britt. & Harr. (4)
Bo. shrubby, hanging, 0.3–1 m lg., **trunk** angular; **shoots** to 40 cm lg., to 2.5 cm br., strongly bristly at first, later glabrous, with shallow notches, with a stem-like base, glossy green; **Fl.** c. 6 mm lg., yellowish-green; **Ov.** oblong, with few Sc.; **Fr.** smoothly spherical, white.—Jamaica (Cockpit County, near Troy). (See also R. ramulosa.)

R. leiophloea Vpl. (4)
Bo. shrubby; **shoots** stem-like below, leaf-like and wider above, outer skin becoming ± detached; **side-shoots** spirally arranged, ± elliptic, shortly "stemmed", sometimes ± lanceolate, to 2.5 cm br., distinctly ribbed; **Fl.** in the upper half of the shoot, c. 1 cm lg., white; **An.** 12–18; **Ov.** with minute Sc.; **Fr.** with a ± annular marking above, with Sc.;—Costa Rica (near San José) (see also R. ramulosa).

R. leucorhaphis K. Sch. (2)
Bo. shrubby, freely branching, to 50 cm lg., with a few holdfast **R.**, also growing on rocks; **shoots** terete, to 7 mm thick, fresh green, then greyish-green, finally grey; **Ar.** small, with brown Sc. with 1–5 Br.-Sp., these appressed, to 4 mm lg., glassy to matt white; **Fl.** subapical, hanging, c. 1.5 cm lg., pure white; **Ov.** weakly angular, with scattered Sc.; **Fr.** spherical, red; **S.** numerous, brown.—Paraguay (Estancia Tagatiya); N. Argentina.

R. lindbergiana K. Sch. (1)

Bo. freely branching, to 2 m lg., hanging, ± woody, branches in whorls or forking; **shoots** to 20 cm lg., to 5 mm thick; **Ar.** crowded, only c. 6 mm apart, mostly very felty, mostly with 2 black Br.-Sp. to 2 mm lg.; **Fl.** lateral, rotate, c. 5 mm lg., pink to white; **Ov.** without Sc.; **Fr.** light red; **S.** to 20.— Brazil (Rio de Janeiro: Serra dos Orgaos) and (?) Africa (Kilimanjaro: R. erythrocarpa occurs here [synonymous, acc. Br. & R.; ?]).

R. linearis K. Sch. (4)
Bo. shrubby, 60–80 cm lg., branching from the sides; **shoots** very narrow, linear, 5–20 cm lg., 4–7 mm br., with a stout M.-Ri., distinctly notched; **Ar.** weakly felty, without Br.-Sp.; **Fl.** lateral, funnelform or rotate, to 1.8 cm lg., white to yellowish; **Ov.** ellipsoid, naked; **Fr.** spherical, translucent, white.—Brazil (in the S., no locality stated); Paraguay (on the Rio Yhu and near Caaguazu); Argentina (Misiones).

R. loefgrenii Br. & R. (1)
Bo. with long thin trunks, freely rooting; **shoots** to 20 cm lg., c. 3 mm thick, pale green to purple, distinctly ribbed; **Ar.** first with appressed Br., later glabrous, with conspicuous Sc., these oblong to 3-sided or often cordate; **Fl.** lateral, to 1.5 cm lg., bellshaped, white; **Ov.** ± 3-sided at first; **Fr.** ± spherical, carmine; **S.** chestnut-brown.—Brazil (São Paulo, near Campinas).

R. lorentziana Gris. (4)
Bo. shrubby; **shoots** branching laterally, lanceolate, 10–30 cm lg., 2–4 cm br., terete below, obtuse above, matt, fresh green, margin not wavy, bluntly dentate, M.-Ri. stout; **Ar.** scarcely felty, without Br.; **Fl.** solitary, white; **Ov.** 4-angled, smooth; **Fr.** indistinctly 4-angled, dark purple; **S.** 1–3, black.—Argentina (Salta: near Oran; Catamarca; Tucuman).
Acc. a drawing of Castellanos, the terminal shoots are ± "stem"-less, the dentation is wavy, the Ar. sometimes have 1 Br.; the Fl. may appear in pairs.

R. lumbricoides (Lem.) Lem. (2)
Bo. shrubby, freely branching, creeping, or clinging to the bark of trees by means of aerial **R.**; **shoots** thin, 4–6 (rarely 8) mm thick, 1 m lg. and more, terete or slightly angular, side-shoots alternate or whorled, 14–20 cm lg., greyish to yellowish-green; **Ar.** crowded, shortly white-felty, with 5–8 stiff horn-coloured Br.-Sp. 3–5 mm lg., spreading, later mostly deciduous; **Fl.** lateral, rotate, c. 2.2 cm lg., 3.75 cm ∅, light straw-coloured, orange-scented (1.2 cm lg., white to cream to greenish-yellow has been reported); **Ov.** ellipsoid, naked; **Fr.** spherical, green, finally deep purple, inside also; **S.** light brown.— Uruguay, Argentina.

R. madagascarensis Web.: see under R. pilosa, which has a greenish Fr. and black S., whereas R. madagascarensis is described as having white Fr. and brown S.; apart from that, the plants in general are similar, also the Fl.

R. mesembryanthemoides Haw. (1)
Bo. shrubby, erect, later hanging, freely branching, to 40 cm lg., with a terete little trunk, this becoming woody; **shoots** dimorphic: terete, to 20 cm lg., to 2 mm thick, or spindle-shaped short shoots 7–15 mm lg., 2–4 mm thick, arranged in dense spirals, light green; **Ar.** on the long shoots with sparse woolly felt and 1–2 small appressed Br.-Sp., those on the short shoots with plentiful felt and 3–4 Br.-Sp.; **Fl.** lateral on the short shoots, c. 8 mm lg., to 1.5 cm ∅, spreading, white to faint pink; **Ov.** ellipsoid, light green; **Fr.** spherical, white or reddish.—Brazil (Rio de Janeiro).

R. micrantha (HBK.) DC. (3)
Bo. ± long, hanging from trees; main St. to 6 mm thick, mostly with 4 angles, rarely with 5; not branching in whorls; **shoots** thin, segmented, in 2's or 3's, mostly 3-angled, to only c, 8 mm br., sometimes flattened, angles somewhat notched, acute, light to washy yellowish-green; **Ar.** weakly felty, with Sc. soon dropping, and often 1–4 Br.; **Fl.** c. 7 mm lg., little opening, white; **Ov.** short-cylindric, glabrous, sometimes with a small Sc. or a Br.-Sp.; **Fr.** spherical to shortly ellipsoid, smooth, white or light yellow to reddish; **S.** very numerous, light brown (acc. Br. & R.: black).—Peru; S. Ecuador.

R. minutiflora K. Sch. (1)
Bo. shrubby, freely branching; **shoots** forking, very slender, to 20 cm lg., scarcely 1 mm thick, light green; **Ar.** minute, shortly felty, sometimes with only 1 Br. rising from the tiny deciduous Sc.; **Fl.** scattered along the terminal shoots, only c. 2 mm lg., rotate, white; **Ov.** ellipsoid, scaly; **Fr.** ?— Surinam (former Dutch Guiana).

R. oblonga Löfgr. (4)
Bo. probably erect at first, later hanging, **main St.** very rarely with 3 angles or wings, mostly like the terminal shoots; **shoots** mostly 1–3(–5) together, leaf-like, thin, oblong-oval, obtuse above, ± indistinctly 3-angled below, 6–12 cm lg., rarely over 3 cm br., with flat indentations and obtuse teeth, light green at first, bordered weakly reddish, M.-Ri. robust; **Ar.** small, with Br. after flowering; **Fl.** solitary, rotate, white to light yellow; **Fr.** spherical, yellowish-green.—Brazil (Rio de Janeiro, Ilha Grande).

R. pachyptera Pfeiff. (4)
Bo. shrubby, freely branching, erect, later hanging, to c. 1 m lg.; **shoots** elliptic to ± circular, coarsely notched, to c. 20 cm lg., to c. 12 cm br., with stout Ri., dark green and ± purplish-red, sometimes 3-angled; **Ar.** very weakly felty; **Fl.** lateral, c. 1.5 cm lg., yellowish, strongly perfumed; **Ov.** shortly cylindric to ± spherical, naked; **Fr.** ellipsoid, red.—Brazil (from Santa Catharina to Rio de Janeiro; São Paulo to the Serra Cantareira).

R. penduliflora N. E. Brown (1)
Bo. bushy, branching, hanging; **shoots** elongated, to 15 cm lg., older ones terete, finely pitted, terminal shoots to 1.2 cm lg., vivid green; **Ar.** with 2 H. to 1 mm lg.; **Fl.** apical, c. 1.2 cm ∅ whitish, tipped reddish; **Ov.** hemispherical to pear-shaped; **Fil.** salmon-coloured below; **Fr.** spherical to ellipsoid, translucent white.—Brazil (Minas Geraes, São Paulo, Rio de Janeiro, Paraná to Santa Catharina).
Br. & R. refer R. cribrata to this spec. although the former shows the following differences from R. penduliflora: Ov. differently shaped, Fil. mid-yellow, rising from a red annulus.

R. pentaptera Pfeiff. (3)
Bo. shrubby, branching, to 40 cm lg. (perhaps more?); **shoots** solitary, paired or in 3's, 7–12 cm lg., 0.6–1.5 cm thick, the 5–6 Ri. ± winged, vivid dark green; **Ar.** c. 4 cm apart, at first with a cluster of fine white H.; **Fl.** also in the upper part of the shoot, in 3's or more, opening in succession, 7–8 mm lg., white; **Ov.** trucate, naked; **Fr.** translucent white, light pinkish-red above.—S. Brazil, Uruguay.

R. pilosa Web., an undescribed name for a Madagascan spec. found growing on gneiss scree; **shoots** shortly hairy; **Fl.** minute, white; **Fr.** greenish, mostly smooth, more rarely bristly; **S.** black. Extraordinarily free-flowering.
R. madagascarensis Web., a similar plant, was described as having white Fr. and brown S.; i.e. Weber correctly saw the plants as two distinct spec. (Fig. 369.)
Since R. fasciculata (Willd.) Haw. was described without Fl. and Fr., and in general with insufficient data, and Rauh collected several plants of the Madagascan spec. (see notes at the end of the genus), these spec. cannot be considered identical. See also R. saxicola.

R. platycarpa (Zucc.) Pfeiff. (4)
Bo. shrubby, freely branching, to 80 cm h.; **shoots** leaf-like, to 30 cm lg., 4–5 cm br., with rounded notches, at first with felt and Sc., mostly soon reddish or bordered thus, with a distinct M.-Ri.; **Fl.**

subapical, 1–3 from one Ar., c. 2 cm lg., scarcely opening, greenish-yellow or matt white; **Ov.** weakly 4-angled, green, angles reddish; **Fr.** similar in shape to the Ov., naked.—Brazil (Organ Mountains) (?).

R. prismatica (Lem.) Rümpl. (1)
Bo. shrubby, freely branching, **main St.** erect to curving, stout, cylindric, 12–30 cm lg.; **shoots** forking or clustered at the apex of the main St., 4–5-angled, c. 1.2–2.2 cm lg., 4 mm thick, terminal shoots thinner, all shoots subterete below, reddish; **Ar.** very close together, Sc. minute, red, with 5–6 spreading Br.; **Fl.** white, Pet. only 5; **Ov.** without Sc.; **Fr.** spherical, pink to white.—Brazil; (Madagascar [?]; R. suareziana Web.—regarded by Roland-Gosselin as being identical with the above spec.—occurs in Madagascar).

R. pulchra Löfgr. (1)
Bo. long, hanging down, sparsely branching, very occasionally in pseudo-whorls of 3–5 branches; **shoots** to 20 cm lg. and more, gradually tapering, ± limp, matt greyish-green; **Ar.** ± sunken, glabrous; **Fl.** lateral, to c. 1.5 cm lg., c. 6 mm ∅, slightly reddish (reddish-purple, acc. Br. & R.); **Fr.** brownish-red; **S.** black.—Brazil (Rio de Janeiro: Organ Mountains, Serra da Mantiqueira, Serra da Cantareira).

R. purpusii Wgt. (4)
Bo. shrubby, hanging, **main St.** terete, with a smooth epidermis; **shoots** of 2 types: at first terete, ± sinuate above, ± leaf-like towards the tip, green, later shoots leaf-like, stout, leathery, flat, lanceolate to elliptic-lanceolate, on a "stalk", 8–20 cm lg., 1–3 cm br., matt dark green, margin with distant flat notches, ± faintly reddish, M.-Ri. sunken; **Fl.** lateral, c. 1.1 cm lg., greenish-white; **An.** 20–30; **Ov.** with semicircular Sc., red; **Fr.** spherical, white, scaly; **S.** glossy black.—Mexico (in the S.); Guatemala (see also R. ramulosa).

R. quellebambensis Johns. n.nud.
Bo. similar to R. cassutha; **Fr.** intense red.—Peru. A good spec. on the basis of these characters alone, so that it merits a full description.

R. ramulosa (SD.) Pfeiff. (4)
Bo. shrubby, main St. terete, woody, c. 30 cm h.; **shoots** numerous, borne at intervals of c. 1 cm along the St., 10–25 cm lg., broadly linear, margin weakly serrate, tip obtuse, tapering below into a "stem" 1–6 cm lg., fresh-green; **Ar.** ± bristly at first, later quite glabrous; **Fl.** subapical, rotate, whitish-green; **Ov.** with 2–3 small Sc.; **Fr.** pea-shaped, green, then almost translucent-white; **S.** numerous,

black.—W. Brazil; Bolivia (Isapuri); Peru (Pozuzo).

Kimnach united here the others of Vaupel's Series "Ramulosae", as mentioned in the introduction to the genus; without any doubt all are more or less closely related, but it must be pointed out that they do vary in the following characters: width and notches of the shoots (the latter forming closely or widely spaced steps of a ladder, or curving), shape of the main St. (terete or angular), and of the Fl. (Pet. in some cases ray-like, sometimes not), as well as the form of the shoots themselves and of the Ri.; in R. angustissima for instance, which has narrow shoots, the Ri. are scarcely discernible in the growing season; in R. leiophloea they are clearly prominent, while in R. purpusii they are just as conspicuously sunken. See my photographs of living plants in "Die Cact.", Fig. 630–632, pp. 673, 675, 1959. The Fr.-form also is not constant: in R. jamaicensis it is smooth and regularly spherical, in R. leiophloea there is a ± urn-shaped or annular widening above. Admittedly Kimnach had a large amount of herbarium material at his disposal; on the other hand I have observed the differences for myself, on living plants.

In Britton & Rose, this problematic group is noticeable for being insufficiently known or studied; Vaupel's observations on the other hand were carefully made. It is undeniable that the spec. he segregated are clearly divergent in their principal forms. Consequently I must give preference here to a separation of the species, to ensure the preservation of differential data. Unification, such as Kimnach proposes, cannot be beneficial. There may indeed be transitional forms within the range of variability, but that is of little consequence when compared with the necessity of bringing the principal differences clearly into relief, and I am thus obliged to maintain Vaupel's delimitation of the species.

See the introductory remarks to Rhipsalis regarding the classification of R. ramulosa etc. under Disocactus.

R. rhombea (SD.) Pfeiff. (4)

Bo. shrubby, erect at first, then hanging, branching, to 80 cm lg., main **St.** terete or with winged angles; **shoots** in 2's, 3's or more, with 2 angles or 3 wings, ovate to lanceolate-rhombic, obtuse above, tapering and stem-like below, 3–12 cm lg., to 5 cm br., deeply notched, M.-Ri. robust, intense to dark green, often reddish; **Ar.** with sparse felt, sometimes with 1 Br.; **Fl.** c. 1 cm lg., light to later canary-yellow, also reported as being whitish-greenish; **Ov.** spherical; **Fr.** dark red.—Brazil (coastal zone, São Paulo and Rio de Janeiro).

R. robusta Lem. (4)

Bo. shrubby, erect to hanging; **shoots** to c. 20 cm lg., c. 10 cm br., elliptic or ovate, rounded above, tapering below, sometimes 3-winged, matt dark green, notches rather deep, M.-Ri. very thick, secondary veins prominent; **Ar.** at first with tiny red L., also nectar-glands secreting clear droplets before anthesis, with 1 or more Br. which are carmine at first; **Fl.** to 6 from an Ar., to c. 1.5 cm lg., 1.8 cm ∅, opening widely, creamy-yellow; **style** white; **Sti.** white, papillose; **Ov.** top-shaped; **Fr.** white, spherical, truncate, with floral remains; **S.** ovoid, brown.—Brazil (Rio de Janeiro, Santa Catharina).

An interesting spec. in which new shoots can also have 5 angles, but more often 3.

R. roseana Berg. (4)

Bo. hanging, bushy, irregularly branching; upper **shoots** ± linear-lanceolate, 6–12 cm lg. and more, 1–1.5 cm br., with regularly alternating notches, smooth, light green, sometimes variable in breadth and notching, other shoots 3-angled, with flat indentations along the borders and prominent notched angles, 4 ± winged angles sometimes present, while the outermost shoots are often only 8–10 mm br.; **Ar.** weakly white-woolly, with 1 short brown Br.; **Fl.** small, yellowish-white; **Fr.** small, whitish.—Costa Rica (?) (acc. Br. & R.: Colombia).

R. russelli Br. & R. (4)

Bo. forming large hanging bushes; **shoots** to 15 cm lg., 5–6 cm br., wedge-shaped below, strongly notched, notches appearing slit-like and the lobes very close together, dark green, sometimes bordered ± purple; **Fl.** often 9 from an Ar., small, cream, only c. 2 mm lg.; **Fr.** spherical, purple.—Brazil (Bahia, near Tonca da Onca).

R. saxicola (A. B. Graf's Exotica, 580. 1963) is a name with Fig. only, and is probably identical with Rauh's spec. M.1298, occurring on crustal granite. This tallies with the specific name, and both are reported from Fort Dauphin, Madagascar.

R. shaferi Br. & R. non Cast. (1)

Bo. at first rigid, erect, later spreading or prostrate; **shoots** terete, 4–5 mm thick, green, ± reddened at the tips; **Ar.** over 1 cm apart, those on new and lower shoots often with a few Br., upper ones without Br. or only 1, appressed; **Fl.** throughout the length of the shoots, mostly solitary, rarely paired, small, rotate, greenish-white; **Fr.** spherical, to 3 mm ∅, white to washed reddish.—Paraguay (near Trinidad and Asunción); Argentina (Misiones: near Posadas).

R. schaferi (incorrect spelling) sensu Castellanos must be referred to Lepismium since he says: "Fl.

and Fr. sunken, in a tuft of white wool, Fr. 7 mm ∅".

R. simmleri Beauv. (1)
Bo. hanging; small main **St.** terete, strongly branching; terminal **shoots** paired, or in whorls of 3–4, with 5 weak angles or Ri., 1–3 cm lg., 1.5–2 mm thick, with long, threadlike, grey, forking aerial R.; **Fl.** solitary, subapical, small, white, red-tipped; **style** 9 mm lg., projecting; **Ov.** obconical, light green; **Fr.** whitish.—Costa Rica.

R. sulcata Web. (3)
Bo. often long, hanging down, main **St.** woody, to 1.5 cm thick; **shoots** elongated, 20–30 cm lg., 5-angled, light green; **Ar.** distant, set in a red mark; **Fl.** solitary, to 1.2 cm lg., rotate, yellowish-white, but white to pink has been reported; **Ov.** naked.—Origin ?

R. teres (Vell.) Steud. (1)
Bo. erect at first, then ± hanging, freely branching; **shoots** solitary, alternating, or several and clustered, cylindric, to over 50 cm lg., to 5 mm thick, newer shoots shorter, thinner; **Ar.** always with grey felt, this later darker, and sometimes with 1–2 dark Br.; **Fl.** lateral on young shoots, to 1.2 cm ∅, spreading, yellowish outside; **Ov.** with 1–2 Br.; **Fr.** spherical, translucent white; **S.** c. 20, elliptic, finely granular.—Brazil (São Paulo and Minas Geraes; Rio de Janeiro).

R. tonduzii Web. (3)
Bo. weakly erect to hanging, branching and bushy, segmented; **shoots** 6–10 cm lg., 1 cm thick, 4–5(–7)-angled, terminal shoots often 3-angled, or sometimes flattened, green, Ri. compressed; **Ar.** bristly at first, becoming glabrous; **Fl.** small, whitish; **Ov.** smooth; **Fr.** spherical, white, glossy; **S.** sickle-shaped, pointed.—Costa Rica. Acc. Britton & Rose, the shoots are arranged in whorls of 2–6.

R. triangularis Werd. (3)
Bo. light green, reddish along the angles; **shoots** mostly 3-ribbed, rarely flattened, primary shoots with to 4 Ri., to 11.5 cm lg., to 3 cm br., with robust Ri. to 2.5 cm h.; **Ar.** set in slight notches, with 3–4 white Br.-Sp.; **Fl.** lateral, 1–3 from an Ar., c. 1.2 cm lg., light green; **Ov.** without Sc.; **Fr.** ?—Brazil (locality not known).

R. virgata Web. (1)
Bo. shrubby, freely branching, ± hanging; main **St.** cylindric, 1 m lg. and more, 4–5 mm thick, green; **main shoots** erect, ± rigid, to 1 m lg.; **side-shoots** rarely whorled, to 3 mm thick, cylindric, tapering towards the tip, **terminal shoots** with small prominent scars (Ar. which have borne Fl.); **Ar.**

crowded; **Fl.** throughout the whole length of the shoot, solitary or paired, 6–8 mm lg. and ∅, white; **Ov.** ovoid, greenish-yellow, rarely scaly; **Fr.** spherical, smooth, green, later white; **S.** dark brown to black.—Brazil (locality not known). Acc. Britton & Rose the Ar. are somewhat hairy, often with a white or reddish Br.

R. warmingiana K. Sch. (4)
Bo. shrubby, freely branching, erect, then hanging; **shoots** broadly linear or narrowly lanceolate, to 30 cm lg., 2 cm br., notched, tapering towards the base or 2-angled or terete and stem-like, sometimes acutely 3–4-angled and then with a robust M.-vein, often suffused reddish; **Ar.** somewhat felty, without Br.; **Fl.** lateral, rotate, c. 2 cm ∅, green outside, white inside; **Ov.** 5–6-angled; **Fr.** blackish-violet; **S.** glossy, reddish-brown.—Brazil (Minas Geraes; São Paulo). Fl. said to be hyacinth-scented.

R. werklei Berg. (4)
Bo. shrubby, branching from the base and higher, hanging, to 1.5 m lg.; **shoots** fresh green, primary shoots mostly 3-angled, robust, spreading and projecting, truncate above, with fairly broad surfaces, in 3's and 5's one above the other at the apex, tipped with 1–2(–3) flattened shoots, these in turn with 1–2 similar shoots, 15(–20) cm lg., linear, rather bluntly tapering to both ends, to 1.8 cm br. at midway, angles little sunken, M.-vein distinct; **Fl.** lateral, to 9 mm ∅, creamy-white; **Ov.** naked or with 1 minute Sc., greenish to yellowish-white.—Costa Rica (near Navarro).

Observations on the identity of New and Old World spec.:
In the course of his 2nd collecting trip in Madagascar, Rauh discovered the following material, which I list under the numbers of the Botanical Institute, Heidelberg; it belongs in part to SG. Rhipsalis, in part to SG. Ophiorhipsalis K. Sch. In the light of these finds, and in view of the discrepancies brought out by these Madagascan members of Rhipsalis alone, identification of similar spec. from the Old or the New World must be postponed until further studies have been made.

016: Shoots light green, terete, without Br., c. 4–5 mm ∅, apparently branching in whorls; Fr. greenish-white at maturity.

017

(+ 020?) Shoots thin, white-bristly; Br. fairly dense at first; Fr. whitish at maturity.

3160

(+ 019?) Shoots to almost 1 cm ∅, ± erect-inclined, bristly at first; Fr. at maturity: not known.

5295 Shoots branching from low down,

reddish at first, fine-bristly, later glabrous, c. 6 mm ⌀; Fr. ?

7494 Shoots weakly white-bristly at first, later glabrous, c. 5 mm ⌀; Fr. ?

7496 Shoots branching from near the base; Fr. at maturity white, glassy, with yellow floral remains.

7497 Shoots terete, glabrous, Ar. crowded at first, with weak Br.; Fr. ?

7528 Shoots with many Ar., new shoots with white Br., reddish at first, later c. 5 mm ⌀; Ar. rather prominent; Fr. ?

7534 Shoots c. 5–6 mm ⌀, new shoots reddish; Ar. crowded, all remaining shortly bristly for a longer time, eventually glabrous; Fr. ?

7554 Shoots terete, c. 6 mm ⌀; Ar. weakly bristly at first, later glabrous; Fr. green at maturity.

7629 Shoots terete, c. 7 mm ⌀; branches not arranged in whorls; new shoots red at first, with a few erect appressed Br.; Fr. ?

For further Rauh discoveries, see under R. coralloides nom.prov. Cf. also text under R. pilosa Web.
For all spec. described as belonging to Rhipsalis, but with a sunken Ov., see under **Lepismium**.

× **Rhipsaphyllopsis** Werd.

× **Rhipsaphyllopsis graeseri** Werd.

A widely cultivated cross between Epiphyllopsis gaertneri (seed-parent) and Rhipsalidopsis rosea, remarkable for the flower-colour which is lacquer-red or carmine, as well as the large number of blooms produced. Mentioned here as an exceptional case, despite its being a hybrid genus, because of its horticultural value.

Rhodocactus (Berg.) Knuth (2)

Bushy to tree-like, leafy plants, with ± stout spination on trunk and branches. Earlier regarded as a subgenus of Peireskia, but segregated by Knuth on account of the inferior ovary. However, the inclusion of all 16 described species is not yet completely clarified in all cases.
Recently, for instance, it was found that "Peireskia conzattii Br. & R." is identical with P. pititache, and that the latter is not a Peireskiopsis; in other instances it has not been possible at this time to check the position of the ovary. Knuth's referals were therefore in part based on probabilities such as are inevitable where genera are separated.
The flowers are solitary or sometimes in shortly pedunculate panicles, or even in clusters; they are white, yellow, reddish or purple. The fruits vary in shape and size, and contain seeds which, as far as known, are black, glossy and have a thin testa.—Distribution: from Mexico and Costa Rica through Haiti to Venezuela and Colombia as well as Brazil. [(R).]

R. antonianus Backbg.—Descr. Cact. Nov. III: 13. 1963.
Bo. shrubby, branches later hanging; **R.** thick-napiform, woody; **St.** to c. 1 cm ⌀, green, becoming greyish-olive, soon branching, secondary shoots thinner, shorter; **Ar.** few, with very short felt; **L.** to 5 cm lg., 3 cm br., alternate, ± spatulate, light green on both surfaces; **Sp.** c. 7, yellowish, 2–12 mm lg., thin to rather stouter, much thickened below; **Fl.** light carmine-pink, 5 mm lg., 2–3 cm ⌀, solitary, apical, sessile; **Tu.** absent; **Sep.** c. 3, pale pink, with a greenish dorsal M.-line; **Pet.** 6, oblong, 18 mm lg., 5 mm br., margins entire; **Ov.** naked, spherical, green, 4 mm lg. and ⌀, with 3 minute L. in the upper part, one of these sometimes 1 cm lg., 3 mm br.; **Fil.** pinkish-carmine, white below; **An.** golden-yellow; **style** 1 cm lg., white; **Sti.** 5, yellowish-green, papillose; **Fr.** small, spherical.—NE. Peru. (Fig. 370, 371.)

R. autumnalis (Eichlam) Knuth
Bo. tree-like, with a large crown, to 9 m h.; **trunk** to 40 cm ⌀; **L.** rather thick, subcircular to oblong, 4–8 cm lg.; **Sp.** 1–3, 3–16 cm lg., grey, tipped brownish, sometimes banded; **Fl.** solitary, shortly pedunculate, to c. 5 cm ⌀, orange, Pet.-margins entire; **Ov.** with leaf-like Sc.; **Fr.** spherical, to 5 cm ⌀, fleshy, with small Sc., glabrous; **S.** glossy, black.—Guatemala, Salvador.

R. bleo (HBK.) Knuth
Bo. tree-like, to 7 m h.; **L.** to 20 cm lg., 5 cm br., long-petiolate, vivid green; **Ar.** sparsely woolly, later naked; **Sp.** mostly 5–6 (or more), sometimes 1–4 at first, robust, black; **Fl.** 2–4 together, shortly pedicellate; **Pet.** 12–15, 3.5 cm lg., ± ovate, pinkish-red; **Fr.** yellow, truncate, 5–6 cm lg., passing over into a massive stem, the flat upperside ± convex in the middle; **S.** black, glossy.—Colombia (near Badillas).

R. colombianus (Br. & R.) Knuth
Bo. tree-like, to 11 m h., **trunk** with clusters of Sp. to 7 cm lg.; **branches** often glabrous; **L.** to 4 cm lg., broadly rounded to ± oblong, short-petiolate; **Fl.** solitary, sessile, c. 4 cm ⌀; **Pet.** not ciliate, light yellow; **Ov.** with small ovate L., these with H. in the Ax.—Colombia (near Sta. Marta).

R. conzattii (Br. & R.) Backbg.: **Peireskia pititache** Karw.

R. corrugatus (Cutak) Backbg.
Bo. shrubby or a small tree, 2.5 m h. (and more); main **trunk** covered with clusters of slender Sp.; **branches** spiny to glabrous, grass-green, smooth, later olive-green, glossy; **L.** petiolate, ± fleshy, distinctly veined, ± lanceolate, wavy, apiculate, grass-green, paler on the underside, 8–32 cm lg., to 7.5 cm br.; **Ar.** prominent, with dirty white felt; **Sp.** 3–25, 5–15 mm lg., sometimes thickened below, blackish; **Fl.** solitary or several together, c. 3.2 cm lg., 2.5 cm ∅, scarlet, orange in the centre, faintly perfumed; **Ov.** truncate, ± 5-angled; **Fr.** ?—Origin ?

R. cubensis (Br. & R.) Knuth
Bo. tree-like, to 4 m h.; **L.** several together, sessile, ± oblanceolate to obconical or oblong, pointed at both ends, 1–4 cm lg., 1–1.2 cm br., glossy green on both surfaces, with 1–3 leaf-like bracts below; **Sp.** 2–3 at first, later to over 25, over 5 cm lg., brownish; **Fl.** solitary, ± terminal, or lateral; **Pet.** rounded, reddish-purple; **Ov.** pear-shaped, naked; **Fr.** spherical, naked; **S.** black.—Cuba (Prov. Oriente and Sta. Clara).

R. grandifolius (Haw.) Knuth (T.)
Bo. shrubby to tree-like, to 5 m h.; **L.** shortly petiolate, oblong, obtuse or acute above, to 15 cm lg., intense green, tuberculate and pitted on the underside; **Sp.** 1–2 at first, later more, to 5 cm lg., black; **Fl.** few together, clustered at the shoot-tips, 3–4 cm ∅, pink inside, also white; **Ov.** with broad L.; **Fr.** large, pear-shaped, leafy; **S.** numerous.—Brazil.

R. guamacho (Web.) Knuth
Bo. shrubby, sometimes tree-like, to 3 m h.; **L.** solitary on young shoots, clustered on older ones, lanceolate to ovate; **Sp.** 1–4 at first, with a few short Ssp., later 20 and more, spreading, rigid, to 4 cm lg.; **Fl.** crowded (but probably solitary), c. 4 cm ∅; **Pet.** not ciliate, yellow; **Ov.** hairy; **Fr.** spherical, later orange, with a few deciduous Sp.—Venezuela (Orinoco valley and Marguerita Island).

R. higueranus (Card.) Backbg. n.comb. (Peireskia higuerana Card., "Cactus", 19: 80–81, 18. 1964).
Bo. shrubby, only 1 m h.; **shoots** c. 1.2 cm ∅ below, flowering shoots 5 cm lg.; **Ar.** 2–3 cm apart, grey, round, 5 mm lg.; **L.** ovate, thick, c. 1.2 × 0.8 cm, sessile; **Sp.** 2–3 on the primary shoots, radiating, 2.5–4 cm lg., black, acicular, those on flowering secondary shoots at the L.-base only 1–2 mm lg., blackish, readily dropping; **Fl.** solitary, apical, c. 3.5 cm lg., 4 cm ∅, yellow; **Pet.** spatulate; **Fil.** inserted at the base of the style, green below, yellow above; **style** thickened below, yellow; **Sti.** 4; **Ov.** inferior, acc. Cardenas's drawing.—Bolivia (Prov.

Valle Grande, Dept. Santa Cruz, near Higuera, 1600 m).

R. lychnidiflorus (DC.) Knuth
Bo. shrubby to tree-like, **branches** cylindric, woody; **L.** without a petiole, fleshy, oval to oblong, to 7 cm lg., apiculate, rounded below, M.-Ri. prominent; **Sp.** 1, 2–5 cm lg., with a few long H.; **Fl.** solitary, c. 6 cm ∅, ± orange; **Pet.** ciliate; **Ov.** pear-shaped, with small L.—Mexico (never re-collected there).

R. nicoyanus (Web.) Knuth
Bo. tree-like, to 8 m h., **branches** rigid, with a smooth brownish cortex; **L.** clustered on old shoots, alternate on younger ones, ± lanceolate, to 7 cm lg., c. 2.5 cm br., ± glossy green; **Sp.** 0–1, straight, rigid, robust, 4–5 cm lg., accompanied at first by white H.; **Fl.** c. 5 cm ∅, ± orange; **Pet.** finely laciniate; **Ov.** pear-shaped, with small L.; **Fr.** medlar-sized, lemon-yellow, filled inside with short H.—Costa Rica.

R. portulacifolius (L.) Knuth
Bo. tree-like, to 6 m h., **branches** terete, very spiny; **L.** alternate on young shoots, at most 1 cm lg., emarginate, wedge-shaped, ± notched above; **Sp.** solitary at first, later in clusters, acicular to ± bristly, c. 2 cm lg., black; **Fl.** solitary at the apex of the shoots, c. 3 cm ∅, pinkish-red; **Ov.** truncate, ± naked; **Fr.** spherical, greenish, umbilicate; **S.** numerous, blackish.—Haiti (Jamaica ?).

R. sacharosa (Griseb.) Backbg. n.comb. (Peireskia sacharosa Griseb., Abh. Ges. Wiss., Göttingen, 24: 141. 1879).
Bo. to 8 m h., shrubby; **shoots** green at first; **L.** ± lanceolate, 8–12 cm lg., fairly stout, glossy green, petiole to 1 cm lg., sometimes less; **Ar.** stout, greyish-white; **Sp.** 1–3 at first, reddish, dark above, very stoutly subulate, 1–5.5 cm lg., one longer than the others, later to c. 7, all or several equal, some fairly short; **Fl.** apical, solitary, ± sunken, or several together, to 8 cm br., purplish-pink, white in the centre; **Ov.** inferior; **Pet.** spatulate, ± apiculate; **Sep.** with longer H. in the Ax.; **Fil.**, **style** and **Sti.** white; **An.** yellow; **Fr.** to 4 cm ∅, ± tapering below, mostly without L., sometimes proliferating; **S.** numerous.—Argentina (Tucuman to Oran) and Paraguay. (Fig. 372.)

R. saipinensis (Card.) Backbg. n.comb. (Peireskia saipinensis Card., "Cactus", 19: 80–81, 17. 1964).
Bo. shrubby, 1–2 m h., branching from the base; **Ar.** c. 7 mm apart, 4 mm lg., pale brown; **L.** to 7 cm lg., to 5 cm br., sessile, circular to elliptic, dark green; **Fl.** apical, in pedicellate clusters, pedicels 5 mm lg., Fl. rotate, 6 cm ∅, with H. in the Ax.; **Sep.**

lanceolate, pale green; **Pet.** lilac-pink, white below, apiculate; **Fil.** thin, white; **style** 2 cm lg., white; **Sti.** yellow; **Ov.** not described.—Bolivia (Prov. Caballero, Dept. Santa Cruz, near Saipina, 1500 m). Resembles R. sacharosa, acc. Cardenas, and therefore included here. Cardenas omitted any description of the Sp.; the illustration shows (2–)3–4 light-coloured ones, twice the length of the broadly subcircular L.

R. tampicanus (Web.) Backbg.
Bo. shrubby, to 1.5 m h. (or more); **branches** fairly thick, green; **L.** oblong-lanceolate to narrowly spatulate, to c. 8 cm lg.; **Sp.** 0–1, to c. 3 cm lg., straight, red to blackish; **Fl.** in panicles, on short pedicels, c. 2.5 cm lg., 2–3 cm ∅, carmine to pinkish-red; **Ov.** with smaller green L. and 2–3 larger lanceolate ones; **Fr.** ?—Mexico (near Tampico).
Acc. N. H. Boke (C. & S. J. [US], XXXV: 1, 3 pp., 1963), this is only a variant of "Peireskia grandifolia" (referable to Rhodocactus). No mention was made as to whether the position of the Ov. tallies with R. tampicanus, and there is still no explanation of the widely separated habitats.

R. zinniaeflorus (DC.) Knuth
Bo. a small tree; **L.** oval, decurrent into a short petiole, wavy, 2–4 cm lg., c. 2 cm br., vivid green; **Sp.** 2 at first, later 3–5, straight, scarcely 1 cm lg., brownish-red; **Fl.** solitary, apical, c. 5 cm ∅, purplish, greenish outside; **Ov.** with leaf-like Sc.; **Fr.** ?—Mexico (no locality given; not re-collected). See also under R. lychnidiflorus.

Ritterocereus Backbg. (153)

Large, shrubby or tree-like columnar Cacti, quite often noticeably frosted. The funnelform flowers open at night but in part remain open the next day, coloured white to pink; tube and ovary scaly, the latter mostly densely so, with ± felt in the axils, without either bristles or spines. On the other hand the juicy and often edible fruits are set with spines which drop at maturity. Seeds brownish or black.—Distribution: Mexico, W. Indies, Curaçao, northern parts of S. America, close to the coast. [(R).]

R. chacalapensis H. Bravo & Th. MacDoug.: see under **Marshallocereus** Backbg.

R. deficiens (O. & Dietr.) Backbg.
Bo. ± tree-like, with a ± distinct **trunk**; **branches** erect, stout, often spineless below, only slightly frosted; **Ri.** 7–8, broad below; **Ar.** rather sunken, with white or brown felt; **Rsp.** c. 8–9, to 1.5 cm lg.,

± spreading to appressed, grey, tipped black, sometimes darker at first; **Csp.** 0–1, to 3 cm lg., ± flattened; **Fl.** only 5–6 cm lg. white; **Fr.** very spiny at first, pulp white or red.—Venezuela (central coast), Curaçao. (Cold-sensitive.)

R. eichlamii (Br. & R.) Backbg.
Bo. little branching, fairly tall; **shoots** deep green, with some frosting at the apex, this persisting in narrow arcs; **Ri.** 8–10, broad below, acute above; **Ar.** with brown or sometimes greyish-white felt; **Rsp.** 4–6, acicular, ± porrect; **Csp.** 0–1, to 2 cm lg., sometimes longer at the apex; **Fl.** to c. 7 cm lg., intense pink; **Tu.** densely set with very convex imbricate Sc., these expanding abruptly in the upper part, passing over into reddish Sep.; **Ov.** with subcircular-oval Tub. and small triangular Sc.; **Fr.** as large as a hen's egg, tessellate, pulp white.—Guatemala (between Rancho San Agustin and Zacapa).

R. fimbriatus (Lam.) Backbg.
Bo. columnar, to 4 m h.; **St.** 8 cm ∅; **Ri.** 10, c. 1.5 cm h.; **Ar.** to 2 cm apart, with reddish-brown felt, later greyish-brown; **Rsp.** mostly 11, 0.6–2 cm lg.; **Csp.** 1; **Sp.** ash-grey, tipped black; **Fl.** c. 8 cm lg.; **Pet.** ± ciliate, reddish to purplish-brown; **Fr.** spherical-ovoid, c. 3.5 cm lg., stoutly spined at first; **S.** pear-shaped, black, ± glossy.—Haiti (Plaine Cul-de-Sac, Massif de la Selle).

R. griseus (Haw.) Backbg.
Bo. to 8 m h., sometimes branching from below, or even with a weak **trunk** to 35 cm thick; **shoots** ± frosted; **Ri.** 8–10; **Rsp.** 10–11; **Csp.** 3; **Sp.** acicular, robust, longest ones to 4 cm lg., grey; **Fl.** c. 7 cm lg., pink outside; **Pet.** white; **style** projecting before the Fl. opens; **Ov.** densely scaly; **Fr.** ± spherical, pulp red.—Venezuela (N. coast of S. America and offshore islands), Mexico (Oaxaca). (Cold-sensitive.)
H. Bravo reports Fr. also with yellowish pulp. In Mexico, the plants are probably only cultivated on account of the edible Fr., and are therefore in part escapes.

R. hystrix (Haw.) Backbg.
Bo. with up to 50 branches, to 8–12 m h., **trunk** short but ± distinct, sometimes to 30 cm ∅; **branches** 7–10 cm ∅; **Ri.** 9–10(–12), with V-notches; **Ar.** with white to grey felt; **Rsp.** c. 10; **Csp.** (1–)3, longest one to 4 cm lg.; **Sp.** grey, brown-tipped; **Fl.** 8–9 cm lg.; **Pet.** white, spreading or revolute; **Ov.** with small oval Sc.; **Fr.** 5–6 cm lg., scarlet, pulp red.—W. Indies.

R. laevigatus (SD.) Backbg.
Bo. tree-like, glossy, leaf to dark green to ± deep

greyish-green, ± frosted at the apex, frosting persisting in arcs; **Ri.** c. 7, broad, ± compressed, rounded; **Ar.** c. 2.5 cm apart; **Rsp.** 8, acicular, thin, to 1 cm lg.; **Csp.** (0–)1, rather longer and stouter, all Sp. at first whitsh-grey or reddish-brown, sometimes darker-tipped; **Fl.** c. 8 cm lg., white; **Ov.** with flat rounded Tub., weakly felty.—Mexico (in the S.) (Fig. 373.)

R. pruinosus (O.) Backbg.
Bo. tree-shaped, to 7 m h., with a distinct **trunk**; **shoot**-tips bluish-green, frosted white; **Ri.** 5–6, with acute lengthwise furrows; **Ar.** c. 4 cm apart, brown-felty (acc. H. Bravo: white-felty); **Rsp.** 5–7(–9), grey, tipped brown to reddish; **Csp.** 1, c. 3 cm lg., stouter; **Fl.** 6–9 cm lg.; **Pet.** white, washed faintly pink; **Ov.** with thick brown felt; **Fr.** ovoid, with light-coloured cushions of felt, these eventually turning red, with lax Sp.-clusters, pulp variously coloured: white, pale pink, light carmine, raspberry-red; **S.** ± yellowish-brown, wrinkled.— Central and S. Mexico.

R. queretaroensis (Web.) Backbg.
Bo. to 6m h., trunk to c. 1 m h., to 35 cm ∅, terete; **shoots** to 15 cm ∅, dark green; **Ri.** 6–8, notched, with acute lengthwise furrows at first; **Ar.** irregularly arranged, deeply sunken, with dark brown finely curly wool, with Gl.; **Rsp.** 6–8, c. 3 cm lg., 2 uppers porrect, shorter; **Csp.** not clearly differentiated, 2–4, to 4 cm lg., porrect; **Sp.** straight, whitish-grey, reddish at first; **Fl.** 8–9 cm lg., light red (?); **Fr.** almost the size of a hen's egg, yellow or red, with light yellow Sp. to 2.5 cm lg.—Mexico (Michoacan and Querétaro to Guanajuato).

R. standleyi (G. Ortega) Backbg. (T.)
Bo. to 4 m h., sometimes with a distinct trunk, light green; **Ri.** (3–)4, 2–3 cm h., notched; **Ar.** c. 3 cm apart, white-felty; **Rsp.** 13–16, 10–15 cm lg.; **Csp.** 4–8, 2–2.5 cm lg.; **Sp.** pink at first, later grey; **Fl.** 6–8 cm lg., to 4 cm ∅; **Sep.** greenish-pink; **Pet.** white, with alternating pink stripes; **Ov.** tuberculate, scaly; **Fr.** spherical, pulp red, sweet; **S.** glossy, black.—Mexico (Guerrero, near Acapulco; Sinaloa, in some areas on the coast).

The following spec. have previously been classified with Lemaireocereus, and must for the time being be left there as they have not yet been fully clarified, i.e. some may belong to Ritterocereus, others to Marshallocereus: Lemaireocereus longispinus, L. martinezii, L. montanus, L. quevedonis, L. schumannii; for descriptions, see under Lemaireocereus.

Rodentiophila Ritt. (120)

A new genus erected by Ritter, but a valid description is still awaited. The plants resemble those of the Genus Eriosyce, even at the seedling-stage, as is clear from my colour-plates, Fig. 3417 and 3453 in "Die Cact.", Vol. VI. 1962. Older plants however are similar not only to those of Eriosyce but also those, for instance, of the stoutly columnar Soehrensia uebelmanniana Lembcke & Backbg.; whereas the Fl. of the latter are bell-shaped to funnelform and to c. 6 cm lg., Ritter states the following for Rodentiophila: "Flowers extremely short"; but the "thick spherical and very juicy berries 2.5 cm ∅" appear similar to those of Soehrensia; Eriosyce has hollow fruits. No information is yet available as to whether any bristles are present on the flower. Regarding the areoles, Ritter says: "enormous and long-felty". The similarity with Soehrensia uebelmanniana, found at an altitude of 3500 m, and the specific name "Rodentiophila atacamensis", lead one to suppose (in the absence of any habitat-data from Ritter) that the latter grows on the Puna de Atacama, and that both genera are from east of the Andes and have penetrated into Chile; this is certainly the case with Soehrensia uebelmanniana. 3 species hitherto listed in Winter's catalogues.—Distribution: Chile (Atacama). [Little known of cultural requirements; perhaps grafting is preferable.]

R. atacamensis Ritt. n.subnud.
Bo. broadly spherical at first, later more elongated, eventually quite large, acc. Ritter; **Ri.** divided into larger oval Tub.; **Ar.** oblong-circular, large, white-felty (in seedling plants); **Sp.** subulate, **Rsp.** to over 10, **Csp.** 1–2, one of these upcurving, at first concolorous brown, later only so in parts, Rsp. either similar or light-coloured, or light brownish, especially the upper ones, all ± equal; **Fl.** short; **Fr.** 2.5 cm ∅, spherical, very juicy.—Chile (Atacama). Varies; some Csp. more porrect and stoutly subulate. (Fig. 374 above, left and right.) Epidermis can be mid-green to bluish-green.

R. megacarpa Ritt. n.subnud.
Bo. similar to the preceding, but the epidermis more yellowish-green (always so ?); apparently only **Rsp.** present, c. 6 (young plants), ± weakly curving, brown at first, shorter than in the preceding spec.; the apex appears to be quite strongly woolly, whereas in the preceding it is not, rather surprisingly; **Fl.** ?; **Fr.** ? (acc. to the name, must be larger than in R. atacamensis).—Chile (no data on locality). (Fig. 374, below.)

R. lanata Ritt. (FR 515) is still listed by Ritter; however Winter's catalogue for 1960 adds no further details, and in more recent issues the name is not even mentioned.

Rooksbya Backbg. (152)

Mostly solitary Cerei; flowers nocturnal, fairly slender funnelform, rather bellshaped above, the perianth at anthesis consisting of a ring of petals around the crowded projecting anthers which form a funnel-shape, closing above to form a sort of annulus. The tube appears to be channelled, because of the long-decurrent scale-bases, then it curves ± strongly upwards and is ± swollen at midway; the fleshy scales only project more clearly in the upper part of the tube. Ovary and seed-cavity are oblong, not recognisably offset; but in the upper part outside several longer bristly and ± projecting spines are present. These may only appear later, sometimes to 6 are present; but acc. Werdermann there may only be 1–2 fine bristles, or these are completely missing, or they appear only as the ovary ripens. The projecting bristly spines on the fruit are ± rigid. In the variety of the type-species, the style appears to be longer. Seeds are glossy brown. The lack of uniform indumentum on the ovary, taken alone, gives this plant a special status; added to this is the curving and somewhat ventricosely swollen tube, the solitary habit and the relatively acute ribs. These characters are also present in "Neobuxbaumia mezcalaensis"; H. Bravo described the flowers as naked but Dawson found—at least in some cases—that bristles were present on the ovary, which agrees with the characters of Rooksbya. Probably this species should more correctly be called Rooksbya mez-calaensis (see also under Neobuxbaumia). 1(–2) species are thus referable here.—Distribution: Mexico (Tamaulipas, Jaumave, and—if N. mez-calaensis is included—from Guerrero to Puebla and Oaxaca). [(R).]

R. euphorbioides (Haw.) Backbg. (T.)
Bo. several meters h., simple, washy greyish to bluish-green; **Ri.** to c. 9(–10), acute; **Sp.** often only 1–2(–3), blackish at first, stout, to c. 2.6 cm lg., sometimes also to 2 shorter ones, directed down-wards; **Ar.** grey, weakly felty; **Csp.** 0, or not recognisable as such; **Fl.** 9.5–10 cm lg., pinkish-red; **Sep.** and **Tu.** ± wine-red, throat cream; **Fr.** yellowish-green, with flat Tub., with bristly Sp., dehiscing above, or the sides disintegrating.—Mexico (Tamaulipas, near Jaumave, and south-wards between El Mate and Antigua Morelos). (Fig. 375.)
   v. **olfersii** (SD.) Backbg.: **Bo.** darker; **Sp.** to 10, fairly long, brown, in projecting tufts, flexible, ± bristly, 1–2 longer ones; **Fl.** as in the type.—Origin ?

Roseocactus Berg. (220)

The species of this genus were earlier classified in Ariocarpus Scheidw., but in the latter Fl. are not central; they arise at the side of the crown from the axils, sometimes several at one time, ± forming a ring; the tubercles are not cleft, i.e. they have no furrow-like and rather woolly depression; areoles, if present, are only small and subcircular, situated below the tip of the areole. In Roseocactus, however, the flowers arise centrally, from the inner end of a furrow-like, woolly depression ± the full length of the tubercles. These characters are quite uniform in all 4 species known today; Roseocactus is thus not only a well-demarcated genus, but despite a distant resemblance to some species of Ariocarpus it is clearly distinguishable by these diagnostic characters. Berger drew attention to this in 1925, and by means of close-up photographs I have shown the considerable divergences of floral insertion and tubercle-character in "Die Cact.", Vol. V, Fig. 2887–2893, 1961. Anderson's renewed attempt (C. & S. J. [US], 4: 122 pp. 1961) to refer Roseocactus to Ariocarpus as a subgenus can only be explained by the absence of a comprehensive principle of systematic arrangement. See also my observations on similar one-sided recombinations under Ariocarpus, Pediocactus and Rebutia.

The species of this genus have a napiform root. The tubercles are ± imbricate, with a horny epidermis, but the shape varies from broadly rounded to triangular or 4-sided. The fruit is a berry which rises from the cranial wool, and after it has dried the seeds remain hidden for a longer time in the wool of the furrow. The most conspicuous diagnostic character was brought out by Engelmann when he gave the type-species of the Genus Roseocactus the specific name "fissuratus" = cleft. The seeds are matt black, the flowers probably all normally ± (light) purplish-red to purplish-pink. Roseocactus kotschoubeyanus v. albiflorus is one of those colourless variants such as occur in normally red-flowered species of Mammillaria, Thelocactus, Krainzia, etc.—Distribution: USA (W. Texas), Mexico (N. Coahuila, Durango, Nuevo León, Zacatecas, San Luis Potosí). [(R); if non-soil mineral composts are used, the spec. can be grown on their own roots, but growth is slow; imported plants can easily be grafted, irrespective of size, and growth and blooming are then improved.]

R. fissuratus (Eng.) Berg. (T.)
Bo. simple or offsetting, depressed-spherical, to over 15 cm ∅; **Tub.** with the upper surface furrowed across, bordered throughout by a furrow and a band; **Fl.** to 4 cm ∅, pinkish-red with a darker centre; **Fr.** white.—USA (SW. Texas), Mexico (Coahuila). (Fig. 376.)

R. intermedius Backbg. & Kil.

Bo. as in the preceding; **Tub.** c. 2.3 cm br., rhomboid, slightly raised towards the middle, transverse wrinkles more apparent, without any band, furrowed almost over the entire length, these furrows 2–3 mm br.; **Fl.** light purplish-pink, to over 4 cm ⌀; **Fr.** elongated-clavate, whitish-pink; **S.** 1.7 mm lg.—N. Mexico.

Erroneously regarded by Anderson as nom. nud. (Latin diagnosis in Kakt. u.a. Sukk. 10: 151. 1960) and despite the difference in furrow-character given as a synonym of "Ariocarpus fissuratus v. lloydii (Rose) Marsh." (C. & S. J. [US], 39. 1965).

R. kotschoubeyanus (Lem.) Berg.

Bo. simple, with a longer cylindric napiform **R.**, only low, to 5 cm ⌀; **Tub.** without any band, spiralled and imbricate, scarcely 7 mm h., to 7 mm br., ± triangular, with a woolly furrow throughout the length, with strong hairy felt towards the base and in the Ax.; **Fl.** to 3 cm lg. and 3(–5) cm ⌀, pinkish-purple to light purple.—Mexico (Durango; Nuevo León; San Luis Potosí). Fl.-⌀ may vary acc. to locality.

v. **albiflorus** Backbg.: **Fl.** pure white, to 5 cm ⌀, often broader than the Bo., only occasionally suffused pink towards the centre.—Mexico (Nuevo León ?);

v. **macdowellii** Backbg.: **R.** more slender, cylindric; **Bo.** smaller; **Tub.** more slender, darker.—Locality? I took the name from a catalogue of Haage & Schmidt (a cactus-nursery in Erfurt which was well known in the early years of the century), in memory of the former successful collector, MacDowell, whose son worked with me when I brought to Hamburg a collection of old Cephalocereus senilis.

R. lloydii (Rose) Berg.

Bo. depressed-spherical, dimensions as in the preceding; **Tub.** ± rhomboid, without any band, ± raised towards the middle, ± wrinkled, the furrow only throughout ± half of the length, and at first very noticeably woolly; **Fl.** ± purplish-red.—Mexico (Coahuila; Durango; Zacatecas).

I have a colour photo from Cullmann showing quite a young plant which has extremely plentiful apical wool from which the Fl. project, as if emerging from a cobweb; three Fl. were open at the one time; Sti. whitish, pink towards the pink style, Pet. with wavy margins and of a brilliant light purple—a picture showing the full beauty of a grafted young plant of Roseocactus, as well as the special position of the genus.

Roseocereus (Backbg.) Backbg. (87)

Erectly shrubby Cerei with very tuberculate ribs;

flowers nocturnal, large, white, the tube towards the ovary set fairly densely with broad scales with much curly axillary hair; fruits with projecting triangular pink scales, with axillary hair. The floral tubes are strongly channelled, primarily because of the long-decurrent bases of the scales. Some of the plants can be of ± tree-like habit. Because of these characteristics, this currently monotypic genus cannot be united with any other.—Distribution: Bolivia (from Cochabamba to Chuquisaca). [(R).]

R. tephracanthus (Lab.) Backbg. (T.)

Bo. shrubby to tree-like, bluish or greyish-green; **branches** to c. 6 cm ⌀; **Ri.** mostly 8, rounded, tuberculately convex below the Ar., particularly on older shoots, new growth less so, or not at all; **Rsp.** 4–7, whitish, tipped brownish, sometimes pale yellowish at first; **Csp.** 1, rather stouter, longer, sometimes brownish at first; **Sp.** lengthening as the shoots age; **Fl.** 18–22 cm lg., greenish-white to white; **Ov.** broadly scaly, with felty H.—Bolivia. (Fig. 377.)

Samaipaticereus Card. (83)

Columnar to tree-like Cerei with relatively few ribs. The principal diagnostic character lies in the nocturnal flowers which do not open wide, the stout tube having short clusters of hairs; the type-species still has a few short bristles whereas in the second species these are quite reduced. Only the fruits of the type-species are known, and these are spherical, salmon-red and reddish-orange inside. The flowers obviously appear in considerable numbers on one side only of the shoots.—Distribution: Bolivia (Prov. Florida and Inquisivi). [(R): the type-species has proved to be strong-growing in cultivation.]

S. corroanus Card. (T.)

Bo. tree-shaped, to 3.5 m h., with a low **trunk** to 15 cm ⌀, green to darker green; **branches** ascending, to c. 4 cm ⌀; **Ri.** 4–6, juveniles sometimes 3–4-angled, later with transverse notching above; **Ar.** with greyish-brown felt at first; **Sp.** c. 5, very short, brownish at first, then greyish-white, one of these to 1 cm lg., others 2–3 mm lg., ± swollen below, all Sp. very thin in juveniles; **Fl.** to 5 cm lg., slightly curving, white, whitish-green outside; **Tu.** with H. and a few Br., all short, brown; **style** white; **Sti.** light yellow; **Fr.** dehiscing longitudinally, tuberculate, salmon-red, orange to flesh-coloured inside, colouring-matter water-soluble; **S.** 1.5 mm lg.—Bolivia (Florida, El Puente de Samaipata). (Fig. 378.)

S. inquisivensis Card.

Bo. columnar, to 4 m h.; **shoots** to 5 cm $\emptyset$; **Ri.** 9, $\pm$ obtuse, with no horizontal notching but somewhat thickened around the Ar.; **Ar.** brownish, becoming grey; **Sp.** 8–11, 0.2–2.5 cm lg., not differentiated; **Fl.** 5 cm lg., white, narrowly funnelform, limb slightly oblique, short, only hairy; **Fr.** ?—Bolivia (Inquisivi, Puente Inquisivi).

S. peruvianus Johns., not described: to 4.5 m h.; shoots 4-angled, with short Sp.; Fl. white; Fr. green, with orange pulp. Acc. to the name, must come from Peru. No further data available.

Schlumbergera Lem. (30)

A genus still scarcely represented in European collections; illustrated by Vaupel in "Die Kakteen", 92. 1926: Fig. 25: A. The main characteristics are as follows: habit resembling that of Zygocactus; flowers regular, quite large diurnal; filaments in 2 series; stigma-lobes capitate, connivent; fruit 4-angled. Only 1 species known.— Distribution: Brazil (Rio de Janeiro). [(R).]

S. russelliana (Gardn.) Br. & R. (T.)
Bo. a shrubby epiphyte, to 1 m lg., main St. terete, segmented; **Seg.** to 3.5 cm lg. and to 2 cm br., light green, with a M.-vein, with very sparse H. at the apex; **Fl.** 5.5 cm lg., dark pink; **Fil.** of the upper Gr. attached to the Tu., and the lower Gr. to the Ov., pinkish-carmine, style and Sti. similarly; **Ov.** dark green, with 4 winged angles, the 1.2 cm lg. berry similarly; **S.** dark chestnut-brown, 1.5 mm lg.— Brazil (Organ Mountains).

S. bridgesii (Lem.) Löfgr.: the plant sometimes found under this name is a hybrid: Fl. red, Ov. only shortly 4-winged.

Schlumbergera SG. Zygocactus (K. Sch.) Moran: see under **Zygocactus** K. Sch.
This combination must be regarded as superfluous and is confusing since Zygocactus was earlier called Epiphyllum, and has in fact continued to be known as such in the trade. Zygocactus has since become more familiar. A new name is not called for since its flowers are quite distinct: zygomorphic, with a longer corolla-tube, the inner group of filaments with a revolute membraneous ring below, the ovary and fruit top-shaped. A combination of this kind tends to allow these differences to be overlooked.

Sclerocactus Br. & R. (192)

Spherical to cylindric plants with $\pm$ interlacing spines, these sometimes longer, flattened and in some species also hooked. The diurnal flowers are $\pm$ bellshaped to funnelform, with only traces of felt, the basally dehiscent fruit similarly. A clearly distinctive group of species.—Distribution: USA (desert areas of the SW.). [(G): difficult plants to grow, i.e. they rarely survive long in collections, and even grafting seldom provides a longer-term solution.]*

S. franklinii Evans (synonym ?)
Bo. spherical to oblong, to 14 cm h., 8 cm $\emptyset$, bluish-green; **Ri.** 8–15, tuberculate; **Ar.** white, with 1–6 pink or yellow Gl. concealed in the wool; **Rsp.** 7–13, radiating and appressed or $\pm$ projecting, terete, straight, or flattened, curving, to 2 cm lg., white or ash-grey; **Csp.** 1–3, 1.5–3 cm lg., black or grey, terete or flattened, straight or curving; **Fl.** to 4.5 cm lg., 3–5 cm $\emptyset$, pink or white; **Fr.** oblong, to 3 cm lg., greenish-pink; **S.** 1–3 mm lg., brown or black, minutely tuberculate.—USA (Colorado, S. Gunnison Valley). In my view, not separable from "Echinocactus glaucus K. Sch.", which Purpus also collected in Gunnison Valley; the plant should therefore be called: **Sclerocactus glaucus** (K. Sch.) Backbg.

S. havasupaiensis Clov.
Bo. fairly slender, cylindric, relatively densely spined; **Sp.** mostly 4 longer ones, 4 medium-long and to 6 shorter, occasionally $\pm$ bent or weakly hooked above (data from herbarium-sheet); **Fl.** 3.5–5.3 cm $\emptyset$, whitish; **Sep.** yellowish-green; **S.** glossy black.—USA (Arizona, in side-canyons of the Grand Canyon).
    v. **roseus** Clov.: **Fl.** flesh-pink, scented: **Sti.** undivided (finely divided in the type); **S.** distinctly tuberculate.—USA (Arizona, only in the Havasupai Canyon).

S. intermedius Peebl.
Bo. ovoid-cylindric, to 20 cm h.; **Ri.** 13, low, slightly spiralled; **Rsp.** c. 12, white, straight or contorted; **Csp.** longer, 4 cruciform, 3–5 cm lg., upper ones flat, sometimes contorted, slightly longitudinally furrowed above, white, other Csp. $\pm$ 4-sided, reddish, often hooked; **Fl.** to 5 cm lg., purple.—USA (Arizona, not far from Pipe Springs).

S. parviflorus Clov. & Jott.
Bo. simple, cylindric, to 45 cm lg., to 9 cm $\emptyset$, erect or curving; **Ri.** 13, distinctly tuberculate; **Rsp.** 14–15, to 3.4 cm lg., compressed, straight; **Csp.** 3, hooked, also one upper 3-sided Sp., not hooked, to 6 cm lg., the 3 lower ones 3–4-angled, to 7.5 cm lg.,

* Translator's note: C. & S.J. (US) XLVIII, 3 : 1976: (Woodruff & Benson). "Changes of Status in Sclerocactus."

purplish-brown; **Fl.** small, to 2.5 cm lg., 2 cm $\emptyset$, purple; **style** purple.—USA (Arizona, Colorado Canyon, above Lees Ferry).

S. polyancistrus (Eng. & Big.) Br. & R. (T.)
Bo. simple, spherical to oblong, to 40 cm h.; **Ri.** 13–17, to 1.5 cm h., very wavy; **Sp.** c. 20, scarcely differentiated, **Rsp.** acicular, white, to 2.5 cm lg., **Csp.** several, unequal, to 12.5 cm lg., upper ones flat, erect, white, others brown, spreading, terete, often hooked; **Fl.** c. 8 cm lg., purple; **style** carmine; **Fr.** light purple, oblong to pear-shaped, with fleshy walls at first, these drying, to 4 cm lg.; **S.** 4 mm lg., black, finely tuberculate.—USA (deserts: California, Nevada and W. Arizona). (Fig. 379.)

S. whipplei (Eng. & Big.) Br. & R.
Bo. simple or somewhat offsetting, to 15 cm lg., to 7.5 cm $\emptyset$; **Ri.** 13–15, spiralled, tuberculate; **Rsp.** 7–11, somewhat flattened, to 18 mm lg., white or black; **Csp.** absent in young Ar., later mostly 4, top one flattened and straight, others brown or black, some or all of them hooked, all to c. 3.5 cm lg.; **Fl.** shortly bellshaped to funnelform, pink to purple; **style** downy, reddish; **Sti.** green; **Fr.** 1.5 cm lg., oblong, red, ± glabrous; **S.** over 3 mm lg., matt, black.—USA (N. Arizona; SE. Utah; W. Colorado).
    v. **pygmaeus** Peebl.: **Bo.** only 5 cm h.; **Sp.** fewer, **Csp.** dark brown, under 2 cm lg., sometimes hooked; **Fl.** ?; **Fr.** 7 mm lg.—USA (Arizona, N. of Ganado);
    v. **spinosior** (Eng.) Boiss.: **Bo.** to over 20 cm h., reputedly more slender than the type; **Rsp.** 12–15.—USA (W. Colorado).

S. wrightiae Bens.
Bo. spherical to ovoid, simple; **Ri.** c. 13, divided into Tub. 12 mm lg., 9 mm br.; **Ar.** 3–4 mm $\emptyset$; **Rsp.** 8–10, white, 6–12 mm lg.; **Csp.** 4, light below, dark brown above, 12–15 mm lg., bottom one hooked; **Fl.** 1.9 cm $\emptyset$ and lg.; **Sep.** lavender-coloured with light borders, c. 1.2 cm lg., 3–6 mm br.; **Pet.** tapering, 1.2 cm lg., 4.5–6 mm br., whitish below; **An.** yellow; **style** yellow with 5 **Sti.**; **Fr.** spherical; **S.** 2 mm lg., 1.5 mm thick.—USA (Utah, near the Fremont River and San Rafael Ridge, at c. 350 m). Named for Mrs. Dorde Wright, who discovered the species in 1961.

Selenicereus (Berg.) Br. & R. (45)

Slender-stemmed clinging or climbing Cerei with aerial roots, ribs low or angular, spines fairly short and sometimes absent. Flowers large, often very large, nocturnal, with longer tubes, these and the ovaries usually with hair and bristles, sometimes without hair but spiny. Inner petals uniformly white and fairly broad, stamens in two series, sometimes very numerous; style long, fairly thick and often hollow. Fruits large, mostly reddish, yellow only in one instance so far as known, with deciduous spines, set with bristles and hairs. Species of this genus are in general more vigorous-growing and easier to flower than Hylocereus in which the flowers, while similar, have no indumentum. Freshly cut stems and flowers of S. grandiflorus, in particular, are used in the preparation of drugs with a spasmolytic effect on the coronary vessels, and to promote blood-circulation; for this purpose cuttings are cultivated in hot-houses.*—Distribution: from S. Texas through E. Mexico, Central America and the W. Indies to the N. coast of S. America; one species, originally reported from Honduras, has been reported from Uruguay and Argentina, and may well have been introduced, while another (which is rather dubious) is said to originate in Paraguay. [(R).]

S. boeckmannii (O.) Br. & R.
Bo. fresh green; **shoots** 2 cm $\emptyset$; **Ri.** 7, rather indented and notched; **Ar.** grey; **Sp.** c. 1 mm lg., thickened below, 3 uppers and 1 Csp. brown, 3 lower ones grey; **Fl.** to 30 cm lg., over 20 cm $\emptyset$, white; **Tu.** and **Ov.** with brown H., with 2–3 stout brown Sp.—E. Mexico; Cuba; Haiti; naturalised in the Bahamas. Fl. not scented.

S. brevispinus Br. & R.
Bo. light green, with white H. at the tip of young shoots; **Ri.** 8–10, slightly indented; **Ar.** brown; **Sp.** 12, 1 mm lg., the 3–4 centrals rather thicker, outer ones ± bent, also 6 or more Br.; **Fl.** 25 cm lg.; **Tu.** and **Ov.** with white H.; **Sep.** yellowish; **Pet.** white.—Cuba.

S. coniflorus (Wgt.) Br. & R.
Bo. matt green, often reddened, St. 4–5-sided; **Ri.** rounded; **Ar.** white; **Sp.** acicular, to c. 6, to 1.3 cm lg. unequal, radiating and projecting, brownish, mostly with 2 appressed brownish Br.; **Fl.** faintly perfumed, white, delicate light green below; **Sep.** sometimes flesh-coloured inside; **Sti.** light green.—Haiti (naturalised in Florida).

S. donkelaari (SD.) Br. & R.
Bo. with very long St. 1 cm $\emptyset$; **Ri.** 9–10, obtuse or indistinct; **Ar.** fairly close together; **Sp.** 10–15, Rsp. appressed, bristly, Csp. 1 or more, 1–2 mm lg.; **Fl.** 18 cm lg.; **Pet.** white; **Sep.** reddish; **Fil.** and **style** greenish below, whitish above.—Mexico (Yucatan).

* See colour-photo: Introduction.

S. grandiflorus (L.) Br. & R. (T.)

Bo. green or bluish-green, climbing; **shoots** to 2.5 cm ∅; **Ri.** 7–8 or fewer, low; **Ar.** not set on prominent Tub., without Br., at first with some H., these later disappearing; **Sp.** acicular, 7–11, 0.4–1 cm lg., yellowish at first; **Fl.** c. 18(–30) cm lg., perfumed; **Tu.** and **Ov.** with H. and Sp.; **Sep.** long, narrow, salmon-coloured; **Pet.** white, forming a beaker-shape; **Fr.** 8 cm lg., ovoid, patterned red and yellowish, with brownish wool and yellowish Sp., edible.—Jamaica and Cuba; Haiti; Mexico (E. lowlands).

(v. **grandiflorus**: Ar.-wool not pure white);

v. **affinis** (SD.) Borg: Ar.-wool pure white at first;

v. **barbadensis** (Eng.) Borg: **shoots** dark green, suffused reddish; **Sp.** longer, always yellowish; **Fl.** with the Sep. more reddish, more strongly recurved.—Barbados, St. Thomas;

v. **irradians** (Lem.) Borg: **Bo.** dark green; **Sp.** clustered, 5 mm lg., whitish, weak; **Fl.** as in the type but rather smaller; **Pet.** more spreading;

v. **ophites** (Lem.) Borg: Ar.-wool dark brown; **Ri.** 6–8; **shoot**-tips reddish at first; **Sp.** very short, thick, whitish;

v. **tellii** (hort.) Borg: **Bo.** more slender, to 1 cm ∅, deep green; **Ri.** mostly 4, rarely 5; **Ar.** brownish; **Sp.** small; **Fl.** as in the type, but smaller.—Mexico (?);

v. **uranos** (Ricc.) Borg: apparently only a form of v. **barbadensis** (Eng.) Borg: lighter green, with similar longer yellowish Sp., with narrower, more spreading Pet.

S. hallensis (Wgt.) Wgt.

Bo. to 3 m lg., pale green; **Ri.** 5–6, sometimes acute; **Ar.** brown, set on small protuberances; **Sp.** 0–2–6, brownish-yellow, thin, 1–3 of these to 1 cm lg., others quite small; **Fl.** 30 cm lg., 28 cm ∅; **Pet.** white, laxly cup-shaped; **Sep.** ochre-yellow; **Tu.** and **Ov.** brownish-red, with H. and Sp. Fl. vanilla-scented.—Colombia.

S. hamatus (Scheidw.) Br. & R.

Bo. very long, light green, glossy; **shoots** to 22 mm ∅; **Ri.** mostly 4-angled, with a nose-shaped spur to 1 cm lg.; **Sp.** bristly at first, or 5–6, upper ones white, bristly, 4–6 mm lg., deciduous, 2–3 lower ones persisting, stouter, brown; **Fl.** 30–40 cm lg.; **Pet.** broad, white; outer **Sep.** reddish, inner ones chrome-yellow; **Tu.** green or brownish, it and the **Ov.** with blackish H. and thin white Sp.—Mexico (Vera Cruz, Jalapa).

S. hondurensis (K. Sch.) Br. & R.

Bo. with shoots to 2.2 cm ∅; **Ri.** 7–10, slightly indented, becoming flatter; **Ar.** brownish, with curly grey H. to 15 mm lg.; **Sp.** 7–9, white, not sharp, brittle; **Csp.** 1 or several, to 6 mm lg.,

reddish-brown; **Fl.** 23 cm lg., 18 cm ∅, yellowish-white; **Sep.** projecting, brown or dark yellow; **Ov.** with plentiful greyish-white H.—Honduras; Guatemala.

S. humilis (DC.) Marsh.: an insufficiently clarified plant: shoots 2.5 cm ∅; Ri. 4–5, compressed; Ar. glabrous or white-felty; Sp. 4–8 mm lg.; Rsp. 8–12, bristly, white; Csp. 3–4, stouter, straw-coloured.—Santo Domingo.

S. inermis (O.) Br. & R.

Bo. glossy, light green; **shoots** to 1.25 cm ∅; **Ri.** 3–5, angular; **Ar.** distant, with a few Br. at first; **Sp.** 0; **Fl.** c. 15 cm lg., white, reddish below; **Sep.** yellowish-green, reddish below; **Tu.** and **Ov.** with one or two Sp., without H.; **style** thick, reddish; **Sti.** yellowish-green.—Venezuela; Colombia.

S. jalapensis (Vpl.) Borg: **Selenicereus pringlei** Rose.

S. kunthianus (O.) Br. & R.

Bo. light green, with robust subterete St.; **Ri.** 7–10, becoming flatter; **Ar.** brown, with curly wool; **Rsp.** 4, cruciform, very small, stiff, brown; **Csp.** 0–1, brownish; **Fl.** 23 cm lg., perfumed, white; **Sep.** narrow, reddish-green; **Tu.** and **Ov.** with greyish-pink H. and white Br.-Sp.; **Fr.** carmine, hairy, spiny.—Honduras (?).

S. macdonaldiae (Hook.) Br. & R.

Bo. dark green at first, **St.** later terete; **shoots** very long, to 1.5 cm ∅; **Ri.** 5, flat, tuberculate; **Ar.** small; **Sp.** several, brown, minute; **Fl.** to 35 cm lg., white or cream; **Sep.** ± recurved, reddish or orange; **Pet.** pure white; **Tu.** and **Ov.** with rusty-brown H., with short brown Sp.; **Sti.** yellowish.—Honduras (perhaps the true homeland?); also reported from Argentina and Uruguay (naturalised?).

v. **grusonianus** (Wgt.) Backbg.: **Bo.** velvety dark green; **Ri.** 6, narrow, becoming flatter; **Ar.** grey, below a small acute Tub.; **Sp.** conical, 3–4, c. 2 mm lg., one directed downwards, reddish-brown, others directed upwards, yellowish-white, tipped reddish-brown, also a few Br.; **Fl.** as in the type but larger; both are vanilla-scented.—Origin: dubious.

Br. & R. hold this to be an ecotype, but Berger regards it as a valid spec.

S. maxonii Rose

Bo. light green (?); **Ri.** 5–6; **Ar.** small; **Sp.** very short, yellowish, stouter, with a few recurved white Br.; **Fl.** 20 cm lg., white; **Sep.** greenish, brownish or pink; **Tu.** with white wool and H., with Br.; **style** cream-coloured.—Cuba (Oriente).

Possibly only a variety of S. urbanianus, with larger Fl., and Sp. straw-coloured at first, later brownish.

S. murrillii Br. & R.
Bo. to over 6 m lg., climbing; **shoots** only 8 mm ∅, dark green, with many aerial R.; **Ri.** 7–8, reddish, very low, thin; **Ar.** white; **Sp.** 5–6, minute, 1–2 bottom ones recurved, longer, 1–2 cm lg., others conical, greenish to black; **Fl.** 15 cm lg. and ∅, white, outer Pet. ± greenish; **Sep.** greenish-yellow, strongly spreading, outermost ones purple on the underside; **Ov.** with only 3 prickles in the Ar., without H.—Mexico (Colima).

S. nelsonii (Wgt.) Br. & R.
Bo. strongly branching; **shoots** thin, weakly glossy, green, to 15 mm ∅, sometimes with aerial R.; **Ri.** 6–7, low, rather tuberculate; **Ar.** small; **Sp.** to c. 12, radiating, acicular, white to yellowish, 5–7 mm lg.; **Fl.** 20 cm lg., white; **Sep.** linear, reddish-brown; **Tu.** and **Ov.** with felt and white Br.; **Fr.** reddish, 2.5 cm ∅, with clusters of Sp. to 1 cm lg.—S. Mexico.

S. pringlei Rose
Bo. climbing high up, yellowish-green, often reddened; **Ri.** 6–7, acute; **Rsp.** 5–6; **Csp.** 1; **Sp.** acicular, spreading, yellow, eventually white, also to 5 white Br.; **Fl.** 20 cm lg., white; **Pet.** rather shorter than the Sep.; **Tu.** and **Ov.** with brown wool.—Mexico (Vera Cruz). (Fig. 380.)

S. pseudospinulosus Wgt.
Bo. resembling that of S. spinulosus, mostly creeping; **shoots** long; **Sp.** differing from those of S. spinulosus in being ± appressed, most **Ar.** having 1 Sp. bent upwards and 1 downwards; **Fl.** white; **Sep.** leather-coloured; **Ov.** larger, longer and less stoutly spiny than in S. spinulosus.—USA (SE. Texas), Mexico (Tamaulipas).

S. pteranthus (Lk. & O.) Br. & R.
Bo. bluish-green, often reddened; **shoots** 1.3–5 cm ∅; **Ri.** 4–6, acute, becoming flatter so that the shoots are eventually terete; **Ar.** with white wool at first; **Sp.** 6–12, to 6 mm lg., yellow, becoming grey; **Fl.** to 30 cm lg., white, unscented; **Sep.** brownish-red; **Tu.** and **Ov.** white-woolly; **style** and **Sti.** whitish; **Fr.** red, spherical, spiny, 6–7 cm ∅.—Mexico (Tamaulipas and Vera Cruz). Said to be naturalised in Florida. The unscented Fl. shows that the perfume is not essential for attracting pollinators to ensure fertilisation. This spec. was earlier better known under the synonym Cereus nycticallus Lk.

S. radicans (DC.) Berg.
Bo. glossy, light green; **shoots** roughened, brittle, to 15 mm ∅; **Ri.** 3–4–5, acute, ·then flatter, shoots

later terete; **Ar.** set on Tub.; **Rsp.** 3–5, red, becoming grey, conical, 3–4 mm lg.; **Csp.** 0–1, rather longer; **Fl.** 32 cm lg., white; **Sep.** red outside, yellow inside; **Ov.** with brown H., with clustered Sp.; **style** white; **Sti.** yellow.—Origin: not known.

S. × "Rettigsche Hybride": a cross with Aporocactus, having pink diurnal Fl.; very rewarding.

S. roseanus (Vpl.) Marsh.: **Selenicereus maxonii** Rose.

S. rostratus (Lem.) Marsh.: **Selenicereus hamatus** (Scheidw.) Br. & R.

S. rothii (Wgt.) Berg.
Bo. bluish to sap-green at first, **St.** later terete; **Ri.** 5–6; **Ar.** prominent, without extra H., mostly with 2 Br.: **Sp.** 4–5, 3–5 mm lg., mostly cruciform; **Fl.** 30 cm lg., 25 cm ∅, faintly scented, white inside; **Pet.** yellowish outside; **Sep.** reddish-green; **Tu.** and **Ov.** with small Sp. and Br.—Paraguay.
Br. and R. referred this spec.—probably on account of its rather remarkable occurrence in Paraguay—to S. macdonaldiae; Berger, however, regarded the 2 spec. as distinct. S. rothii originated with Grosse, in Paraguay, and this is far distant from the main distribution. It has never been established with certainty whether its occurrence there is in fact spontaneous.

S. spinulosus (DC.) Br. & R.
Bo. vivid glossy green; **shoots** long, slender, to 13 mm ∅, with isolated aerial R.; **Ri.** 4–5–(–6), low, more acute at first, becoming obtuse and finally flat; **Ar.** reddish-brown, later greyish-brown; **Rsp.** 6–8, upper ones subulate, stout, short, horn-coloured to whitish, somewhat projecting, 2 bottom ones 5 mm lg., much thinner, bristly, pale; **Csp.** 1, like the upper Rsp.; **Fl.** c. 15 cm lg. and ∅, unperfumed, white; **Sep.** deep to light reddish-brown; **Ov.** with reddish to white Br.; **style** and **Sti.** white.—Mexico (Hidalgo, Rio Tonaltongo).

S. urbanianus (Gürke & Wgt.) Br. & R.
Bo. glossy, later matt, green, often reddened; **shoots** to 5 cm ∅; **Ri.** 5–6, rarely 3–6, acute at first; **Ar.** with rather longer white H. and 1–2 thin Br.; **Sp.** several, spreading, acicular, straw-coloured, later brownish, to 1 cm lg.; **Fl.** to 30 cm lg., yellowish-white; **Sep.** narrow, green, brownish outside, red above; **style** yellowish-green; **Sti.** yellow; **Fr.** spherical.—Haiti; Cuba.

S. vagans (K. Brand.) Br. & R.
Bo. often creeping, freely branching; **shoots** to 1.5 cm ∅; **Ri.** c. 10, low; **Sp.** numerous, acicular, to 1 cm lg., brownish-yellow; **Fl.** 15 cm lg. and ∅,

white, strongly perfumed; **Sep.** brownish to greenish-white, narrow; **style** greenish, cream above.—Mexico (Mazatlan, on the W. coast).

S. vaupelii (Wgt.) Berg.

Bo. light greyish-green, darker at first, sometimes reddened; **shoots** to 18 mm ∅, with a tuft of grey H. at the tip; **Ri.** 5, narrow, scarcely sinuate; **Ar.** small, grey; **Rsp.** 0–5; **Csp.** 1–2; all **Sp.** only 0.5 cm lg., also c. 4 grey H. c. 7 mm lg., and 2–3 small appressed Br.; **Fl.** 25 cm lg., vanilla-scented, white; **Sep.** reddish-green outside, yellow inside; **Ov.** reddish-grey, hairy, with Sp. 3 mm lg.; **Sti.** intense yellow.—Haiti.

S. wercklei (Web.) Br. & R.

Bo. freely branching, pale green; **shoots** thin, subterete, 5–15 mm ∅, with many aerial **R.**; **Ri.** 6–12, weak; **Ar.** with a minute tuft of felt; **Sp.** 0; **Fl.** 15–16 cm lg., light red (to white?); **Sep.** greenish; **Ov.** spiny; **style** green below, pink at midway, whitish above; **Fr.** ovoid, yellow, spiny.—Costa Rica (near Miravalles, Cerro Mogote).

Seleniphyllum Rowl.: a hybrid genus (Selenicereus × Epiphyllum).

Seriocactus Y. Ito: **Brasilicactus** Backbg.

Seticereus Backbg. (72)*

Rather low Cerei, sometimes semi-creeping to shrubby, to ± tree-like, from a restricted area in N. Peru and the extreme S. of Ecuador. Seticereus differs in the following generic characters from Borzicactus, for which the appropriate characters are given in parenthesis for comparison, with "B." indicating Borzicactus): Flowering zone with ± plentiful bristle-development, up to a dense and longer cephalium (B.: not present); floral limb relatively short (B.: longer); tube compressed (B.: terete); hair-development absent from the flower-base (B.: present); fruit up to apple-sized (B.: smaller). These characters are present and uniform in all 4 species described, even in those of a tall-shrubby or ± tree-like habit such as is never found in Borzicactus. To include Seticereus in Borzicactus, as is done by Kimnach, is thus not justifiable; it can only lead to insufficient observation of the distinguishing characters. Ritter's rather similar treatment was still more illogical since his Genus Cephalocleistocactus is differentiated from Cleistocactus **only** by the bristly cephalium; if this is to

be regarded as a diagnostic character in one instance, then it must be uniformly treated as such elsewhere.
Seeds of Seticereus are dull black.—Distribution: S. Ecuador and adjacent N. Peru, at higher altitudes. [(R).]

S. chlorocarpus (HBK.) Backbg.

Bo. ± tree-like with a short **trunk**, to over 1.5 m h., with a fairly dense crown, matt green; **branches** always re-branching above; **Ri.** 9–10, c. 2 cm h.; **Rsp.** c. 8–10, to 1 cm lg., radiating but none in the upper Ar.-margin; **Csp.** (1–)3–4, unequal, subulate, straight, stiff, pungent, to 5 cm lg.; **Sp.** brownish or darker, soon becoming whitish-grey; **Ar.** at first light brownish-white, later sometimes with Br.; **Fl.** (acc. Hutchison) as in the other spec.; **Fr.** described as "green, with robust H.", but this probably refers to an immature Fr., since the specific name means "greenish-yellow".—N. Peru (near Huancabamba and the Olmos valley).

S. ferrugineus Backbg.: **Seticereus icosagonus** v. **ferrugineus** (Backbg.) Backbg.

S. humboldtii (HBK.) Backbg.

Bo. semi-prostrate and ascending, dark green; **Ri.** 10–12, ± tuberculate, transversely furrowed; **Rsp.** numerous, thin; **Csp.** to c. 6, subulate; all **Sp.** chestnut-brown, the bristly **Ceph.** similarly; **Fl.** carmine; **Fil.** violet-red.—S. Ecuador to N. Peru.

S. icosagonus (HBK.) Backbg. (T.)

Bo. semi-prostrate and ascending, freely offsetting, forming colonies; **shoots** to c. 60 cm lg., to over 6 cm ∅; **Ri.** 18–20, low, little tuberculate, in some forms thickened towards the apex, with the Ri. somewhat tuberculate and the Sp. darker; **Sp.** numerous, ± bristly-fine, lighter to deep honey-yellow, **Br.-Ceph.** similarly; **Fl.** light to intense red, sometimes scarlet, to c. 8 cm lg., with whitish to brownish H.; **Fr.** yellowish, to c. 5 cm ∅, Ar. with thin H.—S. Ecuador to N. Peru. (Fig. 381, 383.)

 v. **aurantiaciflorus** Backbg.: **Fl.** light orange-yellow, tipped ± reddish;

 v. **ferrugineus** (Backbg.) Backbg. n.comb. (Seticereus oehmeanus v. ferrugineus (Backbg.) Backbg., "Die Cact.", 982. 1959): **Bo.** darker green; **Sp.** brownish, later grey, a few stouter, all at first brownish; **Fl.** dark carmine; **Fil.** not violet. Perhaps a spontaneous hybrid with S. humboldtii;

 v. **oehmeanus** (Backbg.) Backbg.: **Sp.** light brownish; **Csp.** 1–2, stouter but sometimes absent, otherwise the upper one to 3 cm lg., the lower one to 6 cm lg., obliquely projecting; **Fl.** crimson.—N. Peru.

---

* First Latin diagnosis in Kakt. u.a. Sukk., 3: 37. 1937 (March); Latin diagnosis in BfK. 1937, 7 (July) of what later proved to be the synonymous genus Gymnanthocereus Backbg. (See also under Gymnocereus Backbg.)

S. roezlii (Hge. Jr.) Backbg.
Bo. laxly branching, shrubby, to over 2 m h., greyish-green; **branches** to 7 cm $\varnothing$; **Ri.** to 9, with a transverse notch or V-furrow over the Ar.; **Ar.** yellowish at first; **Rsp.** 9–12, radiating, the bottom one longest, to 1 cm lg., light brown, subulate; **Csp.** 1, 1–4 cm lg., porrect at first, later directed downwards, all later light grey, **Ceph.-Br.** scattered at first, more numerous with increasing age, finally denser and dark at the apex; **Fl.** red, numerous on mature plants.—N. Peru (valley of Bellavista-Olmos, or near Bellavista). (Fig. 382.)
Re-collected by Rauh; I was able to compare his material with plants which had long been in cultivation in European collections, including those of Haage, and all were identical. Unaware of this Kimnach and Hutchison regarded the above name as a synonym of Borzicactus sepium, while Ritter believed that the plants, including those of the spec. seen by Rauh, had not yet been described and called it Borzicactus neoroezlii Ritt. In cases like this it is essential that one should study older collected material in European collections. There is further a variety or form which flowers profusely even when quite small, in which the flowering zone does not develop any bristles for a long time, and even then they are only relatively sparse. Blossfeld Jr. reported plants like this, or collected their seed. Flowering plants are not rare in collections on the Riviera, but I have not named them since I am uncertain whether this is perhaps C. chotaensis (Web.) Vpl., which is probably also a Seticereus: "to 2 m h.; Fl. to 5 cm lg., orange-coloured, 2.5 cm $\varnothing$, with black H.; from Peru (Rio Chota valley)", alternatively it may be a form or variety of S. roezlii. First it is essential to know how tall mature plants can become; if they are only to c. 1 m or slightly more, then they are more likely a variety of S. roezlii. It is also necessary to have some more precise description of C. chotaensis. A good many years ago I saw S. roezlii over 2 m h. in cultivation.

Seticleistocactus Backbg. (74)
Descr. Cact. Nov. III: 13. 1963.

Relatively low-growing slender Cerei, branching from the base or the flanks, and closely related to Cleistocactus; Cardenas described the type-species of the genus as "a remarkable species, diverging from all other species of Cleistocactus by the oblique floral limb with recurved petals, but more especially by the long projecting bristles on the floral tube, ovary and fruit; it must have a position intermediate between Cleistocactus and Bolivicereus". This judgement is sufficient justification in itself for inclusion in a separate genus; in addition, the classificatory principle of my Systematic Survey

leaves a vacant space which Seticleistocactus neatly fills: i.e. the stage of reduction before Cleistocactus. These two genera and Cephalocleistocactus together constitute a "group of reduction", two of the genera having different types of bristle-development: Seticleistocactus with bristles on flower and fruit but none in the areoles of the stem, while Cephalocleistocactus with increasing size develops an increasingly dense bristle-cephalium in the flowering region, with no bristles present on the flower; while in Cleistocactus, bristles are lacking both in the flowering zone and on the flowers.
These grouped genera show clearly that Nature herself has provided, with the line of reduction, the most natural possible principle for classification.
Distribution: Bolivia (Prov. Florida and Valle Grande). [(R).]

S. dependens (Card.) Backbg. n.comb. (Cleistocactus dependens Card., C. & S. J. [US], XXIV: 5, 144. 1952).
Bo. prostrate and ascending; **shoots** to 3.5 cm $\varnothing$; **Ri.** 10–12, low, narrow; **Ar.** whitish-grey above, black-felty below; **Rsp.** 8–12, to 3 mm lg., pungent, reddish-grey at first; **Csp.** 3–4, darker, 1 to 1.5 cm lg., grey, sometimes dark-tipped; **Sp.** all later whitish-grey; **Fl.** numerous, c. 4.5 cm lg.; **Tu.** carmine-pink, slender; **Sep.** and **Pet.** greenish, Sep. pink below, more yellowish above, brownish-tipped; **Br.** on the Tu. (and mostly denser on the bud and Ov.) white, to c. 7 mm lg.; **Fr.** 1.4 cm $\varnothing$, wine-red.—Bolivia (Prov. Florida, La Negra, 1400 m). (Fig. 59 left, 384.)
Cardenas only mentioned S. piraymirensis as being a special case, but since he said the Br. of the above spec. were "long and white", it had to be referred here.

S. piraymirensis (Card.) Backbg. (T.)—Descr. Cact. Nov. III: 13. 1963 (Cleistocactus piraymirensis Card., C. & S. J. [US], XXXIII: 3, 78–79. 1961).
Bo. erectly columnar, to 1 m h., **shoots** to 3 cm $\varnothing$, greyish-green; **Ri.** c. 15, 4 mm h.; **Ar.** 1 cm apart, dark; **Rsp.** 12–18, very fine, 4–10 mm lg.; **Csp.** 1, acicular, to 2.5 cm lg.; all **Sp.** whitish; **Fl.** cylindric, to 6 cm lg., limb $\pm$ oblique, 1.2 cm $\varnothing$; **Tu.** in part $\pm$ curving, bluish-red, with white H.; **Sep.** dark bluish-red, brown-tipped; **Pet.** lighter bluish-red, they and the Sep. $\pm$ revolute; **style** lighter bluish-red below, darker bluish-red above; **Sti.** light green; **An.** bluish-red; **Fr.** reddish to dark green, 1.5 cm lg., with red Sc.; **Br.** on Tu. and Fr. 1–2 cm lg.; **S.** 1 mm lg., glossy, black.—Bolivia (Prov. Valle Grande, Santa Cruz, Rio Piraymirí, 1800 m). (Fig. 385.)

× Setidenmoza icosagonoides: an undescribed yellow-spined hybrid between Seticereus and Denmoza.

Setiechinopsis (Backbg.) De Haas (85)

Slender small-cylindric plants with long, ± scented, nocturnal flowers having a thin tube; the petals are very narrow, the scales on the tube have a bristle-like extension, and bristles are in part present on the ovary; the fruit is spindle-shaped, dry, and splits longitudinally at maturity. Seeds brownish-black. Only 1 species known.— Distribution: Argentina: Santiago del Estero. [(R), but grafted plants grow larger.]

S. mirabilis (Speg.) De Haas (T.)
Bo. mostly simple, to 15 cm h., 2 cm ∅, dark brownish-green; **Ri.** 11–12; **Ar.** minute; **Rsp.** 9–14, whitish, thin; **Csp.** 1, porrect, ± subulate, to 1.5 cm lg., brownish to horn-coloured; all **Sp.** straight; **Fl.** always apical, c. 12 cm lg., white; **Pet.** very narrow, white, tapering; **Tu.** fairly woolly, with black Sc.-Br., **Ov.** also sometimes with Br.; **Fr.** to 4 cm lg., 6 mm ∅; **S.** spherical, 1.5 mm lg.—Argentina (near Colonia Ceres). (Fig. 386.)
v. **gracilior** Backbg.—Descr. Cact. Nov. III: 14. 1963: **Bo.** still darker; **Rsp.** 10–12; **Csp.** 1, also thin, only 0.5(–1) cm lg., light brown above at first, soon white, tipped ± light brown; **Fl.** only 6 cm lg. (when closed, 8.5 cm lg.), c. 2.9 cm ∅; **Pet.** densely capitate and radiating, extremely narrow, greenish-white; **Fr.** 3 cm lg. (Fig. 387). Acc. Spegazzini, the type ("validissimus") has a stout Csp. to 1.5 cm lg. His statement: "Fl. unperfumed", is not accurate; in both type and variety the Fl. are scented, but less strongly during daylight; in the variety, the Fl. is no longer open by the morning and usually it shuts after quite a short time. In the spec., the Fl. can still be open early in the morning; it is sometimes very strongly scented. The style is short, consequently these plants (which are self-fertile) almost always pollinate themselves and are thus autogamous. This character, together with the shape of the perianth, the presence of bristles, and the nature of the spindle-shaped fruit which dries up and dehisces laterally, separates Setiechinopsis from Arthrocereus, and its inclusion in the latter by Marshall and Buxbaum can only be explained by inadequate familiarity with living material of both genera which is, admittedly, rarely available.

Setirebutia (Frič) Krzgr., not described: **Mediolobivia** Backbg.

Soehrensia Backbg. (114)

Large plants which can be oblong to spherical, sometimes large-spherical to stoutly columnar; flowers with moderately long, stout tubes, these only hairy; fruits ± woolly, not dry. Flowers in different shades of red or yellow. These plants occur only at higher altitudes and are rarely seen in Europe: one species is known to the natives as "conical ball", another attains the same size as Echinocactus grusonii, while a third is almost as large as the thickly columnar Helianthocereus poco, with old plants up to 2.5 m high.— Distribution: NW. Argentina (from Mendoza and Tucuman to Los Andes); Chile. [(R).]

S. bruchii (Br. & R.) Backbg. (T.)
Bo. large-spherical, simple, or offsetting to form groups up to 50 cm ∅; **Ri.** to c. 50 or more, tuberculate above; **Ar.** with short white woolly felt, more plentiful at first; **Rsp.** 9–14, spreading, projecting, straight or ± curving, subulate, stout; **Csp.** similarly, to c. 4; **Sp.** darker, Csp. somewhat thickened below; **Fl.** deep red, c. 5 cm ∅, with ± erect Pet.; **Fr.** green, sparsely hairy.—N. Argentina (Tafí del Valle). Fechser has also reported plants with pale red Fl. (Fig. 388.)
This description is based on that of Br. & R., with additions. There are also individual plants with yellowish and more stoutly acicular Sp., all to 2 cm lg., the Csp. scarcely differentiated in thickness, thickened below; Fl. c. 6.5 cm ∅, rather more widely opening, yellowish-red; Fil. red; Sti. green. Br. & R. gave the Sp.-colour as "mostly dark", but gave no data regarding thickness and length. Since Rose collected the plants himself it has to be assumed that he happened to see only those with deeper red Fl. Presumably there are transitional forms, so that the form with lighter Sp. and Fl. (e.g. in the Rivière collection) cannot at the present time be segregated and given varietal status. Since Fechser reported pale red-flowered specimens, Y. Ito's varieties: v. aureorubriflora and v. rosiflora (both 1962) can only be regarded as forms and should be known as such.
v. **nivalis** (Frič) is a form from high altitudes, with denser whitish **Sp.**, collected in 1929 but never re-collected until recently.

S. formosa (Pfeiff.) Backbg.
Bo. thick-spherical at first, later elongated, cylindric in age, to over 50 cm h., mostly simple; **Ri.** 15–35; **epidermis** pale greyish-green; **Rsp.** 8–16, rather thin and flexible; **Csp.** to 8, to 7 cm lg., flexible; **Sp.** variable in colour, mostly whitish but Rsp. also yellowish, and Csp. often darker-tipped, or reddish, all ± translucent; **Fl.** slender bell-shaped to funnelform, to 8 cm lg., varying in ∅,

461

light to golden-yellow; **Tu.** to 2.5 cm $\emptyset$, yellowish-green, laxly hairy.—N. Argentina (Mendoza, Quebrada de Toros, or the lower cordillera of the N. border of Mendoza, to the Cerro Nevado).
Sp. are sometimes also brownish, varying in length and thickness. Spherical plants have not attained flowering-size; this slow-growing spec. needs to be recognisably cylindric before it flowers. Other similar spec. remain spherical, but S. formosa v. maxima can be to 2 m h. (acc. Dodds) and to 40 cm $\emptyset$. The plants seen in some black-and-white photos are difficult to distinguish from Heliantho-cereus poco which also bears apical Fl., and in general both the shape and the indumentum of the Fl. in these 2 genera are very close. Nevertheless the majority of the spec. in the genus—with the exception of very old plants—are cactoid and not cereoid. This example shows that only an exact delimitation, in accordance with narrowly con-ceived genera, can provide clarification (cf. in-troductory remarks to Submatucana).

    v. **maxima** Backbg.: **Bo.** to 40 cm $\emptyset$, to c. 2.5 m h. in age, light and not greyish-green; **Sp.** yellow, brown-tipped; **Fl.** golden-yellow. Discovered by Dodds.—N. Argentina (Mendoza, Cerro de Almohadones, at c. 3000 m);

    v. **polycephala** Backbg.: **Bo.** greyish-green, many-headed, branching from below (in v. maxima also from the flanks); **Sp.** white; **Fl.** golden-yellow. Found by Dodds.—N. Argentina (Cerro de Almohadones, on the Páramo River).

S. grandis (Br. & R.) Backbg.

Bo. spherical to oblong, to 25 cm h.; **Ri.** 14–16, 2 cm h., acute, slightly convex between the Ar.; **Ar.** white at first; **Rsp.** 10–15, yellow, tipped brown, acicular to thin-subulate; **Csp.** indistinctly differen-tiated, $\pm$ thickened below, 2 Sp. often longer, to 8 cm lg.; **Fl.** to 6 cm lg., bellshaped-funnelform, 4 cm $\emptyset$, orange-yellow; **Tu.** to 3.5 cm $\emptyset$, with brownish H.; **Fil.** green; **style** greenish-yellow; **Sti.** yellow; **Fr.** broadly spherical.—N. Argentina (between Andalgalá and Concepción). Younger plants sometimes resemble certain forms of Trichocereus smrzianus (Backbg.) Backbg. which was long considered to be a Soehrensia.

S. ingens Br. & R. ex Backbg.

Bo. eventually a stout and large sphere; **Sp.** projecting, light yellow; **Fl.** to c. 4(–5) cm $\emptyset$, yellow, with brown H.; **Fr.** 3–4 cm $\emptyset$, greenish to brownish-yellow, dehiscing laterally; **S.** small, glossy, black (acc. Fechser).—N. Argentina (be-tween Andalgalá and Concepción, El Molle). (Fig. 389.)
I have examined living plants in the Marnier collection. Colour-photos of Schicketantz show a possible variant of the spec., with rather longer Sp., and Fl. more orange-red.

S. korethroides (Werd.) Backbg.

Bo. simple at first, later $\pm$ caespitose, forming groups of larger-spherical plants, later oblong, to 30 cm $\emptyset$ in age, dull light green to slightly glossy sap-green; **Ri.** over 20, $\pm$ tuberculate at first; **Ar.** with whitish to yellowish felt at first; **Rsp.** 12–20, unequal, whitish to yellowish or horn-coloured, dark-tipped, acicular, to 3 cm lg.; **Csp.** typically 4, yellowish or reddish-brown, often banded, some-times flattened, pungent; **Fl.** to 7 cm lg., 4.5 cm $\emptyset$, intense red, bellshaped-funnelform; **Tu.** with dense greyish-brown H.—N. Argentina (Prov. Los Andes). (Fig. 390.)

S. oreopepon (Speg.) Backbg.

Bo. broadly spherical to elongated-spherical, to 30 cm $\emptyset$, greyish olive-green; **Ri.** c. 18–20–30, 2.5 cm br., slightly notched; **Ar.** 0.8 cm lg., grey; **Sp.** few at first, later to c. 12(–20), 1–5 of these more central, 5–7 cm lg., radials 2–3.5 cm lg., all Sp. thin, flexible, pale yellowish to reddish; **Fl.** (8–)10 cm lg., to 3.5 cm $\emptyset$, golden-yellow, with grey H.; **Tu.** with tapering greenish Sc.; **Fil.** white, inserted through-out the inside of the Tu.; **An.** cream.—N. Argentina (Mendoza, Cacheuta).
Data supplemented from observations made on material in the Marnier collection.

S. smrziana (Backbg.) Backbg.: **Trichocereus smrzianus** (Backbg.) Backbg. Very recently, Ru-bingh of Soestdijk saw the flower for the first time and thus established that this is a spec. of Trichocereus.

S. uebelmanniana Lembcke & Backbg.

Bo. flat-spherical to rounded at first, later col-umnar, to 1.5 m h., to 40 cm $\emptyset$, mid-green; **Ri.** c. 17 at first, later to over 38, thickened around the Ar., $\pm$ tuberculate on new growth; **Rsp.** to 28, 2.5–5 cm lg., $\pm$ interlacing; **Csp.** 2–5, to 15 cm lg.; all Sp. light yellow to golden-brown or reddish, sometimes $\pm$ curving and dark-tipped; **Fl.** bellshaped-funnelform, c. 6 cm lg., yellowish; **Tu.** with dense woolly H.; **Fr.** spherical, 3 cm $\emptyset$, pulp white; **S.** glossy, black, 0.75 mm lg.—Chile (Baños de Puritama and Toconce, 3500 m). A robustly and densely spined plant which has penetrated into Chile from E. of the Andes. The Genus Roden-tiophila Ritt. may be more closely related to it.

Fechser reports another interesting Soehrensia as follows: to c. 1.5 m h., 20 cm $\emptyset$, with yellow Sp., crown $\pm$ obliquely directed towards the N.; Fl. glossy yellow.—N. Argentina (Catamarca). This might possibly be a Helianthocereus.

Solisia Br. & R. (224)

Small solitary plants, strongly resembling Pelecyphora pseudopectinata but with milky sap; like the latter with a napiform extension of the plant-base, compressed tubercles and lengthened areoles, with white pectinate spines; however the flowers of Solisia are not apical but are borne lower down on the body. The fruits are oblong berries which, as in some other genera, are pushed outward when they reach maturity. Inclusion in Mammillaria, as in Moran's treatment, too easily overlooks the interesting and special position of this genus, which Buxbaum correctly recognised in 1951. The fact that he contradicted himself in 1956 when he accepted Moran's views, demonstrates that his systematic method is not firmly based.

Whereas in Mammillaria the flowers always arise from the upper zone of the previous year's growth, in Solisia they are always "lateral" (Br. & R.), and anyone confronted with this plant would be more likely to follow the original author, Stein, in considering it as a relative of Pelecyphora rather than as a Mammillaria.—Distribution: Mexico (Puebla and Oaxaca). [(G); plants on their own R. seldom last long.]

S. pectinata (B. Stein) Br. & R. (T.)
Bo. to 8 cm lg., to 6 cm ∅, mostly set deeper in the soil; **Tub.** small, compressed above, truncate at the tip; **Ar.** elongated; **Ax.** naked; **Sp.** to c. 40, to 2 mm lg., pure white or faintly reddish; **Fl.** c. 2 cm lg., 2.5 cm ∅, bellshaped-funnelform, naked; **Sep.** yellowish-green; **style** white; **Sti.** yellowish-green; **Fr.** an elongated, whitish berry; **S.** 1 mm lg., boat-shaped, black, with a large hilum.—Mexico (Puebla, near Tehuacan; also reported from Oaxaca). (Fig. 391.)

Spegazzinia Backbg.: **Weingartia** Werd.

Stenocactus (K. Sch.) Berg.: **Echinofossulocactus** Lawr.

Stenocereus (Berg.) Ricc. (158)

Moderately stout columnar plants, branching from the base, not tree-like or forming a crown as in the closely related Marginatocereus. In the latter, the flowers are borne in rows running down from the apex, or at intervals on the flanks; in Stenocereus, however, they arise only around the apex, and whereas its buds project from a ring of bristles, and the ovary later shows more numerous and longer bristles, the ovary in Marginatocereus is felty, with a few short bristles only about midway on the floral tube, and then only in some of the

areoles. The floral structure of Stenocereus also differs in that the nectary is more top-shaped, and that of Marginatocereus is oblong; Stenocereus also has the peculiarity that the perianth opens wide at night and closes towards morning, but its pink sepals project for up to a further 3 days (Berger). Consequently the genus was long considered to have diurnal flowers, perhaps because the wide-open flowers could only be seen as such at night. The fruits are spiny and the seeds matt black.—Distribution: Mexico (from Puebla to the Isthmus of Tehuantepec). [(R).]

S. chrysocarpus Sanchez-Mej. 1972
Bo. 5–9 m h., forming a trunk 1.5–3 m h., 25–40 cm ∅; **branches** numerous, ascending, 2–5 m lg., 10–14 cm ∅; **Ri.** 7; **Ar.** 4–6 mm lg., 8–10 mm br.; **Rsp.** 7, 11–15 mm lg.; **Csp.** 0–2, to 17 mm lg.; **Fl.** nocturnal, 8–10 cm lg., 7 cm ∅, white to delicate pink; **Fr.** covered with very spiny Ar., 6 cm lg., 4 cm ∅; **S.** 2.5 mm lg., 1.8 mm br., rough, black.—Mexico (Michoacan, 350 m).

S. stellatus (Pfeiff.) Ricc. (T.)
Bo. erectly columnar, matt, dark green, often reddened, to 3 m h.; **branches** to 8 cm ∅; **Ri.** 8–12, obtuse, low, ± tuberculate; **Ar.** white; **Rsp.** 8–12, to 12 mm lg., spreading; **Csp.** 1–3, one more distinctly central, to 2 cm lg., brown above and below; **Fl.** to 6 cm lg., cylindric-bellshaped, white, pink outside; **Tu.** pink, set with Br. as far up as the nectary; **Fr.** spherical, 3 cm ∅, red, spiny, edible.—Mexico (Puebla; Oaxaca; Tehuantepec). (Fig. 392.)

S. treleasii (Br. & R.) Backbg.
Bo. to 7 m h., sometimes simple, rarely branching somewhat from the flanks (if the growing-tip has been damaged?); **Ri.** to 20, tuberculate, with a ± V-shaped depression; **Sp.** 7–9, short, yellowish, later also 1 longer, more distinctly central Sp.; **Fl.** to 5 cm lg., as in the preceding spec. (H. Bravo); **Fr.** similarly, 5 cm ∅.—Mexico (Oaxaca, road between Mitla and Oaxaca).

Stephanocereus Berg. (185)

A monotypic genus of relatively slender erect Cerei which develop a tuft of bristles at the apex on reaching flowering age; new growth continues through this zone and then another similar apical tuft develops, so that the earlier bristly development persists as an annulus. The Genus Arrojadoa shows quite similar development. In both genera the flowers are nocturnal, and the fruit is naked and set with floral remains. Werdermann referred Stephanocereus to "Pilocereus", presumably only because the fruit, unlike Arrajodoa, has no lid; however it does not have the typical form of the Pilosocereus fruits, being oblong rather than spherical; but the principal character of Stephanocereus lies in a true cephalium always being present, whereas in Pilosocereus the pseudocephalium is not a constant character and can indeed be absent. Stephanocereus is always simple, unless perhaps in some cases where the plant has been damaged and branching has then occurred; the flower is somewhat curving; Stephanocereus is further distinguished from Arrojadoa by its greater height, the umbilicate fruit and the larger, divergent flower.

The only photo of a flowering plant is one I took in the Botanical Garden of Rio de Janeiro, showing the flowers already closed by the morning ("Die Cact.", IV: Fig. 2431, p. 2549, 1960). According to Werdermann, plants of the genus occur only as scattered individuals. The pear-shaped seeds are matt black.—Distribution: Brazil (Bahia). [(R) (G); in Marnier's garden I have seen a fairly large plant raised from seed.]

S. leucostele (Gürke) Berg. (T.)
Bo. mostly solitary, erect, to 3 m h.; **Ri.** 12–18; **Ar.** with H. to 1.5 cm lg., these being only sparse on seedlings; **Rsp.** to c. 20, 0.5–1.5 cm lg., white, thin-acicular, becoming greyish-brown; **Csp.** several, white to golden-yellow, rigid, sharp, 1–2, later often to 4 cm lg.; **Ceph.** of white wool and numerous golden-yellow Br. to 7 cm lg.; **Fl.** to 7 cm lg., white, somewhat curving, yellowish below, greenish towards the limb; **Sti.** cream; **Fr.** spherical to oblong, umbilicate, with floral remains; **S.** almost 2 mm lg.—Brazil (Bahia, S. Catinga). (Fig. 393.)

Stetsonia Br. & R. (63)

Large tree-like Cerei with a stout trunk, of which I have seen very large colonies in the vicinity of Santiago del Estero. The nocturnal flowers are glabrous and slightly curving, with a fairly slender tube, while the ovary is densely set with ± membranous and imbricate scales. The perianth opens widely but the anthers are erectly clustered around the style.—Distribution: Argentina (in the dry NW., on hills and bush-grown parts of the Pampas); Bolivia (acc. Ritter). [(R); head-cuttings sometimes flower in collections.]

S. boliviana Ritt.: only a name.

S. coryne (SD.) Br. & R. (T.)
Bo. forming trees to 8 m h., **trunk** to c. 40 cm ∅; **branches** sometimes to over 100, to 60 cm lg., ± erect; **Ri.** 8–9, 1–1.5 cm h., obtuse, at first vivid bluish-green; **Sp.** 7–9, thickened below, one more central, porrect, to 5 cm lg., rather stout, others to c. 3 cm lg., all brownish-yellow, soon becoming white, blackish-tipped; **Fl.** to 15 cm lg., white; **Tu.** with many membranous Sc.; **Ov.** densely set with imbricate Sc.—NW. Argentina (dry regions).

v. **procera** Ritt.—"Taxon", XIII: 3, 116. 1964: **Bo.** taller, to 10 m h.; **branches** erect (spreading in the type, acc. Ritter), milky-green at first (bluish in the type); **Pet.** pale pink, long-tapering (rounded or short-tapering in the type); **nectary** 1–1.5 cm lg. (0.5–1 cm lg. in the type); **Fr.** ± spherical (oblong in the type); **S.** pale brown (brown in the type).—Bolivia (mountainous terrain in Dept. Tarija, borders of the Provinces Gran Chaco and O'Connor, Palos Blancos; an isolated distribution). (FR 872–873.)

Offered in Winter's catalogue, at first as an independent spec., and also as S. boliviana.

Strombocactus Br. & R. (204)

Simple, flattened-spherical plants, their stout taproots growing down into clefts between steep rocks of argillaceous slate. The flowers resemble Obregonia except that they and the upper part of the fruits have dry-bordered scales; the dry fruits dehisce at maturity by one or two longitudinal tears. The minute dust-fine seeds are brown. The petals are rather variable in both length and width. The unique feature of these plants lies in the rather bent, 4-angled tubercles which are strongly truncate above and arranged in recognisable ribs. Only one species known with all these characters.—Distribution: Central Mexico (Hidalgo). [(R); grafted plants sometimes form offsets.]

S. disciformis (DC.) Br. & R. (T.)
Bo. simple, set disc-like in the ground, sometimes flattened-spherical, bluish to greyish-green or grey, to 8 cm ∅, rarely to over 15 cm ∅; **Ri.** in Isp. 8:13, divided into swollen, bent and distorted-looking Tub.; **Ar.** soon glabrous; **Sp.** at most 4–5 in an Ar., bristle-like, soon dropping, mostly only present close to the crown; **Fl.** 2.5–3.5 cm lg., to 4 cm ∅, white to yellowish-white; **Sti.** similarly coloured; **Fr.** 7 mm lg., dirty brown, thin-walled; **S.** 0.3 mm lg., reddish-brown.—Mexico (Hidalgo, near Ixmiquilpan, Mineral del Monte etc.). (Fig. 394.)

Strophocactus Br. & R. (42)

An interesting genus of epiphytic plants. As in Deamia, the stems clamber up tree-trunks, but here, since they are 2-angled, they lie flat and membranous against their support; the middle-rib is distinct and areoles are present only along the margins. The spines are rather short and fine. The flower, with its long tube, is somewhat reminiscent of Setiechinopsis; the petals are narrow, the tube has some hair-development and probably also bristles; the ovary too is bristly, while the fruit has bristly spines.—Distribution: Brazil (forests of the River Amazon). [Cultivate as an epiphyte.]

S. wittii (K. Sch.) Br. & R. (T.)
Bo. consisting of thin flat shoots to 10 cm br., clinging and climbing, 3–4 times as long as broad, rounded above and below; **Ar.** crowded, with woolly H.; **Sp.** numerous, to 1.2 cm lg., with Br. also present; **Fl.** to 25 cm lg., probably reddish outside, white (to reddish?) inside; **Fr.** long-ovoid; **S.** ear-shaped, black.—Brazil (around Manaos). Acc. H. W. Fittkau, widely distributed in forests subject to flooding, e.g. those of the Rio Negro and other more distant areas of the Amazon basin. (Fig. 395.) The shoots also branch from the flanks.

Submatucana Backbg. (81)*

Spherical plants, either simple or caespitose. The ribs are broader than in Matucana, with fairly large tubercles, while the spination is stouter, except in one species. With its ± curving or zygomorphic and hairy flowers, Submatucana represents the stage of reduction prior to Matucana, with the decisive diagnostic character, according to Britton & Rose, that the "tube and ovary are glabrous". Ritter is not logical in his inclusion of the Submatucana species in Matucana, since he erected the genus Pilocopiapoa Ritt. on the basis of its only species being distinguished from Copiapoa by the hairiness of the flowers. The fruits of Submatucana become dry, and dehisce by longitudinal tears; the seeds are ± black. This genus finally provided a rightful home for "Arequipa aurantiaca (Vpl.) Werd." and "Arequipa myriacantha (Vpl.) Br. & R."; the earlier inclusion of these plants in Arequipa was due to the lack of a better alternative, since at that time no-one knew of any sizeable complex of species with a spherical habit and having hairy and zygomorphic flowers. Kimnach, in his mass-referrals to Borzicactus (erroneously, in my view) also sank Matucana and Submatucana in that genus—i.e. for the very first time globular cacti were included in a genus of which the type-species was columnar. Nature herself confounded him for Hutchison discovered a species of Submatucana which is mostly fairly broadly spherical, and only in age occasionally becomes ± elongated.—Distribution: NE. Peru. [(R) (G).]

* Submatucana and Matucana are now included in Borzicactus by most authors. Translator.

S. aurantiaca (Vpl.) Backbg. (T.)
Bo. simple or caespitose, to 15 cm ∅ and h.; **Ri.** c. 16, divided into oblong Tub.; **Ar.** elliptic; **Sp.** c. 25, reddish-brown, unequal, sometimes to 30 in number, Csp. scarcely distinguishable as such, 3–4 upper Sp. erect, straight, curving, to 2.5 cm lg., centrals 3–7, longer, 2.5–4.5 cm lg.; **Fl.** to c. 9 cm lg., 5–7 cm ∅, quite strongly zygomorphic, hairy, dark red, orange-yellow towards the centre and the throat; **style** with H.-development below brownish-pink; **Sti.** yellowish-green; **Fr.** c. 2 cm ∅, purple to dark brown; **S.** brownish-black to black.—N. Peru (Cajamarca, between Chota and Hualgayoc; Huancabamba, near Sondor).

S. aureiflora (Ritt.) Backbg.
Described by Ritter (KuaS 1965) as Matucana aureiflora and thus referrable to his new SG. Incaica, with the character: "Actinomorphic Fl., remaining open day and night". Backbg. considers that this does not justify subgeneric status and therefore transferred the name here.

S. calvescens (Kimn. & Hutch.) Backbg.
Bo. glossy, dark green, to 15 cm h. and ∅; **Ri.** 16–17, divided into 6-angled Tub.; **Ar.** grey, oblong; **Sp.** c. 25–35, scarcely differentiated, stiff, light brownish-yellow, outer ones 0.5–2 cm lg., 4–8 more central, 1.5–4 cm lg.; **Fl.** to 8 cm lg., 3–5 cm ∅, ± zygomorphic, orange-purple; **Tu.** with white H. to 2.5 mm lg.; **Fr.** spherical; **S.** black, wrinkled.—N. Peru (Santiago de Chuco, 15 km N. of Angasmarca, close to the mine below Arenillas, c. 3700 m).
Ritter's catalogue-name: Matucana megalantha, refers to this plant.

S. currundayensis (Ritt.) Backbg.
Bo. ± spherical; **Ri.** over 12, divided by transverse furrows into rounded Tub.; **Ar.** fairly large, oval, very felty; **Sp.** c. 16–18, subulate; **Rsp.** yellowish, to c. 2 cm lg., **Csp.** stout, yellowish-brown, yellow below at first, to c. 3.5 cm lg.; **Fl.** pale (salmon) pink, **Tu.** fairly long, shortly hairy.—Peru (Cerro Currunday, near Samne). This spec. has not been validly described, but it will need to be re-classified since Ritter lists it as Matucana; this is unusual in botanical practice but it nevertheless remains essential. Ritter publishes his descriptions in several periodicals and his new spec. thus readily escape the notice of any one individual. To avoid this, it is necessary to gather them all together here; some new combinations of still unpublished names of good spec. are thus inevitable.

S. formosa (Ritt.) Backbg.—Descr. Cact. Nov. III: 14. 1963 (Matucana formosa Ritt., "Taxon", XII: 3, 125. 1963).

Bo. hemispherical, to 15 cm ∅; **Ri.** 20–30, divided into Tub. 7–10 mm h.; **Ar.** 3–6 mm ∅, brown; **Sp.** acicular, dark brown; **Rsp.** 6–11; **Csp.** 1–4, 2–5 cm lg.; **Fl.** regular; **Ov.** lacking Br.; **Tu.** with white or grey H.; **Pet.** crimson, blood-red above; **Fr.** 1.5 cm lg., tapering towards the base; **S.** black, 1 mm lg.—Peru (Balsas, Dept. Cajamarca) (FR 658).

> v. **minor** (Ritt.) Backbg.—Descr. Cact. Nov. III: 14. 1963 (Matucana formosa v. minor Ritt., l.c., 125. 1963): **Bo.** smaller, 7–12 cm ∅; **Ri.** 13–21; **Rsp.** 9 at most; **Csp.** 1–2.—Peru (El Chagnal, Dept. La Libertad) (FR 1072).

S. intertexta (Ritt.) Backbg.—Descr. Cact. Nov. III: 14. 1963 (Matucana intertexta Ritt., "Taxon", XII: 3, 125. 1963).
Bo. to 36 cm h., 7–18 cm ∅; **Ri.** 15–25, notched, to 1.5 cm h.; **Ar.** to 8 mm lg.; **Rsp.** 8–12, ± rough, bevelled, 8–20 mm lg., brown; **Csp.** 2–3.5 cm lg., brown, tipped black; **Fl.** 7.5–10.5 cm lg., zygomorphic; **Tu.** to 5.5 cm lg., with flocky white H.; **Pet.** golden-yellow, blood-red above; **Fil.** pale carmine or brown above; **style** pale yellow; **S.** 1.4 mm lg.—Peru (Puente Crisnejas, N. of Cajamarca) (FR 693).

S. madisoniorum (Hutch.) Backbg. n. comb.—(Borzicactus madisoniorum Hutch., C. & S. J. [US], XXXV: 6, 167–172. 1963).
Bo. broadly spherical at first, later ± elongated, simple, greyish-green, epidermis rough; **Ri.** 7–12, quite flat at first, later with the **Ar.** on tuberculate prominences; **Sp.** 0–1–5, to 6 cm lg., ± strongly curving, readily detached, brown, later whitish; **Fl.** scarcely zygomorphic, slender-funnelform, 8–10 cm lg., 4–5.5 cm ∅, mid-red, with brownish H.; **Sti.** yellowish; **Fr.** spherical, 2 cm ∅, shortly hairy, longitudinally dehiscent; **S.** brown, glossy, finely tuberculate.—Peru (Dept. Amazonas, Prov. Bagua, canyon of the Rio Marañon between Km 243 (Rentema) and Km 247 (Campomiento Santa Rosa), E. of Olmos on the Mesones Muro Highway, on cliffs above the road, at 400 m; found by P. Hutchison). (Fig. 396.)
An interesting spec. which, like many of the globular cacti, becomes ± elongated with age; the hairy Fl. clearly puts it within Submatucana, a characteristic group of spec. which is quite distinct from Borzicactus.

S. myriacantha (Vpl.) Backbg. n.comb. (Echinocactus myriacanthus Vpl., Bot. Jahrb. Engler, 50: Beibl. 111: 25. 1913).
Bo. compressed-spherical, to c. 8 cm h., to c. 10 cm ∅; **Ri.** 26, strongly tuberculate, with the Tub. separated by transverse notches; **Ar.** close together, small, shortly felty; **Sp.** numerous, stiffly bristly, yellowish to reddish-brown at first, later blackish-grey or grey; **Rsp.** to 25, 6–18 mm lg.; **Csp.** to c. 10,

to 2.5 cm lg.; **Fl.** borne quite freely, to 6 cm lg., pink; **Tu.** slender, 3 cm lg., with stout H. to 2 cm lg. ("hair-like Br.").—Peru (Chachapoyas, above Balsas). As far as is known at present, this is the only spec. of the G. with finer Sp., but it has the characters differentiating Submatucana from Matucana: Ri. very tuberculate, less so in the crown; moreover the Sp.-count resembles that of the first two spec.

S. paucicostata (Ritt.) Backbg.—Descr. Cact. Nov. III: 14. 1963 (Matucana paucicostata Ritt., "Taxon", XII: 3, 124. 1963).
Bo. to 14 cm h., to 7 cm ∅; **Ri.** 7–11, rather obtuse, 7–15 mm h., notched, with conical Tub.; **Ar.** 10–15 mm apart, grey; **Sp.** chestnut-brown, greying, curving; **Rsp.** 4–8, 0.5–3 cm lg.; **Csp.** 0–1; **Fl.** 6 cm lg., zygomorphic; **Ov.** with white flock and long white H.; **Tu.** 3.5 cm lg., with H. as on the Ov.; **Pet.** dark crimson, bordered violet; **Fil.** white below, purple above; **style** crimson; **Sti.** 4–5; **Fr.** broadly spherical, sparsely hairy, green; **S.** 1.2 mm lg., rhomboid, rough, brown, with a large grey hilum.—Peru (Prov. Huari, Dept. Ancash) (FR 597).

S. ritteri (Buin.) Backbg.
Bo. flattened-spherical to broadly so, to 14 cm ∅, caespitose; **Ri.** 12–22, divided by transverse depressions and constrictions into flat, rather broad Tub.; **Ar.** oblong, light; **Rsp.** 7–10(–14), 1–3 cm lg.; **Csp.** 1–2–5, 2–4 cm lg.; all **Sp.** slightly curving, dark brown at first, upper ones remaining longer thus, others becoming lighter; **Fl.** to 9 cm lg., to 5 cm ∅, crimson-carmine, zygomorphic; **Tu.** with whitish H.; **Fil.** violet; **style** violet; **Sti.** yellowish to reddish-green; **Fr.** 1.5 cm ∅, tuberculate; **S.** black.—Peru (La Libertad, near Otuzco).

Subpilocereus Backbg. (174)

Tree-like Cerei from the coasts and islands of northern S. America where they are often found in company with Ritterocereus griseus and R. deficiens. While Subpilocereus repandus was described in 1753 and has been known for over 200 years, it rather surprisingly took my comprehensive treatment of this group of Cerei in 1938 to draw attention to the fact that here were 7 known species with identical characters of flower and fruit. Britton and Rose regarded them in part as species of Cephalocereus—in itself an argument against the usefulness of such a genus in the wider sense—while Croizat held them to be species of "Pilocereus" because younger areoles show slight hair-development and the flowers are glabrous; however the flowers are divergent in form, likewise the fruits which, in all the Pilosocerei, are uniformly broadly spherical; the seeds of the latter are glossy and not as large as the matt seeds of the above genus. It is easier to understand inclusion of these plants in Cereus Mill., as done by Johnston and Hummelinck, and in one instance by Britton and Rose, since in most cases the authors were not familiar with all the flowers. The following are the uniform generic characters of Subpilocereus: tree-like habit; flowers glabrous, with an oblong ovary, with the tube swollen around the nectary, and then expanding above to bellshaped-funnelform; the oblong fruits are thick-walled and the large seeds are matt black; the flocky hairs at first developed in the areoles hang down to some certain extent and then soon drop.—Distribution: N. Colombia, Curaçao Islands, N. Venezuela, islands of Margarita and Grenada. [(R).]

S. atroviridis (Backbg.) Backbg.

Bo. strongly branching, eventually very tall, with a **trunk**; **branches** to 20 cm $\emptyset$, dark green; **Ri.** c. 8, notched, rounded; **Ar.** weakly felty, with white H.; **Rsp.** c. 8, 0.8–1 cm lg.; **Csp.** 3, one of these to over 2 cm lg.; all **Sp.** white, dark-tipped; **Fl.** ?; **Fr.** oblong, reddish-green, white inside.—N. Colombia (Puerto Colombia).

S. grenadensis (Br. & R.) Backbg.

Bo. to 7 m h., **trunk** to 25 cm $\emptyset$; **branches** greyish-green, to 7 cm $\emptyset$; **Ri.** 7–9, 1 cm h., transversely furrowed; **Sp.** c. 17, to 2 cm lg., scarcely differentiated, subulate, brownish or grey, frosted, shortest ones only 3 mm lg.; **Fl.** c. 7 cm lg., purple; **Sep.** purple above; **Fr.** ellipsoid, to 4 cm lg., green (immature?).—Island of Grenada. Britton and Rose drew attention to the closer affinity with Subpilocereus repandus.

S. horrispinus (Backbg.) Backbg.

Bo. tree-like, to 5 m h., the relatively few **branches** with unfurrowed flanks, bluish-green at first, later olive-green, patterned with vein-like channels, at least in part, the flesh blackening when cut, or yielding a sap which becomes blackish; **Ri.** 4–5, rounded; **Ar.** set somewhat off the vertical, 4 mm apart, strongly felty, oblong, with pendant H., slowly becoming glabrous; **Rsp.** 6–7, to 2.5 cm lg., whitish-grey at first, dark horn-coloured below, later horny-grey, fairly stout; **Csp.** 1 to 10 cm lg., stoutly subulate, flecked at first, whitish-grey, dark below; **Fl.** known only at the bud-stage, yellowish-green, probably pink inside; **Fr.** oblong-spherical, pink, tinged blue; **S.** matt, black, large.—N. Colombia (Puerto Colombia, in the bush). For some time regarded as "Cereus russelianus" or "Cephalocereus russelianus"; but the latter has

thickly subulate Csp. and horizontally furrowed Ri.

S. ottonis Backbg.

Bo. a tall shrub or ± tree-like, sometimes inclined; **branches** bluish-frosted; **Ri.** (4–)5(–6), with furrowed flanks; **Ar.** grey-felty, with pendant flocky woolly H.; **Rsp.** c. 10, stoutly subulate, to 6 cm lg.; **Csp.** 1–3, to 10 cm lg., at first with blackish or dark flecks; **Sp.** ± erect at first; **Fl.** to 9 cm lg., white; **Fr.** oblong, violet-pink, perfumed; **S.** matt, black.—N. Colombia (Goajira Peninsula and westwards); Venezuela (in the NW.). Erroneously held by Britton and Rose to be "Cephalocereus russelianus", and described again by Croizat, as Pilocereus wagenaari Croiz.

S. remolinensis (Backbg.) Backbg.

Bo. tree-like, strongly branching, with a longer **trunk**; **branches** glossy, dark green, at first with curving lines on the flanks above the Ar.; **Ri.** 6–7, acute, fairly narrow; **Ar.** weakly felty, at first with pendant white H.; **Rsp.** 7–13, to 1.5 cm lg.; **Csp.** 1, later to 3 cm lg.; all **Sp.** thinly subulate, blackish-brown at first; **Fl.** to 7 cm lg., creamy-white, tipped lilac-pink; **Fr.** oblong-spherical, yellowish-green; **S.** matt, black, large.—Colombia (in the N., Rio Magdalena, near Remolino).

S. repandus (L.) Backbg.

Bo. tree-like, to 12 m h., strongly branching, **trunk** to 40 cm $\emptyset$; **branches** ascending, to c. 10 cm $\emptyset$; **Ri.** 8–12, notched, greyish or bluish-green; **Ar.** with grey or brown felt and pendant H.; **Sp.** 8–20, scarcely differentiated, all stout, sometimes angular, flattened or twisted, eventually white, dark-tipped; **Csp.** 1–7, 2–6.5 cm lg.; **Rsp.** 7–13; **Fl.** 6–11 cm lg., white, greenish-white or whitish-pink; **Fr.** to 5.5 cm lg., reddish-violet, pulp white or delicate pink; **S.** 2 mm lg., matt, black.—Curaçao Islands. This spec. was earlier often known in collections as "Pilocereus albispinus".

v. **weberi** (Backbg.) Backbg.: **Sp.** shorter; **Fr.** yellowish-green, sometimes tinged faintly pink, the seed-cavity much longer than in the type where it is surrounded moreover by a thicker white layer. (Fig. 397.)

S. russelianus (O.) Backbg. (T.)

Bo. tree-like, to 7 m h., with a longer **trunk** to 2 m lg. and 50 cm $\emptyset$; **branches** squarrose, dark green; **Ri.** 4–5(–6), strongly transversely notched, especially at first; **Ar.** with brown felt and pendant H.; **Rsp.** c. 7, chestnut-brown, strongly tapering to a point; **Csp.** 3, 2 of these projecting, one directed downwards, clavate-subulate, flecked at first; **Fl.** to 9 cm lg., cream-coloured; **Sep.** pink; **Fr.** salmon-coloured, 6 cm lg., pulp white; **S.** matt, black, large.—Venezuela (Puerto Cabello, above La Guayra and as far as the Goajira Peninsula). Synonymous with Cereus margaritensis Johns.

v. **micranthus** (Humlck.) Backbg.: **Sp.** rarely exceeding 1 cm lg., clearly swollen below, flattened on the underside; **Rsp.** recurved, **Csp.** noticeably rather shorter.—Venezuela (near Carúpano, La Pecha, etc.).

S. wagenaari (Croiz.) Backbg.: **Subpilocereus ottonis** Backbg.

Sulcorebutia Backbg. (104)*

An interesting genus from Eastern Bolivia, at first held to be Rebutia on account of the similarity of the flowers. However the development at times of cushions from a stouter taproot, together with the stout spination often observable in the type-species, were just as unusual in Rebutia as the uniformly almost linear areoles. These characters formed the basis of my segregation of the above genus. Then "Rebutia tiraquensis Card." was discovered; with its body up to 12 cm broad and its fairly stout spination it diverged so strongly from Rebutia that it became crystal-clear these were no Rebutias. Subsequently still further species were found which are better classified here than with Rebutia or Lobivia ("Lobivia hoffmanniana Backbg." also proved to be a Sulcorebutia). All species have a narrow oblong areole, and either this is surmounted by a minute depression, or the tubercles taper obliquely upwards and are elongated or not uniformly circular. The flowers resemble those of Rebutia; the fruits can be oblong or spherical, smooth or with small scales. The seeds are small, matt or glossy, black or dark brown. The ribs are quite frequently divided into ± rhomboid tubercles or these are offset. "Rebutia menesesii Card." is clearly referable here because although its areoles are shorter the tubercles are not round as in Rebutia; instead they are exactly twice as broad as long, but still somewhat offset. Further, since this species is undoubtedly very close to "Rebutia candiae Card.", it also must be included here. The bodies are sometimes elongated, in part or in age, as in "Rebutia kruegeri (Card.)" which should certainly be classified here; when grafted, this plant can become quite large and it then offsets from the flanks to form clumps with only a distant

---

* "Die Gattung Sulcorebutia" by Dr. Karlheinz Brinkmann (German language, published by the Deutsche Kakteen-Gesellschaft 1976) contains an extremely useful but uncritical reproduction of all known references in the literature to this genus; it also includes field numbers of the principal collectors, and some notes on cultivation. [Translator's note.]

resemblance to caespitose Rebutias. Against this, I have seen individuals of Sulcorebutia tiraquensis v. electracantha, for instance, which even at c. 7 cm $\emptyset$ have shown no tendency to offset; in general this species becomes relatively large but still does not readily offset, while in Rebutia species of larger diameter this is not so. However the 2 genera are undoubtedly closely related, as indicated by the fact that both flower from relatively low on the plant. A point which seems to me significant is that all currently known species of Sulcorebutia originate in East Bolivia. It would appear that a distinct group of Rebutia-related plants has evolved here, and with their uniform and unique characters as well as other features, they require a special systematic position. Classification of the S. tiraquensis complex is a problem, or at least it calls in some cases for an answer to the question of whether a given plant is a distinct species, a variety or merely a form. For a better understanding of the position I have reproduced the divergences I have noted in this interesting species or complex, but I cannot go at present beyond describing one variety. This species is particularly noticeable for its attractive and variable spination, added to which there is a considerable variety of flower-colour, from light to deep intense red. This genus will be particularly attractive to the private collector. A number of the species have red flowers, and one has yellow blooms; orange colourings also occur, together with transitions between the two colours. The flowers are mostly not as slender-funnelform as Rebutia and they are distinctly, or in part, fairly broadly scaly.—Distribution: NE. Bolivia (Dept. Cochabamba, so far as now known). [(R); grafted plants grow faster and flower more freely.]

S. alba Rausch
Bo. simple, to 2 cm h., 3.5 cm $\emptyset$, green, often suffused violet; **Ri.** to 23, spiralled, Tub. 3–4 mm lg.; **Ar.** 3 mm lg., white-felty; **Rsp.** 20–24, 3–4 mm lg., appressed, interlacing; **Csp.** mostly missing, if present then to 6 in a R. across, 2–3 mm lg.; all **Sp.** white, reddish to black below, with ciliate H.; **Fl.** 30 mm lg. and $\emptyset$, magenta-pink; **Tu.** magenta-pink, with brownish-green Sc., bordered whitish to pink; **Sep.** violet-red, tipped greenish; **Pet.** dark red with a blue sheen, orange to yellow inside; **throat** pink, white below; **Fil.** yellow; **style** green, with 4 yellow **Sti.**—Bolivia (road Sucre-Los Alamos, 2900 m). Species resembling Aylostera heliosa but differentiated by the dark red Fl. and the different habitat. (Fig. 529.)

S. arenacea (Card.) Ritt., comb. nov. in "Cactus", 17: 76, 34. 1962: **Rebutia arenacea** Card. I have left this species in Rebutia since it has neither a stout taproot, stout spines nor linear areoles, nor has it a

± furrow-like prolongation of these; it thus shows none of the Sulcorebutia characters.

S. breviflora Backbg. nom. nov. (Rebutia brachyantha Card., Kakt. u.a. Sukk., 16: 4, 74–75. 1965., non (Wessn.) Buin. & Don., 1963).
Bo. simple, flattened-spherical, to c. 1.5 cm h., 3.5 cm ⌀, brownish-green, crown sunken; **R.** napiform, to 3 cm lg.; **Ri.** c. 11 spiralled, divided into round Tub. 4 mm h., 6 mm ⌀; **Ar.** ± linear, 5 mm lg., 5 mm apart, white-felty; **Sp.** c. 12, bristly, pectinate, to 6 mm lg., upper ones shorter, interlacing, all white and thickened below; **Fl.** c. 2.5 cm lg. and ⌀, yellow; **Sep.** and **Pet.** lanceolate; **Sep.** tipped brownish; **Pet.** strongly recurved at anthesis; **Tu.** to 7 mm lg.; **Ov.** 4 mm ⌀, with brown Sc.; **Fil.** orange-yellow; **An.** light yellow; **style** 1.2 cm lg., whitish, overtopping the **An.**; **Sti.** 4, light yellow; **Fr.** and **S.** unknown.—Bolivia (Dept. Cochabamba, banks of the Rio Caine, 2000 m).

S. caineana: **Rebutia caineana** Card.

S. candiae (Card.) Backbg. n.comb. (Rebutia candiae Card., in C. & S. J. [US], XXXIII: 4, 112. 1961).
Bo. broadly spherical, offsetting, single heads to 3 cm h., to 5 cm ⌀, dark green; **Ri.** 15–20, divided into offset rhomboid Tub.; **Ar.** narrow, long, creamy-white; **Sp.** all radial, pectinate, appressed, 3–7 mm lg., thin, yellowish, some also lighter, upper ones often longest, many of them bent or downcurving; **Fl.** to 3 cm lg., described as somewhat zygomorphic, but this is probably exceptional since a photo in my possession shows Fl. which are more slender than those in Cardenas's illustration; **Sc.** on Tu. and Ov. olive-green; **Pet.** yellow; **Fr.** spherical, 5 mm ⌀; **S.** to 1.4 mm lg., dark brown.—Bolivia (Ayopaya, near Tiquirpaya, 2800 m). (Fig. 398.)

S. canigueralii (Card.) Backbg. n.comb. (Rebutia canigueralii Card., C. & S. J. [US], XXXVI: 1, 26–27, 1964).
Bo. caespitose; **R.** quite long, napiform; **St.** spherical, 1 cm lg., 2 cm ⌀, greyish; **Ri.** in c. 13 spiralled rows of small Tub. 3–4 mm br.; **Ar.** elliptic, narrow, 3 mm lg., white; **Sp.** pectinate, 11–14, bristly, appressed, 1.5–2 mm lg., whitish, brown below; **Csp.** rarely 1–2 present, erect; **Fl.** to 4 cm lg. and ⌀; **Ov.** with green Sc.; **Tu.** reddish-yellow, with green Sc.; **Sep.** brownish-yellow; **Pet.** 2 cm lg., yellow below, orange above; **Fil.** golden-yellow; **style** greenish; **Sti.** 8, light yellow.—Bolivia (Prov. Oropeza, Dept. Chuquisaca, Sucre 2800 m). The spec. shows the narrow areoles and longer taproots typical of Sulcorebutia but unknown in Rebutia.

S. caracarensis (Card.) Don.: see **Rebutia caracarensis** Card.

S. crispata Rausch 1970
Bo. simple to caespitose, 25 mm h., to 35 mm ⌀, epidermis greenish-grey; **R.** napiform; **Ri.** to 13, spiralled, Tub. 5 mm lg.; **Ar.** 4 mm lg.; **Rsp.** to 24, to 8 mm lg., interlacing over the Bo. and web-like, strongly curving, fine, hyaline to pinkish-brown, thickened and yellowish below; **Csp.** 0; **Fl.** c. 30 mm lg. and ⌀, light to dark magenta.—Bolivia (Tomina, c. 10 km from Padilla, at 2400 m). Close to S. verticillacantha but differentiated by the fine-bristly and crisped spination.

S. flavissima Rausch 1970
Bo. simple, to 25 mm h., to 60 mm ⌀, fresh green; **Ri.** to 18, Tub. 10 mm lg., 7 mm h.; **Ar.** to 8 mm lg., with white or yellow felt; **Rsp.** to 24, to 20 mm lg., radiating, curving somewhat to the Bo.; **Csp.** scarcely differentiated, 2–5, to 20 mm lg., projecting, interlacing over the crown, flexible but sharp, brilliant yellow; **Fl.** c. 35 mm lg. and 40–50 mm ⌀; **Ov.** and **Tu.** pink with darker Sc.; **Pet.** spatulate or lanceolate, often apiculate, light to dark magenta with a light M.-stripe; **throat**, **Fil.**, **style** and **Sti.** white.—Bolivia (between Aiquile and Mizque at 2500 m). Belongs to the S. steinbachii group and resembles S. tiraquensis v. electracantha from which it is distinguished by the brilliant yellow Sp. and the magenta Fl. (Fig. 530.)

S. frankiana Rausch 1970
Bo. simple to caespitose, 35 mm h., to 40 mm ⌀, fresh green; **R.** napiform; **Ri.** to 14, spiralled, Tub. 8 mm lg. and br.; **Ar.** 3–4 mm lg., 1–2 mm br., white-felty; **Rsp.** 9–15, to 10 mm lg., curving to the Bo., brown to brownish-red; **Csp.** 0; **Fl.** c. 40 mm lg. and ⌀; **Ov.** and **Tu.** magenta-pink with olive-green Sc.; **Pet.** lanceolate to spatulate, often serrate, light to dark magenta, rarely purple, and yellow inside; **throat** red to magenta; **Fil.** whitish, pink below; **style** and 4 **Sti.** greenish-yellow.—Bolivia (Sucre, road to Los Alamos, 2700 m). Named for Gerhart Frank of Vienna. Fl. sometimes also lilac, without a yellow throat. (Fig. 532.)

S. glomeriseta: see **Rebutia glomeriseta** Card.

S. glomerispina (Card.) Backbg. n.comb. (Rebutia glomerispina Card., C. & S. J. [US], XXXVI: 2, 40. 1964).
Bo. flat, caespitose; **R.** napiform; **St.** 5 mm h. and br. (presumably "cm" was intended?); **Ri.** consist-

ing of 20 rows of Tub. 3 mm h. and 4 mm br., bluish-green; **Ar.** 3 mm apart, elliptic, 3 mm lg., grey; **Sp.** 10–14, spreading sideways, concealing the Bo., 5–20 mm lg., acicular, thickened below, white or orange-brown, or thus at midway; **Fl.** 2.8 cm lg., 2 cm $\varnothing$; **Ov.** white, with emerald-green Sc.; **Tu.** with greenish-yellow Sc. below; **Sep.** deep purple inside, lighter outside; **Pet.** purple; **Fil.** purple; **style** white, the 6 **Sti.** similarly.—Bolivia (Prov. Chapare, Dept. Cochabamba, Huakani, 3200 m).

For the comments of Cardenas regarding Rebutia and Sulcorebutia which he repeats here, see under S. tunariensis. By itself, similarity of the Fl. is unimportant, otherwise what should be done with "Echinopsis kratochviliana" (i.e. a Pseudolobivia) and Lobivia: should all of them be combined or united with Echinopsis?

S. haseltonii (Card.) Don.
Bo. flattened, caespitose, 1.5–2 cm h., 5–6 cm $\varnothing$, greenish-purple; **R.** napiform; **Ri.** c. 20, concealed by the Sp., Tub. 4 mm h., 5–6 mm $\varnothing$; **Ar.** 5 mm apart, elliptic, 4 mm lg., grey-felty; **Sp.** 10–12, pectinate, appressed, 6–15 mm lg., interlacing, light grey or whitish, acicular, stiff, thickened below; **Fl.** basal, funnelform, c. 3 cm lg., 2.5 cm $\varnothing$, slightly curving; **Ov.** spherical, 4 mm $\varnothing$, light purple, with Sc. and white wool-flock; **Tu.** short, purple inside, with acute purple Sc.; **Sep.** lanceolate, 15 mm lg., light yellow, purple above; **Pet.** spatulate, 15 mm lg., light yellow; **An.** 3 mm lg., **Fil.** and **An.** yellow; **style** 1 cm lg., thin, light yellow, with 12–13 yellow **Sti.**—Bolivia (Tarata, Cochabamba, near the Rio Caine, in crevices in red sandstone at 2800 m). Close to S. glomerispina, and named for Scott E. Haselton.

S. hoffmanniana (Backbg.) Backbg. n.comb.: for description, see under Lob. hoffmanniana Backbg., by which name it has hitherto been known; once specimens had been propagated it became clear that while this plant resembled S. kruegeri in habit, plants at the type-locality have stout erect Csp. In view of the linear Ar., it is undoubtedly a Sulcorebutia and is therefore listed here as such (basionym: Lob. hoffmanniana Backbg., Die Cact. III: 1434. 1959).

S. inflexiseta: see **Rebutia inflexiseta** Card.

S. krahnii Rausch 1970
Bo. simple, 30 mm h., to 80 mm $\varnothing$; **Ri.** to 32, spiralled, Tub. 6–8 mm lg.; **Ar.** 4 mm lg. and 3 mm br., with yellowish-brownish or white felt; **Rsp.** 24, 10 mm lg., interlacing over the Bo., bristly-fine, white to brown; **Csp.** scarcely differentiated, 3–7, to 12 mm lg., bristly, $\pm$ sharp, brown to black; **Fl.**

25–30 mm lg., 25 mm $\varnothing$; **Ov.** and **Tu.** greenish-yellow, with reddish-tipped Sc.; **Pet.** yellow, lighter inside, throat white; **Fil.** yellow; **style** and 5 **Sti.** whitish.—Bolivia (N. of Comarapa, Cerro Tukiphalla, at 1900–2300 m). Named for Wolfgang Krahn who brought the first specimens of the species to Europe. These were distributed in the trade as Sulcorebutia weingartioides, said to be a synonym of S. weingartiana. (Fig. 531.)

S. kruegeri (Card.) Ritt.—"Cactus", 17: 76, 36. 1962 (Aylostera kruegeri Card., "Cactus", 12: 57, 260. 1957).
Bo. later oblong but flattened-spherical at first, old specimens more cylindric, offsetting from the flanks to form clumps, lighter to darker green; **R.** conical, napiform; **Ar.** with cream felt, very elongated; **Tub.** narrowly oblong, offset; **Rsp.** pectinate, appressed, to c. 20, thin, to 3 mm lg., whitish, sometimes slightly brownish, $\pm$ thickened below; **Csp.**, if present, 1–2 in the upper part of the Ar., short, fine, brownish, erect; **Fl.** more bellshaped-funnelform, to c. 2.5 cm lg., golden-yellow to orange, or reddish-orange towards the Pet.-margin; **Tu.** with lax broad Sc.; **Fr.** purplish-reddish, 3 mm $\varnothing$, with small Sc.; **S.** 1 mm lg., glossy, black.—Bolivia (Prov. El Cercado, 2568 m). Varies as to presence or absence of Csp.

S. lepida Ritt., without Latin diagnosis in "Cactus" 17: 76, 36. 1962 (with Fig.); final description in Nat. C. & S. J. (England), 17: 13 (March), 1962.
Bo. very dark green, little offsetting, crown sunken; **Ri.** c. 16, completely divided into Tub. c. 3 mm h. and br., several-sided below; **Ar.** narrowly oblong, surmounted by a narrow furrow, to 3 mm lg. and the same distance apart; **Sp.** c. 14–20, 3–7 mm lg., $\pm$ pectinate, radiating sideways and downwards, $\pm$ appressed, black, blackish-red, brown or golden-yellow; **Fl.** crimson to carmine.—Bolivia (locality not known) (FR 369). (Fig. 399.)
I saw this spec. in the Marnier collection with deep carmine or purple Fl. The plant appears more likely to be a smaller and shorter-spined variety of R. tiraquensis, but the latter is not known to have such variability of Fl.-colour as is found, for example, in v. electracantha of the latter spec. See also under S. mentosa.

S. markusii Rausch 1970
Bo. simple, 30 mm h., to 60 mm $\varnothing$, dark green to brownish-violet, with a taproot; **Ri.** 10–17, spiralled, Tub. 5–8 mm lg.; **Ar.** 3–4 mm lg., 1 mm br., white-felty; **Rsp.** 12, to 3 mm lg., claw-like, appressed, brown, white-tipped and black below; **Csp.** rarely 1 to 8 mm lg., $\pm$ subulate, black; **Fl.** c. 35 mm lg. and $\varnothing$; **Ov.** and **Tu.** pink, with brownish-green Sc.; **Pet.** lanceolate to spatulate, dark

magenta or purple; **throat** and **Fil.** whitish; **style** and 6 **Sti.** greenish-yellow.—Bolivia (Mizque, near Vila Vila, at 3000 m). Found by W. Rausch and named for E. Markus of Vienna.

S. menesesii (Card.) Backbg. n. comb. (Rebutia menesesii Card., C. & S. J. [US], XXXIII: 4, 113. 1961).
Bo. broadly spherical, offsetting, to 2 cm h., single heads to 6 cm br., dark greyish-green; **Ri.** 14–18, divided into Tub. to 3 mm lg. and 6 mm br. and ± offset; **Ar.** moderately elongated; **Sp.** 10–12, pectinate, 3–35 mm lg., white or pink, sometimes light brownish at first, roughly hairy, longer ones in particular ± strongly curving to bent; **Fl.** to 4 cm lg., 3.5 cm Ø, pale to golden-yellow; **Tu.** pale yellow, Sc. green, red-tipped; **Sep.** red-tipped; **Fr.** spherical, 6 mm Ø, dark red, with broad Sc.; **S.** 1 mm lg., dark.—Bolivia (Ayopaya, near Naranjito, 1600 m). This spec. is very close to S. candiae. (Fig. 400.)

S. mentosa Ritt.—"Succulenta" 43: 7, 102. 1964.
Bo. flat or hemispherical, fresh green, to 6 cm Ø, crown depressed; **R.** long-napiform; **Ri.** c. 20; **Tub.** 1 cm lg., 5 mm h., chin-shaped; **Ar.** 5–7 mm lg., 2 mm br., white, 6–8 mm apart; **Sp.** thin, ± curving, black or dark red; **Rsp.** 14–18, pectinate, c. 5 mm lg.; **Csp.** 2–4, 5–8 mm lg.; **Fl.** lateral, 3 cm lg., 3.5 cm Ø, purple; **Tu.** 1.5 mm lg.; **Fil.** white or reddish, 2-merous; **style** to 2 mm lg., white; **Sti.** 5–7, pale yellow; **Fr.** spherical, 7–10 mm Ø, brown; **S.** matt, black.—Bolivia (Prov. Campero, Aiquile) (FR 945).
Ov. and Fr. show traces of hairy indumentum, such as has also been observed sometimes in Rebutia; the fact is thus irrelevant as a diagnostic character; traces of felt are only in some instances a proof of the evolutionary process; differentiation on this basis is thus justified only where the indumentum is appreciably stronger, and constant in all species.
S. lepida appears to be closely related to this spec. (see also under that name).

S. mizquensis Rausch 1970
Bo. simple to caespitose, c. 25 mm h., 30 mm Ø, with a taproot; **Ri.** to 17, spiralled, Tub. 4–5 mm lg. and coloured reddish-violet in the lower half; **Ar.** 4 mm lg., 1 mm br., white-felty; **Rsp.** to 20, to 4 mm lg., pressed closely against the Bo., tipped white, pink at midway, black and thickened below; **Csp.** 0; **Fl.** c. 30 mm lg., 25 mm Ø, light to dark magenta, often also with a white **throat**.—Bolivia (near Mizque, at 2600 m). Spination reminiscent of S. kruegeri, but the Fl. are violet-pink and very attractive.

S. muschii Vasquez

Bo. spherical, 6 cm Ø, green; **Ri.** divided into Tub. 6 mm h., 8 mm br.; **Ar.** 7 mm apart, elliptic, 5 mm lg., woolly; **Sp.** stiff, yellow, little curving; **Rsp.** 12–16, the shortest ones 4 mm lg., longest ones 3 cm; **Csp.** mostly 1; **Fl.** numerous, basal, 35 mm lg.; **Ov.** spherical, 5 mm Ø, light red, with reddish-brown Sc. 1 mm br.; **Tu.** short, light red or brownish; **Sep.** lanceolate, 15 mm lg., 4 mm br., yellow; **Pet.** 11 mm lg., 3 mm br., golden-yellow; **style** 14 mm lg., white, with 7 white **Sti.**—Bolivia (Dept. Cochabamba, Prov. Ayopaya near Chicote Grande, at 3400 m). Named for its discoverer, Gerardo Musch. [=Lau 974: a form of S. menesesii, acc. Donald: Ashingtonia II, 7: 138. 1976. Translator.]

S. oenantha Rausch
Bo. simple, flattened-spherical, to 6 cm h., 10 cm Ø, light greyish-green, metallic, often also suffused violet; **Ri.** to 20, spiralled, Tub. 15 mm lg. and to 10 mm h.; **Ar.** to 12 mm lg., wedge-shaped, to 4 mm br. above, tapering below, white-felty; **Rsp.** at first to 16, with 4 Csp., later altogether to 28, c. 12 mm lg., spreading, ± curving, sharp, light yellow, thickened and brownish below; **Fl.** 35 mm lg. and br., orange-brown with green Sc.; **Pet.** dark wine-red, with a pink keel; **Sep.** wine-red, tipped brownish-green; **Fil.** deep pink; **style** yellow with 6 yellow Sti.—Bolivia (in the S. of Totore, Chijmore, at 2900 m). Shape very reminiscent of Weingartia and recognisable by the relatively prominent Tub.

S. pampagrandensis Rausch
[Description not available to Haage, but the following is taken from the original description in KuaS 25: 97, 5. 1974. Translator.]
Bo. simple, broadly spherical, 40 mm h., to 70 mm Ø, light greyish-green, washed violet; **R.** napiform; **Ri.** 18–26, spiralled, Tub. 7–9 mm lg., 5 mm br., flat; **Ar.** furrow-like, 5–8 mm lg., 2 mm br. above, tapering below and narrow, white-felty; **Rsp.** 17–21, arranged in 8–10 pairs and one downwardly directed, 6–10 mm lg., interlacing around the Bo., light brown (sometimes white or yellow); **Csp.** 1(–4), to 15 mm lg., subulate, orange-brown, dark-tipped (also whitish or yellow); **Fl.** 35 mm lg., 45 mm Ø; **Ov.** spherical; **Tu.** short, pink, with brown or greenish Sc.; outer **Pet.** lanceolate (sometimes spatulate), rounded, apiculate, pink with a green M.-stripe, inner ones spatulate-rounded, dark magenta or purple; **throat** 15 mm lg., opening to 10 mm Ø, pink; **Fil.** inserted throughout the Tu., white (or pink); **style** 20 mm lg., thick, greenish-white; **Sti.** 6, white; **Fr.** broadly spherical, 6 mm Ø, yellowish-pink, with broad green naked Sc.; pulp whitish-pink; **S.** ± oblong, 1.5 mm lg., 1 mm Ø, black, covered with residual membranes, hilum broad, basal.—Bolivia (Dept. Cochabamba, S. of Totora, at 2700 m).

This group closely resembles S. hoffmanniana Backbg. or S. glomerispina (Card.) Backbg. in habit, but the Fl. is considerably larger, mostly dark magenta, more rarely lighter. Spination is very variable so that no two plants are really identical; Sp. mostly ± subulate, varying in colour from white through yellow, brown, brownish-red to dark brown. Donald suggests that Ritter's S. weingartioides (FR 944) may be a synonym; he gives the locality as Vila Vila, 2600 m.

S. polymorpha (Card.) Backbg. n.comb. (Rebutia polymorpha Card., Kakt. u.a. Sukk., 16 : 6, 115–116. 1965).
Bo. subspherical to broadly spherical, caespitose, low-growing, single heads to 1 cm lg., 5 cm br., greyish to dark green; **Ri.** 10–15, made up of small hatchet-shaped Tub. to 5 mm h.; **Ar.** to 8 mm apart, to 5 mm lg., elliptic; **Sp.** bristle-like, pectinate, appressed, 3–5 mm lg., grey or dark brown, thin, sharp, to 2 cm lg., upcurving; **Fl.** to 3 cm lg. and ∅, magenta, or reddish outside and orange-yellow inside; **Ov.** varying in colour, acc. Fl.-colour; **Tu.** broadly scaly; **Fil., style** and **Sti.** whitish; **Fr.** 5 mm ∅, spherical.—Bolivia (Prov. Arani, Dept. Cochabamba, near Tiraque, 3200 m). An extremely variable spec., acc. Cardenas; he presumes it to be "descended in part from S. steinbachii, totorensis and tiraquensis which grow in the same area"; little of this is revealed by the description. Perhaps a complex of spontaneous hybrids? There are similarly strong variations in S. tiraquensis, to judge from Rausch's colour-photographs, or Ritter's material which is mentioned thereunder. S. tarabucensis Card. has similar Fl.

S. pulchera (Card.) Don.
(Syn.: Rebutia pulchera Card. 1970)
Bo. spherical, flattened, 2–3 cm h., 4–4.5 cm ∅, light green, crown sunken; **Ar.** 5 mm apart, linear, 5 mm lg., with a little grey felt; **Sp.** pectinate, appressed sideways, thin, bristly, 3–5 mm lg., light grey, black and thickened below, those in the crown shorter and projecting; **Fl.** numerous, basal, funnelform, 5 cm lg., 2.5 cm br.; **Ov.** spherical, 4–6 mm ∅, light green; **Sc.** 2 mm lg., fleshy; **Tu.** curving, 12–14 mm lg., pink, with Sc. 2–3 mm lg.; **Sep.** lanceolate, 25 × 5 mm, light magenta, white below; **Pet.** lanceolate, pointed, 23 × 5 mm, coloured as the Sep., all strongly wavy; **Fil.** inserted at the base of the Tu., 4–5 mm lg., dark magenta; **An.** yellow; **style** 2.5 cm lg., white, with 4 light green **Sti.**—Bolivia (Prov. Zudañez, Chuquisaca, between Rio Grande and Presto, at 2400 m).

S. rauschii Frank
Bo. simple to caespitose, 15 mm h., 30 mm ∅,

blackish-green to violet, with a taproot, crown sunken; **Ri.** to 16, spiralled, Tub. c. 5 mm lg., flat; **Ar.** oblong, to 2 mm lg., with a little white felt; **Rsp.** to 11, 1–1.5 mm lg., subulate, bent downwards, claw-like and appressed, thickened below, black; **Csp.** absent; **pericarpel** spherical, pale green, naked, set with pointed little Sc.; **Per.** light yellowish-green, passing over above into pink; **Sep.** pinkish-brown, narrow; **Pet.** magenta-pink, broadly spatulate; **throat** white; **Fil.** red; **An.** pale yellow; **style** and **Sti.** whitish; **Fr.** spherical, c. 4 mm ∅; **S.** c. 1.5 mm lg., testa finely tuberculate, greyish-brown.—Bolivia (Chuquisaca, near Zudañez, 2700 m). Resembles S. zavaletae, but not identical with this. (Fig. 534.) Named for the plant-hunter, W. Rausch of Vienna.

S. steinbachii (Werd.) Backbg. (T.)
Bo. green, forming ± broad, cushion-like groups from a taproot; **Ri.** indistinct, to c. 13, made up of elongated, ± rhomboid, offset Tub.; **Ar.** very elongated, white-felty; **Sp.** sometimes absent at first on cultivated plants, and then for a long while only Csp. present, but normally-spined specimens have c. 6–8 **Rsp.** to 2.5 cm lg., thin to much stouter, blackish, ± rough; **Csp.** 1–3, darker, becoming whitish, scabrous, sometimes darker-tipped, to stoutly subulate, thickened below, unequal, longest ones to c. 2 cm lg.; **Fl.** c. 3.5 cm lg., scarlet.—Bolivia (Cochabamba, precise locality not known). (Fig. 401.)
v. **gracilior** Backbg. n.v.:
Bo. rather lighter green than in the following varieties; **St.** more slender than in the type and other varieties; **Sp.** light, fine, rather short; **Csp.** mostly absent, or 1 to c. 1 cm lg.; **Fl.** ?—E. Bolivia (Uhlig No. 2205; found by Krahn);
v. **rosiflora** Backbg.—"Cactus" 19, 80–81, 5. 1964: **Bo.** dark bluish-green; **Sp.** blackish-brown, not lighter below, laterals in 3–4 pairs, more projecting, not clearly pectinate; **Csp.** 1–3; **Fl.** 3 cm lg., 4 cm ∅, purplish-pink; **Tu.** 1.5 cm lg., pale greenish-pink; **Fil.** pink, fewer; **style** 2 cm lg. (Fig. 401, left.) Distinguished by the dark colour of Bo. and Sp. as well as the fairly large pink Fl.;
v. **violaciflora** Backbg.—"Cactus" 19, 80–81, 6. 1964: **Bo.** intense green; **Sp.** blackish-brown, light below, laterals distinctly pectinate, **Csp.** 1–2; **Fl.** only 2.3 cm lg., 2.8 cm br., brilliant purple; **Tu.** only 5 mm lg., reddish; **Fil.** white, numerous, crowded; **style** 1.6 cm lg. (Fig. 401, right.) Distinguishable primarily by the short purple Fl. and the divergent Fil.-colour; moreover both varieties are much darker in the Bo. than the type, which is mid-green and has scarlet Fl.

The spelling "violacifera" in "Cactus" was a printer's error.

S. sucrensis (FR 775, 946): possibly identical with S. caracarensis or S. taratensis.

S. tarabucensis Rausch—Kakt. u.a. Sukk., 15 : 5, 92. 1964.
Bo. simple, rarely caespitose, with a napiform **R.**, the head projecting only slightly above the ground, to c. 1.5 cm h., 2 cm $\varnothing$, matt green; **Ri.** 10–11, spiralled, Tub. 6 mm lg., 4 mm br., 2 mm h.; **Ar.** linear, 3 mm lg., 6 mm apart, extended into a furrow above; **Sp.** 6–8(–11), 3–6 mm lg., pectinately curving towards the Bo., thickened below, black to brown; **Csp.** 0; **Fl.** 3 cm lg. and $\varnothing$, dark red, yellow towards the throat; **Pet.** rounded, apiculate; **Tu.** and **Ov.** pinkish-red with olive-green Sc.; **style** 2 cm lg., it and the 7 **Sti.** yellowish; **Fr.** ?.—Bolivia (mountains around Tarabuco, 3500 m; Rausch No. 66).

S. taratensis (Card.) Backbg. n.comb. (Rebutia taratensis Card., C. & S. J. [US], XXXVI: 1, 26. 1964).
Bo. caespitose; **R.** napiform, pink; **St.** c. 2–5 cm h., to 3.5 cm $\varnothing$, dark green to purple, crown sunken; **Ri.** c. 16, spiralled, consisting of small Tub. 4–5 mm lg.; **Ar.** c. 6 mm apart, narrowly elliptic, 5 mm lg.; **Rsp.** 13–16, 3–4 mm lg., pectinate, bristly, hyaline, with a dark brown thickened base; **Csp.** 0(–1); **Fl.** 4 cm lg., 3.5 cm $\varnothing$; **Ov.** with brown pointed Sc.; **Tu.** purplish-brown, with brown Sc.; **Sep.** darker purple inside, lighter purple outside; **Pet.** 2.2 cm lg., magenta; **Fil.** white, **style** similarly; **Sti.** 5, whitish-yellow; **Fr.** 3 mm lg., brownish-red; **S.** glossy, black.—Bolivia (Prov. Tarata, Dept. Cochabamba, on the road Tarata to Rio Caine, 2000 m). (Fig. 402, 403.)
A spec. found by Rausch near Sucre tallies in every respect with the above description. (S. sucrensis Ritt., perhaps only a name?) (Fig. 402.)

S. tiraquensis (Card.) Backbg.
Bo. simple to offsetting, broadly spherical, single heads to 5 cm h., to 12 cm $\varnothing$; **Ri.** 13–26, straight or spiralled, made up of irregularly shaped Tub., these mostly rounded below and $\pm$ prominent; **Ar.** narrowly oblong, whitish, continued above into a small depression which, on account of the elongated base of the Tub. above, often appears like a furrow; **Sp.** sometimes only 12–13 radials on young plants, with 1–2 more central Sp. in the upper part of the Ar., later scarcely differentiated, to over 30, 0.5–3 cm lg., yellowish-brownish at first, becoming dark brown, Csp. sometimes stouter; **Fl.** 3.5 cm lg., 3 cm $\varnothing$, purple; **Fil.** purple below, whitish above; **style** whitish below, purple above; **Sti.** yellowish;

Tu. and **Ov.** scaly, and apparently sometimes also the **Fr.**; **Fr.** 4 mm $\varnothing$, violet-pink.—Bolivia (Carrasco, on the road Cochabamba to Santa Cruz). (Fig. 404, 405, above left.) The Sp. are not appressed but $\pm$ projecting, and not uniform. The type later has dark brown Sp. with the base sometimes yellowish. Spination extremely variable; the dark brown colour sometimes passes over into brilliant violet to reddish-brown, or even to $\pm$ blackish-brown; the colour of the Fl. can vary in the same way from light red to intense red, as I have observed on the floriferous specimens in the Botanical Garden, "Les Cèdres". Furthermore there are plants with much lighter Sp. and others which may perhaps better be considered independent spec. For a clearer survey I will list these below.
In "Cactus" (Paris), 17: 70. 36. 1962, Ritter erroneously repeated the name-transfer.
The following is distinguishable as a good variety:
v. **electracantha** Backbg.—Descr. Cact. Nov. III: 14. 1963: **Bo.** broadly spherical; **Sp.** amber-coloured; **Rsp.** to over 25, acicular, stiff; **Csp.** to over 7, erect, very firm, subulate-acicular, to c. 1.3 cm lg., sometimes reddish below, some Csp. even to 1.6 cm lg., all Sp. densely clothing the Bo., later dirty dark brown; **Fl.** orange-red. (Fig. 404 and 405, right above.)
The following may be referable here, either as forms or varieties; I saw these plants, especially in Buining's collection in Holland; they had been collected by Ritter but not yet clarified:
Sulcorebutia sp.?, var. ?: Bo. green, distinctly translucent; Sp. pale yellowish, projecting laterally, not very dense (referable to S. tiraquensis?);
Sulcorebutia sp. ?, var. ?: Bo. more olive-green; Sp. appressed, yellowish, $\pm$ curving, without any erect longer ones (to S. candiae?);
Sulcorebutia sp. ?, var. ?: Bo. blackish-olive; Sp. rather projecting, strongly interlacing laterally, very pale horn-colour, slightly brownish at first, no Sp. longer than the others;
Sulcorebutia sp. ?, var. ?: Bo. intense dark to mid-green; Sp. projecting, thin-acicular, pale yellowish to creamy-whitish, individuals rather longer (to S. tiraquensis ?);
Sulcorebutia sp. ?, var. ?: Bo. later cylindric in grafted plants, bluish-green; Sp. thin at first, mostly in 4 laterally appressed pairs, later stouter towards the apex and more projecting intermediately, brownish, individuals longer, $\pm$ noticeably obliquely projecting.

S. totorensis (Card.) Ritt.—"Cactus", 17: 76. 36. 1962 (Rebutia totorensis Card., "Cactus", 12. 57, 259–260. 1957).

Bo. depressed-spherical, caespitose, single heads to 2 cm h., to 6 cm ⌀, dark green; **Ri.** 19–21, divided into ± rhomboid Tub.; **Ar.** circular, elongating later to very narrow-elliptic, grey-felty; **Sp.** pectinate, radiating, 0.3–2 cm lg., the longer ones clearly projecting, acicular-thin but sharp, dark brown, some sometimes arranged more as Csp. (in the upper part of the Ar.); **Fl.** 3.5 cm lg., dark purple, still darker above; **style** and **Sti.** pale yellow; **Fr.** and **S.** ?—Bolivia (Carrasco, Lagunillas, or the road Totora to Huerta Molino, 2800 m).

S. tunariensis (Card.) Backbg. n.comb. (Rebutia tunariensis Card., C. & S. J. [US], XXXVI: 2, 1964).
Bo. low-growing, caespitose; **R.** to 15 cm lg. (!); **St.** dark green, 5 mm h., to 1.8 cm ⌀; **Ri.** divided into c. 10 R. of hatchet-shaped Tub. 4 mm lg., 3 mm h.; **Ar.** to 4 mm apart, grey, narrowly elliptic, to 4 mm lg.; **Sp.** pectinate, 10–12, in pairs, bristly, appressed, all 3–5 mm lg., hyaline, brown below; **Fl.** funnelform, 3 cm lg., 2.5 cm ⌀, curving; **Ov.** whitish with white Sc.; **Tu.** narrow, pale purple above, with whitish Sc.; **Sep.** purplish-orange; **Pet.** deep red, golden-yellow below; **Fil.** golden-yellow; **style** white below, green above; **Sti.** 5, yellow.—Bolivia (Prov. Cercado, Dept. Cochabamba, Mount Tunari, 3200 m).
Here Cardenas mentions his "Aylostera kruegeri", and says that the Genus Aylostera and Sulcorebutia should be included in Rebutia; however, he overlooks entirely, or fails to mention, that Aylostera has bristly Sp. on the Fl., the style is united, and the Tu. is stem-like. He also appears to ignore the fact that Rebutia does not show the napiform root-development of Sulcorebutia, and that the latter genus typically has long and narrow areoles. The absence of any comprehensive system of classification provokes just what Cardenas sought to obviate by his statements: a long-continuing confusion. His naming of "Aylostera kruegeri" suggests that he was not sufficiently familiar with the spec. of Aylostera.

S. vasqueziana Rausch 1970
Bo. simple, c. 15 mm h., to 20 mm ⌀, epidermis blackish-green to violet-black; **R.** napiform; **Ri.** to 13, spiralled, Tub. 4 mm lg.; **Ar.** 3 mm lg., with white to yellow felt; **Rsp.** 12–16, to 15 mm lg., spreading, curving, very tangled, weak, golden-yellow, reddish and thickened below; **Csp.** 0; **Fl.** c. 25 mm lg and ⌀, magenta or red, and yellow inside.—Bolivia (Sucre, road to Los Alamos, at 2950 m). Named for the Bolivian plant-hunter, Roberto Vasquez. Close to S. verticillacantha, but distinguished by the smaller size and different spination.

S. verticillacantha Ritt.—"Cactus", 17: 76, 37. 1962, without Latin diagnosis.
Bo. caespitose, deep green, to 3 cm ⌀, oblong; **R.** napiform, 5 cm lg., to 3 cm thick above; **Ri.** 13–21, consisting of Tub. 5 mm lg., 3–5 mm br., 2–4 mm h., connected by a narrow furrow; **Ar.** narrow-oblong, to 4 mm lg., 0.5 mm br., 3–5 mm apart, offset; **Sp.** fully developed in the apex and concealing this, 12–14, 2–4 mm lg., fine, pectinate, appressed, concolorous brown at first, black below, becoming grey; **Fl.** from fairly low on the Bo., light violet-purple to crimson, then orange towards the throat.—Bolivia (no locality mentioned) (FR 752a). (Fig. 533.)
v. **verticosior** Ritt.—l.c.: **Sp.** denser above, concolorous brown. (FR 752).

S. weingartiana is a name without description. These plants were discovered by Krahn and belong within the complex of S. tiraquensis; to a great extent their characters tally with those of the description of the type-species; they can be simple and grow relatively large or they may have a few offsets; Sp. ± ruby-red to brown; Ar. slender, shortly linear.—Bolivia.

S. xanthoantha Backbg. n.sp.
Bo. dark green, soon offsetting quite freely; **Rsp.** 8–12, c. 5 mm lg., yellow, golden-yellow to light brownish, lemon-yellow to whitish, ± curving; **Csp.** 0; **Ar.** 1.5–3 mm lg., 0.5–2 mm br., with short whitish to yellowish felt, extended furrow-like above; **Fl.** 2.5–3 cm ⌀, yellow to golden-yellow; **Tu.** c. 2 cm lg., with green Sc., these more yellowish below; **Sep.** and **Pet.** spatulate, acute above, the former with a green shimmer at the tips; **style** and **Fil.** light yellow; **Sti.** whitish-yellow; **Fr.** ?—Bolivia (FR 774 ?). (Fig. 406.)

Tacinga Br. & R. (19)

Tall, inclined, moderately branching shrubs with terete shoots, of the Subfamily Opuntioideae, which diverge conspicuously in all their characters from any other member of the Cactaceae: the shape of the shoots, the glochids which in older plants drop at a touch, the lack of spines and the unique flowers with their stem-like tube and ovary sections, as well as the recurved petals with considerable hair-development between them and the erect anthers which are for a considerable distance pressed close to the style. Furthermore, the flowers open in the evening or during the night, and the areoles on younger shoots develop tufts of soft hairs. The flowers are not terminal, as stated by Britton and Rose, but arise from close to the apex;

probably the American authors by coincidence saw an apically situated flower. These characters are all so unusual that the plants deserve the rank of an independent tribe. The nocturnal flowers alone are quite unusual among Opuntia and its related genera; some Tacinga flowers are still open for a time during the morning. The hitherto unexplained origin of these plants is one of the most interesting problems of evolution within the Cactaceae, and it cannot be explained by any of the customary solutions. Perhaps the genus is a survivor, the intermediate species or genera having meantime been lost.—Distribution: Brazil (only in the northern Catinga). [(G); grown on Opuntia, the plants develop rapidly and flower readily in cultivation.]

T. atropurpurea Werd.
Bo. over 2 m h.; **branches** 1.4 cm $\varnothing$, greyish-green; **Ar.** with brown wool and grey Glo.; **Fl.** 7 cm lg., dark purple; **Ov.** 5 cm lg., 1 cm $\varnothing$; **Fil.** white; **style** pale green; **Sti.** green.—Brazil (Bahia, between Boa Nova and Conquista).

v. **zehntnerioides** Backbg.: **Fl.** violet-green, with a distinct green tint, 7 cm lg.; **Fl.** only 3 cm lg. have been observed, these having longer Fil. than the varietal type. The Pet. are few, and laxer than in the type of the species. L. are cylindric and vary in length, as in the type. (Fig. 407.)

T. funalis Br. & R. (T.)
Bo. to 12 m lg., with a small woody **trunk**; **branches** sometimes reddish; **Glo.** short; **Fl.** to 8 cm lg.; **Sep.** c. 10; **Pet.** c. 7, greenish, 4 cm lg.; **style** cream; **Sti.** green; **Fr.** to 5 cm lg.; **S.** 3–4 mm $\varnothing$.—Brazil (N. Bahia, Joazeiro). Very floriferous.

T. zehntneri Backbg. & Voll: **Tacinga atropurpurea** Werd.

Tephrocactus Lem. emend. Backbg. (11)*

Members of this genus are by far the most numerous of the Subfamily Opuntioideae in S. America, ranging from Central Peru on both sides of the Andes, to the Argentinian foothills and far southwards. At higher altitudes and above all in drier zones they are often the only representatives of the Subfamily, from little above sea-level right up to 4000 m, occasionally in company with similar or dwarf specimens of the Platyopuntiae, from which they are distinguished by the latter's $\pm$ distinctly flattened shoots. As a result of the vast distribution, the large number of species and the characteristic habit, they had to be put into their own genus, as was done by Lemaire. As so often happens, here too there is a group of transitional forms—or so it would appear—in which the bodies are more oblong, showing a closer relationship with Austrocylindropuntia; but these are either only elongated-spherical forms (T. crassicylindricus) or species forming mounds of segments which, seen from the outside, appear spherical; such mounds are only possible however because of the elongation of the inner shoots; this growth-form is more clearly recognisable in some related and less caespitose plants, while the segments of the typical mound-forming species appear quite spherical on the periphery of the colony, and in part remain so for a longer time. However, a distinction must be drawn between these species and those of Austrocylindropuntia which also shows some spherical forms, because at lower altitudes or in cultivation its shoots become strongly elongated and reveal the genus to which they properly belong; on the other hand Tephrocactus species of the Series "Globulares" never change their growth-form in normal cultivation, even in reduced light. Here too there remain interesting problems of morphology and phylogeny, and it seems preferable to examine these larger questions, rather than those of new combinations of individual and often smaller genera; and in this context the precise classification of the Genus Tephrocactus, seen from the geobotanical point of view, should provide useful information.

The species are divided as follows on the basis of their typical habit:

Series 1: Elongati Backbg.;
Series 2: Globulares Backbg.

The relevant Series is indicated by the figure in brackets after each specific name. No further subdivision appears necessary since the different species can be understood without difficulty.

Lemaire included in Tephrocactus some species which in fact belong to dwarf Series of the Platyopuntiae (e.g. "Airampoae"). The genus was thus restricted to species which could not be associated with the former; Series 1: "Elongati" includes several species which are particularly attractive on account of their generous wool-development, while Series 2: "Globulares" shows interesting forms and body-colours; in the case of T. articulatus, the wealth of forms is unusually impressive, particularly since some of these show unique ribbon-like spines. This species long

---

* Now generally regarded as only a SG. of Opuntia, which includes a number of Backeberg's genera. See "The Subgenus Tephrocactus: a historical survey with notes on cultivation", by Gilbert Leighton-Boyce and James Iliff. Published 1973 by The Succulent Plant Trust, Morden, Surrey, England. [Translator.]

remained misunderstood, and the earliest correct name has not yet regained universal acceptance. Many species growing either at great altitudes or far to the south of the continent are exposed to severe cold. The flowers in general have the typical Opuntia form; the style is often thickened below; the seeds are ± circular; in one case the fruits have glochids inside, which is an unusual phenomenon. The spines show great variety; sometimes they are hair-like or bristly while others are acicular or ± stoutly subulate, alternatively they may be completely absent or only short, sometimes they are flexible. The ovary or pericarp is quite often fairly thick-fleshed, with a relatively small seed-cavity. Some species, particularly those of dry zones in the high mountains, have a stout root-development which is doubtless a factor contributing to the plants' survival in unfavourable climatic conditions.—Distribution: Central to S. Peru, Chile, Bolivia, more western areas of N. to S. Argentina, and down to the Magellan Straits. [(R); grafting recommended for smaller or rare spec. and Austrocylindropuntia subulata readily accepts Tephrocactus, although other species are rarely successful.]

T. albiscoparius Backbg. (2)
Bo. green, forming rather broad and dense groups; **Seg.** ± tapering above, weakly tuberculate; **Ar.** with white felt; **Sp.** 4–8, to c. 5 cm lg., mostly 1 which is shorter, c. 8–9 mm lg., very thin, the others stout, scarcely flexible, all milky-white and projecting ± brush-like beyond the Bo.; **Fl.** ?—Bolivia. Discovered by Frau Wilke.

T. alboareolatus Ritt.—Descr. Cact. Nov. III: 14. 1963 (2)
Bo. greyish-blue to green; **Seg.** c. 5 cm lg., c. 3 cm ∅, ovoid, tapering above; **Ar.** set on weakly tuberculate swellings, circular to oblong, to 6 mm lg., with prominent thick white felt; **Sp.** c. 4, stoutly acicular, irregularly directed, upwards, forwards or downwards, porrect or curving, to 2.5 cm lg., entirely hyaline or with brownish flecks, or light brownish above midway, mostly also with 2 much thinner white Sp. which are appressed and directed downwards; **Fl.** ?—Origin ? (Fig. 408, 409.)

T. alexanderi (Br. & R.) Backbg. (2)
Bo. branching, greyish-green; **Seg.** spherical, to 3 cm ∅, tuberculate; **Ar.** small, circular; **Sp.** 4–12, to 4 cm lg., rougher than in the variety, often downcurving at first, white, later only so below, and then dark above or black-tipped, flexible; **Fl.** ?; **Fr.** red, dry, with longer flexible white Sp. above; **S.** 6 mm lg., white.—Argentina (La Rioja, between Chilenecito and Famatina).
v. **bruchii** (Speg.) Backbg.: **Bo.** as in the type, to

50 cm h., forming groups of similar width; **Seg.** to 9 cm lg., to 5.5 cm ∅, tuberculate; **Ar.** white at first, soon becoming spineless below; **Glo.** yellowish, to 4 mm lg.; **Sp.** 12–15, 1–4 cm lg., only occasionally minutely rough in places, finely pitted, whitish either below or throughout, stouter Sp. violet-grey to bluish-grey, either entirely or in part, outer ones more acicular, inner ones scarcely differentiated, subulate; **Fl.** c. 6 cm lg., pinkish-white.—Argentina (Catamarca, Mazan).
subv. **macracanthus** (Speg.) Backbg.: individual **Sp.** much longer;
subv. **brachyacanthus** (Speg.) Backbg.: all **Sp.** shorter than the longest ones of the type;
v. **subsphaericus** (Backbg.) Backbg.: **Bo.** with oblong Seg.; **Sp.** never rough, 6–15, 3–4 scarcely differentiated Csp., often black to greyish-black, some thin to bristly, individuals longer, all later whitish-grey; **Fl.** ?—Origin: as for the type.

T. andicolus Lem.: **Tephrocactus glomeratus** v. **andicolus** (Pfeiff.) Backbg.

T. aoracanthus Lem.: **Tephrocactus articulatus** v. **ovatus** (Pfeiff.) Backbg.

T. articulatus (Pfeiff. ex O.) Backbg. (2, one variety: 1) (T.: v. diadematus)
Bo. laxly branching, greyish-green; **Seg.** readily detached, oblong to spherical; **Ar.** with little felt; **Glo.** brown, short; **Sp.** 0; **Fl.** white, fading ± to pink; **Fr.** 1.5 cm lg.; **S.** with a coating which is first glassy, then hard and corky.—W. Argentina (Mendoza). Glo. probably present in most Fr.
v. **calvus** (Lem.) Backbg.: **Seg.** spherical or more broadly so, to 3.5 cm h. and ∅, yellowish to greyish-green; **Tub.** more prominent; **Glo.** longer, tufted;
v. **diadematus** (Lem.) Backbg.: **Bo.** forming a low bush; **Seg.** more slender, to 5 cm lg., green to greyish-green; **Sp.** raffia-like, white or bordered brown, 1–4; **Fl.** pale yellow, to 3.5 cm ∅; **Fr.** 2 cm lg.;
v. **inermis** (Speg.) (Backbg.) (1): **Bo.** forming denser groups; **Seg.** green, cylindric, tapering above, to 10 cm lg., to 2.5 cm ∅; **Ar.** white; **Glo.** light to blackish-brown.—W. Argentina (central Provinces);
v. **oligacanthus** (Speg.) Backbg.: **Bo.** low, bushy; **Seg.** bluish, greyish or dark green, to 5 cm lg., to 3.5 cm ∅; **Sp.** only 1–2, or 0, narrower and shorter than in v. diadematus, sometimes very short, light to dark; **Fl.** 3 cm lg., 4 cm ∅, white tinged pink; **style** white;
v. **ovatus** (Pfeiff.) Backbg.: **Bo.** a lax shrub to 50 cm br., ± faded green; **Seg.** large-spherical, to 8 cm ∅, spineless below; **Sp.** 1–7, brown to

blackish, to 13 cm lg., stoutly subulate, sometimes slightly compressed and rather scabrous; **Fl.** white; **Fr.** red, rarely spiny;
v. **papyracanthus** (Phil.) Backbg.: **Bo.** resembling that of v. syringacanthus, colour more greyish-brown; **Sp.** broad, ribbon-like, concolorous white.—W. Argentina (Mendoza, Catamarca);
v. **polyacanthus** (Speg.) Backbg.: **Bo.** low-shrubby, ash-grey; **Seg.** spherical, ovoid or oblong, to 7 cm lg., to 2.5 cm br.; **Sp.** 5–6, rather stiff, brownish, erect, ± keeled, fairly lg., to 10 cm lg., often appearing frosted; **Fl.** white.—W. Argentina (La Rioja; Córdoba);
v. **syringacanthus** (Pfeiff.) Backbg.: **Bo.** erectly bushy, green; **Seg.** spherical, to c. 5 cm $\emptyset$; **Ar.** large; **Glo.** tufted, brown; **Sp.** 1–2, wide, raffia-like, to over 5 cm lg., to over 3 mm br., occasionally to 10 cm lg., greyish-white suffused reddish-brown, occasionally with a few Ssp.; **Fl.** white fading to pink; **Sti.** white; **Fr.** green.—Distribution not precisely known. Differentiated from v. papyracanthus by the Sp.-colour.

T. asplundii Backbg. (2)
Bo. forming cushions, yellowish-green; **Seg.** ovoid, to 5 cm lg., 3.5 cm $\emptyset$; **Glo.** to 4 m lg., inner ones light yellow, outer ones darker; **Sp.** 2–4, to 4 cm lg., subulate, one of these often thinner, shorter; **Fl.** c. 2.5 cm lg., 2.3 cm $\emptyset$, faded reddish-yellow; **Ov.** brownish.—Bolivia (near Ulloma).

T. atacamensis (Phil.) Backbg. (2)
Bo. densely branching, forming groups to 30 cm h., 60 cm br.; **Seg.** pale green, ovoid, c. 2.5 cm lg., 2 cm $\emptyset$, slightly tuberculate above; **L.** light green; lower **Ar.** woolly; **Sp.** 2–4, appressed, 2 cm lg., 1 of these erect, to 2.5 cm lg., yellow to reddish; **Fl.** yellow; **Fr.** green, lacking Sp., 1.5 cm $\emptyset$, **Glo.** uniformly lighter; **S.** flat.—Chile (Profetas and Puquios).
v. **chilensis** (Backbg.) Backbg.: **Bo.** more olive-green; **Seg.** conically tapering, larger; **Sp.** longer, thinner, Csp. 2, flexible, to 5 cm lg., white below, ± reddish-brown above, Rsp. mostly absent or only 1, appressed, to c. 8 mm lg.; **Fr.** small.—Chile (at c. 3000 m).

T. atroglobosus Backbg. (2)
Bo. branching, mostly prostrate to weakly erect; **Seg.** fairly large, ± ovoid to oblong, dark green, ± strongly tuberculate; **Ar.** yellowish-white; **L.** short, reddish to dark green; **Sp.** mostly 2–3(–7), to c. 2 cm lg.; **Fl.** fairly small, numerous, red; **Fr.** flame-coloured, small, smooth.—Origin? Floriferous. (Rivière collection No. 6217). (Fig. 410.)

T. atroviridis (Werd. & Backbg.) Backbg. (1)
Bo. forming high rounded cushions, intense dark green; **Seg.** long remaining subspherical, to 3.5 cm

$\emptyset$, those within the cushion elongated, Tub. rounded; **Ar.** white; **Glo.** light brown, sometimes with 1 small Br.; **Sp.** 3 or more, to 3 cm lg., stiff, sharp, sometimes ± compressed, olive-yellow or darker; **Fl.** yellow, to 3.5 cm lg., 4 cm $\emptyset$.—Central Peru (Yauli, 4000 m). There are also forms with a few small H., the products of spontaneous hybridisation with T. floccosus.
v. **longicylindricus** Rauh & Backbg.: **Bo.** forming cushions 1 m h.; **Seg.** to 30 cm lg., 5–6 cm $\emptyset$; **Ar.** with a few H.; **Sp.** 3–5, stout, sometimes to 3 cm lg., pale amber; **Fl.** yellow; **Fr.** to 3 cm $\emptyset$, with a few H.—Central Peru (Oroya, Mantaro terraces);
v. **parviflorus** Rauh & Backbg.: **Bo.** forming flat compact cushions; **branches** many, short; **Sp.** very short; **Fl.** 2.5 cm lg., 2 cm $\emptyset$, yellow outside, bordered reddish.—Locality as for the preceding variety;
v. **paucispinus** Rauh & Backbg.: **Seg.** to 5 cm lg., 2.5 cm $\emptyset$; **Sp.** only 1–2 (–3–4), to 2.5 cm lg.; **Fl.** 3 cm lg., to 2.5 cm $\emptyset$, with thin yellow Br.-Sp. above; **style** slender.—Locality as for the first variety.

T. bicolor Rauh: see **Tephrocactus fulvicomus** v. **bicolor** Rauh & Backbg.; possibly a good spec.

T. blancii Backbg. (1)
Bo. forming dense small cushions to c. 20 cm br., from a stout underground basal section; **Seg.** spherical, to 3 cm $\emptyset$, with thick swollen Tub.; **Ar.** light; **Sp.** 1–6, irregularly spreading, to 2.5 cm lg., dark, sometimes light-tipped; **Fl.** ?—Peru (Cordillera Negra, c. 4000 m).

T. bolivianus (SD.) Backbg. (2)
Bo. forming cushions 1 m br.; **Seg.** ovoid to oblong, green at first, to 10 cm lg., to 4 cm br., ± tuberculate, later smooth; **Ar.** shortly woolly; **Sp.** only in the upper part of the Seg., 1–5, mostly yellow but variable, to reddish, to 7 cm lg.; **Fl.** to 3 cm lg., 5 cm $\emptyset$, yellow to orange; **Ov.** with Br.-Sp. above; **Fr.** spherical to oblong, yellow, not edible, with a few minute Br.-Sp. above; **S.** 4–5 mm lg., round.—Bolivia (high plateaux). Sp. darker, to blackish, have been reported.

T. bruchii (Speg.) Speg.: **Tephrocactus alexanderi** v. **bruchii** (Speg.) Backbg.

T. calvus Lem.: **Tephrocactus articulatus** v. **calvus** (Lem.) Backbg.

T. camachoi (Esp.) Backbg. (2)
Bo. forming cushions, colonies to 60 cm h., to 1.5 m br., yellowish-green; **Seg.** ± bluish below, ovoid, to 4 cm lg., to 2.5 cm br., finely papillose, weakly

tuberculate; **Ar.** round, white or cream; **L.** ovoid or linear; **Glo.** numerous, honey-coloured; **Sp.** unequal, main Sp. 1–3, stiffer, erect, to 6 cm lg., white below, white with brown flecks above, with 1–2 lower Ssp.; **Fl.** to 6 cm lg., 5 cm $\varnothing$, greenish-yellow.—Chile (Pampa de Antofagasta).

T. catacanthus Backbg.—Descr. Cact. Nov. III: 14. 1963 (2)
Bo. offsetting from below; **Seg.** to c. 4 cm lg., 1.7 cm $\varnothing$, light green, pitted; **Ar.** with flocky felt at first, later with yellowish **Glo.**; **Rsp.** to 7, irregularly curving, appressed, mostly in the lower half of the Ar., horn-coloured or pale pinkish-yellow; **Csp.** 1–2, compressed or flattened, directed strongly downwards, to 1.5 cm lg., whitish horn-coloured; **Fl.**?—N. Argentina (Jujuy, northern mountains; found by Frau Muhr). (Fig. 411.)

T. chichensis Card. (2)
Bo. forming cushions to 60 cm h., 1 m br.; **Seg.** light green to greyish-green, finely pitted, to 9.5 cm lg., to 4.5 cm $\varnothing$, broadly tuberculate; **Ar.** cream; **Glo.** short, yellow; **Sp.** 12–16, 1–5 cm lg., white, projecting, Csp. scarcely differentiated; **Fl.** 4.5 cm lg., light yellow; **Fr.** spherical-elliptic, c. 5 cm lg., with white translucent Sp.; **S.** light brown, 5 mm lg.—Bolivia (Potosí, between Tres Palcas and Escoriani).

v. **colchanus** Card.: **Bo.** forming cushions to 40 cm h., 70 cm br.; **Seg.** light green, ovoid; **Glo.** 6 mm lg., white; **Sp.** c. 11, white, to 3.5 cm lg., upper ones brownish, thicker, shortest ones bristly, the longest Sp. eventually to 6.2 cm lg.; **Fl.** ?; **Fr.** green, scarcely fleshy; **S.** orange-brown, 4 mm lg.—Bolivia (Potosí, above Colcha).

T. chilensis Backbg.: **Tephrocactus atacamensis** v. **chilensis** (Backbg.) Backbg.

T. coloreus Ritt.—Descr. Cact. Nov. III: 14. 1963 (2)
Bo. laxly segmented, light green; **Seg.** to c. 5 cm lg., over 2 cm $\varnothing$, later more greyish-green; **Ar.** brownish-white, prominent, to c. 3 mm lg.; **Glo.** in compact, light brown tufts; **Sp.** mostly c. 5, irregularly directed, unequal, longest ones to 4.5–7 cm lg., usually 1 which is rather thin, of variable length, $\pm$ projecting to appressed, several Sp. $\pm$ downcurving, sometimes $\pm$ sinuate, those in any one Ar. various coloured, even at first, whitish or with a reddish-brownish sheen, occasionally concolorous reddish-brown, all Sp. later fairly long and porrect but flexible; **Fl.** ?—Origin ? (Fig. 412.)

T. conoideus Backbg. non Ritt. (2)
Bo. very small, laxly branching; **Seg.** olive-green, oblong-conical, to 2.5 cm lg., 11 mm $\varnothing$; **Ar.** with brownish felt, more crowded at the apex; **Sp.** to 7 at first, reddish, small, dropping, then 1(–3) rather stouter and appressed or contorted, 1 projecting Sp. to 11 mm lg., whitish-grey, $\pm$ compressed; **Fl.** ?—Chile (Baños de Puritama). Found by Lembcke.

T. corotilla (K. Sch.) Backbg. (2)
Bo. in small, laxly branching groups to 15 cm h., in part prostrate; **Seg.** dull green, reddish at first, spherical to oblong, to 6 cm lg., to 2 cm $\varnothing$; **Ar.** with tufts of erect Glo. to 3 mm lg.; **Sp.** 0–7, to 4 cm lg.; **Fl.** 3.5 cm lg., spiny, creamy-white, fading to pink (only Peruvian spec. with this colour); **Fil.** numerous; **Fr.** with a much-sunken floral scar, 2 cm lg.; **S.** 4 mm lg., $\pm$ oval.—S. Peru (between Airampal and Pampa, 3300 m). (Fig. 413.)

v. **aurantiaciflorus** Rauh & Backbg.: **Seg.** similarly coloured, to 4 cm lg.; **Ar.** whitish-brown, not very prominent; **Glo.** whitish-brown; **Sp.** 0(–1, longer); **Fl.** 3 cm lg., reddish-orange; **Fr.** 2 cm lg., with thin-acicular Sp.—S. Peru (Chiguata, 3200 m).

T. corrugatus (Pfeiff.) Backbg.: **Opuntia longispina** v. **corrugata** (Pfeiff.) Backbg.

T. crassicylindricus Rauh & Backbg. (1)
Bo. squarrosely branching, to c. 30 cm h. or more, in colonies to 1.5 m br., with a napiform main R.; **Seg.** faded greyish-green, $\pm$ cylindric, sometimes to 10–15 cm lg., to 6 cm thick; **Glo.** faded brown, to 5 mm lg., tufted; **Ar.** c. 1 cm apart; **Sp.** in the upper part of the Seg., 3–7, very stout, mostly with 2–3 directed downwards and the others obliquely upwards, the longest one to 5 cm lg., scabrous, all Sp. light grey below, gradually passing over to more reddish to brown, darker-tipped; **Fl.** to 5 cm lg. and $\varnothing$, vivid yellow; **Sep.** greenish-yellow, red-tipped; **Fr.** with a large floral scar, spiny.—S. Peru (Rio Majes, 900–1200 m).

T. crispicrinitus Rauh & Backbg. (1)
Bo. cushion-forming; **Seg.** spherical to oblong, to 4 cm lg., 2 cm $\varnothing$, with moderately broad, oblong Tub.; **Sp.** thin, little projecting, brownish to horn-coloured; **H.** projecting, white, curly; **Fl.** ?—Peru (Cordillera Negra, Punta Caillan). Differentiated by the strongly curly but not very dense H.

v. **cylindraceus** Rauh & Backbg.: **Seg.** to 15 cm lg., to 3 cm $\varnothing$; **Sp.** 1–4, to 2(–4) cm lg.;

subv. **flavicomus** Rauh & Backbg.: **H.** yellow to golden-brown; **Sp.** stouter, 1–3, to 3 cm lg.;

v. **tortispinus** Rauh & Backbg.: **Sp.** as in the type, stouter, brown, bent, often connivent above the apex, to 4, to 3 cm lg.

T. curvispinus Backbg.—Descr. Cact. Nov. III: 14. 1963 (2)

Bo. greyish-green, branching laxly from below to form groups or denser cushions; **Seg.** at first spherical, green, soon greying, c. 2.5 cm lg., 2.2 cm $\emptyset$, noticeably tuberculate; **Ar.** glabrous, depressed; **Sp.** reddish at first, not sharp, flexible, soon leaden-grey, strongly and irregularly curving, 2–5, ± compressed, slightly furrowed or angular, often twisted; **Fl.** ?—N. Argentina (Jujuy, in the mountains; found by Fechser). (Fig. 414.)

T. cylindrarticulatus Card. (2)
Bo. in compact cushions to 20 cm h., 60 cm br., arising from the main **R.**; **Seg.** to 9 cm lg., to 4 cm $\emptyset$, elliptic, newer Seg. cylindric, greyish-green, tuberculate; **Ar.** creamy-white at first; **Sp.** c. 6, projecting, 2–4.5 cm lg., stiff, pointed, brown below, black at midway, light brown above; **Fl.** ?; **Fr.** ellipsoidal, reddish-brown, c. 5 cm lg., 2 cm thick; **S.** light brown, 5 mm lg.—Bolivia (between Tres Palcas and Escoriani).

T. cylindrolanatus Rauh & Backbg. (1)
Bo. forming dense or lax groups; **Seg.** slender-cylindric, relatively small; **H.** dense but sometimes stiffly projecting, white; **Sp.** thin, brownish.—Peru (Cordillera Raura, 4600 m). Differentiated by the slender-cylindric shape, and the sometimes projecting H.

T. dactyliferus (Vpl.) Backbg. (2)
Bo. cushion-forming; **Seg.** spherical to acutely ovoid, faded greyish-green, to 7 cm lg., to 4 cm $\emptyset$, tuberculate above; **Glo.** not numerous; **Sp.** reddish to yellowish-brown, c. 1–5, moderately long; **Fl.** 3 cm lg., orange-yellow, not opening very widely; buds with yellowish Sp. above; **Fr.** c. 5 cm lg.; **S.** yellowish-brown. Old Sp. sometimes blackish-brown.—S. Peru (Azangaro, 3600 m).

T. darwinii (Hensl.) Backbg. (2)
Bo. forming low colonies, probably to only 4 cm h.; **R.** long, woody; **Seg.** subspherical, c. 3 cm $\emptyset$, sometimes oblong, usually few, small, smaller ones to 10 mm $\emptyset$; **Ar.** large, felty; **Sp.** 1–3 in the upper part of the Ar., ± straight, to 3.5 cm lg., yellow or reddish-yellow, flattened; **Fl.** ± the same size as the Seg., yellow.—S. Argentina (close to the Magellan Straits).

T. diadematus Lem.: **Tephrocactus articulatus** v. **diadematus** (Lem.) Backbg.

T. diadematus v. calvus (Lem.) Backbg.: **Tephrocactus articulatus** v. **calvus** (Lem.) Backbg.

T. dimorphus (Först.) Backbg. (2)
Bo. forming lax cushions c. 20 cm h.; **Seg.** brownish-green to green, upper ones ± ovoid, ±

tapering to both ends, c. 2.5 cm lg. and $\emptyset$; **Ar.** white-felty; **Glo.** small, yellow; **Sp.** unequal, 6–8, mostly 2–3 longer ones, brownish, later to 12, to 4.2 cm lg.; **Fl.** light yellow.—S. Peru (Pampa).

v. **pseudorauppianus** (Backbg.) Backbg.: **Bo.** similar to the type; **Ar.** brown-felty; **Glo.** white; **Sp.** c. 7, c. 2 cm lg., brown, some shorter, whitish. **Seg.** subspherical.—Chile (neighbourhood of Coquimbo).

T. duvalioides Backbg.: **Tephrocactus dactyliferus** (Vpl.) Backbg.

T. echinaceus Ritt.—"Taxon", XIII: 4, 145. 1964 (2)
Bo. quite freely branching; **R.** napiform; **Seg.** 4–9 cm lg., 2–4 cm $\emptyset$, tuberculate; **Ar.** white, 1–2 cm apart; **Sp.** 4–10, only in the upper Ar., 1–12(–20) cm lg., straight or curving, reddish-brown, stout, smaller ones thinner; **Fl.** 3.5–5.5 cm lg., pale yellow, with reddish-brown Sp., Pet. obtuse; **style** white; **Sti.** 7, yellowish; **Fr.** yellowish or greenish, spiny above, fairly dry; **S.** brown, bordered white, 3 mm lg.—Chile (road from Arica to Portezuelo Chapiquiña, 2900 m, on the watershed between the Azapa and Lluta gorges). (FR 198.)

T. ferocior Backbg. (2)
Bo. forming cushions or larger mounds; **Seg.** to 8 cm lg., 5.6 cm $\emptyset$, green, with prominent Tub. c. 2 cm lg., 1.5 cm thick; **L.** reddish; **Ar.** with whitish Glo.; **Sp.** very unequal, few at first, later more numerous, cultivated plants may have 0–2 at first, later curving, interlacing or spreading, from whitish to light yellow to brownish, sometimes very stout in habitat, 1–3 more central, sometimes to 6 cm lg.; **Fl.** pale yellow to orange-yellow; **Fr.** to 4.5 cm $\emptyset$, fleshy, spineless, edible; **S.** large, ± 4-sided. In the wild, plants may have to 20 Sp.—Bolivia (Tres Palcas, pampas N. of Tupiza), to N. Argentina (La Quiaca, acc. Frau Muhr).

T. flexispinus Backbg.—Descr. Cact. Nov. III: 14. 1963 (2)
Bo. caespitose, green; **Seg.** elongated, c. 4 cm lg., 1.5 cm $\emptyset$ or rather more, with oblong Tub. to 1.5 cm lg., 5 mm br., ± confluent below; **Ar.** whitish; **Glo.** yellowish; **Sp.** stiffly erect, to c. 8 cm lg., yellowish or pale brownish, sometimes ± curving; **Fl.** ?—N. Argentina (Jujuy, in the mountains; found by Frau Muhr). (Fig. 415.)

T. flexuosus Backbg. (2)
Bo. forming groups; **Seg.** ovoid, pale olive-green, tapering above, to 3 cm lg., 2.5 cm $\emptyset$, sometimes ± spherical, not very distinctly tuberculate; **Ar.** large, felty; **Sp.** yellowish-white, very long, flexible, to 20 cm lg. and more, some twisted, others short,

curving, interlacing sideways; **Fl.** and **Fr.** ?—N. Bolivia (near the Comanche Mine).

T. floccosus (SD.) Backbg. (1)
Bo. forming high rounded or sometimes flatter cushions to 2 m br.; **Seg.** to over 10 cm lg., covered with white **H.**, these tangled and covering the shoots like a cobweb, not clearly curly or brush-like; **Sp.** mostly 1–3, 1–3 cm lg., or shorter, yellow, sharp; **Fl.** 3 cm lg., c. 3.5 cm ∅, yellow or orange; **Fr.** 3 cm ∅, spherical to ovoid, yellowish.—Central Peru to Bolivia (3500–4600 m).
  v. **canispinus** Rauh & Backbg.: **Seg.** smaller, forming denser cushions; **Sp.** grey; **Fr.** green.— Peru (Rimac valley, 1500 m);
  v. **cardenasii** J. Marn.-Lap.: **Bo.** forming cushions, dark green; **Seg.** to 5.5 cm lg., 3 cm ∅; **L.** 1.3 cm lg., 3 mm thick, longer persistent; **H.** felty, dense, yellowish-white; **Sp.** few, fine, sharp, white; **Fl.** and **Fr.** ?—Bolivia (La Paz, Achacachi, 3000 m);
  v. **crassior** Backbg.: **Seg.** thicker, larger, laxer, fewer, spreading.—Central Peru (high plateaux, 4500 m);
    subv. **aurescens** Rauh & Backbg.: **H.** yellow, not white. Rauh gives this varietal status;
  v. **denudatus** (Web.) Backbg.: **H.** only few, possibly a hybrid between T. floccosus and T. atroviridis;
  v. **ovoides** Rauh & Backbg.: **Bo.** in dense flat cushions; **Seg.** elongated-ovoid, to 10 cm lg., 3 cm ∅; **Tub.** very flat, 1.5 cm br.; **Ar.** white-felty; **H.** sparser, not very curly, weak; **Sp.** c. 3–5, 2–3 cm lg., light yellow, 1–2 of these rather darker, longer, projecting.—S. Peru (Nazca-Puquio, on the Atlantic side, 4100 m).

T. fulvicomus Rauh & Backbg. (2)
Bo. in dense groups; **Seg.** to 6 cm lg., to 3 cm ∅, bluish to greyish-green, sometimes suffused purple; **Ar.** light brownish, 3 mm lg.; **Glo.** light, in a ring around the felt-cushion; main **Sp.** 5–7, golden-brown, mostly only slightly bent, ± erect, some decurved, to 4.5 cm lg., also 0–1–2 Ssp., these pointing downwards, ± curving, to 4 mm lg., sometimes also 1–2 quite thin Sp., short, a few mm lg.; **Fl.** yellow, with golden-brown thin Sp. above; **Fr.** 3 cm lg. and ∅, reddish above.—S. Peru (Chala valley):
  v. **bicolor** Rauh & Backbg.: **Seg.** to c. 5 cm lg., brownish-green at first, washed reddish, later greyish to blackish-green, to 3 cm ∅; **Tub.** 5 mm lg. and br., later to 12 mm lg.; **Glo.** tufted, yellowish; **Sp.** 1–3(–8), to 4 cm lg.; **Fl.** carmine outside, yellow inside.—Peru (Nazca-Puquio). Regarded by Rauh as an independent spec.: T. bicolor.

T. geometricus (Cast.) Backbg. (2)
Bo. low, laxly branching, c. 15 cm h.; **Seg.** spherical, 3.5 cm lg. and ∅, light green, later becoming corky; **Tub.** 5–6-angled; **Ar.** brownish, lower ones spineless; **Sp.** 3–5, subulate, black or white, curving above, 5–10 mm lg.; **Fl.** white, 3 cm lg.; **Fr.** dry, depressed-spherical, 17 mm lg., 22 mm br., mostly spineless.—Argentina (Catamarca, Tinogasta, Angostura de Guanchin).

T. glomeratus (Haw.) Backbg. (2)
Bo. forming dense hemispherical cushions in age; **R.** thick; **Seg.** oblong-ovoid, to c. 3 cm lg., 1.5 cm thick, somewhat tuberculate below the Ar.; **Ar.** yellowish-felty; **Glo.** numerous, light yellow, 4 mm lg.; **Sp.** 1, only in the upper Ar., to 4 cm lg., 1.5 mm br., quite flat, decurved immediately above the Ar., whitish-yellow or brown below, often tipped dark brown; **Fl.** and **Fr.** ?; **S.** 5 mm lg., dirty yellow.—N. Argentina (Los Andes). Britton and Rose erroneously used this name for T. articulatus, despite the fact that the two names are clearly descriptive of the typical habit of each plant: "clustered" and "segmented". The type plant has firm Sp. which are bent, ± resembling horns. (Fig. 416.) The varieties sometimes have more than one Sp.:
  v. **andicola** (Pfeiff.) Backbg.: **Sp.** 3–4, slender, white, not firm, 1–2 of these longer, flattened below, lower ones to 5 cm lg., sometimes ± coloured above; **Seg.** 8–12 mm ∅.—Argentina (Mendoza);
  v. **atratospinus** Backbg.—Descr. Cact. Nov. III: 14. 1963: differs as follows from the type: **Seg.** to 4.5 cm lg., 2 cm thick; **Sp.** 1 to several, much stouter, to 4.5 cm lg., 2 mm br., white below, pitch-black above.—N. Argentina (Jujuy; found by Frau Muhr). (Fig. 417.);
  v. **fulvispinus** (Lem.) Backbg.: **Sp.** almost golden-brown.—N. Argentina (Salta);
  v. **gracilior** (SD.) Backbg.: **Sp.** and **Seg.** more slender; downwardly appressed Ssp. not present.—Origin ?;
  v. **longispinus** Backbg.—Descr. Cact. Nov. III: 14. 1963: differs as follows from the type: **Seg.** 4.5 cm lg. but only c. 1.5 cm thick; **Sp.** 1 to several, 7–13(!) cm lg., straight, white below, horn-coloured above, or with flecks of that colour, c. 1 mm br.; **Fr.** glabrous, reddish, almost lacking any pulp; **S.** 4 mm thick, ± flattened.— N. Argentina (Jujuy; discovered by Frau Muhr). (Fig. 418.)
Thanks to the latest discoveries we can now see the whole range of variability of this spec. which was misunderstood by Britton and Rose, and described again by Werdermann as Opuntia hypogaea.

T. glomeratus v. oligacanthus Speg.: **Tephrocactus articulatus** v. **oligacanthus** (Speg.) Backbg.

T. halophilus (Speg.) Backbg.: **Tephrocactus alexanderi** (Br. & R.) Backbg.

T. hegenbartianus Backbg.—Descr. Cact. Nov. III: 15. 1963. (2)
Bo. offsetting from below to form fairly dense groups; **Seg.** c. 2 cm lg., 1.7 cm ∅, leaf-green; **Tub.** c. 7 mm lg., 5 mm br., rounded below, tapering above, crowded or spiralled; **Ar.** small, oblong, somewhat sunken, whitish; **Sp.** almostly bristle-like, flexible, to 7, unequal, ± projecting, white, some to 2 cm lg., others shorter to very short, curving or bent, terete; **L.** only 2 mm lg.; **Glo.** absent at first; **Fl.** ?—Origin ? (Fig. 419.)
Named for Dr. Hegenbart of Marktredwitz who was able to obtain the rare Tephrocactus-material of Ritter's from which this description was made.

T. heteromorphus (Phil.) Backbg. (1)
Bo. branching laxly from the base; **Seg.** bluish-green, shortly cylindric; **Tub.** spiralled, rounded, thickening in the 2nd year; **Ar.** oblong, whitish; **Sp.** bristly, weak, flexible, those lower on the Seg. later much elongated, ± hair-like and fine, pointing obliquely upwards, straight; **Fl.** red (acc. Philippi).—Chile (Tarapaca, Chiquito).

T. hickenii (Br. & R.) Speg. (2)
Bo. forming low, lax groups to 1 m br.; **Seg.** spherical at first, then more oblong, reddish-brown, 3–5 cm ∅, to 4 cm lg., strongly tuberculate; **Ar.** in the lower part of the Seg. mostly spineless, fairly large, round; **Sp.** 2–5, thin, narrow, flat, ± sharp, 5–12 cm lg., silvery to ± black, becoming ash-grey, lighter ones dark-tipped, newest ones mostly dark.—S. Argentina (Chubut, Puerto Madryn; Rio Negro).

T. hirschii Backbg. (1)
Bo. forming small flat cushions to 20 cm br.; **Seg.** light green, shortly spherical to shortly cylindric, 2–3 cm ∅; **Tub.** oblong, little prominent; **L.** 5 mm lg.; **Ar.** small, white; **Sp.** 1–3, to 11 mm lg., brownish, directed towards the apex or bent upwards; **Fl.** carmine, to 3 cm ∅.—Peru (Cordillera Blanca, Quebrada Queshque, 4000 m, together with Puya raimondii).

T. hossei Krainz & Gräs.: **Tephrocactus articulatus** v. **polyacanthus** (Speg.) Backbg.

T. ignescens (Vpl.) Backbg. (2)
Bo. forming large hemispherical cushions over 20 cm h., often with hundreds of heads; **Seg.** bluish-green to yellowish-green, to 10 cm lg., very fleshy, naked below; **Sp.** only in the upper Ar., 6–15, ± equal, 4–5 cm lg. or more, straight, erect, pointed, flexible to rigid, sharp, yellowish-brown; **Fl.** deep red; **Fr.** 7 cm lg., red, spiny and tuberculate above, with a sunken floral scar; **S.** spherical, 5 mm lg.—S. Peru (Sumbay) and N. Chile.
v. **steinianus** Backbg.: **Sp.** thinner, longer, honey-coloured, very flexible, to 20 per Ar.—N. Chile. Seg. also more slender.

T. ignotus (Br. & R.) Backbg.: **Tephrocactus corotilla** (K. Sch.) Backbg.

T. kuehnrichianus (Werd. & Backbg.) Backbg. (2)
Bo. forming larger clumps; **Seg.** spherical to slightly oblong, to 8 cm lg., greyish-green, with fine light dots; **Ar.** fairly distant, white at first; **Glo.** light; **Sp.** mostly only in the upper Ar., 5–12, spreading or ± recurved, whitish-grey, to 3.5 cm lg.; **Fl.** vivid yellow, to 3 cm ∅; **Fr.** broadly spherical, with a sunken floral scar.—Central Peru (800–1200 m).
v. **applanatus** (Werd. & Backbg.) Backbg.: forming dense clumps; **Seg.** compressed-spherical; **Sp.** less fierce, thinner, dirty grey, milky-white at first, to 2.5 cm lg.—Central Peru (Rimac valley).

T. lagopus (K. Sch.) Backbg. (1)
Bo. forming larger colonies; **Seg.** oblong, to c. 10 cm lg., 3.5 cm ∅; **H.** yellowish-white, to 1.5 cm lg., stiffer than in T. floccosus, in part projecting, brush-like; **Sp.** 1, to 2 cm lg., clearly projecting, thickened below, translucent whitish, ± rough, very sharp; **Glo.** sometimes as long as the Sp., to 1.5 cm lg.; **Fl.** orange to red, to 3 cm ∅.—Peru (near Cuzco, Cordillera Raura etc.). Sp. sometimes yellowish.
v. **aureo-penicillatus** Rauh & Backbg.: **Bo.** forming large cushions; **Seg.** ovoid, to 4.5 cm ∅, rather tapering above, tapering below to a slender base, fresh green; **Tub.** large, to 1.5 cm br., 6 mm h.; **Ar.** sunken, oblong, 5 mm lg., yellowish-white, felty; **Sp.** mostly 3–5, 1 of these especially long, to 3 cm lg., subulate, golden-brown, pale yellow above and below, also tufts of golden-yellow **H.** resembling a stiffly erect brush, rarely somewhat curly, to 3 cm lg.; **Fl.** orange-yellow, to 4 cm ∅; **Fr.** spherical, 3.5 cm lg., yellow to wine-red.—Peru (Ticlio Pass, 4700 m);
v. **aureus** Rauh & Backbg.: **H.** mid-yellow; **Sp.** yellow, stout, varying with the locality, longer projecting (Andahuaylas) or inconspicuous (Cordillera Raura); **Fr.** oblong, yellowish as in the type (where it is nearer spherical), 3–4 cm lg., 2.5 cm ∅;
subv. **brachycarpus** Rauh & Backbg.: **Fr.** depressed-spherical, to 2 cm lg., 4 cm ∅, yellowish to reddish, floral scar flat (more sunken in the type);

v. **leucolagopus** Rauh & Backbg.: **H.** pure white; **Fr.** subspherical, green below, yellowish above, floral scar sunken, narrow;

v. **pachycladus** Rauh & Backbg.: **Seg.** larger, to 14 cm lg., 6 cm ⌀; **H.** brush-like and stiff, appressed to projecting, dull to ± satiny-glossy, fairly rigid, yellowish to golden-yellow, at least in the upper part of the Seg.; **Sp.** to 7, to 4 cm lg., brownish-yellow, 1 Sp. always longer; **Fl.** 2 cm ⌀, orange-red.—Peru (summit of the Nazca-Puquio Pass, on the bleak puna at 4400 m, and among tola scrub near Chuquibamba).

T. leoncito (Werd.) Backbg. (2)
Bo. forming large hemispherical cushions to 50 cm h., 1 m br., with rigidly projecting Sp.; **Seg.** oblong-ovoid, c. 4 cm lg., 2 cm ⌀; **Ar.** few; **Glo.** honey-coloured, 7 mm lg.; 1–2 main **Sp.** to 4 cm lg., 1–2 **Ssp.** small, yellowish-brown to whitish, all Sp. much flattened and resembling stiff paper, sharp; **Fl.** yellow, c. 4 cm lg.—Chile (Atacama).
Ritter regards T. reicheanus (Esp.) Backbg. as a variety or form.

T. leoninus (Rümpl.) Backbg. (2)
Bo. forming lax groups; **Seg.** oblong-ovoid, later sometimes more spherical, branching quite freely above; **Ar.** with short felt at first, later with numerous short **Glo.**; **Sp.** variable in number, 6–12 on new Seg., at most 1 cm lg., more numerous on older shoots, Csp. 1–3, to 1.5 cm lg., all Sp. terete, moderately robust, sometimes longer; **Fl.** light yellow, 4 cm ⌀; **Pet.** ± obtuse to rounded above.—Chile.

T. longiarticulatus Backbg.—Descr. Cact. Nov. III: 15, 1963 (2)
Bo. erectly branching; **Seg.** intense green, semi-glossy, to c. 6 cm lg., c. 3 cm ⌀, with oblong prominent Tub. to c. 2 cm lg., 1 cm br.; **Ar.** with thick felt, to 9 mm lg. and almost as broad, yellowish-brownish to white, on cushions c. 5 mm h.; **Sp.** in the upper Ar. mostly erect, later ± projecting, c. 3–6, to c. 3.5 cm lg., unequal, variously arranged, mostly slightly curving, whitish, or only below, reddish-brownish above or concolorously so, some Sp. sometimes directed sharply up or down, or bent; **Fl.**, **Fr.** and **S.** ?—Origin? The epidermis is minutely pitted, and in part ± rough-scaly. (Fig. 420.)
The spec. bears some resemblance to T. zehnderi, but the Seg. are much more elongated, and the Ar.-cushions on new shoots almost twice as large and more whitish-brownish than in T. zehnderi.

T. malyanus Rausch
Bo. forming large cushions, taprooted, the entire plant densely covered with white or yellow woolly felt; **Seg.** to 15 cm lg., 2.5 cm ⌀; young **Ar.** each bear a L.; **Sp.** 0–3, to 2 cm lg., yellow; **Fl.** scarcely emerging from the woolly indumentum, yellow, not opening wide, to 3 cm lg., 2.5 cm ⌀; **Tu.** green, scaly, densely covered with white hairy felt; **style** whitish, with 3 yellow **Sti.**; **Fr.** violet-pink, to 4 cm lg.; **S.** round, c. 5 mm ⌀.—Peru (near Macusani; found by W. Rausch at 4000–4600 m). Named for the Austrian cactus-grower, G. L. Maly.

T. mandragora Backbg. (2)
Bo. forming small groups half-concealed in the soil; **R.** long, thick, to 12 cm lg., to 3 cm ⌀, variously shaped; **Seg.** oblong or ovoid, to c. 2 cm lg., tapering above; **Sp.** very short, thin, 1–3, whitish; **Ar.** set in a depression, or appearing so because they are on an indistinct Tub.; **Fl.** c. 3.5 cm ⌀, glossy, light yellow.—N. Argentina.

T. melanacanthus Backbg.—Descr. Cact. Nov. III: 15. 1963 (2)
Bo. caespitose, laxly segmented; **Seg.** bluish-green, to 6 cm lg., 2.5 cm thick, ± conical; **Tub.** c. 2 cm lg., 5 mm br.; **Ar.** dirty white; **Glo.** yellowish; **Sp.** c. 9–14, to 3.5 cm lg., dark brown, straight but mostly bent below and pointing downwards, sometimes ± sinuate or twisted.—N. Argentina (Jujuy; discovered by Frau Muhr). (Fig. 421.)

T. microclados Backbg. (2)
Bo. branching, mostly underground; **R.** thick-napiform, to 10 cm lg., 6 cm ⌀; **Seg.** minutely spherical, only 7–12 mm ⌀, intense green; **Tub.** minute at first, prominent, later flatter and broader; **Ar.** pale brownish; **L.** scarcely 1.5 mm lg.; **Sp.** very fine, curving downwards at first, c. 2–5 mm lg., later stouter, to 1.3 cm lg., 0–3(–4); **Fl.** yellow or red.—S. Bolivia (Tupiza).

T. microsphaericus Backbg. n.sp. (2)
Bo. articulated and chain-like, little branching, green, to 8 cm lg. has been observed; **Seg.** spherical, c. 1.8 cm lg. and br., rather stouter during the growing period; **Ar.** light brown, 2 mm ⌀, c. 3–4 mm apart; **Glo.** yellow, short at first, later to 4–5 mm lg.; **Sp.** pale horn-coloured, dark below; **Rsp.** to c. 8, thin, soon whitish, to c. 6 mm lg.; **Csp.** c. 3, to c. 2.5 cm lg., projecting; **Fl.** pink, 4 cm lg., 5 mm ⌀; **Fil.** and **An.** yellow; **style** and **Sti.** green; **Ov.** conical, spiny.—N. Argentina (Jujuy, near Maimará) (Coll. Uhlig & Backberg, U 2186; found by Frau Muhr). (Fig. 422.) Clearly distinguished by the unusual chain-like habit.

T. minor Backbg. (2)
Bo. in small lax groups; **Seg.** reddish at first, then bluish to yellowish-green, c. 2.4 cm lg., 2.2 cm ⌀, spherical to tapering above; **Ar.** at first like

prominent pads; **Glo.** later tufted, long, yellow; **Sp.** 1–5, 2 of these usually longer, to 4 cm lg., 3 shorter ones 6–18 mm lg., sometimes only 1–2 Sp. present, longer ones directed ± downwards.—N. Bolivia (4000 m).

T. minusculus Backbg. (2)
Bo. minute, branching; **Seg.** bluish-green, spherical; **Tub.** ± oblong-rounded, prominent, later flatter; **Ar.** eventually depressed, brown-felty at first, circular, fairly large, glabrous later; **Sp.** 0 or 1–2(–6), unequal, ± sharp, to 3 mm lg.; **Fl.** and **Fr.** ? The reddish **L.** on new shoots make them appear, reddish overall.—Bolivia (northern puna, c. 4000 m).

T. minutus Backbg. (2)
Bo. minute, with branches to 2.5 cm lg.; **R.** small, digitate; **Seg.** to 12 mm lg., 8 mm thick, more oblong in cultivation, reddened around the Ar.; **Ar.** broadly circular, 1.5 mm br., very small at first; **L.** very small; **Sp.** mostly absent or very small, scarcely visible, later 1–3–4, very thin, to 1.7 cm lg., often appressed, all grey, sometimes later missing.—N. Argentina (Los Andes).

T. mirus Rauh & Backbg. (2)
Bo. small-shrubby, laxly branching, c. 17 cm h., in groups c. 20 cm br.; **Seg.** leaf-green to greyish-green, spherical at first, later weakly elongated, 2–4 cm ∅; **Ar.** prominent, to c. 4 mm br., light brownish; **Glo.** short, light, set in the upper part of the Ar.; **Sp.** to c. 18, thin and short at first, later longer, stouter, unequal, to 2.5 cm lg., more in the lower part of the upper Ar., whitish (acc. Rauh, also brown at first); **Fl.** yellow, 2.5 cm ∅.—Peru (Nazca valley, 1200 m). In cultivation the Sp. of this attractive spec. do not grow as long.

T. mistiensis Backbg. (2)
Bo. cushion-forming; **Seg.** mid-green, later olive-green, ovoid or elongated; **Tub.** at first large, prominent, oval, soon flatter; **Sp.** mostly absent or 1, rather thin, more bristle-like, c. 4 mm lg.; **Fl.** and **Fr.** ?—S. Peru (Misti Volcano).

T. molfinoi Ritt.: **Maihueniopsis molfinoi** Speg. Ritter classified the plant as Tephrocactus but makes no mention as to whether he really observed shoots which were connected at the base—the most important of the characters given by Spegazzini; in other words it is not certain whether Ritter saw the correct spec. or whether—as in the case of Castellanos—he saw some other plant which he mistook for this spec. Maihueniopsis has not been re-collected at all, or described again.

T. molinensis (Speg.) Backbg. (2)
Bo. forming small clumps, dark green; **Seg.** elliptic to ovoid, sometimes subspherical at first, to 2.5 cm lg., in grafted plants to 4 cm lg., 2.5 cm ∅; **Ar.** with hairlets, these soon dropping but concealing the small new Seg.; **Glo.** tufted, reddish-brown (acc. Borg, sometimes yellow); **Sp.** 0; **Fl.** and **Fr.** ?—N. Argentina (Salta, Molinos, in the Chalchaqui valley).

T. muellerianus Backbg. (2)
Bo. brownish-green, forming groups; **Seg.** c. 2.5 cm lg., 2 cm ∅; **Sp.** 5–9, whitish, dark-tipped, spreading in all directions, 6–17 mm lg., rather longer and stouter on older shoots; **Ar.** white; **Fl.** ?—Origin? Older shoots appear to shrivel soon and become unsightly.

T. multiareolatus Ritt.—"Taxon", XIII: 4, 144. 1964 (2)
Bo. bluish-green, caespitose, forming colonies to 30 cm lg. and br.; **Seg.** 5 cm lg., 3.5 cm ∅, ovoid; **Ar.** large; **Sp.** ± straight; **Rsp.** 8–20, weak, white; **Csp.** 6–8, brown; **Fl.** 3.5 cm lg., yellow; **S.** large.—Peru (Dept. Arequipa, Convento). (FR 275.)

T. neuquensis (Borg) Backbg. (2)
Bo. forming low bushes to 15 cm h., faded green to brownish; **Seg.** ovoid-conical, 2–4 cm lg., 1–1.5 cm ∅, almost smooth; **Tub.** little prominent; **Ar.** small, white; **Glo.** white, short; **Rsp.** 2–3, bristly, white, to 1 cm lg., directed downwards; **Csp.** mostly 1, rarely 2–3, white, flattened, flexible, 2–4.5 cm lg., yellowish or tipped brownish; **Fl.** ?—S. Argentina (near Neuquen). (Fig. 423.)

T. nigrispinus (K. Sch.) Backbg. (1)
Bo. forming small spreading bushes to 20 cm h., dark to reddish or blackish-green; **Seg.** fairly numerous, oblong and slender except on older plants; **Tub.** small, low; **L.** c. 2 mm lg., reddish to dark green; **Ar.** yellowish at first; **Glo.** yellowish; **Sp.** 3–5, mostly from the upper Ar., to 4 cm lg., spreading, straight, subterete, not firm, purplish-black at first, becoming reddish-grey to grey; **Fl.** small, purple, to 2.5 cm lg.; **Fr.** naked, with a much-sunken floral scar.—N. Argentina (bleak uplands of Jujuy and Salta).

T. noodtiae Backbg. & Jacobs. (2)
Bo. cushion-forming, in groups to 20 cm br., greyish-green; **Seg.** to 4 cm lg., 2–3 cm ∅; **Tub.** to 1 cm lg., 7 mm br., flat; **Ar.** small, yellowish; **Sp.** honey-coloured, flexible, not sharp, ± interlacing laterally, 9–10, 6 of these longer, to 2.75 cm lg., 4–5 Ssp., these sometimes weak or thin and flexible, some Sp. curving, often rather darker-tipped, those on cultivated plants becoming translucent, whitish, thinner, sometimes faintly yellowish.—Peru (Lake Titicaca, 3900 m).

T. orutus (FR 1098): no description available.

T. ovallei Remy: a virtually unclarified spec. In the Botanical Garden of Nymphenburg, Munich, I saw plants under this name; they had greyish-green, moderately lg., spineless, conical Seg. with slender tufts of Glo.; **Fl.** yellow, spineless.—Chile (Ovalle).

T. ovatus (Pfeiff.) Backbg. (2)
Bo. forming smaller cushions; **R.** rather thick, branching; **Seg.** spherical, ± tapering above, to ovoid, green, to 4 cm lg.; **Ar.** brown; **Sp.** 7–8, unequal, stiff, erect, brownish at first, later white, 4–10 mm lg.—Argentina (Mendoza). Lower part of Seg. spineless.

T. paediophilus Ritt. (FR 1099).
[Haage states that no description was available to him; **Opuntia paediophila** Backbg. (shown in "The Illustrated Ref. on Cacti & Other Succulents", E. & B. Lamb, III p. 605) clearly corresponds with the plant in the Translator's collection: **Seg.** to 10 cm lg., subterete, c. 4 cm ∅, surface divided into lozenge-shaped Tub., each with an Ar., the latter at first with some white wool; **Glo.** brown to blackish; **Sp.** conspicuously long, 12–15 cm lg. (20–23 cm reported), flat, 3–4 cm br., tapering and sharp, buff to brownish, ± papery, but much firmer than in the "diademata" group, sometimes twisted and variously directed, but mostly 2–4 more centrally arranged, these at first forming an erect tuft, porrect on older Ar., also 1–2 lower Sp., directed ± downwards. **Fl.** and **Fr.** not known to the writer.—Argentina.]

T. parvisetus Backbg.: Descr. Cact. Nov. III: 15. 1963 (2)
Bo. laxly branching, olive-green; **Seg.** 1.5–3 cm lg., 7–8 mm ∅; **Ar.** c. 2–4 mm apart, 1.5 mm ∅ at first, white-felty; **L.** 1 mm lg., reddish; **Glo.** very short, whitish; **Sp.** to c. 12, to 5–8 mm lg., very thin, pale reddish above at first, soon becoming white, spreading, later directed downwards; **Fl.** ?—Chile (in the mountains, but no more precise locality given; found by Lembcke). (Fig. 424.) While clearly related to T. conoideus, it is a valid independent spec.

T. pentlandii (SD.) Backbg. (2)
Bo. forming low cushions; **R.** napiform; **Seg.** small, spherical to slightly tapering to both ends; **Tub.** flat; **Glo.** minute; **Sp.** 4–6, slender, to 8.5 mm lg., whitish, variously recurved; **Fl.** yellow and red, shortly funnelform, 2.5 cm lg., 3.5 cm ∅; **Ov.** broadly compressed; **Fr.** red inside, dry, 1.2 cm lg., with a deep floral scar and a few Br. above.—Bolivia (Tupiza, Pampa Mochara).

v. **adpressus** Backbg. n.v.: Hitherto seen in collections as T. adpressus nom. nud.; similar to T. pentlandii; **Seg.** dark olive-green; **Sp.** 2–3 to 1.25 cm lg., white at first, yellow below, later concolorous white.—Bolivia: locality?
v. **fuauxianus** Backbg.: **Ar.** white, flocky; **Sp.** mostly only 1, straight, rarely decurved, to 5 mm lg.;
v. **rossianus** Heinr. & Backbg.: **Bo.** forming small broad cushions; **R.** very stout and lg.; **Seg.** rather larger; **Tub.** more prominent; **Sp.** 1–3, stouter, also 1–3 pale Ssp., all Sp. ± curving, more spreading; **Fl.** yellow or red, c. 2 cm lg., 3.2–4.2 cm ∅, also reported as brownish-yellow.—Bolivia (Huari-Huari).

T. platyacanthus (SD.) Lem. (2)
Bo. branching to form low bushes; **Seg.** glossy brown, reddish at first, oblong-spherical, soon becoming grey and unsightly; **Tub.** prominent; lower **Sp.** 3–4, more slender, appressed, also 2–3 longer, flattened, stiffly flexible Sp.—Argentina. Not Schumann's spec. of the same name, which has green shoots (v. neoplatyacanthus Backbg.).
v. **angustispinus** Backbg.: **Seg.** more thick-ovoid; **Tub.** several-sided, prominent, clearly defined; **Sp.** narrower, mostly lighter, fairly long, mostly erect, **Ssp.** absent;
v. **deflexispinus** (SD.) Backbg.: **Seg.** tapering to both ends; **Sp.** narrow, long, directed ± downwards;
v. **monvillei** (SD.) Backbg.: **Seg.** more slender; **Sp.** brown; possibly only a form;
v. **neoplatyacanthus** Backbg.: **Seg.** spherical, green(!), to 4.5 cm ∅, often reddish below the Ar.; **Glo.** dirty yellow; **Sp.** 2–4, like thin cardboard, glossy, fawn, with white edges and horizontal bands, to 6 cm lg., flat, Csp. 1, acutely 3-angled, rather shorter, still stiffer, often very twisted, sometimes with 1–2 downwardly directed Ssp.; **Fl.** ?—Argentina.

T. pseudorauppianus Backbg.: **Tephrocactus dimorphus** v. **pseudorauppianus** (Backbg.) Backbg. (Ritter's No. FR 242?), with brownish wool in young Ar.; not to be confused with T. sphaericus v. glaucinus which is bluish-green, with crowded Ar.; the above variety closely resembles the type, T. dimorphus (Ritter's No. FR 553?) with Ar. white at first.

T. pseudo-udonis Rauh & Backbg. (1)
Bo. forming broad cushions, not very tall; **Seg.** to 15 cm lg., 5 cm ∅; **H.** pure white, dense, long-projecting, tangled, scarcely curly (as in T. udonis).—Peru (Cordillera Raura, on the high plateaux).

T. punta-caillan Rauh & Backbg. (1)
Bo. in lax groups; **Seg.** 5–10 cm lg., 2 cm ∅, glossy green; **Tub.** oblong, narrow, apical ones prominent; **L.** to 1 cm lg., semicylindric; **Ar.** small, white; **Sp.** 2–6, projecting sideways or erect, thin, flexible, chestnut-brown; **Fl.** carmine(?).—Peru (Cordillera Negra, Punta Caillan, 4300 m).

T. pyrrhacanthus (K. Sch.) Backbg. (2)
Bo. low, branching, glossy, yellowish-green; **Seg.** ovoid or ellipsoid, to 2 cm lg., 1 cm ∅, tuberculate; **Ar.** white, 3 mm lg.; **Sp.** 5–8, sharp, yellowish-red, to 4 cm lg.; **Glo.** small, golden-yellow; **Fl.** to 3.5 cm lg., 3 cm ∅, golden-yellow; **Sti.** red.—Peru (Tacora and Cerro Tornarape, 4400 m).
  v. **leucoluteus** Backbg.: **Seg.** to 4 cm lg., 3 cm ∅; **Sp.** rather darker; **Fl.** light yellow.—Bolivia (Murillo, Calvario, 4000 m).

T. rarissimus Backbg. (2)
Bo. in lax groups, matt bluish-green; **Seg.** ovoid, tapering above, fairly strongly tuberculate; **Ar.** white; **Sp.** mostly 2–3, rarely more, to 4 cm lg., stiffly bristly, white, not sharp, sometimes with a very small Ssp.; **Fl.** ?—N. Bolivia (between Lake Titicaca and La Paz).

T. rauhii Backbg. (1)
Bo. in lax groups; **Seg.** relatively large, to 25 cm (!) h., to 8 cm ∅, resembling a small Oreocereus; **H.** stiffly projecting, dense, white or greyish-white; **Sp.** pale yellow, scarcely projecting; **Fl.** ?—S. Peru (Nevado Ausangate, Hacienda Lauramarca; probably also in the Cordillera Huaytapallana near Huancayo). (Fig. 425.) The largest and stoutest of the hairy spec. of Series 1: Elongati.

T. rauppianus (K. Sch.) Backbg.: I now regard this as only a rather weakly spined form of T. sphaericus; young shoots of the two plants closely resemble one another.

T. reicheanus (Esp.) Backbg. (2)
Bo. forming cushions to 2 m br., to 80 cm h.; **Seg.** ovoid or oblong-conical, to 5 cm lg., 2.5 cm ∅, green, whitish below, smooth; **Ar.** whitish to straw-coloured; **L.** 5 mm lg., whitish to reddish; **Glo.** numerous, cream to straw-coloured, to 2 cm lg. (!); **Sp.** mostly only in the upper part, unequal, 1–2 longer ones to 5 cm lg., 2 mm br. below, flattened above, often channelled, white or yellowish, sometimes directed sideways, often also 1–3 bristly Ssp. which are compressed, and downcurving or twisted; **Fl.** 8.8 cm lg., to 7.5 cm ∅, greenish-yellow; **style** white and reddish; **Sti.** green; **Fr.** 5 cm ∅, 4 cm lg.; **S.** 4 mm lg., flattened.—Chile (valley of the Rio Toro, 3550 m, and Baños del Toro, Andes of Elqui). Ritter considers the spec. identical

with T. leoncito (Werd.) Backbg.; certainly no great differences are recognisable, but Espinosa does not describe the Sp. as stiffly papery and flattened; instead he says: "Sp. flattened above, often channelled"; Werdermann makes no mention of this latter character.

T. retrospinosus Lem.: **Opuntia retrospinosa** Lem., one of the small spec. of the Series "Airampoae" which resemble Tephrocactus but have flat seg.

T. riojanus (Hoss.) Backbg.: **Tephrocactus alexanderi** (Br. & R.) Backbg.

T. russellii (Br. & R.) Backbg. (2)
Bo. forming small clumps to 20 cm br., dark green to ± reddish-brownish; **Seg.** small, spherical to ovoid, 2–4 cm lg.; **Sp.** in the upper part, 3–6, projecting, yellow, 2–3 cm lg., rather flattened, with 1 to several Ssp. to 1 cm lg.; **Glo.** later numerous, inconspicuous at first, to c. 2 mm lg.; **Fl.** ?; **Fr.** spherical, to 2.5 cm ∅, spineless; **S.** 4 mm lg.—Argentina (Mendoza, Potrillos).

T. schaeferi Ritt., not described: **Tephrocactus conoideus** Backbg. non Ritt.

T. setiger Backbg.: **Tephrocactus weberi** v. **setiger** (Backbg.) Backbg., with specially long, dense and erect Sp.

T. silvestris Backbg. (2)
Bo. almost concealed in the ground, branching, mid-green; **Seg.** minute, spherical, arranged in chains, ± spineless; **Sp.** later rarely 1, spreading, to 17 mm lg., and 1 appressed, to 1 mm lg.—Bolivia (near La Paz). Resembles T. minusculus.

T. sphaericus (Först.) Backbg. (2)
Bo. in colonies which are sometimes very large, prostrate to erect, ± laxly branching, leaf-green; **Seg.** spherical, sometimes ± oblong, to over 7 cm ∅; **Ar.** fairly large, rather prominent, relatively crowded, at first very much so, yellowish; **Sp.** very variable in number, sometimes few, often numerous and enveloping the Seg., brown or darker, greying, to 4 cm lg., sometimes stout, Csp. stouter, often curving, bent or projecting; **Fl.** to 4 cm ∅, (deep orange-) yellow; **Fr.** spherical, often very spiny, sometimes proliferating; **S.** spherical, white, 4 mm ∅, with a thin broad ring.—Peru (Arequipa).
  v. **glaucinus** Backbg.—Descr. Cact. Nov. III: 15. 1963 (2): **Bo.** forming groups by branching; **Seg.** ovoid, ± tapering to both ends, to c. 4 cm lg., 2.5 cm ∅, **epidermis** dull bluish-green, noticeable for its light and fine pitting; **Ar.** 1 cm apart, c. 4 mm lg., raised but flattened-rounded, with light brown felt (T. sphaericus: felt at first

yellowish-white, soon concolorous white); **Glo.** in the upper part of the Ar., little projecting, yellowish (further projecting in T. sphaericus); **Sp.** 10–14, irregularly directed, unequal, to c. 7 downwards, white, others porrect, pointing upwards or curving ± sideways, rarely set in the upper margin of the Ar., or if so, then short, fine, white, 1–2, other Sp. light horn-coloured, brownish above, or in part with brownish flecks, 8–13 mm lg., all thin; **Fl.** ?—Origin ? (S. Peru, Pacific side?). (Fig. 426.) Differentiated by the bluish-green colour, sharp white dots, the brownish coloured or flecked main Sp. and the brownish areolar felt from T. sphaericus in which only the fresh green new growth has indistinct spots;
v. **rauppianus** (K. Sch.) Backbg.: a variety or form with more numerous, weaker, appressed **Sp.**;
v. **unguispinus** (Backbg.) Backbg.: **Seg.** of habitat-plants often reddish-brown; **Sp.** later to 18, whitish-grey, often darker at first; main **Sp.** to c. 2.5 cm lg., mostly very bent and claw-like.— S. Peru (desert of La Joya).

T. **strobiliformis** (Berg.) Backbg.: **Tephrocactus articulatus** v. **inermis** (Speg.) Backbg.

T. subinermis (Backbg.) Backbg. (2)
Bo. forming fairly large groups, green; **Seg.** ovoid, tapering above; **Tub.** very prominent; **Ar.** yellowish-white; **Glo.** eventually in longer clusters, yellow; **Sp.** often missing, or 1–2, mostly spreading sideways, to 2.5 cm lg., horn-coloured or whitish; **Fl.** ?—N. Bolivia (high plateaux, 4000 m).

T. subsphaericus Backbg.: **Tephrocactus alexanderi** v. **subsphaericus** (Backbg.) Backbg.

T. subterraneus (R. E. Fries) Backbg. (2)
Bo. almost concealed in the ground, simple or little branching; **R.** thick, to 12 cm lg.; **Seg.** spherical, 2–4 cm lg.; **Tub.** ± 4-sided, flat, relatively crowded; **Sp.** 1–7, all radials, short, whitish to brownish (at first), thin, recurved, appressed, ± bent; **Fl.** brownish-white with a reddish tinge, c. 2.5 cm ∅; **Sep.** greenish; **Ov.** slender-conical, spiny above; **style** cream; **Sti.** reddish; **Fr.** to 1.5 cm lg.; **S.** 3 mm lg., irregularly shaped—N. Argentina (Jujuy, near Moreno and Javi). (Fig. 427.) Only recently re-collected.

T. tarapacanus (Phil.) Backbg. (2)
Bo. low, made up of many **Seg.**, these small, ovoid, c. 2 cm lg., 1 cm ∅; **Ar.** white-woolly; **Sp.** at the tip of the Seg., usually 3, straight, 12–15 mm lg., white, tipped yellowish; **Fl.** yellow. Schumann added: "**Ar.** small; **Glo.** yellowish-white; **Sp.** 1–2, sub-

ulate, ± compressed, reddish-yellow, to 2 cm lg.; **Fl.** to 3 cm lg., yellow".—Chile (Calaleste). Insufficiently known.

T. tortispinus Ritt., not described: "with dark twisted Sp." (FR 550). No further details available.

T. turpinii Lem.: a name formerly often applied to **Tephrocactus articulatus** v. **syringacanthus** (Pfeiff.) Backbg.

T. udonis (Wgt.) Backbg. (1)
Bo. forming cushions; **Seg.** to 13 cm lg., 6 cm ∅; **Ar.** grey; **H.** dense, tangled, to 7 cm lg., almost "wire"-like, flexible, curly; **Sp.** 2–4, unequal, to 3.5 cm lg., thin, sharp, brownish, later darker, also 1 Ssp. to 7 mm lg., bristly, decurved; **Fl.** ?—Peru (Cordillera Negra, 4300 m). Relatively rare in habitat.

T. unguispinus Backbg.: **Tephrocactus sphaericus** v. **unguispinus** (Backbg.) Backbg.

T. variiflorus Backbg. (2)
Bo. in small lax groups, mid-green; **Seg.** oblong, to c. 1.5 cm ∅; **Tub.** very flat, twice as lg. as br., separated by sinuate lines; **Ar.** yellowish; **Glo.** yellowish; **Sp.** rather small, yellowish, some appressed, others projecting, c. 2–4, unequal, dissimilar; **Fl.** fairly large, with c. 20 broadly linear Pet., ± truncate above, rather laxly radiating, to 18 mm lg., 6–10 mm br., carmine or carmine-pink, to very pale or yellowish-pink.—N. Argentina (pampa, S. of Villazon). Fl. very attractive. Found by Ritter (FR 91).

T. verticosus (Wgt.) Backbg. (1)
Bo. forming compact, flatter to convex cushions; **Seg.** to 10 cm lg., to 3 cm ∅, broad rather than tapering above; **H.** to 4 cm lg., densely tangled, somewhat curly, completely enveloping the Seg.; **Glo.** scarcely recognisable; **Sp.** 1–4, dissimilar, to 3 cm lg., light to darker brown or tipped reddish, projecting beyond the H.; **Fl.** carmine (also crimson?); **Fr.** oblong; **S.** ovate-circular.—Peru (Cordillera Negra, Katai Pass).

T. virgultus Backbg. n.sp. (2)
Bo. a laxly branching, small bush, intense green, later paler; **Seg.** to c. 2.5 cm lg., 1.5 cm ∅, sometimes to only 2 cm lg. at first, 8 mm ∅; **L.** green, c. 3 mm lg.; **Ar.** 5–9 mm apart, small at first, weakly white-felty, later with a compact tuft of felt to 2 mm lg.; **Glo.** whitish, scarcely visible through the felt; **Sp.** 0 at first, later to c. 5–8, straight, fairly firm, slightly spreading or porrect, to 12 mm lg., pale pinkish-white, soon grey; **Fl.** dark pink (acc. Muhr).—Origin ? (Fig. 428.)

T. weberi (Speg.) Backbg. (1)

Bo. forming low bushy colonies to 18 cm h., 30 cm br., yellowish-green; **Seg.** to 6 cm lg., 2 cm $\emptyset$, rather tuberculate above; **Tub.** crowded, spiralled, $\pm$ 4-sided, c. 6 mm br. and lg.; **Sp.** fairly crowded, 5–7, brownish to brown, to 5 cm lg., flexible, irregular, $\pm$ interlacing sideways or more distinctly so, smaller ones mostly lighter; **Fl.** small, yellow, rotate; **Fr.** 1 cm lg., dry (with Glo. inside? Speg.); **S.** hard, smooth, twisted.—Argentina (San Juán; Salta).

v. **dispar** (Cast. & Lelong) Backbg.: **Bo.** sometimes over 15 cm h.; **Seg.** to 7 cm lg., 1.5 cm $\emptyset$; smaller **Sp.** 3–4, white, bristly, spreading downwards, to 5 mm lg., also 4 $\pm$ erect, stiff, projecting **Sp.** c. 2 cm lg., reddish to horn-coloured; **Fl.** 2 cm lg.; **Fr.** spiny (Catamarca, Tucuman);

v. **setiger** (Backbg.) Backbg.: **Sp.** 4–6, to over 3.5 cm lg., horn-coloured to white, crowded, more strongly erect (Córdoba? Tucuman ?).

T. wilkeanus Backbg. (2)

Bo. grouping; **Seg.** c. 2.5 cm lg., 4 cm $\emptyset$, ovoid, tuberculate above; **Sp.** bristle-like, white, sometimes only 1 present; **Fl.** red (Wilke).—N. Bolivia (Viacha). Spination fine, slender; plant rare, never since re-collected.

T. yanganucensis Rauh & Backbg. (1)

Bo. forming flattened-convex cushions to 30 cm br.; **Seg.** crowded, to 5 cm lg., 2.5 cm $\emptyset$, bluish-green; **Tub.** rounded-oblong; **L.** 1 cm lg.; **Ar.** light, c. 2 mm lg.; **Sp.** 1–4, unequal, to c. 2.2 cm lg., light brown to reddish, projecting (in T. hirschii, which resembles this spec. when grafted, Sp. are more strongly appressed or directed upwards); **Fl.** c. 3 cm $\emptyset$, vivid carmine.—Peru (Cordillera Blanca, Quebrada Yanganuco, 3000 m). Seg. much longer in grafted plants.

T. zehnderi Rauh & Backbg. (2)

Bo. forming cushions to 50 cm br., 30 cm h., greyish-green to dark green; main **R.** stout, napiform; **Seg.** to 10 cm lg., to 3 cm $\emptyset$; **Tub.** convex at first; **Ar.** large, oval, white-woolly, to 11 mm lg., 8 mm br.; **Sp.** 3–8, longest ones to 3 cm lg., very stout, weakly curving, reddish-brown, later grey, Sp. on cultivated plants only few, thin, short, white; **Glo.** stoutly tufted and projecting on old Seg.; **Fl.** to 3 cm lg., to 4 cm $\emptyset$, reddish outside, yellow inside; **Fil.** yellow; **Sti.** white; **Fr.** spherical, yellowish, 2 cm lg., 1.5 cm $\emptyset$, spiny, with a deep floral scar.—S. Peru (Sarasassa Volcano, near Incuio, on lava-ash, 3500 m).

Thelocactus (K. Sch.) Br. & R. (199)

Plants spherical to elongated, with distinctly tuberculate ribs, mostly with stouter spination; spines sometimes brightly coloured (white, yellow, red or brown), or roughened and fibrous, sometimes subulate, the centrals in some cases flattened, flexible and longer. The areoles bearing the spines carry an extension, usually called a "long areole", from which the white, yellow or red and very attractive flowers arise; the latter and the fruits are scaly but otherwise glabrous. Some species offset from the base or even from the areoles, and three species show great variability. The seeds are predominantly black; in one case only, so far as known, they are dark brown, but they are probably always matt and never very small.—Distribution: USA (Texas) to Mexico (from the N. frontier to Querétaro, but not in Baja California). [(R); most species grow well.]

T. beguinii (Web.) Berg.: **Gymnocactus beguinii** (Web.) Backbg.

T. bicolor (Gal.) Br. & R.

Bo. mostly simple, spherical to oblong and tapering, varying according to form and locality, quite low or to 20 cm lg. and 10 cm $\emptyset$ (H. Bravo); **Ri.** 8–13, divided transversely into Tub.; **Rsp.** 9–18, to 3 cm lg.; **Csp.** mostly 4, individuals ascending to porrect, to 3–5 cm lg.; **Sp.** yellowish or light red, or red and yellowish, one of these $\pm$ compressed; **Fl.** 5–6 cm lg. and approximately as br., deep purplish-pink; **Ov.** and **Tu.** densely scaly, Sc. ciliate; **Sti.** pale yellow to pinkish-yellow; **Fr.** c. 1 cm lg., dehiscing irregularly from the base; **S.** 2 mm lg.—USA (S. Texas) to Central Mexico.

A variable spec., with the following more clearly distinguishable:

v. **bolansis** (Runge) Knuth: **Bo.** eventually cylindric; **Rsp.** to 25, thin; **Csp.** 3, thickened below; all **Sp.** white; **Fl.** over 7 cm $\emptyset$.—Mexico (Sierra Bola);

v. flavidispinus Backbg.: see **Thelocactus flavidispinus** (Backbg.) Backbg.;

v. **pottsii** (SD.) Backbg.: **Bo.** more spherical, 10–15 cm $\emptyset$; **Ri.** more broadly rounded; **Rsp.** mostly 10–11; **Csp.** strongly subulate, mostly downcurving, one upper **Sp.** flattened.—Mexico (Chihuahua);

v. schottii (Eng.) Davis: acc. Engelmann this is an oblong form, in contrast to the spherical Mexican one; but since the latter is v. pottsii, v. schottii must be regarded as identical with the type;

v. texensis Backbg.: **Bo.** oblong; **Rsp.** 12–13, with red flecks, sub-terete, sometimes also 1 flattened, whitish, to 2.5 cm lg.; **Csp.** c. 4, 3 of these subulate, 1 upper one to 7.3 cm lg., straw-coloured, thin, flattened, one Csp. sometimes flecked red at first.—USA (Texas);

v. **tricolor** (K. Sch.) Knuth: **Bo.** becoming strongly oblong in age; **Sp.** fairly crowded and stout, coloured more strongly red.—NE. Mexico.

T. bueckii (Klein) Br. & R.
Bo. simple, deep green; **Tub.** strongly developed, rather pointed and angular; **Sp.** c. (4–)7, reddish, dissimilar, some curving back or out, the longest ones often strongly elongated, all flexible; **Fl.** dark red; **Pet.** narrow.—Mexico. Plants also reported with stout recurved Sp.

T. conothelos (Reg. & Klein) Knuth
Bo. ± ovoid, to 10 cm h., to c. 7.5 cm ∅, greyish-green; **Ri.** tuberculate, in c. 12 spirals; **Tub.** to c. 2 cm lg.; **Rsp.** 14–16, white, ± appressed, to 1.8 cm lg., sometimes darker below; **Csp.** (1–)2–4, light, unequal and stouter, to over 3.5 cm lg., sometimes curving; **Fl.** 3.5 cm ∅, purplish-violet; **Ov.** scaly; **Fr.** 1.3 cm lg., 9 mm ∅, with Sc. 2 mm lg., greenish below, reddish-violet above—Mexico (Tamaulipas).
In the absence of Fl.-data, previously regarded as belonging to Gymnocactus. De Herdt, of Mortsel-Antwerp, was able to give me the necessary information, so that the spec. can now finally be referred here.

T. crassihamatus (Web.) Marsh.: **Glandulicactus crassihamatus** (Web.) Backbg.

T. ehrenbergii (Pfeiff.) Knuth
Bo. spherical at first, then oblong, offsetting to form mats, single heads to 12 cm h., 7 cm ∅, light green at first, becoming greyish-green; **Ri.** mostly 8–13 R. of spiralled stouter Tub. 1 cm h. and sometimes subdivided by a short transverse notch; **Ar.** yellowish at first; **Rsp.** mostly 6, thin-subulate, spreading, upper ones mostly longest, to 2 cm lg.; **Csp.** 0–1, to 2 cm lg., straight, stiff, yellowish to brownish; **Sp.** all darker at first, later mostly reddish below, finally often dropping; **Fl.** to 4 cm ∅, light carmine-pink to white.—Mexico (Hidalgo, Ixmiquilpan). Very close to T. leucacanthus.

T. flavidispinus (Backbg.) Backbg.
Bo. mostly simple, becoming elongated; **Ri.** fresh green, c. 13, almost completely divided into smaller spiralled Tub.; **Ar.** yellowish; **Rsp.** c. 20, yellowish, all appressed, interlacing, 1.8–2.4 cm lg.; **Csp.** 1, terete, straight, projecting, yellowish, red below, later yellowish-white; **Fl.** purplish-pink with the

throat more violet, c. 5 cm ∅, with a satin-like gloss.—USA (Texas). Grows particularly well when grafted. (Fig. 429.)

T. fossulatus (Scheidw.) Br. & R.: **Thelocactus hexaedrophorus** v. **fossulatus** (Scheidw.) Backbg.

T. gielsdorfianus (Werd.) Werd.: **Gymnocactus gielsdorfianus** (Werd.) (Werd.) Backbg.

T. goldii H. Bravo: **Gymnocactus horripilus** (Lem.) Backbg.

T. hastifer (Werd. & Böd.) Knuth
Bo. spherical at first, seedlings slender-clavate, becoming oblong-ovoid to cylindric, sometimes also ± tapering below; **Ri.** (13–)18–20, to 8 mm h., tuberculate; **Ar.** white at first; **Rsp.** 20–25, hyaline, ± rough, to 15 mm lg.; **Csp.** 4, 3 of these erect, rather brownish at first, the bottom one porrect, to 3 cm lg., pale horn-colour, darker above and below, all soon becoming chalky-white; **Fl.** to 4.5 cm ∅, pale violet-pink.—Mexico.

T. hertrichii (Weinb.) Borg: an insufficiently clarified spec. of Ferocactus, from Arizona.

T. heterochromus (Web.) van Oost.
Bo. depressed-spherical, simple, to 15 cm ∅, bluish to greyish-green; **Ri.** c. 9, with thick rounded Tub., these shrinking appreciably during the dry season; **Ar.** large, round, white; **Rsp.** 7–10, mostly terete, the top one ± broadly compressed, all ± projecting and ± recurved, fairly thick or stout, individuals sometimes more central; **Csp.** 1, equally stout, or much stouter and then sometimes channelled above, to 4 cm lg.; all **Sp.** reddish to brownish, or flecked, very variable in the whitish-reddish patterning or banding; **Fl.** to 6 cm lg., to 10 cm ∅, light violet, the centre often darker; **Fr.** to 1.5 cm ∅.—Mexico (Chihuahua to Coahuila).

T. hexaedrophorus (Lem.) Br. & R. (T.)
Bo. simple, bluish or greyish-green, to 15 cm h. and br.; **Ri.** 13, entirely divided into large, plump, ± 6-sided Tub., with acute transverse depressions; **Ar.** to 3.5 cm apart; **Rsp.** 6–9, dissimilar, projecting, 11–18 mm lg., straight to ± slightly curving; **Csp.** 2–3 cm lg., stouter, erect; **Sp.** yellowish to greyish-pink or brownish-red, ± finely annular; **Fl.** white, c. 6 cm lg. and to 8 cm ∅; **Ov.** with a few fringed Sc.—Mexico (Tamaulipas, San Luis Potosí).

v. **decipiens** Berg.: **Bo.** dark green; **Sp.** bent backwards, appressed, dirty yellowish-brown;

v. **droegeanus** (K. Sch.) Berg.: **Bo.** ash-grey; **Tub.** compressed;

v. **fossulatus** (Scheidw.) Backbg.: **Bo.** broadly

spherical, to 15 cm $\emptyset$; **Ri.** c. 13, often reddish; **Rsp.** (2-)4–5, to 3.5 cm lg., brown to grey; **Csp.** 1, to 4.5 cm lg., often slightly curving; **Sp.** all thickened below, often 4 of these cruciform, one upper Sp. smaller and thinner, centrals sometimes indistinctly banded; **Fl.** whitish or delicate pink; **Sc.** slightly ciliate.—Mexico (San Luis Potosí);
v. labouretianus Berg.: Ri. more coherent; only a form?
v. major (Quehl) Berg.: **Sp.** to 3 cm lg., attractively red; only a form?

T. horripilus (Lem.) Berg.: **Gymnocactus horripilus** (Lem.) Backbg.

T. knuthianus (Böd.) H. Bravo: **Gymnocactus knuthianus** (Böd.) Backbg.

T. krainzianus Oehme
Bo. spherical, caespitose, sometimes forming cushions, glossy, greyish-green, to 8 cm h., to over 6 cm $\emptyset$; **Ri.** 8, entirely divided into conical Tub. to 3 cm lg., the lower Tub. prominent and acute; **Rsp.** 10–13, projecting, to 4.5 cm lg., thickened below; **Csp.** 1, to 5.5 cm lg.; all **Sp.** light grey at first, reddish below; **Fl.** 5.5 cm lg., 9 cm $\emptyset$, glossy, light violet; **Sti.** cream; **S.** matt black.—Mexico.

T. leucacanthus (Zucc.) Br. & R.
Bo. shortly cylindric, to 15 cm lg., later offsetting quite freely from below or from the flanks and forming cushions; **Ri.** 8–13, often spiralled, recognisable as Ri. despite being made tuberculate by transverse constrictions; **Rsp.** 7–20, light yellow at first, then grey, spreading or recurved, sometimes banded; **Csp.** 0–1, blackish at first, later grey, moderately stout; **Fl.** yellow, 5 cm lg.; **Ov.** and **Tu.** with imbricate Sc.—Mexico (Hidalgo, Zimapán and Ixmiquilpan).
v. porrectus (Lem.) Backbg.: **Bo.** bluish-green; **Rsp.** 7–8(–9), appressed, to c. 2 cm lg.; **Csp.** 1, directed obliquely upwards or ± porrect, sometimes gently curving, very long, to c. 4 cm lg.; all **Sp.** dark reddish at first, flecked white, soon light-coloured; **Fl.** coppery.—Mexico (Hidalgo). This name is also applied to a hitherto undescribed plant with large or thick Tub., with acute transverse divisions, offsetting from the lower Ar.; Sp. to c. 9, brownish, ± flecked; Csp. 1, little longer;
v. pseudoporrectus nom. prop.: a plant labelled also T. porrectus, in the collection of Saint-Pie, Asson: Bo. leaf-green; Sp. clustered, spreading; Fl. probably red, but only dried material has been studied, so that no description is possible; however it is worth giving the plant at least a

provisional name so that it does not sink into oblivion;
v. **sanchezmejoradai** (J. Meyr.) Backbg.: only a form of v. schmollii Werd., since the descriptions are so similar. **Fil.** of this variety are purple; **style** pink; **Sti.** 6–9.—Mexico (Querétaro, 15 km E. of Cadereyta);
v. **schmollii** Werd.: **Ri.** c. 12, matt green to light greyish-green, tuberculate; **Rsp.** 13–19, whitish-grey, radiating, appressed, fairly dense, yellowish at first, brownish or red below, to 1.5 cm lg.; **Csp.** 0–1(–3), scarcely longer; **Fl.** 4 cm lg., opening widely, satiny, carmine-violet; **An.** erect; **Fil.** pale yellowish; **style** cream; **Sti.** yellow.—Mexico (Querétaro ?).

T. lloydii Br. & R.
Bo. simple, compressed-spherical, to 12 cm $\emptyset$, pale bluish-green; **Tub.** conspicuous but low, often broader than long, to 4 cm br.; **Ar.** (long Ar.) often extending halfway along the Tub.; **Sp.** mostly 8, sometimes also with one Ssp., terete or angular below, tipped yellowish to carmine, to 6 cm lg.; **Fl.** pale purple; **Sti.** pinkish-yellow.—Mexico (Zacatecas).

T. lophophoroides Werd.: **Turbinicarpus lophophoroides** (Werd.) F. Buxb. & Backbg.

T. lophothele (SD.) Br. & R.
Bo. simple to quite freely caespitose, spherical to elongated; **Ri.** 15–20, spiralled, strongly divided into Tu., these more warty above, connections often only narrow; **Ar.** white to yellowish; **Rsp.** 3–5, to 3 cm lg., subulate, terete, thickened below, sharp, black to light brown or yellowish at first, upper ones ruby-red at first; **Csp.** 0–1, scarcely longer, or only occasionally so; **Fl.** 6 cm lg., 5 cm $\emptyset$, colour varying from yellowish-white to sulphur-yellow, peach-colour to pinkish-red, with a silvery sheen; **style** white; **Sti.** light yellow.—Mexico (Chihuahua).

T. mandragora (Frič) F. Buxb. & Oehme: **Gymnocactus mandragora** (Frič) Backbg.

T. nidulans (Quehl) Br. & R.
Bo. hemispherical, to c. 20 cm $\emptyset$, to 10 cm h., bluish-green at first, later greyish-green, crown white; **Ri.** 20 or more, spiralled, strongly divided into conical, obliquely truncate Tub. c. 2 cm h., narrowly connected; **Ar.** c. 1 cm lg., felty at first; **Sp.** scarcely differentiated, especially later, the lower half of the Ar. with c. 6–8 Sp. 1 cm lg., soon weathering and dropping, the upper part with 3 to 2 cm lg., towards the centre another 4 Sp. to 6 cm lg., all Sp. dark horn-colour at first, frosted, also furrowed and banded, 4–6 larger Sp. finally

persisting, these glossy greyish-white, with disjunctive fibres like asbestos; **Fl.** 4 cm lg., yellowish-whitish; **Ov.** with green ciliate Sc.—Mexico.

T. phymatothelos (Pos.) Br. & R.
Bo. depressed-spherical, with sparse cranial felt, to 10 cm ∅, 5 cm h.; **Ri.** c. 13, with narrowly connected, swollen Tub.; **Ar.** to 2 cm apart; **Sp.** absent or 1–3, straight, subulate, to 2 cm lg., blackish at first, then greying; **Fl.** pink to purplish-pink, c. 5 cm ∅.—Mexico.

T. porrectus (Lem.) Knuth: **Thelocactus leucacanthus** v. **porrectus** (Lem.) Backbg.

T. pottsii (SD.) H. Bravo: **Thelocactus bicolor** v. **pottsii** (SD.) Backbg.—Acc. Br. & R. synonymous with **Thelocactus heterochromus** (Web.) van Oost.

T. rinconensis (rinconadensis) (Pos.) Br. & R.
Bo. simple, to 12 cm ∅, to 8 cm h., greyish to bluish-green, with sparse cranial felt; **Ri.** mostly 13, thick, strongly sinuate, divided into rounded, conical-angular Tub., these narrowly connected; **Ar.** 2.5 cm apart; **Sp.** mostly 4, to 1.5 cm lg., subulate; **Csp.** 0; **Fl.** 4 cm lg. and ∅, white, with a delicate pink dorsal stripe, finally glossy concolorous white; **style** white, pinkish-red above; **Sti.** golden-yellow.—Mexico (Nuevo León).

T. roseanus (Böd.) Berg.: **Escobaria roseana** (Böd.) Backbg.

T. sanchezmejoradai J. Meyr.: **Thelocactus leucacanthus** v. **sanchezmejoradai** (J. Meyr.) Backbg.

T. saueri (Böd.) Berg.: **Gymnocactus saueri** (Böd.) Backbg.

T. saussieri (Web.) Berg.
Bo. broadly spherical, to 20 cm ∅; **Tub.** in c. 20 R., light green, prominent, oblong; **Rsp.** c. 9–11, radiating, white, to 1.5 cm lg.; **Csp.** to 4, ± subulate-acicular, 3–4 cm lg., brown at first; **Fl.** to 4 cm ∅, purple; **Tu.**, **Ov.** and **Fr.** scaly, otherwise as in T. conothelos.—Mexico (San Luis Potosí). Final classification in Thelocactus had to await the results of more recent investigations, i.e. verification of Sc. on Fl. and Fr.

T. schmollii Werd.: **Thelocactus leucacanthus** v. **schmollii** Werd.

T. schwarzii Backbg.
Bo. simple, oblong, to 6 cm h., c. 5.5 cm ∅, bluish-green; **Ri.** c. 13, ± completely resolved into Tub.; **Ar.** oblong, whitish; **Rsp.** 13–14, curving ± towards the Bo., yellowish, sometimes red below at first, 3

upper Sp. flattened, 2 of these to c. 17 mm lg., the uppermost one to 2.7 cm lg., directed towards the crown, more strongly flattened; **Csp.** 0; **Fl.** to 8.5 cm br., reddish-purple, scarlet at the centre; **Sti.** reddish-scarlet; **Fr.** spherical, brownish-violet; **S.** 3 mm lg., matt, dark brown.—Mexico (Tamaulipas).

T. smithii (Muehlpfrdt.) Borg: **Gymnocactus beguinii** v. **smithii** (Muehlpfrdt.) Backbg.

T. stanleyi was only a name used by Schmoll, Cadereyta, Mexico, and never described. Nothing further known of this plant.

T. subterraneus Backbg.: **Gymnocactus subterraneus** (Backbg.) Backbg.

T. tulensis (Pos.) Br. & R.
Bo. simple or offsetting, spherical to elongated, dark green, to c. 12 cm h. and ∅, with short white cranial felt; **Ri.** c. 10, the Ar. set on swollen Tub. with rather narrow, deep connections; **Tub.** plumply conical, to 2 cm h., ± 6-sided; **Ar.** 2.5 cm apart, white; **Rsp.** 6–8, lower ones to 1 cm lg., upper ones to 1.5 cm lg., the latter more bristle-like and ± appressed upwards, others brownish at first, then white; **Csp.** 1(–2), sometimes 3, dissimilar, whitish to horn-coloured, dark-tipped, often rather angular and flattened, straight or curving, to almost 4 cm lg.; **Fl.** c. 4 cm lg., silvery-white suffused delicate pink, with a carmine M.-stripe on both surfaces; **Sti.** pale yellow.—Mexico (Tamaulipas, Tula).

T. uncinatus (Gal.) Marsh.: **Glandulicactus uncinatus** (Gal.) Backbg.

T. valdezianus (Möll.) H. Bravo: **Gymnocactus valdezianus** (Möll.) Backbg.

T. viereckii (Werd.) H. Bravo: **Gymnocactus viereckii** (Werd.) Backbg.

T. wagnerianus Berg.
Bo. oblong to cylindric, to over 20 cm h., to c. 6 cm ∅, often offsetting from below, densely spiny; **Ri.** 13, straight or ± spiralled, obtuse, tuberculate; **Ar.** to 8 mm apart, white at first; **Rsp.** to c. 20, radiating, projecting, ± pectinate, stout, mostly ± reddish-yellow, densely interlacing, the upper ones longest and appearing more like Csp.; **Csp.** 1 at first, later 3–4, straight or slightly curving, bulbously thickened below, to 2 cm lg.; **Sp.** terete, an attractive red on new growth, or all yellow, or yellow and red; **Fl.** red.—E. Mexico. Close to T. bicolor, but the Sp. are not flattened and the habit is more slender; however this spec. could still be regarded as a variety of T. bicolor.

T. ysabelae K. Schlange and v. brevispinus K. Schlange: **Gymnocactus ysabelae** (K. Schlange) Backbg. and v. **brevispinus** (K. Schlange) Backbg.

Thelocephala Y. Ito: **Neochilenia** Backbg. pro parte.

Thelomastus Frič: only a name, applied to a combination of Thelocactus (K. Sch.) Br. & R. with Echinomastus Br. & R., which was also attempted by other authors. More recent investigations have enabled the two genera to be more clearly delimited; in any event, each consists of a characteristic group of species.

Thrixanthocereus Backbg. (178)

Slender Cerei, mostly simple, rarely branching from the base, with numerous finely tuberculate ribs, bearing a long-decurrent, superficial cephalium which even later is only moderately sunken and does not arise from a seam-like depression, or one extending to the stem's axis; this cephalium consists of stiffly erect hairs interspersed with longer bristles; young plants have a basal ring of bristles, as in Micranthocereus Backbg. The berry-like fruits are hairy, and dehisce by means of several longitudinal tears; the seeds vary much in appearance—a further proof of the fact that seeds are an unsatisfactory means towards classification; those of the type-species resemble Astrophytum, i.e. they are brownish, fairly soft and have a large hilum, while in another species they are firm, small and black. The nocturnal flowers remain open for some time during the succeeding day and have a tube with fairly long hairs.—Distribution: N. Peru, at higher altitudes in the Andes. [(R); grafting hastens growth, but the spination then becomes more open.]

T. blossfeldiorum (Werd.) Backbg. (T.)
Bo. simple, rarely branching from below, to c. 3 m h.; **St.** to 7 cm $\varnothing$; **Ri.** 18–25, low, fairly narrow; **Ar.** c. 5 mm apart, with flocky white wool at first; **Rsp.** c. 20–25, thin-acicular, to 8 mm lg., hyaline; **Csp.** typically c. 7, 1–2 of these longer, 1 often to c. 3 cm lg., all dark brown at first, soon in part greying, strong-acicular to thin-subulate, variable, sometimes much lighter to whitish and fine; **Ceph.** with yellowish-white wool interspersed with hyaline Br. and others which are darker, stiffer, to c. 5 cm lg.; **Fl.** c. 6 cm lg., funnelform, rotate, yellowish to cream-coloured, the lowest Sc. with an awn-like extension; **Fr.** greenish.—N. Peru (Huancabamba and Olmos valleys). (Fig. 430–433.)
While the plant is variable, two forms are more clearly distinguishable: f. albidior with dense, fine,

white Sp., the Csp. sometimes bristly-fine and white, at most with slightly reddish tips, the basal hair-like Br. long, fine; this form already shows intermediates to T. cullmannianus, or at least no longer bears a close resemblance to the type-species. In f. paucicostatus the Ri. are more distant and fewer, likewise the hairy Br. at the base of young plants, while the Csp., apart from the longest ones, are shorter.

T. cullmannianus Ritt.
Bo. to over 2 m h., greyish-green, scarcely offsetting from below; **St.** to 6 cm $\varnothing$; **Ri.** 18–24; **Ar.** whitish; **Sp.** not recognisable as Rsp. and Csp., to 90–120, white, very fine, more central ones often red-tipped, mostly 1–2 rather stouter and directed upwards, yellowish or brownish-yellow to brown; **Ceph.** to 4 cm br.; **Ar.** light brown; **Br.-Sp.** hair-fine, mingled with one or two darker ones (acc. photo, Cullmann), sometimes also ± brownish; **Fl.** to 6 cm lg.; **Fr.** to 2.25 cm lg.; **S.** dark brown, as in the type-species.—N. Peru (Cajamarca). (Fig. 434.)
Since the type-spec. is more strongly variable than would appear to be the case from previously published literature, while the seeds of the two preceding spec. also resemble one another, T. cullmannianus is more probably a local form which, together with f. albidior, is referable to the complex of the type-spec.

T. senilis Ritt.
Bo. slender, columnar, completely enveloped in dense fine white Br.; **Ri.** (14–)18, low, slightly tuberculate; **Ar.** crowded, white; **Sp.** not recognisable as Rsp. or Csp., numerous, to over 60, fine, white, apical ones tipped reddish-brown to darker, occasional Csp. later appearing, these longer to fairly long and stout, horn-coloured, developing earlier on plants grafted on a vigorous stock; **Fl.** to 6 cm lg., to 4 cm $\varnothing$, purple; **Ceph.** brown; **S.** black, round, firm, 1.5 mm lg.—N. Peru. (Fig. 435.)
Ritter says the type-spec. has "seeds scattered by the wind", but this is fictitious; if true, why does the second spec. not have them as well? The question remains open as to why quite different types of seeds should occur within one and same genus (as also happens in Gymnocalycium, Parodia, etc.); presumably this is associated with genetic processes and has nothing to do with "suitability for the purpose" of the seed-shape. The same comments are also applicable to Ritter's term "wind-scattered fruits", which he uses elsewhere.

Toumeya Br. & R (206)

Very small plants, mostly solitary, with papery flattened spines which are longer persistent. The bellshaped to cylindric flowers open only moderately wide; the ovaries bear ± scattered little scales, in part also with small spines above, these resembling those on the plant-body. The fruit is fairly dry, spherical, thin-membranous, with 1–2 residual scales above, and dehisces by longitudinal tears. L. Benson has united the rare species of this monotypic genus with Pediocactus (see under the latter), but comparisons of the two plants in flower, with the flowers in Toumeya borne centrally, show so little resemblance that their unification is quite arbitrary (see again under Pediocactus).—Distribution: USA (New Mexico and N. Arizona, occurring only singly, and hard to find). [(G).)

Helia Bravo and Marshall have united Turbinicarpus with this genus, probably because the former also shows flexible spines; but the flowers, and the naked berry-fruits with their different type of dehiscence, are completely dissimilar; unification ignores the fact that Nature has created in Turbinicarpus a clearly distinguishable group of species, with generically identical characters. The Toumeya-combinations of the above authors will thus be found here under Turbinicarpus F. Buxb. & Backbg.

T. krainziana Frank: **Turbinicarpus krainzianus** (Frank) Backbg.

T. papyracantha (Eng.) Br. & R.
Bo. to 10 cm h., 2.5 cm ∅, rarely offsetting from the base or from the Ar. except in grafted plants which sometimes offset very freely; **Ri.** made up entirely of conical Tub.; **Rsp.** c. 5–9, mostly 3–4 mm lg., white, terete or 1 or more flattened and thin; **Csp.** normally 4, cruciform, to 2 cm lg., occasionally to 5 cm lg., papery, flat, sometimes ± furrowed; **Fl.** c. 2.2 cm lg., 1.25 cm ∅, with a satiny sheen, white; **Sti.** 5–6, white; **S.** fairly large, smooth, black, keeled, with a large hilum.—USA (New Mexico; N. Arizona). (Fig. 436.)
The papery Sp. persist, even on old plants; Csp. are at first often slightly brownish, soon becoming greyish-whitish.

Trichocereus (Berg.) Ricc. (86)

A genus of columnar cacti of very variable size, sometimes very large to tree-like, others forming only low colonies. The spination is equally variable. The constant character is the funnelform shape of the nocturnal flowers, this in some cases being fairly long, while others have a stouter tube, but in form and hair-development they quite closely resemble Echinopsis. Since one species of the latter genus is known to attain a height of 1.5 m, while Trichocereus includes quite low-growing

grouping plants, in both cases showing a columnar habit, any generic delimitation based on growth-form and floral characters is difficult (see also the introductory remarks to Echinopsis). Nevertheless the relative groups of species, like those from Chile, are so clearly distinct that a conventional segregation of Echinopsis and Trichocereus became inevitable, in order to overcome the extremely difficult consequences resulting from unification; this consideration should be given due weight in other similar cases. At one time the Helianthocereus species also were included in Trichocereus—the tall-growing species despite their uniformly divergent habit, and the lower-growing ones irrespective of the fact that, like all members of Helianthocereus, they have diurnal flowers which are also brightly coloured; consequently there was continuing uncertainty as to where they should be referred. But here again, segregation has proved beneficial; and a similar delimitation can usefully be carried out within the Genus Trichocereus, since the flowers of the Chilean species, which in some cases remain open for several days, are also more bellshaped-funnelform:

SG.1: Trichocereus: Flower-length averaging 18 cm;

SG.2: Medioeulychnia Backbg.: Flower-length averaging 10 cm, flowers (in part) remaining open for several days.

The figures in brackets after the different specific names refer to the appropriate subgenus. The fruits of Trichocereus are only insignificantly different from those of Echinopsis since, at most, they are only slightly larger, spherical or oblong, almost always green and hairy, rarely reddish—and this too occasionally occurs in Echinopsis. The seeds, so far as known, are black, rarely dark brown.—Distribution: from Ecuador to S. Central Argentina, and in Chile. [(R).] For any specific names not found here, see under Helianthocereus.

T. bridgesii (SD.) Br. & R. (1)
Bo. forming a tall branching shrub to 5 m h., pale green, ± frosted; **branches** to 15 cm ∅; **Ri.** 4–8, rounded, later flatter; **Sp.** 2–6, yellowish, acicular to subulate, dissimilar, to 10 cm lg., shorter in cultivated plants; **Fl.** 18 cm lg., white; **Fr.** oblong, 6 cm lg.—Bolivia (La Paz).

I T. cajasensis (FR 869): no description available.

T. carmarguensis Card. (1)
Bo. columnar, to 50 cm h.; **branches** ± curving, ascending, light green; **Ri.** 14, very low; **Rsp.** 12–13, radiating, to 3 cm lg.; **Csp.** 2–3, to 5 cm lg.; **Sp.** all acicular, yellow or ash-coloured; **Fl.** to 20 cm lg., white; **Sep.** purplish-green; **Tu.** and **Ov.**

with brown and white H.; **Fr.** spherical to ovoid, 2 cm $\varnothing$; **S.** dark brown, glossy.—Bolivia (Cinti, near Camargo). Appears closely to resemble T. strigosus.

T. campos-portoi Werd.: **Arthrocereus campos-portoi** (Werd.) Backbg.

T. candicans (Gill.) Br. & R. (1)
Bo. erect or upcurving, to 75 cm lg., yellowish-green, forming colonies to 3 m br.; **branches** 8–12 cm $\varnothing$ or more; **Ri.** 9–11, broad, low; **Ar.** large, white; **Rsp.** 10–12, to 4 cm lg.; **Csp.** mostly 4 recognisable as such, to 8 cm lg.; all **Sp.** fairly stoutly subulate to stoutly acicular, yellowish or horn-coloured, spreading; **Fl.** to 20 cm lg., strongly perfumed, white; **Fr.** ellipsoid-spherical.—Argentina (Mendoza; Córdoba).
    v. **courantii** K. Sch. (Cereus): see under **Trichocereus courantii** (K. Sch.) Backbg.;
    v. **gladiatus** (Lem.) Berg.: **Bo.** bluish to pale green, to 65 cm h., little branching; **branches** to 14 cm $\varnothing$; **Ri.** to 11; **Ar.** large; **Rsp.** to 13, to 5 cm lg.; **Csp.** 1–4, to over 7.5 cm lg.; **Sp.** more subulate, yellow, often banded red, or red below, sometimes twisted;
    v. roseoflorus Backbg., on the basis of most recent information, is referable to the spec. described here for the first time: Helianthocereus pseudocandicans Backbg. (see under the latter);
    v. **tenuispinus** (Pfeiff.) Backbg.: **Bo.** intense bluish-green, less freely branching, to 85 cm h., to c. 13 cm $\varnothing$; **Ri.** 9–11, to 4 cm br. below; **Rsp.** 12–13; **Csp.** 1(–4); **Sp.** faded yellow, brownish-red below, all thin and rather short; **Fl.** white.

T. cephalomacrostibas (Werd. & Backbg.) Backbg. (2)
Bo. in dense groups to 2 m h.; **St.** to 10 cm $\varnothing$, greyish-green; **Ri.** 8, broad, thickened around the Ar. which are divided by transverse furrows and are to 1.5 cm lg. and br., thickly brown-felty, prominent, very crowded at the apex; **Rsp.** to c. 20, very short, subulate; **Csp.** 1–3(–4), very stout, to 12 cm lg., dark brown at first, later faded grey, sometimes angular and channelled, rather curving and variously projecting, in part interlacing; **Fl.** to c. 12 cm lg., white, c. 10 cm $\varnothing$ (acc. photo, × 0.5 magnification, by Akers in C. & S. J. [US], XX: 9, 131. 1948, Fig. 98); **Fr.** oblong-spherical, reddish or yellowish-orange.—S. Peru (above Mollendo). This spec. has been compared with Weberbauerocereus but the Fl. are much larger or wider. Rauh is correct in stating that this spec. is close to Weberbauerocereus—but the same could be said of all the SG. Medioeulychnia. It is a group within Trichocereus which is intermediate to the closely related Genus Weberbauerocereus.

T. chalaensis Rauh & Backbg. (1)
Bo. with erect branches, to 4 m h.; **branches** swelling during the foggy season to 15 cm $\varnothing$; **Ri.** 8, c. 2 cm br., with a transverse furrow above the Ar., this furrow with a plane surface above and below; **Rsp.** 6–10, to 1 cm lg.; **Csp.** 2–3, to 5 cm lg., dark brown at first, or blackish above; **Fl.** 17 cm lg., 10 cm br.; **Tu.** 2 cm thick, with black H.; **Sep.** wine-red above, green at midway; **Pet.** white; **Sti.** white.—S. Peru (8 km S. of Chala).

T. chilensis (Colla) Br. & R. (2)
Bo. columnar, branching from the base, to over 3 m h.; **branches** numerous, stout; **Ri.** to 16–17, low, broad, tuberculate; **Rsp.** 8–12, to 4 cm lg.; **Csp.** 1, short, to 4–7(–12) cm lg.; **Sp.** amber at first, or blackish, tobacco-brown or intermediate shades, later whitish-grey, often darker-tipped; **Fl.** to 14 cm lg., concolorous white; **Sep.** reddish or brownish-white; **Sti.** cream; **Fr.** spherical.—Chile (Prov. Atacama to Prov. Curico, with a distribution measuring 600 km from N. to S.).
A very variable spec., hence the many synonymous names for forms. The specific name was first written as "chiloensis"; acc. Skottsberg this could be regarded as an incorrect spelling of a geographical name, and could therefore be amended (the plant certainly does not grow in Chiloë); the spelling "chilensis" was used by both Pfeiffer and Schumann.
    v. **eburneus** (Phil.) Marsh. appears to be more justifiable as a variety; **Bo.** stouter; **Sp.** brownish at first, soon becoming ivory-white; **Fl.** pink, or suffused pink (Marshall, Borg).
The spec. has at times been confused with T. litoralis (Joh.) Loos., also from Chile, which it somewhat resembles; T. litoralis has yellowish Sp. which are appreciably shorter, while the Fl. are believed to remain open for several days.

T. chuquisacanus (FR 863A): no description available.

T. coquimbanus (Mol.) Br. & R. (2)
Bo. prostrate or decumbent, forming large colonies; **St.** to 1.2 m lg., to 10 cm $\varnothing$; **Ri.** to 14; **Ar.** large, round, shortly woolly; **Sp.** to c. 20, very dissimilar, **Csp.** scarcely differentiated, sometimes 1 longer, stoutly subulate, to over 5.5 cm lg., shortest Sp. only c. 12 mm lg., all terete, grey, dark-tipped; **Fl.** to 12 cm lg., white, fairly strongly black-hairy; **Fr.** spherical, green, 5 cm $\varnothing$.—Chile (Prov. Coquimbo, along the coast).

T. courantii (K. Sch.) Backbg. (1)
Bo. erectly columnar, to 35 cm h., over 7 cm $\varnothing$, dull green, offsetting from the base; **Ri.** c. 10; **Rsp.** 9–11 and more, finally to c. 20, faded yellow to brownish;

Csp. 1–4, similarly coloured, darker and thickened below; **Fl.** 24 cm lg., rose-scented.—Argentina (Bahia Blanca; Rio Negro; Rio Colorado).

Acc. Spegazzini, old plants can be 1.5 m h.; this spec. is one of the best and most robust grafting-stocks.

T. cuzcoensis B. & R. (1)
Bo. erect, to 6 m h., densely branching, light green at first; **Ri.** 7–8, low, rounded; **Ar.** to only 1.5 cm apart; **Sp.** numerous, to 12, very stout, to 7 cm lg., thickened below, subulate, yellow; **Fl.** c. 14 cm lg., white.—Peru (Cuzco region).

T. damazioi (K. Sch.) Werd.: **Arthrocereus damazioi** (K. Sch.) Berg.

T. deserticolus (Werd.) Loos (2)
Bo. branching from below, becoming 1–1.5 m h.; **Ri.** 8–10, deeply incised, 1.5–2.5 cm h., with distinct furrows above the Ar.; **Ar.** to 1.5 cm apart, covered with dark woolly felt; **Rsp.** irregular, c. 15–25, thin-subulate, 1–1.5 cm lg., dark to grey; **Csp.** 1–3, to 12 cm lg., sometimes rather curving; **Fl.** 7–8 cm lg., pure white, with dark wool outside.—Chile (near Taltal). Acc. Werd.: "related to C. nigripilis". See Tricho. fulvilanus Ritt.

T. escayachensis Card.: **Helianthocereus escayachensis** (Card.) Backbg.

T. fasicularis (Mey.) Br. &R.: **Weberbauerocereus fascicularis** (Mey.) Backg.

T. fulvilanus Ritt.—"Kakt. u.a. Sukk.", 13: 10, 165–167. 1962 (2)
Bo. branching from the base, grass-green to greyish-green, 1–1.5 m h. and more; branches 4–7 cm $\varnothing$; Ri. 8–12(–13), obtuse, notched across half the width; **Ar.** shortly oval, to 1.25 cm lg., with orange to reddish or yellowish felt at first, later brownish black (light brownish in seedlings, then becoming whitish from the base upwards: Backbg.); Sp. dark brown at first, greying; **Rsp.** 9–12, dissimilar, thinner to subulate, mostly 1.5–3 cm lg.; **Csp.** 2–4(–6), spreading, 3–10 cm lg., occasionally to 18 cm lg., stouter-subulate (judging by a photo of Ritter's), later with the upper Sp. often finer (as also in several spec. of SG. Medioeulychnia); **Fl.** apical, 9–12 cm lg., 7–9 cm $\varnothing$, perfumed; **Tu.** with black H.; **Ov.** with grey and black H.; **style** light green; **Fr.** green, spherical, c. 4 cm $\varnothing$; **S.** $\pm$ matt black, 1.2 mm lg.—Chile (Taltal, or from Chañaral to El Cobre).
When one considers that the Chilean spec. can be very variable in form—T. chilensis, indeed, shows wide variablity—then T. fulvilanus cannot be regarded as more than a form of T. deserticolus.

The following characters are common to both spec.: areolar felt becoming darker with age, number and length as well as colour and thickness of spination, transverse notching over the Ar., overall height of mature plants, and above all even the locality; small divergences of Fl.-size and number of Sp. are well within the normal range, and no genuine differences can be recognised. It should also be recalled that Werdermann probably made his description from dried material. Before any description of a new spec., a comparison should obviously have been made with the living type-material, but this is believed to have been destroyed in Dahlem. What is the point of depositing type-material and making a new description unless a check is made as to identity with any previously described spec.? This shows the special effectiveness of the differential diagnosis with its brevity and emphasis on essential data, since similarities are then more speedily recognised than would be possible by means of a long descriptive text. I mention the point here to show why I have never considered the deposition of type-material to be a sufficient answer in itself, without adequate verification. Close-up photographs, especially those in colour, clear differentiation and adequate habitat photographs are, overall, preferable to earlier methods, and this case proves my point. Moreover a descriptive text together with photo, reproduced in printed form, is an insurance against loss, easily understood internationally, and also more readily available to all interested parties.

T. gladiatus (Lem.) Backbg.: **Trichocereus candicans** v. **gladiatus** (Lem.) Berg.

T. glaucus Ritt.—Kakt. u.a. Sukk., 13: 11, 180–181. 1962 (1)
Bo. forming a bush 1–2 m h., branching from the base; **branches** 5–8 cm $\varnothing$, first bluish then greyish-green; **Ri.** 7–9, notched; **Ar.** grey, 1–2 cm apart, to 7.5 mm lg.; **Sp.** black, greying; **Rsp.** 7–10, to 1.5 cm lg., stoutly acicular, somewhat flattened, sometimes also brown; **Csp.** 3–6, 2–8 cm lg., $\pm$ erect; **Fl.** 13–19 cm lg., perfumed, white or delicate pink; **Pet.** to 2 cm br.; **Sep.** pink to $\pm$ blood-red; **Tu.** greyish-green; **nectary** brownish, to 2.3 cm lg.; **style** pale green; **Fil.** white, greenish below; **Fr.** grass-green, 4 cm lg., pulp white; **S.** 1.2 mm lg., weakly glossy, black.—Peru (Dept. Arequipa, along the lower Rio Tambo, on mountains and in the region of Ilo) (FR 270). (T. uyupampensis v. glaucus?).

v. (forma Ritt.) **pendens** Ritt.—l.c.: **Bo.** hanging, or inclined and ascending; **Fl.**, **Fr.** and **S.** unknown.—Chile (coastal cliffs near Arica) (T. uyupampensis Backbg. ?).

Acc. Ritter, this is a survival, only 3 plants having been found. In view of the unusual habit, and the fact that many characters are found in common, these may have been representatives of T. uyupampensis which perhaps once had a much more southerly distribution but, because of the increasing desiccation of the intervening areas (Ritt.), it has since disappeared there; it is the only prostrate or hanging plant of the sort in S. Peru. If my assumption is correct, the type of T. uyupampensis would need to be re-designated a variety, as shown above.

T. grandiflorus Backbg. n.sp. (1)

Somewhat like T. camarguensis. **Bo.** slender, erect; **St.** not as stout as in T. spachianus; **Sp.** concolorous yellowish, ± equal, **Csp.** little projecting; **Fl.** enormous, white, c. 17 cm lg., 23 cm ∅; **Tu.** and **Ov.** with brown H.; **Sep.** linear, brownish-olive; **Pet.** broadly spatulate, c. 3 cm br.; **throat, Fil.** and the lower part of the **style** light green; **Sti.** c. 15, 1.6 cm lg. Nectary absent (!).—Bolivia (no more precise locality known). (Fig. 437.)

The spec. can be seen in the Botanical Garden of "Les Cèdres", St. Jean, Cap Ferrat; it may have been found by Ritter, or it may be the spec. Cardenas regarded as T. lamprochlorus.

T. huascha (Web.) Br. & R.: **Helianthocereus huascha** (Web.) Backbg.

T. knuthianus Backbg. (1)

Bo. eventually tree-like, in age with a longer subterete **trunk,** to 3 m h.; **branches** to 10 cm ∅, frosted, brilliant light bluish-green; **Ri.** c. 7, rounded, to 3 cm br.; **Rsp.** 7; **Csp.** 1, to 10 cm lg., it and the Rsp. soon becoming concolorous whitish-grey although tipped yellowish at first; **Ar.** large, with much felt; **Fl.** large, white.—Peru (upper course of the Rio Marañon).

T. lamprochlorus (Lem.) Backbg. n.comb. (Cereus lamprochlorus Lem., Cact. Aliqu. Nov., 30. 1838, non T. lamprochlorus sensu Britton & Rose) (1).

Acc. the original diagnosis: "**Ri.** 15; **Sp.** stiff, sharp, ± reddish-brown, translucent yellow when young, brown-tipped; **Rsp.** 12–15, 6–9 mm lg.; **Csp.** 4, cruciform, longer, stouter, lowest one downcurving, 2.7–3 cm lg.; **Fl.** and **Fr.** not known".—Bolivia (acc. Rümpler).

Obviously this plant has been confused with T. neolamprochlorus since the time of Salm-Dyck, hence my repeating the description below. Britton and Rose recognised that more than one spec. was involved. In the Botanical Garden at "Les Cedres", I saw the true spec., which has a conspicuously glossy green epidermis (hence the name "lamprochlorus"):

Bo. erect, as robust as T. spachianus, glossy intense green; **Ri.** rounded, c. 11–12 at first; **Rsp.** 7 at first, later more numerous; **Csp.** 1 at first, later 4, cruciform; **Sp.** yellow below at first, brown above, later light-coloured; **Fl.** 15.5 cm lg., 12–14 cm ∅, white; **Sep.** narrow, olive-brown; **Pet.** broader; **Sti.** 2 cm lg., yellowish-greenish; **Tu.** with greyish-brown H.—E. Bolivia (precise locality not known). (Fig. 438.)

The spec. regarded here as the true T. lamprochlorus, which was found by Cardenas and probably also by Ritter, is glossy intense green, with rounded Ri. The Sp. are fewer in number at first, and only 1 Csp. is present. Later the spine-count of the original description is attained, and the Csp. are cruciform. The flowering plant shown in Fig. 1084, in "Die Cact.", II, p. 1127, is another spec., sometimes held to be identical with T. lamprochlorus but in fact differing strongly from it (see also under T. grandiflorus Backbg. n.sp.).

T. litoralis (Joh.) Loos. (2)

Bo. columnar, erect, or arching over and then erect again; **St.** to 12 cm ∅, dark to greyish-green; **Ri.** mostly 21, moderately prominent and ± tuberculate; **Ar.** 1 cm apart; **Rsp.** 9–20, thin-subulate, radiating; **Csp.** (1–)5–8, dissimilar, thicker, to 2 cm lg. or more; **Sp.** honey-coloured at first, later grey; **Fl.** 12–14 cm lg., 10 cm ∅, rather curving, white, with dark H.—Chile (Aconcagua, coast N. of Valparaiso). Fl. said to remain open for 5 days.

T. macrogonus (SD.) Ricc. (1) (T.)

Bo. eventually over 2 m h., bluish-green, branching; **branches** to c. 7 cm ∅, ± frosted at first; **Ri.** mostly 7, rounded, ± depressed over the Ar.; **Ar.** 1.5 cm apart, grey; **Rsp.** 6–9, radiating, subulate, to 2 cm lg.; **Csp.** 1–3, rather stouter and longer; **Sp.** all horn-coloured to brown, later blackish or dark grey or greyish-brown; **Fl.** to 18 cm lg., white; **Fr.** 5 cm ∅, rather broadly spherical; **S.** black, glossy.—Origin? Never re-collected. A robust grafting stock.

T. manguinii Backbg. (1)

Bo. erect, branching freely from below, dark greyish-green; **branches** to 95 cm h., to 11 cm ∅; **Ri.** 18–20; **Ar.** slightly sunken; **Rsp.** c. 11; **Csp.** to 5, to 4 mm lg.; all **Sp.** brownish; **Fl.** to 16 cm lg., very broad, white; **Sep.** reddish-brown.—NE. Argentina or Paraguay?

Earlier often confused with T. schickendantzii, the latter with Fl. (Sep.) green outside; T. shaferi is lighter green, with fewer Ri. and Sp.

T. neolamprochlorus Backbg. (1)

Bo. forming colonies, branching from the base, moderately tall, mostly to c. 50 cm h., glossy, light green, later more dirty green; **stems** to 8 cm ⌀; **Ri.** 9–10, rounded, with transverse depressions; **Sp.** 15–18, radiating in all directions, pale yellow, reddish below; **Rsp.** fine, stiff; 4 Sp. recognisable as **Csp.**, cruciform, stouter, to 2 cm lg.; **Fl.** c. 24 cm lg., 16 cm ⌀, white; **Sep.** narrow, red, recurved; **Fr.** oblong-spherical, green, sparsely hairy.—NW. Argentina (Jujuy [Kuntze] and (?) Mendoza, Córdoba). Long confused with T. lamprochlorus.

T. nigripilis (Phil.) Backbg. (2)
Bo. erect to prostrate and then ascending; **St.** to 1 m lg., to 6–7 cm ⌀; **Ri.** to c. 12; **Ar.** dark grey, 1 cm lg.; **Rsp.** c. 12, radiating, to 11 mm lg., grey, darker above, reddish when seen against the light; **Csp.** 6, laterals to 1.5 cm lg., upper and lower Sp. to 2.8 cm lg., sometimes rather angular below, or more flexible, coloured as the Rsp.; **Fl.** c. 6.5 cm lg., white, with many black H.—Chile (Coquimbo).
[Haage says: T. nigripilis (Phil.) Backbg.: an unclarified species, referred by Ritter in part to T. serenanus Ritt., in part to T. spinibarbis (SD.) Ritt., whereas he amended Eulychnia spinibarbis Br. & R. to Eulychnia longispina (SD.) Ritt.]

T. pachanoi Br. & R. (1)
Bo. ± tree-like, to 6 m h.; **branches** numerous, bluish-green, frosted at first; **Ri.** 6–8, broad, rounded, with transverse depressions over the Ar.; **Sp.** 3–7, dissimilar, to 2 cm lg., dark yellow to brown; **Sp.** mostly completely absent on cultivated plants, which is the reason why this excellent stock is well-liked for grafting; **Fl.** to 23 cm lg., white, with blackish H.—Ecuador (Chanchan valley).
Some 30 years ago I was responsible for introducing this spec., which is now regarded as the best grafting stock.

T. pasacana (Web.) Br. & R.: **Helianthocereus pasacana** (Web.) Backbg.

T. peruvianus Br. & R. (1)
Bo. erect at first, then arching over or even prostrate, to 7 m lg., bluish-green, frosted; **St.** to 20 cm ⌀; **Ri.** 6–8, broadly rounded, with a V-shaped notch over the Ar.; **Ar.** large, brown-woolly; **Rsp.** 6–8, to 1 cm lg.; **Csp.** mostly 1, to 4 cm lg.; **Sp.** honey-coloured below, darker above; **Fl.** very large, white.—Peru (near and above Matucana, on the Central Peruvian Andean railway).

T. puquiensis Rauh & Backbg. (1)
Bo. branching, erect, to 4 m h., bluish-green; **branches** to 15 cm ⌀; **Ri.** 8–10; **Ar.** c. 1 cm lg., not surmounted by a transverse furrow but surrounded by a swelling; **Rsp.** to 10, 1–2 cm lg.; **Csp.** mostly 2, 1 of these more erect, to 10 cm lg., the other directed downwards, to 5–8 cm lg.; **Sp.** chestnut-brown at first; **Fl.** to 15 cm lg., white, with brownish-black H.—Peru (above Puquio).

T. purpureopilosus Wgt. (1)
Bo. forming low colonies, branching from below, semi-prostrate and ascending; **branches** to 32 cm lg., dark leaf-green, to 6.5 cm ⌀; **Ri.** 12, low; **Rsp.** to 20, thin, to 7 mm lg.; **Csp.** mostly 4, cruciform, or 5, 3–7 mm lg.; all **Sp.** light horn-coloured, carmine and thickened below; **Fl.** c. 21 cm lg., white with a pink sheen; **Sep.** carmine.—Argentina (Sierra de Córdoba).

T. randallii Card.: **Helianthocereus randallii** (Card.) Backbg.

T. riomizquensis (FR 856): no description available.

T. rubinghianus Backbg.—Descr. Cact. Nov. III: 15. 1963 (1)
Bo. erect, over 3 m h., dark green; **St.** to c. 8 cm ⌀; **Ri.** c. 16–17, moderately h., not very br., with transverse depressions present also on the flanks; **Sp.** to c. 8, mostly extending sideways and forwards, scarcely overtopping the Ri., some more central, scarcely longer, more clearly porrect, all Sp. acicular, yellowish to horn-coloured; **Fl.** large, numerous, slightly creamy to white; **Pet.** rather broad, apiculate; **Sep.** much narrower, greenish-white, decurved; **Fil.** and **style** white; **Sti.** numerous, thin, long, yellowish; **Tu.** and **Ov.** with blackish H.; **Fr.** oblong, 5 × 4 cm, green; **S.** weakly glossy, black, c. 1.2 mm lg.—Origin ? Material said to have come from the Faust collection at Blanes, Spain, but now no longer there. Plant very vigorous and floriferous. Clearly distinguishable from any other spec. because of its dark green, fairly low and narrow Ri., and the relatively short fine Sp. (Fig. 439.) The plant is illustrated in "Die Cact.", VI, 3708, 1962 (Fig. 3364).

T. santaensis Rauh & Backbg. (1)
Bo. branching from the base, to 5 m h., greyish-green, slightly frosted; **branches** to 15 cm ⌀; **Ri.** 7, broad, flat, with a V-notch over the Ar.; **Rsp.** 2–3, 2–3 cm lg., brownish; **Csp.** mostly 1, to 4 cm lg., coloured similarly; **Fl.** ?; **buds** with black H.—Central Peru (Rio Santa valley, Puente Bedoya, c. 3000 m).

T. santiaguensis (Speg.) Backbg. (1)
Bo. tree-like, to 7 m h., **trunk** cylindric; **branches** ascending, 6–10 cm ⌀, matt yellowish to pale green; **Ar.** white at first, to 1.5 cm apart; **Sp.** slightly recurved, lowest ones to 1 cm lg., upper ones to 0.5 cm lg.; **Csp.** 1, stouter, 1–2 cm lg.; **Fl.** to 20 cm lg., unscented, white.—Argentina (Santiago del Estero, near Icaño, in woodlands).

T. schickendantzii (Web.) Br. & R. (1)
Bo. branching freely from the base to form groups to c. 25 cm h., intense green; **branches** curving upwards, to c. 6 cm ∅; **Ri.** 14–18, only 5 mm h., with slight depressions between the Ar.; **Rsp.** 9 at first, later more; **Csp.** 2–8; all **Sp.** c. 5–10 mm lg., yellowish, flexible; **Fl.** to 22 cm lg., white; **Sep.** green; **Tu.** and **Ov.** with black H.; **Fr.** edible.— NW. Argentina. Differentiated from T. manguinii by its lower habit, lighter epidermis and Fl. which are green outside.

T. schoenii Rauh & Backbg. (1)
Bo. branching irregularly from the base, to 3–4 m h., greyish-green; **branches** 10–15 cm ∅; **Ri.** 7, c. 1.5 cm br. and 1 cm g.; **Ar.** yellowish-grey, 1 cm ∅, 2 cm apart, surmounted by a V-notch; **Rsp.** 6–8, dissimilar, upper ones to 1.5 cm lg., lower ones to 5 cm lg.; **Csp.** 1–2, porrect or directed downwards, stout, to 7 cm lg.; **Sp.** leather-brown at first, later tipped thus but otherwise grey; **Fl.** c. 16 cm lg., white, with blackish-brown H.—S. Peru (valley of the Rio Majes, Chuquibamba, up to 3900 m).

T. scopulicolus Ritt. (FR 991): no description available.

T. shaferi Br. & R. (1)
Bo. quite strongly branching, to c. 50 cm h., light green; **branches** to 12.5 cm ∅; **Ri.** c. 14, 10–15 mm h.; **Ar.** 5–7 mm apart, white at first; **Sp.** c. 10, acicular, to 1.2 cm lg., light yellow, Csp. not clearly distinguishable as such; **Fl.** to 18 cm lg., white, with brown H.—Argentina (Salta, San Lorenzo, 1800 m).

T. skottsbergii Backbg. (2)
Bo. branching from below, to 2 m h., greyish-green; **branches** to 14 cm ∅; **Ri.** to 14; **Ar.** greyish-black, 8 mm lg.; **Rsp.** c. 22–26, to 6.2 cm lg., spreading, flexible, bristly, scarcely sharp, horn-coloured to grey; **Csp.** 3 more clearly recognisable, to 12 cm lg., light brown to grey; **Fl.** to 12 cm lg., white, with dense but not long, mouse-grey H.—Chile (Coquimbo, coast of Talinay; Frai Jorge).
v. **breviatus** Backbg.: **Bo.** to c. 1.6 m h. or rather more; **branches** to 12 cm ∅; **Ri.** to 16; **Sp.** numerous, ± hair-like in flowering Ar., to 40, mostly 1–3 longest ones to 6 cm lg., hair-like ones only 6 mm lg., almost half the Sp. bristle-like, coloured as in the type; **Fl.** c. 8 cm lg., white, with blackish H.—Chile (Coquimbo, Frai Jorge).

T. smrzianus (Backbg.) Backbg. n.comb. (Echinopsis smrziana Backbg., Kaktus-ABC, 219, 412. 1935 (1)
Bo. spherical at first, later cylindric, to c. 16 cm h.

and more, becoming thicker, finally stoutly columnar, younger plants very variable, Sp. either short or longer, epidermis variously coloured, individuals occasionally to 40 cm lg., ± prostrate and then ascending, mostly fresh green at first, later ± greyish-green, to 20 cm ∅ in age; **Ri.** c. 15, later to 3 cm br.; **Sp.** very variable, c. 7–14 at first, irregularly arranged, all thin, sharp, radiating, acicular to finer, from whitish to deep golden-brown, sometimes flecked or dark below; **Fl.** to 12 cm lg., 12 cm ∅, white, Pet. in several series; **Sti.** very long and thin.—N. Argentina (Quebrada Escoipe, upper part). (Fig. 440.)
Flowered for the first time recently in Rubingh's collection, Soestdijk, Holland, to provide the above floral data; this variable spec. was referred for a time to Soehrensia because it closely resembles S. grandis in some characters; however, the Fl. have now been seen to be quite dissimilar. Since the tube of the above spec. is not very stout, it could equally well remain under its first name (Echinopsis), but stouter old St. look more like Trichocereus. The spec. thus belongs to the group which represents a transition from Trichocereus to Echinopsis. A similar situation occurs in some Chilean genera. These problems show that convential differentiation, using established criteria, is sometimes a necessity since Nature—by processes which still remain to be studied—creates every imaginable form, without any "classificatory principle" such as we require for our systematic arrangements. In general, delimitations of this kind reflect the facts of Nature, but demarcation still has to be made in accordance with clear guide-lines. It could also be argued for instance that Echinopsis shaferi—a plant growing to 1.5 m h. and to almost 20 cm ∅, and completely trichocereoid in appearance—should be referred to Trichocereus.

T. spachianoides Ritt. (FR 980): no description available.

T. spachianus (Lem.) Ricc. (1)
Bo. branching from below, to over 2 m h.; **branches** ascending, to over one meter lg., to over 6 cm ∅; **Ri.** 10–15, rounded, fairly low; **Ar.** yellowish at first, later white; **Rsp.** 8–10, 6 mm to 1 cm lg., acicular, stiff, sharp; **Csp.** 1(–3), stouter, longer; **Sp.** amber to brownish; **Fl.** c. 20 cm lg., 15 cm ∅, white.—Argentina (Mendoza; San Juán; La Rioja; San Luis; Jujuy, and found here by Frau Muhr, near León).
For a long time this was the most commonly used grafting stock, and it still is so on the Riviera, etc.; however it is more readily exhausted and more quickly becomes corky than T. pachanoi, which is now preferred because it lacks sharp Sp.; the latter does not lignify, grows in circumference with the

T. strigosus (SD.) Br. & R. (1)
Bo. offsetting from the base to form large colonies to over 1 m br.; **shoots** to 60 cm h., to 6 cm ⌀; **Ri.** 15–18, very low; **Ar.** fairly crowded, with dense white wool at first; **Sp.** scarcely differentiated into Rsp. and Csp., acicular, variable in colour, from white through yellow to pink, reddish-brown or black, numerous, sharp, 1–5 cm lg.; **Fl.** white to delicate pink, to c. 20 cm lg., with brownish H.; **S.** 2 mm lg., glossy black.—W. Argentina (Mendoza; San Juán).
Fl. reported as being either scented or unscented; the probability is that, as known in other spec., they are perfumed only at certain times. To distinguish them from the purely white Fl., those with a ± lilac-pink colour could be described as v. roseoalbus (plants such as those in Monaco's Jardin Exotique).

T. tacaquirensis Vpl.) Card. (1)
Bo. mostly branching from the base, to 2.5 m h.; **branches** fairly crowded, steeply ascending; **Ri.** variable in number, 2 cm h.; **Sp.** numerous, scarcely differentiated into Csp. and Rsp., ± bristle-like, especially at first, ± interlacing, flexible, to 8 cm lg., those in the crown erect; **Ar.** large, round, white-felty; **Fl.** to 20 cm lg., white.— Bolivia (Tacaquira).

T. taquimbalensis Card. (1)
Bo. simple, or branching from below or sometimes from the flank (naturally, or only if damaged?), to 2.5 m h., lacking any trunk; **branches** robust, dark green, to 15 cm ⌀; **Ri.** 9; **Ar.** 1.5 cm apart, 1 cm ⌀, whitish; **Rsp.** 8–13, radiating, subulate, to 2 cm lg.; **Csp.** 1, porrect or directed downwards, stout, to 6 cm lg.; all **Sp.** thickened below, light brown at first, then grey; **Fl.** to 23 cm lg., white, with dark brown H.; **Fr.** 4 cm ⌀, dark green; **S.** ± glossy black, 1.5 mm lg.—Bolivia (Cochabamba, Taquimbala).
v. **wilkeae** Backbg.: **Rsp.** to 2.5 cm lg., subulate, in part stoutly so, appressed, curving, sometimes ± hooked; **Csp.** 4, thick-subulate, sometimes compressed below, much thickened below; **Sp.** sometimes all dark at the base and the tip.— Bolivia (Tupiza).

T. tarmaensis Rauh & Backbg. (1)
Bo. branching from the base, to 2 m h., dark green; **branches** c. 10 cm ⌀; **Ri.** 8, to 2 cm br., rounded; **Ar.** 0.8 cm lg., grey, appearing more sunken above, i.e. with a shallow, obliquely transverse depression; **Rsp.** 2–5, 1–3 cm lg.; **Csp.** mostly 1, to 10 cm lg., projecting horizontally; **Sp.** horn-coloured at first, later grey; **Fl.** white, with long H.; **Fr.** 3–4 cm ⌀; **S.**

small, glossy.—Peru (above Tarma, to 3000 m).

T. tenuispinus (FR 616, 867) and its v. pajanalensis (FR 866, 871): descriptions not available.

T. tephracanthus (Lab.) Borg: **Roseocereus tephracanthus** (Lab.) Backbg.

T. terscheckii (Parm.) Br. & R. (1)
Bo. eventually ± tree-like, to 12 m h., **trunk** to 45 cm ⌀; **branches** parallel, ascending, over 15 cm ⌀, intense green; **Ri.** 8–14, to 4 cm h.; **Ar.** 1.5 cm ⌀, to 3 cm apart; **Sp.** 8–15, subulate, to 8 cm lg., yellow; **Fl.** 15–20 cm lg., c. 12 cm ⌀, white, with brown H.—N. Argentina (Catamarca; La Rioja; Tucuman; Salta; Jujuy).
v. **montanus** Backbg.: **Branches** obliquely ascending, lighter green.—(Salta [Quebrada Escoipe]). Both plants are known to the natives as "Cardón grande" and Cardón del Valle"; some of the habitats listed for the former may thus apply only to the latter.

T. terscheckioides Ritt. (FR 993): no description available.

T. thelegonoides (Speg.) Br. & R. (1)
Bo. with main **St.** to 6 m h., thick-cylindric, to 18 cm ⌀, branching above; **branches** to 8 cm ⌀; **Ri.** 15, low, rounded, strongly tuberculate at first because of the transverse depressions between the small, round **Ar.**; **Sp.** 8–10, 4–8 mm lg., bristly, yellow or brownish; **Fl.** 20–24 cm lg., white, greenish outside.—N. Argentina (Jujuy, on dry hills).

T. thelegonus (Web.) Br. &R. (1)
Bo. prostrate and ± ascending, dark green; **St.** to 2 m lg., to 8 cm ⌀; **Ri.** 12–13, broad, rounded, divided into distinctly 6-sided Tub.; **Ar.** round; **Rsp.** 6–8, acicular, ± spreading, 1–2 cm lg.; **Csp.** 1, porrect, 2–4 cm lg.; **Sp.** brown at first, then grey, sometimes darker, to blackish, sometimes yellowish; **Fl.** c. 20 cm lg., white, with lax light H.; **Fr.** c. 5 cm lg., red, dehiscing laterally.—NW. Argentina (Catamarca; Tucuman).

T. totorensis Ritt. (FR 990): description not available.

T. totorillanus (FR 851), from Bolivia: description not available.

T. trichosus Card. (1)
Bo. columnar, simple, ± clavate, to only 1 m h., greyish or bluish-green; **Ri.** 9, broad, rather obtuse, 2 cm h.; **Ar.** 5 cm apart, triangular, to 2 cm br. (surmounted by a depression?), grey; **Rsp.** 4–6,

1–3.5 cm lg.; **Csp.** 1, projecting, to c. 7 cm lg.; all **Sp.** subulate, grey, brown-tipped, thickened below; **Fl.** to 23 cm lg., white, with white and brown H.; **Sti.** green, 2 cm lg.; **Fr.** with long H.; **S.** 2 mm lg., matt, black.—Bolivia (Santa Cruz, on the road Lagunillas—Santa Cruz, 600 m).

T. tropicus Ritt. n. nud.: **Rauhocereus riosaniensis** Backbg.

T. tulhuayacensis Ochoa (1)

Bo. to 2 m h., branching from low on the Bo., with a short **trunk**, dark green; **branches** to 12 cm ∅; Ri. (7–)8(–9), to 1 cm h., to 3.5 cm br.; **Ar.** to 8 mm lg., yellowish at first, then grey, surmounted by a curving depression, prominences sometimes reddish; **Rsp.** 8, 1.5–2.5 cm lg.; **Csp.** 3–4, to 5.5(–8) cm lg.; **Sp.** mostly directed downwards, longest one more porrect, whitish-grey, otherwise yellowish at first, dark-tipped; **Fl.** fairly large, stoutly funnelform, light pink, ivory-white towards the throat, with black and greyish-brown H.; **Fr.** 4.5 cm ∅, dark green, with brownish H.; **S.** glossy, black.— Peru (10 km from Huancayo, near Huachac, 3400 m).

T. tunariensis Card. (1)

Bo. shrubby, to 3 m h., branching from below, pale green; **branches** erect, to 12 cm ∅ below; Ri. 16–21, 1–1.5 cm h., 1.5–1.7 cm br.; **Ar.** 1 cm apart, to 6 mm ∅, grey; **Sp.** scarcely recognisable as Rsp. and Csp., c. 17, radiating, to 5–6 cm lg., thin-acicular, flexible, longest ones directed downwards, all yellowish; **Fl.** 15–17 cm lg., white; **Sep.** purple; **Tu.** and **Ov.** with brown and black H.; **Sti.** yellowish; **Fr.** spherical, 4 cm lg., 5 cm ∅, dark green, with short, dark brown, black and white H., edible; **S.** 2 mm lg., glossy, black.—Bolivia (Cercado, between Yurac Kkasa and San Miguel, 3800m).

T. uyupampensis Backbg. (1)

Bo. prostrate to pendant, to 2 m lg.; **branches** to c. 3.5 cm ∅; Ri. 9, flat, narrow, slightly raised around the small, light brown Ar.; **Sp.** 8–10, fine, irregularly directed, mostly 2–6 mm lg., darker, pointing up and down; **Fl.** c. 16 cm lg., white, reddish outside.—S. Peru (Uyupampa, c. 3000 m). See also T. glaucus Ritt.

T. validus (Monv.) Backbg. (1)

Bo. becoming tree-like(?), known till now only as stout, erect columns, green; **St.** to 35 cm ∅; Ri. c. 10; **Ar.** fairly large above, to 3 cm apart; **Sp.** few or weak at the apex, developing later in the lower half of the Ar., pale yellow, sometimes darker above; **Rsp.** 7–10, to 3.2 cm lg., the bottom one longest; **Csp.** 1–2, to 7 cm lg.; **Fl.** to 14 cm lg., white, with light greyish-brown H.; **Fr.** ovoid, woolly.—SE.

Bolivia(?). Long known in collections as Echinopsis valida Monv.

T. vollianus Backbg. (1)

Bo. erectly shrubby, branching from the base, glossy, light green; **branches** to 10 cm ∅; Ri. c. 13, rounded, to 7 mm br., 5 mm h.; **Ar.** to 2.5 cm apart; **Rsp.** 8–11, radiating, thin, sharp, to 7 mm lg.; **Csp.** 1, to 2.5 cm lg.; all **Sp.** amber-coloured; **Fl.** to c. 12 cm lg., white; **Fr.** oblong, hairy.—Bolivia (Arque-Cochabamba).

v. **rubrispinus** Backbg.: **Sp.** reddish-brown. Resembles T. spachianus but glossy, and with opener spination; an excellent grafting stock except that the Sp. are very sharp.

T. werdermannianus Backbg. (1)

Bo. forming a large tree, to over 5 m h., with a **trunk** to 1 m lg. and 40 cm ∅; Ri. c. 10 at first, later 14 or more, 2 cm h.; **Ar.** 2.5 cm apart; **Sp.** on new growth c. 10, Csp. scarcely differentiated, to 7 cm lg., later increasing in number, all yellowish, horn-coloured or brownish; **Fl.** to 20 cm lg., white, with black and white H.; **Fr.** 3.5 cm ∅; **S.** 1.3 mm lg., rough.—S. Bolivia (Tupiza, Charcoma valley, probably to Chuquisaca).

There are several large Cerei which cannot with certainty be attributed either to Trichocereus or to Helianthocereus, in the absence of floral data. Some of them have a distant resemblance to Leucostele Backbg., but in Rivière's collection this latter is now enormous, offsetting from the base and developing bristly ovaries and fruits; these characters are not present in Helianthocereus. In the possession of the well-known French botanist Roland-Gosselin, who made a speciality of the succulent plants, there are several of these unclarified plants, with laxer but stronger Sp.; when they flower, they may prove to belong to Helianthocereus. In the absence of any description it is impossible to say now whether they are identical with the Cerei Frič called Trichocereus cephalopasacana, with its v. albicephala; most likely these were members of Helianthocereus. On the other hand Trichocereus pasacana catamarcensis Frič, undescribed, was probably Echinopsis gigantea R. Mey., or Trichocereus terscheckii. T. pasacana inermis Frič, not described, was Echinopsis valida Monv., now Trichocereus validus (Monv.) Backbg.

Mention must be made here of Trichoechinopsis imperialis hort., a hybrid raised by the American breeder Hummel: a cross between a Trichocereus and an Echinopsis (probably E. eyriesii); even small plants bear enormous white Fl., and the plant is unusually quick-growing; it later becomes completely ceroid in habit and grows quite large, the spination resembling Echinopsis eyriesii. It is still found in several European collections and deserves to be more widely cultivated.

Turbinicarpus (Backbg.) F. Buxb. & Backbg. (209)

A genus of small spherical cacti which I referred in 1936 to Strombocactus as a subgenus, because at that time I had not worked out the basis of my later classification. F. Buxbaum then segregated the subgenus and gave it generic rank—absolutely correctly, since these species have a very uniform set of characters: flowers with slender naked tubes or at most with traces of scales on the upper part of the tube, the berries naked, fleshy, all apparently with a tiny lid; see Fig. 2711–2721 in "Die Cact.", V: 2883–2890. 1961; the unification of a larger complex of species such as Toumeya Br. & R. with a monotypic genus is clearly unjustifiable, particularly since the floral structure of the latter is noticeably divergent. L. Benson recently again united Toumeya with Navajoa, Utahia and Pilocanthus in Pediocactus, admittedly without mentioning the inclusion of Turbinicarpus in Toumeya by H. Bravo and Marshall. Surprisingly, F. Buxbaum has again changed his mind because he and Krainz now regard the species of Turbinicarpus as belonging to Toumeya; and recently Frank described a plant, known for a long time but never named, as "Toumeya krainziana". What will these authors do now, when confronted with the Genus Pediocactus Br. & R. sensu lato L. Benson? Since the latter includes species with various types of dehiscence, plants with harder or weak spines, these early deciduous or not, and acc. H. Bravo and Marshall also species with berry-fruits, then logically other genera such as Obregonia, Aztekium and Lophophora should also be included. In a situation like this, where each author is working along his own lines, in his own narrow specialism, the result is utter confusion. The choice is clearly between the narrowly conceived genus, or a continuation without demarcations of the "lumping" process, whereby the concept of a "type-species of a genus" loses all meaning. These attempted combinations start an unwarranted series of chain-reactions. It is worth noting—above all in the face of the homogeneous character of the 9 described species of Turbinicarpus—that the smaller the plant-bodies in any species-complex, the finer the differences must be. It is an important part of the geobotanist's task to make these clear. The phylogeneticist's approach may be quite different. Nevertheless some uniform and logical system of nomenclature is essential so that this can be stabilised. Britton and Rose provided a sound basis. It should be stressed that in the case of the

small genus, it is possible to have a clear mental image of a given group of characters, but an omnibus genus leads to a blurred picture of any diagnostic differences; and since not everyone who is dealing with a given plant-name is able to work through the increasingly complicated literature, everything speaks in favour of the first of the alternatives stated above. For these reasons, I stand by the independent genus which Buxbaum chose in 1937. All the species have relatively weak and ± curving spines. The seeds are small, black, and either glossy or matt.—Distribution: Mexico (Tamaulipas and predominantly in San Luis Potosí). [(R); grafting hastens growth and increases floriferousness.]

T. klinkerianus Backbg. & Jacobs.
Bo. small, to 3 cm h., 4 cm $\emptyset$, ± depressed-spherical, matt, light grey to brownish-green; **crown** ± white-woolly; **Ri.** divided into spiralled Tub., these expanded laterally at the base; **Ar.** with a small tuft of wool, this soon dropping; **Sp.** 3 along the lower margin of the Ar., the bottom one longer, at most 9 mm lg., above that 2 smaller ones, mostly soon dropping, all Sp. curving gently towards the apex, compressed below, fairly weak, with transverse fissures; **Fl.** c. 1.4 cm lg. and br., concolorous white inside, with a dark M.-stripe outside.—Mexico (Tamaulipas). [Haage amends the locality to: San Luis Potosí]. Krainz unites this spec. with T. schmiedickeanus, but the latter is oblong in shape (not broadly spherical), its Sp. are longer and more strongly interlacing, while the Fl. is pink with a violet M.-stripe. The diagnostic characters must be noted with particular care in the case of these dwarf cacti, so as to establish the exact points of divergence and to ensure that the information about them remains available; these purposes are not served by inclusion in larger genera.

T. krainzianus (Frank) Backbg.
Bo. shortly cylindric, dark green, sometimes caespitose, to 4 cm h., 3 cm $\emptyset$; **crown** with white wool; **Ri.** 11, divided into Tub., these spiralled, conical above, rhomboid below; **Sp.** 6–8, ± twisted, 12–30 mm lg., flexible, not sharp, yellowish-brown at first, dark-tipped, finally dropping; **Fl.** 2 cm lg., creamy yellow, greenish-cream outside; **Fr.** 3–5 mm $\emptyset$; **S.** 1 mm lg.—Mexico. This spec. was not described until 25 years after its discovery.

T. lophophoroides (Werd.) F. Buxb. & Backbg.
Bo. depressed-hemispherical, to 3.5 cm h., 4.5 cm $\emptyset$, bluish-green, with a fairly stout **taproot**; grafted plants offset more freely; **crown** with plentiful wool, pierced by Sp.; **Ri.** spiralled, consisting of fairly

flattened-rounded Tub., 4–6-sided below, to 12 mm br., in grafted plants often ± confluent below; **Sp.** 2–3(–4), to 8 mm lg., 1 of these more central, straight, erect, to 1 cm lg., all Sp. black at first, or white, tipped black; **Fl.** 3.5 cm $\varnothing$, whitish, tinged a delicate pink, more so inside towards the centre, the middle of the Pet. of this colour outside; **Fr.** light green.—Mexico (San Luis Potosí, Las Tablas, 1200 m).

T. machrochele (Werd.) F. Buxb. & Backbg.
Bo. simple, depressed-spherical, c. 3 cm h., 4 cm $\varnothing$, matt greyish-green, with a longer R.-section; **crown** with white wool; **Ri.** spiralled, divided into Tub. which are mostly broader than high; **Ar.** dirty white at first; **Sp.** 3–5, mostly 4, to 4 cm lg. or more, curving, mostly compressed below the quite strongly interlacing tips, the upperside flat, grooved, dirty yellow and darker-tipped at first, later grey, rough and bark-like; **Fl.** white, suffused pink; **Fr.** a smooth berry.—Mexico (San Luis Potosí).

T. polaskii Backbg.
Bo. probably mostly simple, broadly spherical, bluish to greyish-green, c. 1 m h., to 2.7 cm $\varnothing$, closely resembling a small Lophophora; **Ri.** not tuberculate but expanded around the Ar. and divided by sinuate lines; **Sp.** mostly only 1, rarely with a shorter Ssp., the larger one to 12 mm lg., yellowish or horn-coloured, weakly annular, weak, curving over the crown, soon dropping; **Fl.** 1 cm lg., 1.5 cm $\varnothing$, white or tinged pale pink, especially in the centre of the Pet.; **Sti.** pink, paler towards the margin; **S.** slightly glossy.—Mexico (50 miles N. of San Luis Potosí, 20 miles N. of Matehuala, on the hills).

T. pseudomacrochele (Backbg.) F. Buxb. & Backbg.
Bo. flattened-spherical, with a cylindric, napiform and extended basal section, to 3 cm $\varnothing$; **Ri.** resolved in Tub., these irregularly angular or square, sometimes compressed; **crown** slightly woolly; **Ar.** white; **Sp.** c. 8, bristly, flexible, unequal, ± projecting to interlacing and bent, yellowish at first, later grey; **Fl.** 3.5 cm $\varnothing$, white with a pink M.-stripe, this darker outside; **Pet.** narrow, long, strongly revolute at anthesis; **Fr.** small.—Mexico (San Luis Potosí). [Haage amends locality to: Mexico (Querétaro).]

T. roseiflorus Backbg.—Descr. Cact. Nov. III:15.1963.
Bo. simple, dull green, broadly subspherical, c. 4 cm $\varnothing$; **crown** white-woolly; **Ri.** consisting of transversely extended, rather prominent Tub., these 4-sided or rounded below, or the surface irregularly flattened or ± angular, also with a

transverse furrow between the Tub., this ± flattened above and below; **Rsp.** on young plants to c. 10(–12), either light horn-colour and darker above, or whitish, to black-tipped, sometimes concolorous white, radiating sideways, later sometimes fewer, unequal, very short, to c. 5 mm lg.; **Csp.** 1 at first, later also 2, one above the other, curving towards the apex, mostly twice as long as the longest Rsp., black; **Fl.** c. 2.5 cm lg., concolorous pink, funnelform; **Pet.** tapering, with a red M.-line outside; **Sep.** shorter, with a broad, brownish central field; **Fr.** ?—Mexico. (Fig. 441.)
Closely related to T. lophophoroides, but Sp. more numerous, Fl. concolorous pink, opening less widely. Plants seen in the collection of Saint-Pie, Asson (France, Basses-Pyrénées).

T. schmiedickeanus (Böd.) F. Buxb. & Backbg. (T.)
Bo. eventually shortly cylindric, to 5 cm h., 3 cm $\varnothing$, vivid matt green, grafted plants are larger; **crown** with white wool, overtopped by Sp.; **Ri.** with Tub. in Isp. 8:13, **Tub.** rounded to shortly conical, 5 mm br. below, 7 mm lg., truncate; **Sp.** 3(–4), to 2.5 cm lg., curving like a ram's horns, bent and interlacing, subterete to (the upper one) blade-like, to 1 mm br., flat on the upperside and often with a fine groove, all Sp. later falling; **Fl.** c. 18 mm $\varnothing$, pink, with a light violet M.-stripe; **Fr.** with rudimentary Sc. or naked.—Mexico (Tamaulipas, near Miquihuana).

T. schwarzii (Shurly) Backbg.
Bo. simple, small, hemispherical, to 3.5 cm $\varnothing$, basal section 3 cm lg.; **Ri.** in 5–8 spirals, tuberculate, brownish to pale green; **Ar.** minutely tufted; **Sp.** 1–2, to 2 cm lg., whitish or yellowish-brown, later dropping; **Fl.** 3 cm lg., 4 cm $\varnothing$, bellshaped-rotate, white, suffused greenish, with a reddish M.-line.—Mexico (E. of San Luis Potosí).

Uebelmannia Buin. (Succulenta, Nov. 1973)

[No generic diagnosis in Haage's addenda. Spherical or shortly columnar plants, occurring in small and isolated populations, often in inaccessible terrain, frequently in rock-crevices, and habitat-photographs frequently show the plants either clad with, or growing among, lichens which indicates high atmospheric humidity. Distribution: Brazil, Minas Geraes.
Cultivated specimens in Britain are mostly imported plants which have shown a discouraging loss-rate as they are very slow to establish and require considerable heat. However both imports and the few available seedlings have been grafted successfully and the natural characters appear unaffected. These related but scattered species provoke in-

teresting questions if Backeberg is correct in attributing to the Amazon basin a key-role in the South American distributions: see "Distribution of the Cactaceae"—p. 517. Translator.]*

U. buiningii Don.
Bo. simple, shortly cylindric, to 8 cm ∅, greenish or reddish-brown, made rough by minute waxy Sc.; **Ri.** 18, straight, c. 15 mm apart, divided into downwardly directed Tub. 5 mm apart; **Ar.** scarcely woolly; **Sp.** reddish-brown, later white, 4 longer ones cruciform, 2–4 shorter ones straight, to 5 mm lg.; **Fl.** to 27 mm lg. and 20 mm br.; **Ov.** white-woolly; **Tu.** 9 mm lg., Sc. with brown Br. in their axils; **Pet.** yellow, lanceolate; **style** with 6–7 **Sti.**; **Fr.** ovoid, yellow, 4 mm ∅; **S.** black, testa tuberculate.—Brazil (Minas Geraes, Serra Negra, on quartz; discovered by A. F. H. Buining and L. Horst on 1.12.66). Resembles U. gummifera, but clearly distinguished by the Bo.-colour. (Fig. 524.)

U. flavispina Buin. & Bred. 1973
Bo. spherical, later short-cylindric, to 35 cm h., 11 cm ∅, light green or green, pitted whitish, especially around the Ar.; **Ri.** to 29, fairly acute, vertical, 1–1.4 cm apart; **Ar.** round, 1–1.5 mm ∅, with greyish-white felt, newer Ar. 2 mm apart, in mature plants confluent, in a continuous white band; **Sp.** to 1 cm lg., 2–5, spreading ± sideways, yellowish, dark yellow to yellowish-brown, later grey to dark grey, to 3.5 cm lg., pectinate, also 1–2 vertical, straight, thin; **Fl.** funnelform, 18 mm lg., 7 mm br., light yellow, with Br. and yellow H. outside; **Sep.** acute, spatulate; **Pet.** similarly; **style** light cream; **Sti.** 6, similarly coloured; **Fr.** 14 mm lg., with a thin red skin and white flesh; **S.** cap-shaped, testa glossy, black.—Brazil (Minas Geraes, W. of Diamantina, on flat rocks and in clefts, growing among bromeliads, grass and lichens at c. 1280 m). (Fig. 525.)
Distinguished from U. pectinifera by the Sp.-colour, number of Ri., and the structure of Fl. and S.

U. gummifera (Backbg. & Voll) Buin.
Bo. simple, elongated-spherical, to 10 cm h., 6 cm ∅, greyish-green; **Ri.** c. 32, tuberculate at first, later narrow and continuous, tuberculate above; **Ar.** small, with thick yellowish-grey wool at first; **Rsp.** 2 shorter side ones, 1 longer Sp. downwardly directed, to 5 mm lg., sometimes 2 minute Ssp.

above; **Csp.** 1, ± subulate, straight, light grey, becoming darker grey, tipped brownish; **Fl.** 2 cm lg., 1.5 cm ∅, sulphur-yellow; **Sti.** dazzling creamy-white; **S.** small, matt, black.—Brazil (Minas Geraes, Serra de Ambrosia).
Old plants resemble U. buiningii, but the Bo.-colour is clearly distinct. U. gummifera was discovered in 1938, when it was classified as a Parodia.

U. meninensis Buin.
Bo. to 50 cm lg., 10 cm br., green; **Ri.** to 40, distinctly tuberculate, Tub. to 8 mm h., to 10 mm apart; **Sp.** 2, rarely more, one directed upwards and the other downwards, to 2 cm lg., blackish-brown, later dark grey; **Fl.** yellow; **S.** twice as large as that of U. gummifera.—Brazil (Minas Geraes, near Pedra Menina, on an isolated mountain-slope, growing on pure white quartzite, among thorn-scrub; discovered by A. F. H. Buining). (Fig. 526.)

U. pectinifera Buin.
Bo. spherical to cylindric, to 15 cm ∅, to 50 cm h.; epidermis dark reddish-brown with a grey waxy coating; **R.** a thin taproot; **Ri.** 15–18, 12 mm h., to 2 cm apart; **crown** with woolly felt; **Sp.** dark brown to black, later black-tipped, 12–15 mm lg., erectly projecting like the crest on a military helmet; **Fl.** greenish-yellow, Pet. acute, 16 mm lg.; **Tu.** with reddish Sc. and white woolly H.; **style** c. 8 mm lg., with 4 **Sti.**; **Fr.** light violet-red, soft-fleshy, with only 9–10 **S.**; hilum flattened, testa reddish-brown, with small convex cells.—Brazil (Minas Geraes, found in 1966 at 1000 m, on white quartz-sand, by L. Horst and Dr. G. Baumhardt). (Fig. 527.)
  v. **pseudopectinifera**: **Bo.** smaller than in the type, epidermis appearing green since it is more weakly white-flocky; **Sp.** not directed vertically upwards nor pectinate, but spreading sideways, variously long; **Fl.**, **Fr.** and **S.** as in the type.—Brazil (Minas Geraes, near Diamantina, at 1200 m, sometimes on sandy debris among bromeliads, at a distance of 40 km as the crow flies from the type-locality).

Utahia Br. & R. (201)

Broadly spherical plants, probably always simple, with fairly dense spines; the apically borne and only moderately large flowers are funnelform to rotate, ± scaly, the tube densely set with dry ciliate scales, the ovary similarly; the seeds are fairly large, skull-shaped, with a sunken hilum. The areoles, seen under a lens, consist of unusually stranded felt; the compressed spines are slightly angular or have fine lengthwise fissures, the centrals being described as almost black at first, although I have

* Photographs and habitat-data with the following first descriptions in the Nat. Cact. & Succ. J. (GB): U. buiningii: March 1968, and U. pectinifera: Dec. 1967. More recently first descriptions of plants in this genus have appeared, with colour photographs, in both the Cactus & Succulent J. (US) and K.u.a.S. (West Germany). Translator.

seen specimens where they were ± white and dark-tipped. I do not know whether there are any intermediate forms; if not, then the white-spined form, in which the spines are also stouter, must be segregated as a variety. It is a remarkable thing that the plants are said to occur mostly on gypsum soils. While once very rare, they have recently been imported from time to time; however, they appear to survive only a short time in cultivation, just as with Coloradoa. In view of the divergent floral characters it is difficult to see why L. Benson referred the genus to Pediocactus Br. & R. (see under that genus) without including Coloradoa, since he also included Toumeya, Navajoa and Pilocanthus.—Distribution: USA (N. Arizona). [No information available regarding cultivation, or whether these plants can be raised from seed and immediately grafted.]

U. sileri (Eng.) Br. & R. (T.)

Bo. mostly broadly spherical, later also ± elongated and then to 15 cm h., 12 cm $\emptyset$; **Ri.** indistinct, 8–16, spiralled, mostly divided into **Tub.**, these rhombic-angular below, more rounded at midway, tapering above, c.1 cm lg. and br.; **Ar.** white, with felty H., to 1.5 cm apart; **Rsp.** 11–13, greyish-white, sometimes brown-tipped, 13–18 mm lg.; **Csp.** 3–4, terete, almost black at first, soon light below, becoming lighter or remaining darker, slender-subulate or stoutly so; **Fl.** 2.8 cm lg., 2.5 cm $\emptyset$, yellowish; **Fr.** green, extensively set with small Sc., c. 1 cm lg. and $\emptyset$; **S.** 4 mm lg., 2.5 mm thick, dark reddish-brown, glossy but appearing matt because of the fine tuberculation.—USA (between Pipe Spring and Ship Rock, close to the border of Utah and somewhat NE. of Fredonia). (Fig. 442.)

Vatricania Backbg. (180)

Cerei which branch somewhat from the base, with a unique type of cephalium; this develops superficially, i.e. not from a groove, at first on one side only, with longer hairy bristles appearing from the aeroles. The tuft-development comes later, encircling the stem above with a constantly enlarging, projecting and furry cap from which the true cephalium extends down the flank. The nocturnal flowers sometimes appear from the lower parts of this cephalium; they are mostly cylindric, expanding somewhat towards the limb, with the widely open perianth yellowish-white inside and reddish outside, projecting only slightly at anthesis beyond the dense silky hairs and bristles of the tube. This monotypic genus was discovered by C. Troll in 1927. F. Buxbaum first attributed this extraordinary plant to the Brazilian genus, Facheiroa, and then put it in SG. Facheiroa of Espostoa Br. & R.;

however the characters of the flowering zones are divergent in all three genera.—Distribution: Bolivia (Chuquisaca). [(R).]

V. guentheri (Kupp.) Backbg. (T.)

Bo. erect, branching from the base, to over 2 m h.; **branches** to 10 cm $\emptyset$, light green; **Ri.** to c. 27, weakly tuberculate, with indistinct transverse furrows over the yellowish-white, felty **Ar.**; **Sp.** on younger plants c. 15, scarcely differentiated, later increasing to c. 25, 0.5–1.5 cm lg., one more central, stouter, to 2.2 cm lg., upwardly directed Sp. shorter and rather stouter than the more numerous, thinner to bristly, downwardly directed ones; **Ceph.** from the flowering zone, with Br. to 6 cm lg., the Ar. with yellowish-white wool to 4 mm lg., the finely bristly cap towards the apex lengthening with age; **Fl.** with a cylindric Tu., expanding slightly, c. 8 cm lg., c. 3 cm $\emptyset$, open for 1 night only; **Pet.** narrow, 1.3 cm lg., 5–6 mm br.; **Tu.** and **Ov.** with ± pinkish silky wool.—Bolivia (Chuquisaca, valley of the Rio Grande, near El Oro). (Fig. 443, 444.)

Vollia was a name I proposed for a form of Zygocactus K. Sch. which flowered from the lateral Ar. (Fig. 459.)

Weberbauerocereus Backbg. (92)

The type-species of this genus was discovered by Meyen, who described it as long ago as 1833. Britton and Rose referred to Trichocereus, the only species known to them, although they did draw attention to the divergent floral structure. In 1942 I segregated this genus of large-shrubby to tree-like Cerei, mainly because of the curving and ± S-shaped floral tube and the rather oblique limb; but it was a long time before this new genus achieved general recognition, which, in turn is largely thanks to Rauh's two journeys to Peru when his finds included a species with strongly bent and oblique-limbed red flowers as well as others with the tube elongated and stout, or the limb broad and ± regular, one such plant having flowers of an unusual brownish colour. Ritter then discovered further species which proved that the genus was not restricted only to S. Peru, but that the overall distribution extended to the Departments of La Libertad and Ancash, as well as the more northerly provinces of the interior: Cajamarca and Lima (Churin). In these new species all the flowers are white to ± pinkish-white, the tube being in general more strongly woolly than in the S. Peruvian species, while the apex of the shoots, or the principal flowering zone, shows noticeably modified spines, i.e. they become finer and bristle-like, longer and more projecting, or tangled, in what Ritter calls a "pseudocephalium"; to me, this name does not appear to be very appropriate since we know some species where there is absolutely no modification of the spines in the flowering zone (e.g. in the type-species); of W. seyboldianus, Rauh says only:—"The radial spines of the flowering zone are bristle-like ... the very stout centrals gradually disappear, and only occasionally longer, very thin ones, are developed"; of W. longicomus, Ritter himself says:—"If the flowering areoles are close together, they appear to form a pseudo-cephalium". It is thus impossible to give a pseudo-cephalium as a diagnostic character of the Genus Weberbauerocereus, but it would be quite justifiable to state that "in a number of species there *may* be considerable modification of spines in the flowering zone"; spine-modification towards the more strongly flowering stem-tip, when these spines become finer and longer, occurs in Lopho-cereus for instance; but once again this is not constant in all species, and is thus not a diagnostic feature of the genus. It is more appropriate to differentiate between "pseudocephalia such as may occur in part in Pilosocereus", and "flowering zones which may have modified spines", since in both cases—unlike Cephalocleistocactus—these are not constant generic characters. Strangely enough, Ritter has not described any species with concolorously red flowers such as Rauh observed, e.g. in W. seyboldianus. It is interesting to note that the zygomorphic flowers of this species look like very stout Loxanthocereus-flowers, with the same red colour, whereas in the other species they are almost completely regular and ± white, with those of W. albus actually being fairly broadly fun-nelform. Weberbauerocereus is thus a natural complex of species intermediate between Tri-chocereus and Loxanthocereus, its flowers some-times resembling the one genus, sometimes the other, but still remaining a very distinctive group in which the flowers are sometimes ± radial, some-times greenish-white, while others are transitional towards zygomorphy (W. fascicularis) or quite strongly zygomorphic, with every conceivable phase of spine-modification, and the flowers not borne exclusively in a modified zone of this kind. Such a variety of forms can only be reflected with sufficient accuracy by a carefully conceived classifi-cation. Weberbauerocereus is thus one of the most interesting genera, and since we now have far more knowledge of this unique Peruvian genus it is a great pleasure to me that I named it for Prof. Dr. Weberbauer, the highly esteemed German botanist who was formerly in the service of the Peruvian Government, and whose great work on the Peruvian Andes is a testimony to his untiring researches; his inability to deal with the cactus-flora of the region in greater detail is undoubtedly because no satisfactory specialised work on the

subject was available to him, so that these plants – the most remarkable subjects of the Peruvian scene—did not receive the same care as he devoted to other plant-families. It is worth mentioning that Rauh observed:—"staminodial hairs sometimes present", as in the flower of W. weberbaueri. As we find with other Andean genera, this feature is not always present and it is thus not a generically diagnostic character, but simply an occasionally observable phenomenon which requires further investigation. The fruits of Weberbauerocereus are not very large—at most 4 cm ∅—and green to red or orange-yellow, sometimes resembling oversized fruits of Cleistocactus, or with more wool present. Seeds are uniformly smaller and glossy black.—Distribution: from the NE. Andean hinterland of Peru to S. Peru, close to the Chilean frontier. [(R).]

W. albus Ritt.—"Kakt. u.a. Sukk.", 13:6, 106–108.1962.
Bo. forming dense tall shrubs to 5 m h., branching from the base to midway; **branches** erect, greyish-green, to 6 cm ∅; **Ri.** 16–20, to c. 8 mm h., little notched; **Ar.** to 5 mm ∅, coffee-coloured; **Sp.** scarcely differentiated, 15–22 radials 2–7 mm lg., hair-like, pale, also 1–2 stoutly subulate Sp., more centrally placed, 0.5–0.75 or 1.5–3.5 cm lg., together with 3–5 finer Csp. c. 0.5 cm lg., all white to ivory; **flowering zone** with enlarged Ar. 7 mm ∅, the Sp. modified, tangled, hair-like, to 4 cm lg., yellowish at first, soon white; **Fl.** to 9.5 cm lg., 7–10 cm ∅, white to light pink, remaining open day and night for several days, with dense brownish and white H.; **Fr.** spherical, to 4 cm ∅, greyish to reddish-green, with brown and light H.—Peru (Dept. Ancash, below San Marcos) (FR 571). (Fig. 445.) Largest Fl. of the genus; style long-projecting.

W. cephalomacrostibas (Backbg.) Ritt.: a catalogue-name of Ritter's for **Trichocereus cepha-lomacrostibas** (Werd. & Backbg.) Backbg. which, for the reasons set out in "Die Cact.", VI: 3707.1962, is close to the Chilean Trichocerei but not, on the basis of flower-type, to the S. Peruvian spec. of Weberbauerocereus, although the two genera are undoubtedly quite closely related.

W. churinensis Ritt.—"Kakt. u.a. Sukk.", 13:8, 133–134.1962.
Bo. bushy, erect, to 2 m h., mostly branching from close to the base; **branches** ± squarrose, to 5 cm ∅; **Ri.** 18–20, weakly notched, obtuse; **Ar.** grey, 3–5 mm lg.; **Sp.** scarcely differentiated, c. 40–60, light to orange-yellow, lower ones hair-like, to 1 cm lg., others fewer, rather stouter, with a few stouter Sp. towards the centre and 1–2 robust Sp. to 3 cm lg.; **flowering zone** sometimes only with thin bristly Sp.

2–4 cm lg.; **Fl.** with a fairly long stout Tu., to 12 cm lg., strongly perfumed, pink above, white below; **Per.** revolute; **Tu.** reddish, with black to blackish-brown H.; **Ov.** with the H. more brownish-black; **Fr.** c. 4 cm lg. and almost as br., blackish-green, with greyish-brown to black H.—Peru (Dept. Lima, below Churin) (FR 685).

W. fascicularis (Meyen) Backbg. (T.)

Bo. tall-shrubby, a few metres h., greyish-green; **branches** to 6 cm ∅ or more; **Ri.** c. 16, low; **Ar.** to 6 mm lg., with light brown or yellow felt; **Rsp.** numerous, mostly to 1 cm lg., fine; **Csp.** several, to 4.6 cm lg., thin, very sharp, mostly ± decurved; all **Sp.** yellow at first, often bristly-acicular, later more robust, Csp. brown, then grey; **Fl.** to 11 cm lg., curving to an approximately S-shape, limb relatively short, not clearly zygomorphic, greenish-white, remaining open during the morning of the following day; **Sep.** ± revolute, reddish-greenish; **style** projecting; **Sti.** greenish; **Fr.** spherical, orange-yellow to reddish, densely set with small Sc., with few H.—S. Peru (near Arequipa). No Sp.-modification present in the flowering zone.

W. horridispinus Rauh & Backbg.

Bo. erectly shrubby, to 2.5 m h., freely branching; **branches** to 15 cm ∅, mid-green; **Ri.** c. 18, ± raised around the Ar. which are surmounted by a transverse notch; **Ar.** very large, to 1.8 cm lg.; **Sp.** in 2 Ser., upper ones stouter, mostly 5–7, dissimilar, some to 8 cm lg., thick-subulate, terete to somewhat compressed or triangular below, ± channelled, straight to bent, twisted or almost claw-like, the lower part of the Ar. with shorter, thinner, more brownish Sp., 1–3, thin-subulate, to 1 cm lg., others very thin, yellowish-brownish, to 20 or more, to 1 cm lg., mostly shorter, the stouter ones all at first light yellowish-brown, then grey and dark-tipped; **Fl.** to 6 cm lg., greenish-brown; **Tu.** with dense brown hairy wool; **Ov.** with dense white wool; **Fr.** (immature) 2 cm ∅, olive-green, with whitish H.—S. Peru (valley of Chala, 2600 m). This is the stoutest St. of any spec. of Weberbauerocereus. Here again, the Sp. of the flowering zone are not modified; however these are probably the most fiercely spined plants in the genus, since the spec. grows in a very dry zone.

W. johnsonii Ritt.—"Kakt. u.a. Sukk.", 13:5, 72–73.1962.

Bo. erect, tree-like, to 6 m h., with a short thick **trunk**, branching from c. 1.5 m up; **branches** erect, parallel, 7–9 cm ∅; **Ri.** 30–35, obtuse, ± tuberculate, to 5 mm h., seedlings have only 17–18 Ri.; **Ar.** brown, to 3 mm ∅; **Sp.** scarcely differentiated, c. 20 more radially placed, fine, to 1.5 cm lg., lower ones more numerous, longer, centrals c. 10–12,

rather stouter, to 1 cm lg., all Sp. flexible, scarcely sharp, glossy, dark golden-yellow; **flowering zone** with erratic modification of the Sp., sometimes ± one-sided, or interrupted, with c. 50 elongated, ± projecting, hair-like, golden-yellow Br. to 6 cm lg., the Ar. larger; **Fl.** to 11 cm lg., faintly perfumed, closing at daybreak, white or a delicate pinkish-white; **Tu.** brownish-green or reddish, with dense short brownish-black wool interspersed with stouter reddish-brown H.; **style** long-projecting, it and the **Sti.** greenish; **Fr.** spherical, green, to 4 cm ∅, with grey and brown H.—Peru (Prov. Cajamarca, Zangal) (FR 570).

W. longicomus Ritt.—"Kakt. u.a. Sukk.", 13:7, 117–119.1962.

Bo. almost tree-like, to 6 m h., branching mostly in the bottom third, greyish-green; **branches** straightly erect, moderately close spaced, to 8 cm ∅; **Ri.** 15–18, very obtuse, to 1 cm h., notched over half the width; **Ar.** brown, to 6 mm lg.; **Rsp.** 15–25, pale to brownish-yellow, to 1 cm lg., lower ones longer, thinner; **Csp.** 1(–2), very stout, subulate, similarly coloured, 1–6 cm lg., also 3–6 finer, shorter Sp. 0.5–1 cm lg., transitional to the Rsp.; **flowering zone** with hair-like Rsp., also thinner but stouter Csp. in the transitional zone, then a discontinuous modification to denser mats of H., the Rsp. concealed and to 10 cm lg., with 1–2 stouter Csp. persisting, these to 6 cm lg., often hidden, the Ar. to 1 cm lg.; **Fl.** to 10 cm lg., 5.5–7.5 cm ∅, somewhat perfumed, still open the following morning, white to pink; **Sep.** pink to carmine; **Tu.** reddish-brown, clad with reddish-brown, ± tufted wool and H.; **style** not projecting, white; **Sti.** light yellow; **Fr.** spherical, to 3 cm ∅, green to reddish, densely clad with wool, this being white above and brown below.—Peru (Prov. Cajamarca, Puente Crisnejas) (FR 656). (Fig. 446.)

W. rauhii Backbg.

Bo. tree-like, with a short **trunk**, to 6 m h.; **branches** vertical, candelabra-like, to 15 cm ∅ below, 8 cm ∅ above; **Ri.** c. 23; **Sp.** below the flowering zone numerous, whitish-grey, to 1 cm lg., in part bristly; **Csp.** often to 6, mostly to 4 cm lg., one more central, 7 cm lg., very stout, ± appressed, yellowish below, dark chocolate-brown above; **Ar.** c. 1 cm lg., with long grey felt; **flowering zone** with only a few elongated, very thin Csp., the Rsp., bristly, elongated, the entire St. then covered with Br.; **Fl.** often only on one side, to 10 cm lg., creamy-brown, Per. ± radial, to 4 cm ∅; **Tu.** densely scaly, with violet-brown H.; **Sti.** green; **Fr.** to 3 cm ∅, brownish-red, more orange at full maturity, white-felty.—S. Peru (Nazca and Pisco valleys, c. 2000 m). Young plants have white Sp. and resemble Cleistocactus strausii.

v. **laticornua** Rauh & Backbg.: **Bo.** lower, to 3 m h., much more freely branching; **branches** more curving and ascending, sometimes rebranching, with fiercer **Sp.** below; **Ar.** smaller; **Fl.** and **Fr.** as in the type.

W. seyboldianus Rauh & Backbg.
Bo. to 3 m h., branching from the base, forming lax bushes; **branches** to 8 cm ∅, vivid green; **Ri.** 15; **Ar.** thick, 8 mm lg., buff at first; **Rsp.** not numerous, ± bristly at the apex, later to 1.5 cm lg., thin, buff; **Csp.** 1–3, similarly coloured, thin, to 7 cm lg.; **Fl.** solitary, subapical, 6–8 cm lg., compressed, strongly zygomorphic, 4.5 cm ∅, deep dark carmine outside, more light wine-coloured inside; **Tu.** strongly bent, thick, reddish-brown, with short reddish-brown H.; **Sep.** recurved; **Fil.** carmine; **An.** pink; **style** reddish; **Sti.** greenish; **Fr.** brownish-red, c. 3.5 cm ∅.—S. Peru (at the foot of Chachani Volcano, above Caima). (Fig. 447, right.) No Sp.-modification present in the flowering zone.

W. weberbaueri (K. Sch.) Backbg.
Bo. to 4 m h., branching from the base to form bushes; **branches** stiffly erect or sometimes ± curving, to 10 cm ∅, greyish-green; **Ri.** 15–22, ± tuberculate at the apex, with a transverse groove; **Ar.** thick, to 8 mm lg., greyish-yellow, with long woolly felt; **Rsp.** to c. 20, 1–1.5 cm lg., thin, yellowish-brown; **Csp.** 6–8, stouter, leather-coloured, to 6 cm lg.; **Fl.** 8–11 cm lg., to 5.5 cm ∅, pale brownish, pale chocolate-brown outside, Per. almost radial; **Tu.** only weakly curving, brownish to olive-green, with short brown H.; **Fil.** greenish below, white above; **style** and **Sti.** greenish; **Fr.** spherical, 4 cm ∅, brilliant orange-yellow, with short woolly H.—S. Peru (near Arequipa). (Fig. 447, left). No modification of Sp. in the flowering zone; Fl. with very curly H. inside below, these extending into the nectary.
v. **aureifuscus** Rauh & Backbg.: **Bo.** to 4 m h.; **branches** obliquely ascending, vivid green, somewhat curving; **Ri.** 17, narrow, with no distinct transverse indentation; **Ar.** grey; **Rsp.** 20–30, to 1.5 cm lg., vivid yellowish-brown; **Csp.** 1–3, brilliant reddish-brown above, later light grey to brownish, 1 of these mostly strongly elongated, to 8 cm lg., flexible, directed obliquely downwards; **H.** on **Fl.** and **Fr.** reddish-brown.—S. Peru (above Caima, near Arequipa, and Cerros de Caldera);
v. **horribilis** Rauh & Backbg.: **Bo.** to 2.5 m h; **branches** stiffly erect, to 15 cm ∅ below, vivid green; **Ri.** c. 17, transversely furrowed above; **Ar.** 1 cm lg., yellowish-brown; **Rsp.** c. 20, stout, sharp, to 1.5 cm lg., yellowish-brown at first, often grey below, later concolorous grey; **Csp.** 1–4, the most central one very stout, to 8 cm lg.,

dark leather-brown; **Fl.** mostly only 7 cm lg.; **Tu.** more strongly white-woolly;
v. **humilior** Rauh & Backbg.: **Bo.** to 2 m h., forming large bushes; **branches** to 10 cm ∅; **Ri.** 16, with an acute transverse indentation; **Ar.** 8 mm lg., light grey; **Rsp.** numerous, to 1.5 cm lg., very stout, light grey; **Csp.** to 8 cm lg., light brown at first, later frosted, grey; **Fl.** ± radial; **Sep.** chocolate-brown.—S. Peru (near Arequipa, western Cerros de Caldera, and at the foot of the volcanoes).

W. winterianus Ritt.—"Kakt. u.a. Sukk.", 13:4, 54–56.1962.
Bo. to 6 m h., with a short **trunk** to almost 2 m h. and then branching; **branches** parallel, ascending, fairly crowded, 5–8 cm ∅; **Ri.** 22–27, to 5 mm h., rather tuberculate, obtuse, seedlings have only 12–14 Ri.; **Ar.** dark to blackish-brown, to 4 mm lg.; **Rsp.** c. 20–30, fine, appressed, 0.5–1.5 cm lg., lower ones longest, numerous, upper ones fewer, shorter, 2–3 times as thick; **Csp.** c. 12–15, acicular, rather stouter than the upper radials, to 1.5 cm lg.; all **Sp.** dark golden-yellow, sometimes light yellow on old plants; **flowering zone** with 30–40 fine, light to golden-yellow Br.-Sp. to 7 cm lg., lower ones shorter, upper part of the Ar. (the point of insertion of the Fl.) enlarged, with longer felt, **buds** with wool the same colour as that of the Ar.; **Fl.** 7.5 cm lg., white or faintly pink inside, pink outside; **Tu.** with blackish-brown wool; **Fil.** and **style** white; **Sti.** light green; **Ov.** more brownish-red; **Fr.** to 4 cm ∅, barrel-shaped, dark green to greenish or reddish-brown, with dense blackish-brown wool.—Peru (Dept. La Libertad, Prov. Otusco, near Samne) (FR 165). (Fig. 448.)
v. **australis** Ritt.: **Branches** to 9 cm ∅; **Ri.** to 33; **Ar.** mostly rather larger; **Sp.** thinner, weaker, those of seedlings lighter; **Fl.** as in the type.— Peru (Dept. Ancash, Quebrada Huécocho, side-gorge of the Quebrada Casma) (FR 1066).
As for v. flavus Ritt., FR 165a, undescribed but listed in Winter's catalogue, Ritter says nothing more. Was it perhaps an early term for v. australis?

Weberocereus Br. & R. (47)

A slender-stemmed clambering or pendant epiphyte, stems mostly 3-angled or terete, rarely flattened or 3-winged at first, with aerial roots. The nocturnal flowers are pink, shortly funnelform or bellshaped-funnelform, the tuberculate ovary set with ± stiff bristly hairs. The hairy fruit is ± tuberculate. The spines are only short, sometimes weak, sometimes rather stouter, in one case missing. It is interesting to note that W. biolleyi, while sometimes only weakly angular, is also terete, and juvenile growths can be 3-winged or sometimes in part flattened. This species alone thus has all the polymorphism of the Hylocereeae. I illustrated anomalous flattening—in what was probably a Nyctocereus species—in "Die Cact.", IV: 2089 (Fig. 1975) 1960. The causes of these unusual forms merit closer investigation. Little information is available regarding the fruits and seeds of this genus, sometimes nothing at all.—Distribution: Costa Rica and Panama. [(R).]

W. biolleyi (Web.) Br. & R.
Bo. growing epiphytically on trees, and hanging down; **St.** thin, only 4–6 mm ∅, new growth sometimes flat, sometimes 3-winged; **Ri.** only very weakly angular, or absent; **Sp.** mostly missing or occasionally 1–3, yellow, short; **Ar.** small, with only traces of felt; **Fl.** 3–5 cm lg., pink inside; **Ov.** tuberculate, hairy.—Costa Rica (near Puerto Limón).
Flowering material in the Botanical Garden, Heidelberg, showed the Fl.-colour to be carmine, acc. Rauh; Britton and Rose say "pinkish", but a deeper colour is sometimes observable.

W. panamensis Br. & R.
Bo. epiphytic, hanging; **St.** distinctly 3-angled but sometimes flat, to 2 cm br.; **Ri.** normally 3, ± rounded or acute; **Ar.** often rather sunken, small, each with a Sc. beneath it; **Sp.** 1–3, very short, weak; **Fl.** 4–7 cm lg., white; **Sep.** yellowish-green; **style** and **Sti.** white, latter also pink; **Ov.** tuberculate, green, with tiny spreading Sc. and 4–8 longer white H.; **Fr.** red, to 3 cm ∅, spherical, tuberculate.—Panama (Rio Fato and Lake Gatun).

W. trichophorus Johns. & Kimn.—C. & S.J. [US] XXXV:6, 203–205. 1963.
Bo. climbing, intense green; **St.** terete or indistinctly 6–7-angled, only 8–12 mm ∅; **Ar.** c. 2–3 cm apart; **Sp.** c. 10, stiff, fairly stout, 3–12 mm lg., also 30–40 ± curly H. 5–20 mm lg.,; **Fl.** bellshaped-funnelform, to 6 cm lg., to 3.5 cm ∅; **Tu.** with dense fine Tub., with fairly long, lax H.; **Ov.** reddish; **Sep.** purple; **Pet.** flesh-coloured; **Fr.** oblong, 3 cm lg., 2.5 cm ∅, purplish-reddish; **pulp** brownish-red; **S.** to 1.75 mm lg., black.—Costa Rica (Prov. Limón, Peralta, c. 100 m).
Readily distinguishable from other spec. on account of the hair-development. Sp. are creamy at first, tipped yellowish, later concolorous yellow, thickened below; old St.-Seg. have to 20 Sp.

W. tunilla (Web.) Br. & R. (T.)
Bo. epiphytic, clambering, with few aerial **R.**; **St.** 1–1.5 cm ∅; **Ri.** rounded or 4-angled on new shoots, later with (2–)4(–5) angles; **Ar.** 3–6 cm

apart, prominent; **Sp.** 6–12, stiff, yellow at first, then brown, to 8 mm lg., swollen below, later mostly dropping; **Fl.** c. 6 cm lg., 4 cm ∅, salmon-pink; **Sep.** brownish, projecting; **Tu.** waxy, firm, tuberculate, with brown Br.-clusters.—Costa Rica (near Cartago or Talbón). Ov. also said to be bristly. (Fig. 449.)
It has still not been established if Cereus gonzalezii Web.—which Britton and Rose considered identical with the above spec.,—is a different spec. The plants had 4–5 brown Sp., rather weak, to only 4 mm lg., and the Ov. was said to be spiny (stiffer Br.?).—Costa Rica (near Pacayas).

Weinbergia cereiformis hort. (Gates): see Lophocereus mieckleyanus (Wgt.) Backbg.

Weingartia Werd. (118)

Simple or caespitose plants, with or without a neck-constriction of the napiform root. Flowers only fairly large, the tube very short, glabrous, scaly; fruit at most 1 cm ∅, glabrous, ± scaly. One remarkable feature of the taprooted species with a neck-constriction is that the roots are sometimes so stout that it is impossible to prise the plants from hard ground with the root intact; as a consequence of this loss of the taproot, experience to date of cultivated plants has shown that the plant-body mostly grows very elongated, becoming almost cereoid in the course of years; I have seen this myself in the case of both Bolivian and N. Argentinian species, particularly where the plants are grafted. A further peculiarity, at least with Weingartia neocumingii Backbg., is that the flowers appear several together from one and the same areole, or together with buds, and then not only on the upper part of the body but also quite low on the side. This does not appear to be constant in all the species, since Ritter does not mention it in connection with the species discovered by him. The Bolivian species all have lighter to deeper yellow flowers, while those of the N. Argentinian species are smaller and orange-yellow to orange-red. Only one species—Weingartia ambigua (Hildm.) Backbg.—with narrow and ± sinuate ribs, has purplish-violet flowers. Unfortunately its origin remains unclarified; Schumann's statement, "Bolivia or Chile" may be justified in that this species perhaps grows outside the previously accepted area of distribution, maybe on paths which are no longer visited by motorised collectors. As far as I know, the fruits contain only a few seeds; the fruits themselves seem mostly to be only slightly juicy and then to dry up; the seeds are matt black. The flowers are never borne centrally, at most near the crown or even lower down on the body. I first called the genus Spegazzinia Backbg., after the Argentinian botanist Dr. Carlos Spegazzini, who was the first man to make a closer study of the cactus-habitats of his homeland. However, this name proved to be a homonym, and it was replaced by Werdermann's name which commemorates Wilhelm Weingart, equally renowned as one of the finest earlier connoisseurs of the Cerei. The species of Weingartia constitute such a uniquely homogeneous group that Hutchison's referral of it to Gymnoclycium Pfeiff. is quite irrelevant and it has not been accepted by any other author. The position is quite different with individual species, where a much better case can be made out for the 'lumping' process which is in general so popular with American authors, and which I attempted in "Die Cact.", e.g. the inclusion of Weingartia pulquinensis in Weingartia neocumingii. The latter is in every respect representative of the E. Bolivian distribution of Weingartia. It must have its origin there, and yet neither Cardenas nor Ritter mentions it, but its identity with W. pulquinensis can scarcely be questioned. It is essential to note that some at least of the species are extremely variable, and I saw in Marnier's collection a specimen of Weingartia riograndensis in which the spines were much more strongly bent towards the apex than those shown in Ritter's photograph to accompany the description, in "Cact. & Succ. Journ. of Gr. Brit.", 23: 1, 11.1961.

Ritter and Cardenas seem to differ about Weingartia pulquinensis Card. since the plant in the Marnier collection which closely resembles Weingartia neocumingii—always bearing in mind the commonly occurring range of variability—bears no resemblance to Ritter's specimen which he sent to Buining in Holland under the same name: the latter has regularly dense, radiating and acicular spines which are interlacing, with several only slightly stouter and slightly longer central spines, all uniformly pale yellow, with just a few of the centrals slightly darker. Many authors probably also regard Weingartia riograndensis Ritt. as referable to Weingartia longigibba Ritt. The distance separating the two distributions is relatively small when one recalls that Neowerdermannia, for instance (which is also referable here), has a range extending from N. Argentina through the entire Bolivian highlands as far as Lake Titicaca. In 1950 I had to change the name of "Echinocactus cumingii SD." (1849–1850) to Weingartia neocumingii Backbg., since Salm-Dyck's name was a homonym of that of Hopfer (1843) which related to an unclarified species with hairy flowers. (W. pulquinensis Card. is regarded as a synonym, with its variety.) In this connection it is important to consider my Fig. 3416, "Die Cact.", VI: 3763. 1962, which shows a plant raised from

seed of Weingartia neocumingii, with very short, rather stout and darker-tipped spines. If a variant such as this were found in habitat, it would doubtless be regarded as a distinct species. Moreover my plants of Weingartia hediniana here in Europe do not develop anything like the very white and woolly crown I have seen on imported plants in the collections of Dölz and the nurseryman Ross—in other words, this may develop earlier or more extensively in other environmental conditions. All these points require consideration when assessing the validity of any species. For all that, the genus is one which well deserves the attention of collectors; indeed it is one of the most floriferous genera of spherical cacti.—Distribution: E. Bolivia, N. Argentina and possibly the frontier region of Chile. (Grafting recommended.) See also Neowerdermannia Frič.

W. ambigua (Hildm.) Backbg.
Bo. simple, spherical, later oblong, light greyish-green, to 15 cm h., 10–12 cm $\varnothing$; **crown** with weak yellowish-white felt; **Ri.** 21, rather sinuate, acute, obtusely swollen around the Ar., to 2 cm h.; **Ar.** 2 cm apart, to 4 mm lg., with some yellowish-white felt; **Rsp.** 8, spreading, stiff, subulate, lowest ones longest, to 1 cm lg., brown to blackish at first; **Csp.** 1, straight, to over 1.5 cm lg., stouter, darker; **Fl.** purplish-violet, c. 3 cm $\varnothing$, glabrous, scaly; **Fr.**?—Bolivia or Chile (K. Schumann).

W. chilensis (Backbg.) Backbg. n. comb. in Descr. Cact. Nov. III, 15. 1963: for description see under Neowerdermannia Frič, since this is the generic name most commonly used for it in collections.

W. chuquichiquensis: resembles W. neocumingii but distinguished by the light yellow rounded Pet. of the Fl.

W. cintiensis n. subnud.: plant branching from the base to form groups, shoots oblong, Sp. dark-coloured; an extremely interesting spec., also collected by Rausch, but not yet described.—Bolivia (Cinti). (Fig. 450.)

W. corroana Card.: **Weingartia neocumingii** v. **corroana** (Card.) Backbg.

W. cumingii (Werd.) Marsh.: **Weingartia neocumingii** Backbg.

W. erinacea Ritt.—C. & S.J. of Gr. Brit., 23:1, 8–9. 1961.
Bo. hemispherical, to 15 cm $\varnothing$, without a taproot; **Ri.** made up of obtuse Tub. 1.5 cm lg.; **Ar.** white, to 1.5 cm lg., the upper floral insertion more thickly woolly; **Rsp.** 10–18, to 1.5 cm lg.; **Csp.** 2–3, even

5–12, to 1.75 cm lg.; all **Sp.** stiff, straight, sharp, yellowish-white, darker-tipped; **Fl.** to 3 cm lg., to 2.75 cm ∅, golden-yellow, darker above; **Pet.** rounded above; **Fil.** pale yellow; **style** greenish; **Sti.** whitish; **Fr.** whitish, broadly scaly; **S.** 1 mm lg.— Bolivia (Cochabamba, S. of Quiroya). Acc. Ritter, related to W. sucrensis Ritt. and W. multispina Ritt.

v. **catarirensis** Ritt.—l.c.: **Bo.** smaller; **Sp.** weaker; **Tub.** smaller; **Ar.** woollier; more freely offsetting (S. of Quiroya, near Catarire).

W. fidaiana (Backbg.) Werd. (T.)

Bo. mostly simple at first, greyish-green, to c. 12 cm ∅ (or more?); **R.** thick, napiform, with a neck-constriction; **Ar.** large, thickly felty; **Ri.** resolved almost completely into round Tub.; **Rsp.** c. 9, to 3 cm lg.; **Csp.** 3–4, to 5 cm lg.; all **Sp.** straw-coloured to violet-black, with transitions between these colours, all curving, mostly upwards, interlacing, projecting ± obliquely upwards, later densely enveloping the Bo.; **Fl.** yellow, to 3 cm lg., remaining open at night, glabrous, scaly; **Fr.** small, oblong-spherical, dehiscing basally; **S.** only few.— S. Bolivia (Tupiza).

The Tub. are not quite round but have 6 ± rounded angles. In the face of the "lumping" process popular with American authors, I consider W. westii (Hutch.) Backbg. more likely to be a straighter-spined variety of the above spec., the Sp. ± concolorous. Admittedly it is oblong, but I have observed this also in W. fidaiana; both plants have the same taproot, with a neck-constriction, the numbers of Sp., both radials and centrals, is approximately the same; true, the Fl. is rather longer—but Ritter has mentioned similar variability in the plants described by him: in W. erinacea, for instance, a difference of 1 cm in length and 1 cm in ∅; moreover the illustration of an older plant shows close similarity to the above spec.

I W. gracilispina (FR 954): no description available.

W. hediniana Backbg.

Bo. simple, rather oblong, without a constricted taproot, to 10 cm h. and 6 cm ∅ has been noted, intense green; **crown** with thick white wool (plants in habitat); **Ri.** c. 16, consisting of roundish Tub., these narrowly connected; **Ar.** white-woolly, thick, wool increasing towards the crown; **Rsp.** 12–14, whitish, brown at first above, spreading sideways, fairly stout but variable in thickness, ± curving, to 2.5 cm lg.; **Csp.** 4 more clearly differentiated, coloured as the Rsp. or rather darker, ± slightly curving; **Fl.** fairly numerous around the crown, to 3 cm lg. and ∅, Sc. few; **Fil.** and **style** white.— Bolivia (road to Sucre? [Card.]).

W. lanata Ritt.—Nat. C. & S.J. (Gr. Brit.), 16:7–8.1961.

Bo. hemispherical, to 17 cm ∅, later somewhat offsetting, without a taproot; **crown** with thicker white wool or with tufts of wool to 1.5 cm lg. in the flowering Ar.; **Ri.** c. 14 distinguishable; **Tub.** to 3.5 cm lg., 2.5 cm br., 2 cm h.; **Ar.** with a somewhat furrow-like extension; **Rsp.** 12–16, 1–4 cm lg., lower ones shorter; **Csp.** very variable in number, length and thickness, c. 10–15, c. 1.5–5 cm lg., yellow to yellowish-brown, little darker above; **Fl.** 2.75–3.75 cm lg., to 3 cm ∅; **Fl.** 2.75–3.75 cm lg., to 3 cm ∅; **Fil.** in 2 Ser., golden-yellow; **style** greenish; **Sti.** white; **Fr.** 8 mm lg., 6 mm br., greenish to reddish-brown; **S.** 1 mm lg.—Bolivia (Chuquisaca, Prov. Oropeza, near Chuquichuqui). Unfortunately no photo was published to accompany the description, so that the relationship with W. hediniana cannot now be verified. Ritter points to the following main differences: in W. hediniana Ar. oblong, Fil. in 2 Ser., style green; in W. lanata Ar. round, Fil. in 1 Ser., style white. Differences in the form of the Ov. are less important since this can be very variable, as I have seen for myself in several Fl.; Fl.-size is not appreciably divergent. Since W. lanata is widespread in the mountains between Rio Grande and Rio Pilcomayo, and the Csp., for instance, are very variable, there is still the possibility of a relationship at subspecific level. In W. neocumingii too the shape of the Ar. differs, being round or oblong. The dimensions given for W. hediniana refer to imported plants I have observed; this does not mean the plants cannot grow larger because often only smaller specimens are collected. Acc. Ritter, W. lanata has the greatest diameter but I cannot exclude the possibility that similarly sized plants may be found in other spec., e.g. W. hediniana.

W. lecoriensis Card.—"Cactus", 19:82, 47–48. 1964.

Bo. spherical, with thick R.; **Ri.** 13–19; **Sp.** 12–14, stiffly acicular, light grey, to 3.5 cm lg.; **Fl.** 3 cm lg., yellow.—Bolivia (Chuquisaca, between Lecori and Sivingamayu, 3200 m).

Cardenas makes a comparison of this spec, with W. westii, but unfortunately not with W. fidaiana. The 3 spec. undoubtedly form a close-knit complex.

W. longigibba Ritt.—C. & S.J. of Gr. Brit., 23:1, 8.1961.

Bo. spherical at first, later oblong, to 9 cm ∅, later offsetting from below, light green, without a thick taproot; **Ri.** c. 10–13 recognisable; **Tub.** to c. 4 cm lg., to 2.5 cm br., without a chin below the Ar.; **Ar.** to 1.25 cm lg., more woolly at the point of floral insertion, but less so than in W. lanata; **Rsp.** c. 7–12, to 2.5 cm lg., lower ones shortest; **Csp.** 3–8, stiff,

1.5–3.5 cm lg.; **Sp.** greyish-brown, rather darker above, straight or only slightly curving; **Fl.** to 3.5 cm lg. and ∅, opening widely, golden-yellow, with spatulate Pet.; **Fil.** light yellow; **style** green; **Sti.** pale yellow; **Fr.** green, 1 cm lg.; **S.** 1 mm lg.—Bolivia (Prov. Oropeza, on the Rio Chico).

W. multispina Ritt.—Nat. C. & S.J. (Gr. Brit.), 16: 7. 1961.
Bo. hemispherical, to over 14 cm ∅, later elongated, green, simple, without a taproot; **Ri.** divided into numerous rather oblong Tub. c. 0.75 cm lg., with a chin-like prominence below the Ar.; **Ar.** with pale brownish felt at first; **Sp.** all alike, concolorous yellowish-brownish to brownish-red, not dark-tipped, straight, ± stiff, sharp, c. 25–30, thin, to 1 cm lg., spreading, passing over into 20–25 Csp., to almost twice as long, 1–2 cm lg.; **Fl.** numerous, c. 2 cm lg., 1.5 cm ∅, golden-yellow with a slight green tinge, Pet. spatulate; **Fil.** pale yellow; **style** greenish-yellow; **Sti.** pale yellow; **Fr.** to 8 mm lg., 7 mm br., yellowish or brownish or mid-green; **S.** c. 0.65 mm lg.—Bolivia (Cochabamba, Aiquile).

W. neocumingii Backbg.
Bo. to 20 cm h. (when grafted), 10 cm ∅, darker or lighter green, simple; **Ri.** divided into c. 16–18 R. of Tub., these ± 4-sided below to ± flat and 6-sided; **Rsp.** to c. 16; **Csp.** to c. 10, the latter rather stouter than the radials; all **Sp.** ± projecting, radiating, whitish-yellow, tipped dark yellow, rather darker in the crown; **Ar.** oblong or round (Berger); **Fl.** appearing from the upper part of the Bo. to far down on the sides, often several simultaneously from one Ar., to 2.5 cm lg., orange-yellow to golden-yellow, reputedly also tending towards brick-colour.—Bolivia (probably Prov. Florida). (Fig. 451, left.)
The type-species stays ± spherical, the Sp. are more brownish and the Fl. are more numerous and borne over a longer period; in v. flavispina hort. the Bo. soon becomes more columnar, strongly over-topped by yellowish, fairly dense Sp., with the Fl. borne only sparingly and not until mid-summer.
At one time both forms were generally known in collections. In the light of the variability of Sp.-colour, Ar.-shape and Fl.-colour as well as the density of the Sp., it seems advisable to study afresh the question of whether Ritter's new descriptions in fact represent valid spec. W. pulquinensis Card. must be regarded as belonging to the above spec.—even after my study of Cardenas's plant in the Botanical Garden of "Les Cèdres"—or at most as one of the range of forms of this spec.; these remarks also apply to the following variety:—
v. brevispina hort.: an unusually short-spined form of W. neocumingii which I saw in Andreae's collection, raised from seed of W.

neocumingii; Sp. fairly firm, only a few mm lg.; v. **corroana** (Card.) Backbg. (W. pulquinensis v. corroana Card.): **Ri.** 11–15, divided into fairly large Tub. to 2 cm br.; **Ar.** 1 cm lg., elliptic; **Rsp.** 18; **Csp.** 1; all **Sp.** subulate, never bristly, 1.5–3 cm lg., grey; **Fl.** 3 cm lg., pale yellow; **Sti.** green.—Bolivia (Florida, Pulquina-Saipina). Since Cardenas himself at first considered this plant to be a variety of some spec. insufficiently differentiated from W. neocumingii, it is obviously very variable; Cardenas erroneously held "Echus. cumingii" to be no longer identifiable, presumably because he was unaware of the numerous specimens in European collections. Since Cardenas re-discovered W. neocumingii (as "W. pulquinensis") and particularly in the light of the known variability, it becomes essential to examine whether or not some of Ritter's spec. are better regarded as varieties of one of the similar plants mentioned above, e.g. W. hediniana-lanata, W. longigibbariograndensis, W. multispina and the plant known as W. pulquinensis in Buining's collection.
In "Cactus", 19: 82, 49. 1964, Cardenas published as a distinct spec.—W. corroana Card.—the plant he had previously described as W. pulquinensis v. corroana Card. In view of the preceding, I cannot regard it as more than a variety of W. neocumingii.

W. neumanniana (Backbg.) Werd.
Bo. to only 7 cm lg., 5 cm ∅, velvety, greyish-green, with a much longer, divided taproot with a neck-constriction; **Ri.** c. 14, made indistinctly tuberculate by the transverse indentations or thickenings above the Ar., but with rather indistinctly 6-angled Tub. towards the crown; **Ar.** c. 1 cm apart; **Rsp.** c. 6, rigid, sharp, spreading, projecting; **Csp.** mostly 1, to 2.2 cm lg., rather longer than the Rsp.; all **Sp.** dark brown to reddish-black; **Fl.** c. 2.5 cm lg. and approximately as br., yellow to reddish-orange.—N. Argentina (N. of Humahuaca).
v. **aurantia** Backbg.—Descr. Cact. Nov. III: 15. 1963: **Bo.** becoming larger, velvety, dull dark olive-green; **Ar.** ± round, white; **Sp.** 1–4, black (or lighter?); **Fl.** reddish-orange, more reddish outside, more orange inside.—N. Argentina? (Fig. 452.)

W. pilcomayoensis Card.—"Cactus", 19: 82, 44–46. 1964.
Bo. spherical or broadly conical, to 13 cm h., to 12 cm ∅, bluish to reddish-green; **Ri.** c. 14, divided into stout, broadly rounded Tub. to 1 cm h., 2 cm br.; **Ar.** on the upper side of the Tub., round or elliptic, to 1 cm lg., grey; **Rsp.** 12–15, rather projecting or appressed sideways, 5–20 mm lg.; **Csp.** 1–4, 2–3 cm lg., those in the upper part of the

Bo. directed towards the crown; all **Sp.** acicular, whitish, tipped grey or brown, thickened below; **Fl.** 4 cm lg., yellow; **Tu.** greenish-yellow; **Ov.** greenish-white, 5 mm lg.; **Fil.**, **style** (above) and **Sti.** yellow.—Bolivia (Prov. Saavedra, Dept. Potosí, on the road from Puente Pilcomayo to Otuyo, 2400 m).

W. platygona Card.—Cactus, 19: 82, 50–51. 1964. **Bo.** cylindric, ± tapering above, to 12 cm lg., 5.5 cm ⌀, suffused deep purple; **Ri.** c. 12, divided into rounded but not prominent Tub.; **Ar.** 1 cm apart, 3 mm lg., grey; **Rsp.** 12–14, ± appressed to rather projecting; **Csp.** 2, directed upwards, to 1.2 cm lg.; all **Sp.** acicular, thin, whitish; **Fl.** 2.5 cm lg., limb ± zygomorphic; **Pet.** golden-yellow; **Sep.** and **Ov.** purple; **Fil.** yellow; style yellowish-green.—Bolivia (Potosí, near Millares, 3000 m). An interesting, clearly differentiated and rare spec., with rather small Fl.

W. pulquinensis Card. and v. corroana Card.: see under **Weingartia neocumingii** Backbg. and v. **corroana** (Card.) Backbg.

W. riograndensis Ritt.—C. & S.J. Gr. Brit., 23: 1, 9–10. 1961. **Bo.** hemispherical, green, lacking a thick taproot, becoming rather oblong; old plants occasionally offset somewhat from the base; **Ri.** tuberculate; **Tub.** to 2 cm lg., 1.5 cm br., 1 cm h., without a chin; **Ar.** 8 mm lg., 4 mm br., with plentiful white wool in the upper part; **Rsp.** c. 5–10, to 2 cm lg.; **Csp.** 3–6, stiffer, to 1.5 cm lg.; all **Sp.** spreading, yellowish-grey to greyish-brown at first, lowest ones shortest; **Fl.** to 3 cm lg., 2.75 cm ⌀, opening widely, golden-yellow, Pet. rounded to tapering, upper Sc. brownish-red, with a light border; **Fil.** white; style pale green; **Sti.** pale yellow; **Ov.** pale green; **Fr.** to 1 cm lg., 0.75 cm ⌀, yellowish to reddish-green; **S.** 1 mm lg.—Bolivia (Rio Grande, near Puente Arce). (Fig. 451, right.) (FR 813.)

W. sucrensis Ritt.—Nat. C. & S.J. (Gr. Brit.), 16: 8. 1961. **Bo.** depressed-spherical, eventually hemispherical, to 15 cm ⌀, always simple, green, with a short **taproot** and a neck-like constriction; **Ri.** numerous, entirely divided into Tub. to 1.5 cm lg., 0.75 cm br., 0.75 cm h., with a small chin-like prominence below the Ar.; **Ar.** white-felty, to 8 mm lg., 4 mm br., felt only short; **Rsp.** 10–15, rather thin, 0.75–2 cm lg., passing over into the Csp., the bottom ones shortest; **Csp.** 6–12, stouter, 1–2 cm lg.; **Sp.** spreading in all directions, light or greyish-brown, dark-tipped; **Fl.** 3.25 cm lg., to 3 cm ⌀, golden-yellow, Pet. tapering above and below, Sc. fairly

dense; **Fil.** golden-yellow **style** greenish; **Sti.** cream; **Ov.** light green, with rounded whitish Sc., green below; **Fr.** c. 6 mm lg., 4 mm ⌀, green to reddish or brownish-green; **S.** 0.75 mm lg.—Bolivia (E. of Sucre, Cuesta del Desmeador, 2500 m).
Acc. Ritter, closely related to W. erinacea.

W. torotorensis Card. **Bo.** spherical, 4 cm h., 7 cm ⌀, fresh green, crown sunken; **Ri.** c. 20, irregularly divided into short, hatchet-shaped, spotted Tub. 10 mm h., 8 mm br. below; **Ar.** 12 mm apart, elliptic, 6–8 mm lg., grey-felty; **Sp.** very unequal, 3–20 mm lg., pectinate, sharp, grey to whitish, some of them curving above; **Fl.** numerous, in a ring, funnel-form, 3.5 cm lg., 3 cm ⌀, light purple; **Ov.** light green with thick Sc. 3 mm lg., with white H. in their axils; **Tu.** very short, with light green Sc.; **Sep.** light purple; **Pet.** purple, whitish below; **Fil.** purple below, whitish above; style white, with 7 light yellow **Sti.**—Bolivia (Bilbao, Dept. Potosí near Toro-Toro, at 2000 m). Named for its place of origin.

W. vilacayensis Card.—"Cactus", 19: 82, 46–47. 1964. **Bo.** subspherical, to 6 cm h., 12 cm ⌀; **Ri.** c. 26, tuberculate; **Ar.** to 2 cm apart, elliptic, 6 mm lg., grey; **Sp.** 17–23, acicular, compressed, mostly pectinate, a few more projecting and clothing the Bo. fairly densely, greyish-white, thickened below, 0.5–3 cm lg.; **Fl.** 5–6 cm lg., yellow; **Tu.**, **Ov.** and style green.—Bolivia (Prov. Linares, near Vilacaya, 3200 m). Spec. of quite strongly divergent habit; Sp. dense and very fine.

W. vorwerkii (Frič) Backbg. and var. n. comb.— Descr. Cact. Nov. III: 16. 1963: for description, see under Neowerdermannia Frič.

W. westii Hutch.: appears more likely to be a form of **Weingartia fidaiana** (Backbg.) Werd. Data as follows: **Bo.** later elongated and cylindric, to 20 cm lg., 8 cm ⌀, dark green or reddish; **R.** with a neck-like construction; **Ri.** 14, divided into 6-sided **Tub.** 1.5 cm br., 1 cm lg.; **Ar.** to 7 mm lg., with whitish or yellowish-brown felt; **Rsp.** 9–11, to 3 cm lg., ± erect or weakly curving; **Csp.** 1–4, scarcely differentiated, to 3.5 cm lg.; all **Sp.** white, tipped brownish, fairly straight, mostly directed upwards; **Fl.** 4 cm lg., 3.5 cm ⌀; **Pet.** yellow; **Sc.** greenish; **Fr.** spherical, to 9 mm ⌀.—Bolivia (Potosí, Cuchu Ingenio). See also under W. fidaiana. Given the divergences mentioned under W. neocumingii as well as those given by Ritter for Fl.-length, the above description is not sufficient evidence for specific rank. (FR 818.)

Werckleocereus Br. & R. (44)

Clambering or epiphytic Cerei with aerial roots, the ribs scarcely or weakly notched, the areoles with short bristles or weak spines. The attractive white flowers are nocturnal and rather shortly funnelform, with an only moderately broad perianth, while the tube is relatively stout. Tube and ovary have black woolly felt and spines. The fruit is spherical and spiny. 2 species described.

The uncertainly based classification on which Kimnach's publications rest is shown by the fact that he—and later Buxbaum—referred "Werckleocereus imitans Kimn. & Hutch." to Werckleocereus, mentioning "habitual convergence" by comparison with similar species of Epiphyllum having dentate flat shoots. Perhaps it was because I drew his attention to the unmistakably cereoid nature of Werckleocereus (making "habitual convergence" an irrelevance since the species has all the characters of Alexander's Genus Cryptocereus) that "W. imitans" was again transferred—this time not to Cryptocereus, however, but (with dubious comparative drawings) to Eccremocactus, even although the latter, according to the original diagnosis, only occasionally shows traces of felt on the ovary, whereas in "Eccremocactus imitans and E. rosei" it is prickly (a divergent character), and the fruit similarly; in Eccremocactus the latter is naked. Details were also provided as to where plant-material had been deposited, and so on. But it did not occur to anyone to send me material for examination, probably because the answer was seen as a foregone conclusion: what sense is there in having a type-species for a genus, with a corresponding generic diagnosis, if one later adds species in which the line of floral reduction shows quite divergent characters so that the differences become obscured, a "genus sensu latiore" is created and this, in turn, is just as dubious as the earlier inclusion of "Werckleocereus imitans" in Werckleocereus; worse still, it ignores the existence of an appropriate genus which is already in being. Every detail could be disputed, but this has little point in the absence of any clearly defined and logical principle of classification for the whole family such as is demonstrated by the story of "Werckleocereus imitans Kimn. & Hutch". This just seems to be a case of "doing something different", without understanding the effects on the family overall.—Distribution: Costa Rica and Guatemala. [Vigorous-growing epiphytes.]

W. glaber (Eichl.) Br. & R.
Bo. clambering, pale green, somewhat frosted; **St.** slender, 3-angled, c. 2 cm $\emptyset$; **Ri.** (or angles) with $\pm$ ladder-like projections at the Ar.; **Ar.** on the prominences, to 4 cm apart, small; **Sp.** 2–4, short,

1–3 mm lg., acicular, swollen below; **Fl.** to over 10 cm lg.; **Tu.** and **Ov.** with tufts of yellow to brown acicular Sp.; **Pet.** white, $\pm$ denticulate; **style** pale yellow, not projecting; **Sti.** white; **Fr.**?—Guatemala (in the W.).

W. tonduzii (Web.) Br. & R. (T.)
Bo. branching and bush-like; **St.** robust, with 3(–4) angles, deep green, not frosted, c. 2.5 cm $\emptyset$; **Ri.** (angles) virtually without notches; **Ar.** small, rather felty; **Sp.** 0, or replaced by weak Br.; **Fl.** to 8 cm lg., creamy-white; **Tu.** and **Ov.** with clusters of dark Sp. arising from the black-felty Ar.; **Fr.** spherical, lemon-yellow, with many Ar. and thin Sp.—Costa Rica (Copey, near Santa Maria de Dota). (Fig. 453.)

Wigginsia D.M. Porter (109)

"Taxon", XIII: 210–211 (July) 1964. (Malacocarpus SD. non Fisch. & Mey.). Salm-Dyck's name, in use for over 100 years, had to be changed because the proposal of R. S. Byles (1957) that Malacocarpus SD. should be declared a nomen conservandum was not admitted. The valid combinations are given here in **Malacocarpus**, with each specific name.

The genius was re-named for Dr. Ira Wiggins, USA.

W. comantii Ritt. (FR 1427): no description available.

W. horstii Ritt. and v. juvenaliformis (FR 1402): no description available.

W. leprosorum Ritt. (FR 1272): no description available.

W. prolifera Ritt. (FR 1403) and v. longispina Ritt. (FR 1403A): no description available.

Wilcoxia Br. & R. (138)

Small to dwarf shrubs with $\pm$ napiform or tuberously thickened roots; the many-ribbed branches are thin, flexible and $\pm$ soft-fleshy, mostly with short or in part fine hair-like or bristle-like spines. The flowers in general open during the day; they are moderately large and funnelform, coloured white, red or purplish-pink, set with bristly spines, and appear high on the flanks of the shoot or apically; there is in fact one species in which the shoot-tip mostly passes directly over to the flower. In one species the flowers are said to be nocturnal, a phenomenon which is parallelled in a few species of the Genus Echinocereus with which Wilcoxia is doubtless fairly closely related. The floral tubes vary in length, being relatively long in part. The ± woolly and bristly fruits are probably always red, and the seeds are glossy black.—Distribution: USA (Texas) to Central Mexico and Baja California. [Some plants can be grown on their own roots, others require grafting.]

W. albiflora Backbg.
Bo. forming a quite freely branching, very small shrub; **branches** smooth, tapering and woody below, to 15 cm lg., to 6 mm ∅, almost terete, light green; **Ar.** minute; **Sp.** c. 9–12, to c. 1 mm lg., very fine, appressed; **Fl.** mostly forming an extension of the shoot-tip, less often high on the sides, c. 2 cm lg.; **Pet.** narrowly lanceolate, tapering, white or a very delicate pink; **Tu.** c. 1.3 cm lg., 3 mm ∅, reddish-green, with to 12 white or brownish small Br.-Sp.; **Fr.**?—Origin unknown, probably Mexico. [Haage adds: Mexico (Sonora).] (Fig. 454.)

W. diguetii (Web.) Peebles: **Peniocereus diguetii** (Web.) Backbg.

W. mariana Gentry: **Peniocereus marianus** (Gentry) H. Sanchez-Mej.

W. nerispina: an undescribed plant, distributed by Schmoll under this name, has longer, projecting, light, dark-tipped Sp., 1–2 of these directed up and/or down, particularly stout, arranged as Csp.; in cultivation these latter Sp. apparently do not become as robust.

W. papillosa Br. & R.
Bo. with a fleshy **taproot** to 7 cm lg., little branching; **branches** minutely papillose, otherwise smooth, to 40 cm lg., 3–5–8 mm ∅; **Ri.** c. 3–5, indistinct; **Ar.** small, white-woolly; **Sp.** clustered, 6–8 together, spreading horizontally, 1–3 mm lg., fine, with a bulbous thickening below, yellowish-brown; **Fl.** 4–5 cm lg., scarlet; **Tu.** with long white wool only (?) above, and several brown Br. 8–12 mm lg.; **Fr.**?—Mexico (Sinaloa: Culiacan, Tinamaxtita, San Ignacio; Guerrero: Cañon del Zopilote).

W. poselgeri (Lem.) Br. & R. (T.)
Bo. with several tuberous black **R.**; **branches** smooth, 30–60 cm lg., 6–10–15 mm ∅, cylindric, ± dark green; **Ri.** 8–10, indistinct; **Ar.** weakly felty; **Rsp.** 9–12, c. 2 mm lg., straight, thin; **Csp.** 1, 5–10 mm lg., thickened below, erect, white to darker, black-tipped; **Fl.** 4–5 cm lg., lateral or terminal, agreeably scented; **Pet.** narrow, denticulate, widely spreading or revolute, light purple with a darker centre; **Tu.** and **Ov.** with white wool and long Br.;

Fr. ovoid.—USA (S. Texas), Mexico (Coahuila).

W. pseudotomentosa Backbg., undescribed: similar to W. tomentosa, with to 10 appressed Sp., rarely thickened below, 3 of these appressed upwards and straw-coloured, 2 laterals, dark, and c. 5 directed downwards, very thin, blackish-brown; **Csp.** 0; **Ar.** with grey curly H. concealing the Sp.-bases, longer-persisting; **Fl.** not known.—Origin?

W. schmollii (Wgt.) Backbg.
Bo. with a napiform **R.** c. 7 cm lg.; **branches** at first very thin in part, later stouter to clavate, weak (to c. 2 cm ∅ if the plant is grafted, which is recommended); **Ri.** 9–10, ± tuberculate; **Sp.** hair-like, unequal, to 7 mm lg., whitish, blackish or violet-blackish; **Fl.** c. 3.5 cm lg., purplish-pink; **Tu.** covered with hair-like Sp.; **Fr.**?—Mexico (Querétaro).

W. striata (Brand.) Br. & R.
Bo. with brownish, deeply penetrating **R.**; **branches** to c. 1 m lg., very thin, smooth, ash-grey to bluish-green; **Ri.** 9, indistinct; **Sp.** c. 9, 1.5–3 mm lg., thin, weak, appressed, coffee-coloured to ± black; **Fl.** 10–12 cm lg., purple; **Fr.** pear-shaped, glossy, scarlet, bristly; **S.** finely pitted.—Mexico (Baja California; acc. Br. & R., also Sonora).

W. tamaulipensis Werd.
Bo. very soft-fleshy, dark green; **branches** to over 20 cm lg., cylindric, to thumb-thickness, new shoots obliquely ascending, tip over-topped at first by whitish to blackish Sp., with little white wool; **Ri.** c. 10. divided by distinct longitudinal furrows; **Rsp.** c. 15–20, to 2.5 mm lg., bristly, upper ones shorter, dark brown or lighter, tipped brown; **Csp.** sometimes scarcely differentiated, 5–10, obliquely spreading, mostly shorter but stouter than the longest Rsp., more thickened below, blackish-brown; **Sp.** ± rough; **Fl.** c. 5 cm lg., pale pink with a darker M.-stripe; **Tu.** with flocky wool and c. 15–20 fine Br.-Sps., those in the upper part of the Tu. to 1 cm lg., concolorous white to blackish-brown; **Fr.**?—Mexico (Tamaulipas).

W. tomentosa H. Bravo
Bo. branching to form a low shrub; **branches** to 1.5 cm ∅, cylindric, greyish-green, strongly tomentose throughout the entire length; **Ri.** c. 7, rounded; **Ar.** 1.5–3 cm apart, round, glabrous; **Rsp.** 8–10, to 6 mm lg., acicular, flattened, stiff, appressed, thickened below; **Csp.** 1, shorter, stouter; **Sp.** black; **Fl.** subapical, c. 9 cm lg.; **Sep.** lanceolate, brownish-pink, tomentose; **Pet.** in 2 Ser., pink suffused purple; **Tu.** weakly curving above the Ov.; **Fr.** ovoid, noticeably tapering to both ends; **S.** pear-shaped.—Mexico (Morelos, near Estacas).

W. viperina (Web.) Br. & R.
Bo. branching to form a lax bush, to 2 m h.; **branches** (lower ones) woody, to 2 cm ∅, velvety, greyish to olive-green; **Ri.** 8–10; **Ar.** 1–2 cm apart, little felty; **Rsp.** 8–9, 3–5 mm lg., thin, thickened below, radiating laterally and appressed, black; **Csp.** 3–4 (or fewer), very short, conical, much thickened below, mostly directed downwards, blackish, all later falling; **Fl.** to 6 cm lg.; **Pet.** slightly ciliate, red; **Tu.** with grey wool and thin Sp.; **Fr.** subspherical, red.—Mexico (Puebla, between Tehuacan and Zapotitlan).

W. zapilotensis Matuda
Bo. to 4 m lg., thin; **Ri.** 16–20, scarcely recognizable; **Sp.** 6–9, minute, appressed, whitish, to 3 mm lg.; **Csp.** 1–2, 2–3 mm lg., reddish-brown with a dark tip; **Fl.** 5 cm lg., reddish-purple.—Mexico (Zapilote Canyon, from the Rio Balsas to approximately 40 km southwards). Named for the source-locality.

W. sp.: with nocturnal subapical Fl.; Pet. brick-red to carmine, inner ones shorter; Tu. conspicuously long.

Wilmattea Br. & R. (48)

An epiphytic, thin-stemmed, clambering Cereus with aerial roots and few short spines. The nocturnal flowers are mostly solitary, moderately large although relatively broad, with a scarcely recognizable tube, and narrow petals. The tube and ovary have traces of felt in the axils of some scales, and up to 4 curly hairy bristles. The fruit is unknown.—Distribution: Guatemala, Honduras. [A vigorously growing epiphyte.]

W. minutiflora (Br. & R.) Br. & R. (T.)
Bo. climbing; **St.** 3-angled, angles acute but not winged, not horny; **Ar.** 2–4 cm apart; **Sp.** 1–3, minute, brownish; **H.** are also said to have been observed; **Fl.** white; **Sep.** linear, with a red M.-line and tip; **Pet.** to 3.5 cm lg., very narrow, tapering; **Fil.** ± erect, attached to the lower part of the Pet.; **An.** cream; **style** white, c. 1.5 cm lg., overtopping the Fil.; **Sti.** c. 12, white below, pink above.—Distribution: see above. (Fig. 455.)

Winterocereus Backbg. nom nov. (69)

(Winteria Ritt., Kakt. u.a. Sukk., 13: 1, 4–8. 1962).

Pendant Cerei, branching freely from the base, with dense, delicate, golden-yellow spines. The clearly differentiating character lies in the slightly curving flowers characterised by a kind of double corolla,

i.e. an outer series of orange-red petals, and an inner one of shorter, white to pink petals. The ± spherical green fruit splits above at maturity. The black seeds are finely tuberculate.—A monotypic genus.—Distribution: Bolivia (Prov. Florida, Fauces Yapacani). Since Gordon Rowley has pointed out (Nat. Cact. & Succ. Journ., 19: 3, 33. 1964) that Winteria Ritt. must be regarded as an orthographic variant of Wintera Murr., and the genus therefore requires a new name, I have chosen Winterocereus as nomen novum, in order to retain the name Ritter intended to commemorate. The genus is close to Bolivicereus. [Referred by Rowley to **Borzicactus**. Translator.]

W. aureispinus (Ritt.) Backbg. n. nov. (T.)
Bo. hanging, green; **St.** to 1.5 m lg., to 2.5 cm ∅; **Ri.** 16–17, with slight indentations between the Ar.; **Ar.** rounded, with light brown felt, 3–5 mm apart; **Rsp.** c. 30, 4–10 mm lg., radiating, lateral ones longer; **Csp.** c. 20, rather stouter, upper ones longer, often elongated on old shoots or on their flowering side; **Sp.** weak, flexible, straight, golden-yellow; **Fl.** lateral, remaining open several days and nights, ± curving, 4–6 cm lg., c. 5 cm ∅, inner Pet. c. 10–12, to 8 mm lg., inclined towards the Fil., outer ones c. 15–20, to 3.5 cm lg., widely spreading and revolute; **Ov.** with numerous Sc. and very sparse short white H.—Distribution: see above. (FR 846). (Fig. 456.)

Wittia K. Sch. (41)

Small epiphytic shrubs, ± freely branching, with flat, leaf-like, oblong, notched, leaf-green stem-segments with a stout middle-rib, without spines. The small cylindric flowers have a relatively long tube and only few petals which are fairly erect (does the limb open more widely at night?); the anthers are arranged in two groups of unequal length. The fruit is strongly angular, with a sunken floral scar; the seeds are numerous, matt, black and finely pitted.—Distribution: Panama, Colombia to N. Peru (Venezuela?). [Nothing is known of the cultural requirements of these plants; they are probably quite vigorous.]

W. amazonica K. Sch. (T.)
Bo. freely branching, shrub-like; **branches** pendant, ± lanceolate, acute or obtuse, ± strongly notched; constricted and stem-like at the base, with a stout M.-rib, 15–40 cm lg., 4.5–9 cm br., leaf-green; **Fl.** slightly bent, c. 2.5 cm lg., wine-red, outer Pet. porrect, inner ones more membranous, shorter; **Ov.** very tuberculate, each Tub. furnished with

stout 3-angled Sc.—Peru (near Leticia and Tarapoto).*

W. costaricensis Br. & R.: **Pseudorhipsalis himantoclada** (Rol.-Goss.) Br. & R.

W. himantoclada (Rol.-Goss.) Woods. & Shery: **Pseudorhipsalis himantoclada** (Rol.-Goss.) Br. & R.

W. panamensis Br. & R.
Bo. with shoots to 1 m lg., 4–7 cm br., weakly notched; **Fl.** very numerous, solitary in the upper half of the shoot, stiff, ± 5-angled, purple, outer **Pet.** obtuse, dorsally ribbed, erect, inner **Pet.** lighter, much smaller than the outer ones, pointed; **Ov.** not tuberculate, with a few membranous Sc.; **Fr.** greenish-white to scarlet.—Panama (near Chepo), Colombia (near Marrangati), Venezuela ? (Fig. 457.) (See footnote to W. amazonica.)

Yungasocereus Ritt. (57)

"Distantly related to Trichocereus and Cleistocactus; branching trees with white bellshaped flowers". Only one species known: **Yungasocereus microcarpus** Ritt. No further details have been made known, and I cannot trace any description. Young plants branch when slender-columnar; they have 7 rounded Ri. 3 mm br. and h.; Ar. round, white, 1 cm apart; Rsp. c. 5, thin, 2–5 mm lg.; Csp. 1, porrect, 8 mm lg. or rather more, dull yellowish-white, faintly reddish above at first. Plant probably becoming relatively large, but the fruit, on the basis of the name, must be small

Zehntnerella Br. & R. (136)

Tree-like plants from NE. Brazil, sometimes with a shorter trunk, branching quite freely from ± close to the base; branches ascending, tapering. The white flowers are small and the petals minute; there is a ring of long white hairs at the base of the tube-interior. The tube is short but recognisable, it and the ovary being furnished with small scales which have white axillary hairs. The small-spherical fruits contain very small, rough-tuberculate, brownish to blackish seeds with a large, basal, slightly sunken

*Translator's note: Interested readers should see the article by W. Barthlott and W. Rauh in Kakt. u.a. Sukk., 27.7: 145–150. 1976, which includes a detailed description, a colour-photo of a flowering shoot, drawings of flower and stamens, and SEM-photos of seed and pollen-grains; recent discoveries have shown the plant to be synonymous with W. panamensis Br. & R. (The plants proved extremely difficult to transport to Europe, so that they are unlikely to become common in our collections!)

hilum. Rare in cultivation.—Distribution: NE. Brazil, States of Piauhy and Joazeiro. [Nothing known of cultural requirements.]

Z. chaetacantha (FR 1229): no description available.

Z. polygona (FR 1228): no description available.

Z. squamulosa Br. & R. (T.)
Bo. sometimes with a trunk, this then to 20 cm ∅; **branches** to 4 m lg. (or more), 5–7 cm ∅, very spiny; **Ri.** 17–20, low, fairly crowded; **Ar.** small, round; **Sp.** 10–15, to 3 cm lg., acicular, nut-brown; **Fl.** c. 3 cm lg.; **Pet.** oblong, c. 4 mm lg., white; **Fr.** c. 2 cm ∅, with dried floral remains; **S.** 1 mm lg.—Distribution: see above. (Fig. 458.)
Werdermann united this genus with Leocereus, but the latter is never tree-like while its flowers are bristly and have no staminodial hairs inside.

Zygocactus K. Sch. (31)

One of the best loved and most widely grown genera of the Cactaceae because the type-species flowers freely, especially around Christmas, so that its popular name is "Christmas Cactus" or in German "Gliederkaktus", because of its short, ± dentate stem-segments. In this case the frequent name-changes go a long way back in time. Pfeiffer described this plant as "Epiphyllum", at a time when the "leaf-cacti" were known throughout the whole world as Phyllocactus. Instead of retaining both names, i.e. declaring them nomen conservandum, which would have been the most appropriate course, and because Haworth had at first understood Epiphyllum to be a "leafy" cactus, this latter name was chosen only for species of that kind, while the plants with small stem-segments, previously generally known as "Epiphyllum", received the name Zygocactus K. Sch.
This re-naming complicated the synonymy unnecessarily because the name Epiphyllum, preferred by Britton and Rose, could perfectly well have been applied to Zygocactus as a nomen conservandum, in the same way as Britton and Rose's "Cactus L." was declared from that time to be validly called Melocactus (Tourn.) Lk. & O., which merely reflected general usage. But this was not an end to the name-changes. R. Moran recently referred Zygocactus K. Sch. as a subgenus to Schlumbergera Lem., the oldest genus for any such re-naming. A good old name was thus quite unnecessarily "sunk" (despite the fact that commercial nurseries and florists mostly still call the plants Epiphyllum), as the internal floral structure

is quite divergent in the two plants (see also under Schlumbergera).

But the line of reduction in shoot-form is not, and cannot be, my sole criterion for delimitation of the genera. Rauh, for instance, says in his writings that classifications mostly overlook vegetative characters, an objection which I have tried to overcome in cases like the Opuntioideae by my threefold division based on body-forms. Nevertheless certain variations in floral structure cannot be ignored in every case, i.e. if the line of reduction is not by itself sufficient for a satisfactory delimitation. Zygocactus belongs to the Subgroup "Epiphylli" which has for a long time been in great confusion, as is shown by the frequent name-changes, principally because of the failure to classify all the species involved strictly according to naturally-occurring external and inner differences, and vegetative form. Because of this failure, many details remained unknown although this is a clear instance where extraordinary variation of numerous characters is observable within a relatively small area. For this reason the present group requires a different treatment, and it is not a satisfactory solution to include Zygocactus under Schlumbergera: a plant with fairly regular flowers, which can scarcely still be found in the wild. This leads all too easily to floral differences being overlooked, and replaces a well-known name with that of a virtually extinct genus. The flowers of Zygocactus diverge in the following characters from those of Schlumbergera: they have a fairly long, true corolla-tube and are strongly zygomorphic, the limb is revolute, the anthers are long-projecting*, the inner series of filaments is united into a short tube at the base of the floral tube, with an inwardly-curving membranous annulus**, the ovary and the fruit are typically top-shaped to spherical. Only a more precise delimitation of this kind can ensure clarity in a case like this. Moreover there are Zygocactus cultivars with a ± angular ovary, where the inner series of filaments does not form a tube and has no folded membrane. Some time ago I saw in Santos a specialist's collection of numerous cultivars, some of them doubtless originating in crosses with genera possessing an angular ovary, from which the plants with a zygocactoid flower had been selected. Natural variations of flower-colour are only present where the ovary is top-shaped to spherical. Even then it is doubtful whether the plant now regarded as v. altensteinii is in fact the true variety, at least if one judges by Pfeiffer's illustration. It is interesting to

*Cf. limb-variations in Epiphyllanthus.
**As in Epiphyllanthus, although here the inner series of filaments does not arise from the base, and is not united into a short tube.

see my Fig. 667 in "Die Cact.", II: 730. 1959, showing a Zygocactus flowering from the lateral areoles, and with a slender, top-shaped to spherical ovary such as is typical of the genus; Berger's drawing of the fruit also deserves attention ("Entwicklgsl., 29. 1926") since the shape is indeed top-shaped but there is a faint longitudinal line which is intended to show a slight (but not winged!) angle, surmounted by a disc-like floral scar (which Knebel maintained was the lid of the fruit, by which it opened), whereas my illustration of a laterally flowering Zygocactus shows a smoothly rounded ovary. Berger's representation may show one of the innumerable hybrids. I suggested that the laterally flowering Zygocactus—a very rare phenomenon which had never previously been seen in Europe—should be called Vollia, in memory of my friend Voll, formerly of the Botanical Garden in Rio de Janeiro, who assisted me for many years with numerous helpful details regarding the problems of classifying the Brazilian Hylocereeae; but after his departure from Rio de Janeiro I received no further material, and could thus not undertake any further observations, so that I did not attempt a description. Nevertheless it seems to me perfectly possible that the apical flowers of this species represent only an evolutionary phenomenon, or that Voll's photo illustrates a more primitive form; in other words the ancestors of Zygocactus may have flowered laterally. The form of stem-segments is somewhat variable, the teeth along the margin being shorter and more rounded, or longer and more acute. Divergent flower-colours, e.g. brick-red with a white tube, represent at most varieties (v. altensteinii, v. delicatus; in the latter the flowers are white only in a shady position; given more light they are pink). Shades of orange suggest hybridisation. These differences have given rise to many different names; the loveliest violet-coloured flower is a brilliant blue-violet. The genus has shown itself to be particularly suitable for the professional grower.—Distribution: Brazil (State of Rio de Janeiro). [Propagation is easy and quick by means of small cuttings in a heated bed. Where plants have been forced, bud and flower-drop is often noticed when the position is altered relative to the light-source; but where plants are kept throughout the summer in the open air or in a cool, shady position, this phenomenon never occurs. The use of an inorganic fertiliser which is low in nitrogen but richer in potassium-phosphate promotes growth and better bud-development.]

Z. truncatus (Haw.) K. Sch. (T.)
Bo. forming bushes or small shrubs, to 30 cm lg.; shoots consisting of several **Seg.**, each of these to 4.5 cm lg., to 2.5 cm br., with 2–4 ± acute teeth along each margin, the upper ones usually larger;

Ar. weakly felty, with c. 1–3 short fine **Br.**, pale to blackish, the apex similarly, on either side of the broad flowering **Ar.**; **Fl.** apical, single or paired, rarely in 3's, to 6.5–8 cm lg., pink to deep or violet-red in different shades; **Ov.** top-shaped, terete, reddish to light carmine, naked; **Tub.** curving close to the **Ov.**, with the **Pet.** arranged in several Ser.; limb very oblique; **Fil.** in 2 Ser., one of these attached to the Tu., the second surrounding the base of the style, with an incurved membranous annulus, all carmine; **style** carmine; **Sti.** 5–6; **Fr.** obovoid or pear-shaped, pinkish-red, translucent, c. 1 cm lg., with a ± distinct floral scar; **S.** smooth, black.—Brazil (mountains in the State of Rio de Janeiro). (Fig. 459.)

v. **altensteinii** (Pfeiff.) Borg: this name is applied to a plant with a whitish Tu. and brick-red Pet.;

v. **crenulatus** Borg: more strongly dentate;

v. **delicatus** (N.E. Brown) Borg: a variety which bears white Fl. if grown in a shady position, but pink ones in stronger light; with a ring of protuberances (instead of a fold) at the base of the Tu.;

v. **violaceus** hort.: probably a hybrid, with Fl. of a stronger brilliant violet.

A number of other names have been erected for hybrids, some of which show attractive Fl.-colours. From France there is the name Epiphyllum bridgesii Lem.: these plants were more yellowish-green, glossy, the Seg. ± ovate, weakly notched, Fl. pink suffused carmine, more regular in shape, with a green angular Ov.; Schumann himself pointed out the relationship with Schlumbergera russeliana, indicating the possibility of hybridisation; however it could also have been a cross with Epiphyllopsis gaertneri since both these genera have angular ovaries. More recently still further hybrids have been raised, including some with salmon-coloured Fl., with variously sized Seg. In general the crosses, most of them recognisable by the angular Ov., have proved robuster, i.e. they need not be grafted as was formerly the custom, especially in the case of the type-species; grafting was also resorted to—quite unnecessarily—for Epiphyllopsis and Rhipsalidopsis.

Distribution of the Cactaceae

The distributions of the different groups are shown on the maps in the following pages. Figures in brackets refer to the relevant maps.

The maps show the distribution of the higher taxa, i.e. those above generic rank, since individual genera can readily be identified by using the classification and the data contained in the introductory notes on each genus.

The maps are also intended as a geographical summary of my Classification since they provide the comparative information necessary for understanding it, as well as showing clearly the basis for certain conclusions.

Study of the different ranges immediately reveals that in each subfamily two separate centres of distribution are recognizable, even in the Peireskioideae (2). Here the basin of the Amazon is not only the limiting factor but this region, because of its early history, explains two facts: the partial overlaying of the major southern area of the Cereoideae by its northern counterpart; and secondly the fragmentation of the western distributions (15). The categories Austrocereeae and Boreocereeae (11 and 14) are vital to an understanding of the dual nature of the respective ranges; only the two higher categories—Semi-Tribes 1 and 2—can adequately represent the phenomenon of the separation of these major distributions, and at the same time the geographical basis of the completely distinct major northern and southern distributions of the spherical cacti (13 and 18). If the history of the Amazon basin is taken as a starting point, then one has to conclude that the tropical belt was once situated far further south than now; and in the present Amazon basin there existed an important distribution of cacti belonging to the northern groups which has now largely disappeared. Although formerly continuous, it is now represented only by the fragmented distributions shown on map 15. In this view, the southern zone must be seen more or less as an outpost, the focal point in the south-west suggesting that more favourable conditions probably once existed in the area of the early Andean elevation, or from there northwards. This explains why genera such as Cleistocactus, Frailea and Wigginsia, at the westward limits of their ranges, penetrated far northwards on a kind of vegetative bridge such as other authors have also felt obliged to assume. Thus the northern zone must at one time have extended far to the south, in a more cohesive distribution than now at first sight seems likely. Quite apart from the Peireskieae (2), vital testimony to this effect is provided by the present range of Pilosocereus (Group Cephalocerei: 15) and of Melocactus (Group Cephalocacti: 17).

Populations like this, once continuous, now lost, provide the only explanation for genera bearing marked similarities but widely separated geographically, such as the Nyctocerei (15), Eriocereus (in S. America) and Harrisia (predominantly in the Greater Antilles and Florida), as well as the existence of other comparable distant partial distributions, e.g. those of Monvillea and

Cereus (Group Gymnocerei: 15). The latter genus must have had its origin more in north-eastern S. America, long before the Amazon region first became a barrier, which explains its occurrence on Fernando Noronha whence it spread only to the southern Antilles. On the other hand map 18 shows how the southerly distribution of Mammillaria crossed the West Indian island-bridge into Colombia.

The distributions of the western S. American Austrocereinae and Austrocactinae stretch far to the north—in other words, along this vegetative bridge—thus explaining the extension of the former to the Galapagos Islands.

A reconstruction of the prehistoric scene, based on the residual populations of our day, supports the view that in the north-west of the S. American continent quite unusual overlapping of the northern and southern distributions within the Cactaceae has taken place, independently of the question of how the endemic taxa of the Galapagos Islands have arisen. This problem has counterparts, for instance in the origin of the extension of Cereus to Fernando Noronha, or the eastwards distribution of the Group Rhipsalides (9) into the Old World. The north-western part of S. America thus poses many interesting questions: how did the "eastern" Monvillea species of Ecuador and N. Peru for instance cross what is admittedly one of the lower parts of the Andean chain and extend almost down to the Pacific coast? While the southern Opuntioideae are separated by a clear lacuna from their northern brethren (see Platyopiuntae: 7), and present a distinctive group of characters, the Opuntias of the Galapagos Islands and the nearest parts of the S. American continent must, on the basis of many similarities, be included within the northern distribution. This

bears an interesting relationship to Dawson's recent report that he had been told of a plant occurring in this archipelago which was almost certainly a Melocactus. These overlapping distributions of north-western S. America are reinforced by the simultaneous occurrence in Colombia of Mammillaria (18), Frailea and Wigginsia—genera of which the present foci are situated respectively well to the north and far to the south of that country. In the New World the overall range of the Hylocereeae (9), which demand more tropical conditions, thus occupies a central position. The "void" in the dense primeval rain-forests of the Amazon basin appears to be explained by their relatively recent development. As for the Cephalocacti, or the Melocacti, it is logical to assume that the little-explored interior of north-western S. America may still contain partial distributions of the kind proved by earlier known finds (17), as well as the newer discoveries of Rauh in the north-west hinterland of N. Peru, where Melocactus was encountered on the right bank of the River Marañon.

The distribution maps—quite apart from their interest in helping to recreate earlier conditions—also show that phylogenetic concepts are not in themselves an adequate basis on which to erect a convincing systematic classification; all the evidence revealed by phytogeography must also be called upon, whatever the family under consideration, and due weight must be given to arguments based on factors of distribution. Until now little attention has been given to geobotanic aspects affecting the Cactaceae. The distribution maps in the following pages show this to be a particularly fascinating aspect of these plants, and one which fully merits much more study than hitherto.

Distribution Maps

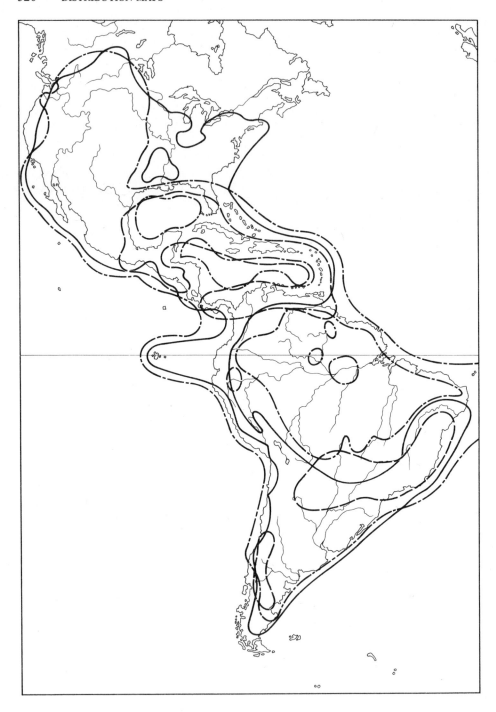

Map 1: Family: Cactaceae
     Distributions of the Subfamilies:
       —— —— Subfamily   I: Peireskioideae
       ———— Subfamily II: Opuntioideae
       —·—·— Subfamily III: Cereoideae

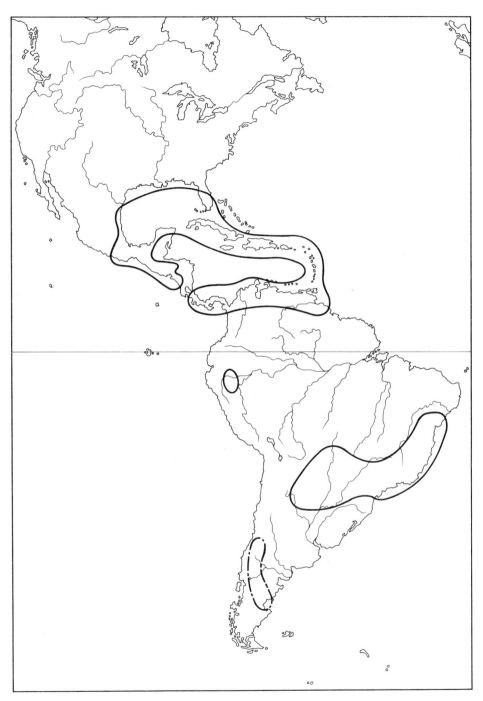

Map 2: Subfamily I: Peireskioideae
Distributions of the Tribes:
——— Tribe 1: Peireskieae*)
·—·—· Tribe 2: Maihuenieae

*) In Florida probably only naturalised.

Map 3: Subfamily II: Opuntioideae
Distributions of the Tribes:
—·— Tribe 1: Phyllopuntieae
——— Tribe 2: Euopuntieae
------- Tribe 3: Pseudopuntieae

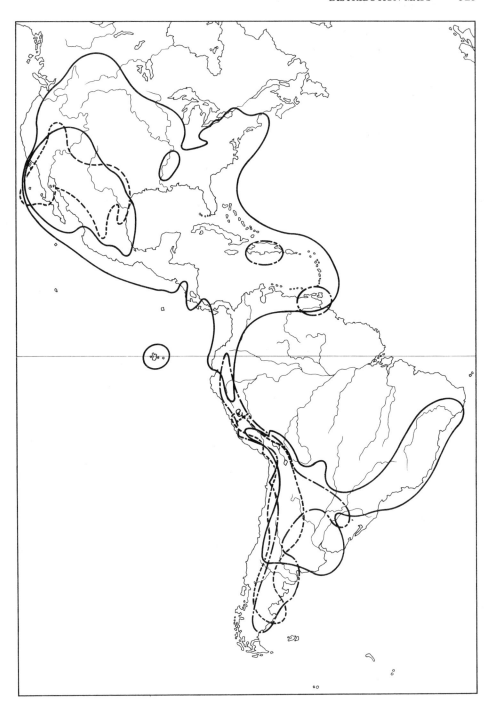

Map 4: Subfamily II: Opuntioideae
Tribe 2: Euopuntieae

Distributions of the Subtribes:
–·–·– Subtribe 1: Cylindropuntiinae
– – – – Subtribe 2: Sphaeropuntiinae
———— Subtribe 3: Platyopuntiinae

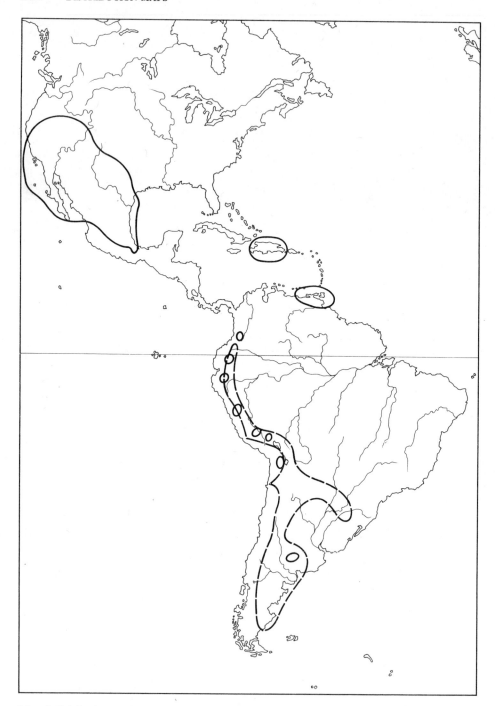

Map 5: Subfamily II: Opuntioideae
    Tribe 2: Euopuntieae
    Subtribe 1: Cylindropuntiinae
    Distributions of the Groups:
        ————— Group 1: Austrocylindropuntiae
        ————— Group 2: Boreocylindropuntiae (Populations in Western S. America: introduced plants)

Map 6: Subfamily II: Opuntioideae
    Tribe 2: Euopuntieae
    Subtribe 2: Sphaeropuntiinae

Distributions of the Groups:
-·—·—Group 1: Austrosphaeropuntiae
————Group 2: Boreosphaeropuntiae

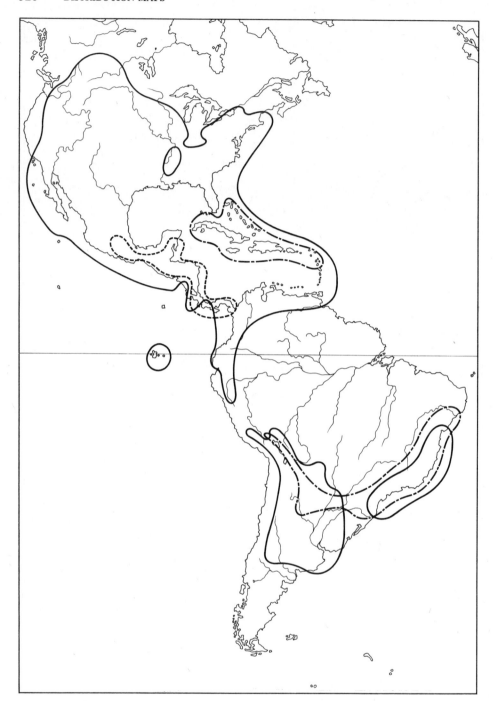

Map 7: Subfamily II: Opuntioideae
　　　Tribe 2: Euopuntieae
　　　Subtribe 3: Platyopuntiinae   Southern Group: Subgroup 1: Brasiliopuntiae
　　　Distributions of the Groups: Northern Group: Subgroup 2: Consoleae
　　　—·—·—Group 1: Cauliopuntiae   —— Group 2: Platyopuntiae
　　　　　　　　　　　　　　　　　　　　　----- Group 3: Nopaleae

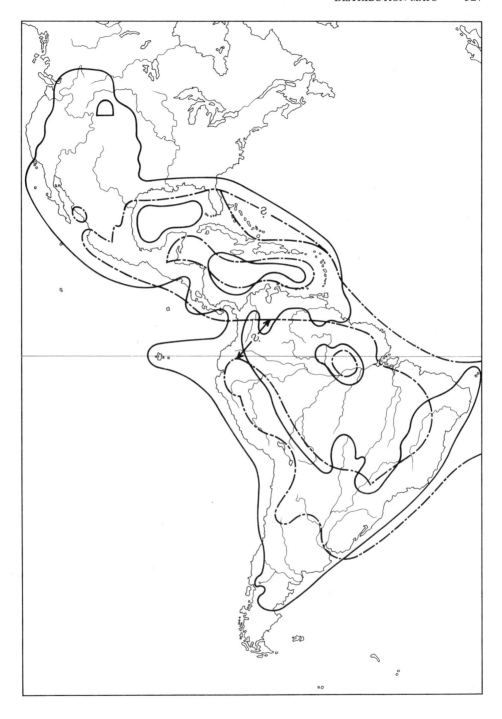

Map 8: Subfamily III: Cereoideae
Distributions of the Tribes:
-·—·—Tribe 1: Hylocereeae
———Tribe 2: Cereeae

Map 9: Subfamily III: Cereoideae
      Tribe 1: Hylocereeae
      Distributions of the Subtribes, with Groups and Subgroups:
      ————Subtribe 1: Rhipsalidinae
            Group 1: Rhipsalides:
                Subgroup 1: Eurhipsalides (Old and New World)
                Subgroup 2: Pseudorhipsalides (Central America and Jamaica,
                      western S. America)
            Group 2: Epiphylloides (only in E. Brazil)
                Subgroup 1: Mediorhipsalides
                Subgroup 2: Epiphyllanthi
                Subgroup 3: Epiphylli
      —·——Subtribe 2: Phyllocactinae
            Group 1: Phyllocacti
                Subgroup 1: Euphyllocacti (Central Mexico to S. America,
                      southernmost Antilles)
                Subgroup 2: Wittiae (north-western S. America)
      -------Subtribe 3: Hylocereinae (south-eastern area in Uruguay: dubious)
            Group 1: Strophocerei
                Subgroup 1: Nyctostrophocerei (inner Brazil)
                Subgroup 2: Heliostrophocerei (Central America to Colombia)
            Group 2: Nyctohylocerei
                Subgroup 1: Selenicerei (southern USA, Central America,
                      W. Indies to S. America)
                Subgroup 2: Hylocerei (Mexico through Central America,
                      northern S. America, western parts of the
                      Amazon basin, almost to the La Plata region)
            Group 3: Heliohylocerei (only in Mexico)

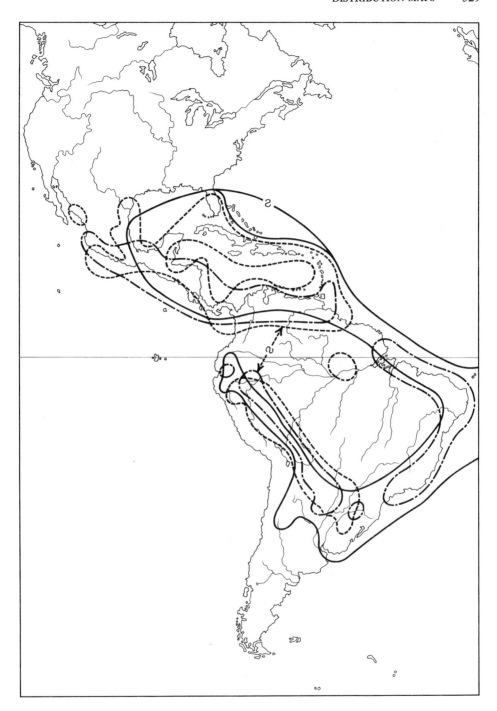

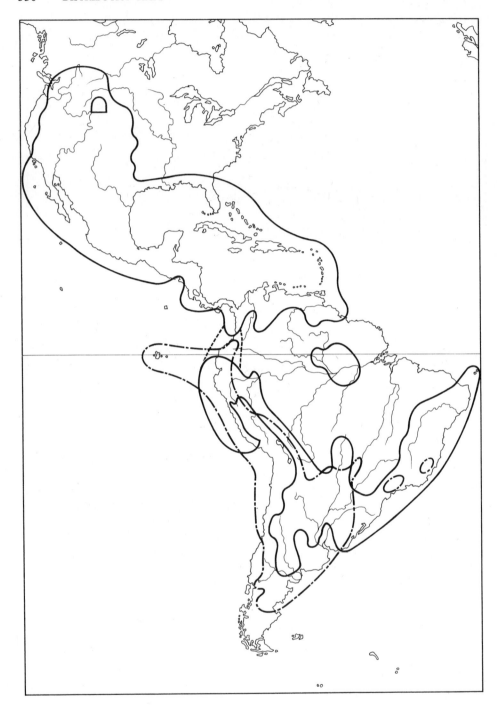

Map 10: Subfamily III: Cereioideae
Tribe 2: Cereeae
Distributions of the Semitribes:
-·—·— Semitribe 1: Austrocereeae
———— Semitribe 2: Boreocereeae

Map 11: Subfamily III: Cereoideae
Tribe 2: Cereeae
Semitribe 1: Austrocereeae
Distributions of the Subtribes:
·—·—Subtribe 1: Austrocereinae
———Subtribe 2: Austrocactinae

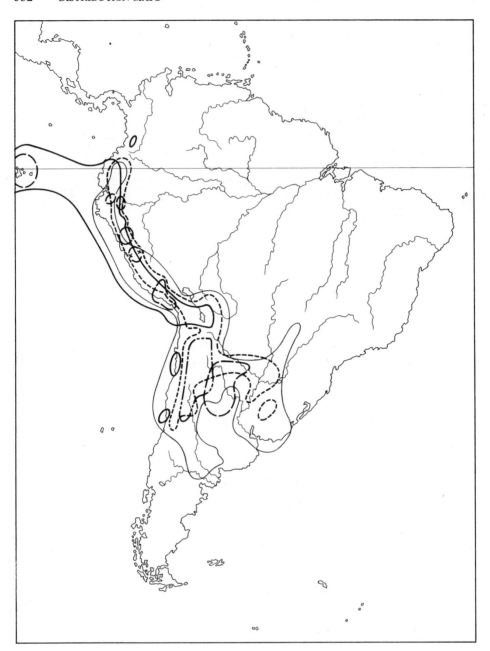

Map 12: Subfamily III: Cereoideae
    Tribe 2: Cereeae
    Semitribe 1: Austrocereeae
    Subtribe 1: Austrocereinae
    Distributions of the Groups:
    –·—·—· Group 1: Pfeifferae
    —×— Group 2: Milae
    ——— Group 3: Corryocerei
        Subgroup 1: Heliocorryocerei

        Subgroup 2: Nyctocorryocerei
    —— Group 4: Gymnanthocerei
    ------- Group 5: Loxanthocerei
        Subgroup 1: Euloxanthocerei
        Subgroup 2: Brachyloxanthocerei
    ——— Group 6: Trichocerei
        Subgroup 1: Nyctotrichocerei
        Subgroup 2: Heliotrichocerei

Map 13: Subfamily III: Cereoideae
     Tribe 2: Cereeae
     Semitribe 1: Austrocereeae
     Subtribe 2: Austrocactinae

Distributions of the Groups:
  —·— Group 7: Lobiviae
     Subgroup 1: Eriolobiviae (these alone
               extending to Peru)
     Subgroup 2: Chaetolobiviae
     Subgroup 3: Gymnolobiviae
  ——— Group 8: Austroechinocacti

Map 14: Subfamily III: Cereoideae
        Tribe 2: Cereeae
        Semitribe 2: Boreocereeae
        Distributions of the Subtribes:
        ·—·— Subtribe 1: Boreocereinae
        ——— Subtribe 2: Boreocactinae
                    (As far as known at present the Cereoideae are missing, in
                    Mexico, from the States Tabasco, Campeche and Quintana-Roo.)

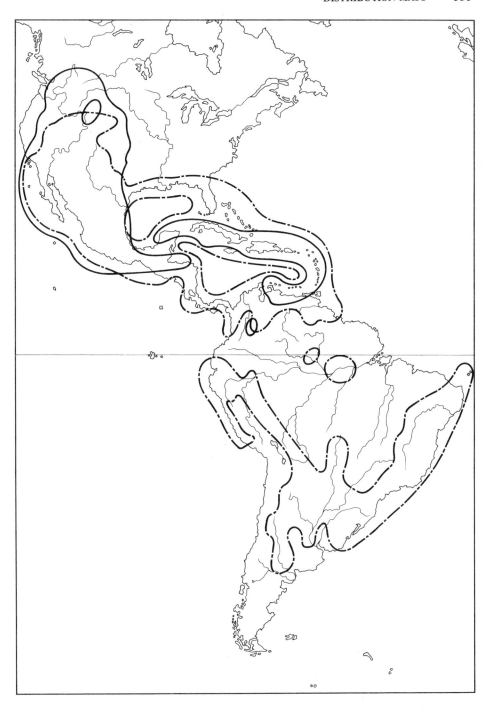

Map 15: Subfamily III: Ceroideae
       Tribe 2: Cereeae
       Semitribe 2: Boreocereeae
       Subtribe 1: Boreocereinae
       Distributions of the Groups (1):
       ·—·— Group 1: Leptocerei
           Subgroup 1: Nyctoleptocerei (Mexico to W. Indies)
           Subgroup 2: Helioleptocerei (W. Indies)
       ··—··· Group 2: Leocerei (Brazil)
       ——— Group 4: Nyctocerei
       ------ Group 8: Gymnocerei
       ——— Group 9: Cephalocerei
           Subgroup 1: Acephalocerei
           Subgroup 2: Hemicephalocerei
           Subgroup 3: Eucephalocerei
       —— Group 10: Cephalocacti (see Map 17)
          (For Groups 3 and 5–7, which are not included here, see Map 16)

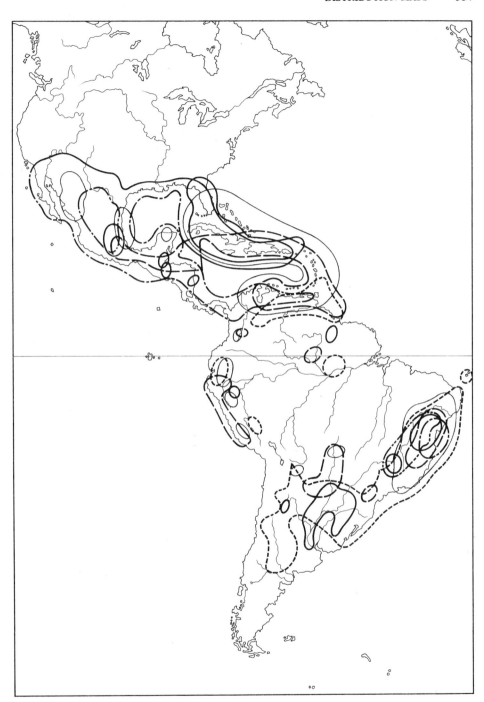

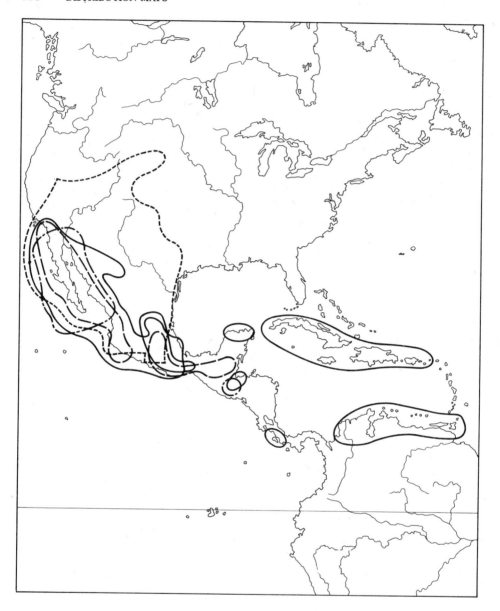

Map 16: Subfamily III: Cereoideae
        Tribe 2: Cereeae
        Semitribe: Boreocereeae
        Subtribe 1: Boreocereinae
        Distributions of the Groups (2):
        ------- Group 3: Echinocerei
        ——— Group 5: Heliocerei
        ——— Group 6: Pachycerei
        ·—·—· Group 7: Polyanthocerei
                Subgroup 1: Heliopolyanthocerei
                Subgroup 2: Nyctopolyanthocerei

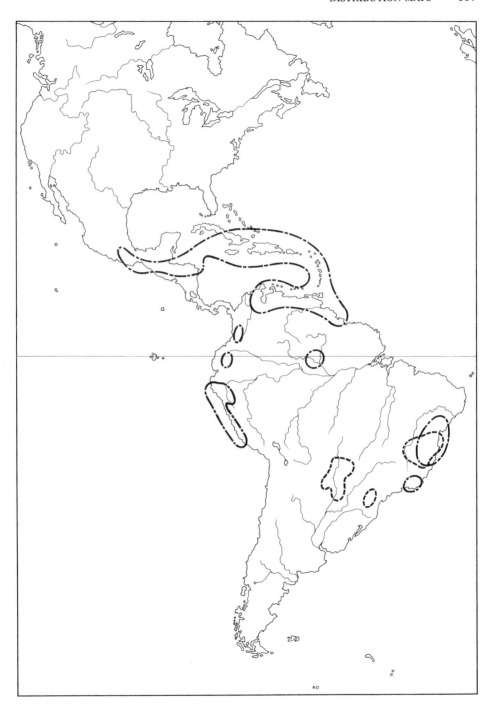

Map 17: Subfamily III: Cereoideae
    Tribe 2: Cereeae
    Semitribe 2: Boreocereeae
    Group 10: Cephalocacti

Distributions of the Subgroups:
—·— Subgroup 1: Heliocephalocacti*)
------ Subgroup 2: Nyctocephalocacti
*) Apparently one species on the
    Galapagos Is. (acc. Dawson)

Map 18: Subfamily III: Cereoideae
        Tribe 2: Cereeae
        Semitribe 2: Boreocereeae
        Subtribe 2: Boreocactinae
        Distributions of the Groups:
        ─ ─ ─ Group 1: Boreoechinocacti*)
                Subgroup 1: Euboreoechinocacti
                Subgroup 2: Mediocoryphanthae
        ─────── Group 2: Mammillariae**)
                Subgroup 1: Coryphanthae
                Subgroup 2: Mediomammillariae
                Subgroup 3: Eumammillariae
      *) Apparently absent in the state of Wyoming, USA;
     **) Absent, so far as known, in the states of Tabasco, Campeche and
         Quintana-Roo, Mexico.

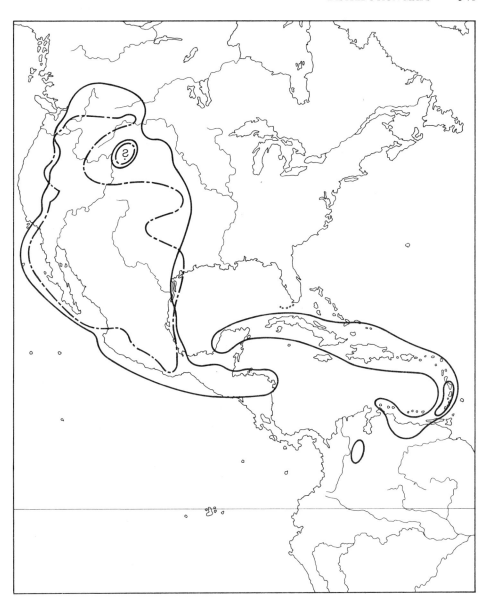

NOTES

NOTES

544

Translator's note

For technical reasons it proved impossible to unite into a single sequence the three different alphabetical sequences of this illustrated section. The reader should therefore note the following:

Figs. 1–459: Acanthocalycium to Zygocactus (from the original Backeberg editions);

Figs. 460–527: Arrojadoa to Uebelmanniana (Haage supplement);

Figs. 528–534: late inclusions to the Haage supplement, covering Rebutia and Sulcorebutia.

Illustrations

Nos. 1–459 Backeberg.
Nos. 460–534 additional supplement.

1. *Acanthocalycium griseum* Backbg. (Photo: Schattat).

2. *Acanthocalycium thionanthum* (Speg.) Backbg. (Photo: De Herdt).

. *Acanthocalycium variiflorum* Backbg.
Above: Flower-colour varies from yellow through orange to red (Photo: Uhlig).
Below: Form with unusually stout and dense spines.

4. *Acanthocereus griseus* Backbg. (Photo J. Marnier-L.).

5. Showing the different forms of the perianth at anthesis in: —
Left: *Acanthocereus griseus* Backbg.
Right: *Peniocereus marnieranus* Backbg.
(Photo: J. Marnier-L.).

6. *Acanthocereus maculatus* *Wgt.*, showing the funnelform inner perianth, unlike *Peniocereus* to which the species is also often referred where the perianth curves downwards (Photo: Schattat).

7. *Acantholobivia incuiensis* (Rauh & Backbg.) Rauh & Backbg.: a genus with nocturnal, mostly autogamous flowers and spiny fruits (left).

8. *Acanthorhipsalis monacantha* (Griseb.) Br. & R.
orange flowers occur in *Hatiora* but never in *Rhipsa
lis*.

9. *Akersia roseiflora* Buin. (Photo:
Buin.).

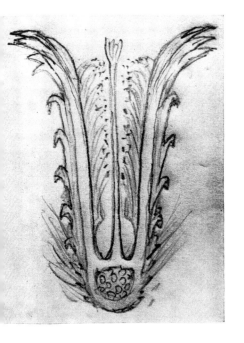

). *Ancistrocactus scheeri* (SD.) Br. & (R. Drawing: Engel-
ıann).

11. *Anisocereus lepidanthus* (Eichl.) Backbg.: longitudinal section of the flower, drawn from the original description.

12. *Aporocactus conzattii* Br. & R.
(Photo: Rose).

13. *Arequipa rettigii* (Quehl) Oehme: younger plants are short-cereoid.

14. *Ariocarpus trigonus* (Web.) K. Sch., with axillary flowers in a circle round the crown. If it is to be united with species flowering from the areoles or from furrows, then logically *Mammillaria* and *Coryphantha* can no longer be segregated (Photo: Runyon).

15. *Armatocereus* flowers [*A. cartwrightianus* (Br. & R.) Backbg.] (Photo: Rauh).

13

14

15

16. *Armatocereus matucanensis* Backbg. (Photo: Rauh).

. *Armatocereus rauhii* Backbg.: showing the symmetrical arrangement of ribs and areoles (Photo: Rauh).

18. *Arrojadoa penicillata* (Gürke) Br. & R. (Photo: Andreae).

19. *Arthrocereus rondonianus* Backbg. & Voll.

20. *Astrophytum capricorne* (Dietr.) Br. & R.

21. *Austrocactus bertinii* (Cels) Br. & R.

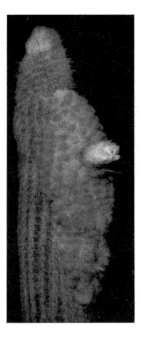

22. *Austrocephalocereus dybowskii* (Goss.)
Backbg.: showing cephalium (Photo: Voll).

23. *Austrocylindropuntia clavarioides* v. *rui
lealii* (Cast.) Backbg. (Drawing: Castellanos

24. *Austrocylindropuntia inarmata* Backbg.: discov
ered by Prof. Herzog of Jena, but not described f
many years (Photo: Rivière).

5. *Austrocylindropuntia subulata* (Muehlpfdt.) Backbg.: form with unusually long leaves (Photo: J. Mar-
ler-L.).

6. *Austrocylindropuntia verschaffeltii* v. *digitalis* (Web.)?: (right) during the growing period, with very long
leaves.

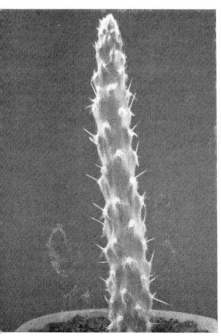
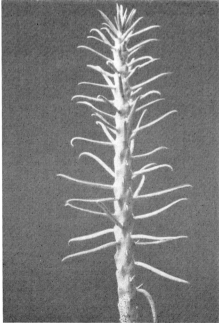

27. *Aylostera albiflora* (Ritt. & Buin.) Backbg. (Photo: Kilian).

28. *Aztekium ritteri* (Böd.) Böd.

30. *Backebergia militaris* (Aud.) H. Bravo: diverges so markedly from *Mitrocereus* in its unique cephalium as well as the flower and fruit, that referral of *Mitrocereus* to *Backebergia* has to be rejected since the generic diagnosis does not apply (Photos: H. Bravo). (Cf. Fig. 238).

29. *Azureocereus viridis* Rauh & Backbg.

31. *Bartschella schumannii* (Hildm.) Br. R.

32. *Bergerocactus emoryi* (Eng.) Br. & R. (Photo: Ethel Bailey Higgins).

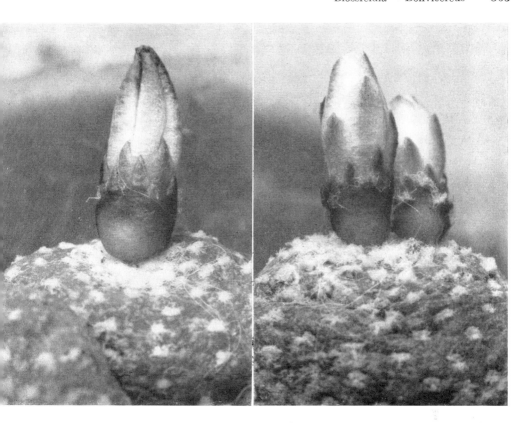

3. *Blossfeldia campaniflora* Backbg. (left), and *Blossfeldia liliputana* Werd. (right): even at the bud-stage
ne inner and outer petals clearly differ in number and shape.

34. *Bolivicereus samaipatanus* Card. (Photo: Cullmann).

35. *Bolivicereus serpens* (HBK.) Backbg.: flowering shoot (left) and close-up of the flower (right) (Photo Rauh).

36. *Borzicactus aequatorialis* Backbg. (Photo: G. Hirtz).

. *Borzicactus pseudothelegonus* (Rauh & Back-
;.) Rauh & Backbg. (Photo: Schattat).

38. *Borzicactus* sp., discovered by Cutak in
Pedregal, Colombia, 91 km from Pasto; listed
here as *B. cutakii* nom. prov. so that it is
not forgotten (Photo: Cutak). The plants are
partly overgrown by *Tillandsia usneoides*.

39. *Brachycalycium tilcarense* (Backbg.) Backbg.: quite a young plant but already of flowering-size.

40. *Brachycalycium tilcarense* (Backbg.) Backbg.: flower in close-up.

1. *Brachycereus nesioticus* (K. Sch.) Backbg.: in habitat (Photo: Förster).

2. *Brasilicactus haselbergii* (Hge.) Backbg.: anomalous elongated flower, clearly a reversion showing the reduction process applying even to the flower, which would normally be small, ± tubeless and spiny (like the fruit) — an evolutionary stage quite distinct from *Notocactus*.

43. *Brasilicereus markgrafii* Backbg. & Voll: showing the typical bell-shaped flower (Photo: Voll).

44. *Brasiliopuntia brasiliensis* (Willd.) Berg. (Photo: Voll).

45. *Browningia candelaris* (Meyen) Br. & R.: habitat view (Photo: Rauh).

46. *Calymmanthium substerile* Ritt.: in habitat (Photo: Rauh).

47. *Calymmanthium substerile* Ritt.: flowering shoot (Photo: Ritter).

8. *Carnegiea gigantea :* seen in habitat (Photo: Polaski).

49. *Carnegiea gigantea* (Eng.) Br. & R.: tip of flowering shoot.

a

b

50. *Castellanosia caineana* Card.: — a) flowering stems; b) elongated spines in the flowering zone (Photos Cardenas).

51. *Cephalocereus senilis* (Haw.) Pfeiff.: flowering cephalium, much extended laterally (Photo: Werdermann).

52. *Cephalocleistocactus pallidus*
Backbg.: —
Left: upper cephalium, showing buds;
Right: lower cephalium, with a yellowish-
green flower (Photos: J. Marnier-L.).

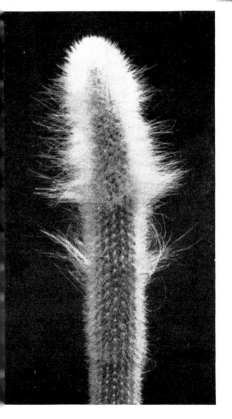

53. *Cephalocleistocactus ritteri* Backbg.: flowering zone
with bristly cephalium.

54. *Cephalocleistocactus schattatianus* Backbg.: in the Marnier Collection.

55. *Cereus insularis* Hemsl., from Fernando Noronha (Photo: Voll).

56. *Chamaecereus silvestrii* f. *crassicaulis* crist. Backbg. (Photo: Maschin).

57. *Chiapasia nelsonii* (Br. & R.) Br. & R.: showing bell-shaped flower. Inclusion in the Genus *Disocactus*, which has a uniformly tubular flower, must therefore be rejected.

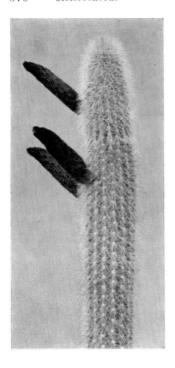

58. Left: *Cleistocactus azerensis* Card.
Right: *Cleistocactus brookei* Card.

59. Left: "*Cleistocactus dependens* Card.": referred, because of the long floral bristles, to *Seticleistocactus* (see also Fig. 384).
Right: *Cleistocactus vallegrandensis* Card. (Photo: Schattat).

60. *Cleistocactus santacruzensis* Backbg. (Photo: J. Marnier-L.).

. Left: *Cleistocactus viridiflorus* Backbg.
ght: *Cleistocactus vulpis-cauda* Ritt. & Cullm. (Photo: Cullmann).

62. *Clistanthocereus tessellatus* (Akers & Buin.) Backbg.: sho
ing the stout, shortly limbed diurnal flower (Photo: Akers).

63. *Cochemiea poselgeri* (Hildm.) Br. & R.

4. *Coleocephalocereus fluminensis* (Miqu.) Backbg.: showing the flower and smooth lidded fruit arising from ıe bristly grooved cephalium (Photo: Knuth).

65. *Coloradoa mesae-verdae* Boiss. & Davids. (Photo: Boissevain).

66. *Consolea rubescens* (SD.) Lem.: the secondary shoots are characteristic of the genus.

67. *Copiapoa chanãralensis* Ritt.

8. *Copiapoa grandiflora* Ritt.: one of the large-flowered species (Photo: J. Marnier-L.).

69. *Copiapoa humilis* (Phil.) Hutch.: type of the species, gathered by Hutchison.

70. *Copiapoa longispina* Ritt.?

71. *Copiapoa streptocaulon* sensu Ritt.; *Copiapoa marginata* (SD.) Br. & R.

72. "*Copiapoa wagenknechtii* Ritt.": now *Copiapoa coquimbana* v. *wagenknechtii* Ritt.

3. *Corryocactus brachypetalus* (Vpl.) Br. & R. (Photo: Rauh).

74. *Corynopuntia planibulbispina* Backbg. (Photo: Rivière).

75. *Coryphantha echinus* (Eng.) Br. & R.

76. *Cryptocereus anthonyanus* Alex. (Photo: Alexander).

77. *Cylindropuntia* species: 1. *C. tetracantha*
(Toumey) Knuth; 2.—5. *C. versicolor* (Eng.)
Knuth; 6. *C. fulgida* (Eng.) Knuth: proliferating
fruits (Plate IX, Br. & R., Vol. I).

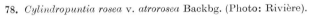

78. *Cylindropuntia rosea* v. *atrorosea* Backbg. (Photo: Rivière).

79. *Deamia testudo* (Karw.) Br. & R.: very free-flowering in cultivation, but seldom seen in collection (Photo: Haage).

80. *Delaetia woutersiana* Backbg. (Photo: Wouters).

81. *Dendrocereus nudiflorus* (Eng.) Br. & R.

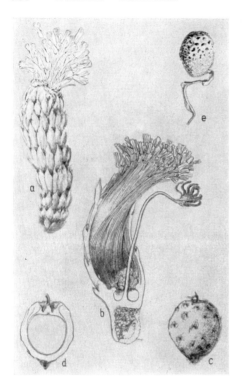

82. *Denmoza* Br. & R.: flowers and fruit, drawn by Castellanos.

83. *Discocactus alteolens* Lem. (left); *D. tricornis* Monv. (right) (Photo: Voll).

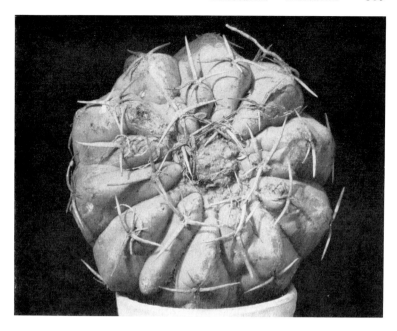

4. *Discocactus boliviensis* Backbg.: cephalium with no stiff bristles.

85. *Disocactus eichlamii* (Wgt.) Br. & R.: in all species of the genus the flower is uniformly tubular, not bell-shaped as in *Chiapasia*.

86. *Dolichothele longimamma* (DC.) Br & R. (Photo: Rose).

87. *Eccremocactus bradei* Br. & R. (Photo: Voll).

8. *Echinocactus grusonii* Hildm.

89. *Echinocereus davisii* A. D. Hought., also known as *E. viridiflorus* v. *davisii* (A. D. Hought.) Marsh.: a rare plant, so distinctive because of its small size and fierce spines that it merits specific status. Grafted plants grow into attractive groups, with small, pale dirty-yellowish flowers.

90. *Echinocereus matthesianus* Backbg.: belongs in the Series "Scheeriani" on the basis of flower shape and length, but the shoots are fairly stout.

1. *Echinocereus pectinatus* v. *rigidissimus* (Eng.) Rümpl.: always one of the most popular species of this ine-flowering genus.

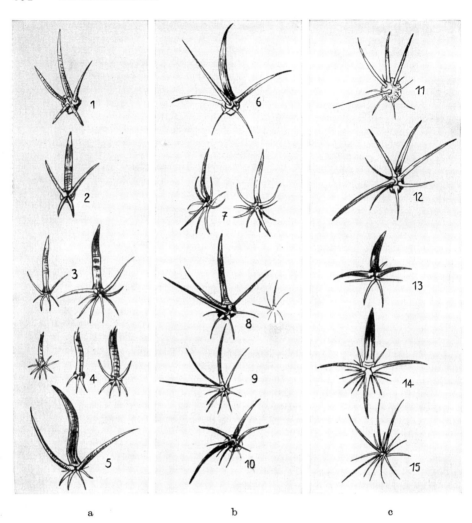

a   b   c

92. *Echinofossulocactus* Lawr.: Key to Spine-Arrangement, according to Oehme: —

a) 1: *E. coptonogonus* (Lem.) Lawr.; 2: *E. pentacanthus* (Lem.) Br. & R.; 3: *E. phyllacanthus* (Mart.) Lawr
4: *E. tricuspidatus* (Scheidw.) Br. & R.; 5: *E. grandicornis* (Lem.) Br. & R. (drawings by H. Oehme, fro
"Key to Spination" by Tiegel and Oehme: Beitr. z. Sukkde. u. -pflege, 78—82. 1938).

b) 6: *E. lamellosus* (Dietr.) Br. & R.; 7: *E. anfractuosus* (Mart.) Lawr.; 8: *E. crispatus* (DC.) Lawr.; 9:
gladiatus (Lk. & O.) Lawr.: 10: *E. dichroacanthus* (Mart.) Br. & R.

c) 11: *E. hastatus* (Hopff.) Br. & R.; 12: *E. obvallatus* (DC.) Lawr.; 13: *E violaciflorus* (Quehl) Br. & R.; 1
E. heteracanthus (Mühlpfrdt.) Br. & R.; 15: *E. albatus* (Dietr.) Br. & R.

d) 16: *E. vaupelianus* (Werd.) Tieg. & Oehme; 17: *E. wippermannii* (Mühlpfrdt.) Br. & R.; 18: *E. tetraxiph*
(O.) Oehme; 19: *E. ochoterenaus* Tieg.

e) 20: *E. arrigens* (Lk.) Br. & R.; 21: *E. lloydii* Br. & R.; 22: *E. zacatecasensis* Br. & R.; 23: *E. multicostat*
(Hildm.) Br. & R.

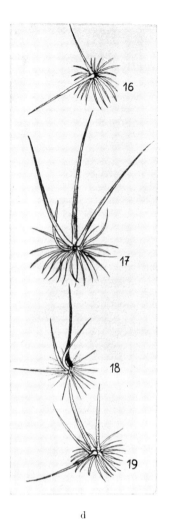

d

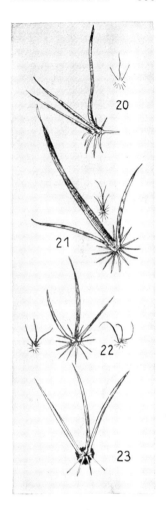

e

93. *Echinofossulocactus ochoterenaus* Tieg
one of the species with colourful spines ar
larger flowers.

94. *Echinomastus kakui* Backbg.: its Japanese discoverer has shown that this name has
precedence over "*E. pallidus* nom. prov.",
as given in "Die Cact." Vol. V.

5. *Echinomastus* sp., apparently related to *E. acunensis* Marsh.; spines reddish-grey at first, later yellowish either dense or open (*E. carrizalensis* Kuenzl; just a name?).

96. *Echinopsis silvestrii* Speg.: elongated in age and sometimes over 1 m high. Since the globose form is retained for a long time, the genus is regarded as covering spherical species, otherwise *Trichocereus* would have to be referred to it, and confusion would inevitably result. It is equally unfortunate when Kimnach and Hutchison include *Submatucana*, of conspicuously spherical habit (see *S. madisoniorum*, Fig. 396) with *Borzicactus*, a genus of slender cerei. Elongated forms are known to occur in very old plants of other spherical cacti, but no-one has felt obliged to unite them with cereoid genera.

98

97

97. "*Echinopsis* sp.": an imported plant which later proved to be an interesting *Pseudolobivia* (*P. luteiflora* Backbg. — see Fig. 341); this had spiny scales on the floral tube as in *Acanthocalycium*, but the diurnal flower lacked any ring of wool at the base of the relatively long and slender tube, so that it could only be referred to *Pseudolobivia*.

98. *Encephalocarpus strobiliformis* (Werd.) Berg.

99. *Epiphyllanthus obtusangulus* (Lindbg.) Berg.
Above: Plant, with fruits (Photo: Voll).
Below: Flower, according to Berger.

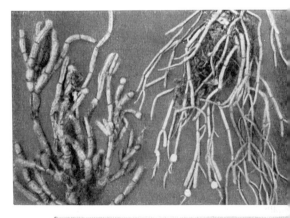

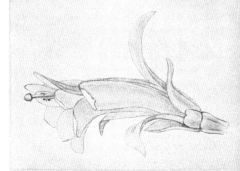

99

100. *Epiphyllopsis gaertneri* (Reg.) Berg.:
flower with spreading stigma-lobes.

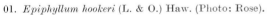

01. *Epiphyllum hookeri* (L. & O.) Haw. (Photo: Rose).

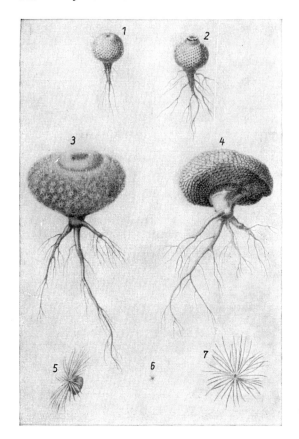

102. *Epithelantha micromeris* (Eng.) Web. (Drawing: Roetter).

103. *Erdisia quadrangularis* Rauh & Backbg. (Photo: Rauh).

104. *Eriocactus leninghausii* (Hge.) Backbg.

105. Split fruit of *Eriocereus bonplandii* (Parm.) Ricc., typical of the genus (Photo: Byles).

936. *Eriosyce ceratistes* (O.) Br. & R.: in flower (Photo: Lembcke).

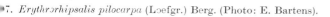

937. *Erythrorhipsalis pilocarpa* (Loefgr.) Berg. (Photo: E. Bartens).

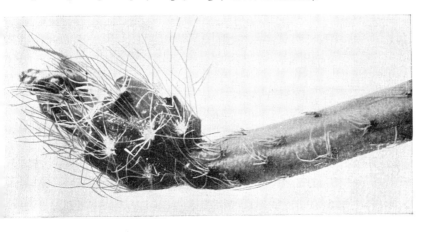

108.― *Escobaria hesteri* (Wright) F. Buxb.

109. *Escobaria nellieae* (Croiz.) Backbg.

10. *Escontria chiotilla* (Web.) Rose: showing the scaly flower and fruit of the tree-like species of this mono-typic genus (Drawing: Br. & R.).

111. *Espostoa lanata* (HBK.) Br. & R.: seam-like early development of the cleft cephalium (cf. Fig. 339).

112. *Espostoa lanata* v. *sericata* (Backbg.) Backbg.: unusual double cephalium and partially anomalou
growth (Photo: Rauh).

113. *Eulychnia iquiquensis* (K. Sch.) Br. & R.: typical
fruits of this mostly tree-like genus.

14. *Eulychnia procumbens* Backbg.: only known reeping species of the genus, showing the characteistic flower (Photo: Lembcke).

115. *Facheiroa ulei* (Gürke) Werd.

116. *Ferocactus acanthodes* (Lem.) Br. & R. (Photo: Polaski).

117. *Frailea carminifilamentosa* Kilian
(Photo: Kilian).

8. *Frailea castanea* Backbg.: a form or variety with white areoles and clustered, downwardly appressed ·ines; the body-colour, as in *F. uhligiana* Backbg., varies from green to brown. Above: an intermediate ·lour.

119. *Frailea chiquitana* Card. (Photo: Kilian).

120. *Frailea pullispina* Backbg. (above), and v. *atrispina* Backbg. (below) with longer spines.

121   122

. *Frailea pullispina* v. *centrispina* Backbg., with one central spine and more conspicuously white areoles.

. *Frailea uhligiana* Backbg., with continuous ribs divided horizontally into flat tubercles; plants reddish-
wn in habitat, becoming green in cultivation.

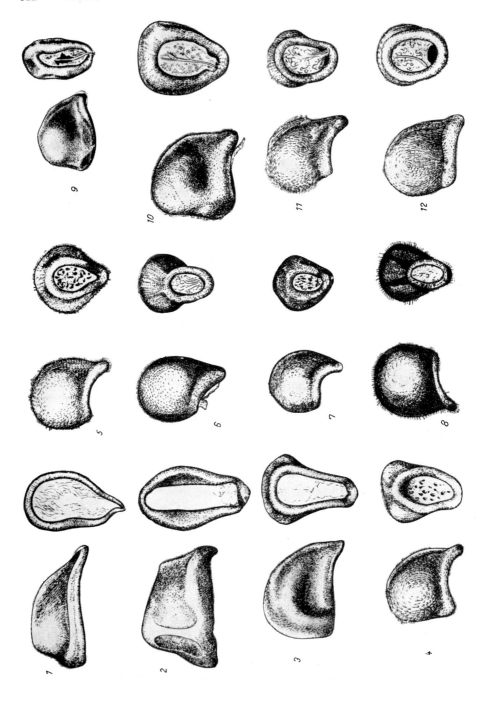

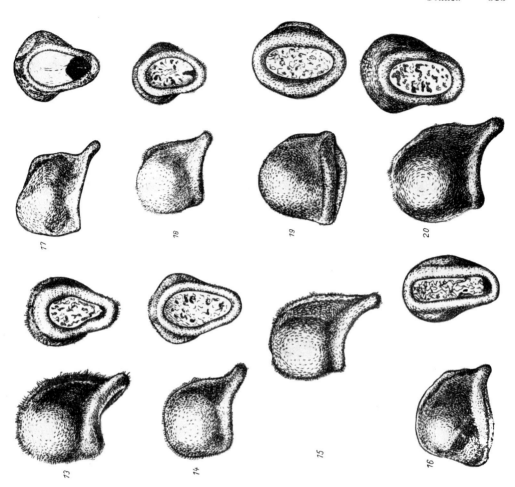

23. Table of Seed-forms in *Frailea :* —

1. *F. cataphracta*
2. *F. castanea*
3. *F. chiquitana*
4. *F. pseudopulcherrima* (1)
5. *F. carminifilamentosa*
6. *F. colombiana*
7. *F. pumila*
8. *F. grahliana*
9. *F. knippeliana*
10. *F. alacriportana* and
    F. gracillima

11. *F.* sp. Simon 1
12. *F. alacriportana* (1): Andreae's form
13. *F. pulcherimma*?
14. *F.* sp. CSR ⫽ 3
15. *F.* sp. ⫽ 8 Kilian — (1)
16. *F. pygmaea* and v. *dadakii*
17. *F. schilinzkyana*
18. *F. pseudopulcherrima* (2)
19. *F. alacriportana* (2) (Ritter)
20. *F.* sp. ⫽ 8 — (2)

This shows the diversity of seed-form and testa-type in this genus, even in different forms of the same species (Nos. 4 and 18; Nos. 12 and 19), proving the dubious value of any deductions based on seed and testa (Drawing: Kilian).

124. *Grandulicactus uncinatus* v. *wrightii* (Eng.) Backb■

125. *Grusonia bradtiana* (Coult.) **Br. & R.** (Photo: Rivière).

126. *Gymnocactus viereckii* (Werd.) Backbg.

127. *Gymnocalycium asterium* v. *paucispinum* Backbg.

128. *Gymnocalycium chiquitanum* Card

129. *Gymnocalycium damsii* v. *centrispinum*
Backbg. (above); v. *rotundulum* Backbg. (below).

30. *Gymnocalycium damsii* v. *torulosum*
Backbg.

131. *Gymnocalycium damsii* v. *tucavocense*
Backbg.

132. *Gymnocalycium griseo-pallidum* Backbg. (Photo: Uhlig).

133. *Gymnocalycium hamatum* Ritt.

134. *Gymnocalycium hammerschmidii*
Backbg.: showing the large flower (Photo:
Till).

135. *Gymnocalycium horridispinum* Frank
(Photo: J. Marnier-L.).

136. *Gymnocalycium hossei* (Hge. Jr.) Berg.: an insufficiently clarified and apparently variable species. This imported plant is unusual in having so few spines; perhaps some other species?

137. Different forms within *Gymnocalycium hybopleurum* (K. Sch.) Backbg.: —

Above: v. *breviflorum* Backbg., flower shorter and smaller;

Centre: v. *ferocior* Backbg., very fiercely spined;

Below: v. *ferox* Backbg., with stout radials but no central spine. (Photo: T. Marnier-L.).

138. *Gymnocalycium intertextum* Backbg.

139. *Gymnocalycium marquezii* v. *argentinense* Backbg.

40. *Gymnocalycium marsoneri* (Frič) Y. Ito: such a variable species that it has produced a proliferation of names.

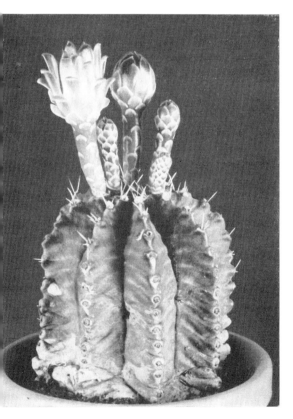

141. *Gymnocalycium mihanovichii* v. *filadelfiense* Backbg.: a variety with a large brownish-green flower. The form illustrated has a slender floral tube, but in other specimens it may be half as thick again (Photo: J. Marnier-L.).

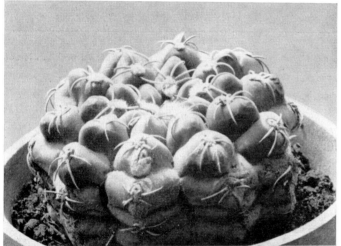

2. *Gymnocalycium ochoterenai* Backbg.: this has proved to be an extremely variable species; apart from v. *ochoterenai*, there are transitional forms linking the following: —

bove: v. *polygonum* Backbg., brownish, with blackish spines;

ntre: v. *tenuispinum*, olive-grey, with whitish-grey spines;

low: v. *variispinum* Backbg., olive-grey, the horn-coloured spines variable in length.

this genus, where descriptions have sometimes been based on a single specimen, not even on an entire ipment, this has led to superfluous names. All 3 varieties shown opposite have 5 spines, but if the plants d been seen on separate occasions, each might have been regarded as a distinct species.

3. *Gymnocalycium pseudo-malacocarpus* Backbg. (Photo: Uhlig).

Backeberg

144. *Gymnocalycium pugionacanthum* Backbg.

145. *Gymnocalycium spegazzinii* Br. & R.: a variable species. The form shown has pink spines, tipped slate grey.

46. *Gymnocalycium vatteri* Buin.
above: type of the species. Below: a form with more strongly bent spines.

147. *Gymnocereus microspermus* (Werd. & Backbg.)
Backbg.

148. *Haageocereus albispinus* (Akers) Backbg.: showing flowers (Photo: Schattat).

49. *Haageocereus clavispinus* Rauh & Backbg.: an erect species, growing in the desert (Photo: Rauh).

50. Flowering Haageocerei: —
Left: *H. horrens* Rauh & Backbg.
Right: *H. olowinskianus* v. *repandus* subv. *erythranthus* Rauh & Backbg. (Photos: Rauh).

151. *Haageocereus repens* Rauh & Backbg.: a creepin species, growing in the desert (Photo: Rauh).

152. *Hamatocactus setispinus* (Eng.) Br. & R. (Drawing: Engelmann).

153. *Harrisia gracilis* (Mill.) Britt.: showing fruit (Photo: Schattat).

154. *Haseltonia columno-trajani* (Karw.)
Backbg.
Left: Growth-form (Photo: Diguet).
Right: Cephalium and flowers (Photo: F.
Schwarz).

155. *Hatiora cylindrica* Br. & R.

156. *Heliabravoa chende* (Goss.) Backbg.: the bud.

57. *Heliabravoa chende* (Goss.) Backbg.: the lower.

158. *Helianthocereus bertramianus* (Backbg.) Backbg.: the close relationship between the tall-growing species and the lower forms of the *H. huascha* complex is demonstrated by the similarity of juvenile plants.

159. *Helianthocereus crassicaulis* Backbg.

160. *Helianthocereus grandiflorus* (Br. & R.) Backbg.: a plant of variable habit.

161. *Helianthocereus huascha* v. *macranthus* Backbg. (Photo: J. Marnier-L.).

162. *Helianthocereus pecheretianus* Backbg.

163. *Helianthocereus pecheretianus* v. *viridio*
Backbg. (Photo: J. Marnier-L.).

164. *Helianthocereus poco* (Backbg.) Backbg. v. *sanguiniflorus* Backbg. with flame-coloured flower (the type
has a light purple flower) (Photo: Muhr).

165. *Helianthocereus pseudo-candicans* Backbg. v. *roseolorus* (Backbg.) Backbg.

166. An attractively flowered *Helianthocereus* (or *Trichocereus*) hybrid: probably *H. grandiflorus* × *T. schickendantzii*.

167. *Heliocereus speciosus* (Cav.) Br. & R.

168. *Hertrichocereus beneckei* (Ehrenbg.) Backbg. (Photo: Schlange).

69. *Homalocephala texensis* (Hopff.) Br. & R.

70. *Horridocactus tuberisulcatus* (Jac.) Y. Ito (left); v. *minor* (Ritt.) (right).

171. *Horridocactus tuberisulcatus:* showing the ± glabrous
flower typical of the genus.

172. *Hylocereus polyrhizus* (Web.)
Br. & R.: the flower, glabrous and
with large scales, is one of the largest in the genus.

73. *Islaya krainziana* Ritt.

Backeberg

174. *Islaya divaricatiflora* Ritt. (*Islaya ros flora* Hoffm.).

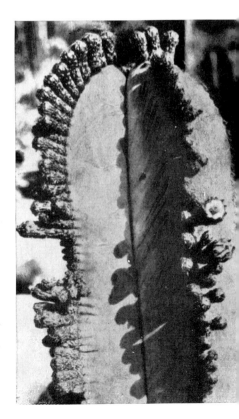

175. *Isolatocereus dumortieri* (Scheidw.) Backbg.: showing the crowded flowers (Photo: Hertrich).

176. *Jasminocereus sclerocarpus* (K. Sch.) Backbg.: showing the white (!) flower (Photo: E. Naundorff).

177. *Jasminocereus thouarsii* v. *chathamensis* Y. Daws. (left) and *J. howellii* v. *delicatus* Y. Daws. (right) (Photo: Dawson).

178. *Krainzia longiflora* (Br. & R.) Backbg.

179. *Lasiocereus rupicola* Ritt. (Photo: Wouters).

180. *Lemaireocereus hollianus* (Web.) Br. & R.: showing the woolly and bristly bell-shaped flower (Photo: Sivilla).

181. *Leocereus bahiensis* Br. & R. (Photo: Kroenlein).

182. *Lepidocoryphantha runyonii* (Br. & R.) Backbg.

183. *Lepismium marnie-nianum* Backbg. during the resting period, and with fruits (below) (Photos: J. Marnier-L.).

184. *Lepismium megalanthum* (Loefgr.) Backbg.: showing the conspicuous scars of the floral cavities.

185. *Leptocereus grantianus* N. L. Britt. (Photo: Poindexter).

186. *Leuchtenbergia principis* Hook.

87. *Leucostele rivierei* Backbg.: flower (Photo: Rivière).

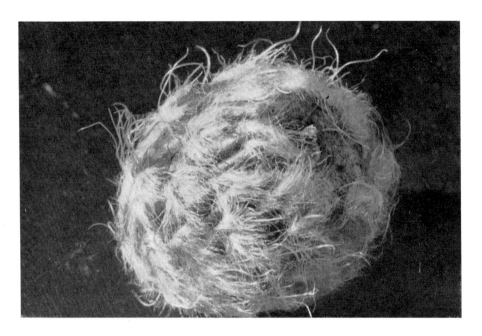

188. *Leucostele rivierei* Backbg.: the fruit, with twisted bristles projecting from the dense covering of white hairy bristles. An astonishingly fast-growing species (Photo: Rivière).

189. *Lobeira macdougallii* Alex. (Photo: Alexander).

0. *Lobivia acanthoplegma* (Backbg.) Backbg.

01. *Lobivia cinnabarina* (Hook.) Br. & R.: the true large-flowered species of the original illustration in Cur-
s' Bot. Mag., 73, pl. 434. 1847. (Photo: Rausch).

192. *Lobivia drijveriana* Backbg.: with an anomalous striped flower.

193. *Lobivia muhriae* Backbg.

4. *Lobivia multicostata* Backbg.

195. *Lobivia neocinnabarina* Backbg.: the flower has a white throat.

196. *Lobivia pentlandii* (Hook.) Br. & R.: t
plant regarded as the type-species of the gen
(Photo: J. Marnier-L.).

197. *Lobivia pseudocinnabarina* Backbg.: the flower has a red throat, the spines are brownish.

198. *Lobivia rigidispina* Backbg.

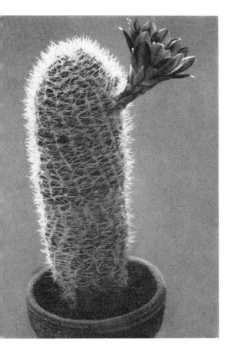

199. *Lobivia schieliana* v. *albescens* Backbg.

200. *Lobivia scopulina* Backbg.: new growth.

201. *Lobivia vanurkiana* Backbg.

2. *Lophocereus* flowers: —
ft: *L. sargentianus* (Orc.) Br. & R.; Right: *L. schottii* (Eng.) Br. & R.

203. *Lophocereus mieckleyanus* (Wgt.) Backbg.
(Photos: Marshall).

204. *Lophophora echinata* Croiz.

05. *Loxanthocereus acanthurus* v. *ferox* Backbg. (Photo: Fuaux).

206. *Loxanthocereus piscoensis* Rauh & Backbg.: first photo of the open flower.

207. *Machaerocereus eruca* (Brand.) Br. & R.

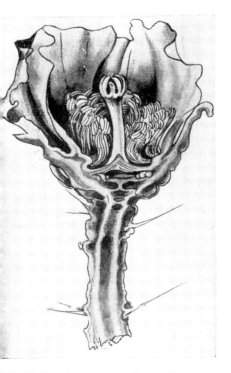

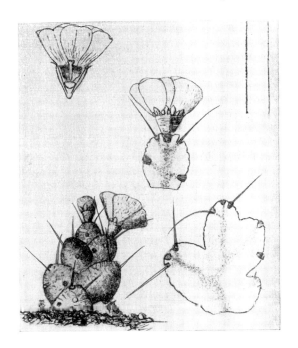

209. *Maihueniopsis molfinoi* Speg.: a genus which has never been re-collected (Drawing: Spegazzini).

208. *Maihuenia valentinii* Speg.: flower in longitudinal section, after Castellanos.

210. "Malacocarpus macrocanthus (Ar.) Hert.", now *Wigginsia macrocantha* (Ar.) D.M. Port.

211. *Mammillaria buchenauii* Backbg.

212. *Mammillaria dixanthocentron* Backbg. (left) and *M. flavicentra* Backbg. (right).

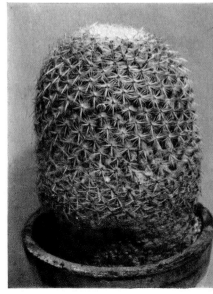

3. *Mammillaria fuscohamata* Backbg.: close-
of the flower.

4. *Mammillaria graessneriana* Böd.: perhaps a hybrid (left); *M. lewisiana* Gat. (right).

215. *Mammillaria nana* Backbg.: before dev-
lopment of any central spines, but already flo-
ering.

216. *Mammillaria pringlei* v. *longicentra* Backbg. (above); *M.
saint-pieana* Backbg. (below).

217. *Mammillaria viperina* J. A. Purpus: one of the species with long or slender stems.

218. *Mammillaria wilcoxii* Toumey: a rarer species with large flowers.

219. *Mamillopsis senilis* Web.

220. *Marenopuntia marenae* (S. H. Parsons) Backbg. (Photo: Parsons).

721. *Marginatocereus* flowers: —
Left: *M. marginatus* (DC.) Backbg. Right: its *v. gemmatus* (Zucc.) Backbg.

222. *Marniera chrysocardium* (Alex.) Backbg. (Photo: Schattat).

223. *Marniera chrysocardium* (Alex.) Backbg.: showing the stiffly bristly ovary, a characteristic of the genus (Photo: Schattat).

224. *Marniera macroptera* (Lem.) Backbg.: ovary with similar stiff bristles (Photo: Schattat).

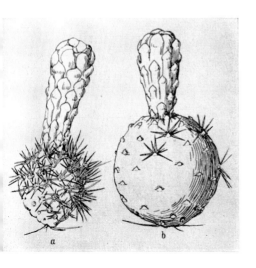

225. *Marshallocereus thurberi* (Eng.) Backbg.: flower with spiny ovary, and the fruit (Drawing: Britton & Rose).

226. *Matucana blancii* Backbg.: a cushion-forming species of this genus of spherical plants (Photo: Rauh).

227. *Mediocactus coccineus* (SD. in DC.) Br. & R. (Photo: Voll).

228. *Mediolobivia euanthema* v. *fričii* Backbg.: a species of the subgenus with slender-oblong bodies (Photo: Andreae).

229. *Mediolobivia spiralisepala* Jajo.

230. *Melocactus communis* Lk. & O.: a colony on one of the islands in the West Indies (Photo: Leguillon)

231. *Micranthocereus polyanthus* (Werd.) Backbg. (from a colour photo by Werdermann).

232. *Micropuntia gracilicylindrica* Wiegd. & Backbg. (Photo: Schattat).

233. *Micropuntia pygmaea* Wiegd. & Backbg.: in flower (Photo: Schattat).

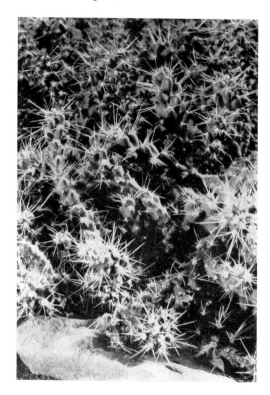

234. *Micropuntia tuberculosirhopalica* Wiegd. &
Backbg. (Photo: Schattat).

235. *Micropuntia wiegandii* Backbg. (Photo: Schattat).

236. *Mila caespitosa* Br. & R. (Photo: Rauh).

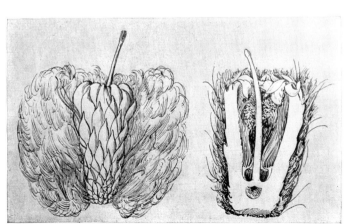

237. *Mitrocereus fulviceps* (Web.) Backbg. (Drawing of the flower: Britton & Rose).

238. *Mitrocereus fulviceps* (Web.) Backbg.: with apical cephalium. The recent referral of the genus to *Backe bergia* H. Bravo, by F. Buxbaum and H. Bravo, has to be rejected because the generic diagnosis is inappli cable (cf. the cephalium above, and the flowers of the two genera).

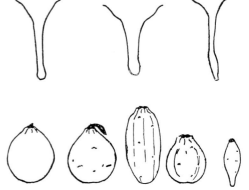

239. *Monvillea* Br. & R.: forms of flower and fruit in the different subgenera: —

Left: SG. 1: *Monvillea*.
Centre: SG. 2: *Hummelia*.
Right: SG. 3: *Ebneria*.

240. *Monvillea haageana* Backbg. (Photo: Haage).

241. *Morawetzia doelziana* Backbg.: the flowers appear from the gradually widening apical cephalium.

242. *Myrtillocactus cochal* (Orc.) Br. & R.

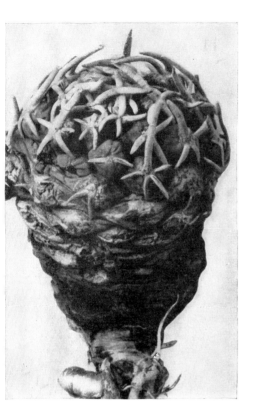 

243. *Navajoa peeblesiana* Croiz. (left); *Navajoa fickeisenii* Backbg. (right). Benson unites these two species in a single genus, the second as a variety of the first, despite the differences of spination; but this is not in keeping with normal methods of segregating plants with such conspicuous differences of habit.

244. *Navajoa peeblesiana* Croiz.: flower (Photo: Wiegand).

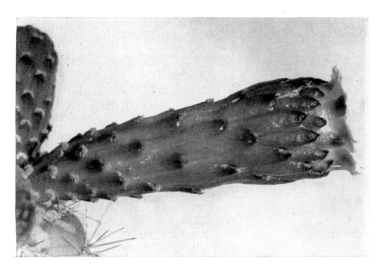

245. *Neoabbottia paniculata* (Lam.) Br. & R.: the flower can apparently arise either from apical felt, or from areoles on the upper flank.

246. *Neobesseya rosiflora* Lahm.

247. *Neobinghamia climaxantha* (Werd.) Backbg.: old flowering zone (Photo: Blossfeld Jr.)

248. *Neobinghamia villigera* Rauh & Backbg.
Left: bud appearing from the apical wool. Right: flower, closing at dawn.

249. *Neobuxbaumia polylopha* (DC.) Backbg.

250. *Neobuxbaumia tetetzo* (Web.) Backbg.: fruits and seeds.

1. *Neocardenasia* Backbg.: the flower of *N. herzogiana* Backbg. bears long bristly spines and appears from ɪrcely thickened areoles; the plant is tree-like and develops a trunk. *Neoraimondia* (cf. Fig. 271) has flow-s without bristly spines, borne on a felty short shoot; no species of the latter genus develops a trunk. ᵉcent attempts to unite these genera reflect the absence of a satisfactory principle for classification (Photo: rdenas).

252. *Neochilenia andreaeana* Backbg.: a species with particularly attractive flowers.

253. *Neochilenia atra* Backbg. (Photo: Schattat).

254. *Neochilenia carneoflora* Kilian (Photo: Kilian).

255. Above: *Neochilenia deherdtiana* Backbg.
Below: *Neochilenia dimorpha* (Ritt.) Backbg.

6. *Neochilenia duripulpa* (**Ritt.**) Backbg.: young
afted plant.

257. *Neochilenia esmeraldana* (Ritt.) Backbg.
(Photo: Krahn).

258. *Neochilenia mitis* (Phil.) Backbg.: resembles *N. napina*, with which Schumann later united it; but the photo shows, the ribs of the former, while flat, are distinct in young plants and the floral hair-develo ment is more marked than in *N. napina* (cf. Fig. 2€0). These illustrations, taken in conjunction, show th *Chileorebutia* Ritt. cannot be maintained.

259. *Neochilenia monteamargensis* Backbg.: later offsetting freely from the base.

60. *Neochilenia napina* (Phil.) Backbg.: the conspicuous tubercles of habitat-plants merge, in older grafted
plants, to form tuberculate ribs (cf. Fig. 258). *Chileorebutia* Ritt. cannot be segregated from *Neochilenia*,
nd Ritter's erection of the former unintentionally demonstrated that *Neochilenia* alone is admissible, while
aising doubts as to his separation of the Chilean species of *"Pyrrhocactus* sensu Ritt.".

61. *Neochilenia pilispina* (Ritt.)
Backbg. (Photo: H. Müller).

262. Left: grafted plants of several low-growing species of *Neochilenia*.
Right: *Neochilenia taltalensis* v. *flaviflora* (Ritt.) Backbg.

263. *Neochilenia residua* (Ritt.) Backbg.

264. *Neodawsonia totolapensis* H. Bravo & MacDoug. [Photos: MacDougall and (right) Sivilla].

265. *Neogomesia agavoides* Castan.: with flowers borne centrally, at the tip of young areoles (see text, regarding the illustration of *Ariocarpus trigonus*).

266. Left: *Neolloydia grandiflora* (O.) Berg. Right: *Neolloydia ceratites* (Quehl) Br. & R.

267. *Neoporteria clavata* (Söhr.) Werd.: showing the flower typical of the genus, with the inner petals curving towards one another throughout flowering; flower-colour is also constant throughout the genus, and the stem-like floral tube is slightly hairy. These strikingly uniform characters are ignored in Hutchison's unification with *Neochilenia*, and the illustrations clearly show the differences of floral features.

268. *Neoporteria gerocephala* Y. Ito.: has a much larger flower than *N. nidus* which it resembles. *N. multicolor* Ritt., with large flowers, is only a form of *N. gerocephala*, and is even more variable than *N. nidus*.

269. *Neoraimondia aticensis* Rauh & Backbg.: the only species of this genus occurring near the sea and with divaricate stems.

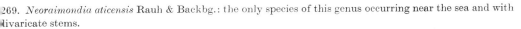

270. *Neoraimondia gigantea* (Werd. & Backbg.) Backbg.

271. *Neoraimondia* flower: petals white, pink or carmine, according to species, the tube without any longer bristly spines, while flowering areoles are modified into short shoots (cf. *Neocardenasia herzogiana*, Fig. 251) Photo: Rauh).

272. *Nopalea nuda* Backbg.

273. *Nopalxochia phyllanthoides* (DC.) **Br. & R.**: has played a significant role in the breeding of many "leaf-like" cultivars.

274. A rare hybrid: Nicolai's cross between *Nopalxochia phyllanthoides* and an *Echinopsis*, or *Pseudolobivia aurea!* Rowley reports that the flowers can be either yellow or white. Buds closely resemble those of *Nopalxochia*.

275. *Notocactus apricus* (Ar.) Berg.

276. *Nyctocereus oaxacensis* Br. & R. (Photo: Schattat).

277. *Obregonia denegrii* Frič.

278. *Opuntia bernichiana* cultivar, showing the great number of flowers and fruits on older flat-stemmed plants.

279. *Opuntia bispinosa* Backbg. (Photo: Rivière).

280. *Opuntia erectoclada* Backbg.: flower in longitudinal section. This is one of the low-growing species from the Series "Airampoae".

281. *Opuntia fragilis* (Nutt.) **Haw.**: a slender form from British Columbia (Pentingtown) (Photo: A. Meyer

282. *Opuntia galapageia* v. *brossetii* Backbg.:
epidermis black, spines whitish to straw-coloured
(Photo: J. Marnier-L.).

283. *Opuntia galapageia* v. *echios* (How.) Backbg. showing flower and fruits (Photo: E. Naundorff).

284. *Opuntia galapageia* v. *myriacantha* subv. *orientalis* (How.) Backbg.: one of the more southerly, trunk-forming varieties (Photo: Dawson).

285. *Opuntia horstii* W. Heinr. (Photo: Heinrich).

286. *Opuntia macbridei* Br. & R.: showing the smaller, ± erect perianth (Series "Macbrideanae") (Photo: Schattat).

287. *Opuntia quipa* Web.: one of the low-growing species of subseries *"Quipae"*, which has relatively small blossoms. The flower shown is not fully open; at anthesis the petals are spreading while the style and the filaments grouped tightly around it are much exserted (Photo: Schattat).

288. *Opuntia schickendantzii* Web.: the long-lost true type, with spherical green fruits (Photo: J. Marnier-L.).

Backeberg

289. *Opuntia stenopetala* Eng.: longitudinal sections of flowers and fruits. This species is one of the Ser. "Stenopetalae" which has unisexual flowers.

920. *Oreocereus trollii* (Kupp.) Backbg.: unlike *Morawetzia*, the flowers are here borne on the flanks.

291. *Oroya laxiareolata* v. *pluricentralis* Backbg. (Photo: De Herdt).

292. *Ortegocactus macdougallii* Alex.: a recently discovered "missing link" in the evolutionary line of the "Mammillariae"; the fairly large flowers arise centrally from the axils, and the ovary is hairy! (Photo: H. Bravo).

293. *Pachycereus pringlei* (S. Wats.) Br. & R.: apex of an older shoot showing the numerous flowers.

294. *Pachycereus* fruits: —
Left: *P. pringlei* (S. Wats.) Br. & R. Right: *P. calvus* (Eng.) Br. & R.

295. *Pachycereus calvus* (Eng.) Br. & R.: fruit after it has split open. Unlike *P. pringlei*, the apical stem-areoles of this species are not confluent.

296

297

298

296. *Parodia atroviridis* Backbg.

297. *Parodia buenekeri* Buin.

298. *Parodia catamarcensis* Backbg. (type): its v.
rubriflorens Backbg. has red flowers.

299. *Parodia dextrohamata* Backbg.

300. *Parodia dextrohamata* v. *stenopetala* Backbg.

301. *Parodia echinus* Ritt.

302. *Parodia elegans* Fechs., not described. Flowers yellow, larger than in *P. erythrantha;* spines white, bu⟨t⟩ reddish-brown at first above midway.

303. *Parodia erythrantha* v. *thionantha* (Speg.) Backbg.: with yellow blooms, while those of the type are
brick-red.

304. *Parodia fechseri* Backbg.: cylindrical when
older.

305. *Parodia fuscato-viridis* Backbg.

306. *Parodia gibbulosa* Ritt.; acc. Haage,
the plant shown is in fact *P. gibbulosoides*.
See also Fig. 504.

307. *Parodia glischrocarpa* Ritt.

308. *Parodia kilianana* Backbg. (Photo: Kilian).

309. Above: *Parodia mairanana* v. *atra* Backbg.: there are forms intermediate between this and the typ
Below: *Parodia otuyensis* Ritt.

10. *Parodia microsperma* v. *cafayatensis* Backbg. (Photo: J. Marnier-L.).

311. *Parodia penicillata* Fechs. & v. d. Steeg (Photo: Uhlig).

312. Above: *Parodia camargensis* v. *prolifera* Ritt. (*Parodia prolifera* Ritt.).
Below: *Parodia pseudostuemeri* Backbg.

13. *Parodia rauschii* Backbg. (Photo: Kilian).

314. Left: *Parodia rigida* Backbg.
Right: *Parodia rubellihamata* Backbg.

315. *Parodia rubriflora* Backbg.

6. *Parodia rubrifuscata* Ritt.: not described.

7. *Parodia sanagasta* v. *viridior* Backbg.

318. Above: *Parodia schwebsiana* v. *applanata* Backbg.
Below: *Parodia setosa* Backbg.

19. *Parodia* sp.: flowers red, hooked spines light rown; said to be from the vicinity of Tarija (Bolia) (Collection: Saint-Pie).

320. *Parodia stuemeri* (Werd.) Backbg.: form with fine spines.

321. Left: *Parodia stuemeri* v. *robustior* Backbg.
Right: *Parodia tafiensis* Backbg.: flower red, with pink stigma-lobes.

322. *Parodia subterranea* Ritt.

23. *Parodia uhligiana* Backbg. (Photo: Kilian).

324. *Pediocactus bradyi* v. *knowltonii* (L. Bens.) Backbg.

325. *Pediocactus simpsonii* (Eng.) Br. & R.: flowers not central, but in a ring round the crown.

326. *Peireskia aculeata* (Plum.) Mill.
(Drawing: Britton & Rose).

327. *Peireskiopsis porteri* (Brand.) Br. &
R.: showing the flower (Photo: H. Bravo).

328. *Pelecyphora pseudopectinata* Backbg.

326

327

328

329. *Peniocereus haackeanus* Backbg.: with the flow
er typical of the genus, the perianth curving down
wards and the stamens erect. (Photo: Schattat).

330. *Peniocereus haackeanus* Backbg.: fruit (Photo: Schattat).

331. *Peniocereus marnieranus* Backbg. (Photo: J. Marnier-L.). The flower is shown in Fig. 5, right.

332. *Pfeiffera ianthothele* (Monv.) Web.

333. *Phellosperma tetrancistra* (Eng.) Br. & R.: according to Buxbaum this has a true floral-tube, a fairly large perianth and seeds with a large corky hilum.

334. *Philippicereus castaneus* (Phil.) Backbg.: with the densely spiny flower and fruit typical of the genus.

35. *Pilocanthus paradinei* (B. W. Bens.) B. W.
Bens. & Backbg.: unusual in having three types
of spines; in age it shows long hairlike spines
which are unique among spherical cacti; the flower is quite large and central. Benson refers the
species to *Pediocactus* in which the blooms form
coronet. Comparison of the relevant illustrations shows that a unification of this kind does
little to clarify divergences.

36. *Pilocopiapoa solaris* Ritt.: flowers similar to *Copiapoa* but hairy; Rümpler described one member of this
complex ("*Echinocactus bridgesii* Pfeiff.") as having floral hairs. It would be interesting to verify whether
the plants are in fact identical (Photo: Wouters).

337. *Pilosocereus sergipensis* (Werd.) Byl. & Rowl.: the prominen
areolar flock and the bell-shaped, funnel-form flowers are characte
ristic of the genus. The fruits are always broadly spherical, wit
persistent floral remains, and the seeds are glossy (Photo: Voll).

338. *Polaskia chichipe* (Goss.) Backbg.: with a
tree-like habit.

39. *Pseudoespostoa melanostele* (Vpl.) Backbg.: branches from the base and does not form a trunk; the cephalium is superficial, not developing from a groove as in *Espostoa* (cf. Fig. 111); the seeds are glossy. Verdermann forst segregated this complex of species, and since the hair-development is similar but not identical, attempted unifications with *Espostoa* have led to confusion (Photo: Rauh).

340. *Pseudolobivia carmineoflora* Hoffm. & Back bg.: the form of body and ribs recalls "*Echi nopsis orozasana* Ritt.", while the rib-notches and diurnal salmon-carmine flower resemble *Lo bivia;* flowers are intermediate in length be tween the two genera. The illustration shows that without the introduction of *Pseudolobivia Echinopsis* and *Lobivia* (and even *Trichocereus* could not be segregated. Flowerlength in *Pseu dolobivia* ranges from "lobivioid-short" t "echinopsoid-long". This segregation makes th different groups of species more readily recogni sable.

341. *Pseudolobivia kratochviliana* (Backbg.) Backbg.: resembling *Echinopsis* but with the relatively shor flowers of *Lobivia*. See also Fig. 97: *Echinopsis* sp.? — a newer *Pseudolobivia* (*P. luteiflora* Backbg. n. sp.)

342. *Pseudolobivia orozasana* (Ritt.) Backbg. (Photo: J. Marnier-L.).

343. *Pseudolobivia poly incistra* (Backbg.) Backbg.: showing changes resulting from overdoses of synthetic fertiliser. The ribs are modified into rows of tubercles, each tipped with a tiny leaf! The spines are now tiny white bristles, the flower has arisen centrally, and the ovary is almost enclosed within the body; only the perianth remains normal. Unless this phenomenon is investigated, existing evolutionary theories about the Cactaceae cannot be regarded as established beyond doubt.

344. *Pseudozygocactus epiphylloides* v. *bradei* (Camp.-Port. & Cast.) Backbg.: part of a plant in habitat showing the crowded long-pendant branches (Photo: Friedrich).

345. *Pterocactus decipiens* Gürke.

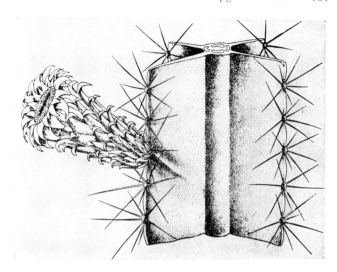

46. *Pterocereus foetidus* MacDoug. & Mir. (Drawing by the authors).

47. *Pygmaeocereus densiaculeatus* Backbg. (left) and a close-up view of the apex with feathery black-tipped new spines (right).

348. *Pygmaeocereus rowleyanus* Backbg. (left) and *P. bylesianus* Backbg. (right) (Photo: Andreae).

9. *Pyrrhocactus atrospinosus* Backbg. (above) and *P. melanacanthus* Backbg. (below) (Photos: Lembcke).

350. *Pyrrhocactus bulbocalyx* (Werd.) Backbg. (Photo: Wouters).

351. *Pyrrhocactus melanacanthus* Backbg.

352. *Pyrrhocactus umadeave* v. *marayesensis* Backbg. (Photo: Lembcke).

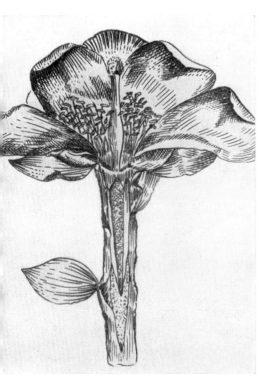

353. *Quiabentia zehntneri* (Br. & R.) Br. & R. (Drawing: Castellanos).

354. *Rathbunia neosonorensis* Backbg.

355. *Rauhocereus riosaniensis* Backbg. (Photo: Rauh).

356. *Rauhocereus riosaniensis* Backbg: flower and longitudinal section (Photo: Schattat).

355

356

357. *Rebutia calliantha* Wessn.: species producing many large flowers.

358. *Rebutia glomeriseta* Card.: referred by many authors to *Sulcorebutia*, but lacking the linear areoles which are a constant feature of the latter genus; this character, together with the presence in some cases of a taproot, or cushion-like habit arising from a main napiform root, and much broader floral scales, constitute the group of characters differentiating *Sulcorebutia* (Photo: J. Marnier-L.).

359. *Rebutia graciliflora* Backbg.: sole species with the central spines sometimes blackish.

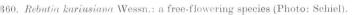

360. *Rebutia kariusiana* Wessn.: a free-flowering species (Photo: Schiel).

361. *Rebutia permutata* W. Heinr. (right) and its v.
gokrausei W. Heinr. (left) (Photo: Heinrich).

362. *Rebutia senilis* Backbg.

363. *Reicheocactus* sp. (from Ritter); erroneously known as "*Lobivia famatimensis* sensu Ritt." (cf. Spegazzini's photo!). The flower (above) has a short tube, quite strongly hairy only below. The longitudinal section of the flower (below) shows that this is not a *Lobivia* (Photos: Buining). Ritter himself stated no locality for this plant.

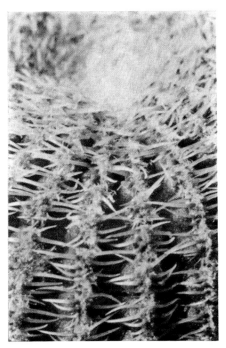

364. *Reicheocactus:* comparative views of spination: —
Left: *Reicheocactus pseudoreicheanus* Backbg.: the spines are not "whitish" as in *Lobivia famatimensis*.
Right: yellowish spination of Ritter-collected material, FR 459. Fechser recently collected *Reicheocactus pseudoreicheanus* near Guandacol, Quebrada de la Troja, Cerro El Cordobés (La Rioja). He states that this species is not found in the Sierra Famatina; its distribution ranges in fact from its western limits to the NE. corner of San Juán.

365. *Reicheocactus pseudoreicheanus* Backbg.: the typical small-barrel form of older stems.

366a. For comparison with *Reicheocactus*, here is *Lobivia famatimensis* (Speg.) Br. & R.; the flowers are variable in length and width; the stems are not barrel-shaped, and the floral tube is longer, stouter and much hairier than Ritter's plant in Fig. 363; the spines, which are differently arranged and more pectinate than in the type of *Reicheocactus*, do bear some resemblance to Ritter's plants, yet the flowers are quite distinct; consequently Britton & Rose's views must be upheld, and Ritter's plants have to be referred to *Reicheocactus*. This photo by Spegazzini, showing the flower as it opens, corresponds to "*Lobivia famatimensis* v. *albolanata*" collected by Blossfeld in the Sierra Famatina, with yellow flowers only 4 cm across, which is now regarded as v. *famatimensis*.

366b. *Lobivia famatimensis* (Speg.) Br. & R. v. *famatimensis*: flower only 4 cm ⌀, re-collected many years ago in the Sierra Famatina by Blossfeld Jr., and described under the synonym *Hymenorebutia albolanata* Bxin.

367. *Rhipsalidopsis rosea* (Lag.) Br. & R.: —
Above: type-plant of the original description.
Below: Colour-photo of the flower in longitudinal section; the filaments are inserted basally.

368. *Rhipsalis houlletiana* Lem.: the only species with nodding flowers; the ovary is acutely angular.

369. *Rhipsalis pilosa* Web.: perhaps only a name? Flowers only $5^1/_2$ mm $\varnothing$. Madagascan species.

370. *Rhodocactus antonianus* Backbg.

371. *Rhodocactus antonianus* Backbg. Left: view of the flower. Right: longitudinal section of the flower in close-up.

2. *Rhodocactus sacharosa* (Griseb.) Backbg.:
th an inferior ovary (Photo: J. Marnier-L.)

373. *Ritterocereus laevigatus* (SD.) Backbg.: showing the flower, which is typical of the genus.

374. *Rodentiophila megacarpa* Ritt. (Photos: Wouters).

375. *Rooksbya euphorbioides* (Haw.) Backbg.: with the spineless flower-form; in this genus the developme
of floral spines varies from species to species (Photo: Rivière).

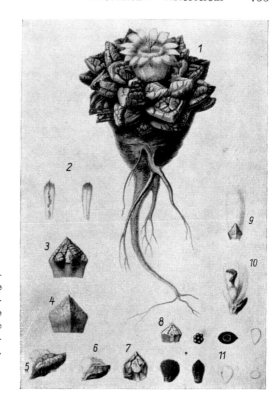

376. *Roseocactus fissuratus* (Eng.) Berg.: in this ge-
us the flowers arise centrally from the furrows of the
newest tubercles. Anderson's unification with *Ariocarpus,* which is not based on any comprehensive
principles of classification, cannot be accepted since
logic would then demand a combination of *Coryphantha* with *Mammillaria* (Drawing: Engelmann).

377. *Roseocereus tephracanthus* (Lab.) Backbg.:
typical indumentum as the fruit starts to develop.

378. *Samaipaticereus corroanus* Card. (Photo: Cardenas).

379. *Sclerocactus polyancistrus* (Eng. & Big.) Br. & R.

380. *Selenicereus pringlei* Rose (Photo: Ha... Jr.).

381. *Seticereus icosagonus* (HBK.) Backbg.: flowering zone with mature bristly cephalium (Photo: Rauh).

382. *Seticereus roezlii* (Hge.) Backbg.: possibly a variety of this free-flowering and laterally branching spe‑
cies. *S. chlorocarpus* (erroneously regarded by Buxbaum as "*Browningia*" or *Gymnanthocereus*) branches
only subapically (Photo: Pallanca).

383. Fruit of *Seticereus icosagonus* (HBK.) Backbg.,
which becomes much larger than that of *Borzicactus*
and *Loxanthocereus;* the flowers of *Seticereus*, unlike
these genera, has a compressed tube.

385

384

386

384. *Seticleistocactus dependens* (Card.) Backbg.: flowers, showing the long bristles characteristic of the genus (Photo: J. Marnier-L.: see also Fig. 59 left).

385. *Seticleistocactus piraymirensis* (Card.) Backbg.: Cardenas shares the view that this genus represents a distinct evolutionary stage (Photo: Cardenas).

386. *Setiechinopsis mirabilis* (Speg.) de Haas: the type-species of the genus. Its spines are stouter than those of its variety, and the strongly perfumed flowers remain open longer in the morning (Photo: Voll).

387. *Setiechinopsis mirabilis* v. *gracilior* Backbg.: the spines are finer, the flower closes sooner and is less scented.

388. *Soehrensia bruchii* (Br. & R.) Backbg. (Photo: Rivière).

889. *Soehrensia ingens* Br. & R. ex Backbg.: —
Above: the type of the species, in flower.
Below: a form with rather longer spines and orange-reddish flowers (Photo: Schicketanz).

390. *Soehrensia korethroides* (Werd.) Backbg.: a form or variety discovered by Rausch, taller in habit o
perhaps an unusually tall mature plant of this usually spherical species which is known in Argentina a
"globe-cactus". Plants in the wild have denser spination than those in cultivation (Photo: Rausch).

391. *Solisia pectinata* (B. Stein) Br. & R.

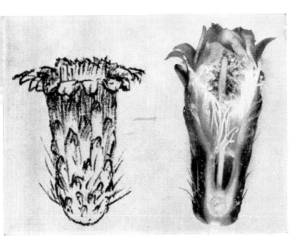

392. *Stenocereus stellatus* (Pfeiff.) Ricc.: the flower of this tall-shrubby species has a fairly densely spined ovary whereas in *Marginatocereus*, which is rather similar, only the tube has small scattered spines.

393. *Stephanocereus leucostele* (Gürke) Berg.

394. *Strombocactus disciformis* (DC.) Br. & R.: showing variable flower-size.

395. *Strophocactus wittii* (K. Sch.) Br. & R. (Photo: Haage Jr.).

396. *Submatucana madisoniorum* (Hutch.) Backbg.: this broadly spherical species, like many other plants of similar habit (*Notocactus*, *Parodia*, etc.), is only rarely more elongated in age. This, together with the different flower-form, shows that Kimnach and Hutchison's combination with *Borzicactus* (a slender-cereoid genus) makes little sense. If these authors are correct in assuming their combination to be necessary, then uniformity of procedure in other cases would lead to unforeseeable consequences and amorphous outsize genera incapable of reflecting natural phenomena (Photo: Schattat).

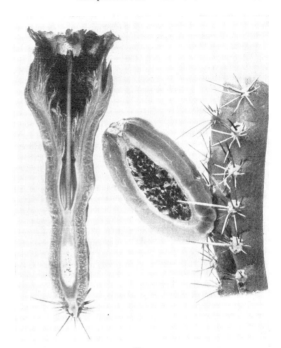

397. *Subpilocereus repandus* v. *weberi* (Backbg.) Backbg.: showing the typical thick-walled fruit and the flower with a double constriction (Photo: Hummelinck).

398. *Sulcorebutia candiae* (Card.) Backbg. (Photo: Schattat).

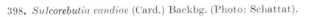

399. *Sulcorebutia lepida* Ritt.: perhaps identical with *S. mentosa* Ritt. (Photo: J. Marnier-L.).

400. *Sulcorebutia menesesii* (Card.) Backbg. (Photo: J. Marnier-L.).

401. *Sulcorebutia steinbachii* (Werd.) Backbg.: deep green varieties with differently coloured flowers. Left: v. *rosiflora* Backbg. Right: v. *violaciflora* Backbg. (Photo: J. Marnier-L.).

402. *Sulcorebutia* sp. "Rausch No. 64": probably *S. taratensis* (cf. Fig. 403) (Photo: Rausch).

403. *Sulcorebutia taratensis* (Card.) Buin. & Don. (Photo: Rausch).

404. *Sulcorebutia tiraquensis* (Card.) Ritt.: a form with particularly stout spines (Photo: Kilian).

05. Above: *Sulcorebutia tiraquensis* (Card.) Ritt. (Photo: Kilian).
eft: v. *tiraquensis*. Right: v. *electracantha* Backbg.
elow: other species and forms of Sulcorebutia.

406. *Sulcorebutia xanthoantha* Backbg. (Photo Kilian).

407. *Tacinga atropurpurea* v. *zehntnerioides* Backbg.

08. *Tephrocactus alboareolatus* Ritt. (Photo: Hegenbart).

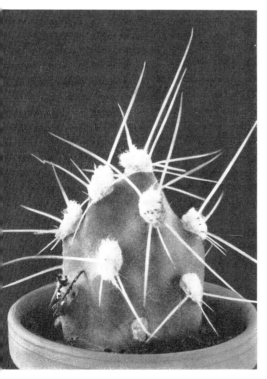

409. *Tephrocactus alboareolatus* Ritt.: a single stem-segment.

410. *Tephrocactus atroglobosus* Backbg. (Photo: Rivière).

411. *Tephrocactus catacanthus* Backbg.   412. *Tephrocactus coloreus* Ritt.

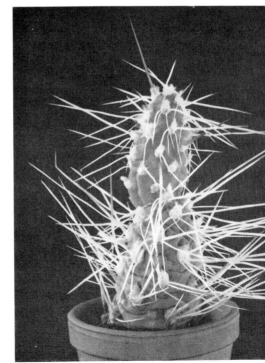

13. *Tephrocactus corotilla* (K. Sch.) Backbg.: longitudinal section of the flower.

14. *Tephrocactus curvispinus* Backbg.

415. *Tephrocactus flexispinus* Backbg.

416. *Tephrocactus glomeratus* (Haw.) Backbg.:
type of the species.

417. *Tephrocactus glomeratus* v. *atratospinus* Backbg.: single shoots (Photo: Kilian).

418. *Tephrocactus glo-meratus* v. *longispinus* Backbg.

419. *Tephrocactus hegenbartianus* Backbg.: freely branching (above) and a single stem-segment (below).

420. *Tephrocactus longiarticulatus* Backbg. (Photo: Hegenbart).

421. *Tephrocactus melanacanthus* Backbg.

422. *Tephrocactus microsphaericus* Backbg.

423. *Tephrocactus neuquensis* (Borg) Backbg. (Photo: J. Marnier-L.).

424. *Tephrocactus parvisetus* Backbg.

425. *Tephrocactus rauhii* Backbg.: in habitat (Photo: Rauh).

426. *Tephrocactus sphaericus* v. *glaucinus* Backbg.

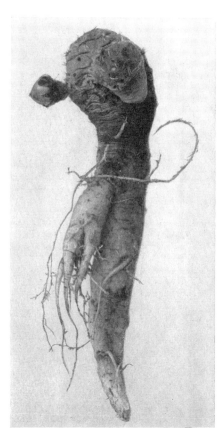

427. *Tephrocactus subterraneus* (R. E. Fries) Backbg.

428. *Tephrocactus virgultus* Backbg. (Photo: J. Marnier-L.).

429. *Thelocactus flavidispinus* (Backbg.) Backbg.

430. *Thrixanthocereus blossfeldiorum* (Werd.) Backbg. flowering stem, showing cephalium.

431. Transverse section through a cephalium-bearing shoot of *Thrixanthocereus blossfeldiorum* (Werd.) Backbg., showing that the cephalium arises from a slight depression — not a cleft, as in *Espostoa* — so that this species cannot be referred to the latter genus (Photo: Cullmann).

432. Variability in *Thrixanthocereus blossfeldiorum* (Werd.) Backbg.
Left: normal form, with finer radial spines and dark shorter centrals.
Right: form with stronger spines, the centrals more robust and longer.

433. Further variability in *Thrixanthocereus blossfeldiorum* (Werd.) Backbg.: another form in which all the spines are medium-long, fine, $\pm$ bristly and pure white (including the thin centrals). Seeds of this variety are the same as those of *Thr. cullmannianus,* so that the latter is probably better regarded as a mere variety.

434. *Thrixanthocereus cullmannianus* Ritt. (Photo: Ritter).

435. *Thrixanthocereus senilis* Ritt. (Photo: Ritter).

436. *Toumeya papyracantha* (Eng.) Br. & R.

437

438

439

437. *Trichocereus grandiflorus* Backbg. (Photo: J. Marnier-L.).

438. *Trichocereus lamprochlorus* (Lem.) Backbg.: the true, glossy, dark green Bolivian species (Photo: J. Marnier-L.).

439. *Trichocereus rubinghianus* Backbg.

440. *Trichocereus smrzianus* (Backbg.) Backbg.: quite recently Rubingh of Holland was able to flower a plant, so that correct diagnosis then became possible (Photo: Rubingh).

441. *Turbinicarpus roseiflorus* Backbg.

442. *Utahia sileri* (Eng.) Br. & R.:
there is also a form with almost
pure white spines.

443. *Vatricania guentheri* (Kupp.) Backbg.: showing the typical flower and early development of the bristly cephalium (Photo: Andreae).

444. *Vatricania guentheri* (Kupp.) Backbg.: the massive cephalium on an old plant. Buxbaum's referral of this genus to *Espostoa* is clearly arbitrary since the flower form and insertion, as well as the cephalia, differ in the two genera; *Espostoa* never has the encircling superficial cephalium seen in mature specimens of *Vatricania*.

445. *Weberbauerocereus albus* Ritt. (Photo: Ritter).

446. *Weberbauerocereus longicomus* Ritt. (Photo: Ritter).

447. *Weberbauerocereus* flowers: —
Left: *W. weberbaueri* (K. Sch.) Backbg.
Right: *W. seyboldianus* Rauh & Backbg. (Photo: Rauh).

448. *Weberbauerocereus winterianus* Ritt. (Photo: Ritter).

449. *Weberocereus tunilla* (Web.) Br. & R.

450. *Weingartia cintiensis* (Card.?) (Photo: Rausch).

451. Left: *Weingartia neocumingii* Backbg., longer-spined form (*W. pulquinensis* Card.).
Right: *W. riograndensis* Ritt. (Photos: Schattat).

452

452. *Weingartia neumanniana* v. *aurantia* Backbg. (Photo: Schattat).

453. *Werckleocereus tonduzii* (Web.) Br. & R

454. *Wilcoxia albiflora* Backbg.

454

453

455. *Wilmattea minutiflora* (Br. & R.)
Br. & R.

456. *Winterocereus (Hildewintera) aureispinus* (Ritt.) Backbg. nom. nov. (Photo: Cullmann).

457. *Wittia panamensis* Br. & R. (Photo: Rose).

458. *Zehntnerella squamulosa* Br. & R.

459. *Zygocactus truncatus* (Haw.) K. Sch.: rare
form, flowering laterally (Photo: Voll).

Illustrations: Supplement

460. *Arrojadoa aureispina* Buin. & Bred.: in habitat (Photo: Buining).

461. *Arrojadoa dinae* Buin. & Bred.: with fruits, in habitat (Photo: Buining).

462. *Arrojadoa eriocaulis* Buin. & Bred. (Photo: Buining).

463. *Austrocephalocereus dybowskii* (Goss.)
Backbg. (Photo: Buining).

464. *Austrocephalocereus purpureus* (Gürke)
Backbg.: in habitat (Photo: Buining).

465. *Aylostera buiningiana* Rausch
(Photo: Buining).

466. *Aylostera heliosa* Rausch
(Photo: Rausch).

467. *Aylostera jujuyana* Rausch
(Photo: Rausch).

8. *Buiningia aurea* (Ritt.) Buxb.: in habitat (Photo: Buining).

469. *Buiningia brevicylindrica* Buin.: in habitat (Photo: Buining).

Backeberg

470. *Buiningia purpurea* Buin.
Bred.: in habitat (Photo: Buining

471. *Lobivia amblayensis* Raus
(Photo: Rausch).

472. *Lobivia cardenasiana* Raus
(Photo: Rausch).

473. *Lobivia cornuta* Rausch
(Photo: Buining).

474. *Lobivia draxleriana* Rausch (Photos: Rausch).

475. *Lobivia fričii* Rausch (Photo Rausch).

476. *Lobivia glauca* v. *paucicostate* Rausch (Photo: Rausch).

477. *Lobivia leptacantha* Rausch (Photo: Rausch).

478. *Lobivia mizquensis* Rausch (Photo: Rausch).

479. *Lobivia pusilla* Ritt. (Photo: Rausch).

480. *Lobivia pusilla* v. *flaviflora* (Photo: Rausch).

481. *Lobivia sicuaniensis* Rausch
(Photo: Rausch).

482. *Lobivia tiegeliana* Wessn.: —
Left:, the type; right, v. *ruberrim[c]*
(Photo: Rausch).

483. *Lobivia zecheri* Rausch
(Photo: Rausch).

484. *(Mediolobivia)* *Rebutia brunescens* Rausch (Photo: Rausch).

485. *Mediolobivia eos* Rausch (Photo: Rausch).

486   *Melocactus albicephalus* Buin. & Bred. (Photo: Buining).

487. *Melocactus azureus* Buin. &
Bred.: in habitat (Photo: Buining).

488. *Melocactus concinnus* Buin. & Bred.: in habitat (Photo: Buining).

489. *Melocactus cremnophilus* Buin. & Bred.: in habitat (Photo: Buining).

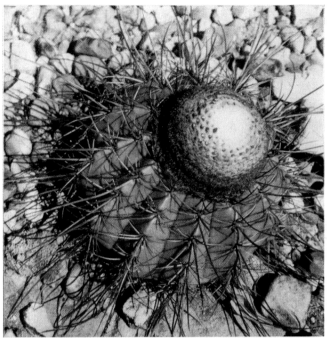

490. *Melocactus erythranthus* Buin. & Bred.: in habitat (Photo: Buining).

491. *Melocactus ferreophilus* Buin. & Bred.: in habitat (Photo: Buining).

492. *Melocactus glaucescens* Buin. & Bred. (Photo: Buining).

493. *Notocactus buiningii* Buxb. (Photo: Buining).

494. *Notocactus carambeiensis* Buin. & Bred. (Photo: Buining).

495. *Notocactus roseoluteus* v. Vliet (Photo: van Vliet).

496. *Notocactus uebelmannianus* Buin.: in habitat (Photo: Buining).

497. *Parodia andreae* Brandt (Photo: Brandt).

498. *Parodia aureispina* Backbg. v. *australis* Brandt (left); *Parodia aureispina* v. *rubriflora* (Backbg.) Brandt (right) (Photos: Brandt).

499. *Parodia aureispina* Backbg. (left); *Parodia aureispina* v. *vulgaris* Brandt (right) (Photos: Brandt).

500   501

500. *Parodia backebergiana* Brandt (Photo: Brandt).

501. *Parodia challamarcana* Brandt (Photo: Brandt).

502. *Parodia culpinensis* Ritt. (Photo: Brandt).

503. *Parodia fričiana* Brandt (Photo: Brandt).

504. *Parodia gibbulosoides* Brandt (Photo: Brandt).

505. *Parodia ignorata* Brandt (Photo: Brandt).

504   505

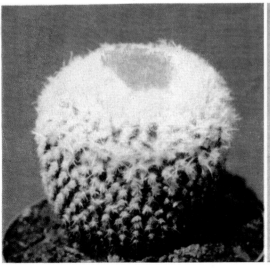

506   507

506. *Parodia kilianana* Backbg. (Photo: Brandt).

507. *Parodia koehresiana* Brandt (Photo: Brandt).

508. *Parodia krasuckana* Brandt (Photo: Brandt).

509. *Parodia laui* Brandt (Photo: Brandt).

508   509

510   511

510. *Parodia neglecta* Brandt (Photo: Brandt).

511. *Parodia neglectoides* Brandt (Photo: Brandt).

512. *Parodia pluricentralis* Backbg. & Brandt (Photo: Brandt).

513. *Parodia pseudoprocera* Brandt (Photo: Brandt).

512   513

514   515

514. *Parodia punae* Card. (Photo: Brandt).

515. *Parodia rostrum-sperma* Brandt (Photo: Brandt).

516. *Parodia salmonea* Brandt (Photo: Brandt).

517. *Parodia spegazziniana* Brandt (Photo: Brandt).

518. *Parodia superba* Brandt (Photo: Brandt).

519. *Parodia thionantha* Brandt (Photo: Brandt).

518

519

520. *Parodia weberiana* Brandt (Photo: Brandt).

521. *Parodia zaletaewana* Brandt (Photo: Brandt).

522   523

522. *Pseudopilocereus fulvilanatus* Buin. & Bred. (Photo: Buining).

523. *Pseudopilocereus magnificus* Buin. & Bred. (Photo: Buining).

524. *Uebelmannia buiningii* Donald: in habitat (Photo: Buining).

525. *Uebelmannia flavispina* Buin. & Bred.: in habitat (Photo: Buining).

(Due to the exigencies of co-editions Figs. 524—527 have been transposed
alphabetically in front of Figs. 528—534.)

526. *Uebelmannia meninensis* Buin.: in habitat (Photo: Buining).

527. *Uebelmannia pectinifera* Buin.: in habitat (Photo: Buining).

528. *Rebutia margarethae* Rausch (Photo: Rausch).

529. *Sulcorebutia alba* Rausch (Photo: Rausch).

530. *Sulcorebutia flavissima* Rausch (Photo: Rausch).

531. *Sulcorebutia krahnii* Rausch (Photo: Rausch).

532. *Sulcorebutia frankiana* Rausch (Photo: Rausch).

533. *Sulcorebutia verticillacantha* v. *aureiflora* Ritt. (Photo: Rausch).

534. *Sulcorebutia rauschii* Frank (Photo: Rausch).